B. Olive 290

1. cloth disclose, conceal · identity · uniform
   cloth as metaphor
3. manufacture; bestowal exchange; author by clothing

CLOTH
AND HUMAN
EXPERIENCE

Smithsonian Series in Ethnographic Inquiry
Ivan Karp and William L. Merrill, Series Editors

Ethnography as fieldwork, analysis, and literary form is the distinguishing feature of modern anthropology. Guided by the assumption that anthropological theory and ethnography are inextricably linked, this series is devoted to exploring the ethnographic enterprise.

ADVISORY BOARD

CLOTH
AND HUMAN
EXPERIENCE

Edited by

Annette B. Weiner & Jane Schneider

Smithsonian Institution Press
Washington and London

This book is published with the assistance of the
Wenner-Gren Foundation for Anthropological
Research

Edited by Allan Forsyth
Designed by Linda McKnight

Library of Congress Cataloging-in-Publication Data
Weiner, Annette B., 1933–
  Cloth and human experience.
  (Smithsonian series in ethnographic inquiry)
  Bibliography: p.
  Includes index.
    1. Costume—Social aspects.   2. Textile fabrics—
Social aspects.   I. Schneider, Jane, 1938–
II. Title.   III. Series.
GT525.W45 1989   391   88–32696
ISBN 0–87474–986–7

British Library Cataloguing-in-Publication Data
available

∞The paper used in this publication meets the minimum requirements of the American National Standard for Permanence of Paper for Printed Library
Materials Z39.48-1984

Contents

Preface

During many years of field research in Western Sicily, Jane Schneider became increasingly impressed by the dedication, time, and effort that Sicilian women direct towards the preparation of their cloth trousseau. Less evident in today's world than in the past, this tradition seemed to call out for study. At about the same time but in another part of the world, Annette Weiner confronted the political importance that Trobrianders and Samoans still attach to "cloth" wealth woven from banana- and pandanus-leaf fibers. These particular experiences convinced us that on a world-wide scale, complex moral and ethical issues related to dominance and autonomy, opulence and poverty, political legitimacy and succession, and gender and sexuality, find ready expression through cloth. Therefore, we organized an interdisciplinary conference, attended by art historians, historians, textile experts, and anthropologists.

The conference, held in 1983 at Troutbeck, New York, was funded by the Wenner-Gren Foundation for Anthropological Research. We are deeply grateful to the participants: Lisa Aaronson, Monni Adams, Susan Bean, Bernard Cohn, Louise Cort, Patricia Darish, Joanne Eicher, Gillian Feeley-Harnik, Diane Owen Hughes, Billie Jean Isbell, H. Leedom Lefferts, Jr., Kathryn March, Matthew Mines, Linda A. Stone, Maude Wahlman, and Ronald Waterbury; to the discussants, T. O. Beidelman, Maurice Bloch, James Boon, Warren D'Azevedo, Shirley Lindenbaum, and Richard C. Trexler; and to the rapporteurs, Ivan Karp and Jason Williams. Each person's particular research interests and intellectual vitality enhanced the conference with a variety of important insights and perspectives. We are particularly grateful to Lita Osmundsen, who was Director of Research for the Wenner-Gren Foundation. Her generous counsel, organizational skills, dedicated staff, and financial support were essential to the conference's success. Her continued assistance with the publication of this volume has enabled us to bring the recognition of cloth's significance before a wider audience.

In preparation for this book, we selected specific themes that would reveal the properties of cloth that underlie its social and political contributions within broad historical time periods. Because we wanted to sharpen our focus in these directions, the volume neither replicates the conference papers nor encompasses the work of all those who participated. Moreover, some essays not presented at the conference have been included in the book. We thank Ivan Karp for his guidance during the publication process. Daniel Goodwin, Editorial Director, and Ruth Spiegel, Managing Editor, of the Smithsonian Institution Press, were splendid working colleagues as was Allan Forsyth, who edited the manuscript. Finally, we are most grateful to the volume contributors, whose enthusiasm for the project made our own endeavors so much more meaningful.

Annette B. Weiner
Jane Schneider

Contributors

SUSAN S. BEAN is Chief Curator and Curator of Ethnology at the Peabody Museum of Salem. Her analyses of the language of social life in south India have appeared in a book, *Symbolic and Pragmatic Semantics: A Kannada System of Address* and in numerous articles. In 1981–82, she was a Mellon Fellow at the Metropolitan Museum of Art. Among the outcomes of her research on Indian textiles are her contribution to this volume and a new permanent exhibit at the Peabody Museum of Salem, " Yankee Traders and Indian Merchants: 1785–1865," created for the 1985–86 Festival of India.

BERNARD S. COHN is Professor of Anthropology and History at the University of Chicago. His primary research interest has been the study of colonial societies, with particular reference to South Asia. His book, *An Anthropologist Among the Historians and Other Essays*, has recently been published.

LOUISE ALLISON CORT is a Museum Specialist for Ceramics at the Freer Gallery of Art and Arthur M. Sackler Gallery within the Smithsonian Institution. She is interested in craft production in Asia and has done extensive research on ceramics and textiles in Japan and India. Her book, *Shigaraki, Potters' Valley* was published in 1979; she is presently preparing for publication her studies of the temple potters of Puri and Orissa, and a seventeenth-century Japanese potter's diary.

PATRICIA DARISH is completing her dissertation in the School of Fine Arts at Indiana University. Her main interest is Central African art traditions. She conducted research among the Kuba of south-central Zaire during 1981 and 1982 and is currently a Research Associate at the University of Missouri–Kansas City, in the department of fine arts.

GILLIAN FEELEY-HARNIK is Professor in the Anthropology Department at The Johns Hopkins University. Her publications include *The Lord's Table: Eucharist and Passover in Early Christianity* (Univ. of Pennsylvania Press, 1981) and a forthcoming book *Death and Development in Madagascar* as well as many articles based on ethnographic and archival research in Madagascar and on research in biblical studies.

JANET HOSKINS is Assistant Professor of Anthropology at the University of Southern California. She has done extensive field work in Kodi, West Sumba, Indonesia and has published articles on traditional poetics, ritual, art, conversion, and emerging historical consciousness among the Kodi people. She has served as a Research Fellow in the Gender Relations Research Group, Research School of Pacific studies, Australian National University, and has collaborated on several films on Sumbanese rituals.

JOHN V. MURRA is President of the Institute of Andean Research. He has taught at Cornell University, the Universidad Nacional de San Marcos (Lima, Peru), Yale University, and Vassar College. He has published *Formaciones economicas y politicas en el mundo andino* (Instituto de Estudios Peruanos, Lima, 1975) and "The Economic Organization of the Inca State" (JAI Press, 1980). He is a corresponding member of the Peruvian Academy of History.

JANE SCHNEIDER is Professor in the Ph.D. Program of Anthropology of the City University of New York. Her long-term fieldwork in Sicily has led to several publications, co-authored by Peter Schneider, including the book, *Culture and Political Economy in Western Sicily*. She has also written about European cloth traditions and is the author of "The Anthropology of Cloth" in the *Annual Review of Anthropology*.

LINDA STONE-FERRIER is currently Associate Professor in the Kress Foundation Department of Art History at the University of Kansas. Her publications include *Images of Textiles: The Weave of 17th-Century Dutch Art and Society*, and an exhibition catalogue, *Dutch Prints of Daily Life: Mirrors of Life or Masks of Morals?* in which she examined the interpretative problems raised by seventeenth-century Dutch everyday scenes.

RONALD WATERBURY, Associate Professor of Anthropology at Queens College, CUNY, has carried out research in Oaxaca, Mexico intermittently since 1965, with an emphasis on economic and political matters. He has also researched, lived, or traveled in many other countries of Latin America, and, in the bargain, has accumulated a considerable collection of popular artisanry.

ANNETTE B. WEINER is David Kriser Distinguished Professor of Anthropology and Chair at New York University. She has conducted ethnographic field research for over a decade in Papua New Guinea and most recently in Western Samoa, Polynesia. She is the author of *Women of Value, Men of Renown: New Perspectives in Trobriand Exchange* and *The Trobrianders of Papua New Guinea.*

1. *Introduction*

JANE SCHNEIDER AND ANNETTE B. WEINER

 Throughout history, cloth has furthered the organization of social and political life. In the form of clothing and adornment, or rolled or piled high for exchange and heirloom conservation, cloth helps social groups to reproduce themselves and to achieve autonomy or advantage in interactions with others. This book brings to light the properties of cloth that underlie its social and political contributions, the ritual and social domains in which people acknowledge these properties and give them meaning, and the transformations of meaning over time.

Malleable and soft, cloth can take many shapes, especially if pieces are cut for architectural assembly. Cloth also lends itself to an extraordinary range of decorative variation, whether through the patterned weaving of colored warps and wefts, or through the embroidery, staining, painting, or dyeing of the whole. These broad possibilities of construction, color, and patterning give cloth an almost limitless potential for communication. Worn or displayed in an emblematic way, cloth can denote variations in age, sex, rank, status, and group affiliation. As much as cloth discloses it can conceal, however, homogenizing difference through uniforms or sackcloth, or superimposing disguised identities through costumes and masks. Cloth can also communicate the wearer's or user's ideological values and claims. Complex moral and ethical issues of dominance and autonomy, opulence and poverty, continence and sexuality, find ready expression through cloth.

In addition to its seemingly endless variability and related semiotic potential, cloth is a repository for prized fibers and dyes, dedicated human labor, and the virtuoso artistry of competitive aesthetic development. As such, it attracts the attention of power holders, including those who would build chiefdoms and states. Throughout history, the architects of centralizing polities have awed spectators with sartorial splendor, strategically distributed beautiful fabrics among clients, and exported the textile output of royal and peasant workshops to earn foreign exchange. Cloth has often become a standard of value, circulating as money, so it should come as no surprise that cloth wealth has enriched the treasuries of many kingdoms and chiefdoms, conferring credibility on political elites along with gold, silver, jewels, and exotic shells.

Another characteristic of cloth, which enhances its social and political roles, is how readily its appearance and that of its constituent fibers can evoke ideas of connectedness or tying. Wrapping individuals to protect them from the malevolent forces of their cultural or natural environment, bark cloths and woven textiles can also envelop more than one person, as in an Indonesian marriage ceremony where a tubular, uncut fabric binds the bride to the groom. A moment's reflection brings to mind any number of instances in which a cloth or thread metaphor illuminates similarly "tied" relations—for example, Anaïs Nin's portrait of love in one of her novels: "She was weaving and sewing and mending because he carried in himself no thread of connection . . . of continuity or repair. . . . She sewed . . . so that the warmth would not seep out of their days together, the soft interskin of their relationship" (1959: 57–58).

Indeed, cloth metaphors echo from many parts of the world, today and in the past. Social scientists and laypersons regularly describe society as fabric, woven or knit together. Cloth as a metaphor for society, thread for social relations, express more than connectedness, however. The softness and ultimate fragility of these materials capture the vulnerability of humans, whose every relationship is transient, subject to the degenerative processes of illness, death, and decay. Weiner (this volume) recalls Homer's description of Penelope, weaving Laertes's shroud by day but then unraveling the same fabric each night, seeking thereby to halt time, neither burying her husband nor marrying a suitor in his absence, and thus preserving the balance between the gods and humans.

To seek the symbolic potentialities of cloth in its material properties is, however, but a preliminary step, and only partially compelling. Equally important are the human actions that make cloth politically and socially salient. The papers in this volume identify various domains of meaning in which people use cloth to consolidate social relations and mobilize political power.

First is the domain of cloth manufacture itself, as spinners, weavers, dyers, and finishers harness the imagined blessings of ancestors and divinities to inspire or animate the product, and draw analogies between weaving or dyeing and the life cycle of birth, maturation, death, and decay. The ritual and discourse that surround its manufacture establish cloth as a convincing analog for the regenerative and degenerative processes of life, and as a great connector, binding humans not only to each other but to the ancestors of their past and the progeny who constitute their future.

A second domain in which cloth acquires social and political significance is that of bestowal and exchange. Participants in life-cycle celebrations in general, and rituals of death in particular, frequently make of cloth a continuous thread, a binding tie between two kinship groups, or three and more generations. The cloth-givers on such occasions generate political power as well, committing recipients to loyalty and obligation in the future.

In a third domain of meaning—ceremonies of investiture and rulership—powerholders or aspirants to power declare that particular cloths transmit the authority of earlier possessors or the sanctity of past traditions, thus constituting a source of legitimacy in the present. A fourth domain involves manipulations of cloth as clothing, the uses of dress and adornment to reveal or conceal identities and values.

The actors who manipulate cloth in one or another domain of meaning vary according to gender. Women are by no means the universal producers of cloth, but in many societies they monopolize all or most of the manufacturing sequence, giving them a larger role than men. Many societies also assign women, rather than men, to exchange or give the cloths that tie the living to the dead, the bride's family to the groom's family, the politically dominant to their dependent clients. In ceremonies of rulership, cloth is generally in the hands of the men, but here, too, women may participate as producers or handlers of sanctified materials. Emblematic and communicative uses of cloth are, finally, as common among women as men; in the fashion system of contemporary Western capitalism, women's dress is elaborated to a uniquely high degree. As this volume suggests, the study of cloth can illuminate women's contributions to social and political organization that are otherwise overlooked.

One can imagine people imbuing cloth with social and political meanings in domains other than the ones just outlined. The domains we describe, however, illuminate with particular precision a theoretical problem posed in a variety of ways by the papers in this book. Capitalist production and its associated cultural values reordered the symbolic potential of cloth in two interrelated ways. First, altering the process of manufacture, capitalism eliminated the opportunity for weavers and dyers to infuse their product with spiritual value and to reflect and pronounce on analogies between reproduction and production. Second, by encouraging the growth of fashion—a consumption system of high-velocity turnover and endless, ever-changing variation—capitalist entrepreneurs vastly inflated dress and adornment as a domain for expression through cloth. Despite these shifts of emphasis and the worldwide expansion of capitalist manufacturing and fashion, ancient cloths and traditions of making them continue to reemerge with political—indeed often subversive—intent, above all in societies emerging from colonial domination. Exploring the domains of manufacture, exchange, and the legitimation of rule, as well as the domain of dress, helps one understand this continuing role of cloth in the reproduction of social life and power.

PART I: CLOTH IN SMALL-SCALE SOCIETIES

Annette B. Weiner's paper, "Why Cloth? Wealth, Gender, and Power in Oceania" introduces Part I, which considers the political significance of cloth in small-scale societies. Focusing on succession to authority, Weiner compares the relatively unstratified Trobriand Islands with Western Samoa, where ranked chiefly titles prevail. In the Trobriands, women gather banana leaves, scrape, dry, and bind them into bundles, or intricately tie them around waist cords to make skirts. At mortuary ceremonies, the female kin of a deceased person amass and distribute these "cloths," valued at hundreds of

U.S. dollars. In Trobriand society, people characteristically attribute death to sorcery, interpreting the loss of a person as a direct attack on the vitality and continuity of his or her kin group as a whole. The more cloth the group's women bestow on others, the better they protect themselves and their kin against continued enmity and political danger. Their distributions simultaneously "untie" the deceased from former social and political obligations.

Where Trobriand women process banana leaves to create a rudimentary form of cloth, women in Samoa soak and dry pandanus, plaiting the narrow fibers into large mats that, when carefully made, feel as soft as linen. Of the two, Samoan "cloth" has more permanence, with some fine mats lasting for as long as 200 years. The oldest mats carry the highest value. Often possessed of individuated histories, these mats are exchanged in all life-cycle ceremonies and at the investitures of chiefs. Relying on these mats to emphasize their associations with ancestors and mythical events of the past, living political actors legitimatize their claims to titles and ranks. In contrast, recently produced wealth circulates at Trobriand mortuary distributions, and new bundles and skirts are considered far more valuable than old ones. A similar contrast separates the ancient polities of Fiji from those of the Hawaiian Islands. Upon the death of a predecessor, the Fijian chief wrapped himself in magnificent rolls of barkcloth, including a train 100 yards long (Kooijman 1972). Although exemplifying the authority of his newly acquired position, these rolls also betrayed the underlying weakness of his succession for, unlike the dynastic cloaks of the substantially more stratified islands of Hawaii, they were not themselves heirlooms.

According to Weiner, the relationship between a greater degree of permanence in cloth and a greater elaboration of political hierarchy is not coincidental. The two go together because a hierarchy depends in part upon sumptuary paraphernalia to objectify rank and, more importantly, to constitute a physical bond between the past and the present. In some Polynesian societies such as Hawaii and Tahiti, it was historically the custom when rulers died to destroy their personal belongings as potentially polluting. But inaugural regalia, in the form of feathered cloaks and girdles, passed from generation to generation as the very substance of dynasty (Henry 1928; Valeri 1985). As Graham Clark (1986) noted for Medieval and Renaissance Europe, the regalia of office transmit ideas of sanctity and majesty as well as social status. Replete with cosmological referents and believed to be seats of spiritual power, such objects have even been said to "rule" in lieu of humans (Heine-Gildern 1956:10).

Weiner observes that once cloth attains a degree of permanence, absorbing value from the passage of time, political elites attempt to hoard and store it, not as capital for eventual deployment or merely for display, but as treasure to be saved in the face of all exigencies that force its dissipation. More than an economic resource or an affirmation of political status, treasure facilitates claims to the past—its names, legends, and events—that justify the transactions and extend the power of living actors. Treasure, of course, also includes valuables of stone, bone, and precious metals with which dynastic elites fill the vaults of state. Hard where cloth is soft, and far more durable, these objects would seem a better vehicle for expressing continuity through time. Weiner argues, however, that all social groups experience contradictory yearnings—for circulation and permanence, for expansion through alliance and conquest, and for rootedness through an internal deepening of authority. Precisely because it wears thin and disintegrates, cloth becomes an apt medium for communicating a central problem of power: Social and political relationships are necessarily fragile in an impermanent, ever-changing world.

The second chapter of Part I, Gillian Feeley-Harnik's "Cloth and the Creation of Ancestors in Madagascar," similarly emphasizes the tendency for cloth to legitimatize power while suggesting the fragility of relationships. The case concerns the Sakalava people of coastal Madagascar, who wrap their dead royalty in cotton cloth, place them in wooden coffins, and bury them in a royal tomb located on a small, offshore island. Unlike the Merina and other peoples of highland Madagascar, the Sakalava do not practice secondary burials in which, as Bloch has described for the Merina (1971), corpses are disinterred to be rewrapped for placement in ancestral tombs. Rather, in Sakalava belief, the dead remain social beings only by returning to possess the living, whom they make ill. In possession episodes, returning spirits disclose their identity by demanding cloths appropriate to their status—cloths that friends and relatives must wrap around the person who is possessed. Most of the returning spirits are of royal ancestry; their high position leads them to ask for *lamba* cloths that, because of age and authenticity, are among the most expensive and difficult to procure. A *lamba* is a rectangular length of silk that also serves as "a common form of dress, a marker of social status, and a valued medium of exchange." Reincarnated through the aid of such fabrics, deceased royalty can pronounce on events of current interest, offering prophesy and vital talk in voices that disguise the politics of the living.

The voices, however, are tenuous. The *lamba* wrapping that clothes a spirit and makes it audible is also like a shroud, demanding silence. Drawing attention to the ambiguity of speech and quiet, revelation and concealment, Feeley-Harnik reflects on the relationship of hard to soft objects in other Sakalava rituals. Besides possession, whose episodic occurence mirrors the distribution of individual illnesses, are events of regional significance, staged collectively at the ancestral tomb. In one such event, a kind of reburial, guardians of the cemetery and the royal capital, assisted by spirit mediums, lead the populace in cleaning the tomb, replacing the fence around it, and weeding the grounds. The activities, Feeley-Harnik suggests, establish an analogy between the skeleton and fleshy corpse, the dead body and its shroud, the tomb and its surrounding greenery, the hardwood fencing and its "wrapping" of leafy branches, hard valuables and the soft silk *lambas*—an interplay of concepts suggesting durability and decay.

Whereas in Madagascar the dead demand cloth from the living after they have been buried, possessing them to make their wishes known, elsewhere negotiations of the deceased for cloth precede burial, constituting a focus of the funeral ritual. Patricia Darish's essay (Chapter 4), "Dressing for the Next Life: Raffia Textile Production and Use among the Kuba of Zaire," illustrates this alternative. Considering a corpse to be nude unless adorned with elaborately embroidered raffia textiles, the Kuba make costly prestations to the dead as a way of ensuring their peaceful transition to an afterlife. The dead, they believe, wish to be buried with cloth of sufficient quantity and quality to facilitate a continued existence as social beings. If disappointed in this request, they will interfere malevolently in the lives of the living.

Darish traces the complexity of fulfilling the sartorial demands of the dead in funerary rituals. The members of the deceased's clan section will have collectively prepared raffia cloth over the years; men weave small squares of it, to which women add a plush-pile embroidery and then assemble the squares into larger garments. At a formal meeting during the mortuary celebration, section members decide which of the various cloths wrapped up in the clan treasury are worthy of bestowal, taking note of the past associations of individual pieces of cloth. Finally, close kin of the deceased observe, evaluate, and criticize or praise the textiles placed on the corpse by more distant relatives and friends. Spousal offerings are especially scrutinized for appropriateness of quantity and workmanship, spouses of course being of a different clan. According to Darish, although the Kuba are an otherwise modern people, who have substantially abandoned raffia cloth in favor of Western dress, their funerals continue to highlight the capacity of cloth to mediate between past and present, the dead and the living, ancestral authority and contemporary political claims.

Janet Hoskins' contribution (Chapter 5), "Why Do Ladies Sing the Blues? Indigo Dyeing, Cloth Production, and Gender Symbolism in Kodi," shifts our attention from death and investiture rituals to textile manufacture and the reproduction of children as domains for attending to the meaning of cloth. Living in western Sumba the Kodi, like other rural Indonesians, give pattern to cloth through the resist dyeing of warp yarns prior to weaving them with plain wefts on the backstrap loom. Known as ikatting, the patterning of the yarns is done by specialists, instructed in the manipulation of various earth tones and indigo. Older Kodi women, past their childbearing years and likely practitioners of herbal medicine, midwifery, tatooing and, more covertly, witchcraft, are the ikat dyers. In communication through sacrificial offerings with the ancestral spirit who introduced indigo to Sumba from the nearby island of Savu, these women alone are in a position to manipulate the color blue.

According to Hoskins, Kodi indigo dyeing involves rituals, songs, laments, and sayings that establish an analog with another process of creation: the conception and birth of a child. Cloth, the Kodi reason, is patterned through the "quickening" and "dampening" of dyestuffs in the blueing bath, whereas children are conceived by the "quickening" of men's sperm and fetuses are nurtured by the "dampening" of the mother's blood. Not only are the most respected and powerful women simultaneously midwives and dyers; they make strikingly parallel ritual offerings on behalf of both dyepot and womb. Fittingly, expectant mothers and older female dyers use the same herbs and barks to enhance their respective forms of productivity, while women's laments compare miscarriages to imperfectly dyed cloths.

Analogous to birth and regeneration, Kodi textile dyeing is also vulnerable to the cycle of death and decay. Hoskins records that practitioners associate the unpleasant smell of the dyebath with the putrefaction of rotting flesh, and consider the bath polluting to gestation. Pregnant women should not look at the dye pots, lest the sight of the dark and churning liquid dissolve the contents of their wombs. Reciprocally, menstruating women are kept from the pots, as the flow of their blood is believed to disrupt the dyeing process. The dependence of birth upon death, gain upon loss, creation upon destruction, is acknowledged by the Kodi in other ways: They model their weddings and funerals after each other, using the same indigo-dyed fabrics to wrap both bride and corpse, and associating blue with the sadness of either separation. Visions of blue add symbolic fuel to both birth and the ikatting process, imbuing them with sacred qualities. From this, Hoskins implies, it is but a short step to the belief that cloth enhances fertility and protects humans from harm.

Kodi rituals and proscriptions are reminiscent of peoples elsewhere who, in the process of making cloth, mythically relate the creation of fabrics to the creation of social progeny. Exemplifying the train of thought that makes one set of processes an analog for the other are taboos that exclude menstruating women from weaving as well as dyeing, and forbid sexually active or pregnant women from seeing or handling the loom (e.g., Emmons 1907; Gustafson 1980; Kent 1983; Messick 1987; Rattray 1927). Also common is the tendency for cloth makers to interact with the spirits and divinities of their homelands and their ancestral pasts, hoping thereby to perfect their skills, acquire inspiration for new motifs, and animate their product with a blessing (e.g., Davis 1982; Tedlock and Tedlock 1985). Besides the Kodi dyers, many peoples believe that weaving skills derive from a mythical diety or ancestor, and are transmitted through dreams or revelations (e.g., Aronson 1983; March 1983). By careful attention to ritual and taboos, the weaver not only demonstrates respect for these sacred sources, but also reactivates the spiritual connection, consecrating the raw materials, the techniques, and the emerging cloth (e.g., Best 1898; Mead 1969; Weiner 1985).

Acknowledging sacred associations in the process of cloth manufacture is like acknowledging historical and mythical past events in the process of cloth bestowal and exchange. Both enhance the affective qualities that are lodged in objects of value. Anthropologists have long puzzled over these qualities. In 1922, for example, Malinowski wrote a poignant account of Trobrianders dangling prized *kula* shells over a dying man as if the shells could inspire him with life (1922: 512–13). Perceiving the power in such objects, Marcel Mauss (1954) emphasized that, in the Trobriands, people encoded *kula* shells with highly significant names and past histories. Ultimately, Malinowski (1926) opted for a rational explanation that equated *kula* valuables with the intense interest of customary exchange, but Mauss held to the idea that the affect elicited by the shells indicated a spiritual force. "One gives away what is in reality a part of one's nature and substance, while to receive something is to receive a part of someone's spiritual essence" (1954:10). The papers in Part I of this book support Mauss's view. Examining the domains of succession, gift exchange, and manufacturing, they show how cloth comes to symbolize such fundamental processes of human experience as biological and social reproduction, the transmittal of authority or legitimation of power, and the vulnerability of people and their relationships to illness and death.

PART II: CAPITALISM AND THE MEANINGS OF CLOTH

On reflection, anyone who lives in a large-scale, industrial capitalist society will agree that cloth is far more than a means to profit in the textile and garment industries and a means to status among fashion-conscious consumers. People under capitalism continue to mark sacred and ceremonial moments with banners, hangings, shrouds, and robes that they carefully conserve from year to year and often over generations. They also acknowledge the birth and maturation of children with gifts of clothing or bedding that are chosen to evoke security, if not a protective power, and they marry with trousseaux of lingerie and linens. Nor do the citizens of capitalist societies refrain from collecting treasured fabrics in heirloom chests, as antiques, or in museums, where they gain in value. Granted, many textile treasures grow threadbare under capitalism, abandoned or abused by owners who see no return—either monetary or sentimental—in them. Equally common, however, is the rediscovery of both sorts of value in one's grandmothers' quilts, or in the hand-crafted cloth of formerly colonized peoples. Finally, notwithstanding the spread of capitalism, political and religious elites still depend upon cloth to mobilize human emotions in support of such large-scale institutions as the nation-state. Flags and military uniforms are two powerful examples.

Yet the roles of cloth have also changed under capitalism. A central difference flows from the vastly expanded scope of fashion that capitalist production and merchandizing encourage. Although not new to the Early Modern period of Western European expansion, the hegemony of fashion in that time and place went so far as to marginalize the idea that cloth constitutes a binding tie to authorities and sacred sources of the past. As Roland Barthes has argued (1967), obsolescence and rapid turnover are the essence of the fashion system, with the result that a disproportionate volume of cloth ends up in the ragbag or as hand-me-downs when compared to non-capitalist circulation.

The changing funeral ceremonies of the seventeenth-century English aristocracy might be seen as heralding a related transformation. As they became increasingly expressive of private loss, these funerals no longer allowed kin groups, through spectacular cloth prestations, to channel death into regeneration and political gain. In earlier times, the mourners had received black drapes from the kin of the deceased; now, to accompany the funeral cortege, they had to supply their own. Cloth no longer expressed the continuity of the groups with ancestral authority and their reproduction through time (Gittings 1984).

The three papers that make up Part II highlight a second difference between the meanings of cloth in capitalist and non-capitalist societies. Under capitalism, the domain of cloth manufacture seems incapable of generating or sustaining ideas of benevolent spiritual or ancestral involvement in the production process, or analogies between this process and the reproduction of offspring. Even when, as in each of the papers, manufacturing is organized through home industries and involves considerable handwork—even when, as in two of the papers, factory production has yet to emerge—market pressures to cheapen and streamline labor prevent spinners and weavers, dyers and finishers, from thinking about or ritually acknowledging the transmission of a sacred ancestry through cloth.

From its inception, capitalist manufacture elevated entrepreneurs whose goals emphasized profit to positions of strategic importance. Merchants or merchant-manufacturers procured the raw materials, structured the production process, supplied equipment or credit for equipment, and arranged for eventual marketing and distribution. Above all, they pressured workers so as to reduce the cost of labor in production. Although factories and well-capitalized machinery represent the extreme of pressure on labor, they were not historically or even today the only alternative. Also common is "putting-out." Where the organization of guilds or unions renders labor more costly, entrepreneurs place textile orders with non-organized producers in rural homes. Here, no less than in factories, the impact of the market is felt. Homeworkers typically experience low piece rates, the fragmentation of the production process among different categories of operatives, the introduction of labor-saving machinery, and the employment of women for less remuneration than men (see Goody 1982; Medick 1981; Schlumbohm 1981).

Entrepreneurs are hardly the only non-producers to have controlled production in the course of textile history. Political and religious elites sponsored the specialized workshops of luxury cloth manufacture in the large-scale agrarian civilizations of Asia, Africa, and the Americas. Here, too, spinners, weavers, and dyers depended upon others to procure their raw materials, organize the labor process, supply equipment, and manage distributions. Luxury industries, however, competed with each other less in the domain of cost than in the domain of aesthetic elaboration, and cloth artisans retained control of aesthetic decisions (see Schneider 1987). Indeed, the luxury cloth of centralized workshops characteristically incorporated not only exotic materials but intensive and highly skilled craftsmanship as well.

Capitalist entrepreneurs sometimes organize productive activity in which aesthetic elaboration is a more salient goal than cutting labor costs. In these situations, the aesthetic judgments, skills, and time of the workers are protected, making possible a continuing role for ritual. But capitalism historically has focused on the manufacture of commodities, defined not simply as goods for sale (for luxury cloth was frequently merchandized), but also as "commodious"—useful, advantageous, beneficial. Such goods strike a middle ground between luxury and deprivation, indulgence and necessity and, if inexpensive enough, permit non-elites to enrich their patterns of consumption. Commodities in the form of commodious textiles, produced in cottages under a putting-out system and eventually in factories, illustrate most dramatically the decline of manufacturing as an arena for imbuing cloth with sacred and ancestral referents, relevant for enhancing its social and political symbolism. As Marx observed, under capitalism it is consumers and not producers who make commodities into fetishes, and in ways that have nothing to do with their manufacture.

Jane Schneider's essay (Chapter 6), "Rumpelstiltskin's Bargain: Folklore and the Merchant Capitalist Intensification of Linen Manufacture in Early Modern Europe," captures an initial phase of what might be called the "disenchantment" of cloth manufacture under capitalism. Schneider outlines how a burgeoning transatlantic trade and domestic fashion market gave an unprecedented spur to linen production in Northern Europe in the seventeenth and eighteenth centuries, leading to the formation of rural "proto-industries" as an alternative to the urban guilds. In some of the industries, peasant households performed all stages of manufacture, selling a finished or nearly finished product to itinerant buyers or at regional fairs. More commonly, merchant-entrepreneurs divided the stages of manufacture, putting out raw materials and semifinished goods to different laboring households, remunerating them by the piece. Either way, entrepreneurs manipulated peasant spinners and weavers by offering premiums for extra work, advancing credit and equipment selectively, and promising opportunities for marriage through participation in manufacture. They also employed women at lower piece rates than men.

In addition to tracing how linen entrepreneurs reshaped cottage industry in Early Modern Europe, Schneider examines a changing folklore of flax and linen production. She describes a new tendency for animistic spirits to take on demonic qualities, as exemplified by the Rumpelstiltskin tale in which a poltergeist offers assistance to a poor spinner, but only at the price of her firstborn child. The negative, malevolent message implicit in such a devil-pact contrasts with the previously widespread idea that spirits impart socially binding protective powers to cloth. There is another transformation as well. In the cloth-making contexts of non-capitalist societies such as that described by Hoskins, women's reproduction is often represented as an analog to dyeing or weaving. The Rumpelstiltskin-type tale, by contrast, pits the goals of production against the goals of reproduction, suggesting that they are inherently contradictory rather than related. Schneider speculates on the possible connections between the merchant capitalist intensification of linen production in seventeenth- and eighteenth-century Europe, and the folkloric transformation of spirit helpers into demons, hostile to women's fertility and reproduction. The transformation, she thinks, was part of the process through which cloth manufacturing ceased to be a setting for thinking about, and articulating, the regenerative power of cloth.

Chapter 7 by Linda Stone-Ferrier, "Spun Virtue, the Lacework of Folly, and the World Wound Upside-Down: Seventeenth-Century Dutch Depictions of Female Handwork," looks at a similar transformation from a different angle, that of the seventeenth-century Dutch artists who interpreted linen cloth production in oils and woodcuts. Painting and drawing at a time when Haarlem and other Dutch cities were becoming centers of linen manufacture for the Atlantic economy, these masters frequently included textile motifs in their art, above all images of spinners and winders of yarn. As Stone-Ferrier points out, in real life the Dutch did not support much flax cultivation or spinning, concentrating instead on the more lucrative stages of the manufacturing process, the weaving and especially the bleaching of imported yarn and cloth. The images of spinners in paintings and prints must therefore be read not as depictions of reality, but as a moral commentary on the subjects as their activities became enmeshed in proto-industry.

According to Stone-Ferrier, seventeenth-century Dutch oils portrayed individual spinners and winders, always female, as proper and virtuous, but poked fun at women who indulged in, or produced for, fashion. Thus, embroiderers and lacemakers were made to appear licentious, as was the fashionably dressed woman, painted with a lover under her skirt. Oil paintings of spinning rooms, as distinct from individual spinners, depicted a raucous and sexually promiscuous world in which women, devoid of all reference to their reproductive role, cavorted with demons and dominated men—a newly intrusive element. This theme of unbridled sexuality and devilish play also typified the spinning rooms shown in woodcuts, a cheaper medium of communication than oils. Popular among the expanding ranks of bourgeois consumers, woodcuts portrayed even individual spinners not as virtuous, but in erotic poses. In their overall effect they, even more than the oils, undermined associations between yarn production and the continuous re-creation of a moral order, promoting instead the lewd and antisocial symbolism of a world turned upside-down by pending change.

The final paper of Part II, "Embroidery for Tourists: A Contemporary Putting-Out System in Oaxaca, Mexico," offers an ironic twist on the problem of cloth manufacture as a symbolic domain under capitalism. In this essay (Chapter 8), Ronald Waterbury examines the traditional Zapotec Indian wedding dress, once offered by grooms to their brides but made today for boutique and tourist markets whose buyers live in, or come from, the industrial United States and Europe. Decorated with colorful inserts of hand-embroidered birds and flowers, the dress is laden with sentiment. To the young Oaxacan women who traditionally received it, the embroidery conferred a religious blessing; to many contemporary North American and European consumers, it represents a nostalgia for lost arts, for the people and crafts that industrial capitalism so brutally pushed aside. Yet the present conditions of manufacture, structured through putting-out, allow no opportunity for reflection or action on these meanings. According to Waterbury, peasant women in the poorest outlying areas embroider the designs on swatches for merchant entrepreneurs, who assemble the pieces using sewing machines. Neither the entrepreneurs, for the most part local women, nor the embroiderers, view their labor as imparting a social meaning to the product, understanding it only in relation to its monetary return in profits or piece rates.

Part I considered domains of meaning in small-scale societies, where political actors attempt to legitimatize their power through displays or transfers of cloth believed to embody associations with authoritative persons of the past, and thus with sacred or ancestral sources. We might wonder whether the changes in manufacturing and the hegemony of fashion that accompanied the emergence of capitalism interfered with this legitimating role of cloth in a substantial way. Diane Owen Hughes (personal communication) has observed that the reliance of fashion on cutting and tailoring challenges the idea that continuous weaving transmits a spiritual force. In relatively uncommercialized areas of the world, taboos on cutting cloth still make this point. Some Indonesians, for example, continue to distinguish between cloth for wearing and cloth for bridewealth, the former being cut and sewn, the latter's endless warp representing "the continuous threads of kinship and descent" (Barnes 1983:17). Similarly the Yoruba (Drewal 1979:198) permit the use of tailored and purchased cloth in Ege/Gelede cult performances that emphasize alliance-making, but insist on "tied, bound or wrapped" fabrics for the Egungun cult in which lineage ancestry and solidarity are celebrated.

Characterized by perpetual mutations, rapid obsolescence, and high-velocity turnover, fashion is propelled through the interaction of designers or "tastemakers" and the changing wants of consumers. Not so the cloth that in small-scale societies binds brides to grooms, the living to the dead, ancestors to heirs, the past to the present and future. At times such binding material is of foreign provenance. According to Feeley-Harnik, many of the expensive *lamba* cloths coveted by Sakalava ancestors in possession episodes are imported silk fabrics that arrived long ago through the precolonial trading networks of the Indian Ocean. But as a rule, the ritual manipulation of particular cloths as symbols of continuity and closeness gains power from the realization that, in their making, they absorbed ancestral authority as well as fibers and dyes. The early ethnographer, Rattray, in his 1929 book on the Ashanti, recorded how kings in investiture rites discarded their luxurious royal robes to don bark cloth, the earliest cloth of their people. It seems fair, in other words, to conclude that the breakthrough to capitalism challenged cloth as a medium of political power. It is the overcoming of this challenge that concerns us in Part III.

PART III: CLOTH IN LARGE-SCALE SOCIETIES

Three large-scale, class-stratified societies, all historically in tension with the expanding markets and institutions of Euro-American industrial capitalism, draw our attention in the final part of this book. Each of them—Peru, India, and Japan—boasts a deep past of interacting textile traditions, some at the level of peasant households, others at the level of state. Identifying these interactions, the papers of Part III also examine the still broader processes that were set in motion by the local appearance of commercial and factory cloth. In each case, certain indigenous handmade cloths persisted despite this pressure, or have been revived, not merely to satisfy boutique and tourist markets as in Waterbury's case study of Oaxaca, but as aspects of the consolidation of cultural identities and the mobilization of political power. By detailing the past meanings and values of cloth in societies of the scale of India or Japan, Part III offers insights into these emotionally charged revivals.

Leading off is Chapter 9, John Murra's revision of his 1962 article, "Cloth and Its Function in the Inka State." Facilitating our com-
prehension of large-scale contexts, Murra disaggregates the peasant
and state levels. Woven with "magical precautions," peasant cloth
was the main ceremonial good, the preferred gift for reciprocal exchanges among kin at funerals and weddings, and a seminal offering, sometimes in diminuitive form, to the dead and to religious
idols. Peasant women, the preeminent weavers, also produced a
surplus for the state. Mobilized through the Inka tribute system, the
cloth of Andean peasant populations was piled so high in the royal
warehouses as to stagger the Spanish conquerors. Although destined for many uses, military attire was among the most important,
soliders being rewarded for distinction in battle and made to feel ritually protected through grants of clothes.

In addition to the peasant surplus, the Inka state relied for cloth
on weavers at court and in administrative centers, including the
well-known cloistered women called *aqlla*. These specialists were the
source of exquisitely fine tapestries, woven from a mixture of cotton
and wool and dyed in many colors. Coveted as items of diplomacy
and foreign exchange, tapestries could not be worn or displayed in
the absence of royal approval, while kings offered them to attract
the loyalty of lords in newly incorporated peripheries. Most valued
for this overtly political purpose were cloths from the royal wardrobe, steeped with associations of past rulers and deeds. An "initial
pump primer of dependency," suggests Murra, cloth of this sort
was hoarded and treasured by the lords of the provinces for four
or more generations, symbolizing at once their obligations to Cuzco,
and Cuzco's bestowal of citizenship in return. Even today, Murra
notes, peasants of the Andean highlands celebrate ancestral tapestries as the standard for beauty and value—a value emphasized by
the pirated dispersal of many ancient weavings into the art markets
of the industrialized world.

In Chapter 10, "Cloth, Clothes, and Colonialism: India in the
Nineteenth Century," Bernard S. Cohn notes a parallel between the
uses of cloth at the state and the domestic levels. Indian village families and the Mughal court both stored gifts of cloth as "emblems
of honor for posterity," letting them mark the events of history and
the cycles of life over several generations. In both rural households
and the royal palace, trunks and chests conserved the textile tracers
of bygone social and political relations. Even more varied than in

the Inka state was the production of cloth at different levels, with specialized industries responsible for renowned traditions in wool, silk, sheer, and painted cotton. Peasant manufacture articulated women's household spinning with the weaving castes. As among the Inka, the Mughal court thrived on cloth accumulated from distant producers, whether as tribute or through markets. According to Cohn, Akbar stockpiled a collection from Indian, European, and other Asian sources, classifying the multitude of textiles in his midst by their weight, color, and day of arrival at court.

Focusing on the nineteenth century, Cohn's paper highlights the misunderstandings that ensued from British rule. As in the small-scale societies analyzed in Part I of this book, the Mughals believed that their garments, handed down through a continuous succession of donors and receivers, served as a medium for the transfer of essential substances, thus constituting political authority, the unity of rule. When British colonial overlords, culturally prepared to anticipate contracts, treated gifts of cloth as bribes, the Mughals were offended. Nor was this the biggest disjuncture. The various constituencies of the Indian population had to negotiate between three conflicting pressures regarding dress. These were their own rules of propriety in relation to social rank, the hegemonic British presence that tempted some to enter the fashion system of Westerners, and the contradictory and changing body of British sumptuary requirements governing what Indians should and should not wear. Although the British disdained "Oriental" clothing, they recognized its capacity to demarcate hierarchically ordered social statuses and, according to Cohn, encouraged its perpetuation, "Orientalizing" the ruled. An especially striking manifestation of this tendency was the turban that the Sikh regiment was urged to adopt as an "Oriental" symbol of military prowess, covering yet harnessing the fierceness of uncut hair.

Complementing Cohn's essay is Susan Bean's Chapter 11, titled "Gandhi and *Khadi*, the Fabric of Indian Independence," in which we follow Gandhi as he arrived at homespun cotton cloth and the peasant woman's spinning wheel as the central, unifying symbols of the national struggle for liberation from British rule. By the late 1880s, Manchester cottons had penetrated much of India, creating a severe trade deficit and artisan unemployment (Bayle 1986:307–09,212). Gandhi's campaign for the renewed production and use in dress of a handspun and handwoven textile is testimony to the potentiality of cloth to unify large-scale societies. Not only did *khadi* displace the trousers, hats, shoes, and tailored coats that English manufacturers were dumping, along with machine-loomed fabrics, on Indian markets; it also challenged British rule and its arrogant imposition of sumptuary codes. Most important, through its ascetic imagery and identification with the poor, *khadi* dissolved the boundaries that divided Indian society. Distinctions of region, religion, gender, and rank were overcome by a simple and colorless textile as Gandhi, the renouncer, summoned up the oldest and most humble traditions of the subcontinent.

In the final essay of this book, "The Changing Fortunes of Three Archaic Japanese Textiles," Louise Cort analyzes rustic and ancient fabrics made from the long fibers of mulberry, *kuzu* vine, and thread-banana leaf. Difficult to collect and necessitating a lengthy soaking, rotting, boiling, and beating process to render them pliable for weaving, these fibers long ago surrendered to the cultivated "grass basts" like ramie and flax, in turn superseded by cotton and, in the famous urban workshops, by silk. Notwithstanding their lowly position in this evolving textile hierarchy, the long-vegetable fibers survived in two "extreme situations,"—in Japan's poorest, most remote regions and as the preferred cloth for sacred state rituals, above all the installation of new emperors. An expression of the "ancient core of Japanese culture," according to Cort, the cloths of rough, uncultivated fibers entered court circles through a process reciprocal to that of royal bestowals. Historically, an expanding Japanese Empire incorporated them as it subdued their producers, seeking not only tribute but a unity of disparate cultural elements in the interest of pacification.

Examining the three "rough" or "thick" cloths of peripheral Japan, Cort addresses themes important to the earlier chapters of this book: The centrality of cloth to gift exchange at marriage and death, the beliefs in its affective, spiritual powers—its capacity to bless and protect—and its evocation of continuities, however fragile, with the past. As a political center of gravity for the Ryukyu island chain, Okinawa even elevated banana leaf cloth to be a courtly textile. Only after the Japanese takeover in the seventeenth century did silk displace this fabric, reducing it to the role of an export to Japan. "Thick" brown cloth of mulberry fiber, woven in the remote mountains of Japan's main island, had long since undergone a parallel transformation, becoming a ritual mainstay of the imperial court.

Like the Ashanti ruler donning bark cloth for ancestral rites, like Gandhi adopting *khadi* in the struggle for Independence, the emperors of Japan forwent their fine silks on occasions of death and investiture, seeking legitimacy from a master symbol of "neolithic" ancestral ties.

Cort's account spans new uses of rustic cloth under modern conditions. Already in the late nineteenth century, mulberry textiles ceased to be used for clothing and ritual purposes. Instead, poor women manufactured food and storage bags from this sturdy material, selling their output for cash. More recently still, an urban movement of craft revival has defined mulberry as a fiber of choice for studio weavers. Comparable but different is cloth of the banana-leaf fiber, promoted today by an Okinawan folk-art movement seeking to establish a cultural identity for the Ryukyu islands independent of Japan—and in competition with the Japanese government's claim that this cloth belongs to the "Living National Treasure." In these and related examples, we see the whole range of cloth symbolism in a complex society, from its ancient beginnings to its myriad uses in rituals of continuity and legitimation, to its mobilization for tribute and, despite the competition of fashion and factory, its contested retention as an anchoring point, a link to real and imagined roots of the past.

CLOTH AND GENDER

The division of labor between men and women in cloth manufacture and distribution, and the assignment of gender symbolism to cloth, emerge as issues in virtually all of the papers in this book. These papers leave us with the impression that, in many societies, cloth is more closely connected with women than with men. As a warning against universalizing this impression, but also as a way to consider its implications, we conclude with a discussion of gender and cloth.

To analyze the gender relations of cloth production, it is essential to acknowledge the multiplicity of steps involved in the manufacture of most fabrics, from the harvesting or collecting of fibers, to soaking, drying, softening, cleaning, and spinning them, to their reconstitution through weaving and their further elaboration through dyeing, bleaching, embroidery, appliqué, and so on. In many cloth traditions, especially those where textiles are associated with ancestral histories, production demands not only technical and artistic skills, but rigorous attention to ritual as well. Men and women may take on some of these tasks in complement to each other, each participating in different stages of the production process, or the preponderance of technical, artistic, and ritual tasks may fall to one gender, excluding the other.

The ethnographic record includes many social groups in which cloth is manufactured wholly or largely by men. In much of Africa, men rather than women, or men as well as women, work at the looms. Among the Lele of Central Africa, women are responsible for food cultivation, leaving men to weave the fine raffia textiles so important to the politics of acquiring wives, settling disputes, and participating in exchange (Douglas 1965:197; 1967). As Darish's paper (this volume) shows, neighbors of the Lele, the Kuba, also assign men to the weaving of raffia, although women add the plush-pile embroidery that gives the material its aesthetic form. In the characteristic "men's" cloths of West Africa, men brocade imported silk or woolen yarn into their weavings but rely on women to spin for the cotton ground. Historically, among the Pueblo Indians, men spun as well as wove and embroidered, all of these activities taking place in the male ritual center, the *kiva*. The weavers and dyers of many urban or courtly textile traditions in large-scale societies were also men. Nevertheless, on a world scale and over several centuries, women have played a larger role than men in cloth production.

It does not necessarily follow that the producers of cloth are the controllers of its distribution. In the Lele case, where men do all of the weaving, women control some raffia exchanges as recipients of especially fine pieces (Douglas 1967:107–09). Yet women's role in production often gives them a larger say in distribution than one might expect. In Samoa, as Weiner (this volume) reports, it was more common for men than for women to hold the highest-ranking titles—but as producers of important textiles, women influenced decisions about bestowals regardless of their rank. Elsewhere, women not only make cloth but also preside over its allocation at major rituals of death and regeneration, marriage and the establishment of new families, investiture and the transmission of ancestral authority.

The predominance of women in cloth production and distribution in many parts of the world is linked to the widespread symbolic systems in which cloth evokes female power. The Kodi of western

Sumba typify this pattern. As Hoskins (this volume) shows, although Kodi women do not participate directly in men's political affairs, their role as skilled dyers renders them fearful, even polluting, to men and gives them command of their own destinies. Like people throughout Indonesia and much of Southeast Asia, they also adhere to symbolic categories that identify cloth with women and "hard" wealth, above all metal, with men. Each set of objects acquires gender-associated values that relate to sexuality, kinship, marriage alliances, and politics.

Upon a Kodi marriage, the groom's kin present gold ornaments along with buffalo and horses to the bride's family, while the kin of the bride give pigs and cloth to the relatives of the groom. Reinforcing the binary code of male and female oppositions are permutations internal to each category. Motifs on Kodi marriage cloths depict the wife-takers' bridewealth offerings, for example buffalos' eyes and horses' tails, while the gold ornaments that grooms offer resemble female genitalia. Both signify the loss of a daughter to her natal lineage and the transfer of her sexuality to her husband's group, a separation that Kodi women compare to death. Yet, according to Hoskins, the secrets of indigo dyeing redress women's subjugation after marriage. Indeed, one finds married women adorning themselves in beautiful ikats as a warning to their in-laws that outstanding bridewealth debts must still be paid.

The Kodi elaboration of a symbolic opposition between cloth and metal, related to each other as "women are to men" and differentially produced by each gender, has parallels among the Iban of Borneo, whose myths juxtapose textiles to sacred traditions of headhunting. "Even in this century," writes Gittinger, "no man's prowess was confirmed until he had taken the head of an enemy, and no woman was fully recognized until she had woven a *pua*" (an elaborate ikat blanket). During the preparation of mordants for the ikat dyeing of yarns, Iban women, like the Kodi, observe the same taboos as those imposed for childbirth and, comparing the laying out of warps for the loom with the taking of heads, call this activity "the warpath of women" (Gittinger 1979:218–19).

Other Southeast Asian symbolic systems balance cloth against writing—the textile and the text. Among the Temang in Nepal (March 1983), women make cloth for bridewealth and funerals, and are depicted as the horizontal weft threads of the loom in contrast to men, symbolized by the vertical warp threads. Whereas the men's texts record the divine oaths that give continuity to ancestral lineages, exchanges of women's cloth at marriage bind the disruptive breaks in lineage solidarity. The contrast extends to an association of men with the right hand, women with the left and, in a mythic past, men with hunting and women with the loom (March 1983; see also Lefferts 1983; Messick 1987).

In societies where women are the main producers of cloth and control its distribution at marriage and death, their contribution to social and political life is considerable. Unfortunately, as Weiner details for one famous instance, ethnographers often overlook this possibility, whether from a disinterest in women's activities, or in fibers and fabrics (as distinct from food), or both. The famous instance is that of Malinowski, whose field research in the Trobriand Islands began in 1915 and led to publications that subsequently influenced theories of "primitive" exchange (notably Firth 1967; Lévi-Strauss 1969; Polanyi 1944; Sahlins 1972). The Trobriand wealth that formed the basis for Malinowski's discussions was produced and exchanged by men. Women's wealth, in the form of banana-leaf bundles and skirts, was obscured by men's production of yams, aesthetically displayed at harvest, and by the shells that men circulated in *kula* exchanges.

As Weiner (1976) asked, would Malinowski have ignored banana-leaf wealth if men had produced it? He did photograph women distributing this "cloth" and in his fieldnotes recorded the Kiriwina term for it as well as its role at death. Yet he overlooked its economic and ritual importance in relation to men's wealth, missing how women leveled the wealth of men (Weiner, this volume). Obligated to contribute to their sisters' accumulations for mortuary payments, men were constrained in the accumulation of "male" wealth, hence in their ability to create and sustain political alliances. Taking a comparative view of the differences between chieftaincy in Melanesia and Polynesia, Weiner (this volume) points out that as political hierarchies gained support from cloth wealth in Polynesian societies, some women achieved political prominence equal to that of men.

What about political formations that transcend chieftaincy, integrating or attempting to integrate a large-scale class society? The cases of Japan, India, and Inka Peru presented in this book are suggestive. In each instance, locally produced cloth, in addition to being the substance of kinship, became a basis for tribute or taxation and an element to be stored in dynastic treasuries. Although women produced this cloth in the Andes and the mountainous peripheries of Japan, in India they often spun for male weavers. In all three societies, courtly and urban textile traditions made use of male artisans, for example the weavers of silk in Japan or the Inka weavers of feathered cloth. Highly skilled female specialists could also play a role in urban or court workshops, however, the cloistered *aqlla* of the Inka state being an outstanding example.

Perhaps the most important conclusion to be drawn from the large-scale societies introduced in this book concerns women's continued affinity for the sacred values that local and rural people historically invested in cloth. These values, derived from concerns about continuity with the past and about transcending the disjunctures of death and marriage, were appropriated, distorted, and at times suppressed as classes and states emerged. Yet they did not go away. Revived during struggles for independence against impinging colonial powers, both the values and the women associated with them enjoyed an elevation of status, at least temporarily. The independence movement of Okinawans against Japanese hegemony (Cort, this volume), and of India against British rule (Bean, this volume), symbolically characterized both women and their role in cloth production as mainstays of the claim to an authentic past and a politically autonomous future.

It is against this backdrop that one might consider the impact on gender of capitalist production and culture. As suggested by the papers in this volume, market pressures to reduce labor costs made women vulnerable to loss of recognition for their contribution to textile wealth. Heavily recruited into the cottage industries of early modern Europe and subsequently into factories, female spinners and weavers were systematically paid at lower piece rates or wages than men. In Europe and perhaps elsewhere, these developments coincided with ideological changes such as those detailed by Stone-Ferrier and Schneider, in which women's manufacturing roles, earlier linked to sexual continence and domestic virtue, were increasingly portrayed as lascivious, demonic, at odds with reproduction. In contrast, the Kodi dyers, although guardians of industrial secrets considered polluting and possessors of such occult powers as witchcraft, command attention; some of these women become priests and even important leaders.

Women's involvement with cloth production exposes in complex ways the complementarity, the domination, and the subversive tactics that together comprise gender relations, forcing us to rethink women's roles in kinship, economic, and political domains. The sacred qualities historically associated with cloth express sexuality as they also transmit notions of biological and social reproductive capabilities, all attributes associated with women. As a master symbol proclaiming the legitimacy of ancestors and succession, the cloth that circulates at births, marriages, and deaths establishes obligations and legitimacy. Such cloth gives women a measure of economic autonomy and even, in some cases, political authority. From these cloth-related perspectives, the analytical categories used to define oppositions between women and men, such as domestic versus public and nature versus culture, are simplistic and inadequate.

CONCLUSION

Perhaps there is a kind of *hubris* in picking up threads from societies so separated in time and space and drawing them together into a meaningful portrayal of the social and political implications of producing and controlling cloth. But the analytical and historical perspectives represented in this book are, by their variety, a powerful testimony to the role of cloth in social transformation. In Part I we saw how, despite the presence of national currencies in societies such as those of Oceania, traditional cloth wealth not only remains an integral part of social and political life, but the continual demand for its presence also integrates its economic value with each nation's inflationary trends. In areas of Madagascar, imported silk textiles, replacing traditional ones, mediate death and relations with ancestors while also constituting symbols of national political importance. Even when vast public displays of cloth are subsequently buried with the dead, as among the Kuba, the continuation of these ancient rituals can subvert the local chiefly ranking system, drawing attention to an economy of equality that levels wealth in contradiction to the hierarchy of regional nobles and chiefs. The attribution to cloth of such a range of symbolic and economic roles reflects more than the labor invested in its production; the connections of its threads and weaving patterns with ancestral or mythical knowledge ultimately make it a political vehicle for transmitting legitimacy, authority, and obligation.

Like language, cloth in its communicative aspect can be used to coerce. In Parts II and III, we see this coercion in situations of complex, socially stratified, capitalist and colonial societies. Whether we view the merchant capitalist cloth manufacturing in early modern Europe or the contemporary Mexican putting-out system, meanings in cloth and the gender division of labor were transformed by those in dominant positions. One society's representations of cloth were misread and misused by another, as the British colonial rule in India so incisively demonstrates. Yet, especially in the examples from India and Japan, we see the political power to be gained through the possession of cloth that symbolizes a sacred past. Cloth as an expression of "keeping while giving" does not articulate the ranking and hierarchy among groups and their chiefs only in small-scale societies. These same principles emerge in different times and places as rallying points for national legitimization. Valued as currency, shroud, ancestor, royalty, or fashion, cloth represents the key dilemmas of social and political life: How to bring the past actively into the present. Ultimately, the opposing properties of cloth—its inalienability and its fragilty—exemplify these universal needs and their contradictions.

REFERENCES CITED

Aronson, Lisa
    1983   Legends, History and Identity Among Akwete Weavers.
            Wenner-Gren Conference, Cloth and Human Experience.

Barnes, Ruth
    1983   Cloth in Lamalera, Indonesia and the Adoption of Patola Patterns. Wenner-Gren Conference, Cloth and Human Experience.

Barthes, Roland
    1967   Système de la Mode. Paris: Seuil.

Bayle, C.A.
    1986   The Origins of Swadeshi (Home Industry): Cloth and Indian Society. In The Social Life of Things. A. Appadurai, ed. Cambridge: Cambridge University Press.

Best, Elsdon
1898　The Art of the Whare Pora: Clothing of the Ancient Maori.
Transactions of the New Zealand Institute 31:625–58.

Bloch, Maurice
1971　Placing the Dead: Tombs, Ancestral Villages, and Kinship Organization in Madagascar. London: Seminar Press.

Clark, Graham
1986　Symbols of Excellence. Cambridge: Cambridge University Press.

Davis, Natalie Zemon
1982　Women in the Crafts in Sixteenth-Century Lyons. Feminist Studies 8:47–80.

Douglas, Mary
1965　The Lele Resistance to Change. *In* Markets in Africa.
P. Bohannan and G. Dalton, eds. New York: Anchor Books.
1967　Raffia Cloth Distribution in the Lele Economy. *In* Tribal and Peasant Economies: Readings in Economic Anthropology. G. Dalton, ed. New York: American Museum of Natural History Press.

Drewel, H.J.
1979　Pagentry and Power in Yoruba Costuming. *In* From the Fabrics of Culture. The Anthropology of Clothing and Adornment. J.M. Corwell and R.A. Schwartz, eds. the Hague: Mouton.

Emmons, G.T.
1907　The Chilkat Blanket. Memoirs of the American Museum of Natural History, Vol. III:329–409.

Firth, Raymond
1967　Introduction. *In* Themes in Economic Anthropology. R.Firth, ed. ASA Monograph No. 6. London: Tavistock.

Gittinger, Mattiebelle
1979　Splendid Symbols: Textiles and Tradition in Indonesia. Washington, D.C.: The Textile Museum.

Gittings, C.
1984　Death, Burial and the Individual in Early Modern England. London: Croom Helm.

Goody, Esther N.
1982　Introduction. *In* From Craft to Industry. The Ethnography of Proto-Industrial Cloth Production. E.N. Goody, ed. Cambridge: Cambridge University Press.

Gustafson, Paula
1980　Salish Weaving. Vancouver: Douglas and McIntyre.

Heine-Geldern, R.
1956　Conceptions of State and Kingship in Southeast Asia. Data Paper #18. Ithaca: University of Cornell, Southeast Asia Program.

Henry, Tevira
  1928   Ancient Tahiti. Honolulu: Bernice P. Bishop Museum Bulletin 48.

Kent, Kate Peck
  1983   Pueblo Indian Textiles: A Living Tradition. Albuquerque: University of New Mexico Press.

Kooijman, Simon
  1972   Tapa In Polynesia. Honolulu: Bernice P. Bishop Museum Bulletin 234.

Lefferts, Leedon H., Jr.
  1983   Textiles, Buddhism, and Society in Northeast Thailand. Wenner-Gren Conference, Cloth and Human Experience.

Lévi-Strauss, Claude
  1969   The Elementary Structures of Kinship. Boston: Beacon Press.

Malinowski, Bronislaw
  1922   Argonauts of the Western Pacific. London: Routledge & Kegan Paul.
  1926   Crime and Custom in Savage Society. New York: International Library of Psychology, Philosophy, and Scientific Method. [Patterson: Littlefield, Adams. 1962]

March, Katherine
  1983   Weaving, Writing, and Gender. Man (n.s.) 18:729–44.

Mauss, Marcel
  1954   The Gift. Ian Cunnison, transl. Glencoe,Il: Free Press.

Mead, Sidney M.
  1969   Traditional Maori Clothing. Wellington: A.H. & A.W. Reed.

Medick Hans
  1981   The Proto-Industrial Family Economy. In Industrialization Before Industrialization. P.Kriedte, H. Medick, and J. Schlumbohm, eds. Cambridge: Cambridge University Press.

Messick, Brinkley
  1987   Subordinate Discourse: Women, Weaving and Gender Relations in North Africa. American Ethnologist 14:210–26.

Murra, John V.
  1962   Cloth and Its Function in the Inca State. American Anthropologist 64:710–28.

Nin, Anaîs
  1959   Ladders to Fire. Chicago: Swallow Press.

Polyani, Karl
  1944   The Great Transformation. New York: Rinehart.

Rattray, R.S.
  1927   Religion and Art in Ashanti. London: Oxford University Press.

Sahlins, Marshall
  1972   Stone Age Economics. Chicago: Aldine.

Schlumbohm, Jürgen
  1981   Relations of Production—Productive Forces—Crises in Proto-
          Industrialization. *In* Industrialization Before Industrialization.
          P.Kriedte, H. Medick, and J. Schlumbohm, eds. Cambridge:
          Cambridge University Press.

Schneider, Jane
  1987   The Anthropology of Cloth. Annual Review of Anthropology
          16:409–48.

Tedlock, Barbara and Dennis Tedlock
  1985   Text and Textile: Language and Technology in the Art of the
          Quiché Maya. Journal of Anthropological Research 41:121–47.

Valeri, Valerio
  1985   Kingship and Sacrifice: Ritual and Society in Ancient Hawaii.
          Chicago: University of Chicago Press.

Weiner, Annette B.
  1976   Women of Value, Men of Renown: New Perspectives on Trobri-
          and Exchange. Austin: University of Texas Press.
  1985   Inalienable Wealth. American Ethnologist 12(2): 210–27.

PART I. *Cloth in Small-Scale Societies*

2. Why Cloth?

Wealth, Gender, and Power in Oceania

ANNETTE B. WEINER

 Poets long ago recognized the power of cloth to symbolize the binding together of social relations. Spinning and weaving form a major theme in Homer's epics, as human destinies are expressed through the threads which gods or fates bind around a person at birth. Poignantly, we remember Penelope weaving Laertes's shroud by day but unraveling her work each night to halt time so she would not be forced to choose a waiting suitor. Hesiod gave women the following advice: "Weave closely; make good cloth, with many woof-threads in a short length of warp." According to the classics scholar Onians (1951:325–26), these references are not metaphoric; they represent explicit imperatives for all manner of fastenings and constructions that sustain the social and cosmological order. Hesiod's advice is echoed in many other societies, past and present. The Tongans of Western Polynesia say that "Humankind is like a mat being woven."[1] This is not only a metaphor for social relations; it is as literal a directive about the nature and complexity of the Tongan social and cosmological order as any expressed in ancient Greece.

In this essay, I take such prescriptions about cloth seriously and analyze cloth as the agent through which kinship identities are translated into political authority. My purpose is to demonstrate that in South Pacific societies with ranked lineages, titles, and chiefs, cloth serves as a major source of wealth and underwrites the political hierarchy. I explore the social and historical conditions in which cloth circulates as wealth in two such societies: the Trobriand Islands of Papua New Guinea and the Samoan Islands of Western Polynesia. Although Samoa and the Trobriands are not the only societies in Oceania where forms of cloth wealth play a central role, they are the societies that I know best through my field research.[2] Because they represent different levels of political organization, they make excellent benchmarks for examining the relation between cloth, rank, and hierarchy in Oceania. Although I take my examples from this part of the world, I believe these relationships have global importance. In general terms, I pursue the issues raised by John Murra (1962; this volume) in his analysis of the significance of Andean cloth production to the rise of Inka civilization. To illustrate my premise that cloth wealth plays a central role in the evolution of political hierarchy,[3] I examine the indigenous understandings about the properties and powers attributed to cloth.

Unlike most Melanesian societies, the Trobriands have a political system in which certain matrilineages are ranked higher than others and where chiefs, by right of birth, are members of such ranking lineages.

In Samoa, too, the rankings of chiefly titles are associated with specific descent groups, but individual access to titles is not necessarily a birthright. Samoan descent groups and the political order differ considerably from those of the Trobriands and these differences are reflected in the cultural and material properties of cloth wealth. By examining cloth wealth as the expression of these differences, I also point out important similarities, establishing a gradient rather than an analytical separation between ranked societies in Melanesia and Polynesia.

For Samoans, as several of my informants told me, fine mats made from pandanus fibers are "more important to us than your gold."[4] The finest of these mats are so delicately plaited that they are soft and pliable as fine linen. "Cloth" of a totally different style is found in the Trobriands, where bundles of banana leaves and women's fibrous skirts are distributed following a person's death. Their importance is apparent; according to an informant, they "show where you belong."

Although mats, bundles and skirts have not been thought of as "cloth," they can and should be analyzed within this category. The technologies of preparing fibers and then plaiting, tying, and binding them together in standardized ways are similar in kind, if not in degree, to weaving. Once we recognize strips of dried leaves as cloth wealth, we find that Oceanic societies with cloth traditions value such wealth not only as a form of currency, but also as a major exchange object, presented to others at births, marriages, deaths, and the inauguration of chiefs. Yet this wealth cannot be understood in all its dynamic properties if it is regarded only as an object eliciting reciprocal returns, for in its circulation it is never a neutral counter.

For example, in Samoa and the Trobriands, women are the producers of cloth wealth and they control its distribution in part or in full.[5] Because the circulation of cloth wealth has political consequences and because women figure in the public aspects of its distribution, cloth and women are an inherent part of political affairs. But though cloth wealth expresses ongoing political actions, such events are rooted in kinship relations, especially between sisters and brothers.[6] While the incest taboo separates a brother and his sister sexually, their relationship remains economically and politically central even after they marry, so that their reproductive potentials are not lost to their natal group. The roots and the importance of this relationship are expressed in major cloth transactions. These efforts to maintain relationships with sisters are reflected in the way some valued cloths are kept rather than given to others.

When an object such as cloth lasts for generations and is identified with the same lineage or descent group, it becomes a treasure that is kept rather than given away. In this sense it becomes inalienable, hidden away and protected from circulation. Even when the treasured cloth must be given to others on loan, or is lost in warfare or some other form of political default, the idea that it should be kept as "the capital stock of substance belonging to a family" (Granet 1975:89), makes keeping the primary locus of value. To keep objects rather than give them to others strengthens an individual's or a group's integrity, but it seriously reduces the value associated with circulation, such as gains in economic and political currency. Conversely, to give and not keep destroys the regenerative potential that brings the force of ancestors, mythological beginnings, and complex genealogies into present concerns. Thus, cloth is not only the means through which rank and hierarchy are expressed in these societies; it also communicates in powerful ways the constraints and limitations on how these relations are regenerated and transformed through time.

Other perceptions about cloth's sacredness add even further to its critical political role. In his classic essay on "value" in Greek myth, Louis Gernet (1981) observed that the legends surrounding precious objects "originate more or less directly in the thematic of magical kingship . . . the well-spring . . . of the different aspects of authority" (p. 144). It is here that we see how deeply the cosmological realm is tied to the economic, as the most sacred cloths are associated with mythical or ancestral events, located in a domain outside daily life. In varying degrees immortal, these ancestors are endowed with an authority that the members of the society respect or hold in awe. Valued cloths demonstrate that their owners have rights to the power of this past and thus they convey authority that is greater than that of the owners themselves. In its association with the past, cloth brings the external, the immortal, into everyday life.[7]

This cosmological connection possessed by certain cloths makes these objects a focal point for this study. How to keep-while-giving is as difficult a societal problem as how death can be transcended or how rank can be preserved. The same problem is reflected in kinship relations, where sisters marry, yet still remain attached to their brothers in important ways. Understanding how societies cope with these never-ending problems of social, political, and cosmological loss, how they attempt to transcend time, to gain permanence when nothing is permanent, to keep sisters and to create treasures, gives us a vital analytical perspective. And this perspective enables us to conjoin categories usually thought of as opposed, such as the material and the ideal, infrastructure and superstructure, the ceremonial and the utilitarian. We can see the political world clearly without losing sight of its cosmological referents, or see the economic necessities amid their context of kinship and gender relationships. Consequently, this perspective enables us to map out and compare how cloth wealth provides the underpinnings of political authority and how this affects the social and political relations between women and men.

To pursue these points I focus closely on significant ethnographic details of the production, exchange, and control of cloth wealth, as these events intersect with gender relations that have political consequences. I begin with a discussion of Trobriand and Samoan kinship from the perspective of the relations between a brother and his sister. Although channeled by the incest taboo and the rules of marrying "out," their combined relationships are central to each others' political successes. In both societies, women as sisters draw on cosmological connections that infuse positions of rank with stability and ultimately, power. Yet at the same time, their actions illuminate the vulnerability of such power for women and men. In structuralist analyses, Polynesian women are often described as playing ambiguous roles, such as symbolizing both fertility and pollution (cf. Sahlins 1985; Shore 1981; Valeri 1985). Unfortunately, these views ignore the ways in which women's roles limit men's power and also give rise to their own political and economic authority.

Because women and cloth form the nexus for this authority, my second section describes the processes of cloth production for both societies, to show how the material objects themselves take on meanings that make them expressions of a range of political alignments. The material properties of cloth, such as its soft yet durable texture and the complexity of its manufacture, illustrate how Samoan fine mats and Trobriand banana-leaf bundles operate as indicators of the level of rank that can be sustained in each society. In the third section, I compare the way differences in the brother-sister relationship enable Samoan women as well as men to achieve power in public politics, in contrast to the Trobriand situation where women's power, also gained through their control over cloth wealth, ultimately undercuts men's power in day-to-day political and economic competition. After presenting these two ethnographic examples, I consider the implications of cloth wealth as an object whose circulation indicates how rank can be meaningfully compared.

WOMEN AND THEIR BROTHERS: THE TROBRIAND SOLUTION

In Samoa and the Trobriands, the social bond between women and their brothers is extremely strong. Although affinity is important, it is made more complex by the vital and never-ending associations and demands within the natal group. For Lévi-Strauss (1969: 12–25), the prohibition of incest was the rule that created the separation between a woman and her brother, thereby establishing a new order of things. Yet in this new order, Lévi-Strauss perceived women's reproductive power as sexual and biological only. The rule of incest was to be understood through the fact that women leaving their brothers, physically and sexually, lost any reproductive role within their own descent or kinship group. The role of women in society became like the role of many objects: to move between men. If, however, we consider the incest prohibition between women and their brothers from the perspective of keeping-while-giving, we find that the incest taboo transforms sexuality into a reproductive force that is expressed in the production of women's wealth. In many societies, even though women marry outside their natal group, their presence and power within it remain essential, tying men's productive work to that of their sisters. Elsewhere I have shown (Weiner 1982) that even in a society where descent is reckoned patrilineally, the significance of sisters to the regeneration of their own patrilineage is critical to the stability of men's sacred rituals.

In the Trobriands, although the incest prohibition between a woman and her brother separates them as sexual partners, the lifelong relationship between them demonstrates the strength of their natal matrilineage—that is, the brother's group. Through their own economic endeavors, and through the processes of giving and transmitting resources to their respective children, brother and sister maintain their natal matrilineage as a forceful social and political presence. For example, when a woman gives things of importance to her brothers' children (see Weiner 1976:133), she is helping to strengthen the lifelong associations and to encourage contributions of those children in their work for her (and her brother's) matrilineage.

The role of women as sisters enters even more profoundly into the reproduction of the matrilineage. Biological reproduction is perceived through a complex set of beliefs that collapse the distinctions we make between biological fact and cultural assumption. After death, a person's spirit continues its existence on an island close enough to the Trobriands to be within sight of Kiriwina, the largest Trobriand Island.[8] At some undesignated time, the spirit is transformed into a spirit child. In this state, it returns to the Trobriands to enter a woman's body, causing conception. Traditional Trobriand belief assumes that the combination of a woman's blood and this ancestral spirit transmits to the infant full identity in its mother's matrilineage and matriclan, and full inheritable rights to the property of its mother's matrilineage.

Although a man's children are not identified through birthright with his matrilineage, he attends to them and lends them things so that from birth, they begin to build up obligations to him and the other members of his matrilineage. Trobrianders claim that a woman's husband plays no part in conception, but they believe that he contributes to the growth of the fetus through repeated sexual intercourse. After the birth of his child, a father continues to provide for its growth by giving the child things from his own matrilineage, such as an ancestral name, decorations, food, and later, use rights to land. Men as fathers take things from their own matrilineage and give them to their children, expanding the potential resources for their children while temporarily depleting the resources of their own matrilineage. But when children become adults they, in turn, support their fathers in economic ways that directly benefit their father and the members of his matrilineage. Through successive generations, those things once given as loans are returned to the members of the father's matrilineage.

Because of these loans, complex sets of exchanges that take place throughout each person's life occur as one's potential for the use of property and access to wealth is augmented by others who are members of different lineages. One's father makes the first effort at these expanding possibilities, followed by one's father's sister, and later one's spouse (see Weiner 1976:123–27; 1988a:51–64 for details). The vast numbers of exchanges made by a person's matrilineage when she or he dies are directed toward the replacement of all that has been given by members of other matrilineages to the dead person during her or his life (see Weiner 1980). During the person's life, she or he had rights to the use of matrilineal properties such as land, ancestral names, and body decorations from the father's matrilineage. Through mortuary exchanges, these properties are incorporated back into the original matrilineage. Although through time, some property may be lost to others, this process of replacement generally makes certain property inalienable within the matrilineage.

Bundles of dried banana leaves and women's fibrous skirts secure the return of some inalienable property, such as lineage (ancestral) names. But even more importantly, this wealth is used by women as sisters in a major distribution each time someone in their natal matrilineage dies. In this one distribution, they disperse thousands of bundles (in total equivalent to several hundred dollars or more) to members of other matrilineages who gave things of value to the dead person during his or her life. In this way, women as sisters expose and reclaim for their own matrilineage all that went into making the dead person more than she or he was at conception. From a societal perspective, these distributions reinforce the relations created through marriages between one matriclan and another, even as they regenerate the purity of matrilineal identity.

In the beliefs associated with conception and in the exchange events at a death, women stand as the controllers of matrilineal identity, in two ways claiming for their brothers and themselves the autonomy and authority of matrilineal regeneration. First, the incest taboo is circumvented by the continued reproductive support a woman gives to her own natal lineage. Incest itself, however, is not totally subverted for it is the ancestral *baloma* spirit that is thought to impregnate a woman. Villagers believe that the spirit child that enters a woman's body has come from a deceased male ancestor of the women's matrilineage, even though its specific identity remains unknown. The notion that women conceive in this way masks an incestuous reproductive cycle that continually creates the essential element of "true" matrilineal identity, dependent upon unnamed ancestors who as classificatory brothers represent a subversive form of incest. The beliefs supporting what anthropologists have called Trobriand "virgin birth" (see e.g., Leach 1966; Spiro 1968; but cf. Delaney 1986) have been interpreted as an attempt to disguise the biological contribution of men as fathers, but in fact they are the means through which the basic problem created by the incest taboo—how to keep while giving—is resolved.

Second, at each death, women's cloth wealth serves as the anchoring matrilineal force, demonstrating the success of regeneration in the face of death and the continued inalienability of matrilineal identity for ranking and non-ranking lineages alike. The numbers of bundles and skirts distributed reveal the strength of members of a lineage as well as the political importance of their relationships with members of other lineages. In purely economic terms, a vast amount of cloth wealth is necessary to make these political statements and, as we will see, therein lie the limitations of Trobriand chiefly rank.

WOMEN AND THEIR BROTHERS: THE SAMOAN SOLUTION

In the Trobriands, the beliefs and practices associated with matrili-
neality serve to keep lineage identity intact while incorporating the
work and support of those from another lineage, such as a man's
children. The Samoan situation is more complex, both in actual
practice and in terms of the histories of kin connections. In Samoa,
the basic unit of descent is not a lineage but rather a multi-branching
group (*'āiga*) with genealogies traced back for ten or fifteen generations.[9] The members of a descent group trace their ancestry
either to a founding woman whose descendants, both male and
female, comprise the *tamafafine* branches, or to a founding man,
usually thought to be the brother of the female founder, whose
descendants comprise the *tamatane* branches (see Shore 1982:
33,91–94). The branches within each descent group own titles,
with specific ones traced through the *tamafafine* lines as well
as the *tamatane* lines. All titles vary in rank, status, and historical
depth.[10]

Titleholders are selected by members of a descent group and
a person may simultaneously hold titles from several branches. Marriage, changes in residence, and adoption all allow individuals to
join or work for several descent groups at the same time and gain
chiefly titles from each of them. With so many possibilities for gaining titles, competition is endemic. The highest titles usually are
traced specifically to the founders of the original title. Titles of lower
rank can be created at any time; one title can be split among several
holders, and some titles are even destroyed. Rights to titles and the
power associated with the bestowal of specific titles shift through
time depending upon the political demands of the moment. Unless
an individual holding a title, even one of the highest rank, receives
the support of the members of his or her descent group, the title
is "empty" and the chief has no power at all.

Despite the complexity that surrounds individual membership
and rights in one or more descent groups, at the very base of *'āiga*
relationships we find a division of interests and duties between a
woman and her brother that is not so different from the Trobriand
brother and sister relationship. To fully understand these similarities
and differences as they apply to the value and meaning of cloth
wealth, we must explore the Samoan relationship between those

who count themselves as *tamatane* and those who are related as *tamafafine*. *Tamatane* members are the primary contenders for the inheritance of descent group property and for the highest titles, although some titles traced through the *tamafafine* are of equally high rank. Those who belong to the *tamafafine* category are treated with the utmost respect by those who identify themselves as *tamatane*. As in the Trobriands, the relationship between those who are *tamatane* and those who are *tamafafine* centers on the continuing relationship between a woman and her brother. Although a growing girl and her brother are isolated from each other within the household in terms of living arrangements and division of labor, a grown man is expected to provide his sister with anything that she needs. A brother is the protector of his sister and he should always treat her with respect throughout her life. A woman has the right to demand this attention from her brother and to aggressively berate him if he is remiss in his duties toward her and her children. Shore (1982:235) points out that when a man is with his sister, he acts shyly and controls the assertive behavior that he usually displays when he is with his male peers. Following his sister's marriage, a man also must accord her husband the same highest respect (see Stuebel 1896:89; Krämer [1902] 1930,II:98).[11]

The force of the brother-sister relationship in Samoa is formally expressed through the roles played by the oldest sister and her oldest brother. Samoans call the oldest sister the *feagaiga* or "sacred" sister. The word *feagaiga* means "perpetual kinship" between the two, which is extended to include their position as *tamatane* and *tamafafine* to each other. *Feagaiga* also means "covenant" or "agreement," and as a verb, it means "to stand opposite" or "to face each other" (Milner 1966:8). A woman's sacred relationship to her brother and his children extends to the sacredness of her son, called *tamasā*, "the sacred child," and to all those who stand as *tamafafine* to her brother. At the same time, the woman's daughter will become the sacred sister to her brother. At every important event in a person's life, the sacred sister, as the representative of those reckoning their ancestral identities back to the founding female, is accorded the highest respect. For example, when a marriage, birth or death occurs, a woman's brother first makes a presentation to her. Called a *sua*, it includes one sample of all the major foods, such as a coconut, a small pig and a yam, plus an exceptionally valuable fine mat. These objects, especially the fine mat, publicly symbolize the respect of the *tamatane* side for this line of *tamafafine* titles, relationships, and ancestors.

The revered position of the oldest sister also indicates her individual power to affect the descent group's affairs. She has the right to veto any decision concerning the conferring of a title on someone within the descent group and she also has the right to arbitrate disagreements within the descent group and to defy her brother.[12] A sacred sister can "throw her weight around the *'āiga* and tell off her brother even if he has a high title," a Samoan informant emphatically told me.[13] The "curse" of the oldest sister is feared because traditionally it was thought that such a curse could destroy those who have the highest priority to titles, especially her brother and his children.

If the sacred powers of a woman as sister give her the potential to cause sickness and death among those kin who stand as *tamatane* to her, these powers also enable her to assist in preventing such calamities. As Huntsman and Hooper (1975:424) point out, too often the cursing power of the sacred sister is emphasized by anthropologists while the other "mystical" powers, which enable her to bless and assist her brother and his children, are seldom noted. Following up on this point, Schoeffel (1981) makes a convincing case for the political importance of Samoan women before missionary influences. She demonstrates that the sacredness surrounding Samoan women as sisters was anchored in cosmological beliefs regarding their sacred powers. Samoans trace this power to the original sister-brother founders, so that when a woman took on the *feagaiga* title she traditionally was thought to assume the sacredness associated with the *mana* (sacred potency) attributed to the original female founder (see Krämer [1902] 1930). By weakening beliefs in the notions of *mana*, the Church effectively weakened the once awesome role of women as sisters. In Schoeffel's view, women who were *feagaiga* not only assisted their brothers who held high titles and were chiefs, but also provided them with *mana* and thereby ensured that the chiefly titles themselves carried a moral, sacred force.

This sacred power associated with the titles and actions of a sacred sister and the chief is equally associated with the best fine mats. Many ancient stories reveal how *mana* was thought to be embedded in fine mats. For example, when a woman was to be married, members of her descent group came without fine mats to the groom's village, where the groom's relatives had a thousand fine mats assembled. When only one fine mat was finally presented by the bride, thunder and lightning ensued. This one fine mat, extremely old yet made just like the thousand others, was far more valued because of its sacred history (Krämer [1902] 1930,I:54).[14] An informant whom I was questioning once stopped and challenged me: "Why do you think Samoans attribute so much significance to strips of pandanus? They have no use at all." It was then that he told me, "A fine mat is protection for life." This sacred value associated with cloth, also seen elsewhere in Polynesia,[15] indicates the vital importance of women and cloth to the political process.[16]

In the past, the sacred sister provided for the well-being of her descent group and she also had the power to destroy it. Today, her role still is vital as she brings together the *tamatane* and *tamafafine* divisions within each descent group. In any generation a sacred sister, in relation to her brother as chief, can weaken or strengthen the status and power of the descent group. This view of sacred protection is a basic value deeply associated with fine mats. Even in contemporary Western or American Samoa, where all commercial enterprises are conducted with national currencies, the economic and symbolic values of fine mats still are of vital consequence. Contemporary events involving violence and potential retribution illustrate the continuing strength of Samoan people's perceptions about a fine mat's sacred power. For example, when a murder occurs, the highest title holder of the murderer's descent group covers himself with a valued fine mat, called for this purpose, *'ie ifoga*, and hurries to the house of the highest title holder of the dead person's descent group in order to forestall vengeance. He then sits outside covered in fine mats (*'ie ifoga*), waiting to be granted forgiveness (see Shore [1982:19] for an actual account). At least one fine mat must be of the highest rank, valued because of its age and aesthetic beauty; by first wearing it and then giving it up to the victim's group, the chief of the guilty man and the other members of his descent group receive "protection for life."

As we have seen, the principles of Samoan descent differ significantly from Trobriand descent principles, yet the basic brother-sister relationship reveals similarities about how the descent group is regenerated through time. In Samoa, despite the vast complexity of ways in which individuals attach themselves to a descent group and the enormous competition to hold a title, the autonomy of the descent group traditionally was maintained by the regenerative, sa-

cred power of women as sisters. So close were the connections between the sacred sister and her brother the chief, that it is not
surprising to find tales of incest among the myths and stories associated with certain ancient sister-brother descent-group founders.
Here again we are reminded of the Trobriand pattern, where the inalienability of matrilineal descent includes the notion that the regeneration of matrilineal identity is achieved by masking the incestuous
relations between a woman and her deceased kinsman.

By contrast, in Samoa the notion of incest is not completely disguised, for at certain times it is given political relevance. Even today,
ancestral cases of brother-sister incest are used as powerful kinds
of knowledge that, when spoken about publicly in political debate,
prove that a chief is the proper and rightful title-holder. In fact,
some of the most powerful spirits (*āitu*) are still believed to return
to the living and are thought to have come into being through
brother-sister incest (Cain 1971:174). Similarly, incest between a
woman and her brother figures in origin stories associated with the
ancient names of the most revered fine mats, giving these mats,
when presented, enormous political advantage. Even the names of
certain fine-mat exchanges evoke the recognition of brother-sister incest. The importance of keeping a sister united with her brother is
enacted through cosmological connections to ancestors, through ongoing political controls, and through the subversive yet powerful
notion of incestuous relations. Elements of each of these features are
transferred to cloth wealth, giving the cloth object power in its own
right and making women an inherent part of that power.

CLOTH AND WOMEN'S PRODUCTION

We must now look critically at the way women are involved in cloth
production. Because the labor involved in cloth production endows
that cloth with certain values, it is important to know the details of
how bundles and fine mats are made. In the Trobriands, although
women may plant yam gardens, men are primarily responsible for
yam production, while only women produce cloth wealth.[17] Bundles, the form of cloth wealth used in the largest quantities, are
made through a long process in which segments of banana leaves
are bleached and dried in the sun and then tied together at one end.
To make skirts to be used as wealth, strips of dried banana leaves

are fringed and dyed red before they are woven between three pieces of cord that form the belt. Decorations of pandanus, cut into geometric designs, are woven into the waist band.[18] While walking through a village, I would often see girls as young as five or six, working on the first stages of scraping the fibers from the recently picked banana leaves. Once the leaves are dried, further work is done by married women and their adolescent unmarried daughters. New bundles have no use value and the technology of their manufacture is hardly complex, yet the labor involved in bundle-making is intricate. After scraping and drying the strips of banana leaves, a woman places about twenty-five strips in a bunch, then tightly ties them together at one end and trims the tied ends into a neat point. Holding the tied end in one hand, she pulls each individual strip outward, as though stretching crepe paper. Then each stiffened strip is pulled back in place to make the bundle's leaves slightly puffed out. The final stage of shaping the bundle takes about fifteen minutes and then it resembles a whisk broom made with flat strips rather than thin bristles.

This final process of puffing out the bundle is important; the extensive labor gives specific value to the newly fabricated object. Without the puffy center, the bundle is considered "old" or "dirty" and it can only be used in inconsequential exchanges (see Weiner 1976:94–95). New cloth bundles and skirts are the most highly valued, and a woman needs thousands of new bundles and as much as twenty to fifty skirts when someone dies in her matrilineage.[19] Even though the distributions following a death are a lineage affair, women work alone at their production, competing with other women who are members of the same matrilineage to be "first" and have the most wealth to give away on the day of a women's mortuary distribution.

In Samoa, making fine mats is infinitely more demanding than producing bundles and skirts, although like bundles, fine mats have no utilitarian value. Preparation of the threads from the pandanus plant requires that the leaves be trimmed and then baked in an earth oven. Next the material is bleached, first by soaking in seawater for a week and then by drying in the sun. Strips of millimeter-wide fibers are separated and the finished plaiting takes from six months to a year. In contemporary Samoa, women sometimes meet together as a group (fale lalaga) to work on fine mat production. Men pool their agricultural resources to provide the women with food each

*Figure 1. A Trobriand woman counting her new bundles in
preparation for the women's mortuary distribution. Photo by
Annette B. Weiner*

day.[20] While plaiting, women are also relieved of child care and as
they work together they gossip, sing, and entertain each other. Although certain women achieve renown for their ability to make exceptionally beautiful fine mats, production does not require unique
skills.

The organization of these women's groups remains part of the
ranking system, for the woman with the highest title in the village
or the wife of the highest title holder controls the group's organization and activities. In contemporary Samoa, this woman has the
right to levy fines for lack of attention to work or for disrespectful
behavior (see Shore 1982:105–06). Before missionaries inflicted
changes on the status of women, the responsibilities and power of
high-ranked women were even more of a monopoly. They con-

trolled the activities of the *aualuma* village groups, comprised of
women and girls who were related by descent or adoption to the
men of a village (Schoeffel 1977). One of their major responsibilities
was the production of fine mats.[21] Women who married into the village came under the authority of the highest woman title-holder,
who generally would be the sacred sister; if widowed, women always returned to live with their natal *aualuma* groups. After the establishment of the first missionary station in 1830, these groups
came under attack and gradually were disbanded. Other women's
organizations have taken their place but now many women work
alone. Because so many fine mats are needed, especially at a death,
Samoans often are forced to buy new ones, which are sold by these
women at the local market in Apia, the capitol of Western Samoa,
for upwards of $150.00.

The fine mats produced by groups rather than women alone are
thought of as '*āiga* property. Each woman stores her own fine mats
and has the right to refuse requests from the chief, although most
informants agreed that this would rarely happen. But the decisions
about which fine mat to give are made by women. Grades are distinguished by the fineness of the pandanus threads, the evenness of
plaiting, and the size and softness of the finished product. The most
important have specific names associated with historical and mythic
events and are carefully, sometimes secretly, saved for important
political occasions.[22]

Like the organization of the descent group itself, control of
property is a complex issue. A woman's fine mats go to support her
husband when he needs such wealth, but they also support her
brother's needs. In addition, she brings fine mats herself to all
events associated with her natal descent group or one from which
she has a title or some other affiliated association. The respect accorded women is further emphasized when a number of fine mats
are completed. At that time, a large celebration is held to which people from many other villages come. The fine mats are paraded
through the village by the women workers, and large quantities of
food are presented by the men whose wives or sisters produced this
wealth. The participation of both husbands and brothers in these exchanges points up an important contrast with the Trobriand situation where, at the end of the women's mortuary distribution, when
women have given away all their bundles and skirts, they receive
gifts of food only from their brothers. While the brother-sister rela-

tionship in both the Trobriands and Samoa is well-defined, in Samoa fine mat production and the food exchanges that "thank" women for their work involve both brothers and husbands. The inclusion of the husband reflects the nonexclusivity of Samoan descent groups as compared with the exclusivity of Trobriand descent groups. These examples of men's food production and women's cloth production, however, are only intimations of how, in both societies, the economic roles of men are tied to cloth production and circulation.

CLOTH AND MEN'S PRODUCTION

In the Trobriands, production of cloth wealth and control over its distribution remain exclusively within the household. Whatever a woman produces belongs to her. She has full rights to sell bundles, but in the selling, men enter into the domain of women's wealth. Because a woman needs many more bundles than she can produce herself, her husband becomes her major source for more cloth wealth. A man takes his own resources, such as yams, pigs, or carved goods, and sells them to other villagers for a specified amount of bundles. Today, men also purchase trade store foods with money and then sell the imported items for bundles. In the circulation of these foods and goods, bundles act as a limited currency, increasing in economic value as inflation raises trade store prices.

A man reduces his own holdings, including money, which is much needed for other things and always in short supply, in order to help his wife accumulate objects with no use value. Yet the exchange value of cloth wealth is essential to maintain the prestige and power of a woman's matrilineage and her brother's political position within that lineage. Thus, men as brothers are equally involved in the cloth exchanges between a woman and her husband. Each year a man makes a special yam garden for his married sister (see Weiner 1976:195–210). He gives the yams to his sister's husband who is obligated, in turn, to contribute to her cloth accumulation as needed.[23] The garden labor of a woman's brother insures that her husband will expend his wealth in ways that ultimately increase her wealth. The obligations a man establishes through his own children are fulfilled after they marry, as they, too, add to his sister's accumulation of wealth. From a societal perspective, the necessity for bundles at each death acts as a leveling device, periodically depleting the wealth of men when gardening, pig raising, craft production and now cash, go toward the support of women's cloth wealth.

In Samoa, anywhere from 500 to 1000 or more fine mats may circulate at births, marriages, deaths, the inauguration of title holders, even the building of a new church or school. In these events there are forty major named categories of distributions, each one referring to the kinship or political relation between the giver and receiver. During these distributions, gifts called 'oloa, which traditionally included food, pigs, and crafted goods, are distributed by the major receivers of fine mats. Today, men present cases of biscuits, bread, tinned meat, pigs, cattle, and cash as 'oloa.[24] In historical sources and even in recent ethnography, Samoan exchanges of fine mats and 'oloa are described as reciprocal returns. For example, Shore (1982:203–08) reported that at marriages or the births of children, the members of a woman's descent group presented fine mats to the members of the groom's descent group who then gave 'oloa in repayment for the fine mats as "balanced reciprocity."

The actual transactions are more complicated; most people who come to the event with fine mats return home with fine mats comparable to those they gave away. Women organize and present the fine mats which are collected from both women and men, and both women and men receive them. At the distribution, a person may receive a better one than she or he brought or even an additional one, which is why a woman rarely refuses her husband's or a chief's request. In each distribution, depending upon the strategies of those who redistribute them, individuals have the possibility of getting back better ones, although sometimes they receive one of lesser value or none at all. Decisions are based on who attends with the highest titles and the kinds of fine mats that are presented. In this way, each distribution is an example of the negotiation and validation of rank and power.

When an event is to take place, the highest title-holder of the descent group collects fine mats from all the other members and also from the members of his wife's descent group. His sister collects fine mats in the same way, calling for support from her husband's relatives and those who are related to her through the tamafafine category. A chief remains indebted to all those who brought fine mats and only the later return of other fine mats cancels the debt. The direction in which the fine mats are given varies with the kind of event as well as where the participants are living.

A few examples will illustrate the procedures. In the exchanges of fine mats and *'oloa* that occur following a murder, the members of the victim's descent group and those from the killer's descent group all bring both *'oloa* and fine mats; they all receive *'oloa* and fine mats in return. At the birth of a child, fine mats are brought by members of the mother's parents' descent groups, if she is living with her husband's relatives, whose responsibility it will be to provide *'oloa*. But if she resides with her own kin, then the responsibility for fine mats falls to those from her husband's descent group. For a funeral, the same conditions of residence apply. If we examine the entire distribution of fine mats at a death, we find that the relationships being defined through each category in which fine mats are presented encompass a huge range of people including kin and in-law relations, branches of the deceased mother's and father's descent groups, the in-laws of the deceased's siblings, title holders within all the descent groups represented, and those holding high titles from all neighboring villages and districts. Who attends, and the value of the fine mats presented, depend upon how high the titles are for the people involved. Within these categories, some fine mats will be presented from members of descent group A to members of descent group B. In other categories, the direction of giving fine mats is reversed.[25]

In contrast, *'oloa* distributions are made expressly to thank people for the work of bringing fine mats and for travelling to the event. In the Trobriands, the response is similar though much less elaborated; when the women's mortuary distribution of bundles and skirts ends, men enter the center of the village and distribute yams to the women who attended the distribution from other villages.[26] The yams thank the women for participating in the event. This example shows that the relationship between *'oloa* and fine mats is not one of "balanced reciprocity" at all. *'Oloa* never cancels the debt of fine mats, for food and fine mats can never be equated.[27] In both societies, the exchanges that define and act on kinship in the most fundamental way are those of cloth wealth. Food, livestock, material goods, and money contribute to the scope and intensity of the circulation of cloth wealth, but they cannot replace such wealth. In the Trobriands, men's garden production increases cloth accumulation.

In Samoa, men's production, by repaying the work of accumulating fine mats, also increases accumulation.

In other Melanesian societies, yams, taro, and pigs take on properties that associate them with ancestral spirits, human relationships, and ritual paraphernalia (see e.g., Young 1971; Kahn 1986; Rappaport 1984 respectively). But these exchanges of food, so immediately consumable, are not durable enough to support the constitution of ranking clans. To view the exchanges of fine mats and 'oloa only as reciprocal elements in an exchange ignores how attempts to create inalienable relationships are rooted in certain kinds of objects, and how the objects themselves express the success of these attempts. As my Samoan informant said, fine mats are statements "for life."

CLOTH AND ITS INALIENABLE PROPERTIES

Cloth wealth not only operates as a defining agent of "life," it also reveals the constraints and limitations within which individuals must negotiate their relations with each other. In traditional Fiji, to mark the end of mourning for a high-ranking chief, enormous quantities of barkcloth, including a train one hundred yards long, were worn by the chief's successor (Kooijman 1972:412). While the billows of cloth added volume to his presence, the cloth's role in masking the chief's vulnerability called attention to it as well, for this barkcloth was not considered a durable heirloom. Thus, while cloth wraps a person with an object that symbolizes the regeneration of authority, it also signals the difficulties of keeping that authority and its history sacrosanct. Because cloth is subject to physical disintegration, keeping an old cloth despite all the ravages of time and the pressures to give it to others adds immeasurably to its value. Old cloths carry the histories of past relationships, making the cloth itself into a material archive that brings the authority of the past into the present. Such objects, which become treasures, are not accumulated for a future investment as capital. Although their owners may need to divest themselves of their most prized possessions, they do so at great loss, regardless of what they gain.

For example, the Maori considered objects made from nephrite as well as flax cloaks (both called taonga) essential for payments for land, peace treaties, services, marriages, and deaths. But certain prized cloaks and jade objects remained inalienable, never to be given to other tribes. *"Taonga* captured history and showed it to the living, and they echoed patterns of the past from first creation to the present" (Salmond 1984:118) as they were passed down from one generation to another. Cloaks no less then nephrite occupied this "fixed point" in the tribal histories because they belonged to specific ancestors and were inherited through specific descent lines. Such inalienability was never achieved in the Trobriands but, in certain circumstances, does occur in Samoa.

In Western Samoa, the fine mats sold in Apia's main market are extremely expensive. But a new fine mat, regardless of the price paid, cannot replace the value of an old mat, even if the old one is patched and faded or brown with age. Ancient fine mats are difficult to find, since the most valued ones remain stored away for years or even generations. In the hundreds of fine mats that circulate for an event, only those presented in certain categories, such as the fine mat of "farewell" when someone dies (see n.25) are extremely valuable. As already noted, Samoans deliberately save special fine mats for important occasions, even for a particular exchange (see n. 22). So important are the strategies in keeping and giving that at times, a person decides to hold his own funeral distributions of fine mats before he dies, thereby insuring that the valuable ones are given to the appropriate people. One man explained his own strategies to me and said that when he dies after the distributions, he will be buried simply without further exchanges.

In all important distributions, when the oldest and, therefore, the most prized fine mats are presented, they are given names that refer to specific legends and historical or mythical events involving the ancestors of a descent group. These names are only used among people with high titles and the stories associated with the names, like the histories of chiefly titles, are considered the secret property of the descent group. When such a fine mat is presented, usually at the death of a high title-holder or at the taking of a high title, as one of my informants said, it is "a kingly event."[28]

In these important exchanges, reciprocity is vital. After a valuable fine mat is given, those who receive it must find one of equivalent or higher value to return, unless they want to belittle the authority of the giver. If the receivers do not have an equivalent fine mat, they must return the very one they just received. In this instance, a fine mat that cannot be replaced by another becomes inalienable and demonstrates the authority of high rank. Today, when especially important fine mats are sent to Samoans living in New Zealand, Hawaii, or the United States for occasions such as marriages and deaths, Samoans usually attach to the fine mat a written history of its previous owners and the dates and places that the fine mat has traveled (Meleisea, personal communication). Without the presence of those who know such histories and can recognize the name of a famous fine mat, a written record is essential to validate its rank.

Trobriand cloth wealth is not associated with individual histories and new bundles are far more valuable than old ones. These differences reflect the dissimilar ways of genealogical reckoning in relation to rank. In the Trobriands, women reproduce lineage identity in direct association with ancestral spirits, without the necessity for long genealogical accounting. The right to chieftaincy comes from being born a member of the appropriate lineage and not, as in the Samoan case, from the competition to gain titles. In Samoa, titles are conferred by members of a descent group through consensus that then must be agreed upon by the sacred sister—or in disputed choices, through her veto. Indeed such controversy now ends in lengthy court cases (see e.g., Tiffany 1974). Conversely, Trobriand chiefs select their successors themselves among members of their matrilineage without consensus or veto rights by others. What changes over time is the actual power of particular Trobriand matrilineages and these shifts are what distributions of cloth wealth expose. Here cloth is not valued because it is an heirloom nor is it imbued with protective and dangerous powers. Yet we can hardly discount the economic and political power of Trobriand cloth since it continually absorbs men's money, pigs, and yams. Although men benefit from the cloth exchanges, their obligations in this respect set limits on how autonomous they can be in using their wealth for more personal political advantage.[29] Trobriand rank remains tied to kinship and death, because even the autonomy of chiefs is curtailed by the necessity to support wives and sisters. While Samoan rank is rooted in kinship, political power shifts constantly, and these changes are revealed and confirmed by extensive exchanges of fine mats. As a result, gender relations regularly shift too, with some men and some women attaining greater political authority at the expense of others.

CLOTH WEALTH, CHIEFS, AND GENDER

Each time someone dies in the Trobriands, the circulation of cloth marks the current state of relationships between the members of one matrilineage and those related primarily through spouses and fathers. On this one day, bundles and skirts are distributed in seventeen categories defined by the specifics of these relationships (see Weiner 1976:103–16). If we could document these events historically, we would see the flux in the strength and weakness of lineages. More or less wealth is given to larger or smaller numbers of people, by the full complement of members of a matrilineage or by those who belong to competitive segments of a matrilineage or only by a few surviving members of a matrilineage that is dying out. Since all deaths, except those of very old people who die in their sleep, are thought to occur through sorcery, each death is seen as a political attack on the growth and stability of a matrilineage. Therefore, the women's distribution of wealth is a defiant act against the reality of aggression—a public assertion that the established political order at that time has not been undermined.

With the help of husbands, brothers, and brothers' children, women counter the threat to the regeneration of matrilineal identity by their ability to show through cloth where each person belongs.[30] For chiefs who are polygynous, the display is essential to maintain connections with the members of their wives' matrilineages and other extended ties. Therefore, men's economic ties to women and their cloth wealth are determined as much by the need for political support as by kinship. Yet, as this support is given, it depletes men's accumulations of their own wealth, so these obligations keep men, including chiefs, economically dependent on women.

Women are not chiefs but their control over cloth wealth supports the strength of matrilineal identity when it is under the most dangerous threat. Even though these distributions are organized around death, they give women their own public domain that is inherently political. But if Trobriand women hold a degree of political power, the use of that power still restricts how much ranking and political autonomy are possible. New wealth must be produced at each death, for genealogical histories are not condensed in cloth. The shallowness of genealogies is affirmed in the notion of

Figure 2. At the end of the women's mortuary distribution, Trobriand women march with the skirts that they will present to the spouse and father of the deceased. Photo by Annette B. Weiner

anonymous conception, vaguely linked to the reproduction of the lineage through brother-sister incest. Unlike Samoa, Trobriand banana-leaf bundles never become heirlooms that make them the agent and symbol of high rank or, as elsewhere in Polynesia, dynastic hierarchies. The histories of matrilineages remain secret knowledge, only revealed publicly in dangerous disputes over land rights (see Weiner 1976:156–67). No objects used in exchange, except bundles and skirts, validate lineage histories (see n.29). Yet unlike Samoan fine mats, Trobriand bundles and skirts do not serve as historical documents or genealogies. Thus, although Trobriand cloth wealth enables women to participate fully in the politics brought into play at a death, ownership of cloth does not entitle them to direct participation in other political affairs. In the same way, while cloth provides the economic base for a level of ranking that gives some men more authority and power over others, it ultimately checks the level of ranking and the scope of men's political engagement.

In contrast, Samoan fine mats are necessary, not only at deaths, but for all major kinship events, such as births and marriages. Moreover this cloth figures centrally in situations that are more singularly political. In traditional warfare, peace could only be declared with a fine mat distribution. In fact, if an acclaimed fine mat was withheld from an expected presentation, this decision alone could precipitate a war (Krämer [1902] 1930,I:377). Fine mats used in these political situations were called '*ie o le malo*, "the fine mat of state" and today they are still presented at the bestowal of a very high title or at the death of a distinguished title-holder.[31]

Yet Samoan political events are still grounded in the internal organization of the descent group. The bestowal of high-ranking titles necessitates approval from major branches of the descent group, measured in fine mats. In the last century, a contender for one of the highest titles defeated another "lawful antagonist" because he had the support of two strong branches, "owing to their wealth in fine mats" (Krämer [1902] 1930,I:26). Another account describes how succession to one of the four highest titles only occurred when eight branches of the descent group came forward with huge piles of fine mats (Krämer [1902] 1930,I:387). When the histories of these special fine mats are read, it becomes clear, as Krämer ([1902] 1930,I:57) emphasized, why certain descent groups and specific titles became so powerful over the last two hundred years.

Marriages are also significant political affairs if they involve high title-holders or the possibility of important alliances. For example, in the 1970s, a young woman from American Samoa married a Western Samoan man and at the wedding, 3,000 fine mats were distributed. These huge presentations occurred not because the couple had especially high titles, but because the marriage consolidated a tie between traditional political districts that had long been separated. According to Krämer ([1902] 1930,I:24), in the last century, not only were the polygynous marriages of chiefs important, but "[m]arriages of daughters of the great chiefs were always affairs of state, which were considered very deliberately." But a marriage was politically important only if the girl's mother was of "noble descent" and came from a descent group wealthy in fine mats.

The political history of Samoa is expressed through fine mats, as these objects demonstrate the economics of wealth, alliances, the histories of titles, and political support. Fine mats are the underpinnings of titles, making kinship negotiations essential for the highest levels of political office. Fine mats not only trace the dynamics of these histories and the statuses of certain titles, but as with Trobriand bundles and skirts, they equally reveal the limits of ranking. Although chiefs eagerly seek out the best fine mats, they cannot keep them for they must give many to those who originally brought them, repay their orators (tulāfale) for their services during the distributions, and give the very best ones to their sacred sisters.[32] The complementary roles of the orator and the sacred sister, at least in the past centuries, indicate how much a chief's autonomy still remains dependent on others. A chief and his orator "sit opposite each other" just as the chief "sits opposite" his sacred sister. The sister surrounds the chief's title with sacred mana, while the secular power of a title depends on the orator's skill and strategic command of situations (see Schoeffel 1981). The orator's importance is his defense of the chief's title in public debates; he must have extensive knowledge of past circumstances and genealogical histories in addition to the proper linguistic form and etiquette involved in speaking for chiefs (see Duranti 1981). The secular power of chiefs can be undermined by other title-holders and their orators. Although a sister no longer keeps her brother's sacred powers intact as she did traditionally, she still is responsible for his support within the internal branches of the descent group. Both the sacred and secular (or internal and external) roles of sisters and orators are sustained with fine mats.

Chiefs' economic demands and obligations never cease and they may hold titles from several descent groups, multiplying their commitments. A man with aspirations for a title has first priorities to the members of his father's descent group, but because his mother, her brother, and her brother's sons give him respect and fine mats, he should support them as well. In doing so, he may eventually succeed to their titles (see Shore 1982:61).[33] This tension between a woman, her children and her brother lies at the core of kinship relations—how to keep a woman's children a strong part of her kin connections despite the importance of their father's kin relations. A statement made to Stuebel in the nineteenth century illustrates the internal politics of descent group organization and the way the political ranking that constitutes its base depends upon these relations.

When a chief is dying he says to his sons: "If one of your children takes a wife, the . . . girdle [fine mat] of the bride is to be
brought to my sister and her son. Also you must continue the
agreement [*feagaiga*] with her son. You are to have a special reverence for him, and your children also. Barkcloths and whatever
you obtain you are to take first to my sister and her son!" A
chief makes presents to his sister's daughters also, who are
called *tamafafine*, but only if they have no brothers . . . (quoted
in Krämer [1902] 1930,II:110,112).

Through fine mats, a man defines his relationship to his sister and
her children. By keeping the very best fine mats flowing to his sister's son as well as her daughter, a man also secures the allegiance
of the next generation, so that they will continue to keep those who
are *tamafafine* (related through the sacred sister) closely allied with
those who are *tamatane* (related through her brother). It now should
be apparent why at a woman's marriage and at the birth of her first
daughter, the very best fine mats are presented in her honor by her
brother; in other events, the woman's sons receive fine mats from
her brother or his sons. When a married woman dies, her brother
presents an exceptionally valued fine mat to her husband's relatives.[34] Usually this is a fine mat that he has kept for many years,
reserving it for an occasion of importance. The fine mat is called,
'ie o le measā. The word, *measā*, according to my informants, means
genitals of either sex and it signifies the fine mat of respect from a
man to his sister. This final element of incest speaks directly to the
importance of the sacred sister in relation to her own and to her
brother's position as the conserving and regenerating links between
the two sides of the descent group.[35]

　　The fine mats that go between a woman and her brother are the
signs of the convenant between them and all those who stand as
tamatane and *tamafafine* to each other. In compressed form, the fine
mat represents the actions necessary to hold the internal organization of the descent group or some of its branches together. The sacred sister always sits opposite the chief, just as her connection to
those who are *tamafafine* is opposite those who are *tamatane*. From
the perspective of individual relationships and the formal descent
group as a whole, the threads of the fine mat keep these divisions
together. Herein lies the political force behind titles. Unlike the Trobriand case, where men cannot escape from the demands of death
and the drain of their own wealth for accumulations of cloth wealth,

Figure 3. Western Samoan women carry fine mats to the house where the funeral distribution will take place. Photo by Annette B. Weiner

Samoan fine mats are the wealth of women and men. In Samoa, the political domain is not completely encumbered by death as it is in the Trobriands, even though ranking still is constituted by the relations between women as sisters and men as brothers.

Because of their political power, some Samoan women have access to the highest titles and political office. In A.D. 1500, one woman, Salamasina, held the four highest titles in Samoa, an achievement that for the first time united the major traditional political districts (see Krämer [1923] 1958). Although women's major political roles have diminished since colonization, some women still gain very high titles. Krämer writing at the turn of the century, recognized the key feature in relation to gender and the political domain. He noted that although girls from lower-ranked descent groups were often treated oppressively, "girls and women of rank enjoyed an almost godlike veneration. It is not only through their prestige that they have great influence over their husbands and relatives and through them, over affairs of state, but titles and offices, even the throne are open to them . . . "([1902] 1930,I:68–69).

Untitled men and women are forbidden participation in village political events, just as they are unable to accumulate fine mats of distinction. Therefore, any discussion of Samoan oppression and domination of women must take into account the oppression and domination of all untitled Samoans. The focus cannot be on gender; it must be on differences created by rank. The politics of titles encompasses gender in its priorities and gives to some women political power that is equal to, and at times greater than, the political power of some men. As rank is equated with greater authority and possibilities for power, gender criteria no longer exclude women from the privileges of political office. In Samoa, we see the beginning outlines of the disengagement of kinship and politics, supported by the ancestral validations that fine mats produce. Samoan women, the symbols and agents for the power believed to be embedded in those sacred heirlooms, the fine mats, provide support for strong titles as some women gain access to these titles themselves.

WHY CLOTH?

The cultural processes surrounding Samoan and Trobriand cloth clearly illustrate how a woman remains a reproductive force within her own natal group even after she marries outside the group. The sexual loss of women as sisters is transcended by the transformation of women's reproductive capacity into an object that maintains the links between kinship and political power. The Samoan fine mat called "genitals" is illuminating; it symbolizes the relationship between sisters and brothers in their efforts to regenerate the most important relationships within their own descent group, despite competing demands and choices. The problem that these societies confront is not how one gives up a sister to obtain a wife, as Lévi-Strauss would have it, for a wife and sister are not equivalents. Rather the dilemma to be resolved is much more existential, yet deeply connected to the practical considerations of economic and political affairs: How is sexuality transformed into social action that remains culturally reproductive for the woman's kin group?

Marriage and death disrupt personal relationships and property, making loss an inherent part of all social action. How these losses are overcome so that a descent group retains its prominence and force through time is the same problem as how titles or dynasties remain sovereign over others. In Oceania, women, death, and cloth come together as the key variables in the regeneration of descent-group identity and by extension, the political authority invested in titles and rank. Cloth is culturally enhanced so that it represents the union of a man and his sister and by extension, kinship solidarity. With this value accorded cloth, it operates as a powerful economic and cosmological resource that symbolizes the abilities of individuals to transcend time, loss, death, and the results of the incest taboo. And because it can be made to last for generations, cloth also exhibits some semblance of immortality.

Cloth is by no means the only object that can outlast a person's life. Bones, stones, and shells (Weiner 1982, 1985) also serve as the material form through which past histories are incorporated into the present. In these Pacific societies, however, "hard wealth" is made by experts, often with imported materials, and thus it is rare. Cloth is locally produced and as "soft wealth," far more abundant. Where the technologies for making it become more complex and where the cloth itself becomes an heirloom, as in Samoa, its preparation becomes highly organized. Not only in Samoa, but elsewhere in Polynesia, certain cloths are thought of as treasures; they are endowed with sacred qualities[37] which enable them to represent the histories and legends associated with important ancestors and mythical dieties. Presentation of such a cloth reveals a person's right to claim the prerogatives and powers evoked by this conjunction of past and present. Although cloths are economic resources, essential to political endeavors, the best ones—the heirlooms—are, if possible, kept out of circulation as inalienable possessions.

To create inalienable possessions is a difficult achievement, yet the need to have something that can last beyond a person's lifetime, and thus allows claims to be made on the past, is a major cultural undertaking. Hocart's (1954:77) well-known dictum, "the first king was a dead king" is pertinent to my point. Inauguration consecrates the past ruler as it transfers sanctions based on the past to the new ruler. A grave site, the bones of the deceased, and even the wealth exchanged at the time of burial, all objectify the sanctity accorded the successor by anchoring her or his newly defined claims to power in objects associated with former power. But where kinship is still the means for political succession, these affinities with the past must incorporate the kin group itself. Objects of cloth can serve these functions because of their profound connections to women, the kinship relations between brothers and sisters, and the sacredness of their ancestors.

In evaluating the differences between Samoan and Trobriand cloth, we find how difficult it is to achieve true inalienability in cloth. Sometimes, as in the Trobriands, cloth never becomes inalienable. Yet bundles and skirts do provide a foundation that regenerates matrilineal identity through successive generations and thereby, this cloth supports a degree of political rank. Samoan cloth has much greater longevity, giving it a measure of inalienability and historical authority which can support more formal levels of rank. These differences in cloth reflect significant differences in gender roles and political influence between Samoa and the Trobriands. While Trobriand women greatly influence the political dynamics surrounding a death, Samoan women's power enters directly into every aspect of political life. Indeed, rights to titles are claimed by some Samoan women, giving titled women and sisters far greater potential for political preeminence. In ancient Hawaii and Tahiti, where cloth production was even more complex and diversified, women ruled over districts, even entire islands.

Throughout Polynesia, cloth wealth provided the economic and cosmological foundation for rank and hierarchy. The Trobriands and Samoa illuminate how difficult this achievement was by showing the centrality of problems associated with death and inalienability. Women and cloth make kinship into a regenerating force that creates a partial solution to the sustainment of rank. Thus, their connections with cloth enable women to enter the political domain. In comparison with men, their roles are limited, but men's participation in both societies is curtailed as well. With all the exchanges, strategies, and investments that people make with cloth, this object reveals the fragile nature of the very relationships deemed by the societies themselves to be of the highest order. The physical characteristics of cloth as it is plaited or woven, unraveled or torn, as it rots and disintegrates, bring to the histories of persons and lineages the reality of life's ultimate incompleteness.

The question for Oceania, "Why Cloth?" exposes the transformations that occur as cloth is culturally imbued with the inalienability of the social group and therefore, the authority attached to rank. The social and political relationships that the use of cloth supports or suppresses are, fundamentally, attempts to make something permanent in a world of change. Defeat through strategy and manipulation, death through human and natural causes, and the loss of women as sisters constitute the continuing degenerative processes inherent in any social system. Keeping an object even for ten years or over a generation demonstrates some success in sustaining permanence. Cloth absorbs time, giving it a visible form, but cloth does not merely describe or circumscribe time. Rather, for these two Oceanic societies, cloth gives to time a range of possibilities while keeping the political world anchored in kinship.

ACKNOWLEDGMENTS

Field research for this paper was supported by the John S. Guggenheim Foundation and an early draft was completed while I was a Member, The Institute for Advanced Study, Princeton. I am grateful to both institutions. This research would not have been possible without the cooperation of the Prime Minister's Department, Western Samoa, the Institute for Papua New Guinea Studies, and the Milne Bay Provincial Government, Papua New Guinea. I am especially grateful to Dr. Horst Cain, Suya and Liki Crichton, Tuala F. Tiresa Malietoa, Leota Pepe, and the Hon. Nomumalo Leulumwenga for their assistance in Samoa and to the many people in Kwaibwaga and Omarakana villages, Kiriwina, Trobriand Islands, who helped me during the years of my research there. I thank T.O. Beidelman, Deborah Battaglia, Gillian Feeley-Harnik, Judith Huntsman, William E. Mitchell, and Jane Schneider for their comments on earlier drafts of this paper and very special thanks to Malama Meleisea and Penelope Schoeffel for sharing information with me.

NOTES

1. This quotation is cited in Rogers 1977.

2. My field work was done on the island of Upolu in Western Samoa during part of 1980 and on northern Kiriwina Island in the Trobriand group in 1971, 1972, 1976, 1980, and 1982.

3. The role of cloth wealth in Oceania has been ignored in studies focusing on gender and hierarchy (e.g., Ortner 1981; Shore 1981) and in two major studies

of Polynesian social stratification (Sahlins 1958; Goldman 1970); more recently, women chiefs and queens have been excluded from studies of Hawaiian divine rulers (Sahlins 1985; Valeri 1985; but cf. Weiner 1987, 1988b). Even the importance of exchange in Polynesia has not been given full recognition, nor have archaeologists considered the importance of cloth in this part of the world (see e.g., Kirch 1984; Terrell 1986). But Leacock (1972), writing from a global perspective, noted that textile production was one of the areas that gave decision-making power to women in precapitalist societies prior to colonization. A recent dissertation focuses on the contemporary importance of Fijian women's economic status, achieved through their production of barkcloth (Teckle 1986). Also see Gailey (1980) on precolonial Tongan women's production of barkcloth.

4. Traditionally, barkcloth was also used as wealth in association with fine mats, but production stopped with colonization and the use of European cloth.

5. Throughout traditional Polynesia, women were the producers of most cloth that was considered wealth. But in special cases, men also produced cloth. For example, in ancient Tahiti, when large quantities of barkcloth were needed, men helped women with production (Henry 1928) and in Hawaii, men made the valued feathered cloaks, but women produced the sacred barkcloths necessary for the most important temple ceremonies, including the installation of the divine king (e.g., Kooijman 1972; Weiner 1987).

6. Margaret Mead (1930) called attention to the importance of Samoan women who, as sisters, had sacred and dangerous powers over their brothers. Huntsman and Hooper (1975) noted the similarity between the sacred sister in Samoa and the covenant between a woman and her brother in the Tokelau Islands. Garth Rogers (1977) analyzed the role of Tongan women, illustrating the significant sacred and political power women had over their brothers. Rogers (1977) suggested that the weaver in the Tongan proverb at the beginning of the essay was the father's eldest sister. See also Hocart (1915;1952) and Mabuchi (1964) on the role of the sacred sister throughout Polynesia.

7. Indonesian textiles, when wrapped around the body, are believed to restrain the natural and cosmological world in the name of social order; when exchanged at marriages or deaths, these same cloths convey a blessing for vitality, fertility, and regeneration (Adams 1980; Fox 1977; Gittinger 1979).

8. Kiriwina also is the most heavily populated island in the Trobriand group and is the ancestral and contemporary home of the highest-ranking chiefs. Unless noted, all references to Trobriand cloth wealth pertain only to Kiriwina, where such wealth is more elaborated than on the other islands.

9. For ease of reading, I translate "'āiga" as "descent group," but in actuality, the group at any one time or event may only be represented by certain branches rather than the entire unit.

10. See Krämer [1923] 1958 on the histories of high titles before Samoa was colonized.

11. But as Shore (1982:235) notes, if a woman is caught with a lover her

brother will react violently. In the same way, if a man squanders his money or is lazy, his sister will berate him publicly for not attending to her and the needs of the family.

12. See Schoeffel 1981 for contemporary examples.

13. Of course, the power of individual women varies; if a woman does not care to enforce her rights, the rights disappear.

14. Krämer ([1902] 1930,I:20) also gives an example of how a title became so powerful that the holder threatened to become dangerous even to his own descent group because the title was thought to have increased in power through the efforts of Nafannu, the goddess of war.

15. The entwined importance of cloth, *mana*, and women also occurs elsewhere in Polynesia, e.g., among the Maori (Weiner 1985); ancient Tahiti and Hawaii (e.g., Kooijman 1972; Weiner 1987) and Fiji (Kooijman 1977).

16. I do not discuss the circumstances of traditional overseas trade in fine mats with Fijian and Tongan chiefs (but see Kaeppler 1978; Hjarnø 1979/80). See Buck (1930) for details on the technology of fine mat production; also Krämer [1902] 1930,II:521–23; and Stair 1897.

17. In the southern Massim, Sabarl women make baskets which are distributed at each death as women's "bulk wealth." (Battaglia 1981) and on Sudest, women's skirts are used in mortuary exchanges (Lepowsky 1981), but only Kiriwina women in the Trobriands make banana-leaf bundles and only here does the general distribution of cloth wealth reach such elaborate proportions.

18. See Weiner 1976:237–41 for additional details on the technology of skirts and bundles.

19. Clean bundles are remade from old ones by untying the bundle and stretching out each leaf. Although they are not equivalent in value to new bundles, clean ones have more value than old ones.

20. Traditionally and in contemporary Western Samoa, men always do the cooking in earth ovens and do all garden work as well. Now that many Samoan households have Western kitchen appliances, women do the stove cooking, but men are still responsible for the yams, taro, and pig roasted in outdoor traditional ovens.

21. Ella (1899:169) observed that "The manufacture of the '*ie* [fine mat] is the work of women and confined to ladies of distinction, and common people dare not infringe the monopoly, which is *sā* [tabu or sacred]."

22. Women also exercise control over fine mats that belong to their husbands. One informant told me that no one else in her family knew that her mother had two very old fine mats. Years later she told her daughter how she had received them when her husband took a chiefly title and periodically, she would air them early in the morning so that no one would see them. Her plans were to keep them for an important event in her own family.

23. Because Malinowski (e.g., 1935) never took women's cloth wealth into account in his studies of Trobriand exchange, he could not understand why men made gardens for their sisters rather than their wives.

24. Krämer ([1902] 1930,II:158) lists all objects made by men as *'oloa*, including anything foreign. The category of fine mats (*ie toga*) traditionally included everything made by women, such as barkcloth, sleeping mats, fans, oil, combs, baskets, etc., as well as fine mats. Even in Kramer's account, nothing is as important and valued as fine mats.

25. For example, if a man dies, the members of his mother's and his father's descent groups present fine mats under the category called *'ie mavaega*, the fine mat of "farewell" to the deceased. When they are presented to members of the dead man's descent group, these people now must respond by presenting other fine mats to each person who originally presented an *'ie mavaega*.

26. The hamlet's name is called out and the senior woman who resides there gathers the yams and then divides them among the other women who live there and attended the distribution.

27. Mauss (1923/4) recognized these differences when he wrote at the beginning of *"Essai sur le Don"* that Samoan fine mats were "feminine" property, "bound up with land, the clan, the family and the person" making them *"immeuble"* ("things that cannot be alienated"; my translation) (see also Weiner 1985).

28. Through marriages between high-ranking Tongan men and Samoan women, many fine mats have become part of Tongan wealth. In the Tongan King's palace today, there are Samoan fine mats stored away that are over three hundred years old (Hau'afa, personal communication).

29. In Kiriwina, stone axe blades, the "hard" wealth of men, are also exchanged at deaths, but this wealth carries the histories of individual men who have owned the blades previously. Here I am only concerned with wealth that symbolizes the kin group and ancestral histories, but see Weiner (1983, 1988a) for a discussion of Trobriand "hard" and "soft" wealth.

30. Even though a man's children are not members of his matrilineage, they still support these people by accumulating wealth for them to give away. In the same way, a man's daughter's husband helps her to get bundles for her father's matrilineage.

31. Even though pigs and other foods as well as money will also be given as *'oloa*, the fine mats are the most valued.

32. The *tulāfale* titles are ranked and each high ranked chief has more than one orator. According to Krämer ([1902] 1930), chiefs themselves often took *tulāfale* titles in addition to their own so they could receive fine mats themselves.

33. In addition, a man must support members of his wife's descent group as well as those from his father's sister's husband's descent group.

34. If the woman is widowed or has never married, then her brother who is

the chief will not present fine mats in her name because the members of her descent group will sponsor her funeral. If she is living with her husband, then the members of her husband's descent group are the sponsor and her brother presents the fine mat (Schoeffel, personal communication).

35. Certain important titles from the *tamatane* and *tamafafine* branches are themselves *feagaiga* to each other, as Schoeffel (1981) has demonstrated. Each title-holder stands as brother and sister to each other with the obligations that a brother and sister have to each other, even though the two chiefs may both be men. When a death occurs, one branch as the "brother" will bring fine mats to the "sister", those who are *tamafafine* (also see Krämer [1902] 1930,I:52 for a similar example).

36. As of 1981, untitled men were not even permitted to vote in the national elections.

37. See e.g., Kooijman 1972; Mead 1969; Weiner 1985.

REFERENCES CITED

Adams, M.
    1980   Structural Aspects of East Sumbanese Art. *In* The Flow of Life: Essays on Eastern Indonesia. J.J. Fox, ed. Cambridge: Harvard University Press.

Battaglia, D.
    1981   Segaya: Commemoration in a Massim Society. Ph.D. thesis. Cambridge University.

Buck, Sir P.H.
    1930   Samoan Material Culture. Honolulu: Bernice P. Bishop Museum Bulletin 75.

Cain, H.
    1971   The Sacred Child and the Origins of Spirit in Samoa. Anthropos 66:173–81.

Delaney, C.
    1986   The Meaning of Paternity and the Virgin Birth Debate. Man 21(3):494–513.

Duranti, A.
    1981   The Samoan Fono: A Sociolinguistic Study. Canberra: Pacific Linguistics.

Ella, Rev. S.
    1899   Polynesian Native Clothing. The Journal of the Polynesian Society 8:165–70.

Fox, J.J.
  1977   Roti, Nada and Savu. *In* Textile Traditions of Indonesia. M.H.
          Kahlenberg, ed. L.A.: County Museum.

Gailey, C.
  1987   Kinship to Kingship: Gender Hierarchy and State Formation in
          the Tongan Islands. Austin: University of Texas Press.

Gernet, L.
  1981   "Value" in Greek Myth. *In* Myth, Religion and Society. R.L. Gor-
          don, ed. London: Cambridge University Press.

Gittinger, M.
  1979   Splendid Symbols: Textiles and Tradition in Indonesia. Washing-
          ton D.C.: The Textile Museum.

Goldman, I
  1970   Ancient Polynesian Society. Chicago: University of Chicago Press.

Granet, M.
  1975   The Religion of the Chinese People. New York: Harper & Row.
          (First published 1922).

Hau'afa, E.
  1980   Personal communication.

Henry, T.
  1928   Ancient Tahiti. Honolulu: Bernice P. Bishop Museum Bulletin 48.

Hjarnø, J.
  1979–80 Social Reproduction: Towards an Understanding of Aboriginal
          Samoa. Folk:21–22.

Hocart, A.M.
  1915   Chieftainship and the Sister's Son in the Pacific. American An-
          thropologist 17(4):631–46.
  1954   The Life-Giving Myth and Other Essays. New York: Harper &
          Row.

Huntsman, J. and A. Hooper
  1975   Male and Female in Tokelau Culture. The Journal of the Polyne-
          sian Society:84(4)415–30.

Kaeppler, A.
  1978   Exchange Partners in Goods and Spouses: Fiji, Tonga and
          Samoa. Mankind:11(2) 246–52.

Kahn, M.
  1986   Always Hungry, Never Greedy: Food and the Expression of
          Gender in a Melanesian Society. Cambridge: Cambridge Univer-
          sity Press.

Kirch, P.
1984   The Evolution of Polynesian Chiefdoms. Cambridge: Cambridge
        University Press.

Kooijman, S.
1972   Tapa in Polynesia. Honolulu: Bernice P. Bishop Museum Bulletin
        234.
1977   Tapa on Moce Island, Fiji. Leiden: E.J. Brill.

Krämer, A.
1930   The Samoan Islands. 2 volumes. Stuttgart. English translation,
        D.H. & M. DeBeer. (Original German publication, 1902).
1958   Salamasina. Stuttgart. English translation, Assn. of the Marist
        Brothers. (Original German publication, 1923).

Leach, E.R.
1966   Virgin birth. Proceedings of the Royal Anthropological Institute,
        pp. 39–50.

Leacock, E.
1972   Introduction In The Origin of the Family, Private Property and
        the State. F. Engels. New York: International Publishers. pp. 7–67.

Lévi-Strauss, C.
1969   The Elementary Structures of Kinship. Boston: Beacon Press.

Lepowsky, M.
1981   Fruit of the Motherland: Gender and Exchange on Vanatinai,
        Papua New Guinea. Ph.D. thesis. University of California,
        Berkeley.

Mabuchi, T.
1964   Spiritual Predominance of the Sister. In Ryukyan Culture and
        Society: A Survey. 10th Pacific Science Congress. Honolulu: Uni-
        versity of Hawaii Press.

Malinowski, B.
1935   Coral Gardens and Their Magic. 2 vols. Bloomington: Indiana
        University Press.

Mauss, M.
1923–24 Essai sur le Don: Form et Raison de l'Echange dans les So-
        ciétés Archaïques. In Année Sociologique. Nouvelle Série 1.
1979   Sociology and Psychology, Essays by Marcel Mauss. London:
        Routledge & Kegan Paul.

Mead, M.
1930   Social Organization of Manu'a. Honolulu: Bernice P. Bishop Mu-
        seum Bulletin 76.

Mead, S.
1969   Traditional Maori Clothing. Wellington: A.H. and A.W. Reed.

Milner, G.
  1966   Samoan Dictionary. Oxford: Oxford University Press.

Murra, J.
  1962   Cloth and Its Function in the Inca State. American Anthropologist 65:710–28.

Onians, R.B.
  1951   The Origins of European Thought About the Body, the Mind, the Soul, the World, Time, and Fate. Cambridge: Cambridge University Press.

Ortner, S.
  1981   Gender and Sexuality in Hierarchical Societies: The Case of Polynesia and Some Comparative Implications. *In* Sexual Meanings, the Cultural Construction of Gender and Sexuality. S. Ortner and H. Whitehead, eds. Cambridge: Cambridge University Press.

Rappaport, R.
  1984   Pigs for the Ancestors. New Haven: Yale University Press. Second edition.

Rogers, G.
  1977   "The Father's Sister is Black," A Consideration of Rank and Power in Tonga. The Journal of the Polynesian Society 86:158–82.

Sahlins, M.
  1958   Social Stratification in Polynesia. Seattle: University of Washington Press.
  1985   Islands of History. Chicago: University of Chicago Press.

Salmond, A.
  1984   Nga Muarahi O Te Ao Maori: Pathways in the Maori World. *In* Te Maori, Maori Art from New Zealand Collections. S. Mead, ed. New York: Harry N. Abrams, Inc.

Schoeffel, P.
  1977   The Origin and Development of Contemporary Women's Associations in Western Samoa. Journal of Pacific Studies 3:1–22.
  1981   Daughters of Sina, A Study of Gender, Status and Power in Western Samoa. Ph.D. thesis, Australian National University.

Shore, B.
  1981   Sexuality and Gender in Samoa: Conceptions and Misconceptions. *In* Sexual Meanings, The Cultural Construction of Gender and Sexuality. S. Ortner and H. Whitehead, eds. Cambridge: Cambridge University Press.
  1982   Sala'ilua. A Samoan Mystery. New York: Columbia University Press.

Spiro, M.
   1968   Virgin Birth, Parthenogenesis, and Physiological Paternity: an
           Essay in Cultural Interpretation. Man, n.s., 3:242–61.

Stair, Rev. J.B.
   1897   Old Samoa, or Flotsam and Jetsam From the Pacific Ocean. Lon-
           don: The Religious Tract Society.

Stuebel, O.
   1896   Samoanische Texte. Berlin: Geographische Verlagshandlung
           Dietrich Reimer.

Teckle, B.
   1986   The Position of Women in Fiji. Ph.D. thesis, University of Sydney.

Tiffany, S.
   1974   The Land and Titles Court and the Regulation of Customary
           Title Successions and Removal in Western Samoa. The Journal of
           the Polynesian Society 83:35–57.

Weiner, A. B.
   1976   Women of Value, Men of Renown: New Perspectives in Trobri-
           and Exchange. Austin: University of Texas Press.
   1980   Reproduction: A Replacement for Reciprocity. American Ethnolo-
           gist 7:71–85.
   1982   Sexuality Among the Anthropologists, Reproduction Among the
           Informants. Social Analysis 12:52–65.
   1983   "A World of Made is Not a World of Born"—Doing Kula in
           Kiriwina. In J.W. Leach and E.R. Leach, eds. The Kula: New
           Perspectives on Massim Exchange. Cambridge: Cambridge Uni-
           versity Press. pp. 147–70.
   1985   Inalienable Wealth. American Ethnologist 12:210–27.
   1987   Towards a Theory of Gender Power: An Evolutionary Perspec-
           tive. In The Gender of Power: A Symposium. M. Leyenaar et.al.,
           eds. Leiden: Vakgroep Vrouwenstudies FSW. pp. 41–77.
   1988a   The Trobrianders of Papua New Guinea. New York: Holt,
           Rinehart and Winston.
   1988b   Dominant Kings and Forgotten Queens. Oceania 58:157–60.

Young, M.
   1971   Fighting With Food. Cambridge: Cambridge University Press.

Valeri, V.
   1985   Kingship and Sacrifice: Ritual and Society in Ancient Hawaii. Chi-
           cago: University of Chicago Press.

3. Cloth and the Creation of Ancestors in Madagascar

GILLIAN FEELEY-HARNIK

 One of the recurrent debates in African ethnology concerns the definition of ancestors and the nature of their authority. Fortes raised these issues in his ethnographies of the Tallensi (1945, 1949), in his essay on "Oedipus and Job in West African Religion" (1959), and in several articles (e.g., 1961, 1965, 1981), to which Kopytoff (1971, 1981), Brain (1973), Calhoun (1980, 1981), and others have since responded. One of their disagreements has to do with meaning. Do the Tallensi (and some other African peoples) actually distinguish between elders and ancestors, as the English terms imply and as Fortes, Brain, and Calhoun argue? Or, like the Suku in Kopytoff's view, do they include elders, ancestors, and perhaps other persons, animals, and things, in the same category of beings?

Another major question concerns the relevance of ideas to social organization. Fortes argued that Tallensi distinctions supported the projection of authority relations among living members of the same lineage onto the dead. To Kopytoff, the primacy of elders rather than ancestors confirms that "horizontal" boundaries between the living and the dead are secondary to "vertical" boundaries between lineage members and outsiders. Both Brain and Calhoun argue that Kopytoff overlooks aspects of relations between progenitors and their descendants that participants themselves find significant and that vary substantially from one group to another. Other scholars have questioned Fortes's own distinction between descent as a jural principle of group formation and kinship as the product of non-jural interpersonal ties, especially where participants emphasize cognate as well as lineal ties when allocating rights and obligations (e.g., Keesing 1978). Kiernan (1982) has reexamined "the problem of evil" in ancestral intervention among the Zulu of southern Africa. Glazier's (1984) essay on the transformation of Mbeere funeral rites in the context of changing land tenure regulations in east central Kenya focuses on historical and material factors that earlier studies did not consider. I have taken a similar approach in analyzing the labor involved in the reconstruction of Sakalava royal tombs (Feeley-Harnik 1990).

The purpose of this paper is to contribute to the general ethnography on relations between ancestors and their descendants from a Malagasy perspective, and to pursue specific questions concerning the role of cloth and other materials in substantiating ancestral claims to authority. What forms do ancestors take? How are they made? What is the role of acts in articulating ideas where, as in the case that follows, speaking is associated with exchanging and thinking with seeing? As Fortes asked in reviewing the African data, "How does parental and lineage authority, as projected in ancestor worship, link up with political authority and its ritual symbolism and representation as in some forms of African kingship?" (1965:140).

Closer attention to the materials with which people apprehend ancestors and communicate with them may clarify how ancestors achieve authority over kin and non-kin. Cloth is central to the creation of ancestors in Madagascar as in many other parts of the world (see Darish and Weiner in this volume, Schneider 1987). In the Malagasy highlands, for example, indigenous silk textiles, handwoven by Merina and Betsileo women, are the focal point of reburial ceremonies (famadihana), in which kin gather every few years to honor important common ancestors by exhuming them, rewrapping them in new shrouds, and reburying them. Among the Sakalava of western Madagascar, where reburial is not practiced, imported silk textiles are central to spirit possession. People wrap their own relatives and friends in shrouds as they are possessed by the spirits of former kings and queens, a process that recurs throughout the year.

I argue that this possession by royal spirits follows the same pattern as the reburial of commoners' ancestors in the highlands, except that Sakalava exhume the dead by invoking them to speak in the bodies of commoners and rebury them by silencing them. Clothing the spirit is essential to the processes of regenerating it and making it speak, thereby identifying itself. Yet shrouding the spirit is also associated with concealment and eventually silence, even as wrapping a corpse is part of burying it. Cloth epitomizes the ambiguity of speaking through mediums, where it is not always clear whether the medium is acting for its spirit or for itself.

The process of clothing spirits to enable them to speak and to silence them resembles other ways in which Sakalava communicate and exchange with royal ancestors, including annual purification services and generational reconstructions of the royal tomb. In these services, different forms of royalty are unwrapped and rewrapped, regenerated and reburied, using materials like trees and stones in addition to bodies, bones, and cloth. The parallels in these processes by which the living and dead interact appear to rest on fundamental assumptions concerning the complex composition of human beings and the contradictory, often conflict-ridden structure of human relations, requiring various indirect as well as direct forms of expression.

THE SAKALAVA

The term "Sakalava" includes different groups of people along the west coast, who make their living by rice farming, animal husbandry, fishing, trading and wage labor. They are linked by their common and continuing respect for the power of the Maroseraña dynasty that ruled over this area until the French conquest of 1896. The Maroseraña dynasty is still represented in the Analalava region of the northwest coast by a living ruler (*ampanjaka*). She rules together with her ancestral predecessors in office. This is in keeping with Sakalava beliefs that the kin groups of royalty and "simple people" (*olo tsotra*) alike include ancestral dead (*razaña*) as well as living members (*olombelo/ño*). Ancestors are considered to have more power than living people and consequently more voice in domestic and political affairs, owing to their age compounded by their death. Their death is celebrated in spirit possession, where they take the form in which they died (Feeley-Harnik 1978).

Sakalava bury their dead in cemeteries attached to local communities. Burying the body and prohibiting the use of the personal name of the dead person are related acts. As one woman explained in response to my unwitting questions about her family:

> I am afraid to say it [her dead father's name], it can't be done. [I would be] ashamed/disgraced [the condition of a person who has not observed the prohibitions entailed by respect]. You cannot utter the names of your parents after they are dead. They would punish you if you did. Your family names are like those of the Hova [Merina] and the Tsimihety, and also the Comorians. All the children get their father's name as well as their own. When Sakalava die, they don't uncover/open (*mañokatra*) the body like the Hova and the Tsimihety. The Hova dig up the body again, if it died somewhere else, and take it back to its ancestral land (*tanindrazaña*). The Tsimihety do the same, burying men in rocks in the mountains, in different coffins from women. Sakalava just leave the body in the place where it died, that's it (*basy*)!

Sakalava observe other prohibitions separating the dead from the living at the burial and afterwards. Nevertheless, ancestors continue to communicate with their living descendants, and thereby influence the changing fortunes of the living. Living people invoke their ancestors by addressing them generically as "Sir" or "Madam" (*Tompokolahy/vavy*), and presenting them with offerings, the materials for which are kept on a shelf in the northeast corner of the house known as the "ancestors' corner" (*zorondrazaña*). Sakalava use the phrase "removing the lock" (*fangala gadra/hidy*) in referring to the opening of a household head's formal speech (*kabary*) to the ancestors. "He opens the mouth of the speech [like a door], unties the knot constricting formal communication" (*mampibihaña ny vavan' ny kabary, mamavatra kabary*), exposing what is on his mind in speaking about it.[1]

When a Sakalava ruler dies, his or her personal name is prohibited along with any other words that resemble it. A praise name such as "The Noble One Who Sustained Thousands" (*Ndramamahañarivo*) is used instead. Teknonyms, like "Soazara's Father" (*Baban' Soazara*) for Ndramamahañarivo, may be used in referring to or addressing the spirit in less formal circumstances, including spirit-possession ceremonies.

Sakalava royalty are buried with elaborate ceremony that lasted a year in the precolonial period (see Dandouau 1912:165–72, Poirier 1939). Royal regalia, perhaps including relics, are kept at the royal capital (*doany*) on the mainland. The corpse, having been reduced to bone, is buried in a royal tomb (*mahabo*) on an island off the coast. Both of these are elaborately fenced. The "royal ancestors' house" at the capital is enclosed within a palisade of pointed stakes, which is itself enclosed within a second fence made of palm fronds around the royal compound, including the house of the living ruler. The royal tomb is enclosed by an inner palisade of pointed stakes with a place that Sakalava call a "door" in the middle of the west side, where two of the posts are taller than the rest, and an outer hedge with a door in the middle of the west side that opens and closes. The plan of the *mahabo*, surrounded by the houses of ex-slaves and spirit mediums, parallels that of the *doany*, where the royal compound is surrounded by the houses of ex-slaves attached to the living ruler.

The royal ancestors are isolated from the living in various ways, but they continue to interact with the living; their influence is considered to be evident in the overall condition of the region. The living communicate with the royal ancestors in annual purification services that Sakalava compare to domestic offerings. They also speak and exchange with them during other "royal services" (*fanompoaña*), the most important of which is the reconstruction of the fence around the royal tomb that a living ruler is obligated to carry out after burying his or her predecessor. These services focus on the acts of unlocking, opening, closing, and relocking the doors implied in communicating with domestic ancestors. Living people and royal ancestors also communicate through spirit possession, in which the ancestors reappear among the living by "coming to govern on people" (*mianjaka amin'olo*) whom the living clothe in royal form. To explore the processes of wrapping and rewrapping that are common to these interactions between the living and the dead, I begin with a brief account of the role of clothing in making and breaking relationships among the living. Then I discuss spirit possession, the commonest form of relationship between the living and the dead, and conclude with a brief outline of services for the royal ancestors that are more infrequent but are regional in scope.

Figure 4. The Ampanjaka *Soazara as a child, dressed in imported red silks and surrounded by followers (ca. 1936). Photo, Service Photo-Cinéma de la Direction de l'Information, Antananarivo, Madagascar*

CLOTHING, SPEAKING, AND LYING

The rectangular piece of cloth known as the *lamba* is one of the most distinctive features of life throughout Madagascar. Draped differently according to age, sex, and circumstances, it is the common form of dress, a mark of social status, and a valued medium of exchange, sometimes serving as money in the context of highland burial rites (Feeley-Harnik and Mack n.d.). The precolonial cloth trade, especially in indigenous and imported silks, was fundamental to the political economy of several Malagasy monarchies (Figure 4). Cloth remains the greatest household expense after food and shelter, and the most important gift besides hospitality (Feeley-Harnik and Mack n.d.). Sakalava women no longer weave, but sewing is an important form of communal work (Figure 5).

Clothing is the product of reciprocity. Sakalava associate nakedness in daily life with poverty, madness, and other forms of social

Figure 5. Relatives by marriage sewing together; the women are also related through the royal spirits that possess them, but photographing the spirits is prohibited. Photo by Gillian Feeley-Harnik, 1973

isolation. Witches who have deliberately cut themselves off from society are recognized by the fact that they dance "naked on top of [tombs of] dead people." The properly social person is clothed, and the clothing itself conveys the nature of people's affiliations and their quality.

"Malagasy clothing" is wrapped around the body; tailoring implies Muslim or European affiliations. Most women in the Analalava region wear cotton body wraps (salovaña, siki/na): One sewn together at the ends to form a tube that covers the torso, a second worn over the shoulders (kisaly, salampy, lamba) and a third covering the head (foloara, kemba), all of which can be draped and folded in various ways. Men wear hip wraps (lambahoany, kitamby). Men and women combine wraps with tailored tops (a(n)kanjo, kazaka). School children and people in their twenties and thirties usually wear European clothing like T-shirts (tirkô), pants (pantalon), shorts (short), dresses

Figure 6. A Sakalava mother and son, in formal and everyday dress. Photo by Gillian Feeley-Harnik, 1981

(*ankanjo, rôbo, seray*) and outfits (*kombinaison*), and most women prize
French underwear, especially bras (*korsaza*).[2] Older men dress up in
suit jackets (*kazaka*) together with a shoulder wrap and cane on the
most formal occasions. Most kinds of European clothing can be purchased from local merchants, but the jackets are usually castoffs, exported from Europe in bulk, distributed through mission churches
or the markets of larger cities (Figure 6).

Indians, Chinese, and Malagasy from the highlands distinguish
themselves in part by wearing European clothing on most occasions.

Highland Malagasy men no longer combine European suits with Malagasy shoulderwraps, as they did during the nineteenth and early twentieth centuries, but Merina and Betsileo women usually complete their finest outfits by adding shawls distinct from those of coastal people in their white color and in the ways they are draped.

Clothing styles express a broad range of opinions concerning relationships among Malagasy and between Malagasy and Europeans, as illustrated in these comments by a young woman concerning characteristic ways of wearing body wraps:

> Tsimihety [her father's affiliation] wear their body wraps only to just below the knees, Sakalava [her mother's affiliation] to the ankles. Girls really start wearing it when they have breasts, though they start practicing earlier. Sakalava say that Tsimihety are naked (*mijalaña*). If the knees stick out (*miboaka*), Sakalava say they look conspicuous, undressed (*miala lamba*). Tsimihety say that if you wear the body wrap to your ankles you can't be strong, you can't move around. People who wear it to the ankles drag along, weak, lethargic, lazy. You can always tell a Sakalava and a Tsimihety seeing them on the road. The Sakalava walks slowly, in a stately and orderly manner. The Tsimihety—man or woman—trots right along, head forward [demonstration]. If a Tsimihety says something is nearby, a Sakalava knows it's far away. If a Tsimihety says it's far away, a Sakalava knows s/he can't make it there on foot. They need to move along calmly, peacefully, in a stately manner.

When I remarked to some Sakalava women that Tsimihety seem to wear shorter body wraps, they nodded and the older woman said "Yes, they're always running away." Later she added:

> They're always in a hurry, going quickly as if they were running away. They don't know how to move in a calm and orderly manner, they're always [she pulled her *salovaña* to her knees, tied it tightly high up under her armpits, and rushed around with a set expression on her face]. We wear it nicely down [she lowered her *salovaña* to her ankles and wrapped it comfortably around her chest], and when we're working, cooking, whatever, we tie it under the chest or around the waist (*mandreritra ambaniaña*). Those who know how to fix it right can tie their *salovaña* around the waist so neatly that it looks like a dress (*rôbo*).

These conflicting perspectives on energy, order, self-possession and modernity, which are quite widespread, probably originated during the early twentieth century, when French administrators distinguished Malagasy groups according to their capacities for work, and thus "progress" along Western lines. However, the name for the branch of the Sakalava monarchy that settled in northwestern Madagascar is *Bemihisatra*, meaning "The many who move forward so slowly as to stop" or, more broadly, "The many rooted in the land." These meanings date back to the early nineteenth century, according to Sakalava oral tradition in the Analalava region (and see Richardson 1885:266).

Sakalava identify themselves most completely as *Bemihisatra* during services for the royal ancestors, where all forms of European clothing are prohibited, including anything sewn rather than wrapped.[3] Men are prohibited from wearing underwear, trousers, belts, shoes, and brimmed hats (brimless *kofia* worn by Muslims are allowed); they must wear hip wraps (Figure 7). Women are prohibited from wearing underpants (bras are allowed), shoes, or sewn body wraps. They must wear a *sambelatra* or *helaka* (literally, "peeled" "skinned", "flayed"), which Sakalava explain as a body wrap without stitching that opens in the front (*lamba mitatatra*). Women are also prohibited from covering the upper parts of their body with head or shoulder wraps. There are special "dressing places" (*ampisikiña*) outside the royal capital and cemetery where people must change their clothes before entering.[4]

Sewing and tailoring have Muslim or European associations, but any clothing that is knotted or tied shut (*miqadra*) is also prohibited at royal centers. This suggests that besides severing foreign relations, Sakalava are required to be open to involvement with royalty. Covering the body can imply that a person is concealing bad thoughts. Evil characters in Sakalava folktales, usually disguised in the ankle-length robes of a Muslim, are revealed when they lift their clothing crossing a stream or let it fall open while drunk, thereby exposing their tails.[5]

The elaboration of clothing to distinguish people according to age, gender, status, and occupation is matched in most circumstances by its capacity for concealment. For example, babies' heads are covered and their bodies heavily wrapped during the first few months of life, even in the most hot and humid weather. The stated purpose is to keep them warm, but the wrapping is also thought

Figure 7. Sakalava men attending a service at the royal cemetery. Wearing the brimmed hat is prohibited for those actually participating in the service. Photo by Gillian Feeley-Harnik, 1973

to protect them from the harm that might come from others' jealous looks. For the same reason, pregnant women always cover their bellies with their shoulder wraps. Their clothing is governed by prohibitions associated with their patrilineal and matrilateral kin groups. It tends to be untailored because ties and knots could impede the birth.[6]

Whenever Sakalava feel uncomfortable they tend to cover their heads and shoulders. Conversely, when they feel relaxed, they loosen, open, or remove their head or shoulder wraps. These processes of wrapping and unwrapping the body are directly associated with speech and silence, familiarity and distance. For example, I was sitting in the courtyard of my "mother-in-law" together with her, her oldest son's wife, the wife's older sister ("Big Daughter-in-law"), and our several children, when another of her sons came in wearing a tiny bathing suit. She scolded him for letting his testicles stick out (*miboaka*) like a Frenchman, and he joked, as he could with his sisters-in-law, saying "Balls make money," at which everyone laughed uproariously.[7]

Personal names are equally revealing from a Sakalava point of view. Just as Needham (1954a,b), Fortes (1955), and Beidelman (1974) noted in Southeast Asian and African contexts, names are associated in Sakalava usage with personal attributes and historical experiences, including interactions between the living and the dead. In familiar circumstances, people of the same generation, and usually of the same sex, are permitted to intrude on the distinctiveness (*anjara*) of one another without disrespect by addressing one another by their personal names. Even so, there is a preference for more indirect forms of reference and address like kin terms, and a decided shift, as soon as a person has descendants of his or her own, to teknonyms. When a person is dead, Sakalava prohibit use of the personal name altogether.

Sakalava mourning customs support the inference that wrapping up, social formality, linguistic restraint, and depersonalization are ultimately associated with death, while speaking asserts the renewal of life and naming establishes familiar relations. When a person dies, the body is washed, pieces of kapok soaked in cologne are put in all the orifices and "places between," and incense is burned to cover the smell of the corpse. The clean body is wrapped in cloth and placed in a plain wooden coffin. Sakalava use all the good *lamba* they have stored in trunks, in contrast to Silamo who are prohibited from using anything but a piece of new white cotton cloth (*bafota malandy*). Sakalava may keep the body in the house for a few days, whereas Silamo must bury it before sundown. Whatever the case, the coffin is covered with another piece of white cloth when it is carried to the cemetery to be buried.[8]

Mourning prohibitions impose an analogous kind of wrapping and silence on the spouse as well, once lasting three months, now four to five weeks; women usually observe these prohibitions longer than men. The prohibitions are summarized in the phrase "to keep closed or locked," which may refer especially to the prohibitions against speaking or leaving the house.[9] The widow or widower "must remain in the house, without speaking to people, without going out." She or he may speak to very close kin of the same sex, but then only in a low voice. Very close kin of the opposite sex may enter the house, but they may neither look at nor speak to the mourning spouse, who may remain behind a curtain even inside the house. Greetings from outside must be answered by clapping. In going outside to the *douche*, he or she must cover up completely, leaving only an opening for an eye to find the way. The spouse announces the end of mourning by dressing up in clean clothing, coming out of the house and speaking to people.

Sakalava are not unusual in seeing cloth as an integrative social substance, interpreting the relations of persons to groups and incorporating them into communities, as exemplified in the power of a famous diviner to transform the dust falling from his hands into cloth. These are social facts that find strong support in everyday terminology concerning cloth. The weft of the *lamba* is its *faha/ña*, a term referring to the provision of sustenance, support, or consistency generally, including nourishment to a child, gifts to a stranger, or prosperity to countless royal subjects, as in Soazara's Father's praise name, Ndramamahañarivo, mentioned above.[10] The verb *mamahaña* refers to weaving, feeding, supporting, restoring or revitalizing others. *Manoratra*, to weave patterns into cloth, is also to write, whence "patterned/written cloth" (*lamba soratra*). The little stripes (Malagasy *lamba* are characteristically striped lengthwise) are the "vowels" (*zanatsoratra*), literally "the children of patterns/ writing" (Richardson 1885:224, 589–90).

Sakalava like clothing with writing on it, expressing their views on such subjects as love, wealth, children, and royal service like "Hang on to what's yours, because people won't give you theirs" (*Tahio ny antena, fa nin-olo tsy omeny*) or "I like the one outside, but I wouldn't trade the one inside the house" (*Tiako ny an-tany fa tsy atakaloko ny an-trano*) or "Children with money don't struggle" (*Zanaka misy vola tsy sahira*).[11] The same principle was used to broadcast loyalty to the PSD (Parti Social Democrate), the majority party in Madagascar prior to the revolution of 1972. Red, white, and green colored cloth, printed with then-President Tsiranana's face in black and white and emblazoned with the party motto, *Anio Rahampitso*

Mandrakizay Tsiranana (Today Tomorrow Forever Tsiranana) and the slogan, *Mirehareha izahay manana anao* (We are proud to have you [as our President]), was sold through local merchants prior to the President's inauguration on May 1, 1972. Functionaries and Indian shopkeepers wore shirts and blouses of Tsiranana cloth to party rallies in Analalava. Others, especially the less wealthy, wore clothing in the national colors.[12]

The political rallies in particular evoked comments that people also dress to mislead, even lie about relationships. Politically appropriate clothing may conceal motives that have nothing to do with party loyalty, or it may belie stated intentions. So many people felt they had to wear the cloth, whether or not they could afford it, that merchants selling Tsiranana cloth were accused privately of profiting in a bad way. By the same token, people may profess Islam and so adopt the distinctive skullcap of Muslim men without observing the proper devotions. They are the "skullcap Muslims" or "people who play at being Muslim" (see also Aujas 1927:33 and Mellis 1938:72). One man remarked in this context that male homosexuals may dress like women without really being women, only "images of women" (Figure 8).

Spirit possession turns on precisely these questions of identity and legitimacy, both during the process in which a person comes to be recognized as possessed by a particular spirit, and subsequently as the person maintains his or her relationship with the spirit as genuine. In each case, clothing and speaking together play a central role in the contradictory processes of substantiating identity and concealing falsity. To examine this connection between clothing and speaking in establishing, maintaining, and severing relations between the living and the dead, we now turn to the subject of spirit possession.

SPIRIT POSSESSION

Spirit possession makes people sick.[13] The sick person goes to a diviner who diagnoses the nature and cause of the problem to establish whether, as one woman explained, "it is a royal spirit [*tromba*] that needs to come out, poison, or your own spirits who are bothering you" (*lolo an-teña miqôdaña anao*). Typically, sickness that has resisted all other forms of treatment, including Western medicines, is

Figure 8. This children's dance group, honoring a visiting government official, is led by a man who dresses as a woman and is also well known as a spirit medium. Photo by Gillian Feeley-Harnik, 1971

interpreted as the work of a spirit that wants to "come out" (*miboaka*). Possession is also suspected when the sickness is accompanied by lost clothes and aching teeth. When I asked, what if someone had simply stolen the clothes, I was told that the diviner would explain that a royal spirit possessing the thief had gotten him or her to steal the clothes. Toothaches may result from eating prohibited foods, since spirits have many food prohibitions. Toothaches are also associated with the overall malaise, centered at the "mouth of the heart" (*vava fo*) just above the stomach, that spirits are commonly thought to cause and cure.

A spirit comes out when it speaks through the body of the sick person, openly declaring its reasons for causing the affliction that will result in the victim's death if not cured. The cure consists in fulfilling the spirit's demands, typically demands that involve its re-incorporation into the world of the living through the body of its host, as described below. That body then supports not only its own living spirit (*jery*) but, periodically, the spirits of one or more ances-tors as well. Despite the intimacy of the relationship between the spirit and its host, often compared to a marriage, Sakalava empha-size that their *jery*, or powers of discernment, are completely differ-ent. This general term for thought, intelligence, or reflection applies equally to the acts of seeing or inspecting something.

The diviner's response depends on the kind of spirit involved. The problem of identity involving clothing and speaking in Sakalava spirit possession is not simply a matter of acknowledging ancestral agency in evaluating a person's behavior. Participants must discover which of several kinds of spirits may be involved, and within each category, which specific spirit. The majority of spirits that possess people are called *tromba*, a term that Sakalava contrast with the term for "living persons" (*olombelo/na*). The broadest distinction that Sa-kalava make within this category is between "good" spirits and "bad" spirits. The former include all the spirits of the royal ancestors (*tromba, tromban-drazaña, zanahary*). The latter include spirits (*lolo*) called *masantoko, njarinintsy, be hondry, be tsioko*, who possess peo-ple in order to murder them.

In contrast to good spirits, who are considered to act on their own, bad spirits are thought to carry out the evil intentions of sor-cerers. The cure consists of taking medicines that will kill them or hiring a living person who knows how to drive them out, since royal spirits are prohibited from doing so. Bad spirits may torment a per-son in a characteristic fashion over a long period of time, but the purpose of the cure is to get rid of the spirit altogether. As long as a bad spirit persists in possessing a person, the cure is not complete. Bad spirits never speak. In fact, if it appears right away, and does not speak, "you already know this thing here [*raha 'ty*] is bad, be-cause it's not speaking," as one medium explained. Bad spirits are identified by bodily gestures like violent punching or uncontrollable shivering, not names and clothing. Perhaps this is because they are not considered human or because they are not incorporated into permanent relations with humans, though some people saw them as the necessary precursors of good spirits.

Sakalava acknowledge that a good spirit can look like a bad one when it is "angry" at its host, perhaps for drinking, breaking an ancestral prohibition, or failing to acknowledge a vow. Royal spirits, like living rulers, are thought to be prone to anger, especially if they feel that people "do not recognize [*mijery*] them," in the fullest sense of the term, that is, see them, reflect on them, respect them. Anger is an important cause of sickness. Many royal rituals concerning both living and dead royalty are intended to assuage their anger, "taking care of them by calming them down, cosseting them" (*mitambesatra azy*) by speaking and singing to them and giving them gifts. Nevertheless, the intentions of good spirits, even when they are angry, are entirely different from those of murderously evil spirits. Their actions will, if ignored, result in death. But their ultimate concern is not with killing but with the host's overall well-being—"Good spirits know how to cure; they like people."

Good spirits include all the Sakalava royal ancestors, distinguished as members of the senior or junior branch of the Maroseraña dynasty, that is as "Descendants of the Gold" or "Descendants of the Silver." If they are immediate ancestors of the local ruler or founding ancestors of the dynasty, they are "big" in contrast to the spirits of more distant or more junior royalty who are "little spirits."

As with bad spirits, the cure consists in "calling" the spirit to state its identity and its intentions, which in the case of good spirits will involve some sort of permanent relationship between the spirit and its host. Sakalava speak here too of "making the spirit come out" or "making it come down [onto the head or into the body]," but in practice they must induce it to speak. Royalty cannot be commanded, so people must cajole the spirit into speaking by bringing gifts, burning incense, and clapping and singing praise songs. As one woman explained it, these are all ways of calling the spirit, "Asking, begging, pleading with the spirit to come, come! We are begging you, just come, speak, say your name! When s/he hears this, s/he will arrive." Some spirits are described as easier to bring out than others, but the process of calling a spirit usually requires several meetings held over weeks, months, and sometimes years.[14]

During this time, when the spirit is on the verge of arriving, it may be addressed as "visitor/stranger" (*vahiny, ampenziky*) like a newborn baby, or as "Sir/Madam" (*Tompoko*), and sometimes referred to as the "difficult one" (*sarotro*) or "thing" (*raha*). It may respond to people's pleas to come out by emerging enough to cause the sick person to shake or cry out inarticulately. It may eventually send one of its "royal slaves," male or female followers, to convey its anger at what is preventing it from revealing itself, for example, polluted surroundings, too few royal relatives in attendance, inferior gifts, the wrong kinds of music, or the persistent disbelief of the sick person's kin, often a husband like the one who kept saying, "It's all lies, no royal spirit is involved."

If the spirit greets the crowd, then some aspects of its identity will be revealed in the way it speaks the royal language—as a man, woman, or child from a particular region. Eventually the spirit may answer the basic question: "Are you a senior or junior member of Sakalava royalty?" The lengthy process culminates in the "utterance" (*toñony*) when the spirit identifies the clothing, stick, and silver ornaments that it requires in keeping with its name. Finally the spirit, fully clothed, reveals itself by stating its name, place of origin, and purpose in rejoining the living at the ceremony called "turning the royal compound upside-down" (*vadiky lapa*) to which we will return.

NAMING AND CLOTHING

The processes of naming and clothing are intertwined. The spirit may hint at its identity, but wait until it has received all it requested before revealing itself fully. The sick person, kin, or friends may recognize the spirit by the nature of its requests, especially if it is one of the little spirits that possess a lot of people. It may still be difficult to find or buy all the clothes at once. Even so, Sakalava emphasize that, in one medium's words, "Until the spirit has been fully clothed, it has not been clearly brought out, the process is not yet complete. When it gets the *lamba* it wants, then it will come out. If it has not yet gotten the *lamba*, then its particular requirements have not been fulfilled, and it will not reveal its name."

The spirit's answer to whether it is a member of the senior or junior branch will already be enough to indicate whether it is big or little. Further hints will reveal whether the sick person is possessed by a royal spirit who ruled in some distant place or by one of the local queen's immediate relatives. These distinctions are economic as well as social. Gifts to royalty should be new; second-hand materials are generally prohibited. Old clothing, like an opened package of cigarettes or a half-empty bottle of rum, is classified in the same category as the leftovers from last night's dinner heated up for breakfast the next morning (*ankera*).[15] Furthermore, the materials worn by big spirits are more elaborate and made of more costly materials like silks and precious metals, compared with those presented to lesser royal spirits.[16]

The term for spirits' clothing (*sarandra, lamba tromba, lambandjanahary*), literally "royal spirits' clothing," refers especially to the mantle.[17] There are no special words in the royal vocabulary for the other garments, which are called by the same terms as their common counterparts. The mantle and the cane are regarded as the most distinctive pieces of clothing and they are typically the most expensive.

The mantle differs in how it is used in the process of possession and how it is worn once the spirit has arrived. When a person starts to shake, and the people around her see that she is becoming possessed, they cover her with a *sarandra* or a large white cloth (*darà*), or a patterned hip wrap (this is not considered proper), as she falls backwards. Holding the four corners, they shake the cloth until the body underneath lies prone on the ground, which indicates that the spirit is there. Then they dress the spirit and uncover it; little spirits usually dress themselves and come out from under the cloth. At the royal cemetery, the host/spirit, still covered by the cloth, may be carried like a corpse into the royal council house just west of the burial compound and dressed there. Once a big spirit is dressed, it is seated upright in its "chair" (*sezy*, from the French word *chaise*), that is, between the legs of a female attendant whose limbs and torso form the arms and back of the chair. The cloth that covered the spirit is not wrapped around its shoulders, but wrapped around the lower part of the body from the waist down and tucked under at the feet, the way a shroud is wrapped around the body of a corpse, except that the upper body and head are left bare.

The red and multicolored silk cloths associated with the senior royal line (*dahalany, sobaiha, tsiampongamena, jakimena*) were once imported along with other silks (*lasoa, hariry, deboan*) by Arab and Comorian merchants from the Arabian peninsula, which Sakalava claim to be the source of most features of the Maroseraña dynasty. Since French colonists curtailed the Arab trade, these cloths have become more rare and expensive than they were reputed to be before.[18]

The stick (*mampingo*) is not sold in stores. It is made from local wood, ideally hard and black like the ebony for which it is named, highly polished and ornamented with silver. The silver differentiates it as a "silver club" (*kobay fanjava*) belonging to a male ruler and often thought of as a weapon, unlike an ordinary man's stick, which is used as a cane. The stick may be purchased, acquired as a gift, or inherited from another person, as long as the person was not a medium. The silver decorations are the work of Indian jewelers, numerous in Analalava during the colonial period, but now found only in the big cities outside the region.

Antique clothing or silver that has been used before must be purified by "washing" it, using mixtures of honey and water to which kaolin and silver have been added. This is how Sakalava purify the royal relics at the capital and the tomb at the royal cemetery every year. One of the several months in which these services are held is devoted to making the liquid. The personal pollution of body and clothing that results from attending a funeral or from breaking a prohibition is cleansed in the same way.[19] Sakalava may also petition royal spirits to relax their clothing requirements, as they do with onerous food prohibitions. A year must pass before appeals concerning food can be made. Such compromises are more difficult to achieve with big spirits than with little ones. Possession is invigorating for the spirit, but still burdensome, sometimes debilitating, for the host even after her or his cure, because of the numerous prohibitions, especially concerning food, and the expenses that are involved in the relationship. The bigger the spirit, the greater the sacrifices are expected to be.

Once these materials have been purchased, or—depending on how difficult it is to find them—*as* they are purchased, they will be presented to the spirit as gifts at the ceremony described as "turning the royal compound upside-down." As one woman, possessed by several spirits, described it:

> The process of urging a spirit to declare itself is called making
> the spirit come out (*mampiboaka tromba*), no matter how many
> times it takes before it finally appears. *Mamadiky lapa* is what it is
> called after a year has passed and it appears (*miboaka*) again and
> reveals all its customary practices (*manambara jiaby ny fomban'azy*).
> *Mamadiky lapa* is when it reveals its prohibitions, to utter its
> name clearly: I am so-and-so, my father is so-and-so, my mother
> is so-and-so, the place where I live is so-and-so.

Another medium explained:

> People who call a royal spirit to turn the royal compound
> upside-down, they are calling [it] again, calling a second time.
> Making a spirit come out (*mampiboaka tromba*) is what [calling the
> spirit] is called when you are first trying to get it out, no matter
> how many times it takes. Turning the royal compound upside-
> down (*mamadiky lapa*) is what [calling the spirit] is called after
> one year has passed. It comes out again and reveals all its cus-
> toms, everything. Until this has happened, you can't heal oth-
> ers. Once that has finished, you can heal or make royal spirits
> come out yourself. [Why is it called *mampiboaka tromba* no matter
> how often or how long it takes?] Because the person is sick! It is
> a sickness after all! You are curing a sickness by making it come
> out!

"To utter the name" (*Manoñono anarany*) is "to raise or reveal the
name" (*manonga anarany*) as Sakalava also express it, using a phrase
that otherwise refers to removing one's clothes. A person's character is expressed not only in his or her name, but in his or her customary ways of acting, especially through clothing. The end of the illness entailed in revealing the name and the character through the
clothing is the beginning of a new relationship between the spirit
and its host, and between the host and his or her kin, to whom the
prohibitions are explained at the same time. A person will still become "sick" in the process of being possessed, but only immediately
prior to the act of possession, not interminably. On the contrary,
provided that the host observes the spirit's prohibitions, the relationship is considered to be a source of good health and fortune,
including the financial benefits of curing others in turn.[20]

The income from such activities, like the clothing and other
things involved in possession—the offering dish, silver coins, ornaments and charms, kaolin, incense and incense burner—are considered to belong to the spirit, not its host. The spirit's clothes,
wrapped in cloth or stored in a plastic bag, are kept with the rest
of its things on a set of shelves hung on the eastern wall of the
house, opposite the ancestor's corner in the southern corner or in
the northeast corner of the southern room. The shelf (*taky*), like the
shelf with the same name and purpose in the ancestors' house at
the royal capital, is covered with a piece of plain white cotton cloth
(*gora, bafota*) called a *lamba* or *darà* in commoners' houses, but a

tsafoday/tafonday in the case of the ancestors' house. The stick and other special possessions, for example, a spirit's folding chair, propped against the wall below the shelf, are likewise covered with white cloths (and they are usually kept covered that way when they are carried to meetings). They must be given to the ancestors' attendants at the royal cemetery when the host dies, although kin may later petition to get them back. These objects, covered in white, serve to bring the spirit not only into the body of its host, but also into its house. Their presence transforms the host's house, like her body, into a shrine honoring the royal ancestors, comparable to the royal capital and royal tomb and requiring many of the same prohibitions, especially concerning pollution.

SUBSTANTIATING IDENTITY AND CONCEALING FALSITY

Clothing, naming, and speaking are the central issues in spirit possession. Specific royal spirits possess people in order to be able to speak out and be spoken to in ways they could not if they remained buried. Frequently they speak to express their anger at something that has happened and their demands for changing it. Their way of speaking is compared to the bellowing of a bull. Their words, uttered in the royal language, are referred to as "ancestors' orders," a phrase that also emphasizes their commanding aspect.[21]

Sakalava acknowledge the role of economic power in political expression when they explain that rulers, not commoners, speak after death because a ruler is buried with coins in his or her mouth, whereas it is prohibited to put money in the mouths of commoners. The money is what gives royal spirits a voice, even as money buys the clothing that creates the forms through which they speak, substantiating their identity.[22] Still, the mouths of royalty are tied shut like those of commoners when they are buried. Royalty speak only when wrapped in the bodies of commoners who are wearing the clothing that identifies them, which includes the shroud that silenced them in the first place. Furthermore, once the intertwined processes of clothing and speaking have revealed the spirit's identity and the host's cure, the relationship between the two is to some extent reversed. People usually refer to their relationships with spirits by saying "Government sits on me" (*Fanjakaña mipetraka aminakahy*) rather than the spirit's praise name or teknonym. Furthermore they emphasize the spirit's autonomy, saying that you can never know when the spirit might possess you "because your minds (*jery*) are not the same."

However, in giving its name, the spirit has relinquished some of its power to its host. Sakalava women converted to Islam regularly prevent their spirits from speaking during Ramadan. They do this by "tying their mouths shut," as one woman put it. They disagree with the orthodox Muslim view that *tromba* are evil spirits (*setoan*), arguing that spirit possession is a serious illness. Yet they are careful to observe the prohibition against possession during the month of Ramadan, dedicated to purification through fasting and prayers. They call the spirit and say, as the same woman continued: "I am tying myself up!" (*Zaho mifehy!*—"I am fasting!" in the context of Ramadan). "Keep silent and don't make me sick!" Once this is done, they can attend spirit-possession meetings during Ramadan, and their spirits will neither speak nor make them sick in their efforts to speak. Sakalava "tie up" (*mifehy*) the mouth of a corpse before it is wrapped and buried. The term also applies to governing, whence the name of the royal district administrators (*mpifehy*, literally, "tiers-up") and the districts over which they have jurisdiction (*fehezina*, "tied bundles") in Sakalava monarchy.

People silence the dead by tying their mouths shut, wrapping them in shrouds and burying them. They make them speak by clothing them in the bodies of commoners, but clothing them in part as if they were unwrapping and rewrapping them again in shrouds. The spirit's clothing is just as articulate as that of any living person. Indeed, people often explain the differences among spirits by comparing them to the living, but periodically the mantle covers it all. The act of wrapping the spirit in its shroud, rewrapping it every time it reappears, seems to be instrumental in bringing it into the living body of the medium and identifying its voice. Spirits are rewrapped *to* reappear, *to* speak. But at the same time, their speech is veiled by having to emerge from the body of another as it is veiled by their death recalled in the mantle that serves first as a shroud.

Irvine's (1982) comparative analysis of spirit mediumship and possession from a sociolinguistic perspective highlights the complexity of the creative process by which spirits are identified. She argues that semantic analysis alone is insufficient because the meaning attributed to behavioral forms, even if generally agreed upon, may vary according to the context in which they occur, the personal interests of participants, and the histories of their relations with one another. Irvine suggests that the attribution or declaration of identity in spirit possession is simply a specific instance of a more general social process, and that comparable factors may be involved in participants' interpretations of identity on a broader scale. The Sakalava data confirm Irvine's observations. Moreover, they suggest that in this case at least, much of the participants' own sense of the complexities involved in substantiating identity lies in their perceptions of the spirit's clothing.

Someone may appear to be possessed, but people will say, "only the clothes possess her" or "the spirit is not doing it, the body is doing it," suggesting, without having to say so directly, that the person is a "lying medium" or even a sorcerer. For example, one woman said about the group of little spirits from Betsioko that possess people the most frequently:

> There are so many of them. All the things about them (*ley raha jiaby amin'azy*) possess everyone, but the real them (*ley teñan'izy*) seldom does. Their things, their handkerchiefs (*mouchoir*), possess people, but only a very few are actually possessed by the real thing. In every village, almost everyone in the place is possessed by one of those royal spirits. A lot of people just get possessed so that people will see. It's appearance (*fizahaña*), few people really have it (*misy azy vantaña*). [How do you know the real thing?] They chronicle (*mitantara*) what happened before they died. The ones that aren't really it can't *say* much about it [her emphasis]. If the real one comes when the others are there, then the others will leave. But there are too many that just appear to have it. [What about the living ruler's ancestors? The Father and Son possess so many mediums.] If a person dares to become possessed at the royal cemetery, it's it (*izy*)! If it doesn't go to the royal cemetery, it's not it. If it comes there, this one's really it (*izy ankitiny 'ty ê*)! They have a trial (*fitsaraña*) for it there. There's questions they ask in case of deception (*mihaboka*). *Mihaboka* concerns possessions (*fañanana*). It means to claim you have things you don't have. The true ones (*ley marigny*) are ordered to go to the royal cemetery, ordered by the royal spirit possessing them. The false ones just need to get possessed. When they get there, people see.[23]

The *vadiky lapa*, when a spirit comes out and declares its name, the names of its parents, its place of origin, its prohibitions, and other customary observances, is compared to the trial at the royal cemetery. It is a validation, but on a lesser scale. As one man explained, speaking about the little spirits associated with the junior branch of Sakalava royalty,

> Little spirits, Kotomena, Fotsy, Ley Sarotro, don't go through a trial. They *mamadiky lapa*. Ampela Be [an elder father's sister in the junior branch]—she might pronounce her name before, but at Andampy [their royal center] she really does it all. They elevate her/reveal her name (*mampanonga azy*). Zafinimena [members of the senior branch] don't go through the *vadiky lapa*, just the trial.

Big spirits must undergo the trial at the royal cemetery before they can live there all year round. The process of legitimation is considered suspect in certain cases. Yet even here, people will explain that "the spirit just hasn't come out clearly yet." Whereas an outsider like a Muslim shopkeeper may say bluntly, "Spirit possession is nothing but deception (*politique*), lies, foolishness," Sakalava rarely challenge false mediums openly; they simply avoid them (see also Ottino 1965:92). Indeed, these suspicions about possession appear to be unresolvable. The alternatives are clear. Everyone is aware of divided loyalties, commonly expressed in terms of insides and outsides. People try to sort them out by distinguishing good from bad spirits, big ones from little ones, and the "real ones" from the "appearances." It is not so much the alternatives as the "turning" (*mivadiky*) from one to the other, the inevitable consequence of conflicting obligations, that preoccupy people when they examine their relationships with one another. As one man said,

> To turn against a blood brother (*mamadiky fatidra*) is very bad. For example, he comes asking for something, and you say you don't have it. You have taken an oath, "If I could help, but don't, may I become air, ashes, dust. May I cease to exist here above," like that. In turning away from a friend, you face scrutiny (*mivadiky amin' ny namana, astrikanao ny zavàna*). Turning against someone is like committing sorcery, murder. God sees it and sends sickness to that person.

Sakalava describe the transformation of a famous spirit/medium into a sorcerer in the same terms: "He was famous, but in the end he turned" [and would be destroyed for it].

"Turning" (*vadiky*), the commonest expression for deceiving or betraying someone, has its counterpart in the Sakalava royal vocabulary, where "to roll or turn over like a canoe" (*mihilaña*) is the term for dying, and "turning" is the root of the Merina term for reburials, *famadihana*.[24] Perhaps the *vadiky lapa* is so named because it begins to turn over the relationship between the spirit and its host. But all social relationships are thought to have the potential to turn, and this enduring indeterminacy in human affairs seems vested in the very materials with which the tromba is clothed. The generative force of the cloth brings the spirit—its voice—to life, but also shrouds its pronouncements with uncertainty, so that it can never be clear whether the spirit speaks for itself or for its medium, for Sakalava as a whole or for some restricted group within it.[25]

In fact, there are no sharp distinctions between host and spirit, living and dead, kin and non-kin (in that one can "get kin" by means like blood brotherhood) to facilitate people's understanding of how relations become transformed. The resolution must be worked out through time and space. There is an historical dimension to the contrast between inside and outside—knowing the genealogical relationships and the events in which people participate—that cannot be separated from the geographical dimensions of the process by which people are drawn into the royal centers, especially the royal cemetery.

I will amplify these points by describing the kinds of Sakalava royal service that I see as variations on the themes of burying, exhuming, rewrapping, and reburying the dead as a means of speaking to them and silencing them. Sakalava do not make the same explicit comparison between clothing and architecture that Murra (1983:1–2) noted among contemporary descendants of the Inkas. Nevertheless, these royal services raise the question of how other combinations of hard and soft materials besides bones and cloth, sticks and mantles, are used to convey the complexity of human beings, their opposed and common interests, and their different ways of talking about the contradictions of politics. This work focuses on the fences enclosing the royal residence and relic house at the capital and the royal tomb at the cemetery, the doors with which they are opened and closed, and the procedures by which these doors and fences are periodically removed and rebuilt.

CLOTHING SPIRITS, PURIFYING RELICS, AND
RECONSTRUCTING TOMBS

Sakalava celebrate the beginning of every lunar new year by opening the doors in the enclosures around the royal ancestors, purifying
the relics and regalia and the tomb within, and then closing the
doors. These procedures, extending over six months of every year,
begin toward the end of the rainy season. Around April, the doors
in the fences separating people from the royal ancestors are opened
and the courtyards surrounding the relic house at the capital and the
inner fence and tomb at the cemetery are cleaned in the "weeding
service."

The weeding service is followed in the next month by the preparation of mead, which is allowed to ferment during an intervening
"dead" month, when the doors are closed and royal ritual is prohibited. Services resume with the first month of the new year, around
July. The doors are reopened, and the weeding service is repeated,
after which the relics and regalia at the capital and the tomb at the
cemetery are cleaned, using the mead. This service concludes with
a formal obeisance to the living ruler and the royal ancestors, attended by people from the surrounding countryside, during which
people drink the mead that remains. The doors are closed for the
following month, considered inauspicious, and reopened in the
next month, when people may again pay their respects, make or
fulfill vows, and listen to royal spirits speak through mediums on
current events. The doors are then closed for the remainder of the
year.

"We beg for a door" (*mangataka varavara*) is one of the songs that
people sing in making offerings to the royal ancestors. When they
"receive a door" (*mahazo varavara*), when the doors are open, communication is open between the living and the dead, whether it
takes place through spirit mediums, now in full residence at the
cemetery, or through the "supplicator" who intercedes for people
at the entrance to the burial compound. "At the door" (*ambaravara*)
or "at the mouth" (*ambava*), the two procedures are considered
equivalent. Sakalava pay their respects to the royal ancestors
(*mikoezy*); they make vows (*mañano vava*); fulfill vows or otherwise explain their actions (*mamantoko*); beg pardon for their wrongs
(*mañanto, mamonjy, malilo*) and entreat the spirits' blessings (*man-*

gataka, mangataka hatsarana, mangataka radỳ, milamalama, mivalovalo).
Here, as with domestic ancestors, these various acts of speaking are
accompanied by many different kinds of giving. People give money,
cloth, and cattle, and they receive the spirits' blessing in the mark
of kaolin that the supplicator puts on their faces. They sing royal
praise songs and present entertainments to assuage the spirits'
anger, and they receive the spirits' commentary through mediums
on current affairs. When the doors are closed, communication
ceases.

The function of opening and closing the doors in this elaborate
manner is to regulate communication with the royal ancestors. By
undoing, cleaning, and refurbishing the materials in which royalty
are reenveloped every year, Sakalava clarify the nature of the relationships that connect people with the monarchy. By opening and
closing the doors, they continue to unwrap and rewrap the dead in
complex materials that articulate their current opinion of the
politico-religious and economic principles embodied in monarchy,
in the context of alternative forms of government.

Periodically, the fences are removed and replaced. The most important of these royal services involves the replacement of the innermost fence around the tomb. The old posts of the inner fence are
taken down, the tomb is cleaned, the area around it is weeded, and
a new fence is put up around it. The service held in the Analalava
region in 1972–76 was carried out by the guardians of the royal cemetery, assisted by the guardians of the royal capital and the populace
as a whole, under the leadership of spirit mediums representing the
royalty buried in the tomb and a young boy representing the living
ruler, who is prohibited from direct association with the dead.

Participants said that the work took a long time, six to eight
years, during the precolonial period, because of the care required
to select and prepare the materials. The actual construction should
take no more than a day (even as the original burial, following the
year required to reduce the corpse to bone, takes no more than a
night). The posts must be made from certain species of hardwood
tress, ideally trees that have caught fire and died while still standing
in the forest. Soft, green, fallen, or rotten woods are prohibited. The
trees are then debarked, so that only the hard cores remain. They
are then implanted in the ground around the tomb.

People are recruited to work as individuals rather than members
of kin groups. They are organized according to spatial, temporal,

and occupational principles and practices associated with the royal capital and cemetery rather than commoners' villages or administrative centers. The reorientation of participants is achieved primarily through indirect, largely nonverbal means; talk about royal corpses or burials is—as always—prohibited.

The reconstruction of the tomb is essentially a reburial. The data show that the transformation of the trees into posts stuck back in the ground around the tomb exactly parallels the transformation of the fleshy corpse into a skeleton, enclosed in a tree trunk and buried in the tomb itself. The difference is that the royal corpse is multiplied several hundred-fold in the course of being reburied in the form of these posts. And in taking this form, it has become embodied in the labor of commoners, stripped of their associations with kin in the process of reorganizing as individual citizens around the body of royalty (Feeley-Harnik 1990).[26]

The reconstruction of the royal tomb is intended to repair the damage done when participants at the original funeral broke through the fence to bury the corpse in the royal tomb. The spirit of the dead ruler is thought to move the pallbearers on that occasion, so they could crash through the fence at any point. Dandouau (1911:171–2) and Poirier (1939:104) report that both the inner and outer fences of the royal tomb are repaired or rebuilt at that time. Mellis, long resident in northwestern Madagascar, says that the break in the innermost fence is first covered with a white cloth. The fence is reconstructed only when the dead ruler reappears in the body of a commoner who is recognized as his or her legitimate medium (1938:61, photographs 62,67). In other words, the reconstruction of the royal tomb coincides with the reemergence of his or her voice in political affairs.

My data on the Analalava region support Mellis's account, suggesting that the logic of "reclothing" the royal tomb through the labor of commoners in the reconstruction service matches the logic of reclothing spirits in the bodies of commoners through spirit possession. Both actions give discreet but persistent voice to Sakalava political opinion. Because the Sakalava were denied that voice throughout the colonial period and early independence, permission to undertake the service following the death of the queen's father in 1925 was consistently refused. Only with the change of government in 1972, when the Sakalava voice counted quite literally in elections, was permission granted by General Gabriel Ramanantsoa, who received the benefit of their voices. Apparent consensus at the national level was achieved by tacitly permitting alternative views to flourish locally.

WRAPPING ANCESTORS AND CLAIMING POWER

Sakalava spirit possession, like the Sakalava royal rituals for celebrating the new year and reconstructing the fence around the royal tomb, are comparable to procedures for stripping and reclothing the dead found throughout Madagascar, the best known being the reburials (famadihana) celebrated by the Merina and Betsileo. As Malagasy ethnology indicates, there are many ways of understanding the significance of these rites. The parallels among them suggest that they would benefit from comparative analysis in a regional or national context. To do so would expand Kottak's (1980) argument about the involvement of Betsileo funerals in political-economic relations among the Betsileo and between the Betsileo and the Merina. Such analysis might also modify Bloch's (1971, 1982) arguments about Merina reburial as a refuge from change, affirming an enduring ancestral order associated with men in the face of human mortality associated with women. Bloch generalizes this interpretation to all Madagascar without taking into account the cloth, the ostensible focus of Merina reburials, which is in part the product of women's work and arguably a form of women's wealth.

From a regional perspective, Malagasy reburials are all ways of making ancestors, wrapping them to make them speak, and wrapping them to separate people with ancestors and descendants from those without, people with the history embodied in those generations from people without, and thus people with political power and authority in this life from people without. Malagasy burial ceremonies raise the question of whose *voice* counts in political affairs. In pluralistic societies, the answer is inevitably equivocal.

To rewrap the dead is to speak about the distribution of power and authority among specific contending parties in specific circumstances. The revelation of identity seems to be a crucial issue in the creation of ancestors, but so is the concealment of peoples' affiliations and opinions. Openness and hiddenness operate simultaneously, not because of any mystery or confusion about the nature of the tensions and contradictions in the political process, but because none of the participants exercises full control in all circumstances. The circumstances are always turning. From the Sakalava point of view, however, people who do not continue to recognize their ancestors are "lost to their ancestors" (*very razana*), just as people taken as slaves are "lost" to their communities, and with the same result. They become subject to the domination of others.

People express political loyalty to regional authorities as they conceal their loyalties to domestic groups and vice versa. Among the Merina and Betsileo, they persist in burying their own dead, while honoring royalty. In the very process of cloaking them, hiding them, they single them out and honor them. Men appear to bury their dead oratorically, while women bring them to renewed life in their shrouds.

Among Sakalava in the Analalava region, the ambiguity of political expression is also embodied in the shroud. Rewrapping the royal tomb in the hard cores of trees multiplies royalty, but it also extols the collective power of commoners. It calls into question the single voice of royalty by making it the creation of commoners. In spirit possession, royalty are brought to life in the very bodies of commoners, typically women, aided by men. Enshrouding these mediums makes them speak, but they may speak as much for themselves and their own kin as for others, a potential source of trouble for monarchy in the precolonial period that the Sakalava may have turned to their advantage in protecting monarchical institutions from the French.[27]

The ambiguity, the potential for turning, inherent in all social situations, is embodied in the materials with which spirits are wrapped: Combinations of soft and hard materials like cloth and sticks, trees and stones, cores and bark, trunks and leafy branches, analogs of shrouds and corpses, tombs and bodies, the bones and flesh of human beings, both female and male. The interconnections of these different materials, and their transformations back and forth in time between fragile and more enduring states, is the root of Malagasy burial rites. In their transformations, they are commentaries on the complex composition of human beings and of human relations, especially relations of domination and subordination that call for silence as well as speech, concealment as well as open confrontation. Strategies like these have drawn on both the strengths and the weaknesses attributed to men and women in ever-changing combinations throughout the precolonial, colonial, and postcolonial periods in Madagascar.

Sakalava in the Analalava region now question whether to rebuild the royal tomb in perishable tree trunks and branches that will decay like cloth, or whether to switch to harder materials, cement and tin, as Sakalava elsewhere on the west coast have already done. In other words, they question whether to rewrap the ancestors in substances that embody the continuing involvement of local people in principles and practices associated with monarchy or whether to bury them forever, to relinquish these institutions and become supporters of national government. Indeed, it is unclear whether these choices are absolutely opposed. Perhaps there is still some value in maintaining political alternatives for parties on both sides, given the currently inadequate capacities of either to achieve more than partial political integration of the region and nation respectively. Covell's recent assessment of patron-client relationships in Malagasy bureaucracy concludes bleakly:

> . . . the system persists *because* [my emphasis] the bulk of the
> population is only partially incorporated in it. The general popu-
> lation of a country like Madagascar enjoyed a brief period of po-
> litical relevance at the time of the pre-independence elections
> and before the consolidation of a one-party or military regime.
> Since then the system has shrunk, as has the number of people
> whose opinions must be taken into account by the political elite.
> It is within this group that reliable channels of communication
> are necessary; for the partially integrated, partial channels suffice
> (n.d. [c. 1978]:32).

Covell's data suggest that former President Tsiranana made some effort to organize development schemes along the lines of traditional reburial ceremonies. Nevertheless, tax-collecting has remained the dominant model for communication between the national government and the people (Covell n.d.:23–4; see Covell 1974). Without the reembodiment of political ideals in material relations of exchange on a national level, interest in regional alternatives will continue to flourish.

Royal spirits speaking through mediums have consistently rejected the use of these new materials. Despite their resistance, the materials were bought in the 1950s, but they were never used, and finally they were resold. The outsider who bought them to build a house is said to have died as a consequence. The tomb, when it was finally reconstructed in 1972–76, was wrapped in trees that would eventually rot, requiring the attention of Sakalava again in the future.

DEATH, LIFE, AND POLITICS

I have described the role of cloth in Sakalava spirit possession, arguing that the process of clothing the spirit is essential to creating it, by inducing it to identify itself and state its intentions concerning its host. This is the immediate objective of the procedures surrounding spirit possession. Once the relationship between the spirit and its host is regularized, clothing the body serves, together with calling the spirit, to bring it back into its host to speak on various issues, including current affairs. The processes of clothing, naming, and speaking are associated in the recreation or revival of the dead but also in their reburial, in the revelation of political opinion but also in its concealment.

I have pointed out the parallels in the Analalava area between spirit possession and other forms of royal service, suggesting that they are all variations of practices involving the exhumation and reburial of the dead found in other parts of Madagascar. The way in which these practices are handled and their regional distribution suggest that they make the expression of political opinion possible under pluralistic circumstances on a broader scale.

The many forms of ancestors in Madagascar and the diverse materials with which they are revived and reburied, ranging from cloth to trees to cement, raise questions about the relationship of materials to ideas and behavior that merit further research. How do hand production (women's work) and commercial exchange affect the evaluation and use of different kinds of cloth in Malagasy funeral rituals? What accounts for the analogies between cloth and other materials or, perhaps more accurately, the combination of cloth and other "hard" materials like sticks and bones with other complex combinations of materials like fenced tombs? What is the relationship between these materials of wealth and power and the regionally and historically varied kinds of human bodies they constitute or represent? A closer examination of the relations between the living and the dead helps to elucidate differing conceptions of the very substance and value of human beings in the context of changing political-economic circumstances.

ACKNOWLEDGMENTS

This paper is based on 21 months of ethnographic field research in the Analalava region of northwestern Madagascar, from July, 1971 to November, 1973 and briefly in 1981, funded by a Predoctoral Research Grant from the National Institute of Mental Health and a Grant-in-Aid from the Wenner-Gren Foundation for Anthropological Research. I am grateful to these institutions for their support and to the members of the Wenner-Gren Foundation Symposium on "Cloth and Human Experience" for their comments on an earlier draft of this paper. I especially thank Jane Schneider and Annette B. Weiner, organizers of the conference, and T.O. Beidelman, George Bond, Pamela Feldman, Alan Harnik, Ward Keeler, and Michael Lambek for their helpful comments on later drafts.

NOTES

1. Because of the importance of cloth in exchange relations throughout Madagascar and the possibility of historical connections between trade and the exchange of ideas, I have drawn attention here and in the footnotes below to some comparable data from other Malagasy contexts, past and present, as well as some additional data concerning the Analalava region.

The opening words of a Betsileo funeral oration for a commoner in the late nineteenth century link speaking to weaving: "It is true that to have something to warp is to have something to weave; to have a dead person is to have to speak. When an ox is dead, it is cut up with a knife; when a person is dead, s/he is cut up with the tongue [in detailing his or her life]" (cited in Dubois 1938:684–5). *Mamelon-tenona*, "to stretch out the warp on the loom for weaving" is one of a group of words derived from the root *velatra*, which have to do with exposing the inside of something by spreading it out, including *mivelatra*, which also means "to begin a formal speech" (see Richardson 1885:748–49). The truthfulness and generosity associated with opening to expose the insides of things is directly opposed to the deceit and avarice associated with the actions of closing or covering so that only the outside or back shows.

2. *A(n)kanjo* probably derives from the Swahili *kanjo* (see French *canezou*). Other commonly used French terms include *tricot, pantalon, robe, [serrée], combinaison, corsage, casaque.*

3. This prohibition sometimes includes Merina and European speech and, at the royal cemetery, European objects like iron bedsteads and kerosene lamps. Similar prohibitions were enforced by Merina monarchs. European clothing came into common use among Merina nobility during the reign of Radama I (1792–1828). As on the coasts, it was always combined with Malagasy clothing, especially the mantle (e.g., Ellis 1835, 1867 *passim*, Guillain 1845:191). European clothing was prohibited in the course of reactions to close European involvement in Malagasy affairs, for example, during the reign the Merina queen Rasoherina ("Silkworm Chrysalis") following the assassination of Radama II in 1863 (Ellis 1867:319, 384–5).

Sakalava prohibitions do not include European textiles, though fabrics do have important politico-historical implications. For example, *dongimena, sobahiya* and other silks from "Araby," which are now rare if not impossible to find, are associated with the former resplendence of the precolonial monarchy. *Sotema* (from SOTEMA, the acronym of the French cloth factory in Majunga, nationalized after 1972), seen as wearing poorly and fading quickly, epitomizes the costliness and miseries of daily life. *Tergal*, imported French polyester, seen as attractive and long-lasting, exemplifies modernity.

4. The principal entertainment during services for the royal ancestors is a war dance in which Sakalava dress like former Sakalava rulers and reenact the battles between them that brought the senior "Descendants of the Gold/Red" (*Zafinimena*) to power over the junior "Descendants of the Silver/White" (*Zafinifotsy*). The clothing of the two rulers is identical except in color. They wear red and white versions of an outfit including a tall stiff hat with a train, a bandolier, and a hip wrap made from royal silks, and they carry a weapon, either a wooden rifle or a long stick, sometimes decorated with silver. The dance is not currently considered to be a form of possession. People compete to see who is the best, while spectators throw money to spur them on. Nevertheless, spirit mediums who put on the rulers' clothing inevitably become possessed in the course of dancing (Feeley-Harnik 1988).

5. In other Malagasy contexts, notably the oratory attributed to the Merina king Andriapoinimerina, covering the body is potentially treasonous. Merina subjects were exhorted to be like a cloth that presents the same face inside and out. Otherwise the "good side" (*vadi-tsarany*, from the root *vadiky* discussed below) is distinguished from the other side (Feeley-Harnik and Mack n.d.).

6. Dandouau (1908:163) reports similar prohibitions against tight, tied, and knotted clothing for pregnant women in the Analalava region. At that time, childbirth occurred in a cloth enclosure inside the house.

7. Concerning clothing and speaking on formal occasions, Ellis, a member of the London Missionary Society in Madagascar during the second half of the nineteenth century, describes a Merina oration in which body wrapping and unwrapping played a prominent role. This form of speech (*kabary*), associated with men, relies heavily on indirect means of expression.

> When anyone from the people came forward to speak [at a royal
> gathering of the people to hear the laws of a new sovereign], he
> stepped out in front of his party, with the *lamba* over his shoul-

ders gathered together in front by his left hand on his breast, while he used his right arm by stretching it forward when he began to speak, with the folds of his lamba depending from it.

The speaker usually began in a quiet clear voice, and in a short time moved gently backwards and forwards in front of his companions while speaking, his language being correct, and his utterance easy and free. As he went on his voice became louder, his speech more rapid, his step quicker, both his arms moving as he spoke; and then as he still walked to and fro, he took off his *lamba* from his shoulders, wound it round his waist, fastened it with a bow or knot on his hip, allowing the ends to hang down like the ends of a sash reaching to his ankles [sic], and then, both his arms being at liberty, he would continue his speech with increased action until it ended in a climax. This would generally elicit applause from his friends, into the midst of whom he would rush, untie his *lamba* and cover up his person (Ellis 1867:323).

8. Malagasy speakers in Mayotte are descendants of followers of the Maroseraña ruler Andriantsoly who migrated there from northwestern Madagascar toward the mid-nineteenth century. Lambek (1986) notes that although they are Muslim, there are some points of comparison. A cloth screen is usually put up around the bed of a dying person, and sometimes kept there when the corpse is washed. "Extreme care is taken to wash the corpse through a cloth covering and never to expose any of the flesh. I think this must have to do with protecting the integrity of the self, even when deceased; at the same time it obliterates their personal identity. Immediately after a death the face is covered with a cloth."

9. The Malagasy phrase is *mitaña hidy*, "to grasp the lock." *Hidy* refers to anything used to shut or lock something; to the state of being locked or closed "comme les dents d'un mort;" and to anything prohibited. The reduplicative *hidihidy* refers to clenched teeth, obstinate silence, or angry words. The verb *mihidy vava* (literally, "to close/lock the mouth") means to have the mouth clenched shut without being able to open it, or, figuratively, to keep an obstinate silence (Abinal and Malzac 1970:244-45).

10. Although I never heard Sakalava use *faha/ña* in this context, the Bara of highland Madagascar use the term to refer to the vital energy, associated especially with women, that is celebrated in the songs, dances, and cattle-wrestling contests involved in Bara funerals (Huntington and Metcalf 1979:109-16). Bara speak of their participation in the all-night pre-burial vigils in which these events take place as "going to await *faha*." Otherwise they use the term in referring to a thin cow (lacking *faha*) or to curing ceremonies intended to strengthen people (Huntington 1979:111).

11. COTONA and SOTEMA, the two major cloth manufacturers in Madagascar, send representatives throughout the island to find out which patterns and sayings sell best (Rick Huntington, personal communication). The popularity of "I like the one outside but . . . " may relate to the fact that if a man has an "out-

side child" (*zanaka an-tany*), then he should "cloth [his] wife" (*fampisikinambady*), as the compensation is known among Bemihisatra-Sakalava in the Nosy Be region, by giving her money or jewelry (Ottino 1964:243,n.1).

12. Lambek (1986), noting that cloth is the most important gift that a man gives a woman in Mayotte and that a bride's value to her husband is judged by the number of pieces of cloth he brings on their wedding day, says that the inability to wear the latest styles at public gatherings indicates lack of male support. This applies in the Analalava region as well.

The entertainment on the occasion of Tsiranana's visit to Analalava consisted of dancing by a *troupe folklorique* made up of prisoners from the nearby national penitentiary: Men wearing highland-style pants and sashed tunics in the national colors.

13. What follows is an outline of some salient features of the process by which people come to be recognized as possessed by royal spirits. More detailed descriptions of specific cases will be published elsewhere.

14. The process of "making a tromba come out" (*mampiboaka tromba*) is guided by a person known as a *fondy*, a Swahili word also used to refer to teachers of the Koran. Sakalava are aware the Muslims and Christians belittle them because they have no sacred texts. The *fondy* may be assisted by a "supplicator" (*ampangataka*) or "doorkeeper" (*ampitanambaravarana*), the same terms used to refer to the royal officials (ex-royal slaves) who intercede between the living and the royal ancestors at royal rituals such as those described below. The supplicator is often one of the sick person's relatives, but the *fondy* must be a royal spirit. As one medium said, "Anyone can talk to a royal spirit, but only a royal spirit can make a new royal spirit come out."

Sakalava spirit possession strikingly resembles *pepo* (or *sheitani*) spirit possession among Swahili speakers along the East African coast as described by Skene (1917:420–34) and Giles (1987). Here, too, spirit possession causes sickness. A male or female specialist, known as a *fundi* (or *mganga*), is hired to cure the patient by bringing the spirit out. The spirits have personal names characteristic of other members of the different "tribes" to which they are thought to belong. They are recognized by the language they speak through the person they possess. The "first step [in treating possession] . . . is to get the spirit to 'come into the head' and speak to the *fundi*," explaining what it wants in exchange for leaving the patient. Medicines are used together with music, singing, dancing, food, and drink, to induce the spirit to speak. In speaking, the spirit will name itself, but stating its name does not appear to be the main issue. The goal may be exorcism or continued interaction. When the spirit's identity has been determined, new clothes appropriate to its tribal membership must be purchased for the decisive ceremony (Skene 1917:420–23, Giles 1987:240–41).

The Swahili word *pepo* is "the equivalent of the Arab word *jin*, or devil or evil spirit (Skene 1917:420); Silamo in northwestern Madagascar refer to evil spirits, including the spirits that possess people, as *setoan* (viz. *sheitani*). Sakalava use *pepo* (From Swahili *upepo*) to refer to the wind. *Tsiny/tsigny*, referring to usually malevolent non-human spirits may derive from *jin*. *Tsigny* is also the term for the curse of Sakalava royalty; in the highlands, it means "blame, fault."

15. In fact, *ankera* is what most people eat for breakfast, even as the used

clothing sold by the Catholic Church and in the marketplaces of every large town and city is a part of everyday dress.

16. The complete outfit of the living ruler's father, an important spirit in the Analalava region, includes a tan pith helmet, dark glasses, tan sports coat like that of a French colonial functionary (sometimes called a *trois poches* or "three pockets"), white shirt, striped hip wrap, belt, silver chain bracelet, gold rings, a white cloth to wipe the sweat from his face, and a silk *lamba* (Sakalava also say *darà*) known as *sobaiha*, having purple and yellow stripes down the middle, red stripes at the edges, and red fringes. He may also carry a cigarette case and a staff. Estrade (1977:59) describes his clothing when he made a surprise visit as a "new royal spirit" at the Doany Andriamisara, the Sakalava royal center near Majunga, during the new year's service there in July 1972: "colonial pith helmet, khaki Administrator's vest, dark glasses, and cigarettes."

His son, buried in the same royal tomb though he never ruled, wears a felt hat with a brim, white jacket, white nylon shirt open at the neck, vest pocket hankerchief, striped hip wrap, silver link bracelet, gold rings, and a *sobaiha*, and he carries a gold cigarette case. The son's illegitimate half-brother wears clothing very similar to his, except for the jewelry, because the clothing is meant to indicate the kin relationships among the spirits as well as their own identities.

The clothing of the grandfather and great grandfather are less elaborate because they were so weak when they died, and thus when they possess people, it is said to be difficult to get anything on them before they collapse. Nevertheless, they are the only ones allowed to wear the finest silk cloth known as *dalahany*, which is predominantly red with black and yellow stripes and red fringes.

Lesser *trombas* wear correspondingly simpler clothing. A group of young Zafinimena rulers from Betsioko near Majunga who possess people in the Analalava region wear ordinary cotton hip wraps, undershirts or short-sleeved T-shirts, and brimmed straw hats. The spirits are further distinguished by their tastes and prohibitions in food and drink and other characteristic modes of behavior that, including manner of dress, are known collectively as their *fomba* or "customs."

17. Ellis (1835, I:280) provides some historical data on the *sarandra* in one of his many descriptions of Merina courtly dress: "The *serandrana* (sic), or sash, is used by the nobles and others for binding the salaka or other undergarments to the person of the wearer. This article is often of costly materials and rich in its appearances, being frequently of red silk with beautifully variegated borders." Sakalava in the Analalava region currently identify *sarandra* as a large "cloth from the old days (*lamba taloha*) placed on top of a big spirit possessing someone (*saha mianjaka*)."

18. *Sobaiha*, of which there were three pieces in the seven Indian merchants' shops in Analalava in 1972, then cost the equivalent of $10 = $24. At that time, a woman's body wrap, shoulder wrap, and head wrap cost about $7, and the average salary for occasional labor was $0.50 per day. *Dalahany* was no longer available. *Kikoy*, a white cotton and silk cloth with blue and yellow stripes along the edges and white fringes, worn by Zafinifotsy rulers, was also no longer

available, though a *kikoy*-like cloth made from rayon could be bought for $4 a piece. Some of the *sobaiha*, though made of silk, may have been Indian copies. Indians gradually replaced Arabs as traders on the west coast during the late nineteenth century (Rasoamiarimanana 1981:83, 88). They also may have replaced them in the trade involving Sakalava royal silks.

19. Richardson (1885:721) describes "turning clothing inside out" (*mamadilamba*), from the root *vadiky* discussed below, as "an ancient method of purification after being present at a funeral."

20. Naming is also the focus of Dandouau's (1912) description of Sakalava spirit possession in the Analalava region, attributing the appearance of possession to drunkenness. A "bad spirit"(he includes angry "good spirits" in this category) is exorcised by forcing it to say its name: "When a *tromba* has said its name, it is considered as no longer dangerous. One can invoke it personally, give it offerings and sacrifices that it is known to like" (*ibid*.: 11). Rason (1968) paraphrases Dandouau's (1912) account without acknowledging it.

Rusillon's (1912) description of "the four main stages" in which a Sakalava royal spirit appears, based on data from the Majunga region, reflects this same emphasis on speaking. "The *Misafosafo* ['the coaxing']: the *Tromba* is flattered, enticed, urged to come; the *Vakim-bava* ['the breaking into speech']: the *Tromba* gives signs of its presence; l'*Ampitononina* ['the making to speak']: the *Tromba* is made to speak; it is invoked for all possible purposes; finally the *Valy-hataka* ['the response to the request'] or rejoicing with sacrifice in gratitude (1912:117–18). Lambek also draws attention to the climactic moment in spirit possession among Malagasy speakers in Mayotte (Sakalava refugees from the Merina during the nineteenth century) when the spirit first reveals its name in public, which he sees as an act of "investiture," though he does not deal with the spirits' clothing (1981:126–27,140–50). Lambek's analysis, inspired by Geertz and Ricoeur, focuses on possession as "a system of communication."

21. "To speak" (*mikoraña*) in ordinary languages is *misaonty* in the royal vocabulary; royal persons also "roar like bulls" (*mitregny*). Sakalava explain the term *beko* in "ancestors' orders" (*bekondrazana*) as "orders." It also refers to foreign words, especially those used in drilling soldiers (Richardson 1885:77).

22. Dandouau (1911:167) says the mouth is filled with silver coins, then bound with thin strips of royal silk (*dalahany*) instead of raffia, as in the case of commoners. Two gold coins were put into the jaws of Soazara's Father's body after it had been reduced to bone (Poirier 1939:104). *Fehy vava*, the term for the cord used to tie the mouth shut, also means to impose silence on someone (see below and Richardson 1885:176–7). Among Malagasy speakers in Mayotte, "*Tromba* often have a silver coin pressed between their lips in order to get them to speak" (Lambek 1986). The words for "money" (*vola*) and "speech" (*vola/na*) may be cognates in Malagasy.

23. Estrade (1977:307) cites a Sakalava saying applied to government functionaries who act only after being bribed: "Teta's royal spirit: money appears" (*Tromban'i Teta: vola miboaka*). In referring to the money of those whom Teta has duped, the saying also acknowledges the existence of people who fake posses-

sion for financial gain. Among Malagasy speakers in Mayotte, "The ambiguity of spirits' speech . . . lies less with who is speaking—though the contrast between host and spirit always adds a level of meaning—than with whether the spirit can be trusted" (Lambek 1986).

24. Scholars of Merina reburials interpret *famadihana* (turning over) as referring to the process of turning the body over in the course of wrapping it or moving it from one tomb to another, without considering the connection that Malagasy make between inverting or reversing and subverting or betraying. The counterpart of "turning over" (*mihilaña*) for dying in the Sakalava royal vocabulary was "turning one's back" (*misamboho*) in the Merina royal vocabulary.

25. Lambek (1986) comments: "The inside/outside contrast, often expressed as that one can never know how someone 'really' feels 'inside' is also central in Mayotte experience. It's often symbolized by the *añatin trañu/an tany* opposition [inside the house/outside]. I guess the cloth wrapping of the interior of the house of the newly married couple fits this—to create a unified new interior domain. I wonder whether this concern over what you call the 'enduring indeterminancy in human relations' is related to the lack of unilineal descent and prescriptive marriage rules?"

26. Sakalava also wrap trees with cloth directly. On the northwest coast, as elsewhere in Madagascar (Aujas 1927:32; Renel 1920–21:118–27), spirits are associated with trees, especially tamarind (*madiro*) and *Dracaena* species (*hasina*). In the Analalava region, there is usually one such tree dedicated to a particular spirit that may also possess a member of the village. The tree is often surrounded by a fence to keep it from being profaned. Spirits' trees are also located in the countryside, usually near well-traveled roads. Sakalava make vows to the spirits identified with these trees in the same way that they make vows to spirits embodied in mediums or to the spirits at the royal cemetery through the 'supplicator' at the door. The fulfillment of these vows (*tsakafara*) involves wrapping the trunk of the tree in white cloth or tying pieces of white cloth to the branches.

27. The attitudes of the French to Sakalava spirit possession will be described elsewhere. I will simply note here that, confronted by the spirit's cloth and stick, colonial administrators saw only the stick. They could never decide whether it was a cane or a weapon, just as they could never decide whether the phenomenon was ceremonial or political, harmless or threatening. At best, spirit possession exemplified marked differences in linguistic style, or as Mellis put it, explaining the Sakalava preference for speaking through mediums: "the horror of Malagasy for direct discussion, for the brutal response: yes or no" (1938:71). At worst, it epitomized the natives' capacity for concealment, for lying outright. Rusillon is typical in dismissing a pile of tromba cloths as "a whole wardrobe *de demi-sauvage*" (1912:113). I think that it was precisely the "invisibility" of the soft enveloping cloth and the predominance of women involved in possession (albeit as "men") that contributed to the indecision of French officials and thus their inconsistent and ultimately inconsequential efforts at suppression. Sakalava spirit possession spread rather than diminished under colonial rule.

REFERENCES CITED

Abinal, R.P. and R.P. Malzac
1970   Dictionnaire Malgache-Français. Paris: Editions maritimes et d'outre-mer.

Aujas, L.
1927   Les Rites du Sacrifice à Madagascar. Mémoires de l'Académie Malgache II:3–88.

Beidelman, T.O.
1974   Kaguru Names and Naming. Journal of Anthropological Research 30:281–93.

Bloch, M.
1971   Placing the Dead: Tombs, Ancestral Villages, and Kinship Organization in Madagascar. London: Seminar Press.
1982   Death, Women, and Power. In Death and the Regeneration of Life. M. Bloch and J. Parry, eds. pp.211–30. Cambridge: Cambridge University Press.

Brain, J.L.
1973   Ancestors as elders in Africa—further thoughts. Africa 43:122–33.

Calhoun, C.J.
1980   The Authority of Ancestors: a Sociological Reconsideration of Fortes's Tallensi in Response to Fortes's Critiques. Man (n.s.) 15:304–19.
1981   Correspondence. Man (n.s.) 16:137–38.

Covell, M.
1974   Local Politics and National Integration in the Malagasy Republic. Ann Arbor: University Microfilms International.
n.d.   [c. 1978] Linkage or Line of Defence? Patron-client Relationships in the Malagasy Bureaucracy. ms.

Dandouau, A.
1911   Coutumes Funéraires dans le Nord-ouest de Madagascar. Bulletin de l'Académie Malgache IX:157–72.
1912   Le *Tromba*. La Tribune de Madagascar, Octobre, pp. 8,11,15.

Dubois, H.-M.
1938   Monographie des Betsileo (Madagascar). Paris: Institut d'Ethnologie.

Ellis, W.
1835   History of Madagascar. 2 vol. London: Fisher.
1867   Madagascar Revisited, Describing the Events of a New Reign, and the Revolution Which Followed. London: John Murray.

Estrade, J.-M.
1977   Un Culte de Possession à Madagascar—le Tromba. Paris: Editions Anthropos.

Feeley-Harnik, G.
1978   Divine Kingship and the Meaning of History among the
        Sakalava (Madagascar). Man (n.s.) 13: 402–17.
1988   Dancing Battles: Representations of Conflict in Sakalava Royal
        Work. Anthropos 83:65–85.
1990   A Green Estate: Land, Labor, and Ancestors among the Sakalava
        of Northwestern Madagascar. Washington, D.C.: Smithsonian In-
        stitution Press, forthcoming.

Feeley-Harnik, G. and J. Mack
n.d.   Cloth Production in Madagascar: A Preliminary Inquiry. British
        Museum Occasional Papers. London: British Museum Publica-
        tions.

Fortes, M.
1945   The Dynamics of Clanship among the Tallensi. Oxford: Oxford
        University Press.
1949   The Web of Kinship among the Tallensi. Oxford: Oxford Univer-
        sity Press.
1955   Names among the Tallensi of the Gold Coast. In Afrikanistische
        Studien Diedrich Westermann zum 80. Geburtstag gewidmet. J.
        Lukas, ed. pp.337–49. Institute für Orientforschung
        Veröffentlichung nr. 26. Berlin: Akademie-Verlag.
1959   Oedipus and Job in West African Religion. Cambridge: Cam-
        bridge University Press.
1961   Pietas in Ancestor Worship. Journal of the Royal Anthropologi-
        cal Institute 91:166–91.
1965   Some Reflections on Ancestor Worship in Africa. In African Sys-
        tems of Thought. M. Fortes and G. Dieterlen, eds. pp. 122–44.
        Oxford: Oxford University Press for the International African In-
        stitute.
1981   Correspondence. Man (n.s.) 16:300–02.

Giles, L.L.
1987   Possession Cults on the Swahili Coast: A Reexamination of
        Theories of Marginality. Africa 57:234–58.

Glazier, J.
1984   Mbeere Ancestors and the Domestication of Death. Man (n.s.)
        19:133–48.

Guillain, C.
1845   Documents sur l'Histoire, la Géographie et le Commerce de la
        Partie Occidentale de Madagascar. Paris: Imprimerie Royale.

Irvine, J.
1982   The Creation of Identity in Spirit Mediumship and Possession. In
        Semantic Anthropology. D. Parkin, ed. pp.241–60. New York:
        Academic Press.

Keesing, R.M.
1970   Shrines, Ancestors, and Cognatic Descent: the Kwaio and
        Tallensi. American Anthropologist 72:755–75.

Kiernan, J.P.
1982   The 'Problem of Evil' in the Context of Ancestral Intervention in
        the Affairs of the Living in Africa. Man (n.s.) 17:287–301.

Kopytoff, I.
1971   Ancestors as Elders in Africa. Africa 41:129–42.
1981   Correspondence. Man (n.s.) 16:135–7.

Kottak, C.P.
1980   The Past in the Present: History, Ecology and Cultural Variation
        in Highland Madagascar. Ann Arbor: University of Michigan
        Press.

Lambek, M.
1981   Human Spirits: A Cultural Account of Trance in Mayotte. Cam-
        bridge: Cambridge University Press.
1986   Letter of August 28, 1986.

Mellis, J.V.
1938   Nord et Nord-ouest de Madagascar. Tananarive: Imprimerie
        Moderne de l'Emyrne.

Murra, J.V.
1983   The Role of Cloth in Andean Civilization. Footnote to the 1962
        article: "Cloth and Its Function in the Inca State". Paper contrib-
        uted to the Wenner-Gren Foundation symposium on "Cloth and
        the Human Experience," September 28 - October 5, 1983.

Needham, R.
1954a   Reference to the Dead among the Penan. Man 54:10, art. 6.
1954b   The System of Teknonyms and Death-Names among the Penan.
        Southwestern Journal of Anthropology 10:416–31.

Ottino, P.
1964   La Crise du Système Familial et Matrimonial des Sakalava de
        Nosy Be. Civilisation Malgache 1:225–48.
1965   Le *Tromba* (Madagascar). L'Homme 5:84–93.

Poirier, C.
1939   Notes d'Ethnographie et d'Histoire Malgaches: Les Royaumes
        Sakalava Bemihisatra de la Côte Nord-ouest de Madagascar.
        Mémoires de l'Académie Malgache 28:41–104.

Rasoamiarimanana, M.
1981   Un Grand Port de l'Ouest: Majunga (1862–1881). Recherche,
        Pédagogie et Culture 9:78–89.

Rason, R.
1968   Le *Tromba* chez les Sakalava. Civilisation Malgache 2:207–14.

Renel, C.
    1920–21   Ancêtres et Dieux. Bulletin de l'Académie Malgache (n.s.)
               5:1–261.

Rusillon, H.
    1912   Un Culte Dynastique avec Evocation des Morts chez les Sakalava
               de Madagascar. Le "Tromba". Paris: A. Picard.

Schneider, J.
    1987   The Anthropology of Cloth. Annual Review of Anthropology
               16:409–48.

Skene, R.
    1917   Arab and Swahili Dances and Ceremonies. Journal of the Royal
               Anthropological Institute 47:413–34.

4. Dressing for the Next Life

*Raffia Textile Production and Use
among the Kuba of Zaire*

PATRICIA DARISH

 Kuba raffia textiles are recognized as one of the great decorative art traditions of Subsaharan Africa. Their combinations of two-dimensional designs and decorative techniques are renowned. Yet discussion of Kuba textiles has centered on their rich surface design, whereas questions concerning the uses and meanings of these textiles for the Kuba have largely been ignored. Beyond aesthetic appreciation, most accounts have stressed the importance of these textiles as emblems of rank or as indicators of social prestige. But the social significance of Kuba textiles is more complex than these analyses conclude. My research among the Kuba suggests that the meaning of these textiles for the Kuba emerges from the dynamics of their production and their use.

Kuba textiles exist not solely as aesthetic objects, but also as products of a sociocultural framework that places a high value on the making of textiles. Kuba textile production is in sharp contrast to other areas of the world, such as the Pacific, where the use of special textiles is relegated to certain social strata and where exchange and recirculation of textiles dominates the social history of cloth. Instead, textile production among the Kuba requires the interdependent contributions of men and women. This complementarity of the sexes is revealed in textile production and ownership and is vis-ually expressed in the most important context of use: the display of textiles at funerals and their subsequent use as burial goods. Traditional Kuba textiles persist to the present because textile production and use patterns are linked to Kuba ideas regarding social responsibility, ethnic identity, and religious belief.[1]

THE KUBA: ETHNIC DIVERSITY

"Kuba" is a name given by neighboring peoples, and later adopted by Europeans and Americans, to a consolidation of seventeen or more ethnic groups that organized into a kingdom as early as the seventeenth century.[2] Collectively, the Kuba are sedentary agriculturists who live in the Western Kasai region of south-central Zaire, approximately seven hundred miles east of the Atlantic Ocean. Fishing competes with agriculture as the primary occupation along the major tributaries of the region's rivers.

The historical Kuba kingdom corresponds roughly to the present-day administrative zone of Mweka. Mweka zone is bounded on the north by the Sankuru River and on the west and southwest by the Kasai and the Lulua Rivers respectively. To the north live various Mongo groups, among them the Ndengese and Nkucu directly north of the Sankuru River. To the east are the Songo Meno and the Binji, to the south live other Kete and Lulua groups, and west of the Kasai River live the Lele.

The Kuba have been subdivided into ethnic groupings according to shared cultural, linguistic, and historical traits (see Vansina 1964:6–7; 1978:5). The "central Kuba" grouping includes the Bushoong, the Ngeende, the Pyaang and the Bulaang; they constitute more than 75 percent of the total population of the Kuba kingdom. All share a single tradition of migration into their present area and speak a variant of the Bushoong language. The Bushoong, who dominate the kingdom politically, are the most numerous.[3]

The "peripheral Kuba" grouping includes the Kel, the Shoowa, and the Ngongo. Although today they share social and cultural institutions with the central Kuba, their languages and traditions of migration are different. The Northern Kete constitute still another Kuba grouping. Some of these Northern Kete, along with the Cwa (pygmies), are the autochthonous inhabitants of the region.[4]

According to the latest evidence, all of the Kuba groups except for some Northern Kete and Cwa migrated to this region from the north (Vansina 1978). Following protracted struggles between these migrating groups, the Bushoong eventually achieved dominance in the area. Beginning in the seventeenth century, the kingdom was ruled from a capital village called Nsheng by a paramount ruler or *nyim*, who is traditionally chosen from one Bushoong clan.[5] While most Kuba-related ethnic groups are organized into independent chiefdoms, to this day they recognize the traditional authority invested in the Kuba paramount ruler.

From the seventeenth century through the nineteenth century the capital village of Nsheng developed into a bureaucratic center as the kingdom was divided into provinces and chiefdoms, each represented at the capital by a titleholder appointed by the *nyim* (Vansina 1964:167). Paralleling elaborate developments at the capital, titleholding evolved in most Kuba villages. A system of titleholding, which continues to the present day, is common throughout the region.

Kuba ethnic groups are organized into chiefdoms consisting of several villages, except for the Northern Kete, for whom each village is an independent chiefdom. Except for the Cwa, Coofa, and Mbeengi, the Kuba are matrilineal (Vansina 1978:6). Most Kuba villages are composed of "clan sections" made up of matrilineages. A clan section is defined as ". . .the localized expression of the lineage. It comprised only a handful of lineage members but many spouses and children, married or not, and its composition fluctuated over time" (Vansina 1978:6). Marriage follows a virilocal pattern of residence. Vansina writes elsewhere that nearly 50 percent of married people did not live in the village where they should live according to the "rules" (Vansina 1964:58–59; 1978:6). An average village contains two to four hundred people in three to six clan sections, although there are some larger villages with upwards of a thousand people.

Although village structure varies somewhat according to ethnic group, the village council (*malaang*) is the local governing body. Vansina describes this council as an outgrowth of clan section organization (Vansina 1978:111). Originally comprised of clan section chiefs, today it is composed of titled individuals. Most titleholders are male. There are two female titleholders who act as representatives for the women of the village, but do not attend council meetings on a regular basis.

Most titles are hereditary, although the means by which one achieves a title varies from ethnic group to ethnic group. In most Bushoong villages the most important title is that of *kubol* or village headman. This title is usually given to the oldest man in the village. Among the Shoowa the village headman is called *itaka* (Shoowa); as in all chiefdoms in the kingdom, he is selected from an aristocratic clan (*mbaangt*, Bushoong). Many other important village titleholders are also selected from these aristocratic clans. Historically it appears that certain titles have been conferred for life (Vansina 1978:135), while others may be vacated by dismissal or elevation to a higher title. The title will then be filled from the ranks below.

A titleholder's rank is given visible form by the right to wear certain insignia of office. For many titleholders, this includes the right to wear specific bird feathers, as certain feathers correspond directly to certain titled positions. For example, the highest ranked titles in the chiefdoms are the "eagle feather chiefs" (*kum apoong*). These chiefs are found among all of the Kuba groupings. Other emblems of regalia, such as special hat forms, belts, or staffs, may correspond directly to specific titles, or may simply indicate that those wearing or carrying such items are prominent titleholders. For example, the hat *ncok* is worn by the titleholder *Mbeem* at his funeral and appears to be worn only by this titleholder, while the belt *mwaandaan* may be worn by a number of titleholders who hold high office.

Research indicates that in the past, certain styles of men's and women's raffia skirts may have been worn only by high-ranking titleholders. Precise information on this is lacking, and although informants from aristocratic clans insist that this was true in the past, it is not current practice. Moreover, I found that patterns and styles of skirts identified by informants as only made or owned by important families were evenly distributed among people of all classes. The only time that textiles per se designate rank or title is when "eagle feather chiefs" (*kum apoong*) add decorative embellishments, such as cowrie shells or brass repoussé, to their costumes.

RAFFIA TEXTILES: COMPLEMENTARITY IN PRODUCTION

Throughout the Kuba area (and indeed throughout Zaire), the cultivation of the raffia palm and the weaving of raffia cloth is exclusively men's activity. Even the onlookers who congregate under the shed while weaving is in process are always boys and men.

Raffia cloth is woven on a single-heddle loom that utilizes untwisted single lengths of raffia fiber for both warp and weft. The size of one woven unit of raffia cloth (*mbala*) varies according to the length of the original raffia leaflet, but a typical piece of woven raffia cloth as it is cut from the loom averages 26 by 28 inches.

Once the warp has been set on the loom, weaving a piece of cloth requires about two and one-half to three hours for an experienced weaver to complete. A man usually completes a piece of cloth in an afternoon (Figure 9).

There are three kinds of woven raffia cloth. A plain woven cloth (*mbala*) is used for most kinds of skirts and is by far the most common variety produced in the region. *Mbala badinga*, woven with an extra design stick, introduces a pattern in the cloth and is used for certain men's and women's skirts. The third kind of cloth is a very coarse weave, employed for utilitarian purposes such as storage sacks or clothing worn exclusively for hunting and other work in the forest.

Woven raffia cloth is part of a labor-intensive continuum that transforms raffia fiber into a medium for the creation of ceremonial skirts. When a piece of raffia cloth is cut from the loom, it is selvageless, stiff, and coarsely textured. If the cloth is used for women's skirts, it undergoes pounding in a mortar and other softening processes before it is hemmed, dyed, and decorated. These treatments change the stiff raffia cloth into a flexible and supple cloth approaching the quality of fine linen.[6] During research in 1981 and 1982, only women were observed treating cloth this way, although in some villages there were mortars similar in style to the one Torday found employed by men. (1910:pl.XXI).

The fabrication of skirts is for the most part gender-specific; only men assemble and decorate men's skirts, and only women assemble and decorate women's skirts. Several kinds of decorative techniques are utilized by both men and women. These include various embroidery stitches, appliqué and reverse appliqué, patchwork, dyeing, stitch-dyeing, and tie-dyeing. Only women, however, practice certain embroidery techniques such as openwork and cut-pile.

It is the length, configuration of skirt panels, and style of the borders that differentiates men's from women's skirts. A woman's

Figure 9. A Northern Kete man cutting a completed unit of raffia cloth (mbala) *off the loom. Photo by Patricia Darish, 1981*

long ceremonial skirt may be six to nine yards in length and is essentially unbordered. It is worn wrapped around the body three to four times and secured with a belt. Much shorter "overskirts," approximately one and a half yards in length, are worn over the longer skirts. Men's raffia skirts are usually half again to twice as long as women's skirts. Generally, men's skirts are assembled with square central sections, framed by narrower, composite borders completed with a raffia bobble fringe. Men's skirts are worn so that the length is fully gathered around the waist and hips and the top border folds downwards over a belt.

Many younger women presently wear imported cloth for daily wear, in much the same manner as do women in larger African cities. Younger men prefer to wear western-style trousers and shirts. Wearing plain, undecorated raffia cloth skirts is now a habit of the older generation. However, some older Kuba men and women mimic the traditional style of skirts by purchasing imported cotton cloth and machine-hemming it in the same style as raffia skirts. Even though changes in the style and fabric used for everyday attire are apparent in the region, the weaving of raffia cloth and the production of raffia textiles are still important daily activities.

THE DYNAMICS OF TEXTILE FABRICATION

Raffia weaving and skirt fabrication and decoration are not relegated to specialists or restricted to certain clans or lineages. Traditional decorated raffia skirts and cut-pile cloths are considered tangible wealth that everyone wants to accumulate, so the participation of every adult is expected. One Bushoong informant told me that textile fabrication is just as important as hunting.

Many proverbs underline the importance of raffia textile production in everyday life. For example, an older Northern Kete man or woman may say to an unmarried woman, "If you want to marry [well], consult the diviner so that you will find a man who will make you a skirt" (that is, weave raffia cloth). This proverb illustrates that knowledge about textile fabrication is both appropriate and valued in Kuba culture. Other Bushoong proverbs affirm the integrity and importance of traditional work, such as, "A calabash without a purpose is hanging over the hearth," and, "A man without work? We'll give him black mushrooms to eat." Black mushrooms belong to a category of wild foods consumed by women and children; they are not considered "proper" food to serve to men. Both proverbs imply that a person without work to do is considered useless.[7]

For most adults, work on textiles is both a part-time activity and a part of daily routine. Thus, the processes of weaving cloth and decorating textiles typically are relegated to short work periods. Some men prepare the fiber, set the warp, or complete one of the preliminary stages of weaving or dyeing early in the day, before they go to the fields or visit their traps. Many women are able to sit down and relax for a short period after returning from their fields. During this interval, they may embroider or complete another stage of skirt decoration or construction before they prepare the evening meal. Other women only have time during the two days a week (Fridays and Sundays) when they do not usually work in their fields.

Some individuals, by the nature of their talents and preferences, regularly weave raffia cloth or specialize in certain details of fabrication. Other individuals, due to infirmity or old age, are confined to the village and therefore restricted in their activities. These individuals also spend a proportionately larger part of their time in textile production. In one Bushoong village, a woman with an arthritic hip spent most of the day embroidering cloth and caring for small children. The number of hours she spent sewing was many times that of the average woman, as she was not able to work in the fields, draw water, or pound flour.

There are certain occasions when people regularly spend more time working on textiles. During the first half of the dry season, both men and women are able to devote more attention to textile production, because they are not busy clearing fields, planting or harvesting. During periods of mourning, the immediate family of the deceased is confined to the village and the women remain in their houses from dawn to dusk. During this period, which may last anywhere from three to nine months, much time is devoted to sewing and embroidering. This labor is required to replenish the family's supply of textiles, which is depleted at the funeral (Figure 10).

OWNERSHIP OF TEXTILES

During my research, especially among the Bushoong, I found that most decorated raffia skirts are neither fabricated nor owned by a single individual, but result from the cooperative efforts of the men and women of the clan section of a matrilineage. For example, the

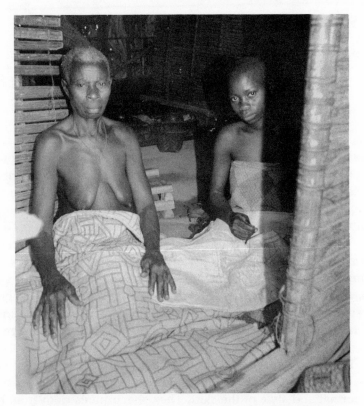

Figure 10. Two Bushoong women, restricted to their home during a mourning period, are embroidering and assembling the panels of a skirt (ncaka nsueha). *Photo by Patricia Darish, 1981*

construction of a long woman's skirt may be the work of half a dozen women of various ages. This fact alone challenges the Western notion of "artisanship" and "ownership;" a single raffia skirt may be interpreted as a chart of social relations and of communal artistry. While individuals may be singled out for the quality of their work, it is exceptional to find a long, elaborately decorated textile made by only one individual. Even textiles that are obviously the work of only one person are never considered the property of that person.

Several Bushoong proverbs collected by the author illustrate this assumption of group ownership:

One person can weave cloth, many can wear them.

There is no one else who can weave cloth as well as this man,
but when someone in his family died, they buried him nude.
His cloth is only for sale (to someone outside of the clan section).

The weaver is weaving, the blacksmith's helper is working the
bellows, but they are all wearing leaves!

These last two proverbs refer to the individual who does not fulfill
his (and by implication her) social responsibility—that of contributing to the group effort of textile fabrication. Thus, while the role of
individuals in the production of raffia textiles may be important, it
is often disguised and must be discussed in relationship to production within the clan section. This is especially true for women's
skirts, due to the time-consuming fine embroidery and appliqué
technique. For example, a particular Bushoong long woman's skirt
(nsueha) may be composed of more than thirty individually embroidered units, each consisting of black embroidered designs finely
stitched on doubled sections of raffia cloth. It would take one person
several years to complete a long skirt such as this.

The female head of the clan section typically directs the cloth
production of several women in her clan section. First, she chooses
the format and style of the skirt. Then she acquires cloth from her
husband or another male relative, or purchases it outright. After the
cloth has been softened, she determines the dimensions for a section of the skirt desired, doubles over the cloth, and hems it. Any
holes in the cloth resulting from the pounding process are covered
with appliqué. At this point, she may furnish one or more prepared
sections of cloth to other members of her clan to embroider.

If she supplies cloth to a novice or less skilled embroiderer, she
may baste the lines of the design onto the cloth beforehand. She
may also do this for married women living at some distance from
their matriclan. For example, the author observed a Bushoong
woman, living in another Bushoong village two days distance from
her natal home, embroider a section of a skirt her mother had given
to her to complete. In this way, completion of the textile is hastened
as large and small sections of a skirt are simultaneously worked by
several women at the same time.

As each unit of embroidered cloth is completed, it is returned
to the clan section head and sewn to other sections of the skirt al-

ready completed. Thus, the assembly of the skirt proceeds in an organic fashion over a period that may extend for several years. Aesthetically, the finished textile documents the varying skills and the repertoire of traditional designs at the disposal of the women who contributed to its fabrication.

The combination of style and decorative techniques utilized in the assembly and decoration of men's skirts dictates a working sequence different from that for women's skirts. Unlike the latter, in which each section is compositionally different, most men's skirts repeat the same design or designs throughout the entire length of the central panels and the skirt borders. Because of this linear repetition, individuals usually create men's skirts in an assembly-line fashion.

This does not mean that men's skirts require significantly less time to fabricate. Because so many separate units of decorated raffia cloth are needed to complete a man's skirt, it may take several years to acquire sufficient cloth to construct an entire skirt. This procurement is more difficult if the man fabricating the skirt does not weave raffia cloth himself.[8]

RAFFIA TEXTILES AND THEIR USES

For centuries, raffia cloth has been woven across a wide region of Central Africa (see distribution map 1, Loir 1933). In addition to its use as clothing, from the sixteenth century onward the use of raffia cloth as currency has been documented among various societies in Central Africa (Birmingham 1983; Douglas 1963; Martin 1984; Vansina 1962). It appears that in the Kuba area, raffia cloth squares were the principal currency initially and were replaced later by the cowrie imported by the Imbangala and Chokwe groups living to the south and west of the Kuba.[9] During this period, ten raffia squares or the approximate length of a skirt formed a larger unit of value (Vansina 1962:197). That cloth has retained its association with wealth or value in the Kuba area can readily be seen in the several other uses for which it has been employed.

Vansina notes that raffia cloth, among other items (including dried foodstuffs, salt, iron, utilitarian and decorative objects), formed a part of the annual tribute of many villages at the end of the dry season. Exact amounts of cloth given to the *nyim* are unknown but one village is mentioned as paying one raffia cloth for each adult man. In addition, special tribute could also be imposed whenever there was a need for certain items at the capital. Quantities of raffia cloth were also given to the *nyim* by subject chiefdoms at the death and installation of eagle feather chiefs (Vansina 1978:140–42).

Among some Kuba groups in the nineteenth century, raffia cloth and decorated skirts figured in marital contracts. For the Bushoong the bride-price was composed of both material goods and services. These services might include clearing a field, or building a house for the future mother-in-law. The future bridegroom might also weave a skirt, which his mother or sister would embroider, so that he could offer it to his mother-in-law. The actual items of the bride-price, payable at the time of marriage or even later, included cowries in bulk or in the form of *mabiim* (320 cowries sewn to a raffia cloth backing), camwood, raw raffia cloth (*mbala*), or decorated mats.[10] In the case of divorce, the spouse who initiates the divorce is responsible for the repayment of the bride-price to the other family (Vansina 1964:31–34).

Another type of marriage formerly practiced among the Bushoong calls for a bride-price much higher than that of an ordinary marriage. In this marriage the woman (*ngady akan*) was considered a "pawn" of the lineage and any children that resulted from the marriage were negotiated between lineages, according to the contract (Vansina 1978:6) Recorded bride-prices for this form of marriage listed several men's skirts as well as women's skirts, *mabiim*, beaded bracelets, necklaces, and hats. Even though among some Kuba groups, such as the Northern Kete, the payment was less, raffia cloth was always mentioned as a component of the bride-price (Vansina 1964:40–41).

Raffia cloth and skirts have also formed a required part of many legal settlements. One account mentions the loan of raffia cloth by one man to another to repay a debt (Hilton-Simpson 1912:110). In a case of adultery, a man was required to give the village tribunal 300 cowries, a man's skirt (*mapel*), and a ceremonial knife to the injured husband. After a fight that resulted in bodily harm, the guilty party was heavily fined. This fine included iron gongs, spears, swords, and raffia cloth (Vansina 1964:147).

One of the most frequently cited uses for decorated raffia textiles concerns their appearance during public events. A number of festive occasions are mentioned by early visitors to the region, although more often than not, the reason for the event is not given. Hilton-Simpson describes large dances, held frequently at Misumba (an important Ngongo chiefdom), in which women dressed similarly in either red or white skirts (1912:110–11). Hilton-Simpson also describes a dance held at the end of mourning for the *nyim's* sister. He was so fascinated by the visual impact of Kuba dress that he published a color illustration of this event on the cover of his book.

> As the sun was beginning to sink a little and the great heat of the afternoon became rather less oppressive, the elders assembled in the dancing-ground attired in all their ceremonial finery. This consisted of voluminous loin-cloths of raphia fibre bordered by strips of the same material elaborately embroidered in patterns, and in some cases ornamented by fringes of innumerable small tassels; around their waists they wore belts covered with beads or cowrie shells, and upon their heads nodded plumes of gaily coloured feathers (Hilton-Simpson 1912:201).

Torday describes the funeral of a high-ranked titleholder at the capital as follows: "A funeral dance took place the same evening, and all the elders turned up to it in their best finery. Their skirts were of rich embroidered cloth, and in their bonnets they wore bunches of gaily colored feathers" (1925:157).

Other important occasions requiring the display of elaborate dress are the *itul* rituals (described by Vansina 1964, Cornet 1980) and the funeral of a paramount ruler and subsequent installation of his successor (Vansina 1964:111–16). But these events occur infrequently and only at the capital.

Today, the most common occasion for the display of Kuba textiles is at funerals. This was true historically throughout the Kuba region, although only royal funerals are mentioned in early accounts. Torday (1925:197) described the funeral of the mother of a titleholder at the capital: "When we arrived it (the coffin) had not yet been closed and we could see the corpse, thickly painted with camwood paste and enveloped in fine cloth." Wharton (1927:128–29) states that the casket of the *nyim* Mbop aMbweeky was lined with embroidered raffia cloth, and that:

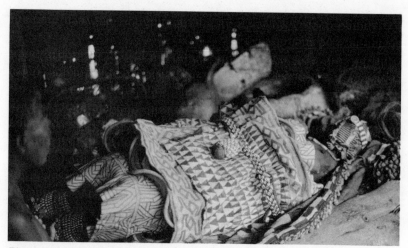

Figure 11. The body of a deceased female Bushoong titleholder, lying in state. Photo by Patricia Darish, 1981

. . . great quantities of cowrie-shell money were placed near the body so that the king might not want for funds on his long journey. Lest he hunger or thirst, meats of every description and many molds of bread, together with gourd on gourd of palm-wine were disposed within the casket. At the king's feet space was reserved for a trunk, in which were laid piece on piece of the rarest examples of the Bakuba art of cloth-weaving and embroidery.

THE CONTEXT OF USE: RAFFIA TEXTILE DISPLAY AT FUNERALS

Today, the display of elaborately decorated raffia textiles most typically occurs at funerals, when the body of the deceased is dressed with a prerequisite number of textiles and related costume accessories, including hats, bracelets, belts, and anklets. In this state the deceased is presented to mourners for several days and then buried with the textiles and other gifts (Figure 11).

The majority of textiles and costume accessories displayed on the corpse belong to the clan section of the deceased. As discussed earlier, most raffia skirts are neither owned nor fabricated by a single individual, but are the result of a cooperative effort by several people. As property of the clan section, textiles are placed on the body following a formal meeting of the section members. During this meeting, decisions are made as to precisely which textiles and other gifts will be placed on the corpse and buried with it. The textiles possessed by the clan section are unwrapped and each piece is closely examined for the quality of its workmanship. Any damage since the last examination is noted and taken into account when making the final selection. At all other times, these textiles are securely wrapped and stored with one or more leaders of the clan section.

While meetings are restricted to members, aspects of the decision-making process were gathered from interviews with numerous clan section heads and from examinations of their textile holdings. These informants often related aspects of the history of specific raffia textiles and of the individuals who created them. For example, in one Bushoong store of textiles, I was shown a short overskirt (*ncaka ishyeen*) which had a border much older than its central panel. The informant explained that the original central panel had been detached from the border and buried with a family member a number of years previously. The older border (which had been made approximately fifty years earlier by her great-grandmother) had been kept because of its age and the quality of its workmanship. She also kept the border because she wanted to show her children and her grandchildren how finely embroidered textiles used to be.

Other informants told the author that they were putting aside very old textiles for their own funerals. For example, one Bushoong woman had an extremely fine and old example of a decorated overskirt made by a relative who lived during the reign of the Kuba paramount ruler Kot aPe (ruled 1902–16). This woman was in her late seventies and could still recall the relative who had sewn the textile.

Textiles placed on the body of the deceased may also come from other sources. The spouse of the deceased (whether male or female) must also contribute one or more textiles of appropriate value to the clan section of the deceased. The type of textile given by the spouse follows the gender of the spouse, not that of the deceased; thus a widow contributes one or more women's skirts while a widower provides one or more men's skirts. These skirts are usually displayed with the corpse and subsequently buried with it.

The value and aesthetic merit of the textile given by the spouse is determined by the clan section of the deceased. Decisions may be reached after much heated discussion. At one meeting held in a Southern Bushoong village in 1982, the widow of the deceased brought a textile which was immediately rejected. The clan argued that the textile was not suitable because it was not long enough and the quality and quantity of embroidery was insufficient. The widow angrily left the meeting but later returned with a longer and more completely embroidered textile, which was accepted, subsequently displayed, and buried with the body of the deceased.

At another funeral in a Northern Kete village, I observed a man offering an incomplete man's skirt (in this case the borders of the skirt were missing) to the head of the deceased's clan section. The man was criticized and rebuffed; he was reminded that one would never wear an unfinished skirt, so why would he offer one as a gift to the deceased?

Friends are also free to contribute textiles or other gifts to the clan section of the deceased. These gifts (*labaam*) from individuals outside of the clan section of the deceased insure the giver a reciprocal and equivalent exchange between clan sections upon his or her own death. *Labaam* may consist of textiles as well as contemporary currency (Zaires), cowrie and beaded bracelets or anklets (*mabiim*), and necklaces or decorated belts. The bracelets, anklets, and necklaces usually adorn the deceased while he or she lies in state. These gifts may be buried with the deceased or stored in the coffers of the clan section until needed at a future occasion. Gifts of money also may be used by the clan section to defray funeral expenditures, such as those incurred for the food and palm wine consumed by relatives and friends while they attend the funeral.

While many of the gifts displayed with the deceased are traditional and customary in nature, other items relate directly to the individual's rank. Certain hat forms and other elements of regalia may also correspond directly to titleholding and therefore will be prominently displayed. As discussed earlier, this includes the types of feathers that indicate the title the deceased held in life. For example, one deceased Bushoong man held the important title of *Mbeem* in his village. A conical shaped hat (*ncok*) and guinea fowl feathers are the prerogative of this titleholder, so this special hat and feathers were included in his funeral attire. But a modern symbol of success was also included. This man had been an agricultural purchasing agent, in charge of the collection of corn, manioc, and coffee from local farmers. To represent this aspect of his rank and achieved status, the deceased was displayed and later buried with his attaché case.

PRESENTATION OF THE BODY AT FUNERALS

After the death of an adult, the women of the clan section wash the body of the deceased, then anoint it with red camwood powder.[11] The body is then dressed for display and subsequent burial.

Among all the ethnic groups in the area, a series of textiles varying in size, style, and gender are wrapped around the body in a prescribed order. Generally, the first textile encircling the body is a red-dyed raffia skirt, *mapel nshuip* (for men) or *ncak nkaana* (for women), which is devoid of surface decoration. These skirts are the simplest in design of all long Kuba skirts. Informants likened this textile to an undergarment.

Included with this first skirt is a small packet of cowries tied to a corner, just as Kuba men and women secure money or other small valuables into a knot in the corner of a skirt. Cowries are included because it is believed the deceased will use them to pay for river transport to the next world (*ilueemy*), discussed below.

Several different styles of textile may be placed on the deceased over this first skirt. With a woman, two styles of long, embroidered, and appliquéd skirts (*nsueha* or *mhahla*) are added next. Both are about six yards long. *Nsueha* and *mhahla* are similar in form and design except for two distinctive characteristics. The former is embroidered with black thread on undyed raffia cloth; the latter is first embroidered with undyed raffia thread and when completely assembled, the entire skirt is dyed red.

In Bushoong practice, these two skirts are the minimum requirement. However, the number of skirts on the body increases in proportion to the importance or wealth of the deceased. For this reason, multiples of long, embroidered textiles may also be added. Shorter women's overskirts are also employed as the top layer of the ensemble.

For a deceased man, several different skirt styles may be added over the underskirt. A very popular choice is a red-dyed skirt with a patchwork black-and-white rectangular border and bobble fringe (*kot'a laam'a mbokihey*). It is made and used all over the region. There are other styles of long men's skirts which may also be added (*ndono kwey, masheshela,* and *kumishinga*).

Some Kuba-related ethnic groups elect to add additional textiles as the final covering. For example, the Shoowa add sections of cut-pile and embroidered cloth (*winu*) as a final covering over the displayed body. Research indicates that this is the primary, traditional purpose of these cut-pile cloths.

As noted above, in addition to textiles there are many other costume accessories made by the Kuba, consisting of strands of beads or beaded raffia bracelets, belts, and anklets. These are rarely worn except as costume elements at the time of burial. Other items, such as hats, feathers, and belts, differentiate titled men and women from non-titled individuals. The total ensemble, the multiples of textiles and costume accessories, is of overriding importance to the Kuba aesthetic at funerals.

When the body is completely dressed it is displayed, usually sitting upright on a wooden support bier, for several days under an open shed. Three days seems to be the usual number in contemporary practice. Women of both clan section and village maintain a vigil under the shed with the body during the entire time it is displayed. Men gather under a shed some distance away. If the deceased was an initiated man, prescribed rituals, including songs, dances, and possibly masquerade performances, may take place during this time (Binkley 1987a).

Shortly before burial, the men of the clan section oversee construction of a coffin made from large decorated mats secured to a bamboo framework. The coffin may be fabricated in imitation of a pitched-roof house, and is often meticulous in its attention to architectural detail. Other coffins are fashioned in the same manner but with a flat roof. At the time of burial, the corpse is placed in the coffin and taken to the cemetery. Just before it is lowered into the ground, additional items such as currency, drinking cups, or costume elements, may be placed in the coffin. At one Bushoong funeral, a relative lifted the edge of the coffin and placed the tattered everyday hat worn by the deceased inside.

DRESSING FOR THE NEXT LIFE

The dressing of the corpse reflects both individual and group beliefs about proper burial. Although ideas concerning life after death are not systematically codified, there is a general belief in *ilueemy*, the land of the dead. The deceased is thought to travel to this land by crossing a river and to reside there until his or her spirit returns to the land of the living, usually after one or two generations.[12] For this reason coffins are fabricated in imitation of house construction while currency—both modern, in the form of Zaires, and traditional, in the form of cowries—is included with the body. Although Vansina (1978a:199) states that belief in *ilueemy* is archaic, I found it prevalent in the Kuba area in 1981 and 1982. I met individuals in many villages who were believed to be reborn (*nshaang*). One informant commented upon the depth of knowledge and other unusual talents of a young man as proof of his *nshaang* status.

Because of the pervasive belief in *ilueemy*, there is overwhelming concern that the deceased be dressed properly at burial. The Kuba believe that only raffia textiles are an appropriate mode of dress for burial. Several informants noted that they would not be recognized by deceased relatives in *ilueemy* if they were not dressed in traditional textiles. In addition they were concerned with ethnicity; they wished to be recognized by relatives and visitors to the funeral and in the afterlife as being a Bushoong, a Kete, or a Shoowa person, replete with all emblems of attained title or status.

In the Kuba area, to be buried in anything but traditional attire is tantamount to being buried nude. Even individuals who have not worn raffia skirts for twenty years or more have stated that when they die, they will be buried in traditional dress. Another Bushoong proverb expressed this attitude succinctly: "As bamboo does not lack roots, a man cannot dismiss his origins." To Bushoong (or Kete or Shoowa) men and women, it is imperative to express this belief in cultural heritage, especially at funerals and in visual form through the display of traditional attire. This is not an archaism or a revival but rather a conscious preservation of cultural values.

If individuals are concerned with the appropriate self-presentation at their own funerals, the clan section also is concerned about the proper burial of its members for several reasons. It is widely believed that deceased people have a malevolent spirit (*mween*), and that this spirit may become angered if all due respect is not paid to the deceased at the funeral. It is believed that the *mween* is particularly concerned that respect due his or her rank and achieved status be recognized by the clan section at the funeral (Binkley 1987a).

Fear of reprisals from the slighted *mween* acts as a strong motivating force on the clan section. A slighted *mween* may cause problems ranging from unsuccessful hunting or fishing to illness, infertility, or death for members of the clan section. The malevolent spirit of a deceased titleholder is considered far more powerful than that of an untitled individual; if an important titleholder's *mween* is angered, the entire village may be harmed. In order not to offend a powerful *mween*, there may be protracted discussions among clan section members to make certain that burial arrangements have been properly made.

Concern for prestige provides another motive for displaying the appropriate number and quality of textiles on the deceased. If the clan section of the deceased presents the proper textiles in sufficient number and quality, it shows the village that the clan section acknowledges its responsibilities and honors and respects its members at the time of death, and thus allows the clan section to enhance its prestige. Understandably, a public funeral provides an open forum for gossip and unsolicited criticism. At one Bushoong funeral, a woman outside the clan section criticized the textiles displayed on the corpse. She said that the quality of a certain textile was insufficient as it did not have enough embroidery, and that the clan section should have placed a greater quantity of textiles on the body. Another Bushoong informant stated that gossip such as this is the primary activity at funerals.

Following most adult deaths, a crucial ritual is conducted at the grave site before the coffin is fully lowered into the ground and covered with earth. This ritual is performed by the surviving spouse and a member of the opposite sex from the clan section of the deceased. Kneeling on opposite sides of the coffin, each marks the little finger of the other's right hand with white clay or kaolin. This gesture severs the social bonds of marriage and kinship ties between the deceased and the living. If this ritual is not performed, the deceased will appear in dreams (especially to the spouse) and may also be a source of harm to other members of the clan section. For surviving clan-section members, this ritual shows the deceased that the clan section has fulfilled its responsibilities to the deceased and should be left in peace.

WHY THE DEAD WEAR DECORATED RAFFIA TEXTILES

In Kuba villages today, the use of undecorated raffia cloth for every-day clothing has been largely supplanted by western dress such as shirts and trousers for men, and blouses and printed cotton wrappers for women. But despite this adoption of modern dress, the display of decorated raffia textiles continues to be a central element in the ritual surrounding death. Undoubtedly, the aesthetic appeal of these textiles in ceremonial and funeral contexts is strong. But the Kuba have many reasons in addition to aesthetics for giving decorated raffia textiles such a major role at funerals. The persistence of this tradition is fundamentally linked to the burial of textiles at funerals, because the Kuba believe that the process of making textiles is as important as the textiles themselves.

As we have seen, both male and female members of the clan section are essential participants in all of the stages of textile production. Thus, the display of textiles at funerals powerfully reaffirms the enduring social relationships that encompass the complementary and interdependent efforts of the men and women of the clan section. These relationships are acknowledged and reproduced in the social arena of the funeral. Both men's and women's skirts are placed on the body of the deceased when it is displayed in the village. These textiles are made and given by clan section members and others who expect the same tributes in return at their funerals. In this respect, exchange of textiles is a one-way process, moving from the living to the dead as the textiles are buried with the deceased. Yet this very process supports Kuba assertions of ethnic identity and adherence to traditional beliefs in the afterlife.

Even though Kuba textiles do not recirculate, burying them is not seen as a depletion of the system. Members of the clan section are constantly renewing this aesthetic and unifying resource as part of their everyday work. A Bushoong proverb states: "You can take from a raffia palm, but you can never deplete its supply."[13] For the Kuba, both the decorated textiles and the material from which they are made are powerful symbols of abundance and wealth. The raffia palm has been an inexhaustible resource for centuries, exploited not only for decorated and plain clothing, but also for shelter, palm wine, and food. Moreover, raffia cloth squares have been a principal currency and have formed a major portion of the wealth of the Kuba paramount ruler. The burial of these labor-intensive raffia skirts at funerals recalls these ancient ideas of abundance and wealth. Thus the Kuba still choose raffia cloth for funerals because it is a potent symbol of security and continuity, actively linking the living to one another as well as to the community of the recently deceased.

ACKNOWLEDGMENTS

Research among the Bushoong, Shoowa, and several Northern Kete peoples residing in Mweka zone, Republic of Zaire was supported by the Fulbright-Hays Doctoral Dissertation Research Abroad Program through Indiana University for 21 months during 1981 and 1982. This paper is dedicated to Norm Schrag, whose scholarship, friendship, and sense of humor are an enduring memory to his Indiana University colleagues. I would like to thank Mary Jo Arnoldi, David Binkley, Ivan Karp, Doran Ross, Jane Schneider, Jan Vansina, and Annette Weiner for reading previous versions of this paper.

NOTES

1. Except for the Lele (Douglas 1963), we do not have precise ethnographic details of past or current use patterns for raffia textiles among neighboring peoples.

2. See Emil Torday (1910;1925) and especially Jan Vansina (1954;1964;1978a) for detailed accounts of Kuba history, ethnography, and linguistics.

3. The last census taken of all the Kuba people was in 1950, when the population was estimated to be over 70,000 (Vansina 1964:8).

4. These groupings have been outlined by Vansina (1964:6–7;1978:5).

5. All terms are cited in the Bushoong language, unless otherwise noted.

6. Some decorated textiles, such as the cut-pile and embroidered Shoowa *winu*, the Bushoong *ncaka buiin*, and the raffia cloth employed for the borders of men's skirts, do not utlilize softened cloth.

7. These proverbs were collected in Kete and Bushoong villages by the author during 1981–82.

8. I returned to one Bushoong village a year later to find the production of the center sections of a man's skirt at the same stage I had observed a year earlier.

9. According to Jan Vansina, personal communication, 1987.

10. In the late nineteenth century and into the twentieth, bride-prices in cowries and francs rose tremendously, because young men did not want to work for their mothers-in-law and the reduction in services caused the amount to rise (Vansina 1964:31–34). Though I do not have data for contemporary practices, I suspect that even the custom of bride-price has been dropped by many of the Kuba groups.

11. Camwood powder is used as a cosmetic in Central Africa; it is still favored by many older Kuba women today.

12. Vansina (1978:198–99) states that the "proto-Kuba" practiced ancestor worship, but adopted some of the religious beliefs of the Kete, in this case the concepts of *nshaang* and *ilueemy*, when they moved south of the Sankuru River. These concepts are more thoroughly discussed in Vansina 1958.

13. Recorded at a Southern Bushoong funeral in 1981 (Binkley 1987b).

REFERENCES CITED

Adams, Marie Jeanne
    1978   Kuba Embroidered Cloth. African Arts, 12(1):24–39,106–07.

Binkley, David Aaron
    1987a   Avatar of Power: Southern Kuba Masquerade Figures in a Funerary Context. Africa, Journal of the International African Institute, 57(1):75–97.
    1987b   Personal communication.

Birmingham, David
    1983   Society and Economy before A.D. 1400. In History of Central Africa, Vol. I. David Birmingham and Phyllis M. Martin, eds. pp. 1–29. London: Longman Group Limited.

Cornet, Joseph
    1980   The Itul Celebration of the Kuba. African Arts, 13(3):28–33,92.

Douglas, Mary
    1963   The Lele of the Kasai. London: Oxford University Press.

Hilton-Simpson, M.N.
    1911   Land and Peoples of the Kasai. London: Constable and Company Ltd.

Loir, Helene
    1935   Le tissage du raphia au Congo belge, Musée Royal de l'Afrique Centrale, Anthropology and Ethnography, Sér.3, Vol. 3, No. 1. Brussels.

Mack, John
1980   Bakuba Embroidery Patterns: a Commentary on their Social and
Political Implications. *In* Textiles of Africa, Dale Idiens and K.G.
Ponting, eds. Bath: The Pasold Research Fund Ltd.

Martin, Phyllis M.
1984   Power, Cloth and Currency Among the Societies of the Loango
Coast. Paper presented at the annual meeting of the African
Studies Association, New Orleans, 1984.

Picton, John and John Mack
1979   African Textiles, Looms, Weaving and Design. London: British
Museum Publications Ltd.

Torday, Emil and T.A. Joyce
1910   Notes ethnographiques sur les peuples communement appelés
Bakuba, ainsi que sur les peuplades apparentées: les
Bushongo. Musée Royal de l'Afrique Centrale, Anthropology
and Ethnography, Sér. 4, No. 2. Tervuren.
1925   On the Trail of the Bushongo. London: Seeley Service and Co.

Vansina, Jan
1954   Les tribus Ba-Kuba et les peuplades apparentées. Musée Royal
de l'Afrique Centrale, Ethnographic Monographs, No. 1,
Tervuren.
1954   Les valeurs culturelles des Bushong. *Zaire* 8:899–910.
1958   Les croyances religeuses des Kuba. *Zaire* 12:725–58.
1962   Trade and Markets Among the Kuba. *In* Markets in Africa, Paul
Bohannan and George Dalton, eds. Evanston: Northwestern University.
1964   Le Royaume Kuba. Musée Royal de l'Afrique Centrale, Anthropology and Ethnography, No. 49. Tervuren.
1978   The Children of Woot, A History of the Kuba Peoples. Madison,
Wisconsin: University of Wisconsin Press.

Wharton, Conway
1927   The Leopard Hunts Alone. New York: Fleming H. Revell.

5. Why Do Ladies Sing the Blues?

Indigo Dyeing, Cloth Production, and Gender Symbolism in Kodi

JANET HOSKINS

 The unusually large, bold patterns and rich blues and rusts of Sumbanese warp ikat cloth have attracted foreign buyers for over a century, making the textile traditions of this isolated Eastern Indonesian island the focus of an important export trade. To European visitors, the cloths appear as objects of ostentatious display and public presentation. Worn as ceremonial costume by both men and women, they form part of marriage payments from the bride's family, are used as "sails" on the "ships" that drag stones for megalithic graves, and as banners in feasts, processions, and welcoming ceremonies for important officials. Suspended from the walls or ceiling on ceremonial occasions, warp ikats also make sumptuous funeral shrouds, wrapping the corpse in as many as a hundred different layers (Adams 1969, Hoskins 1986).

The exuberant unfolding of several meters of color-saturated textiles, patterned with plant, animal, and human designs, is the public face that Sumbanese cloth producers present to the outside world. In isolated huts secluded in the bush, another face of cloth production is hidden: Here, indigo dyeing is conducted as a cult of female secrets. Hedged by a system of taboos that forbid access to all men, and to women at certain stages in their reproductive cycles, older women practice an occult art that is associated with herbalism, midwifery, tattooing, and (more covertly) witchcraft. Soaking in the indigo bath, threads take on sacred powers that make obligations binding, proffer blessings, and enclose fertility in a sheltered bundle. In the bath, tied clusters of thread define the white outlines of motifs that will appear, like a photographic negative, against the blue background of the finished cloth. The design is created when the dye is applied, etching out shapes reminiscent of the bridewealth objects and animals controlled by men, in a pattern that will assume its final form once the weft threads are interwoven to produce the cloth.

The art of traditional dyeing is merged with the production of herbal medicines, poisons, abortifacients, and fertility potions in a body of occult knowledge known as *moro*, "blueness," which is the exclusive possession of a few female specialists. In its magical aspects, as a series of mysteries that only cult initiates may penetrate, this "blue art" is a ritual as well as a technological process. Associated with myths about a witch ancestress from the neighboring island of Savu, the production of Sumbanese textiles is also linked to theories of human conception and the growth of the fetus within the womb. A metaphoric parallel between the production of children and the production of cloth informs exchange relations established through the transfer of cloth and the transfer of women from one ancestral village to another. Finally, cloth itself becomes the medium for an inarticulate protest against perceived injustices that afflict women and give their sorrow its particularly "blue" coloring.

THE SUMBANESE "BLUES": INDIGO DYEING IN CONTEXT

Sumba is the fourth island east of Bali, lying south of the Lesser Sunda Island chain which stretches out toward Timor and eventually Australia. With an arid climate and an often-precarious agricultural base, the Sumbanese subsist on a mixture of garden-grown rice and corn, pastoralism (raising cattle, buffalo, and small spirited horses for export), and trade. Slaves, livestock, and textiles were the most important items of trade in the nineteenth century, both between traditional domains and to ships from Holland, Makassar, Java, and Sumbawa. Many of the finest cloths from this period ended up in Dutch homes as blankets and wallhangings, because their appealing variety of shapes and representational forms was dramatically different from the stripe patterning of textiles produced on neighboring islands. Export of Sumbanese textiles continued after the Dutch took political control of the island in 1913, and has intensified since independence in 1949.

Warp ikat cloths are produced along the coastal areas, where wild indigo plants grow, and the most famous cloths are those from Kanatang and Kaliurang, in the eastern half of the island. Kodi, at the farthest western tip, produces a distinctive style of ikat-patterned textile, whose more abstract, geometric design shows a greater influence from imported Indian *patola* cloths. Kodi is the major textile-producing area for the western part of the island. During the "hungry season" of October to December, indigo-dyed Kodi textiles are often traded for food from the more fertile interior regions.

Fieldwork in Kodi, undertaken over a period of three years (from 1979 to 1981, with return visits in 1984, 1985, and 1986) revealed a still-lively production of traditional cloths, despite the increased use of commercial threads and dyes, especially for the reddish colors. Indigo-dyed cloths remain the only ones that are acceptable for the most important ritual and ceremonial occasions. Virtually all Kodi women learn to bind the threads into patterns for ikat dyeing, and to weave on a backstrap loom. Only a few, however, become initiated into the mysteries of indigo dyeing, which is part of a complex of magical and technical skills usually passed down the maternal descent lines.

When young, unmarried girls are introduced to the cults, they learn to chew up the herbal preparations used to make the dyes. They are not allowed to bring cloths to be dyed until they have reached sexual maturity—but then they are excluded from the dyeing process for long periods of time, because it is seen as dangerous to menstruating or pregnant women. Regular practitioners of indigo dyeing are all women past menopause, who have already borne children and acquired the tattoos on the forearm and calf that mark female achievement of wifehood and motherhood. Thus, participation in cloth production marks stages in the female life cycle, and creates a "rite of maturity," celebrating the culmination of a woman's career by her acquisition of hidden knowledge and greater control over the processes not only of dyeing, but also of childbirth, menstruation, and menopause.

Indigo dyeing serves to define boundaries: Between men and

women, between those who have learned its mysteries and those who have not, and between degrees of competence and knowledge of the herbal preparations used. It creates a hierarchical order, in that participants in indigo dyeing and the "blue arts" are not only transformed but gain status. Dyeing also involves some degree of danger, suffering and pain. The indigo bath is seen as polluting to women at certain stages in the reproductive cycle, and its unpleasant smell evokes (for the Kodi) the odor of corpses, decay, and putrefaction.

Overcoming such fears and learning the secrets of the indigo dye bath may also qualify a woman to practice as a midwife and healer (*tou tangu moro*, literally a "person who applies blueness"— referring here to herbal medicines). After she has passed the age of childbearing herself, a woman may transform her passive role as a "receptacle" for the growing fetus into the more active one of controlling and regulating the fertility of others. She acquires knowledge which gives her greater control over physiological functions, and wears indigo-colored tattoos on her forearms as a badge of her reproductive success. Differences between men and women are elaborated as a contrast between durable, male objects such as metal and stone, and female vitality and production of semidurables (cloth and children) in a mysterious domain of their own. The very secrecy of these rites is presented to men as part of the "mystery" of the reproductive process, which women are believed to affect through occult techniques.

Kodi belief emphasizes similarities between indigo dyeing and the processes of pregnancy and childbirth. The "binding medicines" used in the dye bath to make colors fast are also administered to women after childbirth to control bleeding. However, the degree of control possible in indigo dyeing is greater than in the dangerous and often-unpredictable practice of midwifery. The transfer of substances from one domain to another reflects a conscious effort to marshal "the blue arts" as a form of control over the body, as well as female ornamentation.

In addition to its association with the production of children, the logic of exchange, and the life cycle, indigo dyeing finds expression in women's most developed form of the verbal arts: The singing of formalized songs of lament (*hoyo*) at funerals and other situations where misfortunes are recalled and shared. The songs use metaphors taken from textile production to reflect on situations of loss—bereavement, serious illness, the departure of a loved one to prison or exile. They are most often performed at mortuary ceremonies, but also treat the painful separation of the bride from her natal home at marriage. The transfer of brides and of corpses, both wrapped in textiles and reduced to a state of passive detachment, is part of a larger pattern in which weddings and funerals are modeled after one another. Feelings of detachment and separation are the focus of the songs, which speak of the heart (*ate dalo*, literally, "liver") as tinged with the blueness of affliction. Like the tradition of "blues" in our own society, they show a kinship of suffering among persons who consider themselves powerless.[1]

Kodi indigo cults are distinct from male cultic preoccupations with ancestors, headhunting, and warfare. They show that female arts and weapons are distinct from those of men, and have a darker and more mysterious coloring, directly grounded in the bodily experience of childbearing. I will explore the meanings of these differences, their implications for an understanding of the female resentment, and the development of alternate arenas of power. My portrait of the "blue arts" has six sections: (1) the place of indigo dyeing in relation to patrilineal ancestral villages and matrilineal clans; (2) the dangers of "blueness"; (3) the metaphoric and metonymic relations between cloth production and the production of children; (4) cloth in mythology and song; (5) the social meanings of the exchange of cloth and the exchange of women; and (6) the tattooing of textile designs on the body, to enclose female reproduction within the partrilineage and celebrate the legitimate sexuality of mature women. Finally, I will consider how these themes relate to differences established between women at varying points in the life cycle, the fragile and ephemeral character of cloth valuables and human children, and the linkages established between women and cloth in this and other societies.

PATRILINEAGES, MATRICLANS, AND THE SECRETS OF INDIGO

About 50,000 Kodi live in scattered hamlets near their gardens, returning to large ancestral villages along the coast for calendrical ceremonies, funerals, and feasts. The prestige economy of feasting, bridewealth payments, and fines is based on the circulation of large numbers of horses and buffalo, although ownership of herds is concentrated in the hands of a few wealthy men. The agricultural work of planting and harvesting garden crops of dry rice, corn, and tubers is shared by both sexes, but men have exclusive control of the public domain of exchange. They negotiate transfers of land and livestock, marriages, mortuary payments, and feasting obligations. The most prominent men may attain the ceremonial title of *rato*, "great feast giver," which assures them of a permanent place in ancestral genealogies. A few women, famous priestesses and singers, were also said to have become *rato* in the past, but none were living at the time of my research.[2]

Alongside the competitive system of prestige feasting which creates "Big Man" leaders, ideas of hierarchy and complementarity are developed through a diarchic division of ceremonial tasks. Notions of rank and precedence define the holders of important priestly offices from among the descendants of particular ancestral villages. Noble families in the past had large numbers of slaves, transferred along with brides at marriage and attached to their houses as dependents, working in the gardens or tending livestock for absent owners. Many of the most sacred heirloom objects are still stored in cult houses inhabited only by slaves, who guard these objects at considerable risk to their lives because of the taboos associated with them. Three-fourths of the population describe themselves to government census takers as followers of the traditional system of spirit worship, called *marapu*, while about 13 percent are Protestant and 9 percent Catholic.

Kodi has long been known for its unusual system of "double descent" (Van Wouden 1956, Needham 1980) where membership in "houses" (*uma*) and villages is established around a core of agnates, and women are recruited into them through the exchange of marriage gifts. Inalienable ties of birth and blood are traced along the matriline (*walla*), establishing strict rules against incest within the female bloodline. Members of a house worship patrilineal ancestors and other guardian deities (*marapu*) dwelling in the house tower and pillar, and also share rights to land, ritual office, livestock, and the heirloom objects making up its sacred patrimony. Even when they live for much of the year in isolated garden hamlets, they return to their ancestral villages for major rituals and funerals.

In contrast to the corporate rights and obligations transmitted along the patriline, members of a matriline share a common bodily substance, and are believed to show similarities of personality and character. They have no collective functions to bring them together, nor are female ancestresses named and propitiated separately from their husbands.

While the name of a given patriclan is often taken from the tree that is planted in the center of the ancestral village and serves as a communal altar, the name of a matriclan is a personal name or the name of a region. The term *walla* means "flower," and refers to the "flowering" of a woman's descendants like blossoms along the boughs of the great trees planted in the village squares. But the seeds and sprouts of future clansmen are identified as male children. (*Ha wu wallada*, literally the "seeds and flowers," is translated as male and female children, while *kahinye mono katulla*, the "sprouts and shoots," are male descendants who will continue the patriline.)

There is no official ritual associated with the matriclans, but secrets such as those used in dyeing thread, preparing certain herbal medicines, and assisting childbirth or abortion may be passed along the female line. Blood ties between members of the same matriclan can surface as important in situations where factions form across clan boundaries, and these ties are often blamed for divisiveness within ancestral groupings. Some specific matriclans are associated with the hereditary transmission of witchcraft and sorcery.

Because of such negative associations, people's matriclans are often kept secret from all but their closest relatives. They may not be openly discussed until marriage negotiations, when rules of matriclan exogamy make it necessary to reveal those bloodlines. Although both matriclans and patriclans are exogamous, incest within the matriclan is much more dangerous. It can result in immediate hemorrhaging, miscarriages, or even death, and cannot be ritually mediated. In contrast, persons from different houses who wish to marry within the patriclan can do so by arranging an adoption and a change in marriage payments.

Women's bodies are seen as vessels for the transmission of immutable substances, whereas men's bodies contribute form, social position, and membership in agnatic groups which must be verified by exchange payments. Kodi theories of conception stress the necessity of both male and female contributions, but acknowledge that women have more control over pregnancy and childbirth, and that the infants born to them remain "of the mother's substance" until adulthood.

Indigo-dyeing secrets are passed on as part of the lore of matriclans, but are seen as having an exogenous origin: The bringer of the art of indigo dyeing was a woman from the neighboring island of Savu (*warico haghu*), who migrated to Sumba at some point in the distant past. Current Savunese inhabitants of Sumba are usually credited with considerable occult knowledge, but are also known as witches and practitioners of a kind of "black magic," locally associated with the color blue.[3] Some accounts say that the ancestress of dyeing was accompanied by her husband (*mone haghu*) who was a metalworker. Metalworking and textile dyeing are associated in a couplet that refers to both of these imported arts (*beti kyamba, buri bahi*, "dipping cloth, pouring iron"), and must be repeated in invocations to their respective ancestral spirits whenever the arts are practiced.

The two arts are also associated in the couplet name for the Creator, a double-gendered deity addressed as the Mother Binder of the Forelock, Father Smelter of the Crown (*Inya wolo lindu, Bapa rawi ura*). The female aspect of creation is presented as a parallel to the female crafts of binding and dyeing thread (here, the hairs at the forelock, seat of the vulnerable life force or *hamaghu*), while the male aspect smelts the harder skull at the crown (seat of destiny, the enduring soul or *ndewa*). Each of these traditional crafts establishes gender boundaries in a rigorous and exclusive fashion: It is forbidden for women to witness the process of metal smelting, just as it is forbidden for men to see the indigo bath for dyeing thread.

Both Sumba and Savu are famous for their elaborately decorated textiles, which have been exported to foreign markets since the nineteenth century. The motifs used on Savunese textiles are primarily floral and ornamental, although traditionally they indicated membership in a matrilineal moiety system called the "greater" or "lesser" blossom (Fox 1977). In East Sumba, representations of horses, deer, crocodiles, roosters, snakes and skulltrees fill the horizontal panels with symbols of wealth and male animals. In West Sumba, and particularly Kodi, more geometric motifs depict animal parts (the "buffalo eye" and "horse's tail") as well as wealth items like the gold omega-shaped ear pendants used in bridewealth payments (*hamoli*).

THE DANGERS OF "BLUENESS"

Textiles are the most important wealth items produced by women, and they are also the best way for modern women to enter the cash economy. Most cloths sold at local markets are of inferior quality and use modern thread and dyes, but valuable pieces are privately bought or exchanged at the price of a large pig, horse, or buffalo. Because of the constant demand for quality indigo-dyed cloth for ritual exchange, the "blue-handed women" (*warico kabahu moro* or *tou betingo*, "indigo dippers") of Kodi are highly respected and enjoy a certain economic independence.[4]

The advantages of acquiring skills in textile dyeing are hedged by the dangers involved in the process, and its associations with witchcraft, death, and the acrid smell of corpses. The term for the color produced by indigo (*moro*) designates a range of colors from blue to green, and is also used to mean raw or uncooked. The darkest shades, a kind of blue-black, are the most valued. Among the mysteries associated with indigo dyers, their secrets for making the dye as dark and heavily saturated as possible receive special attention. Descendants of two specific *walla* (Walla Kyula and Walla Cubbe) are said to have acquired these secrets from the indigenous peoples of the area. Significantly, these *walla* are also the ones most commonly associated with the hereditary transmission of witchcraft.

Witches, who can be either male or female, are believed to have extensive knowledge of local herbs and medicines, and to eat their foods raw, since their ancestors did not know how to make fire, cook food, or plant crops at the time that the Kodi arrived. Folk etymology links their name, *tou hamarango*, to either the "eaters of raw foods" (from *mu moro*) or the "eaters of blue substances," depending on how the term *moro* is used. Witchcraft can be detected through bluish marks at the navel, fingertips, or eye sockets, and victims of witch attacks often complain of seeing a bluish color moving around them, interrupted by flashes of a red light.

A death caused by a violent accident, murder, or drowning is called a "blue death" (*mate moro*), and the soul of the victim is said to fly off into the sky. Relatives cannot bury the body within the stone tombs of the ancestral village until a special ceremony has been performed to "call back" the lost soul. As the corpse waits, rotting, for a temporary earthen burial, its putrefying smell is said to be particularly intense and reminiscent of the indigo dye bath.

The association of death and indigo makes the dye bath dangerous for women who are in the process of creating a new life within their bodies. Pregnant women may not look at the dye pots, because it is believed that the sight of churning, dark liquids within the pot would dissolve the contents of their wombs and cause an immediate abortion. Conversely, menstruating women are barred from the indigo dyeing, since the flow of their blood would make the dyes "run" irregularly. The two-directional magical effect is interesting: Female fertility that is not being used to produce children is dangerous to the indigo bath, but once conception has occurred it is the indigo which has the dangerous power to dissolve the fetus.[5]

I interpret the idea that indigo dyeing threatens normal female fertility as an effort to create a conceptual separation between two forms of creative production: The coagulation of blood within the womb (caused by the father's contribution of sperm) and the coagulation of dyeing agents in the textile bath. A metaphoric parallel is obviously established between womb and dyeing pot, and the use of some of the same herbs and barks reinforces the association metonymically. Kodi theories of human conception refer to the father's sperm as the form-giving agent, comparing the male role to the metalworker who smelts a vat of molten liquids into an enduring shape. The lime that is added to the indigo pot, called the "male ingredient" or the "husband" (*laghi*) of the indigo plant, is the chemically active substance, the mordant, that causes the color to "take."

Kodi theories of sexual reproduction also follow a betel metaphor. As in the quickening process of pregnancy, the lime is added to the betel quid, producing a reddish liquid from the green pulp of the areca nut and betel catkin that gives a caustic "bite." Betel chewing has a clear role in courtship, usually as a preliminary to sexual relations. A girl indicates her willingness to sleep with a suitor by agreeing to chew betel with him, and a neglected wife may complain to her relatives if her husband does not "give her betel" in order to produce a child. The exchange of betel is a public activity initiated by men, whereas in textile dyeing women procure their own lime and combine it themselves in secret. The cloth "child" that they produce is created independently of men, and quickened by their own powers.

Betel and cloth differ in other ways as well, which define male and female domains of creative activity. The betel quid is a blue-green mixture of fresh nuts and leaves or catkin, which is made red by the addition of lime. The indigo bath, in contrast, is an originally muddy reddish-brown mixture of ash, barks, and roots, which is "quickened" into a deep blue by the fermenting action of lime. Betel is the marker of public social interactions and visiting, which may lead to marriage and childbirth. Textile dyeing presents once again an inverse pattern: It is secret, restricted to women, and carried on in the privacy of secluded huts. I propose that indigo dyeing is dangerous to men because it represents an independent female creation, an appropriation of male "quickening" substances without male control, and a process similar to childbirth that is outside of the ancestral value system.

CLOTH PRODUCTION AND THE PRODUCTION OF CHILDREN

The metaphoric parallels Kodi women establish between the dyeing of cloth and the formation of a child in the womb can be discerned in the language used to describe the two processes, and their sharing of certain taboos. First, there is the "quickening" (*pa kati*, "the bite") induced by the male lime when it is added to the mud bath in which stems and leaves of the indigo plant (*rou kanabu*) have been soaking along with various plant nutrients (among them tamarind, ironwood, and rice straw). This is akin to the conception of the child, as it allows for the chemical reduction of fermentation. Second, there is the stage of soaking the thread (bound into bundles with gewang leaf or commercial twine) in the dissolved and fermented indigo (yellow or light green in color) so that the soluble indigo can penetrate the fibers. Only after the pale liquid has saturated the threads evenly can they be taken out of the bath and exposed to the air for oxidation. An insoluble compound is formed on the thread during this period, which eventually defines the shapes and patterns of the motifs bound into the lengths of thread. The Kodi term for this is "dampening" (*mbaha*), also the name of the stage of a fetus in the womb when it is believed to absorb a great amount of the mother's blood, but does not yet have a firm skeleton or shape. Threads removed from the dye bath at this stage are not yet fast in color, just as a fetus born during the first few months of pregnancy is not viable outside the womb.

Considerable skill is needed to determine when the almost colorless soluble indigo has penetrated all of the thread, and it can be taken out and shaken for a few minutes to separate individual strands for oxidation.[6] As the threads hang on the branches of a nearby tree, the pale greenish color oxidizes to a deep blue. The thread is then immersed in the dye bath again, the stages of dye saturation and oxidation being repeated at least four times to get the deepest possible hue. The repeated "dipping" (betingo) uses the same fermented bath, the mixture of alkali, tannin, and nutrients being maintained, but without new additions of lime. The dye bath should not be stirred vigorously or turned even when threads are removed, because stirring would cause a premature oxidation. Women who described the process noted that when a fetus is in the final stages of its development, a husband is also not allowed to disturb the contents of his wife's womb, for fear of stirring up the delicate mixture and causing a miscarriage.

If the chemical interactions within the bath are not properly controlled, or the threads are incompletely penetrated by the indigo solution, then the blue produced may become brownish, greenish, or grayish as it is woven into cloth. In similar fashion, birth defects and breech births are often traced to male violations of the taboo on sex in the last month or two before birth. However, maternal death in childbirth is always explained not by male violations but by incest or adultery on the part of the mother. As in the taboos associated with access to dyeing sites, male transgressions endanger the "product" (the thread being dyed, the fetus), while a woman's immorality is violence inflicted against herself, the container (the indigo dye bath, the female womb).

Once properly saturated, oxidized, and dried, indigo on cotton thread is fast to water and its blue is brightened with each washing. The precise combinations of chalk, ash, herbs, and roots used in preparing dyes are all "secrets of the trade," which cannot be revealed to men or to other women who have not made offerings to the spirit of the Savunese ancestress who first brought these practices to Kodi. Also secret are the locations of the best indigo plants along the sea-

Figure 12. *An older Kodi woman shakes out freshly dyed
threads from the indigo pot and hangs them up to dry.
Photo by Laura Scheerer, 1985*

shore, the other roots used to "bind" the color, and the time needed
for the mixture to ferment.[7]

Two other expressions used to describe childbirth difficulties
draw on the vocabulary of indigo dyeing: An aborted fetus (*manuho*)
during the first six months of pregnancy is said to have been ex-
pelled when it was "incompletely saturated" (*njaha mbaha ndaha
pango*, literally, "not yet fully dampened") with the life-giving substances of its mother's body. If a women dies while pregnant, she
is said to "bring along the funeral shroud in her womb" (*ngandi
ghabuho ela kambu dalo*)—showing that the placental envelope is associated with the textiles used to wrap corpses. The metaphoric cloth
that shields the infant in the womb is also made to serve as the mortuary bundle for its voyage to another world.

The ritual surrounding the preparation of the dye pot is similar
in many respects to the rites that a midwife performs at childbirth:
A chicken must be sacrificed before each dye pot is prepared, its soul
dedicated to the Savunese ancestress who introduced dyeing (the
mori ghuro, mori nggilingo, "mistress of the dye pot, mistress of the

indigo") and its entrails examined to determine whether or not she has given her consent for the secrets to be shared. The same ritual preparations are made for the two women who normally assist in births—the "one who pushes" (*tou pa tunda*) massaging the child out of the womb, and the "one who receives" (*tou pa himbia*) holding the child as it emerges.

Similar offerings are made to the objects that are used to ease both childbirth and dyeing. At birth, the strip of barkcloth that a woman grasps in her labor receives an offering of betel, cooked rice, and cooked meat from the chicken killed for the ritual specialists. In indigo dyeing, this offering is usually set in front of the pot as the dye is prepared. Men cannot be present at either childbirth or dyeing, nor can they hear the chants that are pronounced to ease childbirth or quicken the dyes. The names of the ingredients used in women's herbal medicines and the spirits of the places where they were collected also must remain secret.

The metaphoric association between the process of conception in the womb and the "fixing" of indigo dyes in secret production centers is reinforced by a metonymic one, because some of the same herbal potions are used to control both processes. Such potions can be either drunk by the expectant mother or used in a healing bath after childbirth. They are intended to cleanse the "dirty blood" that may remain after labor and to stop excessive bleeding. Herbalism and massage were used by midwives to detect problems with the fetus before birth. Specific foods might be prescribed to treat "softness" of the spine, or to help "turn around" a breech birth through massage. A root (*amo ghaiyo*) identified to me along the seashore was said to be useful in "closing" both colors and the womb. The running of poorly dyed sarungs when they are washed is also linguistically linked to irregular female bleeding, a symptom of reproductive disorders.

In a broader sense, women are seen as dangerous when they are "open," their reproductive energies not properly channeled and contained, the flow of their blood unregulated by the flow of prestations between patrilineally defined groups. The perforated "openings" in women must be bound, sealed, and controlled, "locking" their blood into their bodies just as indigo dyes are "locked into" threads. These ideas are reflected in the steps taken by the most respected and powerful women to control and contain both colors and reproductive substances. Such women spend a large part of their days binding threads stretched across a wooden frame. Patterns are tied off with *gewang* fibers that protect the threads from successive dye baths. The tighter the leaf fiber is tied, the less likely that the colors will "bleed" into one another, thus allowing white, yellow, and red motifs to be distinguished through different saturations of the reddish *kombu* dye. The final stage is alway the indigo bath that seeps into all of the unbound threads and provides the dark background for the whole cloth. Through these stages, "binding" is equated with sexual restraint and the production of healthy children.

Unmarried women wear their hair loose and unparted, but married women part it in the center and bind it in a bun at the back of the head. Their hair is never publically unbound again until the husband's death, when it is loosened for the period of mourning and keening as the widow guards the corpse inside the house. During mourning, a woman is forbidden to wear the bright patterns of ikat textiles, although she will receive gifts of cloth (contributions to the funeral shroud, *ghabuho*) from each person who attends the funeral. The textiles that a woman produces and wears do not become her "inalienable wealth" (Weiner 1985), until they are bound around her body at her own funeral and transformed into the garments that she will take with her to the afterworld.

CLOTH IN MYTHOLOGY AND SONG

The use of cloth to replace the normal organs of female reproduction is a theme in a number of mythic accounts, which present a model of a knowledgeable older woman who is able to substitute a textile bundle for a uterus. Adams (1970:96) has published a myth from Kapunduk, East Sumba, in which a miscarried fetus, the ancestor of the first royal line, is brought to life by being wrapped in cotton and stored in a sacred gong by an ancient noblewoman.

I collected a similar myth in Kodi. A princess who lives in the upper world first summons her suitor to the heavenly kingdom by sending down her spindle, inviting him to climb up the thread into her bedroom. Her unrestrained sexuality is signaled by the loose, undyed thread which instead of being prepared for the loom, is used to snare a bridegroom from the world below. Once she has conceived, her child falls to the earth as a blood clot, torn out of her body by the thunder of a heavy rainfall. It falls into a stalk of white millet, where it is found by a wise older woman who stores it in fine textiles in the attic of her house, near the family heirlooms, until it grows into a beautiful young man.

Enveloping the fetal blood in cloth creates a false womb, a concentration of fertility for an older woman who would herself be unable to bear a child. In some older versions, she also fetches bananas and papayas for the infant to suckle, since she cannot offer him her breasts. A solution of rice water and cucumber juice is fed to the newborn, who grows as tall and pale as the millet stalk where he was found. Significantly, birth is less miraculous than nurturing the blood clot outside the womb: The child produced is not an artificial child but a real one, endowed with unusual abilities. Similarly, a post-menopausal woman well versed in herbalism and indigo dyeing has the skills and knowledge that allow her to preserve a life under unusual circumstances, even if she cannot bear children herself. Her occult knowledge of plants and cloth is used to bind people to her by these services.

Miscarriages, mourned as reproductive failures, are compared to imperfectly dyed cloths in lament songs, linking indistinct motifs to the child born too soon, before the limbs and organs are fully formed. Here is one woman's lament, addressing the creator deity, which asks that the spirit of the lost child be called back to reenter her womb, so that she can conceive the same child a second time, and carry it to term more successfully:

Here is the child aborted like	*Henya a ana manuhu*
the cucumber flower	*wala karere*
Whose birthday never came	*Na dadi inja dukingo*
Here is the one fallen like	*Henya a ana kanabu*
the gourd flower	*wala karabu*
Whose appearance never arrived	*Na hunga inja tomango*
Let him return to the barkcloth of	*Pa kambala waingo kiyo*
the father's lap	*ela baba bapa*
Let him roll back to	*Pa maliti waingo kinggolo*
the mother's breast	*ela huhu inya*
You who carved the straight limbs	*Yo na hanganto timbu rowa*
Who separated crooked chicken feet	*Yo na katara witti myanu*

So he can return to the mother's   *Tanaka bali kingo ela*
breast of cucumber milk   *huhu inya wei karere*
So he can go back to the father's   *Tanaka bali kingo la*
lap of wide thighs   *baba bapa kalu kenga*
To be poured without spilling   *Buri nja kahaghara*
To be smelted with no faults   *Lala nja ta nibyuro*

The fetus is dispatched to be reimmersed in the creative juices of the mother's dyeing and binding, and reformed by the father's metal working skills.

A kind of reincarnation for the souls of children who die shortly after birth is believed to be possible through eating certain herbs and vegetables, which may store the child's spirit for a short time after its death. Here, once again, the art of herbalism links textile processing to birth and healing. Only certain plants are appropriate, and the woman concerned may consult a midwife for advice in this matter. A song such as the following one can be interpreted as a prayer asking for reincarnation through a vegetable intermediary. It directly addresses the spirit of the dead child, who must have died within four days of birth (that is, before the naming ceremony that would fix his ancestral identity):

Why were you born into the light   *Pangu bu dadi la manggawango*
Why did you appear to our senses   *Pangu bu hunga la mandendo*
When like wilted sirih leaves   *Bu inja kuta mate baka*
You dissolved in the layers of   *La taneikya lipu*
my rotting intestine   *njamu nggu*
When like dried areca nut   *Bu inja winyo mate note baka*
You fell apart like rice in   *La hambule pare*
the stomach cavity   *moyo nggu*
Why once born didn't you   *Pena bu dadi inde*
leap over the danger   *pada tongo nyahi*
Why once evident didn't you   *Pena bu hunga inde*
slip past the abyss   *tombe longo reyeda*
When the rain begins to fall   *Ba na kawunga a ura*
Wait at the bud of   *No kalungguka ela hangula*
red-tailed reeds   *kiku laka*
When the year starts anew   *Ba na kabondi a ndoyo*

> Wait at the sprouts of   *No kalungguka ela kapundu*
> black-tipped ferns   *mandi myete*

When the child is still unnamed, it has not yet acquired the spirit name (*ngara marapu*) or ancestral destiny (*ndewa*) that secures its fate, and it can still be reformed and reborn. A fetus or unnamed child must be wrapped in a simple cloth and buried underneath the floorboards of the house, so that its spirit will not leave. Relatives are not permitted to express sorrow through a funeral sacrifice or using fine textiles for the shroud, as this would place the child in the category of ancestors rather than incompletely processed raw spirit material.

The textile shroud, finally, evokes regeneration. In the myths reviewed above, we saw how a magical child was gestated in the artificial womb of an old woman's cloth. Similarly, the tying, binding and dressing of a corpse is a preparation for a later rebirth. The textiles that wrap the body will provide a splendid costume for the deceased in a new life in the village of the dead. The soul of a dead person is explicitly compared to a bride, and the rites of marriage and burial are self-consciously modeled after one another. The sorrow that women express in funeral dirges is a reflection on the trauma of detachment which they first experienced as brides, forced to leave their natal homes to marry into another village. They lament this separation as a characteristic of the "female condition" which binds them to passive acquiescence in many endeavors, and defines their mode of action as more constrained than that of men (Hoskins 1987a).

THE EXCHANGE OF CLOTH AND THE EXCHANGE OF WOMEN

The bride who is transferred to another ancestral village is enveloped in many layers of fine *sarungs* and dyed indigo shoulder cloths, contributing to her sexual attractiveness. But the erotic appeal of the cloth also lies in its objectification of the woman: Through motifs that enclose her first on the textile surface and are later (in tattooing) transferred to her skin, she is made into an exchange valuable, representing the wealth that must be given to her patrilineage by her husband's ancestral village. The new daughter-in-law is even described as the *wei haranga*, the "water received for the livestock," whose fertile liquids are acquired in exchange for livestock and used to reproduce the male line.

The motifs on textiles exchanged at weddings are icons of the wealth offered up as the brideprice. Each marriage payment must include a basic "price" of at least ten horses and buffalo, paid by the wife-takers (*nobo vinye*, literally, "sister-takers"). It is reciprocated by an equivalent counterpayment in cloth (equal amounts of male cloths and female *sarungs*) and pigs. Since one large pig and a pair of cloths is given for each ten head of livestock, the wife-giver's payment may seem lighter economically, but in social terms, the gift of a woman is seen as superior and more encompassing, as is evident from an analysis of textile motifs.

In both East and West Sumba, textiles depict symbols of wealth and prestige that are given by the wife-takers. In East Sumba, these include horses, deer, roosters, and dogs. The more geometric designs characteristic of Kodi cloth contain references to body parts of these animals. A common motif on women's *sarungs* is the *mata karimbyoyo* or "buffalo eye," and some also contain "horses' tails" (*kiku ndara*), An undulating zigzag line is identified as the "scales of a python's skin" (*karaha kaboko*), and small white dots refer to decorations on spears (*kambora nambu*) or the crosshatch footprint of a buffalo hoof (*kadanga karimbyoyo*). Significantly, pigs are never depicted on textiles because they are given along with the bride and must come from the wife-giver.

The textile motif could be said to offer a "miniaturization" (Lévi-Strauss 1966:23) of the marriage payments from both sides, since the representation of decomposed animal parts in a geometric pattern provides visual evidence that the obligation to give has been fulfilled. The women's cloths are marked with the buffalo's eye and the horse's tail because in a procession of marriage gifts, the most expensive and prestigious gifts (usually gold and buffalo) are generally presented before the more humble ones (horses). The buffalo's eye marks the beginning of the presentations; the horse's tail their completion. When a new wife first moves into her husband's house, her ceremonial transfer marks a finished exchange transaction, and she must wear the textiles and gold brought from her parent's house. As these contain representations of brideprice cattle, the gifts given for her continue to parade across her hips and thighs, reduced to miniature artistic depictions. Thus, the new daughter-in-law clothes her reproductive organs with textiles given by her family as emblems of her properly legitimated status within her new home.

The names of the geometric motifs are well known to women, but often obscure to men—who do almost none of the work of tying the patterns into thread, and refuse to weave. Moreover, the bride's mother-in-law (*inya yanto*) receives the gift of textiles that accompanies the bride, judging its appropriateness and equivalent value. (If the counterpayment as a whole does not include textiles of fine quality, it can be refused—although this occurs rarely.)

If the new wife seems "objectified" by the representations of exchange gifts on her clothing, the husband dresses in garments that recall marriage prestations as well. The border area of many men's cloths is lined with images of the *hamoli* gold ear pendant, given to the bride's parents "to replace the glimmer of the girl's dark eyes" (*ndali ha mata mete a lakeda minye*). A single gold piece must accompany each ten head of livestock, and here the play of mirrors, reflections and rereflections, becomes even more complex: The form of the pendant is a kind of omega shape with an opening in the middle and two tube-like extensions that curve up on either side. Most observers, including the Kodi, recognize it as a stylized presentation of female genitalia. The bride's father must receive this pendant to console him for the loss of his daughter, substituting a metal emblem of the value of her sexuality for the real person.

The extended tips of the *hamoli* pendant may be elaborated with the heads of animals—horses or pythons being the most common. Thus, in this object, the girl's sexuality is surrounded and contained by male animals. The female wealth object is itself bounded by the male wedding gifts of livestock and authority. (Although pythons are never given as part of the brideprice, they appear as wild spirits who can magically help a young man to acquire such goods.) By these symbols, the opening through which a woman's blood would flow to her descendants is shown as being enclosed and regulated by male control.

The symbolism of marriage gifts in Eastern Indonesia usually opposes the "male goods" (livestock and gold) paid by the wife-takers to the "female goods" (pigs and cloth) with which the wife-givers reciprocate. In Kodi, this association is not made terminologically explicit. However, both pigs and cloth can only be produced by women, and livestock are only tended and traded by men, so the

Figure 13. A young woman weaves a sarung, *which incorporates both the omega-shaped ear-pendant design and the buffalo-eye motif. Photo by Janet Hoskins, 1980*

categories do seem to apply. But the motifs on cloth also encapsulate and depict the pattern of exchanges of which they are a part: Male cloths are covered with emblems of female sexuality, while female *sarungs* are spotted with the male buffalo eye and horse's tail. The two can only exist in tandem, as part of a balanced transaction, so each partial image reminds the owner of its missing counterpart.

Wearing a fine *sarung* can also serve as a visual mnemonic for an unfulfilled obligation. If the groom's parents had promised a brideprice of thirty head, ten delivered at the time of the bride's move to her husband's village and twenty to be delivered over the years, then when the daughter-in-law wears her wedding textiles at a funeral or feast, her husband's family is reminded of their promise to make additional payments. There is no exact correspondence between the number of animal eyes and tails depicted and the brideprice established, but the finer clothes usually contain more

densely detailed work. If a schedule of livestock payments cannot
be kept, then an extension must be requested from the wife-givers
by giving them an additional small textile gift along with an explanation. The textile does not replace the animal owed. It is simply a kind
of interest paid on the loan of the daughter's fertility.

FROM CLOTH TO SKIN:
FEMALE TATTOOING AS A RITE OF MATURITY

Tattooing is a female rite restricted to women who have proven their
ability to reproduce. A young bride, just conceiving her first child,
may have her forearms tattooed, but she cannot have her calves and
thighs tattooed until she has produced several healthy children. The
tattooing is done by an older woman, often one who is also a midwife and herbalist, rubbing candlenut and ash into a series of tiny
puncture wounds made with citrus thorns. Women are tattooed individually, after a small ceremonial offering of a chicken to the spirit
of her maternal village (the *lete binye*, or "doorway and steps" that
she came out of) to assure the consent of her ancestors.

The motifs tattooed onto the skin are the same as the ones used
on textiles. In East Sumba, these are representational–pythons,
horses, roosters and dogs. In West Sumba, they are geometric, decomposed representations of the exchange items given in bride-
price payments (horse tails, buffalo eyes, omega ear ornaments).
Their permanence on the skin reflects the more permanent position
of the married woman within her husband's patrilineage. She has
already been incorporated with a sacrifice to introduce her to his ancestors. If she has danced at feasts sponsored by her husband's village, she may have already received a special gold payment made
for "stepping down onto the dancing ground" (*ndali nataro*), given
by her natal house/lineage to the house of her husband. Above all,
by bearing children for her husband's line, she acquires an enhanced rank and status, qualifying her to serve as a representative
of the house in public settings such as bride-price negotiations.

The process of tattooing is painful. Older women who described it to me stressed how much they had suffered and cried as
the thorns dug into their skin, and the bleeding wounds stung with
the application of ground candlenut and other herbs. But they felt
that the tattoos themselves were badges of accomplishment. One

very old woman told me that she had been tattooed just before the Dutch took control of the area in 1911. Her husband's family was afraid that the foreign invaders might rape the younger women, and assumed that tattoo markings showing that they were already wives and mothers would provide some sort of protection.

Although most women over the age of fifty have elaborate tattoos on their forearms, and some all the way up the thigh, the practice has now died out. Older courtship songs reveal that the thigh tattoo had a strong erotic lure: As the upper thighs were always covered by clothing, only a secret lover could know what patterns were represented there. Children still exchange insults by crying out to a friend "Your mother has no tattoos on her thighs!"—implying that intimate knowledge of her body had become common. While the tattoo was designed to be the private secret of the conjugal pair, its existence was also used to provoke the speculation of others. A man told me that his mother was kidnapped by another man, who eventually made her his wife, because he had heard stories of the beauty of her tattooed thighs.

The cessation of tattooing as a marker of female maturity came at about the same time as the cessation of circumcision as a male rite. Circumcision, like tattooing, has been performed in Kodi as a secret, individual operation carried out in seclusion by an older man. Boys were circumcised shortly before marrying, but their sexual initiation was the task of an older woman or a slave attached to the house, because the first semen ejaculated after the operation was dangerous "water from the knife" (*wei kioto*) and could sear a female womb. Tattooing and circumcision are classified together by the Kodi because they are both rites of "sharpness" (*lakiyo*), the key characteristic of a violent and inauspiscious death (*mate pa lakiyo*).

The violence of ritualized sharpness is, however, made auspicious by its intentional infliction. Boys who willingly submit to the circumciser's knife become "clean" enough to marry. Mature women who submit to the lengthier agonies of tattooing establish their public virtue as wives and mothers. Their resistance to pain dignifies them as the survivors of childbirth—although the more intimate tattoos on the upper thighs seem to have been motivated mainly by personal vanity. Hidden by their daily *sarungs*, these designs remained an enticing mystery to the men who could not gaze on them, enhancing a woman's appeal through suggestion.

The dangerous heat of the circumciser's knife suggests that

there may exist a parallel complex of men's crafts, centered on met-
alwork and similarly marked by dangerous and polluting periods of
creative activity. Headhunting is defined as a response to the seeth-
ing heat of the skull tree, which steams and burns with anger at an
unavenged killing.[8] Warfare, feuding, and high murder rates in contemporary Kodi are all attributed to "hot blood," which rises in men
at certain times and enflames their passions to violence. The influence of cloth is usually portrayed as cooling and soothing, while
metal objects are formed through a hot smelting process and remain
charged with ritual heat if they are misused.

All important social events require a conjunction of the sharp
heat of metal and the conciliatory softness of textiles. In negotiating
a peace in front of the ancestral spirits, the divination spear is first
used to "cut through" to the source of ancestral anger, after which
the litigating parties exchange cloth to cool their anger and provide
the proper atmosphere for peace-making. Yet the complementary
balance of male and female elements is also slightly asymmetric in
its consequences on the lives of men and women—as the meaning
of indigo "blueness" can show us.

"BLUENESS," CLOTH, AND GENDER IDENTITY

Indigo dyeing and the color blue constitute important symbolic associations for women in their reproductive functions, their exchange
as wives between partrilineages, and their achievement of maturity
and enhanced status in old age. The residual meaning underlying
each of these contexts is an emotion of resentment, a sadness and
negativity that appears almost antisocial. I argue that when Kodi
women "sing the blues," they are expressing an ambivalence towards the process of female creation. This creation is expressed by
metaphoric extension in a number of domains—the creation of infants within the body, of cloth within the dye bath, of daughters
in the home—but it is always accompanied by knowledge of an incipient loss. Infants will come out of the body, cloth will be exchanged
and traded by male intermediaries, daughters will be separated
from the house and sent to live in another village at marriage.

Kodi women are symbolically identified with the cloths that
they produce. Indigo-dyed textiles are both the evidence of their labors and the envelopes that enclose them and show them to be so-

cially legitimated wives and mothers. Throughout the lifecycle, transitions between stages of female identity are linked to participation in or exclusion from textile production, and the secrets associated with it. Initiation into indigo dyeing is in a sense an initiation into womanhood—but it is not accomplished at or around menarche. Instead, initiation extends throughout the lifespan, to be completed only upon burial in the indigo funeral shroud that most women dye and weave for themselves.

Young girls are taught to bind the threads for textile dyeing, often assisting at the dye bath by chewing the various barks and herbs added to the mixture of chalk and ash to prepare the dye. The rules prescribe that herbal ingredients and copra base be chewed by unmarried girls, who have not yet accepted the betel quid of courtship. Once a girl enters adolescence, she is excluded from the dyeing hut, sent home to practice weaving on the backstrap loom, and encouraged to produce *sarungs* that may be used for her own wedding costume.

At her marriage, a girl's family matches the value of the livestock and gold given for her with a counter-gift of pigs, jewelry, and cloth. The cloth produced in her home village and taken to her husband's village thus epitomizes her own personal history, and is referred to as the "companion" (*ole*) that she brings with her into a strange home. As a new daughter-in-law, she wears textiles that remind her husband's family of their obligation to keep bringing livestock payments to her village of birth. She also produces children—sons who will be descendants or "fruit" of her husband's "house," and daughters who will be exchanged with other villages as "flowers" sent to bloom in other lands. Married women spend four or five hours a day tying thread bundles and weaving textiles for sale or exchange.

When a woman grows past childbearing age, she may begin to practice one of the traditional female arts of midwifery, herbalism, or indigo dyeing. In doing so, she achieves a greater degree of knowledge and control over bodily processes, and learns from other women the secrets of which plants can be used to prevent excessive bleeding at childbirth or leaking in the dye bath. She wears tattoos on her arms and legs that display the motifs that she has already portrayed on a textile surface, and that have now become part of her body.

Cloth is a master symbol for the transitions of a woman's life, wrapping her as an infant, a bride, and a corpse. Men also wear cloths with indigo coloring, but they are never identified with the processes and substances that go into their production. Instead, theirs is the world of public exchange, feasting, and the distribution of raw meat at ceremonies to fulfill past obligations. The world of indigo dyeing is conceptually opposed to that of the male activity of feasting. It is taboo to come close to an indigo pot carrying blood or raw meat, and no woman can cook food for men at the same time that she prepares the ingredients of the dye bath. The male blood of feasting and headhunting can never come in contact with the female blood of reproduction, or the blue substances that magically control and aid this process.

The contrast between metal goods and textiles plays on more pervasive themes in Kodi gender symbolism. It is not simply that women are seen as "things," exchange goods, while men are not. On the contrary, for both sexes, the link between persons and possessions is rather indistinct and hard to define. Men are identified with named gold valuables that are stored in lineage house attics. Like metal objects in general, gold is part of a sacred patrimony which is passed vertically, down through the generations of a single agnatic clan, rather than horizontally, in affinal exchanges that follow the paths of women. The ancestry of men can be traced in the ancestry of swords, spears, and knives, a metaphorical skeleton of metal that symbolizes the indestructible relatedness of the patrilineage.

In contrast, women are linked to the more ephemeral life cycle of cloth, known to tear and disintegrate over time, fragile but often poignantly beautiful. Both cloth and children are only semidurable: They assure their creators of a certain semblance of immortality, but they are ultimately also subject to the processes of aging, fading, and falling apart. It is the difference in durability between metal goods and textiles that defines their symbolic values. When men exchange land or gold in formal transactions, they refer to these forms of indestructible wealth as the "cloth that does not tear, the pig that will not get sick" (*kamba nja madiryako, wawi nja kapore*)— acknowledging only too clearly the contrasts with organic objects, subject to the same frailty as human beings.

Cloth is portrayed in myths and prayers as offering protection and blessings, a shelter from life's dangers. Promises can be made binding by the ceremonial presentation of a textile, said to provide an "umbrella against the sun, a block from the rain" (*kada ngindi lodo, haluri tipu ura*). But it is clear that the shielding, binding power of cloth is not eternal: It offers only the shadow of an obligation, the memory of a convenant. As long as this is honored, the cloth will provide a cooling and refreshing shade to its new owner. But it cannot be allowed to rot before the proper payments are made. Like the mother's womb, it offers a refuge which must be left behind, a mantle of protection which can be pierced by human weakness, illness and mortality.

The vulnerability of cloth represents the vulnerability of women, exchanged along with their textiles. But the secrets of indigo form an occult tradition of resistance to the forcible alienation of women from the products of their labors. Women do not like to lose their daughters, their cloths, their powers to the male world. They also feel the sting of male disdain for their association with the messy business of birth and death—the handling of bloody infants and rotting corpses. What to the male world is a fearful and polluting activity (the dyeing of thread with indigo dyes) becomes for older women a way of regaining control over their own destinies, and also often a source of additional wealth.

Women both subscribe to and resent many of the restrictions placed on them. When indigo dyeing or funeral songs present a note of protest, it is largely inarticulate. The enforced secrecy of female indigo cults is a response to the constraints of the male world and an effort to police their own in reproductive matters. In clandestine meetings, women share knowledge of herbal preparations used not only for successful childbirth recovery, but also for abortion and contraception. They may apply "binding" roots to treat irregular menstrual bleeding or hasten menopause. It was unclear to me, and to most of my male informants, how effective these preparations were. Gheru Wallu, my first Kodi landlady and a skilled herbalist and midwife, told me, "Men will never know women's secrets about these things, and they will always think that we can control even more than we can."

Older women consciously cloak their secret knowledge of reproductive matters in a mystique that not only excludes men but disciplines their sisters: Kodi word play links "loose dyes" and "loose morals" through the image of a "leaking woman" who cannot control her sexuality. Magical herbal preparations can be used by jealous wives or fearful mothers to cause a woman's own body to rebel against her wayward behavior. A fetus will "leak out" of an unfaithful bride before it is brought to term. An adultress who refuses to confess will have the placenta bound inside her, and can die if she does not relent. Incest, as noted, produces a huge gush of maternal blood that must be treated with binding roots. Inappropriate actions create a physical syndrome of "incomplete closure" in the body, and are often life-threatening.

The model of textile production presents a way of understanding Kodi notions about the creation of gender identity through a temporal process: "Womanhood" is not given at birth as a "natural" attribute, nor is it automatically assumed at puberty, with the onset of menses. Instead women, like the textile they produce, must be created through stages such as the one in which their bodies are "opened" in childbirth and then closed again by the application of the proper medicines. Their movement from one patrilineage to another, marked by the exchange of valuables, is represented first on the textiles which they wrap around their bodies and later directly on the skin of their calves and forearms. These valuables are also seen as "enclosing" their sexuality and reproductive potential within the confines of the new descent group. It is the movement from one lineage house to another, the partial severing of ties of birth and their replacement by ties of marriage, that defines the shared attributes of Kodi womanhood.

There is no separate "sisterhood" characterized by female solidarity, and in fact herbalism, midwifery, and indigo dyeing are all arenas for intense female rivalry. The complex of "blue arts" is concerned with reproduction and fertility, but does not promote these arts exclusively, or present any public moral instruction to cult members. These members work at the periphery of the male world, neither opposing it or nor imitating it directly. Although the secrets of the woman's world in Kodi may intimidate or intrigue certain men, they do not threaten the larger social order. Moreover, the policing of sexual behavior lends tacit support to the normative order established by male ancestors. Nonetheless, across the generational and hierarchical divisions of Kodi society, women share a common experience of loss, the painful detachment from loved ones. And these female feelings have a place of refuge. Indigo cults articulate the emotions of displacement and separation experienced as both children and textiles slip away, with parts of the person attached.

Evoking women's painful move to another home at marriage, the secluded cults also help them produce valuables that provide an inalienable link to their place of origin, and to their personal history.

ACKNOWLEDGMENTS

Doctoral research in 1979–81 was supported by the Fulbright Commission, the Social Science Research Council, and the National Science Foundation, under the auspices of the Indonesian Academy of Sciences (LIPI) and Universitas Nusa Cendana of Kupang. Return visits in 1984, 1985, and 1986 were funded by the Research School of Pacific Studies, Australian National University and the Faculty Research and Innovation Fund of the University of Southern California. I would like to thank Marie Jeanne Adams, James J. Fox, Nancy Lutkehaus, Jane Schneider, Annette Weiner, Valerio Valeri, and members of the ASAO panel on "Female Initiation in the Pacific" for their comments on an earlier version of this paper.

NOTES

1. Sources that associate women and the color blue proliferate throughout the Pacific, but I will cite only a few. Uli, the goddess of sorcery and also of the sea water, is an important example from aboriginal Hawaii. Uli is defined in the Pukui and Elbert *Hawaiian Dictionary* as referring to "any dark color, including the deep blue of the sea, the ordinary green of vegetation, and the dark of black clouds; the black and blue of a bruise" (1971:340). It is also the name of the goddess of sorcery, said to come from Kahiki, the land of origins, and can refer to an early stage in the development of a fetus, as the body begins to form.

In other parts of Polynesia, its cognates refer to darkness and dampness. In Samoa, *uri* means the darkness of clouds and the deep blue sea, and also malevolent feelings and emotions (Tregear 1969:578). In Tahitian, it suggests that which is "deep, unfathomable, as in the sea," and also obscure. In Tongan, the associations are most negative; *uli* is "filth, contamination, nastiness, dirty, polluted" and terrifying (Tregear 1967:578). Firth (1970:103) speaks of a "Dark God called Atua Pouri" who receives the victims of sorcery and is in contact with the spirits of miscarried foetuses. In some areas, specific goddesses are associated with the magical powers of blueness; in others, the color is more generally associated with stories of sorceresses and witches.

Lila Abu-Lughod's *Veiled Sentiments* discusses another tradition of women's laments, also with certain similarities to the American blues, among the Awlad

'Ali Bedouins of Egypt. Messick's (1987) analysis of women's weaving in North Africa also suggests that it is a "subordinate discourse" which embeds a distinctively female worldview.

2. The disappearance of female priestesses seems related to historical reinterpretations of the diarchic division of power between ancestral villages and lineages which came after the imposition of Dutch colonial control. These reinterpretations are discussed in Hoskins (1987b, 1988a).

3. On the island of Roti, the origin of weaving and metalworking is also traced to a neighboring island, that of Ndao (Fox 1980). It is possible that Sumbanese theories of "Savunese" dyers and metalworkers also refer to Ndao (Hoskins 1988b). Neighboring Indonesian societies make similar links between indigo dyeing and spiritual malevolence, as the cloths are almost universally used as funeral shrouds (Schulte-Nordholt 1971, Traube 1983, Fox 1973). On Roti, a folk etymology associates the local name for indigo (tau) with the words for "fear" or "frighten," and the terrifying spirits of the outside are conceived of as "darkening" or "blueing" their victims (Fox 1973:350). Wild indigo plants, called the "indigo of the spirits" (Fox 1973:351), are thought to be used by spirits for nefarious purposes. But such powers can also be used to ward off dangerous spirits. After someone dies a "bad death," an entire pot of indigo dye must be poured on his grave before the funeral is finished (Fox 1973:360). The dark dye serves to "fix" him in the grave and keep his soul from wandering. A similar ambivalence is reflected in the description of sorcerers as having the power to poison or to cure through the use of "blue powers" (mana-momodo).

4. Dyeing is the most remunerative of the stages of textile production, particularly in relation to the time invested. In 1980, I collected the following fee scale for tasks involved in the production of a sarung commissioned by an outsider: Tying the threads to create the ikat pattern (wolo) cost Rp. 2000 and took about a week; dyeing the threads in the indigo bath (betingo) cost Rp. 3000 and took four or five days once the bath was prepared; weaving the thread on a backstrap loom (tanungo) cost Rp. 1500 and took from two weeks to a month of labor. Weaving is a tiring process, but it involves little specialized knowledge or creativity in design, so it is often delegated to younger, less skilled women.

5. The dangerous effects of contact with the dye bath on a pregnant woman can be reversed if the mistress of the dyeing shack (mori kareke nggilingo) calls out a warning to her visitor. In so doing, she sacrifices the contents of the dye pot, which are ruined, but saves the life of the fetus. A pregnant woman who unexpectedly finds herself near a secret dyeing site may also recite the following prayer addressed to the female spirit of indigo, hoping to placate her anger and save the contents of her womb:

From your throat and	Wali kyoko
from your liver	wali ate kinyani
Mistress of the pot,	Mori ghuro,
mistress of indigo	mori nggilingo
Foreign woman,	Minye dawa,
Savunese woman	minye haghu

Surely you know yourself	*Angga peghe do kinyaka*
I did not mean to obscure the liquid	*Nja ku kabaro tonoma*
Surely you saw yourself	*Angga ice do kiyaka*
I did not want to soil the cloth	*Nja ku pyunakao taloki*
Clouding the swampy source	*Myata rende kabaro*
Polluting the head of the river	*Kataku loko mbunako*
So turn friendly eyes toward me	*Maka marere mata nuri*
As we chew betel together	*Moka la hamama*
So open your mouth in laughter	*Maka wiala ghoaba ndeha*
As we eat tobacco	*Moka la mu mbaku*

Her prayer must be accompanied by an offering of betel and areca nut, and a promise to later sacrifice a chicken and a pig to atone for the violation.

If a man should happen by, such procedures are not necessary: It will be the dye pot that is ruined, because he does not have the same "reproductive vulnerability" as women. However, the textile-dyeing women would certainly retaliate by sending him the "blue sickness" of witchcraft. Each sex has its own weaknesses, and its own weapons.

6. Proper indigo dyeing involves a combination of chemistry and technology, acquired through long practical experience. Dyers monitor the timing of chemical interactions through smelling, feeling, tasting, and examining their materials at every stage of the process. As Kajitani (1980:307) notes: "Each dye compound with its impurities is unique in its ability to bond or react with fibers . . . . So the good traditional dyer, like the medieval alchemist, develops his or her own preferred materials and techniques, which become guarded secrets that often disappear upon the dyer's death."

7. Taboos regulated by the Kodi traditional calendar restrict the gathering of wild indigo plants to the time when the quality of indican in the leaves of these plants reaches it maximum level, shortly after the rainy season begins. It is forbidden to pick wild indigo or prepare the dye bath during the "bitter months" (*wulla padu*), which usually fall in October and November on the lunar system. Technical processes (all of them usually carried out by women) that involve white substances—dyeing thread, baking lime, and boiling sea salt—are said to be particularly dangerous because their light color attracts the lightning bolts and strong winds of the beginning of the rains. After a ceremony in January to "make the tips of the young plants bland" (*kaba wei kapoke*), women are permitted to begin dyeing thread in preparation for the large-scale festivals that greet the swarming of the sea worms (*nale*) in February.

8. Headhunting is often paired with textile production and childbearing in other areas of Indonesia. Among the Iban, the same taboos apply to the preparation of thread for dyeing and to childbirth within the longhouse (Freeman 1970:125), and the laying out of the thread is called "the warpath of the women" (Gittinger 1979:219). Among the Belu of Timor, a new mother coming out of seclusion after childbirth is ceremonially dressed in the textiles and head decora-

tions of a headhunter (Gittinger 1979:33). In Kodi, both freshly taken heads and freshly dyed threads are hung on trees to dry, but these associations are not made as explicitly as the links to metalworking (See Hoskins 1987b). The skull tree is often depicted on East Sumbanese textiles, but there is no special use of textiles in headhunting ritual. Rogers (1985) notes that the opposition of textile production to metal work (associated with the opposition of female to male) is important among the Batak of Sumatra, the Ngaju of Borneo, the Lamaholot peoples of Flores, and the Tanimbarese of the Moluccas.

REFERENCES

Abu-Lughod, Lila
    1986   Veiled Sentiments. Berkeley: University of California Press.

Adams, Marie Jeanne
    1969   System and Meaning in East Sumba Textile Design: A Study in Traditional Indonesian Art. Southeast Asia Studies Cultural Report Series No. 16. New Haven: Yale University.
    1970   Myth and Self Image among the Kapunduku People of Sumba. Indonesia 10:81–106.

Fox, James J.
    1973   On Bad Death and the Left Hand: A Study of Rotinese Symbolic Inversions. In Right and Left: Essays on Dual Symbolic Classification. Rodney Needham, ed. Chicago: University of Chicago Press.
    1977   Roti, Ndau and Savu. In Textile Traditions of Indonesia. Mary Hunt Kahlenberg, ed. Los Angeles: County Museum of Art.
    1980   Figure Shark and Pattern Crocodile: The Foundations of the Textile Traditions of Roti and Ndao. In Indonesian Textiles. Mattiebelle Gittinger, ed. Washington D.C.: The Textile Museum.

Firth, Raymond
    1970   Rank and Religion in Tikopia. London: George Allen Unwin.

Freeman, Derek
    1970   Report on the Iban. New York: Humanities Press.

Gittinger, Mattiebelle
    1979   Splendid Symbols: Textile and Tradition in Indonesia. Washington D.C.: The Textile Museum.

Hoskins, Janet
    1986   So My Name Shall Live: Stone Dragging and Grave-Building in Kodi, West Sumba. Bijdragen tot de Taal-, Land en Volkenkunde 142:31–51.
    1987a   Complementarity in this World and the Next: Gender and Agency in Kodi Mortuary Ceremonies. In Dealing with Inequality: Analyzing Gender Relations in Melanesia and Beyond. Marilyn Strathern, ed. Cambridge: Cambridge University Press.

1987b   The Headhunter as Hero: Local Traditions and Their Reinterpre-
         tation as Natural History. American Ethnologist 14(4).
1988a   Matriarchy and Diarchy: Indonesian Variations on the Domesti-
         cation of the Savage Woman *In* Myths of Matriarchy Reconsid-
         ered. Deborah Gewertz, ed. Sydney, Australia: Oceania Mono-
         graphs, University of Sydney Press.
1988b   Arts and Cultures of Sumba. *In* Islands and Ancestors: Indig-
         enous Styles of Southeast Asia. Jean Paul Barbier and Douglas
         Newton, eds. Catalog for an exhibit at the Metropolitan Museum
         in New York. Geneva: Barbier-Muller Museum.

Kajitani, Noboko
1980   Traditional Dyes in Indonesia. *In* Indonesian Textiles. Mattiebelle
         Gittinger, ed. Washington, D.C.: Textile Museum.

Lévi-Strauss, Claude
1966   The Savage Mind. Chicago: University of Chicago Press.

Messick, Brinkley
1987   Subordinate Discourse: Women, Weaving and Gender Relations
         in North Africa. American Ethnologist 14(2):210–26.

Needham, Rodney
1980   Principles and Variations in the Structure of Sumbanese Society.
         In The Flow of Life. James J. Fox, ed. Cambridge: Harvard Uni-
         versity Press.

Pukui, Mark K., and Samuel Elbert
1971   Hawaiian Dictionary. Honolulu: University of Hawaii Press.

Rogers, Susan
1985   Power and Gold: Jewelry from Indonesia, Malaysia and the
         Phillipines. Geneva: Barbier-Muller Museum.

Schulte-Nordholte, H.G.
1971   The Political System of the Atoni of Timor. The Hague: Martinus
         Nijhoff.

Traube, Elizabeth G.
1980   Affines and the Dead: Mambai Rituals of Alliance. Bijdragen tot
         de Taal-,Land- en Volkekunde 136(1):90–115.

Treager, Edgar
1969   The Maori-Polynesian Comparative Dictionary. Oosterhout:
         Netherlands Anthropological Publications.

Van Wouden, F.A.E.
1956   Locale groepen en dubbel afstamming in Kodi, West Sumba.
         Bijdragen tot de Taal-, Land- en Volkenkunde. 11:204–46.

Weiner, Annette
1985   Inalienable Wealth. American Ethnologist 12(2):210–27.

PART II. *Capitalism and the Meanings of Cloth*

6. *Rumpelstiltskin's Bargain:*

Folklore and the Merchant Capitalist Intensification of Linen Manufacture in Early Modern Europe

JANE SCHNEIDER

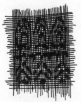 According to the folklorist Ruth Bottigheimer, many of the European folktales collected in the late eighteenth and early nineteenth centuries portray spinning as "highly undesirable despite the surface message that it will lead to riches" (1982:142,150). These tales present spinning as a form of subjugation or punishment for women, whose occupational hazards include "hips . . . too wide to pass through a doorway, lips licked away from . . . moistening the thread," noses engorged from lint dust, a thumb grown to grotesque proportions (Bottigheimer 146). Moreover, "although many tales declare that spinning mediates wealth in the form of gold, it is primarily associated with poverty . . . above all it is the archetypical employment of domesticated, poverty-stricken womanhood" (Bottigheimer 150; also Ferguson 1979:83).

The tales also suggest that malevolent spirits can heighten the perils of spinning. For example, in the Briar Rose and Sleeping Beauty stories, spinning implements or rough flax fibers are the instruments of a curse: A mere scratch puts whole kingdoms to sleep for a hundred years. Even more to the point is the tale of Rumpelstiltskin, in which a poor miller tells the king that his daughter can spin straw into gold, whereupon the king invites her to his castle,

177

a veritable warehouse of fiber. As she despairs over her impossible situation, a dwarfed and crippled poltergeist appears and, in exchange for gifts of a necklace, a bracelet, and the promise of her firstborn child, does the spinning for her, ensuring her marriage to the king. In some versions of the story, she is ultimately spared from handing over her child by a messenger who, at "a high mountain near the edge of the forest, where foxes and hares say good night to each other," overhears the little demon say the name (Rumpelstiltskin) that, if she can guess it, will release her from the bargain. In other versions, the child cannot be saved. Similar is the story of the Three Crones, or the Three Old Women, in which a poor mother slaps her daughter for her lazy neglect of spinning. The mother then explains the girl's tears to the passing queen as the consequence of the family's inability to supply her with sufficient flax, so much does she love to spin. The queen, delighted, announces that the castle is full of flax; once the girl spins it, she is welcome to marry the prince. Three old women magically appear to assist the terrified maiden, in exchange demanding to be presented as aunts at her wedding.

In Rumpelstiltskin-like tales, achieving status through marriage carries a negative evaluation. These girls achieve status not from their own industriousness, but from their willingness to risk their lives in a devilish pact with spirit helpers, often at the instigation of desperate or ambitious parents. Curiously, this negative evaluation is linked to a demonized view of spirits who, in other contexts of European folklore, appear benign. In many stories, for example, fairies do housework or thresh grain out of a desire to create a trusting relationship with humans, and disappear if humans attempt to repay them with clothes or food. If such helpers exact a price, it is explicitly to give reproductive potential to the spirit world, for in folk belief, fairies cannot reproduce without human wombs to carry their offspring and human midwives to deliver them. In contrast to such generous spirits, and to spirits whose requests are well justified, the assistance of a Rumpelstiltskin entails dangerous bargains. Fear of such danger found daily expression in spinning communities, where it was the custom to place carded flax under a weight and remove the belt from the spinning wheel before retiring for the night, to discourage unsolicited spirit help (Evans 1957:305).

Bottigheimer contrasts the infanticidal Rumpelstiltskin with elves and dwarfs who, like the generous Frau Holle, assisted spinners in their tasks without extorting a reward in return. She suggests that elves and dwarfs underwent a transformation from benign to demonic in the period preceding the late eighteenth century, when collectors like the Grimms began recording folktales (1982). When they identify a fiber, the spinning tales generally refer to flax (or hemp, which is closely related). This suggests that these stories, with their demonization of spirit helpers and their painful marriage bargains, bore some relation to the intensification of linen manufacture in the seventeenth and eighteenth centuries. Spurred by the opening of the New World economy and the related explosion of fashion-driven consumption in Europe, this intensified activity engaged rural communities in a merchant-organized putting-out system of linen cloth production. In this paper, I consider the possible connections between this system and the Rumpelstiltskin story, looking first at the entrepreneurial promotion of linen manufacture, then at how the linen promoters mobilized labor, and finally at the environmental impact of the industry as a whole—an impact of special relevance for spirit beings.

If the Rumpelstiltskin tale mirrored the experience of linen producers in Early Modern Europe, it did so as a sociological and moral reflection on the ambivalence of spinners and flax growers, as they weighed the contradictory implications of a new mode of production. As Rebel (1988:5) shows for a group of Hessian tales of the same period, the peasant voice was one of uncertain accommodations, "a disturbing and open-ended meditation on the desperate choices of the poor, on the temptation to advance socially by serving the rich. . . ." Far from offering "banal and homiletic conclusions," Rebel argues, the tales confront us "with paradoxes that demand reflection . . . ." A ubiquitous example is the dilemma of superfluous children, often expressed in the motif of parents misrepresenting their daughters to get them married off. As we shall see, marriage was precisely the institution on which the intensification of linen manufacturing turned.

LINEN IN EUROPEAN HISTORY

In the history of European textiles, cotton and linen played interchangeable roles. Unlike silk and the finer wools, both were relatively inexpensive to produce, and unlike coarser wool fabrics, they

were comfortable to handle and wear. Both are composed of cellulose fibers, making them amenable to bleaching rather than the
more involved and costly process of dyeing. Until their latter-day
experiments with imitation chintz and calicos, Europeans rarely
elaborated either cottons or linens through the complex resist-dye
techniques of Islamic and Asian civilizations. As Mazzaoui has suggested, they concentrated instead on a "diverse line of service-
able, attractive and low priced products," mostly "light-to-medium
weight cloth suitable for undergarments, bedding and summer
clothing" (Mazzaoui 1981:89–90). Included in this diverse line was
a mixed cloth, called fustian, with a linen warp and a cotton weft.
Linens, cottons, and fustians enhanced the living standards of the
urban middle and lower classes, and displaced coarse homespuns in
peasant households as well.

Although similar in terms of appearance and markets, cotton
and linen followed substantially different production paths. Cotton,
a tropical plant, could not be cultivated in temperate Europe, where
the cultivation of flax was widespread. This distinction underlay the
far greater role of accumulated capital in the organization of cotton
manufacture when compared with linen, and its closer association
with urban craft guilds. Most of the linen industries were less
capital-intensive and more rural. Cotton production was also the
first to undergo technological innovation. The shift from distaff and
spindle to the Indian-invented, foot-pedaled spinning wheel, and
from the vertical to the horizontal loom, transformed this industry
in the twelfth century. In the eighteenth century, cotton manufacture ushered in the industrial revolution. Linen entrepreneurs, by
contrast, did not promote wheel spinning, with its threefold increase in capacity, until the early modern period, and even then the
changeover was never quite complete (Endrei 1968:85–91; Grant
1961:220–27).

Maureen Mazzaoui's (1981) book on the medieval Italian cotton
industry divides Europe's involvement with cotton into three great
periods. The first, from the twelfth through the fifteenth centuries,
was a period of substantial growth when Italian merchants, assisted
by advances in shipping and navigation, imported cotton from the
Eastern Mediterranean, Sicily, and Spain, putting the fiber out to
thousands of producers in the Po Valley and Tuscany. The second
was a period of uncertainty, from the sixteenth to the eighteenth
centuries, during which Italian cotton entered a steep decline. In

part its undoing was at the hands of transalpine cotton manufacturers, who had gotten their start importing cotton or cotton yarn from Italy, and then imitated Italian wares. The Fugger-financed South German fustian industry, which flourished in the sixteenth century, represents the most powerful instance of such competition. Equally damaging was the rising cost of imported raw cotton, as the Ottoman Empire consolidated its hold over primary products on behalf of Ottoman industries, spurring in Europe a search for new sources of supply. The third great phase of European cotton history, in the eighteenth century, was marked by slavery in the New World plantation zones of cotton production, ever-cheaper transport costs for moving the raw material, and a staggering technological breakthrough in manufacture.

Linen history complemented the history of cotton. During the first phase, it was produced on two levels: in peasant households as a homespun, and in urban workshops as a luxury. The former was widely diffused, the latter quite concentrated, above all in Northern France and Flanders where towns like Ypres, Cambrai, and Laon gave names to such well-known fabrics as Diaper, Cambric, and Lawn. Here, hand spinning with saliva-moistened fingers and weaving in damp, stone vaults, enhanced the value of the precisely cultivated and carefully tended local flax crop (Endrei 1968:85–91; Horner 1920:317–28). Neither this industry nor the peasant household industry kept up with cotton in the already expanding market for "decent cloth"—the cloth that provided a comfortable, inexpensive, and hygenic material for underwear, tablewear, and bed clothes. Starting in the late eighteenth century, cotton once again outdistanced linen in the competition for this mass market.

What about the middle period, between the two cotton booms? I have noted these booms precisely to highlight the dynamism of linen in these intervening centuries when the spinning tales were told. For, despite the decline in cotton manufacture in this period, the market for decent cloth had not contracted. On the contrary, a growing population and the hegemony of a fashion-conscious Renaissance culture guaranteed its continued expansion. Especially important was the growth in demand that followed the opening of the Atlantic economy (Kriedte 1983:32). As early as 1594, Brittany sent nearly a million linen cloths to the West Indies, while in 1601 it was confessed in Rouen that "linen cloths are the true gold and silver mines of this kingdom, because they are developed only to be trans-

Figure 14. Linen served as a comfortable, inexpensive, and hygienic material for underwear, tablewear, and bedclothes. Painting, "Le Lever de Fanchon," by Nicolas-Bernard Lépicié; Musée Hotel Sandelin: Pas-de-Calais, France

ported to countries where gold and silver are obtained" (quoted in Kriedte 1981a:35). Echoed in the Hessian declaration that linen exports were the "main channel through which Spanish gold and silver flows into our coffers" (quoted in Kreidte 1981a:36), this pronouncement underscores the importance of linen manufacture from 1600 until the cotton revolution.

MERCANTILIST DOCTRINE AND THE LINEN PROMOTERS

The intermediate centuries saw more linen intensification in some European regions than in others. Generally, peasants made the greatest commitment to flax and linen manufacture in areas that had not been dominated by the manorial system, with its emphasis on cereals and mixed husbandry. Most favorable to linen production were the Celtic western edge of feudal development and the Germanic and Slavic frontiers, where subsistence strategies focused on dairy cattle or other livestock. The pattern conforms to Joan Thirsk's analysis of industrial location, according to which the most welcoming environments were those where the predominance of pastoral pursuits ensured a surplus of labor, especially in the winter season (Thirsk 1961; but see Spencely 1973). Within these broad zones of linen manufacture there was considerable variation, dedication to linen being more pronounced in some localities than in others (see Mendels 1981; Tilly 1964; Kriedte 1981:17–20; Kisch 1981:179–81).

By the seventeenth century, a few places—above all Haarlem—had emerged as specialized centers of cloth export without a supporting base of flax cultivation and yarn production. That is, they concentrated on the more lucrative end of the trade—the weaving, bleaching, and finishing of cloth—while importing the fiber, usually in its spun form, from Celtic or Baltic Europe, where regional weavers lamented the competition for yarn. For Haarlem, the special water of the town's lake provided such a strategic advantage for bleaching that the Dutch exported as "Hollands" a linen cloth that was spun, and often woven, outside of Holland (Horner 1920:350–65). Manchester and Nuremberg also exported cloths that underwent the initial stages of the manufacturing process elsewhere. Nevertheless, because flax cultivation was widely diffused in Europe, commerce in flax and linen yarn was less developed than in other textiles. A common pattern was for each linen district to organize its own manufacturing, from planting the (possibly imported) flax seed to bleaching and finishing the cloth. It is these specialized regions of "proto-industrial" linen manufacture that concern us here.

I have attempted to reconstruct the process of intensification in these regions, using both secondary sources and a series of letters, pamphlets, and broadsides written in the seventeenth and eighteenth centuries by men who called themselves "promoters" or "undertakers" of linen manufacture. Although most of my primary source material is from the British Isles, its themes are consistent with documents quoted in secondary sources that trace the development of linen on the continent. Most of the authors of the primary sources were merchants and landlords who stood to accumulate either profit or rent from cloth production schemes. In the Scottish lowlands, Silesia, and the non-black-earth areas of Russia, rent was often at stake, taking one of two forms: in kind (as yarn or cloth) or in cash (e.g. Horner 1920:472–77; Kisch 1981:179–81; Smout 1969:127–28).

Regardless of the type of exaction, rent and profit were not the linen promoters' sole objectives. On the contrary, some claimed to be unfairly victimized by the rancor of others who, out of envy, failed to see how their innovations and initiatives served the public good (Haines 1677:4,14–15; Hill 1817:Preface). Linen manufacture, they all seemed to feel, could solve the most pressing problems of the mercantile state.

First among these problems was the foreign exchange of the nation, earned through manufactured exports, lost through importing the manufactures of others. The promoters argued that if indigenous producers could supply indigenous markets as well as penetrate colonial and foreign markets, they would alleviate the "exhaustion of the treasury," reversing the drain of bullion to purchase linens abroad.

A second mercantilist problem amenable to solution through the intensification of linen manufacture was the alarming impoverishment of rural populations, due to a convergence of demographic growth, staggering price inflation, and the incipient commoditization of land resources (Kriedte 1983:52–54). The specter of a falling standard of living for much of the peasantry loomed large in the promotion literature which, in virtually every case I reviewed, mentioned beggars and vagrants, children whose parents could not afford to keep them, and the "idle" poor. Unable to pay their rents without selling the family cow, tenants and cottagers were slipping precariously toward dependence on public or religious charity.

Linen promoters took a dim view of charity, which they thought of as "pernicious" (one of their favorite words)—a parasitic burden on those who worked. Gifts to the poor, they argued, would encourage nonchalance and reinforce habits of mendacity and sloth. This vocabulary is reminiscent of Protestant culture, which many of the promoters embraced. Guignet's detailed account of linen manufacture in Valenciennes in northern France, however, quotes Catholics voicing similar concerns (1976:407–53). Whatever their religion, the promoters advocated an expansion of flax cultivation and linen manufacture as an alternative to charity for poorer peasants. They anticipated that such developments would sort out the "worthy and industrious" poor, who were victims of genuine adversity in their own or their parents' lives, from those who lazily abused the guilt of others. Such an expectation came across clearly in the sermon which an English vicar delivered to his "lambs" in 1715, commemorating a merchant's gift of a linen workhouse to the community. Unlike distributions of money, he preached, the workhouse had transformed a "barren wilderness" into a "well-watered green" (Acres 1715).

The promotion of linen manufacture as an alternative to charity spoke to the quality and quantity of population—cornerstones of the mercantile state. An eighteenth-century Scottish merchant provided a representative view of quality when he wrote that the discontented and turbulent idle poor made bad soldiers. Seditious or mutinous in wartime, impossible to disarm in peace, they contrasted markedly with the "working poor" who, even though they had no property, "cheerfully [risked] their lives in war." This was in itself a reason to invest in linen (Lindesay 1736:6–9). As Guignet suggests, the promoters believed that work, no less than property, was morally redemptive and that the working poor could be saved (1976:30–52,420–34).

In addition to quality of population, mercantilist doctrine also emphasized numbers. The strength of a nation derived not from its silver and gold mines, but from the density of its active population. Given that for many of the promoters, a root cause of pauperism was an excess of population manifest in over-large families, a populationist argument on behalf of linen seems contradictory. An Irish landlord-undertaker acknowledged as much when he described as his country's "fatal problem" that "we want people, and yet we have more than we know how to Employ" (Anon 1729:10). Flax cultivation and linen manufacture were his proposed solution. He shared with other promoters the conviction that these activities would not only occupy the vagrant and dispossessed, but also increase the rate of population growth. So prevalent was this idea that promoters aware of military planning proposed linen schemes for coastal areas in need of better defenses (Haines 1677:9).

There were three ways in which linen manufacturing was expected to enhance population. By providing employment, it would stem the migration of the poor and indigent to the colonies. Industrial areas could also be expected to attract immigrants, particularly skilled craftsmen. Most important, employment opportunities would encourage fertility through an increase in mating and marriage. As one promoter put it, when the "multitudes of poor are starving, they are frightened from marriage;" by contrast their "natural inclinations, which are heightened by Plenty and Satisfaction, prompt them to marry and beget Children." Their happiness, moreover, also "prompts foreigners to come" (Anon 1738:52). When, in 1677, A. Haines proposed that linen workhouses be established in every county of England, his rationale was that then there would no longer "be need of so great caution to prevent the Marriages of the meaner sort, since now the Parishes need not so much fear a Charge, knowing a means how to employ all their Children. . . " Far from "causing any depopulation," the scheme, he said, "may increase our Inhabitants; and the more the better, since we know how to dispose of them in such laudable Employment" (Haines 1677:10–11).

Hindsight suggests that the linen promoters were correct. Several well-known studies not only have shown an association between rural "proto-industry" and rising population, but also have identified the principal mechanism of this demographic increase as a shift to younger and more universal marriage (Braun 1978; Crawford 1968:32; Guignet 1976:335–55,622–23; Medick 1981; C. Tilly 1978; L. Tilly 1984:307–10). In Franklin Mendel's somewhat over-determined characterization of the linen districts of interior Flanders, "an improvement in the relative price of linen produced surges in the number of marriages" (1981:176).

The populationism implicit in the linen promotion schemes takes us part way toward understanding the moral and sociological issues raised by the spinning tales. In both the tales and the schemes, marriage was portrayed as a pivotal institution of rural life. Both also identified poverty and unemployment as the primary obstacles to marriage, while presenting the manufacture of linen as the main way out. The equation does not, however, tell us why the spinning tales present such ambivalent messages about this solution. Why did the inventors and transmitters of this folklore not declare a wholehearted enthusiasm for the industry that would save women from spinsterhood? To better grasp this ambivalence, two more steps are necessary: a closer look at the promotion schemes to discover how capital mobilized labor, and a look at the ecology of the manufacture within its agricultural setting. In the first instance, we will learn how the linen promoters played upon the motivations of producers, including their motivation to marry. In the second, the task is to uncover something intelligible to our modern secular consciousness about the dwarf demon, Rumpelstiltskin.

LINEN PROMOTION AND THE MOBILIZATION OF LABOR

There were two basic modes of textile production in Early Modern Europe. In the first, which German scholars call the *kauf* system, households organized the production of handicrafts. Although pressed to manufacture a surplus to meet their need for cash, they controlled and integrated the production process from the raw material to the finished cloth, which they then sold to merchants or used to pay their rent. The second, *verlag* system, based on putting-out, opened the door to a division of labor among the various stages of production, and to merchant ownership of the raw materials and semifinished goods as they moved from stage to stage.

Because flax cultivation was widespread among Europe's peasant households, the linen industry naturally gravitated toward the *kauf* pattern—much as peasant households in the cotton-growing areas of China organized production, from planting the fiber to the finished textile (Chao 1977). The German historian Jürgen Schlumbohm attributes the marked seasonal variation in the marketing of cloth in Osnabruck, Hanover, to the *kauf* system. Cloth came to market mainly in the summer months because, as contemporaries observed, it took nearly a year to cultivate and harvest the flax, and to process, spin, weave, bleach, and finish it. Because all of these steps occurred within individual households, they had to be sequential, so the time of planting the fiber determined the time of eventually selling the cloth (Schlumbohm 1983).

In describing the *kauf* system of Osnabruck, Schlumbohm emphasizes that it was not a retrograde movement. Like its Chinese cotton counterpart, it generated a substantial export trade, evident in the large number of "Osnabrucks" that clothed New World slaves. Yet, except for the fact that adult women managed most of the weaving, the system discouraged a division of labor, whether between agriculture and industry, or, within households, between men and women, adults and children, all of whom labored on the crops, and all of whom spun (Schlumbohm:104–08; also see Guignet 1976:204–14; L. Tilly 1984:303–07).

Some observers praised the system for its close articulation of activities, such that "the disadvantages of bad spinning soon became apparent in the weaving" and could be corrected. Others, however, blamed the decline of Osnabruck linens on the seasonal, part-time commitment of the rural population and their inefficiency in the assignment of tasks. Most important, Osnabruck was but an island in a larger sea of linen production that struck a balance between household manufacture and putting-out. In nearby Bielefeld, in Prussia, for example, spinning, weaving, bleaching, and finishing developed as separate industries, integrated by merchants. The result was not fully a putting-out system, because flax was locally produced and the spinners, if they did not cultivate it themselves, could purchase the processed fiber from local farmers and brokers, selling the yarn "in small quantities to the weavers or the yarn dealer . . . " (Schlumbohm 1983:107–15). Nevertheless it bore the stamp of the linen promotion schemes.

Several features were common to these schemes. The promoters generally had capital which they invested in one or more of the following ways: To advance credit for flax seed, sowers, spinning wheels, reels, or looms to producers; to construct or rehabilitate buildings for processing the fiber and for spinning, weaving, and bleaching the cloth; and to purchase housing and other amenities that would attract skilled textile craftsmen. The diasporas of religious persecution, of which the Huguenots were a particularly relevant example, provided many of these craftsmen.

Most of the promotion literature also marshaled arguments in favor of government intervention in linen development, whether through tariff legislation against competitive imports, through capital investment, or through the maintenance of a regulatory apparatus to control quality without stifling the production schemes. The pamphlets and broadsides that the promoters wrote were, in fact, often addressed to government bodies.

Of all the plans for investment capital, whether public or private, the most interesting were proposals for prizes and bounties to reward initiative and industriousness among the producers. These rewards and punishments reflect a view of the rural population as so many actors "naturally" distinguishable by their "unequal skills" and "differential capacities." The promoters' rewards were designed to play upon these distinctions in order to increase productivity (e.g., Guignet 1976:562–81). Credit was an important tool of social engineering. Advances against flax, yarn, or cloth expanded or contracted in relation to personal assessments of a debtor's honesty, cheerfulness, reliability, zeal, sobriety, or dedication to work. Additional loans helped favored clients pay their rent and purchase such household and personal "decencies" as silver plate, drapes, utensils, furnishings, ornaments, and apparel. Under special circumstances, credit made possible the repurchase of items that had earlier been pawned (Guignet 1976:585–91; Anon 1729).

Premiums and bounties augmented credit in the structuring of rewards and punishments. For example, the Irish landlord Sir Richard Cox in 1749 advertised as a "sure method to Establish the Linen Manufacture" his annual distribution of a dozen monetary prizes to those tenants who raised and dressed the most flax, spun the most and the best yarn, spun diligently for two years in a row, wove the most and the best cloth, and kept the most looms in operation. In addition, he boasted of setting aside an equal number of premiums for immigrant Protestant weavers who agreed to settle in his town, which between 1735 and 1749 had grown from 87 to 117 households, with 226 flax wheels. "I am persuaded," Cox wrote of the gold-lettered plaque that he had hung on the master weaver's house in honor of his "superior industry," that "the Invention has forwarded the Work, more than all the Money I have expended. It is a Natural Vanity to desire to be distinguished . . . And surely ought to be indulged, since it is productive to much Good" (Cox 1749:23–26). Elsewhere (1749:21) Cox described himself as "stirring up"—his French counterparts used the word "animating"—a "generous and useful Emulation between the new comers, which of them shall first become rich," and recommended this strategy for creating "in a short time different Classes of Rivals," until all become rich. "I forsaw," he wrote "that these good effects . . . would make others ashamed of their indolence, and stir up a Spirit of Industry" (1749:23).

Cox's promotion scheme included an overhaul of the ritual calendar; he discouraged his tenants from celebrating their traditional feast days and transformed May Day into "the joyous season of Determining the Premiums" (1749:32). Then, a full assembly gathered for the applauses and demerits that each deserved. In determining who got what, firsthand "Acquaintenance" and "Observation" were essential, for it was Cox's view that the "Undertaker must attend personally the growth of the Undertaking" (1749:48). He should not "receive Reports from others; For those will often be partial, through Love, Malice, or Envy; and then his Favours will be refused to the Deserving, and unprofitably conferred on those who will not deserve them. He must himself be the Witness and the Judge of Merit as well as the Distributor of Rewards" (1749: 29–30). Acknowledging that competition among producers could be in itself a source of envy, Cox also recommended that the Undertaker keep his inhabitants from "litigiousness and contention," using "a strong hand, watchful eye and resolute heart" against those who "grow rich under the Pretense of procuring Right, but are indeed even doing Wrong." Allowing free rein to their machinations would be as if a Cheesemonger were "rearing and cherishing Rats in his Shop" (1749:35).

Cox described his promotion scheme in a letter to a fellow undertaker, whom he thought could use it in the publication of how-to-do-it manuals. Other schemes, while less detailed, reveal the same understanding of promotion: One had to "stir-up" or "animate" the producers' ambitions and vanity; hold out to them examples of a better standard of living that they would want to emulate; attend to the talent, "capacities, genius and inclinations" of individuals (Lindesay 1736:52); encourage the right attitude with bounties and premiums while punishing obstinacy, carelessness and sloth. Having set the producers in competition with one another, each one "striving to excell the rest" (Haines 1677:6–7), a good undertaker had then to calm disputes (Bailey 1758). At cross-purposes with such peace-making was the system of remuneration for piecework, whose rates varied according to producers' "unequal skills" and "differential capabilities." As Guignet shows for lace makers, the "rapidity of work and quality of execution" were "naturally factors of social differentiation" and affected the price that was paid (1976:571–56).

From the accounts I have seen, it is fair to say that the promoters who energized flax cultivation and linen manufacture in seventeenth- and eighteenth-century Europe thought that spinning was the "bottleneck" of textile production, yarn the "strategic material," and spinners the "infantry"—it took up to eight spinners to keep a weaver in work (Guignet 1976:42,126–38,392; Deman 1852:90–91). In a *kauf* system of household manufacturing, everyone spun while the women wove. But in their schemes, the linen promoters singled out children and young women as the most promising candidates for the spinning task. Many of them justified this emphasis with the mercantilist arguments that female spinners "conserved the sinews" of the adult male for war, or tapped the greatest reservoir of rural idleness (Anon 1735:23; Bailey 1758:47). They also feminized the production of thread and yarn through the claim that small and delicate hands did it better. An English promoter on a visit to Ireland felt enthused by his discovery that "no women are apter to spin [flax] well than the Irish, who, labouring little in any kind with their hands, have fingers more supple and soft than other women of the poorer condition amongst us" (quoted in Horner 1920:21–21; Warner 1864:390). To a Scottish promoter, it was in the interest of all governments "to teach tender fingers as soon as tongues" (Anon 1715:1–8).

Schemes that feminized spinning did not necessarily envision mobilizing the spinners through the authority structure of the peasant household. On the contrary, many promoters advocated the organization of autonomous spinning institutions, free of parental control. Their argument included the observation that youthful women, when at home, were unruly. Unless sent out to be servants or chambermaids, their idleness led to "tearing hedges, robbing orchards, beggaring their fathers" (Anon 1715:14–19). If gathered to spin away from home, they might be more productive, for "when so many are employed in sight of each other" and with proper encouragement, "small and great" will strive to excel (Haines 1677:14). Of course, the fathers would also benefit. Without linen manufacturing, a man with many children was desperate; with it, he who had the most children lived the best (Acres 1715:14–19). Indeed, the daughter who spun was a "treasure," the more so because she could also spin her own clothes (Anon 1735:23).

Orphanages and workhouses that taught spinning represented the greatest separation of work from family and the most rigorous application of work discipline. Somewhat more relaxed were the spinning schools that the promoters organized and staffed with skilled instructors. An English traveler of the late seventeenth century recorded an example from Silesia. The mistress, holding a wand, stood at a pulpit in the center of the room, around which some 200 boys and girls, aged eight and older, sat spinning with distaff and spindle (the wheel was yet to arrive). The children produced yarn from flax supplied by their parents, graduating to higher benches, and eventually from the school, according to their proficiency. When one of them had spun all the flax on a distaff, the mistress rang a bell, and an assistant appeared to store the bobbin and deliver another distaff. The spinning mistress also summoned this assistant to mete out humiliations and floggings for idleness and sloth (Horner 1920:402–03; Warden 1864:365).

In addition to the spinning schools, the linen promoters encouraged the formation of a vast network of spinning mistresses, "fanning out" from a few source points to teach wheel spinning and improved techniques to the "most docile," who would in turn teach others. As with linen promotion generally, premiums "animated" this network. Another source of animation was the conscious recruitment of elite women to participate in spinning demonstrations because "Examples of this kind would stir up the lower Sort of People to practice and delight in an Employment so beneficial to themselves and the Public" (Bailey 1758:66). Seeing women of the "best Distinction" at the wheel, they would understand that "to spin is looked upon to be the greatest Honour and Perfection of the female sex" (quoted in Horner 1920:83). Other promoters characterized spinning as "the most genteel [occupation] for the delicate sex," and as "delightful and intellectual" (e.g. Deman 1852:90–91). One could, thought a Scottish merchant, solve the yarn problem by "prevailing on a Wise Woman in each parish to set an example." He also argued for a continuation of spinning premiums "which have already had so good effect that most of them are won by Ladies, whose Bread does not depend upon their Labour" (Anon 1734:20).

To some of the linen promoters (e.g., Acres 1715; Cox 1749), female spinners were like the enterprising woman in Proverbs Chapter 31, who chose flax, toiled at her work, and "like a ship laden with merchandise . . . [brought] home food from far off." Working through the night, never allowing her candle to expire, this "capable wife" even purchased land and planted a vineyard. Other promoters, however, wrote disparagingly of spinners who had become too enterprising. Valenciennes merchants, for example, claimed that the spinners of their district "perniciously" bypassed the local weavers, selling their yarn to itinerate bandits and interlopers, from whence it entered an international trade (Guignet 1976:42). Obsessed with the shortage of yarn, and with foreign (especially Dutch) competition for it, many promoters argued for the creation of a yarn market to reduce the spinners' options and control what they called the "hemorrhage" of yarn (1976:130–31). Some, however, attributed the young spinners' participation in contraband to their position at the bottom of the textile hierarchy, where remuneration was pitiful and the risk of indebtedness through advances dangerously high (1976:133).

Whether their remarks were couched in a language of sympathy, admiration, or mistrust, it is clear that the linen promoters considered the female spinners to be self-motivated persons, capable of diligent work if only their ambitions could be "kindled." And what were these ambitions if not marriage? The Scottish minister who preached the commemorative sermon for the merchant-donated workhouse in his parish alerted the "virgins" of his congregation that "the wheel and the distaff are an human nuptial wagon" (Acres 1715:14). His words were strongly echoed in the spinning bees, the nodule that formed throughout the vast network of "fanned-out" spinning instruction and that, even more than the schools and orphanages, structured the intensification of yarn production in the linen districts. For descriptions of this institution, we have Hans Medick's synthesis and interpretation of German language sources on the *Spinnstube* (1984).

Spinning technology, whether with distaff and spindle or with the pedal-operated wheel, was portable. Thus, when the work was a by-occupation of the long winter evenings, it made sense for neighbors to assemble in one place, save on light and fuel, and spin together. As we have seen, the promoters favored such collective spinning, claiming—contrary to the opinion of some—that when young women worked away from their families, their productivity improved (e.g., Acres 1715:13–18). However, the spinning bees, or *spinnstuben*, were controversial, because the assembled company lightened the burden of a tedious and repetitive activity with frivolity and entertainment. According to Medick, this fact did not deter the enthusiasm of the "defenders of mercantile performance" who, unlike contemporary religious and moral reformers, emphasized,". . . the economic usefulness and productivity of the specific forms of sociability and 'merriment' of the *Spinnstube*. The special connection between work and free time appeared to offer advantages as over against the tiring work inside household and family." Noting that "there was a clear connection of *Spinnstuben* work and sociability with the intensification of rural commodity production in textiles since the seventeenth century," Medick quotes an observer of the time who claimed that the "merriments" of the bees were "originally connected by our wise forefathers with this kind

*Figure 15. Painting, "Removing Flax from the Lint Hole, County Antrim";
Ulster Folk and Transport Museum, Holywood, County Down, Ireland*

of spinning, and that it chiefly caused the spinning of thread to become the most widespread and continuous manufacture, indeed a
real national industry"(Medick 1984:326–29).

Spinnstube entertainment typically involved courtship play for,
as Medick shows, the institution was closely tied to "youth sexual
culture" and rural mating (1984:318). In the course of a typical evening, young men dropped by to flirt. Although they also devoted
much of their leisure to card-playing and smoking tobacco, they ate,
drank, and danced with the girls and, carrying their wheels, es-
corted them home. Flandrin, describing how French rural spinners
gathered in barns where the body heat of the cows kept their fingers
moving, quotes a contemporary to the effect that "a great many
striplings and lovers" regularly attended (quoted in 1976:109). So
much did the spinning bees nurture courtship that religious reformers, both Protestant and Catholic, attacked them as dens of vice, se-

duction, and immodesty where youths enjoyed too much autonomy from parental chaperoning (Medick 1984).

Some accounts of the spinning bees suggest an atmosphere of antagonism between the sexes that ranged from play to violence. For example, in the linen district of the Scottish lowlands, coy young women were reported to have used the rocks that weighted their spindles to batter unworthy suitors and escorts, as matrons sometimes battered their husbands, and the spinning assemblies in barns or houses were called "rockins" (Warden 1864:246). Similarly, Medick reports the mid-eighteenth-century severe beating of a weaver-journeyman with a distaff by the female company of a *spinnstube*, because he "visited unwanted attentions" on one of them (Medick 1984:331). Yet to characterize the work culture of spinning in terms of female solidarity is to miss the competitive relationships that flourished among young girls as they entered the mating game.

Redfern Mason describes the typical Irish spinning song as "an impromptu dialogue on the love affairs of the young people present," with nonsense verses inserted to punctuate the repartee of matching names (Mason 1911:118–24). A singer's keen wits and sharp tongue entertained the group as she dangerously skirted the edge of malicious ridicule and "saucy gossip." A line such as "you mannerless girl, he's your match," could make its subject feel "struck in the face" should the beau named be taken by another. "If the man is worth it, don't let her take him," was a possible retort—or, "There is no tree in the wood that I could not find its equal" (Mason 1911).

When a young girl's name became coupled with the name of an acceptable man, the sharp-witted dialogue shifted to the household furnishings that the newlyweds would try to acquire: "A twelve hundred tick with white feathers filled; white linen sheets and white baskets abundant; a quilt of fine silk, the dearest in Limerick; candlesticks of gold upon tables-a-glistening; Good gold and silver in their pockets-a-jingling . . . " (Mason 1911). Lists of this sort, as well as the taunting dialogue over names, suggest a double association between the spinning circles and courtship. The circles encouraged encounters between youths outside of parental sponsorship, and they drew attention to girls' chances for status mobility through marriage. Indeed, men hung around the gatherings not only to flirt, but also to evaluate the industriousness and skill of the women. According to numerous contemporaries, spinning skills contributed to marriageability and the better the spinner, the better the mate she might catch.

According to Medick, the mercantile defenders of the spinning bees were explicit on the link between marriage chances and spinning output. Finding value in what the moralists berated, they praised "the gatherings of both sexes in the *Spinnstube* and the competition of the women in terms of the village marriage market as a motive which could be used for the national economy." In the words of a contemporary, this arrangement "encourages work in a large society of compeers, especially when many young males are there to cast a watchful eye on the industry and quickness of the girls who would be their future wives. This is much better than when a girl spins alone with her mother or sister" (quoted in 1984:329). Medick concludes that neither the market nor the rulers gave "form or impetus to the rhythm of production of linen thread"; rather "the village marriage market" organized the "necessary coercion" (1984:332).

Should we wonder then, that competition in love and status mobility through marriage were central themes in the spinning tales? As Bottigheimer notes, it was in spinning bees that countless of these tales were invented, rearranged, and retold (1982:143).

We have seen that the linen promotion schemes typically had a populationist bent. Their authors claimed that the expansion of this industry would increase the rate of marriage in the countryside, multiplying the citizenry of their nation. Now it is apparent that this emphasis on marriage fit into their strategy for intensifying production—the strategy that deployed capital to animate labor through a system of punishments and rewards. Among the promised rewards for good spinning were prizes, decencies, and a decent husband.

The spinning tales, I think, commented with ambivalence on this structure of "capital penetration," expressing neither unqualified support nor clear opposition. In their juxtaposition of fabulous marriage opportunities with impossible spinning tasks, they warned of risk to the daughters of the poor who overcommitted their labor to marry up, or had it overcommitted by their parents. This ambivalence, it seems, reveals a sociological understanding of the manipulative aspects of the promotion schemes which, as Guignet suggests, created a pattern of subordination that was simultaneously "cordial" and "conflictual." Contacts between spinners or their parents and the agents of these schemes were, as we have seen, solicitous yet potentially dangerous. Even as the puppeteers of promotion dangled the hope that "superfluous children" could marry and even climb, they initiated debts, obligations, and potential legal entanglements that engulfed the spinners, to use Guignet's expression, "in quicksand" (1976:577–81). The Rumpelstiltkskin-type tale underscores this contradiction by weighing a strategy for marriage and mobility through rural textile manufacture against the costs to a future generation.

FLAX, FAIRIES, AND THE DEMONIZATION OF SPIRITS

According to the spinning tales, it was, despite appearances, spirits rather than the spirit of industry that animated spinners. Nor were spirits far removed from the spinners' world. Writing of the silk-reeling equivalent of the linen *spinnstube* in Lyons, Natalie Davis recreates an atmosphere that in rural settings could only have been more enchanted: "a broken thread meant a quarrel; a man crossing a thread stretched at the doorsill . . . bore the same name as one's future husband." The water for washing threads "laughed" instead of boiled. And there were night visitors who came to finish the spinning or steal the spindles (Davis 1982:61). In the linen areas, spirit helpers participated in all the stages of production. Dwarfs and fairies could weave and bleach; from a single hank of yarn they could make the sails for an entire ship. Similarly, they were known to tailor shirts from miniscule fabrics, three inches square. Most impressive was their ability to spin, converting mountains of flax into yarn or gold at night. But fairies could also wreak mischief. For example, they fashioned horses and boats for the fairy kingdom from stalks of hemp or flax that they stole from mortal's fields. A flax crop with stunted plants was understood to have provided a means of fairy transportation.

On the whole, European peasants portrayed fairies, dwarfs, and trolls as "little people," no less worthy of the good things of life than humans. Indeed, it was common for folk tales to describe agreements between these spirits and humans, and to justify fairy pique when humans failed to live up to their part of the bargain. The animistic belief system underlying this perspective included the idea that the little people had inhabited the land first, but had yielded it, however unwillingly, to settle in rocks and caves, woods and streams, as human populations and agricultural activities expanded. Thus deprived of space, the fairy societies came to depend upon human contributions to ensure their perpetuation. It was widely held that fairy children could not be born except with the assistance of human midwives, and that, to maintain their numbers, fairies would at times kidnap a mortal woman of childbearing age, or rob a human cradle, leaving behind a changeling. In exchange, however, they offered the powers of magic on behalf of human goals, often without thought of repayment. If they occasionally stole from the flax field, perhaps it was because they had once lived under its soil.

Beliefs about fairies, trolls, and dwarfs shaded subtly into a set of ideas about evil spirits and witches, yet these concepts were not the same. Evil or witchlike spirits were thought to be motivated by envy and spite, and therefore quick to distort their side of the relationship with humans. Fairy tricks and shakedowns could ultimately find justification in an overall balance of give and take, particularly in the context of the fairies' prior claim to the land. But the very same acts when attributed to witches violated the model of reciprocity. Witches would stunt your flax crop, not to acquire the raw materials for a boat that they needed, but because they hated you and relished seeing you ruined.

Apparently, witches were after flax in the linen districts of the Celtic fringe, the Germanies, Switzerland, and Eastern Europe. Frazer collected for *The Golden Bough* (1890) many stories linking this crop to the ritual fires that peasants lit, whether to give light to reciprocating spirits or to destroy witches and vampires. On the eve of May Day, in conjunction with the midsummer solstice, and again on All Hallow's eve, peasants typically celebrated the transitions in the agricultural cycle with great bonfires (originally bone fires). Young people, impersonating spirits or magically transformed through spiritual intervention, mummed and begged for pieces of wood and brush to use as fuel. It was risky not to contribute, for a good fire was the best defense against personal and household misfortune in the form of hailstorms, crop failures, and the wasting diseases so prevalent among the peasants' livestock and their children. The idea that fire could destroy malevolent spirits led neighboring villages to vie for the largest conflagration, and to burn their most hated enemies in effigy. The fires were also believed to promote fertility. Young unmarried couples—perhaps the same couples who flirted in the *spinnstuben*—leapt over the glowing embers, celebrating the pending marriages and procreative yearnings of sexually maturing youth.

Flax figured importantly in bonfire rituals, especially the midsummer fires of June 24, which the Church assimilated to the feast of Saint John the Baptist. One belief focused on height through imitative magic; the height of the flames foretold how tall the crop would grow. More commonly, it was held that the higher a young couple jumped in the air when leaping over the still-burning embers, the taller their eventual flax stalks. Parents of the youth who leapt the highest could count on the tallest crop, unless they had failed to contribute fuel to the fire. In some apparently more Christianized villages, nubile girls climbed the bell tower to ward off witches through bell-ringing, and it was said that the girl who swung highest on the bell rope would have the tallest crop (Frazer 1980:247–48).

In addition to staging fertility campaigns based on imitative magic, peasants attempted to harness energy from the spirits they were destroying and channel it into fecundity and renewal. In Bavaria, for example, they slew a dragon-monster during the Midsummer ritual, spreading the blood-soaked (linen) cloths on their flax fields. Almost everywhere, the charred sticks from the bonfires were considered prophylactic for witchcraft; people took them home, fashioned cattle prods from them, and planted them along with their flax. The flames, too, were protective; in planting decisions one took account of the direction in which the wind blew them.

The idea that witches threatened the flax crop is closely related to the idea that the spirits who showed up to help spin it were dangerous to human reproduction. The Rumpelstiltskins, intensely interested in the offspring of those they helped, were also witch-like. By what process did the "little people" become so demonized? How were the rocky or forested peripheries of settled areas transformed into redoubts of spiritual danger? Part of the answer undoubtably lies in the witch-hunt that tore up rural Europe in the sixteenth and seventeenth centuries.

Subjecting peasants to an elite demonology that assimilated all earth spirits and spirits of the dead to the Christian devil, both Catholic and Protestant reformers spread witch-hunt propaganda with the newly available printing press and a state-supported apparatus of courts and itinerant prosecutors. Yet peasants must also have contributed to the transformation, their vision of the demonic becoming more elaborate as linen production intensified. According to peasant belief, the dairy cattle that provided the food staple in so many of the linen districts had already displaced the spirit dwellers of fields and meadows, and thus were constant targets of witchcraft and vindictive spirit tricks. People not only prodded their cattle with charred sticks snatched from the midsummer fires, but drove them through these fires for greater protection. Where flax cultivation and linen manufacture overlaid subsistence agriculture, the environmental impact was many times greater than that of cattle alone. Keeping in mind the "little people"—the prior inhabitants of the landscape—let us see how dramatic, and unwelcome, the linen intrusion was.

THE ENVIRONMENTAL IMPACT OF FLAX PRODUCTION

The climate range that flax can endure is broad; the best-known fields were as far apart as the Nile valley and the deltas of northern Russia. Yet since the industrial revolution unleashed the unrelenting competition of cotton, 96 percent of the world's flax supply has come to be grown between 49 and 53 degrees latitude, with more than 82 percent of the acreage now in the Soviet Union (Dempsey 1975:3,6–7). The reason is that flax is a "long day" crop which benefits from northern light. In addition, it thrives in moderate temperatures, evenly distributed rainfall, and moist winds. Most important is the quality of nutrition it receives, with both the yield and fineness of the crop enhanced by well-drained alluvial or loam soils, located in river deltas or near the shores of lakes, where the water table is high (Dempsey 1975:7–10). The plant sinks deep roots, so these soils must be pulverized through several plowings. They should also be weeded, because flax competes poorly with weeds and is exceptionally vulnerable to fungal diseases introduced through spores. Finally, flax is sown broadcast so that weeding is a hands-and-knees operation, conducted when the flax plants are still young enough to be crushed and stand up again (Dempsey 1975:14–26; Warden 1864:4–17,33–34). According to estimates from Flanders, to harvest an acre of flax took twelve to fifteen adult workers while eighty-two "woman" days were necessary to weed it (Mendels 1981:175–76).

Like cotton, flax exhausts the soil. In virtually all rotation systems, cultivators allow five to ten years between flax crops (Dempsey 1975:14; Horner 1920:449–50). According to Slicher van Bath, it had already become apparent to north Italians by the late Middle Ages that too much flax was a threat to their grain crops, which also taxed the soil. Their solution, adopted as well by south German manufacturers of fustian, was in some ways a harbinger of eighteenth- and nineteenth-century British imperialism: Import cotton from the tropics and conserve temperate soils for food (Slicher van Bath 1963).

In addition to causing soil exhaustion, flax requires a heavy burden of labor to prepare it for textile manufacture. A ton of dried flax straw yields no more than 400 pounds of long linen fibers and another hundred pounds of short fibers or "tow." The crop must be pulled, not cut; left in place, its roots would injure successive cultigens (Horner 1920:450). Having dried out for two to three days, it must then be steeped or retted—arranged in one layer and anchored with stones just below the surface of a slowly flowing stream or pond. This process, which takes from ten days to two weeks, loosens the cellulose fibers from the plant's woody core and surrounding bark. The water ferments the resins and gums that hold these parts together, yielding as its byproduct a fetid, pungent-smelling scum and sediment that is capable of killing fish. This explains the many laws that governed the disposal of retting water, as well as the places where retting could take place (Warden 1864:36–40).

Once retted, the flax crop is carefully lifted from the water, using hands rather than rakes, which would injure the fibers, and laid out on a meadow to be "grassed." The more thinly it is spread, the less the need to turn it during the week or more that it spends distended and exposed to air. An exposure of three weeks to a month can substitute for submerged retting in some moister climates, the fermentation taking place from the action of dew (Kirby 1963:25).

Grassing is followed by breaking and scutching, operations that today take place in mills, but before the late eighteenth century were performed with a simple wooden press that fragmented the bark and core. This was followed by several twists with the hands to dislodge the fragments, and finally, by shaking and beating with a wooden knife. One last step before spinning was to "hackle" or "heckle" the fibers, removing all remnants of gum and resin as well as the short fibers or tow, with combs of several grades made by the village blacksmith. To remove impurities without shredding the long fibers took considerable skill, and in many flax-growing regions, itinerant combers did the job. Elsewhere, it was thought to be women's work and men had to learn an "artificial weakness" to do it (Horner 1920:379). In such areas, women owned hatchels and combs as well as spinning wheels, reels, and yarns.

Once spun and woven into cloth, linen was usually bleached, both to remove residual impurities and because, as a cellulose vegetable fiber, it was hard to dye. Degrees of whiteness, rather than hues of color, were (in addition to fineness) the index of a linen cloth's reputation. The bleaching process did not become efficient until after 1760, when Irish bleachers developed a chloride of lime, or slaked lime, powder that allowed them to eliminate steps without jeopardizing the fibers. Before then, the multiple steps could take up to seven months. The cloth was first washed in soap and water, then rinsed and steeped or boiled in a cauldron with lye, potash, bone ash, or cow dung. After a 48-hour soak came more washing and beating, followed by two days of "grassing." Then the fabric was laid on a "bleach green" to air, being watered periodically. These operations were repeated several times before souring, usually in a vat of buttermilk, for up to three weeks. After souring came more washing, beating, and grassing. The souring and grassing series, like the preceding series of alternate lye steeps and airings, was repeated five or six times, until the desired whiteness was obtained. Attempts to shorten this process through the use of pure lime or acids ran the risk of over-oxidizing the delicate fibers (Coons and Koob 1980:62; Horner 1920:40–41; Trotman and Trotman 1948:124–25).

Clearly, a linen industry brought many sources of irritation to other users of the land. Its impact can be heard in the strident voices

Figure 16. Before Irish bleachers developed slaked lime in 1760, fabrics were spread out on "bleaching greens." Painting, "Bleaching Ground," by David Teniers; Semper Galerie: Dresden

of the agricultural improvers (another kind of promoter in the eighteenth century), and seen in the dilemmas faced by peasants who worried about their cows.

The improvers could rightly be concerned about soil exhaustion, the pollution of ponds and streams, the absorption of rural labor for harvesting, processing, and spinning, and the tendency of both flax and cloth to overrun good meadows. Fields for grassing and bleaching, abundant in regions of linen manufacture, were often as large as seven acres. Dew retting, common east of the Elbe, took up especially large areas "which [could] not be used for any other purpose" while the fermentation took place (Kirby 1963:25). Hence the argument that perservering with flax would "prove destructive both to the tenant and to the soil." Note the contempt of the late eighteenth-century agricultural reformer, Arthur Young:

> View the north of Ireland and you behold a whole province
> peopled by weavers; it is they who cultivate, or rather beggar,

the soil, as well as work the looms. Agriculture is there in ruins;
it is cut up by the roots, extirpated, annihilated. The whole region is the disgrace of the kingdom. All the crops you can see
are contemptible, are nothing but filth and weeds; no other part
of Ireland can exhibit the soil in such a state of poverty and des-
olation. But the cause of all those evils, which are absolute ex-
ceptions to everything else on the face of the globe, is easily
found. A most prosperous manufacture, so contrived as to be
the destruction of agriculture, is certainly a spectacle for which
we must go to Ireland. It is owing to the fabric spreading all
over the country, instead of being confined to towns. There, literally speaking, is not a farmer in a hundred miles of the linen
country of Ireland. The lands are infinitely subdivided (and the)
weaver . . . has always a piece of potatoes, a piece of oats, a
patch of flax, and grass for a cow . . . If I had an estate in the
south of Ireland, I would as soon introduce pestilence and famine upon it as the linen-manufacture . . . (quoted in Horner
1920:52).

The voices of tenants and cottagers came through less clearly than
the voices of improvers like Arthur Young, not only because they
were illiterate, but also because their relationship to linen was more
complicated. After all, the manufacture began as their by-
occupation, a welcome source of income to make ends meet. Moreover, up to a certain point, linen was compatible with—even complementary to—the cattle husbandry that ensured subsistence in
many of the linen districts. Did not cloth makers sour this textile
in several successive buttermilk baths (sometimes also in cattle
dung), while linseed (flax seed) and linseed cake made excellent cattle fodder? Did not the body heat of cows keep the fingers of the
spinners warm? In 1736, Stephen Bennet, an English promoter visiting Sweden, argued for raising more cattle in a linen district "for
without milk whey for the perfection of the bleaching, all labour is
in vain . . . " (Geijer 1979:175). Buttermilk, however, was also an
ideal substance on which to wean calves, whose removal from their
mothers was essential to milk production for the farm. And linseed
was not known as cattle feed until a Norfolk farmer of the mid-
nineteenth century discovered this possibility. Furthermore, to raise
flax as a fodder required a different technique than to raise it as a
fiber. One had to sow the crop widely to encourage branching and

leave it in the field until the seeds had thoroughly ripened, by which time the stalks were tough. When intended as a fiber, flax plants were sown thickly and pulled green, just after they had flowered. One could still remove their seeds, through a process called rippling, and allow them to ripen thereafter, but they would not then excel as feed. Moreover, some producers claimed that if flax were retted with the seeds still attached, it would come out finer (Warden 1864:17ff).

Surely, the greatest losses to cattle from having linen in their midst came from "grassing." The very word suggests competition for grazing areas, above all the bottomland meadows enriched from the overflow of rivers and streams. As one promoter put it in describing the proper conditions for bleaching greens and airing the retted plants, it was important to select "short, thick pasture ground . . . clean and free from cattle" (Warden 1864:36,47), that is, level ground, safe from wind and floods, and "not in danger of being disordered by Cattle, Fowl or Vermin" (Bailey 1758:51–64). Finally, in the complex rotation cycles developed to incorporate flax, it often replaced clover or hay or shared a divided field with them. (Warden 1864:33). It is no accident, therefore, that in the tiny area of Flanders, famous for early improvements in *both* dairying and flax cultivation, there developed an internal division between maritime agricultural and internal textile zones (Mendels 1981). Such a division was paralleled in the Vendée where, as Tilly has shown, the plains and valleys became devoted to commercial farming, while subsistence farming coupled with rural textile industries characterized much of the Bocage (Tilly 1964:33–35). Similar descriptions exist for the Scottish lowlands (Smout 1969:127–28), and for the microenvironments of Silesia (Kisch 1981).

At the same time that linen manufacture undermined local agricultural resources, posing a particular challenge to cattle, it contributed to population pressure on the land. This in turn caused many of the linen districts to import food, rendering their inhabitants more vulnerable than before to price inflation and periodic shortages (Schlumbohm 1981:117–25). The resulting subsistence crises reinforced the perception that what linen added by way of additional income could quickly disappear because of the new dependencies it created. Particularly destabilizing were the crises in which food shortages and sagging textile markets coincided, threatening the return of pauperism (e.g., Kisch 1981). Yet, despite the dangerous implications of linen intensification for subsistence farming (and over the objections of the agricultural improvers), the linen promoters held firm.

It was not a problem, they argued, that the land became fragmented and more densely populated, for this increased its value to the lords who collected the rents (Cox 1749:40). Besides, an expanding population could clear or drain the forest and bog, creating enclosures on these once communal resources (1749:41–43). Of course, critics would label flax as "pernicious," but the retting water killed beasts and fish only if it were left to stagnate. Allowed to evaporate on the fields, it provided a fertilizer (Crommelin 1705:11; Hyndman 1774:26). Most important, the "great aversion" to flax could be explained away. Perhaps it grew out of the pastoral bias of the ancestors, who wanted the land for grazing and clothed themselves in wool. Perhaps it was merely the propaganda of the already successful flax farmers who sought to monopolize this most valuable source of "wealth and grandeur" (Bailey 1758:51; Hyndman 1774:33). For some promoters, the aversion was attributable to the "venom and rancour" of landlords who made their living by "settling the land with dairies and poor cottagers," and to whom "able tenants" and industrious immigrants were a threat. Anticipating the "eternal objections" of those who forever "discouraged any new venture," the linen promoters felt confident of the contribution their projects would make to the cottagers' standard of living and the "publick Good" (Cox 1749:46–48). Needless to say, they preferred numerous prizes and premiums to "induce individuals" to expand their flax fields and bleaching greens, and advocated considering only the dryness of the ground, not the position of the moon and other superstitious indications, when planting the crop (Hill 1817:20; Hyndman 1774:8).

It seems to me that the fairies and trolls, dwarfs and green men of the linen districts became demonic to the degree that linen production intruded on their living space, over and above the prior intrusion of subsistence crops and livestock. For, while promising love and money, the linen promotion schemes undermined not only an earlier autonomy and earlier social ties, but also earlier uses and users of the land. It matters little that some of the prior users were ancestors (dressed in wool, perhaps), and some were earth spirits;

these two categories of spirit often merged. What does seem significant was their resentment of the new activity and their motivation to sabotage those who benefited from it.

PROMOTERS, PEASANTS, AND RUMPELSTILTSKINS

I have attempted to show that the intensification of the rural linen industry in Early Modern Europe met neither unmitigated opposition nor unbounded support from the peasant producers of yarn and flax. During times of high food prices and rising unemployment, riots sometimes broke out. But as recent scholarship demonstrates, the food riot was a long way from expressing the solidarity and consciousness of a "producing class" (Reddy 1984). More revealing of the ambivalent positions of the flax growers and spinners was their folk ideology as encoded in customs, tales, and songs. The linen-related motifs of this folklore offer clues to the producers' moral and sociological assessment of merchant capitalism as it organized linen manufacture. I have emphasized that their assessment raised, without ever being able to resolve, a series of troubling contradictions in the intensification process. The process brought improved marriage chances and jeopardy to one's offspring; money or "riches" and the shift from trusting to litigious social relations; material rewards in the form of "decent" apparel and furnishings and vulnerability to periodic crises in which these items were pawned. It is no wonder that the intensified uses of the landscape would also transform fairies into devil-like Rumpelstiltskins.

Note that the demonized spirits of the spinning tales did not seek to eliminate linen manufacture. On the contrary, Rumpelstiltskin and the witch-like crones contributed to its development, magically producing yarn and facilitating the status mobility through marriage that the linen schemes promised as the reward for diligent spinning. The spirits did, however, claim a piece of the action through their malicious sabotage of human reproduction. As such they splendidly dramatized the core dilemma of the linen "proto-industry." Inextricably mixing opportunity with danger, it rescued poor women from celibacy, shame, or migration only to jeopardize their and their children's social support and health. Caught in this dilemma, the producers crystallized their ambivalence toward the promotion of linen in tales of misfits like Rumpelstiltskin, who were nasty and yet helpful at the same time.

REFERENCES CITED

Bottigheimer, Ruth B.
    1981   Tale Spinners: Submerged Voices in Grimms' Fairy Tales. New German Critique 27:141–50.

Chao, Kang
    1977   The Development of Cotton Textile Production in China. Cambridge, Mass. and London: Harvard University Press.

Coleman, D.C.
    1969   An Innovation and its Diffusion: the "New Draperies." Economic History Review (Second Series) 22:417–29.

Coons, Martha and Katherine Koob
    1980   All Sorts of Good and Sufficient Cloth. Linen Making in New England 1640–1860. North Andover, Mass.: Merrimack Valley Textile Museum.

Crawford, W.H.
    1968   The Rise of the Linen Industry. In L.M. Cullen, ed. The Formation of the Irish Economy. Cork: The Mercier Press.

Cullen, L.M. and T.C. Smout
    n.d.   Comparative Aspects of Scottish and Irish Economic and Social History, 1600–1900. Edinburgh: John Donald Publishers.

Davis, Natalie Zemon
    1982   Women in the Crafts in Sixteenth-Century Lyon. Feminist Studies 1:47–80.

Dempsey, James M.
    1975   Fiber Crops. Gainsville: University of Florida Press.

Endrei, Walter
    1968   L'évolution des techniques du filage et du tissage du moyen age à la révolution industrielle. Paris and Le Haye: Mouton.
    1971   Changements dans la productivité de l'industrie lainière au moyen age. Annales E.S.C. 26:1291–99.

Evans, E. Estyn
    1957   Irish Folk Ways. New York: Devin-Adair.

Flandrin, Jean-Louis
    1980   Families in Former Times: Kinship, Household and Sexuality. Cambridge and New York: Cambridge University Press.

Frazer, Sir James George
    1890   The Golden Bough. New York: Macmillan.

Geijer, Agnes
    1979   A History of Textile Art. London: Philip Wilson.

Grant, I.F.
    1961   Highland Folk Ways. London: Routledge and Kegan Paul.

Guignet, Philippe
    1976   Mines, Manufactures et Ouvriers du Valenciennois au XVIIIe
            Siècle. Contribution à l'histoire du Travail dans l'ancienne
            France. 2 Vol. 1977 edition, New York: Arno Press, Dissertations
            in European Economic History.

Horner, John
    1920   The Linen Trade of Europe During the Spinning-Wheel Period.
            Belfast: M'Caw, Stevenson and Orr.

Kellenbenz, Hermann
    1976   The Rise of the European Economy: An Economic History of the
            Continent of Europe, 1500–1700. New York: Holmes and Meier.

Kirby, Richard Henry
    1963   Vegetable Fibers: Botany, Cultivation and Utilization. London:
            Leonard Hill Books.

Kisch, Herbert
    1981   The Textile Industries in Silesia and the Rhineland: A Compara-
            tive Study in Industrialization (with a postscriptum). *In* Peter
            Kriedte, Hans Medick, and Jürgen Schlumbohm, eds. Industriali-
            zation before Industrialization. Cambridge and New York: Cam-
            bridge University Press.

Kriedte, Peter
    1981a   The Origins, the Agrarian Context, and the Conditions in the
            World Market. *In* Peter Krietde, Hans Medick, and Jürgen
            Schlumbohm, eds. Industrialization before Industrialization.
            Cambridge and New York: Cambridge University Press. pp.12–38.
    1981b   Proto-industrialization between Industrialization and De-
            industrialization. *In* Ibid. pp.135–61.
    1983   Peasants, Landlords and Merchant Capitalists: Europe and the
            World Economy, 1500–1800. Cambridge: Cambridge University
            Press.

Leggett, William F.
    1945   The Story of Linen. Brooklyn, New York: The Chemical Publish-
            ing Company.

Lythe, S.G.E.
    1960   The Economy of Scotland in its European Setting, 1550–1625.
            Edinburgh and London: Oliver and Boyd.

Mazzaoui, Maureen Fennell
1981   The Italian Cotton Industry in the Later Middle Ages, 1100–1600.
        Cambridge: Cambridge University Press.

Medick, Hans
1981   The Proto-industrial Family Economy. In Peter Kriedte, Hans
        Medick, and Jürgen Schlumbohm, eds. Industrialization before
        Industrialization. Cambridge and New York: Cambridge Univer-
        sity Press. pp.38–74.
1984   Village Spinning Bees: Sexual Culture and Free Time among
        Rural Youth in Early Modern Germany. In H. Medick and D. Sa-
        bean, eds. Interest and Emotion; Essays on the Study of Family
        and Kinship. Cambridge: Cambridge University Press.

Mendels, Franklin F.
1981   Agriculture and Peasant Industry in Eighteenth Century Flan-
        ders. In Peter Kriedte, Hans Medick, and Jürgen Schlumbohm,
        eds. Industrialization before Industrialization. Cambridge: Cam-
        bridge University Press.

Nicholas, David
1976   Economic Reorientation and Social Change in Fourteenth Cen-
        tury Flanders. Past and Present 70:3–29.

Rae, Gordon and Charles E. Brown
1968   Geography of Scotland, General and Regional. London: G. Bell
        and Sons.

Rebel, Hermann
1988   Why Not "Old Marie"—Or Someone Very Much Like Her? A
        Reassessment of the Question about the Grimm's Contributors
        from a Social Historical Perspective. Social History 13:1–24.

Reddy, William M.
1984   The Rise of Market Culture: The Textile Trade and French Soci-
        ety, 1750–1900. Cambridge: Cambridge University Press.

Sabean, David
1975   German Agrarian Institutions at the Beginning of the Sixteenth
        Century. Upper Swabia as an Example. The Journal of Peasant
        Studies 3:76–89.

Schlumbohm, Jürgen
1981   Relations of Production—Productive Forces—Crises in Proto-
        industrialization. In Peter Kriedte, Hans Medick, and Jürgen
        Schlumbohm, eds. Industrialization before Industrialization.
        Cambridge and New York: Cambridge University Press. pp.94–126.
1983   Seasonal fluctuations and social division of labour: rural linen
        production in the Osnabrück and Bielefeld regions and the
        urban woollen industry in the Niederlausitz (c. 1770–c. 1850). In

Maxine Berg, et al, eds. Manufacture in town and country before the factory. Cambridge: Cambridge University Press.

Sharp, Buchanan
1980   In Contempt of all Authority. Rural Artisans and Riot in the West of England, 1586–1660. Berkeley and Los Angeles: University of California Press.

Slicher van Bath, B.H.
1963   The Agrarian History of Western Europe A.D. 500–1850. London: Edward Arnold.

Smout, T.C.
1969   A History of the Scottish People, 1560–1830. New York: Charles Scribner's Sons.

Spenceley, G.F.R.
1973   The Origins of the English Pillow Lace Industry. Agriculture History Review 21:81–94.

Taylor, Peter and Hermann Rebel
1981   Hessian Peasant Women, their Families and the Draft: A Social Historical Interpretation of Four Tales from the Grimm Collection. Journal of Family History 6.

Thirsk, Joan
1961   Industries in the Countryside. *In* F.J. Fisher, ed., Essays in the Economic and Social History of Tudor and Stuart England. pp.70–88. Cambridge: Cambridge University Press

Tilly, Charles
1964   The Vendée; a Sociological Analysis of the Counterrevolution of 1793. New York: John Wiley and Sons.
1978   The Historical Study of Vital Processes. *In* C. Tilly, ed. Historical Studies of Changing Fertility. Princeton: Princeton University Press.

Tilly, Louise
1984   Linen was their life: family survival strategies and parent-child relations in nineteenth-century France. *In* H. Medick and D.W. Sabean, eds. Interest and Emotion: Essays on the Study of Family and Kinship. Cambridge: Cambridge University Press.

Tits-Dieuaide, M.J.
1980   L'évolution des techniques agricoles en Flandre et en Brabant du XIVe au XVIe siècle. Annales E.S.C. 35:362–81.

Trotman, S.R. and E.R. Trotman
1948   The Bleaching, Dyeing, and Chemical Technology of Textile Fibers. London: Charles Griffin.

Warden, Alex J.
 1864   The Linen Trade, Ancient and Modern. London: Longman, Rob-
          erts and Green.

Primary Documents from the Seligman Collection, Columbia University Libraries

Anon. 1700. A Letter from a Merchant in Scotland to his Correspondent in London Relating to the Duty upon Scotch-Linnen. Printer unnamed. (L569)

Anon. 1729. A Scheme for Supplying Industrious Men with Money to Carry on their Trades, and for better Providing for the Poor of Ireland. 2nd edition. Dublin: Printed by Thomas Hume, opposite Essex Bridge. (B513)

Anon. 1734. A Letter to the Author of the Interest of Scotland Considered; Containing some Hints about the Linnen Manufactures. Edinburgh: Printed for Gavin Hamilton by R. Flemming. (L564)

Anon. 1735. Some Considerations on the Improvement of the Linen Manufacture in Ireland, particularly with Relation to the Raising and Dressing of Flax and Flax-Seed. Dublin: Printed by R. Reilly on Cork Hill. (R73)

Anon. 1739. Some Thoughts on the Importance of the Linnen-Manufacture to Ireland and How to Lessen the Expense of it. Dublin: Printed by and for George Faulkner. (S052)

Anon. 1740. The Rules to be Observed by the Flax-Raisers appointed by the Trustees for the Manufactures, and by all others who Apply to Them for a Premium for Raising Lint, etc. No publisher. (R86)

Anon. 1753 (orig. 1738). A Letter from a Merchant Who has left the Trade, to a Member of Parliament, in which The Case of the British and Irish Manufacture of Linen, Thread, and Tapes is fairly stated; and all the Objections against the Encouragement proposed to be given to that Manufacture fully answered. London. (B512)

Anon. 1762. A Review of the Evils that have Prevailed in the Linen Manufacture of Ireland. Dublin: Printed for Peter Wilson.

Anon. 1778. A Linen Draper's Letter to the Friends of Ireland. Dublin: no printer named. (L64)

Acres, Joseph, 1715. The Linen Manufacture. A Sermon Preach'd at Blewbury Sept. 19, 1715. Being the Day appointed for an Anniversary Sermon, upon the Account of the Large Charity given to the Poor of that Village, by William Malthus, late Citizen and Merchant of London. London: Printed for J. Baker in Pater-Noster-Row. (AC76)

Bailey, William. 1758. A Treatise on the Better Employment and More Comfortable Support of the Poor in Workhouses, Together with some Observations on the Growth and Culture of Flax with diverse new Inventions, neatly engraved on copper, for the Improvement of the Linen Manufacture of which the Importance and Advantages are Considered and Evinced. London: Printed for and Sold by the Author at the Corner of Castle Cort in the Strand. (B15)

Cox, Sir Richard. Bart., 1749. A Letter to Thomas Prior, Esq. Shewing, from Experience, a Sure Method to Establish the Linen-Manufacture, and the Beneficial Effects, it will immediately produce. Dublin: Printed for Peter Wilson. (C839)

Crommelin, Louis, Overseer of the Royal Linnen-Manufacture. 1734 (Orig. 1705). An Essay Towards the Improving of the Hempen and Flaxen Manufactures in the Kingdom of Ireland. Dublin: Reprinted for R. Owen, Bookseller in Skinner Row. (C88)

Distaff, Jenny. 1720. The Linen Spinster, in defense of the Linen Manufactures No. One. London: Printed for F. Roberts at the Oxford Arms in Warrwick Lane.

Haines, R. 1677. Proposals for Building in every County a Working-Alms-House or Hospital; as the Best Expedient to perfect the Trade and Manufactory of Linnen Cloth. London: Printed by W.G. for R. Harford. (H127)

Hill, Samuel Esq. 1817. A Plan for Reducing the Poor's Rate by Giving Permanent Employment to the Labouring Classes with Some Observations on the Cultivation of Flax and Hemp and an Account of a new process for dressing and preparing flax and Hemp without water-steeping and dew-retting. London: printed for J. Harding, St. James Street. (H55)

Hyndman, C. 1774. A new method of Raising Flax; by which it is Proved that Ireland may raise annually many Thousand Pounds Worth more Flax than the usual Quantity of Land, and from one Fourth less seed than by the Common Method. With Tables, Shewing what Quantity of Seed will sow any Lot of Ground. The whole Containing Many useful and Curious Remarks on that Valuable Plant, never before made Publick. Belfast: Printed by James Magee for the Author. (H99)

Laing, Alexander. 1872. Lecture on the History of the Linen Manufacture in Newburgh (Fife). Newburgh on Tay: James Wood.

Lindesay, Patrick. 1735. Reasons for Encouraging the Linnen Manufacture of Scotland and other parts of Great Britain. Humbly submitted to Parliament. London: Printed for John Peele. (L64)

Lindesay, Patrick 1736. The Interest of Scotland Considered with Regard to its Policy in Employing of the Poor, its Agriculture, its Trade, its Manufactures, and Fisheries. London: Printed for T. Woodward and J. Peele. (L645)

Merchant, C.S. 1760. Information to the People of Ireland Concerning the Linen Trade of Spain, Portugal and the Spanish West Indies. Dublin: Printed for Richard Watts. (In3)

7. Spun Virtue, the Lacework of Folly, and the World Wound Upside-Down

Seventeenth-Century Dutch Depictions of Female Handwork

LINDA STONE-FERRIER

Pictures of everyday scenes from seventeenth-century Holland—the Golden Age of Dutch art—have often been interpreted as superficial reflections of daily life. In actuality, such scenes were not just casual depictions; they embodied traditional attitudes towards societal roles. Moreover, popular attitudes towards certain important roles were not reflected in artistic imagery because no appropriate pictorial conventions existed. Brewers, for example, were highly admired in the seventeenth century, particularly in Haarlem, where brewing represented the most important industry and was praised in city histories. The success of brewing, however, did not inspire images of the brewer at work because there was no pictorial precedent for such a depiction. Conversely, certain earlier conventions, such as depictions of religious figures, were untapped by most Dutch seventeenth-century artists because of the contemporary prohibition against iconic religious imagery.

The numerous seventeenth-century Dutch paintings and prints

of spinners and winders differ from other scenes of daily life. They represent one popular subject in the history of art that not only retained its favor in Holland, but also appeared in newly conceived pictorial contexts. As in earlier imagery, the traditionally female occupations of spinning and winding were shown in many paintings and prints of domestic interiors, exemplifying the roles for ladies that were recommended in contemporary treatises and handbooks. When these traditionally female activities were shown performed by men, spinning and winding represented a symptom of the world-turned-upside-down—the folly resulting from women gaining the upper hand in their domestic domain.

These time-honored scenes of virtuous females and foolish males, spinning in domestic interiors, expanded in the mid-seventeenth century to include unprecedented paintings by Haarlem artists of female winders in the traditionally male milieu of professional weavers. The depictions of female and male spinners and winders in domestic interiors had their roots in literary sources—either moralizing or satirical. But the paintings of female winders in weavers' workshops reflected the extraordinary economic success and international fame enjoyed by seventeenth-century linen producers in Haarlem. The traditionally popular image of the virtuous female spinner or winder in a domestic interior provided the pictorial vocabulary for a new context; the positive associations of this female activity were transferred to the male professional arena.

EXEMPLARY FEMALE SPINNERS AND WINDERS

The view of spinning and winding as appropriate women's work had been accepted in many cultures for countless generations. The terms "distaff side," meaning the female side of a family, "spinster" and *Spindelseite* all derive from the traditionally female occupation of spinning (Ciba Review 28:983).

Sixteenth- and seventeenth-century Dutch paintings of female spinners and winders showed them consistently in their traditionally virtuous roles. Innumerable examples abound, both in portraits and in images of anonymous women in domestic interiors. To show a woman spinning in a portrait was to illustrate her moral character rather than her profession (Bruyn 1955:31). Maerten van Heemskerck's portrait of Anna Codde from 1529 is only one example of many (Amsterdam, Rijksmuseum). The spinning performed by the sitter does not allude to her family's profession, wine marketing, nor to her husband's profession, brewing (Bruyn 1955:27). Instead, the spinning image gives the viewer vital information regarding Anna Codde's character.[1]

Paintings and prints of anonymous spinners in domestic settings outnumber even the spinners in portraits. The sheer numbers testify to the popularity of the image. The depicted spinners were young and old, rich and poor, and rendered in both paint and prints throughout the seventeenth century by many Dutch artists. Quirijn Brekelenkam's "The Bible Lecture" (Private Collection) and Esaias Bourse's "Woman at a Spinning Wheel" (Amsterdam, Rijksmuseum:1661) capture the warmth of the Dutch home in two paintings of the female spinner. Other examples focus on the spinner or winder, using various pictorial devices: Brekelenkam framed a winder in a niche in one painting (Private Collection, Frederik Muller), and spotlit her with streaming light beside an open door in another (London, Alfred Brod Gallery). In two paintings of old women spinning (Amsterdam, Rijksmuseum), Nicholas Maes combined deep shadows with an unidentifiable light source, which embraced the spinners and imparted a warm, homey ambience to the images. Gerard Ter Borch painted his sister as a well-to-do spinner elegantly dressed in a fur-trimmed satin jacket (Rotterdam, Museum Boymans-van Beuningen) (Figure 17). In an early seventeenth-century pen drawing, Jacob de Gheyn captured the old spinner carefully adjusting the thread on the wheel's spindle (Private Collection, G. Bainbridge). In a 1667 painting by J. Toorenvliet, the elderly spinner studiously examines the flax being spun (Karlsruhe, Gemälde-galerie). Still another celebration of the spinner appears in a mid-seventeenth century print series of female virtues by Geertruydt Roghman (Atlas van Stolk #1031).

What these images of spinning women have in common is a decisively domestic level of production. There is no suggestion that the spinners are part of a textile production team; that would have been indicated by several accompanying weavers or spinners. The spinners' production is actually limited by their status as housewives. Such assumptions concerning their behavior and activities were voiced in sixteenth- and seventeenth-century books written for women by men. Several different treatises existed, but invariably

*Figure 17. "Spinner," painted by Gerard Ter Borch, shows
the artist's sister performing what was considered to be a
virtuous woman's work. Museum Boymans-van Beuningen,
Stichting Willem van der Worm: Rotterdam*

four topics were discussed: the war of the sexes; the training and
duties of a wife; love and beauty; and the court (Kelso 1956:2). The
advice applied to all women, regardless of rank.

In these treatises, the only occupation recommended to the
female readers was that of housewifery (Kelso 1956:4), and their
appropriate tasks or arts were needlework, spinning, and weaving (Kelso 1956:46).[2] The purpose of such tasks was to fill a lady's
leisure hours in order to preserve her virtue (Kelso 1956:45).
Needlework, spinning, and weaving were appropriate ways in
which women could "reveal their own sharp and pregnant wit"

which required "great knowledge, pains and skill," a sixteenth-
century Englishman wrote, whereas men showed their wit by
strenuous toil.[3]

In a similar book by Vives, the author defended sewing, cooking, weaving, and spinning from attacks by those who regarded
them as base exercises performed only because of poverty. To Vives,
those with the latter opinion were merely ignorant. Noble and rich
women had to busy themselves in this way so as to fill their hours
profitably (Kelso 1956:46).

In still another book on the subject, Torquato Tasso added that
a highborn lady should occasionally perform domestic tasks, although not in the kitchen, where she might soil her clothes. The
spinning wheel and loom were the appropriate tools of the noble
matron (Kelso 1956:112). Such industriousness was, according to
one Englishman, a source of national pride:

> The labours that be both decent and profitable for gentlewomen
> are these, most meete in my minde, and also in daylye use with
> many, as spinning of Wooll on the greate compasse Wheele, and
> on the rocke or distaffe, wherewith I would not that any should
> be so daintee, as to be offended thereat but rather commende
> and use them as an ornament, and benefit of god bestowed
> upon oure flourishing countrey, surpassing all our princely
> neyghbours.[4]

The popular association between spinning and women had ancient
roots. The most renowned female spinners included Lachesis, one
of the Three Fates who spun the thread of life, subsequently cut by
another Fate (Hall 1974:288); the Virgin, spinner of the thread of life;
and the mythological Minerva and Arachne.[5] Numerous images of
these famous spinners preceded the seventeenth-century Dutch
paintings. Sixteenth-century prints of the Three Fates, such as
Hans Baldung's 1513 engraving (Hollstein 1954,II:138) and Joris
Hoefnagel's 1589 engraving (Vignau-Schuurmän 1969,II:Fig.128),
exemplify the popularity of the mythological imagery, which came
to symbolize *memento mori*, the fleeting quality of life. An emblem from Jani Jacobi Boissardi's 1593 *Emblemata, Auss dem Latein verteutscht* (Frankfurt) shows four women, one of whom spins while
another cuts the thread. A grinning skeleton carrying an hourglass
watches a third woman as she inscribes on a slab, "*sola virtus est
funeris expers*" (Valor alone is spared the grave). The image clearly

stems from the story of Lachesis and the Fates (Boissardi 1593:95).

Seventeenth-century emblematic images that symbolize *memento mori* demonstrate the enduring strength of the original associations with Lachesis and the Three Fates.[6] An emblem in Andreas Friedrichen's 1617 *Emblemata Nova* (Frankfurt) shows a woman spinning with an hourglass resting on her head. A skeleton, also holding an hourglass, advances toward her in what appears to be an attempt to cut the spun thread. Above them is written, *"Das Leben hangt an ein Faden"* (Life hangs on a thread) (Friedrichen 1617:165). On the title page of Hieremias Drexelius' *Nuntius Mortus, Aeternitatis Prodromus Mortis Nuntius Quem Sanis Aegrotis Moribundus*, 1629, a woman spins on the left, facing a skeleton on the right. A large hourglass separates them.

The specific association between spinning and *virtuous* women, seen in seventeenth-century Dutch paintings and recommended in contemporary handbooks, stemmed originally from the image of the Virgin as the spinner of the thread of life.[7] As the model of female virtue, the spinning Virgin traditionally represented the paradigm for the religious woman's emulation, as in Jacob de Gheyn's 1593 engraving (Amsterdam, Prentenkabinet, Holls. 32g II/Pass. 200:II). St. Elisabeth was similarly depicted spinning by Hans Baldung in the sixteenth century (Hollstein 1954,II:125). Spinning as a metaphor for domestic industriousness was also explicitly set forth in the Bible; Proverbs 31:10–13, 19, and 24:

> Who can find a capable wife?
> Her worth is far beyond coral.
> Her husband's whole trust is in her,
> and children are not lacking.
> She repays him with food, not evil,
> all her life long.
> She chooses wool and flax
> and toils at her work . . . .
> She holds the distaff in her hand,
> and her fingers grasp the spindle . . . .
> She weaves linen and sells it,
> and supplies merchants with their sashes.
> (*New English Bible 1971*).

In the seventeenth century, the biblical image of the virtuous female spinner was adopted in Johannes de Brune's 1624 *Emblemata of Zinnewerck, voorghestelt in Beelden, ghedicten* (Amsterdam) in which a woman spins while her husband carves by their hearth. The association with the Virgin's traditional role is reinforced here by the fact that Joseph was a carpenter. An inscription accompanies the image:

> What rest and profit give little loss. How exquisite is it for God, how sweet for us to behold it! That man and woman together maintain themselves from her handwork, and by watching over by the Lord. Now what the world gives, much unrest, good and honor, but with a cheerful heart, based on rocky ground from God's truth and oath, and on her duty bound. Of the heavens rest and desire, trusting that the man, who seeks God's kingdom, never can be lacking (De Brune 1624:318).[8]

An emblem in *Emblemata Selectiora* (Amsterdam 1704) continues the visual tradition of the virtuous female spinner who follows the Virgin's example. A well-dressed young woman spins on a wheel before a hearth, with a dog and a cat resting at her feet. Beneath is written: "Domesticity is women's crown jewel, such a crown to ornament a woman as dutifully running the peaceful house" (Anonymous 1704:4).[9]

On the evidence presented so far, the image of the clearly virtuous female spinner or winder in seventeenth-century Dutch paintings appears to reflect both the contemporary treatises and handbooks for women, and the pictorial precedents in which the female spinner represented the Virgin's virtue. Although there were negative literary and pictorial contexts associated with the spinner, apparently these did not affect the seventeenth-century *painted* view of her. The negative views of women spinning and winding appeared only in prints. In contrast, both prints and paintings showed both virtuous and lascivious embroiderers and lacemakers, despite their literary and pictorial associations with spinners and winders.

FEMALE HANDWORK AS AN EROTIC METAPHOR

What negative didactic contexts were associated with traditionally female tasks in the production of textiles? Seventeenth-century

Dutch emblems of spinning, embroidering, and lacemaking presented erotic visual plays, based on popular Dutch metaphors for
copulation derived from the motion of the textile professions' tools.[10]
Such erotic images clashed with the ideal of the sober industriousness of Dutch society. In the emblem book *Nova Poemata ante hac
nunquam* (Leiden 1624), a young woman is shown spinning while
she gazes out a window. The accompanying inscription presents a
licentious double meaning for the woman's relationship to the
spindle:

> I am stretched long, white—so you see—and fragile. At the up-
> permost am I the head, slightly big. My mistress wishes me
> steady, often has me in her lap; or instead, she lays me nearby
> her side. She holds me many times—yes, daily, may I say, with
> her hands. She pulls her knees up, and in a rough place, now
> she sticks my top. Now she pulls it out again. Now she goes to
> place it again (Anonymous 1972 (1624):71).[11]

In another emblem book, *Nederduytsche Poemata* (Leiden 1621), under
the section *Het Ambacht van Cupido* (The Occupation of Cupid), a
cupid spins before an elegantly dressed young woman (Heinsius
1621:3). Therefore, spinning could be one of love's occupations.

Similarly, three other emblems depict the correspondence between lovemaking and needlework and embroidery. An example by
Jacob Cats in *Sinn-en-Minne-Beelden en Emblemata Amores Morelqüe
Spectantia* (Amsterdam 1622) presents an explicit reference to lovemaking. A young, well-dressed woman sews in the company of her
well-dressed suitor. The inscription beneath the image reads, "I
spoke last with my love, while she sat and sewed. I placed her before my grief; hear, yet, how she captured me. Watch what I am
doing, she spoke, notice how it all goes. First, the needle makes a
hole that is filled with the thread . . ." (Cats 1622:171).[12]

Another emblem by Jacob Cats from the same emblem book depicts a fashionably dressed young woman embroidering while a
cupid sits watching her. Again the inscription presents an explicit
lovemaking analogy: ". . . Your needle bores a hole; your thread
makes the stitch. Love, treat me in the same way; keep all the same
strokes. You know I am wounded by your sweet mouth. Go on, heal
the pain there where you gave me the wound" (Cats 1622:54–55).[13]
The association was still strong by the end of the seventeenth
century, as reflected in an emblem from Willem den Elger's *Zinne-*

Beelden der Liefde (Elger 1703:149). Here a cupid actually assists the young woman in her embroidering.

The erotic associations of the female spinner in prints, as well as the virtuous image of her in paintings, were shared by embroiderers and lacemakers, although the latter two were depicted positively and negatively in both media. Mid-seventeenth-century paintings of lacemakers and embroiderers by Jan Vermeer (Paris, Louvre), Nicolaes Maes (Vienna, Liechtensteingalerie; London, National Gallery of Art) and Gabriel Metsu (Vienna, Gemäldegalerie) picture the female worker as a figure of domestic industriousness, similar to the spinner in paintings. Nothing intrudes on the virtuous ambience in these examples.

Just as common, however, were painted images of embroiderers and lacemakers that reflect the erotic love play seen in emblematic prints. Seated working women are interrupted by courting men, who woo them with varying degrees of explicit behavior. In a mid-seventeenth-century painting by Jan Steen, a young, cloaked suitor bows slightly and doffs his hat to a woman who sews in her bedroom (Private collection, Stephenson Clark). In a painting by Quirijn Brekelenkam, the young caller advances towards the embroiderer, his cloak over one arm, and he gestures with the other (Hamburg, Kunsthalle). In a second example by Brekelenkam, the cloaked and hatted suitor reads to the young lacemaker, possibly from a love-song book (Amsterdam, Rijksmuseum). A lacemaker depicted by Gabriel Metsu is closely watched by her suitor who leans over her table, a wine glass in his hand (Dresden, Gemäldegalerie). In another painting by Jan Steen, a cocky caller is seated with a woman sewing (Private English collection). His legs are flung apart; one fist is planted on his knee and there is a leer on his face. In two of these paintings, the figures are drinking—an activity less conducive to lace production than to lovemaking. In three of these paintings, the young woman has discarded one of her shoes, which sits prominently in the foreground. Clearly this is an allusion to her abandonment and vulnerability in her suitor's presence. [14]

The consistent portrayal of virtuous women spinning and winding stands in contrast to the ambivalent portrayals of female embroiderers and lacemakers. The female spinner or winder may have been consistently depicted as virtuous in paintings—a medium more expensive and more seriously regarded than prints—because spinning and winding constituted the vital steps of clothmaking.

Embroiderers and lacemakers, who were depicted in both virtuous and lascivious contexts, produced ornamentation that was valued by many but was considered a superfluous and condemnable luxury by others.

Various moralizing sermons, tracts, and emblems from the seventeenth century express the criticism that such ornamentation and fancy apparel often received. Such elegantly made clothing was associated with prodigality, lasciviousness, vanity, foolishness, and *memento mori*. In Johannes Stalpaert's *Vrouwelick cieraet van Sint Agnes versmaedt* of 1622, and J. de Decker's *Lof der Geldsucht*, c. 1640, all female ornamentation was condemned. In the former tract, St. Agnes was held to be a model of sober dress (Van der Heijden 1966:9). An emblem in Iohannem à Nyenborg's 1660 emblem book, *Variarum Lectionum Selecta Figuris aeneis applicata* (Groningen), shows female clothing piled atop a pedestal in a niche decorated with garlands, heraldry, accouterments of civilization, and a mirror. Beneath the image is inscribed, "*de usu & abusu vestium, & de superbia*" (The use and abuse of clothing, and vanity) (Nyenborg 1660:79). The layering of this pile of clothing clearly recreates its relationship with the wearer. The skirt on the bottom spills over the pedestal's edge; the bodice with its stiff sleeves extends outward; the wide ruff and the lacy, spiked cap are perched upright. The assembled clothing symbolizes the superficiality of such fashion in the way the outfit has collapsed. Finally, the noticeably faceless cap further underlines both a literal and figurative lack of character in the potential wearer.

The specific relationship between fine apparel, ornamentation such as lace or embroidery, and lasciviousness was also recognized and proclaimed by sixteenth- and seventeenth-century moralists. Vives, in his advice to ladies, insisted the clothes should be woven of clean, coarse wool or linen, unadorned with jewels. They should be worn without perfume in order to maintain one's humility. Rich dress served only to attract men, which endangered a lady's chastity (Kelso 1956:47).

The earliest pictorial association between elegant dress and love play occurred in moralizing satirical prints, and also in various engraved and painted five-part series on the senses. In a sixteenth-century Dutch print satirizing fashionable attire, a lady hides her lover under her skirt, while two other women and a man hit her skirts in an attempt to reveal the lover.[15] Thus, the indulgence associated with fashionable dress encompasses lovemaking literally and metaphorically. Similarly, moralizing pictorial series of the senses often showed elegantly dressed young couples in various amorous occupations. The popularity of such associations between dress and lovemaking in seventeenth-century paintings became widespread. Thus, the popular metaphors comparing the movement of tools used in lacemaking and embroidery to copulation were joined by similar associations between lace or embroidery and their alluring appeal to the opposite sex.

THE MALE SPINNER AND WINDER: THE TOPSY-TURVY WORLD

The consistently positive *painted* image of the female spinner or winder, which contrasts with the painted image of the embroiderer and lacemaker, can be regarded in yet another context. Whereas there were not depictions of male lacemakers or embroiderers, male spinners and winders represented the predominant negative image of those activities. Foisting men into the female role of spinning or winding was a function of *omnia vincit amor* (love conquers all), or a reversal of roles referred to as "women-on-top."[16]

Seventeenth-century emblems show that such role reversals were the ancient fate of Hercules and Sardanapalus. In the 1601 *Emblemata Moralia* (Horozcii 1601:Plate 43), the 1612 *Minerva Britanna*, and the 1653 *Devises et Emblesmes d'Amour Moralisez* (Flamen 1653:37). Hercules spins in response to the whims of his love, Omphale. The inscription beneath the 1612 emblem informs the reader of Hercules' folly:

> Alicides heere, hath thrown his Clubbe away,
> And weares a Mantle, for his Lions skinne
> Thus better liking for to passe the day,
> With *Omphale*, and with her maids to spinne,
> To card, to reele, and doe such daily taske
> What ere it pleased, *Omphale* to aske.
>
> That all his conquests woune him not such Fame,
> For which as God, the world did him adore,

As loves affection, did disgrace and shame,
His virtues partes. How many are there more,
Who having Honor, and a worthy name,
By actions base, and lewdness loose the fame.
(Peacham 1973 (1612):95).

Similarly, King Sardanapalus was undone by love. His spinning testifies to his weakness in the face of womanly wiles, as depicted in emblems by Ian Moerman in *De Cleyn Werelt: Daer in claerlijcken door seer schoone Poetische, Moralische en Historische exempelen betoont wort* (Amsterdam 1608), L. Haechtanus in *Paruus Mundus* (Frankfurt 1618), and Henricum Oraem Assenheim in *Viridarium Hieroglyphico-Morale* (Frankfurt 1619). The inscription beneath the 1608 emblem reads, "Here sits the king of the Assyrians, whom he has forsaken by spinning out of love" (Moerman 1608:27).[17]

This demeaning image of the spinning leader doubtless inspired the early seventeenth-century German and Netherlandish political broadsheets that satirized the Spanish invading general, Ambrosio Spínola, during the Eighty Years' War. The first depiction of Spínola in a political broadsheet was, in fact, praiseworthy, as the accompanying text makes clear. A 1607 German sheet celebrated his victories against the Dutch by depicting him spinning the weapons from his distaff. The image of spinning was a visual pun on his name, Spínola. His assistant to the right grabs Time or Fortune by the hair. The political uneasiness of the Dutch leader, Maurice of Nassau, is represented by the thorns piercing his soles (Coupe 1966–67:156).

By 1620, the spinning Spínola had acquired pejorative connotations. In the German political print entitled *"Spanische Spinnstuben oder Rockenfahrt,"* the Pope blesses the Jesuits as they card flax from which Spínola spins weapons. Three *"dapffer Deutsche Knecht"* (brave German youths) on the left gather the spun swords and arrows in order to tangle Spínola's murderous thread (Coupe 1966–67:156).

The German engraving was apparently influenced by a similar 1617 Dutch broadsheet satirizing spinning Jesuits, *"Een arge verward Maienschel ende quaet Gespin der Iesuwijt"* (A very confused man and evil spinning Jesuit) (Coupe 1966–67:156) (Figure 18). Good Intention, seated on the left, spins from a distaff with flax prepared by

Figure 18. This 1617 Dutch political broadsheet, "Spinning Jesuits," satirizes Jesuits by showing them in the negative, reversed role of male spinners. Stichting Atlas van Stolk: Rotterdam, no. 1325

a devil on the far right. Another small devil tangles the yarn spun by Good Intention. Lady Discord oversees the sabotage. Across the bottom of the image a spider creeps, wearing a cardinal's hat which is connected by the spider's spun thread to the pile of twisted yarn. Against the back wall, a caricature of Spínola is stuffed into a hunting horn (a member of the Stichting Atlas van Stolk staff in Rotterdam pointed this out to me). Fighting troops can be seen through the open window.

The depiction of a common man spinning also represented a slanderous image of male subservience to women. In P. Adrianus Poirters' emblem book, *Het Masker Van de Wereldt* (Antwerp 1588), a woman beats a man above an image (by Pieter Quast) of a woman spinning and a man winding, with a devil between them. Beneath the image is an inscription that reads, *"Quaet Huysgesin, Duyvels gespin"* (Devils spin in an evil household) (Poirters 1588: 333).[18]

A later version of the same threesome appears in a copy by Salomon Savery (1594–1664?), part of a series entitled *Siet 't verwarde gaernes* (This is how things turn out when the threads of life are tangled). The seated woman now has snakes in her hair as she spins, beneath the label "*Bedroch*" (Deceit). A devil, labelled "*Quaet Ingeven*" (Suggest Evil), holds the spun thread to her left. To the devil's left, a man with a codpiece winds the yarn. Above him is written, "*Geveldt d' uijt wercker*" (Overpower the one who does the work). The winder has been undone by his own folly, presumably love.

Significantly, such demonic imagery associated with spinning or winding commented on a social order rather than on the real Dutch textile industry. Jane Schneider has shown (Chapter 6, this volume) that elsewhere in early modern Europe, competition and tension between the rural textile industry and the agricultural sector contributed to the demonization of folkloric figures. Two pieces of evidence suggest that similar tensions did not exist in seventeenth-century Holland. First, the linen industry—specifically, bleaching outside Haarlem—depended on the dairy industry for buttermilk, a discard product, that was the secret of the *Haarlemmer bleek* (Haarlem bleach) (Van Ysselsteyn 1946:27), introduced to the Dutch by the Flemish émigrés in the late sixteenth century (Horner 1920:348–50; Van Ysselsteyn 1946:327). Most of the polder lands served for dairy-cattle grazing beyond the Haarlem dunes where the linen was bleached. The great satisfaction and pride taken in both the bleaching and the dairying industries are manifested in two groups of paintings that enjoyed great popularity at mid-century: The landscape views of the linen-bleaching fields outside of Haarlem and neighboring communities by Jacob van Ruisdael and his followers,[19] and the monumental paintings of cows, most notably by Paulus Potter and Aelbert Cuyp.

The second piece of evidence that the textile industry and the agricultural sector were in harmony in Holland, even though they were a threat to each other elsewhere in Europe, is the notable absence of witch hunts and trials in the seventeenth-century Netherlands. Among the European nations, the Dutch were the first to ban the execution of witches. The last witch burning occurred in 1595 in Utrecht. In 1610, the last recorded witch trial in the United Provinces took place; it ended in acquittal (Huizinga 1941:59). This is precisely when an enormous influx of Flemish émigrés to Haarlem brought with them the secrets of the full-milk or buttermilk bleaching, which led to the subsequent success and fame of the linen-production industry.

SPINNING ROOMS AND "WOMEN-ON-TOP"

In addition to the pictures of spinning or winding men surrounded by demonic figures, the common male winder was depicted in the specific context of the spinning room. The *Rockenstube* or spinning room, was an important center for yarn production in German villages from the late fifteenth through the seventeenth centuries. It was economically advantageous for women to spin in one room because it saved on light and heat (Coupe 1966–67:155). Although the spinning room was intended to be a working place for women only, it evolved into a center for village social life when men began to join the women after working hours (*Ciba Review* 28:1012–13). The festive racousness and sexual promiscuity that often ensued cast the spinning rooms into ill repute. In the seventeenth century, such spinning rooms did not play the same role in the production of textiles in the Netherlands as they did in Germany. The production of linen in Haarlem, for example, depended upon the import of spun flax from Silesia (Horner 1920:353). Thus, depictions of spinning rooms by Dutch artists may have been based more on German pictorial precedents than on real Dutch spinning rooms.

Sixteenth- and seventeenth-century Dutch artists gave spinning-room festivities a particular emphasis. The raucousness of the revelry and sexual promiscuity were well presented; the artists captured the turbulence of a world-turned-upside-down. The women clearly held the upper hand—after all, the spinning room was their domain—and the men were kept winding or spinning.

When discussing such images, art historians have traditionally focused on the disorder of this world in which women dominate. It has been shown that such domestic chaos was a popular comic mode in the Netherlands and the rest of Europe, in literary farces, poems, proverbs, and prints. Besides spinning, a submissive man was also forced to kiss his mistress' thumb and kneel before her; he had furniture thrown at him, and faced the ignominy of the woman literally donning the trousers (Gibson 1978:677–78). Almost invaria-

Figure 19. In Barthel Beham's 1524 woodcut "The Spinning Room," sexual promiscuity and disorder are rampant in the topsy-turvy world where women have the upper hand. Graphischen Sammlung "Albertina": Vienna

bly, these diverse humiliations and comic variations of the "women-on-top" took place in spinning rooms, those female strongholds that were alien territory to men.

Various examples suggest this theme's popularity. Barthel Beham's woodcut of a spinning room (1542) highlights the sexual promiscuity (Figure 19). The scene is littered with spinning paraphernalia, and couples cavort in various sexual positions (Hollstein 1954:2,245).[20]

In the later sixteenth-century anonymous engraving of a spinning room printed by Boscher, the emphasis shifts to the power of women in their own domain.[21] A female spinner in the left background waves a banner embellished with the picture of a hand and the words, *D'Overhant* (the upper hand), while her sister spinners lambaste the male intruders into submission. In the foreground two men beg for mercy, while another male resentfully winds thread in the left background. Tools of the spinning trade are strewn over the floor.

The early-seventeenth-century painting of the spinning room by Pieter de Bloot (RKD) follows in the tradition of the Boscher engraving. A female spinner carries a banner decorated with pictures of a hand, a winder, a spindle, and the words, *Voer 'Hant* (the upper hand). Spinners on the left thrash a male intruder's bottom. In the middle a male holding a winder is beaten, while on the right a female offers a kneeling, supplicant male something to eat, as though giving communion to a repentant sinner.

In a mid-seventeenth-century painting by Jacob van Loo, the imagery of the spinning room assumed a morally tempered ambiguity (Leningrad: Hermitage). In the background, two couples engage in the traditional spinning-room love play. Musical instruments and a wine glass are near at hand. In the foreground, an elderly spinner at her spinning wheel offers a contrast to the frivolity. Bent forward, her hand held at her lips and her brow furrowed, she looks directly at the viewer, obviously concerned about the activity behind her. The virtuous image of the female spinner, as found in portraiture and genre scenes, is contrasted with the promiscuity of the two background couples. Because of this juxtaposition, the subdued love play in the background appears more erotically provocative than the comic spinning room scenes with their explicit and unrestrained display of sexual escapades.

In J. Toorenvliet's painting of a spinning room from the mid-seventeenth century, the tradition of sexual promiscuity and female dominance is expressed less forcefully (RKD). In the background, a female spinner bends over a male who looks up at her fondly. In the foreground, a second female spinner stands beside a seated, pipe-smoking male visitor who has laid his satchel at his feet. Smiling, the foreground female spinner holds a distaff in one hand while offering the spindle to the man with her other hand. He leans on the table top, clearly less interested in the spindle than in what the offering of the spindle suggests. The love play of this spinning-room scene is mild in comparison with our previous examples, and it lacks the titillation seen in the Jacob van Loo painting.

Perhaps the image of "women-on-top" lacks force in the Toorenvliet painting because mid-seventeenth-century Dutch spinning rooms were not meeting places of the sexes. By that time they had become houses of correction for female harlots, drunks, and other offenders of social propriety (Amsterdam, Amsterdams Historisch Museum 1972:20; Haley 1972:159).[22] The degree to which the Dutch spinning house came to be regarded as a center for exemplary behavior and productivity by the end of the seventeenth century is demonstrated by prints of working women in C. Arnold's *Waare Afbeelding der Eerste Christenen* (Amsterdam 1701); by P. Fouquet, Jr.'s, *"Het vrouwen Tuchthuys of Spinhuys van Binne, tot Amsterdam"* (Amsterdam Atlas); and by Feullantines' *"t' Spinn-huis, La Maison des Feullantines."*[23] A portrait by Bartholomeus van der Helst of the Amsterdam Spinhuis regentesses (Amsterdams Historisch Museum) includes elegant, engraved, ceremonial glassware—evidence of the institutional respectability the Dutch spinning house had acquired by the end of the century.

A NEW PICTORIAL CONTEXT FOR THE FEMALE WINDER

When women who wound entered the textile domain that was traditionally male—the weaving workshop—they were not depicted as fools, unlike the men who entered the traditional domain of the woman, the spinning room. Women remained respectable because winding and spinning were traditionally female tasks, regardless of the milieu.

In an unprecedented group of paintings, produced around the mid-seventeenth century only by Haarlem artists, women are depicted winding in the company of male weavers who work at large looms. Twenty-five examples of these paintings are represented by photographs in the Rijksbureau voor Kunsthistorische Documentatie in the Hague, which suggests that a much larger number of such paintings were on the market in the seventeenth century.[24]

These Haarlem scenes depict a weaver's cottage. The walls of the workplace are wood-beamed; the floor is strewn with straw, tools of the weaving profession, and household utensils: a broom, a pump, a bucket, a basket, a barrel. Light entering from a window illuminates the weaver's prominent loom. Paintings by J.D. Oudenrooge (RKD) and Cornelis Beelt (The Hague, Haags Gemeentemuseum) show the weaver at his loom in the company of female workers. A 1653 example from a group of paintings by Cornelis Decker depicts a male weaver who is working at his loom accompanied by a woman who sews in front of her winder (The Hague, Dienst Verspreide Rijkscollecties).

These mid-century paintings of female winders and male weavers in a workshop have no pictorial precedents. A market for these paintings appears to have been inspired by the extraordinary success of the Haarlem linen industry, a success which was celebrated in seventeenth-century poems and histories of the city. To satisfy the market's demand for visual celebrations of the linen industry's success, the traditional view of the domestic spinner or winder was transformed into a new pictorial context, in which the female artisan retained her traditional virtuous associations.

The public's high regard for both the Haarlem linen workers and the product of their labors is reflected as early as 1588 in Hadrianus Junius' *Batavia*. Junius praised the whiteness and fineness of Haarlem linen (Six 1913:87).[25] In 1596, Karel van Mander celebrated *'t Hollants lijnwaet de werelt door bekent* (Holland's world-famous linen goods) (Van der Loeff 1911). In *Des Crizione de Tutti i Paesi Bassi* 1567 (published in 1612 as *Beschrijvinge van alle de Nederlanden*, that is, *Description of all the Netherlands*), Guicciardini described Haarlem linen as ". . . having been woven very well for a long time . . . so that the city appears to have returned to its former bloom" (Guicciardini 1612 (orginally 1567):201).[26]

By 1621, the praise of Haarlem's linen production had escalated to a new level. In Samuel Ampzing's *Het Lof der Stadt Haerlem in Hollandt* (In praise of the city of Haarlem in Holland) (Haarlem 1621), we find the following passage:

> Due to our citizens' art and spirit, she (Haarlem) holds up her
> head, and with her name and fame bursts through the heavens,
> by which our city and citizen are known, as far on the globe as
> he has sent his arts. Has he no good things? So good is he in
> this art, excellently skilled! It is a wonder what amount and vari-
> ety of very artful works he prepares on his loom. His linen re-
> flects a lot of light even as it competes in its perfection with
> silk's delicacy. The rest is so artistically colored with patterns it
> is unpredictable what his spool is able to create. So
> Tradesmanship, here, was also pursued with fervor, and most of
> them there have weaving as their main concern; from thread,
> and from flax, and all linen goods, by which the trade of our city
> exists (Cited in Van Ysselsteyn 1946:31).[27]

In a second version from 1628, *Beschrijvinge ende lof der Stad Haerlem in Holland* (Description and praise of the city of Haarlem in Holland), Ampzing praised Haarlem's linen by comparing it with Italy's production:

> The Italian has indeed invented silk-damask, and because of it, fame has sent her name everywhere. But Haarlem has reflected that even further in linen, even the Italian thought it better than his own. Here is the correct school to learn the art well. And respect is not a little, but hold it, indeed, in honor (Heppner 1938:9).[28]

It is no accident that Italy's silk-damask and linen production was Ampzing's poetic foil. Dutch painting and craftsmanship stood in the shadow of Italian artistic renown. Thus, Ampzing could not have made his point more emphatically.

Praise of Haarlem's linen came from foreign countries as well. In *Des wereldts proef-steen, ofte de Ydelheydt door de Waerheyd* (The world's touchstone, or vanity through truth) (Antwerp 1643), A. à Burgundia wrote:

> Holland sends us very fine yarn, and the finest linen wares. Kamerijk and Kortrai show us also the same, and we make great pleasures with that nicely woven cloth, because through the firm thread it is comfortable to wear and to sew, so that often someone wished that the finest spider webs hanging there in the corner were better than Holland's cloth (Burgundia 1643:3–4).[29]

These seventeenth-century statements about Haarlem linen and damask weaving have a decidedly chauvinistic tone. It is Haarlem linen and Haarlem linen workers that are being extolled. The literary statements reflect societal pride in the linen professions, a pride that fostered a market for the paintings of weavers and winders by Haarlem artists. Although linen was produced elsewhere in seventeenth-century Europe, paintings of weavers and winders appeared only in Haarlem, where the most famous and desirable linen was woven and bleached.

This unique group of Haarlem paintings depicts the production of linen in Haarlem with some inaccuracies. Much of Haarlem's linen was woven in large, rented rooms, which contained several looms owned by wealthy entrepreneurs. With the exception of one painting by J.D. Oudenrogge, in which two looms are depicted

(RKD), the Haarlem paintings of weavers' workshops showed only one loom. They are images of peaceful domesticity and suggest only limited production for personal use, rather than large-scale commercial output. In reality, weaving was a commercial venture, and cloth was not woven at home for personal use. Seventeenth-century rural Dutch inventories of domestic possessions, written at the time of a death, never include a loom, although they often include a spinning wheel (De Vries 1974:224). However, the artists depicted the weavers and winders in a domestic context in order to exploit the positive associations of the milieu.

The depiction of winders rather than spinners in the painted weaving scenes does represent accurately one aspect of linen production. Only for a short time after the advent of the Flemish émigrés at the end of the sixteenth century was high-quality yarn spun in Holland (Horner 1920:353). The coarse yarns used for the bulk of Dutch linen came mostly from Silesia where they had been spun. The flax was then wound by Haarlem workers. Evidence of the importation of spun flax to Haarlem was mentioned as early as 1567 in Guicciardini's account of Haarlem's linen production in *Des Crizione de Tutti i Paesi-Bassi* (published in 1612 as *Beschrijvinge van alle de Neder-landen*): ". . . trading various handcrafts especially all kinds of woven works as linen cloths, dyes, silks, and cloth mixtures; through which the shipping and the merchant trade of the long yarn from Silesia, exported to here, have been woven well for a long time" (Guicciardini 1612 [1567]:201).[30] Such facts alone do not explain the depiction of winding as a respectable, seemingly domestic task. Winders could be presented in this way because the positive connotations of the industrious spinner also were suggested by depictions of the winder. Thus, the exemplary painted image of the winder in the mid-seventeenth century Haarlem weaving scenes continues the traditionally respectful depiction of female spinners and winders in earlier sixteenth- and seventeenth-century paintings.

NOTES

1. Heemskerck painted other portraits of women spinning (Bruyn 1955:27–35).

2. Such advice was given as early as in Jerome's writing, (Kelso 1956:274).

3. A Booke of Curious and Strange Inventions, 1596 (cited in Kelso 1956:46).

4. John Jones, The Arte and Science of Preserving Bodie and Soule, 1579:20 (cited in Kelso 1956:2). The writers of these treatises ignored national distinctions in this womanly advice. All the authors apparently drew on the same original sources: Aristotle, Plato, Cicero, Jerome, and Paul (Kelso 1956:267).

5. For a fuller account, see Duke University Museum of Art 1972 and Ciba Review 1939,28:986.

6. Emblem books contained proverbs, aphorisms, and biblical quotations juxtaposed with pictorial images. The inscriptions in combination with the pictures presented intellectual puzzles which, when solved, revealed a moralizing meaning. Emblem books were extremely popular throughout Europe in the seventeenth century, in various languages (See Praz 1939–47).

7. In the sixteenth-century theater, the spinner's distaff also was used as an attribute of virtue, which was personified by a woman. (De Jongh 1967:65).

8. (Wat rust en ghewin gheeft luttel onderwin./ Hoe kost'lick is't, voor God, hoe zoet, voor ons, t'aen -schouwen!/ Dat man en vrouw to zaem haer zelven onderhouwen,/ Van haerer handen werck, en wachten, van de Heer,/ Niet wat de weereld geeft, veel onrust, goed en eer,/ maer met een vrolick hert, gevest op rotsche gronden/ Van Godes trouw en eed, en aen haer plicht verbonden,/ Des hemels rust en lust; vertrouwend' dat de man,/ Die Godes rijcke zoeckt, noyt yet ontbreken kan.)

9. (Huislykheid is't vrouwen kroon cieraad/ Wat kroon zoo em een vrouw te cieren/ Als 't neerstig vreedzaam huis bestieren!) Virtually the same message was dictated in the early seventeenth century by Jacob Cats, although without an accompanying image (Cats 1776, I:370). For a discussion of the housewife's pictorial role in the Netherlands since the seventeenth century, see Boot 1978:168ff.

10. The metaphors for copulation included the needle piercing a hole in cloth and the loom's shuttle driving the woof threads through the warp.

11. (Ick been een spanne lang/ wit/ so ghy siet/ en teeder/ Aen't upterste ben ick het hooft een weynich groot/ Of anders leyt sy my by hare zijde neder. Sy grijpt my menichmael ja dag'lijer mach ick segghen/ Met hare handen aen/ sy doet haer knein op/ En in ruyge plaets steeckt sy nu mijnen top/ Nu trecktser hem weer uyt/ nu gaetser hem weer leeghen.)

12. (Ick sprack lest met mijn Lief, terwijl sy sat en naeyde,/ Ick steld' haer voor mijn smert, hoort doch, hoe sy my paeyde,/ Let eens, op't geen ick doe, (sprack sy)/ merckt hoe't al gaet,/ Eerst maeckt de naeld' een gat, dat stopt/ daer na den draet.)

13. (. . . U naelde boort een gat, u draet vervult de steke:/ Lief, handelt soomet my, hoet al de selve streke;/ Ghy weet, ick ben gequetst door uwen soetten mont;/ Wel aen, gheneest de smert daer me ghy gaeft de wont.)

14. The image of the barefoot young woman suggests a movement towards undress. The erotic implications of this image are corroborated by more explicit seventeenth-century paintings in which a young woman's shoes lie prominently

in the foreground. E. de Jongh has shown in his analyses of Jan Steen's painting "Morning Toilet", ca 1663 (Amsterdam, Rijksmuseum and London, Buckingham Palace) and Adriaen van de Venne's *"Geckie met de kous"* (Warsaw, Museum Narodowe) that the image of a young woman pulling her stocking on or off plays on the meaning of that stocking as a metaphor for an immoral woman or a woman's genitals, and of the foot as a phallic symbol. (Amsterdam, Rijksmuseum 1976:245,259–61). Shoes flung off obviously may anticipate both real and metaphorical love play.

15. *Spotprent* on fashionable clothing, sixteenth-century Dutch. *In* Veth n.d.:Fig.16.

16. "In hierarchical and conflictful societies that loved to reflect on the world-turned-upside-down, the *topos* of the woman-on-top was one of the most enjoyed. Indeed, sexual inversion—that is, switches in sex roles—was a widespread form of cultural play in literature, in art, and in festivity . . . . Erhard Schoen's woodcuts (early sixteenth century) portray huge women distributing fools' caps to men. This is what happens when women are given the upper hand; and yet in some sense the men deserve it" (Davis 1975:129,136).

17. (*Hier sit den Coninck der Assyriers verheven, Die hem ovt liefden tot spinnen heeft begheven.*)

18. E. de Jongh states that the author of the emblem book was as well known in the northern Netherlands as was Jacob Cats (Brussels, Koninklijk Museum voor Schone Kunsten 1971:145).

19. The paintings of Haarlem's linen-bleaching fields are discussed in chapter 4 of my revised Ph. D. dissertation, published in 1985 by UMI Research Press as Images of Textiles: The Weave of Seventeenth-Century Dutch Art and Society, and in my article, Views of Haarlem: a Reconsideration of Ruisdael and Rembrandt, Art Bulletin 67 (3): 418–36.

20. Earlier pictures of humiliated spinning men include a late Gothic engraving by Israhel van Mechenem, and an early sixteenth-century Netherlandish sculpture for a choir stall (Hollstein 1954:II:678,No.27).

21. For a discussion of the engraving's attribution and the identity of the publisher, Boscher, see Gibson 1978:679.

22. The *Rasphuis* was the corresponding house of correction for male petty thieves, cheats, tricksters, and perpetrators of minor violent crimes. There the men were forced to rasp a weekly quota of brazilwood, which was used in dyeing (Haley 1972:159).

23. See: C. Arnold, engraving in: *Waare Afbeelding der Eerste Christenen*, 1701; P. Fouquet, Jr., "*Het Vrouwen Tuchthuys of Spinhuys van Binne, tot Amsterdam*," Amsterdam Atlas, engraving, n.d., Atlas van Stolk #3853; Feullantines, "*t'Spinn-huis, La Maison des Feullantines*," engraving, n.d., Atlas van Stolk #3852.

24. These paintings are discussed in chapter 2 of my book *Images of Textiles: The Weave of Seventeenth-Century Dutch Art and Society*, UMI Research Press, 1985.

25. Damask is not mentioned because it had yet to be introduced into Haarlem (Six 1913:87).

26. (. . . *lange tijdt seer goet is gheweeft* . . . *Soo dat de stadt scheen weder in den ouden fleur to gheraken* . . . .)

27. *(Ons' Burg'ren konst, en geest, waer door sy't hooft opsteken,/ En met haer naem en faem den Sterren-tent verbreken,/ Waer door dat onse Stadt en Burger is bekent/ So wijdt op d'Aerden-kloot als hy zun konsten sendt./ Heeft hy geen goedt verstandt van alderley te* Weven?/ *Wel is hy in dees' konst uyt nemend wel bedreven!/ 't Is wonder wat hy al, en wat verscheydenheydt/ Van wercken op zijn boom seer konstlich toebereydt./ Syn lijwaet sal veel-licht self Indien wel lyden/ In fijnheydt met haer syd' en sachticheydt te strijden:/ De rest is konsten-rijck met verwen so doorschaekt,/ Dat niet om seggen is wat voorts sijn spoel al maeckt./ So werdt oock hier met macht de* Koopmanschap *gedreven,/ En meest wel die daer heeft haer opsicht op het Weven,/ Van Garen, en van Vlas, en allen Linne-waedt:/ Waer by de nering meest van onse Stadt bestaet.)*

28. *(Italian heeft wel het Sij-damast gevonden/ En over-al hierdoor den roem haers naems gesonden:/ Maer Haerlem heeft dat voords in 't lywaet nagedacht,/ Dat selfs Italien meer dan 't haere acht./ Hier is de rechte school die konste wel te leeren:/ En achtze ook niet kleijn, maer houdze wel in eren.)*

29. *(Hollandt seyndt ons heel fijn gaeren./ En de fijnste lijnwaet-waeren/ Camerijck en Corterijck/ Toonen ons oock desghelijck/ En wy scheppen groot vermaecken/ In dat net-gheweefde laecken,/ Want het door den vasten draet/ Is bequaem tot dracht en naet./ Maer oft iemandt wilde hebben/ Dat de fijnste Spinnewebben/ Die daer hanghen in den hoeck/ Beter zijn als Hollandts doeck?)*

30. (. . . *handelende verscheyden handtwercken/ besonder alderley gheweven wercken/ soo van Lynen lacekenen Coleuren/ Smallekens ende Noppen: waer door de reedinge ende den koophandel van het lanck garen/ uyt* Silesien *herwaerts over ghevoert/ langhe tijdt seer goet is gheweeft.)*

REFERENCES CITED

Ampzing, Samuel
    1628   Beschryvinge ende Lof der Stad Haerlem in Holland. Haerlem: Adriean Rooman.

Ampzing, Samuel
    1621   Het Lof der Stadt Haerlem in Hollandt. Haerlem: Adriean Rooman.

Amsterdam, Amsterdams Historisch Museum
    1972   Regenten en Regentessen Overlieden en Chirurguijns, Amsterdamse groepportretten van 1600 tot 1835 (exhibition catalog).

Amsterdam, Rijksmuseum
    1976   Tot Lering en Vermaak (exhibition catalog).

Anonymous
1704   Emblemata Selectiora. Amsterdam: Apud Franciscum van der Plaats.

Anonymous
1972   Nova Poemata ante hac nunquam edita, Nieuwe Nederduytsche, Gedichten ende Raedtselen. Soest, Holland: Davaco Publishers. (Original text, 1624).

Assenheim, Henricum Oraem
1619   Viridarium Hieroglyphico-Morale. Frankfurt: Lucam Iennis.

Boissardi, Jani Jacobi
1593   Emblemata, Auss dem Latein verteutscht. Frankfurt: Dieterich Brn von Lüttich.

Boot, Marjan
1978   'Huislykheid is 't Vrouwen Kroon Cieraad. Openbaar Kunstbezit Kunst Schrift 22(4):168ff.

Brussels, Koninklijk Museum voor Schone Kunsten
1971   Rembrandt en zijn tijd (exhibition catalog).

Bruyn, J.
1955   Vroege portretten van Maerten van Heemskerck. Bulletin van het Rijksmuseum, 27–35.

Burgundia, A. à.
1643   Des wereldt proef-steen, ofte de ydele-heydt door waerheyd. Antwerp: Petrus Gheschier.

Cats, Jacob
1622   Sinn-en-Minne-Beelden & Emblemata Amores Morelqüe spectantia. Amsterdam: Willem Iansz Blaeuw.
1776   Alle de wercken van den Heere Jacob Cats. Amsterdam: J. Ratelband.

Ciba Review
1–141   1961–69,Basel, Gesellshaft für Chemische Industrie.

Coupe, W.A.
1966–67 The German Illustrated Broadsheet in the Seventeenth Century, Historical and Iconographical Studies. Bibliotheca Bibliographica Aureliana Series, 20, Baden-Baden: Heitz.

Davis, Natalie
1975   Society and Culture in Early Modern France: Eight Essays. Stanford; Stanford University Press.

De Brune, Johannis
1624   Emblemata of Zinnewerck. Amsterdam: J.E. Kloppenburch.

De Jongh, Eddy
    1967   Zinne-en minnebeelden in de schilderkunst van de zeventiende
            eeuw. Nederlandse Stichting Openbaar Kunstbezit en Openbaar
            Kunstbezit in Vlaanderen in samenwerking met het Prins
            Bernhard Fonds.

De Vries, Jan
    1974   The Dutch Rural Economy in the Golden Age, 1500–1700. New
            Haven and London: Yale University Press.

Drexelius, Hieremias
    1629   Nuntius Mortus; Aeternitatis Prodromus Mortis Nuntius Quem
            Sanis Aegrotis Moribundis. Baltalaris Belleri.

Duke University Museum of Art, comp.
    1972   Recent Tapestries (exhibition catalog). Durham, North Carolina.

Elger, Willem den
    1703   Zinne-Beelden der Liefde. Leyden.

Flamen
    1653   Devises et Emblesmes d'Amour Moralisez. Paris: Chez Louis
            Boissevin.

Friedrichen, Andreas
    1617   Emblemata Nova. Frankfurt: Lucam Iennis.

Gibson, Walter S.
    1978   Some Flemish Popular Prints from Hieronymus Cock and His
            Contemporaries. Art Bulletin 60 (4):673–81.

Guicciardini, Lodovico
    1567   Des Crizione de Tutti i Paesi-Bassi. Dutch 1612 translation:
            Beschrijvinge van alle de Nederlanden. Amsterdam.

Haechtanus, L.
    1618   Paruus Mundus. Frankfurt: Apud Lucam Iennis.

Haley, K.H.D.
    1972   The Dutch in the Seventeenth Century. New York: Harcourt,
            Brace, Jovanovich.

Hall, James
    1974   Dictionary of Subjects and Symbols in Art. Introduction by
            Kenneth Clark. Great Britain: J. Murray.

Heinsius, Daniel
    1621   Nederduytsche Poemata. Leyden: Hernien van Westerhuisen.

Heppner, A.
    1938   Wevers Werkplaatsen Geschilderd door Haarlemsche Meesters
            der 17 eeuw, A. van Ostade, C. Decker, G. Rombouts, C. Beelt,
            J. Oudenrogge, Th. Wijck. Haarlem: De Erven F. Bohn N.V.

Hollstein, F.W.H.
 1949   Dutch and Flemish Etchings, Engravings, and Woodcuts. 20
         Vols. Amsterdam: Menno Hertsberger.
 1954   German Engravings, Etchings, and Woodcuts, ca. 1400–1700. 22
         Vols. Amsterdam: Menno Hertsberger.

Horner, John
 1920   The Linen Trade of Europe during the Spinning Wheel Period.
         Belfast: M'Caw, Stevenson & Orr, Limited.

Horozcii, D.D.IO.
 1601   Emblemata Moralia. Agrigenti.

Huizinga, J.H.
 1941   Dutch Civilization in the Seventeenth Century and Other Es-
         says. Arnold J. Pomerans. Collins, Transl. London.

Kelso, Ruth
 1956   Doctrine for the Lady of the Renaissance. Illinois: University of
         Illinois Press.

Moerman, Ian
 1608   De Cleyn Werelt: Daer in claerlijcken door seer schoone
         Poetische, Moralische en Historische exempelen betoont wort.
         Amsterdam: Dirck Pietersz.

The New English Bible with the Apocrypha
 1971   New York: Oxford University Press.

Nyenborg, Iohannem à.
 1660   Variarum Lectionum Selecta Figuris aeneis applicata. Groningen:
         Jacobum Sipkes.

Peacham, Henry
 1973   Minerva Britanna, English Emblem Books. No 5. John Horden,
         Ed. London: Scholar Press. (Original text, 1612).

Poirters, P. Adrianus
 1588   Het Masker van de Wereldt, afgetrocken door . . . Antwerp: Jo-
         hannes Stichter in den Bergh Calvarien.

Praz, Mario
 1939–47 Studies in Seventeenth Century Imagery. Two Vols. London: The
         Warburg Institute.

RKD   (Rijksbureau voor Kunsthistorische Documentatie): The Hague.

Six, Jhr. J.
 1913   Paschier Lamertijn. Oud Holland 31:85–109.

Van der Heijden, M.C.A.
 1966   Johannes Stalpaert van der Wiele, Bloemlezing met inleiding en
         aantekening. Zutphen: N.V.W.J. Thieme & Cie.

Van der Loeff, J.D. Rutgers, Ed.
1911   Drie Lofdichten op Haarlem, Het Middelnederlandsch Gedicht van Dirk Mathijszen en Karel van Mander's Twee Beelden van Haarlem voor Vereeniging "Haerlem." Haarlem.

Van Ysselsteyn, G.T.
1946   Van Linnen en Linnenkasten. Amsterdam: P.N. van Kampen & Zoon N.V.

Veth, Cornelis
n.d.   De Mode in de Caricature. Amsterdam: van Munster's Uitgevers-Maatschappij.

Vignau-Schuurmän, Th. A.G. Wilberg
1969   Die Emblematischen elemente im werke Joris Hoefnagels. 2 Vols. Leiden: U. pers Leiden.

8. Embroidery for Tourists

A Contemporary Putting-Out System in Oaxaca, Mexico

RONALD WATERBURY

 If you wander through the bustling Friday market-place of Ocotlán in Mexico's Valley of Oaxaca, you will see many women vendors seated on the ground next to their produce, occupying the time between clients by embroidering multicolored pansies, roses, and birds entwined in leafy branches onto finger-smudged swatches of cloth. If you go farther afield, into any of the many villages of the district, you will encounter other women, sitting in doorways or under a mesquite tree in their patios, busily embroidering. Back in the marketplace again, you may notice a number of women—some at produce stands, others sitting under the portals of the buildings that surround the central square—receiving pieces of embroidered cloth from peasant women. After examining the embroiderer's work, these women hand back a small roll of money, another cut of cotton cloth, and several skeins of thread.

What you have witnessed is but a small part of the extensive putting-out system that has grown up spontaneously over the last two decades in the Valley of Oaxaca, especially in the Ocotlán branch of the valley. The end-products of the process are the colorfully embroidered blouses or dresses of the type most people call Mexican wedding dresses. To those who know Mexican needlework, they are "San Antonino" dresses, after the community in which this particular style originated and in which the putting-out system is organized.[1]

243

Most San Antonino dresses end up in the wardrobes of North American or European women, who purchase them for reasons that include nostalgia for handicrafts. In the real world of Oaxaca, however, the economics of their production is far from romantic. In 1978, a common-quality dress sold for $50 in the import boutiques of North America, but the peasant woman who embroidered it earned less than 10 cents an hour for her labor. The goal of this paper is to describe the development and organization of this less-than-romantic production system, and to analyze its social and economic significance for San Antonino and the region as a whole.

In a putting-out system, merchant-entrepreneurs mobilize labor to produce commodities without incurring much risk, and with a minimal investment in fixed capital. Such systems represent an intermediate stage between precapitalist and capitalist forms of production. Putting-out entrepreneurs exercise only partial domination over labor by controlling the supply of raw or semiprocessed materials, and by controlling the marketing of the completed product. Historically, putting-out systems functioned to augment production under preindustrial technological conditions. In Europe, they expanded significantly in rural areas during the seventeenth and eighteenth centuries, creating what some authorities call the "proto-industrialization" stage in the evolution of industrial capitalism (Kriedte and Schlumbohm 1977; Mendels 1972).

Putting-out systems were eventually replaced by full-fledged industrialism for the production of most commodities. But under certain conditions they have survived: or, as the example presented here will illustrate, they can be spontaneously reborn. (For some contemporary cases in Mexico and elsewhere see Brown 1983; Charlton 1988; de Mauro 1983; Cook 1982b,1984; Ferretti 1983; Hopkins 1978; Lamphere 1979; Littlefield 1978,1979; Swallow 1982.) One necessary condition for their survival or rebirth is sufficient consumer demand for handmade or quasi-handmade goods. Another is the presence of a population compelled by economic circumstances to sell its labor cheaply.

Despite the hegemony of industrial production, demand for handcrafted artifacts endures. Garcia Canclini (1981:72–75) attributes this to "nostalgic fascination for the rustic or the natural." There is also the aesthetic judgment of some consumers that industrial goods are without personality. Being the product of anonymous labor, they are mere commodities that lack individuality, artistic merit, or cultural meaning. By comparison, a handcrafted object evokes the aura of human tradition, the sweat and skill of its individual maker, and—since craftsmanship avoids the repetitive precision of a stamping machine—uniqueness and originality.

One of the most effective ways to project a distinctly personal image is to wear clothes that are not mass-produced. In industrial society, members of the artistic or Bohemian subculture have long worn "folk" or "ethnic" clothing as a way of rejecting factory standardization. This interest in handmade ethnic clothing diffused more widely following World War II, influenced by the expanding number of tourists who traveled to remote and exotic places and brought back pieces of folk art and craft, among them handmade or hand-adorned clothes. The greatest demand for "ethnic" garb, however, grew out of the American counterculture movement of the 1960s and early 1970s. Among other things, its ideology rejected narrow patriotism in favor of cultural pluralism, and forswore mainstream materialist values. One symbol of this ideology was the wearing of peasant dress. Since then, many elements of counterculture dress style have become incorporated into Euro-American mass popular culture. The style has also diffused into the upper-middle class.

In addition to the new demand for "ethnic" dress in the postwar United States, many Third World governments have grown to appreciate the multiple uses to which folk artisanry can be put. (See Garcia Canclini 1977, 1981; Graburn 1976; and Smith 1977.) Among the most active countries in this regard is Mexico, whose past and present Indian cultures are officially venerated as a critical component of the nation's cultural patrimony and as a unique symbol of national identity. Several Mexican government agencies, the most important of which is FONART (the National Fund for Artisanry), actively stimulate the production and distribution of traditional and quasi-traditional arts and crafts. These agencies hold that folk arts bring a multiplicity of economic benefits, as advertisements to attract tourism, as a major source of foreign currency from direct sales to tourists and from exports, and as a way of lifting the standard of living of the rural producers, thereby presumably diminishing the tide of urban immigration. Substantial returns flow to the public treasury through taxes, to store operators and exporters through profits, and to the eventual consumers through the availability of moderately priced handmade goods. The actual producers, however, benefit hardly at all (Cook 1982a, 1982b; Garcia Canclini 1981; Littlefield 1979; Novelo 1976).

In addition to demand, a putting-out system requires a population compelled by poverty to sell its labor cheaply. In preindustrial Europe, the principal font of outworkers was rural households for whom piecework, often performed by women, provided a welcome supplement to inadequate agricultural incomes (Goody 1982; Hobsbawn 1965; Jones 1968; Klima 1974; Klima and Macurek 1960; Mendels 1975; Scott and Tilly 1975; Thirsk 1961). Similar conditions prevail in the contemporary Third World. Exploitation of this labor force, as this study demonstrates, need not always be carried out directly by urban merchants, although they take the largest cut of the surplus value by the time the product reaches its eventual consumers. Rather, when the outworkers are rural peasants, the product of local peasant origin, and the capital requirements low, a putting-out system lends itself well to peasant entrepreneurship—the direct exploitation of peasants by peasants.[2]

THE ORIGINS OF EMBROIDERING IN SAN ANTONINO

The state of Oaxaca is touted in political speeches, in the press, and by the tourist industry as a wellspring of the nation's indigenous cultural patrimony. Among Mexico's states it has the largest variety of indigenous ethnic communities, and is perhaps the richest in traditional and quasi-traditional crafts. The state's annual government-sponsored folkdance festival, Lunes del Cerro, is shown on national television, several of its master artisans are periodically featured in the media, and photographs of its monumental precolombian ruins and picturesque peasant marketplaces decorate travel posters and tourist advertising. Paradoxically, Oaxaca's Indian peasants, the source of all this national pride, are among the poorest people in the nation (See also Cook 1982a, 1982b).

The central Valley of Oaxaca, in which San Antonino lies, is dotted by over 250 peasant communities, many of which specialize in specific crops, crafts, or trade. The bulk of the region's peasant products are exchanged in the centuries-old and still vigorous system of periodic marketplaces (Beals 1975; Cook and Diskin 1975; Malinowski and de la Fuente 1982).

San Antonino is adjacent to Ocotlán, the district headtown,

some 30 kilometers south of Oaxaca City, to which it is linked by a paved road. The community is relatively large (population c. 4000) and, by local standards, relatively prosperous. Its inhabitants are of Zapotec descent, and most adults speak both Spanish and the indigenous tongue. Most of the community's residents are farmers, involved in intensive cash-crop horticulture on small plots, and most of these households supplement their agricultural income with earnings from other activities such as butchering, baking, and petty marketplace trading. Thus, the ways of the market, at least on a regional basis, are not new to *Tonineros*, as the people from San Antonino often call themselves (Waterbury and Turkenik 1975).

Exactly when the craft of embroidery began in San Antonino is not known, although it probably was introduced by Dominican friars during the colonial period. Certainly, the cut of the blouse, with its yoke and sewn-in sleeves, is post-conquest. According to elderly informants, embroidering has long been a common female pastime, devoted predominantly to the decoration of women's clothing. Traditional dress customs mandated the use of embroidered blouses, simple ones for daily wear and ornate ones for fiestas. Most women embroidered only for their own families, but a few especially skillful needleworkers occasionally made blouses for others as a part-time, income-producing activity. Their most frequent customers were the parents of young husbands-to-be, who were expected to present the bride with a complete fiesta outfit including an elaborately embroidered blouse.

Although the wearing and making of embroidered blouses began to decline in the late 1930s as part of the general shift from Indian to *mestizo* peasant dress style, the craft did not die out completely. It was preserved by a handful of women who continued to make traditional blouses on special order and who occasionally sold blouses to the two or three tourist shops in Oaxaca City.

The revival of embroidery in San Antonino began in the 1950s, sparked by the growth of post–World War II tourism to Oaxaca which increased the market for all of the region's crafts. This augmented demand was communicated to the village by city tourist shop operators, who began coming to San Antonino in search of merchandise. Some of the village women who had continued to make and sell blouses on a small scale stepped up their production. The women who still remembered how to embroider began teaching young girls, and a few *Tonineras* established themselves as interme-

Figure 20. A modern-style blouse worn with traditional
fiesta-style garb by the late Doña Sabina Sánchez, one of the
women responsible for adapting the blouse for the tourist
market. Photo by Ronald Waterbury

diary traders by purchasing completed garments from other *Tonineras* and reselling them to tourist shops in the city. By the mid-1960s,
embroidering had again become a common female activity in San
Antonino.

Throughout this period demand increased steadily, but the actual production process remained traditional. Factory-made cloth
and thread were used, as they had been for many years, and the
tasks of cutting, embroidering, and assembling of blouses were not
yet differentiated; each woman made the entire garment herself.
Then in the late 1960s tourism to Oaxaca increased dramatically and,
more importantly, the demand for peasant and ethnic clothing
spread beyond tourists into the general international market. Not

only did purchases by the growing number of Oaxaca City tourist shops increase, but buyers from Mexico City and abroad also began to come directly to San Antonino in search of embroidered dresses. The traditional organization of production could no longer keep pace and several village women initiated putting-out operations.

THE RISE OF PUTTING-OUT OPERATIONS

Putting-out arrangements were not unknown to San Antonino, as a few men already sewed trousers as piece-rate outworkers for Oaxaca City clothing merchants. In fact, the wives of two of these men were among the first putters-out of embroidered dresses. For labor, the new putting-out merchants recruited young, predominantly unmarried girls in San Antonino, particularly those from poorer families. The money derived from piecework provided these girls with a small supplement to household income or, in some cases, savings for the cash portion of the girl's dowry.

Beginning about 1970, the pool of outworkers in San Antonino became insufficient. To meet ever-rising demand and to keep costs down, the putting-out merchants—who were also growing in number—sought pieceworkers beyond their own community. The greatest need was for embroiderers, that being the most time-consuming of the steps in making a dress and thus the one requiring the greatest number of workers. The putting-out merchants were obliged to search for embroiderers outside of San Antonino, not only because the number of *Tonineras* able to embroider was insufficient to meet production needs, but also because the *Tonineras* were reluctant to accept the low fees they were offering. The long tradition of marketplace trading in San Antonino's women made alternative occupations available to them—and in this relatively prosperous community, many households did not need to engage in the self-exploitation that piecework embroidery entails.

In their quest for outworkers, San Antonino dress merchants first looked to nearby villages in which some women already knew how to embroider. Based on his independent survey of the economics of craft production in the region, conducted between 1978 and 1980, Scott Cook states (1982a:64,fn.11) that of Ocotlán district's twenty municipalities:

only three or four . . . have little or no embroidery; 11 of the 12
communities surveyed . . . had a significant incidence of families
engaged in this work—ranging from 100% of the households
censused in one community to a low of 16% in another, with the
average incidence being 56% of the 467 households censused in
the eleven communities.

By then the network of outworkers had already spread to other districts, mostly to the south of Ocotlán, and included communities
more than 40 kilometers away. Most of the more distant communities were agricultural villages that produced no crafts and in which
the women had never embroidered. This expansion was technically
possible because embroidering, at the level of expertise necessary
to satisfy mass wholesale standards, demands the least skill of all the
steps and is relatively easy to learn. It was economically possible because most of these villages are located in marginal agricultural
zones where the soil is too poor to sustain an acceptable living. Indeed, permanent emigration is common from these villages, and
among the remaining households most of the adult males migrated
seasonally in search of work. For households that comprised mainly
women and children with few alternative sources of income, self-
exploitation through embroidery was almost welcome. In fact, even
at the risk of appearing effeminate, a few men in the outlying villages became embroiderers too.

Most embroidery on commercial-grade dresses is now performed by women in communities other than San Antonino. However, those phases of the production process such as crocheting or
pattern-drawing, which require greater skill and are somewhat better paid, are still largely performed by *Toninera* outworkers or in the
merchants' own households.

THE ORGANIZATION OF THE WORK

Although the putting-out system has fundamentally changed the
organization of production, the product itself has changed only su-
perficially. The traditional garment was a short-sleeved white blouse
embroidered in white. Presently most garments are dress length
and are embroidered with colored thread, sometimes on colored
cloth. A band of embroidery down the front has been added and

some models now have long sleeves with embroidered cuffs. The basic construction of the garment has remained the same, as have the embroidery designs.

The tasks required to produce an embroidered dress are identical, whether made by a single artisan or through the putting-out system. There are seven steps: (1) cutting the cloth to form the parts of the dress (yoke, sleeves, and body); (2) drawing the embroidery design on the cloth; (3) embroidering the parts; (4) smocking a narrow strip across the top of the body in a pattern of *monitos* (small figures); (5) crocheting the edge of the neck and sleeves; (6) sewing the parts together into a dress; and (7) washing and ironing the completed garment.

The tools used by outworkers, which they supply themselves, are simple and inexpensive: a ballpoint pen for drawing the embroidery pattern, sewing needles and a hoop (which not all embroiderers use), and crochet hooks. The putting-out household needs a sewing machine to assemble the dresses, and a washtub and iron to prepare them for final sale. Sewing machines are common possessions in San Antonino because they have long been given as wedding presents to brides by their parents. A new electric Singer (with zigzag capability) cost P/7,270 ($320) in 1978 and could be purchased on credit.[3] Many women continued to use their old treadle machines, more often due to preference rather than price. An electric iron cost about P/250 ($11).

Under the putting-out system, the merchant assigns each task to a different outworker, who usually specializes in only one step of the process. All San Antonino merchants provide the cloth, pay their outworkers, collect the completed pieces, and sell the finished product. Early in the development of the system, piecework embroiderers were required to provide their own thread. However, as many of them—particularly those from outside San Antonino—skimped on the amount of thread used or chose color combinations considered inappropriate by buyers, the dress merchants soon undertook to supply the thread.

The major variation in the work process is the number of steps carried out in the merchant's own household. Small-scale merchants usually perform many of the tasks themselves, thereby compensating for limited volume by investing more of their own labor. One informant, for example, put out only the drawing and embroidering; she and her 13-year-old daughter did all the rest. Large-scale producers, in contrast, put out everything except cutting and final assembly, and a portion of the latter was often put out too, if the volume of work surpassed the household's own sewing capacity. In 1978, all but one of the merchants distributed and collected all the parts themselves at each phase of the process. The notable exception was the largest merchant who, because of the volume of his business and the size of his network of outworkers, subcontracted out some of the embroidery distribution to agents in two different towns.

COSTS AND RETURNS

Production costs to San Antonino putting-out merchants for a commercial-quality dress in 1978 are itemized in Table 1. Since assembling, washing, and ironing of dresses are usually performed in the merchant's own household, figures for those phases are not included in the table. When those tasks were also put out, additional costs of P/8 and P/5 respectively were incurred, raising the total to approximately P/245 (U.S. $10.92).

Fees paid to pieceworkers are quite standardized because the number of actual and potential outworkers is vast compared to the limited number of merchants, most of whom are from a single community. Among San Antonino's dress merchants, however, formal collusion to control wages is definitely not practiced. Unlike the butchers, bakers, and petty marketplace traders, who are organized, no formal association of dress merchants exists. Nonetheless, information derived from outworkers and buyers and from the village's universal espionage corps—the children—makes costs and prices common knowledge.

Wages earned by outworkers differ according to the level of skill associated with the task and the time required to complete it. Our calculations reveal that on an hourly basis, embroidery paid the least of all: approximately P/2 per hour (U.S. $0.09).[4] Crocheting yielded P/3 to P/6 per hour ($0.13 to $0.27); smocking (making the *monitos*) earned P/6 to P/8 per hour ($0.27 to $0.35); drawing the embroidery design returned the most, at least P/8 per hour (U.S. $.35).[5] In mid-1978, wholesale buyers were paying an average of P/300 ($13.25) per dress, which provided a 30 percent markup for the San Antonino merchants. By the time the garments reached retail shops in the United States they had increased in price a minimum of 400 per-

TABLE 1

Dress Production Costs to San Antonino
Putting-Out Merchants in 1978

Item	Cost	
	Pesos	Dollars
Materials		
Cloth (approx. 3.5 m. at 20)	70.00	3.10
Thread (10 skeins at 2.50)	25.00	1.11
Labor		
Design drawing	10.00	.44
Embroidery	100.00	4.42
Smocking and *monitos*	12.00	.53
Crochet	12.00	.53
Miscellaneous (soap, electricity, travel, etc.)	2.50	.11
Total	230.00	10.25

Note: *Pesos are converted to U.S. dollars at the rate of 22.60 to 1, which was in effect in mid-1978. The totals have been rounded to the nearest 5 pesos and 5 U.S. cents.*

cent, selling there for at least $50 each.[6]

Since most garments are exported or purchased by foreign tourists, devaluation of the peso and subsequent price inflation also affected the embroidered dress trade. As is evident from Table 2, between 1970 and 1978 the already miserably paid outworkers absorbed a disproportionate share of the effects of the devalued peso, while all others—must notably the cloth manufacturers—managed to keep their selling prices ahead of the rising value of the dollar.

The size of putting-out networks varies considerably. The smallest merchants in 1978 employed no more than 10, whereas the largest operator in San Antonino estimated that he put out to about 900 workers in 15 different communities. But as the scale increases, so do organizational problems. Accounting becomes increasingly onerous (especially for those merchants who are functionally illiterate), quality less controllable, and distributing and collecting the parts less manageable, more time-consuming, and more costly. Fur-

TABLE 2
Inflation 1970–78
In Pesos

Item	1970	1978	Percentage Rise
Cost of factory-made cloth (per sq. meter)	5	21	300
Selling price of quality dress	250	900	260
Selling price of commercial-grade dress	150	300	100
Value of U.S. dollar	12.50	22.60	81
Wages paid by putting-out merchants per dress for:			
Embroidering	60	100	67
Design drawing	7	10	43
Smocking and *monitos*	10	12	20
Crocheting	10	12	20

thermore, the expansion of the system to distant villages engendered some theft. The utilization of subcontractors in other communities by San Antonino's largest trader was an attempt to minimize this problem.

PRODUCT QUALITY

Despite the dress merchants' attempts at quality control, modifications in the production process brought about by the putting-out system were accompanied by a perceptible deterioration in the quality of the garments. The newer pieceworkers tended not only to be less skilled but also less aesthetically motivated, as they never saw nor had any relationship to the completed garment. But as the market became more generalized, wholesale buyers became more interested in low price than high quality and what might be called a "commercial-grade" garment evolved.

Nonetheless, high quality embroidery is still appreciated by discriminating individual purchasers as well as by museum and exhibition buyers. In fact, demand for quality dresses has also risen, although to a much more modest degree than for the commercial-grade dresses. As might be expected, given their greater labor input, better materials, and short supply, quality dresses fetch much higher prices. In fact, from 1970 to 1978 they ran well ahead of the inflating value of the dollar (Table 2).

A few San Antonino women have continued to specialize in making and/or trading of the finer garments. One such woman, Doña Sabina Sanchez, was among those craftspersons elevated by the Mexican press and government agencies (such as the Tourism Ministry and FONART) to the status of national "artisan celebrity" (Cook 1982a:60). Prior to her untimely death in an automobile accident in 1981, she was wooed by exhibitors, featured on national television, and honored with diplomas and awards. She was also the subject of a documentary by a North American filmmaker and was taken to California to demonstrate her craft at a showing of the film at a Los Angeles museum.

MARKETING

Most commercial-grade dresses are marketed through wholesale buyers who purchase directly in the village. A modest proportion of garments, perhaps 10 percent, is taken by San Antonino dress merchants to tourist shops in Oaxaca City, and an even smaller amount to shops in Mexico City. Agents from FONART also occasionally buy, but the volume is insignificant compared to that handled by private intermediaries. Least important of all are direct sales to consumers. San Antonino, lacking exotic attractions, is not on the tourist circuit; anyone who ventures into the village in quest of embroidery must search to find it as there are no retail shops, and putting-out merchants do not put out signs.

The most important marketing agents, the traveling wholesale buyers, are of two types: professionals who come regularly, and amateurs or quasi-professionals who come sporadically. The professionals can be divided into large-volume buyers, nearly all of whom are North Americans or Europeans, and moderate- to small-volume buyers, some of whom are Mexicans. The amateurs and quasi-professionals, mostly foreigners, make purchases in the moderate to small range.

San Antonino putting-out merchants and their customers dis-

TABLE 3

Sales Volume and Net Income per Month of San Antonino
Putting-Out Merchants in 1978

Scale	Households (n=40) No. %	Volume of Dresses Sold	Net Income[1] in Pesos	Equivalent[2] in Dollars
1	1 2.5	300-400	18,000-24,000	800-1,060
2	5 12.5	150-250	10,500-17,500	465- 775
3	15 37.5	25-149	1,750-10,430	75- 460
4	19 47.5	5- 24	350- 1,680	15- 75

1. Net income is calculated by assuming a profit of 70 pesos per garment for all but
the largest operation. For that case, because of somewhat higher costs (subcon-
tractor's commissions, some putting-out of final assembly, and greater transport
costs), I estimate 60 pesos per dress. (See the discussion and Table 1 of the previous section.)
2. Pesos converted to dollars at the prevalent exchange rate at that time of 22.60
to 1, rounded to nearest $5.

play a certain affinity of scale. The large-volume professional buyers, who purchase hundreds of dresses per trip, prefer the efficiency
and convenience of dealing with the largest San Antonino merchants (principally those in Scales I and II of Table 3). Conversely,
the top San Antonino merchants were able to establish and maintain
favored client relations with large buyers by proving themselves to
be reliable volume suppliers. Therefore they sell to smaller buyers
only if they have stock in excess of that committed to their preferred
customers, or if immediate cash is needed. Hence the smaller buyers, even the professional ones, are usually required to make the
rounds of the smaller putting-out merchants.

Although most transactions are on a cash basis, the large professional buyers sometimes leave sizable deposits with trusted San
Antonino suppliers, to provide them with some of the capital necessary to complete the order. The history of the top putting-out business in 1978 is a case in point. According to the husband's account,
several years before a European buyer, to whom they had been periodically supplying a moderate number of dresses, offered a substantial cash advance if they could complete an exceptionally large order
within six months. The wife, who until that time had managed the
putting-out network while the husband sewed dresses, hesitated for

fear of being unable to fulfill the commitment. The husband, how-ever, accepted the challenge, took over and expanded the network of outworkers, and successfully completed the order. The gains from that achievement permitted them to purchase an automobile which, along with referrals to other volume buyers, facilitated fur-ther expansion of the business.

GOVERNMENT INVOLVEMENT

In all of these developments, the government's role has been mini-mal. FONART's purchases are of little importance. The advertising effect of the publicity accorded Doña Sabina and the government-sponsored artisanry exhibitions primarily affects Mexican nationals, whereas the vast majority of San Antonino dresses are sold to for-eign tourists or are exported. A representative of the national bank for the development of cooperatives once initiated conversations with a few San Antonino dress merchants, but none expressed inter-est in organizing because they saw no advantage in doing so. No effort has ever been made to organize pieceworkers.

EMBROIDERY IN SAN ANTONINO'S SOCIOECONOMIC STRUCTURE

The commercialization of embroidery has made an important addi-tion to San Antonino's already complex occupational mix and has substantially improved the standard of living of some but not all of the 40 putting-out households. For the multitude of outworkers in and out of San Antonino, its economic contribution has been minimal, though considered worthwhile given the poverty of pieceworking households. Its effect on gender roles has been nil, de-spite the fact that all but one of the putting-out businesses are man-aged by women. Nor has the political status of the putting-out households reflected their rising economic fortunes.

As I noted earlier, for decades most of San Antonino's house-holds have combined agriculture with one or more other occu-pations. In 1978, the most numerous non-agricultural activities, excluding embroidery, were petty marketplace trading (380 house-holds), making tortillas (75 households), baking bread (25 house-holds), and butchering beef (15 households). Although insignificant in 1965, by 1978 embroidery involved 40 households as putting-out merchants and many more as pieceworkers, and thus formed a major addition to the occupational matrix. Nonetheless, it was still just one occupation of many. Indeed, only two of the putting-out households relied solely upon the dress business for subsistence.

The contribution the putting-out system has made to household incomes is shown in Table 3, which places dress-merchant households in four categories according to their monthly sales volumes and net incomes. As this table demonstrates, the income range among the 40 putting-out operations was great. And as Table 4 shows, there was a wide range in the number of dresses sold by different households. The six households operating at Scales 1 and 2 (Table 4) represented 15 percent of the merchants but nearly half (46.2 percent) of the sales. By village standards, they were growing rich. In fact, their putting-out operations allowed them to enjoy a standard of living comparable to that of Oaxaca City's middle class. That is, most of them had built or were building multi-roomed brick and cement houses, complete with tile floors and indoor plumbing (two eschewed ostentatious displays for reasons that will be made apparent shortly). Furthermore, their homes were furnished and equipped with most of the material conveniences and symbols of the modern lifestyle: plastic-covered upholstered couches and chairs, beds with box springs and mattresses, gas stoves, electric refrigerators, television sets, and radio-phonograph consoles. They also possessed ample wardrobes and an array of personal gadgets such as cameras, pocket calculators, and cassette tape recorders, and spent large amounts on public and private fiestas.

The single Scale 1 dress merchant, who himself represented only 2.5 percent of all the merchants but sold 12 percent of the dresses (Table 5), earned over P/18,000 per month in 1978, which matched the income of most urban professionals. That permitted his family to enjoy not only all the modern amenities listed above but also one of the community's three private cars and the luxury of sending their only child, a son, to the university. Moreover, one of the households that operated at Scale 2 in 1978 had by 1982 risen to even greater heights. In the summer of that year, they inaugurated a brand new Chevrolet Citation with festivities that included live music, fireworks, and a priest to bestow blessings and sprinkle holy water on the car. That vehicle was an addition to the full inventory

TABLE 4
Distribution of Estimated Monthly Sales of San Antonino
Putting-Out Merchants in 1978

Scale	Merchants		Dresses Sold	
	No.	%	No.	%
1	1	2.5	350	12.0
2	5	12.5	1000	34.2
3	15	37.5	1300	44.4
4	19	47.5	275	9.4
	40	100.0	2925	100.0

of domestic appliances and consumer goods they had already accumulated and to the pickup truck they had purchased two years before.

The lifestyle of most of the pieceworkers, especially those from outside San Antonino, is worlds apart. They travel on foot, donkey, or second-class bus; live in dirt-floored, one-room, adobe houses or mud-daubed cane huts; sleep on mats on the floor; own a few pieces of crude wood furniture and no modern appliances; rarely possess more than one change of clothing; bathe outdoors by ladling water over themselves from a bucket; and relieve themselves on the ground.

San Antonino's fifteen Scale 3 putting-out operations, representing 37.5 percent of the merchants producing 44.4 percent of the dresses, earned returns that were much more modest than those of the top six. Though considerable by village standards, this income alone would not permit anything approximating a middle-class lifestyle. Where dress income was combined with substantial earnings from agriculture and other occupations, however, it did permit a few Scale 3 households—especially those at the upper end of the scale—to approach that level, albeit minus the motor vehicles and university education.

The combined average monthly sales of all nineteen Scale 4 putting-out businesses (comprising nearly half the total) was less than 10 percent of the combined sales of all dress merchants, and even less than the production of the one household in Scale 1. The incomes derived were meager. As an extreme example, in 1978 the smallest putting-out merchant sold but five dresses per month, netting her only P/350, about one quarter of the earnings of the average female petty marketplace trader. As one might expect, turnover is high among Scale 4 dress merchants because insufficient capital and the competition from larger more established businesses for outworkers and especially for buyers makes their chances of expansion slim.

Nonetheless, women continue in the activity for several reasons. First, as a supplemental source of income, it is less onerous and requires less time out of the house than does marketplace trading, the principal alternative occupation for women. For the few Scale 4 households that enjoy substantial incomes from other sources, it provides women with an independent source of petty cash. But for most Scale 4 putters-out, the principal reason is that the earnings, although miniscule, are important because these households are very poor, sometimes as poor as their pieceworkers. In fact, many Scale 4 dress merchants are pieceworkers just trying to break into the putting-out business.

THE WEALTH RANKING OF PUTTING-OUT HOUSEHOLDS

The economic significance of the dress trade can also be appreciated by comparing the wealth ranking of putting-out households to that of the general population.[7] Discarding the single putting-out household in Wealth Rank I (the case is anomalous and the numbers are not statistically reliable),[8] Table 5 shows a significantly greater representation of putting-out households in the community's upper wealth ranks (II and III), and a lesser representation in the lower ranks (IV and V). Because only two putting-out households rely on the dress business as their sole income source, it is not possible to specify what proportion of a household's economic standing is directly attributable to its putting-out activities. Nonetheless, the information in Table 5 is highly suggestive.

These inferences from Table 5 can be corroborated by including landholding data in the matrix, as agriculture is the one income source common to virtually the entire community and land ownership was given the greatest weight in wealth ranking by all informants. Again disregarding the one putting-out household in Wealth

TABLE 5

*Wealth Rank of Putting-Out Households Compared to
the General Population of San Antonino in 1978*

Wealth Rank	Putting-Out Households		General Population	
	No.	%	No.	%
I (VERY RICH)	1	2.5	5	8.5
II (RICH)	7	17.5	39	4.1
III (ORDINARY)	16	40.0	184	19.3
IV (POOR)	13	32.5	554	58.1
V (VERY POOR)	3	7.5	173	18.0
	40	100.0	955	100.0

Rank I, Table 6 indicates that putting-out households were not pulled up in the ranking by land ownership since their mean land holding was either equal to (Rank IV) or less than (Ranks II, III, and V) that of the general population in the same wealth ranks.

In sum, although the size of the operations varies widely, the embroidery trade has been economically important to all of the 40 households with putting-out businesses. In qualitative terms and by village standards, for a few it has meant riches (Scales 1 and 2 of Table 3); for others (Scale 3) it has made a substantial contribution towards attainment of a comfortable standard of living. Even for the many who earn minimal or at best modest returns (Scale 4), it has provided welcome supplemental income.

GENDER RELATIONS AND THE PUTTING-OUT BUSINESS

Because putting-out has become such an important addition to the community's occupational repertory, and because all but one of these businesses are managed by women, we must ask the obvious question: Why have these changes had no effect on the position of women in the community?

A cardinal precept in San Antonino's gender ideology holds that male and female roles should be complementary and based upon the "natural" propensities of each sex.[9] In this scheme of

TABLE 6
*Landholdings in Hectares of Putting-Out Households by Wealth Rank
Compared to
General Population of San Antonino in 1978*

Wealth Rank	Putting-Out Households		General Population	
	No.	Mean Landholding	No.	Mean Landholding
I	1	16.7	5	7.9
II	7	2.0	39	3.8
III	16	1.3	184	1.6
IV	13	0.5	554	0.5
V	3	0.0	173	0.06

things, embroidering has long been associated with females, not only because it is allegedly suited to their more delicate hands, but also because it can be performed in the spare time between other naturally appropriate female tasks such as cooking, washing, child-rearing, or selling in the marketplace—and, of course, because the finished garment itself is an item of female attire.[10] Therefore, being simply an entrepreneurial extension of embroidery, the management of putting-out systems was classified as appropriate women's work. This permitted a significant number of households to take advantage of a new economic niche without contravening the "natural" complementarity of male and female work tasks.

However, the strong representation of women in the putting-out business limited their capacity to expand, because the development of large-scale operations infringed upon the time women had to devote to their domestic duties. Only where surrogates, in the form of daughters or servants, were pressed into domestic service did a few large-scale putting-out businesses headed by women emerge. In such cases, the affected households could not conceal the fact that their major source of income was female-generated—a mark of shame in San Antonino, which ridicules a subordinate husband.

Ideally, the Oaxacan family balances women with men. The

wife-mother role in the domestic domain is recognized as indispensable, and accorded full respect. In the many households for which we have intimate information, women participate in virtually all decisions regarding household economic strategies. (Indeed, children's views are considered as well, depending on their age and economic importance.) In fact, it is not uncommon that the wife's is the dominant voice. Yet, however forceful her role, it should not spill over into the public sphere, lest her husband's image as a man, and his legitimate jural authority over the family, be compromised. In public, even the most dominant wife will show deference to her husband; otherwise, they will both become targets of gossip and ridicule, because the public arena is considered the "natural" location of male dominance.

Three of the top six putting-out businesses in 1978 (Scales 1 and 2) posed no problems for men because the largest operation was managed by the husband, and the other two were operated by spinsters residing with a single elderly parent. Two other households in the top group, which were potential targets of gossip, deflected serious criticism in two ways. First, they followed the age-old method of maintaining a relatively humble lifestyle in order to hide some of their material success. Second, the husbands distanced themselves from the putting-out operations by referring to them as "my wife's *negocito*" (little business), thus deemphasizing the economic importance of the new source of income. They also conspicuously pursued manly agricultural pursuits, leaving all aspects of the putting-out management to their wives.

The household that had risen to first place among the putting-out businesses by 1982 became the butt of numerous jokes, because the husband had become "nothing but a *costurera* (seamstress) and errand boy" for his wife's business, which—judging from the family's ostentatious displays of wealth—was obviously successful. During expansion of the business, the husband all but abandoned his agricultural pursuits. He learned how to sew and dedicated himself to assisting his wife, who clearly remained in charge. An additional humiliation was that he did not know how to drive; the couple's sons chauffeured the wife around.

If the gender ideology of separate domains for women and men constrained the development of putting-out businesses within San Antonino, it also limited the expansion of these businesses at the regional level. It is not considered proper for women to travel unaccompanied beyond the marketplaces of the valley, and even there, they are generally accompanied by children, their husbands, or other San Antonino vendors. The few women who do make frequent unaccompanied trips outside those boundaries, regardless of how legitimate their reasons (legitimate reasons include commercial activity and schooling), are gossiped about as loose women and probable prostitutes. This restriction does not hinder the marketing of garments because they can be delivered to shops in Oaxaca City or sold to the buyers who come directly to the village. Furthermore, a substantial network of outworkers can be managed from the local marketplaces that are within the respectable female traveling range. The very largest operations, however, entail traveling farther afield, which for women means delegating the traveling to men, or mobilizing male family members as escorts. Reinforcing this pattern is the fact that women do not drive. Given that buses run infrequently, are often unreliable, and serve only some of the communities, men with motor vehicles have an edge over women in the efficient management of a large network of pieceworkers.

It follows then, that the largest dress business in 1978 was managed by a husband using an automobile. In the household that had gained the top spot by 1982, the wife was driven around in a pickup truck by her sons. In contrast, the only woman dress merchant who regularly traveled alone to Mexico City to sell garments to tourist shops was subjected to malicious gossip concerning her sexual morality. When her teenage daughter began to accompany her because she had no sons, it was rumored that they were both prostitutes.

It also follows that the rising economic position of putting-out households has not seen a parallel rise in their political status. Since at least the late 1930s, the office of municipal president has been held by men whose households were relatively wealthy, although not always the wealthiest, and whose incomes usually derived from non-agricultural sources such as milling, butchering, baking, and wholesale marketing of produce. Even though putting-out has become one of the most important non-agricultural sources of income and has bestowed on several families more than enough wealth to make their heads eligible for the presidency, not a single male from those households has been mentioned as having presidential caliber. The male managers of putting-out businesses would be considered fully eligible, but in 1982 there was only one male manager and he was a foreigner. In San Antonino foreigners, like women, are considered unfit for public trust.

CONSEQUENCES OF THE PUTTING-OUT SYSTEM

In San Antonino, the "tourist" demand for hand-embroidered "peasant" garments outstripped the capacity of a traditional, undifferentiated organization of production to make them. In response, a number of peasant women became entrepreneurs, initiating a putting-out system. This system expanded output through an increased division of labor, but with little reliance on mechanization and capital investment. Notwithstanding these limitations, putting-out has had impressive effects on the local population. The product has been commoditized (Cook 1982a; Greenwood 1977; Hart 1982), the labor that produces it is alienated, and social inequality is more pervasive now than in the past.

Even in San Antonino, the embroidered blouse that goes by this name has lost its use value, both in the practical and in the symbolic sense. In practical terms, almost nobody wears it. In fact, only a few elderly women still wore the simpler version of the blouse by the time the putting-out system was organized. Similarly, the practice of giving elaborately embroidered blouses as wedding presents has ended, terminating their use to symbolize the alliance between intermarrying families.

Perhaps the only remaining symbolic use for embroidered blouses is as part of the costume worn by San Antonino's delegation to the annual state-sponsored folkdance extravaganza, *Lunes del Cerro*. During the performance, the blouses serve to identify the community. As this elaborate event is staged largely for tourists and national television, the spectacle takes on aspects of a commercial advertisement. In short, even this vestige of use value is overshadowed by the value of exchange. The San Antonino embroidered blouse is today more a trademark than an authentic cultural form.[11]

For the vast majority of consumers, the ethnic association of the San Antonino blouse with the community of this name is irrelevant, having been obliterated by what Garcia Canclini (1981:94–99) calls "commodity unification." As circulation and consumption remove products farther from their point of origin, their specific ethnic iden-

tities become homogenized as simply "typical." Thus, only some of
the Oaxaca City tourist shops label San Antonino dresses correctly;
everywhere else, wholesalers, retailers, and consumers refer to
them as "Mexican wedding dresses." Even the large Mexico City
FONART outlet dedicated to Oaxaca artisanry homogenizes its merchandise in this way. On several visits to the store, I observed the
San Antonino garments labeled as "Ocotlán," after the district in
which San Antonino is located.

Along with the loss of symbolic and ethnic identity, the putting-
out system has been accompanied by labor alienation. Previously
the San Antonino dress was made by a San Antonino craftswoman
who purchased the materials, performed all the steps at her own
pace and with her own tools, and sold or presented the finished garment herself. Now, even though most putting-out merchants perform the final assembly phase in their own households, on their
own sewing machines, using the labor of their own families, the
phase of the process that gives the garment its distinction and mar-
ketability, the embroidery phase, is performed by alienated pieceworkers. Although they work in their own homes, at their own pace,
and use their own tools, they have no control over the raw materials, the design and colors of the embroidery, the shape of the final
dress, or its ultimate disposition. Residing for the most part in the
outlying villages, rather than in San Antonino, the outworkers also
lack a communal basis for identifying with what they make.

As we have seen, financial remuneration to outworkers is
miniscule, and has reinforced the direction of change in the community and regional class structures of the Ocotlán district. To San
Antonino, putting-out has meant the formation of a new cash-
producing economic sector consisting of the putting-out households. The households involved now constitute an important element in the subclass of peasant-merchants, whose wealthiest and
most successful members are politically influential. Because embroidery is associated with women, however, and because the community discriminates against women in politics, the putting-out households have yet to gain political prominence commensurate with
their entrepreneurial standing, or on a level with the butchers, bakers, and produce wholesalers.

From the wider perspective of the region, wealth differentials
between central and peripheral villages are not new. But the
putting-out merchants of San Antonino have exploited this differen-

tial, taking advantage of cheap labor in the poorer rural communities and enhancing the favorable economic position of their own village in the process.

Finally, the most far-reaching consequence of the putting-out system has been its effects on social relationships in the work process itself. Most other peasant merchants and processor-vendors in San Antonino, as well as in other rural communities of the region, still rely exclusively on in-house family labor for the tasks that must be performed. Only a minority resorts to the hiring of wage labor, and then seldom more than one or two persons who are employed episodically. Moreover, the relationship between these peasant merchants and their employees is still basically familial. Although the workers are paid, they always take their meals with the family and often live with the family as well. By contrast, the relationship between the putting-out dress merchants and their non-San Antonino outworkers is strictly business—and indeed it is only slightly less businesslike between these merchants and the outworkers who are their fellow villagers.

The new relationship of social inequality in the Ocotlán district, together with the changed meanings of the wedding dress and the increasing alienation of labor, mean that the richly embroidered San Antonino garments of today bear no real relationship to the cloth that circulated in the Oaxacan marriage exchange system of the past. Ironically, the embroidered blouse is still linked to marriage and the embroidery motifs, although dictated by the putters-out, are anchored in tradition. The putting-out structure, however, has transformed what the embroiderers do, both materially and symbolically, substituting for the earlier intimacy between production and use a pyramid of market relations. One wonders if the consumers of "ethnic" clothing understand this transformation any better than the pieceworking embroiderers comprehend all of the steps that intervene between their hands and the final disposition of what these hands create.

ACKNOWLEDGMENTS

This paper is one result of a long-term research project in San Antonino that began in 1965 and, through the summer of 1988, had accumulated over 54 months in the field. I appreciate the direct and indirect support the project has received over the years from the National Science Foundation, the Social Science Research Council, and the PSC/CUNY Faculty Award Program of the City University of New York. I would especially like to thank my wife and research associate, Carole Turkenik, who collected much of the data on which this paper is based, and who provided invaluable editorial criticism. The paper also benefited from comments on earlier drafts by Edward Hansen, Jane Schneider, and Eric Wolf.

NOTES

1. Although the style originated in San Antonino, the dresses are no longer exclusively embroidered there, nor are all putting-out merchants who deal in the dresses from this community. It is still, however, the principal center of operations.

2. Peasant putting-out merchants or agents also existed in historical Europe; e.g., see Klima 1974.

3. The symbol "P/" will be used for Mexican pesos.

4. In the independent survey mentioned previously, Scott Cook arrived at the identical hourly wage for embroidering (Cook 1982a:64,fn.11). This not only corroborates our wage figure but also supports our statement that fees paid by merchants tend to be standardized.

5. For comparison, the wage paid to male agricultural day-laborers in San Antonino at that time, including the value of meals provided, was about P/7.50 per hour ($0.33). Most field hands employed in San Antonino come from other communities, which is further evidence of San Antonino's relative economic prosperity.

6. The U.S. prices derive from our own informal survey of several stores in New York City and Los Angeles, from a knowledgeable Oaxaca City artisanry wholesaler, and from a North American wholesale buyer.

7. The wealth rankings were constructed by utilizing a modification of Silverman's (1966) card-sort technique. A number of key informants, known to be reliable and perceptive, were asked to rate all households according to wealth. A point system was then devised by which we ranked the households. We settled on five categories because that best represented the consensus of our informants and our own observations.

8. The case is anomalous because, although the wife operates a putting-out system at the lower end of Scale 3, the household would occupy Wealth Rank I without her activities. The bulk of their wealth derives from their bakery and the 17 hectares of land they work, one of the two largest holdings in the community.

9. I purposely use the term sex rather than gender here because it is widely believed in San Antonino—by both women and men—that the behavioral differences most social scientists would attribute to socialization are in fact genetically determined.

10. The for-cash production of all clothing in San Antonino is traditionally gender-specific: *costureras* (seamstresses) of women's garments are always women, and *sastres* (tailors) of men's clothing are always men. For home use, however, it is acceptable for women to sew men's pants and shirts.

11. The young San Antonino girls who dance at *Lunes del Cerro* nearly always borrow the blouses they perform in, and would never wear one at any other time.

REFERENCES CITED

Beals, R.
  1975   The Peasant Marketing System of Oaxaca, Mexico. Berkeley: University of California Press.

Brown, E.
  1983   Shetlands to Protect Knitting Tradition. The New York Times, Feb. 25.

Charlton, L.
  1980   Gloveresses Still Stitch in the Cotswolds. The New York Times, April 30.

Cook, S.
  1982a   Crafts, Capitalist Development, and Cultural Property in Oaxaca, Mexico. Inter-American Economic Affairs 353(3):53–68.
  1982b   Craft production in Oaxaca, Mexico, Cultural Survival Quarterly 6(4):18–20.
  1984   The "Managerial" vs. the "Labor" Function, Capital Accumulation, and the Dynamics of Simple Commodity Production in Rural Oaxaca, Mexico. *In* Entrepreneurship and Social Change. Sidney Greenfield and Arnold Strickon, eds. pp. 45–95. Lanham: University Press of America.

Cook, S and M. Diskin, eds.
  1975   Markets in Oaxaca. Austin: University of Texas Press.

De Mauro, L.
  1983   Irish Sweaters to Last Forever, The New York Times, Aug. 28.

Ferretti, F.
  1983   Mystery: the Night Knitters. The New York Times, Aug. 14.

Garcia Canclini, N.
  1977   Arte Popular y Sociedad en America Latina. Mexico: Grijalbo.

1981   Las Culturas Populares en el Capitalismo. Havana: Casa de Las
Americas.

Goody, E.
1982   Introduction. *In* From Craft to Industry: the Ethnography of
Proto-Industrial Cloth Production. E. Goody, ed. pp 1–37. London: Cambridge University Press.

Graburn, N. ed.
1976   Ethnic and Tourist Arts: Cultural Expression from the Fourth
World. Berkeley: University of California Press.

Greenwood, D.
1977   Culture by the Pound: an Anthropological Perspective on Tourism as Cultural Commoditization. *In* Smith 1977, pp. 129–38.

Gullickson, G.
1982   Proto-Industrialization, Demographic Behavior and the Sexual
Divisions of Labor in Auffay, France, 1750-1850. Peasant Studies
9(2):106–118.

Hart, K.
1982   Commoditization. *In* From Craft to Industry: the Ethnography of
Proto-Industrial Cloth Production. E. Goody, ed. pp. 38–49. London: Cambridge University Press.

Hobsbawm, E.
1965   The Crisis of the 17th Century. *In* Crisis in Europe 1560-1660.
Trevor Aston, ed. pp. 5–58. London: Routledge & Kegan Paul.

Hopkins, N.
1978   The Articulation of the Modes of Production: Tailoring in Tunisia. American Ethnologist 5(3):468–83.

Jones, E.
1968   Agricultural Origins of Industry. Past and Present 40:58–71.

Klima, A.
1974   The Role of Rural Domestic Industries in Bohemia in the 18th
Century. Economic Historical Review 27:48–56.

Klima, A. and J. Macurek
1960   La Question de la Transition du Féodalisme au Capitalisme en
Europe Centrale (16e-18e siècles). International Congress of Historical Sciences, Stockholm.

Kriedte, P. and J. Schlumbohm
1977   Industrialisierung vor der Industrialisierung. Gottingen:
VandenHoeck & Ruprecht.

Lamphere, L.
1979   Fighting the Piece-rate System: New Dimensions of an old Strug-

gle in the Apparel Industry. *In* Case Studies on the Labor Process. New York: Monthly Review Press.

Littlefield, A.
1978   Exploitation and the Expansion of Capitalism: the Case of the Hammock Industry of Yucatan. American Ethnologist 5:495–508.
1979   The Expansion of Capitalist Relations of Production in Mexican Crafts. Journal of Peasant Studies 6:471–88.

Malinowski, B. and J. de la Fuente
1982   The Economics of a Mexican Market System. London: Routledge & Kegan Paul.

Mendels, F.F.
1972   Proto-Industrialization: the First Stage of the Industrialization Process. Journal of Economic History 32(1):241–61.
1975   Agriculture and Peasant Industry in 18th Century Flanders. *In* European Peasants and their Markets: Essays in Agrarian Economic History. W.N. Parker and E.L. Jones, eds. pp. 179–204. Princeton: Princeton University Press.

Novelo, V.
1976   Artesania y Capitalismo en México. Mexico: SEP/INAH.

Scott, J. and L. Tilly
1975   Women's Work and the Family in Nineteenth Century Europe. Comparative Studies in Society and History 17(1):36–64.

Silverman, S.
1977   An Ethnographic Approach to Social Stratification: Prestige in a Central Italian Community. American Anthropologist 68:899–921.

Smith, V.
1977   Hosts and Guests: the Anthropology of Tourism. University of Pennsylvania Press.

Swallow, D.
1982   Production and Control in the Indian Garment Export Industry. *In* From Craft to Industry: the Ethnography of Proto-Industrial Cloth Production. E. Goody, ed. pp. 133–65. London: Cambridge University Press.

Thirsk, J.
1961   Industries in the Countryside. *In* Essays in the Economic and Social History of Tudor and Stuart England. F.J. Fisher, ed. pp. 70–88. Cambridge: Cambridge University Press.

Waterbury, R. and C. Turkenik
1975   The Marketplace Traders of San Antonino: a Quantitative Analysis. *In* Markets in Oaxaca. S. Cook and M. Diskin, eds. Austin: University of Texas Press. pp. 209–29.

PART III. *Cloth in Large-Scale Societies*

9. Cloth and Its Function in the Inka State[1]

JOHN V. MURRA

 Inka rulers used cloth in dealing with defeated ethnic lords but also with peasants and soldiers throughout their realm. Intensive cloth production went on at both levels—state workshops, even manufactures, were kept weaving full time while peasant textiles were hoarded in ethnic treasuries. Cloth from both state and peasant looms was frequently offered, expected, confiscated or sacrificed; the study of textile circulation helps archaeologists, historians and ethnologists to understand how Andean societies functioned in pre-European times.

ANDEAN TEXTILES: AN INTRODUCTION

Years of full-time devotion have been lavished by some students on the description and analysis of the variety and technical excellence of Andean textiles. As Junius Bird, the leading modern student of the craft, has indicated, some of these fabrics "rank high among the finest ever produced."[2] Andean interest in cloth can be documented archaeologically to have endured for millennia, long before the coming of the Inka. Recent ethnohistoric studies show that the extraordinary imagination in creating a multiplicity of fabrics was functionally matched by the many unexpected political and religious contexts in which cloth was used.

The major fibers spun and woven in the ancient Andes were cotton in the lowlands and deserts and the wool of camelids in the highlands. Cotton is found in some of the earliest strata (pre-2000 B.C.), long before the appearance of maize on the Coast. Its twining and later weaving reached excellence very early,[3] and throughout coastal history it remained the important fiber; Bird goes so far as to say that the whole "Peruvian textile craft is based on the use of cotton and not on wool or any other fiber."[4] It is unfortunate that our sixteenth-century historical sources said so little about cotton cultivation, and it is curious that coastal ceramics, which so frequently illustrate cultivated plants and fruits, rarely if ever show cotton.[5]

In the highlands, archaeology tells us little, since textiles do not keep well in Andean conditions; this fact sometimes leads to neglect of the cultural significance and technical quality of highland fabrics, so evident from the early European sources. Although the excavations of Augusto Cardich[6] show that camelids had been hunted for many thousands of years, it has been impossible so far to date the beginning of llama domestication. Judging by camelids as represented on pottery and by sacrificed llama burials found on the Coast as early as Cupisnique times, we can assume that these animals were already domesticated by 1000 B.C. Bird suggests that a growing interest in wool by coastal weavers was possibly the major incentive for the domestication of camelids,[7] but at the present stage of highland studies, the taming of the guanaco and vicuña by those who had hunted them for 5,000 years and who first cultivated the potato is a more likely possibility.

In time, the use of wool increased even on the Coast and it became widespread with Inka expansion,[8] but apparently it had not penetrated everywhere, even in the highlands. Santillán reported in the 1570s that some highlanders carried burdens on their backs as they had no llamas, and even in very cold country their clothes were woven "like a net" from maguey fibers.[9] Garcilaso de la Vega also points to regions where maguey thread was woven into cloth, as wool and cotton were lacking.[10] Although neither source localizes these regions, tradition recorded by modern folkloric research describes some of the early inhabitants of the Callejón de Huaylas as

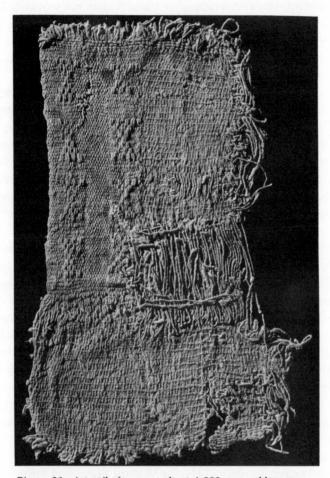

*Figure 21. A textile fragment about 4,000 years old, exca-
vated at Huaca Prieta on the north coast of Peru by Junius
Bird; it is unique in the way in which it combines the techniques of twining and weaving. Photo by Junius Bird,
American Museum of Natural History*

karapishtu, maguey leaf wearers.[11] Felipe Waman Puma, an early
seventeenth-century petitioner to the king of Spain, who reports
and illustrates an ingenious four-stage evolutionary sequence for
highland cultures, claimed that before people learned to weave they
went through a period when they were dressed in "leaves" and

later, through another wrapped in furs.[12] While the wool of vicuñas and alpacas may have been used even before domestication, it was in Inka times that llama-herding expanded as a state policy, much as it encouraged the cultivation of maize and coca-leaf,[13] through the use of *mitmaq* colonists.

The most systematic historical description of Inka looms and classification of fabrics has been recorded by the Jesuit Bernabé Cobo.[14] Although each fabric and weaving or ornamenting technique must have had its own name, European chroniclers were content with a dual classification: (1) *awasqa*, the cloth produced for domestic purposes, which was rather rough, indifferently colored and thick,[15] and (2) *kumpi*, a finer fabric, woven on a different loom. All early observers agreed the *kumpi* blankets and clothes were wonderfully soft, "like silk," frequently dyed in gay colors or ornamented with feathers or shell beads. The weave was smooth and continuous; "no thread could be seen."[16] Comparisons in those early days of the invasion were all unfavorable to European manufactures; only eighteen years later Cieza speaks of it as a lost treasure.[17]

Even today the peasant inhabitants of the Andean *altiplano* recognize ancestral textiles as the standard for beauty and high value. The authorities of Coroma, in the state of Potosí, were until recently the custodians of ten bundles (*q'epi*) of ancient and colonial weavings, one for each lineage. The local middle classes became aware of the high value of these hereditary bundles when some United States pirates took advantage of the 1982–83 drought and "bought" sixteen out of fifty-two garments. The price of each weaving on the illegal market is now in the thousands of dollars.

The Peruvian architect Héctor Velarde suggested once that the startling masonry at Machu Picchu or Huánuco Pampa reminded him of rows of stone that had been woven together. Years later, Bolivia's senior archaeologist, Maks Portugal Zamora, noted that the "peasants at Ojje (near the shrine of Copacabana) call this place *chchuku perqa* or 'sewn wall,' the . . . aboriginal vision building the wall of stones 'united as if sewn together' . . ." (p. 296).[18]

In pre-European times clothing was not tailored but left the looms virtually fully fashioned. The most detailed ethnohistoric description of peasant clothing will be found in Cobo.[19] According to Cieza there were no status differences in the tailoring of garments but only in the cloth and ornamentation used.[20] This is easily noted in the quality of archaeological textiles, since some graves display elegant, new, unused garments which must have required considerable expenditure of time and effort, while others contain ordinary clothes. Ethnic and regional differences in clothing are predictable but cannot yet be mapped beyond the varieties of *llawtu* headdresses, the hairdo, and frequently the type of cranial deformation.[21]

PEASANT USES OF CLOTH

The uses to which textiles were put by the Andean peasant should not be taken for granted. People do have to keep warm when living at 10,000 or 13,000 feet, and clothes are always important psychologically, but in the Andes the functions of cloth went far beyond such universals. Cloth emerges as the main ceremonial good and, on the personal level, the preferred gift, highlighting all crisis points in the life cycle and providing otherwise unavailable insights into the reciprocal relations of kinfolk.

Shortly after a child was weaned, he or she was given a new name at a feast to which many relatives, lineal and affinal, were invited. An "uncle" acted as sponsor and cut the first lock from the child's hair. The kinfolk followed: all who sheared hair were expected to offer gifts. Polo de Ondegardo enumerates silver, cloth, wool, cotton, and "other things." Garcilaso states that some brought clothes while others gave weapons.[22]

Initiation came at puberty for girls and at age fourteen or fifteen for boys. The boys were issued a *wara*, a loincloth woven for the occasion by their mothers. Receiving new clothes woven with magic precautions and wearing them ceremonially was an important part of change in status but details of it for the peasantry have been neglected by the European observers who have concentrated on the initiation of the young from the royal lineages. An inkling into the kind of detail we are missing comes from modern ethnology: as late as the 1920s at Quiquijana, in the Cusco area, pairs of youths would race ceremonially, their clothing fancy and new from head to foot.[23] Special clothes were still woven and all garments ceremonially washed for the young men assuming religious office thirty years ago on the island of Taquile, in Lake Titicaca.[24]

While some chroniclers and modern commentators have accepted some version of the account that marriage in the Andes depended on royal sanction, late sixteenth-century sources like Román, Murúa, and Waman Puma indicated that at the peasant household level, marriage took place on local initiative with textile gifts presented by the groom and his kin. Román, who had never been in the Andes but was widely read, mentioned llamas, but Murúa argued that only *señores*, the lords, could offer these beasts; peasant marriages were preceded by gifts of food, guinea pigs, and cloth.[25] One of the qualifications of a desirable wife was her ability to weave, and we are told that the several wives of a prominent man would compete as to who could "embroider a better blanket."[26]

Of all life's crises and their association with cloth, death is the best documented in archaeology, the early chronicles, and in ethnology. Polo, one of the best of the early observers, points out that the dead were dressed in new clothes, with additional garments placed in the grave along with sandals, bags, and headdresses.[27] This was not only an Inka custom but a pan-Andean preference, going back thousands of years. Coastal archaeology, which has at its disposal a fuller statement of the culture owing to the marvelous preservation of all remains in the desert, reveals that the dead were wrapped in numerous layers of cloth. Confirming Polo's observation, many mummies enclosed scores of garments, some of them diminutive in size and woven especially as mortuary offerings.[28] Yacovleff and his associates have tried to calculate the amount of cotton needed to make a single mummy's shroud from Paracas: it measured about 300 square yards and we are told that this size was not unique; it required the product of more than two irrigated acres planted to cotton. How many woman-hours of spinning and weaving time were involved Yacovleff thought was uncalculable.[29]

Recent ethnological work by Núñez del Prado and Morote Best clarifies the identification of persons with clothing while confirming the utility of checking colonial accounts against modern ethnology: within eight days after death, the relatives of the deceased accompanied by their friends, amidst drinking and singing, should wash every piece of the dead man's clothing, since the soul would return and complain if one garment remained unwashed. If an item be carried away by the water during the ceremonial washing, the soul would sorrow at the place where the garment gets caught in the river; to find and release it, the crowd follows the weeping sounds until the garment is located.[30]

Peasant and ethnic community worship in the Inka state has never been adequately studied since no European bothered to describe it in the early decades after the invasion. Only at the beginning of the seventeenth century when idol-burners like Avila, Arriaga, Teruel, and Albornóz reported on their vandalism do we get a hint of what local, ethnic religion may have been like, as contrasted with the activities of the state church. Arriaga, for example, was proud of having brought back to Lima and burned six hundred "idols, many of them with their clothes and ornaments and very curious *kumpi* blankets." They also burned the *mallki*, bones of "ancestors who were sons of the local shrines . . . dressed in costly feather or *kumpi* shirts."[31] If the ancestor was a woman, her shrine included her spindle and a handful of cotton. These tools had to be protected in case of an eclipse when a comet was believed to threaten the moon (another woman). The spindles were in danger of turning into vipers, the looms into bears and tigers.[32]

Sacrifices are another measure of a culture's values. Santillán tells us that the main offerings of the Inka were cloth and llamas, both of which were burned. The Jesuit Cobo claimed that the offering of fine cloth "was no less common and esteemed (than the llamas), as there was hardly any important sacrifice in which it did not enter." Some of these garments were male, others female; some were life-size, others miniature. Cobo, who frequently copied Polo's now-lost memoranda, reproduces the information that at Mantoca-lla, near Cusco, wooden reproductions of corncobs, dressed as if men and women, were fed to the sacrificial pyre at maize-shucking time.[33]

CLAIMS ON PEASANT AND ETHNIC CLOTH

There is a standard, much-quoted portrait of the never idle Andean peasant woman spinning endlessly as she stood, sat, or even walked.[34] She spun the thread and made most of the clothes in which she dressed herself and her family; she took the spindle into her grave as a symbol of womanly activity.

In practice, the sexual division of labor was less rigidly defined. Spinning and weaving skills were learned in childhood by both girls and boys. While wives and mothers were expected to tend to their families' clothing needs, all those "exempted from *mit'a* labor services"—old men and cripples and children—helped out by spinning and making rope, weaving sacks and "rough stuff" according to strength and ability.[35] Modern ethnographic research confirms this impression: both sexes weave but different fabrics.[36]

In the Andes, all households had claims to community fibers, from which the women wove cloth: "this wool was distributed from the community; to everyone whatever he needed for his clothes and those of his wives and children . . . ."[37] However, not all villages or ethnic groups had their own alpacas or cotton fields. In that case, housewives got their fibers through barter and other forms of exchange. Iñigo Ortiz's wonderfully detailed description of Huánuco village life in 1562 records various transactions: potatoes and *ch'arki* meat for cotton, peppers for wool.[38]

Still, to say that claims could be made on community resources is a formal statement masking a shortage of useful data on the provenience of the lowland woman's raw materials for weaving. Although coastal archaeology seems to tell us so much about textiles, we know almost nothing about cotton-growing practices and the economics of cotton. For example, it would be interesting to know where coastal households and villages harvested the fibers for their own use. Perhaps each village had its own cotton patch, corresponding to the highland local herd; this seems to be suggested by Ortiz's material from Huánuco. At Machque he found a cotton field "which was of all these Indians" and at Huanacaura there was a hamlet settled "communally to cultivate the cottonfields nearby."[39] But Ortiz was talking of a rather low-lying, dry highland on the eastern slopes of the Andes. On the Coast, our studies of land tenures [40] would suggest that irrigated acreage (and thus cotton fields) were subject to a variety of rights and claims that may not have operated for food crops and pastures in the highlands.

Recent research has stressed not only the contrast between the peasant community and the Inka state, but also the intermediate role of the ethnic lord, the *kuraka*.[41] He was, at the lower echelons, so frequently a member of the community, his authority and expectations reinforced by so many kin ties and obligations, that the weaving contributions of the *kuraka* partake of the reciprocal arrangements prevailing at all levels of village economic life.

The weaving claims of a minor lord like those of Huánuco included automatic access to community wool and cotton. The inspection of 1562 emphasized their claims to labor by enumerating the shirts and sandals the lord "received," the headdresses and carrying bags woven for him by "his Indians." Some of the garments were made by men, others by women, and they did it, according to a formula quoted by the inspector, "when he begged them." We still do not know if these were ordinary villagers whose ties to the *kuraka* were "reciprocal," or if they devoted full time to his service, like one Liquira, a retainer of the Yacha lord. They may have been his several wives, whom the Europeans, ignoring polygyny, called women "de servicio."[42]

Some clarification can be gained from the testimony of lawyers like Polo and Falcón: it is true, claimed the first, that the lords "received" much cloth but the weavers were their own wives.[43] Falcón recorded independently two contradictory versions: the lords insisted that before 1532 they had "received" cloth, which the peasants interviewed by the lawyer denied. Falcón thought that both told the truth: cloth, which was needed by the lord for a multitude of purposes, was mostly woven for him by his many wives but since the invaders had prohibited polygyny, there was by the 1560s a shortage of weaving hands.[44] All sources agreed that all weaving was done with the lord's fibers.

Further understanding comes when we gain access to a description of the arrangements existing in the Lupaqa kingdom, a major polity near Lake Titicaca, with some 20,000 households distributed over a wide territory that spilled west as far as the Pacific shore and to the coca-leaf gardens in the lowlands to the east.[45] In 1567, the European inspector recorded weaving and cloth-gifting obligations, always in a context of rights in land and in human energy. Qhari, lord of the polity's whole upper moiety, testified that in his home province,

> each year they weave for him five garments for which he provides the wool, while in the other six provinces they give him one garment each and some (give) two and sometimes even six or seven as each province decides of its own free will . . . all these are of *auasca* (ordinary cloth) . . . and when this witness

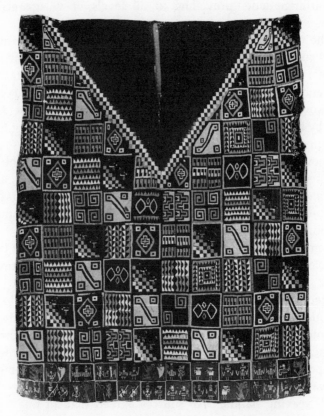

*Figure 22. This complex Inka tunic from the Lake Titicaca
area may have been created early in the Spanish Colonial
period. Photo, American Museum of Natural History*

needs a garment of good *cumpi* for personal use, he requests it
from the lords of the said towns and they weave it. . . .

The European inspector checked such statements by the lords
against the testimony of their subjects. Those of the lower moiety
declared that they "gave" their lord, Kusi,

thirty service Indians to herd his cattle (camelids) . . . and to
plant for him 20 *tupu* of land which are 60 (European) *hanegas* of
potatoes and quinoa and cañagua while he provides the
seed . . . and some years they weave him two garments and in

others three and these are of *cumpi* and the said lord gives them
the wool for it . . . and also each year they weave 8 ordinary
garments and sometimes 9 so that he will be able to give them
away according to his wishes to Indians or persons (*sic*) who
come through this town. . . .[46]

Even these very brief quotations convey the significant features of
cloth production and use: the beneficiary of weaving prestations always provided the fibers, much as he issued the seed to those planting his acreage. The primary purpose of most weaving duties, be
they of elegant or ordinary clothing, was their being "offered" or
"given away."

TEXTILES AT COURT AND IN THE ARMY

The perception above is reinforced when we come to peasant-state
relations as expressed in cloth. In Inka thinking there were two main
economic obligations the citizen had toward the state, and to each
of them corresponded an enduring pre-Inka right guaranteeing subsistence and traditional self-sufficiency to the peasant community,
a right that the Inka found it convenient to respect:

Obligation to work the crown and church lands	Right to continue to plant and harvest one's own crops on *ayllu* lands
Obligation to weave cloth for crown and church needs	Right to wool or cotton from community stocks for the making of one's own clothes

This Andean definition of equivalence between weaving and food
production as the peasantry's main obligations to the crown is confirmed by two independent but contemporaneous statements about
tasks considered important enough by the state to give the "Indians
time off." Lawyer Polo argued that such time off was granted only
to work the peasant lands and to weave the family's clothes; otherwise they were always kept busy "with one task or another."[47]
Sarmiento de Gamboa was even more rigid and specific: only three
months were "granted to the Indians"; the rest of the time was spent
toiling for the Sun, the shrines, and the king. The actual work sched-
ules need not be considered accurate; what matters are the implicit
priorities. These are confirmed by the few Andean writers: Garcilaso

is categorical. The "compulsory tribute" consisted only in the delivery of food produced on state lands and of cloth made of Inka wool.[48] Salcamayhua described one of the kings as "a friend of cultivated fields and of cloth making."[49]

Much as the ethnic lords had to provide the fibers that were worked up for them into cloth, the Inka state did not expect the peasantry to use its own raw materials for the weaving *mit'a*. As Polo recorded it elsewhere, "no Indian contributed (to the state) the cloth he had woven from the community's wool for his own garments."[50]

In some ways, lawyer Polo de Ondegardo was the European most knowledgeable about Inka statecraft. However, in one of his statements involving textiles he claimed that "they were inspected to see if they had made it into cloth and they punished the careless; thus all went around clothed . . . . "[51]

Why would inspection be necessary to enforce the making of *one's own* clothing? Polo argued: to insure that people went around dressed. But I feel that this was a manifestation of the perennial preoccupation with the nakedness of "savages." All Andean peoples wore clothes for the simple reason that it was cold; archaeology tells us they did so long before Inka times. Also, the setting up of a bureaucratic system capable of as much "inspection and punishment" as claimed by the European chroniclers is unlikely. Given the compulsory nature of the allotment ("they never took into account if the person receiving wool already had some from their own llamas"),[52] Polo's threat of "inspection" most likely refers to issues of state fibers made routinely to the housewife to be woven into garments for state purposes.

However, such distribution of state fibers to the citizenry does contribute to a misunderstanding of the Inka economy that has haunted Andean studies since the 1570s. Andean writers like Blas Valera, in their nostalgia for ancient rights that contrasted so visibly with European exactions, interpret such compulsory issues of state wool and cotton as welfare features by a diligent paterfamilias.[53] There were "welfare" measures in the Inka state, but they consisted of the enduring pre-Inka reciprocal duties and privileges incumbent on local kin and ethnic units.

The amount to be woven by each household is a matter of some controversy. Cieza claimed that each household owed a blanket per year and each person, one shirt.[54] Three other sources insist that there was no limit or accounting: "they simply wove what they were ordered and were always at it."[55] Interestingly enough, two of the three insist elsewhere, somewhat like Cieza, that each household owed only one garment per year.[56] They may be confusing different sets of obligations—one garment to the state, a uniform, verifiable, quantity, but also an unspecified amount to the ethnic lords, since this obligation was governed by tradition and local reciprocities.[57]

At the state level, some quantitative impressions are available. At the time of the European invasion, state warehouses were located throughout the kingdom, and virtually every eyewitness has indicated his amazement at their number and size.[58] Some contained food, others weapons and ornaments or tools, but the startling and peculiarly Andean aspect was the large number holding wool and cotton, cloth and garments.

Among the participants in the invasion, Xérez reported that at Caxamarca there were houses filled to the ceiling with clothes tied into bundles. Even after the "Christians took all they wanted," no dent was made in the pile.[59] "There was so much clothing of wool and cotton that it seemed to me that many ships could have been filled with them."[60] As Pizarro's cavalry proceeded across the Inka realm, similar stores were found at Xauxa and in Cusco. In the capital, we are told, it was "incredible" to see the number of separate warehouses filled with rope, wool, cloth both fine and rough, garments of many kinds, feathers, and sandals. Pedro Pizarro, musing some forty years later about what he had witnessed as a youth observes, "I cannot say about the storehouses I saw, of cloth and all kinds of garments which were made and used in this kingdom, as there was no time to see it, nor sense to understand so many things."[61]

Later observers added some information on the bookkeeping procedures by which the Inka state administration kept track of all the textiles that had been "tributed" by the people or woven by the state's own craftsmen. Cieza de León reports that in each provincial capital there were khipu kamayuq who took care of all accounts, including textile matters. At Maracavilca, near the provincial center at Xauxa, Cieza interviewed one "gentleman," Guacaropora by name, who had kept full records of everything looted from the storehouses in his charge, including cloth, during the eighteen years that had elapsed since the invasion.[62]

One gathers from the eyewitness accounts that warfare and the army were major consumers of fabrics. The military on the move expected to find blankets, clothes, and tent-making equipment on their route. Waman Puma heard in his youth that young men, aged eighteen to twenty, who acted as the army's carriers and messengers, would be issued some hominy and thick clothes as "a great gift."[63] Soldiers who had distinguished themselves in battle were given cloth, and Estete was told that the vast storehouses of "new clothing" found at the king's encampment at Caxamarca were to be issued to his troops on his formal accession to the throne.[64]

Even the royal kin were susceptible to offers of textiles. During the reconquest of Ecuador by Wayna Qhapaq, the king was confronted with a rebellion of his relatives who resented the unprecedented gifts and privileges granted to the Kañari, a local ethnic group promoted to act as an incipient standing army. Sarmiento reports that the king soothed his rebel relatives with clothes and food, in that order.[65] In Salcamayhua's independent report of the same incident, the king had to offer "for grabs" much cloth and food and other, unnamed, valuable things.[66] The much-debated historical sequence of Montesinos may be imaginary but his account that during the reign of one Titu Yupanqui, the soldiers rebelled because they were hungry and had not received the two suits of clothing owed them annually, has a culturally authentic ring. "The king ordered the granaries repaired and the clothing mit'a revived; only then were the troops satisfied.[67]

There were other ways of indicating the extraordinary attachment displayed by the army toward textiles. In describing the occupation of Xauxa by the Europeans, P. Sancho says that general Quizquiz's retreating army burned at least one and maybe several warehouses full of "many clothes and maize," in that order.[68] In describing the same events, Zárate tells us that when Quizquiz had to withdraw suddenly, he left behind 15,000 llamas and 4,000 prisoners but burned all the cloth which he could not carry.[69] The enemy was not deprived of the men (who, according to Garcilaso, joined the European army), but of cloth. To the north, in Ecuador, Rumiñ awi, retreating before Sebastián de Benalcazar's invasion, burned down a room full of fine garments kept there since Wayna Qhapaq's time.[70]

None of these attitudes can be understood in terms of matter-of-fact clothing or ornamental needs. Here archaeology is more helpful than alien observers: we find evidence of the magicomilitary importance of cloth back in Mochica times, two thousand years ago. Battle scenes painted on North Coast pottery show prisoners being undressed and their clothes carried off by the victor.[71] These attitudes endured beyond the fall of the Inka state: during the civil wars among the Europeans, their Andean troops believed that the enemy could be harmed or killed by getting hold of his clothes and using them to dress an effigy which was hanged and spat upon.[72] When the Almagristas lost the battle of Salinas, the Indians who accompanied both armies proceeded to undress the dead and even the wounded.[73] One eyewitness claims that during Manco Inka's withdrawal to resistance headquarters in the forest, in the 1540s, a skirmish took place in the highlands; even if details of the encounter were distorted, his statement that the victorious Indians took all the Europeans' clothes [74] is likely to reflect cultural norms. More than two centuries later, in 1781, the European dead were undressed during the Andean rebellions which culminated in the sieges of Cusco and La Paz.[75]

Feather-ornamented cloth seems to have a special association with soldiers and war. The feathers collected by children while herding were used in *kumpi* and "other military and imperial needs."[76] In describing the military warehouses he saw in the fortress near Cusco, Sancho reports one containing 100,000 dried birds whose feathers were used for uniforms.[77]

Since our written accounts are post-European, it is difficult to find accounts of productive processes involved in state weaving as distinct from peasant weaving. Among the few suggestive reports is one from the Bolivian National Archives, recording the presence in Inka times of a manufacture employing "a thousand" full-time male weavers of fine, feathered cloth. The lords of Huancané, near the shores of Lake Titicaca, petitioned the colonial court to help them evict these resettled "aliens." One Martin Chuca testified that "his father was an accountant for the Inka and sometimes (the witness) had accompanied his father to the said town of Milliraya and had seen the thousand *cumbi* weavers . . . and his father counted all the people, who had been resettled there."[78]

While we need not take such decimal accounts literally, a manufacturing center of several hundred craftsmen resettled away from their homes requires organizational and supply arrangements which imply macro-organizational structures archaeology should help us unravel in the future.

Figure 23. Aqlla *state weavers, "selected" from their ethnic communities, are shown in this drawing from about 1614 which appears in Felipe Guaman Pomo de Ayala's book,* El primer nueva corónica y buen gobierno, *written in the early seventeenth century*

A parallel feature of state weaving were the *aqlla* women found at many Inka administrative centers and also at the capital. According to sketchy sixteenth-century accounts, the *aqlla* spent their lives weaving for the state,[79] after having been "selected" out of their ethnic and lineage homes. The Andean writer Waman Puma mentions that there were six kinds of *aqlla*, from princesses of the blood to peasant women. Beyond their weaving duties, what they all had in common was that they were lost to their lineages of origin, a burden the conquered Lupaqa lords, for example, found very taxing. The sketchy accounts left us by the European eyewitnesses stress the analogy to nuns, since they are said to have been selected and guarded by old ex-soldiers. Archaeology has helped: in his study of a major administrative center at Huánuco Pampa, Craig Morris has located and studied an *aqlla wasi*, the house of the chosen. The uniformity of the buildings within the walled enclosure, the tiny gate, the many looms and spindle whorls excellently preserved, have been described and illustrated.[80] Morris thinks the *aqlla* performed other duties beyond weaving, like cooking for the troops coming through the administrative center. We know from the inspection of 1549, conducted only seven years after the European intrusion into Huánuco, that forty men were annually assigned "to guard the women of the Inka."[81]

THE POWER OF CLOTH IN EXCHANGE

The extraordinary value placed on textiles in the Andes cultures and the existence of class differences allowed the manipulative use of this commodity in a variety of political and social contexts. We have seen the compulsory nature of peasant weaving for the lords and for the state. The *kuraka*, in turn, provided "gifts" for the Cusco representatives, including clothes, from the populations to be enumerated and administered.[82] When Wayna Qhapaq passed through Xauxa and organized one of the many wakes for his mother, he was showered with gifts of fine cloth so well worked "the king himself dressed in it."[83]

Since traditional reciprocity was the model of Inka state revenues, an ideologic attempt was made to complement such massive textile exactions through a redistributive policy that exalted the institutionalized generosity of the crown. The simple fact that a fine cloth like *tokapu* or *kumpi* had come to be defined as a royal privilege meant that grants of it were highly valued by the recipient, to the point that unauthorized wear of vicuña cloth is reported to have been a capital offence.[84] On important occasions, such as accession to the throne or at the death of a king, when large crowds gathered at Cusco, the crown distributed among those attending as many as a thousand llamas, women, the right to be borne in litters—and, inevitably, cloth.[85]

Everybody from a humble peasant working for his *kuraka* to a lofty royal who was being removed from the succession race "considered themselves well rewarded" by a grant of garments, particularly if these had belonged to the lord or the king.[86] Anyone who had carried "tribute" or an idol or had come to Cusco on an official errand was given something "in return," depending on status, but always including cloth.[87] Sons of the *kuraka*, who were hostages in Cusco, had their exile sweetened by grants of clothes from the royal wardrobe which they sent home, a sign of royal pleasure.[88]

When an area was incorporated into the kingdom, the new citizens were granted "clothes to wear . . . which among them is highly valued," according to Blas Valera.[89] Recently, we gained additional insights into Inka political grants: soon after the European invasion, one Alonso de Montemayor received in *encomienda* one of the major Aymara polities, the Charka.[90] A record of what Montemayor "received" has been located in the Archive of the Indies in Sevilla: vast quantities of marketable coca-leaf, llamas, cloth, and timber.

Litigation over this early pillaging of Charka resources reveals that their knot-record keepers recorded everything extorted. Among the treasures in custody of lord Ayawiri was one he was reluctant to turn over but after having been threatened with hanging, "having nothing else to give him and to save himself, gave him 35 garments of very fine *cumbi* . . . which the Inka had given to his predecessors . . . ."[91] Such a hoard of dynastic cloth, accumulated over four or five generations is one side of the exchanges between the ethnic lords and their Cusco kings. There is no hope of locating archaeologically hoards that would have survived the exactions of the Europeans (Montemayor sold the thirty-five garments at the Potosí fair) given the rainy climate in the highlands. But on the desert coast, where other Aymara polities had their outliers, we may well want to look for them, once the archaeological study of particular ethnic groups becomes the norm.

Understanding the functions of cloth in such political and military contexts may lead to major new insights into Inka economic and state organization. The sources quoted hint strongly at the compulsory nature of these "gifts" of cloth. Several chroniclers, particularly

Garcilaso, have been greatly impressed with what they see as campaigns of peaceful penetration, the paradox of the gift-laden conqueror. They see in this a further example of the "generosity" of the Inka state.

There is another way of viewing such ceremonial grants to the vanquished, at the moment of their defeat: the compulsory issue of culturally valued commodities, in a society without money and only marginal markets, can be viewed as the initial pump-priming step in a dependent relationship. The "generosity" of the conqueror obligated one to reciprocate, to deliver on a regular, periodic basis, the results of one's workmanship to the Cusco warehouses.

To the Andean peasant, the Inka "gift" could be stated as doubly valuable: as cloth and as a crown grant. The state was doubly served: the supply of cloth was ensured and the onerous nature of the weaving *mit'a* could be phased in terms of culturally sanctioned reciprocity. But one can also see in this textile "gift" the issuing of Inka citizenship papers, a coercive and yet symbolic reiteration of the peasant's obligations to the state, of his or her conquered status.

A primary source of state revenues, an annual chore among peasant obligations, a common sacrificial offering, cloth could also serve at different times and occasions as a status symbol or a token of enforced citizenship, as burial furniture, bride-wealth, or armistice sealer. No political, military, social, or religious event was complete without textiles volunteered or bestowed, burned, exchanged, or sacrificed. In time, weaving became a growing state burden on the peasant household, a major occupational specialty, and eventually a factor in the emergence of retainer craft groups like the *aqlla*, the weaving women, a social category inconsistent with the prevailing Cusco claim that services to the state were no more than peasant reciprocity writ large.[92]

NOTES

The dates in square brackets following the names of sixteenth- and seventeenth-century authors refer to the year of first publication or writing; the second, modern date indicates the edition used by the writer for this chapter.

1. Earlier versions of this paper were read at the Boston meeting of the Ameri-

can Anthropological Association in 1955 and the Second Congress of Peruvian History in Lima in 1958. The research was aided by a faculty fellowship from Vassar College and a grant-in-aid from the Social Science Research Council. A first published version of it appeared in Murra 1962.

2. Bennett and Bird 1949:256. See also O'Neale (1949:105), who felt that "on their primitive looms they produced extraordinarily fine textiles [textures?], and in addition they had imagination, ingenuity and the technical proficiency to develop unknown numbers of simple and complex weave variants. Design and color harmonies exhibit a confident sense of proportion which never fails to arouse admiration." See also A.P. Rowe 1986.

3. Carrión 1931. Also Bennett 1946:29.

4. Bennett and Bird 1949:258. Also Bird 1952; Bird and Bellinger 1954. There is an excellent summary of technical information on Andean textiles in Bird 1949:256–93. This discussion, based on archaeological data, dealt mostly with coastal fabrics; my own, relying heavily on ethno-historical material, is primarily about highland woolens.

5. Yacovleff and Herrera 1934:257.

6. Cardich 1958.

7. Bennett and Bird 1949:260; Bird and Bellinger 1954:3.

8. An example: at Pachacamac where cotton was six to eight times more abundant than wool and the latter was found concentrated in the strata with Inka pottery (Bennett and Bird 1949:21).

9. Santillan [1563–64] 1968:99–149.

10. Garcilaso de la Vega [1609] 1960. See Bk. 14, ch. 13, pp. 309-310.

11. Angeles Caballero 1955.

12. Waman Puma de Ayala [1615] 1980:48–56.

13. Murra 1960:400.

14. Cobo [1653] 1956:258–59. Another early reference guide to Quechua phrases on weaving and weavers is the dictionary of Gonzalez Holguin ([1608] 1952).

15. However, from Gonzalez's dictionary ([1608] 1952:17-18) we learn that *ahua* was the weave of the cloth, *ahuani*, to weave, and *ahuac*, the weaver, without any implication about quality. In modern Cusco Quechua, cloth is *away* (Morote Best 1951).

16. Pizarro [1572] 1965:195.

17. Cieza de León [1553] Bk. I, chs. xliv, xciv; 1984:64, 119.

18. O'Neale 1949:106; Bird and Bellinger 1954:15.

19. Cobo [1653] Bk. XIV, ch. ii; 1956:192–93. See also the systematic, modern discussion of Inka clothing by J.H. Rowe 1946:233-35.

20. Cieza de León [1553] Bk. II, ch. xix; 1967:64.

21. Pizarro [1572] 1965:192–93; Murúa [1590] Bk. III, chs. xi, xxxiii; 1946:187, 242; Salcamayhua [1613] 1927:144.

22. Polo [1561] 1940:181; Polo [1571] 1916c:200-201; Garcilaso [1609] Bk. IV, ch. xi; 1960:130-31; Gonzalez [1608] 1952:323.

23. Muñiz 1926.

24. Matos Mar 1958.

25. Romàn y Zamora [1575] Bk. II, ch. x; 1879:287, 290; Waman Puma [1615] 1980:87; Murúa [1590] Bk. III, ch. xxxiii; 1946:240.

26. Ibidem.

27. Polo [1559] 1916a:8; [1567] 1916b:194.

28. O'Neale 1935.

29. Yacovleff and Muelle 1932; Yacovleff and Muelle 1934.

30. Nuñez del Prado 1952; Morote Best 1951:151.

31. Arriaga [1621] chs. 1, 2, 9; 1920:5, 25, 98.

32. Montesinos [1644] Bk. II, chs. xiv, xxii; 1882:48–49.

33. Cobo [1653] Bk. XIII, chs. xiv, xxii; 1956:176, 203.

34. Murúa [1590] Bk. III, ch. xxix; 1946:233; Garcilaso [1609] Bk. IV, ch. xiii; 1960:133–34; Cobo [1653] Bk. XIV, ch. vii; 1956:22.

35. Xerex [1534] 1947:327, 330; Polo de Ondegardo [1571] 1916c:131; Waman Puma [1615] 1980:201–224; Cobo [1653] Bk. XI, ch. vii; 1956:22.

36. Morote Best 1951:15; Franquemont 1986:309-330.

37. Polo [1571] 1916c:66.

38. Ortiz de Zúñiga [1562] 1967:f. 17v.

39. Ortiz de Zúñiga [1562] 1967:f. 144r.

40. Murra 1980.

41. J. H. Rowe 1955; J. H. Rowe 1957; Núñez Anavitarte 1955; Moore 1958.

42. Ortiz de Zúñiga [1562] 1967:f. 128v.

43. Polo [1561] 1940:141.

44. Falcón [1565?] 1916:154.

45. Diez de San Miguel [1567] 1964:f. 94.

46. Ibidem.

47. Polo [1561] 1940:140–41; [1571] 1916c:131.

48. Sarmiento de Gamboa [1572] 1943;117–18.

49. Garcilaso [1609] Bk. V, ch. vi; 1960:155–56.

50. Salcamayhua [1613] 1927:147

51. Polo [1571] 1916c:127. See also [1561] 1940:136, 178. Thirty years after the invasion, the peasants of the Huánuco area still remembered that the Inka crown had issued them wool to be woven for the state warehouses and contrasted with the European exactions in kind.

52. Polo [1571] 1916c:65–66.

53. Ibidem.

54. Cieza [1553] Bk. II, ch. xviii; 1967:59–61.

55. Castro and Ortega [1558] 1974:91–104; Polo [1561] 1940:165; Polo [1571] 1916c:66, 127; Santillán [1563] ch. xli; 1968:115.

56. Castro and Ortega [1558] 1974:102; compare with Santillán [1563] ch. xliii; 1968:115 with ch. lxviii; 1968:126.

57. See also the indignant protests of Waman Puma [1615] 1980:499, 501, 530, 910, and drawings, 578, 668.

58. Morris 1967. See also Morris 1981:327–75.

59. Xerez [1534] 1947:334.

60. Estete [1535] 1918.

61. Pizarro [1572] 1965:195.

62. Cieza [1553] Bk. II, ch. xii; 1967:36–37; see also Espinoza Soriano 1971. Also Murra 1975.

63. Waman Puma [1615] 1980:499.

64. Estete [1535] 1918:f. 8v.

65. Sarmiento de Gamboa [1572] 1943:126.

66. Salcamayhua [1613] 1927:213–14. See also Cabello Valboa [1586] Bk. III, ch. xxi; 1951:375–76.

67. Montesinos [1644] Bk. II, ch. x; 1882:58.

68. Sancho de la Hoz [1535] 1927?:141. See also letter to the king from the *cabildo* of Xauxa, the first European capital (Porras Barrenechea 1959:124–31).

69. Zárate [1555] Bk. II, ch. xii; 1947:491.

70. Zárate [1555] Bk. II, ch. ix; 1947:481.

71. Muelle 1936.

72. Murua [1590] Bk. III, ch. lviii; 1946:306.

73. Zárate [1555] Bk. II, ch. xi; 1947:491.

74. Cusi Yupanqui [1565?] 1916:83.

75. Villanueva 1948.

76. Waman Puma [1615] 1980:209.

77. Sancho [1535] ch. xvii; 1917:194.

78. Murra 1978:415–23.

79. Murra 1980:chs. IV, VIII.

80. Murra and Morris 1976.

81. See the inspection of 1549, included in Ortiz de Zúñiga ([1562] 1967:289–310.

82. Sarmiento de Gamboa [1572] 1943:88.

83. Cobo [1653] Bk. XII, ch. xvi; 1956:89.

84. Garcilaso [1609] Bk. VI, ch. vi; 1960:201.

85. Cabello Valboa [1586] Bk. III, ch. xx; 1951:359; Murúa [1590] Bk. III, ch. xliv; 1946:266; Cobo [1653] Bk. XII, ch. vi; 1956:69.

86. Cabello Valboa [1586] Bk. II, ch. xx; 1951:197.

87. Falcón [1565?] 1918:153-54; see also the excellent description in Cobo [1653] Bk. XII, ch. xxx; 1956:125.

88. Garcilaso [1609] Bk. VII, ch. ii; 1960:248.

89. Ibidem.

90. Archivo General de Indias, Sevilla: Justicia section, 653.

91. Ibidem.

92. Murra 1980, ch. VIII.

REFERENCES CITED

The dates in square brackets following the names of sixteenth- and seventeenth-century authors refer to the year of first publication or writing; the second, modern date indicates the edition used by the writer for this chapter.

Arriaga, Pablo José de
[1621]   Extirpacion de la idolatria en el Peru. *In* Colección de
1920   libros y documentos referentes a la historia del Perú, Serie II, Vol. 1. Lima.

Angeles Caballero, César A.
1955   Archivos Peruanos de Folklore 1 (1). Lima.

Bennett, Wendell C., and Junius Bird
1946   The Archaeology of the Central Andes. *In* Handbook of South
        American Indians. J. Steward, ed. 2:61–147. Smithsonian Institu-
        tion, Bureau of American Ethnology, Bulletin 143. Washington
        D.C.: U.S. Government Printing Office.
1949   Andean Culture History. Handbook No. 5. New York:
        American Museum of Natural History.

Betanzos, Juan de
[1551] Suma y narracion de los incas. Biblioteca de Autores
1968   Españoles, Vol. 209. Madrid: Ediciones Atlas.

Bird, Junius B
1952   Fechas de radiocarbono para Sud América. Revista del Museo
        Nacional, 21:8–34. Lima.

Bird, Junius B., and Louisa Bellinger
1954   Paracas Fabrics and Nasca Needlework, 3rd century B.C.—3rd
        century A.D. The Textile Museum, Catalogue Raisonné. Wash-
        ington, D.C.: The Textile Museum.

Cabello Valboa, Miguel
[1586] Miscelanea antartica. Lima: Universidad Nacional Mayor
1951   de San Marcos.

Cardich, Augusto
1958   Los yacimientos de Lauricocha. Buenos Aires: Centro Argentino
        de Estudios Prehistóricos.

Carrión Cachot, Rebeca
1931   La indumentaria en la antigua cultura de Paracas. Wira Kocha:
        Revista Peruana de Estudios Antropológicos, 1 (1):37–86.

Castro, Cristobal de, and Diego Ortega Morejon
[1558] Relacion y declaracion del modo que en este valle de
1974   Chincha . . . .Historia y Cultura, (8):91–104. Lima.

Cieza de León, Pedro
[1553] La crónica del Peru. *In* Obras Completas, Book 1. Madrid:
1984   Monumento Hispano-Indiana.
[1553] El señorio de los Incas, Book II. Lima: Instituto de Estu-
1967   dios Peruanos.

Cobo, Bernabé
[1653] Historia del Nuevo Mundo. Biblioteca de Auto res
1964   Españoles, Vols. 91–92. Madrid: Ediciones Atlas.

Cusi, Yupanqui, Titu
[1565?] Relacion de la conquista del Peru. *In* Colección de libros
1916   y documentos referentes a la historia del Perú, Serie I,
        Vol. 2. Lima.

Diez de San Miguel, Garci
[1567]   Visita hecha a la provincia de Chucuito. Lima: Casa de la
1964   Cultura del Perú.

Espinoza Soriano, Waldemar
1971   Los Huancas, aliados en la conquista. Huancayo.

Estete, Miguel de
[1535]   Noticia del Peru, Boletín 1 (3):300–50, f. 1–12. (Facsimile
1918   ed.) Quito: Sociedad Ecuatoriana de Estudios Históricos
    Americanos.

Falcón, Francisco
[1565?]   Representacion hecha en Concilio Provincia . . . . *In* Co-
1918   lección de libros y documentos referentes a la historia del
    Perú, Serie I, Vol. 11. Lima.

Franquemont, Edward M.
1986   Cloth Production Rates in Chinchero, Perú. *In* Junius B. Bird
    Conference on Andean Textiles. A. Rowe, ed. pp. 309–29. Wash-
    ington, D.C.: The Textile Museum.

Garcilaso de la Vega
[1609]   Comentarios reales de los Incas. Biblioteca de Autores
1960   Españoles, Vol. 133. Madrid: Ediciones Atlas.

Gonzalez Holguin, Diego
[1608]   Vocabulario de la lengua general de todo el Peru. Edición
1952   del Instituto de Historia de la Facultad de Letras. Lima:
    Universidad Nacional Mayor de San Marcos.

Jesuita Anónimo [Garcia de Toledo?]
[1575]   Relacion de las costumbres antiguas. *In* Los Pequeños
1945   Grandes Libros de la Historia Americana. Lima.

Matos Mar, José
1958   La Estructura Económica de una Comunidad Andina. Ph.D. dis-
    sertation. Universidad Nacional Mayor de San Marcos.

Molina "del Cuzco," Cristobal de
[1575]   Relacion de las fabulas y ritos de los incas. *In* Los
1943   Pequeños Grandes Libros de la Historia Americana. Lima.

Montesinos, Fernando de
[1644]   Memorias antiguas historiales y politicas del Peru. *In*
1882   Colección de libros españoles raros y curiosos. Madrid.

Moore, Sally Falk
1958   Power and Property in Inca Peru. New York: Columbia Univer-
    sity Press.

Morote Best, Efraín
1951   La vivienda campesina en Sallaq. Tradición (7–10). Cusco.

Morris, Craig
    1967   Storage in Tawantinsuyu. Ph.D. dissertation. University of Chicago.
    1981   Tecnología y organización Inca del almacenamiento de víveres en la sierra. In Runakunap Kawsayninkupaq Rurasqankunaqa: La tecnología en el mundo andino. H. Lechtman and A. M. Soldi, eds., pp. 327–75. México, D.F.: Universidad Nacional Autónoma.

Muelle, Jorge C.
    1936   Chalchalcha—un análisis de los dibujos Muchik. Revista del Museo Nacional 4:65–88.

Muñiz, César A.
    1926   Del folklore indígena. Revista Universitaria 16(52). Cusco.

Murra, John V.
    1962   Cloth and its functions in the Inca State. American Anthropologist, 64(4):710–28.
    1960   Rite and Crop in the Inca State. In Culture in History: Essays in Honor of Paul Radin. S. Diamond, ed., pp.393–407. New York: Columbia University Press.
    1975   Las etnocategorías de un khipu estatal. In Formaciones económicas y políticas del mundo andino. J. V. Murra, ed., pp. 243–54. Lima: Instituto de Estudios Peruanos.
    1978   Los olleros del Inka: hacia una historia y arqueología del Qollasuyu. In Historia, promesa y problema: Homenaje a Jorge Basadre. 1:415–23. Lima.
    1980   The Economic Organization of the Inka State. Greenwich, Conn: JAI Press.

Murra, John V., and Craig Morris
    1976   Dynastic oral tradition, administrative records and archaeology in the Andes. World Archaeology 7(3):270–79.

Murúa, Martin de
    [1590]   Historia y genealogia real de los reyes Incas del Perú. C.
    1946   Bayle, ed. Book III. Madrid: Biblioteca Missionalia Hispanica.

Núñez Anavitarte, Carlos
    1955   El cacicazgo como supervivencia 'esclavista-patriarcal' en el seno de la sociedad colonial. Cusco.

Núñez del Prado, Oscar
    1952   La vida i muerte en Chinchero. Cusco.

O'Neale, Lila M.
    1949   Weaving. In Handbook of South American Indians. J. Steward, ed. Vol 6:97–148. Smithsonian Instituion, Bureau of American Ethnology, Bulletin 143. Washington, D.C.: U.S. Government Printing Office.

Pequeñas prendas ceremoniales de Paracas. Revista del Museo Nacional 4(2):245–66. Lima.

Ortiz de Zúñiga, Iñigo
[1562]   Visita de la provincia de León de Huánuco. Huánuco:
1968   Universidad Nacional Hermilio Valdizán.

Pizarro, Pedro
[1572]   Relacion del descubrimiento y conquista de los reynos del
1965   Peru. Biblioteca de Autores Españoles, Vol. 168. Madrid: Ediciones Atlas.

Polo de Ondegardo, Juan
[1559]   Instruccion contra las ceremonias y ritos. *In* Colección de
1916a   libros y documentos referentes a la historia del Perú, Serie I, Vol. 3. Lima.
[1567]   De los errores y supersticiones de los Indios, sacadas del
1916b   tratado y averiguacion que hizo el Licenciado Polo. *In* Colección de libros y documentos referents a la historia del Perú, Serie I, Vol. 3. Lima
[1571]   Relacion de los fundamentos acerca del notable daño que
1916c   resulta de no guardar a los indios sus fuero . . . . *In* Colección de libros y documentos referentes a la historia del Perú, Serie I, Vol. 3. Lima
[1561]   Informe al licenciado Briviesca de Muñatones. Revista His-
1940   tórica 13:128–96. Lima.

Porras Barrenechea, Raúl, ed.,
[1534] 1959   Cartas del Perú. Lima.

Portugal Zamora, Maks
1980   Estudio arqueológico de Copacabana. Mesa redonda de arqueología boliviana y surperuana 2:285–323.

Roman y Zamora, Jeronimo
[1575]   Republica de Indias. *In* Colección de libros raros y curio-
1879   sos que tratan de América, Vols. 13–14. Madrid.

Rowe, Ann Pollard, ed.
1986   The Junius B. Bird Conference on Andean Textiles. Washington, D.C.: The Textile Museum.

Rowe, John H.
1946   Inca Culture at the Time of the Spanish Conquest. *In* Handbook of South American Indians. J. Steward, ed. 2:183–330. Smithsonian Institution, Bureau of American Ethnology, Bulletin 143. Washington, D.C.: U.S. Government Printing Office.
1955   Movimiento nacional Inca del siglo XVIII. Revista Universitaria (107). Cusco.
1957   The Incas under Spanish colonial institutions. Hispanic American Historical Review 37 (2).

Salcamayhua, Juan de Santa Cruz Pachacuti Yamqui
[1613]   Relacion de antiguedades deste reyno del Piru. *In*
1927   Colección de libros y documentos referentes a la historia
         del Perú, Serie II, Vol. 9. Lima.

Sancho de la Hoz, Pedro
[1535]   Relacion para Su Majestad de lo sucedido en la conquis-
1927?   to . . . de la Nueva Castilla. *In* Colección de libros y do-
         cumentos referentes a la historia del Perú, Serie II, Vol. 9.
         Lima.

Santillan, Hernando de
[1563-64] Relación de origen, descendencia política y gobierno de
1968   los Incas. Biblioteca de Autores Españoles, Vol. 209. Ma-
           drid: Ediciones Atlas.

Sarmiento de Gamboa, Pedro
[1572] 1943   Historia Indica. Buenos Aires: Biblioteca Emece.

Waman Puma de Ayala, Felipe
[1615]   El primer nueva corónica y buen gobierno. J.V. Murra and
1980   R. Adorno, eds. México, D.F.:Siglo XXI.

Villanueva, Horacio
1948   Los padres betlemitas del Cuzco y la rebelión de Tupaj Amaru.
         Revista del instituto y Museo Arqueológico (12):73–84. Cusco.

Xerex, Francisco de
[1534]   Verdadera relacion de la conquista del Peru. Biblioteca de
1947   Autores Españoles. Vol. 26. Madrid: Ediciones Atlas.

Yacovleff, Eugenio and Fortunato Herrera
1934   El mundo vegetal de los antiguos peruanos. Revista del Museo
         Nacional 3(3):241–332 and 4(1):29–102. Lima.

Yacovleff, Eugenio and Jorge C. Muelle
1932   Una exploración en Cerro Colorado. Revista del Museo Nacional
         1(2):31–59. Lima.
1934   Un fardo funerario de Paracas. Revista del Museo Nacional·
         3(1–2):63–153.

Zarate, Agustin de
[1555]   Historia del descubrimiento y conquista del Peru. Biblio-
1947   teca de Autores Españoles, Vol. 26. Madrid: Ediciones Atlas.

10. Cloth, Clothes, and Colonialism

India in the Nineteenth Century

BERNARD S. COHN

 In 1959, Mr. G.S. Sagar, a Sikh, applied for a position as a bus conductor with Manchester Transport. His application was rejected because he insisted that he wanted to wear his turban rather than the uniform cap prescribed by the municipality for all its transport workers. Sagar argued that the wearing of the turban "was an essential part of his religious beliefs" (Beetham 1970:20). He didn't understand why, if thousands of Sikhs who had fought and died for the empire in the two World Wars could wear their turbans, he couldn't do so. The transport authorities argued that "if an exception to the rules of wearing the proper uniform were allowed there was no telling where the process would end. The uniform could only be maintained if there were no exceptions" (Beetham 1970:19).

At its most obvious level, this was a dispute about an employer's power to impose rules concerning employee's dress and appearance, and the employee's right to follow the injunctions of his religion. Early in the dispute, which was to last seven years, a distinction was made between such items of attire, as the kilt of a Scotsman, which were expressions of national identities—a "national costume" that could be legally prescribed for workers—and those items of dress that were worn as the result of a religious injunction. The advocates of allowing the Sikhs to wear their turbans on the job said that to prevent them from doing so was an act of religious discrimination. The Transport worker's union supported management in the dispute, on the grounds that an individual worker could not set the terms of his own employment, which they saw as a matter of union-management negotiation.

At another level the dispute was about working-class whites' resentment of dark-skinned, exotically dressed strangers, whom they saw as "cheap" labor allowed into their country, to drive down wages and take pay packets out of the hands of honest English workingmen. The fact that many of these British workers preferred easier, cleaner, or higher-paying jobs did not lessen their xenophobic reactions. Similarly, some of the middle class saw the immigrants from the "new" commonwealth as a threat to an assumed homogeneity of British culture. The turban, the dark skin, and the sari of Indian and Pakistani women were simply outward manifestations of this threat.

In short, the dispute over the Sikh's turban can be seen as a symbolic displacement of economic, political, and cultural issues, rooted in two hundred years of tangled relationships between Indians and their British conquerors. In order to understand this conflict, I will explore the meaning of clothes for Indians and British in the nineteenth century; the establishment of the categorical separation between dark subjects and fair-skinned rulers; the search for representations of the inherent and necessary differences between rulers and ruled as constructed by the British; and the creation of a uniform of rebellion by the Indians in the twentieth century.

TURBANS OF IDENTITY

The dispute over Mr. Sagar's turban also echoed the growing sense of loss of power being felt by the British as they rapidly divested themselves of the Empire in Asia and Africa, and heard their former subjects demanding their independence and some form of equity with their former rulers. The whole social order at home also appeared to the middle and upper classes to be changing, with the revolution being acted out in terms of clothes. The youth of the under class was setting the styles for their elders and betters, and mocking many former emblems of high status by turning them into kitsch and fads for an increasingly assertive new generation.

There is an irony that a Sikh's turban should be involved in the final act of a long-playing drama in which the costumes of the British rulers and their Indian subjects played a crucial role. For the British in nineteenth-century India had played a major part in making the turban into a salient feature of Sikh self-identity.

Sikhism was a religious movement that grew out of syncretic tendencies in theology and worship among Hindus and Muslims in North India in the fifteenth century. Guru Nanak, its founder, whose writings and sayings were codified in a holy book called the *Granth Sahib*, established a line of successors as leaders and interpreters of his creed. Through much of the sixteenth and seventeenth centuries, the Sikhs faced increasing persecution from their political overlords, the Mughals, as much for their strategic location across the traditional invasion route of India in the Punjab as for their growing religious militancy.

This militancy was codified and restructured by the tenth and last in succession of the Gurus, Gobind Singh. He created a series of distinctive emblems for those Sikhs who rallied into a reformed community of the pure, the *Khalsa*, from among the wider population, which continued to follow many Hindu and Muslim customs. In a dramatic series of events in 1699, Guru Gobind Singh chose five of his followers as founding members of this new brotherhood. Those selected had shown their willingness to have their heads cut off as an act of devotion to their guru.

Guru Gobind Singh issued a call for large-scale participation in the celebration of the New Year in 1699. Those Sikh males attending were enjoined to appear with their hair and beards uncut. As the festivities developed, there was no sign of the Guru, who was waiting in a tent, until he suddenly appeared brandishing a sword, and called upon the assembled Sikhs to volunteer to have their heads cut off as a sign of their devotion. One volunteered and accompanied his Guru back to the tent. A thud was heard and the Guru reappeared with a bloody sword. The apparent sacrifice was repeated with four other volunteers, and then the side of the tent was folded back to reveal the five still alive and the severed heads of goats on the ground.

These five were declared the nucleus of the *Khalsa*. They went through an initiation ritual in which they all drank from the same bowl, symbolizing their equality, and then the chosen five initiated the Guru. Next, they promulgated rules: Sikh males would wear

their hair unshorn; they would abstain from using alcohol and tobacco, eating meat butchered in the Muslim fashion, and having
sexual intercourse with Muslim women. Henceforth they would all
bear the surname Singh. In addition to unshorn hair (*kes*), they
would wear a comb in their hair (*kangha*), knee-length breeches
(*kach*), and a steel bracelet on their right wrist (*kara*), and they would
carry a sword (*kirpan*) (MacLeod 1976:14–15; K. Singh 1963:83–84).

J.P. Oberoi has analyzed these symbols as well as an unex-
pressed sixth one, the injuction against circumcision, as establishing
the total separation of the Sikhs from Hindus and Muslims. In addition he sees them as two opposed triple sets: The unshorn hair,
sword, and uncircumcised penis representing "amoral", even dangerous power; the comb, breeches, and bracelet expressing constraint. In the totality of the two sets, he sees an affirmation of the
power and constraint inherent in humanness (Oberoi 1967:97).

Note that this excursus on the formation of the Sikhs and their
symbology does not mention the turban as part of their distinctive
costume and appearance. Most scholars who have written about the
history of the Sikhs and their religion are silent on the question of
when and how the turban became part of the representational canon
of the community. M.A. Macauliffe, translator of and commentator
on the sacred writings of the Gurus, noted in a footnote, "Although
the Guru [Gobind Singh] allowed his Sikhs to adopt the dress of
every country they inhabited, yet they must not wear hats but turbans to confine their long hair which they are strictly enjoined to
preserve" (1909,V:215). W.H. MacLeod notes that the turban is the
one post-eighteenth-century symbol added to the "*Khalsa* code of
discipline" (1976:53). The wearing of turbans, though lacking "formal sanction . . . during the nineteenth and twentieth centuries has
been accorded an increasing importance in the endless quest for self
identification" (1976:53).

Early nineteenth-century representations by European and Indian artists of the "distinctive" headdress of the Sikhs showed two
different types. One was a tightly wrapped turban of plain cloth,
which was either thin enough or loose enough on the crown to accommodate the topknot of the Sikh's hair. The second type of turban worn by the Sikhs in the early nineteenth century was associated with rulership. This turban was elaborately wrapped and had
a *jigha*, a plume with a jewel attached, and a *sairpaich*, a cluster of
jewels in a gold or silver setting. As will be discussed below, these

ornamental devices were symbols of royalty, popularized in India by the Mughals.

In the eighteenth century, Mughal political and military power declined. The Punjab went through a period of invasions and the emergence of contending Sikh polities, which were combined under the leadership of Ranjit Singh by the early nineteenth century into a powerful state. With the death of Ranjit Singh in 1839, the state came under increasing pressure from the East India Company, which in a series of wars finally conquered and annexed the former Sikh state in 1849.

Although the Sikh state was fragmenting, the Sikh armies proved formidable; despite their defeat by the East India Company, Sikhs were treated more as worthy adversaries than as a defeated nation. Those British who fought against the Sikhs were highly impressed by their martial qualities. Unlike many of their conquered subjects, who struck the British as superstitious and effeminate, the Sikhs were considered manly and brave. Their religion prohibited "idolatry, hypocrisy, caste exclusiveness . . . the immurement of women" and immolation of widows, and infanticide (Macauliffe 1909, I:xxiii). Captain R.W. Falcon, author of a handbook for British officers in the Indian army, described the Sikh as "manly in his war-like creed, in his love of sports and in being a true son of the soil; a buffalo, not quick in understanding, but brave, strong and true" (1896:Preface). In short the Sikhs, like a few other groups in South Asia (the Hill peoples of Nepal, the Gurkhas, and the Pathans of the Northwest Frontier) who came close to defeating the British, were to become perfect recruits for the Indian army.

Within a year of their defeat, Sikhs were being actively recruited for the East India Company's army, and the officers who had just fought the Sikhs "insisted on the Sikh recruits being "*Kesadhari*," from among the *Khalsa* Sikhs who were unshorn (Singh 1953:83). Only those Sikhs who looked like Sikhs—wearing those badges of wildness, the beard and unshorn hair—were to be enrolled. It was also official policy to provide every means for the Sikhs to keep their "freedom from the bigoted prejudices of caste . . . and to preserve intact the distinctive characteristics of their race and peculiar conventions and social customs" (Singh 1953:83 and 1966, II:111–15).

The effectiveness of the British decision, made in 1850, to raise Sikh units for their army was borne out in 1857–58. The bulk of their native army in North India rebelled. The Sikhs enthusiastically and

effectively participated in the defeat of their hated enemies, the remnants of the Mughals and their despised Hindu neighbors of the
Ganges Valley.

With the reorganization of the British Army in India after 1860,
the British came to rely increasingly on the Punjabis in general and
Sikhs in particular to man their army. The Punjab, with 8 percent
of the population of India, provided half of their army in 1911. The
Sikhs, who were 1 percent of the Indian population, accounted for
20 percent of the total number of Indians in the military service (GOI
The Army in India Committee, 1913 IA:156).

By the late nineteenth century a standardized Sikh turban, as distinct from the turban of the Punjabi Muslims and Hindu Dogras,
had emerged and had become the hallmark of the Sikhs in the army.
This turban, large and neatly wrapped to cover the whole head and
ears, became the visible badge of those the British had recruited.
The Sikh turban and neatly trimmed beard were to stand until 1947
as the outward sign of those qualities for which they were recruited
and trained: Their wildness, controlled by the turban, and their
fierceness, translated into dogged courage and stolid "buffalo"-like
willingness to obey and follow their British officers.

During World War I, the British army replaced the great variety
of headgear of both their own troops and their colonials with steel
helmets, but by now "the Sikhs had come to associate their uniform
pagri (turban) with their religion," and the argument that the turban
as such was not prescribed by their religious code was to no avail
(T.A. Heathcote 1974:103).

Thus, the current significance of the distinctive turban of the
Sikhs was constructed out of the colonial context, in which British
rulers sought to objectify qualities they thought appropriate to roles
that various groups in India were to play. The British sought to
maintain the conditions that, they believed, produced the warrior
qualities of the Sikhs' religion. In any post-eighteenth-century European army a uniform, in which each individual is dressed like every
other one of the same rank and unit, symbolizes the discipline and
obedience required for that unit to act on command. A distinctive
style of turban, worn only by Sikhs and serving in companies made
up of Sikhs, was the crucial item of their uniform, which represented and helped constitute the obedience that the British expected
of their loyal Indian followers.

Over time the military-style turban became general, although far from universal, among the Sikhs. The Sikh has now come "home" to the British Isles, but the turban no longer symbolizes loyalty to an old military code identified with their former rulers. Instead, the turban now plays a part in the Sikhs' effort to maintain their unique identity in the face of hostility and pressure to conform to "normal" or expected dress in mass society.

The struggle to maintain the very difference that had been encouraged by their past rulers now is seen as a form of obstinacy. The pressure to conform to the rules of dress for bus conductors has been followed by a long legal struggle over whether Sikhs could ignore the law in England that motorcycle drivers and passengers had to wear crash helmets. The battleground has more recently shifted to the question of whether a Sikh boy could be barred from a private school because he and his father "insisted on his wearing uncut hair and a turban above his blazer" (Wallman 1982:4). This case was settled in 1983, when the House of Lords reversed a lower court, which had found the the Headmaster had "unlawfully discriminated against the Sikh . . . by requiring him to remove his turban and cut his hair" (*RAIN* 1983:16).

THE BRITISH AS THEY WISHED TO BE SEEN

While the British established themselves as the new rulers of India, they constructed a system of codes of conduct which constantly distanced them—physically, socially, and culturally—from their Indian subjects. From the founding of their first trading station in Surat in the early seventeenth century, the employees of the East India Company lived a quasi-cloistered life. Although dependent on the Mughal and his local official for protection, on the knowledge and skills of Indian merchants for their profits, and on Indian servants for their health and well being, they lived as a society of sojourners. In their dress and demeanor they constantly symbolized their separateness from their Indian superiors, equals, and inferiors. Paintings by Indians of Europeans in the seventeenth and eighteenth centuries emphasized the differences in costume, which apparently made little concession to the Indian environment culturally or physically. At home, in the office, in the field hunting, or when representing the majesty and authority of the Company, the British dressed in their own fashions.

The one exception to the cultural imperative of wearing European dress was among those whose careers were spent up-country as British representatives in Muslim royal courts, where it was usual for some of them to live openly with Indian mistresses and to acknowledge their Indian children. These semi-Mughalized Europeans, although wearing European clothes in their public functions, affected Muslim dress in the privacy of their homes. The wearing of Indian dress in public functions by employees of the Company was officially banned in 1830. The Regulation was directed against Frederick John Shore, a judge in Upper India who wore Indian clothes while sitting in his court. Shore was a persistent critic of the systematic degradation of Indians, particularly local notables, intelligentsia, and Indians employed in responsible jobs in the revenue and judicial services. He argued strenuously not just for better understanding of the natives, but also for their full employment in the governance of their own country (Shore 1837).

The practice of maintaining their Englishness in dealing with Indians goes back to the royal embassy sent by King James the First to negotiate a treaty to "procure commodities of saftie and profit" in the Mughal's realm in 1615. The English ambassador, Sir Thomas Roe, was instructed by his ruler: "To be careful of the preservation of our honor and dignity, both as wee are soverign prince, and a professed Christian, as well in your speeches and presentation of our letters as in all other circumstances as far as it standeth with the customs of these Countries" (Foster 1899,I:552). Roe was not comfortable in conforming to the proper behavior expected of an Ambassador at an Indian court. The Mughal, Jahangir, despised merchants as inferior to warriors and rulers. Although amused by Roe, and personally polite and accommodating to his peculiarities, he was sceptical about an ambassador representing a powerful European who seemed so interested in trade. Roe's explicit concern with establishing the means to increase "the utility and profits" of the subjects of King James was not shared by Jahangir.

The English effort to obtain a trade treaty was based on their own ideas about trade, which involved defining certain cultural objects as commodities. Increasingly in the seventeenth and eighteenth centuries, the commodities they sought in India were a wide variety of textiles, to be shipped to England or traded in Southeast Asia for spices and other valued objects to be sent to England. A major problem arose because the Indians were not much interested in the manufactured goods that the British had available—woolens, metal goods, and various "curiosities." What the Indians wanted was silver, copper, and gold. Another problem arose because the British persisted in viewing textiles as practical or utilitarian objects, suitable for providing profit for the shareholders and officials of the Company. The textiles and clothes made by Indians did indeed have a market and a practical value, but there were many other significations involved in the production and use of these objects, which the British defined as commodities.

Roe and his small party, which included the Reverend Terry as his chaplin, began to realize that the clothes worn—and particularly the use of cloth and clothes as prestations in the Mughal's court— had meaning far beyond any "practical use." Jahangir did allow Roe to follow his own customs of bowing and removing his hat, rather than using the various forms of prostration that were the usual means of offering respect to the Mughal. Through the three years that he traveled with Jahangir, Roe and his followers always wore English dress, "made light and cool as possibly we could have them; his waiters in Red Taffata cloakes" Terry, the chaplin, always wore "a long black cassock" (Foster 1899:I:106)

Roe had brought with him to the Mughal Court a considerable number of gifts, among which was a bolt of scarlet cloth that was perhaps more appropriate for the natives of North America than a sophisticated Indian ruler. Roe substituted for the cloth his own sword and sash. This gift was greatly appreciated by Jahangir, who asked Roe to send his servant to tie it on properly and then began to stride up and down, drawing the sword and waving it about. Roe reported that on a number of occasions Jahangir and some of his nobles, wishing to honor Roe, wanted to present him with clothes, jewels, and turbans. Although Roe, in his account, does not explain why he tried to avoid receiving these gifts, I can infer that he probably understood their significance. This kind of gift was the means by which authoritative relations were established and would, in the eyes of the Indians, make Roe into a subordinate or companion of the Mughals. In order to understand why Jahangir was pleased with Roe's sword and sash and why Roe was leery of accepting clothes and jewels, I will now explore the constitution of authority in Mughal India.

CLOTHES AND THE CONSTITUTION OF AUTHORITY

By the fifteenth century, the idea that the King was the maintainer of a temporal as well as a sacred order was shared by Muslims and Hindus in India (Hasan 1937:55–57). Royal functions were centered on the idea of protection and the increase of the prosperity of the ruled. "If royalty did not exist," wrote Abu al Fazl, the chronicler of Akbar's greatness, "the storm of strife would never subside, nor selfish ambition disappear. Mankind being under the burden of lawlessness and lust would sink into the pit of destruction, the world, this great market place would lose its prosperity and the whole earth become a barren waste" (1927,I:2).

The Mughals, who had established suzerainty over northern India in the early sixteenth century, were a Turkic-speaking people from Central Asia who traced their descent to Ghengiz Khan and Tammerlane. They based their authority on a divine relationship with God. The *Padshah* (Emperor), wrote Abu al Fazl, was "a light emanating from God" (I:2). In constituting their authority, the Mughals also drew upon their descent from Ghengiz Khan as a world conqueror. Under the Mongols, the Mughals were a ruling family that was part of a particular clan (*ulus*), which produced the legitimate ruler or Khan. Therefore, the Mughals claimed authority on a historical basis as descendents of the Ghengiz Khan (Khan 1972:11–12 and Tripathi 1959:105–06).

Under Ghengiz Khan and his immediate successors, "the power of the tribe over its members . . . was apparently transferred bodily to the Khan" (I.A. Khan 1972:12). Some of this sense of the embodiment of authority in the person of the ruler, not just of the tribe but of the state, was built upon by Akbar and his successors. In this they were expressing a widespread and older theory of kingship, found in Central Asia, Persia, and India, in which "the king stands for a system of rule of which he is the incarnation, incorporating into his own body by means of symbolic acts, the person of those who share his rule. They are regarded as being parts of his body, and in their district or their sphere of activity they are the King himself" (Buckler 1927/28:239).

This substantial nature of authority in the Indic World is crucial for any understanding of the widespread significance of cloth and clothes, as they are a medium through which substances can be transferred. Clothes are not just body coverings and adornments, nor can they be understood only as metaphors of power and authority, nor as symbols; in many contexts, clothes literally *are* authority. The constitution of authoritative relationships, of rulership, of hierarchy in India cannot be reduced to the sociological construction of leaders and followers, patrons and clients, subordination and superordination alone. Authority is literally part of the body of those who possess it. It can be transferred from person to person through acts of incorporation, which not only create followers or subordinates, but a body of companions of the ruler who have shared some of his substance.

The most literal representation of the act of incorporation into the body of the Mughal *Padshah* was through the offering of *nazr* (gold coins) by a subordinate of the ruler and the ruler's presentation of a *khilat* (clothes, weapons, horses, and elephants). Philologically, *khilat* can be traced in both Persian and Arabic to an Aramaic and Hebrew root *halaf*, "to be passed on," which is central to the Arabic idea *Khilafat*, the succesor to the title of the head of the Muslim community. Narrowly, in Arabic, *khilat* derives from the word for "a garment cast off." By the sixteenth century in India, the term *khilat* came to involve the idea that a king, as a special honor, would take off his robe and put it on a subject. F.W. Buckler suggests that there is a special significance involved in this act, as robes worn by the King could transmit his authority (Buckler 1922:197;1927: 240). Buckler goes on to state: "Robes of Honour are symbols of some idea of continuity or succession," which "rests on a physical basis, depending on the contact of the body of the recipient with the body of the donor through the medium of the clothing. Or to put it rather differently, the donor includes the recipient within his own person through the medium of the wardrobe" (Buckler 1927/28:24).

The sets of clothes through which the substance of authority was transmitted became known as *khilats*, glossed in English as "robes of honor," in French *cap à pied*, "head to feet." In Mughal India the *khilats* were divided into classes consisting of three, five, or seven pieces. A seven-piece *khilat* might include, among other things, a turban, a long coat with full skirt (*jamah,*) a long gown (*ka'bah*), a close-fitting coat (*alkhaliq*), one or more *kamrbands*, trousers, a shirt, and a scarf. Along with the actual clothes, other articles were included.

The most powerful *khilat* was a robe or garment that the Mughal himself had worn, and on occasion he would literally take off a robe and place it on one of his subjects, as a particular honor. Next to such a robe, the garment of most significance was a turban and its associated ornaments.

All forms of salutations in Indian society relate to the head, hands, and feet. In Akbar's court there were three major forms of salutation which entailed manifest acts of obeisance; these were termed the *kornish*, *taslim*, and *sijda*. Abu'l Fazl states: "Kings in their wisdom have made regulations for the manner in which people are to show their obedience . . . His Majesty (Akbar) has commanded the palm of the right hand to be placed on the forehead and the head to be bent downwards . . . . This is called the *kornish*, and signified that the saluter has placed his head (which is the seat of the senses and mind) into the hand of humility, giving it to the royal assembly as a present and has made himself in obedience ready for any service that may be required of him" (Fazl:166-67).

The *taslim* "consists in placing the back of the right hand on the ground, and then raising it gently till the person stands erect, when he puts the palm of his hand upon the crown of his head, which pleasing manner of saluting signifies that he is ready to give himself as an offering" (Fazl 166-67).

The *sijda*, or complete prostration, was objected to by the orthodox Muslims in Akbar's court as it is one of the positions of prayer. Akbar therefore ordered that it be done only in private, but it appears to have been used in subsequent rulers' courts (Islam 1970:321-2).

Abu'l Fazl makes it clear that in the context of the court, the person offering the salute is offering himself as a sacrifice; his head is being offered to the Mughal. In warfare, this sacrifice was literal. In a famous painting, The Emperor Akbar (1542-1605) is shown receiving the heads of his enemies, some being held by his warriors or piled up at the feet of his elephant. His defeated foe wears neither a helmet nor a turban as, head lowered, he is brought before the victor. (Gascoigne 1971:71-72).

In the eighteenth and nineteenth centuries, an Indian would place his turban at the feet of his conqueror as a sign of complete surrender. This was also used in a metaphoric sense to ask a great favor of someone, indicating a willingness to become their slave. Nineteenth-century guide books written for Englishmen traveling to India warned their readers never to touch a Hindu's or a Muslim's turban, as this was considered a grave insult.

The Sind in Western India, conquered by the British in the 1840s, was a region of Muslim chieftains among whom the turban meant sovereignty. E.B. Eastwick, a company official with an excellent knowledge of Persian and Sindhi, writes of the turban "descending," "succeeded to" and being "aimed at." The Governor General, Lord Ellenborough, in writing to General Napier, commented about the need to support a particular ruler and underlined the substantial nature of the turban: "I have little doubt, that once established in the possession of the turban . . . Ali Murad will be able to establish the more natural and reasonable line of succession to the turban, and clothe the measure with the firms of legality" (Eastwick 1849:277).

For the Mughal rulers of India, the turban and its associated ornaments had the powerful and mystical qualities that crowns had in medieval Europe. The jewels attached to the turban included the *kalghi*, an aigrete of peacock or heron feathers with a jewel attached to it. This was only conferred on the highest nobles. The *jigha* consisted of a cluster of jewels set in gold with a feather. The *sarpech* and *sarband* were strings of jewels or filigree work of gold or silver, stitched onto the turban. There was also a string or diadem of pearls worn as a garland around the turban, the *sirha*. Kings in the medieval Hindu tradition were the controllers of the earth and its products, and in cosmographic terms jewels were the essence of the earth, its most pure and concentrated substance. Thus the cloth turban with its associated jewels brought together all the powers of the earth.

Akbar, the Mughal Emperor, delighted in innovative patterns or designs of clothes and created a new vocabulary for talking about them. Like all rulers of the period, he had special warehouses and treasuries for the maintenance and storage of clothes, arms, and jewels. He also decreed changes in the basic design of some articles of clothes. According to Abu'l Fazl, the author of the "Ain-i Akbari," a general description of Mughal rule during the period of Akbar, the Emperor took an inordinate interest in every aspect of the production of cloth. There were imperial workshops in major cities of the empire which could "turn out many master pieces of workmanship: and the figures and patterns, knots and variety of fashion which now prevail astonish experienced travelers" (Fazl I:94). Akbar collected cloth from other Asian countries and Europe, as well as India.

Cloth and clothes received as presents, or commissioned or bought in the open market, were carefully kept and classified by the day of the week and the day in the month on which they arrived at court, as well as by price, color, and weight. There was a rank order of clothes and cloth: Those received on the first day of the month of *Farwardin* "provided they be of good quality, have a higher rank assigned to them then pieces arriving on other days; and if pieces are equal in value, their precedence or otherwise, is determined by the character of the day of their entry; and if pieces are equal as far as the character of the day is concerned, they put the lighter stuff higher in rank; and if pieces have the same weight, they arrange them according to colour" (Fazl I:97). The author lists 39 colors, most of which refer to the colors of fruits, flowers, and birds. Given the variety of colors and fabrics, the almost infinite variations of design motifs in the textiles, and the great variation possible by folding, cutting, and sewing into garments, one can imagine the possibilities for originality and uniqueness. Some sense of this creativity and great variation was demonstrated in the recent exhibition of Indian textiles organized by Mattiebelle Gittinger (Gittinger, 1982)

Akbar, like his successor, lived in a world of textiles, clothes, and jewels, and created elaborate rules restricting the wearing of some emblems, jewels, and types of clothes to certain ranks in Mughal society. As the British in the nineteenth century steadily extended their control over their subjects and their allied Princes, they ordered and simplified those emblems of sovereignty and began to act as the Sovereign in India.

FROM ROBES OF HONOR TO MANTLES OF SUBORDINATION

The significations entailed in the receipt of *khilats* were not lost on the British from the days of Sir Thomas Roe's visit. In the second half of the eighteenth century, as the Company's military power grew, the British transformed themselves from merchants dependent on the good will and protection of Indian monarchs into rulers of a territorially based state. As part of this process, the British officials of the Company sought to be honored with Mughal titles and *khilats*. In Bengal, as the Company's leaders gradually began to act as Indian sovereigns, they in turn began to grant *khilats* to their Indian subordinates and to use their influence with the Mughal Emperor to obtain titles for their allies and employees. In the early decades of the nineteenth century, a visit to Delhi and the Mughal Emperor and ennoblement at his hands had become a kind of tourist attraction for high-status Europeans. Captain Mundy, who accompanied Lord Combermere, the Commander in Chief of the Army in India, on an inspection tour through North India from 1827 to 1829, visited Delhi. The offering of *nazr* (gold coins) and receipt of *khilat* was on the itinerary. Mundy describes the enrobement, and his reaction to it:

> On receiving Lord Combermere's offering, the King placed a turban, similar to his own, upon his head, and his lordship was conducted, retiring with his face sedulously turned towards the throne, to an outer apartment, to be invested with a khillât, or dress of honour. In about five minutes he returned to the presence, attired in a spangled muslin robe and tunic; salaamed, and presented another nuzzar. The staff were then led across the quadrangle by the "grooms of robes" to the "green room," where a quarter of an hour was sufficiently disagreeably employed by us in arraying ourselves, with the material tastily bound round our cocked-hats. Never did I behold a group so ludicrous as we presented when our toilette was accomplished; we wanted nothing but a "Jacik i' the Green" to qualify us for a May-day exhibition of the most exaggerated order. In my gravest moments, the recollection of the scene provokes an irresistible fit of laughter. As soon as we had been decked out in this satisfactory guise, we were marched back again through the Lâl Purdar and crowds of spectators, and re-conducted to the Dewânee Khâs, where we again separately approached His Majesty to receive from him a tiara of gold and false stones, which he placed with his own hands upon our hats (Mundy 1832:172).

The officials of the East India Company exchanged what they defined as "presents" with Indian rulers and some of their subjects, but changed the nature and signification of this act. Company officials could not accept "gifts" and when protocol required officials to accept a *khilat*, weapons, or jewels, they had to deposit them in the Company's *toshakhana* (treasury). These gifts were recycled, given in turn to some Indian ruler at a durbar or other official meeting when it was deemed appropriate for the Company to exchange gifts with Indians. According to the rule that the Company followed, and which they imposed not only on their own subjects but on the allied Princes when presents were exchanged, it was prearranged that the value offered by each party must be equal. In short, prestation and counter-prestation had become a contractual exchange. The British were aware of the contradiction inherent in the practice in terms of Indian theories of prestation. In India a superior always gives more than he receives, yet as an "economic man," the nineteenth-century Englishman was not about to enhance his honor by giving more than he received.

The basis of British authority in India in the first half of the nineteenth century was ambiguous. In their own eyes they ruled by right of conquest. Yet their own Monarch was not the Monarch of India; the agency of rule was a chartered Company, supervised by Parliament. In the wake of the Great Revolt of 1857–58, the Company was abolished, their Queen was declared ruler of India, and India became part of the Empire in constitutional terms. The Crown of Great Britain became the ultimate source of authority for British and Indians. As part of the signalizing of this new legal arrangement, an Order of Knighthood, "The Star of India," was established (Cohn 1983).

The intentions of the Queen and her advisors in establishing this new Order were spelled out in its "Letter Patent and Constitution" published July 6, 1861:

> . . . It hath been the custom of Princes to distinguish merit, virtue and loyalty by public marks of honor in order that eminent services may be acknowledged and to create in others a laudable emulation, and we being desirous of affording public and signal testimony of our regard by the institution of an order of knighthood, whereby our resolution to take upon ourselves the government of our territories in India (India Office Library and Records, L/P & S/15/1:215).

Initially the Order was restricted to 25 members, British and Indian, the Highest British Officials of Government and the most important of the Indian Princes being invested with the mantle and insignia of the Order. Four years after its establishment, the Order was reorganized into the three ranked classes of Knight Grand Commander (KGCSI), Knight Commander (KCSI), and Companion (CSI), and the numbers who could be awarded the honor were greatly increased.

The light blue mantle of the Order was lined in white silk and fully covered the body. It fastened with a white silk cord decorated with blue and silver tassels. On the left side of the robe, over the heart, was embroidered in gold thread the rays of the sun, and superimposed in diamonds was the motto, "Heaven's light our guide" and a star. The collar was a large necklace made of a gold chain with palm fronds and lotuses; in its center was an emblem of the Crown of Great Britain, from which hung a pendant with a portrait of the Queen of England.

The mantle, insignia, collar, and pendant were distinctly European in their form and content. The recipients of the knighthood had to sign a pledge that the mantle, and its attachments would be returned at the death of the recipient, as the knighthood was not hereditary. This provision offended most Indian recipients, as Indians of all statuses stored gifts and emblems of honor that they received for their posterity. The *toshakana* (treasure room) of a Prince was an archive of objects whose origin and receipt embodied his status and honor. They could be taken out on occasion to be worn, used, or displayed, but they would be held from generation to generation to mark the constitutive events in the history of the family or the State. Shawls, robes, clothes, and pieces of cloth received in ritual contexts embodied those contexts. Even a peasant family will have several trunks full of cloth, saris, dhotis, and piece goods that have been received at weddings or in other ritual contexts, which are seldom worn but are displayed and discussed on solemn occasions. In a very direct way, these objects constitute the relationships between individuals, families, and groups.

The Nizam of Hyderabad, the most important allied Prince of the British, objected strenuously, not to the honor the knighthood bestowed on him by the Queen, but to the mantle and the jeweled insignia. The Nizam through his Prime Minister Salar Jang pointed out to the Viceroy that the "people of this country have a particular antipathy to wearing costumes different from their own." This, Salar Jang stated, was especially true of Princes, "who have always been tenacious of the the costume of their ancestors," and he pointed out that "the wearing of the robe of the new order, would probably be ridiculed by his people." If the robe were made out of velvet or silk it would be in contravention of Mohammedan law. The Nizam also

raised an issue about the wearing of the pendant which had a portrait of the Queen, as proper Muslims were "prohibited from wearing the likeness of any created being on their person" (India Office
Library and Records, L/P & S/15/3:80–82). The Viceroy sternly informed the Resident at Hyderabad, who had forwarded the objections of the Nizam and his Prime Minister, that the statutes and constitution of the Star of India were not to be questioned. The Nizam
had to accept the regalia as is, or refuse to accept the honor.

In 1861, the British in India had yet to develop a formal investiture ceremony for the induction of knights into the order. Hence
when the patent and regalia reached the Nizam, although he made
proper reverence both to the patent and to the insignia, he did not
put the mantle on, and the whole matter was quietly dropped. But
by the end of the nineteenth century, the Nizams as well as all other
recipients of knighthood seemed pleased enough to wear the robe
and associated insignia.

By 1869, at the time of the first visit of a member of the royal
family, the Duke of Edinburgh, the pages wore a seventeenth-century cavalier costume. At the Imperial Assemblage of 1877, a full-
dress version of Victorian "feudal" was utilized for the design motif
of the ceremony at which Queen Victoria was made Empress of
India. From 1870 to World War I, the number of occasions at which
Indians, depending on their status, roles, and regional origins, had
to appear in their assigned "costumes," increased enormously.

With the advent of the railroad, the Viceroy and his suite, the
Governors, and other high officials and their retinues traveled more
and more frequently. The Central Government and each of the
major provinces had a cool-season and hot-season capital. The seasonal trips between these capitals provided occasions for an increasing number of meetings between the top rulers and Princes, landlords, rich merchants, and an army of lower Indian officials. The
Monarch's birthday, Jubilees, the crowning of Edward VII and
George V King-Emperors of India, all provided occasions for the displaying of Empire at home and in India.

With the opening of the Suez Canal in 1869, the trip to and from
India was cut from months to a matter of weeks, facilitating the flow
of royalty and aristocrats visiting India, and of Indian princes visiting
the Continent and England. Indians as part of their tours would be
presented at Victoria's court, at Windsor or at her "cottage,"
Osbourne House on the Isle of Wight. Here she had a "durbar

room" built and decorated for receiving the homage of her loyal Indian feudatories. Indians were required on such occasions to appear in their "traditional" Indian royal dress rather than Western clothes (V.C. Chaudhuri 1980:344).

"ORIENTALIZING" INDIA

The establishment of the Star of India and its investiture evoked in its intent and regalia British Victorian conceptions of a feudal past. It was part of the general process of enhancing the image of the monarchy and the aristocracy to symbolize a simpler past, in contrast to the rapid social, economic, and political change that characterized contemporary reality. This past was seen as the source of Britain's liberties, its legal system, and its natural order, which grew from an organic relationship between rulers and ruled. This was more than mere nostalgia for a past that might have never been. It was a powerful symbolic statement by the ruling classes (who themselves were not necessarily aristocratic) about order, deference, and hierarchy as the prerequisites for maintaining political and social stability during a period of economic and technological change (Burrow 1981; Strong 1978; Hobsbawm and Ranger 1983).

As Britain had a feudal past, so did India, particularly the India of the Princes and the great mass of the Indian peasantry. The application of social evolutionary theories to India by a wide range of British officials and scholars yielded a crucial ruling paradigm: The Indian present was the European past (Maine 1871). This construction of a universal history enabled the British to control the Indian past, as they too had been feudal but were now advanced out of this stage. But since the British were still in a position through their own history to direct the future course for India, it made the British part of India in their role as rulers.

India was seen through British beneficence as being capable of being changed. They had created the conditions for the Indians' advance up the social evolutionary ladder by introducing the ideas of private property and modern education, the English language and its thought and literature, railroads, irrigation systems, modern sanitation and medicine, and authoritarian yet rational bureaucratic government, and the form of British justice. The British also knew the dangers of too rapid a move out of the feudal stage—the unleash-

ing of disorder, dislocation, and potentially dangerous revolution-
ary forces that, if not controlled and checked, could lead to anarchy.
To prevent this dangerous outcome, Indians had to be controlled,
made to conform to the British conception of appropriate thought
and action, for their own future good. India had a future, but its
present had to be an "Oriental one" to prevent a too rapid and hence
disruptive entry into the modern world. What might be thought of
as the Orientalization of the clothes of British rule in India began,
as did the westernization of clothing in the army.

During the Great Uprising, the British quickly shed their heavy,
tight, redcoated uniforms. W.H. Russell, who was sent by the Times
to report on the war, wrote in one of his letters:

> . . . I have often thought how astonished, and something more,
> the Horse-guards, or the authorities, or the clothing depart-
> ments, or whatever or whoever it may be that is interested in
> the weighty matters of uniform, and decides on the breadth of
> cuffs, the size of lace, the nature of trowser-straps, and the cut
> of buttons, would be at the aspect of this British army in India!
> How good Sir George Brown, for instance, would stand aghast
> at the sight of these sunburnt "bashi-bazouks," who, from heel
> to head and upwards, set at defiance the sacred injunctions of
> her majesty's regulations! Except the highlanders . . . not a corps
> that I have seen sport a morsel of pink, or show a fragment of
> English scarlet. The highlanders wear eccentric shades of gray
> linen over their bonnets; the kilt is discarded. . . . Lord Cardi-
> gan, in his most sagacious moments, would never light on the
> fact that those dark-faced, bearded horsemen, clad in snowy
> white, with flagless lances glittering in the sun, are the war-
> hardened troopers of her majesty's 9th lancers; or that yonder
> gray tunicked cavaliers, with ill-defined head-dresses, belong to
> the Queen's bays . . . . Among the officers, individual taste and
> phantasy have full play. The infantry regiments, for the most
> part, are dressed in linen frocks, dyed carky or gray slate colour—
> slate-blue trowsers, and shakoes protected by puggeries, or linen
> covers, from the sun . . . . It is really wonderful what fecundity
> or invention in dress there is, after all, in the British mind when
> its talents can be properly developed. To begin with the head-
> dress. The favourite wear is a helmet of varying shape, but of
> uniform ugliness. In a moment of inspiration some Calcutta hat-
> ter conceived, after a close study of the antique models, the
> great idea of reviving, for every-day use, the awe-inspiring

head-piece of Pallas Athene; and that remarkably unbecoming affair . . . became the prototype of the Indian tope in which the wisest and greatest of mankind looks simply ridiculous and ludicrous. Whatever it might be in polished steel or burnished metal, the helmet is a decided failure in felt or wickerwork, or pith, as far as external effect is concerned. It is variously fabricated, with many varieties of interior ducts and passages leading to escape-holes for imaginary hot air in the front or top, and around it are twisted infinite colours and forms of turbans with fringed ends and laced fringes. When a peacock's feather, with the iris end displayed, is inserted in the hole in the top of the helmet, or is stuck in the puggery around it, the effect of the covering is much enhanced . . . . I have seen more than one pistol in one of the cummerbunds, or long sashes, which some of our officers wear round the stomach in the oriental fashion (Russell, quoted in Ball 1859,II:325–27).

With the reestablishment of social order in Upper India, the army was reorganized. What had been the Bengal Army was in effect dissolved. European soldiers who had enlisted in the Company service were pensioned and/or repatriated to Great Britain, and henceforth all of the European troops serving in the Indian army would be from regular Royal battalions, which were rotated through India. The British officers of the Indian army were now commissioned by the King and would be permanently assigned to units made up of Indians, who were recruited from "the martial races:" Sikhs, who accounted for 20 percent of the army in 1912; Punjabi Muslims (16 percent); Gurkhas (12 percent); Rajputs, mainly from Rajasthan (8 percent); Dogras and Garhwalis (7.5 percent); Pathans (8 percent); Jats (6 percent). The remaining soldiers in the army were made up of Marathas, Brahmans, Hindustani Muslims, and "other Hindus," of whom the only significant number were Telagus and Tamils (GOI, Army in India Committee 1913,IA:156).

In addition to the "class composition" of the new army, its dress was transformed as well, for both Indian soldiers and British officers. Over the second half of the nineteenth century, the service uniform for Europeans and Indians was much the same—cotton khaki trousers and shirt, with a jacket added in cold weather. Indians were given "exotic" headgear, the Sikh turban as previously discussed, and each of the other major martial races had their distinctive turban in terms of wrapping and color. The Gurkhas began to be recruited after the Gurka wars of 1814–15 and took readily to European-style uniforms, which they have continued to wear in the British and Indian army to the present. Their distinctive headdress in the second half of the nineteenth century was the Kilmarnock cap, a visorless, brimless pillbox. For service in the Boxer Rebellion they were issued broad-brimmed felt hats, which they wore up to World War I in the Australian style with one side turned up. Subsequently they have worn it with the brim down and at a "jaunty angle." Their uniforms, with jacket and trousers, have been dark blue or green.

Vansittart, the author of the handbook on the Gurkhas for use by their officers, described them as having a strong aversion to wearing a turban, as they associate it with the Plainsmen whom they "despise." Vansittart goes on to eulogize the Gurkhas, "as delighting in all manly sports, shooting, fishing . . . and as bold, enduring, faithful, frank, independent and self reliant . . . they look up to and fraternise with the British whom they admire for their superior knowledge, strength and courage, and whom they imitate in dress and habits." (Vansittart, quoted in Tuker 1957:92-93; Bolt 1975:57, 63). The Gurkhas had a "traditional" weapon, the kukri, a 20-inch curved knife carried in the waistband which became their trademark.

It was in designing the dress uniforms for the officers and men that the British exercised their fantasy of what an "oriental" warrior should like. As was common in the second half of the nineteenth century, the cavalry units got the most colorful and dramatic uniforms. As was noted, during the Mutiny the British began to add cummerbunds and *puggrees*—linen covers wrapped around their wicker helmets or cloth caps and hats. A few British went all the way and began to wear full turbans, which were recognized as having some protective function. A full turban could be made up of 30 or 40 feet of cloth and, when thickly wrapped over the whole head and down the ears, could protect the head from a glancing sabre blow. General Hearsey, who commanded a division of the Bengal army, came from a family which had long provided officers, and many British thought he had Indian "blood." After the Mutiny, Hearsey had his portrait painted in a long black oriental-style robe, wearing a richly brocaded cummerbund and holding a scimitar. Could he have been seeking to appropriate part of his enemies' powers through using his clothes?

By the end of the nineteenth century, the dress uniform of the

British officers of the cavalry had become fully "orientalized;" it included a knee-length tunic in bright color, breeches and high boots, and a fully wrapped colorful turban. The Indian non-commissioned officers and troopers were similarly attired for dress parades and the increasing number of ceremonial functions.

The change in uniform for both European and Indian emphasized a basic conceptual change. One of the results of the Mutiny was to rigidify the already considerable differences between Indians and British. The Indians, seen by the British in the first half of the nineteenth century as misguided children, had been revealed by their actions in 1857–59 to be treacherous and unchangeable. Outwardly they might conform to the sahib's expectation but they could never be trusted. At any time their deep-seated, irrational superstitions could break forth in violence and overturn all the painful efforts of the conquerors to lead them in proper directions. Policies based on an assumption of change were proven wrong, so what was required was a strong hand capable of smashing any "sedition" or disloyalty, combined with an acceptance of Indians. Henceforth, the British should rule in an "oriental manner," with strength and with the expectation of instant obedience.

For this reason, Indians more than ever should look like Indians; those the British most depended on to provide the strength to keep India, the soldiers, should appear as the British idea of what Mughal troopers looked like, with their officers dressed as Mughal grandees. Another characteristic believed to be quintessentially Indian or oriental was a love of show, of pageantry, of occasions to dress up in beautiful or gaudy clothes. Indians, it was believed, were susceptible to show and drama, and hence more occasions were found where rulers and subjects could play their appointed parts and could act their "traditions" through costume. Hence the insistence that the Chiefs and their retinues should always appear in their most colorful (if outmoded) clothes. The first major demonstration of this new ruling paradigm was during the visit of the Prince of Wales to India in 1876.

The Prince and his large suite traveled widely throughout India, arriving in Bombay, then proceeding to Ceylon and Madras, and reaching Calcutta in November of 1876. There he was treated to a month-long round of entertainments, balls, and levees, culminating in a large investiture ceremony for the Star of India. The trip was well reported in England by correspondents from leading newspapers. *The Graphic* and the *Illustrated London Weekly* sent artists who recorded all the events for the home audience. In their drawings, the artists dwelt upon the exotic quality of Indian life and dress, such as the "wild" Naga tribesmen and women brought down to Calcutta to entertain the Prince and British high society with their barbarous dances. The Prince was also treated to a *nautch*—a dance by young women which was a popular entertainment for eighteenth century Nabobs. The dancers' beautiful and colorful dresses and their sensuous movements were anything but Victorian (Annual Register 1782:36).

At center stage throughout the Prince of Wales' visit were the Princes of India, in all their splendor. Neither the pen of the journalists nor the black-and-white line drawings of the artists could adequately capture the variety and color of the clothes, nor the extraordinary display of precious stones and jewelry with which the figures of the Indian rulers were decked. The intent of the whole visit was to inspire the prince's loyalty by the presence of the eldest son of their English queen, and to affirm their central role in the maintenance of the Empire.

Everywhere he went, the Prince of Wales was showered with valuable gifts by his mother's loyal Indian feudatories. Princes vied to outdo their competitors with the value, ingenuity, and brilliance of jewels, paintings, antique weapons, live animals, richly embroidered brocades, and other art works which they presented to him. What he collected in six months of touring in India literally filled the large converted troop ship, the *Serapis*. When he returned, his trophies and gifts went on traveling exhibition throughout England and eventually wound up in a quasi-museum in London at the Lambeth Palace. In return for their gifts, the Prince of Wales presented the Princes with copies of Max Muller's English translation of the *Rig-Veda*.

It was not only the Princes themselves who enthralled the Prince and his suite as they traveled, but also their exotic retainers, dressed in a dazzling variety of costumes. The editors of *The Graphic* pulled out all stops in trying to describe for their readers the impression that these "military fossils" made on the Europeans.

One of the chief features of the Maharajah of Cashmere's reception of the Prince of Wales was the wonderfully heterogeneous character of the troops who lined the route from the river to the

Palace. Never on record has such a miscellaneous army been collected together. The troops wore uniforms of all countries and all
ages, and carried as many different weapons, ranging from
chain armour and Saracenic javelins to the scarlet uniforms and
muskets of British soldiers half a century ago, the 12th and the
19th centuries being thus, as our artist remarks, face to face.
There were troops in veritable native costume, turbaned, and
carrying blunderbusses or flint-and-steel muskets; next to them
would be a red-coated company, with white, blue, or black
knickerbockers, and striped worsted stockings; then would come
a detachment in chain-mail and breastplates, and steel caps with
high tufts; while others again wore brass helmets, and were clad
in brass breast and back-plates, not unlike our own Household
Cavalry. One corporal particularly attracted our artist's attention,
being clad in a new tunic of cloth, on which the mark "superfine" had been left, a badge of distinction of which the wearer
appeared highly proud. He bore an old trigger gun, with a bayo-
net with a broad-leaved blade. Notwithstanding the semi-
European clothing and armament of many of the troops, however, very little of European discipline, or drill, apparently
existed, and our sketch of "Charge!" will give an idea of the
helter-skelter ruck—so characteristic of Eastern warfare—with
which a squadron of cavalry obeyed the word of command. Our
artist writes: "This regiment wore a green uniform with red
facings—some were shod and others barefoot—their trousers
were reefed up to their knees, while their sleeves were exceed-
ingly lengthy. As for the horses, they had ropes for bridles, and
in appearance were veritable descendants of Rozinants (*The
Graphic*, March 4, 1876:222).

Through the first half of the nineteenth century, the British seemed
to eschew competing with the splendors of Indian royal clothes. Unlike their eighteenth century counterparts who wore vividly colored
silks and satins, they wore fairly informal coats, dark or muted in
color, straight and at times baggy trousers, and plain shirtwaists and
vests. Until the middle of the nineteenth century, when the *sola topi*
(pith helmet) became ubiquitous, their headgear was a beaver stove-
pipe hat or a cap. The white ruling elite must have appeared dowdy
in comparison with their Indian underlings, who dressed in a version of Mughal court dress while carrying out their official functions.
The British appeared to have given up the sartorial struggle of trying
to outdress the pageant of Oriental splendor they sought to control.

It was Queen Victoria herself who suggested that the Civil servants in India should have an official dress uniform, as did their counterparts in the Colonial Service. The administration of India was completely separate from the ruling of the other colonials, one being run through the India Office and the other through the Colonial Office. Although the question of a special uniform was raised several times after the Queen expressed interest, the Council of India decided that prescribing a dress uniform would be an undue expense for their officials (Davies 1937:487).

Lord Lytton, Viceroy from 1876 to 1880 and a great believer in the power of ceremony and display as an integral part of ruling India, complained to his Queen that "official functions" in India looked like "fancy dress balls," because there was no check on the "sartorial fancies of the civil service" (Davies 1937:488). Although no uniform was prescribed for the Indian Civil Service until the early twentieth century, "some civil officers had provided themselves with one which was similar . . . to the levee dress of the 3rd and 5th class civil servants at home and in the colonies" (Earle, India Office Library and Records Memo 1876, Euro Mss. F86/163). The only civilians allowed a "dress uniform" by regulations were those who had "distinct duties of a political kind to perform, and who are thereby brought into frequent and direct personal intercourse with native princes." This uniform included a blue coat with gold embroidery, a black velvet lining, collar and cuffs, blue cloth trousers with gold and lace two inches wide, a beaver cocked hat with black silk cockade and ostrich feathers, and a sword (V.C. Chaudhuri 1980:373).

THE GAEKWAR AND THE KING

An incident occurred during the Imperial Durbar of 1911 that illustrates the official British concern with conformity of dress and manners expected of the Indian Princes. In 1911, King George V and his Queen traveled to India for his formal crowning as the King-Emperor of India. This was to be the only time that a reigning Monarch of Great Britain was to visit India before Independence. All three Imperial Durbars took place at the same site. In the first two, the structure marking the ritual center was a dais on which the Viceroy proclaimed the new titles of the Emperor. In 1911 the focal point of the event was a large platform, covered by velvet awnings and drapery and dubbed the homage pavilion, on which the King and his Princess sat on thrones. In previous Durbars, the Indian Royalty and nobles had been more or less passive bystanders; this time, it was decided that the leading Princes would individually offer "homage" as an expression of fealty and respect to their Imperial majesties.

The Gaekwar of Baroda was highly westernized, and generally considered by the British to be a "progressive" ruler, but too friendly with a number of prominent Indian nationalists. Baroda was ranked second behind Hyderabad in the official order of precedence at the Imperial Durbar established by the Government of India for Indian states. Therefore, the Gaekwar was to follow the Nizam in offering homage. The day before the actual ceremony a rehearsal was held to instruct the Princes in the proper form of offering homage to the King-Emperor and his consort. They were told to walk up the steps of the platform, bow low before each of their majesties, and then walk backwards down the steps in such a fashion as never to show their back to the Royal couple. The Gaekwar of Baroda was unable to attend the rehearsal and sent his brother to take notes for him.

On the day of the offering of homage, the Gaekwar was dressed in a plain white knee-length jacket and his "traditional" red turban. He wore white European trousers and carried an English style walking stick. He did not wear, as was expected, the sash of the Order of the Star of India. The Gaekwar approached the King, bowed once, omitting any obeisance to the Princess, took several steps backward, then turned and walked down the steps swinging his cane. It appears that at the time nothing was said about his behavior; subsequently however, led by the *Times* reporter, his behavior was interpreted as seditious. A major row ensued in the English language Press of India as well as in England itself over what was defined as a studied, purposeful, and seditious insult. The storm was revived three weeks after the event, when the newsreels taken at the Durbar reached England. The *Illustrated London News* of January 29 reproduced a page of sequential stills from the film showing "very clearly the way in which the Gaekwar of Baroda, carrying a stick, entered the Presence, bowed curtly, and walked off with his back to the King-Emperor" (Jan. 29, 1912:67). In addition to the pictures of the Gaekwar they printed pictures of two other ruling chiefs paying homage with deep bows of reverence. The Gaekwar and members of his court protested that, for personal reasons, the Gaekwar was distressed on the day of the ritual, was confused as to what was proper behavior, and intended no insult or lack of manners by what had happened (Rice 1931:16–22; Sergeant 1928:127–41).

The intentions of the Gaekwar are less relevant than his failure to maintain the dress code expected of Indian Princes. The most seditious touch of all would seem to have been the Gaekwar's use of a walking stick, an accouterment of the white Sahibs, military and civilian, which marked the insouciance they displayed in the presence of the Indian masses. It was also used on occasion to thrash Indians whose actions, manners, or appearance irritated them.

In India, the military "orientalized" to overawe the Indian Princes and the heathen masses; at home, the ruling classes archaized their ceremonial dress to overawe the new middle classes and the potentially dangerous lower orders of society. From the middle of the nineteenth century, the British at home increasingly invented or reinvented civic rituals at all levels of the polity. These rituals called for the creation of costumes, regalia, and accouterments to mark them as special and hallowed by tradition. They were designed to evoke in participants and audience, from the Lord Mayors of small cities to wealthy merchants and bankers in London, to the Royal family, to Union officials, a collective conception of the past (Cannadine 1983). The use of costumes and accouterments developed for such civic rituals were transported to India by the British to hierarchize the grandeur of their Indian princes. As a writer in the *Illustrated London News*, summing up what for him was the success of the Imperial Durbar of 1911, explained;

Despite the oft-repeated statement that this age is a very drab
one sartorially so far as the West is concerned, there are various
occasions on which Europe is able to show the Orient that it,
too, can display itself in brilliant plumage. Such instances as the
Coronation of King George and Queen Mary and that of King
Edward VII and Queen Alexandra jump to the mind at once:
and to these memories of glittering kaleidoscopic state pagentry
must now be added those of the Great Durbar held so recently
at Delhi. There Europeans vied with Asiatics with excellent effect
(Jan. 27, 1912:11).

INDIANS IN EVERYDAY CLOTHES

One of the first impressions formed by British travelers to India in the nineteenth century was of the nakedness of most of the Indians whom they encountered on their arrival. Most British travelers to India from the eighteenth century to the early nineteenth century arrived either in Madras or at Diamond Harbour, down river from Calcutta. Madras was an open roadstead where British passengers had to disembark from their ships into open row boats manned by Indian boatment. At Diamond Harbour many travelers transferred to barges or small sailing boats for the remainder of the trip to Calcutta. The boatman was usually the first Indian they were able to observe closely. James Johnson, a surgeon in the Royal Navy who was in India in the late eighteenth century, records his impressions of the dress of the Bengali boatmen (*dandi*):

> The habilment of the Bengal *dandy*, or waterman who rows or drags our *budjrow* (barge), up the Ganges, consists in a small narrow piece of cloth (*doty*), passed between the thighs, and fastened before and behind to a piece of stout packthread, that encircles the waist. In this dress, or undress, corresponding pretty nearly to the figleaf of our great progenitor, he exposes his skin to the action of the tropical sun, a deluge of rain, or a piercing northwester, with equal indifference! (Johnson 1813:420–21).

British women newly arrived in India recorded their shock not only at the seminakedness of lower status Indian household servants, who seemed constantly underfoot, dusting, sweeping, lounging about, or playing with the *babalog* (white children), but also at their free access to the bedrooms of the *Memsahibs* as if they were non-males. The traveler or sojourner in India quickly adjusted to the near nakedness of the Indian males, which after a while did not shock British sensibilities "owing to the dark colour of the skin, which as it is unusual to European eyes has the effect of dress" (Calcott 1812:2). They then began to discern great variation, based on region, caste, sect, and wealth, in Indian dress.

Indian Hindu male dress consists of three large pieces of cloth. One the *dhoti*, is wrapped and folded in various ways, and covers the lower half of the body. A second piece, worn in cooler weather, is a cotton shawl, or *chadar*. The third piece, a long, narrow strip of cloth which is wrapped around the head, is the turban or *pagri*. The usual textile for these cloths was cotton, but on occasion silk would be worn. There is, however, enormous variation in how parts of the *dhoti* are tucked into the waist and in the length of draping. Such details frequently indicate the occupation or status of the wearer. Most Hindu *dhotis* were white and without seams. Even Hindus whose work required them to wear Muslim-style stitched clothes, and later European jackets or coats of various kinds, would change into a *dhoti* when arriving home.

The basic difference between Hindu and Muslim clothes was that Muslim clothes were tailored, which involved the cutting and sewing of cloth, but Hindu clothes were of uncut pieces, formed into garments by folding, tucking, and draping. Although it was frequently asserted that in ritual and domestic contexts in the nineteenth century, uncut and unsewn clothing was invariably worn, I have found no adequate explanation of this injunction to use only uncut cloth when performing *puja* worship. This is certainly a common habit today among more orthodox Hindu males, who will bathe and then put on a fresh *dhoti*; on most auspicious ritual occasions such a *dhoti* will be of silk.

My speculation is that the use of unsewn cloth or a *dhoti* for males performing *puja*, or the use of *sets* of specified cloth and clothes as prestations, reflects an underlying concept of the necessity of completeness, or unpenetratedness, of totality, which is congruent with Hindu ideas of cosmogony. Parallel to the male wearing only an unsewn garment during *puja* were women who, by the late nineteenth century, had taken to wearing a *choli*, a sewn blouse or petticoat, which they removed while cooking food. Cooking had to be done in a specially designated and ritually cleansed area of the house.

N.C. Chaudhuri has described how males who worked in Mughal courts or in British offices would wear Muslim dress, but followed the rule that such garments were "worn for work only, and never in personal life. . . . Hindus who put on Muslim costume for public appearance scrupulously put them off when going into the inner house, and for religious observances, and they would never dream of wearing anything but orthodox Hindu clothes" (N.C. Chaudhuri 1976:53). The mansions of wealthy Calcutta Hindus in the late nineteenth century frequently had a western-style dressing room, complete with a wardrobe made in England, adjacent to the master's bedroom in the outer apartment of the house. There the master would change into Hindu clothes before entering the inner apartment and courtyard, the province of the women and the deities of the house. (N.C. Chaudhuri 1976:57).

The exception to the rule of eschewing sewn clothing at home in pre-nineteenth-century India was in the Punjab and Rajasthan. The Rajputs appear to have taken to wearing a *jama* (sewn coat) before the advent of the Mughals (Verma 1978:47). What was conventionally thought of as Mughal court dress adapted major elements of Rajput dress during the time of Akbar (Buschan 1958:30). It was also during this period that marking features were established to differentiate Hindu from Muslim attire, even when they were wearing the same type of coat (a *jama* or *angarakha*). The *jama* has ties that fix the flap of the upper half of the garment under the armpit and across the chest; Muslims wear their *jama* tied to the right, Hindus to the left. The *jama* became reduced to a shirt-like garment for cold weather wear among peasants of Upper India in the nineteenth and twentieth centuries, but the custom of tieing continued to follow the old pattern of left for Hindus, right for Muslims (Ghurye 1966:129).

The Mughal rulers prescribed a form of their own dress for Hindus associated with them or employed in their offices and as officials. However, the British tried to have Hindus who worked for them—whether as domestic servants or as clerks, writers, and revenue and judicial officials—continue to wear the Mughal-style dress appropriate to their functions (N.C. Chaudhuri 1976:57–58). Writing about British attitudes toward Indians wearing European clothes, N.C. Chaudhuri trenchantly sums up the situation: "They, the British, were violently repelled by English in our mouths and even more violently by English clothes on our backs" (1976:58).

By the mid-nineteenth century, increasing numbers of urban Indians, particularly in Calcutta and Bombay, began to wear articles of European clothing. In Bombay the lead was taken by the Parsis, a group descended from the Zoroastrians, who had fled from Persia when the Islamic rulers began to persecute them for maintaining their religion. The Parsis settled in coastal areas of Gujarat, and by the eighteenth century were an important component of the population of Bombay, as carpenters, builders, and boat builders. By the early nineteenth century, some had become successful merchants, bankers, and European-style businessmen. Although they maintained a distinctive style of dress, particularly in the caps they wore, trousers, shoes, and an adaptation of a long English frock coat became new elements of their distinctive costume.

By the 1880s many successful, wealthy Indians and Western-educated Indian males had taken to wearing European clothes in public. Even those who normally wore a complete Western outfit, however, did not take to Western headgear. Many Indians continued to wear a turban with European clothes, particularly in the cold season. They also took to wearing a great variety of caps, from military forage caps to a wide range of brimless skull caps. The one type of hat that Indians did not wear was the pith helmet.

By the eighteenth century, the Europeans were aware of rules governing where Indians could wear footcoverings, and before whom they could appear in slippers. During a visit in 1804 to the Peshwa in Poona, the head of the Maratha Confederacy, Lord Valentia, who was touring India collecting botanical specimens, observed the expected behavior. Accompanied by the long-time British Resident Colonel Close and his retinue, he entered the courtyard of the palace in a palanquin, but from there had to continue on foot. He entered the Durbar room, and before stepping on the white cloth covering of the floor, took off his slippers. Lord Valentia was met by the Peshwa's *Dewan* (prime minister), and after a few minutes the Peshwa entered and remained standing by his throne (*gaddi*, literally a cushion). Valentia approached, flanked by the Dewan and the Resident, and was lightly embraced by the Peshwa. Then, after the Peshwa seated himself, Valentia had to sit on the floor crosslegged as "we had no chairs or cushions, and were not permitted to put out our feet, as showing the sole of the foot is considered disrespectful" (Valentia 1809, II:120–21). After formal conversation, done through an interpreter who spoke only to the Dewan, who in turn spoke to the Peshwa, Valentia was invited to have a private conversation with the Peshwa in a small room adjacent to the Durbar. Here, seated on a small "Turkey" rug next to the Peshwa, they spoke more informally for over an hour before returning to the Durbar room for dismissal. Valentia recorded, "I was extremely tired with my position, that it was with some difficulty that I could rise, and for a few minutes was obliged to rest against the wall" (II:122).

In portraits, successful and rich Europeans in India frequently are portrayed in their offices with several of their Indian employees or associates. The crucial Indians for the Europeans were their *Banians*, a title minimally translated as "cash keeper." These were men who ran both official and commercial activities of the British. They secured credit, dealt with most Indians on the *Sahibs'* behalf, kept their books, and were their factotums in all their public dealings. Another employee of high status was the *Munshi*, inadequately described as a "scribe." The *munshi* frequently were highly educated Muslims who acted in the initial phases of a European's career as his teacher of Persian and Urdu, and later as a confidential secretary responsible for his correspondence with Indian officials and rulers. In eighteenth-century paintings, the *Munshi* and *Banian* have their slippers on while the bearer or *hukkah bardar* is barefoot. This is obviously a concession on the part of the European to the high status of these employees. Captain Thomas Williamson spent upwards of twenty years in India in the 1780s and 1790s. His *East India Vade Mecum* (1810), the first guidebook for Europeans to provide detailed instructions on managing a household and observing proper manners, observed that:

> A Banian invariably rides in his palanquin attended by several
> underlings. . . . He, to a certain degree, rules the office, entering
> it generally with little ceremony, making a slight obeisance, and
> never divesting himself of his slippers: a privilege which, in the
> eyes of the natives, at once places him on a footing of equality
> with his employer (Williamson 1810:189–90).

In the 1830's F.J. Shore, a judge in Upper India, complained that "natives of rank" walk into the rooms of Englishmen with their shoes on. He attributed this practice to a combination of the bad manners of the natives of Calcutta "who are of an inferior order" and the ignorance and carelessness of Europeans who do not know eastern etiquette (Shore 1837, I:79–80). Shore, who was highly critical of his countrymen's lack of knowledge and their disdain for the people of India, explained to his European readers they should not allow Indians in their presence with shoes. If Indians did so, the *sahib* should explain to them that:

> "Nations have different customs; ours is to uncover the head—
> yours to uncover the feet, as a token of respect. You would not
> presume to walk into the sitting-room of another native with
> your shoes on; why then do you treat me with a disrespect
> which you would not show to one of your own countrymen? I

am not prejudiced, and it is quite immaterial to me which practice you choose to adopt. You can either take off your shoes or
your turban, but I must insist on one or the other mark of civil-
ity if you wish me to receive your visits." This is unanswerable
by the native; and those English who have acted in this manner,
have been decidedly more respected by the people" (Shore 1837
I:80).

By 1854, so many Indians in Bengal, particularly in Calcutta, had
taken to wearing European shoes and stockings, that the Governor
General in Council passed a resolution allowing native gentlemen
"on official and semi-official occasions . . . to appear in the presence
of the servants of the British government" wearing European boots
or shoes (V.C. Chaudhuri 1980:425). Twenty years later, the rule was
made general throughout India and now included Government
courts, as the practice of wearing European dress had spread up-
country, among "educated native gentlemen accustomed to European habits." The rule was to apply only to the public parts of
courts, and not the chambers of the judge. His rooms were "private"
and hence he could there enforce whatever rules he wished.

There were several issues lurking beneath the seemingly trivial
question of which Indians of what status could wear what kinds of
shoes, and where. Indian Christians always were allowed to wear
their shoes wherever Europeans would normally wear their shoes.
Europeans had long objected to removing their shoes when entering
an Indian temple or when appearing in the durbar of an Indian
ruler. The British construction of the rules governing the wearing
or non-wearing of shoes was that Europeans did not have to conform to Indian custom, but Indians had to conform to European
ideas of what was proper Indian behavior. The Europeans could
also decide when an Indian practice had changed sufficiently to
allow their subjects to follow new rules. The "victory" of the Bengalis, in getting rules regarding the wearing of shoes changed, encouraged some of them to try to have changed the rule that they must
wear turbans while they were in government offices.

A group of Bengali officials in the 1870s petitioned the Lieutenant
Governor of Bengal to allow them "to adopt the European custom
of uncovering the head in token of respect in durbars and courts of
justice, and on all other official occasions and places" (Chaudhuri
1980:429). The petitioners pointed out that the "wearing of the *pagri*

(turban) is at present not a national custom of the Bengalis." Many Bengalis, they wrote, think the *pagri* an unreasonable headdress, as "it does not act as sufficient protection from the glare and heat of the sun," and is inappropriate to "active occupations." As a result of the decline in the use of the *pagri*, they claimed that Indians who work in government offices are forced to keep two headdresses: A *pagri*, which they carry in boxes or store in their offices, and a "light cap" which they actually wear. When a European superior approaches them while they are working in the office, they remove their caps and put on the *pagri*.

The Indians suggested a simple solution to the question: "We think that the best course is to wear caps and to uncover the head as token of respect." They pointed out that this would not prevent those Indians who continued to wear *pagris* from doing so, but those who by inference were more progressive in their dress and manners should not be forced to continue a custom they thought old-fashioned. In making their request, the petitioners felt they were acting in concert with the rulings about shoes, as that question was settled by the acceptance of the fact that Indians could wear shoes while the rest of their dress was "Oriental," and did not require Indians to fully adopt European dress. Hence, substituting the wearing of a cap indoors rather than going bareheaded in the European fashion could seem appropriate. To continue to be forced to wear a *pagri* in the presence of Europeans rather than wearing brimless caps could act "as a cause of moral depression on the people."

The Lieutenant Governor was strongly opposed to the suggested innovation. He did not think the petitioners represented "even the middle class of the natives of Bengal." It was proper for native gentlemen to wear whatever they wanted in private life, he wrote, but the use of the cap "was a very slovenly and unbecoming style of dress for public occasions." The Lieutenant Governor declared that "No European of respectability would appear in such caps." They were not "western" nor were they "Oriental," and hence by implication they were some kind of bastard concoction, which furthered a tendency he abhored towards laxity in dress and manners—and dress and manners were the means by which Indians showed proper respect in the office and on public occasions. Sir Ashley Eden then went on to lecture those Indians seeking to change current dress codes:

If any change in the rules is to be made it should not in the Lieutenant-Governor's opinion, take the shape of further relaxation of existing customs. Indeed, the Lieutenant-Governor thinks that the chief change required, is that some of the Native gentlemen, especially native officials, who attend levees and durbars should pay greater attention than heretofore to their customs, and should in this way imitate the European custom of showing respect by not appearing on such occasions in the ordinary clothes in which they have just left their desks or court-houses. The new prevailing laxity in this matter may possibly have some bearing on the want of cordiality in the relations between Europeans and Natives, of which such frequent complaint is made by those who remember a different state of things. Attention to costume was a form of respect in which the forefathers of the present generation were never deficient. In giving up the customs of appearing with the head covered on public occasions, Native gentlemen are adopting neither the customs of the West nor of the East, and the movement is one which the Lieutenant-Governor deprecates and which he is certainly in no way prepared to encourage (Chaudhuri 1980:436).

THE UNIFORM OF THE INDIAN NATIONAL CONGRESS

By the last decades of the nineteenth century, there was increasing documentation of the declining production of fine cotton textiles in India. Muslins of Dacca, printed cloths of the South of India, palampores, fine woolen shawls of Kashmir and the Punjab, had all but disappeared (Havell 1888:18–20; Havell 1890:9–15; Birdwood 1880:244–58); Murkherjee 1888:317–98; Irwin 1973). While the demise of fine weaving and printing was being decried, it was also noted that cheaper and coarser cotton cloth, frequently woven out of imported thread, continued to be in demand as it was cheaper and sturdier than Lancashire-made *dhotis* and *saris*. The effects of European imports on the production of Indian textiles were highly differentiated on a regional basis, and reflected ritual imperatives, changing social statuses, and taste. E.B. Havell, Superintendent of the School of Arts in Madras and subsequently of the Government Art School in Calcutta, who was the most influential of the Europeans concerned with the restoration of Indian fine arts and crafts, described the complexities of the situation in regard to Indian textiles in Madras:

The European goods have their great advantage in point of
cheapness, and consequently the native manufacturer who supplies the wants of the low caste and poorer classes has suffered
most.

White Cloths - for Male Wear. Two kinds of white cloth for
personal wear are produced by the native weaver: first, a plain
white cloth with a narrow border of coloured cotton, and sometimes with a broader band woven across each end, which are
worn by the low caste poor; and, secondly, superior cloths of
fine texture in which the borders are broader and of silk, and
generally embroidered with a simple pattern, and the bands at
each end either of silk or of silver lace. These cloths, originally
intended for Brahmins only, are now indiscriminately worn by
the wealthier classes of every caste. The first of these has been
almost entirely superseded for general wear by English long
cloth, which is cheaper than the native cloth by about one half.
Still, the manufacture is carried on throughout the districts on a
very small scale, for the native cloth is always worn, by those
who can afford it, on occasions of ceremony, and by some it is
preferred on account of its superior durability and thicker texture. The manufacture of the finer cloths still occupies a very
large proportion of the weavers, and is extensively carried on in
and around about Madura and Salem. The prosperity of this industry has also been affected to a less extent by the cheapness of
European goods, in a similar way, that whereas a well-to-do native would formerly have four to six country cloths in constant
wear, many now reserve the more expensive costume for the religious and domestic ceremonies at which a Hindu would expose
himself to ridicule if he appeared in other than his traditional
dress. But as these cloths are only within the reach of the
wealthier classes, it is probable that the spread of Western ideas
and mode of dress has had more prejudicial effect on the industry than the mere cheapness of European goods. Both in the
fine, but more especially in the inferior cloths, the profits of the
weaver seem to be reduced to a very low margin.

Cloth for Female Wear. The manufacture of cloths for female
wear is carried on on a very extensive scale, and has not declined to such an extent as the other, for though the industry
has suffered considerably in the inferior kinds by the competition of English and French cheap printed cotton goods, European manufacturers have not hitherto produced anything which
can at all compete with the finer cloths of Tanjore, Kuttálam and
Kuranád, and other places. While the more gorgeous beauties of

the textile manufactures of the north, such as those of Benares,
Surat and Gujerat, have been fully recognised, it is a pity that
the more sober, though none the less remarkable, artistic
qualities of these fine cloths and their adaptability in many ways
to decorative purposes have not been better appreciated. Artisti-
cally speaking, a decline is only noticeable in the cotton cloths,
most of which have lost their characteristic beauty by the use of
European dyed thread. The Madura cloths, however, are an exception (Havell 1888).

The decline of the craft production of Indian cloth, used for dress,
decoration, and rituals, was caused by a combination of price and
the changing of taste of Indian consumers. In the 1860s European
manufacturers had not yet developed an adequate knowledge of the
varied tastes of Indians or the functions of cloth in India. James
Forbes Watson, Reporter of Economic Products at the India Office
in London and Director of the India Museum, was a lifetime student
of Indian textiles who produced 18 volumes containing 700 samples
of Indian textiles. Twenty sets of what Watson thought of as portable
"textile museums" were distributed in Great Britain and India. His
goal was to acquaint manufacturers with the "tastes and needs of
their Indian customers." In addition to his sample books, he wrote
what remains today the most extensive single-volume study of Indian dress and textiles, *The Textile Manufactures and the Costumes
of the People of India*, London 1866. In this work he explained
that to be successful, the manufacturer producing cloth for the Indian market had to know "how the garment was worn, by which
sex and for what purpose." Above all, he had to grasp "the
relationship between the size of cloth, its decoration and use, if
he were to be successful in selling textiles in India." The European manufacturer might produce a cloth that was correct in size,
length, and breadth for a turban or *lungi* (loincloth) but it might
prove "unsaleable because its decoration is unsuitable . . . or
because it is not in good taste from an Indian point of view"
(Watson 1866:5).

Watson cheerfully stated that increased consumption of European cloth in India would be good for both the Manchester manufacturers and the people of India. Indians were underclothed and
hence cheap textiles would be a boon for them. If the Indian weavers
couldn't compete, it wouldn't necessarily be a bad thing as:

In a great productive country like India it is certain that *she* will
gain; for if supplies from Britain set labour free there, it will only
be to divert it at once into other and perhaps more profitable
channels. It might be otherwise if India were not a country
whose strength in raw products is great and far from developed;
but as it is, her resources in this direction are known to be capable of a vast expansion and to be sufficient to occupy the energies of her whole people (Watson 1866:8).

As can be seen by the exchange between the Lieutenant Governor
of Bengal and his Bengali underlings, Indian tastes in clothes were
rapidly changing. The thousands of clerks and functionaries who
worked in the Government and commercial offices of Calcutta and
Bombay had by the late nineteenth century developed a distinctive
form of dress, a mixture of Indian and European. They wore an un-
ironed white European shirt with tails out, covering the top of their
finely draped white *dhoti*; their legs were bare to midcalf, showing
white socks held up by garters, and their feet were shod in patent
leather pumps or short boots produced by Chinese bootmakers in
Calcutta (Thurston 1906:519).

Some of the wealthier and more flashily dressed Bengalis were
described by S.C. Bose as thinking that an adaptation of the European style of dress could bring them the benefit of "modern civilization" by "wearing tight pantaloons, tight shirts and black coats of
alpaca or broadcloth." They would top this costume with "a coquet-
tish embossed cap or a thin folded shawl turban" (S.C. Bose
1881:192).

The wealthy of Calcutta sought to modernize not only their
dress, but their home furnishings as well. I noted above the separation of the large Calcutta mansions into two sections: A domestic
one of the women which was private, and a public set of rooms used
by males for entertaining their Indian and occasional European
guests. The drawing rooms were furnished in a mixed "Oriental"
and "Western" style.

A Canadian visitor, Anna Leonwens, described a visit to the
home of a wealthy gentleman, Ram Chunder, in Bombay. She described him as "educated in all the learning of the East as well as
in English, but never the less a pure Hindoo in mind and character."
The occasion was for an evening of Indian dance, drama, and music.
Her host was dressed in a "rich and strikingly picturesque" manner.

He wore deep crimson satin trousers, a white muslin *"angraka"* or tunic, a purple vest with gold embroidery, a fine Cashmere cummerbund, white European stockings, and embroidered antique Indian slippers (Leonwens 1884:175). The entertainment took place in a large room, furnished in the Oriental style, with *kincob* (brocade) wall hangings decorated with peacock feathers. The floors were a fine tile mosaic, and around the walls on tables and shelves were a "melange of European ornaments, clocks, antique pictures, statues, celestial and terrestrial globes and a profusion of common glass wear of the most brilliant colors" (Leonwens 1884:174).

It was not only the wealthy, Western-educated, or urban middle classes whose dress was beginning to change, but more common folk as well. Tribesmen recruited from the hills of Southern India as labor on tea and coffee plantations spent some of their wages on turbans and caps (innovations for them) and woven coats "of English cut" for festival clothes (Thurston 1906:520). An Indian working for Edgar Thurston, Superintendent of the Madras Government Museum and head of the Ethnographic Survey of Madras, appeared wearing a white patchwork shirt, adorned "with no less than six individual and distinct trademarks representing the King-Emperor, Brittania and an elephant, etc." The inclusion of the printed trademarks was generally popular; soldiers of the Maharaja of Kashmir wear jackets blazoned with the manufacturer's identification of "superfine" (*The Graphic*, March 4, 1876:229). European manufacturers were supplying cloth with all sorts of designs, which according to Thurston met the "Indians' love of the grotesque," a taste nurtured by exposure to the "carvings on Hindu temples and mythological paintings" (Thurston 1906:522). One of the most popular patterns in cloth manufactured for use in women's petticoats had a border "composed of an endless procession of white bicycles of ancient pattern with green gearing and treadles, separated from each other by upright stems with green and gold fronts . . ." (Thurston 1906:522).

While a few Europeans were proselytizing for better taste and seeking to "direct progress in a right groove and to prevent the decline of Indian art," some early Indian nationalist writers were developing a critique of the Government of India's policies furthering the destruction of Indian "manufactures," which they claimed advantaged British manufacturers to the detriment of incipient Indian efforts to establish modern industry. The early nationalists also argued that Government revenue policies were contributing to the continued misery of the mass of Indian cultivators (Buck 1886:i; Tarapor 1978, 1980, 1981; Chandra 1966; Sarkar 1973, Ch. III; for a counter-argument see Morris, 1963 and 1968).

Thus there were two streams of thought: the aesthetic and moral concern of Europeans influenced by the art and craft movement in Great Britain and their Indian experience, and the early Indian nationalist critique of government policies leading to the continued impoverishment of India. These two streams of thought provided a major part of the ideology of the *swadeshi* movement in Bengal, 1903–08. The movement's goals were complex, but one aim was to encourage the development and use of indigenously produced goods through a boycott of European manufactures. As the movement developed, there was increasing discussion and propaganda to encourage Indian weavers and to revive the hand spinning of cotton thread (Sarkar 1973:94–108). These ideas were taken up and formalized by Mahatma Gandhi through the next decade. Gandhi had been much influenced by Ruskin's and Morris's critiques of modern industrial society and its destructive and alienating effects on the bodies, minds, and morals of the European working classes (Chatterjee 1984). Gandhi continually articulated and elaborated on the theme that the Indian people would only be free from European domination, both politically and economically, when the masses took to spinning, weaving, and wearing homespun cotton cloth, *khadi*. To give substance to these theories, he created the enduring symbols of the Indian nationalist movement; the *chakra* (spinning wheel), which appeared on the Indian National Congress flag and continues to be ambiguously represented on the Republic of India's flag, and the wearing of a *khadi* "uniform," a white handspun cotton *dhoti*, *sari*, or *pajama*, *kurta* and a small white cap.

In 1908, when he was still in South Africa, Gandhi began to advocate handspinning and weaving as the panacea for the growing pauperization of India. (Decades later, Gandhi could not recall ever having seen a spinning wheel when he began to advocate their use) (Gandhi 1968, II:730). In 1916, after his return to India, he established an *ashram*, where a small group of his followers were to begin practicing what Gandhi had been preaching. The first order of business was to find or develop a *chakra* to implement his call, not only to boycott foreign-made cloth and thread, but to make and wear their own *khadi*. At first they had to make do with cloth which was handwoven, but made of mill-made thread produced by Indian mills. It was not until 1917 or 1918 that one of his loyal followers, Gangabehn Majumdar, located some spinning wheels in Baraoda and encouraged some weavers to spin and weave cloth for the *ashram*. The next step was to try to produce their own cloth at the *ashram*: the first result was a cloth 30 inches wide, which was too narrow for an adequate *dhoti*. The first piece of cloth produced cost 17 annas per yard, grossly expensive for the time. Finally Gangabehn was successful in getting cloth of adequate width, 45 inches, made so that Gandhi was not "forced to wear a coarse short *dhoti* (Gandhi 1968:735–37).

I have been unable to find out when and how Gandhi created the uniform of the Indian National Congress, but it was clearly between 1918 and 1920. During the First Non-Cooperative Movement of 1920–21, the wearing of *khadi* and especially the cap, by now dubbed a "Gandhi cap," was widespread and became the symbolic focus, once again, of the British-Indian battle over headdress. In March of 1921, Gandhi reported that some European employers were ordering that the white *khadi* caps not be worn in the office. Gandhi commented that "Under of rule of Ravana," the villain in the Ramayana, "keeping a picture of Vishnu in one's house was an offence, [so] it should not be surprising if in this *Ravanarajya* [Raj of Ravana] wearing a white cap . . . not using foreign cloth, or plying the spinning wheel came to be considered offences" (Gandhi 1964–65, XIX:482).

A month later, the Collector of Allahabad in Eastern Uttar Pradesh forbade government employees from wearing "the beautiful, light inoffensive caps" (XX:105). A few months later in Simla, Indians in government service said they risked dismissal if they wore *khadi* dress and caps (XX:223). A lawyer in Gujarat was fined 200 rupees and ordered out of court for wearing the cap; when he returned an hour later still wearing the cap, another 200 rupees were added to his fine (XX:204). The campaign, as far as Gandhi was concerned, was highly successful. When an English businessman dismissed a young clerk for wearing the offending hat, he declared "the manager by his simple act of dismissal of a poor Indian employee had given political color to the transaction." The British were falling for Gandhi's symbolic transformation of the *khadi* cap into a sign of rebellion. He urged Indians everywhere, by the simple act of wearing a hat, to bring the Raj to its knees (XX:378–79, 487–88). The British, Gandhi argued, were confusing Non-Cooperation with the use of *khadi*, thereby reinforcing the power of the movement. If they were so frightened by the mere wearing of a *khadi* cap, which was a "convenience and symbol of *swadeshi*," what might happen if he, Gandhi, asked Government employees to stop working, and not just wear *khadi*?

The Chief Justice of the High Court of Bombay issued a letter to all judges under his jurisdiction to bar pleaders in their courts from wearing the Gandhi cap; if they continued to do so, he said, they were to be charged with contempt of court for having been disrespectful to the judge. The Chief Justice went on to state, "No pleader should appear in Court if he wears any headdress *except* a turban" (Gandhi, XXII:15). Gandhi also reported that a Muslim youth was shot by a European youth for selling or wearing a Gandhi cap (Gandhi XXII:175).

HEADS AND FEET: TURBANS AND SHOES

From the eighteenth to the twentieth century, the British and Indians fought out a battle about the proper forms of respectful behavior, centered on heads and feet. But to say that turbans, caps, and shoes were symbolically charged for both groups tells us little. What were the underlying meanings of this battle?

Europeans explained the nature of Indian headdress in functionalist and materialist terms: the turban was for the protection of the head. Watson described the Indian turban as providing "protection from the heat of the sun, it is usually of a fine muslin-like texture, which when folded, is at once bulky and porous—this admirably fulfilling its main purpose . . . [the light cloth] is a good non-conductor" and "allows the free escape of perspiration" (Watson 1866:13). Indians clearly did not share the idea that the turban or other headdresses were primarily for protection from the sun. The elaborate decoration of the caps, the jewel-bedecked turbans of the rulers, and the choice of a hat as a major symbol of the Nationalist movement all indicate that hats are much more than a form of protection from the heat or the rays of the sun.

I can only sketch some of the possibilities that might help explain the significance of head coverings for Indians. Clearly, there is no simple answer to the question of the significance of the head for Indians. Fazl wrote that for Muslims the head is the seat of the senses, (Fazl 1927:167). For Hindus the head is the locus of the eyes, including the third or inner eye in the center of the forehead. Lawrence Babb has persuasively argued that sight is the crucial sense cosmographically for Hindus. "Hindus wish to see their deities" (Babb 1981:387). Today, Hindus live in constant sight of the deities, in the form of ubiquitous colored lithographs, which emphasize and accentuate the face and eyes of the deities. Indians wish to see and be seen, to be in the sight of, to have the glance of, not only their deities, but persons of power. The concept of *darshan*, to see and be seen, includes going to a temple, visiting a holy man or guru, or waiting for a glimpse of a movie star or the Prime Minister.

Babb stresses that the Hindu conception of "seeing" is not "just a passive product" of "sensory data originating in the outer world;" it involves the observer directly with the person or deity seen. Hindus live in a substantive world in which there are constant flows of various forms of matter, among them emanations from "the inner person, outward through eyes to engage directly with objects seen, and to bring something of these objects back to the seer" (Babb 1981:396). Not only is the head the seat of sight, but it is also the part of the body that concentrates positive flows of substances and powers within the body. In the practice of raj yoga, for example, one seeks to concentrate through exercise and meditation the power of the whole body in the head.

As the head is the locus of power and superior forms of knowledge, the feet become the opposite. The feet are "the sources of downward and outward currents of inferior matter" (Babb 1981:395). When a Hindu visits a guru, a parent, a patron, a landlord, a government official, or a god, he or she will touch their feet. This is an "act of submission or surrender" but it is also a reciprocal act, as one is obliged to offer "shelter and protection to the one who has surrendered." By touching the feet one is taking what is ostensibly base and "impure" from a superior being and treating it as valuable and "pure" (Babb 1981:395).

I think Babb's exegesis and analysis, which draws on the work of Wadley and Marriott in their discussions of power and substantive flows, provides an explanation for the significance of the head and feet, and hence their coverings. It explains why Lord Valentia was correct in surmising that his feet, if pointed towards the Peshwa, would have defiled him; they were the source of impurity. Shoes and slippers were dirty, not just from being used to walk around in, but as the repositories of base substances flowing from the wearer's body. This is why it was an Indian custom not only to take off one's dirty shoes or slippers when entering the space of a superior, but more importantly, to sit so that the feet would not imperil the well-being of others.

The solution worked out in Indian courts to accomodate the inability of Europeans to sit for long periods on a rug or a cushion with their feet tucked under them was to allow them to sit on chairs; thus their feet, covered or uncovered, would be facing downward. Today, or at least yesterday—35 years ago when I was doing field work in a village—the few villagers who had chairs would sit on them, particularly if they had provided me with a chair, but with their feet off the ground and tucked up under them.

A painting by Thomas Daniel, based on sketches by James Wales, shows Sir Charles Malet delivering a ratified treaty to the Peshwa in Poona in 1792; we see almost all the Indians and Europeans sitting or kneeling on a large rug, while the Peshwa sits on a slightly raised platform, supported by large cushions. Of the fifty-odd figures depicted, all but two have their feet placed so that they cannot be seen. Some of the English appear to have lap cloths or cummerbunds covering their feet; one English military officer is wearing boots, but the sole of his boot is on the ground. One Indian soldier is kneeling in such a fashion that one bare foot can be seen, but he too has the sole of his foot firmly on the rug (Archer 1979, Pl.261).

The writers of guide books who advised British travelers never to touch an Indian on his turban or head were correct, but this was not merely politeness in observing yet another peculiar Indian custom; because the hands, like the feet and mouth, are sources of impurities, touching the head would threaten the well-being of the Indian being touched.

In the conceptual scheme which the British created to understand and to act in India, they constantly followed the same logic; they reduced vastly complex codes and their associated meanings to a few metonyms. If Indians wore shoes in the presence of *Sahibs*, they were being disrespectful in the early nineteenth century. But to Indians, the proper wearing of slippers or shoes stood for a whole difference in cosmology.

The European concepts of custom and superstition were a means to encompass and explain behavior and thought. They allowed the British to save themselves the effort of understanding or adequately explaining the subtle or not-too-subtle meanings attached to the actions of their subjects. Once the British had defined something as an Indian custom, or traditional dress, or the proper form of salutation, any deviation from it was defined as rebellion and an act to be punished. India was redefined by the British to be a place of rules and orders; once the British had defined to their own satisfaction what they construed as Indian rules and customs, then the Indians had to conform to these constructions. Wearing the Gandhi cap thus was a metonym for disorder. To the Indian this cap was indeed a symbol, but a highly complex one. Involving a cosmological system which set the meaning of the head and its covering, it had as well an ideological referent as a critique of British rule in India, and embodied to its wearer a protest against the insults and deprivations of 150 years of colonial rule.

ACKNOWLEDGMENTS

This paper was written while I was the holder of a fellowship for independent study and research awarded by the National Endowment for the Humanities. The paper is based on my continuing research on the British construction of a colonial sociology and its representations in eighteenth- and nineteenth-century India. This work over the past ten years has been supported by the National Science Foundation, the American Council of Learned Societies and Social Science Research Council Joint Committee on South Asia, the American Institute of Indian Studies, and the Lichtstern Research Fund of the Department of Anthropology of the University of Chicago.

In writing this paper, my greatest debt is owed to the South Asia Collection of the Regenstein Library of the University of Chicago and to its creator, Maureen L. P. Patterson. The paper reflects the influence of Anthony King, of the Sociology Department of Brunel University, whose writings, conversations, and "guided architectural tours," taught me that one can read the past in objects, museum collections, buildings, and landscapes, as well as in documents and books. While I was writing the paper I learned much about the significance of clothes in conversations with my colleague Jean Comaroff. The paper would not have been completed without

Lois Bisek's skill, patience, and uncanny ability to make sense out of my ungrammatical, misspelled, and wretchedly typed draft.

REFERENCES CITED

Archer, Mildred
    1972   Company Drawings in the India Office Library. London: H.M. Stationary Office.
    1979   India and British Portraiture, 1770–1825. New York: Sotheby Parke Bernet.

Babb, Lawrence
    1981   Glancing: Visual Interaction in Hinduism. Journal of Anthropological Research 37:387–401.

Ball, Charles
    1859   The History of the Indian Mutiny, 2 vols. London: London Printing and Publishing Co.

Beetham, David
    1970   Transport and Turbans: A Comparative Study in Local Politics. London: Oxford University Press.

Birdwood, George
    1880   The Industrial Arts of India. London: Chapman and Hall, Ltd.

Bolt, David
    1975   Gurkhas. London: White Lion Publishers.

Buck, E.C.
    1886   Preface. Journal of Indian Arts 1 (1):i-iv.

Burrow, J.W.
    1981   A Liberal Descent: Victorian Historians and the English Past. Cambridge: Cambridge University Press.

Bhushan, J.B.
    1958   The Costumes and Textiles of India. Bombay: D.B. Taraporevala.

Buckler, F.W.
    1927–28 The Oriental Despot. Angelican Theological Review 10 (3):238–49.
    1922   Two Instances of Khilat in the Bible. Journal of Theological Studies 23:197–99.

Callcott, Maria Graham
    1812   Journal of a Residence in India. Edinburgh: A. Constable.

Cannadine, David
    1983   The Context, Performance and Meaning of Ritual: The British Monarchy and the "Invention of Tradition," c. 1820–1977. *In* The

Invention of Tradition, Eric Hobsbawn and Terence Ranger, eds. pp. 101–64. Cambridge: Cambridge University Press.

Chandra, Bipan
1960   The Rise and Growth of Economic Nationalism in India. New Delhi: People's Publishing House.

Chaudhuri, N.C.
1976   Culture in a Vanity Bag. Bombay: Jaico Publishing House.

Chaudhuri, V.C.
1980   Imperial Honeymoon with Indian Aristocracy. Patna: K.P. Jayswal Research Institute.

Cohn, Bernard
1983   Representing Authority in Victorian India. In The Invention of Tradition, Eric Hobsbawm and Terence Ranger, eds., pp. 165–209. Cambridge: Cambridge University Press.

Davies, C.C.
1937   India and Queen Victoria. Asiatic Review (n.s.) 33:482–504.

Eastwick, E.B.
1849   A Galance at the Sind Before Napier or Dry Leaves from Young Egypt. Karachi: Oxford University Press.

Falcon, R.W.
1896   Handbook on the Sikhs for the use of Regimental Officers. Allahabad: The Pioneer Press.

Fazl, Abu'l
1927   The Ain-i-Akabari, Vol. I. Calcutta: Asiatic Society of Bengal.

Foster, William ed.,
1899   The Embassy of Sir Thomas Roe to the Court of the Great Mughal. 1615–19, Vol. I. London: Hakluyt Society.

Gandhi, M.K.
1966   An Autobiography: The Story of My Experiments with Truth. Boston: Beacon Press.
1964–65 Collected Works. Dehli: Publications Division, Ministry of Information and Broadcasting, Government of India.

Gascoigne, Bamber
1971   The Great Mughuls. London: Cape.

Ghurye, G.S.
1966   Indian Costume. Bombay: Popular Prakashan.

Gittinger, Mattiebelle
1982   Master Dyers to the World. Washington: Textile Museum.

Gopal, S.
1976   Jawaharalal Nehru: a Biography, Vol. I. Cambridge, Mass.: Harvard University Press.

India, Government of (GOI)
  1913   Proceedings of the Committee on the Obligations Devolving on the Army in India, Its Strength and Cost. Vol 1-A, Minority Report. Simla: Government Central Branch Press.

Hasan, Ibn
  1936   The Central Structure of the Moghul Empire and Its Practical Working up to the Year 1657. London: Oxford University Press.

Havell, E.B.
  1888   The Printed Cotton Industry of India. Journal of Indian Art 2(19): 18–20.
  1890   The Industries of Madras. Journal of Indian Art 3(26):9–16.

Heathcote, T.A.
  1975   The Indian Army: The Garrison of British Imperial India, 1822–1922. New York: Hippocrene Books.

Hobsbawm, Eric and Terence Ranger
  1983   The Invention of Tradition. Cambridge: Cambridge University Press.

Hutchins, Frances
  1967   The Illusion of Permanence: British Imperialism in India. Princeton: Princeton University Press.

Irwin, John
  1973   The Kashmir Shawl. London: Her Majesty's Stationary Office.

Islam, Riazul
  1970   Indo-Persian Relations: A Study of the Political and Diplomatic Relations between the Mughal Empire and Iran. Teheran: Iranian Culture Foundation

Iyer, Anantha Krishna
  1935   The Mysore Tribes and Castes, Vol. I. Mysore: Published under the auspices of Mysore University.

Johnson, James
  1813   The Influence of Tropical Climates. London: J.J. Stockdale.

Khan, I.A.
  1972   The Turko-Mongol Theory of Kingship. Medieval India: A Miscellany 2:9–18.

Leonowens, Anna H.
  1884   Life and Travel in India. Philadelphia: Porter and Coates.

Macauliffe, M.A.
  1909   The Sikh Religion: Its Gurus, Sacred Writings, and Authors, VI Vols. Oxford: Clarendon Press.

Macleod, W.H.
  1976   The Evolution of the Sikh Community. Oxford: Clarendon Press.

Mereweather, J.W.B. and F. Smith
1919   The Indian Army Corps in France. London: J. Murray.

Moore, Joseph Sr.
1886   The Queen's Empire and her Pearls. Philadelphia: J.B. Lippincott.

Morris, Morris D.
1963   Towards a Reinterpretation of Nineteenth Century Indian Economic History. Journal of Economic History 23(3):606–618.

Morris, Morris D. et at.
1968   Reinterpretation of Nineteenth Century Indian Economic History. Indian Economic and Social History Review 5(1):1–15.
Royal Anthropological Institute Newsletter (RAIN) (56)1983.

Rice, Stanley
1981   The Life of Sayaji Rao III, Maharaja of Baroda, Vol. II. London: Oxford University Press.

Sarkar, Sumit
1973   The Swadeshi Movement in Bengal, 1903–08. New Delhi: Peoples Pub. House.

Sergeant, Philip W.
1928   The Ruler of Baroda: An Account of the Life and Work of the Maharaja Gaekwar Sayajirao III. London: J. Murray.

Shore, F.J.
1837   Notes on Indian Affairs, Vol. I. London: J.W. Parker.

Singh, Khushwant
1953   The Sikhs. London: G. Allen and Unwin.
1963–66 A History of the Sikhs, Vols. I and II. Princeton: Princeton University Press.

Strong, Roy C.
1978   Recreating the Past: British History and the Victorian Painter. New York: Thames and Hudson.

Tarapor, Mahrukh
1978   Indian and the Arts and Crafts Movement. Paper read at the Victorian Studies Conference, Birmingham.
1980   John Lockwood, Kipling, and British Art Education in India. Victorian Studies 23(21):53–81.
1981   Art Education in Imperial India: The Indian Schools of Art. Paper read at the Seventh European Conference on Modern South Asia Studies, July 1981. SOAS, London.

Thurston, Edgar
1908   Ethnographic Notes in Southern India. Madras: Printed by the Superintendent, Government Press.

Tripathi, R.P.
    1956   Some Aspects of Muslim Administration. Allahabad: Central
              Book Depot.

Tuker, Francis
    1957   Gorkha: The Story of the Gurkhas of Nepal. London: Constable.

Uberoi, J.P. Singh
    1967   On Being Unshorn. Transactions of the Indian Institute of Ad-
              vanced Study 4:87–100. Simla: Pooran Press.

Lord Valentia, George Annesley Mountnorris
    1909   Voyages and Travels in India, Ceylon . . . , Vol II. London:
              printed for W. Miller.

Verma, Som Prakash
    1978   Art and Material Culture in the Paintings of Akbar's Court. New
              Delhi: Vikas.

Wallman, Sandra
    1982   Turbans, Identities, and Racial Categories. Royal Anthropological
              Institute Newsletter (October) (52)2.

Watson, J. Forbes
    1866   The Textile Manufacturers and the Costumes of the People of
              India. London: G.E. Eyre and W. Spottiswoode.

Watson, J. Forbes and John Kaye
    1868–75 The People of India, 8 Vols. London:India Museum.

Williamson, Thomas
    1810   The East-India Vade Mecum, 2 Vols. London: Black, Parry and
              Kingsbury.

11. *Gandhi and* Khadi, *the Fabric of Indian Independence*

SUSAN S. BEAN

 Cloth was central to the Indian struggle for national self-government—cloth as an economic product and cloth as a medium of communication. Cloth was officially incorporated into the nationalist program in 1921 when the Indian National Congress resolved to campaign for the boycott of foreign cloth, to require its officers and workers to spin cotton yarn and wear hand-spun, hand-woven cloth (*khadi*), and to adopt a flag with the spinning wheel in the center. Mahatma Gandhi was the force behind the adoption of these resolutions, but they were successful because Gandhi had achieved an understanding of the role of cloth in Indian life, the culmination of decades of experimentation with cloth as a medium of communication and means of livelihood.

Gandhi's changing sociopolitical identity can be traced through his costume changes as well as through his speeches, writings, and activities. As he came to appreciate the semiotic properties of cloth, he learned to use it to communicate his most important messages to followers and opponents and to manipulate social events. Once he had appreciated the economic importance of cloth in India, he made it the centerpiece of his program for independence and self-government. The development of Gandhi's thought and practice, which is explored in the following pages, is illuminated by the historical and cultural context provided in Cohn (this volume) and Bayly (1986). Cohn analyzes the use of costume in the reorganization and management of hierarchical relations during the British Raj. Bayly provides valuable insights into the role of cloth in Indian culture, emphasizing its moral nature—its capacity to embody and transmit social value—a characteristic of cloth which Gandhi appreciated.

LESSONS IN THE SOCIAL MEANING OF COSTUME

When Mohandas K. Gandhi disembarked at Southampton in 1888, he was wearing white flannels given to him by a friend and saved especially for the occasion, because he "thought that white clothes would suit [him] better when [he] stepped ashore" (Gandhi 1957:43). On his arrival at Southampton he realized that white flannels were not worn in late September. Later he replaced his Bombay-style clothing, which he thought "unsuitable for English society" (Gandhi 1957:50), with an evening suit from Bond Street, patent leather shoes with spats, and a high silk hat, "clothes regarded as the very acme of fashion" (Fischer 1982:37). Gandhi was sensitive to the connection between costume and social status, and perceived that changes in social position required changes in costume. His sensitivity became self-consciousness because Gandhi, the student from India, was so ignorant of how Gandhi, the London barrister, should appear.

In 1891 when Gandhi returned home to Rajkot, a barrister, he promoted the westernization of his household, begun for him by his brother, by adding items of European dress (Gandhi 1957:92). Gandhi believed his success was dependent on westernization. Later, in the harsher, more repressive, and openly racist South Africa where he went to work as a barrister in 1893, he confronted his indelible Indianness.

On this third day in South Africa, he visited the Durban court. It was explained to him that Hindus had to remove their turbans in court, though Muslim Indians were permitted to keep their turbans on. Turbans were not like hats: In this context, removal was not deferential, it was demeaning (see Cohn, this volume). Gandhi thought he could solve the problem by wearing an English hat, but his employer warned him that he would be undermining efforts for recognition of the Indian meaning of the turban and for permission to keep it on in court. His employer added, in appreciation of Indian dress: "An Indian turban sits well on your head." Besides, he said, "If you wear an English hat you will pass for a waiter" (Gandhi 1957:108). (Most waiters in South Africa were Indian converts to Christianity who wore English dress.)

Gandhi kept his turban and began to appreciate the limits of his Englishness—limits imposed by the colonial regime and by his pride as an Indian and a Hindu. But still he thought he could make his Indianness compatible with Englishness. He wore a fashionable frock coat, pressed trousers, and shining shoes with his turban (Fischer 1982:57). After he was thrown off the train to Pretoria for traveling first class, he reapplied for a first-class ticket, presenting himself to the station master "in faultless English dress" (Gandhi 1957:116). He succeeded. The station master said, "I can see you are a gentleman" (Gandhi 1957:117).

Gandhi later also succeeded in persuading the railway authorities to issue first- and second-class tickets to Indians "who were properly dressed" (Gandhi 1957:128). He sought to demonstrate that Indians could be as civilized as Englishmen and therefore were entitled to the same rights and privileges as citizens of the British Empire. This belief seemed to be supported by the Empress Victoria herself, who stated that there was a distinction between "aliens and subjects of Her Majesty [and] between the most ignorant and the most enlightened of the natives of India. Among the latter class there are to be found gentlemen whose position and attainments fully qualify them for all the duties and privileges of citizenship" (Queen Victoria, quoted in Erikson 1969:172–3).

When Gandhi brought his family to South Africa in 1896 he believed "that in order to look civilized, our dress and manners had as far as possible to approximate to the European standard. Because, I thought, only thus could we have some influence, and without influence it would not be possible to serve the community. I therefore determined the style of dress for my wife and children. How could I like them to be known as Kathiawad Banias? The Parsis used then to be regarded as the most civilized people amongst Indians, and so, when the complete European style seemed to be unsuited, we adopted the Parsi style. Accordingly my wife wore the Parsi sari, and the boys the Parsi coat and trousers. Of course no one could be without shoes and stockings. It was long before my wife and children could get used to them. The shoes cramped their feet and the stockings stank with perspiration" (Gandhi 1957:186).

Soon the prospect began to fade that one could be an Indian and a full citizen of the British empire by wearing Indian headgear with an English suit. For one thing, it had become clear that the color of one's skin was as much a part of one's costume as a frock coat, and this fundamental Indianness Gandhi would not have changed even if he could. He began to admire Indian dress. In 1901, back in India for a visit, he met some rulers of Indian states at the India Club in Calcutta. Gandhi recalls, "In the Club I always found them wearing fine Bengalee *dhotis* [Hindu garments of seamless cloth, wrapped and folded around the lower body] and shirts and scarves. On the darbar day [Viceroy's audience] they put on trousers befitting *khansamas* [waiters] and shining boots. I was pained and inquired of one of them the reason for the change. "We alone know our unfortunate condition [began the reply]. We alone know the insults we have to put up with, in order that we may possess our wealth and titles. . . .' 'But what about these *khansama* turbans and these shining boots?' I asked. 'Do you see any difference between *khansamas* and us?' he replied, and added, 'They are our *khansamas*, we are Lord Curzon's *khansamas*. If I were to absent myself from the levee, I should have to suffer the consequences. If I were to attend it in my usual dress, it would be an offence'" (Gandhi 1957:230). As in the Durban court, the sartorial dictates of the Empire were demeaning for its Indian citizens (see Cohn, this volume). During the same visit he remarked on his mentor, Gokhale: "In the Congress I had seen him in a coat and trousers, but I was glad to find him wearing a Bengal *dhoti* and shirt [at home]. I liked his simple mode of dress though I myself then wore a Parsi coat and trousers" (Gandhi 1957:234). Gandhi began to experiment with his own costume. Soon he embarked on a tour of India to learn about its people; he traveled third class. For clothing he took a long woolen coat, a *dhoti*, and a shirt. But on his return to Bombay in 1902 he resumed the life of the well-dressed, well-housed barrister riding first class on the trains.

Gandhi's responses to the costumes of others and his experiments with his own attire indicate a growing awareness of the meaning of clothes—their importance as indicators of status, group identity, social stratification, and political beliefs. He had begun to doubt the possibility of being both a dignified Indian and an English gentleman. The sartorial requirements of the Empire forced Indians to humiliate themselves, and revealed the true relationship—of master and slave—between the English and the Indians. Gandhi's experiments with simple, inexpensive Indian garments expressed his growing disdain for possessions and his growing identification with the poor.

By 1908 he had come to believe that Indians could not be Englishmen and that India should be ruled for the benefit of India by Indians. He set forth these views in *Hind Swaraj* (*Indian Home Rule*) (1908), where he also said: "If people of a certain country, who have hitherto not been in the habit of wearing much clothing, boots, etc., adopt European clothing, they are supposed to have become civilized out of savagery" (Gandhi 1922:32). He himself had believed this when in 1893 he appealed to the railroad authorities to allow Indians in European dress to ride first class, and in 1896 when he brought his family to South Africa and insisted on the further westernization of their dress. By 1908, he no longer believed that European garments were an index of civilization and Indian ones of its lack.

In *Hind Swaraj*, Gandhi first articulated the importance for India of the economics of cloth. For fifty years, an economic nationalism (whose roots were in fact much older) had been evolving in India. British rule had not benefited India, as the British maintained. On the contrary, British rule had destroyed the economy of India by taking its wealth back to England, by overtaxing its farmers, and by destroying Indian industries that might compete with English ones, thus causing poverty, famine, and disease. Cloth manufacture had been the premier industry of India and its decline was a chief cause of Indian poverty. These views were set out in detail in R.C. Dutt's two-volume *Economic History of India* (Dutt 1901 & 1903). Gandhi commented in *Hind Swaraj*: "When I read Mr. Dutt's *Economic History of India* I wept; and, as I think of it, again my heart sickens. . . . It is difficult to measure the harm that Manchester [the seat of the English mechanized textile industry] has done to us. It is due to Manchester that Indian handicraft has all but disappeared" (Gandhi 1922:105).

From 1908 on, these two elements—the economics of cloth and the semiotics of cloth—united in Gandhi's thought. By 1921, *khadi* (homespun cloth) had become central to his politics. The interven-

ing years were full of experiments with costume and with the production of handmade cloth.

CLOTH IN ECONOMIC NATIONALISM

Gandhi's campaign for *khadi* was a product of economic nationalism.
Gandhi's views on cloth and clothing were unique, but the elements
of which they were composed were not. According to the economic
nationalists, India's decline was due largely to British destruction of
Indian manufactures beginning in the late eighteenth century. Cotton textiles had been India's premier industry. Weavers and dyers
so excelled in producing both coarse , inexpensive textiles and fine,
exquisitely dyed, luxury textiles that Indian cloth was prized in
Rome, China, Egypt, and Southeast Asia.

> As early as 200 B.C. the Romans used a Sanskrit word for cotton
> (Latin, *carbasina*, from Sanskrit *karpasa*). In Nero's reign, deli-
> cately translucent Indian muslins were fashionable in Rome
> under such names as *nebula* and *venti* textiles (woven winds) the
> latter exactly translating the technical name of a special type of
> muslin woven in Bengal up to the modern period. . . .The qual-
> ity of Indian dyeing, too, was proverbial in the Roman world, as
> we know from a reference in St. Jerome's fourth century Latin
> translation of the Bible, Job being made to say that wisdom is
> even more enduring than the "dyed colors of India" (Irwin 1962).

In the fifth century A.D. an Indonesian diplomatic mission carried
textiles from India and Gandhara to China. In the eleventh century,
"500 Jewish families on their way to settle in the Northern Sung capital of China, bought cotton goods in India to take as gifts" (Gittinger
1982:13). Fifteenth-century fragments of Indian cloth found at Fostat,
near Cairo, show that the trade was not exclusively in fine textiles.
The fragments are "often lacking in care or precision [in dye crafts-
manship] and only occasionally showing exceptional skill. Inescapa-
ble is the sense that these were made for a modest clientele and do
not represent elements of a 'luxury' trade" (Gittinger 1982:33).

Until the sixteenth century, Indian and Arab merchants dominated the trade in Indian cottons. From the late sixteenth century,
Europeans gained increasing control of the world trade in Indian
cottons (Chaudhuri 1978). At first European traders were interested

in Indian cottons as trade goods which could be exchanged in Southeast Asia for spices. By the middle of the seventeenth century, the traders had discovered that if they supervised the design of the textiles made in India, these could be sold at a reasonable profit in London. At the end of the seventeenth century, the demand for Indian painted cottons had become so great that France banned chintz imports to protect its own silk industry (Irwin and Brett 1970:3,4). England followed suit a few years later. So popular were these fabrics that the prohibitions were ignored. In 1720 "a second prohibition was introduced . . . to forbid 'the Use and Wearing in Apparel' of imported chintz, and also its 'use or wear in or about any Bed, Chair, Cushion, or other Household furniture'" (Irwin and Brett 1970:5).

The great popularity of Indian cottons was due both to the cheapness and to the superiority of Indian products. Indian handspun yarns were superior to those produced in England and were imported for the weaving of fine cloth. Indian dyers were expert in the technology of mordant dyeing, which produced washable cottons in vibrant colors (Chaudhuri 1978:237ff). While the competition from Indian cloth could be fought with duties and prohibitions, the technological superiority remained unchallenged until the industrial revolution.

From the late eighteenth century, with the development and growth of machine spinning and weaving and the adoption and modification of Indian cotton-dyeing technology (Gittinger 1982:19), England began to produce quantities of inexpensive cotton textiles. English political control of India permitted adjustments in tariffs (and import prohibitions) to assure the advantage of Lancashire cottons in trade. English cotton-spinning mills secured supplies of raw cotton from India, and British traders succeeded in competing in India with the local hand-loom industry, thus opening a vast new market for the products of the Lancashire mills. The hand-spinning of cotton yarns had virtually died out in India by 1825. Only the highest counts of cotton yarns could not be reproduced by machinery. Even Indian hand-loom weavers used the cotton yarns produced in Lancashire. During the nineteenth century, exports fell drastically and the world's greatest exporter of cottons became a major importer of cotton yarns and piece goods. "In the first four years of the nineteenth century, in spite of all prohibitions and restrictive duties, six to fifteen thousand bales [of cotton piece-goods]

were annually shipped from Calcutta to the United Kingdom.
. . . After 1820 the manufacture of cotton piece-goods declined
steadily, never to rise again" (Dutt 1906:296). Between 1849 and
1889, the value of British cotton cloth exports to India increased from
just over 2 million pounds a year to just less than 27 million pounds
a year (Chandra 1968:55). At the end of the nineteenth century, the
development in Europe of inexpensive, easier-to-apply chemical
dyes dealt the final blow to Indian technological superiority in textile
production.

The interpretation of these changes has long been a subject of
heated debate among historians and economists. Did British cloth
destroy the demand for Indian hand-looms or supplement it? Did
indigenous production really decline or was it simply consumed in
the domestic market? Did British policy destroy Indian manufactures or was the demise of Indian industry the inevitable result of
the competition between artisans and machines? Did India fail to in-
dustrialize because British policy prevented it or because Indian society was infertile soil for industrialization?

During the late nineteenth century, an interpretation of England's economic relations with India evolved that became the economic basis of Indian nationalism. In this economic nationalism, the
history of cotton production and trade was central. Especially significant was the transformation of India from the world's most advanced producer of cotton textiles to an exporter of raw cotton and
an importer of cloth.

Dadabhai Naoroji was the recognized leader of this movement
and codified the theory of economic nationalism. In his view, "the
continuous impoverishment and exhaustion of the country" (Naoroji 1887) was unquestionably the result of British rule. Wealth was
taken from India to pay the Englishmen in London who ruled India
and to pay large salaries and pensions to English civil servants, who
spent much of this wealth in England. Grinding poverty and severe
famines resulted from the enormous tax burden on the cultivators.
British protection of English industries, through trade advantages
in the structure of tariffs, destroyed indigenous artisanry and prevented the development of machine industry.

Naoroji and other early nationalists (e.g., Ranade, Tilak,
Gokhale) believed that the low tariffs on British yarns and cloth com-
ing into India and the high tariffs on Indian textiles taken out of
India caused the decline of the textile industry, forced more people

onto the land, and created an unbalanced economy that exacerbated the poverty of India. Furthermore, they believed that the tariff structure on cotton goods revealed the true nature of British rule:

> Be that as it may, as regards this question of the cotton duties, the mask has now fallen off the foreign English administration of India. The highest officials in the country, nay the entire official body and the leading newspapers in England, have had to make the humiliating confession—The boast in which we have been so long indulging, the boast that we govern India in the interest and for the welfare of the Indians, is perfectly unfounded; India is held and governed in the interests of the English merchants (*The Bangabasi*, 17 March 1894, quoted in Chandra 1966:235).

The national leadership united on this issue, and on the importance of protection for India's artisans and nascent industries. Moreover, for the first time they united in action, around the issue of cotton tariffs. In 1896 they urged the boycott of foreign goods (Chandra 1966:250). The tactic of appealing to the English government of India to practice what it preached—just government—had begun to give way to active opposition. The seeds of opposition, the idea of *swadeshi* (the promotion of indigenous products), had already been planted:

> In 1872 Justice Ranade delivered a series of public lectures at Poona on economic topics, in which he popularized "the idea of *swadeshi*, of preferring the goods produced in one's own country even though they may prove to be dearer or less satisfactory than finer foreign products." These celebrated lectures so inspired the listeners that several of them including Ganesh Vasudeo Joshi . . . and Vasudeo Phadke . . . enthusiastically "vowed to wear and use only swadeshi articles." Joshi used to spin yarn daily for his own *dhoti*, shirt and turban; he started shops at several places to popularise and propagate *swadeshi* goods, and, at the Delhi Durbar of 1877 and in the midst of pageantry and flamboyancy, he represented the Sarvajanik Sabha dressed in pure self-spun khadi (Chandra 1966:122–3).

Indians could fight the destructive power of the English government by using Indian products in preference to foreign ones. The ideology and practice of *swadeshi* grew among nationalists and then, when the English government of India imposed excise duties on Indian cloth, *swadeshi* promoters turned to their most powerful weapon, boycott. In 1896, many people in Dacca resolved to boycott Manchester cloth and to patronize Indian mills (Chandra 1966:126). The center of activity was the Bombay Presidency, home of the nascent textile industry (the first mill opened only in the 1850s). Indians showed their opposition to English clothing by refusing to buy it or wear it, and by burning it. "According to the *Nyaya Sindu* of 2 March 1896 huge bundles of English clothing were thrown into the Holi fire that year" (Chandra 1966:130,n.167). A *Times* correspondent reported that "It was impossible for a respectable citizen to go with a new English piece of cloth without being asked a hundred perplexing questions" (Chandra 1966:130). Even though agitation subsided in subsequent years, *swadeshi*, the promotion of indigenous products, with cloth as its main platform, became a permanent feature of the nationalist movement.

English cloth had become the most potent symbol of English political domination and economic exploitation. As cloth is used mainly in clothing, the results of English exploitation—the demise of indigenous industry—were constantly there for all to see, on the backs of Indians who wore Manchester cloth made into British-style garments, and on Indians who used Manchester cloth for turbans, *kurtas* (shirts), *saris*, and other Indian garments. *Swadeshi*, an attempt to revive and promote Indian industry, required that each person be counted as a patriot-nationalist or a supporter of English domination and exploitation. An individual's political views, encoded in his or her costume, were exposed to public view.

Indeed, part of the reason for the decline of the *swadeshi* movement was the difficulty in procuring, and resistance to wearing, *swadeshi* costume. In the late nineteenth century, the Indian mills and handloom weavers together did not have the capability to clothe the nation. More significantly, most nationalist leaders, including Gokhale and Naoroji (but not the more militant Tilak), continued to wear English costumes with Indian headgear in public. They still believed that the way to gain a just administration of India was to show the English rulers the errors of their ways, so that English fair play and justice would prevail, Indians would be given a greater voice in the government of their land, and artisanry and industry would be revived. Like Gandhi when he appealed to the railway authorities in South Africa in 1893, they seemed to believe that they had to show their English rulers that they were like the English, that they were

English gentlemen, and were entitled to all that the English government would give to its own people.

Thus a fascinating paradox was generated from the semiotic and economic characteristics of cloth. These early nationalists wanted to revive and modernize Indian manufactures, especially the textile industry. But their political beliefs stood in the way of utilizing its products. Cloth is made to be worn and to express the social identity of its wearer. They expressed their belief in English values and their right to English justice by comporting themselves as English gentlemen in English dress (albeit with a special hat or turban to signify a slight cultural distinctiveness). Because they were still committed to this Englishness of dress, they were incapable of carrying out their own program of *swadeshi*.

Gandhi, following the lead of Tilak, Joshi and others, came to the more radical position that to promote Indian industry, foreign notions of civilization and gentlemanliness would have to be discarded. Economic Indianization was intrinsically connected to socio-cultural Indianization. One could not promote the Indian textile industry without wearing its products and one could not wear its products and remain a proper Englishman. And if one gave up frock coats and morning suits, one would no longer be an English gentleman entitled to treatment as such. A new strategy would be required to achieve the nationalists' goals for India, a strategy based more on confrontation and opposition than on persuasion and cooperation.

THE MAHATMA AS SEMIOTICIAN

Gandhi began his conscious experimentation with costume on his trip to India in 1901. He had begun to question the political efficacy of gentlemanly dress. The experiments intensified during the *satyagraha* (truth force) campaign of militant non-violence in South Africa, from the 1906 opposition to the Black Act until his departure in 1914. In 1909, when Gandhi settled at Tolstoy Farm, he is said to have put on "laborer's dress"—workman's trousers and shirt in the European style, which were adapted from prison uniform (Nanda 1958:109). There is a photograph of him during the *satyagraha* campaign wearing *lungi* (South Indian wrapped lower garment), *kurta* and coat. His head and feet are bare; he carries a staff and a bag slung across his shoulders. This costume was similar to the one he wore on his third-class pilgrimage through India in 1901. The transformation was so radical and unfamiliar that the Reverend Andrews, who arrived to join the movement in 1913, did not recognize the "man in a *lungi* and *kurta* with close cropped head and a staff in hand," reported Prabhudas Gandhi who added "probably he took him for a *sadhu* (ascetic holy man)" (Gandhi, P. 1957:176).

That same year, after being released from jail, he attended a meeting in Durban in a *dhoti* (perhaps a *lungi*). His feet were bare and he had shaved his moustache. He was in mourning for the dead coal strikers (Ashe 1968:124). However, when he sailed for England in 1914 he was dressed as an Englishman (Fischer 1982:151), and when he landed in India the following year he was dressed as a Kathiawari (Gujarat) peasant, in *dhoti*, *angarkha* (robe), upper cloth, and turban, the most thoroughly Indian of his costumes. His *satyagrahi* garb was his own design, and expressed simplicity, asceticism, and identity with the masses. His Kathiawari dress was more formal. It identified his region of origin and presented him as a totally Indian gentleman. In his autobiography he comments on this costume "with my Kathiawadi cloak, turban and *dhoti*, I looked somewhat more civilized than I do today" (1982:374). The costume was an attempt to provide an Indian resolution for the contradiction between being civilized and being Indian.

His colleagues were not sure what to make of him. He "was an eccentric figure, with his huge white turban and white clothing, among the western attired delegates" (Gold 1983:63). By appearing in this eccentric fashion he forced his colleagues to notice and accommodate his view of a truly Indian nationalism. He deliberately used costume not only to express his sociopolitical identity, but to manipulate social occasions to elicit acceptance of, if not agreement with, his position.

Despite the thoroughgoing Indianness of his Kathiawari costume (actually because of it) it was inadequate for Gandhi's purposes because it indicated region, class, and religion. Gandhi's program called for the unity of all Indians throughout the subcontinent, rich and poor, Hindu, Sikh, and Muslim. He needed a costume that transcended these distinctions. His experiments continued. He arrived in Madras in 1915 traveling third class and wearing a loose shirt and pair of trousers (Erikson 1969:279). He was photographed in Karachi in 1916 wearing a dark-colored hat similar in shape to what has become known as a "Gandhi cap" (Gold 1983:59). Again during the Kheda *satyagraha* in 1918 he was photographed in his Kathiawari turban. At the 1919 Amritsar Congress he first wore the white homespun "Gandhi cap." Some believe it was derived from South African prison garb (Ashe 1968:199). The cap also resembles some worn by Muslims and it may be important that Gandhi began to wear it during the campaign to support the Caliph of Turkey, a campaign important to Gandhi for its promotion of Hindu-Muslim unity. The cap, which Gandhi discarded two years later, was to become part of the uniform of Indian nationalists (see Cohn, this volume).

Gandhi's final costume change took place in 1921 when he began his national program for the revival of handmade cloth. *Khadi* (homespun) was scarce and expensive, so he urged his followers to wear as little cloth as possible:

> I know that many will find it difficult to replace their foreign cloth all at once. . . . Let them be satisfied with a mere loin cloth. . . . India has never insisted on full covering of the body for the males as a test of culture. . . . In order, therefore, to set the example, I propose to discard at least up to the 31st of October my *topi* (cap) and vest, and to content myself with only a loin cloth, and a *chaddar* (shawl) whenever found necessary for the protection of the body. I adopt the change, because I have always hesitated to advise anything I may not myself be prepared to follow. . . . I consider the renunciation to be also necessary for me as a sign of mourning, and a bare head and bare body is such a sign in my part of the country. . . . I do not expect co-workers to renounce the use of the vest and the *topi* unless they find it necessary. . . . (29 September 1921, quoted in Jaju 1951:98).

Later recalling the same event, Gandhi added he "divest[ed] [him] self of every inch of clothing [he] decently could and thus to a still greater extent [brought himself] in line with the ill-clad masses . . . in so far as the loin cloth also spells simplicity let it represent Indian civilization" (quoted in Jaju 1951:99). Gandhi had completely rejected the English gentleman and replaced him with the Indian ascetic, the renouncer, the holy man. When he visited the Viceroy in 1921 (and still later, when he attended the Round Table Conference in London in 1931 and visited King George and Queen Mary at Buckingham Palace) wearing his *mahatma* garb, nothing could match the communicative power of a photograph of Gandhi in loincloth and *chadar* sitting among the formally attired Englishmen. He communicated his disdain for civilization as it is understood in the West, his disdain for material possessions, his pride in Indian civilization, as well as his power—an ordinary man would not have been granted entry. By dealing openly with a man in *mahatma* garb, the British accepted his political position and revealed their loss of power.

The communicative power of Gandhi's costume was, however, uniquely Indian. Paradoxically, as his popularity grew, the messages he brought to the Indian public in his speeches and writings had increasingly limited range. Gatherings were huge, running to a hundred thousand or more. Only in the cities were public address systems available to him. Most people who went to see him could not hear him. Even if they could hear him the Gujarati or Hindustani or English in which he spoke could not be understood by many, sometimes most, of his audience. In a nation about three-quarters illiterate, his writings were available to still fewer.

Gandhi needed another medium through which to communicate with the people of India. He used his appearance to communicate his most important messages in a form comprehensible to all Indians. Engaged in the simple labor of spinning, dressed as one of the poor in loincloth and *chadar*, this important and powerful man communicated the dignity of poverty, the dignity of labor, the equality of all Indians, and the greatness of Indian civilization, as well as his own saintliness. The communicative power of costume transcended the limitations of language in multilingual and illiterate India. The image transcended cultural boundaries as well. His impact on the West was enhanced by his resemblance, in his simplicity of dress and his saintly manner, to Christ on the Cross.

In India, visual communication has a unique force. The sight of the eminent or holy blesses and purifies the viewer; the experience is called *darshan*. People came, literally, to *see* Gandhi. Through *darshan*, the power of Gandhi's appearance surpassed his message in words. "For the next quarter of a century, it was not only for his message that people came to him, but for the merit of seeing him. The sacred sight of the *Mahatma*, his *darshan*, was almost equivalent to a pilgrimage to holy Banaras" (Nanda 1958:213).

During this same period, Gandhi was experimenting with the economics of cloth production. Gandhi recalled: "It was in London in 1908 that I discovered the wheel. . . . I saw in a flash that without the spinning wheel there was no *Swaraj* [self-government]. But I did not then know the distinction between the loom and the wheel, and in *Hind Swaraj* used the word loom to mean the wheel" (quoted in Jaju 1951:1). "I do not remember to have seen a handloom or a spinning wheel when in 1908 I described it in *Hind Swaraj* as the panacea for the growing pauperism of India. In that book I took it as understood that anything that helped India to get rid of the grinding poverty of her masses would in the same process also establish *Swaraj*. Even in 1915 when I returned to India from South Africa, I had not actually seen a spinning wheel" (Gandhi 1957:489). By the time Gandhi returned to India in 1915, cloth production had become central to his program.

Like most leaders of the nationalist movement, Gandhi thought the reindustrialization of India to be of paramount importance, but unlike most of them he was opposed to mechanized industry, which he viewed as a sin perpetrated on the world by the West. He wanted to revive artisanry. From the establishment of Phoenix farm in 1904, Gandhi had committed himself to the simple life of labor. Machines were labor-saving devices that put thousands of laborers out of work, unthinkable in India where the masses were underemployed. Factory production facilitated the concentration of wealth in the hands of a few big capitalists, and transformed workers into "utter slaves."

Gandhi selected Ahmedabad, the Manchester of India, as the site for his settlement because this "great textile center was best suited for experiments in hand-spinning and weaving which appeared to him the only practicable supplementary occupations for the underworked and underfed masses in the villages of India" (Nanda 1958:134), and ". . . as Ahmedabad was [also] an ancient centre of hand-loom weaving, it was likely to be the most favourable field for the revival of the cottage industry of hand-spinning" (Gandhi 1957:395). Erikson, who has written so brilliantly on the early years in Ahmedabad, observes that "Gandhi blamed the disruption of native crafts [not only for the poverty of India, but also] for the deterioration of Indian identity. He was soon to elevate the spinning wheel to significance as an economic necessity, a religious ritual and a national symbol . . . Gandhi wanted to settle down where both tradition and available materials would permit him and his followers to build a community around the cultivation of spinning and weaving" (Erikson 1969:260).

By the time he settled at Ahmedabad his goal for India was the achievement, through *satyagraha*, of the reduction of poverty, disease, and immorality, and the restoration of dignity. Spinning offered solutions to all these problems. The English had destroyed the greatest cotton producer in the world in order to protect their own industries from competition, to create a source of raw materials not available in the British isles, and to make a ready market for their finished products. Gandhi sought to restore India's lost supremacy, to revive this "second lung" of India (the first was agriculture). His reasoning was simple: If Indians returned to the production of their own cloth there would be work for millions of unemployed, Indian wealth would not be taken to England and Japan, and Indians would again be their own masters (See Jaju 1915:8). "*Swadeshi* is the soul of *Swaraj*, *Khadi* is the essence of *Swadeshi*" (Gandhi quoted in Jaju 1951:12).

Until its demise in the 1820s, spinning had been a supplementary occupation of women all over the country. Weaving, by contrast, had always been a caste occupation. Though at first Gandhi concentrated on reviving spinning among women, he soon broadened his program. Spinning would become the leisure pursuit of all. The wealthy would spin as service; the poor to supplement their incomes. Through spinning, India would be able to clothe itself, and thereby free itself from foreign exploitation and domination. Through spinning, all Indians, rich and poor, educated and illiterate, would be laborers, equal and united through their labor (see Bean 1988):

> Originally there was one specific objective: to give work and clothing to the half-starved women of India. To this was related from the beginning the larger objective of khadi—the cloth itself as a means of economic self-sufficiency (*swadeshi*) which in turn must inevitably produce self-government (*swaraj*). This progression, *Khadi* = *swadeshi* = *swaraj*, was Gandhi's incessant preachment for the rest of his life. . . . His genius had found a tremendous symbol which was at the same time a practical weapon . . . for the liberation of India. . . . The symbol he had found, the wheel itself, assumed enormous importance with the passage of time: it related itself to the whole of life, to God, to the pilgrimage of the spirit. . . (Sheean 1949:154,157,158, see also Bayly 1986).

Gandhi had returned from South Africa determined to wear hand-made cloth. He brought a weaver to the ashram, but there was no hand-spun yarn available for the loom, so Gandhi began looking for a spinner. It was not until 1917 that his associate Gangabehn located spinners who would produce yarn to be woven at the ashram—if slivers, carded cotton for spinning, could be supplied to them. Until then, Gandhi had relied on machine-spun yarn from Ahmedabad mills for his looms, but he still had to get the slivers for hand-spinning from the mills. Gandhi's *khadi* had to be entirely hand-made, so he asked Gangabehn to find carders who could provide the slivers. Gandhi "begged for [the raw] cotton in Bombay" (Gandhi 1957:492). Finally the entire process of making cloth could be done by hand.

At this time, Gandhi's *dhoti* was still of Indian mill cloth. The *khadi* manufactured at the ashram was only 30 inches wide. Gandhi "gave notice to Gangabehn that, unless she provided . . . a *khadi dhoti* of 45 inches width within a month, [he] would do with coarse, short *khadi dhoti*. . . . well within the month she sent [him] a pair of *khadi dhotis* of 45 inches width, and thus relieved [him] from what would then have been a difficult situation. . . ." (Gandhi 1957:493). Perhaps Gandhi was looking for an opportunity to change to a loin-cloth, a change he accomplished two years later. From 1919 on, he was clothed entirely in *khadi*, and instead of the turban, he began wearing the white *khadi* "Gandhi cap." *Khadi* was much too coarse for wrapping as a Gujarati turban.

In 1920 as part of the Non-cooperation Movement, the leaders of the Indian National Congress endorsed hand spinning and weaving, to supply cloth to replace boycotted foreign cloth and to engage the masses in the nationalist cause. In this they followed Gandhi, but they were by no means in full agreement with him. "Tagore argued that trying to liberate three hundred million people by making them all spinners was like urging them to drown the English by all spitting together: it was 'too simple for human beings.' Complaints came in against *khadi* as a material in the conditions of modern living. It wouldn't stand up to the wear and tear of a factory. It was too heavy. It was hard to launder and therefore unsuitable for children. Gandhi's answer was that with more skill there would be better *khadi*" (Ashe 1968:249).

Most nationalists disagreed with Gandhi's opposition to mecha-

Figure 24. Children dressed in khadi *display a chromolithograph, of the sort used in India for veneration and worship, showing the stages of Gandhi's life expressed in sartorial transformations. Clockwise, starting from the lower left, we see Gandhi as a law student in London and next, still in Western dress, during the early years of his stay in South Africa. For his* satyaghraha *campaign in South Africa, he devised his first non-Western costume. At the upper left, Gandhi wears the turban of the Gujarati peasant as part of the distinctly Indian garb he chose for his return to India. He soon replaced the turban with a non-regional "Gandhi cap," adopted by his followers but abandoned by Gandhi in favor of the ascetic garb he wore from 1921 until the end of his life. Photo by Brian Brake from Magnum*

nized industry. Many, including Jawaharlal Nehru, believed industrialization crucial for India's economic well-being. Few felt Gandhi's love for the purity and simplicity of coarse white *khadi*. Jawaharlal Nehru's sister Vijayalakshmi Pandit thought *khadi* rough and drab. She felt deprived to have to wear a wedding sari of *khadi*, though it had been spun and woven by Kasturbai Gandhi and dyed the traditional Kashmiri pink. Their father Motilal Nehru, at the meeting of the Congress Working Committee in Delhi during November 1921, burst out laughing when he heard Gandhi say that a person must know hand-spinning in order to participate in civil disobedience (Nanda 1958:235). In a letter to his son, the elder Nehru spoke of the *khadi* movement as one of Gandhi's hobbies.

Despite their disagreement, the Nehrus and other nationalist leaders supported hand-spinning and *khadi* because they recognized its symbolic and economic importance in the programs of *swadeshi*, boycott, and noncooperation. Mrs. Pandit noted the effects of wearing *khadi* "Gandhi caps," *kurtas*, and *dhotis*: She could no longer detect the social class of the visitors to her family's home. The uniform was a leveler, all Congressmen were the same (Pandit 1979:82). Accommodations were made for intranational variation: *dhotis* for Hindus, *pyjamas* (trousers) for Muslims, turbans distinctive for Sikhs or southern Brahmins. *Khadi*, the fabric of nationalism, transcended and encompassed these distinctions. Gandhi had taught his followers that costume can transform social and political identities. When Gandhi, clothed in loincloth and *chadar*, was received by the Viceroy Lord Reading in 1921, his followers (and his opponents) also saw that costume can be used to dominate and structure a social event. The most important result of those meetings was that Gandhi, wearing his opposition to English values and representing the people of India, was accepted to negotiate as an equal with the representatives of the British Empire in India. Gandhi forced the Empire to compromise its standards and thus demonstrated the power of the freedom movement he led.

By 1921, all Congressmen were dressed in *khadi*. The Governor of Bombay Presidency, C.R. Das, made *khadi* the uniform of civic employees. From July 1922, no member of Congress was allowed to wear imported cloth, and dues were to be paid in hand-spun yarn instead of cash. Hand-spinning and *khadi* had become a fixture in the freedom movement. Economic revitalization and self-government would be accomplished through mass organization, carried on by *khadi*-clad Congress workers promoting indigenous industries and mass action by teaching spinning to everyone, spreading the boycott of foreign products to the most remote villages, and preparing the way for mass civil disobedience.

Khadi had become, in Nehru's words, "the livery of freedom."

REFERENCES CITED

Ashe, Geoffrey
    1968   Gandhi. New York: Stein and Day.

Bayly, C.A.
    1986   The Origins of Swadeshi (Home Industry): Cloth and Indian So-
              ciety, 1700-1930. In The Social Life of Things. Arjun Appadurai,
              ed. Cambridge: Cambridge University Press.

Bean, Susan S.
    1988   Spinning Independence. In Making Things in South Asia:
              Proceedings of the South Asia Regional Studies Seminar.
              Michael Meister, ed. Philadelphia: University of Pennsylvania.

Chandra, Bipin
    1965   Indian Nationalists and the Drain, 1880-1905. Indian Economic
              and Social History Review 2(2):103-44.
    1966   The Rise and Growth of Economic Nationalism in India. New
              Delhi.
    1968   Reinterpretations of Nineteenth Century Indian Economic His-
              tory. Indian Economic and Social History Review 5:35-75.

Chatterji, Basudev
    1980   The Abolition of the Cotton Excise, 1925: A Study in Imperial
              Priorities. Indian Economic and Social History Review
              17(4):355-80.
    1981   Business and Politics in the 1930s: Lancashire and the Making of
              the Indo-British Trade Agreement. Modern Asian Studies
              15:527-74.

Chaudhuri, K.N.
    1968   India's International Economy in the 19th Century. Modern
              Asian Studies 2:31-50.
    1978   The Trading World of Asia and the English East India Company
              1660-1760. Cambridge: Cambridge University Press.

Cohn, Bernard
    1988   Cloth, Clothes, and Colonialism: India in the Nineteenth Cen-
              tury. (This volume).

Dewey, Clive
    1978   The Eclipse of the Lancashire Lobby and the Concession of Fiscal
              Autonomy to India. In C. Dewey and A.G. Hopkins, eds. The
              Imperial Impact. London: Althone Press.

Dutt, Romesh Chunder
    1968   Romesh Chunder Dutt. Delhi: Government of India, Ministry of
              Information and Broadcasting.
    1901,1903 The Economic History of India, 2 vols. London.
    1906   India Under Early British Rule. London: Kegan Paul

Erikson, Erik
  1969   Gandi's Truth. New York: W.W. Norton.

Fischer, Louis
  1982(1951) The Life of Mahatma Gandhi. London: Granada.

Gadgil, D.R.
  1942   The Industrial Evolution of India in Recent Times. Calcutta.

Gandhi. M.K.
  1922(1908) Indian Home Rule. Madras: Ganesh & Co.
  1941   Economics of Khadi. Ahmedabad: Navajivan Press.
  1957   An Autobiography: the Story of My Experiments with
  (1927-29) Truth. Boston: Beacon Press.

Gandhi, Prabudas
  1957   My Childhood with Gandhiji. Ahmedabad: Navajivan Press.

Ganguli, B.N.
  1965   Dadabhai Naoroji and the Mechanism of External Drain. Indian
          Economic and Social History Review 2(2):85–102.

Gittinger, Mattiebelle
  1982   Master Dyers to the World. Washington, D.C.: Textile Museum.

Gold, Gerald
  1983   Gandhi: A Pictorial Biography. New York: New Market Press.

Irwin, John
  1962   Indian Textiles in Historical Perspective. Marg XV(4).

Irwin, John and K. Brett
  1970   The Origins of Chintz. London: Victoria and Albert Museum.

Jaju, Shrikrishnadas
  1951   The Ideology of Charka. Tirupur.

Masani, Rustom Pestonji
  1939   Dadabhai Naoroji: The Grand Old Man of India. London: Allen &
          Unwin.

Mehta, Ved
  1977   Mahatma Gandhi and His Apostles. New York: Penguin Books.

Nanda, B.R.
  1958   Mahatma Gandhi. Boston: Beacon Press.

Naoroji, Dadabhai
  1887   Essays, Speeches and Writings. C.L. Parekh, ed.
          Bombay.

Pandit, Vijayalakshmi
  1979   The Scope of Happiness. New York: Crown.

Pradhan, G.P. and A.K. Bhagwat
  1958   Lokamanya Tilak. Bombay.

Sarkar, Sumit
    1973   The Swadeshi Movement in Bengal, 1903–1908. Calcutta.

Sharma, Jagadish
    1955,1968   Mahatma Gandhi: A Descriptive Bibliography.

Sheean, Vincent
    1949   Lead Kindly Light. New York: Random House.

Sitaramayya, Pattabhi
    1969   History of the Indian National Congress, vol. 1 (1885–1935).
            Delhi: S. Chand.

Wolpert, Stanley
    1962   Tilak and Gokhale. Berkeley: University of California Press.

12. The Changing Fortunes of Three Archaic Japanese Textiles

LOUISE ALLISON CORT

 This paper traces the history and present uses of three long vegetable fibers[1] in Japanese and Okinawan cloth production, exploring their survival in the poorest and most remote mountain regions, their symbolic value in sacred state rituals, and their current role in nationalist and folkloric revivals. By situating the three fibers in their historical and ecological context, and by describing the labor process through which they are produced, the relationship between their symbolic and their material aspects becomes evident. Central to this relationship are the long traditions of female processors and weavers of such fibers, the honor accruing to women for participation in these tasks, and the belief that, through the textile arts, women mediate the spiritual well-being of the larger communities.

Mention the textiles of Japan, and the fibers that come to mind immediately are silk (an animal fiber) and cotton (a seed fiber), not the long vegetable fibers that will be discussed here. During the heyday of textile production in Japan throughout the Edo period (A.D. 1615–1868), the efforts of professional weavers and dyers, supported by an elaborate system of raw-material procurement and finished-product distribution, created an array of fine silk and cotton fabrics.[2]

NOTE: A glossary of Japanese written forms of critical textile terminology is printed on p. 415.

No less appealing than the sumptuously tinted and patterned silks were the cottons, characteristically dyed with indigo augmented by other vegetable dyes in solids, stripes, and plaids, and patterns produced by ikat-dying (kasuri)[3] or stencil-dyeing. While silks were reserved for luxury garments, cottons made up the work clothes and everyday costumes of most Japanese.

Silk had been known in Japan from the bronze age (Yayoi period, circa 200 B.C.–A.D. 250), but cotton began to be cultivated in Japan only in the fifteenth century. Until that time, the staple fiber for commoners' clothing was the bast fiber[4] called asa. Asa is a generic term, often translated erroneously as "flax" or "linen," that embraces a range of varieties of grass-bast fibers, of which the most common in Japan were hemp and ramie or "China grass."[5] The fiber known as "linen" or "flax"[6] was not brought to Japan until the eighteenth century (Akashi 1976:123). Even asa was a relative latecomer to Japan, arriving perhaps by the end of the neolithic period. During the ten millennia of Japan's neolithic age, coarser fibers had been exploited as the earliest material for cords, ropes, nets, baskets and—finally—woven cloth. Those fibers were the bast fibers of various wild trees and vines that grew on the slopes of Japan's abundant mountains. It may be that weaving was practiced only after the introduction of asa, the technique and the new fiber arriving simultaneously, and was than applied to the older tree-bast fibers, which had been used until then only in baskets, mats, and nets.[7]

The introduction of asa cultivation, processing, and weaving techniques, probably from the Korean peninsula, quickly made the tree-bast fibers less desirable for cloth-making. The grass-bast fibers of the asa group could be cultivated from seed in fields and, when harvested, could be split, softened, and spun into thread in a comparatively simple way. The tougher fibers of the tree-bast group required not only the physical effort of gathering them from mountain slopes but also a longer process of soaking, rotting, boiling with wood-ash (lye), and occasionally beating before the tough fibers could be extracted.[8] At that stage, moreover, the truly time-consuming task began: As the stiff fibers could not be spun into a continuous thread, the individual fibers had to be split and then joined end to end, by twisting or tying, to make a thread. (An individual fiber might, however, be as much as twelve feet long.) When the tree-bast fibers could at last be woven, they produced fabrics that were usually darker in color and rougher to the touch than asa.

Logically, the tedious processing of tree-bast fibers should have been abandoned at the earliest possible moment. Yet, some two millenia after the introduction of *asa* to Japan, tree-bast fibers are still used. While *asa* and then cotton replaced them as clothing for commoners, the tree-bast fibers and related leaf fibers survived in two extreme situations. At one extreme, they were retained for their symbolic value in the most sacred state rituals, especially the rites for installing a new emperor. At the other, they continued to serve in clothing for inhabitants of the poorest and most remote mountain regions, where restricted land area and severe climate precluded cultivation of other fibers, where hard labor required rough, durable garments, and where wild materials were important sources of cash income. In recent decades, just as they seemed about to lose even those tenuous identities, their use has been revived in contexts that recall the association of certain long vegetable fibers with the most ancient core of Japanese culture. Their symbolic power has revived amid a widespread prosperity that has obliterated their last claim to practical usefulness.

In this paper, I will focus on three of these traditional long vegetable fibers.[9] I have selected these three fibers because I have had field contact with the people who still gather, process, and weave them. The first fiber I consider is that produced either from *kōzo* (*Broussonetia kazinoki*) or from *kaji* (*Broussonetia papyrifera*). From a very early time the two fibers, both from plants of the mulberry family, were considered to be interchangeable, especially as sources of fiber for the utility cloth called *tafu*, meaning simply "thick cloth." Yet mulberry-plant fibers were indispensable for imperial rituals as well.

The second fiber I discuss is *kuzu* (*Pueraria hirsuta*), a vine yielding a lustrous fiber that became important for use in various ceremonial garments.[10] The third fiber is *bashō* (thread banana, *Musa liukiuensis*). Properly speaking, thread-banana fiber is not a tree-bast but a leaf fiber, although the two types of long vegetable fibers are closely related on the basis of morphology.[11] In the hierarchy of Okinawan textiles, thread-banana cloth occupied the same low position with regard to *asa*, cotton, and silk as did the mulberry-plant fibers in Japan. After a long period under Japanese trade influence, the independent kingdom of Okinawa became a Japanese domain in the seventeenth century, and thread-banana cloth became tribute cloth. The post–World War II revival of this fabric has a specifically political context: Reassertion of the independence of Okinawan culture from that of Japan.

MULBERRY-PLANT FIBERS AS SACRED THREADS
AND SACRED CLOTH

Japanese mythology and early literature show a range of conceptions concerning bast fiber and cloth that were embodied in early patterns of worship. The contrasting properties of the various tree-bast and grass-bast fibers, and the various stages of processing the fibers as thread and as cloth, were expressed in ritual pairings of white (mulberry-fiber) and blue-green (*asa*) "cloth offerings" or of mulberry-plant thread and woven cloth. The two-color "cloth offerings" adorned the Shinto altar and were indispensable components of imperial accession rituals. The latter pair, held during private worship performed by women for their households, suggests that both thread and woven cloth from the humble tree-bast fibers were understood as essential to human welfare.[12]

Of the two plants in the mulberry family, botanists believe that *kōzo* is indigenous to Japan, since it grows wild throughout the islands. *Kaji*, however, seems to have been introduced at some point, since it is found wild only in the two southerly islands of Kyushu and Shikoku. (*Kaji* grows wild throughout Southeast Asia and the Pacific Islands.) The *Kogoshūi* ("Gleanings from Old Tales"), a document written in A.D. 807 by an advocate of the Imbe (Imibe) family of hereditary court ritualists, alleges that both *asa* (hemp, ramie, etc.) and *kaji* were introduced to Japan by the founders of the Imbe clan; presumably the clan ancestors migrated from the continent into Kyushu toward the end of the neolithic period (Okamura 1977:251). Since the fibers of both *kōzo* and *kaji* can be used for both weaving and papermaking, from an early date they were thought of as interchangeable, and the term *kōzo* is often used to indicate both.

The most informative early source on the uses of textiles in Japan is the *Manyōshū*, the first anthology of Japanese verse, completed around A.D. 759 and containing some 4500 poems, mostly from the seventh and early eighth centuries. The *Manyōshū* poems, rich in allusions to details of everyday life, indicate that silk, whether imported or locally made, had become the desired luxury cloth. *Asa*, not to mention other bast-fibers, had been relegated to commoners' clothing and papermaking.[13] Yet the *Manyōshū* also shows that bast-fiber fabrics were far from unimportant, whether as ordinary clothing or in special ritual use. The complex of textile- and garment-related terms that appears in the *Manyōshū* suggests that *asa* and the tree-bast-fiber cloths were often paired and were thought of as complementary elements of a set.

Fabric woven from the mulberry-plant fibers was called "*taku* cloth," (*takununo*; in compound words, pronounced *tae*), from the early term for the fiber, *taku*. One *Manyōshū* poem (XVI:3791–3) describes a man wearing "the cloth of *tae* tissue" and "the handwoven cloth of sun-dried hemp" wrapped "like a double skirt" that proved attractive to "many a country lass from her lowly cottage"[14] (whereas his imported silk garments attracted the notice of the court ladies).

Manyōshū poems mention various kinds of *taku* fabrics, cords and ropes, caps, and bedding. Through the literary device called the pillow word,[15] all such *taku* products were associated with the word "white" or with other white objects. Bleached mulberry-fiber cloth was known more specifically as *shirotae*, "white *taku* cloth," and was likened in poetry to snow, clouds, waves, and feathers. At the other end of the spectrum was *aratae* or "rough *taku* cloth." In fact *aratae* designated tree-bast fibers other than mulberry, such as mountain wisteria, which even with bleaching did not lose their brownish cast (Okamura 1977:118).

A second pair of opposites emerging in *Manyōshū* usage consisted of *nigitae*, "smooth cloth," and *aratae*, "rough cloth." The word *nigitae* was written with the character meaning "peace" or "harmony"—the same character that also appeared in Yamato, the name of the state that developed by the seventh century through the "harmonization" of various rival clans. The similarity of the two terms is probably not coincidental. *Nigitae* signifies finely-woven fabric made soft and lustrous by fulling—prolonged beating with a wooden mallet (the "pacification" of the cloth?). According to the *Kogoshūi* of A.D. 807, *nigitae* could be woven from either *asa* or mulberry fiber, and it was used specifically for sacred garments (Okamura 1977:252).

Closely related to *nigitae* is the term *nigite*, meaning folded fiber or cloth offerings. *Nigite* offerings were an indispensable element in the basic form of the Shinto altar. An altar was constructed on any site that was to be used to perform a sacred act. A coarse mat was spread over the clean-swept ground and a special eight-legged table placed upon it. A branch of a glossy-leaved evergreen tree was stood upright on the table, enclosed by a rope tied to posts at the four corners of the table, and draped with the cloth offerings, or *nigite*. These offerings were of two types, white and blue-green.[16]

The *Kogoshūi* makes clear that the white cloth offerings were made from mulberry fiber (*kaji*), while the blue-green cloths were made of *asa*.[17] It seems probable that at first both types of "cloth offerings" were made out of unwoven strands of fiber, although later they came to be made of woven cloth or of paper made from the same fibers (Okamura 1977:86–89). The paired fiber offerings appear on the archetypal altar, the one described in one of the most important Shinto myths. After the unruly male deity Susanoō disrupted with various acts of desecration the work of his sister, the sun goddess Amaterasu—planting the rice fields, performing the harvest festival, and weaving the garments for all the gods—the angry goddess retreated into a cave, plunging the world into darkness. The efforts of the other gods to placate her wrath began with setting up a great altar using a five-hundred-branched evergreen tree ornamented with a necklace of sacred jewels, a sacred mirror, and the special white and blue green cloth offerings. The cloth offerings are said to have been supplied by the god Ama no Hiwashi, divine ancestor of the Imbe clan which became associated with ritual production of sacred cloth for the imperial court (Tsunoda, de Bary, and Keene 1958:30–31).

Yet another term found in *Manyōshū* verses is *yū*, literally, "tree batting."[18] Like the term for "cloth offerings," *yū* seems to have designated not woven cloth but thread—specifically, according to the *Kogoshūi*, the thread of the mulberry fiber *kaji* from which *nigitae* cloth was produced. The term *yū* meaning "tree batting" is related to a character with the same pronunciation meaning "pure, sacred" (sometimes used to write the name of the Imbe clan, hereditary producers of *nigitae* cloth as detailed in the *Kogoshūi*). *Yū* is also related to another homophone meaning "to tie," which was not only the function of a length of fiber or thread, but also a term appearing in the names of gods associated with growth and fecundity (Okamura 1977:66). *Manyōshū* poems indicate that a loop of this mulberry-fiber thread was always worn to tie back garment sleeves when worshipping the gods.[19] One poem (III:443) tells of a woman worshipping while holding the thread in one hand and the woven cloth in the other. The presence of the thread may indicate at once her "pure" state as she performs the worship and the nature of her ritual request.

Other *Manyōshū* poems confirm that household worship was a responsibility of the senior woman of the house. When the first fruits were offered on the night of a special harvest ritual (*Niinamesai*, "Festival for the First Tasting"), men were shut outside (Ellwood 1973:72). (By contrast, worship at the state level was conducted by hereditary male priests.) To hold up thread and cloth for worship was to offer the fruits of women's work. Various tribute laws of the early Yamato state exacted a certain quantity of woven cloth—varieties of bast-fiber cloth—and a certain amount of rice from each household, and the "loom duty" was specifically the woman's (Toyota 1965:249). (Again, by contrast, luxury silks for use in the court were woven by male weavers at government-operated provincial or central workshops.) Just as the goddess Amaterasu wove to make garments for all the gods, so each woman wove to clothe her family (and to pay the tax).

HARMONIZING OF OPPOSING ELEMENTS IN SACRED CLOTH

The various pairings of tree-bast and grass-bast fibers in early literature and in religious ritual show a conscious mingling of ancient and recent, indigenous and continental elements in the material culture. At the political level, the unification of Japan was achieved by a clan known as Yamato. The Yamato state, arising in western Japan and strengthened by close contact with continental technology, succeeded in winning the allegiance of several dozen independent tribal groups. The special accession ritual performed by each new Yamato emperor incorporated the pairings of cloth fibers and other materials in a manner that underscored the emperor's power to unify those disparate cultural elements.

Women's responsibility for both household weaving and household worship reflected an ancient order—the order of the neolithic period. This same encapsulation of neolithic patterns appeared at the state level, in the harvest festivals that were part of the cycle of annual rituals performed for the welfare of the Yamato state. The most important was the annual offering of the first fruits (*Niinamesai*). At the beginning of each emperor's reign, however, the first-fruits ritual was replaced once only by the *Daijōsai*, "Great Offering Ritual," wherein the new emperor asserted his authority by undertaking the ritual usually performed by priests. Cloth figured importantly in the items that were offered. The *Kogoshūi* claimed that the Imbe clan's responsibility for providing sacred cloth began with the god Ama no Hiwashi's hanging the two kinds of cloth offerings on the lower branches of the archetypal altar. Subsequently, according to that text, certain Imbe-clan descendants of Ama no Hiwashi were charged with the responsibility of producing cloth from mulberry-plant fiber and *asa*. As fertile ground on which to cultivate the plants, those clan members were given the province of Awa (now Tokushima Prefecture, on the island of Shikoku). In the years when the imperial accession ritual occurred, they supplied cloth to the court (Okamura 1977:253).

In this manner the *Kogoshūi* of A.D. 807 asserted the ancient prerogatives of the Awa branch of the Imbe clan. That text was written, however, to defend the family rights against the rise in stature of the other major priestly house, the Nakatomi, following reorganization of the government by the Taihō code of A.D. 702. The Nakatomi clan and the Imbe clan supposedly shared responsibilities in the Department of Worship, the members of the Nakatomi clan reciting prayers and the members of the Imbe clan providing all materials for ritual use. But by the time of the accession ceremony of A.D. 927, the Imbe clan was supplying only mulberry-fiber cloth, while the Nakatomi clan was providing the cloth woven from *asa*. By the time of that ceremony, moreover, a shift in terminology had occurred, reflecting a further loss of status by the Imbe clan and the cloth that they produced. The term *aratae*, "rough cloth," had come to include mulberry-fiber cloth together with other coarser cloths made from tree-bast fibers, while *nigitae*, "smooth cloth," excluded mulberry-fiber cloth and referred to *asa* alone.

The *Daijōsai* ceremony took place during one night in late autumn, following months of preparation.[20] Two identical buildings were constructed within the imperial palace grounds, using unpeeled logs and thatch recalling ancient forms of architecture. They were the Yuki Hall to the east and the Suki Hall to the west. Meanwhile, two ritually-designated fields (the eastern Yuki Field and the western Suki Field) were used to grow the offertory rice and other grain. Some of the rice was offered as grain; the rest was fermented to make rice wine. Of the wine, half was left white and half was tinted black with ash of a certain bitter wood. Elsewhere, craftspeople chosen by divination prepared the mulberry-fiber thread and woven cloth to be provided by members of the Imbe clan[21] and the *asa* to be sent by the Nakatomi clan.

Before the ceremony, within the inner chamber of the Yuki and Suki Halls, couches were constructed of piled mats. At the head of each couch stood two lamps, one black and one white, and two baskets of cloth, a black one containing "rough cloth" and a white one holding "smooth cloth." A dais held offerings of cooked rice and millet (a major foodstuff prior to the introduction of rice at the close of the neolithic period), placed on oak leaves, and of white and black sake. The emperor performed identical rituals of offering within each hall, but he went first to the Yuki Hall as night was deepening, then to the Suki Hall when dawn was approaching.[22]

The new emperor's offering of paired "rough cloth" and "smooth cloth" suggests a multilevel symbolism at work in the ritual for the harmonizing of the contrasting worlds of rough and smooth, dark and light, east and west, even native and continental.[23] The ultimate purpose of the *Daijōsai* was to "pacify" through harmonizing the "rough spirit" (*aramitama*) and the "smooth spirit" (*nigimitama*), whether those counterbalancing forces were interpreted as resting within an individual, or within the nation, or in the characters of the major gods, the rough male deity Susanoō and the serene sun goddess Amaterasu. Each of the two types of cloth belonged to a cluster of associated objects and concepts. *Aratae*, coarse tree-bast cloth, was linked to black rice wine, millet, black basket, black lamp, the Yuki Hall, night, the east, the unruly Susanoō, the rough spirit. In the context of Japan, where advanced clans spread from west to east, the east always connoted the holdout of unconverted barbarians. Contrasting images were associated with *nigitae*, fine bleached and fulled grass-bast cloth: white rice wine, rice, white basket, white lamp, the Suki Hall, morning, the west, the calm and radiant Amaterasu, the smooth spirit. The Yamato state, personified in the emperor, owed its power to having harmonized two groups of opposing elements: The older indigenous elements of the neolithic society (rough tree-bast fibers, millet) and the advanced continental elements (including rice and *asa*) brought by the Yayoi cultural invasion, which spread over Japan from west to east.

While the *Daijōsai* ceremony served, on the ritual level, to reestablish the desired balance, on the cultural level it continued the process whereby the old elements were gradually overwhelmed and obliterated by the new. By the time of the accession ceremony held in A.D. 927, the members of the ancient Imbe clan had already lost their right to present *asa*, as we have seen. Eventually the Imbe clan lost even its right to offer "rough cloth" of mulberry fiber; the last presentation of *aratae* from the Imbe of Awa is recorded for the *Daijōsai* ceremony of 1339. Thereafter all offertory cloth came from the Nakatomi (by then known as the Fujiwara) domain.[24]

In 1915, and again in 1928, the *Daijōsai* ceremony was enacted according to the ancient records, and the old Awa province was called upon once again to supply the appropriate "rough cloth." A special weaving shed was constructed on the grounds of the shrine honoring the ancestral deity of the Imbe clan, Ama no Hiwashi, and unmarried girls were selected as weavers.

Apparently no effort was made to weave with mulberry fiber, however: in 1915 bleached hemp (coarse *asa*) was supplied, and in 1928 the warp had to be changed to finer *asa* in the form of spun ramie, because the hemp was unmanageable for the young weavers whose experience was limited to silk and cotton (Okamura 1977: 263–68).

"THICK CLOTH" AND RURAL SURVIVAL

At the other extreme from its incorporation into imperial ritual, mulberry-plant fiber continued to be processed and woven in the most mountainous and resource-poor areas of Japan. Production of utilitarian "thick cloth" was women's work. In this century, mountain women have found "thick cloth" to be a means of participating in an engulfing cash economy and, more recently, a way to cope emotionally with the gradual depopulation and economic devaluation of mountain communities.

Despite the gradual disappearance of mulberry-fiber cloth from ritual use, the need for it never disappeared entirely from everyday life. Even the court required a copious supply of what is simply termed "cloth" (*nuno*) in records of tribute being sent from the sixty-two provinces. Thirty provinces sent "cloth" (presumably indicating tree-bast fibers, since *asa* is listed separately), and those provinces lay mainly in the east, far from the capital of Kyoto and relatively backward in economic development (Toyota 1965:248–51). By the

Edo period the standard term for such cloth was "thick cloth".[25] The actual fiber used to make this "thick cloth" depended upon the region, and even coarse *asa* or coarse cotton cloth was sometimes designated by the term (Yanagida 1976:24; Gotō 1976). One characteristic common to all varieties of "thick cloth" was that it was woven on a simple body-tension or backstrap loom, whereas commercial weaving carried on in urban workshops used the floor loom. The floor loom was less tiring to the weaver and more efficient, but it was unsuited to weaving "thick cloth" because the loom's constant tension and the long distance between beams tended to pull apart twist-joined warp threads.

The rustic "thick cloth" attracted the attention of local scholars of the late eighteenth and early nineteenth centuries who traveled extensively to document regional rural culture.[26] The Shinto scholar Motoori Norinaga (1730–1801), aware of ancient ritual uses of the fiber called *yū*, was pleased to find the same fiber still being used to make "thick cloth" in the province of Awa. He wrote admiringly, "The color is white and the thread is strong. When the cloth is washed, it does not need starching, and with every washing it becomes whiter" (Gotō 1974:122). In the mid-nineteenth century, a local Awa scholar elaborated on the cloth's virtues:

> . . . [T]afu is made from mulberry bast and is not a kind of *asa* cloth. It is woven in [several counties in Awa province] and is also produced in quantities within Tosa province. In my youth it was bleached and dyed with family crests and was used commonly for clothing, but the taste of today's world has turned to gorgeousness, and "thick cloth" is worn by young people only when they are learning fencing. One does not see people wearing it regularly. It is used only for bags to hold rice and barley, or for edgings on tatami mats, or for doorway banners. . . .
>
> In the mountain district of Iya, people who are now elderly wore "thick cloth" both summer and winter in the days of their youth. An extremely cold winter was expressed by the fact that one had to layer five or seven "thick cloth" garments for warmth, and in the dialect of that area occur references to "six-layer chill" and "seven-layer chill." On my visit to those mountains in the ninth month of 1842, I saw that most people have now changed to cotton garments. . . .(Gotō 1974:122).

Such texts show that, by the early nineteenth century, the use of cotton for commoners' garments had become so commonplace that the very name "thick cloth" was unknown to most people. One of the last areas where "thick cloth" continued to be woven for garments was the mountainous interior of Awa province (now Tokushima prefecture). One such locale was the Kitō district, comprised of small, isolated hamlets lining the narrow valley of the Naka river which flows around the south flank of Shikoku's tallest peak, Mount Tsurugi. Out of Kitō's present area of 232.08 square kilometers, only 0.7% is arable land. Mountain products, including timber and charcoal, have always been the main items for tribute or cash income.

Throughout the Edo period, the Kitō district was controlled by the Hachisuka domain, based in the coastal city of Tokushima. Aside from the meager area set aside for slash-and-burn cultivation to support the local population, the land was domain-owned forest, and the residents lived in extreme poverty. Over half were landless, and their numbers increased as the domain steadily attempted to turn more land into forest. In addition, mulberry fibers were claimed by the domain for use in papermaking and were collected as a tax item from every household. An undated document from Kitō local officials warned the domain that any further increase in demand for mulberry fiber would deprive the residents of fiber even for essential clothing, without which they could not work in the domain forests (Takeuchi 1982:8).

Gotō Shōichi (1897–1980), the noted textile historian born in Tokushima, remembered during his childhood—when all urban commoners wore indigo-dyed cotton garments—seeing the "strange sight" of mountain men coming to town in their stiff brown costumes (Gotō 1976). Cotton could never replace "thick cloth" for work clothing in the mountains, where the costume of "thick cloth" jacket tied at the waist with a straw rope and "thick cloth" trousers or leggings repelled brambles and twigs. Much-washed "thick cloth" became soft and felted; the older fabric was used for inner garments, and examples are known of "thick cloth" loincloths passed down for three generations (Kawabata 1982). Mulberry fiber was also used for all other fabric requirements of the mountain household, including bedding and mosquito nets (urban households used indigo-dyed *asa* mosquito nets). Perhaps most important were the "thick cloth" bags used to transport precious grain and seed on foot, using shoulder poles, over steep, slippery mountain paths. Grain bags were the last "thick cloth" items used in the mountains.[27] The ability to process and weave "thick cloth" was a

Figure 25. Mountain work clothing from Tokushima prefecture, made of mulberry (kōzo) fiber in the early twentieth century. Photo by Mary Dusenbury

prerequisite for marriage. Girls began learning to prepare thread around the age of ten, and by the age of fifteen they were weaving (Horiuchi 1982:98).

Statistics for "thick cloth" production in the Kitō area are available from the mid-nineteenth century onward; they show that, from the turn of the century, the production of the cloth actually increased, despite the decline in its use for garments.[28] This increase in "thick cloth" production was caused, paradoxically, by the introduction of cotton cloth to the area by itinerant merchants, who were willing to trade cotton (produced in workshops in Tokushima) for "thick cloth." The merchants sold the "thick cloth" to urban consumers for use as storage and food processing bags and as indigo-dyed tatami edging. At certain times, "thick cloth" was worth more, measure for measure, than cotton, so that the women who wove it received in exchange not only the equivalent length of cotton but also a few coins as well. The opportunity of earning cash held a powerful attraction for the residents of the resource-poor mountain villages. The entire recorded production for 1912, 1800 bolts of "thick cloth," was sent out of the region (Takeuchi 1982:11). The women used the cotton mainly for their own clothing, while continuing to weave sturdy "thick cloth" workclothes for the men in the household.[29] Not vanity but poverty forced them to do so.

Sakakibara Asa, a Kitō woman born in 1891, grew up in the era when "thick cloth" production was increasing. Like many other girls of the region, she was sent to town to work as a nanny for the children of a middle-class family. A year's service netted her only twenty yen, and Asa realized that she would never prosper through such work. She used her twenty yen to buy bolts of striped cotton from a merchant in a coastal town, and then she peddled the cotton in the mountain villages through which she passed on her way back to Kitō. With the cash earned in that way she bought "thick cloth" in Kitō and sold it to the same merchant.[30] After three years of trading, she had saved 360 yen (Takeuchi 1982:17–18).

Asa also wove "thick cloth" herself. The thread was prepared at night, by the light of the fire in the open hearth, or in spare moments between daytime chores. Some women were even able to twist the thread while walking the mountain paths on their way to the fields. Working steadily every night, it took two weeks to prepare enough thread to weave one bolt of cloth, and two or three days more to weave it (Takeuchi 1982:18–19).

Trading of "thick cloth" for cotton continued into the 1920s; thereafter, women continued to weave it for their own household use, primarily for bags. But production was dying out when World War II created acute shortages of mill cloth and brought "thick cloth" garments back into use. With the return of prosperity in the mid-1950s, "thick cloth" weaving in Kitō seemed to end altogether. But in the 1970s, Sakakibara Asa—whose son was now the mayor of Kitō—was instrumental in reviving the craft one last time. This revival took the form of a village-sponsored social-service program "to make life worth living" for elderly people had lost their integral role in household-based economies, since most of the male heads of households went into the towns and cities to work. Asa and other people old enough to remember the process gathered at the new Hall of Creative Crafts built at the edge of the Naka river. Their students were housewives in their forties and fifties who were also idle now that their children were grown (Takeuchi 1982:12).

At the same time that "thick cloth" weaving was reviving in its original mountain context, it was also transmitted for the first time to an urban setting by the Tokushima weaver Kawabata Fumi (born

1928). Trained in western-style tailoring, Fumi happened to read about Kitō "thick cloth" while recuperating from a serious accident. Once she regained the use of her hands, she went to Kitō to learn mulberry-fiber processing and weaving from one of the elderly women in the village. Fumi's husband became involved in cultivating both *kaji* for fiber and indigo for dye. Fumi weaves mainly *obis*, finding the stiff cloth well suited to use for the wide kimono sash. She exhibits her ikat-dyed pieces in the annual Traditional Crafts Exhibitions sponsored by the Ministry of Cultural Affairs. Her customers are middle-class women who enjoy the occasional luxury of wearing a kimono instead of Western garments and who take an interest in patronizing traditional crafts. Some of them are also her students (Kawabata 1982). Thus it seems likely that the "thick cloth" tradition will continue as a curiosity practiced by a few studio weavers. The poverty of its mountain weavers forced it out of use there; the affluence of urban housewives may underwrite its continuation.[31]

SILKEN *KUZU* CLOTH: FROM LUXURY FABRIC TO WALLPAPER

Similar in appearance to silk, cloth made from bast fiber of the *kuzu* vine was produced, like silk, on a commercial rather than household scale, although the labor was done by women. For centuries tied to the economy of the warrior class, *kuzu* cloth producers made a successful transition to the modern economy, only to falter when they could not compete with Korea because of the cost of labor-intensive raw-materials processing. Even the discovery of *kuzu* cloth by the Folk Craft Movement has not managed to secure its survival.

Whereas mulberry-fiber textiles never escaped their association with a primitive standard of living—even when incorporated into the *Daijōsai* ritual of imperial accession—the cloth woven from *kuzu* (called *kuzufu*, *kappu*, or *kuzununo*) was identified early on as a luxury fabric. When finely split, using a needle, the fiber looks almost like raw silk. It shows to best advantage when used as weft only and allowed to lie flat within a fine warp of silk, grass-bast fiber, or cotton. (At an early time *kuzu* was used for both warp and weft,[32] but that technique soon died out, as *kuzu* does not lend itself to the spinning necessary for strong warp threads.)

Crisp and lustrous *kuzu* cloth was the desired fabric for tailoring

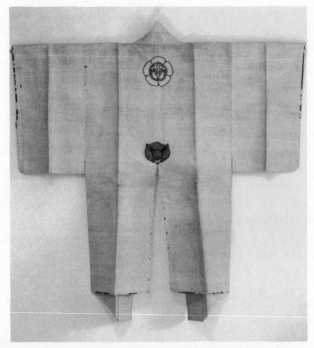

Figure 26. An Edo-period warrior's parade jacket made of kuzufu, from the mid-nineteenth century; the family crest of a domain leader is outlined in black silk cord, overlapping the back seam. Photo by Louise Allison Cort

special skirt-like trousers (*sashinuki*, gathered at the ankles with silk cords) worn by male courtiers when playing a kind of kickball called *kemari*. The game was a social grace in the court of the Heian period (A.D. 795–1185), and it continued to be popular among the Kyoto nobility. *Kuzu* cloth was also used by warriors for hunting costumes, as lining for chain-mail armor jackets, and for trousers to be worn on horseback. *Kuzu*-cloth trousers worn for travel were dyed with a special black dye that made them water-repellent. *Kuzu* cloth was ideal for the straight-lined silhouette of the sleeveless jacket and trouser combination (*kamishimo*) worn by warriors on formal occasions (grass-bast fibers could also be used for such garments) and for the crisp, crest-emblazoned jackets worn in summer processions.

Kuzu cloth became associated centuries ago with the town of

Kakegawa in ancient Tōtōmi province (now Shizuoka prefecture). The first known mention of the fabric in connection with the place occurs in a poem by the courtier Fujiwara no Tamesuke (1260–1328):

00.7501.25
> This too is a skill of the place—
> In every gateway they are preparing *kuzu* cloth:
> The town of Kakegawa.

The mere availability of *kuzu* was not a deciding factor, as the vine grows wild throughout the Japanese Islands. However, the town of Kakegawa lay along the coastal trunk road (*Tōkaidō*) connecting the imperial capital of Kyoto to the eastern provinces—to the important city of Kamakura, headquarters for the military government (A.D. 1185–1333), and later to the capital at Edo. Tamesuke was on his way to Kamakura when he composed his poem. Kakegawa was a "station" along the highway where travellers could expect to find food and shelter. They could also find protection. At the beginning of the fifteenth century, a powerful local warrior built a fortified residence there. It was replaced by a larger scale castle erected at the end of the sixteenth century. During the Edo period, the castle was occupied by a succession of warrior families (Takahashi 1975:5).

Under the policy of the Tokugawa government, designed to keep its rivals off guard, all domain leaders were obliged to spend fixed periods of time in Edo. On their journeys to and from the capital many used the *Tōkaidō*. Commoners going on pilgrimages also traversed the road. In Kakegawa they replaced their worn-out traveling trousers or bought bolts of cloth as souvenirs and distributed them throughout the country. *Kuzu* cloth is listed as a noteworthy Kakegawa product in the 1712 compendium of famous local products from various provinces, *Wakan Sansai Zue* (Kodama 1965:240–41). Woodblock prints of the early nineteenth century show *kuzu*-cloth shops lining both sides of the road through Kakegawa; those shops are still there, although the cloth business has diminished.

Production of *kuzu* cloth during the Edo period was controlled by the Kakegawa domain as an important source of income, as well as for use in regular presentations to the government and to other domain leaders. An economic survey of 208 villages within the domain, carried out in 1805–06, listed as the sources of *kuzu* fiber the villages of Kamisaigō and Kurami. Both villages lay in the mountainous interior. The *kuzu* harvested there was sent to Kakegawa, where townswomen prepared the fiber and wove the cloth (Saida 1973:56–57,74).

The *kuzu* plant with all its uses was the subject of a special study, *Seikatsuroku* ("Record of Processing *Kuzu*"), published in 1828 by the agricultural advocate Ōgura Nagatsune. While Ōgura recorded the use of *kuzu* fiber for cloth, he focused on the edible starch processed from the root as an emergency food in famine years. *Kuzu* starch had long been a staple in Japanese cooking, especially for sweets, since it did not become gummy when cold and, according to principles of Chinese medicine, its yin root nature was believed to counteract the yang acidity of sugar.[33] A sweet made from *kuzu* had been a famous product of the station-town of Nissaka, not far from Kakegawa, since the sixteenth century.

Ōgura's tract gives detailed instruction for processing *kuzu* fiber for weaving, as it was done in Kakegawa, noting that fiber preparation is the key to the quality of the finished cloth. Cotton was the usual warp fiber. Cloth of different weaves and grades was woven in lengths suitable for trousers, for formal jacket-and-trouser sets, for procession jackets, and for other specialized garments, and it could be purchased plain or dyed. Lavender was the popular color in 1828, but nineteenth-century sample books show that blue-green, gray, brown, and beige were also available. *Kuzu* cloth intended for children's summer trousers was woven in a striped pattern. Cheap grades of *kuzu* cloth were dyed with stencils to imitate the woven stripes.

The abolition of the warrior domains in 1871 had disastrous effects on the *kuzu*-cloth industry as it was so dependent upon the warrior class. Many merchants went out of business, some selling their remaining stock to lacquerers for use as undercoating on lacquered wooden objects, a function usually served by cheap coarse cloth. The few merchants who hung on tried desperately to discover new uses for their product.

Someone remembered the traditional use of *kuzu* cloth to reinforce the area around the handles of the paper-covered sliding door (*fusuma*) used as room divider and closet door, and had *kuzu* cloth woven in bolts wide enough to cover the door itself. The idea was successful, and cloth for these doors sustained the Kakegawa workshops until around 1900, when the wide cloth was further adapted to use as wallpaper—"grass cloth"—for export to Europe and North

America. That enormously popular product was the mainstay of production until 1960. Experiments with dyes developed methods for using powdered mineral pigments that would not fade. In the prewar years, and again after the war, annual production reached 100,000 bolts.

After the Japanese occupation of Korea in 1910, the *kuzu* plant had been introduced to check erosion on deforested slopes, and Korea also began processing the fiber and supplying it for use in Kakegawa. A booklet printed in 1954 by the Kakegawa *kuzu*-cloth merchants' association reflects uneasiness at being dependent upon Korea to supply the bulk of *kuzu* fiber (Anon. 1954:3). The booklet was designed to instruct farmers who wanted to undertake *kuzu* processing as a side-business, with the hope of increasing the numbers of local producers. The move came too late, however, for Korea had already begun producing its own "grass cloth," and a strike by Korean fiber suppliers against the Kakegawa merchants dealt a fatal blow to the Japanese grass-cloth business. Only a handful of Kakegawa shops continue to operate, producing *kuzu* cloth for obis, handbags, and souvenir items in the "folk craft" idiom.[34]

Kuzu fiber is still processed in the villages mentioned in the survey of 1805. The work is done by elderly farm women who receive extremely low pay. (In 1976 the women who split and knotted the fibers into threads received only 20 yen per bundle, but one kilogram of treated *kuzu* fiber—perhaps one hundred bundles—cost 18,000 yen from the retail merchant.) The merchant is responsible for organizing the production process: He hires women to gather and prepare the fiber, purchases it and distributes it to other women who prepare the thread,[35] pays for the thread, and has it woven in his workshop.

In the 1930s, the beauty of *kuzu* cloth came to the attention of the small group of connoisseurs of traditional Japanese "folk crafts" known as the Folk Craft Movement. Their leader, Yanagi Sōetsu (1889–1961), eulogized *kuzu* cloth as follows:

There are few fabrics in which nature itself appears so artlessly. One must acknowledge that people prepare it and people weave it, but human strength is only a small part of it. This cloth was born precisely because *kuzu* has a character that cannot easily be controlled. People do no more than lend their skills in order to articulate its beauty. As a result, one might say that their work commemorates nature's beauty. In weaving, value is determined by the extent to which the qualities of the given fiber can be brought to life. The work of the weaver is to serve that effort. The most respectful weaver makes the best *kuzu* fabric.

Everyone remarks on the special luster of *kuzu* cloth. It is this luster that identifies the cloth as *kuzu* cloth. It differs from the luster of silk or *asa*. In that respect *kuzu* has more integrity. It dislikes being twisted. The woven cloth has an essential straightness, and it is somehow masculine. It is different from supple silk. It does not roughen like cotton. For these reasons, it was welcomed for garments that required a well-defined line, such as *hakama* trousers or *kamishimo* outfits. For the same reasons, it was also fitting as the covering of a flat, vertical *fusuma* panel or even more so for the wall of a Western-style room. Few people have yet discovered how appropriate it is for bookbinding. There must be many new ways to use its particular beauty and firmness to the best advantage.

. . . Pieces made in the past tell us how beautifully *kuzu* grew, was dyed, was woven, and was tailored. Nowadays, unfortunately, demand has fallen off, and only *fusuma* coverings continue to be made. Those fabrics are plain white for the most part, and since they are inexpensive the weaving is hasty and coarse. One cannot expect to find anything that bears comparison with the work of the past (Yanagi 1981:271–72).

A number of issues of Yanagi's monthly magazine *Kōgei* (Craft), issued from 1931 to 1951, were bound with varieties of striped and plaid *kuzu* cloth especially woven by Yanagi's nephew, Yanagi Yoshitaka, who took a particular interest in that cloth among the many traditional types that he wove. No one has yet emerged, however, to take a role comparable to that of Kawabata Fumi for "thick cloth." Unless such a person appears and generates new interest in the cloth, its production will probably die out naturally with the generation of elderly women who presently process the fiber.

BANANA-FIBER CLOTH AND OKINAWAN CULTURAL IDENTITY

In the earliest Okinawan hierarchy, different grades of cloth produced from thread-banana fiber served as royal garments, ritual robes, and utilitarian clothing. When Okinawa became a Japanese tributary, silk and grass-bast cloths replaced the finest banana-fiber cloth in a superimposed hierarchy of desirability. In this century, the Folk Craft Movement has helped identify banana-fiber cloth as a "National Treasure," whose production now sustains the sense of identity of Okinawan weavers resisting a new wave of Japanese cultural dominance.

The cloth known as *bashōfu* in Japanese, *haji* in Okinawan, is woven from leaf fiber of the thread-banana plant.[36] This species of banana differs from the two others also found throughout the Ryukyu archipelago, one producing ornamental flowers and the other edible fruit. Specialists disagree as to whether the thread banana is native to the Ryukus or was introduced from the outside and—if so—from where (Walker 1976:324).[37] No one knows when Okinawan banana-fiber cloth began to be produced, but until the mid-twentieth century it was being woven throughout the islands.

The Ryukyu archipelago is a chain of some 140 small islands stretching between the Japanese island of Kyushu to the northeast and Taiwan to the southwest. Okinawa, lying midway along the chain, is the largest island. The islands further south, known collectively as the outer islands (Sakishima), are closest to Taiwan. The island of Okinawa has always been the center of development in the Ryukyus, and its name is often used to designate the entire archipelago. Its location, roughly equidistant from Taiwan, the South China coast, and the Philippines, made it a key transfer point on maritime trade routes, and its culture was influenced by a complex intermingling of various outside cultures. The process of unifying rival, independent clans that led to the formation of the Yamato state in Japan by the seventh century A.D. was echoed on Okinawa beginning in the twelfth century and in Sakishima about two centuries later. In 1429, Shō Hashi unified three independent feudal states and established a kingdom closely patterned on Chinese models, with its capital on Okinawa at Shuri, adjacent to modern Naha. The Chinese cultural influence continued to predominate even after the Ryukyus were conquered in 1609 by the Shimazu domain, based in Satsuma province at the southern tip of Kyushu. With Japan closed to outside contact by government decree, Satsuma exploited the Ryukyus as an avenue for illegal trade. After the fall of the Tokugawa government and the dethronement of the last Shō king, the Ryukyus became the Japanese prefecture of Okinawa in 1879. The islands were lost to Japan at the close of World War II and remained under United States jurisdiction until they reverted to Japan in 1972.

Most of the early documentary evidence regarding banana-fiber cloth occurs in Chinese records. The earliest mention is found in a document dated 1372, which notes banana fiber and grass-bast fibers as the plant fibers being woven into cloth and sewn into garments by the local population (Akashi 1976:373). Another Chinese document, from 1532, specifies that banana-fiber garments were worn in summer and the grass-bast fiber ramie (called *bu* in Okinawan) was preferred for winter (Akashi 1976:373). The same fibers were reported as being woven by women and sold in the marketplaces by a Japanese document of 1603 (Akashi 1976:372).

While these records seem to indicate that neither cotton nor silk was being processed or woven in the Ryukyus prior to the early seventeenth century, a Chinese text of 1534 lists a variety of silks and cottons being sold in the Shuri markets (Akashi 1976:372). Presumably those textiles were trade goods brought from India or China. Japanese tradition insists that techniques for raising silkworms and cultivating cotton were introduced from Satsuma in the seventeenth century, but local lore maintains that both silk and cotton had been brought from China about a century earlier (Miyagi 1973:115,122).

Whatever the source of the silks and cottons, they figured importantly in the strict Chinese-style hierarchy of costumes and colors that was established by the beginning of the sixteenth century as a corollary to the ranking system, and revised in 1639. According to that system, members of the royal family and the court wore lined silk garments in winter and on all formal occasions and unlined ramie garments in summer. Warriors wore cotton for ordinary use and lined silk for formal occasions in winter; in summer, they wore banana-fiber cloth for ordinary dress and unlined ramie for formal occasions. Commoners wore cotton in winter and banana fiber in summer; they were not permitted to wear silk (Tsujiai 1973:20–23).

The classification system implies that ramie was considered superior to banana-fiber cloth, but the unequal status of the two fabrics may not have been established until the seventeenth-century revision and may reflect a Japanese viewpoint. Earlier records showing the use of banana-fiber cloth as tribute cloth suggest that it was highly desirable. In the late sixteenth century, the finest grade of

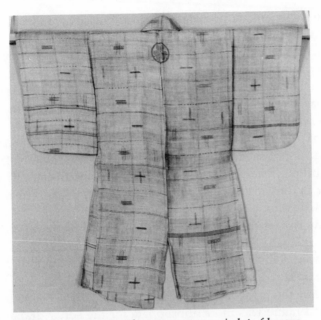

*Figure 27. A seventeenth-century summer jacket of banana-
fiber cloth from Okinawa, probably made of tribute cloth tailored in Japan. It is believed to have been worn by the third
head of the Owari Tokugawa house, Tsunanari (1652–99).
Tokugawa Reimeikai collection: Tokyo*

banana-fiber cloth (*niigashi,* "boiled skeins," for which the thread
was boiled with lye before weaving in order to increase its pliability
and luster) was being sent to China together with horses, mother-of-
pearl inlaid lacquer, conch, and sulphur (Tsujiai 1978:4). The 1616
record of the estate of the first Tokugawa shogun, Ieyasu
(1542–1616), lists thirty-three bolts of banana-fiber cloth (Tokugawa
1977:644). Another Japanese document shows that, on the occasion
of the birth of a Japanese imperial prince in 1644, King Shō Ken sent
gifts of a sword, a horse, thirty rolls of velvet, thirty bolts of *niigashi*
banana-fiber cloth, fifty bolts of "ribbed" (gauze-weave?) banana-fiber
cloth, thirty bolts of thin banana-fiber cloth, one hundred bundles
of cotton, and five vats of wine (Tokugawa 1977:690). The 1644 list
also indicates the diversity of banana-fiber cloths.

However, ramie predominates in tribute records from the seventeenth century on.[38] The annual tribute established by the Shimazu clan in 1611 included six thousand bolts of fine ramie and ten thousand bolts of coarse ramie but only three thousand bolts of banana-fiber cloth (Tonaki 1977:36). Quality control of ramie production was assured by the establishment in every village, in 1619, of a supervised workshop for fiber preparation and weaving (Miyagi 1973:121). Except for the banana-fiber cloth woven in Shuri, that cloth does not seem to have been subject to the same restrictions. Later tribute records suggest that most banana-fiber cloth was replaced by unwoven banana-fiber (Miyagi 1973:121), but how that was used is not clear.

The rise of ramie's importance may be directly related to the needs of Japan. Banana-fiber garments with their stiffness and porosity were ideally suited to summer wear in hot, humid Okinawa, since they stood away from the body and allowed moisture to evaporate, but the Japanese climate is more temperate.[39] Fine-textured, bleached ramie was more appropriate for the softer drape of Japanese garments, and it was better suited than most grades of banana-fiber cloth to the subtle dye colors and hand-painted and stencil-dyed decoration fashionable in Japan. For some time, ramie had been established in Japan as the most desirable fabric for summer wear.

Within Okinawa itself, however—despite the implication of the official dress rules—certain kinds of banana-fiber cloth seem to have maintained a high status. A 1711 dictionary of the Ryukyuan language relates that "in the past" the formal garment for women had been the *hiranuki*: It was made from either banana fiber or ramie, was dyed blue-black with indigo, and was lined (Tsujiai 1973:22). The stipulation of lining recalls the formal winter dress of the upper classes and hints that before silk became available, banana fiber was an equal alternative to ramie for formal garments. (Indeed, it was customary, upon the birth of a princess to the Shō family, to assign to her use a specially-cultivated grove of thread-banana plants or field of ramie [Okamura 1977:398]). The same dictionary also describes a dark-blue indigo-dyed robe called *chōginu* ("court robe") or *kurochō* ("black court") worn by noblemen on formal occasions (Tonaki 1977:36). An 1829 administrative report from Amami Oshima, north of Okinawa, describes the painstaking process by which the *chōginu* robe was made:

> The best-quality banana fiber is split as finely as possible, and
> the thread is dyed numerous times in indigo, over a five-day
> period, until it is saturated. The family members take turns full-
> ing the woven cloth over two or three days. The finished cloth is
> lustrous. . . . It is sewn into wide-sleeved garments and worn
> with a wide sash (Shigeno 1976:98).

The term *kurochō* was also given to a dark blue robe worn until recently by women at weddings, although the cut differed from that
of the man's robe worn at court (Okamura 1977:399). The woman's
kurochō would appear to be the descendent of the ancient *hiranuki*.

The description of using the "best-quality fiber" for fabricating
the man's *chōginu* robe implies a high degree of refinement in techniques of preparing banana fiber, a further indication of the importance of both the fiber and the cloth. As early as 1546, a Korean document recorded that three different grades of cloth were made from
the varying qualities of fiber in the inner and outer section of the
trunk: "The finest grade is white as snow, smooth and flawless as
a beautiful woman's skin" (Tonaki 1977:36). Each piece of the
thread-banana stalk—formed of leaf sheaths wrapped tightly in concentric layers, opening into "leaves" only at the very top— has fiber
on both surfaces, sandwiching a pulpy center, but only the long fibers on the outer surface are used for weaving (the short fibers of
the inner surface formerly were used by papermakers). Furthermore, the quality of the fiber is best on the innermost layers, where
it is protected from the elements. An 1872 report on banana-fiber
cloth production differentiated six grades of fiber altogether. The
three outer grades were used only for heavy thread, cords, and
ropes. The fourth layer from the outside was used for work clothes,
the fifth for everyday garments, and the sixth for garments for formal occasions (including all the garments mentioned above). Only
three leaf sheaths of the finest grade occurred on a given plant.

The qualities of the different grades of fiber were expressed in
terms of the quantity of rice for which they could be traded; work-
clothing grade was called "3 *shō*" (5.76 quarts), whereas the finest
grade was called "1 *tō* 3 *shō*" (almost 25 quarts). The relative fineness
of the grades of cloth was expressed in terms of *yomi*, a unit of eighty
warp ends. In a standard width of slightly more than one foot,
work-clothing cloth would have seven to nine *yomi*, cloth for everyday wear ten to twelve *yomi*, and the finest cloth twenty *yomi* (1600

warp ends) (Tonaki 1977:35; Tsujiai 1973:25). Finally, the overall quality of fiber was improved by careful trimming of the plant to make it grow straight and branchless. Thread-banana plants intended for twenty-*yomi* garments were usually grown inside the walled courtyard that surrounded the Okinawan dwelling, protected from the wind until they reached their ideal thickness after three years.

Regional differences—including subtle variations in soil and climate—created further levels of distinction. The finest quality of banana-fiber cloth—the *niigashi* mentioned above—was woven in the royal capital, Shuri, a center for all types of textile production. Shuri banana-fiber cloth was not traded on the market but sent to the court. The Japanese scholar Arai Hakuseki, visiting Okinawa in 1719, acknowledged that the finest banana-fiber cloth was "better than hemp or ramie" (Uemura 1971:67). Shuri banana-fiber cloth was dyed in brilliant colors; one surviving garment is striped with dark and medium blue, rust-red, and white on a mustard-yellow ground. It is a man's robe; women's garments usually had red grounds. Various ikat patterns were employed, as were complex woven designs—gauze weaves and floating-warp patterns— probably borrowed from Chinese silks. Plain-weave banana-fiber cloth was patterned colorfully with the Okinawan stencil-resist technique called *bingata*, "red pattern."

In contrast to the gorgeous variety of the banana-fiber cloth from Shuri, the commoners' banana-fiber cloth was severely restricted. Only plain-weave cloth was permitted. Only simple stripes (narrower for men than for women and for elders than for young people), dyed in blue or reddish-brown, could be worn. Women were allowed to wear dark, small-figured printed patterns for formal occasions. The effect of such rules was to make status distinguishable at a glance (Nihon Minzoku Gakkai 1973:114–15). Only after the end of Tokugawa rule were commoners free to use the full range of Okinawan textile-decorating techniques, and they developed their own hierarchy: ikat for formal garments; simple ikat, checks, and stripes for everyday ware; and stripes or plain cloth for work clothes (Tonaki 1977:34).

With the demise of Shimazu control and the end of the tribute-cloth system in 1903, the ramie textiles from the southern Ryukyus (Sakishima) became important commercial goods on the open market. They were already famous as "Satsuma ramie" in the Japanese market, and they became a major source of income. Banana-fiber cloth, however, was not well known outside the Ryukyus. In 1923, for example, out of 81,000 bolts produced, only 251 were sent to Japan. With cheap mill cloth available in Okinawa, and with the growing popularity of Western-style garments, production of banana-fiber cloth declined steadily: 135,000 bolts had been woven in 1895, but only 27,000 were woven in 1940.

An exception to the overall decline occurred in the village of Kijōka, one of the two areas in northern Okinawa (Yambaru) that had long had a reputation for its commoner-class banana-fiber cloth, known as "Yambaru banana-fiber cloth." In Kijōka, ikat-dyed banana-fiber cloth was redeveloped and the Japanese-style floor loom was introduced by a local man, Taira Shinshō. Shinshō's son Shinji, as mayor of the village, continued the effort to improve quality by inviting specialists to give instruction. In 1939 he arranged for the first exhibition of banana-fiber cloth at a department store in Tokyo (Tonaki 1977:37).

At just that moment the leader of the Folk Craft Movement, Yanagi Sōetsu, published an article in praise of banana-fiber cloth in his monthly magazine *Kōgei*. Yanagi had first become familiar with the cloth when he made several study trips to the Ryukyus in the 1920s. Yanagi was deeply sympathetic to the cause of Okinawan cultural identity, and he championed such issues as the campaign to allow Okinawan language to be used alongside Japanese. In his article, Yanagi praised banana-fiber cloth because it had to be prepared from beginning to end by hand and did not lend itself to mechanization, and because it was worn by all classes from high to low. He said that banana-fiber cloth presented an opportunity to approach the very "wellsprings of beauty" (Yanagi 1954:188).

Only a few years after Yanagi wrote, the destruction of war swept over the islands, bringing the weaving of banana-fiber cloth to a halt. However, a number of Kijōka girls had been sent to the Japanese city of Kurashiki to work in an airplane factory. Among them was Taira Toshiko (born 1921), eldest daughter of Shinji. With the war's end, the plant closed, and its owner—Ōhara Sōichirō, an ardent supporter of Yanagi's Folk Craft Movement—became concerned about the Okinawan girls. When he heard that they had some familiarity with weaving, he arranged for them to be trained by the weaver Tonomura Kichinosuke (now director of the Kurashiki Folk Craft Museum, established with Ōhara's backing).

Toshiko returned to Okinawa in 1946 with exhortations from Yanagi and Ōhara to preserve Okinawa's textile tradition. She started by recruiting war widows and gradually developed a group of women that called itself the "Society for the Preservation of Kijōka Banana-fiber Cloth." At first the society's income was so meager that Toshiko operated a general store to support herself, but with the backing of influential women among the American occupation forces and of the Folk Craft Movement members in Japan, the group's work gradually became known. In 1974 the society, with Toshiko as its representative, was designated an Important Intangible Cultural Property ("Living National Treasure") by the Japanese government (Tonaki 1977:37–38). This honor guarantees financial support for the society so long as it conforms to strictly-defined standards of the "traditional" procedures within the production of banana-fiber cloth.[40]

Production of banana-fiber cloth continues elsewhere in Okinawa, with similar cultural motives but without the official support of the Japanese government. On the island of Iriomote, in the western Yaeyama group, women under the guidance of a young Kyoto-trained weaver named Ishigaki Akiko process and weave thread-banana fiber as part of a movement to preserve the economic and cultural independence of their island in the face of increasing dependence on the Japanese economy and intensive development of Okinawa as a Japanese resort. Their concern for perpetuating the production of banana-fiber cloth is part of a larger concern for preserving the cultural fabric of which it is a part, including the songs that accompany its processing and the festivals and rituals in which it is meant to be worn. At the same time, the Iriomote weavers are ready to modernize their product in order to make it economically viable. Unlike the women of Kijōka, they are not committed to following certain rules defining the nature of banana-fiber cloth. Their goal is to experiment with new dyes, designs, and uses, allowing the cloth to keep step with an affluent modern culture that appreciates and searches out "traditional" materials.

The accomplishment of the women of Kijōka and Iriomote is admirable, but it is supported by a long tradition that not only required women to weave but also endowed that activity with primary importance. A Japanese visitor to the Ryukyus in 1876 remarked that "there is no woman—even in the royal family—who is ignorant of the skills of spinning, reeling, weaving, and stitching" (Miyagi

1973:275). That complex of skills was further urged upon women by Japanese government edicts such as the one of 1834 that proclaimed: "A woman's foremost accomplishment is not to purchase a single garment for either summer or winter but to prepare them all by her own hands" (Miyagi 1973:116).

Behind the edict lay, of course, the obligation to submit cloth in payment of annual taxes as well as to clothe all the members of the family. But various traditions, no doubt older than the edicts, encouraged the production of banana-fiber cloth and even made it pleasurable. In the arduous task of preparing the banana fiber, women were supported by the community custom of gathering in the evenings at a bonfire-lit crossroads to sing and talk as they worked together. Since young men tended the bonfires, such gatherings were opportunities for matchmaking. The young woman about to marry, faced with the responsibility of weaving twenty-*yomi* banana-fiber garments for herself and her groom, was aided by her friends, who contributed their thread to her (Tonaki 1977:36).

The Okinawan woman weaving for her lover or her family expressed affection through her work. Folk songs from every village record the deep emotion that underlay the work: "I wind on the skeins of twenty-*yomi* thread to make my beloved a formal robe like a dragonfly wing" (Miyagi 1973:184). But the work of weaving also had another powerful symbolic meaning: The woman did not just adorn her family and keep them warm, she also protected them spiritually. According to Okinawan belief, the living person is activated by the presence of a spirit located in the chest, called *mabui*. That spirit withdraws from the body at the time of death, but it can also be stolen or lost. When the *mabui* is thought to have escaped, a woman member of the victim's family is responsible for performing the rites that will reinstall it. The ritual for returning the *mabui* begins with collecting three pebbles from a particular place and binding them inside the garment behind the neck (Lebra 1966:22,25,61). The body of the standard Okinawan garment is formed by two narrow loom-widths of banana-fiber cloth joined by a central back seam; the well-sewn back seam keeps the *mabui* in place. (A corpse is dressed in a kimono having the back seam slightly opened, so that the *mabui* may exit [Tonaki 1977:34].)

Both affection and spiritual power are embodied in the capacity of the banana-fiber or cotton towel called *tisaji* to protect the man for whom it was made. Women wove elaborately-worked *umui* (remembrance) towels for their lovers. Sisters wove *uminai* towels for their brothers to take on long sea voyages, reflecting the Okinawan belief in a sister's unique power to protect her brother. This belief sprang from the founding myth involving a sister and brother and was incorporated in the custom of having a sister and brother share leadership of a kingdom (Lebra 1966:101; see also Weiner, this volume).

The Okinawan woman's role as leader was centered in the spiritual realm, while the man's role was political. At every level—state, community, kin group, and household—it was the responsibility of senior women to enact the rituals. Priestesses at the higher levels of society were chosen for their manifest ability, believed to be an inborn aspect of their character, to attract and secure the favor of the gods (Lebra 1966:26). By tradition they remained unmarried, and they lived on the grounds of the main village shrine. Their badge of office was a white robe, now of ramie or cotton but formerly of banana-fiber cloth (Tonaki 1977:36). When not in use, the robe was kept in the shrine. In some places it was the custom to burn the robe every twelve years (Lebra 1966:76).

In Okinawa, where dark indigo-dyed garments were the customary garb for formal and auspicious occasions, white was worn only by priestesses or by participants in funerals. The mourning garment was woven with stripes of white cotton within the banana fiber warp, and at the funeral it was turned inside out and draped over the head (Tonaki 1977:34), marking the exceptional occasion by a reverse of usual practice. So too the precincts of village shrines or other sacred places were marked off by ropes twisted to the left rather than to the right, as was usual (Lebra 1966:53). So too did the priestess's white robe—the robe of banana-fiber cloth— set her apart from ordinary society, as someone who operated in a realm of special spiritual power.

CHANGE AND SURVIVAL

The three long vegetable fibers, and the elements of ancient material culture they represent, have survived within drastically altered contexts by fulfilling specific needs in sacred ritual, trade and commerce, or isolated peripheral economies. In each tradition, women have always contributed the intensive labor necessary to collect, process, and prepare the fibers, although both their positions within the economy of production and their rewards for participation have varied. Mulberry-fiber cloths were used both for imperial accession rituals and for utilitarian purposes in remote mountainous regions. In the royal courts, the cloth contributed to the ritual perpetuation of the state; in the mountains, the woman's skill in producing such cloth was vital to the survival of her household. From an early date, *kuzu* cloth was produced as a commercial product, and the labor of women was an invisible element controlled by the merchant who sold the cloth. Banana-fiber cloth was both produced by women (whether for household, royal court, or trade) and worn by women in their roles as religious authorities. The role of women as processors and weavers of the fiber was honored and supported by community custom.

In recent decades, just as all three fibers have seemed about to be abandoned for good, they have drawn the attention of groups concerned with defining and preserving elements of Japanese traditional culture, especially the Folk Craft Movement led by Yanagi Sōetsu. But this attention has helped to assure the continuing survival of only one kind of cloth. In 1974, after Okinawa had reverted to Japanese control, the Japanese government claimed banana-fiber cloth as a Japanese "National Treasure" and began to give economic support to the group of women that still produces it. Simultaneously, however, another group of Okinawan weavers began producing banana-fiber cloth as part of an effort to resist Japanese cultural and economic dominance.

Cloth of mulberry-plant fiber is still produced, thanks to the determination of mountain women to resist the boredom of enforced idleness resulting from a transformed economy—and thanks also to the curiosity of an urban weaver (with her students, resisting the boredom of middle-class urban life). *Kuzu* cloth survives because the lifetime habits of hard-working, elderly farm women, who continue to gather and process the fiber, allows *kuzu* cloth production to continue. For both kinds of cloth, survival is tenuous, but it is significant. Sheer sentimentality does not have the power to perpetuate fiber cloths known and used continuously since the late neolithic period, now that they are no longer economic necessities; but stronger emotions may yet preserve them.

NOTES

1. The designation "long vegetable fibers" is used to distinguish the bast or stem fibers (such as the mulberry-plant fibers *kōzo* and *kaji*, and the fiber of the *kuzu* vine, to be discussed in this paper) and the structural or leaf fibers (such as *bashō*, the third fiber to be discussed) from other, shorter fibers or nonfibrous plant components, including wood, seed fibers, and the soft tissues of leaves, pith, and green bark (Weindling 1947:13–15). Thanks to Amanda Mayer Stinchecum for introducing me to this term as being more precise than the commonly-used "bast fibers."

2. Much cotton fabric was also produced on a noncommercial basis for home consumption, but the distinctive feature of Edo-period textile production was the range of fine-quality commercial goods.

3. The resist-dye process generally known by its Indonesian name, ikat, is called *kasuri* in Japanese. The process involves wrapping bundles of warp and/or weft threads before dyeing in such a way as to produce patterns that become visible when the cloth is woven.

4. Based upon the cellulose polymer (empirical formula $C_6H_{10}O_5$) as are all vegetable fibers, bast or stem fibers are the fibrous bundles occurring in the inner bark (bast or phloem) of the stems of dicotyledenous plants. The cells are typically long and thick-walled and overlap one another; they are cemented together by noncellulosic materials to form continuous strands that may run the entire length of the plant. The bast fibers are released from the cellular and woody tissues of the stem, and are broken down into constituent cells, by the process of controlled rotting called retting (Weindling 1947:15; Cook 1968:3–4).

5. *Taima* (*Cannabis sativa*) and *choma* or *karamushi*.

6. *Ama* (*Linum usitatissimum*).

7. Almost no fiber objects survive from the neolithic period, but their traces appear as impressions left on pottery, the famous "cord-patterned" (*jōmon*) earthenware that gives its name to Japan's neolithic period (?–ca. 200 B.C.). Twisted cords were coiled around sticks and rolled over the pot's damp surface to consolidate and decorate it; baskets and cloth were spread under the pot as it was being constructed. There is no way of detecting which fibers might have left their marks on the pots.

8. To be precise, the processing of hemp and ramie was far from easy, and the chief advantage of these plants over the tree-bast fibers was that they could be cultivated and harvested within four or five months. Ramie in particular required scraping or pounding to remove the outer bark before the retting process could be effective, although the resultant fiber was a natural white comparable to bleached cotton, as contrasted to the darker hue of hemp (Weindling 1947:276 and 293).

9. Other wild tree-bast fibers still used in Japan and the Ryukyus include

yamafuji ("mountain wisteria," *Wisteria brachybotrys*), *shina* (*Tilia japonica*), and *atsushi* (*Ulmus laciniata*) (Gotō 1964).

10. Although *kuzu* is commonly translated as "arrowroot," the Japanese plant is not identical to the arrowroot plant, which comes from the tropical West Indies. *Kuzu* was introduced to the United States at the Philadelphia Centennial Exposition of 1876 and now flourishes throughout the Southeast, where it is known—and cursed for its invasive qualities—as kudzu (Shurtleff and Aoyagi 1977:9 and 12ff.).

11. Like the bast or stem fibers, the leaf fibers are long, strong, and firmly bound into filaments by a natural gum. They traverse the leaves, forming their supporting and strengthening structure (Weindling 1947:13–14).

12. Yanagida remarked upon the ancient Shinto concept that the proper offerings to the gods are not luxury goods but the best of each person's everyday necessities (Yanagida 1976:31).

13. *Asa* paper was used for inscribing imperial edicts and, dyed various colors, for copying Buddhist sacred texts. The reddish-brown paper called *kokushi*, made from either one of the mulberry plant fibers, was used for ordinary documents (Toyota 1965:272).

14. Translations from Nippon Gakujitsu Shinkōkai 1965:75.

15. A "pillow word" is a conventional epithet used in Japanese poetry to modify certain fixed words.

16. *Shironigite* and *aonigite*.

17. The Japanese term *ao* can mean either "green" or "blue". It is not clear whether the term indicates in this case that the *asa* cloth offerings were dyed blue with indigo or that they simply had the greenish cast of freshly-cut vegetation. I tend to feel the latter was meant, since in modern shrine usage the strands of *asa* are undyed.

18. The same characters used to write *yū* were later read as *momen*, the word for "cotton".

19. The loop of thread was called *yūdasuki*. The custom persists in the Ryukyus, where a loop of fiber is slung over the right shoulder of the priestess who approaches the shrine, to invoke the protection of the gods. The general term for the sleeve-loop, *tasuki*, is related to the verb *tasukeru*, "to aid" (Okamura 1977:89).

20. The description of the ritual that follows is based on Ellwood 1973, although the interpretation is my own.

21. The Imbe clan members were responsible for sending one bolt of mulberry-fiber cloth (*aratae*) and six *kin* (almost eight pounds) of mulberry-fiber thread (*yū*) (Okamura 1977:257).

22. The terms for the offertory cloth, *yū* and *asa*, here allude to their homophones meaning "evening" and "morning."

23. Ellwood notes that the formulation of the ritual was influenced by continental (Taoist and Confucian) ideas regarding the necessity of the proper adjustment between contrasting opposites, yin and yang (Ellwood 1973:155).

24. Records of subsequent *Daijōsai* ceremonies even indicate that the baskets of *aratae* actually contained bleached *asa* cloth (Okamura 1977:263).

25. *Tafu*, written with the characters meaning "thick cloth" but possibly simply a colloquial corruption of the ancient term *tae*.

26. Production of "thick cloth" was documented in the interior of Shinano province (modern Nagano prefecture) (Gotō 1974:122).

27. Motor vehicles entered the district only in the 1930s (Takeuchi 1982:9). All rice—a luxury item reserved for festival days—used in Kitō had to be carried in from the coast, as did salt. The local diet, typical of mountainous regions, was based on millet or barley and greens. In the mid-1950s, Gotō collected twenty-two "thick cloth" items from Kitō: fifteen were grain bags, two were lunch-box bags, two were bags for storing bedding, only one was a garment. Three of the grain bags had been dyed with persimmon tannin to waterproof them (Gotō 1974:126).

28. Production for 1896 was 450 bolts; for 1900, 750 bolts; for 1904, 800 bolts; for 1912, 1800 bolts. A Kitō village office report of 1905 mentions that some three hundred households were involved in "thick cloth" production, with an average of one woman per household weaving the cloth (Takeuchi 1982:11).

29. A survey of 1897 noted that, whereas in the past both men and women had worn "thick cloth" jackets and trousers as their usual costume, it was now rare to find women wearing "thick cloth" (Gotō 1974:123).

30. Around 1910, a bolt of striped cotton sold for 1 yen 60 sen, while a bolt of "thick cloth" was worth 1 yen 70–80 sen (Takeuchi 1982:17).

31. In the summer of 1988 I visited Kitō and met three of the women who have chosen to carry on the skills they learned from the preceding generation of mountain women. Having mastered the basic skills, they are now intent upon finding new designs and uses for the *tafu* that they weave on both backstrap and frame looms (the latter using cotton warps). Although they say that most Kitō citizens do not understand what they are doing or why, they find inspiration from occasional meetings with women in other mountainous areas of Japan who are attempting to continue their own regional traditions of tree-bast fiber cloths.

32. The oldest example of *kuzu* cloth known in Japan was found adhering to the front of a bronze mirror excavated from a tomb in Fukuoka Prefecture, northern Kyushu, dating to the third or fourth century A.D. Both warp and weft threads were of S-twisted *kuzu* fiber (Nunome 1983:46–47).

33. The manifold uses of *kuzu* starch as food and medicine are outlined in Shurtleff and Aoyagi 1977:10–12, 52–56.

34. In 1987 I was surprised to encounter a display of handsome "sunshades,"

distributed by a San Francisco importer, made with *kuzu* fiber wefts (although the publicity did not name it as such). The importer's color brochure illustrated Kakegawa women—some of whom I had met—gathering, processing, and weaving *kuzu* fiber.

35. Collecting the *kuzu* vines in the mountains and removing the fiber by soaking the coiled vines and washing them in running stream water requires physical stamina and can only be done by women in good health, although the women I met doing such work were in their seventies. Preparing the thread tends to be done by women of frailer health, who work indoors while sitting.

36. Japanese *bashō*, Okinawan *bashaa*.

37. The Okinawan plant is closely related to the cultivated species, *Musa textilis*, that is indigenous to the Philippine archipelago and is the source of the textile fiber known as Manila hemp or abaca (Weindling 1947:38–43).

38. The bulk of tribute was sent as rice, reflecting standard practice in Japan, but the rice-poor islands of Miyako and Yaeyama were permitted to send a portion of their due as cloth. Okinawan ramie was distributed throughout Japan as "Satsuma ramie" (Tonaki 1977:36).

39. An unlined jacket for mid-summer use, tailored from striped and ikat-patterned banana-fiber cloth of exquisite quality, is said to have been worn by the third head of the Owari branch of the Tokugawa house, Tsunanari (1652–99). It may be one of the oldest surviving examples of banana-fiber cloth. The Japanese name for a jacket with this cut and fabric was *shimabaori*, which may mean either "striped jacket" or "island jacket"—referring to the source of the fabric (Tokugawa *et al.* 1983: catalogue no. 245; see Fig. 27 here).

40. The impact of the system of designating "Living National Treasures" upon textile production is examined at length by Amanda Mayer Stinchecum in an unpublished paper, "Growth, Continuance or Decline: Japan's Traditional Textile Arts," presented to the University Seminar on Modern Japan, Columbia University, November 14, 1986.

REFERENCES CITED

Akashi Kunisuke
    1976   Senshoku Monyōshi no Kenkyū (Research on the History
    [1931]   of Design Motifs). Kyoto: Shibunkaku.

Anoymous
    1954   Kuzuō Seizō no Tebiki (Handbook on Kuzu Processing).
                [Kakegawa: not given].

Cook, J. Gordon
    1968   Handbook of Textile Fibers—Natural Fibers. Watford, Herts:
                Merrow. 4th ed.

Ellwood, Robert S.
   1973   The Feast of Kingship: Accession Ceremonies in Ancient Japan.
           Toyko: Sophia University.

Gotō Shōichi
   1964   Asa Izen (Before Asa). *In* Nihon Minzoku Gakkai Kaihō 32:43–47.
   1974   Awa no Tafu wo Kataru (Speaking of Awa Tafu). *In* Senshoku to
           Seikatsu 5:122–26.
   1976   3 April: interview
   1979   24 March: interview

Horiuchi Toshiko
   1982   Genshi Sen'i (Primitive Fibers). *In* Senshoku no Bi 16:97–105.

Kawabata Fumi
   1982   9 July: Interview.

Kodama Kota, ed.
   1965   Sangyōshi II (History of Industry II). Taikei Nihonshi Sōshō 11.
           Tokyo: Yamakawa Shuppan.

Lebra, William P.
   1966   Okinawan Religion: Belief, Ritual, and Social Structure. Hono-
           lulu: University of Hawaii Press.

Miyagi Eisho
   1973   Okinawa Joseishi (History of Okinawan Women). Naha:
   [1967] Okinawa Taimuzusha.

Nihon Minzoku Gakkai
   1973   Okinawa no Minzokugakuteki Kenkyū (Ethnographic Research
           on Okinawa). Tokyo: Minzokugaku Shinkōkai.

Nippon Gakujutsu Shinkōkai
   1965   The Manyōshū. New York and London: Columbia University
           Press.

Nunome Yoshio
   1983   Shōbugaura Kofungun Daiichigofun Shutto no Hiraginu to
           Kuzufu ni Tsuite (Concerning the Plainweave Silk and Kuzu
           Cloth Excavated from Tomb No. 1 in the Shōbugaura Tumulus
           Group). *In* Kodaigaku Kenkyū 99:46–47.

Ōgura Nagatsune
   1944   Seikatsuroku (Record of Processing Kuzu). *In* Nihon
   [1828] Kagaku Koten Zenshū 11. Tokyo: Asahi Shimbunsha.

Okamura Kichiemon
   1977   Nihon Genshi Orimono no Kenkyū (Research on Japanese Primi-
           tive Weaving). Tokyo: Bunka Shuppankyoku.

Saida Shigetoki, ed.
   1973   Kakegawa Shikō (Kakegawa Records). Tokyo: Meicho
   [1811] Shuppan.

Shigeno Yuko
1976   Amami Senshoku Kō (Thoughts on Amami Textiles). *In* Senshoku to Seikatsu 13:98–101.

Shurtleff, William and Aoyagi, Akiko
1977   The Book of Kuzu; A Culinary and Healing Guide. Brookline, Mass.: Autumn Press.

Takahashi Nobutoshi
1976   Tōtōmi Kakegawajō (Tōtōmi Kakegawa Castle). Fujiidera: Nihon Kojō Tomonokai.

Takeuchi Junko
1982   Ki no Nuno, Kusa no Nuno (Cloth from Trees, Cloth from Grass). *In* Aruku-miru-kiku 184:4–31.

Tokugawa Yoshinobu
1977   Sumpu Onwakemonocho ni Mirareru Senshokuhin ni Tsuite (Concerning the Textiles Recorded in the Sumpu Record of Bequests). *In* Kinko Sōsho 4:607–716.

Tokugawa Yoshinobu et. al.
1983   The Shogun Age Exhibition; From the Tokugawa Art Museum, Japan. Tokyo: The Shogun Age Executive Committee.

Tonaki Akira
1977   Kijōka no Bashōfu (Banana-fiber Cloth of Kijōka). *In* Kijōka no Bashōfu. Ningen Kokuhō Shiriizu 41:34–40. Tokyo: Kōdansha.

Toyota Takeshi ed.
1965   Sangyōshi I (History of Industry I). Taikei Nihonshi Sōshō 10. Tokyo: Yamakawa Shuppan.

Tsunoda, Ryusaku; Wm. T. de Bary; and Donald Keene
1958   Sources of Japanese Tradition. New York: Columbia University Press.

Tsujiai Kiyotarō
1973   Ryukyu Bashōfu (Banana-fiber Cloth of the Ryukyus). Kyoto: Kyoto Shoin.
1978   Ryukyu no Bashōfu (Banana-fiber Cloth of the Ryukyus). Kyoto: Tambaya.

Uemura Rokurō
1971   Okinawa no Shikisai oyobi Senshoku to Minzoku (Okinawa's Color Sense and its Textiles and People). Tokyo: Iseikatsu Kenkyūjo.

Walker, Egbert H.
1976   Flora of Okinawa and the Southern Ryukyu Islands. Washington, D.C.: Smithsonian.

Weindling, Ludwig
    1947   Long Vegetable Fibers. New York: Columbia University Press.

Yanagi Sōetsu
    1954   Bashōfu Monogatari (Tale of Banana-fiber Cloth). *In* Yanagi
            Sōetsu Senshū V:147–90. Tokyo: Nihon Mingei Kyōkai.
    1981   Watashi no Nengan (My Resolve). *In* Yanagi Sōetsu Shūshū
            Mingei Taikai 3:271–72. Tokyo: Chikuma Shobō.

Yanagida Kunio
    1976   Momen Izen no Koto (Before Cotton). Tokyo: Ōbunsha.
    (1939)

GLOSSARY OF JAPANESE WRITTEN FORMS

ama	亜麻
aramitama	荒御魂
aratae	荒妙
asa	麻
bashō	芭蕉
choma	苧麻
imbe	斎部
kaji	構
karamushi	苧
kōzo	楮
kuzu	葛
kuzufu (kappu, kuzununo)	葛布
nigimitama	和御魂
nigitae	和妙
nigite	和幣
shirotae	白妙　白栲
tafu	太布
taima	大麻
taku	栲
takununo	栲布
yamato	大和
yū	木綿 or 斎 or 結

Index

we take into consideration not only the reasons cited above but also the fact that the modern road to Monastir, repaired after the first World War, has changed directions in many points so that it became shorter than it was before the repairs.

These considerations will enable us to maintain without hesitation that all three *miliaria* were found in the original position in which they stood. We may indicate these positions on the map, fig. 1, by the

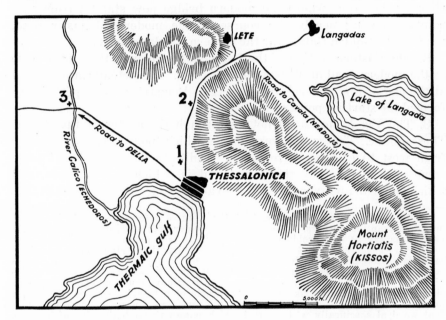

Figure 1. Thessalonike and its environs. 1, 2, 3 positions where *miliaria* have been found.

numbers of the miliaria and study the possibility that the *Via Egnatia* in its course from Pella, passing the Echedoros (Galico) river, instead of going in a straight line to Thessalonike swerved to the northeast and by-passing the low coastal areas, that were subjected to floods, proceeded to the city by the positions marked by *miliaria* 2 and 1. This conception is logical but unacceptable for two reasons: a) the formation of the ground is such that it was not necessary to introduce such a large by-passing curve, and b) the distance between the spots of *miliaria* 3 and 2 is about 7-8 miles and therefore if the course of the *Via* were as assumed above we would expect to find recorded on *miliarium* no. 3 twelve-thirteen miles instead of the nine. We must consequently accept the fact that *miliaria* no. 1 and 2 belong to the eastern section of the *Via Egnatia* that led from Thessalonike to Neapolis, that that section followed almost the course of the modern Langada road, which passes through the straits of Derveni and proceeds thence to Kavala.

Summarizing our observations we can draw the following conclusions:

A. The *Via Egnatia*, in its course from Pella, crossed the Echedoros river at the point where the modern bridge now stands; from that point, following nearly the course of the modern Monastir road, reached the Golden Gate, near the modern Vardar square.

B. The Eastern section of the *Via Egnatia* followed the same course as the modern road of Thessalonike-Kavala. The Letean Gate, located at the end of the modern street of Agios Demetrios, in all probability formed the starting point of that section.

C. The *Via Egnatia* did not go through the center of the city of Thessalonike. The great thoroughfare which today traverses the city from west to east nowhere in our traditions is referred to by the name of Egnatia;[23] by the name, that is, which it now bears, and which is due to an error that has prevailed to our own days.

---

23. It has been noted already, that the relative references are to be found only in Byzantine authors. I believe that an older reference, used repeatedly, is neutral as far as our problem is concerned. It is a passage from Cicero (*De provinciis consularibus* 2, 4), from which we learn that "Macedonia . . . sic a barbaris . . . vexatur, ut Thessalonicenses positi in gremio imperii nostri, relinquere oppidum et arcem munire coganur, ut via illa nostra, quae per Macedoniam est usque ad Hellespontum militaris, non solum excursionibus barbarorum sit infesta sed etiam castris Thraeciis distincta et notata." The "via illa nostra militaris" is certainly the Egnatia, but the text does not permit us to assume that we deal specifically with a road which passes through the city of Thessalonike where the barbarians were predominant, which, it seems, that Schönebeck believes when he states (*op.cit.* 480) "Nun schreibt Cicero, dass im Jahre 55 v. Chr. Thessalonike von den Einwohnern verlassen wurde, so dass die Seeräuber (?) selbst die via Egnatia beherrschten."

ROMA QUADRATA

Ferdinando Castagnoli
Roma

Questo nome, che evoca il sacro ricordo della nascita di Roma, presenta oscuri e dibattuti problemi: perchè la città del Palatino sia detta quadrata; se dobbiamo supporre un perimetro della città a forma di quadrato intorno al colle (Tacito) o sulla sommità (Solino); se questo quadrato abbia il valore di un templum e se dobbiamo perciò collegarlo con la disciplina etrusca o addirittura con le terremare; infine quale sia il significato di un luogo sacro di fronte al tempio di Apollo, che portava, al pari della città, il nome di Roma Quadrata.[1]

---

1. Della Roma Quadrata parlano i seguenti testi:

Fest. 310 L.: Quadrata Roma <locus> (Lindsay[2]) in Palatio ante templum Apollinis dicitur, ubi reposita sunt quae solent bona ominis gratia in urbe condenda adhiberi, quia saxo m<u>nitus est initio in speciem quadratam. Eius loci Ennius meminit cum ait (*Ann.* 157): "et quis est erat Romae regnare quadratae."

Dion. Hal. 2,65: il tempio di Vesta τῆς τετραγώνου καλουμένης Ῥώμης, ἣν ἐκεῖνος ἐτείχισεν, ἐκτός ἐστιν. Cfr. 1, 88: Romolo περιγράφει τετράγωνον σχῆμα τῷ λόφῳ.

Plut. *Rom.* 9: Ῥωμύλος μὲν οὖν τὴν καλουμένην Ῥώμην κουαδράταν, ὅπερ ἐστὶ τετράγωνον, ἔκτισε.

Appian. *Frg.* 1a, 9 . . . . πόλιν ἔκτισαν . . ., ἣν καὶ ὠνόμασαν Ῥώμην, τὸ τηνικάδε τετράγωνον λεγομένην ὅτι δέχα ἓξ σταδίων ἦν αὐτῆς ἡ περίμετρος, ἑκάστης πλευρᾶς τέσσαρα στάδια ἐχούσης.

Solin. 1,17: Nam. ut adfirmat Varro auctor diligentissimus, Romam condidit Romulus, Marte genitus et Rea Silvia, vel ut nonnulli Marte et Ilia: dictaque primum est Roma quadrata, quod ad aequilibrium foret posita. ea incipit a silva quae est in area Apollinis, et ad supercilium scalarum Caci habet terminum, ubi tugurium fuit Faustuli. ibi Romulus mansitavit, qui auspicato murorum fundamenta iecit. . . .

Tzetzes *ad Lycofr.* 1232: πρὸ δὲ τῆς μεγάλης ταύτης Ῥώμης, ἣν ἔκτισε Ῥωμύλος, περὶ τὴν Φαιστύλου οἰκίαν ἐν ὄρει Παλατίῳ ἑτέρα τετράγωνος ἐκτίσθη Ῥώμη παρὰ Ῥώμου καὶ Ῥωμύλου παλαιοτέρων τούτων (porrei una virgola prima di περί, non prima di ἑτέρα, come gli editori).

Pap. Oxyr. 2088, 8-17: Servius Tullius rex belli stip[end – – –] causa exercitum conscripsit co[– – –] cum finitumis belligerabat deinde o[– – –]u perdito divisit pagosque in tribu[– – –]ea in oppido quo qui[[.o]]sque pago civis ha[bitabat –] exque pagis milites conquirebantu[r – – –] pagis cogebatur primoque in pago [– – –]dita est eaque Roma muro [– – –]quis at Romam quadrata r[– – –]aput Romam quad[rat]am.

C.I.L. VI, 32327 (atti dei ludi secolari severiani): un *tribunal* fu posto *ad Romam quadratam.*

Tra gli scritti meno antichi intorno alla Roma Quadrata e al mundus cito i seguenti: Fowler, W. Warde, "Mundus patet," *JRS* 2 (1912), 25-33; Frothingham, A. L., "Circular Templum and Mundus," *AJA* 18 (1914), 302-320; Leopold, H. M., R., "Il mundus e la Roma quadrata," *Bull. Paletn. Ital.* 44 (1924), 193-206; Täubler, E., "Roma Quadrata und mundus," *RM* 41 (1926), 212-226; "Terramare und Rom." *Sitzungsb. Heidelb.*, 1931-32; Kroll, W., "Mundus u. Verwandtes," *Festschrift Kretschmer*, 184-190; Du Jardin, L., "Mundus, Roma Quadrata e Lapis Niger," *Rend. Pont. Acc. Arch.* s. 3, 6 (1927-9), 47-76; Weinstock, S., "Mundus patet," *RM* 45 (1930), 111-123; e cfr. ib. 47 (1932), 120 n. 1; Rose, H. J., "The Mundus," *Studi e mater. st. relig.* 7 (1931), 115-127; Deubner, L., "Mundus,"

Alla città si riferisce evidentemente (per quanto non sia ammesso
da tutti) Ennio (ciò non fu compreso da Verrio Flacco) ; così anche
Solino, Dionigi, Appiano, Plutarco, Tzetzes e, a quanto sembra, il
papiro di Ossirinco. Al luogo sacro, invece, Festo e gli atti dei ludi
secolari.

Esaminiamo anzitutto questo secondo problema. Colla notizia di
Festo sulle cose riposte *ominis gratia in urbe condenda* sono stati
naturalmente collegati, per l'analogo contenuto, Ov., *Fast.* 4, 819 sgg.[2]
e Plut., *Rom.* 11.[3] E poichè Plutarco, a questo proposito, parla di un
mundus, si sono collegate le notizie che Festo e Macrobio[4] (senza
riferirsi però al rito delle origini della città) hanno lasciato sul mundus
(o *mundus Cereris*), e con questo mundus si è identificato la Roma
Quadrata di Festo. Dato infine che Plutarco pone il mundus non come
si attenderebbe sul Palatino ma nel Comizio, molte difficoltà si sono
annodate, molte soluzioni si sono proposte. Alcuni pensano che il
riferimento di Plutarco al Comizio sia errato; e le notizie vadano
riferite al Palatino: in questo caso (secondo i più) mundus e Roma
Quadrata sarebbero in rapporto. E cioè: o si identificherebbero
(Wissowa, Hülsen, Kroll, ecc.) (potendo il monumento essere circolare
nella parte sotterranea, quadrato nella superiore; ovvero quadrato
solo in origine: le due spiegazioni si riportano all' *initio*[5] di Festo; o
anche i due nomi possono riferirsi ad un monumento circolare e qua-

---

Hermes 68 (1933), 276-287; Szabó, A., "Roma Quadrata," *Rhein.Mus.* 37 (1938)
160-169; Müller, W., *Kreis und Kreuz*, 59-62; Basanoff, V., "Pomerium Palatinum,"
Mem.Acc. Linc. s. 6, 9, 3-109; C. G. Jung e K. Kerényi, *Einführung in das Wesen
der Mythologie*, 20-22; Altheim, F., *Italien und Rom*, 1, 242 n. 66; Blumenthal,
A. v., "Roma Quadrata," *Klio* 35 (1942), 181-188.

2. Apta dies legitur, qua moenia signet aratro. | Sacra Palis suberant: inde
movetur opus. | Fossa fit ad solidum, fruges iaciuntur in ima | et de vicino terra
petita solo. | Fossa repletur humo, plenaeque imponitur ara, | et novus accenso
fungitur igne focus. | Inde premens stivam designat moenia sulco . . .

3. Ὁ δὲ Ῥωμύλος . . . ᾤκιζε τὴν πόλιν, ἐκ Τυρρηνίας μεταπεμψάμενος ἄνδρας
. . . Βόθρος γὰρ ὠρύγη περὶ τὸ νῦν Κομίτιον κυκλοτερής, ἀπαρχαί τε πάντων, ὅσοις
νόμῳ μὲν ὡς καλοῖς ἐχρῶντο, φύσει δ' ὡς ἀναγκαίοις, ἀπετέθησαν ἐνταῦθα. Καὶ
τέλος ἐξ ἧς ἀφῖκτο γῆς ἕκαστος ὀλίγην κομίζων μοῖραν ἔβαλλον εἰς ταῦτα καὶ
συνεμείγνυον. Καλοῦσι δὲ τὸν βόθρον τοῦτον ᾧ καὶ τὸν ὄλυμπον ὀνόματι μοῦνδον.
εἶθ' ὥσπερ κύκλον κέντρῳ περιέγραψαν τὴν πόλιν . . .

4. Fest. 144: Mundus, ut ait Capito Ateius . . ., ter in anno patere solet, diebus
his . . . sic refert Cato . . .: "Mundo nomen inpositum est ab eo mundo, qui supra
nos est: forma enim eius est, ut ex is qui intravere cognoscere potui, adsimilis
illae": eius inferiorem partem veluti consecratam Dis Manibus clausam omni
tempore nisi his diebus . . .; quos dies etiam religiosos iudicaverunt ea de causa,
quod quo tempore ea, quae occultae et abditae religionis Deorum Manium essent,
veluti in lucem . . . patefierent, nihil eo tempore in republica geri voluerunt . . .;
126: Cereris qui mundus appellatur . . .; Macr. 1, 16: mundo, quod sacrum Diti
patri et Proserpinae dicatum est . . . et Varro ita scribit: mundus cum patet,
deorum tristium atque inferum quasi ianua patet . . . Cfr. anche Schol. Bern.
ad Verg. *Ecl.* 3, 105.

5. In senso spaziale è inteso, per es., dal Täubler, in senso temporale dal Kroll.
La spiegazione in rapporto al linguaggio dei misteri (Täubler, *RM* 1926, 220)
è da escludersi. *Indicio* propone di leggere il Blumenthal, l.c. 184.

dripartito = *quadratus*),[6] o il mundus sarebbe coperto dalla Roma Quadrata (Boni, Frothingham, Leopold, Du Jardin: con relativa identificazione con la cisterna sotto il palazzo dei Flavi ed una lastra di tufo), o l'uno incluso nell'altra, che sarebbe un'area quadrata (K. O. Müller, Thulin, Weinstock, Deubner), colla funzione di templum (Täubler). Per lo più si pensa che questo mundus fosse al centro del colle (possibilmente all'incrocio del cardine e del decumano) e, secondo alcuni (Täubler, Deubner, ecc.) avrebbe un precedente nelle fosse riscontrate nel centro di alcune terremare.

Ovvero l'indicazione di Plutarco non è errata, e si è pensato allora: che mundus e R. Q. siano cose del tutto distinte (il mundus, circolare, del Comizio, sarebbe il centro dell'ager Romanus a forma circolare, mentre la R. Q. sarebbe il centro della città quadrata del Palatino: così il Blumenthal; secondo il Weinstock e altri, il mundus del Comizio sarebbe stato originariamente sacro a Cerere, e secondariamente connesso (da Ovidio e Plutarco) con le origini di Roma; o anche si è pensato (Leopold, Du Jardin) che i due monumenti esistettero prima sul Palatino e poi (dopo che furono sepolti dal palazzo di Domiziano) nel Comizio (la R. Q. del Comizio sarebbe il niger lapis).[7]

Quanto ai rapporti col mundus Cereris mi sembrano certe le conclusioni del Rose, e soprattutto, dello Hedlund, che il mundus sacro ai Mani e a Cerere, comunicazione con l'oltretomba (i tre giorni dell' anno in cui era aperto, sono *religiosi*) non abbia nulla a che vedere con quello relativo al rito della fondazione di Roma.[8] Ciò è evidente per il concetto cultuale completamente diverso: è mai possibile che il luogo sacro all'origine di Roma sia al tempo stesso la *ianua deorum tristium atque inferum?* e come è ammissibile, che Festo nella sua esaurientissima trattazione sul mundus, e parimenti Macrobio, non facciano parola di un suo rapporto alle origini della città? Già osservata è la incompatibilità di alcuni particolari: il mundus nel quale si poteva entrare, con una volta che richiama il cielo, è ben diverso dalla fossa ricolma di terra di cui parla Ovidio. Esso era una costruzione (o una grotta, secondo lo Hedlund) con una cavità inferiore;[9] è ipotesi incerta se esso fosse nel santuario di Cerere sull'Aventino;[10] la connessione con Cerere può essere secondaria, come sviluppo di un'impersonale culto ai Mani (Hedlund) ma potrebbe anche essere origi-

---

6. Müller, *loc. cit.*, 62 (v. sotto).

7. Sotto il niger lapis cercavano il mundus già il Milani e lo Studniczka.

8. Alla identità delle due cose crede invece ancora il Deubner.

9. Lo Hedlund pensa, mi pare a torto, che le due parti fossero allo stesso livello.

10. La testimonianza dello Schol. Bern. ad Verg. *Ecl.* 3,105 *mundus in sacro Cereris* può infatti essere un autoschediasma da Festo 124, come nota il Deubner, pag. 283.

naria[11] e in rapporto (come il nome suggerisce) a Panda Cela (indigitazione di Cerere) (Altheim).[12] Quello che è indiscutibile, in base alle fonti, è che il culto del mundus è un culto dell'oltretomba (escluderei anche, col Weinstock, la teoria della riserva di grano, sostenuta particolarmente dal Fowler). In base a tale concetto sembra probabile l'etimologia del mundus (in questo senso) dall'etrusco munθ, che forse significa "morto," e in genere dalla radice mun-, il cui significato ctonio sembra certo.[13] Quanto all'origine si sono supposti dei rapporti con la Grecia (Altheim) o l'Etruria (Rose) (è invece da escludersi, come vedremo, una derivazione dalle terremare).

Questo era l'unico mundus in Roma, come è da ricavarsi dalle testimonianze (cfr. nota 4), che ne parlano chiaramente in questo senso, e non solo era originariamente estraneo alle origini della città (come già fu merito del Weinstock di mostrare), ma non si può dire che esso vi fosse connesso nemmeno secondariamente. A parte la grandissima improbabilità che il mundus quale è descritto da Festo (con le sue strutture sotterranee) fosse nel Comizio (come il Weinstock e altri[14] pensano), è infatti da ritenersi (con lo Hedlund) che il rapporto tra il rito della fondazione e il mundus sia nato semplicemente da un arbitrio di Plutarco. Ritengo anche che sia abbastanza facile ammettere l'origine di questo arbitrio nella attribuzione, inesatta, del termine mundus a tutti i luoghi di culto sotterranei: attribuzione che è nota anche a Servio[15] ed è originata dal parallelismo con una definizione greca.[16] Quanto a Ovidio, un'allusione al mundus nelle parole *inde movetur opus* (vista dal Kroll per il raffronto a Fest. 126)[17] è ipotesi rischiosa. In tutta la sua descrizione non c'è assolutamente nulla che abbia rapporti col mundus. (Egli parla di una fossa aperta prima di iniziare coll'aratro il solco primigenio e riempita di messi e di terra; sopra alla fossa così riempita è posta un'ara.)

Ovidio e Plutarco non hanno dato che una "ricostruzione" del rito della fondazione della città, in base ad analogie con riti usati nelle fon-

---

11. Per un possibile raffronto etrusco in questo senso, v. Kroll, l.c., pag. 122, n. 1. Non mi sembra giusto negare (come fa lo Hedlund) il rapporto tra il mundus e Cerere nell'iscrizione di Capua *CIL* 10, 3926.

12. *Terra Mater*, 113 sgg.

13. Cfr. Ernout, A., *Bull. de la Soc. de Linguist.* 30 (1929), 107; Leifer, F., "Studien zum antiken Aemterwesen," *Klio Bh* 23 (1931), 198, n. 7, 206, n. 2.

14. Per es. Altheim, l.c.

15. Serv., ad Aen. 3,134: Quidam aras superorum deorum volunt esse, medioximorum id est marinorum focos, inferorum vero mundos.

16. Porph., *antr. nymph.* 6 (p. 60 n.): ὡς γὰρ τοῖς μὲν Ὀλυμπίοις θεοῖς ναούς τε καὶ ἕδη καὶ βωμοὺς ἱδρύσαντο, χθονίοις δὲ καὶ ἥρωσιν ἐσχάρας, ὑποχθονίοις δὲ βόθρους καὶ μέγαρα.. Al contrario Paul. Fest. 27 parla di *altaria* anche *in effossa terra*. E' improprio perciò definire *mundi* il Tarentum, il lacus Curtius, ecc.

17. *dictus est quod terra movetur*.

dazioni delle colonie, che essi evidentemente dovevano tener presenti (così il focus di Ovidio ricorda il costume dei coloni greci: Hedlund) ; inoltre ispirazioni furono suggerite dal rito della collocazione dei termini,[18] come pensa il Thulin (seguito dal Kroll, dal Täubler, dal Deubner).[19]

L'ultimo argomento in favore del mundus sul Palatino, l'analogia con le terremare, ha perduto ogni valore dopo il recente lavoro di revisione sulle terremare.[20]

Rimane da vedere ora il contrasto topografico dato dalla collocazione (secondo Plutarco) nel Comizio del βόθρος della fondazione.[21] Plutarco segue evidentemente una tradizione di una Roma primitiva comprendente anche il Foro.[22] Non c'è poi alcun motivo per ritenere (come il Weinstock e altri fanno) che anche Ovidio si riferisca al Comizio; in armonia col resto della sua narrazione dobbiamo credere che si riferisca al Palatino. I due autori hanno dato dunque dello stesso rito (oggetto, probabilmente, di ricostruzioni antiquarie, più che di antiche tradizione) due diverse localizzazioni, in relazione a due teorie sulla città primitiva, e più precisamente hanno pensato (si può ciò ritenere probabile) di poter fissare i ricordi del rito della fondazione, l'uno nei monumenti antichissimi (dei quali si avevano conoscenze confuse) sepolti sotto il niger lapis nel Comizio (così già lo Schwegler), l'altro (in accordo, come in altri casi, con Verrio Flacco) nella *Roma Quadrata ante templum Apollinis*.

Siamo così ricondotti alla Roma Quadrata. Esclusa l'identità e anzi qualunque rapporto col mundus, non rimane che definirla, con Festo, come un *locus* nel quale si ritenevano poste *quae solent bona ominis gratia in urbe condenda adhiberi*. Esso era *ante templum Apollinis*.

Tra i testi relativi alla Roma Quadrata città, quello di Solino offre elementi di difficilissima soluzione. E' stata fin da principio notata la stranezza della indicazione di un quadrato per mezzo di due soli punti (*area Apollinis, supercilium scalarum Caci*). La questione

---

18. Cfr. Sicul. Fl. 141 Th.

19. Non ha perciò interesse storico, ma solo storiografico, l'esame sul significato del riempimento con la terra della fossa (su cui parla anche Lydus, *de mens.* 4,73, p. 125 W.), simbolo di dominio ovvero di sinecismo. Il Müller vi vede un simbolo cosmico.

20. Cfr. in particolare Patroni, G., "Terremare e Palatino," *Rendic. Acc. Italia* s. 7, 1 (1939-40), pag. 108; e in genere la rassegna di P. Barocelli, *Bull. Com.* 70 (1942), 131 sgg.

21. Vedi anche la spiegazione del Blumenthal sopra ricordata.

22. Al cap. 17 il Campidoglio risulta posseduto de Romolo. In vari testi con Romolo viene connesso oltre il Campidoglio (dove si mostrava un'altra sua *casa*), il Quirinale, l'Esquilino, o addirittura i sette colli (Verg., *Aen.* 6,783; Serv. *ad.* 1). Nel Comizio stesso era il fico Ruminale (altro caso di duplice collocazione, nel Comizio e sul Palatino).

poi è enormemente complicata dalle diverse ipotesi sul tempio di
Apollo. Si è pensato che i due punti indicassero gli estremi della
diagonale di un quadrato (dall'angolo orientale, cioè dalla zona di
S. Bonaventura — dove da alcuni si colloca il tempio di Apollo —
all'angolo occidentale, dove erano le scalae Caci). La spiegazione è
un semplice ripiego: Solino dice che la R. Q. *incipit* e *habet terminum*
nei due punti; sono indicazioni concrete, ed è perciò un arbitrio pensare alla astrattezza geometrica di una diagonale di un quadrato: con
due punti è impossibile indicare un quadrato. Accettando invece
l'identificazione del tempio di Apollo con quello di Giove Vincitore si
ha, oltre queste difficoltà, anche il risultato di un quadrato molto
esiguo, come è indotto a ricostruire il Richmond.[23] Voler vedere, infine,
in questa linea il decumano della città è un'arbitraria interpretazione
del testo.

Occorre anzitutto determinare la paternità di Varrone nel passo di
Solino. A Varrone per lo più si attribuisce non solo la prima proposizione, ma anche la seconda, poichè di questo autore è propria una
siffatta ricerca antiquaria; la terza proposizione viene da molti
ritenuta un'aggiunta di Solino, poichè Varrone, morto nel 27, molto
difficilmente poteva avere menzionato il tempio di Apollo, il quale fu
dedicato nel 28 (anche l'espressione *habet terminum* è forse non con-
veniente a Varrone).

Questa duplicità di composizione rende possibile la seguente ipotesi:
che Solino nella sua aggiunta al passo di Varrone non alludesse alla
città del Palatino, ma al luogo davanti al tempio di Apollo. Questo
tempio è quello volgarmente detto di Giove Vincitore.[24] Ora è da
considerarsi l'indicazione di Solino, della *silva quae est in area Apol-*
linis e il *supercilium scalarum Caci*: questa *area Apollinis* si suole
mettere per lo più nella parte posteriore del tempio, e si identifica
anche con la *area Palatina*;[25] ma è molto più naturale che essa fosse
sul fronte, davanti ai portici e alle grandiose gradinate. Ristretta
l'indicazione di Solino nel luogo davanti al tempio di Apollo (le Scalae
Caci infatti erano lì vicine) si ha motivo di ritenere che Solino parli
della stessa Roma Quadrata di cui parla Festo, e di abbandonare il

---

23. *JRS* 4 (1914), 181-188.

24. E' questa infatti l'unica identificazione possibile, e anzi da ritenersi, per
molti argomenti, sicura. Cfr. Richmond, A. J., *JRS* 4 (1914), 193 sgg.; Lugli, G.,
Roma antica, 438 sgg.

25. Un argomento a ciò si vuol vedere in Ov., Trist. 3,32 e in Joseph. Fl., *Ant.*
Jud. 19,3,2. Nel primo testo dopo la menzione della *porta Palati* e di Giove Statore
è detto: *hoc primum condita Roma loco est;* ma può riferirsi genericamente al
Palatino meglio che a un punto isolato (del resto il tempio di Giove Statore è
molto lontano da quello di Apollo); lo stesso si può dire per il secondo testo:
ἐν εὐρυχωρίᾳ τοῦ Παλατίου . . . . Πρῶτον δὲ οἰκηθῆναι τῆς Ῥωμαίων πόλεως τοῦτο
παραδίδωσιν ὁ περὶ αὐτῆς λόγος.

significato di Roma Quadrata-città, che (come si è visto sopra) presenta difficoltà insormontabili. Secondo questa interpretazione si viene a dover ammettere che Solino sia caduto in una confusione analoga a quella che riscontriamo in Festo, contaminando i due concetti di Roma Quadrata: tale confusione era facile, perchè il senso corrente doveva essere quello della ristretta località, non della pianta della città romulea.

O forse meglio la ristretta località davanti al tempio di Apollo era da Solino considerata la città fondata da Romolo.[26] Induce a crederlo il passo di Tzetzes (cfr. anche Zon. 7,3[27]), che parla di due Rome, romulee entrambi, delle quali la più antica era quadrata, fondata presso la casa di Faustolo: dunque in questo passo la Roma Quadrata è un luogo ristretto, presso la casa di Faustolo, lo stesso perciò che Solino indica tra il tugurium Faustuli e la selva del (vicinissimo) tempio di Apollo, e perciò identico al *locus ante templum Apollinis* di Festo; questo infatti era il luogo che conservava vivo il toponimo;[28] e la notizia della città di questo nome fondata da Romolo si riferì a questa ristretta località (Solino, sembra anche Zonara), magari supponendo (per conciliare la divergenza) due città romulee (Tzetzes).

Questo *locus*, dice Festo, era *saxo munitus*,[29] *in speciem quadratam*. Benchè ogni ipotesi al riguardo sia arrischiata, penserei ad una sostruzione o meglio anche ad un tratto delle mura del Palatino, che molto probabilmente correvano sotto il tempio di Apollo: un tratto che si estendesse (Solino) dalla *silva quae est in area Apollinis* fino al vicino *supercilium scalarum Caci*. Forse uno scavo potrebbe dare una conferma o una smentita all'ipotesi.[30]

Perchè questa R. Q. avesse tal nome è discusso: alcuni vedono una figurazione in piccolo della città (ed in particolare coloro che danno ad ambedue le cose la forma di un cerchio quadripartito); il Blumenthal, ricorrendo ad una etimologia dalla stessa radice dell'ai. rädati "scavato," pensa ad una forma *rodma poi confusa con Roma. Io penserei che questo termine, che gli antichi collegavano con la primitiva città, si sia attribuito artificiosamente a questo *locus*, dove la vicinanza con molti monumenti della leggenda romulea (casa Romuli e il sacro

---

26. Così anche Pais, E., *Ancient Legends*, cap. XII. Diversa è però l'impostazione della sua teoria: egli pensa a due R. Q., che sarebbero due tappe successive dello sviluppo della città; il nome di Roma sarebbe derivato dal fico *(rumis)* vicino alla prima R. Q.

27. ἔκτισε δὲ αὐτὴν περὶ τὴν τοῦ Φαυστύλου οἴκησιν· ὠνόμαστο δ᾽ ὁ χῶρος Παλάτιον.

28. Ancora negli atti severiani dei ludi secolari.

29. Quanto all'*initio* di Festo (cfr. anche n. 5) potrebbe spiegarsi semplicemente come riferimento al principio della città.

30. Il Blumenthal, escludendo sia il significato di città sia quello dato da Festo, pensa ad una strada che ai tempi di Solino portasse tal nome.

albero sorto dal colpo di lancia di Romolo, ambedue presso le scalae Caci, e non lungi il Lupercale, ecc.) poteva fare imaginare il punto di inizio della costruzione della città, consacrato da offerte rituali.

Possiamo finalmente venire alla Roma Quadrata nel significato di città. In un primo tempo nessuno aveva dubitato che il termine si riferisse alla forma quadrata o quadrangolare della città del Palatino: ciononostante tutti notavano come il colle, soprattutto prima delle costruzioni imperiali, non avesse in realtà una forma tale da giustificare il termine. E' vero che una forma quadrangolare ha il tracciato del pomerio della città del Palatino descritto da Tacito (*Ann.* 12, 24): ma che valore dobbiamo attribuire a questa descrizione? Le mura dovevano stare (e stanno) sui fianchi del colle, il pomerio di Tacito segue il fondo delle valli, mentre originariamente il pomerio è una linea strettamente connessa colle mura.[31] Inoltre quali basi poteva avere Tacito a sua disposizione? Non certo dei cippi; come si è creduto ricavare dal *certis spatiis interiecti lapides.* Che questo tracciato sia una semplice induzione si ricava dalle stesse parole: *noscere haud absurdum reor.* Un saggio dei criteri sui quali egli si appoggia è dato a proposito dell'*initium condendi: a Foro Boario, ubi aereum tauri simulacrum aspicimus, quia id genus animalium aratro subditur, sulcus designandi oppidi coeptus.* . . . Il fatto che la città di un tal pomerio, abbia una forma non molto lontana dal quadrato, potrebbe essere semplicemente la conseguenza della interpretazione del termine Roma Quadrata. Un argomento rilevante infine è il fatto che Varrone per spiegare il significato di quadrato non si riferisce, come sarebbe stato ovvio, ad una forma quadrata della città, ma ricorre alla teoria della divisione augurale del templum (v. anche la strana spiegazione di Appiano).

Secondo Varrone dunque la città sarebbe *ad aequilibrium posita,* costituita cioè con la divisione gromatica; perciò sarebbe stata divisa per mezzo del cardine e del decumano; e sarebbe stata detta quadrata in quanto divisa come le colonie, le quali hanno una forma quadrata.[32] (Cfr. la divisione augurale di Romolo, che col litus *regiones direxit:* Cic., *de div.* 1, 17, 30.)

Alcuni, particolarmente il Täubler, hanno presa per buona la spiegazione di Varrone. Le difficoltà nascono quando si tenta di rintracciare sul Palatino un cardine e un decumano. Uno di essi si vuol vedere

---

31. Perciò non si può seguire nemmeno Messalla, ap. Gell. 13,14,2: . . . *pomerium . . . Palatini montis radicibus terminabatur;* e comunque con esso non si accorda Tacito, che vi include anche l'ara Massima di Ercole.

32. Perciò non è necessario leggere in Varrone (come propone il Blumenthal p. 186) *dictaque primum est Groma* (o *a groma*) *quadrata.* . . .

nelle indicazioni date da Solino, della selva del tempio di Apollo e del
supercilium scalarum Caci: ma il testo non autorizza una tale interpretazione; e perchè non sarebbe ricordata anche l'altra linea? Del
resto la traduzione topografica di questo templum non trova nessuna
rispondenza nella realtà.[33] E poi, come lo stesso Täubler osserva, non
alla città del Palatino ma a quella etrusca delle quattro regioni si può
ragionevolmente attribuire, per motivi cronologici, il rito etrusco della
divisione augurale del templum.

La teoria del templum ha ricevuto tuttavia un forte sostegno nella
nuova spiegazione intuita da F. Altheim, del termine *quadrata* nel
senso di "quadripartita." In base a questa spiegazione il Müller con-
fronta la pianta della città e il cielo nella dottrina etrusca: entrambi
sono cerchi divisi in quattro parti dal cardine e dal decumano: perciò
si spiega insieme la città circolare di Plutarco e quella quadrata.
Contemporaneamente il problema è studiato da S. Szabò, che porta vari
esempi di *quadratus* in questo senso, e approfondisce questa "quadra-
tura del cerchio." La teoria è accolta anche da F. Dornseiff,[34] da Jung
e Kerenyi; è invece respinta dal Blumenthal. Il quale ritiene (mi
pare a torto) che la città circolare ricordata da Plutarco in rapporto
al mundus del Comizio sia diversa dalla Roma Quadrata: non trova
perciò un problema di una città rotonda e quadrata al tempo stesso;
nega fondamento alla spiegazione data da Varrone; ritorna alla
spiegazione della forma quadrata del pomerio della città del Palatino
attestato da Tacito.

Il significato di quadratus per quadripartito è solidamente fondato:[35]
il *versus quadratus* è il τετράμετρον; la *legio quadrata* è composta di
quattro unità minori (Paul. Fest. 336) (nello stesso senso, τετράγωνος
in Aristoph., *Ucc.* 1005). Ritengo però che il termine non sia da
riferirsi al templum. Infatti sembra da escludersi che Roma abbia
avuto cardini e decumani per la complessa conformazione del suolo:
certo non ve ne è rimasta la minima traccia anche indiretta e ogni
tentativo in proposito è sempre caduto nell'insuccesso. Per la città
di Romolo sono già state viste inoltre le difficoltà cronologiche, poichè
il concetto del templum è etrusco. Penso perciò che quadripartita si
dicesse la città che Servio Tullio divise in quattro regioni (Liv. 1, 43
quadrifariam enim urbe divisa). E troviamo assai naturale che tale
determinazione venisse posta alla Roma di Servio Tullio, la quale

33. Sono giochi di fantasia la ricostruzione del Täubler, *RM* 1926, 218, e del
Basanoff, *op. cit.*

34. *Rhein. Mus.* 38 (1939), 192 (con riferimenti al mondo orientale).

35. Cfr. Immisch, O., *Sitzungsb. Heidelb.* 1923, pag. 31 sg.; Altheim, *Glotta*
XIX (1930), pag. 32 sgg.; e i sopra citati Szabò, Blumenthal.

rappresenta una fase della storia della città di radicale mutamento, per l'aggregazione di stanziamenti sino allora separati (e dato anche il fatto che questa divisione aveva il suo importante riflesso costituzionale della divisione in tribù del popolo). In un secondo tempo dovette andar perduto il vero senso del termine (ciò non meraviglia: Festo confonde addirittura, nella citazione di Ennio, la città col luogo ante templum Apollinis), e fu attribuito il termine alla città di Romolo e perciò al Palatino, almeno da parte dei più;[36] e l'erudizione della fine della repubblica e dell'impero cercò un senso nella spiegazione gromatica (con Varrone) o forse (con Tacito) in una ricostruzione del pomerio (e v. poi anche Appiano). Ma nel documento più antico, il verso di Ennio, non è improbabile che fosse adoperato nel giusto senso. La lettura più probabile[37] è: *et qui sextus erat Romae regnare quadratae*, e il Vahlen non esita a riferire il passo a Servio Tullio: è probabile perciò un riferimento alla città delle quattro regioni. Lo stesso accade (almeno è molto verosimile) nel papiro di Ossirinco dove a proposito dell'opera di Servio Tullio si parla (in un rapporto indeterminabile[38] per le lacune del testo) di Roma Quadrata.

Le testimonianze sulle più antiche fasi della città in parte si fondano su un contenuto di realtà storica, in parte sono applicazioni a questo contenuto di schemi estranei ispirati per lo più al mondo etrusco, in parte sono elaborazioni erudite. Tra i contenuti reali che emergono nelle tradizioni intorno alla Roma Quadrata, sono: da un lato l'antico ed importante villaggio del Palatino, che, per una sua preminenza tra gli altri stanziamenti, si doveva e quasi certamente si deve ritenere la più antica Roma; dall'altro la costituzione della città delle quattro regioni: questa rappresenta una riorganizzazione radicale, e alcuni elementi dovettero perciò sembrare propri della fondazione e si riportarono alle origini, a Romolo. Così il nome di *Roma Quadrata*. Una trasposizione di questa città delle quattro regioni è forse anche la città di Romolo (in Plutarco) che ha il suo centro nel Comizio. Applicazioni di schemi estranei sono la forma circolare della città (in Plutarco), derivazione dalla città teorizzata dagli Etruschi (ai quali si ispirano tutte queste versioni sul rito della fondazione) in relazione anche all'etimologia di *urbs* da *orbis* (Varro, *L.L.* V, 143), e la considerazione del Comizio come centro, ispirata da principi teorici (cfr.

---

36. In Plutarco ciò sembra de escludersi. Se la fondazione di cui parla al cap. 11 è la stessa di cui al cap. 9, la Roma Quadrata comprende anche il Comizio.

37. V. anche Lindsay nella 2a edizione di Festo. Il Blumenthal, l. c., 184 propone: *et quis* (cioè *quibus*) *est* <*et*> *erat.* . . .

38. Tentativi di integrazione furono fatti da Levi, M. A., *Riv. Filol. Class.* 56 (1928), 511 e da Piganiol, A., "Le papyrus de Servius Tullius," *Scritti in onore di B. Nogara*, 373 sg.

il già citato Arist., *Ucc.* 1005: ὁ κύκλος γένηταί σοι τετράγωνος, κἂν μέσῳ ἀγορά . . . e anche da confronti reali, di città col foro nel centro). Dall'esigenza di spiegare il nome *Roma Quadrata* deriva la teoria del templum (Varrone), dei quattro stadi (Appiano), e forse il tracciato del pomerio palatino (Tacito) ; il nome non compreso fu attribuito anche ad un luogo ristretto, forse in epoca recente (in questo senso la testimonianza più antica è di Verrio Flacco, mentre nel senso di città risaliamo ad Ennio), e la localizzazione fu ispirata dalle memorie romulee della zona. In questo luogo si pensava esser poste offerte di auspicio alla fondazione della città (Festo e Ovidio; e in un secondo tempo il luogo fu spiegato come città: probabilmente Solino e Zonara, certo la fonte di Tzetzes).

PNYX AND COMITIUM

ERIK SJÖQVIST
Swedish School, Rome

The Comitium, the traditional meeting place of the comitia in Rome, has lately been the subject of two important studies. Gjerstad[1] followed with modern stratigraphical criteria the last excavations on the site of the ancient Rostra and the so-called Tomb of Romulus, carried out by Bartoli in 1939, and was thus able to demonstrate the remarkable exactitude of the observations made in 1899 by Boni,[2] the first explorer of the site. Further, he tried to establish, with additional information gained in new excavations, both a relative and an absolute chronology of the fragmentary remains of the monuments laid bare; to reconstruct them; to identify them, and to place them within their historical contexts. His contribution is very valuable, though limited to a central but minor part of the Comitium: the Rostra and their immediate vicinity.

Lugli[3] approaches the problem from a different point of view. He is a topographer and employs a strictly topographical method, collecting in a most useful way the essential literary material from ancient sources; he discusses it with reference to the scattered existing archaeological remains, and tries to produce a reconstruction of the Comitium and adjacent buildings during the Republic, surveying at the same time the abundant scholarly literature on the subject. He expresses his scepticism regarding the stratigraphical results and disagrees with the absolute dates proposed by Gjerstad, attributing earlier dates to the lower layers and certain monuments discussed by Gjerstad.

The present paper, though accepting Gjerstad's initial date of the Rostra stratigraphy, is not primarily concerned with the stratigraphical problems, nor with the topographical identification of non-existing buildings or monuments. My aim is to draw attention to such elements in the general topography of the site as may contribute to a more comprehensive understanding of the arrangement of the Comitium in Republican times. Such an attempt must necessarily lead to dissension in minor or major points with previous authors in the

---

1. Gjerstad, E., *Il Comizio romano dell'età repubblicana*, Skrifter utgivna av Svenska Institutet i Rom, 5, Opuscula Archaeologica, 2, Lund & Leipzig, 1941, 97-158.
2. Boni G., "Esplorazioni del Comizio," *Not.Sc.* 1900, 295-340.
3. Lugli, G., *Monumenti minori del Foro Romano*, chapt. 1., *La topografia del Comizio nell'età repubblicana*, 1-27 and pl. II. All essential bibliography is quoted there.

field, but I have dispensed with a detailed discussion of the various earlier theories and proposals, in the interests of a short presentation of some essential features in the plan and function of the place, hitherto not observed.

The configuration of the place where the Comitium was to come into being was determined by certain elements much older than the beginning of the urbanization of the Forum area. From the north came an ancient road—later to be known as *Clivus Argentarius*—leading from the Campus Martius and passing along the foot of the Capitoline Hill. On the Campus Martius it was identical with the later *Via Flaminia*, a natural artery of commerce and traffic running from the Tiber valley and its rich hinterland toward the stronghold of the Seven Hills, which guarded the passage over the river and protected its navigable lower tract. Just before reaching its end at the Forum valley the road had to pass over a considerable elevation of the ground created by the foot hill of the Capitoline *arx;* here since early times were located the local quarries, the *Lautumiae*, which may also have given their name to this last stretch of the road. After a fairly steep gradient of not less than 10 meters on a total distance of about 50 meters it reached the low ground of the Forum. The levels are necessarily approximate. I have taken as the datum point the level 21.84 on Reina's map *Media pars Urbis*, fol.1, marked at the lowest step of the church of SS.Martina e Luca, taking into due consideration the fact that the flight of steps has been rebuilt in late years. The level of the original lowest step is, however, clearly traceable on the wall of the church to the left of the present stair. The upper point has been given me by the courtesy of Professor A. M. Colini who conducted the excavations carried out in connection with the isolation of the same church in 1941. In his notes he states that close to the church between the same and the Carcer "emerge un frammento di tufo vergine del livello attuale della strada". The actual street level is 1.20 meters lower than the datum point. That means that it would carry the level 20.64 expressed in the same scale used by Reina.[4]

The lowest floor level at the Rostra varies, according to Gjerstad

---

4. I am told by Prof. Colini that the original level may have been even higher, and that the soft surface rock (cappellaccio) which rests on a virgin clay layer probably may have been worn off and dug through at a relatively early stage. This was doubtless the case between the church of SS. Martina e Luca and the Forum Julium, where Republican walls, still visible close to the present entrance of the Forum Julium, are footed on a lower level. A massive curved retaining wall was left *in situ* under the present street Via del Tulliano and its level was still lower than the visible remains just referred to. Cf. also Conferenze del Museo dell'Impero, venerdi 27 giugno 1941, Colini, A. M., "Scoperte tra il Foro di Cesare ed il Carcere," *Bullettino Comm. Archeol.* 69 (1941) (*Bull, del. Museo dell'Imp.Rom.* 12), 91-92.

(*op. cit.*, Pl. 3, p. 112), from 10.17 to 10.36. The difference would thus be maximum 10.47 and minimum 10.28 meters.

The orientation of the last stretch of the *Clivus Argentarius* is fortunately very well defined by the still existing façade of the Carcer. The irregular shape of its upper room and the oblique cutting of the lower room which originally was circular show that the Carcer was planned with due consideration of the orientation of the ancient street.[5]

Converging toward the same point in the Forum there came from the northeast another road, *Argiletum*, the mere name of which testifies to its great antiquity.[6] It now ends in the Forum area at a level with it, but that is the effect of the levelling off and planning of the area in Caesar's time and still more of the time when Domitian monumentalized the zone by transforming a tract of *Argiletum* into his *Forum Transitorium*. The road came from the Esquiline hill, crossing the sloping quarters of the *Subura*, and must have ended in a slope toward the lowest point of the valley where it met the *Clivus Argentarius* at an angle of about 58°. Ancient and modern levelling off of the ground prevent us, however, from giving any even such approximate figures for the levels of the declivity, as it was possible to produce in the case of the *Clivus Argentarius*.[7]

This sector of a hill slope was to become the political meeting place of the Roman people. Its lowest point, where the two bordering streets met, was from the very beginning of the history of the Comitium the place of the speaker's platform, the *suggestus*, later known as the Rostra. It faced at a somewhat diverging angle the gentle concavity of the hillslope where the participants in the comitia had their seats. This diverging angle disturbs the symmetry of the layout, and is not easy to explain. It may, however, be kept in mind that the front of the Rostra faces straight North and is thus oriented in the same way as all the earliest monuments in the Forum area, which in their orientation seem to have respected the four cardinal points. This was particularly valid for sanctuaries, and the Rostra

---

5. It should be observed that the present façade of the Carcer in travertine which dates from the time of Tiberius is not quite parallel to the original one, the orientation of which is traceable in a wall of Grotta Oscura tufa in the lower chamber. Cf. Frank, T., *Roman Buildings of the Republic*, 40, fig. 5. In reconstructing the original orientation one has evidently to follow the earlier wall.

6. *Varro, de lin.lat.* 5, 157 cannot decide upon any safe etymology of the archaic name.

7. Lugli, *Roma Antica, il centro monumentale*, 78, presumes that before Basilica Aemilia was built in 179 B. C. the *Argiletum* followed a direction more straightly oriented East-West, thus meeting the *Clivus Argentarius* at an almost right angle. It seems however more likely that the shape of the NW end of the basilica was in fact determined by the pre-existing street. Its striking irregularity remains otherwise unexplained and unexplainable.

was for several reasons considered a holy place. Even Cicero refers to it as *templum auguratum* (in *Vatin.* 24).

Pliny's well known notice (*nat.hist.* 7, 60, 212), concerning the herald who had to proclaim the hour of noon from the steps of the Curia when the sun was between the Rostra and the Graecostasis, may also reflect the ritual necessity of this traditional orientation. It should further be noted that the Rostra façade forms a right angle with the lower stretch of the *Clivus Argentarius,* thus connecting these two elements in an architecturally satisfactory way. Finally, the queer obtuse angle at the back of the Rostra, a feature as yet essentially unexplained,[8] lies in the prolongation of the *Argiletum,* a fact that seems to link the platform to the bordering street on this side (fig. 2). The impression remains that the architect of the assembly place was not entirely free in his planning, but that, within the limits of a rigid ritual orientation, he made the best of the possibilities offered by the natural configuration of the terrain and the pre-existing streets.

The speaker on the Rostra thus turned his back to the Forum and addressed the crowd seated in the theatre-like area limited by the two streets just mentioned. Ancient tradition (Cic. *de rep.* 2, 17, 31) affirms that the Comitium was *saeptum,* enclosed, a technical term which should not be interpreted as "walled in", but which merely refers to the religious ceremony of its inauguration when the place was marked out by *cippi,* boundary stones. It had its natural border-lines and needed no enclosure except toward the South where the long speaker's platform, on which there was also ample space for the magistrates, effectively screened it off from the Forum area.

Such was the primitive shape of the Comitium, which remained essentially the same as long as it functioned as an important political meeting place. It was ideally suited to an assembly, allowing the crowd to see and hear the speaker well, and the speaker to survey his audience and follow its reactions as an actor on the stage the audience in the *cavea* of a theatre.[9]

The ancient literary evidence referring to the Comitium does not in any point contradict such a view. It seems on the contrary to give an easy and satisfactory explanation of some of the passages of the ancient authors that are patently difficult to reconcile with the pre-

---

8. Cf. Gjerstad, *op. cit.,* 142.

9. It should be noted that Colini suggests a similar original shape of the Comitium in C. Ricci, A. M. Colini & V. Mariani, *Via dell'Impero,* Itinerari dei Musei e monumenti d'Italia, Vol. 24, 50: "Le falde del Campidoglio disposte a guisa di cavea, offrivano a questa piazza famosa il terreno piu acconcio". Similarly A. Boëthius in his Swedish book "*Hur Rom byggdes under antiken*", 46. His passage reads in translation: "In the hill-slope of the Capitolium above the Rostra was apparently the old meeting place of the popular assembly".

vailing ideas of the general layout and shape of the place. Some of these have to be discussed here.

1. Pliny, *nat.hist.* 34, 26, speaking about various statues in Rome, says: "invenio et Pythagorae et Alcibiadi in cornibus comitii positas" which were still standing there until "Sulla dictator ibi curiam faceret". Petersen has rightly understood the meaning of *cornua* as an architectural term.[10] It is not the corners of a square or rectangular building, nor the extremities of a piazza, nor the entrance to a square, as has been put forward by various authors, but the flanking ends of a semicircular building and particularly the flanks of a theatre *cavea* facing the stage.[11] Vitruvius always uses it in this sense, as becomes especially clear in his prescription of how to dispose the "sounding vessels" designed to improve the acoustics of the cavea (*de arch.* 5,5,2) and how to place flanking entrances to the orchestra (*ibid.* 5,6,5). Petersen was led astray in his further conclusions mainly by his false preconception that the theatre-shaped area, at the ends of which the statues stood, was the Rostra, not the Comitium itself. This led him to topographical absurdities, which have rightly been discarded by subsequent writers, but unfortunately his basically correct linguistic interpretation of *cornua comitii* has also been overlooked, and no one has undertaken a closer analysis of the passage quoted.

Taking into consideration the shape of the assembly place, the commanding position of the two statues becomes immediately clear: they were flanking—one on each side—the curved concavity of the Comitium area, and there they remained until the Curia Cornelia succeeded the old Curia Hostilia.

2. Livy, 1,36, tells the story of the miracle performed by the augur Attus Navius in the time of Tarquinius Priscus and of a statue of him put up on the place where he accomplished the miraculous act "in comitio in gradibus ipsis ad laevam curiae" (1,36,5). This phrase has invariably been understood as locating the statue to the left on the flight of steps leading up to the Curia, whereas it more correctly should be translated: "on the very steps in the Comitium to the left of the Curia". The expression seems to indicate that Livy imagined the Comitium provided with steps like the *cavea* of a theatre, particularly as *gradus* is a specific term for the seats in a theatre.[12]

Comparing this with the very non-committal localization given to the statue by Dionysius of Halicarnassus (3,71,5), who testifies to

---

10. Petersen, E., *Comitium, Rostra, Grab des Romulus*, 17, n. 14.

11. All the relevant instances are presented in *Thesaurus L. L.*, s.v. (vol. 4, col. 970-971).

12. *Thesaurus L. L.*, s.v. (6.2 col. 2150, 2, specialia).

having seen the statue with his own eyes "in front of the Curia near the sacred fig tree", one finds that its presumed place on the stair-case of the Curia itself seems excluded. It is localized by the refer-ence to the holy fig tree which surely must have grown in the Comi-tium area, not in the staircase of the Senate-house.

3. Dion.Hal. 4,38,5. tells the well known story of the death of Servius Tullius at the hand of his son-in-law Tarquinius Superbus. Tarquinius throws Servius κατὰ τῶν κρηπίδων τοῦ βουλευτηρίου τῶν εἰς τὸ ἐκκλησιαστήριον φερουσῶν. The meaning is quite clear. The old king was thrown down the steps of the Curia that descended to the Comitium, but attention should be called to the use of the word κρηπίδες. Κρηπίς as an architectural term signifies the substructure, basement or foundation of a building in general. Herodotus (1,185) uses it more specifically as the stepped quay of the river Euphrates. On an inscription from Delos (*IG* XI(2),203 A 95), dating from the third century B. C., it is used as the technical term for the seats of the theatre (τὰς κρηπίδας τὰς ἐν τῷ θεάτρῳ), while it never occurs in the sense of "flight of steps leading up to a building". The correct word there would rather be κλίμαξ, ἀναβαθμός or ἀναβάσεις.[13]

The use of κρηπίδες to signify the steps, as well as the fatal effect of the fall, seem best explained by presuming that Dionysius imag-ined the scene as taking place at the door of the Curia overlooking the theatrically sloping "cavea" of the Comitium, at the bottom of which Servius Tullius met his death.

4. Livy, 1,48,3 tells the same story using the phrase ". . . e curia in inferiorem partem per gradus deiecit". Here, from the mere sequence of the phrase, it seems abundantly clear that the *gradus* cannot refer to the steps of the Curia, but to the *pars inferior* which is the sloping area of the seating place of the Comitium, where again the use of the word *gradus* suggests an analogy with the seats in a theatre.

The general conclusions to which the evidence here presented leads us can be summarized as follows.

The arrangement and planning of the Comitium was from the be-ginning determined by the configuration of the terrain. The hillslope to the North of the Forum was limited by two converging roads and formed a concave theatre-like sector. This was the seating place of the people, covering an area of about 2,900 square meters and thus accommodating more than 5.800 people. To judge from independent literary evidence the *cavea* must—at least during some period of its long life—have been partly or totally provided with steps for the

13. Cfr. Liddell-Scott, s.v.

comfort of the audience. We know also that on certain occasions it could temporarily be partly roofed in, probably by large awnings (Livy 27,368), a system well known from later evidence regarding theatre performances.

In the "cavea" there were several statues and monuments of historical importance. Particularly noteworthy were the statues of Pythagoras and Alcibiades "in cornibus comitii".

Dominating the Comitium, at the top of the cavea and probably oriented North-South lay the old Curia, looking down over the meeting place and facing the Rostra to the South. The long stepped platform with the old *sacellum* at the tomb of Romulus and the ships' beaks from Antium provided ample space for the speaker, seating space for the magistrates and a special platform for foreign embassies, the "Graecostasis."

The *cappellaccio* blocks and Republican walls, unearthed by recent excavations and again partly covered between the Carcer and the *tabernae* of the Forum Julium, may have belonged to the original Curia Hostilia or to some other adjacent building, as Lugli very appropriately suggests.[14]

The Comitium was easily accessible from the Forum area and from the two main arteries bordering the "saeptum", probably by an open entrance on each side of the Rostra, placed like the "parodoi" of a theatre. The area could of course also be reached from above by way of the Curia, which was in direct communication with the Comitium.

A negative conclusion has also to be drawn. All topographical reconstructions—made mainly at the writing desk—which place buildings of various types and names in the area occupied by the *cavea*, have to be ruled out as contradicting the main layout of the Comitium and its proper functioning, as well as lacking convincing literary arguments in their favor. There is no place for a *Basilica Porcia*, nor for a *Tribunal Praetoris*, nor for a *Graecostasis* in the seating space itself. They have to be relegated to unknown sites in the immediate vicinity.

Between this meeting place of the Roman popular assembly and its Athenian counterpart, the Pnyx, there are striking similarities. Thanks to the excavations carried out by Kourouniotes and Thompson in 1930-1931 and published in 1932 we are well informed about the history and the architectural development of the site.[15]

---

14. Lugli, *Roma Antica*, 95.

15. K. Kourouniotes and Homer A. Thompson, "The Pnyx in Athens, A Study Based on Excavations Conducted by the Greek Archaeological Service," *Hesperia*, 1 (1932) 90-217, pl. I-IV. An able discussion of the material including later bibliography is found in McDonald, W. A., *The Political Meeting Places of the Greeks*, 67-80.

The Athenian assembly place went through three main periods of development, of which only Period 1 concerns us here. From a chronological viewpoint its *terminus ante quem* is very convincingly fixed by Thompson to the year of the Thirty Tyrants in 404/03 B. C., and it seems highly probable that it was laid out at the very beginning of the fifth century. It is, thus, the political meeting place of the Athenian hegemony and of the great fifth century.[16] How was it constructed?

The natural slope of the Pnyx hill was carefully dressed and cut so as to form a gently sloping, theatre-like concavity, and at the centre, at its lowest point, a platform was built to serve as the speaker's podium, flanked by long retaining walls on each side. The place was otherwise not walled in, but marked out by boundary stones, one of which came to light in the excavations. The entrance was from the East, at the end of the retaining wall on the left of the speaker's platform (fig.1). The total area covered about 2.400 square meters and could easily accommodate about 5.000 persons, a figure rarely reached in the assembly before the Peloponnesian war (Thuc.8,72).

There were no cuttings for seats and the audience had either to sit directly on the sloping rock floor or bring their own cushions or seats, following the same system used in the early days of the Athenian theatre.

The long walls on each side of the speaker's platform functioned as a terrace wall retaining a low horizontal podium of stamped and hard packed earth on which seats could evidently be placed for the presiding magistrates or for foreign delegations pleading their causes.

With the exception of the fact — conditioned by natural premises — that the assembly place in Rome covers a narrower and deeper sector than that in Athens and the rigid orientation of the Roman Rostra, the identity in planning and layout between the two seems obvious (see reconstructive sketches, figs. 1 and 2). The differences are to be found in details: the Athenian assembly was surely not stepped; the Roman one possibly was so. The former seems to have had few or no commemorative monuments — at least there is no evidence for this; the latter was in the early Republic the favorite place for statues and historical monuments; the Curia was situated in close contact with the Comitium, whereas the bouleuterion was in the agora. But these differences cannot obscure the fundamental identity in plan of the two most famous assembly places in the Ancient World.

I am quite convinced that the likeness between the two is based on historical relations.

16. *Hesperia, loc. cit.*, 109, 216.

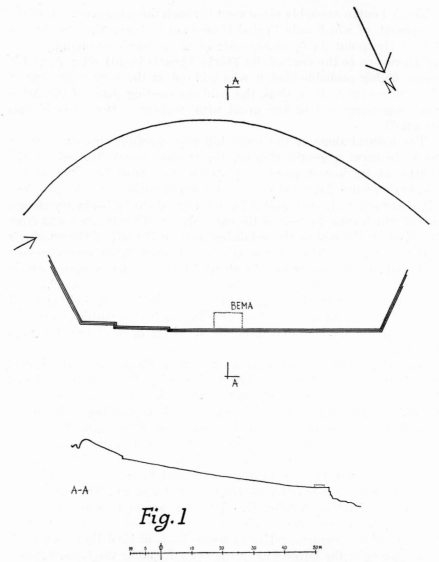

Figure 1. Reconstructive sketch of the Athenian Pnyx during Period I.
Plan and section. (After H. Thompson.)

Gjerstad[17] has shown that the first traces of the Roman Comitium
are dateable to the year of the fall of the decemvirs, i.e. 449/48 B.C.
In 449 B.C. the assembly place was still at the altar of Vulcanus above
the Forum Romanum; from then onwards it became the Comitium.

17. Gjerstad, *op. cit.*, 148.

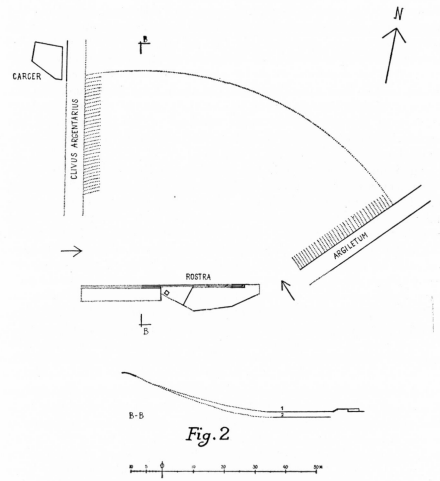

CARCER

CLIVUS ARGENTARIUS

N

B

ARGILETUM

ROSTRA

B

B-B

Fig. 2

Figure 2. Reconstructive sketch of the Roman Comitium.

This was a year of singular importance in the social and constitutional history of Rome. The new bill of rights, as reflected in the laws of the Twelve Tables, was codified and took effect that year. The Valerio-Horatian laws opened a new chapter in the long history of the struggle for the sovereignty of the magistrature and the popular assembly. With the fall of the decemvirs and their handing over of the executive power to the regular magistrature and the supreme power to the comitia, the Comitium was born as a political meeting place.

The tradition of how the Laws of the Twelve Tables were prepared and compiled is unanimous and clear. Both Livy (3,31,8) and Dionysius of Halicarnassus (10,52,4) tell us that in the year 453 B.C. the

Romans sent a committee of three men, Sp.Postumius, A.Manlius and P.Sulpicius (the latter called by Dionysius Servius Sulpicius), with the special task of studying "the famous laws of Solon, and to learn the institutions, way of life, and laws of other Greek city-states" (Livy). They remained away for almost three years and returned to Rome in 451 B.C. after having spent their time in Athens and the cities of Magna Graecia (Dion.Hal.10,54,3), and as respected experts in foreign law were called in as members of the committee of the decemvirs (Livy 3,33,5), the plenipotentiary body that ruled Rome until the plebeian revolution of 449 B.C.

The influence of Athenian law on this early Roman legislation must have been strong and direct.[18] Cicero (*de leg.* 2,25) testifies to that effect, regarding the Solonian law against luxuries in tombs and burial rites "quam legem eisdem prope verbis nostri decemviri in decimam tabulam coniecerunt." A statue of Hermodorus, philosopher and law-giver of Ephesus in the fifth century, is said to have been dedicated at an early date in the Comitium as a token of the Roman acknowledgement of their debt. "There was also in the Comitium a publicly dedicated statue of Hermodorus of Ephesus, the interpreter of the laws that the decemvirs wrote" says Pliny (*nat.hist.* 34,21).[19]

With the laws and the constitutional influence came also the architectural plan of the political meeting place from Athens to Rome. The intimate bond between the new laws and the new assembly place, which together came into being in the same year, was further emphasized when the Romans fixed the twelve bronze tables on the central monument of the Comitium, the Rostra. "After the legislation they had undertaken had been concluded, the consuls engraved the laws on twelve bronze tablets and affixed them to the Rostra before the Curia" says Diodorus Siculus (12,26,1), and there they were admired down to his own day.[20] The tablets, the laws and the Comitium itself were a reminder to the Romans of the early Republic, of their obligations to the oldest democracy of the world, and should historically be re-

---

18. Cfr. Boesch, F., *De XII tabularum lege a Graecis petita* (Diss.Göttingen) 1893, a book that I have had no opportunity of consulting.

19. Regarding the identity of Hermodorus and other literary sources referring to his Roman connections, see Münzer, s.v., in *RE* vol. 8.1, col. 859-861.

20. Diodorus calls the speaker's platform by its later denomination, Rostra, οἱ ἔμβολοι, though that name was attached to the platform only after 338 B. C. when the Antiate ships' beaks were fixed on the old "suggestus". This is a slight and easily understandable anachronism of no importance.

garded by us as a rare but clear instance of direct contact between
Athens and Rome, manifest in an important architectural creation,
before the great influx of Greek ideas and art in the Hellenistic
period.[21]

21. Professor Boethius points out to me how well this tallies with his ideas
of the Hippodamian influence on Italic town planning in the fifth century, as
expressed in his paper *Roman and Greek Town Architecture*, Göteborgs Högskolas
årsskrift, Vol. 54, 1948:3, 7.

THE AGGER OF SERVIUS TULLIUS

EINAR GJERSTAD
University of Lund

Plates 22-24

It was my intention to contribute with a paper on the city-wall of
the kings of Rome but, as sometimes happens, the article expanded far
beyond the limit of a contribution of this kind and I had therefore to
confine myself to one single problem of those connected with that
subject. After some days of deliberation I have chosen to discuss the
question, whether there is evidence for a continuous agger across the
Quirinal, Viminal, and Esquiline earlier than that of the Republican
city-wall, or in other words, whether there is some historical reality
behind the tradition of the agger built by Servius Tullius.

In 1907, when the foundations were laid for the new building of the
Ministero dell'Agricoltura, several remains of the Republican city-
wall of Rome were discovered and destroyed. A general report on
these discoveries has been published by Vaglieri[1] and Boni has devoted
a careful study[2] to that particular section of the city-wall still extant
in the garden of the Ministero dell'Agricoltura, where only the external revetment of Grotta Oscura tufa is preserved,[3] the earth of the
agger abutting against it at the time of its discovery having been
removed to fill in the depression between Pincio and Giardino del Lago.
Boni arrived on the spot at the last moment when the explosions of
the bursting charges had already damaged those walls which, doomed
to destruction, awaited the finishing blow of the picks, and he was
therefore only able to examine the piece of the wall mentioned. We
must be grateful that this important remnant of antiquity happened
to be investigated by Boni who was much ahead of his time in archaeological method, a scrupulous observer, the pioneer of stratigraphical
excavation in Italy. It seems that this part of agger was the last one
available for study. In view of the fact that the parts of the agger
removed before that time had not been examined in such a way that
their history had been made clear (cf. below), our knowledge of this
subject would probably always have remained hypothetical if Boni
had not succeeded in saving the last piece of evidence.

---

1. *NSc* 1907, 504 ff.
2. *Ibid.*, 1910, 509 ff.
3. This piece of the city-wall is Quir. G. in the classification of G. Säflund,
"Le mura di Roma repubblicana," *Acta Inst. Rom. Regni Sueciae* I, 1932, 82 ff.
The other pieces of the wall now disappeared are Quir. h[I-IV] in Säflund's classification (*op. cit.*, 84 f.).

From Boni's description and graphical documentation (pl. 22, a) we learn that the agger abutting against the facing wall of Grotta Oscura blocks consisted of five strata.[4] Of these, strata 1 and 2 are similar to each other, consisting of compact tufa earth in somewhat intermingled layers mixed with scoriae and coarse *ejectamenta*. These layers of uniform consistency contained ceramic material partly homogeneous (cf. below), and there is nothing to indicate that they represented different building-periods; they are evidently to be interpreted as successive fillings of the same agger. Stratum 3, on the other hand, is of a different kind, is composed of dark-grey pozzolana, and it represents a heightening of the agger added on a later occasion. Stratum 4 was less compact than the subjacent layers, and as regards stratum 5, the top layer, Boni is uncertain whether it belonged to the undisturbed filling of the agger or not, and it is therefore left out of account by him.

Examining the relation of the agger to the revetment wall of Grotta Oscura tufa we observe the important fact that only strata 4 and 5 abut against the wall, while strata 1-3 have been cut through down to the bottom level of the blocks, stratum 4 filling up the interstice between the wall and the cut of strata 1-3; only the blocks of the bottom course abut against the cut of stratum 1. The explanation of this stratigraphical situation is very simple and evident: strata 1-3 are remains of an agger earlier than the wall of Grotta Oscura, which has been built into this earlier agger, the upper front part of which was cut away for the purpose.[5] On top of the early agger the earth of the later one was accumulated abutting against the inside of the tufa wall. There is a characteristic difference between the top level of the two *aggeres*: the surface of the late agger is horizontal, while that of the early agger is slightly convex.[6] The dimensions of the early agger are unknown, both its width and height. Only by digging to the bottom of the agger information in the matter could have been obtained, but such digging was apparently not carried out.[6a]

---

4. The layers are counted from the bottom.

5. Boni himself suggested this explanation, *op. cit.*, 510: In questa zoccolatura di tufo incoerente e rimescolato (probabilmente avanzo del *murus terreus* di un vallo più antico) contro la quale sono addossati i blocchi interni dei due primi strati . . . ." etc. It appears from his words that he considered only stratum 1 as a probable relic of an earlier agger. This is apparently a misinterpretation of his own graphical evidence.

6. Of course I disregard the very curved top of stratum 3, which is not an original shape but obtained by the digging of the foundation pit for the tufa-wall. The surface of stratum 2 shows, however, the slightly convex top of the original agger.

6a. At least it is not mentioned by Boni, nor recorded by his graphical documentation. Boni states only that the blocks of the Grotta Oscura wall were founded in a vertical cut of the agger, on the compact earth of its filling, but not how far this filling continued beneath the foundation level of the blocks.

The date of the later agger is given by the date of the Grotta Oscura wall, which with good reason has been assigned to 378 B. C.[7] An approximate date for the earlier agger is afforded by the pottery found in the earth. In the stratum 3 no finds are reported. In strata 1 and 2 Boni discovered fragments of a type of tile, which he assigns to the beginning of the Republican period. In stratum 1 he found fragments of advanced red impasto jars and some painted pottery, which from the description cannot be exactly dated but seem to belong to the 6th century B. C.[8] In stratum 2 a potsherd of a more significant kind came to light: "un frammento di vaso attico del V secolo av. Cr., a figure nere, delle quali non è però dato di riconoscere la rappresentanza."[9]

This black-figured fragment intrigued me. Where was it? I hunted for it for a long time but in vain, until one day, while working in the store-room of the Forum Museum, I came across a parcel with the annotation: "Da vari luoghi di Roma." I opened the parcel and among others found an envelope with the following label: Mure urbane a S.Susanna. II strato.—On the envelope there was also a sketch of the wall and agger in the garden of Ministero del'Agricoltura (pl. 23, a). The find-spot and identity of objects enclosed in the envelope cannot therefore be doubted.[9a] These objects are (pl. 23, b, c, d): fragments of flat and semicircular tiles, as described by Boni, and a fragment of an Attic early Red figured kylix, not a Black figured fragment as stated by Boni. It is thus evident that Boni made a *lapsus calami,* writing "figure nere" instead of "figure rosse." Sir John Beazley, whose expert knowledge of the subject I have consulted, is of the opinion that the sherd dates from 490-470 B. C.; though to put the limits as wide as possible we should say 520-470 B. C.[10] Since we must reckon with a time of about 20 years between the production of the vase and the occurrence of one of its fragments in the filling of the agger, the conclusion would be that, on the one hand, the agger must be earlier than 378 B. C., on the other hand, it cannot be earlier than the first half of the 5th century B. C. Until contradicted by other evidence we may suppose that the earliest possible date of the agger is really that

7. Säflund, *op. cit.,* 231 ff.

8. *NSc* 1910, 511: Altri cocci di pasta più fine, uno dei quali color rossiccio e un altro bianco-gialliccio, adorno esternamente di fascietta scura a filettatura gialla che ricorda la tecnica dei vasi protocorinzi." This seems to refer to painted Italo-geometric pottery.

9. *Loc. cit.*

9a. So far I have not been able to find the pottery fragments of Stratum 1. For kind permission to publish the finds from the agger I wish to express my great gratitude to Professor P. Romanelli.

10. I quote from a letter of Sir John Beazley: "The rf. fragment. This must be 520-470 B. C. I set the limits as wide as possible. My impression is that it is 490-470."

of its construction, and I am therefore inclined to consider it to have formed part of the agger of Servius Tullius.

This last statement needs explanation. We know that ancient speculation has fixed the reign of Servius Tullius at 578-538 B. C. Though no critical scholar would accept these dates as reliable, very few would place the end of his reign later than, say c. 525-520 B. C., in view of the fact that the subsequent reign of Tarquinius Superbus ceased with the introduction of the Republic which is usually considered to have happened in 509 B. C.[11] During my studies in the early history of Rome I have, however, come to the conclusion that both the initial and final dates of the Regal period should be somewhat revised. This is not the proper place for a full discussion of the problem, which would transgress the limits of this paper, and I must therefore confine myself to a few statements and limits of evidence.[12]

The evidence for fixing the date of the foundation of Rome is purely archaeological. Boni's stratigraphical excavations near Equus Domitiani and other places in the Forum Romanum[13] and my own stratigraphical soundings in the Forum Romanum have proved that the foundation of Rome, i.e. the *synoikismos* of the earlier villages into a city, may be assigned to c. 575 B. C. *Ab urbe condita* is thus the time after c. 575 B. C., which at the same time is the initial date of the period of the kings of Rome.

The end of the Regal period can be chronologically determined on the basis of both archaeological and literary material. Generally it is believed that we are informed about the introduction of the Republic by the *Fasti*, the first year of the Fasti being considered as the year of the Republic. This is a fundamental misinterpretation of the Fasti, which tell us nothing about the initial date of the Republic but only about the initial date of the introduction of the eponym system of counting years.[14] The synchronization of the first year of Fasti with that of the first year of the Republic is due to an inference by the Roman annalists, but such an inference is too hasty. The introduction of an eponym system of counting years is not identical with a change of the form of government: we have, as pointed out by Hanell, many instances of eponym magistrates during a monarchical govern-

---

11. For the sake of convenience I use the Varronian dates.

12. Meanwhile I refer to an article (in Swedish) published in *Historisk Tidskrift*, 1949, 321 ff.: Roms grundläggning och dess kungar (The Foundation of Rome and Its Kings).

13. The results of these excavations are still unpublished but will be published by me before very long together with the results of my supplementary excavations.

14. Hanell, K., "Das traditionelle Anfangsjahr der römischen Republik," in *Dragma Martino P. Nilsson* (*Acta Inst. Rom. Regni Sueciae*, Series altera, I), 1939, 256 ff.; "Das altröm. eponyme Amt" (*Acta Inst. Rom Regni Sueciae*, Series altera, II), 1946, 96 ff.

ment. There are strong indications that the monarchy was not abolished before the middle of the 5th century B. C. Already Pais[15] has expressed such ideas, as well as Kornemann[16] and more recently Hanell.[17] I am convinced that this dating is approximately correct and wish to point out some indication in favor of it.

During the Archaic period Rome was politically and culturally incorporated into the Etruscan sphere of dominion. 500 B. C. marks no change of the cultural situation. Etruscan culture continues to flourish in Rome until c. 450 B. C., when the cultural contact with Etruria was broken. This is also confirmed by my excavations in the Forum Romanum: a monumental building of tufa blocks from the Regal period was intentionally destroyed c. 450 B. C. and on top of it, and on the last floor of the period of the kings, a new floor was laid, which is contemporary with the first Republican floor in the Comitium.[18]

Further, we have indications referring to foreign politics. The Etruscan dominion in Campania was unbroken until 474 B. C. when it received a severe blow through the victory of Hieron at Cumae, but it was not crushed until 445 B. C. through the Samnite invasion.[19] It is hard to believe that Rome would have been able to liberate itself from the Etruscan domination while this was unbroken, but it is easy to understand if the liberation took place in connexion with the disintegration of the Etruscan domination South of Rome.

One should also pay attention to the indication of inner politics. So far as we know, 509 B. C. was a tranquil year in Rome, while the middle of the 5th century B. C. was an agitated time. I may recall the following facts: the codification of the actual law, *lex XII tabularum*, established in 451 and 450 B. C.; the second *secessio* of the plebeians in 449 and the extension of the authority for the *tribuni plebis* effected in the same year; *lex Canuleia* made in 445; the military tribunate established in 444 and the censorship in 443 B. C. All this indicates conflicts, a social crisis, in the middle of the 5th Cent., a situation that is much more likely to give rise to a change of the mode of government than the tranquil years around 509 B. C.[20]

---

15. Pais, E., *Storia critica de Roma* I, 1913, 602; *id., Storia di Roma*[3] II, 1926, 241.

16. Kornemann, E., "Die Anfänge der röm. Republik," *Internat. Monatschr. f. Wiss. Kunst u. Techn.* 14, 1920, 481 ff.; in his *Röm. Gesch.* I, 1938, 72 ff. he has so far modified his opinion that he dates the introduction of the Roman Republic to the period between 500 and 474 B. C.

17. Hanell, *Das altröm. eponyme Amt*, 206.

18. Cf. *Opusc. archaeol.* II (*Acta Inst. Rom. Regni Sueciae* V), 1941, 112 ff., 146 ff.

19. *CAH* VII, 584.

20. Not until 15 years later, viz. 495 (new territorial division in tribes and the first institution of centuries) and 494 (the first *secessio* of the plebeians and

These are indications of a general kind, but there are also others of a more particular character referring to individual kings reigning after 509 B. C.[20a] The temple of Jupiter Optimus Maximus was dedicated in 509 B. C. Tradition tells us that Tarquinius Priscus started building this temple which was completed by Tarquinius Superbus, but there is no tradition connecting Servius Tullius with the erection of the temple.[21] As it cannot reasonably be supposed that the building of the temple was interrupted during the whole reign of Servius Tullius, the original and true tradition seems to have been distorted, and it is not difficult to understand how this happened. The original tradition mentioned a king Tarquinius viz. Priscus, as the builder of the temple. As the date of the dedication of the temple fixed by the Fasti at 509 B. C. could not be changed, Tarquinius Superbus, the last king, had also to be connected with the building of the temple when in current opinion that year became the first year of the Republic. According to the original tradition we may assume that Tarquinius Priscus was still reigning in 509 B. C. The conquest of Crustumerium was made by him.[22] I believe that he was still reigning in 500 B. C. In Livy 2, 19 we find the following notice regarding the events of 500 B. C.: *Fidenae obsessae, Crustumeria capta.* Already Niebuhr[23] has seen that we have here an annalistic notice attached to the *Fasti,* a notice that has been preserved in its original, laconic form.[24] By combining the tradition of Tarquinius Priscus as the conqueror of Crustumerium with the notice of the *Fasti* about the time of that conquest, we may draw the conclusion that Tarquinius Priscus still reigned in 500 B. C.; but soon afterwards he must have died, because Servius Tullius had taken over the government in 495 B. C. Tradition connects him, as we know, with the institution of centuries and the new division of the Roman territory in tribes. These were originally 21 in number.[25] If we read Livy II, 21, we detect two notices of fact

---

the institution of the plebeian tribunate) we observe the earliest and clear symptoms of the social tension culminating in the middle of the century and causing that social transformation during which the Republic was born.

20a. For the kings reigning before 509 B. C. there are no such references simply because the *Fasti* were not then existing.

21. Only Tacitus, *Hist.* 3, 72 mentions also Servius Tullius as having had charge of the construction of the temple, a late and worthless notice evidently created on account of the surprising omission by tradition of this king as a builder of the temple.

22. Livy, I, 38, 4; Dionysius III, 49.

23. Niebuhr, G., *Röm. Geschichte* II, 1873, 5.

24. A systematic and critical excerption of such early annalistic notices preserved in the later historic literature will provide us with much valuable research material and help us to regain a part of the true tradition.

25. Hirschfeld, O., *Kleine Schriften*, 1913, 248 ff. These 21 tribes consisted of the 4 urban tribes and the 17 earliest rustic tribes, the sixteen with gentilic names and Tribus Clustumina, erected on the territory of Crustumerium conquered 5 years earlier as mentioned above.

referring to the year 495 B. C.: *Romae tribus una et viginti factae. Aedes Mercuri dedicata est idibus Maiis.* We can recognize the laconic annalistic style. The tradition of Servius Tullius as originator of the centuries and the new tribes is true, but only if his reign is assigned to the early part of the 5th century B. C.

When Servius Tullius died, we do not know, but we are not without fixed points for a chronological determination of the reign of his successor. Tradition states that Tarquinius Superbus built a temple to Semo Sancus, which was dedicated 466 B. C.[26] In this temple was preserved the *foedus Gabinum,* the treaty settling the relations between Rome and Gabii, which had been conquered by Tarquinius Superbus.[27] We may therefore conclude that he reigned in the sixties of the 5th cent. B. C. A certain L. Tarquinius is mentioned as *Magister equitum* in 458 B. C.,[28] but when we approach the middle of the 5th cent. B. C. the name Tarquinius disappears from Roman history.

To these indications mentioned above we may now add the date of the agger here examined. The tradition of Servius Tullius as the constructor of an agger across the Quirinal, Viminal, and Esquiline has every sign of being genuine[29] nor is there any reason to doubt the statement that Tarquinius Superbus reinforced the agger.[30] In view of this we have to consider the fact that there is evidence of an agger earlier than the first Republican city-wall but not earlier than the beginning of the 5th Cent. B. C. and that this agger seems to have been heightened and widened subsequently. We have seen that the tradition of the Servian constitution is true if assigned to the beginning of the 5th cent. B. C. and in the same way the tradition of the Servian agger is true if assigned to that period.

The agger of Servius Tullius extended from the Quirinal to the Esquiline. Are there any more traces of it? In 1862 Bergau and Pinder published a paper on "Gli avanzi dell'aggere e del muro di Servio Tullio scoperti nella Villa Negroni,"[31] containing a report of the discoveries of important parts of the city-wall and its agger made in 1861 during the works for the railway station of Rome. These observations by Bergau and Pinder were subsequently confirmed by

---

26. Dionysius IX, 60.
27. Dionysius IV, 58.
28. Livy 3, 27, 1. In the *Fasti* he is called Tarquitius. This form occurs also among the inscriptions of the tomb of the Tarquinians in Caere (*CIL*, XI, 3626-34).
29. Livy 1, 44, 3: Addit duos colles, Quirinalem Viminalemque inde deinceps auget Esquilias, ibique ipse, ut loco dignitas fieret, habitat. Aggere et fossis et muro circumdat urbem; *De vir. ill.* 7, 6: Collem Quirinalem et Viminalem et Esquilias urbi addidit; aggerem fossasque fecit.
30. Dionysius IV, 54, 2.
31. *Annali Inst. Corrisp. Archeol.* 1862, 126 ff.

Lanciani and supplemented by him in other parts of the agger.[32] Finally some of the photographs included in Parker's Collection and taken during the course of excavation are important testimonies of evidence.[33]

Bergau and Pinder distinguished two building-periods in the construction of the agger (fig. 1)[33a] and a study of stratification as shown by a photograph,[34] seems to verify their opinion: the agger of stratum 1 composed of yellowish tufa earth has a distinct outline both on top and along the inner escarpment, i.e. there is a clear line of demarcation between this and stratum 2 which consists of darker earth and forms both a lateral and vertical addition to the original

Figure 1. Section of the Agger and its revetting wall near the railway station (Agger i^I). (*Annali Inst. Corrisp. Archeol.* 1862, Tav. d' Agg. k, fig. 2.)

agger.[35] On the other hand, the photograph reveals the schematical rendering of the stratification in the drawing of Bergau and Pinder, and it should be observed that the top of the strata was not exactly horizontal but slightly convex, which is also confirmed by the photograph (pl. 23, e).[36] The top width of the original agger is 9.30 m,[37] its exact base width and height are unknown, as the excavation did not proceed to the bottom of the agger, but the approximate depth of the

---

32. *Op. cit.*, 1871, 59 ff.; *Bull. Com.* II, 1874, 199 ff. Some of Lanciani's rough-drawings (published by Säflund, *op. cit.*, pls. 11: 1 Agger c), 14:2 (porta Viminalis) give valuable information.

33. In particular photos nos. 151, 793 and 3005 (here pls. 22b, 23e, 24a).

33a. The section as stated by Bergau and Pinder is cut at an oblique angle of 42°. A reconstruction of the section cut at right angles is shown fig. 2.

34. Parker, photo no. 151, here pl. 22b (Agger i^I, Säflund, *op. cit.*, 49 ff. fig. 22).

35. Lanciani (*Annali Inst. Corrisp. Archeol.* 1871, 61 f. and *Bull. Com.* II, 1874, 200) has pointed out that the earth of the agger was found stratified in reversed sequence to that found when digging the fossa: cultivated soil is found close to the revetment wall, then follows a layer of tufa earth and finally a layer of dark pozzolana, forming the bottom of the soil dug for the fossa. Thus it is evident that the soil dug for the fossa was used for the accumulation of the agger but it affords no counter-evidence of the probability of the two building-periods of the agger.

36. Parker, photo no. 793.

37. The measurements given here are those of the agger cut at right angles (cf. note 33a); the restored measurements given by Bergau and Pinder (*op. cit.*, Tav. d'Agg. K: 3) and repeated by Säflund (*op. cit.*, 51) are slightly incorrect.

unexcavated part is said to be 1 m. The part excavated has a base width of 13.60 m. and a height of 4.50 m. The top width of the raised agger is 13.05 m. Thus the addition amounts to 3.75 m. At the base the increase in width was still larger, owing to the fact that the escarpment was less steep than that of the original agger, but for the same reason as mentioned the exact base width is unknown. In height the agger was raised 0.90 m. A reconstructed section of the agger based on the drawing of Bergau and Pinder and on the photographic records is given in figure 2.

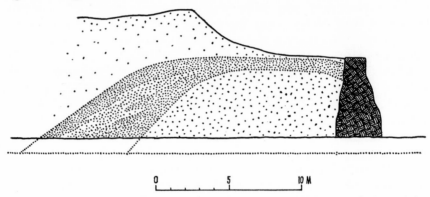

Figure 2. Reconstructed section of the Agger shown in figure 1 and plate 22, b.

On the top of the agger now described there was a heavy filling of earth by which the agger was considerably raised and widened to obtain a final width of 42 m., as shown by the recent discoveries in connection with the works for the new railway station.[38] This enlargement of the agger is well illustrated by fig. 1 and pl. 22, b, where a part of the subsequent filling has been left on top of the earlier agger, but still better by pl. 24, a,[39] which clearly shows the difference in composition between the earth of the lower agger and that of the later addition.

Bergau and Pinder identified stratum 1 of the original agger with that of Servius Tullius and stratum 2 with that of Tarquinius Superbus. As will be shown presently they were probably right, though their premises were false. Like everybody at that time they considered the revetting tufa wall to be that originally built by Servius Tullius and thought the agger in question to be contemporary with the tufa wall. When that was proved to date from the 4th century B. C., the agger, if contemporary with the erection of the wall, would date

38. Information kindly given by Sopraintendente Aurigemma.
39. Parker, photo no. 3005 (Agger E, Piazza Fanti, Säflund, *op. cit.*, 46, fig. 21).

from the same century. Säflund has, however, proposed to assign this agger to an earlier period than the revetting wall and to consider it as remains of a primitive agger, probably without revetment and identical with the one which tradition ascribed to Servius Tullius.[40] He was right, though he could not prove the case, as pointed out by me some time ago.[41] It could not be proved, because the relation of the agger to the revetting wall was unknown. Bergau and Pinder as well as Lanciani and everyone else who had the opportunity of studying the agger before its removal were of the opinion that wall and agger were contemporary and there was nothing to prove the contrary. Though it was evident that the agger must be of an earlier period than the filling on the top of it, both might have belonged to successive building-periods of the tufa wall.

At this critical moment evidence is provided by the agger on the Quirinal examined by Boni. Its original part shows the same structural characteristics as the original agger on the Esquiline: both consist of two distinct strata indicating two periods of construction, a heavy bottom stratum of yellowish tufa earth and a thinner top stratum of darker pozzolana earth; both have a slightly convex top and both are embedded and covered by the later filling of the agger. On account of this structural similarity it cannot be doubted that the original earth-walls on the Quirinal and the Esquiline form parts of the same agger, and as the part on the Quirinal is earlier than revetting tufa wall of 378 B. C. and may be identified with the agger built by Servius Tullius and reinforced by Tarquinius Superbus, the same must hold good for the parts on the Esquiline. The correspondence between the two *aggeres* on the Quirinal and the Esquiline is not, however, only restricted to the original earth-wall but also the later filling of the Republican period accumulated on top of the original agger on the Esquiline, by which it finally obtained a width of 42 m., as mentioned above.

We may thus conclude that the agger of Servius Tullius is a historical fact; it formed the nucleus of the later Republican agger, running along the same line as that across the Quirinal, Viminal, and Esquiline. Outside the agger was a fossa; the earth of the digging of that was accumulated into the agger; the subsequent deepening of the fossa resulted in a raising and enlargement of the agger. Was the Servian agger revetted by a stone-wall like that of the Republican period? There is no evidence for it.[42] Very likely it was an agger

40. Säflund, *op. cit.*, 122 ff., 163 ff., 231, 248 f.
41. *Boll. Assoc. Internaz. Studi Mediterranei* III, 1933, Num. 6, 27.

provided with a wooden palisade but without stone-revetment, similar
to the early earth-walls of Ardea, and Satricum[43] only the gates were
more probably revetted by stone blocks, as we can see, e.g. in Ardea;
but this question must be treated in connection with the problem of the
whole fortification system of Regal Rome, a problem to which I shall
return before very long.

42. Along the line of the agger here discussed or not far from it some cappellaccio walls have been discovered which have been considered, and by some scholars
are still considered, to have formed part of the city-wall of the kings (G. Lugli,
Le mura di Servio Tullio e le cosi dette mura serviane in Historia VII, 1933, 24 ff.;
id. *I monumenti antichi di Roma e Suburbio* II, 1934, 102 ff.). I shall examine this
question in my forthcoming paper on the city-wall of Regal Rome but wish to
state now that none of the cappellaccio walls referred to can be proved to be of
the period of the kings.

43. The agger of Antium (Lugli, "Saggio sulla topografia dell'antica Antium,"
Riv. Ist. d'Arch. e Storia dell'Arte VII, 1940, 153 ff.), may contain remains of
an early earth-wall, but the agger now visible does not seem to be later than
the 4th cent. B. C. Its construction needs further examination.

OECUS AEGYPTIUS

AMEDEO MAIURI
Direttore degli scavi di Pompei e di Ercolano

Tavole 25-26

Tra le più belle case dei nuovi scavi di Ercolano è la "Casa dell'Atrio a mosaico" che, al pari della "Casa dei cervi," della "Casa della gemma" e della "Casa del rilievo di Telefo," aperta con verande, terrazze e stanze di siesta e di soggiorno verso la veduta del mare, riassume meglio d'ogni altra il gusto, le abitudini, il costume di vita della classe signorile ercolanese negli ultimi anni di vita della città.[1] Sottoposta alle stesse gravi conseguenze del terremoto dell'anno 63/2 d.C., subì anch'essa, in quegli ultimi sedici anni, più o meno radicali trasformazioni di strutture e di decorazione.[2]

Nella "Casa dell'Atrio a mosaico" apparve, fin dai primi momenti dello scavo, la forma del tablino chiuso al fondo, sviluppandosi il quartiere del peristilio di fianco e non nell'asse dell'atrio. Di tablini chiusi che costituiscono a volte l'ambiente più nobile dell'abitazione, non mancano esempi nell'edilizia pompeiana ed ercolanese in case di proporzioni modeste e con scarsa e ridotta possibilità di sviluppo; ma in questa casa il tablino si presentò di un tipo affatto nuovo.

Eseguiti lo scavo ed i restauri con la maggiore diligenza, ne è risultata una sala quadrangolare (m. 6,80 x m. 8,20) divisa da una doppia serie di pilastri in tre navate, di cui la maggiore costituisce la vera e propria area della sala con soffitto alto, mentre le minori, assai più strette e con soffitto basso e piano, non possono avere che funzione di semplici ambulacri laterali.[3] La poca elevazione dei pilastri (m. 2,40) e la notevole differenza di livello fra soffitto centrale e soffitti laterali, apparivano giustificate dalle finestre che si aprono, tre da ogni lato, al di sopra di ciascun intercolunnio e delle quali si rinvennero chiare e sufficienti tracce; anzi di una di esse, verso l'angolo sud-est, erano interamente conservati l'altezza e il vano di apertura. Quel

---

1. Per la descrizione di queste case e i caratteri dell'edilizia ercolanese vedi cenni preliminari in A. Maiuri, *Ercolano — Itinerari dei Musei e Monumenti d'Italia*, 3ˆ ed., Roma, 1946.

2. Delle conseguenze che ebbe il terremoto sugli edifici di Pompei ho trattato in A. Maiuri, *L'ultima fase edilizia di Pompei*, Istituto di Studi Romani, 1942; delle conseguenze sugli edifici di Ercolano, dirò particolarmente nella pubblicazione in preparazione sui nuovi scavi. Sulla data controversa del terremoto (63 o 62 d. C.) vedi A. Van Buren in Pauly-Wissowa, *R.E.* s.v., *Pompeji*; *AJP* 68 (1947) 383; Onoroto, O. in *RendLinc* 1949, 544.

3. Lo scavo ed i restauri di questa abitazione ebbero luogo dal giugno dell'anno 1929 al luglio 1930.

tablino, come si disse nei primi brevi cenni descrittivi, aveva una vera e propria pianta basilicale, in cui la maggiore elevazione delle pareti della navata centrale era utilizzata per l'apertura dei vani di luce.[4] Era un indiretto richiamo agli *oeci aegyptii* che Vitruvio accomuna alle basiliche (lib. VI, 3, 9), e tale richiamo fu fatto esplicitamente dallo Harsh.[5]

Ma poichè il tablino ercolanese resta ancora unico esempio di tal genere di *oeci* e le vicende di guerra hanno ritardato la pubblicazione dei nuovi scavi di Ercolano, mi è gradito di illustrare, in onore del benemerito scavatore ed illustratore di Olynthos, questa singolare e preziosa testimonianza delle ultime influenze ellenistiche sulla casa romana (tavv. 25-26 e figg. 1-2).[6]

Il carattere lussuoso dell'ambiente ci è rivelato oltre che dalla sua singolarità architettonica, dalle semicolonne che decorano gli stipiti del vano centrale, e dai pochi residui della pavimentazione che i precedenti scavatori dell'età borbonica lasciarono *in situ*. Il mosaico dell'atrio s'interrompe per dar luogo ad un ricco pavimento in *opus sectile* di marmi policromi che ricopriva peraltro la sola area centrale: nelle navate minori si ha invece un pavimento in signino decorato di segmenti di marmo. La decorazione è nello stile dell'ultima fase pompeiana. I pilastri a sezione quadrata (m. 0,40 circa di lato), due al centro e due mezzi pilastri alle estremità, decorati di baccellature, terminano con elegante capitello a palmette e foglie di acanto a basso e piatto rilievo, accentuato dalla policromia dello stucco bianco su fondo azzurro. Di fine ed elegante esecuzione è la decorazione delle pareti su fondo bianco, di cui resta buona parte sul muro di fondo e qualche frammento sui muri laterali; il pavimento in marmo così caldo di colore, doveva dare maggior spicco al tono chiaro e luminoso delle pareti. Nulla invece resta della decorazione del soffitto che, a differenza degli atri tetrastili e corintii, doveva essere piano o leggermente carenato in corrispondenza della navata centrale.[7]

Il "tablinum-oecus" di questa casa ercolanese rende perfettamente ragione della distinzione che Vitruvio fa tra "oeci corintii", "tetrastyli"

---

4. Maiuri, A., *Ercolano*, 71; id. *Ercolano-Itinerari dei Musei e Monumenti*, I^ ed., 42; cfr. 3^ ed., 26.

5. Harsh, Ph., "The origins of the Insulae at Ostia" in *Memoirs of the Americ. Acad. in Rome* 12 (1935) 33, nota 2: "there is a modified Egyptian oecus behind the atrium, while the enclosed peristyle is located at the side of the atrium"; cfr. *ibid.*, 35, nota 1; cfr. A. Van Buren in Pauly-Wissowa, *R.E.* XVII, 2, col. 2121 s.

6. Alla copiosa bibliografia su tale argomento, è da aggiungere A. Maiuri *Portico e peristilio: contributo allo studio della casa romana* in "La Parola del passato," Napoli, 1946, fasc. III, p. 306 ff.

7. La distinzione tra i due sistemi di copertura si ricava dal testo di Vitruvio (l.c.); mentre per gli *oeci* corinti si parla di "*curva lacunaria ad circinum delumbata*," per gli *oeci* egizi si dice solo degli *ornamenta* da apporre ai *lacunaria*.

ed "aegyptii," sovrattutto se si tengono presenti i classici esempi degli "oeci" pompeiani.[8] Mentre cioè gli *oeci* corintii e tetrastili hanno un solo ordine di colonne, o rialzate su basamento ("Casa delle Nozze d'argento," "Casa di Meleagro"), o poggiate sul pavimento ("Casa del Labirinto"), ed hanno architrave e cornice o in legno o in stucco e da ultimo un soffitto ricurvo a volta (Casa delle Nozze d'argento[9]), negli "oeci aegyptii" si hanno invece due ordini. All'altezza dell'epistilio dell'ordine inferiore si stende tra l'epistilio e la parete esterna dell'ambiente una travatura tutta in giro e su questa si getta il masso del pavimento, in modo da poter restare allo scoperto, cioè in *opus signinum* e con appositi scoli d'acqua. Inoltre sull'epistilio e sull'appiombo delle colonne sottoposte si alza un secondo ordine di colonne di modulo minore (di un quarto), anch'esso completo di epistilio e cornice e tra queste colonne si aprono delle finestre. Salvo lievi e non sostanziali semplificazioni, il "tablinum-oecus" ercolanese risponde esattamente al canone vitruviano (figg. 1-2) : solo, in luogo delle colonne, per maggiore robustezza, si hanno bassi pilastri; le finestre, anzichè aprirsi fra gli intercolunni di un ordine superiore, si aprono sulla parete liscia, ma sempre in corrispondenza degli intercolunni dell'ordine inferiore; infine, per non restringer troppo l'area, si dovè rinunciare alle navate dei lati di est e di ovest, per modo che non si ebbe al piano superiore l'intero circuito deambulatorio *(pavimentum subdiu ut sit circumitus)*. Pur così modificato, risponde questo "oecus" alle finalità essenziali dello schema vitruviano: la luce che filtra dall'alto delle tre coppie di finestre è sufficiente ad illuminare gradevolmente l'ambiente.

Ma soprattutto istruttiva nei riguardi dell'interpretazione del testo vitruviano, è la presenza delle intercapedini che si osservano tra le pareti esterne dell'ambiente *(parietes qui sunt circa)* e le pareti

---

8. Contrariamente all'avviso dei primi commentatori che ritenevano gli oeci tetrastili fossero tutt'uno con i corinzi (Barbaro) o con gli egizi (Galiani), si ritiene concordemente che Vitruvio (l.c.) distingua tre specie di *oeci* (corinzi, tetrastili, egizi) oltre ai ciziceni *non italicae consuetudinis*. Trascrivo qui appresso il testo vitruviano relativo alle forme dell'oecus egizio *De Arch., VI, 3, 9*: Inter corinthios autem et aegyptios hoc erit discrimen. corinthii simplices habent columnas aut in podio positas aut in imo; supraque habent epistylia et coronas aut ex intestino opere aut albario, praeterea supra coronas curva lacunaria ad circinum delumbata. in aegyptiis autem supra columnas epistylia et ab epistyliis ad parietes, qui sunt circa, imponenda est contignatio, supra coaxationem pavimentum, subdiu ut sit circumitus. deinde supra epistylium ad perpendiculum inferiorum columnarum imponendae sunt minores quarta parte columnae. supra earum epistylia et ornamenta lacunariis ornantur, et inter columnas superiores fenestrae conlocantur; ita basilicarum ea similitudo, non corinthiorum tricliniorum videtur esse.

9. Per la "Casa delle Nozze d'argento" Sogliano, A., *Not.Scavi*, 1910, p. 319 ss. fig. 2, Delbruck, R., *Hellen.Bauten in Latium*, II, 143; per la "Casa di Meleagro" Delbruck, R., *op. cit.*, 144, fig. 76; per la "Casa del Labirinto" Overbeck-Mau, *Pompeji*, 4ᵃ ed., 342.

sopraelevate della navata centrale.[10] Mentre nei disegni ricostruttivi degli architetti commentatori di Vitruvio, fin da A. Palladio, le pareti esterne dell'ambiente si arrestano all'altezza del I° ordine e le finestre dell'ordine superiore si aprono in pien'aria alla luce diretta, qui invece necessariamente, le pareti esterne sono anch'esse sopraelevate in modo da formare due intercapedini.[11] Quelle due intercapedini (figg. 1-2)

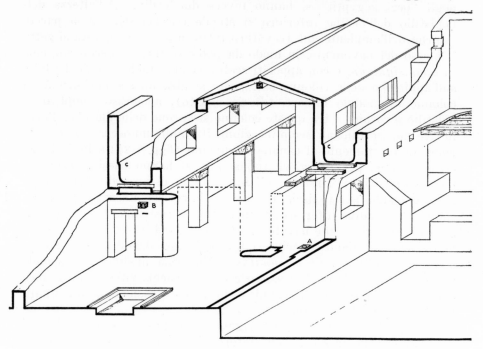

Fig. 1. Ercolano. Casa dell'atrio a mosaico. (Sezione assonometrica.)

vennero sistemate a terrazza per poter ricevere e discaricare le acque di gronda: uno spesso intonaco di signino riveste ancora le superfici dei muri con accurato arrotondamento degli angoli e degli spigoli e con il piano di scorrimento rivolto verso la parete dell'atrio: nell'angolo A si apre infatti nel pavimento sottostante una vaschetta (m. 0,32 x 0,33 x 0,27) destinata alla raccolta delle acque di scolo e munita di una fistula (diametro m. 0,05) che le discaricava nel bacino dell'im-

10. Non è rettamente inteso da Jo. H. Schneider nel suo commento a Vitruvio, Lipsia, 1807, I, p. 464 che si oppone alla giusta interpretazione di un *"paries interior"* ed *"exterior."*

11. Si veda il grandioso oecus egizio disegnato da A. Palladio, *I quattro libri dell'architettura*, lib. 2° p. 41, Venezia, 1570, da cui derivano più o meno ridotti i disegni dei successivi commentatori, ad es. L. Marini, 1836, tav. CIV, fig. 5-6.

pluvio; indubbiamente un'altra vaschetta simile, andata distrutta, doveva essere dall'opposto lato (fig. 1).

Pienamente giustificato appare in questa casa ercolanese l'adozione dello schema dell' "oecus aegyptius" in luogo dell' "oecus corinthius." L'*oecus* tetrastilo o corintio, a quattro o più colonne, ci si presenta a Pompei come una più o meno profonda exedra *columnata* illuminata

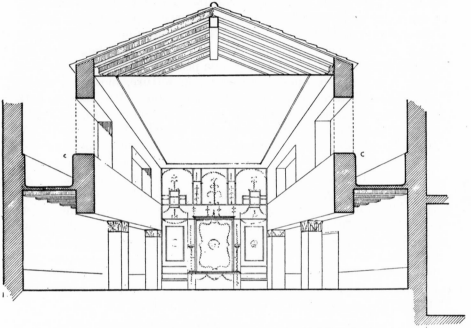

Fig. 2. Ercolano. Casa dell'atrio a mosaico-Tablino (sezione).

dalla luce che veniva dal grande vano di apertura schermata e temperata da cortinaggi sospesi; si aprono infatti tutti nei peristili, su vaste e luminose aree di giardino ed è ovvio pensare che servissero da sale di soggiorno e da triclini estivi. Ad Ercolano invece questo tablino, già atrofizzato nella sua vera funzione perchè chiuso al fondo dalla parete divisoria con la casa attigua, poteva trarre la sua luce solo dall'atrio, che, a sua volta, con il tablino cieco e l'apertura del compluvio assai angusta, appare oggi piuttosto oscuro e più doveva apparire in antico con i vani delle porte chiuse. Da ciò la necessità di derivare la luce dal tablino stesso; e non potendo derivarla dalle pareti perimetrali (chiuse a nord e ad est da case limitrofe, a sud da altri ambienti della stessa abitazione), si ricorse all'espediente delle due intercapedini da servire come veri e propri pozzi di luce; l' "oecus aegyptius" risolveva architettonicamente il non facile problema di illuminare un ambiente chiuso tutt'intorno da muri di altre abitazioni.

Ma per ben comprendere l'uso a cui poteva essere destinato questo oecus-tablinum è necessario osservarne il sistema di chiusura.

Delle tre porte con cui s'apre sull'atrio, le due minori di lato erano chiuse da battenti monovalvi (una di esse conserva la soglia con il cardine dell'imposta) ; il vano centrale invece, pur conservando la soglia, non reca alcun segno nè di cardine nè di risalto per l'appoggio dei battenti : la semicolonna di destra conserva peraltro nel rivestimento a stucco il solco di un listone di legno inserito e immorsato nello spessore del'intonaco. Era pertanto quel vano, a somiglianza dei tablini delle case ricche,[12] munito di una pesante tenda assicurata a un robusto telaio ligneo, quali si scorgono in pitture, mosaici e rilievi con vedute d'interni della casa greco-romana. Ma poichè, data l'ubicazione di quell'*oecus* nell'asse della fauce d'ingresso, occorreva meglio difenderlo dalle indiscrezioni dei viandanti e dalle correnti d'aria, si provvide a munirlo d'una chiusura più solida e permanente.

Nello spazio tra le porticine laterali e il vano centrale, si osservano (tav. 25, fig. 1), all'altezza di m. 2.17 dal pavimento, due grossi monconi di travi carbonizzati inseriti nella grossezza del muro entro alveoli fasciati di laterizio, i quali, sporgendo convenientemente dalle pareti di almeno m. 0,70-0,80, dovevano servire di appoggio a qualche cosa di più pesante e robusto che non fosse il cortinaggio di una tenda (tav. 25-26). L'esempio miracolosamente conservato che abbiamo nella "Casa del Tramezzo di legno" suggerisce la sola spiegazione possibile:[13] quei due robusti travi servivano anche qui di appoggio a un tramezzo di legno che, con una o più porte bivalvi, chiudeva il tablino trasformato in *oecus:* l'altezza del tramezzo della "Casa dell'Atrio a mosaico" è presso a poco quella della "Casa del Tramezzo di legno," ed è ovvio dedurre che la trasformazione di quei due tablini in "oeci" si dovesse ad analoghe esigenze familiari.

Tali esigenze ci sono chiaramente rivelate nella "Casa dell'Atrio a mosaico" dall'ubicazione della cucina. In un'abitazione così estesa e che ha il suo vero e proprio quartiere di rappresentanza nelle sale che si affacciano sulla loggia panoramica aperta verso la veduta del golfo, la *culina* si trova invece nell'atrio a fianco della fauce d'ingresso ; si è costretti a pensare che, pur riservando per ospiti e convitati, il grande e sontuoso *oecus* tricliniare sulla loggia, il triclinio consueto della famiglia fosse precisamente nel tablino. Così, pur avendo trasformato il *tablinum* in un elegante *oecus* ellenistico, il proprietario di

---

12. Ad esempio nella "Casa del Menandro": Maiuri, A., *La Casa del Menandro e il suo tesoro di argenteria*, I, 54 s.

13. Maiuri, A., *Ercolano*, 58 s. fig. a p. 56; id. *Ercolano-Itinerario*, 3^ ed. 31, tav. XIV.

questa ricca abitazione restava fedele all'uso tradizionale della casa romana, secondo quanto attesta Varrone (apud Nonium p. 83) : *ad focum hieme ac frigoribus cenitabant, aestivo tempore in propatulo, rure in corte, in urbe in tabulino.*[14] Ma come i ricchi proprietari delle case pompeiane, anche il nostro ricco ercolanese aveva più triclini: quotidianamente e d'inverno, nell'ambiente chiuso e raccolto del tablino; *aestivo tempore,* nell'exedra del giardino al rezzo delle piante e al grato rumore del saliente della piscina; per ospiti di riguardo nell'oecus tricliniare della loggia innanzi all'ampio panorama della marina e del golfo.

Ercolano dunque ci offre il primo ed unico esempio di uno di quegli "oeci aegyptii" i quali richiamavano a Vitruvio più l'immagine di basiliche che di triclinii *(ita basilicarum ea similitudo, non Corinthiorum tricliniorum videtur esse).* E' un richiamo degno di attenzione e che induce a rimeditare in questo minuscolo modello ercolanese il grave e complesso problema della Basilica di Pompei.

---

14. Tralascio di proposito l'ultimo inciso (l.c.) : *quod moenianum possumus intellegere tabulis fabricatum,* su cui più si discute e che, non senza ragione, Patroni, G. ("L'origine della domus ed un frammento varroniano male inteso," in *RendLinc* 11 [1942] 490) ritiene dovuta ad un'interpolazione esplicativa dello stesso grammatico Nonio Marcello.

DER TRAJANSBOGEN IN PUTEOLI

HEINZ KÄHLER
München

Tafeln 27-30

Im vorletzten Jahr seiner Regierung vollendete Domitian die nach ihm benannte Küstenstrasse, die, über Linternum und Cumae führend, Sinuessa mit Puteoli verband. Sümpfe wurden ausgetrocknet, Flussläufe beglichen, Berge durchschnitten. Der sandige, mühsame Landweg verwandelte sich in die feste gerade Strasse, die Statius mit dem Ruhm ihres Erbauers besungen hat.[1] Ihre Spuren findet der Wanderer noch heute an manchen Stellen, das Pflaster am Fuss der Weinberge, die Ruinen der Grabbauten, die sie in der Nähe der Städte säumten, den gemauerten Tunnel, in dem sie das Gebirge östlich von Cumae durchquerte.

Als der Kaiser im Jahre nach der Beendigung der Strasse ermordet wurde, beschloss der Senat den Namen des verhassten Tyrannen aus der Geschichte zu löschen. Seine Standbilder wurden von den Postamenten gestürzt, in den Inschriften seiner Regierungszeit sein Name und seine Titel getilgt. So fand man auch keinen Meilenstein der von ihm gebauten Strasse. Der Bogen, der sie an der Brücke über den Volturnus überspannte, mag wie die zahlreichen Denkmäler dieser Art in der Hauptstadt zerstört worden sein.[2] Die Statuen in Sinuessa, Cumae und Puteoli, von dankbaren Bürgern kurz vorher errichtet, wurden von den gleichen Leuten in den Staub gestürzt und nur aus dem Lied des Dichters klingt nach fast zweitausend Jahren ungeschmälert der Dank des Landes in den Worten des gelben Flussgottes und vernimmt man aus dem Mund der Sibylle von Cumae die Weissagung von des Kaisers ewigem Ruhm.[3]

Vor etwa vierzig Jahren fand man in der Oberstadt von Pozzuoli, hundertfünfzig Meter südwestlich des Amphitheaters, neben dem Pflaster einer von Westen nach Osten führenden Strasse eine Inschrifttafel aus Marmor, die einen römischen Fuss stark und fünfeinhalb Fuss hoch war (Taf. 27, a).[4] An der Breite von vier Fuss fehlten nicht ganz vier Zentimeter, da bei der zweiten Verwendung der Platte ein schmaler Streifen fortgearbeitet worden war. Der Stein, der in vier

1. *RE*. 6, 2579; Statius, *Silvae* 4, 3.
2. Statius a.O. v. 95ff. *RE* 7, A1, 413 A II Nr. 29.
3. Statius a.O. v. 124ff.
4. Gabrici, E., *NSc.* 1909, 212. Cagiano de Azevedo, M., *Bull.Mus.Imp.* 10. 1939, 45 mit Zusammenstellung der wichtigsten Literatur. Die Aufnahme zu Taf. 27a verdanke ich der Freundlichkeit von Mrs. Edith Hall Dohan in Philadelphia, die jetzt verstorben ist.

Stücke zersprungen war, hatte einmal die Front eines Statuensockels
gebildet. Er war mit ihm, dessen Kern aus einem weniger wert-
vollen Material bestand, durch zwei Klammern auf der Oberseite verbunden gewesen. Die etwas vertiefte Inschrifttafel ist mit einer
schlichten Welle und einer schmalen Leiste gerahmt, die rechts der
Inschrift bei der Wiederverwendung der Platte beseitigt wurde. Die
Tafel trug elf Zeilen, die getilgt worden sind, als man die auf dem
hohen Sockel stehende Statue herabwarf. Noch ist aus den Spuren
des Breiteisens, das die Buchstaben zerstörte, zu erkennen, wie der
Arbeiter, der auf die Stufen der Basis getreten war, die oberen drei
Zeilen fast mit senkrecht auf die Fläche treffenden Schlägen beseitigte,
wie er dann in den nächsten drei Zeilen das Werkzeug schräger von
oben herab führte, so dass die Kerben die Buchstaben in der Diagonalen durchschnitten, und wie er schliesslich in den untersten
Zeilen die breite Schneide, da er nun von oben nach unten arbeitend
das Eisen in immer spitzerem Winkel zur Fläche des Steines stellen
musste, fast waagerecht hielt, wie es sich ergibt, wenn man die
Schneide nicht über eine Ecke einsetzen und beschädigen will. Da
der Arbeiter seinen Zweck nicht voll erreichte, hat er sich auf die
Stufen des Denkmals gesetzt, um mit diagonalen Schlägen seine zer-
störende Tätigkeit in der linken Hälfte der sechs untersten Zeilen
wirkungsvoller fortzusetzen.

Die Unterschiede in der Führung des Werkzeugs lassen den Schluss
zu, dass der Sockel noch aufrecht stand, als die Inschrift beseitigt
wurde. Man hätte sich die Mühe der Auslöschung wohl auch erspart,
wenn man die Absicht gehabt hätte, das Denkmal sogleich ganz zu
beseitigen. Die Tilgung war jedoch nicht so vollständig, dass man
bei näherem Hinsehen nicht doch noch Spuren der Buchstaben erkannte. Wer beobachtet hat, wie das Werkzeug in den verschiedenen
Zeilen mit verschiedenen Schlägen geführt wurde, der wird die
Formen der Buchstaben in dem Stein trotz der Vernichtung wahr-
nehmen und so ist es denn auch gelungen, die Inschrift trotz ihrer
Zerstörung annähernd wieder zu entziffern. Nach ihrem Wortlaut
hat die römische Colonie Puteoli dem Kaiser Domitian zum Dank für
eine von ihm erfahrene Wohltat das Denkmal errichtet, ähnlich wie
ihm auch andere Körperschaften der Stadt Statuen errichtet haben.[5]

Ob die Bürger von Puteoli das Standbild Domitians, das auf dem
Sockel mit der Inschriftplatte sich erhob, aufgestellt haben, als der
Kaiser die Küstenstrasse von Sinuessa nach Puteoli anlegen liess,
lässt sich nicht mehr entscheiden. Sicher gab es auch andere Ur-

---

5. Die Entzifferung bei Cagiano de Azevedo a.O. 48 Abb. 6, die im wesentlichen überzeugt: nur die letzte der elf Zeilen ist unwahrscheinlich. Vorgeschlagen
sei hier: VICTORIS ACCEPTA.

sachen, den Kaiser zu feiern, dessen Vater die Colonia Flavia Puteolana unter anderem mit einem Amphitheater beschenkt hatte, dem
drittgrössten unter allen erhaltenen Bauten dieser Gattung. Lange
wird auch der seiner Inschrift und Statue beraubte Sockel nicht gestanden haben. Nach der Zerstörung des Sockels wurden die kost-
baren Marmorplatten der Verkleidung für andere Zwecke benutzt.
Die Inschriftplatte wurde umgedreht, sodass die Rückseite Ansichts-
fläche wurde. Sie fand an einem grossen Denkmal Verwendung, das
mit Reliefs geschmückt wurde (Taf. 28). Johannes Sieveking[6] wird
die Beobachtung verdankt, dass an die Darstellung auf der Rückseite
der Inschriftplatte, die bald nach ihrer Auffindung in den Besitz des
Universitätsmuseums von Philadelphia gelangt ist, eine Reliefplatte
im alten Museum in Berlin (Taf. 29) im rechten Winkel anschloss, die
Bunsen 1830 im römischen Kunsthandel aus Puteoli erworben hatte,
wo sie um 1800 gefunden worden war (Taf. 30).

Die Darstellung auf der Rückseite der Inschriftplatte (Taf. 28)
zeigt rechts in einer muldenförmigen Nische einen frontal dargestellten ruhig stehenden Soldaten in Tunica und Paenula, mit einem
kleinen Ovalschild in der einen, der Lanze in der anderen Hand. An
seiner Rechten hängt das Schwert in rankengeschmückter Scheide.
Unter dem Bausch der Tunica wird das Ende des breiten Ledergürtels
sichtbar. An den Füssen trägt er bis über die Knöchel reichende
stiefelartige Sandalen. Der Soldat auf der anschliessenden Berliner
Platte (Taf. 29), deren Oberfläche bei der Ausflickung der Beschädigungen etwas geputzt ist, unterscheidet sich von dem auf dem Relief
in Philadelphia nur dadurch, dass er dass rechte Bein statt des linken
entlastet und dass bei ihm statt des rechten die linke Hälfte des
Mantels über die Schulter geschlagen ist. Aus der linken Hälfte der
Rückseite der Inschriftplatte ist ein Teil eines flacheren Reliefs gearbeitet, das zwei Soldaten darstellt in gleicher Tracht wie die beiden
Figuren an der Ecke. Sie marschieren nach links. Der vordere von
ihnen schultert die Lanze, der hintere trägt einen grossen Schild an
einer Schlinge über den Rücken, in die er den Zeigefinger gehängt
hat. Nach dem Skorpion im Rankenschmuck des Metallschildes
dürften die Soldaten Prätorianer sein.[7]

Wie der linke Teil des Reliefs in Philadelphia gegen die mulden-
förmige Nische mit ihrem kräftigen Rahmenprofil um etwa 4 cm
zurückweicht, so findet sich auch an der rechten Nebenseite der

---

6. Sieveking, J., *SBMünch.* 1919, 6. Abb. Die Aufnahme der Platte in Philadelphia verdanke ich Mrs. Hall Dohan, die der Platte in Berlin C. Weickert, Berlin.
Zur Zusammenfügung und Interpretation vgl. Cagiano de Azevedo a.O. 45ff.

7. *RE* Bd. 12, 1375. v. Domaszewski, A., *Arch. epigr.Mitt.* 15, 1902, 13. Die
Vorlage für Taf. 30 verdanke ich der Leitung der Mostra Augustea in Rom.

Berliner Platte, die eine Dicke von 22 cm hat, im gleichen Abstand von der Vorderkante und parallel mit diesen eine Ritzlinie mit zwei etwas stärker eingearbeiteten Kerben oben und unten. Rechts von dieser Linie ist ein 14 cm breiter Streifen für den Anschluss einer weiteren Platte geglättet, links von ihr zeigt die Oberfläche Spuren des Zahneisens und der Verwitterung. Es schloss sich also rechts an das Berliner Relief eine etwa 14 cm starke Platte an, die ebenso wie der linke Teil der Platte in Philadelphia gegenüber dem Relief an der Ecke des Denkmals etwas zurücktrat. Es ist ziemlich wahrscheinlich, dass die ursprünglich an das Berliner Relief anschliessende Platte, die mit 14 cm höchstens 17 cm Dicke mindestens um 8 cm dünner war als der linke Teil des Reliefs in Amerika, bei ihrer geringen Stärke unverziert geblieben ist. Der Reliefgrund hätte bei einer dem anderen Relief entsprechenden Höhe der Ausladungen nur eine Dicke von höchstens 8 cm, wahrscheinlich nur 5 cm erhalten können, was bei den Maßen der Platte, selbst wenn das Relief am Bau ausgeführt wäre, auffallend dünn wäre. Doch muss man annehmen, dass eine Ausarbeitung irgendwelcher Darstellung in jedem Fall vor dem Versetzen der Platte hätte stattfinden müssen, da die Prellschläge den Stein allmählich aus dem Verband mit dem Mörtel seiner Hintermauerung hätten lösen müssen. Das Denkmal, zu dem die beiden Platten aus Pozzuoli gehörten, unterschied also offenbar zwischen reliefgeschmückter Front und schlichterer Nebenseite. In seinem Aufbau war die Ecke besonders betont.

Sieveking wollte die beiden Platten, in deren Reliefs er Arbeiten trajanischer Zeit erkannte, mit der Basis einer Reiterstatue Trajans verbinden, deren vier Ecken durch Schildwacht haltende Soldaten besonders ausgezeichnet wären. Schweitzer[8] hat in einer Besprechung des Aufsatzes von Sieveking eingewendet, dass die aus den beiden Platten zu errechnenden Maßen für die Basis eines Reiterdenkmals zu gross seien. Einen Vorschlag für die ursprüngliche Verwendung der Platten wusste auch er nicht zu machen. M. Cagiano de Azevedo[9] und F. Magi[10] setzen die Platten an die Attika eines Bogens, ohne dass sie von der Gestalt des Denkmals eine rechte Vorstellung geben können. Offenbar wurden ihre Ueberlegungen bestimmt durch die Attika der Umfassungsmauer des Nervaforums, wo Minerva in einer ähnlichen muldenförmigen Nische wie die Soldaten an der Ecke unseres Monumentes steht.[11] Wenn der Kopf der Figur hier wie dort sich zu

---

8. *PhW* 1920, 438.
9. Cagiano de Azevedo a.O. S.55.
10. Magi, F., *"i rilievi flavi del Palazzo della Cancelleria,"* Mon. Vaticani di *archeologia e d'arte* 6 (1945), 163.
11. von Blankenhagen, P. H., *Flavische Architektur und ihre Dekoration,* 116 Taf. 38.

vollerer Körperlichkeit gegen den Grund rundet als die unteren Teile, so ist das eine primitive und simple Eigenart eines jeden Hochreliefs; sie wird ganz unabhängig von dem Standort des Reliefs zunächst gefordert durch das Volumen als solches, das die Masse von Leib und Gewand stärker als Fläche und Relief, die Körperform des Kopfes stärker als Plastik erscheinen lässt; es bedarf zunächst nicht der Erklärung durch die Stellung des Reliefs im Verhältnis zu einem Beschauer und kann über die Höhe der Anbringung nichts besagen.

Aber es dürfte nicht allzu schwer sein, sich eine Vorstellung von der ursprünglichen Form des Denkmals zu machen, zu dem die beiden Platten gehört haben.[12] Die Besonderheiten der Anordnung, bei der die Ecken gegenüber den Feldern zwischen ihnen betont werden, finden sich am Sockel des Bogens von Ancona, der im Jahre 115 n. Chr. geweiht worden ist (Taf. 27, b).[13] Die beiden Fronten dieses Denkmals sind durch Halbsäulen zunächst dem Durchgang und Dreiviertelsäulen an den Ecken gegliedert. Diese Säulen stehen weder wie beim Titusbogen in Rom[14] oder beim Trajansbogen in Benevent[15] auf einer schlichten gemeinsamen Bank noch auf Einzelsockeln wie beim Gavierbogen in Verona.[16] Vielmehr zeigt der Sockel eine Art von Zwischenform, indem die einheitliche Bank unter den einzelnen Säulen flach vorkröpft. Zu einem derartigen Bau müssen auch die beiden Reliefplatten aus Pozzuoli gehört haben. Zum Unterschied von allen übrigen bekannten trajanischen Bögen aber hatte der Bogen in Puteoli reliefgeschmückte Sockel, wie sie schon der nur durch Münzen bekannt gewordene Nerobogen in Rom[17] hatte und wie sie dann im dritten Jahrhundert beliebt waren.[18] Gleich dem Nerobogen und den

---

12. Die hier vorgetragene Deutung der Reliefs wurde bereits 1939 ohne nähere Begründung von mir vertreten in *RE* 7, A1, 413 A II Nr. 18 a. Sie wurde übernommen von Blümel, C., *Römische Skulpturen*, 43 bei der Interpretation der Berliner Platte.

13. Noack, F., *Triumph und Triumphbogen*, Vortr. Bibl.Warburg 5, 1925/6, 189 Taf. 19. Rossini, *Gli archi trionfali* 1836, Taf. 44ff. RE 7 A1, 403 A II Nr. 1a. Aufnahme des Sockels bei Galli, E., *Boll.d'arte* 30, 1936/37, 323 Abb. 3.

14. Rossini a.O. Taf. 31ff. Noack a.O. 183 Taf. 18. Lehmann-Hartleben, K., *BullCom.* 62 (1934), 89. *RE* 7, A1, 386 A I Nr. 23.

15. Meomartini, A., *I monumenti e le opere d'arte della cittá di Benevento* 1889 Taf. 2ff. Noack a.O. 189 Taf. 20/21. *RE* 7, A1, 404 A II Nr. 4a.

16. Kähler, *RM*. 50 (1935) 208 Abb. 20. *RE* 7, A1, 413 A II Nr. 28 a.

17. Mattingly, *Coins of the Roman Empire* I: Nero 183-190, 211, 329-334. Noack a.O. Taf. 38 Abb. 5-10. *RE* 7, A1, 385 A I Nr. 21.

18. Dütschke, H., *Antike Bildwerke in Oberitalien* 3 Nr. 397. Cagiano de Azevedo a.O. Abb. 2. Hübner, *Arch.Zeitung* 28, 1870, 29 Taf. 29. Das Relief, dessen eigenartige Fussleiste modern ist (Dütschke), wird datiert, ausser durch die Büste Hadrians, durch Beziehungen zu den späthadrianischen Tondi des Konstantinsbogens, die qualitativ besser sind, jedoch eine sehr verwandte Reliefauffassung zeigen, etwa in der Art, wie von dem Pferd nur der vordere Teil dargestellt wird (Vgl. besonders H. P. L'Orange u.A. von Gerkan, *Der spätantike Bildschmuck des Konstantinsbogens* Taf. 41, 2). Es bedürfte der Untersuchung, zu welchem Bogen das Florentiner Relief gehört haben kann. Zeitlich würde am

späteren Bögen muss auch der Bau in Puteoli über und über mit Reliefs bedeckt gewesen sein, da man kaum die Wandteile zwischen den Säulen ungeschmückt gelassen haben wird, wenn man sogar die Säulensockel und die Flächen zwischen ihnen zu Reliefträgern machte.

Der tektonischen Funktion der Sockel unter den Säulen entsprechend waren die Reliefs hier von denen auf den Flächen zwischen den Säulen in ihrem künstlerischen Ausdruck unterschieden. Während unter den Säulen Figuren in Vorderansicht und in ziemlich starker Erhebung stehen, sind die Darstellungen zwischen den Säulensockeln flacher gehalten. Ihre Gestalten bewegen sich im Profil von beiden Seiten gegen die Mitte des Denkmals. Die architektonische Bindung bestimmte offenbar die Form des Reliefs. Die der architektonischen Gliederung innewohnende Vertikalität und Frontalität zwingt gleichsam die Einzelfiguren unter den Säulen in die reine Vorderansicht im Unterschied zu den späteren Bögen, bei denen sich die Figuren der Säulensockel ebenfalls der Mitte des Denkmals, dem den Bogen durchziehenden Kaiser, zuwenden. Die Ausrichtung auf die geistige Mitte überlagert bei Bauten wie dem Diokletiansbogen[19] und Konstantinsbogen[20] die ursprüngliche Bindung der Darstellung in den tektonischen Aufbau des Denkmals. Wenn die Gestalten zwischen den Säulensockeln des Bogens in Puteoli dagegen in einer flächenhaften Bewegung ins Profil gewendet sind und gegen die Mitte des Baues ziehen, kommt darin der Wandcharakter der sich zwischen den Säulen ausspannenden Felder zum Ausdruck.

Der Bogen von Puteoli war kein massiver Steinbau. Der Kern bestand wie beim Bogen von Benevent aus Ziegel oder Mörtelmauerwerk, das mit Marmorplatten verkleidet war. Aus den beiden erhaltenen Platten liesse sich, da die Gliederung des Baues einer klassischen Säulenordnung unterworfen war, auch der annähernde Aufbau in seinen ungefähren Maßen erschliessen. Die Breite des Sockels muss mit dem Breitenmass der Plinthe unter der Säulenbasis auf ihm ungefähr übereingestimmt haben. Aus ihr wieder könnte das Maß des Gebälks annähernd festgestellt werden. Der Abstand der Säulen neben dem Durchgang von den Ecksäulen dürfte sich annähernd durch Verdopplung des links an den Sockel der Ecksäule anschliessenden Reliefs ergeben, wenn man annimmt, dass die Ver-

---

ehesten der Arco di Portogallo passen, der zwischen 136 und 138 errichtet sein muss (*RE* 7, A1, 338 A I Nr. 30), also gleichzeitig etwa mit dem Jagdmonument Hadrians, von dem die Tondi am Konstantinsbogen stammen. Aber es ist nach dem, was von diesem Bogen, vor allem von seiner Sockelform bekannt ist (Lanciani, R., *BullCom.* 1891, 19) mehr als unwahrscheinlich, dass das Relief zu diesem Denkmal gehört hat.

19. *RE*. 7, A1, 479 Abschnitt d.

20. Kähler, 96. *Berlin Winckm. Prgr.* 1936.

kürzung der Inschriftplatte um wenige Zentimeter deshalb erfolgt
sei, damit die Fuge annähernd in der Mitte des Feldes zwischen den
beiden Säulensockeln sässe. Unbekannt bliebe die Weite der Durchfahrt und die Tiefe des Denkmals.

Da es unwahrscheinlich ist, dass der Sockel nach Tilgung der Inschrift und Beseitigung der Domitianstatue Jahre hindurch stehen
blieb, und da es auch nicht sehr wahrscheinlich ist, dass die Platten
nach Zerstörung des Sockels lange gelagert haben, kann man vermuten, dass die aus dem Material des Domitiandenkmals gearbeiteten Reliefs zu einem Bogen gehört haben, der am Anfang des
zweiten Jahrhunderts errichtet wurde. Der einstige Standort dieses
Baues in Pozzuoli ist nicht ganz sicher zu ermitteln. Die Platte in
Philadelphia wurde mit anderen Bauresten südwestlich des Amphitheaters auf dem Pflaster einer römischen Strasse, doch ohne Verbindung mit anderen zum Bogen gehörigen Bauresten gefunden.[21]
Es ist allerdings unwahrscheinlich, dass sie bei ihren grossen Aus-
maßen sehr weit verschleppt worden ist, etwa von dem tiefer gelegenen Hafen herauf, dessen Erweiterung durch den Kaiser Trajan
im Jahre 106 n. Chr. beendet wurde.[22] In dem Raume, wo man die
Platte fand, südlich des Amphitheaters, ausserhalb der antiken Stadt,
muss die Via Antiniana ihren Anfang genommen haben, die Puteoli
mit Neapel verband.[23] Die Strasse, mit deren Erbauung unter Nerva
begonnen wurde, ist unter Trajan im Jahre 102 fertig gestellt
worden.[24] Es ist nach Fundort und Darstellung bestechend, die Reliefs mit einem Bogen zu verbinden, der zum Gedächtnis an die kaiserliche Wohltat die Strasse an ihrem Anfang überspannte, wie der
Bogen am Anfang der Via Trajana, die von Benevent nach Brindisi
führte, oder der Bogen auf der Mole des unter Trajan ausgebauten
Hafens von Ancona dem Optimus Princeps errichtet worden sind.

Denn dass auch das Denkmal in Puteoli, zu dem die beiden Platten
gehört haben, den Kaiser in erster Linie nicht als den siegreichen
Feldherrn gefeiert hat, sondern als den Optimus Princeps, ist der
Darstellung ohne weiteres zu entnehmen. Nicht Soldaten mit Ge-
fangenen erscheinen — gleichsam Relief gewordener Ausschnitt aus
dem Triumphzug — an dem Sockel des Baues wie an den Bögen des
Septimius Severus, Diokletian und Konstantin, Prätorianer, die stän-
digen Begleiter des Kaisers, eskortieren hier im Bild die Gestalt
dessen, dem zu Ehren der Bogen errichtet ist. Ihm, durch dessen
leibhaftige Erscheinung in der Durchfahrt das Denkmal erst seinen

---

21. L'Orange a.O. Taf. 24ff.
22. Vgl. Anm. 4.
23. Beloch, *Campanien*₂ 1890, 92.142.144.
24. CIL. X 6926-6928.

eigentlichen Sinn erhält, wenden sich seine Garden zu. Erst in den Reliefs der darüber befindlichen Wandfelder darf man, wie beim Beneventer Bogen auch den Kaiser selbst dargestellt erwarten, sicher, da schon die Sockel nicht auf die Idee des Triumphes anspielen, nicht als Soldat sondern als den besorgten Landesvater. So ordnet sich der Bau in Puteoli in die Reihe der Bögen von Benevent und Ancona ein und wird auch wie diese eine Stiftung von römischem Senat und Volk sein.

In den Anfang des zweiten Jahrhunderts gehören die Reliefs aus Pozzuoli auch nach ihrem Stil, wie der Vergleich mit den beiden vor kurzem an der Cancelleria in Rom gefundenen monumentalen Friesen deutlich macht.[25] Diese Reliefs, darstellend die Begegnung zwischen Domitian und seinem Vater Vespasian bei dessen Rückkehr aus dem Orient im Jahre 71 und den Aufbruch Domitians zum Chattenkrieg im Jahre 83, haben in der Vorhalle eines von Domitian wahrscheinlich im Marsfeld errichteten Tempels links und rechts neben der Tür gesessen.[26] Sie dürften gegen die Mitte der neunziger Jahre entstanden sein, ja die Tatsache, dass in dem einen Fries das Bildnis Domitians unbeschädigt blieb, im anderen der Kopf des nach seinem Tode geächteten Kaisers nicht abgeschlagen sondern in ein Bildnis seines Nachfolgers umgearbeitet wurde, lässt daran denken, dass der Bau im Jahre 96 noch eingerüstet und der Oeffentlichkeit unzugänglich war. Zur Ausführung der beiden Reliefs hatte man zwei Werkstätten herangezogen. Die des ersten Bildes[27] reiht ihre Gestalten in einem ausdrucksarmen Klassizismus aneinander, gibt ihnen abgesehen von den beiden Kaiserporträts, deren Ausführung einem besonderen Meister überlassen blieb,[28] Köpfe, die mit ihren verblasenen griechischen Profilen und ihrer leblosen Glätte einen wenig erfreulichen leeren Manierismus erkennen lassen. Bedeutender ist die Werkstätte, der die Profectio übertragen wurde.[29] In ihrer Arbeit spürt man etwas von der lebensvollen Wärme, die die Durchgangsreliefs des Titusbogen erfüllte, obwohl sie deren Qualitäten weder als Gesamtkomposition noch im Detail erreicht und sicher nicht mit der Werkstätte dieser Bilder identisch ist.[30] In der unorganischen Ueberlängung der Figuren und der manierierten Verkleinerung der Köpfe gegenüber den seltsam unstatischen und substanzlosen Körpern steht dieses Relief dem Gegenstück vom gleichen Bau näher als den Kom-

25. Magi, a.O. Taf. 1ff.
26. Kähler, *Gnomon* 22 (1950) 30.
27. Magi, Taf. 1 B. 4. 5. 7. 8. 19-22.
28. Magi, 149 Taf. 23. 24.
29. Magi, Taf. 1 A. 2. 3. 6. 9-11, 13-18.
30. Vgl. vor allem Strong, E., *Scultura romana* I, 111 Abb. 73.

positionen des Titusbogens. Dagegen weist die Arbeit des Profec-
tiomeisters so deutliche Uebereinstimmungen mit den Sockelbildern
aus Pozzuoli auf, dass man einen engeren Zusammenhang zwischen
den Arbeiten hier und dort annehmen möchte, wenn auch nicht die
gleiche Hand in den beiden Schöpfungen zu erkennen ist. Dazu finden
sich zwischen den sicher nur wenige Jahre voneinander getrennten
Reliefs auch wieder zu auffällige Unterschiede. So fehlt den Gestalten des Bogens von Puteoli die labile Unruhe des römischen Reliefs, mag vielleicht auch die Standfestigkeit der frontal dargestellten
Soldaten an den Sockeln unter den Säulen bis zu einem gewissen
Grade durch ihre Funktion im Aufbau des Denkmals gefordert sein.
Weitgehende Uebereinstimmung zeigt vor allem das Detail. Der etwas
geputzte und darum erstarrte Kopf des Berliner Prätorianers (Taf.
29) hat einen nahen Verwandten in dem Kopf des dem Kriegsgott
vorauseilenden Liktoren des römischen Reliefs,[31] der Schildträger
mit der domitianischen Haartracht im Hintergrunde des Reliefs in
Philadelphia (Taf. 28 links), der ähnlich hinter seinem Vordermann
verschwindet wie der letzte Legionär auf dem Profectiorelief in Rom,[32]
lässt enge Beziehungen erkennen zu dem Kopf des Soldaten vor dem
Genius des Senats in diesem Relief.[33]

Die Verbindung der Reliefs des Trajansbogens von Puteoli mit dem
Kreis der Werkstatt, die in Rom um die Mitte der neunziger Jahre
den rechten der beiden grossen Friese in der Vorhalle des domitianischen Tempels ausführte, setzt voraus, dass das Denkmal in Puteoli
stadtrömischen Arbeitern übertragen wurde. Das aber würde soviel
bedeuten, dass der Auftraggeber nicht die Colonia Flavia Puteolana
war sondern der römische Senat. Auf den Staat als Auftraggeber
möchte man schon aus dem wenigen schliessen, was von den Darstellungen des Denkmals erhalten blieb. Aehnlich wie der Senat 114 in
Benevent anlässlich der Eröffnung der Via Trajana, 115 in Ancona
anlässlich des Ausbaues des Hafens dem providentissimus Princeps
Bögen erbauen liess, die sich schon durch ihre vom Titusbogen abge-
leitete Form als Werke einer stadtrömischen Bauhütte zu erkennen
geben, hat er offenbar schon dreizehn Jahre früher aus einem ähnlichen Anlass in Puteoli ein Denkmal errichten lassen, das ebenfalls
in der Tradition der stadtrömischen und senatseigenen Bögen steht,
einen Vorläufer des Bogens von Ancona bildend, wie der Titusbogen
dem Bogen von Benevent als Vorbild diente. Die Werkstätte mag
eine der römischen Baufirmen gewesen sein, die sich wie die Haterier

---

31. Magi, Taf. 9.
32. Magi, Taf. 3.
33. Magi, Taf. 15, 1. Vgl. dazu auch Taf. 16, 1. 17, 1.

in domitianischer Zeit auf diese Gattung von Denkmälern spezialisiert hatten,[34] damals als nach Sueton[35] der Kaiser in allen Regionen der Stadt so viel Triumphbögen errichten liess, dass ein Spassvogel auf einen von ihnen mit griechischen Buchstaben schrieb ἀρκεῖ, was mit einem nicht ganz geglückten Wortspiel in Angleichung an das lateinische Wort arcus — Bogen — heisst: "Jetzt aber Schluss!"

34. Castagnoli, F., *BullComm.* 69 (1941) 59ff. Taf. 1-4.
35. Sueton, *Domitian* 13, 2.

NOTES FROM OSTIA

Axel Boethius

PLANS AND SECTIONS
BY HANS NEUMÜLLER

Göteborg

Plate 31

"If you wish to have a just notion of the magnitude of this city, you must not be satisfied with seeing its great streets and squares, but must survey the innumerable little lanes and courts. It is not in the showy evolutions of buildings, but in the multiplicity of human habitations which are crowded together, that the wonderful immensity of London consists." Dr. Johnson about London, Boswell, Johnson 1763 5/7.

Studying Olynthus and David Robinson's great work, which recalls Dr. Johnson's words, quoted above, I have tried to call attention to the fundamental difference between a town like late republican and Imperial Rome on the one hand and on the other hand towns with an obvious tendency to separate bazaar- and living-quarters like old Pompeii, Priene, Olynthus or any old Greek and Oriental town right down to our own times.[1] It is typical of the Roman system and also of Pompeii from the third century onwards that the workshops, the typical *tabernae*—ἐργαστήρια—for trade, handicraft and also proletarian living, were spread out all over the town. In addition, in Rome upper stories were added, accessible by direct staircases. These *insulae*, as I have pointed out several times, can be safely traced back to the third century B. C. They were obviously—not less than legions and city walls—an expression of "the unlimited crowding of citizens" (Vitruvius 2, 8, 17) and founded on special social and economic function, "the social and commercial system," as I put it. Vitruvius *l. c.* shows that this very untidy and unsafe town architecture had already improved in the first century B. C. The Rome and Ostia of the late first and the second centuries A. D. as well as remains from the last years of Pompeii show us brickfaced *insulae*, standardized in type with well-arranged rows of windows, balconies or porticoes along the façades, direct staircases of concrete, *tabernae* with barrel vaults, etc.

While for a few weeks in Ostia, 1949-50,[2] I have, after some years,

---

1. *Roman and Greek Town Architecture*. Göteborgs Högskolas Arsskrift 54. 1948: 3.
2. I wish to express my most sincere thanks to Professor P. Romanelli and the great expert in the field of Roman town architecture Italo Gismondi for the splendid weeks I spent in Ostia and all their generosity and information of the greatest value.

revised the classification of these *insulae* suggested by me as an easily intelligible way to distinguish in international discussion the different types of planning of these uniform tenement houses, and also of the fragments of the Forma Urbis. The suggested system may—even if it proves to be only provisory and personal—help in this paper to detach from crowds of *insulae* a special type, which I wish to discuss and illustrate. Referring to my previous studies and my illustrations in the *Scritti in onore di B. Nogara*,[3] I here only mention *insulae* built on one row of *tabernae* interrupted by staircases to the upper stories (type I)[4] and *insulae* constructed on two rows of *tabernae*, built back to back (type II).[5]

Together with these types go several less simple combinations, such as for instance the cluster of shops, facing three sides, left of the entrance to the Macellum of Ostia from the Decumanus (Taberna dei Pescivendoli. To the right: type II). Such a conglomeration corresponds exactly to the house with shops facing four sides on the Forma Urbis fgm. 62, discussed by P. Zicans in his study *Ueber die Haustypen der Forma Urbis*.[6] The Caseggiato del Temistocle in Ostia shows how a row of shops (type I) can get shut in by a surrounding wall and transformed to an isolated mercato or bazaar. Forma Urbis fgm. 158 illustrates this, as also Zicans somewhat vaguely explains (p. 191, pl. 3: 2). Referring to Zicans' very useful attempt to understand the house-types of the Forma Urbis with the help of archaeological material I would note in passing that almost all the combinations of shops, corridors, courts, storehouses and so on on the Forma Urbis can be illustrated from the remains in Ostia. On the other hand, as G. Lugli[7]

---

3. Roma, 1937, P. 12 ff. "Appunti sul carattere razionale e sull'importanza del'architettura domestica in Roma imperiale."—For illustrations also *Den romerska storstadens hyreshusarkitektur*. Göteborgs Högskolas Arsskrift 50. 1944: 4, pp. 11, 18, 20, 22.

4. For instance *tabernae* along the Cardo or the Cardine degli aurighi. Forma Urbis fgm. 187 shows a row with the most striking resemblance to the *tabernae* of the Cardine degli aurighi. For type I cf. otherwise Forma Urbis fgm. 109, 179, 192, 319, etc.

5. For instance in Ostia the *tabernae* along the Decumanus belonging to the Terme di Nettuno, the bazaar (with *tabernae* finestrate) between the Cardo and the Semita dei Cippi etc. Forma Urbis: 169, 321, 170, 230, 324, 244, 269, 273, etc.; 184 (= G. Lugli, "Nuove osservazioni sul valore topografico e catastale dell' 'Insula' in Roma antica," (*Rivista del Catasto e dei Servizi Tecnici Erariali N. S.* Anno 1, N. 1 [1946] Tav. 1, 25, 26, 27) contains another good example, though split up by Lugli, who adds one half of it to the *tabernae* of an *insula* of type IV on the other side of a narrow street (27). Together with Lugli's Osservazioni goes his study "Il valore topografico e giuridico dell' 'Insula' in Roma antica," *Atti della Pontificia accademia romana di archeologia, Rendiconti*, 18 (1941-42), 191 ff.

6. "Acta instituti romani regni Sueciae 5," *Opuscula archeologica* 2 (1941), 188, fig. 2:10.

7. *Osservazioni*, 4.

remarks and as for instance Forma Urbis fgm. 306, 18 (= Zicans pl. 3: 8, 9) and many others confirm, it seems evident that parts of Rome were much more irregular and crowded than what we see today in Ostia, though the type of architecture became in principle the same after the end of the first century A. D. Romanelli's and Gismondi's extremely important new excavations establish that before that date Ostia had large atrium and peristyle houses, thus more resembling a town like Pompeii than the descriptions of late republican and Augustan Rome, given us by Cicero, *De lege agraria* 2, 96, Vitruvius 2, 8, 17, and other sources, as being already a town with high tenement houses. We should of course not forget that late republican and Augustan Ostia had rows of *tabernae* (type I), as is shown, for instance, by the Via dei Molini[8] and the Horrea of Hortensius with its colonnade toward the Decumanus, but all the same it now seems evident that only toward 100 A. D. and especially in the second century did Ostia become an integral part of Rome with the same architecture.

To type III I assign great buildings with street-fronts of *tabernae*, such as for instance the Terme di Nettuno, the Horrea, the Scuola di Traiano in Ostia.[9] This group may seem unnecessary or even illogical, because the surrounding rows of *tabernae* are nothing but type I or II, but it is perhaps useful to make a distinction between types I and II as isolated buildings and the same types used as screens. Together with type III go also the isolated bazaars or mercati with shops facing on to inner courts, in which the Romans often concentrated trade or manufacture, for instance the Casa del Larario or the Piccolo Mercato in Ostia.[10] They belong to the series of Roman endeavors to create consolidated blocks such as the Roman theater, libraries like the Templum Pacis or the library of Hadrian in Athens, the Imperial fora or the tenement-houses, which Calza called "palazzi di tutti," such as for instance the Casa di Diana, the Insula degli aurighi and the Insula del Serapide.[11] These great house-blocks, combining the usual façade with *tabernae* and staircases toward the street and inner courts with peristyles in 2-3 stories were classified by me as type IV.

Of course there is much to add to the types I-IV, even if they help one through most of the *immensus numerus insularum*, which Sue-

---

8. "Acta instituti romani regni Sueciae 4," *Opuscula archeologica* 1 (1935) 173 ff. The first period of this row of shops evidently belongs to the earlier periods and levels of Ostia, characterized by very coarse *opus incertum* with biggish blocks, resembling rubble work.

9. Forma Urbis 37, 176, 169, 62, etc.

10. Forma Urbis 179, 170, 171.

11. Forma Urbis 184, 179, 109. Cf. Harsh, *Memoirs of the American Academy in Rome*, 12 (1935), 55; Zicans, *op. cit.*, 192, pl. 3:11, pl. 4:1, 4.

tonius (*Nero* 38) contrasts to the *domus priscorum ducum.* Even leaving aside the atrium and peristyle houses such as the Domus della nicchia a mosaico and the Domus di Giove fulminatore in Ostia,[12] we have, as Calza always pointed out,[13] the *insulae* with flats (and not *tabernae*) on the bottom floor. It would be a most important task to study these flats, which no doubt show what the upper floors were like, and also afford us much evidence for the use of wooden roofs (*contignationes*) in the *insulae.*[14]

The aim of this paper is to study another type of house, where the system of the *insulae* with *tabernae* is reduced to a narrow strip-house with only one or two *tabernae* and staircases toward the street. Lugli has called attention to this kind of house, which became quite a characteristic feature of medieval Rome.[15] This reduction of the Roman *insula* of types I-IV is of course perfectly easy to understand from an architectural point of view for those who realize that the *insulae* originated in a row of *tabernae* without any necessary connection with central court or *atrium,* the courts, etc., of types III and IV being an obvious combination of shop-houses "in the office of a wall" and inner premises. On the other hand, a study of Ostia or the Forma Urbis shows that narrow-fronted houses were, as far as we can see, by no means frequent in Imperial tenement-house architecture. Large houses with a row of *tabernae* toward the street (or even toward inner courts) do in any case form the majority in the material available to us. It would all the same be dogmatic rationalization to deny that narrow-fronted houses could easily develop out of *insulae* of the types characterized above, and it is, as a matter of fact, easy to show that such a development actually took place.

As Gismondi has pointed out, building lots in the town of the Imperial age determined by atrium and peristyle houses on the lower, late republican level, directly invited to the building of strip-houses. Typical, for instance, is the *insula* between the Angiporto delle Taberne finestrate and the Vico cieco, though connected with the Taberne finestrate by a vault over the angiporto. This building has two *tabernae* toward the Decumanus with a staircase behind, accessible

---

12. Forma Urbis 386/309, 173, 336, 200, 338, 45, 188. Zicans, *op. cit.,* 194, pl. 4:2, 5-10.

13. Cf. the new edition of his *Guide Ostia* (Rome 1949), 18 f.

14. For instance: Insula di Bacco fanciullo and insula di Giove e Ganimede, Insula del graffito, Caseggiato del Sole, Casa delle trifore, etc. It seems evident that wooden roofs were frequently used in upper storeys. Though the Ara Caeli house affords us an instance of barrel vaults, we have to reckon with *contignationes* and lower upper-storeys, when estimating the capacity of the *insulae.*

15. "Il valore topografico e giuridico dell' 'Insula' in Roma antica," p. 205 f. Osservazioni p. 12 ff. Cf. also my study *Den romerska storstadens hyreshusarkitektur* p. 19 ff., fig. 5, 6.

from the Angiporto delle Taberne finestrate as in one *insula* on Forma
Urbis fgm. 178 (fig. 1), 324 and others. The *insula* C below the
Basilica cristiana in Ostia might also be compared.[16] These structures,
though having their main entrances on their narrow front, could easily
change into type I or II, as Forma Urbis fgm. 324 shows.

    More specific and typical are narrow-fronted houses built on scraps
of ground at the angles of blocks, and of course whole streets, where
we see a clear tendency to split up the *insulae* in the medieval way. A
good example of the former group is the house at the angle of the Via
della casa di Diana and the Via di Molini. It consists of two *tabernae*
and a staircase facing the narrow street west of the Via di Molini
leading from the Via della casa di Diana to the Decumanus (fig. 2).
In the first period a wide door from the same alley gave access to the
shops. The façade was thus of exactly the same type as that of the
medieval narrow-fronted houses. Later the door to the *tabernae* was
blocked. The two *tabernae* retained doors only toward the Via della
casa di Diana; the plan of the house was in this way changed also:
two shops with staircase situated at the back leading from the side
road (like the house at the Angiporto delle Taberne finestrate). This
type of narrow-fronted house with two or three *tabernae* toward the
street meets us on the Decumanus itself east of the Tempio collegiale
(fig. 3). As Gismondi points out, the northern part of an elegant
house has here been used for two *tabernae* with "retrobotteghe" toward the Decumanus and the portico along it. The staircase to the
upper stories starts directly from the portico in the left *taberna*, as
we see it on the Forma Urbis for instance fgm. 169 a, 170 (fig. 4).
The same kind of house with two *tabernae* and a staircase inside one
of them is met with also north of the so-called Casette tipo in front of
a rectangular store-house (fig. 5). At the corner of the Via delle case
repubblicane and the Via del Larario is a small house with one *taberna*
and a staircase towards the Via del Larario (fig. 6), which seems to
me to be a most typical narrow-fronted house, though Gismondi believes that it was united by a vault with the portico and the shops on
the other side of the alley leading to the Via degli Horrea Epagathiana.
To me the two parallel vaults seem rather improbable, but with the
house to the left, in any case, we come to typical narrow façades with
one *taberna* and staircase.

    The best example seen by me until now is to be found at the Semita
dei Cippi (fig. 7). A narrow-fronted house with staircase, *taberna*
and "retrobottega" has to the right a corridor that leads to a portico

---

    16. *Atti della Pontificia accademia romana di archeologia. Rendiconti*, 18
(1941-42), 134 ff., pl. 1.

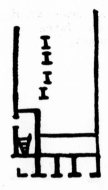

178

Fig. 1. Forma Urbis fgm. 178. Narrow-fronted house with staircase behind the *tabernae*.

CASA STRETTA   ALLA VIA DELLA CASA DI DIANA

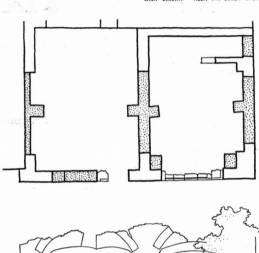

Fig. 2. *Insula* at the Via della Casa di Diana. 1) Plan. 2) Façade toward the Via della Casa di Diana. 3) Façade toward the alley leading to Decumanus with door to *taberna* (blocked in the second period of the building) and staircase.

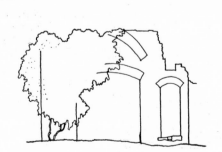

CASA STRETTA AL DECUMANO (AD EST DEL TEMPIO COLLEGIALE)

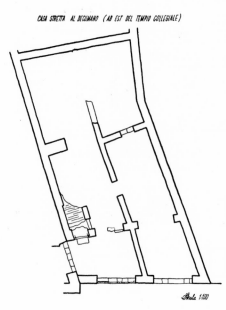

Scala 1:100

Fig. 3. Narrow-fronted house east of the Tempio collegiale, facing the Decumanus.

 169 a

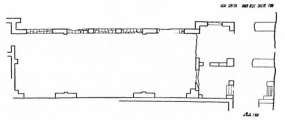

Fig. 4. Forma Urbis fgm. 169 a. *Insula* of type II with staircase in *tabernae*.

Fig. 5. Strip house north of the Casette tipo with two *tabernae* and staircase in the left one (cf. fig. 4).

CASA STRETTA   NORD DELLE CASETTE TIPO

Scala 1:100

ANGELO DELLE VIE DEL LARARIO E DELLE CASA REPUBBLICANA

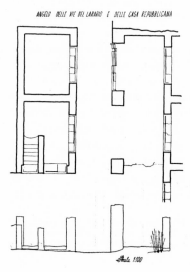

Scala 1:100

Fig. 6. Narrow-fronted house between the Via del Larario and the Via degli Horrea Epagathiana. *Taberna* with staircase.

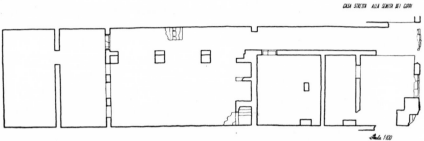

Fig. 7. Narrow-fronted house at the Semita dei Cippi. Facing the street: staircase, *taberna* and entrance to corridor.

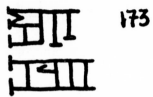

Fig. 8. Forma Urbis fgm. 173. From left, facing the street: staircase, *taberna*, entrance to corridor, neighboring house.

running along a small light court. Behind the court is a small residential house. Very likely this plot contained two *insulae* from the administrative point of view, the narrow-fronted house toward the Semita dei Cippi and the court and house at the end of the corridor. Exactly the same arrangement is to be seen on Forma Urbis fgm. 173 (fig. 8).[17] The opus listatum of the narrow-fronted house dates it to the late third or fourth century. In this case the resemblance with medieval and later narrow-fronted and strip-houses is complete (pl. 31, a).

As Gismondi points out, there is in the narrow street running south from the Via della Fortuna annonaria, between the Semita dei Cippi and the Via delle Ermete, a building plot which is split up in an almost medieval way (fig. 9). Starting from the left we see first an *insula* with staircase, entrance corridor and two *tabernae;* then follows a typical narrow-fronted house with one *taberna* and entrance, and further a narrow *domus* with entrance and two windows, in width resembling the narrow but elegant *domus* west of the Casa dei pesci at the Via della Caupona. I might perhaps suggest the name "Via delle case strette" for this street, to emphasize its special interest and also

17. Zicans, *op. cit.,* 189 has in my opinion misunderstood this fragment, not seeing that it shows two narrow-fronted houses divided by a corridor leading to inner parts of the building lot. Cf. *Den romerska storstadens hyreshusarkitektur,* fig. 2 (n:o 4), p. 11, 19 ff.

its obvious affinity with a number of fragments of the Forma Urbis, for instance 173 (*Den romerska storstadens hyreshusarkitektur*, fig. 2, p. 11), 176 (Lugli, *Osservazioni*, Pl. 1, 19-24, Fig. 10). Here the process of splitting up the house-block into narrow-fronted houses with one *taberna* and staircase is evident.

As remarked by Lugli and myself, it often happens that two such houses are coupled together in medieval and later tenement-house architecture as shown in pl. 31, b (cf Lugli, *Osservazioni*, fig. 8-9). They thus get a very characteristic façade with closely-connected windows in the center and windows at the corners. The *insula* which is to be found in the Aurelian wall between Porta Maggiore and Porta Tiburtina exhibits this disposition of the windows (pl. 31, c). In Ostia the Casa della Capella d'Iside has this type (figs. 11 and 12), which is also to be traced on the Forma Urbis.

In conclusion, we have to add to the four main types of *insulae*, called by me I-IV, to the *domus* and the *insulae* with flats on the bottom floors, the narrow-fronted houses, discussed in this paper, with two *tabernae* toward the street (including staircase or with staircase

Fig. 9. "Via delle Case strette." I *Insula* with staircase, entrance and two *tabernae*, II *Insula* with entrance and *taberna*, III narrow *domus*, IV large *insula*.

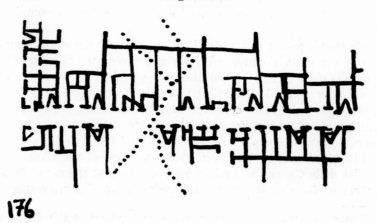

176

Fig. 10. Forma Urbis fgm. 176. Street with a row of narrow-fronted houses with *tabernae* and staircases.

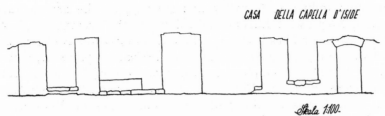

CASA DELLA CAPELLA D'ISIDE

Scala 1:100.

Fig. 11. Casa della Capella d'Iside. Façade with staircase,
two *tabernae* and staircase (as in 1, cf. fig. 12).

behind) or with one *taberna* and staircase. This kind of house does by
no means dominate as it does in later times, but it is of importance not
to forget them in Imperial Rome. As J. Ward Perkins recently
summed the matter up in a review of my *Roman and Greek Town
Architecture* (*JRS* 1949, 175 f.), "few will dispute that the characteristically Roman tenement-house with *tabernae* on the ground floor,
revived and resurrected by the architects of the Renaissance, has had

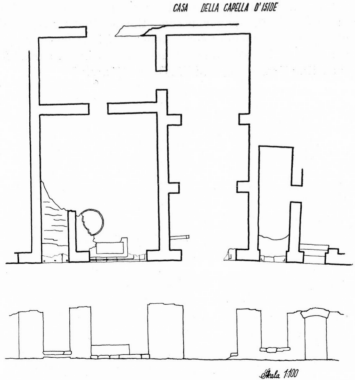

CASA DELLA CAPELLA D'ISIDE

Scala 1:100

Fig. 12. Casa della Capella d'Iside.

a profound influence, formally and socially, on the architecture of Italy and North-west Europe right down to the present day." Ward Perkins' review makes it clear to me that I ought to have been careful —as I was in my Swedish book *Den romerska storstadens hyreshusar-kitektur*, p. 44—to emphasize still more clearly that the Roman *insulae* were typical of Rome and, at least from about 100 A. D., of Ostia; that I was speaking of "the main types of Mediterranean towns" (and not of England); and that there is no evidence for Roman *insulae* in Gaul and Spain. Roman infiltration reached Pompeii and might thus have affected other greater provincial towns all over Italy and even—why not?—towns like Marseilles. I wished, however, to point out only the contrast between this Roman system of Italy, destined to dominate Western Europe from medieval times, and Eastern towns with bazaar-quarters. A journey from Rome to Athens revealed the same fundamental difference in urban, local tradition as today. Having established this we have to face two most important and interesting questions. When did the Roman system become dominant in N. Italy, France, Switzerland, Corfu, etc.? Did it have any effect on Constantinople? And further: when did the narrow-fronted houses, discussed in this paper, become the dominating type and when did they solve the problem of town house-architecture as we see it on all the old plans of Rome and still trace it today in old parts of Italian towns, including Trastevere and the Campo Marzio?

ZUM PROBLEM DER BRITTENBURG BEI KATWIJK

Franz Oelmann
Bonn

Tafel 24

Beim Congress of Roman Frontier Studies, der im Juli 1949 in Newcastle upon Tyne veranstaltet wurde, hatte ich Gelegenheit, über den Stand der Forschung am Rheinlimes des spätrömischen Reiches zu berichten und dabei zu dem Problem seines Anfangspunktes an der Mündung des Stromes Stellung zu nehmen. Die vorgetragenen Gedanken werden hier weiter ausgeführt und zur Diskussion gestellt.

Spätestens seit dem frühen 16. Jahrhundert bis um die Mitte des 18. Jahrhunderts waren am Strande bei Katwijk aan Zee gleich südlich der alten Rheinmündung bei Ebbe merkwürdige Fundamentmauern zu sehen, die unter verschiedenen Bezeichnungen wie arx Britannica, burcht te Britten oder Brittenburg und ähnlich von den holländischen Antiquaren viel beachtet und in Ansichten bzw. Plänen festgehalten wurden.[1] So erscheint die Ruine auf einem Kupferstich des A. Ortelius vom Jahre 1567 oder 1568 (Taf. 24, b) als ein etwa quadratisches Mauerviereck von 240 pedes, also etwa 72 m Seitenlänge, das an zwei Seiten mit mächtigen Halbrundtürmen bewehrt ist. Dieser äussere Mauergürtel umschliesst ein kleineres Mauerviereck und dieses einen dritten, wieder kleineren Bau von quadratischem Grundriss, der durch eine Quermauer geteilt und aussen durch Mauervorsprünge verstärkt ist. Vor dem äusseren Mauerring sind noch einige schräg dazu verlaufende Mauerstücke sichtbar, sie scheinen nicht organisch damit verbunden und daher nicht zugehörig, vielmehr von älteren, vor Errichtung des Kastells zerstörten Gebäuden herzurühren. Wenn auch die übrigen Darstellungen der Ruine im Einzelnen voneinander abweichen, so stimmen sie doch in den wesentlichen Elementen überein bis auf ein Aquarell von P. Coos v.J. 1667, in dem die Ruine überhaupt nicht wiederzuerkennen ist und neben einem geschlossenen Rechteckbau wieder schräg dazu liegende Mauerzüge von ansehnlicher Länge erscheinen, sowie eine Federzeichnung von 1749, wo nur noch der Pfahlrost eines Mauerwinkels mit zwei Rundtürmen zu sehen ist.[2]

---

1. A. W. Bijvanck, *Nederland in den romeinschen tijd* II (1943) 420f. mit Litt.; seine *Excerpta Romana, de bronnen der romeinsche geschiedenis van Nederland*, 3 (1947) waren mir bisher nicht zugänglich.

2. J. H. Holwerda, *Oudheidkundige mededeelingen van het Rijksmuseum van oudheden te Leiden N.R.* 8 (1927) 1ff.

Die Ruine ist wegen der zahlreichen römischen Altertümer, die hier bzw. in der Umgebung gefunden und mit ihr zusammen abgebildet wurden, immer für römisch gehalten worden und zeigt in der Tat weitgehende Verwandtschaft mit spätrömischen Festungsbauten. Erst J. H. Holwerda jr., hat seit 1908 mehrfach die These verfochten, dass die Brittenburg nicht römisch, sondern späteren und zwar karolingischen Ursprungs sei.[3] Er begründet diese These zunächst damit, dass die angeblich von der Brittenburg stammenden Altertümer überhaupt nicht dort, sondern zumeist in etwa 1 km Entfernung bei Anlage des Nieuw Vliet oder Mallegat i.J. 1571 gefunden worden seien, dass sie auch, soweit datierbar, ausschliesslich der mittleren Kaiserzeit angehörten und daher zu dem spätzeitlichen Charakter der Befestigung nicht passten. Vor allem aber sei die Anlage von den sonst bekannten Kastellen spätrömischer Zeit am Rhein wesentlich verschieden, wogegen sich im mittelalterlichen Festungsbau bessere Analogien fänden. Dazu werden u.a. karolingische Curtes verglichen und eine Nachricht bei Einhard herangezogen, wonach Karl d.Gr. die Flussmündungen an der Nordsee zum Schutze gegen die Normannengefahr befestigt habe. Hinzu kommen schliesslich Ueberlegungen zur Frage der spätrömischen Reichsgrenze in Holland überhaupt: Holwerda war nämlich der Ansicht, die Rheinlinie unterhalb Nijmegen sei damals ganz aufgegeben gewesen, denn es fehle im Tieflande der Betuwe völlig an spätrömischen Funden. Dagegen hat zwar A. G. Roos 1923 den spätrömischen Ursprung der Brittenburg mit dem Hinweis auf die Ueberlieferung bei Historikern und Panegyrikern des 4. Jahrhunderts sowie auf archäologische Befunde ähnlicher Art an anderen Stützpunkten des spätrömischen Rheinlimes wieder verteidigt, jedoch bei Holwerda nur erneuten Widerspruch gefunden.[4] Auch A. W. Bijvanck hält in seiner Gesamtdarstellung von 1943 (vgl. Anm. 1) trotz gewissen Bedenken an dem spätrömischen Ursprung fest, ohne indessen näher auf das Problem einzugehen. Eine erneute Stellungnahme dazu dürfte daher gerechtfertigt sein, wenn neue Argumente in einem oder dem anderen Sinne beigebracht werden können.

Da ist zunächst unter rein methologischem Gesichtspunkt darauf hinzuweisen, dass das Fehlen spätrömischer Funde am alten Rhein in Holland sehr wohl auf einem Mangel an Beobachtungen, also einer Forschungslücke, beruhen kann und dass Schlüsse ex silentio oft sehr

---

3. *Bijdragen voor vaderlandsche geschiedenis en oudheidkunde 4.R.* 7 (1909) 1ff.; 341ff.; *IV.* Bericht der *Röm.-Germ. Komm.* 1908 (1910) 82f.; *Nederlands vroegste geschiedenis* (1918) 103; 2. Aufl. (1925) 190f.; *Oudheidkundige mededeelingen N.R.* VIII (1927) 25ff.; ferner bei H. Brugmans, *Geschiedenis van Nederland* I (1935) 98.

4. A. G. Roos, *Mnemosyne N.S.* 51 (1923) 327ff.

fragwürdig sind. Das wird in diesem Falle bestätigt durch die Veränderungen, die die archäologische Fundstatistik inzwischen erfahren hat: in Utrecht hat A. E. van Giffen die spätrömische Schicht im Kastell unter dem Domplein neuerdings gefunden,[5] und nach mündlicher Mitteilung, die ich ebenfalls van Giffen verdanke, hat die Durcharbeitung der Münzfunde von Vechten die Fortdauer der Belegung dieses Platzes auch in spätrömischer Zeit mit Sicherheit ergeben. Erwarten musste man das ohnehin auf Grund der historischen Ueberlieferung, worauf noch zurückzukommen ist.

Was dann die Nachricht über die Befestigung der Flussmündungen durch Karl d.Gr. betrifft, so ist an der Tatsache gewiss nicht zu zweifeln, aber einmal braucht die Brittenburg nicht unbedingt damit zusammenzuhängen und zwar umso weniger, als ihre Datierung in Karls Zeit durch Kleinfunde ebenso wenig gesichert ist wie die Datierung in spätrömische Zeit, um Holwerdas erstes Argument im Gegensinne zu verwenden. Trotzdem lässt sich die Ueberlieferung sehr wohl auf die Brittenburg beziehen, ohne deren spätrömischen Ursprung auszuschliessen. Denn wenn hier an der Rheinmündung bereits eine römische Festung vermutlich im mehr oder weniger fortgeschrittenen Zustande des Verfalls bestand, so lag es für Karl viel näher, diese nach Ausbesserung der Schäden wieder in Benutzung zu nehmen, als einen Neubau zu errichten. Dass römische Mauerringe im frühen Mittelalter nicht etwa abgebrochen, sondern gern weiter oder wieder benutzt wurden, ist eine bekannte Tatsache. Für Holland sei nur erinnert an Utrecht, wo durch eine Schenkungsurkunde v.J. 723 ein "monasterium, quod est infra muros Trajecto castro situm constructum" bezeugt ist.[6] Auch in Nijmegen ist die karolingische Pfalz, der heutige Valkhof, an der Stelle des spätrömischen Kastells, möglicherweise unter Benutzung von dessen Mauern, errichtet worden, und nicht anders wird es in Vechten gewesen sein, denn in der eben genannten Urkunde von 723 wird auch eine "villa Fethnam castro" erwähnt.

So sind wir für die Datierung der Brittenburg allein auf den überlieferten Grundriss angewiesen. Dieser darf freilich nicht allzu wörtlich genommen werden, denn er beruht ja nicht wie ein moderner Ausgrabungsplan auf exakter Vermessung des Befundes, vielmehr muss mit einer Interpretation im Sinne des zeitgenössischen Festungsbaues und entsprechenden Veränderungen oder Ergänzungen gerechnet werden. Das ist umso wahrscheinlicher, als die Ueber-

---

5. A. E. van Giffen, *Nieuw Utrechts Dagblad* V 6. u. 23. 5. 1949.
6. Gosses-Japikse, *Handboek tot de staatkundige geschiedenis von Nederland* (1927) 24f. mit Litt. Den Hinweis verdanke ich F. Petri.

lieferung nicht gleichmässig und damit eindeutig ist, worauf schon
hingewiesen wurde. Zunächst darf festgestellt werden, dass Holwerda
allen Bemühungen zum Trotz schlagende Analogien aus karolingischer Zeit nicht hat beibringen können. Denn die von ihm verglichenen Curtes sind zwar rechteckige Anlagen, aber in der Bautechnik
ganz verschieden. Sie haben Erdwälle oder Erdmauern mit Holzver-
steifung, wie sie bezeichnenderweise im karolingischen castrum
Dorestad von Holwerda selber nachgewiesen worden sind, und sie
entbehren vor allem der vorspringenden Halbrundtürme oder Basti-
onen. Diese letzteren sind zwar im späteren Festungsbau des Mittelalters ganz geläufig, aber die Brittenburg ist nach der Ueberlieferung
in der sog. Divisiekroniek schon im Zusammenhang mit der Flut-
katastrophe v.J. 860, als Strand und Dünenkette sich landeinwärts
verschoben, untergegangen. Dagegen sind vorspringende Halbrundtürme auch im spätrömischen Festungsbau nicht ungewöhnlich, und
auch die Bewehrung der Ecken eines Mauervierecks mit einem Paar
divergierender Türme lässt sich belegen.[7]

Mehr noch aber hilft vielleicht zum besseren Verständnis des Brit-
tenburggrundrisses der Vergleich mit einem anderen spätrömischen
Kastell, das in Jublains (Noviodunum Diablintum, Dép. de la
Mayenne) bis heute in teilweise ansehnlicher Höhe erhalten geblieben
ist.[8] Diese Ruine (Abb. 1) besteht ebenfalls aus drei ineinanderge-
schachtelten Mauervierecken, dessen äusserstes mit vorspringenden
Halbrundtürmen bewehrt ist. Die Abmessungen sind etwas grösser
als bei der Brittenburg, der äussere Mauerring misst rund 115 x 126
m, doch ist der Unterschied nicht so erheblich, dass ein Vergleich der
beiden Anlagen sinnlos wäre. Hier ist nun ganz deutlich und auch
immer angenommen worden, dass die Baulichkeiten, wie sie heute auf
engem Raume vereint erscheinen, nicht etwa in einem Zuge errichtet
worden sind, sondern das Ergebnis einer baulichen Entwicklung
bilden, bei der ein immer mehr gesteigertes Bedürfnis nach Sicherheit
massgebend gewesen ist. Am spätesten ist zweifellos der äussere
Mauerring mit seinen vorspringenden Türmen und einer Mauerstärke
von 4,70 m. Das sind deutliche Kennzeichen der Spätzeit und vor dem
4. Jahrhundert nicht denkbar, frühestens z.Zt. Constantins, eher aber
später und zwar in der 2. Hälfte des Jahrhunderts. Das mittlere
Viereck ist ein mächtiger Erdwall mit abgerundeten Ecken ohne
Türme, nicht einmal an der Innenseite. Wenn eine solche Befestigung
am obergermanisch-raetischen Limes gefunden und damit ins 2. oder

---

7. Vgl. etwa R. Cagnat, *L'armee romaine d'Afrique* (1892) 651 (Stadtmauer
von Thiaret). Spätantike Stadtbefestigungen bei A. Blanchet, *Les enceintes
romaines de la Gaule* (1907) passim.

8. A. Grenier, *Manuel d'archéologie gallo-romaine* (1931) 455ff. mit Litt.

die erste Hälfte des 3. Jahrhunderts datiert wäre, so würde das gar nicht auffallen, denn sie trägt die typischen Kennzeichen von Befestigungen dieser Zeit, später dürfte sie ohne Analogie sein. Dasselbe gilt von dem Kernbau der Anlage: ein Mauerviereck von rund 20 x 30 m lichter Weite mit einem Impluvium von rund 7 m in Geviert in der Mitte, also ein grosser Hallenraum mit Oberlicht, ein Atrium compluviatum oder besser corinthium von ungewöhnlichen Abmessungen, das an den Ecken der Nord- und Südseite noch durch kleinere Anbauten teilweise späterer Zeit bereichert ist. Die Mauerstärke beträgt rund 2 m, also weit weniger als im spätrömischen Festungsbau üblich, aber wohl ein Hinweis auf eine ansehnliche Höhe des Gebäudes.

Eine völlige Analogie zu diesem Gebäude ist mir nicht bekannt, weitgehende Aehnlichkeit zeigt immerhin eine merkwürdige Bauanlage am raetischen Limes, der Burgus in der Harlach bei Weissenburg (Abb. 2).[9] Er bildet ein Mauerviereck von rund 32 m im Geviert,

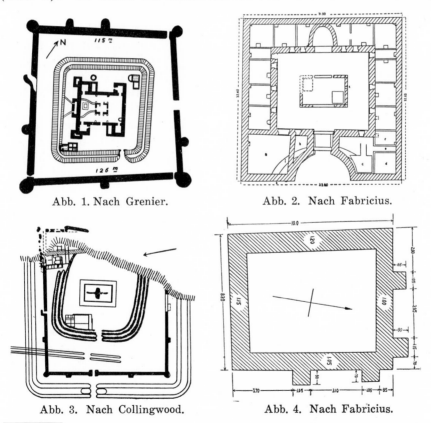

Abb. 1. Nach Grenier.   Abb. 2. Nach Fabricius.

Abb. 3. Nach Collingwood.   Abb. 4. Nach Fabricius.

9. *Der obergermanisch-raetische Limes des Römerreiches* A 7 (1933) 120f. (E. Fabricius).

auch mit einem Impluvium in der Mitte, dazu aber mit einer Flucht von Zimmern ringsum ausgestattet. Ich möchte darin keinen grundsätzlichen Unterschied sehen, sondern nur eine Bereicherung desselben Bautypus, der in Jublains in einfacherer, ursprünglicher Form vertreten ist. Der Bau am raetischen Limes ist nun zweifellos ein Burgus gewesen, die feste Unterkunft, einer militärischen Einheit mit der Aufgabe der Strassenpolizei. Dieselbe Deutung ergibt sich zwanglos für den Kernbau der Ruinen von Jublains, wie sie schon Grenier gegeben hat, d.h. als fester Polizeiposten neben der offenen Zivilstadt, der civitas Diablintum.

Auch Grenier datiert das Erdkastell in die Zeit vor der Mitte des 3. Jahrhunderts und vergleicht es zutreffend mit ähnlichen Erdbefestigungen, wie sie als Polizeiposten der mittleren Kaiserzeit etwa an den grossen Strassen von Köln nach Bavai und von Köln nach Trier, ebenso auch in Raetien an der Strasse von Augsburg nach Bregenz bekannt sind.[10] Die Steinbauten, d.h. den Atriumbau in der Mitte und den äusseren Mauerring, hält er dann für etwa gleichzeitig, entstanden infolge des ersten Frankeneinfalles i.J. 256 und zerstört sowie endgültig verlassen schon beim zweiten Einfall v.J. 275, so dass die Bauten also nur rund 20 Jahre in Benutzung gewesen wären. Das ist indessen wenig wahrscheinlich. Denn wenn Grenier zunächst damit argumentiert, dass beim Bau des Atriums in der Mitte, des corps de logis, wie er es nennt, ebenso wie in dem äusseren Mauerring zahlreiche Spolien, wohl sicher aus der zerstörten Zivilstadt stammend, mit verwendet sind, so gibt diese Tatsache doch lediglich einen terminus post quem, sagen wir nach 256, aber auch beliebig später. Schwerer wiegt das Argument, das sich aus der Münzreihe ergibt: die innerhalb des Kastells gefundenen Münzen gehören zum weitaus grössen Teile der Zeit von 253 bis 273 an, von 151 Stück gehören allein 110 dem Tetricus, und mit einem Stück des Aurelian von 275 bricht die Reihe ab. Aber auch dieses Argument scheint mir nicht unbedingt stichhaltig, denn die Zusammensetzung der Münzreihe legt den Verdacht nahe, dass es sich um einen Schatzfund handelt, der nur nicht als solcher erkannt worden ist. Er würde dann nur beweisen, dass i.J. 275 Gefahr im Verzuge war, für die Baugeschichte und vor allem für die Zeitdauer der Benutzung der Anlage würde er nichts beweisen, so dass eine Datierung des äusseren Mauerringes ins 4. Jahrhundert, wie sie sich aus der Bautechnik ergibt, durchaus möglich erscheint. Denn dass die Datierung mit Münzfunden Vorsicht erfordert, ist schon

---

10. Grenier .a.O., 267ff.; J. Hagen, *Die Römerstrassen der Rheinprovinz* 2, Aufl. (1931) 139ff.; 200ff.; L. Ohlenroth im XXIX. Bericht der *RGK* 1939 (1941) 122ff.; H. van de Weerd, *Inleiding tot de gallo-romeinsche archeologie der Nederlanden* (1944) 78.

mehrfach bemerkt worden,[11] und dass vor allem Schlüsse ex silentio leicht anfechtbar sind, trifft auch in diesem Falle zu. Es sei nur daran erinnert, dass bei der Ausgrabung des Burgus in der Harlach durch die Reichslimeskommission in den Jahren 1916/17 überhaupt keine Münze gefunden wurde, woraus gewiss niemand den Schluss ziehen wird, dass dieser Burgus nie benutzt worden sei.

Die Analogie, die das Kastell Jublains bietet, legt nun den Gedanken nahe, dass auch bei der Brittenburg die drei Mauerringe nicht in einem Zuge errichtet worden sind, sondern verschiedenen Zeiten angehören. Am spätesten dürfte auch hier der äussere Mauerring mit seinen vorspringenden Rundtürmen sein. Der mittlere Mauerring könnte zeitlich dazu gehören wie etwa in den rheinischen Kastellen valentinianischer Zeit vom Typus Alzey und in den Kastellen des syrischen und arabischen Limes aus der Zeit Diocletians und später, wo die Kasernen an die Innenseite der Ringmauer angelehnt sind. Doch ist das gewiss nur eine Möglichkeit. Am ältesten dürfte jedenfalls der quadratische Bau in der Mitte sein, und wenn man nach seiner Bedeutung fragt, so lassen die regelmässig angeordneten Mauervorsprünge an der Aussenseite zunächst an ein Horreum denken. Doch scheint mir der Bau für diesen Zweck reichlich klein, auch wäre der quadratische Grundriss dafür ganz ungewöhnlich. Wenn man dagegen die ungewöhnliche Lage an der Mündung eines grossen Stromes und Schiffahrtsweges ins Meer beachtet, so liegt gewiss nichts näher, als hier einen Leuchtturm zu vermuten, denn gerade einen solchen unentbehrlichen Wegweiser für die Schiffahrt muss man hier unbedingt erwarten und das umso mehr, als auch die gegenüberliegende Themsemündung zum mindesten einen solchen Leuchtturm in Richborough, gleichfalls später durch ein Steinkastell mit Rundtürmen gesichert (Abb. 3), besessen hat, um gar nicht zu reden von den Leuchttürmen in Boulogne einerseits und Dover andererseits.[12] Zu einem turmartigen Gebäude würden im übrigen auch die Mauervorsprünge gut passen, die am ehesten als Strebepfeiler verständlich sind und auf eine ansehnliche Mauerhöhe schliessen lassen wie etwa bei einem kleineren Burgus von 8,45 x 10,00 m Aussenmassen am obergermanischen Limes in der Talschlucht des Emsbaches unweit des Feldbergkastells (Abb. 4).[13]

Einen solchen Leuchtturm, der natürlich an der Rheinmündung nicht erst in der Spätzeit, im 4. Jahrhundert, erwartet werden darf, wird man somit auch baugeschichtlich als den Kern der Brittenburg

---

11. z.B. Gordon Home, *Roman London* (1926) 8ff.

12. R. C. Collingwood, *The archaeology of Roman Britain* (1930) 51 fig. 12 a; Grenier, *Manuel* I (1931) 471; II, 2 (1934) 529.

13. *Der obergerm.-raet. Limes* A 2, 1 (1936) 98 u. Taf. 7 Fig. 3c (E. Fabricius).

ansehen dürfen, während der äussere Mauerring mit seinen vorspringenden Türmen sich leicht als das Endglied der Kette fortifi-
katorische Anlagen verstehen lässt, die für den Rheinlimes in spätrömischer Zeit durch die Ueberlieferung bezeugt sind. So spricht
Eumenius in einer Rede v.J. 296, also unter Constantius, von "alarum
et cohortium castra toto Rheni et Histri et Euphratis limite restituta,"
und im Panegyricus auf Constantin v.J. 310 heisst es: "totus armatis
navibus Rhenus instructus sit et ripis omnibus usque ad oceanum
dispositus miles immineat." Dann wissen wir durch Libanios und
Ammianus Marcellinus, dass Julian in den Jahren 358-360 am "limes
Germaniae secundae" gewesen ist, dass er die Rheinschiffahrt wieder
in Gang gebracht hat, um den Getreideinport aus Britannien zu
sichern, dass zu ihrem Schutze zahlreiche Grenzplätze neu befestigt
wurden und dass er selber bis zum Ozean vorgestossen ist. Wie
Ammian weiter berichtet, hat Valentinian I. diese Politik fortgesetzt:
"Rhenum omnem a Raetiarum exordio ad usque fretalem oceanum
magnis molibus communiebat."[14] Diese Nachrichten bezeugen über-
einstimmend die grosse Bedeutung, die der Rheinlimes auch in spätrömischer Zeit gehabt hat und zwar bis zur Mündung des Stromes ins
Meer, sodass hier bei Katwijk nach einem Kastell dieser Zeit sogar
gesucht werden müsste, wenn es nicht in Gestalt der Brittenburg
schon bekannt wäre. Welchem der genannten Kaiser die Anlage des
Kastells dann zuzuschreiben ist, bleibt unsicher, doch werden Julian
oder Valentinian den Vorzug verdienen, weil vor ihrer Zeit der Rhein
als militärische Grenze verloren gegangen war und von zahlreichen
Neuanlagen danach ausdrücklich die Rede ist.

Kurz zu erörtern bleibt schliesslich noch die Frage, wie diese kleine,
aber starke Festung im Altertum geheissen hat, ob sie überhaupt einen
besonderen Namen geführt hat. Denn hier an der Mündung des
Rheins lag nach der Ueberlieferung eine grössere Siedlung zivilen
Charakters namens Lugdunum, vermutlich auch schon früh durch ein
Kastell geschützt ebenso wie die übrigen Grenzplätze am Rhein. Die
römischen Siedlungsfunde von Klein-Duin, rund 1½ km südöstlich
der Brittenburg und identisch mit der Fundstelle römischer Altertümer von 1571, sind wohl mit Recht darauf bezogen worden.[15] Doch
sind daneben noch mindestens drei weitere Fundplätze im Raume von
Katwijk aan Zee bis nach Katwijk aan den Rijn bekannt, die sich über

14. Vgl. A. Riese, *Das rheinische Germanien in der antiken Litteratur* (1892)
227; 234; 284f.; 291; 295; 307; Bijvanck, *Excerpta Romana* I (1931) 376; 379;
412 431 433 435.
15. H. van de Weerd a.a.O. 46; Bijvanck, *Nederland i. d. rom. tijd* 2 (1943) 420;
ders., *Mnemosyne* N.S. 46 (1918) 83f. Genaue Angaben über die Lage der bisher
bekannten Fundplätze römischer Altertümer im Raume von Katwijk verdanke ich
der Güte A. E. van Giffens.

eine Strecke von mehr als 2 km Länge oder, wenn man die Brittenburg mitrechnet, sogar mehr als 3 km Länge verteilen, und dabei scheint mir die Frage der siedlungsgeographischen Selbständigkeit des Praetorium Agrippinae der Peutingerkarte (nur 1½ km stromaufwärts in Valkenburg?) noch keineswegs geklärt. Es wird also hier im Falle von Lugdunum nicht anders gewesen sein als an zahlreichen anderen Grenzplätzen an Rhein und Donau, wo die militärische und zivile Besiedlung sich oft mehrere Kilometer weit am Ufer entlang zog, so in Batavodurum-Noviomagus, Vetera-Tricesima-Colonia Traiana, Novaesium, Carnuntum, Aquincum und sonst. Doch sind dabei Sonderbezeichnungen für bauliche Anlagen mit besonderer Zweckbestimmung wie etwa für ein Truppenlager, einen Vicus, auch eine Colonia oder etwa einen Leuchtturm, natürlich nicht ausgeschlossen, und es sind daher auch hier mehrere Möglichkeiten zu prüfen.

Wenn die Ruine im 16. und 17. Jahrhundert bald castrum Britannicum oder arx Brittonum, bald burcht van Brittanie, burcht te Britten, huys van Britten, huys te Britten, auch château de Britten oder Brittenburg genannt wird — vielleicht ist auch eine im 14. Jahrhundert erwähnte borch te Bretten darauf zu beziehen —, so liegt gewiss der Verdacht nahe, dass die lateinischen Formen gelehrten Ursprungs, also jünger sind als die niederdeutschen Formen. Zwar hat Holwerda gemeint, dass castrum Britannicum als Bezeichung eines wichtigen Punktes am limes Britannicus karolingischer Zeit ungewöhnlich gut gepasst hätte, doch scheint mir dabei nicht genügend beachtet, dass mit dem limes Britannicus bei Einhard immer nur die Bretagne bzw. eine Militärgrenze gegen die dort sesshaft gewordenen Bretonen gemeint und daher die Uebertragung des Begriffs auf andere der Insel Britannien gegenüberliegende Küstenstrecken des Festlandes kaum zulässig ist. Man wird also annehmen dürfen, dass die Namensform Britten die ältere ist, und das um so mehr, als sie auch im oberdeutschen Sprachgebiet nicht selten begegnet. So gibt es ein Britten im Kreise Merzig, südlich Trier, ferner gehört hierher Bretzenheim bei Mainz, das in Urkunden des 8. Jahrhunderts als Brittenheim — latinisiert Brittanorum (auch Brettanorum oder Prittonorum) villa — erscheint, dann Britheim am Neckar (Britihaim a. 782), auch Brutten im Thurgau, das im 9. und 10. Jahrhundert Pritta, Britta oder Brittona heisst, sowie möglicherweise die Orte Bretten, Brettenbach, Brettnach usw.[16] Die Namen im Einzelnen zu erklären, muss der Eigennamenforschung überlassen

16. E. Förstemann, *Altdeutsches Namenbuch* II (Ortsnamen) 3. Aufl. (1913) 576f.; Henius, *Grosses Ortsnamenlexikon für das Deutsche Reich* (1928) *s.v.*

bleiben. Immerhin darf man sagen, dass in vielen Fällen wahrscheinlich der Personnenname Britto den Kern des Ortsnamens bildet. Er
erscheint nicht nur als Cognomen in römischen Inschriften der Kaiserzeit, aus der auch ein Trierer Bischof dieses Namens und Zeitgenosse
Gratians bekannt ist, sondern er ist ebenso im Mittelalter bis mindestens ins 11. Jahrhundert gebräuchlich gewesen.[17] Im Falle der Britt-
tenburg wäre auch die Anknüpfung an den Volksnamen der Brittones
nicht undenkbar, wenn das Kastell von einer militärischen Einheit
dieses Namens gebaut worden oder mit ihr belegt gewesen wäre. Denn
für die Benennung eines Ortes nach dem dort stationierten Truppen-
teil lassen sich Beispiele namhalft machen wie etwa am Donaulimes
Asturis-Klosterneuburg, Comagenis-Tulln und Batavis-Passau, wo
der Name sich sogar bis heute gehalten hat.[18] Man müsste dann eine
spätrömische Ortsbezeichnung mit dem Bestandteil Brittonum voraussetzen und annehmen, dass dieses Wort allein in die Volksprache
übergegangen wäre, um erst sekundär durch den Zusatz "burg"
wieder erweitert zu werden. So ist es offenbar auch bei dem benachbarten Forum Hadriani gewesen, dessen Name nicht nur in Voorburg
oder Foreburg, sondern auch in den einfachen Formen Fore und Veur
weiterlebt.[19] Für die Anknüpfung an den Brittonennamen könnte
angeführt werden, dass sich in der Sammlung Chevalier zu Utrecht
ein Ziegel mit dem Stempel VEX (illariorum) BRIT (tonum) mit
der Herkunftsangabe "château de Britten" befand. Doch ist die
Fundangabe dieses sonst in Nijmegen häufigen Stempels äusserst
suspekt, sodass die entsprechende Erklärung des Ortsnamens darin
kaum eine Stütze finden dürfte.[20]

Zu erwähnen ist in diesem Zusammenhange noch eine Ansicht, die
R. Müller in einer Arbeit über "Die Geographie der Peutingerschen
Tafel" 1926 geäussert hat, vermutlich ohne Kenntnis des archäologischen Befundes.[21] Er leitet den heutigen Ortsnamen Katwijk ab
von caput vicus und setzt diese hypothetische Namensform gleich mit
dem caput Germaniarum, das im Itinerarium Antonini am Beginn der
Rheinuferstrasse genannt ist. Dagegen ist zunächst unter wortge-
schichtlichem Gesichtspunkt einzuwenden, dass Katwijk als Ortsname auch sonst vorkommt, wo eine Anknüpfung an caput vicus nicht
möglich ist, so z.B Katwijk an der Maas und Kettwig an der Ruhr,

17. A. Holder, *Altceltischer Sprachschatz* I (1896) 609; Förstemann, *Namen-buch I (Personennamen)* 2. Aufl. (1900) 336.

18. F. Wagner, *Die Römer in Bayern* (1924) 51f.; A. Schober, *Die Römer in Oesterreich* (1935) 32f.

19. Bijvanck, *Mnemosyne* N.S. 46 (1918) 97.

20. Zuletzt *CIL* 13 pars VI (1933) 12557; Bijvanck, *Excerpta Romana* 2 (1935) 203 Nr. 348.

21. R. Müller, *Geographischer Anzeiger* 27 (1926) 216.

das im 11. und 12. Jahrhundert Katwik oder Katwig geschrieben wird.[22] Trotzdem wäre die Gleichsetzung, rein topographisch gesehen, sehr wohl denkbar, wenn caput Germaniarum im Itinerar wirklich als Ortsname gemeint wäre. Das ist aber auch nicht der Fall. Veranlasst ist das Missverständnis vermutlich dadurch, dass Parthey und Pinder in ihrer Ausgabe des Itinerars von 1848 der Lesart in zwei jüngeren Handschriften gefolgt sind, wo es heisst: "caput Germaniarum a Lugduno Argentorato mpm CCCXXV sic." Sie haben caput Germaniarum offenbar als Ueberschrift eines neuen Abschnittes verstanden, worin die Strassen in den beiden germanischen Provinzen verzeichnet sind. Die Ausgabe von O. Cuntz von 1929 lehrt aber, dass im Archetypus aller erhaltenen Handschriften gestanden hat: "a Lugduno caput Germaniarum Argentorato . . .," wobei in der Urschrift capite statt caput anzunehmen ist. Hier kann caput Germaniarum nur als Erläuterung zu Lugdunum gemeint sein, das am Anfang der Rheinstrasse lag, also tatsächlich das caput (limitis) Germaniarum bildete und auch von Ptolemaios durch den Zusatz Βαταυῶν von gleichnamigen Städten Galliens und Aquitaniens unterschieden ist. Zwar begegnet caput im Itinerar sonst nur als wirklicher Ortsname, wie z.B. Caput Cilani, Caput Tyrsi usw., so wie es in der römischen Ortsnamengebung überhaupt ganz geläufig ist. Auch ein Caput Germaniarum wäre als Ortsname also keineswegs ungewöhnlich, darf vielmehr gerade hier durchaus erwartet werden. Aber die handschriftliche Ueberlieferung spricht dagegen, und überdies sind ähnliche Erläuterungen bei Ortsnamen im Itinerar gar nicht selten. Man vergleiche etwa das Wort fines, das nicht nur als Ortsname mehrfach erscheint, sondern ebenso häufig als Erläuterung eines Ortsnamens wie z.B. Cyrene fines Marmariae, Catabathmos fines Alexandriae usw. Dasselbe gilt von den Worten traiectus und portus, die gleichfalls als Ortsnamen vorkommen, daneben aber wieder zur Erläuterung von Ortsnamen verwendet werden und als Zusatz zu Lugdunum in der Form von traiectus Britanniae oder portus Germaniarum sehr wohl denkbar wären. Schliesslich gehören hierher auch die Worte colonia, municipium, vicus, villa, praetorium, legio, ala, castra, castellum, praesidium, die sich auf die Rechtsstellung oder den militärischen Charakter eines Ortes beziehen und alle sowohl als Namen desselben wie auch als erläuternder Zusatz verwendet werden.[23] So bleibt das Namenproblem bei der Brittenburg einstweilen offen, nur der glückliche Fund einer Inschrift mag vielleicht einmal die Lösung bringen.

---

22. W. Kaspers, *Zeitschr. f. Ortsnamenforschung* 13 (1927) 213f.
23. Alle Belege sind dem Index zum Text der *Itineraria Romana* I ed. O. Cuntz (1929) zu entnehmen.

LEBENDIGES ALTERTUM

Erich Swoboda

Graz, Austria

Bereits 1 Stunde östlich von Wien liegt beiderseits der breit und ruhig dahinströmenden Donau mit ihrem Steilhang im Süden und dem davor gelagerten, ungehemmt wuchernden Auengürtel eine Landschaft erfüllt von bewegtem und bewegendem Geschehen, voll geschichtlicher Erinnerungen. Für den Historiker des Altertums gewinnt sie Bedeutung, sobald im Verfolg augusteischer Sicherungspolitik römische Truppen im 6.Jh.n.Chr. die Donau in diesem Raum überquerten und nordwärts gegen das Reich Marbods vorstiessen; denn in diesem Zusammenhang wird in der antiken Literatur zum ersten Male der Name Carnuntum als der eines strategisch günstigen und wichtigen Platzes genannt (Vell.Pat.2, 109,5), am Schnittpunkt zweier Hauptverkehrslinien gelegen und von der Natur in gleicher Weise zum Angriff wie zur Verteidigung bestimmt. Als der Aufstand der pannonisch-dalmatischen Völkerschaften im Rücken der die March aufwärts marschierenden Armee, das *gravissimum omnium externorum bellorum post Punica* (Suet.*Tib.* 16), Tiberius zur Umkehr zwang, und das spätere politische Programm des ersten Princeps hinsichtlich der Reichsgrenzen (Tac. *Ann.* 1, 11 *consilium coercendi intra terminos imperii*) die Abkehr von allen Offensivplänen zur Folge hatte, ging der Name der illyrisch-keltischen Siedlung auch auf das Lager über, das jetzt hier erbaut wurde. Von nun an zählte die Festung Carnuntum bis in die letzten Tage römischer Herrschaft zu den bedeutendsten militärischen Punkten an der Nordgrenze des Reiches, während die Zivilsiedlung, die hier wie anderswo neben dem *castrum* emporwuchs, seit ihrer Stadtwerdung unter Hadrian (*municipium Aelium Carnuntum*) als kulturelles und wirtschaftliches Zentrum inmitten barbarischer Distrikte den Gedanken des universalen Rom verwirklichte. Durch ihre Grenzlage von den Germanen jenseits der Donau wiederholt angegriffen und überrannt — zum ersten Male mit verheerender Wucht zur Zeit der Markomannenkriege unter Marc Aurel[1] — sind über Lager und Zivilstadt während ihres 400-jährigen Bestandes alle Schicksale hinweggegangen, die einer Siedlung widerfahren können und haben, seitdem vom 3. Jahrhundert an auch der Verfall der politischen und wirtschaftlichen Kapazität

---

1. W. Zwikker, "Studien zur Markussäule" (*Allard Pierson Stichting* 8) 1941; hiezu die Besprechung R. Eggers im *Gnomon* 1942, 327 ff.

des Reiches mit brutaler Energie in seine Geschicke eingegriffen hat, aus dem einstigen Vorort von Pannonia sup. schrittweise ein *oppidum . . . desertum quidem nunc et squalens* (Amm.Marc.30, 5,2) gemacht.[2]

Bei dem völligen Mangel an jeder schriftlichen Ueberlieferung, welche über die Geschichte Carnuntums orientieren könnte, blieben allein Ausgrabungen, die zunächst allerdings nur die Erforschung des Lagers und seiner Bauten zum Ziele hatten und dort so gut wie abgeschlossen sind;[3] unsere Kenntnis von der Zivilstadt schöpfte bis zum Jahre 1926, das die erste Veröffentlichung über das Amphitheater der Zivilstadt von R. Egger brachte,[4] mehr oder weniger lediglich aus Zufallsfunden, und erst 1938 wurden auch auf dem Areal der Zivilsiedlung systematische Grabungen in entscheidendem Maße in Angriff genommen.[5] Der Ausbruch des 2. Weltkrieges setzte im Jahr darauf hinter den vielversprechenden Anfang den Schlußpunkt, doch kaum ging das Leben wieder einigermaßen seine gewohnten Bahnen, so wurde von der NOe-Landesregierung, Kulturreferat (Hofrat Dr. Hans Rintersbacher), der Plan zur Freilegung Carnuntums wieder diskutiert und im Herbst 1948 mit seiner praktischen Durchführung begonnen. Aus der Reihe überraschender Ergebnisse dieser Campagne und der des Jahres 1949 sei in Kürze ein Komplex erörtert, dessen Grundriß keiner der sonst geläufigen antiken Raumgruppierungen folgt und sich in einem bestimmten Typ des Bauernhauses des ostalpinen Raumes über die Jahrhunderte hinweg bis in die Gegenwart erhalten hat.

Die Geschichte des Bauwerks (Abb. 1) ist, unter Außerachtlassung einiger noch ungeklärter Fragen, die in diesem Zusammenhang jedoch ohne Bedeutung sind, im wesentlichen folgende: seine erste Anlage fällt aller Wahrscheinlichkeit nach in die Blütezeit der Zivilstadt Carnuntum, d.s. die Jahre etwa von 120 bis zum Ausbruch der Markomannenkriege, eine Zeitspanne, die zum mindesten für die beiden Mosaike gilt, welche auf den Boden der zwei südlichsten Räume gelegt sind. Wie ausgedehnte Brandspuren, Münzfunde, Mauer- und Dachziegelschutt, sowie eine deutlich erkennbare zweite Bauperiode, die Werkstücke einer früheren Epoche verwendet, lehren, ist die erste Anlage im Verlaufe des Markomannenkrieges ein Opfer der Kämpfe geworden. Nach der

---

2. Swoboda, E., *Carnuntum, seine Geschichte und seine Denkmäler*, 1949; vgl. auch R. Egger, "Die Ostalpen in der Spätantike" (*Das Neue Bild der Antike 2*, 1942) S. 395 ff.
3. *RLiOe* 1-10, 12, 16-18 (1900-1937).
4. *RLiOe* 16, 69 ff.; der Bericht wurde von Miltner, F., *RLiOe* 17, 1933, 1 ff. fortgesetzt.
5. Vgl. H. Vetters, *AJA* 52, 1948, 230 ff.

CARNVNTVM – AVSGRABVNG MCMIL
»LAVBENHAVS«

GRVNDRISZ

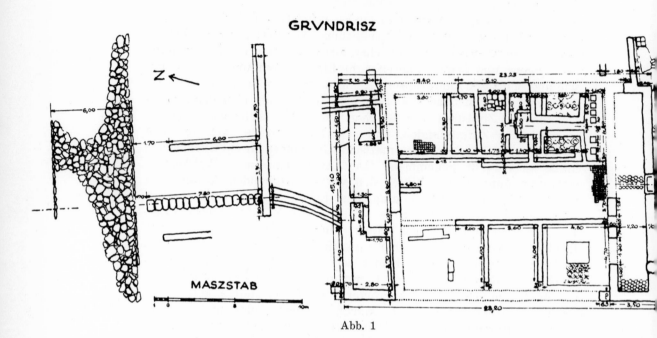

Abb. 1

Wiederkehr beruhigter Verhältnisse schritt man, vielleicht noch im 2., eher aber erst im 3. Jahrhundert an den Wiederaufbau, wobei man von der ersten Anlage verwendete, was noch zu verwenden war, z.Bsp. die Fundamente, den Bau im Norden um eine 2.80 m. tiefe Vorhalle vergrößerte und in den südöstlichen Raum, dessen Mosaik, zerstört und von Brandspuren verunziert, seinen Sinn als Dekoration verloren hatte, eine Hypokaustanlage einbaute. Wie lange der Bau in dieser Form stand, ist nicht zu sagen; vermuten läßt sich, daß er, da spätere Umbauten nicht festgestellt werden konnten und aus seinem Bereich noch eine Münze des Valens (364 — 378) zutage kam, bis in die letzten Tage Carnuntums seiner Bestimmung gedient hat.

 Nun ein Wort zum Grundriß. Die Außenmauern des Baus, die im allgemeinen bereits 40 cm unter der Oberfläche erscheinen, 70 cm breit und stellenweise noch bis zu 1,00 m hoch erhalten sind (Aufgehendes und Fundament), schließen sich zu einem Rechteck von 23,20 x 15,20 m zusammen, dessen Innengliederung durch einen etwas aus dem Zentrum gerückten, rund 4 m breiten und

15,50 m langen Korridor bestimmt ist, von dem aus sich westwärts
3, nach Osten zu 4 Räume öffnen; die Böden der beiden südlichsten trugen Mosaiken, die, wie bereits erwähnt, der ersten
Bauperiode angehören. Derselben Epoche zuzuzählen ist die im
Süden dem Korridor quer vorgelegte Halle, 2,20 m tief und 13,80
m lang (Innenmaße) und mit kleinen, sechseckigen Ziegeln ge-
pflastert (6 cm Dm), in deren Giebelseite die Türschwelle des Eingangs versetzt ist, der Lage des Korridors entsprechend ebenfalls
aus der Mittelachse gerückt. Die Halle im Norden mit Keller,
Abfluß zum Kanal und Hypokaustum ist, wie die Fundumstände
erweisen, ein späterer Annex, nicht der ursprünglichen Planung
zugehörig.

Der erste Grundriß präsentiert sich demnach als ein Rechteck
mit vorgelegter Halle und bewahrt damit einen Typus des Wohn-
baus, der entweder als Rechteck allein oder mit Türlaube in vorgeschichtliche Zeit zurückreicht und während dieser überall dort
in Uebung war, wo genügend Wald gestanden ist, der Mensch
bereits seßhafter Bauer geworden war und gelernt hatte, mit
seinen primitiven Werkzeugen Bäume zu fällen. Ist nun in der
Architektur der Zweck das Primäre und die Form das Sekundäre,
und ist das Rechteck neben dem Rund eine der beiden möglichen
Komponenten räumlicher Gestaltung und daher als Element des
urgeschichtlichen Hausbaus in ganz Nord- und Mitteleuropa, aber
auch in den tropischen Zonen anzutreffen,[6] so ist damit zugleich
gesagt, daß unser Haus in seinen Umrißlinien über das Primäre,
mit anderen Worten: über das Primitive, Elementare, nicht hinausgekommen ist, daß der Baumeister trotz der Entwicklungsmög-
lichkeiten, welche das Rechteck als Raumelement gibt, an dem
überkommenen Grundriß festgehalten hat. Und da auch die Dach-
form geblieben ist, wie sie in der Urzeit gewesen war, das steile
Pfetten- oder Firstdach, das der Niederschlagsreichtum unserer
Breiten bereits in der Steinzeit ausgebildet hatte,[7] so haben wir
den Vorläufer des Carnuntiner Hauses so zu denken, wie ihn Abb.
2 zeigt: dem rechteckigen Wohn- und Herdraum ist giebelseitig
durch Verlängerung der Firstpfette über die Front des Wohnraumes
eine Türlaube angegliedert, die zunächst, von zwei Pfosten ge-

---

6. Ebert, *Reallexiken d. Vorgesch.* 5, 1926, S. 160 ff.; Oelmann, F., *Haus und
Hof im Altertum*, 1927, S. 41 ff. Die Formulierung "nordisches Tiefhaus," der
man in der volkskundlichen und urgeschichtlichen Literatur immer wieder
begegnet, ist falsch, ein Schlagwort, dem auch ich noch in der Monographie
Carnuntum, S. 49 erlegen bin; man kann nur von Tief- oder Rechteckhaus sprechen,
das aber ist durchaus nicht nur auf den Norden beschränkt. Vgl. auch O. Paret,
Das neue Bild der Vorgeschichte, 1948, S. 117 ff.

7. Radig, W., *Der Wohnbau im jungsteinzeitlichen Deutschland.* 1930, S. 40 ff.

tragen, offen bleibt, später aber über die Zwischenstufe des "Antenhauses" an allen 3 Seiten eingewandet wird. Diese Laube ist jedoch nicht als ein Annex im Sinne einer Raumdifferenzierung zu verstehen, sie dient lediglich dem Zweck, Schutz vor den Unbilden der Witterung zu bieten, den Eingang in den Wohn- und Herdraum vor der unmittelbaren Berührung mit der Außenwelt zu isolieren. Sie ist also, um nur einige Beispiele zu nennen, durchaus verschieden von der jeweils zweiten Zelle der bandkeramischen Rechteckhäuser bei Köln-Lindenthal[8] und in der Harth,[9] zu unterscheiden von den Raumteilungen der bisher bekannten Rechteckhäuser in der Zivilstadt Carnuntum[10] und in Donnerskirchen,[11] von der Disposition des römischen Bauernhauses bei Gleisdorf,[12] und durchaus anderer Bestimmung als der "kammerartige Anbau" bei einigen Häusern auf der Stellerburg,[13] wo z.Bsp. an einem ca 3 x 5 m großen Haus eine Erweiterung in der Art vorgenommen wurde, daß, wie deutlich erkennbar ist, zu einem späteren Zeitpunkt "in gleicher Breite des alten Hauses ein kammerartiger Anbau von etwa 6 Fuß Länge an den Ostgiebel angesetzt wurde", um "ein neu hinzutretendes Raumbedürfnis auf einfachste Art zu befriedigen." Denn in den zuerst genannten Fällen handelt es sich um Raumteilung innerhalb des ursprünglich einzelligen Rechteckhauses ohne Laube, bzw. um Einbeziehung der Laube in den Wohnraum, wie sie wirtschaftliche und kulturelle Entwicklung, die erst Wunsch und Bedürfnis nach vermehrter Differenzierung wachrufen, mit sich bringen, auf der Stellerburg um Raumteilung durch Addition. Unser Haus hat diese Entwicklung nur insoferne mitgemacht als durch den Korridor eine harmonische und rationelle Aufteilung des Wohnraumes geschaffen, der Laube aber ihre ursprüngliche Bestimmung belassen wurde, wodurch das Haus auch nach seiner Umsetzung in Stein seine erste Form bewahrte. Die Einwirkung römischen Bauwillens erfaßte also nur das Konstruktive, nicht die Grundform. Dieses Beharren am Ueberkommenen wurde auch dann nicht gelockert, als die Befriedigung gesteigerter Bedürfnisse weitere Räume erforderte; man wurde ihnen durch einen Zubau, durch die Nordhalle, gerecht.

Es liegt nahe, in dem Grundriß unseres Hauses die Bautradition

---

8. Buttler-Haberey, "Die bandkeramische Ansiedlung bei Köln-Lindenthal," *Röm.German. Forsch.* 2. 1936.

9. Tackenberg, K., *Germania.* 21, 1937, S. 217 ff.

10. *RLiOe* 8, 1907, Sp. 9.35.37; Fig.3.17.19; *RLiOe* 7, 1906, Sp. 97; Fig.51 K.

11. Kubitschek, W., "Römerfunde von Eisenstadt" (*Sonderschr.d.Oesterr. Arch. Instituts* 11) 1926, S. 49.

12. Schmid, W., "Archaeologische Forschungen in der Steiermark," *JOAI* 25, 1929, Sp. 67 ff.

13. Rudolph, M. V., *Die Ausgrabung der Stellerburg*, 1942, S. 87.

der einheimischen illyrisch-keltischen Bevölkerung zu sehen; sie
vergegenwärtigt den Typus des Hauses der Handwerker und Kauf-
leute wie ihn Oelmann für die gallisch-römischen Straßensied-

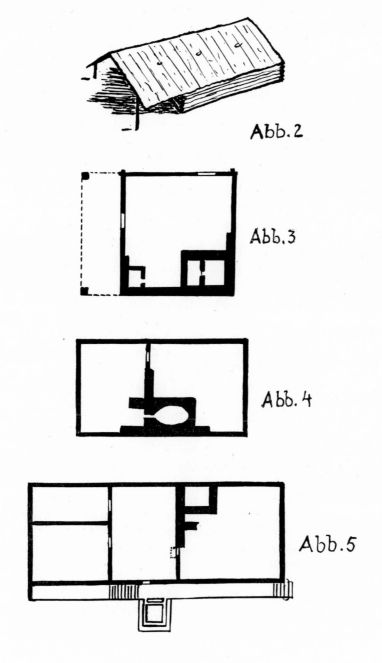

Abb. 2

Abb. 3

Abb. 4

Abb. 5

lungen in Deutschland und England nachgewiesen hat.[14] Ob
freilich Oelmanns Beobachtung, daß diese Rechteckhäuser (taber-
nae, canabae) mit und ohne ambitus in den beiden britannischen
Landstädten Calleva und Venta Silurum nahezu alle entlang der
Hauptstraße liegen, während die vornehmeren und weitläufigen
Gebäude die Seitenstraßen umsäumen — eine Tatsache, aus der
Oelmann, gewiß richtig, die Entwicklung vom Straßenvicus zur
Stadt abliest—, auch für Carnuntum gelten wird, kann beim gegen-
wärtigen Stand der Grabung nicht gesagt werden; es scheint jeden-
falls fraglich, da unser Haus, vor allem im Osten, an vielräumige
Gebäude grenzt, und die Straße nördlich des Hauses kaum die
Hauptstraße sein dürfte.

Aber wie dem auch sein mag, der Haustyp ist sicher vorrömisch.
Es ist nun interessant festzustellen, daß sich dieser Typus, der
durch seine Enge und Abgeschlossenheit den Bedingungen entspricht, die an das Stadthaus gestellt werden, im kärntnerisch-
steirischen Bauernhaus, dem sogen. Rauchstubenhaus, bis heute
erhalten hat. Die Abb. 3,4 und 5 zeigen die Entwicklung, welche
diese Bauform genommen hat; sie geht aus vom Rechteckhaus
mit offener Laube (Abb. 3) und führt über die geschlossene (Abb.
4) zum ausgebauten Rauchstubenhaus des ostalpinen Raumes (Abb.
5), in dem sich zwei vorgeschichtliche Feuerstätten schneiden, das
westliche Herdgebiet und das östliche Kochofengebiet. "Der Haupt-
und Herdraum hatte schon in vorindogermanischer Zeit eine Vorhalle, die im ostgermanisch-slavischen Raume und daher auch beim
Rauchstubenhaus lange offen blieb und deshalb Laube ("Labn")
heißt. Noch heute findet man in Kärnten und im angrenzenden
obersteirischen Murgebiet Lauben ohne traufseitige Wände, und
wenn diese im übrigen Bereich des Rauchstubenhauses oft gemauert
sind, so ist das eine verhältnismäßig junge Erscheinung. Jenseits
der Labn lag und liegt oft noch heute der Speicher oder die daraus
gebildete Kammer oder Kachelstube."[15]

Das Carnuntiner Haus ist ein weiteres Beispiel dafür, daß die
Architektur die Tradition nicht minder zäh bewahrt wie etwa das
Religiöse, daß bis in unsere Tage weiterlebt, was vor vielen Jahrhunderten gebaut wurde, und daß es falsch wäre, wenn der Ausgräber auf provinzialrömischem Boden nur die "klassische" Raumord-
nung betrachten wollte.

---

14. *Bonner Jahrb.*1923, S. 77 ff.

15. Geramb, V. v., "Vom Werden und von der Würde unserer Bauernhöfe"
(*Heimatliches Bauen im Ostalpenraum*, 1941) S. 78.

POLYBIUS ON THE PONTUS AND THE BOSPHORUS

(iv. 39-42)

F. W. WALBANK
The University of Liverpool

Five hundred years before Constantine founded his New Rome, the unique virtues of its site had engaged the attention of Polybius, who analysed them in one of his most characteristic digressions. The geographical excursus was a traditional feature of Greek and Roman historiography, designed to contribute to the entertainment of the reader;[1] but the seven chapters in which Polybius discusses the hydrography of the Pontic area, the course and causes of the Bosphorus current, and the position of Byzantium, illustrate rather that historian's earnest desire to instruct. A recent study of Polybius' work on the east Balkans[2] by Ch. Danov suggests that Polybius' account here is highly original, and based on information gathered on the spot. The intention of the present paper is to consider afresh Polybius' discussion of the Pontus and Bosphorus in the light of this and other theories about his sources, and taking into account recent oceanographical work. In offering his results to Professor D. M. Robinson, *qui nihil Graecum a se alienum putat*, the writer takes the opportunity to wish him πολλὰ ἔτη.[2a]

I.

Danov assumes that Polybius visited Byzantium and the Pontus, quoting three passages, iv.38.12; 39.6; 43.2. In fact, not one of these will support such an interpretation,[3] and the first presupposes the very opposite. For both here and in iv.40.1-3 Polybius had an excellent opportunity to mention his visit, but omits to do so; and since he was the kind of man we know him to be, an *argumentum*

---

1. Cf. *ClMed* 9 (1948) 156ff.

2. Danov, Ch. M., *Polybios u. seine Nachrichten über den Ostbalkan* (Sonderschr. des bulgar. arch. Inst., No. 2, Sofia, 1942), 63. For the loan of a copy of this work, in Bulgarian and therefore (unfortunately) comprehensible to me only in the German summary on pp.61-4, I am indebted to the kindness of Dr. Marcus N. Tod.

2a. The subject seems appropriate to the occasion since Professor Robinson's first publication was a monograph on Sinope on the Pontus, where he cites Polybius' accurate and detailed geographic description of that city.

3. In 38.12 and 39.6 Danov appears to be misled by φασι, which he takes as referring to native informants; it means of course *on dit;* cf.43.6 or 59.5 (subject οἱ μῦθοι).

ex silentio in such a context acquires great weight.[4] Indeed it may be assumed that Polybius never visited Byzantium and the Pontus, because he carefully does not claim to have done so; in which case his account must be based on information gained from others, written or oral. In support of this conclusion is the fact that Polybius, the habitual exponent and defender of autopsy against the armchair historian, is here at pains to assert the superiority of scientific deduction *(ἐκ τῆς κατὰ φύσιν θεωρίας)*—which, as we shall see, means Peripatetic speculation—over the account of some unnamed predecessor whose description of the Pontic currents drew on "merchants' yarns."[5]

For the central section of this digression (39.7-42.8), with its theoretical speculations on the origin and ultimate fate of the land and water masses of the Pontic area, Polybius' source (as Danov agrees)[6] is clearly literary. But it is sandwiched between two 'topographical' passages of quite different character (39.1-6; 43.1-44. 10), which are closely linked by the mention of *τὸ καλούμενον Ἱερόν* at the Pontus end of the Bosphorus (39.6), and the reference back to this with the resumption of the same source in 43.1. What this source was will be considered below; but first it is convenient to pay some attention to the hydrographical section, the digression within the digression.

II.

For the constant current from the Maeotis through the Pontus and Propontis into the Aegean Polybius gives two reasons (39.7-10); the large number of inflowing rivers, the water of which must find an exit, and the displacement of sea-water by alluvial matter deposited by these. The interest of the Peripatetic school in this type

4. So, correctly, Thommen, *Hermes* 20 (1885) 218. I missed this point in *ClMed* 9 (1948) 160 n.8. Polybius drew on official Byzantine documents for his account of the treaties between Byzantium and Rhodes, and Byzantium and Prusias in iv.52. Von Scala's reference to the Rhodian record office (*Studien des Polybios*, i 268) is off the mark, for this would not have contained the treaty with Prusias; but Danov is not therefore justified in assuming that Polybius consulted the Byzantine record office. For he admits Polybius' use of local Byzantine historians, such as Demetrius of Byzantium, and the consultation of the documents may well go back to one of these. The argument in the text is in my opinion the overriding one.

5. iv.39.11; 42.7; cf. *ClMed* 9 (1948) 161-2. Polybius' virulence in these passages against *ἐμπορικὰ διηγήματα* and *ἡ τῶν πλοϊζομένων ψευδολογία καὶ τερατεία* undoubtedly represents polemic against some rival account, perhaps the work of some Byzantine Pytheas, who had ventured to carry his explorations further than the Achaean 'Odysseus', and is not simply a general attack on merchants. But we are not in a position to give this rival a name. Von Scala, *op.cit.* 200 thinks this polemic is copied from Polybius' source. This is most improbable: it is precisely in his style.

6. *op.cit.* 62.

of problem is well established.[7] Aristotle wrote of the ταλάντωσις
of the sea in straits;[8] Theophrastus compared the change of the current to the change of the winds *(παλιμπνόη . . . . πνεύματος).*[9] But
the closest parallel to Polybius' argument is that attributed by Strabo
(i.3.4. c.49) to Theophrastus' pupil, Strato of Lampsacus, the head
of the Peripatetic school from 287 to 269 B. C. Following Aristotle
(*Meteor*.ii.1.12), Strato explained the Bosphorus as having been
burst apart[10] by the force of waters piled up from the rivers dis-
charging into the Pontus. Polybius mentions the rivers but not the
break-through. This omission is not, however, significant, since the
break-through was irrelevant to his case. His other point—the
gradual silting-up—is also in Strato, but combined with a curious
error, for which he incurs the reproof of Strabo. Because, as a result
of mud-deposits from the rivers, the Pontus is shallower than the
Propontis, Strato argues, there is naturally a flow of water from the
one into the other—therein, comments Strabo scornfully, likening the
sea to a river.[11] But Strato's error was not new. Aristotle himself
wrote of the downward slope of the sea-bed from the Maeotis by
successive stages to the Atlantic (*Meteor.* ii, 1, 12f), which is shallow, but at a lower level *(ἐν κοίλῳ).* Moreover, he, like Strato,
attributes the slope to silting in the higher regions: ὥστε τὰ μὲν διὰ
τὴν ἔκχυσιν οὐ βαθέα, τὰ δ' ἔξω πελάγη βαθέα μᾶλλον (p.354a,
26-7). Both current and silting are increased by the unparalleled
number of rivers debouching in the Pontus and Maeotis (p.354a,
16-18).[12]

Polybius accepts the argument about silting, but neglects the view
that seas behave like rivers and run in the direction of the lowest
sea-floor. Whether he saw through the fallacy or merely omitted it
(like the reference to the break-through) from his own simplified

7. cf. Berger, H., *Die geog. Fragm. des Eratosthenes*, 61-3. Aristotle himself
was interested in the currents of the Euripus and, according to Procopius, *de
bellis*, viii.6.19ff. lost heart and died when he failed to solve the problem. Still
earlier Diogenes of Apollonia, the last of the Ionian physicists, connected the
Bosphoran current with the scorching of the southern regions by the sun, and the
attraction of the moisture from the north as if along a lamp-wick (Seneca,
*Quaest.nat.*iv.2; Lyd. *de mensibus*, p.262; schol.ad Apoll. Rhod.iv.269).

8. *Meteor.* ii.1.11.

9. *De vent.frag.*v.4.26.

10. For a Samothracian legend about this break-through see Diod. Sic.v.47.3-4.

11. i.3.5 c.51. Berger, *op.cit.* 64-5, argues that the Stoic Strabo is here misrepresenting the views of a Peripatetic, and that Strato cannot have committed
this egregious error; but a comparison with Aristotle, *Meteor.* ii.1.12f. disposes
of this objection.

12. Aristotle's argument is complicated and confused by his taking over from
οἱ ἀρχαῖοι μετεωρολόγοι the notion that the northern parts of the earth are
'higher', and therefore naturally cause rivers to flow southward. But the commentaries of Olympiodorus and Alexander of Aphrodisias leave no doubt about
his meaning.

account, is not clear. But either explanation would plausibly account for the discrepancy, on the assumption that Polybius' source for this section was Strato.[13]

III.

Having established the causes of the current, Polybius draws his conclusions (40.4-42.8). Since the silting up of the Pontus and Maeotis has gone on from time immemorial, both must ultimately become dry land; for time is infinite, and the sea-basins are finite, and "it is a law of nature that if a finite quantity continually grows or decreases in infinite time . . . . the process must in the end be completed" (40.6). The general thesis implies that both time and the material world are infinite in duration; and both assumptions are made by the Peripatetic school. Aristotle accepted infinite time both in the past and in the future;[14] and ps.-Philo, *de aeternitate mundi,* 264.12, records the thesis as specifically aimed at the Stoics, who denied that the world was infinite in time.[15] Strato, it is true, disagreed with Aristotle's definition of time;[16] but this is no reason for thinking that he differed from his school in respect to its infinite duration. Moreover he discussed the particular application of the thesis to the Pontus area in terms almost identical with those of Polybius; and like Polybius[17] he saw evidence of the silting process in the sandbanks along the western coast of the Pontus, including

13. As Berger first suggested: *op.cit.* 9ff.; 62; followed by Von Scala, *op.cit.* 189-200, and by Danov, *op.cit.* 62. W. Capelle, *RE* s.v. "Straton" cols.287-301, doubts whether Polybius used Strato.

14. cf. *Meteor.* i.14.353a.15: ἐπεὶ ὅ τε χρόνος οὐχ ὑπολείπει καὶ τὸ ὅλον ἀΐδιον, where Nile and Tanais now run was once dry land; *Physics* iv.13.222a.29ff.: time without end. For the infinite duration of the material world cf. *Meteor.* i. 14.352b.17 . . . . μὴ μέντοι γένεσιν καὶ φθοράν, εἴπερ μένει τὸ πᾶν. See also Von Scala, *op.cit.* 192.

15. For the views of Chrysippus and Poseidonius see Stobaeus, *Ecl.*i.8.42. Whether the Peripatetic quoted in ps.-Philo was Theophrastus (Zeller, *Hermes.* 11 (1876) 422-9) or Critolaus (Diels, *Doxog.gr.*106ff) is disputed.

16. See Simplicius *ad Phys.* 788, 3ff.D. *(Corollarium de tempore):* Aristotle made time the ἀριθμός of movement, but Strato argues that an ἀριθμός is a διωρισμένον ποσόν whereas time and movement are continuous—τὸ δὲ συνεχὲς οὐκ ἀριθμητόν. Moreover an ἀριθμός does not (like time) come into existence and perish. Strato therefore defines time as τὸ ἐν ταῖς πράξεσι ποσόν; but Simplicius justly asks what this ποσόν really is.

17. Strato *ap. Strabo,* i.3.4 c50 δοκεῖν δὲ κἂν χωσθῆναι τὸν Πόντον ὅλον εἰς ὕστερον, ἂν μένωσιν αἱ ἐπιρρύσεις τοιαῦται. Cf. Polyb. iv.40.4: φαμὲν δὴ χώννυσθαι μέν καὶ πάλαι καὶ νῦν τὸν Πόντον, χρόνῳ γε μὴν ὁλοσχερῶς ἐγχωσθήσεσθαι τήν τε Μαιῶτιν καὶ τοῦτον, μενούσης γε δὴ τῆς αὐτῆς τάξεως περὶ τοὺς τόπους, καὶ τῶν αἰτίων τῆς ἐγχώσεως ἐνεργούντων κατὰ τὸ συνεχές. Aristotle, *Meteor.,* i.14.353a asserts that the Maeotis now takes smaller vessels than sixty years ago—a statement criticised somewhat caustically by Gillius, *De Bosporo Thracio (Geog.graec. min.*ii.17). The *Black Sea Pilot* (British Admiralty, 1920, ed.7) records a reported decrease in depth of six feet in the Gulf of Taganrog between 1706 and 1833, but without any confidence. Shifting sand, without any over-all silting, would explain both Aristotle's statement and the soundings recorded in the *Pilot.*

τὰ καλούμενα **Στήθη** ὑπὸ τῶν ναυτικῶν.[18] Strabo goes on to enquire why the alluvium brought down by the rivers accumulates off the coast, instead of reaching the open sea, and finds his solution in the refluent movement of the sea itself. Unfortunately he does not state whether this question and answer are from Strato, whom he has mentioned just before; if they are, they form the complementary half to the query in Polybius, who asks (41.3ff) why the silt, instead of being deposited close to the land, is projected a day's journey out to sea, and explains this as due to the continued force of the river. It is a plausible hypothesis that both aspects were originally discussed by Strato, and that Polybius has recorded one and Strabo the other.

Finally, Polybius discusses the salt content of the Maeotis (40.9) and Pontus (42.3-5), of which the former is now a λίμνη γλυκεῖα, and γλυκυτέρα τῆς Ποντικῆς θαλάττης. According to Strabo (i.3. 4. c.50), Strato said that γλυκυτάτην εἶναι τὴν Ποντικὴν θάλατταν, and he may well have said the same of the Maeotis.[19] Both Polybius and Strato took this relative freshness as evidence for the forcing out of the sea water, and for the eventual conversion of the Pontus, like the Maeotis, into a fresh-water lake as a step towards complete silting-up.[20]

The above analysis has shown sufficient divergences between the arguments of Polybius and Strato to admit of some doubt about their relationship. Strato mentions points omitted by Polybius (the bursting through of the Bosphorus, the parallelism between seas and a river), and omits one which Polybius mentions (the conclusion of any finite process in infinite time); though both refer to the Στήθη, they discuss the situation of this sandbank from different aspects; and though they argue from low salinity to ultimate silting-up, Polybius alone mentions the Maeotis separately. On the other hand, we only know Strato's arguments via Strabo, who had them through Eratosthenes,[21] and if we possessed a fuller account, many of these

18. cf. Polyb. iv.40.2 καλοῦσι δ' αὐτοὺς οἱ ναυτικοὶ Στήθη. (It is odd that Danov, op.cit. 63, despite his attribution of these chapters to Strato, claims the reference to the Στήθη in Polybius for an oral source.)

19. The low salt content of the Maeotis is often referred to; it helped to cause Polycleitus' confusion of the Maeotis with the Caspian (=Aral): Fr.gr.Hist. 128 F.7 (=Strabo, xi.7.4. c. 509): cf. Curt. vi.4.18: some argue that the Maeotis Palus empties into the "Caspian" (on the confusion of Aral and Caspian see Tarn, Alexander the Great, ii, 13 n.) et argumentum afferant aquam, quod dulcior sit quam cetera maria. On the sweet water of the Pontus see Dion.Byz. (ed. Güngerich) p.2, lines 6-8; Sallust. Hist. fg. 65; Arrian, Peripl.pont.Eux. 10, who states that the coastal peoples water their cattle in the sea. The Black Sea Pilot (ed. 7), 4, records that "each square mile of its surface receives the drainage of 5⅓ square miles. . . . The specific gravity of the surface compared with that of fresh water is as 1014 to 1000."

20. cf. Polyb. iv.42.3.

21. cf. Capelle, RE, s.v. "Strato" col. 300.

divergencies might well disappear. It is certain that Polybius follows some Peripatetic source, that Strato is the Peripatetic author most closely concerned with this type of problem, and that nothing we know of Strato contradicts the view that Polybius was following him here.[22] It may therefore be taken as a strong working hypothesis that Strato was Polybius' source for his hydrographical chapters.

IV.

We may now turn to the 'topographical' sections (39.1-6; 43.1-44. 10), which are of a different character. From the time of Herodotus there existed literary accounts of the Pontic area, either separate or parts of a larger work, embodying material derived from *periploi*, marine handbooks designed to serve the practical needs of pilots.[23] The character of the *periplous* was laid down by its purpose. It contained a list of coastal towns and harbors, with distances given originally in 'days' and 'nights,' and later in stades, the names of capes and temples, and occasional mythological and historical information. Like the passage of Herodotus, iv, 85-6,[24] Polybius' account here clearly links up with this literature,[25] though he may well be drawing on a literary predecessor as his intermediate source. We know of at least two third century writers, Diophantus and Demetrius of Callatis, who wrote on the Black Sea and probably incorporated *periplous* material,[26] though neither can be established as

22. For Polybius' acquaintance with Strato see xii.25c.3: that he is praised as a critic rather than a constructive thinker is no argument against his use by Polybius. Danov, *op.cit.* 63 claims iv.40.8 (large ships no longer navigate the Maeotis without a pilot) for an oral source; it may well come from Strato (cf. n.17 above for a similar observation in Aristotle).

23. See Gisinger, F., *RE* s.v. "Periplous" cols. 843-8; *ibid.* s.v. "Skylax" cols. 635-40; Rostovtzeff, M., *Skythien u. der Bosporus*, 25-40; texts in Müller, *Geog. graec.min.* 2 vols., 1882, and Baschmakoff, L., *La synthèse des périples pontiques*. On the relation of the *periploi* to the Italian and Greek *portolani* of the Middle Ages, see Kretschmer, K., *Die italienischen Portolane des Mittelalters* (Veröffent. des Inst. für Meereskunde . . . an der Univ. Berlin, Heft 13, 1909) and Delatte, A., *Les portolans grecs* (Bibl. de la fac. de philos. et des lettres de l'univ. de Liége, fasc. cvii) Paris, 1947. An important example of the literary treatment of the *periplous*, comparable to Pausanias' treatment of the *periegesis*, is the *Anaplus Bospori* of Dionysius of Byzantium (ed. Güngerich, Berlin, 1927), who knew and used this passage of Polybius.

24. Herodotus' debt to the *periplous* is revealed in his measurements, given in days and nights of sailing converted into stades; on these successive methods of measuring distances see Gisinger, *RE* s.v. "Periplous" cols. 843 ff.

25. See for example the measurements in stades (39.1—probably calculated from voyages originally; 39.3.4.5.6; 43.1.2), names of capes (43.2.5.6), and temples (39.2; 43.2), mythological (39.6; 43.6) and historical (43.2; 44.4) references, and details of actual navigation (44.3-10).

26. Diophantus' Ποντικαὶ ἱστορίαι was used by Alexander Polyhistor (Steph. s.v. Ἄβιοι) and mentioned by Agatharchides of Cnidos (*de mari Erythr.* 64); on the importance of Demetrius' Περὶ Ἀσίας καὶ Εὐρώπης (which also drew on

Polybius' source. Whatever this was,[27] it had access to remarkably accurate information.

Comparison of Polybius' description of the Bosphorus current (iv, 43-4) with those of Gillius, the *Black Sea Pilot,* and Merz-Möller,[28] confirms his accuracy for the part south of Roumeli Hissar (Hermaeum). But between the Pontus and the Hermaeum the current, he alleges, is uniform, a flagrant error, pointed out by Gillius, who knows from his own experience and the testimony of fishermen of two rebounds before this.[29] Polybius' misstatement, whether his own or drawn from his immediate source, covers the lack of any real knowledge of what happened in the northern part of the Straits; and this distinction points to the immediate or ultimate use of a source which interested itself in the area immediately around Byzantium, and probably had access to information accumulated by Byzantine fishermen.[30]

In one other respect Polybius' account is at fault. He makes no reference to any but surface currents; and since the existence of a highly saline under-water current flowing from the Propontis towards the Black Sea is very relevant to any speculations on the conversion of the latter into a fresh-water lake, his silence must indicate ignorance concerning it. When the existence of this current was first suspected is not known; but it was far earlier than is usually as-

Diophantus: cf. Rostovtzeff, *Skythien u. der Bosporus,* 25ff.) for the Pontic area cf. Agatharchides *ibid.* and Scymnus 719.

27. Whether it was the same Byzantine source as Polybius used in 46 ff., we cannot say. See above, n.4.

28. See the appended table of comparison. References: Gillius, P., *De Bosporo Thracio,* i.4 (*Geog.Graec.min.* ii, pp. 14-18): he uses Dionysius of Byzantium (cf. Dion. Byz. (ed. Güngerich) 3.1 f.) and Polybius, but supplements both with personal experience; *Black Sea Pilot,* ed. 7, 1920, 26-7; Möller, A. Merz-L., *Hydrographische Untersuchungen in Bosporus u. Dardanellen* (Veröffentl. des Inst. für Meereskunde . . . an der Univ. Berlin, N. F. Geog.-naturwissenschaftl. Reihe, Heft 18, 1928), 127 ff. (with separate maps, which I have not seen). I am indebted to my colleague Prof. J. Proudman for a reference to this work.

29. The current strikes the European coast at Dikaia Petra (Kireç Burnu) and the Asiatic at Glarium (Paşa Bahçe). Gillius, *loc.cit.* "id quod ego iterum et saepius uidi, et piscatores testantur"; and he quotes Dion. Byz. (Güngerich 31.11; 32.10) for the promontories 'Οξύϱϱους and Πεϱίϱϱους, "ita nuncupata a uehementi defluxu Bospori."

30. Strabo vii.6.2 c.320 refers to the Bosphorus current in connection with the route followed by the tunnies coming from the Pontus; and Von Scala *op.cit.* i.196 suggests that Polybius' source was also concerned with the tunnies, but that Polybius adapted the account to his own interest—the advantage of the situation of Byzantium. Certainly Polybius was well acquainted with the tunny-routes: cf. xxxiv.2.14 (=Strabo, i.2.15 c.25); and Dionysius of Byzantium, who deals with the Bosphorus in great detail, drawing on information available to him at home, constantly discusses the taking of the tunny and pelamys. cf. Dion. Byz. 3.5f (Güngerich) κατὰ δ' ὀξὺ ὑηγνυμένου πεϱὶ αὐτὴν τοῦ ϱεύματος τὸ μὲν πολὺ καὶ βίαιον ὠθεῖ κατὰ τῆς Πϱοποντίδος, ὅσον δὲ πϱαῦ καὶ θήϱας ἰχθύων ἀγωγόν, ὑποδέχεται τῷ καλουμένῳ Κέϱατι. Cf. too Gillius (quoted in the last note); Tac. *Ann.* 12.63.2. Cf. also Robinson, D. M., *AJP* 27 (1906) 140.

The Bosphorus from the Hermaeum to Byzantium

Polybius iv	Gillius (*Geog.gr.min.* ii.14-15)
43.4 ἐπὰν εἰς τὸ τῆς Εὐρώπης ῾Ερμαῖον . . . φερόμενος . . . ὁ ῥοῦς βίᾳ προσπέσῃ . . . . ὥσπερ ἀπὸ πληγῆς ἐμπίπτει τοῖς ἀντίπερας τῆς ᾿Ασίας τόποις.	Tertius in Europam contra Hermaeum promonturium. . . . Quartus decursus defertur in Asiae promonturium uulgo nominatum Moletrinum.
43.5 ἐκεῖθεν δὲ πάλιν . . . τὴν ἀνταπόδοσιν ποιεῖται πρὸς τὰ περὶ τὰς ῾Εστίας ἄκρα καλούμενα τῆς Εὐρώπης.	Quintus in Europam ad promonturium Hestias, a quo uiolenter reiectus
43.6 ὅθεν αὖθις ὁρμήσας προσπίπτει πρὸς τὴν Βοῦν καλουμένην. (For the identity of the Βοῦς promontory with the Leander Tower (Kys kulessi) on a small island off Scutari cf. Oberhummer, *RE* s.v. ῾Bosporos (1)᾽ cols. 754-5.)	ita fertur in Asiam, ut exiliter deinde repulsus ab Europa iactetur fluctuans iuxta Asiam, primo ad utrumque promonturium claudens uicum Chrysoceranum, postea ad promonturium dictum Bouem siue Damalim.
43.7 τὸ τελευταῖον ὁρμήσας ἀπὸ τῆς Βοὸς ἐπ᾿ αὐτὸ φέρεται τὸ Βυζάντιον, περισχισθεὶς δὲ περὶ τὴν πόλιν βραχὺ μὲν εἰς τὸν κόλπον αὐτοῦ διορίζει τὸν καλούμενον Κέρας, τὸ δὲ πλεῖον πάλιν ἀπονεύει. . . 43.10 ἀπολιπὼν τὴν τῶν Καλχηδονίων πόλιν φέρεται διὰ πόρου.	Septimus repulsus rapidus fertur ad promonturium Bosporium siue Byzantium nuncupatum. Cuius mucrone discissus defluit in duas partes, quarum rapidior praecipitat in fretum ad Propontidem uersus, altera debilior exsilit in sinum Cornu appellatum. Cf. Dion.Byz. (Güngerich), 3. 5f. (quoted in n.30).

The Bosphorus from the Hermaeum to Byzantium

Black Sea Pilot, ed.7, 26-7	Merz-Möller, p.128
It there turns towards the European coast, and runs along Roumeli Hissar, and strikes on Kandili point.	Im Nord-Süd gerichteten Teil der Enge setzt der Strom an Rumeli-Hisar, mit grösserer Geschwindigkeit im NE-SW gerichteten am Kandeli-Leuchtturm des asiatischen Ufers vorbei.
The mainstream strikes the western shore at Arnaut point. From Arnaut point the main current sets towards the Asiatic shore, along which it runs as far as Leander tower.	Bis Tschengel-Köi verläuft die Rinne annähernd nord-südlich, der Stromstrich zieht hier mit zunehmenden Geschwindigkeiten . . . in der Mitte des Stromes entlang. . . . In den Strom hinein reichen die Küstenvorsprünge von Arnaut Köi, Defterdar Burnu auf der europäischen . . . von Wani Köi, Tschengel Köi auf der asiatischen Seite . . . Südlich Tschengel Köi stellt sich das nach Südwest umbiegende asiatische Ufer dem rasch fliessenden Strom entgegen, der Stromstrich nähert sich wieder diesem Ufer und ist bis Skutari hin zu verfolgen.
The main current . . . sets strongly on to Old Seraglio point, and divides into two branches; the southern and larger flows into the sea of Marmara, and the western into the Golden Horn.	Der Stromstrich wechselt daher wiederum auf das europäische Ufer hinüber, ist aber weiterhin nur wenig ausgeprägt vorhandden . . . Zwischen Galata und Tschiragan Palast nimmt die für die Schiffahrt wichtige Grosse Neer fast die halbe Breite des Strombettes ein. Sie wird von den Stromfäden gespeist, die an Alte Serai Burnu abkurven und das Goldene Horn durchfliessen, und von Galata bis südlich Tschiragan auch beständig vom Hauptstrom selbst.

sumed. Modern authorities frequently write[31] as if the earliest reference was that in Count L. F. Marsigli's *Osservazioni intorno al Bosporo Thracio ovvero Canale di Constantinopoli*, published in Rome in 1681 in the form of letters to ex-Queen Christina of Sweden; and as late as 1870 Spratt[32] was still questioning its existence. Yet both Macrobius and Procopius (in a passage which Gillius adapts without acknowledgement)[33] assume the reverse under-water current as a matter of common knowledge, and both argue scientifically from the fate of nets and other objects dropped into the lower water of the channel. At what date between Polybius and Macrobius the discovery was made is not known, for it may clearly have been a commonplace among fishermen before it came to the attention of learned speculation.

Modern soundings have confirmed the existence of this current, which, however, according to the recent researches of Ullyott and Ilgaz,[34] does not reach the Black Sea (as Merz and other previous writers had assumed),[35] but is absorbed by the turbulent surface current, which returns to the Marmara all the highly saline water flowing towards the Pontus, before it can cross the threshold of the inner sea. These findings are confirmed practically by the very moderate salinity of the lower levels inside the Black Sea, a situation which contradicts the assumption required by Merz's hypothesis, viz. that some 200 km. of strongly saline water have been pouring annually into the Black Sea from the Mediterranean over at least the last 5000 years.

V.

Despite certain shortcomings, which are partly due to the limitations in the knowledge available at that time, Polybius' chapters represent an important contribution to the study of the geography of the Black Sea area, especially in their practical discussion of the implications of the surface current in the Bosphorus, which, as Polybius shows, has been a real factor in history. But the speculation on

---

31. Cf. Merz, *op.cit.* 11, who knows of no hydrographical work on the Bosphorus prior to Marsigli; Oberhummer, *RE* s.v. "Bosporos (1)" col. 745: "Neu ist die Feststellung eines Unterstromes" (and he mentions no early speculation on this subject).

32. *Proc.RoyalGeog.Soc.* 1870-71, 528.

33. Macrob. *Sat.* vii.12.31 ff; Procop. *de bell.* viii.6.27-8; paraphrased by Gillius i.4 (*Geog.Graec.min.* ii.16-17).

34. P. Ullyott and Orhan Ilgaz, *Researches on the Bosphorus, II. A new hypothesis concerning the water movements in the Bosphorus channel* (Türk cografiya dergisi: Istanbul Boganzinda Arastirmalar, Ankara, 1944): in Turkish pp. 85-114, English summary, pp. 115-118. I am grateful to Mr. W. K. C. Guthrie for the loan of a copy of this work.

35. Merz-Möller, *op.cit.* with bibliography of previous work.

the drying up of the Black Sea, though derivative and unconvincing, and seriously out in its estimate of the time required for the completion of geological processes, also has its place in the history of human thought. It is difficult, however, to follow Danov[36] in the view that for his discussion of either the hydrography of the Pontus or the currents of the Bosphorus Polybius based his account on knowledge obtained by personal experience or enquiry on the spot. We must rather conclude that his account in iv, 39-42, which, like the longer geographical discussion in Book xxxiv, combines straightforward descriptive geography with theoretical discussion, is a well-organised but none the less "armchair" compilation, dependent on the theorising, probably of Strato, certainly of some Peripatetic source, and on an account of the Bosphorus and the Black Sea, which incorporated 'periplous' material and the experience of the fishermen of Byzantium.

---

36. *op.cit.* 63.

THERMOPYLAE AND CALLIDROMOS

A. R. BURN

University of Glasgow

To Xerxes and his officers, looking south from Lamia, the grey cliffs of Trachis rose like a wall, in which the dark line of the Asopos chasm was conspicuously in view. Those experienced and enterprising soldiers did not need a local traitor to show them that much; but, as Munro has shown though Herodotus does not mention it, the gorge must have been held. It was commanded by the Greek citadel (of Trachis ?) of which traces remain on the cliff-top by Delphinon. A much-used route, via Doris, which the Persians used after forcing Thermopylae (Herodotus VIII, 31-2), probably went through the gorge, as it did in Grundy's time (1899) ; but the gorge, 1000 feet deep and only 12 feet wide in places, was such an obvious death-trap that against opposition neither Persians nor Gauls nor Romans ever even attempted it.

There are however plenty of other physically possible ways up the hills from Malis; several of them are followed by modern mule-tracks. When Herodotus describes the hills as ἄβατα (VII, 176 and 198) his language is more picturesque than accurate. In particular, the spur or projection of the hills from the monastery of Damasta to the Alamanna Bridge—the scene of Athanasios Diakos' gallant defence in 1821—affords easy access; even the crags at its top, though not unimpressive, can be passed, left, right or centre, without climbing. It was here that a German mountain division attacked (unsuccessfully) in the last battle of Thermopylae, the rear-guard action of the New Zealanders in April, 1941.

What *was* true—emphatically true then, when the hills were forested and when fighting was best done in close formation—was that the mountain paths were useless for purposes of overt attack on a forewarned enemy. If a path is rough, and broad enough for only one man, like any Greek *monopáti*, then for the 1000th man to be less than a mile behind the leader is a notable achievement. The reason is that the lapse of time between the first man's and the last man's arrival at any point is increased by the second or so's delay at every awkward step, multiplied by the number of such steps, multiplied by the number of men in the column. To attempt to advance up a rough, wooded mountainside *off* the paths would have meant much slower movement and worse straggling still. To arrive at the enemy's position straggling like that would have been much worse than useless;

and to halt often enough for the rear files to come up and form line of battle, *before* reaching the enemy, would have meant that the leading men needed to come down for more food and (especially) more water before they got anywhere. Modern weapons, with skirmishing formations and covering fire, have by no means abolished the problem of supply by dirt tracks, but they have altered its character. This is the reason why there is so little actual mountain fighting in ancient and mediaeval warfare, as compared with the present day.

The only possible use of mountain paths for an attack on Thermopylae, then, was for a surprise move, if a practicable path could be found unwatched; a *tactical* outflanking movement, not a general invasion of Greece over the mountains, ignoring Thermopylae, for the above-mentioned reason, that considerable forces could not be maintained over a mountain *monopáti*. As Napoleon said of Spain, a large force would have starved and a small force would have been beaten. It was necessary to clear either the citadel above the gorge, or the coast road; and of the two, the coast road looked the less unattractive.

Marinatos' excavations of 1939 have settled the topography of the battlefield on the coast road. The Phocian Wall was excavated along its whole length, and the hillock of the last stand identified by the dramatic discovery of "quantities of bronze or iron missiles, all or almost all of fifth century types.... Only one, probably Persian, spearhead was found, and one spear-butt, certainly Greek" (Martin Robertson, in *JHS* 59 [1939] 200). There is, however, one point whose interest has perhaps not been brought out: this is the fact that the Phocian Wall, on its little spur, crosses the road, not at right-angles, but at forty-five degrees. It thus gave exactly the "text-book" post of vantage beloved of all Greeks when setting defences: an elevated position from which to shoot at an enemy advancing along the beach, from his unshielded side. The position also sheds light on Herodotus' story of the Spartans' feigned flights to draw the enemy on. Such withdrawals would have the effect of drawing the enemy *into the angle* between the marshy shore and the hillside with the Phocian Wall. Here, caught in front and flank, both with missiles and by the assault probably of fresh troops from the spur, it may well be believed that their losses were very heavy.

But the Persians, as a soldierly mountain people, must surely have had their eyes, from the first, upon possible ways over the hills. I cannot believe that they were surprised, though they were no doubt relieved, when Ephialtes the Malian said that he could show them an insufficiently guarded path. They had probably been interrogating every well-disposed Thessalian or local native for days. This brings us to the problem, where was that path?

Grundy, whose *Great Persian War* (pp. 300 ff.) has been followed by almost all later writers, took a route up the Asopos Gorge, up a side gully, over a shoulder to the Damasta Monastery, and thence up the Great Ravine, whose precipitous east wall covers the flank of the Hot Springs position. Of this route he says (page 301) "it is absolutely certain that this is the original path of the Anopaea, for the very good reason that it traverses the only line which *can* be traversed in that very difficult country." In reality, far from being the only possible line, it is not even the best; and moreover, the paths which Grundy used exist chiefly to connect the monastery with the Old Drakospiliá chapel and with the Elevtherokhori. Without the monastery and the chapel, they would not exist; and without the paths a good deal of his route would be, not perhaps impossible, but extremely bad going.

Let us consider what Herodotus says about the path (VII, 216);

"It starts from the River Asopos, the river which runs through the gorge; and it has the same name as the name of the mountain, Anopaia. This Anopaia runs along the ridge (κατὰ ῥάχιν, literally 'along the backbone') of the mountain, and ends near the city of Alpenos, the first city in Locris on the side towards Malis, and by the so-called 'rock of Melampygos' and by the seats of the Kerkôpes, where also the narrowest part is." This I take to mean the narrowest part *of the coast road* (cf. chap. 176), and not of the path; though the latter is also true.

The path came down, then, to the "East Gate," using, practically certainly, the obvious valley by Drakospiliá; though it has also an alternative ending via Anávra. Whether Herodotus means to say that it had alternative endings, is not quite clear.

As to its middle course, Herodotus is vague. Pretty clearly he had not been over it. But he does say explicitly that the path ran "along the ridge" of the mountain, and that the name of the mountain was the same as that of the path, Anopaia, meaning perhaps something like the "upper way" (cf. Eustathius on the similar word in *Odyssey* I, 320). That the name of the mountain was the same as that of the path presumably means that the path went over the top of it.

Much more intriguing however is the later name of the mountain, Callidromos, the Fair Way. It is a curious name for a mountain, and one whose significance seems never to have been explained. A visit to the "ridge of the mountain," however,—which is at the *top* of the steep rocks above Grundy's route—shows that the name really is very appropriate.

A fundamental point about the geology of Trachinia and Callidromos is that the strata "dip" slightly from north to south, producing under erosion rugged cliffs facing north—the broken ends of the strata—and longer, more gentle slopes to the south. Both slopes, but especially the northern cliffs, are naturally much cut about by torrent-beds. But this "lie of the land" produces, where not interrupted by water-action or faulting, *comparative ease of movement in directions parallel to the exposed edges of the strata, i.e. east and west.* A most spectacular example of this is to be found at the top of Callidromos; Dr. Grundy did not find it, through nervousness as to the predatory propensities of Vlach shepherds (see his p. 302); but they, though still present, are by now as friendly as any other Greek country-folk.

The fact is that the ridge of Callidromos culminates not in one but in two parallel rock "sills," between which quantities of débris washed down from the sills, have, at least in the western part of Callidromos, filled up the intervening groove almost completely. This produces a fantastic effect. A stream—one of the head-waters of the Asopos— flows from east to west, it is no exaggeration to say, *along the top of the mountain.* It runs through a long, narrow, deep-soiled mountain plain, carpeted in spring with white and purple crocuses, between rounded ridges with remains of oak and fir forest, rising perhaps 200 feet above the stream on the north side and still less on the south; and it runs so slowly that it has cut meanders, as in an English water-meadow, through the soft soil. The place is called Nevropolis; in the time of Dodwell, circa 1806 (*Classical Tour,* II, 126) and of Leake (*Travels in Northern Greece,* II, 31), there was a village of this name somewhere hereabouts. It is evidently a Slav name ending in -polye, field. This plain is some 300 yards wide from ridge to ridge, and about a mile long, from the top of the rapids at the west end of the mountain, to a grey rock pyramid, the southwest corner of the rocky summit of Lithitsa. Below the pyramid, in April 1946, a little circular lake reflected the trees. It is not marked on the maps; possibly it fills, through the blocking of some *katavothra,* the crater-like "circular vale" in which Dodwell found the village. South of the lake a cart-track rises just perceptibly and then goes down to Palaiokhori on the main road. British and New Zealand drivers are reported actually to have taken trucks over the mountain by this route during the retreat in 1941, when the main road was blocked by bombing near Elevtherokhori. Their ascent from Elevtherokhori was made possible by the existence of a modern revetted path, which our enginers blew up

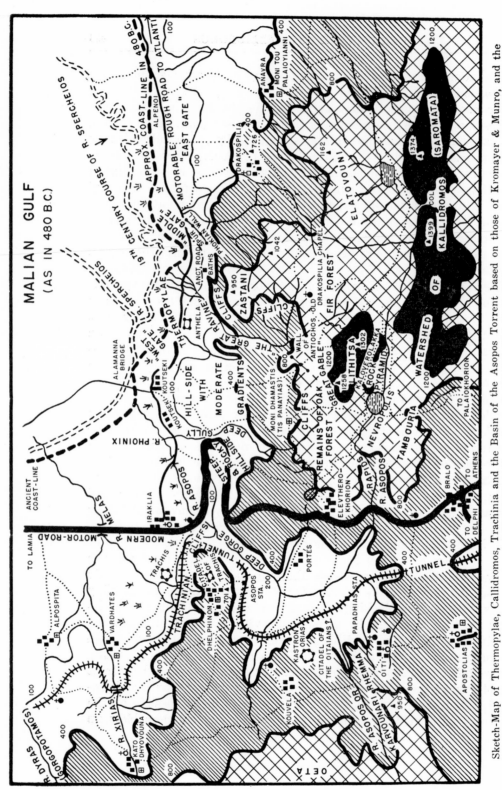

Sketch-Map of Thermopylae, Callidromos, Trachinia and the Basin of the Asopos Torrent based on those of Kromayer & Munro, and the 1: 100,000 Staff Map. SCALE, 1: 102,960. Heights in Metres.

Ground over 400 metres | Paths shown are modern (from the 1: 100,000 map). | Athens-Salonica Road

Ground over 800 metres | Approximate sea-coast in 480 B. C. | Remains of ancient fortifications

Ground over 1200 metres | Athens-Salonica Railway | Churches | Chapels | Monasteries behind them; but in the plain or valley of Nevropolis no "made" road exists, nor is necessary.

Passing the lake and rock pyramid, a right and left turn brings one into a similar but smaller plain or reach of valley; and then at last we come to hummocky ground, with fir forest, near the main summit of Callidromos. The Drakospiliá track, which in 1946 was being much used for timber-hauling, here turns northwards, rises slightly to a col, and descends via the old chapel to the modern village. This plain, surely was the *Kalòs Dromos* that gave the mountain its name; and here was the weakness by which Thermopylae fell, more than once or twice. Once an enemy reached the ridge of Callidromos *at any point,* there was no physical difficulty between him and the head of the Great Ravine, where his arrival turned the defences of Thermopylae itself.

Where and how did the outflanking parties get up?

Obviously they did not all necessarily reach Nevropolis by the same route. The weakness of Thermopylae is precisely that the cliffs west of it, though in appearance formidable, can be passed by many points; so the defenders, whose man-power was always limited (that was why they were holding the pass) had both to keep adequate forces at Thermopylae and at Trachis, and to patrol or hold some miles of rocky but not impossible hillside between the two. Careful reconnaissance with the help of local inhabitants more than once revealed to an enterprising enemy a feasible route, not watched by sentries at night; and what always followed—the liability of ancient citizen soldiers to panic in a dawn surprise—has a certain melancholy sameness.

Of the four captures of Thermopylae by way of Anopaia, the first, by the Thessalians, is recorded for us only in a few words (Hdt. VII, 215), without details. The most clearly recorded is the last, described by Plutarch, no doubt from Cato's memoirs (*Cato the Elder,* chap. 13).

Cato with 2000 men (Livy 36, 17) and a prisoner of war as guide entered the hills on a moonless night. The guide lost his way (perhaps not wholly unintentionally?) and they found themselves blundering about in "pathless and rocky places" to no purpose. Cato halted the column and went on a personal reconnaissance with one companion, L. Manlius, "a skilled mountaineer." After some awkward scrambling in the dark they "came into a path which they supposed to lead down to the enemy camp." They left marks upon "some conspicuous projecting rocks," went back and brought up the column, and followed the path, but were held up again by a ravine. By now it was nearly daybreak; but the first light showed that they had penetrated just far enough. "At the bottom of the rocks" was the Greek position, held by 600 Aetolians. A raid on an outlying picket secured a prisoner, and exact information about strengths and dispositions; a dawn attack, "with trumpets and shouting," led by Cato in person, scattered the Aetolians; and the appearance, as the sun rose high, of Roman troops on the hills behind them led to the panic flight of the main Seleucid army.

It is at least consistent with this narrative to suggest that Cato ascended by the Damasta "spur." Its lower reaches had no doubt been a good deal deforested since Xerxes' days, and the defenders' nervousness about it is shown by the existence of fortifications there, including a wall, (the "τεῖχος of Callidromos") cutting off the upper reaches of the Great Ravine. Cato's intention may have been to turn the western end of the cliffs at the top of the spur; and these will have been the rocks into which they blundered when the guide lost his way. Cato however found and marked a possible line—perhaps that marked on the staff-map as a path due south of the monastery. (I have not followed it.) The column thus reached Nevropolis, and continued probably by way of the narrow but easy ravine, now known as the Hermit's Hollow (Kaloyerolakka), north of the above-mentioned rock-pyramid. (To wheel right and go round the rocks was actually a better route, but would not have seemed so in the dark.) This route led Cato to the edge of the Great Ravine; the outpost which he surprised will have been on the edge of it, (perhaps at its head) and the 600 Aetolians encamped "below the rocks" will have been the garrison of the wall whose remains still stand.

The positions of the forts of Teichious and Rhoduntia, which baffled Cato's colleague Flaccus, cannot be discussed here for lack of space.

Finally, the flank march of the Gauls and that of the Persians hang together, since Pausanias (X, 22), our only authority on the route of the Gauls, says that both went the same way.

Pausanias says (loc. cit., §5) that this was not the "precipitous and formidably steep path above Trachis" which they had unsuccessfully attempted some days before, in the hope of sacking a temple on the cliffs above. (This path might well be the route up the corner of the cliffs, just west of the Asopos Gorge). Hydarnes' path, he adds, was "an easier route, through the land of the Aenianes"; and this phrase has often been combined with Herodotus' statement (VII, 218) that the Persians having crossed the Asopos, marched *"having on their right the mountains of the Oetaeans and on their left those of the Trachinians."* "The mountains of the Trachinians" should, it would seem, mean the Trachinian Cliffs; and the Aenianes were, in classical times, the people of the upper Spercheios basin. Hence it has been argued that the unguarded path must have started west of the cliffs, near modern Vardhátes; passed over the high ground west of Delphino; crossed the Asopos near Portés and reached Nevropolis via Elevtherokhori. This view is supported by Munro (*JHS* 22, 313-4), and by Sir John Myres, to whom I am indebted for much fruitful discussion of this subject and for permission to quote his views in advance of his own projected publication.* It would certainly, as Herodotus says (ch. 223), make "the way round and up" much longer than the way down from Lithitsa; indeed, from Vardhátes to Nevropolis by this route is not less than twelve miles, a long way for a column strung out on a *monopáti* to cover on a summer night. But there is one worse objection to it: this is that Herodotus most explicitly says (VII, 216) that the path *starts from the Asopos,* and (217) that the Persians *crossed* the Asopos at the beginning of their march. None of the attempts of past writers to evade this difficulty (such as that the path west of the Asopos was not part of the Anopaia) seems to me better than special pleading. What Herodotus says, is that the *Persians' night march* started by crossing the Asopos "the river that flows through the gorge"; the name Anopaia is only added casually. And the only way by which a route from Malis to Nevropolis would be likely to *start by crossing* the Asopos (not by going a mile up its gorge!) is, surely, by way of the Damasta spur.

If so, however, how did the Persians have "on their right the mountains of the Oetaeans and on their left those of the Trachinians"? And what about Pausanias' expression "through the Aenianes"?

These difficulties are not so serious as they might seem, and as I, for one, long thought them. The Aenianes included the Oetaeans; even the acropolis at Kastron Oreias, it has been suggested, was probably theirs—perhaps, indeed, that "Oeta" which the Gauls tried to reach, as described in Pausanias X, 22, 1. At one point, according to Strabo, (IX, 427) their territory even touched that of the Locrians, though for the most part a corner of Doris came between. The "hinterland," so to speak, of the Trachinian Cliffs therefore probably *was* Oetaean, and in any case the main mass of Oeta was conspicuous on the right; while the forward slopes of Callidromos certainly belonged to Trachis. Moreover, by Strabo's time *(loc. cit.)* the Aenianes had ceased to exist as a separate people. Pausanias, 150 years later still, may be pardoned, then, even if his phrase here was positively mistaken. It may be noticed that when he describes, in the same chapter, the Gallic raid on Callion, which *did* pass through Aeniania, he uses the aston-

---

* See additional note at end of this article.

ishing expression "back through Thessaly"; evidently regarding
Thessaly as extending to the Spercheios.

I would suggest, then, that the Persians with Ephialtes, "having
crossed the Asopos" went up the Damasta "spur," probably turning
the cliffs by their west end, where today the path from the monastery
crosses a grassy col to reach Elevtherokhori. This would be the "way
round" emphasized by Herodotus, chap. 223. The "peak of the mountain" where the Phocians were encamped would be (as Munro has it)
Lithitsa. Surprised at dawn, the Phocians "pulled in" to their rocky
"keep"; but the Persians with their local guide by-passed them on
the south and by way of the level ground east of Nevropolis reached
the col near Old Drakospiliá.

Why was there a way up unguarded? A thousand Phocians, it will
be agreed, were few to hold the hills from the Asopos to the Great
Ravine. But why, then, had not Leonidas detached more men? Because, I think, of the fierce frontal attacks, in which some critics
gratuitously disbelieve. Who, one might naturally ask, would attack
like that if reconnaissance had given him hope of "finding a flank"?
So Leonidas kept the mass of his troops "where they were needed"
at the Hot Springs, reckoning that there would be time to reinforce
Callidromos if the Persians showed signs of moving that way. He
was deceived, and the speed and silence of Hydarnes' march completed his undoing.

Nevertheless, Leonidas keeps his place among the heroes. No
Thermopylae, no Artemisium; and no Artemisium—with the losses
by storm and battle which the Persians suffered, while bringing up
and concentrating their fleet in face of the enemy—no Salamis. But
Leonidas did not know that. All he can have seen was that his line
had been broken after three days. The Persians were up; with the
summit secured, their reinforcements must have been streaming up
the spur; no need for secrecy now. There was not a hope, with the
route by Anavra available as well as that by Drakospiliá, of stopping
them getting down. There were just a few hours to go, while Hydarnes' rear companies closed up; time for the bulk of the Greek army
to get a good start (for the Persians had cavalry) while a sacrificed
rearguard held on for as long as might be.

ADDENDUM

Sir John Myres, in a letter to the writer, argues against a Persian advance up the Damasta spur, and in favor of a longer, western route *to* the Asopos, on the grounds that:

(1) The Damasta route makes Herodotus describe as "the mountains of the Trachinians" the part of the range where Trachis town is *not;* while (2) it describes the range on which Trachis *is* as "the mountains of the Oetaeans." (3) "The Persians would surely be risking much by crossing the Asopus in the plain. Were there no Greek scouts as far as the river?" (4) "It is not the whole route but the mountain as far as Alpenus that is called Anopaea, and this section of the whole route (which is what matters to the Greeks) *begins from the Asopus.*" (5) The first part of the Damasta route is transverse to the ὄρος, not κατὰ ῥάχιν. Also in ch. 223 "Herodotus puts the *periodos* before the *anabasis;* whereas if the Persians came your way, they went *up* before they went *round.*" (6) "The Persians only reached the ἀκρωτήριον τοῦ ὄρεος at dawn; did it take them all night to climb the Damasta spur?"

These are powerful arguments; and though I still feel a difficulty about Herodotus' words in ch. 217, τὸν ᾽Ασωπὸν διαβάντες ἐπορεύοντο πᾶσαν τὴν νύκτα, I feel it best to give them fully, agreeing that there is at least a strong case for the western approach-march.

BIBLIOGRAPHY

Ancient texts: Herodotus, VII, 175-7, 198-225; Strabo, IX, pp. 427-8; Livy, 36, 15-18; Plutarch, *Cato the Elder*, chap. 13; Pausanias, X, 22. Of these, Strabo and Livy, like Appian, *Syrian War*, 17, take their local topography at second hand, and make a sad mess of it.

Modern studies: Leake, W. M., *Travels in Northern Greece* (London, 1835), II, 22-65

Major-General Gordon, *Two Visits to the Anopaea* (Athens, 1838). The only modern writer hitherto who gives sufficient attention to Nevropolis.

Grundy, G. B., *The Great Persian War*, 257-317 (London, 1901). Generally excellent on topography, but unfortunately omits the top of the mountain.

Munro, J. A. R., *Observations on the Persian Wars*, in *JHS* 22 (1902), 312-9. Classic, and not wholly superseded by the same writer's Chapter IX, § iv (pp. 291-301) in *Cambridge Ancient History*, IV (Cambridge, 1926), which however has a good map (after Kromayer).

Kromayer, J., *Antike Schlachtfelder*, II, 134-154 and Map 5 (Berlin, 1907). On the campaign of 192 B. C. Gives a much better map than Grundy, but follows him in the text.

Harmening, L. & F., in Kromayer, *op. cit.*, IV, 21-63 (1924), on the campaign of 480, give a good summary of the earlier topographical literature.

On Marinatos' excavations of 1939, I have seen only the summary account in *JHS* 59 (1939) 189-209. Cf. Marinatos, *Bericht über den VI. Intern. Kongress für Arch.* (1940) 333-341; *AA* (1940) 194-201.

Sir J. L. Myres hopes shortly to publish his views on the campaign of 480 B. C.

ZUM STADTBILD DES SPAETROEMISCHEN TRIER: CARDO UND DECUMANUS

†WILHELM VON MASSOW

Das Strassennetz des antiken Trier entsprach dem üblichen Schema der römischen Kolonie, die Strassen schnitten sich rechtwinklig[1] und bildeten verschieden grosse Häuserblocks, sogenannte insulae. Auf den Grundplan des römischen Lagers zurückgehend, wird die normale Anlage der Colonia durch die beiden Hauptachsen gegliedert. Von Süden nach Norden verläuft der Cardo, den der Decumanus von Osten nach Westen überquert. Ueber dem Schnittpunkt dieser beiden Hauptstrassen pflegt sich das Forum auszubreiten, der Mittelpunkt des politischen Lebens, auf dem sich dann auch der Tempel des Stadt-gründers erhebt.

Mit einer gewissen Selbstverständlichkeit wird in Trier bisher die vom Südtor an der Kreuzung der jetzigen Ziegel- und Saarstrasse unter der letzteren nach Norden führende Römerstrasse als Cardo angesehen, während die zwischen der Brücke und dem Amphitheater sich am Südrande der Kaiserthermen unter der jetzigen Kaiser-strasse hinziehende Römerstrasse als Decumanus gilt. Dass sich da-bei allerhand Unstimmigkeiten ergeben, ist wohl bemerkt worden, die letzten Folgerungen daraus wurden aber bisher nicht gezogen.

Nord- und Südtor der spätrömischen Stadtbefestigung sind, das erste in Gestalt der Porta Nigra fast vollständig, das zweite wenig-stens im Fundament einwandfrei erhalten. Aber die vom Südtor nach Norden führende Strasse trifft keineswegs auf die Porta Nigra, sondern erst die östliche Parallelstrasse führt durch dieses Tor und auch nicht in gerader Linie, sondern nachdem sie etwa 200 m davor einen Knick nach Nordosten gemacht hat, die einzige uns bekannte Abweichung von dem sonst streng beobachteten Rechteckschema. Ein durchgehender Cardo hat also im spätrömischen Trier gefehlt.

Der Grund für diese Achsenverschiebung ist leicht zu finden. Der Umfang der noch unbefestigten Stadt hatte sich offenbar nach den verschiedenen Seiten im Lauf zweier Jahrhunderte unregelmässig erweitert, sodass schliesslich keine Möglichkeit vorhanden war, das ehemals im Zentrum gelegene Forum genau in der Mitte zu lassen. Als man sich entschloss, bei der Errichtung der Stadtmauer kurz nach 200 das Amphitheater und einen Teil des Bergabhanges, ver-mutlich um des daran gelegenen Circus willen, mit einzubeziehen, da

---

† Deceased.

1. Der Strassenplan ist der Hippodamische den David M. Robinson in Olynth entdeckt hat, vgl. *Olynthus*, 8, 29-35: 12, 170-178.

ergab sich aus zwingenden fortifikatorischen Gründen, dass die grossen Torburgen als militärische Hauptstützpunkte möglichst in die Mitte jeder Stadtseite gelegt wurden. Das ist an der Südseite klar zu erkennen. An der Nordseite, die an sich schon breiter ist, musste nicht nur aus diesem Grunde das Tor weiter nach Osten gelegt werden, sondern das vom jetzigen Standpunkt der Porta nach der Mosel zu stark abfallende Gelände zwang den Erbauer, das Tor auf den Rand der Terrasse zu setzen, also ziemlich weit aus der Nord-Südachse heraus. Um diese aber nicht allzusehr auseinanderzuzerren, entschloss man sich, sie vom Forum aus nur um einen Häuserblock nach Osten zu verschieben und den weiteren Ausgleich durch den Knick nach Nordosten zu suchen. An dem Strassenknie dürfte, wie Harald Koethe vermutete, ein grosses Ehrenportal gestanden haben, wie solche in römischen Städten nicht selten waren und wovon auch in Trier Reste zutage gekommen sind. Ist somit der nördliche Teil des Cardo bestimmt nicht identisch mit dem ursprünglichen, so scheint mir auch der südliche nicht unbedingt sicher mit seinem Vorgänger übereinzustimmen. Es wäre m. E. durchaus denkbar, dass im Trier des 1. Jahrhunderts der Cardo in der westlichen Parallelstrasse zu dem späteren gesucht werden muss. Denn diese Strasse läge in der Mittelachse des älteren Trier und führte auf die Mitte des Forums. Dann müsste freilich die jetzige grosse Ausfallstrasse nach Süden in älterer Zeit auch um so viel weiter westlich gelegen haben. Eine Bodenuntersuchung ausserhalb der Stadtmauer würde diese Frage leicht klären können.

Wenn der vermeintliche Decumanus das römische Trier in eine ungleich grössere nördliche und eine viel kleinere südliche Hälfte teilt, so wird nach dem eben Gesagten diese Unregelmässigkeit der Veränderung des Stadtumfangs zuzuschreiben sein. Aber kann die bisher als Decumanus angesehene Strasse wirklich dafür in Frage kommen? Gewiss, die prunkvollen Kaiserthermen liegen daran, aber mit ihrer wahrscheinlich höchst langweiligen südlichen Längswand der Palaestra. Und für das Forum bildet die Strasse ja nur die südliche Begrenzung, die an der Rückseite der Kaufläden entlang führt. Schliesslich aber läuft sie sich an der Nordostecke der Barbarathermen tot. Hier musste man um die Ecke biegen, wenn man zur Brücke gelangen wollte. Diese war also keinesfalls ihr Ausgangs- oder Endpunkt, vielmehr war sie weder im ersten noch im zweiten Zustand irgendwie auf diesen vermeintlichen Decumanus ausgerichtet. Das aber scheint mir das entscheidende Kriterium zu sein. Denn wenn die Brücke, ganz gleich in welchem Winkel, auf die ursprüngliche Stadtmitte trifft, so

muss man erwarten, dass ihr Strassenzug sich in der Querachse der
Stadt, eben im Decumanus, fortsetzt.

Wir kennen zwei römische Brücken in Trier. Die jüngere von beiden wird noch heute benutzt, wenigstens sind die Pfeiler bis auf zwei
antik. Wann sie gebaut ist, kann nicht mit Gewissheit gesagt werden.
Dass sie erst von Konstantin d. Gr. errichtet worden sei, wie E. Krüger auf Grund einer Goldmünze vermutete,[2] ist nicht mehr überzeugend, nachdem sich herausgestellt hat, dass die Porta Nigra und mit
ihr die Stadtbefestigung bereits im Anfang des 3. Jahrhunderts entstanden ist.[3] Man möchte den Brückenneubau gern mit der gewaltigen Mauerplanung in Zusammenhang wissen. Aber für unsere Fragen spielt die genaue Datierung keine Rolle. Wichtiger ist das Verhältnis beider Brücken zueinander. Die ältere Moselbrücke, vermutlich die gleiche, auf der im Jahre 70 Cerialis den nächtlichen Angriff
der Treverer zurückschlug, wurde bei dem tiefen Wasserstand der
Mosel im Sommer 1921 unterhalb der jüngeren Brücke wiederent-
deckt.[4] Beide Brücken laufen nicht parallel, sondern nähern sich einander der Stadt zu. Ihre verschiedene Richtung bietet uns einen er-
wünschten und bisher viel zu wenig beachteten Anhaltspunkt für den
Ansatz des Brückentores, von dem ja beide ihren Ausgang nehmen,
bzw. in dem sie sich treffen mussten. Nachdem Kutzbach nachgewiesen hatte,[5] dass im Ufer noch zwei weitere Pfeiler der jüngeren
Brücke verborgen liegen, wobei herauskam, dass der noch heute
durch die Kreuzigungsgruppe betonte dritte Pfeiler vom Stadtufer
aus ehemals der fünfte und demnach der Mittelpfeiler war, kann über
die Lage des Brückentores eigentlich kein Zweifel mehr bestehen. Die
Stadtmauer springt hier erheblich zurück, wohl um einen von der
Brücke her angreifenden Feind besser in der Flanke packen zu können. Sie läuft am Fluss entlang genau nach Norden und ist bis zu
dem westlich von der Mitte der Barbarathermen liegenden Turm
durch Grabungen festgestellt worden. Von diesem Turm an scheint
sie tatsächlich nach Nordosten umzubiegen.

Das Strassennetz Triers ist im wesentlichen Jahrhunderte hindurch dasselbe geblieben. Wenn nach grösseren Zerstörungen durch
Einebnen der Boden erhöht wurde, haben die darauf entstehenden
neuen Strassen die Richtung der älteren eingehalten. Jedenfalls steht

2. E. Krüger, "Die Zeitstellung der Porta Nigra zu Trier," *Trierer Zeitschr.*
8, 1933, 93 ff. Vgl auch zur römischen Moselbrücke, *Trierer Zeitschr.* 7, 1932,
172 ff.

3. Harald Koethe, "Die Stadtmauer des römischen Trier," *Trierer Zeitschr.*
11, 1936, 46 ff.

4. Siegfr. Loeschcke, *Trierer Jahresber.* 13, 1921, 66 ff.

5. Friedr. Kutzbach, "Archäologische Untersuchungen an der Moselbrücke in
Trier," *Nachrichtenblatt f. rhein. Heimatpflege* 3, 1931/32, 220 ff.

fest, das weder die erste noch die zweite Brücke in eine der rechtwinklig angeordneten Strassen einmündet. Da sie aber nicht auf eine
Häuserwand stossen konnte, muss eine andere Erklärung gefunden
werden. Sie scheint sich mir aus der Lage und dem Charakter des
Forums zu ergeben.

Ueber das Forum Triers ist noch wenig bekannt. Immerhin genügen die auf dem Grundstück des Trier Bürgervereins ausgegrabenen
Fundamentreste, um zu sagen, dass der Platz von einer Säulenhalle
mit Kaufläden umgeben war und in seiner Anlage dem Forum von
August[6] so sehr ähnelt, dass wir geradezu berechtigt sind anzunehmen,
auch in Trier habe die Mitte des Forums ein Augustustempel eingenommen. Die letzte Bestätigung kann natürlich erst eine Grabung
erbringen. Wie dem auch sei, jedenfalls scheint es mir kein Zufall zu
sein, dass die Verlängerung der Achse der älteren Moselbrücke genau
auf den Mittelpunkt des Forums führt. Der schiefen Richtung dieser
Strasse passt sich übrigens die Nordfront des Vorhofes der Barbarathermen an.

Die spätrömische Brücke jedoch ist anders orientiert. Ihre stärkere Abweichung von der Richtung des Strassennetzes lässt ihre
Achse die durch das Forum gegebene Mittelachse der Stadt schon
früher schneiden und scheint zunächst gar keine Beziehung zu ihr zu
haben. Aber das Gegenteil ist der Fall, wie wir sehen werden.

Die beiden Strassen, die das Forum nördlich und südlich begrenzen,
sind weiter von einander entfernt als alle übrigen Parallelstrassen
innerhalb des sonstigen römischen Trier. Die scheinbar grösseren
aber nicht erforschten Insulae westlich des Tempelbezirks dürften
unterteilt gewesen sein. Der ganze Streifen über der Ost-Westachse
ist also schon durch die Breite seiner Insulae vor andern hervorgehoben. Es wundert uns nicht, dass er so bedeutende Bauten wie die
Kaiserthermen und jenen palastartigen Komplex enthält, der westlich an das Forum anschliessend, wenigstens in seinen Fundamenten
beim Bau der Hindenburgschule festgestellt werden konnte. Bei dem
Versuch, die Bedeutung dieses "Palastes" zu ergründen, bleiben wir
vorläufig in vagen Vermutungen stecken. Es muss uns genügen, dass
es sich um einen repräsentativen Grossbau handelt, der höchst wahrscheinlich einem öffentlichen Zweck diente oder einem hohen Würden-
träger gehörte. Bemerkenswert ist nun, dass dieser Baukomplex in
der Mitte durch eine Strasse geteilt wurde, wobei man sich vorstellen
mag, dass über diese hinweg Bogengänge von einem Teil zum andern
geführt haben können. Diese Strasse aber nimmt genau die Mittelachse ein, und genau auf den Punkt, wo sie aus dem Palastkomplex

---

6. Felix Stähelin, *Die Schweiz in römischer Zeit*, Basel 1927, Planbeilage II.

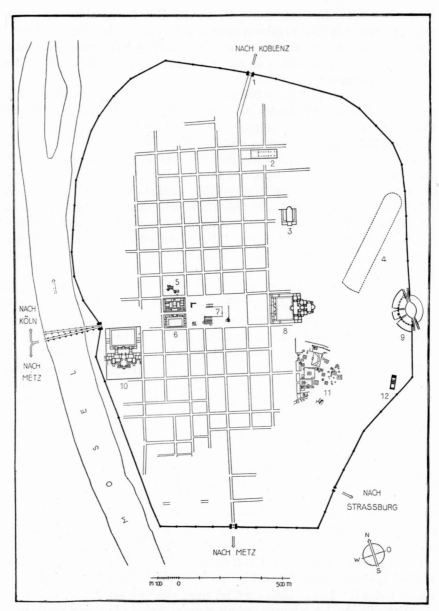

Abb. 1. Stadtplan des römischen Trier mit Eintragung der wichtigsten Bauten.
— 1. Porta nigra. 2. Dom. 3. Basilika. 4. Circus (?). 5. Palast des Victorinus.
6. Palastanlage. 7. Forum. 8. Kaiserthermen. 9. Amphitheater. 10. Barbarathermen. 11. Tempelbezirk am Altbach. 12. Tempel am Herrenbrünnchen.

heraustritt, ist die Achse der jüngeren Moselbrücke ausgerichtet. Die von ihr in die Stadt führende Strasse geht also von da ab in die allgemeine Richtung über. Diese und keine andere muss als Decumanus angesehen werden. Noch haben wir sie erst bis zum Forum verfolgt, wo sie geradeswegs auf den vermuteten Augustustempel zuläuft, dessen Front wohl nach Osten zu lag mit dem Altar davor. Aber die Mittelachse ist architektonisch noch weiter ausgestaltet worden. Das Forum hat wenigstens zweieinhalb, wahrscheinlich drei Insulae eingenommen. Ueber die dann folgende Insula ist noch nichts bekannt. Dass auch sie interessante Bauten enthalten muss, ist anzunehmen. Umso genauer kennen wir den östlichen Abschluss. Hier liegen, wie schon erwähnt, den ganzen Raum einer übergrossen Insula in der Breite füllend, die Kaiserthermen. Diese sind nicht nur als Bauwerk wegen ihrer gewaltigen und straff gegliederten Formen zu bewundern, sondern lassen allein durch die Stelle, an der sie liegen, auf einen genialen Städtebauer schliessen. Sie bilden zweifellos den markanten östlichen Abschluss der über das Forum, und wie wir nun wissen, von der Brücke her durch den "Palast" führenden Mittelachse. Es ist nicht ausgeschlossen, dass der Erbauer der Thermen auf einen älteren Gedanken zurückgegriffen hat. Denn schon vor der grossen Zerstörung Triers in der zweiten Hälfte des 3. Jahrhunderts hat, wie die Ausgrabung unter der Agnetenkaserne ergeben hat, in der Mittelachse eine reichgeschmückte Badeanlage bestanden, die vielleicht auch schon eine öffentliche Therme war. Aber wie grosszügig wird nun die neue Grosstherme in den zur Verfügung stehenden Raum hineinkomponiert! Es ist bis jetzt immer nur nebenbei bemerkt worden, dass die Kaiserthermen eigentlich falsch orientiert sind. Bei jeder normalen Therme, u. a. auch bei den Barbarathermen, liegt das Caldarium nach Süden zu, einfach um dem Warmbad auch ein Höchstmass von Sonnenbestrahlung zukommen zu lassen.[7] Und wie wichtig war diese auch von Vitruv geforderte Ausrichtung besonders in unserem Klima! Die Abweichung von diesem wohlbegründeten Brauch kann nicht einer blossen Laune entspringen. Der Gestalter des neuen Stadtbildes hielt diesen monumentalen Abschluss seiner Achse für so unentbehrlich, dass er diesem Gedanken die praktischen Gesichtspunkte bedenkenlos opferte. Für die richtige Orientierung war die Insula zu schmal, so wurden die Thermen um 90° gedreht und mit ihrer Schmalseite zwischen die beiden Strassen gestellt.

Die Kaiserthermen wurden in ihrer Eigenschaft als Bäderpalast bekanntlich niemals vollendet. Nach längerem Stilliegen wurde die

---

7. Heinz Kähler, "Die Südfassade der Barbarathermen in Trier," *Trierer Zeitschr.* 18, 1949, 20 ff.

gesamte Anlage durch Umbau wesentlich verändert. Das Frigidarium
wurde niedergelegt, der Kuppelsaal des Tepidariums zur Vorhalle
umgewandelt, vor allem aber die Palaestra unter Hinzunahme des
ehemaligen Frigidariumraumes zu einem ungewöhnlich grossen, von
Hallen umgebenen Hofe ausgestaltet. Ueber den Benutzungszweck
der neugeschaffenen Anlage haben sich bisher keine Anhaltspunke
ergeben, sodass wir über Vermutungen nicht hinausgekommen sind.
Diese hat Daniel Krencker zusammengestellt.[8] Der Gedanke an die
Umwandlung in ein Prätorium scheint ihm, ohne dass er sich für
diese Deutung entschieden hätte, danach am meisten gelegen zu
haben, während er die Deutung als Forum, wobei das ehemalige Caldarium die forensische Basilika geworden wäre, auf Grund von Vergleichen mit andern Forumsbasiliken abzulehnen geneigt ist. Er
selbst sagt aber S. 161: "Bei der Vergleichung mit andern Beispielen
wird man sich immer sagen müssen, dass ein feststehender Raum
eines für ganz andere Zwecke errichteten Gebäudes übernommen
worden ist. Man muss mit einer dadurch bedingten gewissen Unfrei-
heit des betreffenden Baumeisters rechnen. Da aber der Umbau mit
grossen Mitteln und auf ganz radikale Art vorgenommen wurde, so
müssen doch die stehengebliebenen und mitbenutzten Teile für die
Zweckbestimmung des Neubaues hervorragend geeignet gewesen
sein." Ich habe die Deutung der umgebauten Anlage als Kaiserforum
trotz der vorgebrachten Bedenken von jeher für die wahrscheinlich
richtige gehalten. Nicht nur die eben zitierten Sätze von Krencker
erlauben es, sich mit der ungewöhnlichen Form der forensischen Basilika abzufinden, sondern es verdient betont zu werden, dass das
Trier des 3. und 4. Jahrhunderts voller schöpferischer künstlerischer
Gedanken war, sodass uns ein Abweichen von sonst üblichen Formen
nicht zu befremden braucht. Allein die sogenannte Basilika und der
römische Vorgänger des Domes, dessen Bild sich dank der Entdeck-
ungen seit 1943 bedeutend geklärt hat, sind dafür Beweise.[9] Der Auf-
schwung, den die Residenz namentlich unter der zielsicheren Regierung Valentinians I. genommen hat, möchte das Bedürfnis nach einem
repräsentativen Forum gesteigert haben. Immerhin dürfte die Umwandlung der Thermen in ein Kaiserforum an überzeugender Kraft
gewinnen, wenn wir sehen, wie es sich fast logisch an das alte Forum
anschliesst, was ja auch bei den Kaiserforen Roms der Fall war.
Freilich wissen wir von der dazwischen liegenden Insula vorläufig
nichts. Enthielt sie eine Ost-West-Durchgangsstrasse oder aber einen
einstöckigen Bau, über den im Osten die mächtigen Hallen der Ther-

---

8. Daniel Krencker [u. a.] "Die Trierer Kaiserthermen," Augsburg 1929, 161 ff.
9. Th. Konrad Kempf, "Die Deutung des römischen Kerns im Trierer Dom
nach den Ausgrabungen von 1943-1946," *Das Münster*, I, 1947, 129 ff.

men aufragten? Jedenfalls wird diese Insula nicht als einzige des gesamten Mittelstreifens belanglos bebaut gewesen sein. Vielleicht war sie auch platzartig gestaltet. Das gerade dort stärker ansteigende Gelände bot sogar zu Freitreppen Gelegenheit.

So formt sich uns ein ziemlich anschauliches Bild von einem der Glanzteile des römischen Trier, und es gehört nicht allzuviel Phantasie dazu, es sich näher auszumalen. Ueber die auf neun Steinpfeilern lagernde Holzbrücke näherte man sich dem Brückentor, das an wuchtiger Kraft und baulicher Ausgestaltung sicher nicht hinter den andern Toren zurückstand. Denn es lag an der repräsentativsten Stelle. Möglicherweise gehören in der Nähe seines vermutlichen Standortes gefundene skulpierte Quader zu seinem künstlerischen Schmuck. Zu beiden Seiten breitete sich die 6 m hohe Stadtmauer aus, zinnenbewehrt und stellenweise von Türmen unterbrochen. Links lag der Hafen mit ankernden Schiffen, rechts ragten die mächtigen Hallen der Barbarathermen über die Mauer. Hatte man das Brückentor durchschritten, so traf der Blick auf den Durchgang zwischen den beiden Teilen des palastartigen Baues. Zwischen ihnen gehend sah man vor sich vermutlich den Tempel auf dem säulenumstandenen Forum. War man um ihn herumgegangen, so stand man an dem Altar und blickte zurück auf die Front des Tempels, den man sich auf einem Podium mit Freitreppe vorzustellen hat. Im Osten erblickte man dann von weitem die dekorative Westfront der Thermen mit ihrem grossartigen Säulenvorbau in Art eines Nymphaeums und sah dann darüber das ehemalige Tepidarium, nunmehr die Vorhalle aufragen, die in das einstige Caldarium, die Forumsbasilika, überleitete.

Wie frei man übrigens in der Spätzeit mit der Bezeichnung Basilica umging, beweist eine Stelle der Villenbeschreibung von Sidonius Apollinaris, Epist. II 2, 4, wo damit offenbar nur der Begriff Halle gemeint ist.[10] Man hat den Ausdruck Basilica bisher nur auf den im 19. Jahrhundert zur evangelischen Kirche umgestalteten Römerbau angewandt nach den Worten der Preisrede auf Constantin vom Jahre 310, worin der Redner sagt: video basilicas usw. Er sah also mehrere "Basiliken." So ist es durchaus wahrscheinlich, daß der genannte Römerbau eine von diesen ist. Er entspricht nicht dem üblichen Basilikatypus, würde also auch im übertragenen Sinne nur "Halle" bedeuten. Da liegt es nahe anzunehmen, daß der Redner unter den erwähnten Basiliken auch die Hallen der Thermen mitgemeint hat, die ja damals bestimmt schon bestanden und sonderbarerweise trotz ihrer Größe sonst verschwiegen worden wären. Dann aber wäre die Bezeichnung Basilika für das Caldarium schon im Anfang des 4.

---

10. Krencker, *Kaiserthermen a. a. O.* 327 Anm. 2 [H. Wachtler].

Jahrhunderts ortsbekannt gewesen. Umso leichter konnte sich die Umgestaltung in eine wirkliche Forumsbasilika vollziehen.

Diese Ausführungen legen Gedanken nieder, die dem Verfasser in mehreren Jahren der Beschäftigung mit dem römischen Trier gekommen sind und beanspruchen nicht, als unbedingt sichere Lösung betrachtet zu werden. Wenn sie Anregung zu weiterer Forschung geben und das Bild der alten römischen Kaiserresidenz wiederbeleben helfen, ist ihr Zweck erfüllt.

DEATH

That full and final hour, may it welcome be
    That comes to close mine eyes forevermore.
Now? Tomorrow? Indifferent to me,
    If it but come not like the tempest's roar,
But on some day of spring, even like today,
    A quiet sunset on a shining sea,
When a light wind begins its gentle play,
    My white-robed soul fall fluttering to the grave
Like an apple blossom, and whatever the tide
    Bearing it down the stream that flows beside
Orchards and hedges to a greater deep,
    Wherever borne or if it linger near
Of old familiar voices may it hear
    Only the farewell that the fountain then shall weep.

John Gryparis

Translated by
John B. Edwards

DER URBAU DER KIRCHE ST. GEREON IN KOELN

ARMIN VON GERKAN
Bonn

Die schweren Beschädigungen, die in Köln auch die Kirche St. Gereon erlitten hat, gaben allerdings die Möglichkeit, einen gründlichen Einblick in ihr bauliches Gefüge zu nehmen. Sowohl die Landesregierung von Nordrhein-Westfalen, wie auch das Deutsche Archäologische Institut beschafften dafür die Mittel, und ich hatte den Vorzug, den Forschungsauftrag zu erhalten, worüber ich hier den ersten, noch vorläufigen Bericht vorlege. Die Untersuchung erfolgte im Sommer und im Herbst 1949, ist aber noch nicht abgeschlossen und soll im Frühjahr 1950 zu Ende geführt werden. Das Gesamtresultat kann aber nur noch in Einzelheiten verändert werden.

Ueber die früheste Baugeschichte der Kirche standen sich bisher zwei Ansichten gegenüber. Die amtliche Veröffentlichung von P. Clemen, besorgt von H. Rathgens, in Band II, 1 der *Kunstdenkmäler der Stadt Köln*, 1911, erklärt dem Urbau für ein fränkisches Monument, möglicherweise auf spätantiker Grundlage, muss aber jetzt als überholt gelten. Bewährt hat sich die öffentliche Meinung, die sich auf die legendäre Tradition stützte und den Bau für spätkonstantinisch hielt, vermutlich eine Stiftung der Kaiserin Helena zum Gedächtnis der Märtyrer der thebäischen Legion. Diese Ansicht vertritt auch die Monographie St. Gereon zu Köln von Dr. G. Gretz und O. Koch, 1939, jedoch ihre zwar geistreiche, aber viel zu weitgehende Rekonstruktion, bei dem damals intakten und deshalb unzugänglichen Bauzustand, ist nicht aufrecht zu erhalten. Dasselbe gilt vom vermuteten fränkischen Umbau. Nur eine Fensteröffnung in der Tambourmauer über dem südlichen Triumphbogenpfeiler, die allerdings kein Bogen zu einem antiken Emporenumgang ist, und die Vermutung von römischen Treppentürmen an der Westseite bestehen zu Recht.

Ein Dutzend Gräben, die meistenteils an den Wänden und Pfeilern des Zentralbaues angelegt worden sind, ergaben nur wenig Reste einer früheren Bebauung des Nekropolengebietes, auf dem die Kirche errichtet worden ist. Vor beiden Westpfeilern liegen geradlinige ältere Mauerzüge von 0.45 m Stärke, die unter der Türschwelle einen rechten Winkel bilden und die bekannte suburbane Orientierung der Stadt einhalten; in der östlichsten Konche der Nordseite fand sich eine dritte, parallel zum nördlichen Schenkel des Winkels, die eine noch ältere, jedoch auch schon spätantike Bestattung überquert. Sie alle sind nur ganz flach fundamentiert, kaum 0.50 in den gewachsenen Boden, aber auch die Kirche selbst, die jene Mauern, nach Bedarf verstärkt, als Fundament benutzt, hat gleich flache Fundamente. Die Fundamente sind etwa 1.50 m hoch geführt und dann angeschüttet: eine recht bedenkliche Konstruktion, die allein schon die Annahme einer massiven Ueberwölbung des Urbaues nicht gestattet. Noch verwunderlicher ist es, dass auf die gleichen, wenn auch erweiterten Fundamente ebenfalls der mittelalterliche Wölbbau gesetzt worden ist. Die Füllerde enthält, wenn auch nicht sehr zahlreich, Einschlüsse und Scherben aus der ganzen Kaiserzeit, ist aber auch im Mittelalter stark durchwühlt, durch Beisetzungen und Reliquiensucherei, wobei sowohl späte Keramik, wie Bauschutt hineingeraten sind. In den tiefsten unberührten Schichten und in der Füllung der Baugrube lag, als terminus a quo, Keramik der spätantiken Zeit und die beiden einzigen Bronzemünzen: eine umgeprägte Tetrarchenmünze und eine der Kaiserin Helena (Cohen Nr.6). Es fehlen jüngere Funde, die eine spätere Datierung ermöglichen könnten. Bis auf die Bankette, die die Baugrube füllen, sind alle Fundamente als Freimauern mit der üblichen Verkleidung aus flachen Tuffschichten erbaut und als solche dann angeschüttet worden.

Die entscheidende Datierung gibt der Grabstein eines römischen Soldaten, der im 4. Jahrh. an der Westseite der Atriumsmauer bestattet war, die südlich an der Narthexfront anschliesst und bei der Beisetzung schon gestanden haben musste.

Die Vermessung des Zentralraumes ergab natürlich keine Ellipse, sondern einen Korbbogen aus vier Mittelpunkten, mit einer langen Achse von 80 Fuss. Für die Querachse war der Betrag von 60 Fuss vorgesehen, aber nicht eingehalten: man nahm für die Radien, die die Zentren verbinden, die Richtung von 45° an, steckte aber das Zentrum auf der Querachse nicht, wie nötig wäre, in 17,2, sondern in nur 15 Fuss Abstand vom Mittelpunkt ab, und dadurch wurde die Querachse nach Süden bereits ein wenig zu lang. Für den nördlichen Bogen wurde — offenbar ein Versehen — das Zentrum in nur 13 Fuss Abstand genommen, weshalb der Nordbogen erheblich stärker gekrümmt ist (Abb. 1 u. 2).

Die vier Konchen auf beiden Seiten liegen noch im Bereich der flachen Bögen. Abgesehen von Unregelmässigkeiten der Ausführung, sind sie folgendermassen konstruiert. Die Tambourmauer ist 4 Fuss (1.17 m) stark und wird von Gurtbögen zwischen den Pfeilern getragen. Auf ihrem äusseren Umriss liegen die Zentren der Konchen, deren Radius 8 Fuss (2,35 m) beträgt, bei 2½ Fuss (0,72 m) Wandstärke. Dabei erhalten die Nischen ihre hufeisenförmige Ueberhöhung und eine Weite von 14½ Fuss, die sich aus der radialen

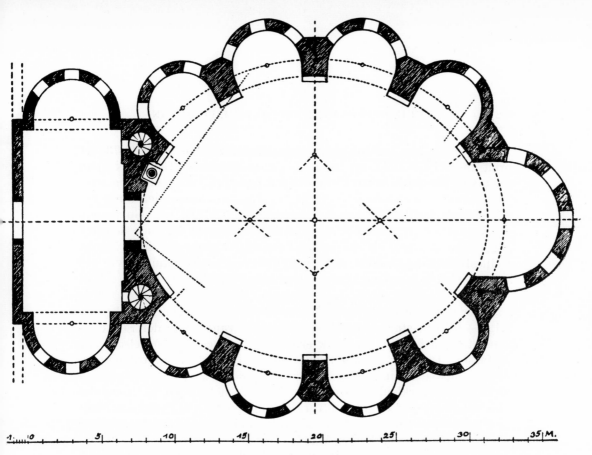

Abb. 1. Grundplan.

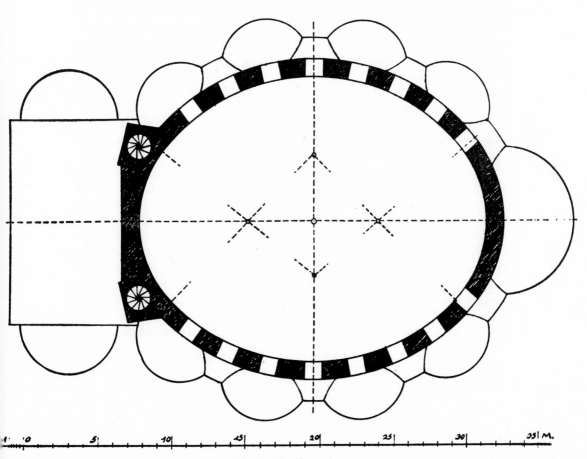

Abb. 2. Tambourplan.

Verengerung von selbst ergibt. Die Pfeiler sind 6 Fuss (1,73 m) breit und 9 Fuss (2,65 m) tief; wie der beschädigte Pfeiler erkennen liess, war die Stirn mit 0,45 m starken Quadern verkleidet. Da aber die Schwelle noch um 0,33 m weiter vortritt, kann hier auch ein Säulenpaar gestanden haben, über dessen Gebälk der Gurtbogen wieder zurücktritt: der Kämpferquader des Bogens ist auch deutlich abgehauen worden, als die mittelalterliche Vorlage errichtet wurde. Keinesfalls aber standen seitlich von den Pfeilern Säulen, wie gelegentlich angenommen worden ist, da Fundamente dafür fehlen (Abb. 3).

Unter dem heutigen Fussboden ist hier und an anderen Stellen die 0,12 — 0,15 m starke Mörtelschicht und darauf Reste der Sockelinkrustation in üblicher Technik erhalten, die auch die Sockelschwelle umfasste. Darüber ist die flachere Wandinkrustation anzunehmen, welche entweder hinter den Säulen durchlief oder gegen die vortretende Quaderverkleidung stiess. In Kämpferhöhe wird die Inkrustation aufgehört und die Mosaikverkleidung der Gewölbe und des Tambours begonnen haben. Vom Mosaik sind allenthalben zahlreiche Steinchen gefunden, kleine Würfel aus verschiedenfarbigem Glasfluss, wie auch farblose mit einer Goldschicht unter einer dünnen Glasauflage. Das bestätigt die von Gregor von Tour überlieferte Bezeichnung "Sancti Aurei", und ein Stück ungestörter Brandschicht mit vielen solchen Resten im Zentralraum selbst beweist, dass das Mosaik nicht allein auf die Konchengewölbe beschränkt war. Man möchte fast vermuten, dass die Benennung und die bei Gregor überlieferte Zahl von nur 50 Märtyrern auf einen Figurenfries hinweist, der aber nur an der Tambourwand anstelle der oberen Fensterreihe unterzubringen wäre.

Die Inkrustationsreste haben keinen gleichmässigen unteren Rand, sondern eine deutliche Abnutzung lässt erkennen, dass gegen sie der Fussboden stiess, nur 0.35 m unter dem heutigen. Es handelt sich um einen Mosaikboden, der in gleicher Höhe den Zentralraum und die Nischen bedeckte. Leider ist davon nichts in situ gefunden, aber doch zahlreiche Reste, auf einer festen Betonschicht schmale Streifen, die in abwechselnd schwarze und bunte Dreiecke geteilt sind und merkwürdigerweise von Ziegelstreifen eingerahmt sind. Weit seltener sind Reste von Rankenformen. Auch von der Inkrustation sind viele Bruchstücke gefunden, aber sie gestatten keine Wiederherstellung.

Die Tragebögen und Halbkuppeln begannen in 5,07 m Höhe. Ihre heutige flach-elliptische Form haben die Bögen erst dadurch erhalten, dass die mittelalterlichen Vorlagen die Oeffnungen zwar nicht stark, aber doch so einengen, dass die Laibungen senkrecht höher aufsteigen

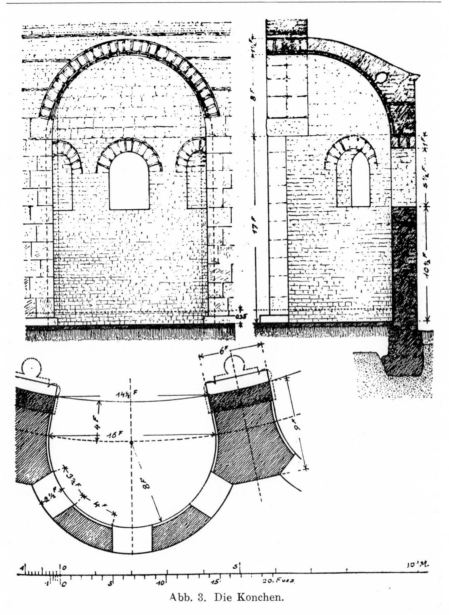

Abb. 3. Die Konchen.

und der Uebergang zum antiken Rundbogen dann ausgerundet worden ist. — Das Tambourmauerwerk, heute noch neben den Bögen und in Tastungen unter dem Emporenfussboden sichtbar, besteht aus sorgfältigen Flachschichten mit gelegentlichem doppelten Ziegeldurchschuss, während die Konchenmauern viel unregelmässiger und

fast ohne Ziegel gebaut sind. Die Gurtbögen zeigen einen Wechsel
von Tuffsteinen und je 2 Ziegeln, mit einer Ziegelabdeckung; kleinere
Bögen haben zwischen den Keilsteinen nur einen Ziegel. Die Gurtbögen sitzen über einer doppelten Bipedalschicht, die im Konchengewölbe in eine Doppelschicht aus kleineren Ziegeln übergeht. Das
Gewölbe selbst besteht aus horizontalem Bruchsteinmauerwerk in
Mörtel, das in der Kämpferzone in spätrömischer Technik durch
eingemauerte grosse Töpfe erleichtert wird. Aussen sind sowohl
Mauern wie Gewölbe glatt verputzt gewesen. Bemerkenswert sind
die grossen Quadern in den Bogenkämpfern, die eine innige Verbindung mit der Pfeilerstirn ergaben, im staufischen Umbau aber
abgehauen und in die neuen Vorlagen einbezogen worden sind.

Die Konchen (Abb. 3) haben in der Regel je 3 Fenster, 3,12 m über
dem Fussboden, 1.05 m breit und hoch, mit Halbkreisbögen von 0,35 m
Stärke, die bis an den Kuppelansatz reichen. Die seitlichen Fenster
sind so weit abgerückt, als dies die Zwischenpfeiler gestatten. Auffällig ist, dass beide Ostkonchen nur je 1 Fenster haben: man möchte
vermuten, dass irgend ein Baukörper im Osten die Anlage der letzten
Fenster verhinderte, aber es hat sich bisher keine Bestätigung dafür
ergeben.

Von der heutigen Türwand gehört nichts mehr dem antiken Bestand
an. Doch liegt in tieferer Lage eine grosse Kalksteinschwelle von
3,75 m Länge und 1,15m Breite, leider mit abgespaltener Oberfläche.
Sie muss die Türgewände getragen haben, und das Portal mag etwa
die heutige Weite von 2,65 m gehabt haben; es hätte dabei gut Raum
in einer überwölbten Nische von gleicher Höhe, wie die Konchen. —
Nördlich vom Portal steht heute in einer engen Nische die sogenannte
Blutsäule. Napoleon I. liess den Säulenstumpf in den Louvre schaffen,
doch soll er unterwegs liegen geblieben sein und ist angeblich im
Wald von Brauweiler wiedergefunden und 1925 zur Kirche gebracht
worden. Nur ist dieser Säulenstumpf sicher nicht authentisch, da er
mit 0.54 m Durchmesser nicht einmal auf den oberen Rand der
Marmorbasis von 0.495 m passt. Die Basis war über dem Fussboden
kaum sichtbar und wurde erst jetzt zusammen mit der Sandstein-
plinthe, die dabei leider stark verkleinert wurde, um 0,50 m gehoben.
Beide sind ringsum bis zur Formlosigkeit abgetreten. Es muss also
vor dem staufischen Umbau der Ritus eines Umschreitens der Säule
bestanden haben, und zwar in einer allerdings geräumigeren Nische,
denn sonst wäre die Basis nicht so stark beschädigt und von der
Plinthe nicht der erhöhte, durch die Nachbarschaft der Wand ge-
schützte Rand stehen geblieben sein. Folglich gehört die Säule zum
Bestand des Urbaues, jedoch als Einzelstück, denn südlich vom Portal

gab es keine Nische, und da hier in nächster Nähe die ältere Mauer in einem tieferen Niveau liegt, kann die Säule hier auch nicht schon vor der Kirche gestanden haben.

Die mittelalterliche, fast quadratische Vorhalle ersetzt die antike, die etwas länger, aber viel weniger tief war: ihre Westwand ist im Fundament gefunden, das noch den Abdruck der Türschwelle zeigt. Die aufgehende Wand war 0,71 m stark und konnte auch kein Gewölbe tragen. Dagegen sind die beiden Nebenräume im Norden und Süden in Lage und Grösse durch die einstigen Apsiden bedingt, von denen die Fundamente der nördlichen festgestellt sind. Ein Graben südlich ausserhalb der Kirche zeigte, dass die Westwand der Vorhalle sich weiter fortsetzte: hier lag ein umfangreiches Atrium, von dem Reste schon während des Krieges auf dem Platz vor der Kirche bei der Anlage eines Löschteiches zu Tage traten.

Anders als die übrigen Pfeiler, tragen die beiden westlichen keine abgesetzten Strebepfeiler, sondern breite und flache Lisenen aus flachgeschichtetem Mauerwerk, das an sich ebensogut antik wie mittelalterlich sein könnte. Im Bereich der südlichen durchbricht der Verbindungsgang vom staufischen Treppenturm zum ersten Umgang über der Empore hinter dem Pfeiler eine frühere Wendeltreppe. Er folgt hier ihrer engen Krümmung. Sichtbar sind die Spindel, das steigende Gewölbe darüber und 3 Stufen; zwei tiefere konnten freigelegt werden. Die Stufen bestehen aus flachen Steinschichten und römischen Ziegeln: hier lag also ein älteres, aufgegebenes Treppenhaus, das römisch sein muss, weil es nicht vor dem antiken Mauerwerk liegt, sondern in den Mauerkörper des Pfeilers und der anschliessenden Konche eingebettet ist. Ein gleicher Treppenturm ist im Norden zu ergänzen, aber bisher nicht sichtbar, weil hier der Verbindungsgang fehlt, die Stelle aber wegen der Zerstörung ohne Baugerüst noch nicht zugänglich ist. Aber zu ihm dürfte ein bisher undeutbarer Mauerrest gehören, der sich hier zwischen dem Gurtbogen und der Konchenkuppel einschiebt. Die Treppen führten auf keinen Umgang, sondern dienten zur Pflege des Daches, und führten noch eine volle Windung höher, wie das Gewölbe über den Stufen im Süden beweist: das wären etwa 4 m, wodurch die Höhe des Tambours bis zu 16 m Höhe nachgewiesen ist. Bei der sonst elliptischen Form des Tambours muss die Front zwischen den Treppentürmen gerade angenommen werden.

Am Ostende der südlichen Empore ist von Dr. G. Gretz eine Bogenöffnung in der Tambourmauer entdeckt worden, die in üblicher römischer Technik aus Keilsteinen und Ziegeln, mit einer doppelten Ziegelverkleidung und einer einfachen Abdeckung erbaut ist. Die

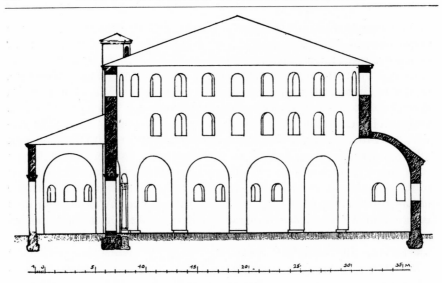

Abb. 4. Schnitt.

Stelle ist weiter freigelegt worden und ergab eine Spannweite von 1,20 m: es ist aber ein Fenster, das den Boden der Empore nicht erreicht. Das Fenster ist ebenso, wie alle Konchenfenster, einmal zugesetzt und verputzt worden, wohl erst im Mittelalter, als die Kirche baufällig geworden war, aber noch vor 1060, da die annonische Chorwand gegen den Fensterputz stösst. Ein entsprechendes Fenster konnte auch an der Nordseite festgestellt werden. Die Fenster nehmen nicht mehr auf die Pfeilerstellung Rücksicht, sondern gehören der ungegliederten Hochmauer an. Sie sind wohl symmetrisch zu der Querachse zu ergänzen, mit Abständen von wenig über Fensterbreite, was für den Umfang 24 Fenster ergeben würde, aber in dieser Höhe allerdings unterbrochen war: im Osten durch das Apsisgewölbe, im Westen durch die Treppen und das Vorhallendach. Die Höhe der Mauer gestattet aber eine zweite Fensterzone, wenn hier nicht der Märtyrerfries angenommen werden muss.

Wie schon erwähnt, konnte der Tambour kein Gewölbe tragen, sondern nur ein hölzernes Zeltdach mit vermutlich offenem Dachstuhl. Die genannte Dissertation Dr. G. Gretz — O. Koch nahm eine doppelte Tambourwand und darüber eine Kuppel an, aber der Befund lässt die Ergänzung einer zweiten Mauerschale schlechterdings nicht zu (Abb. 4).

Die genaue Gestalt der Hauptapsis konnte noch nicht nachgewiesen werden. Nischenreste in beiden Chorwänden schienen Anhaltspunkte zu bieten, erwiesen sich aber als mittelalterlich, dann barock und im 19. Jahrhundert mehrfach verändert, schliesslich zugemauert, aber nicht aufgezeichnet und völlig in Vergessenheit geraten. Allein zwei Quadern, die hinten in den Triumphbogenpfeilern wieder in Kämpferhöhe sitzen und die letzten Steine von der Aussenhaut des Tambours sind, geben wohl die Stelle, wo auch die Aussenhaut der Apsismauern angesetzt haben wird, und die Weite der Apsis mag durch die Weite des Triumphbogens selbst ungefähr gegeben sein, denn die Pfeiler enthalten römisches Mauerwerk. Bei der Rekonstruktion ist, wie bei den Konchen, das Zentrum im Scheitel der Tambourmauer angenommen, so dass auch hier eine überhöhte Nische entsteht, aber von einer Hufeisenform allerdings abgesehen ist. Obwohl die tiefe mittelalterliche Confessio die Apsisfundamente grösstenteils beseitigt haben dürfte und auch eine Grabung hier untunlich erscheinen lässt, ist zu hoffen, dass ein kurzer Graben in der Krypta selbst die Bestätigung bringen wird. Er war im Herbst noch nicht möglich, weil die Krypta als Notkirche diente.

Die Untersuchungen haben natürlich auch manche Ergebnisse für die mittelalterlichen Perioden ergeben, die hier aber nicht behandelt werden sollen. Es sei nur gesagt, dass die Datierungen sich gut bestätigt haben und kaum revidiert zu werden brauchen; wichtig ist nur, dass eine bisher allgemein vorausgesetzte fränkische Bauperiode nicht vorhanden war. Das ist aber ein wichtiges negatives Ergebnis und sollte warnen, der frühfränkischen Zeit wirklich monumentale Bauten zuzuschreiben. In die fränkische Zeit gehören jedoch mehrere Beisetzungen in grossen, glatten und schmucklosen Sandsteinsarkophagen, von denen im Inneren der Kirche jetzt drei gefunden worden sind, drei andere in der Vorhalle, einer im Südgraben ausserhalb, also im Atrium. Alle waren geöffnet und leer, wie das auch von früheren Funden bekannt ist. Dagegen scheinen zwei Sarkophage in der Nordapsis der Vorhalle noch unberührt zu sein, gewiss aber ein dritter ebenda in sehr tiefer Lage, der noch spätantik sein könnte. Die Hebung aller erreichbaren Gebeine ist wohl der Zeit des hl. Norbert 1121 zuzuschreiben, der systematisch und gutgläubig nach den Reliquien der Märtyrer forschte und jede Beisetzung aus früher und vergessener Zeit dafür ansah. Aber die Durchwühlung des Zentralraumes war offenbar so gründlich, dass dieser eigentliche Hauptteil der Kirche arg verwüstet gewesen sein muss, und die erwähnte Brandschicht mit Resten des Mosaiks lag gerade auf dem erhaltenen Teil des Deckels des einen Sarkophages gleich südlich vom Portal: damals lag also der Sarkophag offen, das Dach der Kirche aber war zerstört, und die Herrichtung erfolgte erst in der staufischen Zeit bis 1227. Vorher bestand offenbar ein Zustand, der dem heutigen stark ähnelte: der hohe Chor, erbaut von Anno II. um 1069 und erweitert von Arnold II. hundert Jahre später, diente als Kirche, während der alte Zentralbau als Ruine davor stand. Der staufische Neubau mag eine ebenso dringende Wiederherstellung gewesen sein, wie sie gegenwärtig geboten ist.

A PICTURE

The village hangs high up on the mountain side,
    One move—and it were dashed down into the sea.
The little white houses flakes of foam might be
    Flung up and scattered there by the tossing tide.

And my heart dances seeing they are so fair,
    Facing the sunset there as they flash along;
With glorious colours the Sun fills all the air,
    But keeps his keenest ray to gem each far-flashing pane.

Athanas

Translated by
John B. Edwards

THE ILLUSTRIOUS ANCESTRY OF THE NEWLY EXCAVATED VIKING CASTLES TRELLEBORG AND AGGERSBORG

H. P. L'ORANGE
Oslo

Plates 32-35

In the course of the last few years Danish archeology has discovered and interpreted for us a remarkable camp or castle type of the 10th and 11th centuries, which offers us a completely new picture of the military character of the Viking empires of the North. The director of the National Museum in Copenhagen, Poul Nörlund, with his Danish colleagues, has excavated the Viking camp at Trelleborg and published it in *Nordiske Fortidsminner*, Vol. IV, 1, 1948: "Trelleborg." And C. G. Schultz has given a preliminary report on the results of his first examination of a similar camp in Aggersborg in *Fra National-museets Arbeidsmark*, 1949, 91 seqq.: "Vikingeleiren ved Limfjorden."

Trelleborg and Aggersborg are characterized by their strongly geometrical character: a concentric system of mighty walls and ditches confine a mathematically circular area; two gate- and axis-streets intersecting each other at right angles in the centre of the circle, divide it in 4 congruent quarters. In these four quarters the houses are arranged in the same severe geometrical manner.

Trelleborg lies in West Seeland only 3-4 kilometers from the coast of the Great Belt (pl. 32).

"It consists of two parts, a very strong fortified main defence work and a more weakly fortified outer defence work. Part of the latter's area is laid out as a burial ground. The main ward, which is surrounded by a massive circular rampart, is situated at the extreme end of a promontory. On the open sides the terrain falls away steeply to the surrounding meadows, previously the lake, and here there is only quite a narrow approach of firm ground around the rampart. This circular ward is cut off from the hinterland and the outer ward by a wide and deep ditch which extends right across the promontory. Its course follows that of the circular rampart itself and describes an arc with the same centre."

"The outer ward also is covered by vallum and fosse, which, like the large inner ditch, cut off the stronghold's terrain from the hinterland. Both to the North and to the South they extend to where the ground slopes down to the swampy meadows. On their longest expanse they, too, form concentric arcs and follow the vallum and fosse of the main defence work at the same interval. But the northern section bends at right angles to enclose the burial ground mentioned already, which must have existed before the outer defences were constructed. This bend is the only thing that disrupts in a striking manner the severe geometric character of the construction."

"The two main streets are axis-streets or gate-streets, which, at right angles to each other, connected the East gate with the West gate and the North with the South. There are also traces of a rampart-street along the inner side of the circular rampart."[1]

The inner diameter is 136 m. The length of the radius (68m.) is that of the distance between the two ditches. The circular rampart is 17,6m. thick, and the large ditch is apparently traced out to the same width. As in Aggersborg, the rampart must be defined as a wooden wall filled with earth.[2] The streets were paved with wood. It must have been the large number of inhabitants that made this necessary.

Trelleborg's sister fortress, Aggersborg lies on the Limfjord which traverses the northern part of Jutland (pl. 33, a). In the winter of 1945-46 C. G. Schultz succeeded in finding within a circular vallum traces of a structure with houses of the same shape as those of Trelleborg and divided into similar blocks. The lay-out is even larger than that of Trelleborg—Schultz gives the inner diameter as 240 m.— and there is a possibility that it is also richer and more developed. As was the case in Trelleborg, the 4 gates seem to have been defended by wooden towers.[3]

Nörlund's historical interpretation of Trelleborg-Aggersborg is perfectly convincing:

"The character of the houses is such that they cannot have been intended for ordinary habitation. The many uniform buildings with the enormous central hall are not family houses, but rather barracks for an army. Altogether a force of between 1000 and 1500 men could without doubt have been provided with sleeping quarters in the fortress."

"The date of the finds in Trelleborg lies quite definitely within the period of about a century 950-1050. In all probability we may be able to assert that the date of the fortress' foundation falls within the first

---

1. Nörlund, P., *op. cit.*, 265 ff.
2. Schultz, C. G., *op. cit.*, 91 ff.
3. Nörlund, *op. cit.*, 285 ff.; Schultz, *op. cit.*, 91 ff.

part of the reign of Sweyn Forkbeard, immediately before 1000, and
that it was in use until the middle of the following century."[4]

"It is now a very great help in the understanding of Trelleborg as
a historical phenomenon that a fortress of a quite corresponding char-
acter has been found inside Danish frontiers. Aggersborg lies on the
Limfjord and here in this fjord was the assembly point for the Danish
Viking fleets, before they set out on their forays on England or the
Frankish coasts."

"If one wishes to understand Trelleborg, it is very necessary to see
it in relation to Aggersborg. They are two links in the same chain.
They lay on the great sea-route used by the Viking fleets to the Baltic
and to England. Trelleborg was not a local phenomenon, but a matter
of national importance. After an interval of some generations, King
Sweyn resumed Viking expeditions to Western Europe. He is described with good reason as the great organiser of Viking expeditions.
When he undertook his great push in his last years and conquered
England, he had made full preparations for it."[5]

"It is most obvious to designate the king himself, Sweyn Forkbeard,
the mighty Viking prince, conqueror of England, as the builder of
Trelleborg. In any case the fortress must have been built at the king's
command."[6]

ORIGIN OF THE TRELLEBORG-AGGERSBORG CASTLE TYPE

"Besides the great Nordic towns and fortifications of the Viking
Age—Danevirke, Hedeby and Birka—a completely new phenomenon
is brought to light in the case of Trelleborg: a circular fortress like
so many at home and abroad, but remarkably characterized by its
geometrical system and by its mathematical precision. In contrast to
the casual, haphazard building in the towns we find here the disposition of the buildings planned in advance, a town plan of which the
strict scheme is carried out with a striking relentlessness. There is
something highly developed about this fortress which cannot as a
matter of course be admitted into an ordinary Danish milieu of the
period c.1000, and it is strikingly apparent that Danes just at this
time in the Viking Period had rich occasion to make observations and
gain experience in widely different parts of the world. It will be
expedient now to go right back and ask the question: To what extent
can it be taken that Roman military technique lies behind Trelleborg's
characteristic structure? In a lay-out which to such an extent as

---

4. Nörlund, *op. cit.*, 280 ff.
5. Nörlund, *op. cit.*, 285 ff.
6. *Ibid.*, 280.

Trelleborg is stamped with order and system, it is inevitable to ask if these features so alien to the North can be due to Roman influence, in spite of the many centuries which separate the Vikings from the Roman period."[7]

The great Western military tradition which we meet with in the Roman *castra* seems, however, to have had its day long before the castles of Trelleborg and Aggersborg were built. The Frankish square redoubts, although having in some way preserved the outline, had given up the inner organisation of the Roman *castra*. Another ancient tradition of fortification, however, the military tradition of the Ancient Orient, was still alive, vital even to the very centuries of the Viking age, maintained by the greatest military power of the early medieval period, the Arabs. And while the plan of Trelleborg-Aggersborg essentially differs from the Roman *castra*—in the first place by its circular outline (in contrast to the rectangular Roman), in the second place by its completed axis cross (in contrast to the axis cross of the Roman, which was broken by the prætorium)—it repeats in all the essential features the oriental fortification plan which Sassanian Persia had handed over to the great Southern expansionistic power of that time, the Arabian "Vikings" of the Mediterranean. The contrast between the Oriental and Western plan is an essential one, as Roman military theory forbade as a principle the round camp and only allowed it where it was imposed by the terrain.[8] Since this Viking study leads us back thus to Antiquity, it may not be out of place, I hope, to offer it as a tribute to the great classical archaeologist to whom this volume is dedicated.

The military empire of the Assyrians seems to have given a definite, fully crystallized form to the camp fortification of the Ancient Orient. It is very often met with on the great Assyrian palace reliefs. As in Trelleborg—Aggersborg the outline of the Assyrian camp is circular, and itself divided by two gate- and axis-streets intersecting each other at right angles in the centre of the circle.[9] A detail of a relief from the palace of Ashurnazirpal the 3rd (884-859) in Nimrūd-Kalach, now in the British Museum, is reproduced in plate 33, b. On the Balawat gate reliefs of Salmanassar the 2nd (858-824) only one gate- and axis-street divides the camp,[10] (pl. 33, c). From the Assyr-

7. Nörlund, *op. cit.*, 281 ff.

8. Grosse, R., in F. Sarre - E. Herzfeld, *Archäologische Reise im Euphrat- und Tigrisgebiet*, 133, Note 1.

9. A great number of examples is quoted by F. Sarre - E. Herzfeld, *op. cit.*, p. 132 f.

10. A. Billerbeck - Fr. Delitzsch, "Die Palasttore Salmanassars II von Balawat," *Beiträge zur Assyriologie und semit. Sprachwiss.* 6 (1909) Pl.A₁C₁D₁M₁ show this camp (C₁ reproduced in pl. 33, c).

ians this camp was passed on to the succeeding peoples of the East. In the fourth century A.D. the army of Julian the Apostate in the neighborhood of Hatra takes over a camp *in orbiculatam figuram*.[11]

The fortification of the cities of the Ancient East follows the system of the Assyrian camp to be seen in the old reliefs. Long before the Assyrians had established their empire the double walls of Zendjirli trace the circular outline of a city of 700 m.'s diameter in a manner as near to exactness as could be expected at that time.[12] In Hatra the tendency toward a circular city wall is sufficiently marked to permit this type of plan to be called a round city.[13] The walls of the old city of Ctesiphon which probably follow the outlines of the Parthian wall, were also almost circular. These cities illustrate the oriental tradition, in contrast to the Graeco-Hippodamian system as represented by Seleucia on the Tigris.[14]

The mathematically circular city outlines and mathematically axial gate-way cross are met with in three dominant cities, tracing the route whereby the fortification system of the Ancient Orient was passed on to the Arabs: the Parthian Dārābjird, the Sassanian Fīrūzābād, the Abbasid Baghdad.

In Dārābjird (pl. 35, b) the wall and fosse form an exact circle, with an inner wall marking a concentric circle, the diameter of which was about half that of the circle described by the outer wall.[15] There was a gate at each of the main points of the compass and an axial street-cross connecting them; evenly spaced around the wall there were still four gates, probably with radial streets.[16]

Fīrūzābād, the oldest Sassanian city, situated in the very heart of Persia (pl. 34, a) was originally the fortified residence of the new dynasty, before its transference to Ctesiphon. Before Ardeshir had made himself a king, he was a governor of Dārābjird. But after the revolt in this city and Ardeshir's massacre of the population, he could not trust it any more. Then he built a replica of Dārābjird in a valley in the neighborhood, but smaller and better defended by the mountains. It has "l'aspect d'un camp retranché," writes R. Ghirshman. "Elle est construite suivant un plan circulaire parfait avec deux murs

---

11. Ammian. Marcell. 24, 8, 7.

12. Sarre - Herzfeld, *op. cit.*, 132 ff.

13. Andrae, W., "Hatra," *Wissenschaftl. Veröffentlichungen der Deutschen Orientgesellschaft* 21 (1912) plan Pl. 1; 9 (1908) plan Pl. 1.

14. Reuter, O. in Pope, *A survey of Persian Art*, I, 441; 575.

15. Diameter of outer wall 1274 m., breadth of wall 10 m., of fosse 27 m., of *intervallum* 420 m., diameter of inner wall 630 m.

16. E. N. Flandin - P. Coste, *Voyage en Perse*, Pl. 31. Le Strange, G., *The Lands of the Eastern Caliphate*, 289. Sarre - Herzfeld, *op. cit.*, 132 ff. Reuter, *op. cit.* 441.

de terre séparés par un fossé. Ce plan, qui imite celui de la ville Parthe de Darabgird située à l'Est de Firuzabad, doit s'expliquer par le souci de la sécurité et de la défense de la ville. Ses origines remontent très haut dans l'art des fortifications de l'Asie occidentale."[17] There was a gate at each of the main points of the compass and, undoubtedly, an axial street-cross connecting them. Istakhri writes of it in the tenth century: "It is almost as great as Istakhr, Shāpur, and Dārābjird. It is surrounded by a well preserved wall of earth and by a fosse. It has four gates: in the east Bab Mihr, in the west Bab Bahram, in the north Bab Hormizd, and in the south Bab Ardeshir." In the 12th century Ibn al-Balkhi says: "The city is round as a circle traced with a compass."[18]

This Parthian and Sassanian fortification plan has been the prototype of the most famous of all the "round cities" of the East: Baghdad, "The Round City" of Mansur (pl. 34, b), the second caliph of the Abbasid dynasty. The idea of building *ex novo* a great city—Baghdad was founded in 762—which would at the same time both strengthen and glorify the power of the new dynasty, is the same as in the history of Ardeshir, the Seleucids, the Diadochs, and Alexander. Originally Baghdad was planned, more than the great metropolis of the Abbasids, to be the fortified center for the troops of the caliph: the circular form and whole inner disposition sprang from this conception of its function. A double wall, the outer one somewhat less high, battlemented and with bastions about every 55 meters circumscribed the city with two concentric circles. Each wall was surrounded by its fosse, and each had four gates corresponding to the axial street-cross. These four main streets were vaulted in a double passage-way, and widened into a square at either end. In addition there was a roadway immediately inside the city wall, a *Ringstrasse*.[19] In the "round cities" of the East this intramural *Ringstrasse* is often met with.[20] In the centre of the circle lay the palace of the caliph.

The severe and schematic partition of the cities into quadrants and sections, transferred from the military camp, correspond also to the organisation of social and urban life. "The custom of segregating classes and crafts in Oriental cities imposed some system on the layout

17. Ghirshman, R., "Firuzabad," *Bulletin de l'Institut Français d'Archéologie Orientale* 46 (1947) 13 f.; 18.

18. After the quotation by Ghirshman *l.c.*

19. E. E. Beaudouin - A. U. Pope, in Pope, *A Survey of Persian Art* II, p. 1394. Sarre - Herzfeld, *op. cit.* 106 ff. Le Strange, G.. *Baghdad During the Abbasid Caliphate*, 15 ff. I would here express my indebtedness to my colleague and friend A. Bugge who at an early stage of this work drew my attention to Mansur's "Round City" in Baghdad.

20. Beaudouin - Pope, *op. cit.*, 1396.

of quarters and streets at a very early time, and at least by the first
Islamic period, and probably long before, the principle was established
of dividing the circle defined by the city wall into quadrants. In such
a plan, two principal roadways cut through the entire town, intersecting at right angles in the centre, the citadel frequently marking
this intersection. These main streets connected the four city gates,
which were often more or less exactly at the points of the compass,
though naturally their location was determined primarily by the major
roads of approach."[21] The plan with four gates corresponding to the
points of the compass was used also in Central Asia and is still to be
seen in Eastern Tibet.[22]

Thus the Assyrian army encampments live on in the fortification
systems of the great city foundations of the Parthian, Sassanian, and
Abbasid Empires. The theory that army encampments determined
city plans is especially well demonstrated at Ctesiphon, which was
established by the Arsacids as a camp for their troops opposite
Seleucia; and Hatra also must have owed its plan to an original tent
encampment of its first nomadic citizens.[23] In this connexion the utterance of Tabari is significant: that the gates of the Round City (Baghdad) are laid out as in war encampments. "Ueberall und immer
wieder haben Heerlager das Muster für Städtegründungen abge-
geben."[24]

Under the domination of the great dynastic centers and the influence of a mighty military tradition, cities and castles of the "Round
City" type grew up throughout the East.[25] The Arab expansion in
the Mediterranean must evidently have brought this fortification plan
to Western countries, such as Italy, Spain, France, Algeria, and
Morocco.

Has it also influenced Eastern Europe? How, for instance, is the
enormous Avarian castle between the Danube and the Theiss, stormed
by the Franks in 796, to be understood? It was of circular form surrounded by seven mighty concentric wall-"rings." And do the innumerable ring-forts all over the extensive Slav area originate in the
round castle of the Orient? Have we, in fact, in the Saxon ringforts
and Frankish square redoubts, which confronted one another in the
center of medieval Europe, the very descendants of the two great
military traditions of Antiquity? In a comment upon the Western

---

21. Beaudouin - Pope, *op. cit.*, 1393.
22. Learner, F. D., "Eastern Tibet: its Lamas and its Temples," *Journ. of the
Royal Central Asian Society* 23 (1936) 45. Beaudouin - Pope, *op. cit.*, 1393 Note 1.
23. Reuter, *op. cit.*, 441.
24. Sarre - Herzfeld, *op. cit.*, 133.
25. Beaudouin - Pope, *op. cit.*, 1394 ff.

Slavs dating from 973 we read: "When they are going to build a castle they mark out a round or a square place, corresponding to the form and size they wish to give the castle."[26]

This comparison between the Arab fortifications and the Viking castles Trelleborg-Aggersborg has made it clear that in both cases we are dealing with an identical type. They belong also to the same historical epoch. The last great tribal migrations sweep over our continent: the mighty movement of the Viking raids from north to southwest and southeast; the explosive expansion of the Arabs over the Mediterranean. These movements both as pirate raids and as colonising enterprises have a clear inner and outer similarity. In the Western Mediterranean, in Italy, Spain, the Carolingian Empire, they intersect. It suffices to recall the rivalry and infiltration of Normans and Saracenes in Sicily. The Viking empires in these meetings gained a sound knowledge of the highly developed fortification plan of the Arabs.

At the same time Baghdad, the Caliphate's unsurpassable incarnation of this primeval oriental city-concept, shone with a splendor and magnificence not possessed by any other city in the world of that age. It was in these very centuries that the Abbasids made Mansur's "Round City" the most splendid urban centre of the Middle Ages, the focus of world trade and intellectual life. Baghdad is by far the greatest city of the contemporary world; the population is reported to have been one and a half million. The West dreams of its magnificence, fairy-tales, and fables add color to the picture. It is not merely a coincidence that on a Norwegian design from the 13th century appears Holy Jerusalem (Jorsalaborg) with the ideal ground-plan of Mansūr's Baghdad[27] (pl. 35, a). This city plan, as Nörlund has pointed out, with two crossroads meeting in the center of a circle, seems to have set the urban ideal for the Middle Ages. It is Baghdad which has inspired this ideal.

For matters of practical life direct contact had long been established between the Western world and Baghdad. Not only was there official political contact, as when the Carolingians sent their embassies to the Caliph. First of all there was direct commercial intercourse. In the middle of the 9th century Ibn Khordadhbeh testifies that the Northern Viking empires had such trade contact with Baghdad (here quoted in de Goeje's translation):

26. Jakobsens, Abraham, "Bericht über die Slavenlande," *Die Geschichtsschreiber der Deutschen Vorzeit*, 10. jh., 1, p. 2.

27. Fett, H., *Norges Malerkunsti Middelalderen*, 216, fig. p. 218.

ITINÉRAIRE DES MARCHANDS RUSSES

Les Russes, qui appartiennent aux peuples slaves, se rendent, des régions les plus éloignées de Caklaba (le pays des Slaves), vers la mer romaine, et y vendent des peaux de castor et de renard noir, ainsi que des épées. Le prince des Romains prélève un dixième sur leurs marchandises. — Ou bien, ils descendent le Tanaïs (Don), le fleuve des Slaves, et passent par Khamlydj, la capitale des Khazares, où le souverain du pays prélève sur eux un dixième. Là ils s'embarquent sur la mer de Djordjân (la Caspienne) et se dirigent sur tel point de la côte qu'ils ont en vue. Cette mer a 500 parasanges de diamètre. Quelquefois ils transportent leurs marchandises, à dos de chameau, de la ville de Djordjân à Bagdad. Ici les eunuques slaves leur servent d'interprètes. Ils prétendent être chrétiens et payent la capitation comme tels.[28]

THE COSMIC CITY OF THE EAST AND ITS WESTERN RADIATIONS

In "The Laws" Plato explains how the ideal city in the ideal state is to be laid out.[29] The legislator shall build a temple for Hestia, Zeus, and Athene on the castle in the middle of the city, draw a circle around it and on the basis of this circle divide the city itself and the whole country into 12 parts *(κύκλον περιβάλλοντα, ἀφ' οὗ τὰ δώδεκα μέρη τέμνειν τήν τε πόλιν αὐτὴν καὶ πᾶσαν τὴν χώραν)*.[29] The temple being put in the axis of the wheel and the area divided into 12 parts, cosmic laws and proportions penetrate the city. The inhabitants live under this cosmic law. The number of the families is 5040 which is divisible by 12 times 12, thus allowing a division into 12 tribes, each with 12 clans. "Now we must think of each part as being holy, as a gift from God, which follows the movement of the months and the revolution of the All. So the whole state is directed by its relationship to the All and this sanctifies its separate parts" *(ἑκάστην δὴ τὴν μοῖραν διανοεῖσθαι χρεὼν ὡς οὖσαν ἱεράν, θεοῦ δῶρον, ἑπομένην τοῖς μησὶν καὶ τῇ τοῦ παντὸς περιόδῳ. διὸ καὶ πᾶσαν πόλιν ἄγει μὲν τὸ σύμφυτον ἱεροῦν αὐτάς . . . .).*[30]

The similarity between Plato's ideal city and the round cities of the East is obvious. And also in the form of the Eastern cities the cosmic reflection must have been vividly felt. In the first place this is true of the residential cities such as Fīrūzābād and Baghdad.[31] The king amongst his vassals and satraps was a reflection of the heavenly hierarchy; he was "the King of the Universe," "The Axis and Pole

---

28. Ibn Khordadhbeh, *Liber Viarum et Regnorum*, Bibliotheca Geogr. Arab. VI (Ed. M. J. De Goeje, 1889) 115 *seq.* f. H. Arbman has drawn my attention to this paragraph. The name *Rūs, Ros* was related to the tribe of Swedish Vikings that from 862 dominated the Slav Nowgorod area; only later it was transferred to the Eastern Slavs and their country generally.

29. *The Laws*, 745 f., 771.

30. *The Laws*, 771.

31. Baghdad should have signified the city "founded by God," Le Strange, *op. cit.*, 11.

of the World," "The King of the four quadrants of the world."[32]
Therefore his round city, with the palace in the centre and very axis
of it, between the four city quadrants, is an image of the world. It
is the wheel of the Universe, a sort of οὐρανόπολις. Thus in the royal
city we are face to face with the same cosmic symbolism as that which
surrounded the Eastern king in his throne room.[33]

Are the revolving castles and fortresses of Western lore[34] inspired
by these "round cities" of the East? Do they in the world of myth
and poesy correspond to Trelleborg-Aggersborg in that of reality?
Are they the legendary accompaniment of this new, exotic and overwhelming fortress type?

> "Dar umbe gienc ein tiefer grabe. . .
> Dar inne ein tiefez wazzer ran;
> Dâ was ein grôz wunder an,
> Daz ez die mûre umbe treip,
> Daz sie dehein wîle bleip:
> Sie lief alsô snelle
> Umb und umbe, als ein welle
> Sie treip, daz sie nie entwelt,
> Reht als ein mül, diu dâ melt,
> Alsô diu âventure zelt."

32. Herzfeld, E., *Iran and the Ancient East*, 320.

33. L'Orange, H. P., "Domus Aurea—Der Sonnenpalast," *Serta Eitremiana*, 1942, 68 ff. The cosmic symbolism of the "round city" will be more thoroughly treated in my new book, *Iconography of Cosmic Kingship*.

34. Weston, J. L., "A Hitherto Unconsidered Aspect of the Round Table," *Mélanges M. Wilmotte*, 1910, 2, 888. The verses cited are from "Diu Crone," Ed. Scholl, p. 159, vv. 12954 ff.

EIN ARCHAISCHER GEFAESSDECKEL

CARL WEICKERT
Berlin

Tafel 36

Der Gefäßdeckel, der hier vorgelegt wird, besteht aus parischem Marmor. Er ist, wenn man die Verletzungen außer Betracht läßt, kreisrund mit einem Durchmesser von 25,5 cm. Am Rand seiner Unterfläche bildet ein 4,5 cm breiter, um 4 mm vertiefter Streifen das Auflager für die Wandung des Gefäßes, das der Deckel zu verschließen hatte. Die im Inneren der Unterseite stehengebliebene, flache, kreisrunde Erhebung hat einen Durchmesser von 16,5 cm, sie ist ganz erhalten und hielt den Deckel in der zu schließenden Oeffnung des Gefäßes fest. Leider ist die Form dieses Gefäßes nicht mit Sicherheit zu bestimmen. Als der Deckel für das Berliner Museum aus dem Kunsthandel mit einer Provenienzangabe Eleusis erworben wurde, berichtete man von einem bauchigen Marmorgefäß mit geknicktem Fuß und niedrigem, weitem unprofiliertem Hals, das zu dem Deckel gehören solle. Der Bauch dieses Gefäßes trägt flüchtige Reliefdarstellung, die nach einer kleinen, unzureichenden Fotografie nicht zu deuten ist. Die Halsform des Gefäßes würde aber eher einen Stülpdeckel erfordern. Leider sind die Maße des Gefäßes, das nicht erworben werden konnte, unbekannt. Sollten Gefäß und Deckel wirklich zusammengehören, müsste dieser mit dem 4,5 cm breiten Auflager auf dem Hals des Gefäßes ruhen, mit der flachen Erhöhung der Unterseite aber in dessen Mündung eingreifen. Hals und Deckel würden dann bündig zu liegen kommen.

Die Oberfläche des Deckels wird von einem Gorgoneion gebildet, dessen kräftiges Relief heute noch 9 cm hoch ist. Als die breite stumpfe Nase noch erhalten war, die man sich wohl mit Falten auf dem Rücken denken muß, wird es nicht viel höher gewesen sein. Die plastisch behandelte Form des Gorgoneions setzt erst über einem 1 cm hohen, geglätteten Saumstreifen ein. Das Relief ist stark bestoßen und der ursprünglich kreisförmige Rand des Auflagers nur vom linken Ohr bis etwa zum Scheitel erhalten. Nach dem ersten Eindruck möchte es scheinen, als seien Reste von Bemalung erhalten, doch hat die Untersuchung, besonders die unter der Quarzlampe gezeigt, daß dies wohl eine Täuschung ist. An verschiedenen Stellen, besonders an den Zähnen und Ohren zu beobachtende grünliche Verfärbung, die übrigens auch über Bruchstellen hinweggeht, ist wohl erst beim

Liegen in der Erde entstanden, verursacht vielleicht durch irgend-
welche in der Nähe liegende Bronze. Professor Brittner vom
Chemischen Laboratorium der Berliner Museen, dem für die Untersuchung des Stückes zu danken ist, hat festgestellt, daß die zart-
grün gefärbten und pastos aufsitzenden Teilchen in der Hauptsache
aus kohlensaurem Kalk mit Kupfersalzen vermengt bestehen. Diese
letzteren sind der grünfärbende Bestandteil. Auch nach Professor
Brittners Ansicht ist das Wahrscheinlichere, daß das Zusammen-
lagern des Deckels mit kupferhaltigen Gegenständen in feuchter Erde
die Verfärbung verursacht haben könnte. Doch macht er ausdrücklich
darauf aufmerksam, daß eine Abwanderung von Farbteilchen einer
originalen Bemalung beim Lagern in der Erde auch auf Bruchstellen
möglich ist.

Die Bildung der wenig schräg gestellten Augen, der muldenförmigen
Oberlider und der in recht altertümlicher Weise noch fast ornamental
gehaltenen Ohren, die Buckellocken, die die Stirn umrahmen, die in
Form konzentrischer Kreisabschnitte verlaufenden Stirnfalten, die
kräftigen Bäckchen und das weit auseinandergezogene Maul, aus
dessen abgerundeten Ecken je ein Paar spitzer Hauer über die einge-
ritzten Zahnreihen hervorstehen, erweisen das Gorgoneion als spätarchaisch, dem letzten Viertel des 6. Jh.v.Chr. angehörend. Die Abbildung lässt leider die Zähne nicht deutlich erkennen. Aus dem Unter-
kiefer richtet sich je ein Hauer schräg nach oben zur Nase hin, die
Hauer des Oberkiefers stehen in umgekehrter Richtung. Daß das
Schreckgebilde nicht wie üblich die Zunge herausstreckt, hat gewiss
seinen Grund darin, daß diese unten mit dem Kreisrande in Konflikt
gekommen wäre. Folgerichtig sind deshalb die Zahnreihen zwischen
den geöffneten Lippen geschlossen. Aus demselben Grunde fehlt auch
die sonst übliche Ausbildung des Kinns. Ferner wünschte der Bildhauer von dem flachen Dreieck, das sich in Gorgonengesichtern über
der Oberlippe zur Nase bildet, einen Anschluß an das Rund des Deckels
zu finden. Er rückte daher die Backen höher und ließ das Mund —
Nasenfeld bis zum Rande ausgreifen. Vielleicht hat er auch deshalb
entgegen dem gebräuchlicheren Typus den unteren Hauer nach außen
gestellt, um den Mundwinkel zu betonen.

Die zeitliche Stellung des Deckels wird durch den Vergleich mit
dem Kopf der marmornen Gorgone ermöglicht, die als Akroter den
älteren Porostempel der Athena auf der Burg von Athen krönte, der
nach neuerer Forschung bereits wie sein marmorner Nachfolger von
Säulen umgeben war.[1] Dieses prachtvolle Antlitz ist mit seiner dro-

---

1. Schuchhardt, W. H., *AM* 60-61, 1935/36, 86ff.
2. Beste Abbildung bei H. Payne, *Archaic Marble Sculpture* Taf. 1. Vgl. auch
H. Schrader, *Archaische Marmorbildwerke* Taf. 184.

henden Furchtbarkeit das Zeugnis noch unerschüttert archaisch-sachlichen Empfindens.[2] Der Porostempel wurde zu Beginn der Tyrannenherrschaft des Peisistratos oder kurz vorher erbaut, also um 560 v.Chr. Das breite, fast freundliche Grinsen der Gorgone des Deckels ist mit dem wuchtigen Ausdruck der athenischen nicht zu vergleichen, von dem Abstand in der Qualität einmal ganz abgesehen. Dieses Grinsen entsteht nicht etwa durch das breitgezogene Maul, das zum Typus des Gorgoneions gehört und sich schon an einem Porosrelief aus Dreros auf Kreta aus dem späten 7. Jh. findet,[3] son-dern durch die rundlichen Bäckchen und die Fläche, die sich zwischen ihnen und dem Maule bildet und durch die Schrägstellung der Augen, die der Richtung des Mundes entspricht, die ihrerseits wieder dem Kreisrund des Deckels folgt. Auch die schematischen Falten der Stirn, die wieder dieselbe Richtung aufnehmen, tragen zu diesem Ausdruck bei. Aehnliche Falten zeigen die Gorgoneia tönerner Stirn-ziegel, ebenfalls von der Burg in Athen.[4] Nur die unterste Falte des Deckel-Gorgoneions nimmt ein wenig den weiterhin dem Auge folgenden Schwung der Falten des tönernen Gorgoneions auf. Der Dachschmuck, dem das tönerne Gorgoneion angehörte, ist um 510 v.Chr., also gegen das Ende der peisistratidischen Zeit anzusetzen. Seine Gorgone entfernt sich noch weiter von der marmornen Gorgone des Athena-Tempels. Die Backen sind hier nicht weniger rundlich als bei der Gorgone des Deckels, verlieren aber an plastischer Fülle und streichen breit und ungegliedert zum Maule hin. An den äußeren Augenwinkeln bilden sich hier fröhliche Fältchen, die den weit auf-gerissenen Augen, die doch furchtbar sein sollen, wunderlich wider-sprechen. Die Qualität dieser Stirnziegel ist durchaus nicht etwa gering, sodaß die Veränderung des Ausdruckes nicht mangelndem künstlerischem Können zugeschrieben werden darf. Leider lässt sich der Bau, von dem sie stammen, nicht mehr bestimmen.[5] Zwischen diesen beiden Beispielen aus Athen steht der Deckel des Marmorge-fäßes und zwar näher dem tönernen. Während dieses den beabsich-tigten furchtbaren Ausdruck nicht mehr erreicht, wirken die schräg-gestellten Augen hier wenigstens auf den heutigen Betrachter wie tückisch, sodaß ein eigentümlich zwiespältiger Eindruck ensteht. Doch muß man sich hüten, zuviel hineinzusehen. Weist doch eine ganze Anzahl der Mädchenstatuen auf der Burg diese Augenstellung auf, sodaß sie sich als ein Zeichen des Zeitstiles, nicht aber als Aus-

---

3. *AA* 1937, 245 Abb. 1.
4. Buschor, E., *Tondächer* II, 40, Taf. 5.
5. Nach Buschor gehört dazu die Sima *a.O.* I 17 Abb. 17.

druck eines besonderen Charakters zeigt.[6] Diese Augenstellung findet sich noch um 500 v.Chr. an einer herrlichen Kore, die mit dem tiefen Ernst ihres schönen Frauenantlitzes alle anderen Koren zu übertreffen scheint und in denkbar größtem Gegensatz zu der Fratze des Deckels steht.[7] Auch die Frisur mit den Buckellöckchen kommt bei Koren vor.[8] Am ähnlichsten ist die Kore Nr. 673.

Wenn es auch dem Verfertiger des Marmorgefäßes nicht gelang, mit seiner bildhauerischen Begabung einen überzeugenden Ausdruck abschreckender Furchtbarkeit zu erreichen, ernst ist es ihm bestimmt damit gewesen. Wie der Deckel des Gefäßes zum Verschließen dient, so soll gewiss das Gorgoneion ihn nicht lediglich schmücken, sondern vom unberechtigten Oeffen des Gefäßes abschrecken. Die antike Bezeichnung als Apotropaion darf hier voll angewendet werden.[9] Im wesentlichen auch in diesem Sinne erscheint die Gorgone mit mythischen Beifiguren ausgestattet im Artemistempel von Korfu,[10] und auch das oben genannte Marmorkroter des Porostempels ist in diesem Sinne zu verstehen. Das grauenerregende Antlitz der Gorgone

6. Wir finden die schrägen Augen z.B. an der Kore des Akropolismuseums Nr. 682, die um 530 anzusetzen ist (Payne *a.O.* Taf. 40-43. Schrader *a.O.* Taf 53-56), an Nr. 675 (Payne Taf. 49-50. Schrader Taf. 60-61), Nr. 680 (Payne Taf. 54-55. Schrader Taf. 68-69), Nr. 673 (Payne Taf. 62-64. Schrader Taf. 16, 74, 75), Nr. 670 (Payne Taf. 65-67. Schrader Taf. 14-16), die beiden letzteren um 520 v.Chr. entstanden.

7. Akropolismuseum Nr. 674. (Payne Taf. 75-78. Schrader Taf. 62-66.)

8. Akropolismuseum Nr. 682 und 673 (Payne Taf. 40-43; 62-64). Einen guten Ueberblick über die Abwandlungen des Gorgoneions gewinnt man an griechischen Münzen bei K. Regling, *Die antike Münze als Kunstwerk*, die vom frühen 6. Jh. bis tief in das 4. Jh. v.Chr. reichen : Nr. 6, 88, 130, 159, 216, 283, 357, 452, 487, 503, 715. Das älteste Stück, ein Elektron-Halbstater aus Kleinasien, zeigt den in archaischer Zeit seltenen Fall eines Gorgoneions ohne herausgestreckte Zunge. Nr. 88, ein silbernes attisches Tetradrachmon, steht zeitlich dem Deckel am nächsten. Dann geht die Entwicklung über äußerliche und daher grotesk wirkende Bildungen, Nr. 130-357, zu gemilderten über, die sich immer mehr bemühen, die grauenhafte Fratze in ein schönes Antlitz zu verwandeln, so Nr. 452-715; Daß endlich das schöne Antlitz der Gorgo, wie das der Medusa Rondanini in München, die Zunge nicht mehr zeigt, ist selbstverständlich. Wie ein Gorgoneion aussieht, das archaisch wirken möchte, ohne es zu sein, kann man an dem Marmorkroter beobachten, das wahrscheinlich zum Apollontempel in Kyrene gehört (*AA* 1929, 415 Abb. 23; L. Pernier, *Africa Italiana* 1, 1927, 137). Die Medusa auf einem böotischen Reliefpithos des frühen 7. Jahrhunderts (R. Hampe, *Frühe griechische Sagenbilder* Taf. 38) streckt ebenfalls die Zunge nicht heraus. Hier ist die Medusa noch nicht mit dem Typus der Gorgone vereinigt, den in einem frühen Stadium die zeitlich von dem Reliefpithos nicht sehr verschiedenen Masken aus Tiryns zeigen (R. Hampe *a.O.* Taf 42). Keinesfalls darf aus der Eigentümlichkeit der nicht herausgestreckten Zunge für den Deckel ein besonders frühes Datum erschlossen werden. Vgl. im allgemeinen H. Besig, *Gorgo und Gorgoneion*, Diss. Berlin 1937 passim. — Ferner: J. D. Beazley, *JHS* 67 (1947) 2 Anm. 1: Robinson, *Olynthus* 6,86-87: 9,288-289 (Münzen von Neapolis in Makedonien): 10,39-40 (C. Bronzen); Seltman, *Athens and its Coinage*, 50 ff.; Robinson, *AJA* 43 (1939) 71, Abb. 26 (Terrakotta aus Olynth).

9. Jahn, O., *Berichte der Sächs.Ges.d.Wiss.* 1854, 47 und 1855, 59.

10. Rodenwaldt, G., *Korkyra* II Taf. 1ff.

schützt vor allem Bösen im Großen wie im Kleinen, vor der Einwirkung böser Geister und des bösen Blickes. Unter seinem dämo-
nischen Schutz stand auch der Inhalt des von dem Deckel verschlos-
senen Gefäßes. Ob dieser Inhalt einen realen oder ideellen Wert hatte,
ist unbekannt und nicht zu erchließen. Für Kostbarkeiten fehlt es
an einer Sicherung des Verschlusses. Das Gewicht des Deckels allein
reicht dazu nicht aus. Man könnte sonst an ein Thesauros, einen
Schatzbehälter denken, wie solche im Fußboden des Apollontempels
von Gortyn auf Kreta[11] und des Apollontempels von Kyrene[12] einge-
baut waren.[13] Oder aber in dem Gefäß waren der profanen Berührung entzogene Kultgeräte aufbewahrt. Daß es in einem Heiligtum
aufgestellt war, ist wohl mit Sicherheit anzunehmen.

Man könnte erwägen, ob in dem Antlitz des Deckels nicht etwa die
männliche Schreckgestalt des Phobos zu erkennen wäre, den nach
Ilias 11, 37 der Schild des Agamemnon trug, freilich, wie auch die
Aegis der Athena, *Ilias* 5, 739, in Verbindung mit der Maske der
Gorgo. Das Gorgoantlitz kann sehr wohl für männliche Gestalten verwendet werden und ist dann mit Sicherheit Phobos zu nennen.[14]
Da aber bei dem Deckel das Geschlecht der Schreckgestalt nicht zu
erkennen ist, bleibt die Frage besser unentschieden. Die Gestalt der
Gorgo war verbreiteter und so ist sie mit größerer Wahrscheinlichkeit auch auf diesem Deckel gemeint. Wie leicht ein der Gorgo ähnlicher Kopf als männlich verwendet werden konnte, zeigt der von vorn
gesehene Kopf eines Kentauren auf einer schwarzfigurigen Amphora
von der Athener Agora.[15] Hier umgibt ein struppiger Bart das Gesicht. Wenn er in diesem Falle das sonst nicht angegebene Geschlecht
des Unholdes gut charakterisiert, tut er das bei der Gorgone nicht.
Sie ist von früher Zeit noch bis ins 6. Jh. häufig mit einem ganz ähnlichen Bart ausgestattet, ohne daß deshalb in ihr Phobos erkannt
werden müsste.[16] Diese Eigentümlichkeit geht auf den sehr wahr-
scheinlichen Ursprung des Gorgoneions aus einem Tiergesicht zurück.

---

11. Savignoni, L., *Monumenti antichi* 18, 1907, 227 Abb. 3, 15, 23.

12. Pernier, L., *a.O.* 140.

13. Ein im Delphinion zu Milet gefundenes, beckenartiges Marmorgefäß (Th.
Wiegand, *Milet* I 3, 157 Abb. 46 u. 47; zur Aufstellung des Gefäßes Taf. 1, 4 und
7) ist seiner eiförmigen Gestalt wegen wohl eher ein Mischgefäß gewesen (a.O.
411.).

14. Jahn, O., *a.O.* 1855, 57. P. Wolters, *Bonner Jahrbücher* 118, 1909, 269ff.

15. *AA* 1938, 555 Abb. 9. *Hesperia* 8, 1939, 233.

16. Vgl. Bronzeplatte vom Kabirion bei Theben: de Ridder, *Bronzes antiques du
Louvre* I Nr. 96 Taf. 11; H. Payne, *Necrocorinthia* 80 Abb. 23ff. Plastisch H.
Payne, *Archaic Marble Sculpture* Taf. 121, 4.

Da der Marmor des Deckels parisch ist, ist es recht wohl möglich, daß dieser auf Paros gearbeitet wurde. Stilistisch scheint er nicht schlecht zu dem zu stimmen, was Ernst Langlotz als parisch angesprochen hat,[17] man vergleiche etwa einen Kopf aus Thasos in Wien.[18]

17. Langlotz, E., *Frühgriechische Bildhauerschulen* 132 ff.

18. *JOAI* 11, 1908, Taf. 1 und 2. Ueber Marmorindustrie in Paros vgl Rubensohn, *RE*. 18, 1857-1758 (Marmorgefäße) ; Robinson, *Olynthus* 12, 246-247; Besig, *op. cit.*, 161 (Marmorrelief mit Gorgo in Paros). Für Medusakopf auf Münzen von Neapolis gegründet von Thasos vgl. Robinson, *Olynthus* 6,86-87; 9,288-289.

THE OLIVE TREE

Twisted old olive, the bees take for their nest
   Thy hollow trunk now that thou'st got so old,
   With but few tufts of green still to enfold
Thee there as if for burial thinly dressed,
And every little bird puffs out his chest
   With love's intoxication making bold
   An amorous chase along thy limbs to hold,
Thy limbs that barren of green shall rest.
How cheerful they will make thy final hours
   With their enchanting murmurings around,
Those pretty creatures with love's plenteous powers,
   Like memories in thy heart their tumults sound.
Oh, that like thee might pass to their decline
Even other souls that sisters are to thine.

Lorentsos Mavilis

Translated by
John B. Edwards

DIE UNGLEICHEN ZWILLINGE

GUIDO KASCHNITZ-WEINBERG
Frankfurt a. M.

Tafel 41

Das Weihgeschenk des Polymedes von Argos in Delphi,[1] in dem wir seit von Premersteins glänzender Untersuchung[2] eine Darstellung des Brüderpaares Kleobis und Biton erkennen dürfen, gilt mit Recht neben dem Kuros von Tenea als bedeutendstes Werk der Peloponnesischen Rundplastik aus Archaischer Zeit. Dass diese Beurteilung im strengen Sinn aber nur für die besser erhaltene Statue A zustrifft, die wir hier der Bequemlichkeit halber Kleobis benennen, glaube ich in der folgenden Skizze nachweisen zu können. Da mir das Studium der Originale derzeit nicht möglich ist, beruhen meine Beobachtungen ausschliesslich auf Eindrücken, die die Aufnahmen in dem schönen Buch *Delphes* von De La Coste-Messelière und G. de Miré vermitteln, (Taf. 41, a).[3] Eine Ueberprüfung dieser Beobachtungen durch eine Untersuchung an Ort und Stelle wäre daher wünschenswert und würde wahrscheinlich noch sehr wesentliche Ergänzungen bringen.

Die zweite, schlechter erhaltene Statue des Weihgeschenkes (B), in der wir vielleicht das Bild des Biton vermuten dürfen, ist seit ihrer Auffindung wenig beachtet worden. In der Annahme, sie sei, ihrem Zwillingscharakter entsprechend, als Doppel vom Meister verfertigt worden, hat man sogar bei dem Versuch einer photographischen Rekonstruktion des Monuments kurzerhand zwei Aufnahmen des Kleobis zusammengestellt.[4] Bei genauerem Vergleich der beiden Statuen zeigt sich jedoch, dass der Biton weder der Hand des Polymedes entstammen kann, noch im stilistischen Sinn als Kopie des Kleobis bezeichnet werden darf, obwohl an der Absicht, ein Ebenbild des Zwillingsbruders zu liefern, nicht gezweifelt werden kann. Der Umstand, dass die beiden Statuen teilweise nicht unerhebliche Verschiedenheiten aufweisen, wie Gisela Richter festgestellt hat,[5] spielt im Zusammenhang dieser Ueberlegungen kaum eine Rolle. Etwas anderes ist es, wenn man neben diesen Verschiedenheiten in den Maßen und

1. Literatur: *Fouilles de Delphes* IV,1 (1909) 17f.; *BCH* 24 (1900) S.445ff.; Richter, G. M. A., *Kouroi* 78ff.
2. *JOAI* 13 (1910) 41ff.
3. P.De La Coste-Messelière u. G. de Miré, *Delphes*, Taf. 34-37.
4. Vgl. Schrader, *Archaische Plastik*, 99, Abb. 6.
5. Richter, *op. cit.*, 79 u.82.

in der Gestaltung von Einzelheiten[6] auch solche der plastischen Struktur, des Stils und der allgemeinen Qualität wahrzunehmen vermeint. Stimmt diese Beobachtung, dann muss man den Biton der Hand eines anderen Meisters zuschreiben, der trotz seiner unzweifelhaften Bemühungen den Kleobis nachzuahmen, der Einstellung jener Zeit entsprechend, garnicht auf den Gedanken kam, seinen persönlichen Stil zu unterdrücken. Dass die Qualität seines Werkes wesentlich geringer war als die der Kleobisstatue wird der folgende Vergleich beider Standbilder, wie ich glaube, gleichfalls mit Sicherheit ergeben.

Zunächst wird der Vergleich durch die schlechte Erhaltung des Biton beträchtlich erschwert und es mag sein, dass man seit jeher geneigt war, in ihr die Ursache einer zweifelsohne schon längst beobachteten Verschiedenheit in der Präzision des formalen Ausdrucks beider Werke zu sehen. Tatsächlich ist die Oberfläche der Bitonstatue besonders am Kopf und an der Brust stark abgeschlagen und verrieben, so dass die beim Kleobis stark hervortretenden Begrenzungen der Gesichtsformen, Muskel und Locken hier undeutlich werden und verschwimmen. Aber schon die Photographien lassen bei genauerer Prüfung erkennen, dass auch vor der Auswirkung zerstörender Elemente der Formenaufbau dieser Statue nicht jenen klaren und gleichsam architektonisch gefügten Charakter besessen haben kann, der beim Kleobis seit jeher die Bewunderung der Betrachter gefunden hat. Ist einmal die Aufmerksamkeit auf diese, bisher nicht betretene, Fährte gelenkt, dann tauchen bald auch in der allgemeinen Anlage von Körper und Gesicht Verschiedenheiten auf, die erkennen lassen, dass Grundschema und Aufbau der Bitonstatue, bei aller äusserer Uebereinstimmung von Bewegung und Haltung, mit dem Schema und der Architektonik des Kleobis nichts Gemeinsames haben vgl. Abb. 1. Dieser ist in der Klarheit und Logik seiner plastischen Struktur echt peloponnesisch. Wie Säulen wachsen die schlanken und doch kräftigen Beine auf, in mässig straffer Schwellung gehen die Oberschenkel in die schlanken Hüften über und nehmen den keilförmigen, zwischen sie hineingeschobenen Rumpf auf.

---

6. Die Statue B besitzt nur 6 Spirallocken über der Stirne, A dagegen 8. A weist 6 Haarsträhne im Rücken auf, B dagegen 8. Nach Homolle *FdD* IV,1,S.11 ist das Schamhaar bei A durch eine Art von Schachbrettmuster angegeben "remplis par de petits traits droits ou courbes qui figurent les poils" vgl. auch Deonna, Les "Apollons archaïques" S.86 u.Taf.V,125. Ob diese Angabe bei B überhaupt niemals vorhanden war oder jetzt vollständig abgerieben ist, kann nach Homolle nicht mehr festgestellt werden. Aus der Beschreibung Homolles S.6f. geht nicht mit Sicherheit hervor, ob das Glied der Statue B angesetzt war wie bei A oder nicht. Homolle erwähnt *BCH* 24 (1900) 446 "Très légères variantes, pour la pose et les formes, autant que la matière et le travail", die die Statue B von A unterscheiden, ohne weiter darauf zurückzukommen.

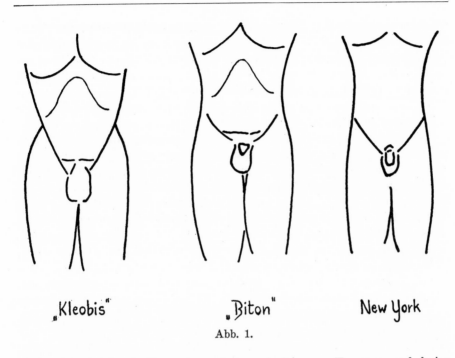

„Kleobis"   „Biton"   New York

Abb. 1.

Es ist der gleiche Aufbau, den wir in primitiveren Formen auch beim
Dreros-Apoll beobachten können, derselbe, der das Schema der peloponnesischen Jünglingsfigur auch in der Zukunft bestimmt, wie die
hervorragendste Schöpfung dieses Kunstkreises in den nächsten
Jahrzehnten, der teneatische Kuros beweist.

Obwohl der Biton die Kleobisstatue nachahmt, lehrt eine genauere
Untersuchung, dass sein Verfertiger in einer Tradition aufgewachsen
sein muss, der dieses peloponnesische Schema fremd war. Die Nachahmung bleibt auf die ungefähren und äusserlichsten Züge beschränkt. Von der oben beschriebenen Tektonik tragender und
lastender Glieder ist kaum eine oberflächliche Andeutung übrigge-
blieben. Das Gegliederte tritt hier viel weniger hervor. Die Ueber-
gänge sind nicht klar markiert, sondern sanft, ja verschwommen.
Der Bauch ist weich gebildet und besonders gegen das Geschlecht zu
gerundet. Die Formen entbehren der straffen Spannung, die in der
stereometrischen Grundlage ihren Ansatz findet. Von der keilförmigen Gestalt des Rumpfes beim Kleobis ist hier ebensowenig zu
spüren wie von der klaren Einfügung in die Ansatzflächen der
tragenden Schenkel. Die Linie des seitlichen Konturs, die beim
Kleobis als Folge der strengen Stereometrie gerade zu den Weichen
verläuft und in einem klar herausgearbeiteten stumpfen Winkel zur
Umrisslinie der Schenkel geführt ist, wird beim Biton zum sanft ein-

wärts geschwungenen Bogen, der in den Achseln beginnt und ohne deutlichen Absatz in die Hüftlinie und damit in die Begrenzung der Oberschenkel übergeht. Dem bogenförmigen Abschluss des Rumpfes nach unten entspricht beim Biton eine ebensolche nach aufwärts gerichtete Begrenzung der abfallenden Schulterpartien, die sich auch darin sehr auffallend von der viel wagrechter ausgerichteten breitschultrigen Anlage des Kleobis unterscheidet.

Es kann kaum einem Zweifel unterliegen, dass die Verwendung eines so konsequent durchgebildeten, aber vom peloponnesischen ganz verschiedenen Grundschemas nur so zu erklären ist, dass der Bitonmeister gewohnt war, seinen eigenen Schöpfungen ein Schema zu unterlegen, das sich von dem des Polymedes grundsätzlich unterschied. Die sichtlichen Schwächen der Biton-Statue zeigen sich ja nicht so sehr in einer Verflauung oder Deformierung des Aufbaus der Kleobis-Statue, sondern entspringen vielmehr zum grössten Teil einem ganz allgemein hervortretenden wesentlich geringeren Talent. Davon abgeschen wird aber der Versuch deutlich, den Aufbau des Kleobis in die Form des eigenen gewohnten Schemas zu übersetzen, was dem Bitonmeister in den Grenzen seiner beschränkten Fähigkeiten leidlich gelingt.

Wenn wir uns fragen, welchem Kunstkreis das von Bitonmeister benützte Schema der Jünglingsfigur entstammt, dann werden wir ganz unzweifelhaft nach dem Osten gewiesen. Wir finden den spulenförmigen Grundriss des Rumpfes, der oben und unten durch nach aussen schwingende, an den Seiten aber durch einwärts gerichtete Bogen gebildet wird, an der attischen Suniongruppe wieder, die dieses Schema ebenso wie der Meister des New Yorker Kuros, Vgl. Abb. 1 vielleicht von den Inseln bezogen hat, die ihrerseits wiederum diese Grundform mit rhodisch-naukratischen Schöpfungen gemeinsam haben.[7]

Weist uns schon das Grundschema des Biton nach dem Osten, so gilt das Gleiche auch für die eigentlich plastische Struktur der Statue. Die weichen, wie aufgeblasen wirkenden Formen des Bauches, denen auch die plastische Konsistenz der Schenkel entspricht, haben wir bereits erwähnt. Vergleicht man die Köpfe der beiden Statuen, dann tritt dieser strukturelle Gegensatz noch deutlicher hervor. Wie der Körper so ist auch der Kopf des Kleobis nach streng tektonischen Prinzipien aufgebaut. Das Stereometrische der Anlage zeigt sich in der keilförmigen Grundgestalt des Gesichtes, die von der flach gewölbten Kalotte des Schädels überdeckt wird. Unter den muskulösen

---

7. Vgl. Deonna, *a.a.O.* 232f. nr. 135, AAb. 157 (Statuette aus Rhodos in London) u. G. M. A. Richter, *a.a.O.* S57.

Fleischteilen wird das statische Wesen des Knochengerüstes deutlich fühlbar und diesem im organischen Sinne klaren Ausdruck der funktionellen Verbindung statisch-stereometrischer und dynamisch-spannender Elemente entspricht die klare Herausformung von Augenpartien, Nase und Mund, die fest in die Architektonik der Gesamtanlage des Kopfes verankert sind und in ihr eine wichtige gliedernde Funktion innehaben.

Dagegen wirkt der Kopf des Biton kugelig und massig; darin nähert er sich den Köpfen östlicher Figuren. Er ist zwar bewegt aber ungegliedert. Die Modellierung der Masse tritt hier an die Stelle des Gebauten und Konstruierten beim Kleobis und nähert sich einer plastischen Ausdrucksweise, die wir an östlichen Köpfen wiederfinden, unter denen ich in diesem Zusammenhang einen Kopf aus Kamiros auf Rhodos besonders hervorheben möchte (Taf. 41, b).[8] Die Formen der Augenpartien, der Nase und des Mundes sind flau und wulstig. Sie sind nicht in die Architektonik des Kopfes eingelassen und scharf als eigene Bildungen geformt, denen eine tektonische Funktion im Aufbau des Kopfes zukommt, wie beim Kleobis, sondern sitzen an der Oberfläche der bewegten Masse, die als solche die ganze Struktur des Kopfes bestimmt. Der Ausdruck des Gesichtes ist durch den ersten für uns fassbaren Versuch, ein Lächeln wiederzugeben, vollständig verändert. Der Mund spitzt sich zu, die Mundwinkel sind emporgezogen, ebenso die im Lächeln angespannten Wangen. Dadurch wird das Gesicht an dieser Stelle stark verbreitert, Schläfen und Schädelkalotte treten demgegenüber zurück, während sie beim Kleobis als Basis des Dreiecks, in das die Gesichtsform hineinkomponiert ist, den ganzen Aufbau beherrschen. Dadurch verändert sich nicht nur die Anlage des Gesichts, sondern auch sein Ausdruck. Im Mienenspiel des Lächelns scheint sich alles gegen die Mitte, also gegen die Nase zu, zusammenzuziehen und zuzuspitzen. Die monumentale heitere Ruhe im Gesichtsausdruck des Kleobis scheint einer plumpen aber fröhlichen Schalkhaftigkeit gewichen, der ein ganz anderes Temperament zugrundeliegt. Die Haarflechten sind, auch wenn man die starke Verreibung der Oberfläche berücksichtigt, rundlicher modelliert als beim Kleobis, wo das Gegliederte und Abgeteilte viel stärker wirkt. Besonders lehrreich ist der Vergleich der Gegend oberhalb der Brustmuskel an der Ansatzstelle des Halses. Beim Kleobis treten die Schlüsselbeine klar und getrennt hervor, sie lassen den Ansatz der Linea alba, die hier beginnt, deutlich erkennen. Beim Biton ist diese Gliederung völlig vernachlässigt. Die Schlüsselbeine bilden hier einen ganz unnatürlichen kragenförmigen Absatz,

---

8. *Clara Rhodos* 6/7, 260ff. Abb. 50-53.

aus dem der Hals aufwächst. Alles ist hier unverstanden nachgeahmt, bleibt flau und unbestimmt. Man sieht, der Künstler interessiert sich nicht für die Struktur des Knochengerüstes und noch weniger für dessen Verhältnis zu der darüberliegenden Haut oder den hier ansetzenden Muskeln. Der Bauch ist, wie schon angedeutet, als ungegliederte Masse aufgefasst, die eingegrabene Linie an der unteren Grenze des Brustkorbes hat nicht den lebendigen Schwung, den sie beim Kleobis aufweist, sie wird auch oben gegen die Linea alba in einer schmäleren und spitzeren Schleife geführt, der Nabel sitzt wiederum ganz an der Oberfläche und bleibt ungegliedert.

All dies sind Eigenheiten der Struktur und des Stils, die in die gleiche Richtung weisen, wie vorhin schon das besondere Schema der Gestalt und die plastische Formung des Kopfes: nach dem jonischen Osten.[9] In der Statue des Biton besitzen wir das älteste festländische Zeugnis für eine ganz bestimmte jonische festländische Auffassung des Kuros, die hier an der Nachahmung des argivischen Meisterwerkes und geschaffen von einer sehr mittelmässigen Hand sichtbar wird, aber im Verlauf des 6. Jahrhunderts sich sehr bedeutend auswirkt. Die Heimat dieses Meisters, der vielleicht als Gehilfe in der Werkstatt des Polymedes arbeitete, wird man auf den Inseln suchen dürfen. Als Kopie wird man den Biton nicht bezeichnen können, er war wohl auch kaum als solche gemeint. Eher ist er eine, wenn auch nicht ganz freiwillige oder bewusste Umstilisierung. Der Meister suchte wohl sein Bestes zu geben in dem Bestreben, der Polymedesstatue ein brüderliches Ebenbild zur Seite zu stellen. Dem Polymedes, der mit der Schöpfung des Vorbildes seine Aufgabe erfüllt sah, wird vielleicht die stilistische Verschiedenheit, wenn er sie überhaupt beachtete, kaum unwillkommen gewesen sein, stellte sie doch ein sehr diskretes Mittel dar, die persönliche Individualität des Zwillings zum Ausdruck zu bringen, ohne die Einheit des Werkes und der Idee zu gefährden. Aber auch diese Ueberlegung sollte vielleicht hier besser ausgeschaltet bleiben, da sie wohl allzusehr einem modernen Empfinden entspricht. Wegen der geringeren Qualität des Gehilfenwerkes machte sich der Meister wohl keine Gedanken. Derartige Sorgen lagen, wie noch viel spätere Gemeinschaftswerke zeigen, nicht im Bereich griechischer Denkungsart.

---

9. Auf einen "léger souffle ionien", der sich im schwachen Lächeln beim Biton ausdrücke, weist schon Deonna a.a.O. S.306 hin und fügt dazu die Bemerkung: "que dès la première moitié du VIe siècle, des sculpteurs ioniens purent venir dans le Péloponnèse et que l'influence ionienne commença à agir sur l'art dorien". De Ridder, *REG* 1902, S.384f. hat von ganz anderen Voraussetzungen ausgehend und ohne besonderen Bezug auf die Statue B den jonischen Charakter des ganzen Monuments betont; in dem Zusammenhang, den er dort im Auge hat, sicher mit Unrecht, vgl. Deonna *a.a.O* S.178, Anm. 3.

Kunstgeschichtlich ist das Wirken eines jonischen Meisters zu Anfang des 6. Jahrhunderts im peloponnesischen Bereich nicht ohne Interesse. Ein konkreter Fall zeigt uns, wie dieses Eindringen östlicher Auffassungen durch wandernde Bildhauer gefördert wurde, die wie der Bitonmeister in den Werkstätten angesehener Plastiker sich verdingt haben mochten. Ist das Zusammenwirken jonischer und peloponnesischer Formungstendenzen beim Biton infolge des geringen schöpferischen Talentes seines Verfertigers, der das Wesen des plastischen Aufbaus im festländisch-peloponnesischen Sinn kaum verstand, noch auf das Oberflächlichste beschränkt, so entfaltet es sich nur wenige Jahrzehnte später im teneatischen Kuros zur vollständigen Durchdringung. Der Sinn für die weiche aber bewegte Modellierung der Masse mildert nicht nur die Härten der peloponnesischen Tektonik, er bereitet auch den Boden für die Differenzierungsmöglichkeiten des plastischen Ausdrucks im naturalistischen Sinn und bildet so eine der Voraussetzungen für die Schöpfungen des Polyklet, dessen Klassik, wie die Klassik des 5. Jahrhunderts überhaupt, auf einer Vereinigung östlicher und festländischer Strukturprinzipien beruht.

THE DISSEMINATION OF A GREEK DRAPERY PATTERN

A. W. Lawrence

Cambridge

Plates 37-38

The purpose of this note is to call attention to a concatenation of data in objects made over the duration of two thousand years in most of the countries from Britain to Japan. My excuse for rushing into this venture lies in the fact that their joint significance is liable to escape the notice of specialists in widely separated fields of research, through whose cooperation it should be possible to link the evidence more precisely.

The pattern in question originated in the drapery of Greek female figures before the middle of the sixth century B. C., in accordance with a growing taste for decorative elaboration, and is seen at its best in the Attic *korai*. These wear voluminous rectangular garments which are gathered on the shoulders, with the result that they hang in a series of perpendicular folds which overlap one another along each edge. The Greek innovation consisted in arranging these overlaps to form a regular zigzag pattern, emphasised by flattened folds, and setting such edges in pairs which diverge from the gathering in perfectly symmetrical duplication (pl. 37, a). This device was a stock feature all through the later archaic period, till about 480 B.C.

Shortly before it became unfashionable in Greece, Darius I ordained the creation of a Persian art and fetched Ionian sculptors to carve for him; they introduced the trick in the sleeves and skirts of men's "Median robes."[1] Change was not permitted in Persian official sculpture, and it therefore recurs constantly in the reliefs of Persepolis and in gems for a hundred and fifty years, making its final appearance in reliefs of Artaxerxes III, 359-338. It never occurs again in this region.

In Greece, after the end of the archaic period, all the progressive artists abandoned symmetrical design, but their old-fashioned colleagues continued for a while to work in the archaic style, which in their hands turned into mannerism. Even after the transition, a limited demand for such work persisted, to avoid a break with tradition, e.g. in figures of deities reminiscent of old idols, and these are still more mannered; zigzag edges, being the most recognizable

---

1. Frankfort and Richter, *AJA* 50 (1946) 6, 15, figs. on pp. 8, 13, 16, 24.

archaic feature, were indispensable.[2] Probably a few figures of this sort were produced in each generation from the end of the Archaic period to the Roman conquest, but as a rule with no pretension to aesthetic value. When sculptors of repute began to work in imitation of the Old Masters, the aim was to recapture past grandeur rather than past quaintness, so that the prototypes chosen were usually of the later fifth century; very few statues older than 100 B.C. imitate the archaic. In the finest of these, a statue from Pergamon, the zigzag edges are turned into scallops by rounding the folds.[3] But in all the arts a more accurate reproduction of archaic models became frequent in the first century B.C. The figures are purely decorative; zigzag edges to the drapery seem almost an essential feature, and are flattened even more than in real archaic drapery. The Artemis from Pompeii (pl. 37, b),[4] a statue half life-size, may be taken as a fair representative of the figures comparatively true to the prototype. This archaistic work retained its popularity into the Christian Era only for a few decades, after which instances are rare and of a different character. The design becomes very free; the zigzag pattern and similar mannerisms provide the archaic flavor while the figure as a whole bears no resemblance to any archaic original.[5] Eventually the production of archaistic figures in any medium ceased, apparently about 150 A.D.

Again the zigzag pattern was adopted by an Oriental people just when it lost favor in the Mediterranean. This time it went straight to the North West frontier of India (or rather Pakistan), to become an element in the Buddhist art of Gandhara. Here it is very commonly used in a single row of overlaps, though cases of symmetrical duplication are by no means rare. The statuette which I illustrate (pl. 38, a) represents a Bodhisattva; it stands 102 cm. high, and is carved in the usual greenish schist. It belongs to the Central Asian Antiquities Museum, New Delhi, and was found at Taxila in the ruins of the monastery of Mora Moradu.[6] Stucco groups from the monastery and from an adjoining *stupa* are modelled in the same style and include

2. Bulle, *Archaisierende Rundplastik* (*Abh. Bayer. Akad., phil. u. hist. Kl.*, 30, 1918); Schmidt, E., *Archaistische Kunst in Griechenland u. Rom.*

3. Bulle, *op. cit.*, 21, no. 42a, pl. 5; *Altertümer von Pergamon* 7, no. 43, Bleiblatt 8.

4. Naples *Guida* 106; Bulle, *op. cit.*, 11, no. 10a.

5. E.g. the Tyche at Munich (no. 49) which is apparently Antonine; Bulle, *op. cit.*, 26, no 50, pl. 7.

6. *Archaeological Survey of India, Annual Report* 1915-16, 30, pl. XXIVa; Exhibition, Royal Academy, London, 1947-48, Cat. no. 103 ("Provenance unknown"). Identified by Mr. Ronald Smith, to whom I owe practically all my Gandharan material. Other examples in *ASI Report* 1911-12, pl. XL; 1912-13, pl. VII*d*; 1925-26, pl. LXVI*a, b*.

other examples of the duplicated zigzag pattern.[7] The stuccoes in the monastery were assumed by the excavator to date from a late reconstruction of the building, but they stood in parts which had remained unaltered, and the figures may confidently be attributed to a fairly early stage in Gandharan art. There are comparable zigzags at the foot of the dress in a group found not far away (at Charsada near Peshawar) which bears an inscribed date, 89.[8] The year is almost certainly reckoned by Kanishka's era and so should correspond to roughly 230 A.D. Such a date agrees well enough with the evidence of a figure stylistically similar to the Mora Moradu statuette, in which however the hanging ends of drapery are rounded and corrugated with folds, precisely as in Roman togate statues.[9] In some Gandharan figures these rounded ends are found in conjunction with a zigzag arrangement elsewhere on the body.[10]

The Mora Moradu statuette and its relatives must have been inspired by some Greco-Roman archaistic statuette, no doubt in bronze or silver.[11] Apparently such figures ceased to be produced approximately when Gandharan art began, in the middle of the second century A.D., a couple of generations before the Charsada dedication. The area had, of course, been in contact with Greek art through Bactria in the first century B. C., when it became familiar with an archaistic Athena on the coins of Menander of Kabul.[12] But there can be only a negligible chance that relics of that period might have had any effect upon Gandharan art; the classical influence which infuses it appears to have come invariably from almost contemporary art of the Roman Empire.[13] Assuming that to hold good in this case, the zigzag pattern would seem likely to have been introduced into Gandharan art practically at the start, unless the hypothetical import was already an antique (of an outmoded style and therefore sent abroad to fetch a higher price). The pattern must have remained in vogue in Gandhara to 400, on the evidence of further exportation.

Zigzag edging, both used singly and duplicated, spread from Gandhara as an integral feature of Buddhist iconography. First, no doubt, it reached the lower Ganges Valley, where it relieves the austerity of fifth-century Gupta sculpture. But it was naturalized in China well

7. *ASI Report* 1915-16, pl. XXIIIb; 1927-28, p. XXXIXd.

8. *ASI Report* 1928-29, 142; *Epigraphica Indica* 22 (1933-34) 14, with 2 pls.

9. *ASI Report* 1909-10, pl. XIXd; *cf.* 1903-04, pl. LXVIIIc.

10. *ASI Report* 1912-13, pl. VIIIc.

11. E.g. Hill, Dorothy K., *Cat. of Classical Bronze Sculpture in the Walters Art Gallery*, no. 188, pl. 39; British Museum, *Cat. Bronzes*, no. 192, pl. I = Seltman, *Approach to Greek Art*, pl. 89.

12. British Museum, *Cat. Indian Coins, Greek and Scythic Kinges*, pl. XI.

13. Wheeler, *Antiquity* 23 (1949) 4, discusses the classical sources and dating.

before 500. There may have been examples of the pattern among the images which Fa-Hien brought from India at the very beginning of the fifth century; at any rate Chinese sculptors were using it lavishly a bare hundred years later.[14] And from China it spread, with Buddhism, to Korea and thence to Japan; it constantly appears in the seventh-century sculpture of those countries, still in practically its original form. Later the artists of the Far East adapted it to their own notions by curving the lines, the more sinuously as time went on, but clearly recognizable derivatives persist to the final decay of sculpture around 1300. In the minor arts its influence lingers there to this day. Other Buddhist peoples, such as the Tibetans and the Burmese, have retained the pattern virtually unaltered, though coarsened.

Almost simultaneously with its introduction to China, the pattern was revived, with slight modifications, in the Byzantine Empire. In the third and fourth centuries, although the archaistic fashion had long since died, artists had occasionally chosen to show an overlapping edge of drapery in a form approximating to the zigzag, though with rounded folds and no symmetrical duplication. But commercial craftsmen of the third and fourth centuries, when they carved figures in relief on ivory or bone plaques, naturally flattened any overlapping folds.[15] The center of work in these materials was Alexandria; most of it is crude, but perhaps the supreme importance of that city in early Christianity furthered the adoption of the mannerism in Italy and Constantinople. In a good ivory which could be as early as the fourth century and has no obviously Alexandrian features, the panel of the Symmachi, the edges of the dress again diverge in semi-symmetrical zigzags, and a single zigzag of rounded folds is found in Christian sarcophagi of the fourth century.[16] In the mosaics of Sant' Apollinare Nuovo at Ravenna, which date from the beginning of the sixth century, the dress of most figures opens to one side of the waist in a large zigzag, which in a few figures is symmetrically repeated on the other side. Pairs of symmetrical zigzags occur in Byzantine carving sporadically from this time onward; they are usually on a diminutive scale in relation to the figure, as in a book cover of the twelfth century in the Bodleian Library (pl. 38, b). The larger Byzantine zigzags, whether single or double, tend to be more or less rounded.

14. Most easily studied at the Museum of Fine Arts, Boston, which has notable sculptures inscribed with dates in the early sixth century as well as more primitive figures. Cf. for illustrations *Museum Journal*, Philadelphia, 7 (1916) 152.

15. Cecchelli, *La Cattedra di Massimiano*, 161, illustrates an unusually clear example.

16. A fairly well-dated example is the sarcophagus believed to have been made for the Archbishop Liberius who died in 378 (Lawrence, Marion, *Sarcophagi of Ravenna*, 13, figs. 25-26).

Zigzag folding leapt to the opposite end of Europe at some time in the seventh century, perhaps not till Theodore of Tarsus became Archbishop of Canterbury. The Anglo-Saxon Chronicle records that in the year of his arrival, 669, the King of Kent gave the old Roman fort at Reculver for the site of a monastery; the foundations of its church are laid around those of a sculptured cross, which presumably was erected first of all, and some of its figures seem to imitate archaic Greek work (pl. 38, c, d).[17] Henceforth the zigzag edging of drapery was often used in the Anglo-Saxon parts of England and Scotland,[18] and it crossed to the continent when Charlemagne introduced English and Byzantine artists. It recurs in mediaeval Europe whenever and wherever Byzantine influence was felt. Used singly or symmetrically repeated, it appears in the semi-Byzantine Norman mosaics of Sicily, and in every branch of Romanesque and Gothic art. It is habitually found in masterpieces of Russian religious paintings till the seventeenth century and in popular icons of the Orthodox Church to the present day; in the West it may have ended by inspiring the linenfold panelling of Tudor mansions.

17. Peers, *Archaeologia* 77 (1927) 241, pls. LXII-LXIV.
18. Examples are collected by Clapham, *English Romanesque Architecture* I; Kendrick, *Anglo-Saxon Art* and *Later Anglo-Saxon and Viking Art*.

THE AEGINA HERACLES

WALTER R. AGARD
The University of Wisconsin

Plates 39-40

Few if any Greek sculptures of the Fifth Century, B.C., have been so underestimated by archaeologists and historians and critics of art as the Heracles from the east pediment of the temple of Aphaia at Aegina (pl. 39, c).[1] Furtwängler[2] paid it no special attention, beyond including two nondescript illustrations and two sketches by Haller; Rodenwaldt,[3] Michaelis and Wolters,[4] Buschor,[5] and Karo[6] gave it neither analysis nor illustration. Among French scholars, Collingnon[7] devoted a few approving words to the head; Reinach[8] and Faure[9] ignored the figure; Picard[10] used a photograph taken from the wrong side, and commented merely that "La joie d'Héraclès combattant semble même chargée d'expression: elle marquerait à la fois le défi, la curiosité, l'orgueil de la victoire assurée"; Pierre Devambez[11] included a good illustration and the following cursory praise: "On admire surtout la vigueur contenue . . . une impression de force qui n'avait pas été obtenue encore par la ronde-bosse."

Many of these scholars chose as their outstanding example of the figures from Aegina the fallen warrior in the opposite corner of the east pediment, being more concerned, apparently, with the technical problems solved in that figure than with its artistic merit, although that merit, one must grant, is considerable. Such was also the attitude of Ernest Gardner,[12] of H. B. Walters,[13] who termed the fallen warrior a masterpiece but, like Gardner, ignored the Heracles,

---

1. The photograph, by Clarence Kennedy, shows the figure as viewed in its position on the pediment. For pl. 39, a, Furtwängler's restoration, I am indebted to the Munich Glyptothek, for pl. 39, b to Mr. Stowitz, and for pl. 40 to Mr. Kennedy. Cf. also Agard, *The Greek Tradition in Sculpture*, 11, fig. 6.

2. *Aegina.*

3. *Propyläen-Kunstgeschichte.*

4. *Die Kunst des Altertums.*

5. *Die Plastik der Griechen.*

6. *Greek Personality in Archaic Sculpture.*

7. *Histoire de la sculpture grecque*, I, 295.

8. *Apollo.*

9. *Histoire de l'art.*

10. *La sculpture antique*, Fig. 94.

11. *La sculpture grecque* 35.

12. *Handbook of Greek Sculpture.*

13. *The Art of the Greeks.*

and of Lawrence.[14] A similar attitude was taken by Tarbell,[15] by Chase,[16] by Miss Richter,[17] and by Robb and Garrison.[18] Among American scholars, only R. B. Richardson,[19] who called it "one of the finest of all the (Aegina) figures," and Helen Gardner[20] devoted any attention to it; Miss Gardner's brief analysis is detailed and just. But the comment which I wish to take as the text of this paper is J. D. Beazley's: "If a single figure had to be chosen to represent the ripe archaic sculpture, would it not be the archer Heracles, himself tense as a drawn bow?"[21] Beazley must be accounted among our most sensitive and discerning critics of ancient art. His judgment is, I am sure, sounder in this instance than that of the scholars who casually passed the figure by.

Why does this Heracles represent so well ripe archaic sculpture? Because it achieves that synthesis of adequately naturalistic form, fine geometric design, and refinement of detail which makes the best work of that period so distinguished. Let us examine each of these points.

The first is easily dealt with. The figure gives the impression of a normal, healthy human body; no obvious distortion or pronounced archaic conventions intrude to make the spectator adjust himself to a bizarre rendition of the human form. But of course art requires no such degree of naturalism, and the presence of it is only one element in the artistic value of this statue.

Far more important is the design, which deserves as careful attention on the part of the spectator as undoubtedly the sculptor devoted to planning and executing it.

This is architectural sculpture, therefore it had to be planned in relation to the triangular pediment and the total façade. As a kneeling figure it fits nicely into the low space near the end of the triangle, and leads the eye of the spectator forward toward the center (pl. 39, a). It is interesting to note that in both sculpture and vase painting Heracles is hardly ever pictured as kneeling; he usually strides forward as he shoots, engages an opponent in violent action, or stands or sits in repose. Here the sculptor adapted the pose to the architectural requirements.

---

14. *Classical Sculpture.*
15. *History of Greek Art.*
16. In *A History of Sculpture*, although an illustration of the archer appears in his *Greek and Roman Sculpture in American Collections.*
17. *The Sculpture and Sculptors of the Greeks.*
18. *Art in the Western World.*
19. *History of Greek Sculpture*, 108.
20. *Art Through the Ages*, 100.
21. *Cambridge Ancient History*, V, 422.

The main masses, repeating the structure of the building, are, in order of importance, horizontal, vertical, and diagonal. Horizontal are the flat-topped lion's-head helmet, the extended left arm (the line continued across the top of the jerkin), the right upper arm, the nearly horizontal line of the left thigh (continued across the bottom of the jerkin), and the lower edge of the chiton. Vertical are the torso and the sharply-defined outer lines of the jerkin. The diagonals are very subtly planned to echo the thrusts of the pediment: the left thigh repeats the ascending line of the triangle twice, above gently, below with greater urgency; the left lower leg accentuates the diagonal of the opposite side of the pediment, and the right lower leg repeats the oblique direction twice at descending angles. That this was not accidental, but definitely designed, is indicated by the fact that the right knee is elevated on a base of its own instead of resting on the plinth; if the knee were placed on the plinth the diagonals would be much less varied in their contrasting directions. Slight curves then serve to redeem the figure from rigidity: the right lower arm bends down, the front of the left foot is slightly raised, and the right foot, resting on the ball, curves gracefully upward, giving elasticity to the pose.

A further instance of planning is the checkerboard pattern carved across part of the jerkin. Here the prevailing horizontals and verticals are repeated, but each square is cut in an oblique plane, flush with the surface on the left, carved in depth toward the right, so that the shadows cast bring out the pattern strongly. It should also be noted that the pattern does not continue far enough on either side to weaken the solid form.

Once the essential masses were established, details were added, as in architecture, to soften abrupt transitions. The neckpiece of the helmet curves into the hard line of the shoulder; a bit of drapery under the arm connects arm and torso; the jerkin flaps make a series of diagonals leading steadily from the horizontal thigh to the vertical back, and this transition is in turn softened by the folds of the chiton, which ripple away until they repeat in minor rhythm the vertical lines of the flaps.

That such analysis is more than fanciful can be demonstrated, I think, by comparing the sculptural figure with the photograph of an actual person kneeling to shoot a bow. Some years ago Mr. Stowitz, Pavlowa's dancing partner, asked me for pictures of Greek sculpture and vases which he might adapt for dance poses, and later sent me a photograph of his imitation of the Aegina archer (pl. 39, b). A comparison of his figure with the sculptured one will indicate how radically different are straight realism and the artistic design worked out by the sculptor.[22]

The application of color (the accessories were blocked in with contrasting red and blue against the blue background of the pediment) doubtless also served a useful purpose in emphasizing the design of the figures and enlivening the total effect.

The Aegina Heracles is, however, more than mere decoration for a building. In its own right it deserves a high place among masterpieces of classical sculpture. In addition to its dynamic design, conveying the sense of power effectively disciplined and directed, it has the refinement of detail which distinguishes art from sheer geometry and superior sculpture from the commonplace.

Fortunately the figure suffered little restoration by Thorwaldsen (he contributed the tip of the nose, the left lower leg, part of the right foot, and the bow), so that here we have an original statue, nearly intact, by which to judge the refinement of detail.

First we must note the rather broader modeling than in most of the Aeginetan sculpture, giving a less nervous, more monumental effect. But the characteristic Aeginetan crispness and clarity are present in the carving of the lion's head, the sharply-defined eyes, brows, lips, and ears. The narrowed eyes and protruding lips indicate the tension of the archer. There is no attempt at a detailed anatomical study, as a comparison with an actual human body (pl. 39, b) makes clear; only the few muscles and tendons that serve to suggest the energy summoned by the action are rendered, in arm and leg, but these are carved with sure precision. The loving devotion of the sculptor to his craft is evidenced by the careful finish given every part of the body (pl. 40), although only one side of it would be seen, and that from a great distance.

We must conclude, I believe, that this Heracles is more than representative of ripe archaic art. It is a masterpiece of classical sculpture: the healthy human form worked into a subtly varied, monumental design, with sensitive modeling and refinement of detail.

---

22. Cf. Watts, Diana, *The Renaissance of the Greek Ideal,* 3-5 pl. 1 (Aegina archer); pl. III (girl assuming this position as a gymnastic exercise, Cinema series, no. 1).

ZUR ENTSTEHUNG DES PARTHENONFRIESES

WALTER-HERWIG SCHUCHHARDT
Freiburg i. Br.

Tafeln 42-43

Da, wo der Parthenonfries an den Langseiten der Cella sich der Ostfront nähert, geht seine Darstellung vom Sturm der Reiterscharen, vom Donnern der Wagen und Viergespanne zur stilleren Reihung menschlicher Gruppen über, die — bald dicht gedrängt, bald locker verteilt — das vordere Drittel jeder Langseite füllen. Mit diesen Gruppen von Männern und Jünglingen beginnt recht eigentlich erst die feierliche Prozession. Doch ist es nicht einfach das Volk von Athen, nicht jedermann, der sich hier zum Zuge formiert. Ausgewählte, mit besonderen Funktionen versehene Vertreter politischer und religiöser Gemeinschaften sind es, die hier in den abgekürzten Formeln kleiner Gruppen an uns vorüberziehen. Im Süden zunächst die Hekatombe der Stadt Athen, deren ausgebreitete Schilderung zwei Drittel des Abschnittes der Fußgänger einnimmt. Fügt man auf der verlorenen Platte XLIII[1] eine Kuh ein, zu der sich notwendigerweise

Abb. 1. Nordfries des Parthenons.

ein Führer, wahrscheinlich noch ein Geleitsmann gesellt, so besteht der Zug aus zehn Kühen;[2] das ist aber der zehnte Teil einer Hekatombe im wörtlichen Sinne. Die Tiere werden dann von zehn Führern und zehn Geleitsmännern[3] begleitet, zu denen 7 Festordner[4] kommen; vielleicht ist ein achter als vierte Figur der Platte XLIII einzufügen, was bei dem weiten Abstand des Jünglings 111 von 112 möglich, ja ratsam erscheint (Abb. 3).

1. *JDAI* 45 (1930) 244, Abb. 27 (Schuchhardt).
2. Smith, *Sculptures* 64 f., Abb. 125; Premerstein, *JOAI* 15 (1917) 8; Deubner, *Attische Feste* 25, Anm. 10.
3. Schuchhardt a.O. Abb. 27-28; *Führer:* 108, 110. *Fehlender,* 112, 115, 118, 121, 124, 126, 129; *Geleiter:* 109, 111. *Fehlender,* 113, 116, 119, 122, 125, 127, 130.
4. 107, 114, 117, 120, 123, 128, 131.

Es folgen[5] drei Skaphephoren (Platte XXXVII*), vier Kitharaspieler[6] (102-105) und — in dichtgedrängter Schar — 18 ältere Männer. Obwohl diese drei Gruppen insgesamt 35 Figuren aufweisen, sind sie doch so eng zusammengeschoben, daß sie nur ein Drittel des Fußgängerabschnittes einnehmen, während die Hekatombe zwei Drittel beherrscht (Abb. 2).

Am Nordfries dagegen ist die gleiche Friesstrecke reicher und gleichmäßiger gegliedert. Nicht weniger als sieben verschiedene Themen werden hier in ebenso vielen Gruppen vorgetragen. Wieder eröffnen Opferrinder den Zug, vier Kühe, von vier Führern (N 2, 4, 6, 8) geleitet. Auf der andern Seite der Rinder schreiten, ganz wie am Südfries, begleitende Jünglinge; drei an der Zahl, da man die erste, dem Zuge sich entgegenwendende, nach Stuarts Angabe (Michaelis 242) eine Binde tragende Figur eher als Festordner ansehen wird. Den Rindern folgen vier Schafe, stattliche Tiere mit wolligem Vlies

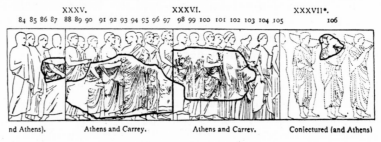

XXXV.   XXXVI.   XXXVII*.
84 85 86 87   88 89 90   91 92 93 94 95 96 97   98 99 100   101 102 103 104 105   106

nd Athens).   Athens and Carrey.   Athens and Carrey.   Coniectured (and Athens)

Abb. 2. Südfries des Parthenons.

und gerieftem Gehörn, demnach als weiblich anzusprechen (Michaelis 243), $\tau \acute{\epsilon} \lambda \epsilon \iota \alpha \ \hat{\iota} \epsilon \varrho \acute{\alpha}$, Prachtexemplare als Gabe für die Gottheit. Gegenüber der großen Staatshekatombe, von 10 Kühen an der Südseite repräsentiert, erscheint in diesen Gruppen von je vier Tieren die bescheidenere, aber altehrwürdige Opfergabe der vier Phylen,[7] deren Fleischanteile nur den profanen und sakralen Beamten des Staates zustanden. Scharf abgewandt von dem letzten Begleiter der Schafe, die Trennung von der folgenden Gruppe betonend, in ungewöhnlicher Form sich über eine Fuge schiebend steht der Festordner N 12 in gelassener Haltung da, den heranschreitenden Opferträgern entgegenblickend. Es sind drei Jünglinge, die auf der linken Schulter, breit dem Beschauer zugewandt, je einen trog- oder wannenartigen Behälter tragen, ein metallenes[8] Schaff, $\sigma \varkappa \acute{\alpha} \varphi o \varsigma$ (Höhlung, Mulde). Der

---

5. Schuchhardt 243, Abb. 26.
6. Zur Benennung s. Michaelis, *Parthenon* 239.
7. Pfuhl, *De pompis* 16; Deubner, *Att. Feste* 25 ff.
8. Eherne und silberne werden bei Photios *(σκάφος)* genannt, nicht goldene, wie Deubner (28) will.

Inhalt, Honigwaben und Backwerk, scheint eine bedeutende Last auszumachen, die von den Jünglingen, mit beiden Händen, auf der Schulter getragen wird. Der mittlere hat sich für dieses Geschäft den Mantel hoch geschürzt.

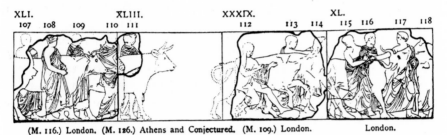

XLI.   XLIII.   XXXIX.   XL.
107 108   109   110 111   112   113 114   115 116   117   118

(M. 116.) London.   (M. 126.) Athens and Conjectured.   (M. 109.) London.   London.

Abb. 3. Südseite des Parthenonfrieses.

Den drei Skaphephoren folgen drei ganz entsprechend schreitende, große Krüge tragende Jünglinge (Abb. 1). Auch ihre Last drückt schwer, zumal die metallenen Hydrien, mit Wein gefüllt, nur mühsam auf der linken Achsel gehalten werden können. Ein vierter (19) hat sein Gefäß für einen Augenblick zu Boden gesetzt. Nun hebt er es mit beiden Händen an, es wieder aufzuladen und den Anschluß an seine Gruppe nicht zu verlieren. Ueber seiner gebückten Gestalt streckt der erste der Flötenbläser sein Instrument vor. Doch ist von ihm nur diese Doppelflöte, ein Teil der linken Hand und des Mantels erhalten. Eine ungefähre Vorstellung von den Figuren der Flötenspieler (20-23) gibt Carreys Zeichnung. Auch die Gruppe der Kitharisten ist stark zerstört (24-27). Vier Figuren erscheinen weit auseinandergezogen, lebhaft bewegt, vielleicht in rhapsodischem Gesang begriffen als Kitharoden (Michaelis 244).

Unmittelbar auf den vierten Musiker (27) folgt eine Schar älterer Männer. Es sind 17 gegenüber den 18 des Südfrieses. Sie drängen sich ganz wie dort — fast alle (oder alle?) bärtig — in dichtester Häufung zusammen, nur um eine Figur (28) den Raum von zwei Platten überschreitend. Genau die gleiche Ausdehnung besitzen die Männer am Südfries (84-101); doch mischen sich hier, wenn wir Carreys Zeichnung folgen dürfen, Bärtige und Unbärtige durcheinander. Ihr Zug geht ununterscheidbar über in eine Gruppe von vier Figuren, die vor ihnen einherschreiten und — nach Carreys Zeichnungen — tafelähnliche Gegenstände in der Hand (103) oder unter dem Arm (?104) tragen. In diesen Gegenständen den Schallkasten einer Kithara zu erkennen (Michaelis 239), will nach ihrer Form und der Art, wie sie gehalten werden, schwer gelingen. Eher möchte man an Schreibtafeln (Diptycha) oder Pinakes mit Aufzeichnungen

denken. Von den drei (?) Skaphephoren der Platte XXXVII
(Schuchhardt 243 Abb. 26) ist nur eine Figur (106) fragmentarisch
erhalten, so daß wenigstens Motiv und Thema gesichert sind.

In ganzen gesehen ist die Thematik des Fußgängerabschnittes im
Norden doppelt so reich: zweifach sind die Opfertiere vertreten
(Kühe und Schafe), zweifach die Opferträger (Skaphe- und Hy-
driaphoren), zweifach die Musiker (Flötenspieler und Kitharisten).
Im Süden erscheinen dieselben Themen nur einfach, Opferträger und
Kitharisten nehmen einen bescheideneren Raum ein. Die Hekatombe
dagegen breitet sich über den größten Teil des südlichen Abschnittes
aus. Die Greise sind nach Zahl, Ausdehnung, Anordnung denen am
Nordfriese fast gleich.

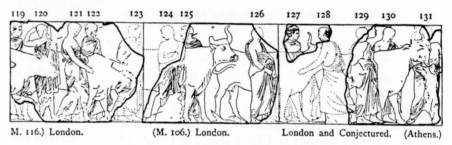

M. 116.) London.   (M. 106.) London.   London and Conjectured.   (Athens.)

Abb. 4. Südseite des Parthenonfrieses.

Trotz seiner reicheren Thematik erscheint der betrachtete Abschnitt im Norden ruhiger, einheitlicher und gleichmäßiger als der
des Südfrieses. Länger ist der Zug feierlich schreitender Festteil-
nehmer gedehnt, ruhiger und gedämpfter klingt der Rhythmus der
einherziehenden Tiere und ihrer Begleiter. Im Süden (Abb. 4) dagegen zeigt die breite Darstellung der Hekatombe stärkere Ausbrüche
von Unruhe und Bewegung, die ihrerseits Anlaß geben zu Gegenak-
tionen (Abb. 3) der Kuhführer (112, 115),[9] zu Gegenbewegungen,
Wendungen, Gebärden der Begleiter und Festordner.[10] Auffallen muß,
wie dieser stärkeren Unruhe, dieser von Spannungen und Kontrasten
erfüllten Bewegtheit der K o m p o s i t i o n ein lebhafter Wechsel
im Stil der A u s f ü h r u n g entspricht. Dieser Stil trägt bald rasch
und flüchtig (Abb. 2), fast skizzenhaft vor (98-103), bald laut und
plastisch (110, 114, 121); er dient ebenso der Charakterisierung
heftiger, jäher Bewegung (109, 112), wie er durchscheinend-zart mit

---

9. Wie milde ist dagegen die Haltung des einzigen bewegten Kuhführers im
Norden (N 5), zumal wenn man sie ergänzt (Schweitzer II, 12, Abb. 7).

10. 113, 114, 117, 120, 124, 125, 128, 131.

Ernst und Stille schildert (107-111).[11] So scheint es, als ob solcher
Reichtum an vielfältig-gegensätzlichen Worten schon durch Reichtum
und Vielfalt des zugrundeliegenden Satzbaues bedingt, ursächlich mit
ihm verknüpft sei.

Entsprechend dem ruhigen Fluß der Erzählung ist im Norden
auch das System der Ausarbeitung letzter Hand, die Abgrenzung
verschiedener Bildhauer und ihrer persönlichen Handschrift verhältnismäßig klar zu erkennen. Wurde zunächst der gesamte Abschnitt der Fußgänger auf fünf ausführende Bildhauer verteilt,[12] so
hat Schweitzer den Zug der Rinder (N 1-8) von dem der Schafe (N 9-
11) getrennt (Abb. 5 u. 1) und zwei — freilich eng verwandte —
Meister angenommen (I 17 und Anm. 1). Eine Entscheidung ist
schwer zu fällen; des Verbindenden scheint mir fast mehr als des
Trennenden, zumal der gesamte Abschnitt N 1-11 gewichtige Beziehungen zu der Metope SII einerseits, der Apollonplatte andererseits
aufweist.[13] Eine Zweiteilung kann hier nur Nuancen treffen.

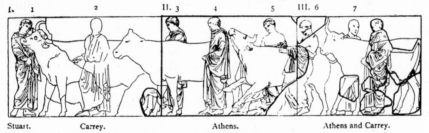

Abb. 5. Nordfries des Parthenons.

11. Die Verwandtschaft dieser zarten Gestalten mit dem schönen Weihrelief im
Brocklesby Park (Ashmole, *Antike Plastik Walther Amelung*, 13 ff.; E. A. 3006)
ist so groß daß man denselben Meister etwa 15 Jahre später am Werk sehen
möchte. Vielleicht ist das Akropolisfragment Walter no. 41 dazuzustellen, wie
Ashmole (a.O. 15) vorschlägt. Dagegen hat das Asklepiosrelief Nat.Mus. 1346
(Papaspiridi 230 ff.) weder zeitlich (Süsserott 110: 390-80) noch stilistisch (wie
Fr. Poulsen, E. A., 3006 will) etwas mit unserer Gruppe zu tun.

12. Schuchhardt a.O. 230 ff.: 1) N 1-11; 2) N 17-19; 3) N 20-27; 4) N 28-37;
5) 38-43.

13. Ist nicht der Kopf des Schafführers 10 (Schuchhardt 255, Abb. 46-7)
dem des Kentauren der Südmetope II (Rodenwaldt, *Abh.Berl.* 1945/6 No. 7 Taf. 8)
eng verwandt in Form und Umrahmung des Auges, in den breiten kräftigen
Locken! Auch der Kopf des Kuhführers N3 steht nicht fern (Schuchhardt 255,
Abb. 44; Hege-Rodenwaldt, *Akropolis* Taf. 50; Gerke, *Griech. Plastik* Taf. 168),
und man ist versucht, seinen und seiner Gefährten klassischen Gewandstil nur
wenig strenger im Mantel des Lapithen von SII wiederzufinden (Rodenwaldt
Taf. 7). Die festen Faltenzüge, die schön gerollten Säume seines Mantels kehren
beim mittleren Jüngling (N 4) wieder; die gleiche Saekante wie dort lagert auf
der Kruppe des Kentauren; weitere verwandte Züge lassen sich finden. Die
kräftig-fleischige Bildung von N 6 ist sehr wohl den Leibern der Metope zu
vergleichen. Und darf man von hier zur Apollonplatte des Ostfrieses springen?
Schon Kjellberg hatte den Apollonkopf (Hege-Rodenwaldt Taf. 54) mit N 5
(Schuchhardt 219 Ab.) verglichen. Wie eng darf man, auch auf Grund der
Gewandbehandlung, O 38 — 42 mit N 1 — 11, beide Abschnitte mit SII ver-
knüpfen?

Sodann wurden von Langlotz die Gestalten N 3-5 und 13 (Taf. 43, a) dem Agorakritos zugeschrieben,[14] was in dieser Gemeinsamkeit nicht angeht, da die Figurentypen N 1-11 sich von den folgenden N 13-19 grundsätzlich wie in allen Einzelheiten unterscheiden. Später[15] wird der Skaphephor N 13 in seiner Gewandbehandlung "von den benachbarten Figuren" unterschieden, eine Feststellung, die zunächst überraschen und befremden muß. Denn nicht nur im Motiv sind die sechs mit Opfergaben beladenen Jünglinge (N 13-18) gleichartig. Auch in der künstlerischen Durchführung dieses Motivs, ja bis in Einzelheiten der Ausführung sind sie überaus gleichartig. So wurde denn auch ihre Zusammengehörigkeit im engsten Sinne der Ausführung von e i n e m Meister angenommen.[16] Ueberprüft man jedoch die Frage erneut, so zeigt sich, daß N 13 sich in der Tat von den andern Opfergabenträgern abhebt.[17] So ähnlich in der Gesamtanlage das Gewand dem der Hydrophoren N 16-18 (Taf. 42, a) ist, so anders ist seine Ausführung im einzelnen. Reicher und doch gleichmäßiger ist das Netz der Falten über die ganze Gestalt gespannt. Weich gerundet, wie Adern über der Hautfläche, wölben sich die Faltenrücken; ihre sanfte Schwingung und stete Wiederholung erinnert an die dekorative Abfolge von Schnüren und Gehängen. Sparsamer und markanter sind demgegenüber bei den Hydrophoren die Falten verwendet; schärfer, plastischer ziehen sie als Grate über die ruhige Fläche des Gewandes, dessen breite Bahnen in flacher, aber fester Modellierung das Relief des Körpers geben. Die Kraft und Eigenart dieses Reliefstils wird in einzelnen Zügen besonders deutlich; an den glatten Streifen der Mantelsäume, die vor der ersten Gestalt (N 16) von oben nach unten ausgebreitet sind, bei der dritten (N 18) ähnlich geplättet von der linken Hand herabstreichen (besonders deutlich bei Gerke, Taf. 167); an der gepreßten Form, in welcher der linke Arm des mittleren Jünglings (N 17), die Gewandmasse vor Schulter und Brust des dritten die vordere Reliefebene hält. Zarter und reicher klingt dagegen die Formensprache des Skaphephoren; um ein Weniges schwächer und schwanker wirkt auch seine Haltung. Kein Zweifel, eine andere Hand hat hier den Meißel geführt. Ihr mag auch der Festordner N 12, mögen die folgenden beiden Schaffträger N 14-15 zuzuschreiben sein. In dem wiedergefundenen Kopf des dritten (N 15)[18] glaubt man jetzt

---

14. *Scritti in onore di Nogara* 227[1].

15. Langlotz, *Phidias-Probleme* 100[3], wo freilich der Text nicht ganz klar ist, da N 13 keinen Kopf besitzt.

16. Kjellberg, *Studien* 52; Schuchhardt 232; Schweitzer I 17.

17. Außer den großen Parthenonwerken vergleiche etwa G. v. Lücken, *Parthenonskulpturen* Taf. 19 (N 13) mit Hege-Rodenwaldt, Taf. 47 (N 16-18).

18. *RM* 46 (1931) 81 ff., Taf. 11 (Technau); Deubner, *Att. Feste* 28 Anm. 7, Taf. 1, 2.

etwas von der größeren Weichheit dieses Meisters zu spüren gegenüber der knapperen, längeren Dreiecksform der Gesichter von N 16-18[19] (Taf. 42, a).

Also ein weiterer Meister an der Ausführung, für die schon so viele bewiesen oder behauptet sind.[20] Der Nachweis könnte nur geringes Interesse beanspruchen. Aber es handelt sich bei allen diesen Bemühungen nicht um den Einzelfall, sondern um ein Prinzip; um das sehr praktische und reale Prinzip, nach welchem die riesige Aufgabe des Parthenonfrieses in wenigen Jahren vom ersten Entwurf zur letzten Ausführung getrieben wurde.

Für die Erkenntnis dieses Prinzips aber und die Verfestigung unserer Vorstellungen scheint mir die angeschnittene Stelle einige Aufschlüsse zu geben. Hat man die Verschiedenheit der verglichenen Figuren (N 13 und N 16-18) verfolgt und zur Kenntnis genommen und sich auf Grund dieser Feststellung entschlossen, zwei verschiedene Hände am Werke zu sehen, so tritt nach solcher Aufspaltung umso mächtiger und gebieterischer die Forderung wiederum auf, das Gemeinsame und Gleichartige der Figuren zu sehen und zu erklären. Deutlich tritt es zu Tage: in dem eigentümlichen Umriß der Gestalten, in ihrer gelängten Proportion, ihrem gehemmten Stand; in der etwas mühsamen Darlegung von Motiv und Vorgang; in dem leisen Zwang, der Gebundenheit, die über der Reliefgebung liegen. Gemeinsamkeiten, die so gerade diese beiden Platten (V und VI des Nordfrieses) eng zusammenschließen. Auf der anderen Seite steht der Meister von N 13 durch die Feinheit seiner Handschrift, den Reichtum des Details dem der Hydrophoren nicht nach; mag dieser auch kraftvoller, markiger sein, jener ist nicht einfach Schüler und Adept. Die Unterschiede sind nicht solche der Qualität, sondern solche der Individualität; die Gemeinsamkeiten nicht Folge einer Abhängigkeit voneinander sondern von einer beide bindenden Vorlage. Alle Gemeinsamkeiten wurzeln in dieser Vorlage, einer Vorstufe im Gang der Arbeit. Hinter der Schicht der letzten Ausführung wird eine zweite vorletzte Stufe deutlich. Sie kann nicht in Umriß und Zeichnungen allein bestanden haben; ihr muß auch die plastische Grundform des Reliefstiles, die den Figuren eigentümliche gebundene Reliefanlange zueigen gewesen sein. Auch das System der langgeschwungenen, gegabelten Faltenzüge war schon gegeben, vielleicht in der sparsamen und kräftigen Form des Hydrophoren-Meisters, die sein Nachbar bereicherte und verfeinerte.

Nun findet sich vier Platten weiter gegen Westen (X) bei den alten

---

19. Schuchhardt 257, Abb. 48-49; Hege-Rodenwaldt, Taf. 52-53.
20. s. zuletzt Langlotz, *Phidias-Probleme* 100[3].

Männern mancher gemeinsame Zug in dem gewinkelten Umriß des vorgeschobenen Beines (N 41-43) mit seinem ungeschickten Uebergang zum Oberkörper; in dem Grätensystem der Falten; in der flachen Anlage der Gestalten, wie des Stoffes. Trockener, spröder hat hier die ausführende Hand gebildet; die gemeinsame Grundlage ist als verbindendes Element dennoch deutlich.

Schweitzer hat diese Verbindungen schon hervorgehoben.[21] Sein Vorschlag, die verschiedenen "Hände" zu Werkgruppen (a.O. 11 ff.) zusammenzufassen, bestätigt sich vollkommen. Das Maß der gemeinsamen Bindung wie der persönlichen Freiheit wird bei den tragenden Jünglingen im Vergleich von N 13 mit N 16-18 vollkommen greifbar. Mag das gleiche Motiv eine Gemeinsamkeit des Stiles besonders ermöglicht oder besonders deutlich gemacht haben, die Unterschiede sind es nicht weniger.

So werden wir mit Schweitzer die Figuren N 12-43 zu einer Werkgruppe zusammenfassen, die nach der neuesten Zählung von fünf Meistern ausgeführt wurde.

Es ist anzunehmen, daß der ganze Abschnitt von dem Hauptmeister vorgebildet, jede Figur in den großen Zügen ihrer P r o p o r t i o n , ihrer R e l i e f g e b u n g und des F a l t e n s y s t e m s festgelegt wurde. Die deutliche Gemeinsamkeit dieser drei Elemente bei den tragenden Jünglingen und den Greisen spricht dafür, zumal der Typus des frontal Gesehenen sich bei N 38, 31 und 26 in genau gleichem Abstand sehr gleichartig wiederholt. Aber auch der Hauptmeister ist nicht der primäre Urheber und Schöpfer seines Friesteiles. Offenkundig ist er seinerseits an einen größeren, allgemeingültigen Entwurf gebunden. Dieser bestimmte die Abfolge des Zuges seinem Inhalt nach, darüber hinaus seinen Rhythmus im Ganzen, seine Gliederung im Einzelnen. Doch war nicht nur die Aufteilung der Gruppen bis in die letzten Glieder geleistet, sodaß jede Figur in einem bestimmten Verhältnis zu ihrer Gruppe und mit dieser zum Ganzen stand. Es war auch diese so weit durchgedachte und durchgegliederte Komposition in einem letzten Schritt vor ihrer plastischen Verwirklichung mit den Blöcken, die sie tragen sollten, in Beziehung und Verhältnis gesetzt worden. Denn die — ungleiche — Abfolge der senkrechten Fugen dieser Blöcke ist mit den inhaltlichen Abschnitten, mit der Abfolge der Figuren und dem künstlerischen Rhythmus des Ganzen in einen natürlichen Einklang gebracht. Diese überraschende und bewundernswerte Abstimmung bedeutet den entscheidenden Schritt von der letzten zeichnerischen Klärung der Komposition zur

---

21. Schweitzer I, 17, Tabelle zu Platte I-X.

ersten praktischen Verbindung mit dem Stein. In diesem Vorgang der Skizzierung auf dem Stein, der endgültigen Umreißung einer Komposition, die ihr Schöpfer ebenso im Ganzen überschaute, wie er sie im Einzelnen nunmehr festlegte, wird die dritte Schicht in der Entstehung des Parthenonfrieses deutlich, die erste im gesamten Vorgang, die einzige, die mit dem Namen Phidias legitim verbunden werden kann.

THE PARTHENON

Crowned by a cloud, all-radiant,
　　Upon a winter dawn,
A white and dreamlike loveliness
　　Uprose the Parthenon.

A magic veil encircling it
　　Would half the sun obscure;
Cleaving the cloud it called to me:
　　"I am the symbol pure

In the expanse of the infinite
　　Of Beauty, the far-flung gleam,
Making cold white marble etherial
　　As the white mist of dreams."

Kostes Palamas

Translated by
John B. Edwards

THE PROBLEM OF THE ELGIN MARBLES

GEORGE KARO

Pomona College

Since Byron hurled his *Curse of Minerva* against Lord Elgin in 1811, the despoiling of the Parthenon and Erechtheion has never quite ceased to be discussed.[1] Again and again, the innate British love of fair play has demanded that the precious marbles be returned to Greece. The latest, and as far as I know the most authoritative treatment of this thorny question is Harald Nicolson's article in the *New York Times Magazine* of March, 27, 1949. Doubly competent, as Foreign Office specialist for Greek Affairs and as author of the best book on Byron's last year of life, he felt very keenly that at least a partial restitution should be made on the centenary of the poet's death at Missolonghi, April 19, 1824. He enlisted the sympathy of his chief, Ramsay MacDonald, and suggested that at least the most glaring gaps in the Erechtheion be closed by returning the Caryatid and the Ionic column from the British Museum to their original places. Nothing came of it, and Nicolson eloquently stresses the weakness of the arguments with which what actually were depredations have been justified or excused, for a century and a half. Fully aware of the peculiar sensitiveness of public opinion which may be suddenly aroused by such restitutions, Nicolson mentions a well-known case in point: the bronze horses on the front of St. Mark's, restored to Venice from Paris in 1816. A far more recent case is almost unknown. Some twenty-five years ago the Egyptian government asked the German Republic to exchange the fine polychrome head of Queen Nofretete, the wife of Amenophis IV, acquired quite legally by the Berlin Museum, for two Early Kingdom statues of the highest quality. The museum authorities felt that the bargain would be very favorable, the German government was eager to improve relations with Egypt. But a sudden wave of sentimental revolt defeated the plan. People who had never bothered about works of art waxed indignant, gushing ladies laid bunches of violets beside the charming young queen's portrait. The government dared not ignore public emotion. The deal was called off, to the irritated surprise of Cairo.

As the Elgin marbles were acquired for the British Museum by an Act of Parliament, another such Act would be necessary before any

---

1. Smith, A. H., "Lord Elgin and His Collections," *JHS* 36 (1916) 279 ff. Gennadios, John G., *Lord Elgin and His Predecessors in the Archaeological Invasion of Greece and Especially Athens, 1440-1837*. Archaeological Society Publications No. 25, 1930 (In Greek).

part of the collection could be restored (Nicolson, p. 12). That it would hardly have a chance is proved by the fate of the only practical and practicable attempt at a solution known to me. And as I am the only survivor among the people concerned, there seems no reason to keep it secret.

It sprang from the enlightened and realistic mind of Panajotis Kavvadias, the eminent Professor of Classics who for so many years ruled the Archaeological Department in the Greek Ministry of Education, and contributed more than anybody else to that spirit of mutual trust and friendship which has produced such fruitful scholarly collaboration between Greek and foreign archaeologists, as well as among the various foreign Archaeological Schools at Athens. If Greece has, for more than half a century, been a model to all countries, in her generous attitude towards their scholars, this is due, next to the almost universal and admirable Hellenic φιλοξενία, to no single person more than to Kavvadias. Perhaps I am the last of those who knew and fully realized the difficulties which beset his path, but never caused him to swerve from it.

When he heard that I was going to Paris and London, in the summer of 1912, he asked me to submit a proposal to two old friends of mine: Émile Pottier, *Conservateur* of Greek and Roman Pottery in the Louvre, and Frederick Kenyon, Director of the British Museum. Both of these leading scholars were justly renowned for their unselfish generosity. Kavvadias and I were confident that they would treat the problems involved with every consideration.

For the Louvre, it seemed a very simple problem. The old French *Expédition de Morée* had, in 1829, brought back fragments of several metopes from the temple of Zeus at Olympia, fruits of a short and necessarily premature excavation. These marbles had been in the Louvre ever since, and when the great German excavations of 1876-1881 recovered many further pieces, plaster casts of the Parisian fragments were used to complete, as far as possible, the metopes in the Olympia Museum. All illustrations are based upon these combinations of marble and plaster.[2]

Kavvadias proposed an exchange. Where the Louvre possessed a major portion, the missing part should be sent from Olympia to Paris, and *vice versâ*. Thus the Louvre would *e.g.* gain the complete relief of the Stymphalian birds, Olympia the complete Cretan bull, and so on. Nothing could be fairer.

As for the Elgin marbles, an exactly similar method could be fol-

---

2. Blouet, Abel, *Expédition de Morée* I, pls. 74-78, cf. 62, 67. *Olympia* III, 138-181, especially 140 ff.

lowed. If the head of a figure in London had been found during the
Greek excavations on the Acropolis, it would be sent to the British
Museum, and *vice versâ*. Apart from various cases concerning the
metopes and frieze of the Parthenon, this solution would have proved
especially beneficent for the statues of the West pediment, most of
all for Athena and Poseidon, whose shattered remnants are distributed between the British Museum and the Acropolis Museum, in a
truly deplorable manner.[3]

Kavvadias asked me to say that as soon as Pottier and Kenyon
had agreed on principle official diplomatic negotiations would be
started by Greece. And he stressed his resolution not to let any suggestions of restitutions or gifts intrude upon those strictly practical
negotiations. When I put in a plea for a return of the Erechtheion
column from the British Museum, he at once turned this down, emphasizing that nothing of the kind should raise the slightest suspicion,
in Paris or London, that an agreement reached would not be final,
might appear as the thin edge of a wedge.

I started for Paris with high hopes; they were promptly dashed to
the ground. With a sharp decisiveness unusual in so courteous and
warmly understanding a man, M. Pottier at once declared that he
could not even submit the Greek proposal to his *Directeur Général,*
or to the Minister concerned. Clear-cut regulations made anything
of the sort absolutely impossible. He himself had encountered great
difficulties when he had tried to get an Attic vase by Sotades, recovered by the French *Délégation en Perse,* from the Persian rooms
of the Louvre to his own part of the great palace, the Gallery of Greek
vases, where other works by Sotades and his colleagues are exhibited.[4]
I could do no more, and bowed silently to such super-bureaucracy,
against which a generous, highminded scholar of world-wide fame
was powerless.

Nor did I fare any better in London. Sir Frederick Kenyon and
his wife, with whom I stayed in their house beside the British Museum, were the friendliest of hosts. But at the first word about my
mission Kenyon cut me short. Nothing could be done or even attempted. The Trustees of the Museum were very sore on a subject
which had repeatedly brought them attacks in the press and individual
expressions of public opinion. Not a single piece could be taken from
the Museum, let alone anything as long and as sharply discussed as
fragments from the Parthenon. All I could do was to drop the subject

3. Smith, A. H., *The Sculptures of the Parthenon.* Prandtl, A., *AM* 33 (1908)
1-16, pls. 1-4. Carpenter, Rhys, *Hesperia* 1 (1932) 1-30; 2 (1933) 1-88.
4. Pottier, E., *CRAI* 1902, p. 428; Louvre, CA 1526. Hoppin, *Blackfigured
Vases,* 475.

and return crestfallen to Greece, where Kavvadias smiled regretfully and closed the chapter of the Elgin marbles and the Olympian metopes.

Forty years will soon have elapsed since then. Conditions have changed, very much for the worse, as far as museums—and everything else—are concerned. One cannot say any longer that those precious relics are safer in London or Paris than in the capital of a small and militarily weak country surrounded by enemies. It is almost a miracle that the treasures of the Museums have escaped the unprecedented ruthlessness of bombing and looting by the Nazis. What even more hideous destruction the future may bring cannot be foreseen, surmises would be futile. One can only devoutly hope that the Acropolis may be spared.

But recent discussions have their importance in another field. The problems of restoring or not restoring ancient monuments have entered a new phrase. Here the Acropolis presents most important evidence of almost every question involved. There can be no doubt that after the establishment of Greek independence it was right and proper to demolish Turkish buildings on the Acropolis, including the mosque within the Parthenon, that Hoffer and Ross did a splendid pioneer job when they cleared the great temple from late encumbrances, removed the Turkish bastions in the West and caused the Propylaea to emerge radiantly from the dismantled XVIIIth century fortifications.[5] Ross earned the finest recompense when the blocks, columns and reliefs of the Nike temple were found almost complete within the southern bastion, and his restoration of the dainty little building, in 1836, remains an amazingly successful first step in a century's successive enterprises.[6] When the Greek architect A. Orlandos had to take the Nike temple to pieces once more, and reerected it, according to the best methods of modern archaeology, only minor mistakes by Ross were discovered and corrected.

From 1837 to 1850 small repairs were made on the ruins of the Parthenon and Erechtheion; they consisted mainly in the removal of unsightly additions in brick. But the ugly brick arch which had defaced the west entrance to the Parthenon, ever since late Roman

---

5. Hoffer, who was the first of all to discover the curvatures of the Parthenon, has apparently been ignored by both earlier and recent writers (including Goessler and Riemann, see below) though W. H. Goodyear had repaired this injustice in his *Greek Refinements* (1912), nearly forty years ago. The excavations conducted by W. Kolbe and the architect A. Tschira in 1938 have proved that similar curvatures already appear in the foundations of the earlier Parthenon, begun, but soon abandoned, under Themistokles or Kimon. See Kolbe, *JDAI* 51 (1936) 1 ff.; *Forsch. u. Fortschr.* 1939, 393 f., 427 f. Tschira, *AA*, 1939, 38 ff. Riemann, H., *Antike* 16 (1940) 142-154.

6. Ross-Schaubert-Hansen, *Der Tempel d. Athena Nike*, 1838. Orlandos, A. K., *AM* 40 (1915) 27 ff. Cf. Goessler, P., *Ephemeris* 1937, 69-82.

times, was retained and extensively repaired in 1872. It is fortunate that no funds were available for costly reconstructions during what may be called the Viollet-le-Duc period.

A new epoch set in with the new century: Nikolaos Balanos, the leading archaeological architect of Greece, commenced his comprehensive program of restoring the Acropolis. What he did for the Erechtheion (1902-1909) and even more successfully for the Propylaea (1908-1912, 1915-1917) is too well known to need discussion here.[7] Hardly any new blocks were used, and the reconstructions were so soberly restrained that informed and fairminded observers could not fail to approve of them. Both buildings had been vastly improved without irritating effects of modernity.

As for the Parthenon, on which Balanos had worked, so to speak in a minor key, between 1898 and 1902, the great lintel block of concrete substituted for the Roman brick arch gave the great western portal so much of its old stately dignity that the whole ruin seemed transfigured here. Thus all but the impenitent adversaries of any restoration accompanied Balanos' efforts with high hopes.

But here a curious experience was in store for us. At first we greeted the rebuilding of the northern colonnade which seemed to promise a far more complete appearance of the great temple. And this promise is actually fulfilled in a three-quarter view from the West: the overlapping columns add to the plastic impression. But as one walks along the colonnade, this impression is destroyed by a contrary one. Where the cella wall is missing the columns seem aimlessly to stand in a vacuum, the cubic mass of the building dissolves before one's eyes. This is not due to any lack of skill or conscientious endeavor on the architect's part. Balanos had lived with and for the Parthenon for many years, and his great book[8] shows how meticulously he studied, and tried to reproduce, the infinite delicacy with which perfect harmony had been obtained, by minutest deviations from the exact regularity of a normal temple. He was so familiar with every detail that he could actually visualize the ancient aspect of the whole. But, with such important parts missing, and the impos-

---

7. Karo, "Denkmalpflege a.d. Akropolis," *Antike* 4 (1928) 66-84. My wholehearted approval, even of Balanos' work on the Parthenon, is tempered in my later reports and finally replaced by warnings which the International Congress for the Preservation of Monuments of 1932 echoed on the Acropolis itself. Cf. *AA* 1919, 315 ff.; 1925, 309 ff.; 1932, 104; 1933, 192, and especially 1934, 124; 1936, 94 f. They reflect the natural evolution of such problems during a generation, as well as the irresistible lure to do too much to which almost all restoring architects gradually succumb.

8. *Les monuments de l' Acropole*, Paris, 1938, 147 plates 20 folded diagrams. It remains the foundation of detailed knowledge concerning the structure and the refinements of the Parthenon.

sibility of even closely approaching the unrivalled refinements of the Parthenon, in modern workmanship, in an inferior material like concrete, the supreme harmony is broken, as if pages of a perfect symphony score had been torn out. And this disappointing result was increased when Balanos replaced by concrete casts the two southern figures of the East pediment, Helios and Dionysos. It was to have been an experiment, but the scaffolding was taken down and funds were not available for either reerecting it, or for protecting the West frieze by a glass roof, one of the most urgent measures of conservation. We may hope that in the course of a tidying-up, which the Acropolis needs after the years of terror, both these desiderata will be fulfilled and that American help will not fail here, just as it contributed to Nicolaos Balanos' best endeavors.

NIKE

A tremor of life flits by,
  The marble feels a thrill,
The sleeping Victories awake—
  Their wings with rapture fill;

They lace their sandals light,
  Soft-fluttering robes they bind;
For some far distant flight
  They spread their wings to the wind.

George Drosines

Translated by
John B. Edwards

PERSONIFICATION OF CLOUDS

MARGARETE BIEBER
Columbia University

Plate 44

During the American excavations in the Athenian Agora in 1934, T. Leslie Shear discovered in a well, cut in the rock below the east front of the Hephaistion, the body of a woman carrying another on her back (pl. 44). Then in 1936 he found in a well on the Hephaistion plateau the head of a woman which fitted this group.[1] Shear suggested at once the temple as its provenience. Homer A. Thompson, in his recent ingenious reconstruction of the east pediment of the temple, declares the group to be the acroterion from the east front of the temple.[2] While this is possible, his interpretations as two Hesperides, who hand down an apple to Herakles, standing before Zeus in the pediment, is open to serious doubt.

Acroteria on the roofs of archaic and classical temples, as far as they are preserved, represent single figures or groups which belong in the air and to whom it is therefore natural to appear above the roofs: Gorgo, the symbol of thunder, Nike, the victory sent down from Olympos by Zeus; Zeus carrying Ganymede to Olympos, in the terracotta group found in Olympia;[3] the Dioscouri, being representations of stars, abducting the daughters of Leukippos, on the Nereid monument;[4] Eos, the dawn, carrying away Kephalos, and Boreas, the north wind, carrying away Oreithyia, on the temple of the Athenians at Delos.[5] The Aurae or breezes of Epidauros, the salubrious winds helping Asklepios in his miraculous cures, are also appropriate.[6] The Hesperides are indeed the daughters of Hesperos, the evening star,

---

1. Shear, T. L., "The American Excavations in the Athenian Agora, Twelfth Report," *Hesperia* 6 (1937) 376 ff., Fig. 42; id. in *AJA* 40 (1936) 409.

2. Thompson, Homer, *Hesperia* 18 (1949) 241 ff., Pls. 53-55.

3. Kunze, E., *Hundertstes Winckelmannsprogramm der archäologischen Gesellschaft zu Berlin*, 1940, colored frontispiece and Pls. I-X.

4. Smith, A. H., British Museum *Catalogue of Sculpture* II p. 40. Picard, Ch., *Manuel d'archéologie grecque, La Sculpture*, Période classique III, 1, p. 859 f., Fig. 345. Charbonneaux, J., *La Sculpture grecque classique* Pl. 41. Picard rightly gives a question mark to the explanation "Peleus abducting Thetis."

5. Courby, F., *Exploration de Délos* XII (1931) Pl. XXVII; Appendix on acroteria p. 237 ff., Figs. 270 f. Picard, *op. cit.*, II, 2, 789 ff., Figs. 316 f.

6. Athens, National Museum, Nos. 156-7. Staïs, V., *Marbres et Bronzes* I, 40, No. 157. Kavvadias, *Fouilles d'Épidaure*, 20 f., Pl. VIII, Figs. 2-3; Pl. XI, Figs. 16-17. Defrasse and Lechat, *Épidaure*, 174 f. Charbonneaux, *op. cit.*, Fig. 62. Brunn-Bruckmann, *Denkmäler*, Pl. 19 and text to Pl. 648, Figs. 4-6 (head). Neugebauer, K. A., in *Arch. Jahrb.* 41 (1926) 89 ff. Richter, G., *Sculpture and Sculptors of the Greeks*, 104 and 277, Figs. 710 ff.

but they belong in the garden on an island in the middle of the ocean from which Herakles has to bring the apples. That they pluck them on a roof and hand them down to Herakles, who holds them already in his hand in a metope on the east façade and has already brought them to Zeus in the pediment, seems unlikely to me. The korai of the temple of Aegina stand indeed under what may be interpreted as a stylized tree, but the composition of palmettes and scrolls here is just a finial, as on so many tomb stelae, and not an actual plant.

The date of the group has been assumed by Shear as well as by Thompson to be the same as the architecture, friezes, and pediments, that is about 450-440 B. C. I believe that it belongs to the same period as the cult statues of Hephaistos and Athena made by Alkamenes in 421-416 according to the inscription,[7] just as in Olympia the cult statue of Zeus by Phidias and the acroterion by Paionios were later than the sculptural decoration of the temple.

I believe that the group represents the personification of Clouds. Shortly before, in 423 B. C., Aristophanes presented his *Clouds* in the theater of Dionysos at Athens. The title is taken from the chorus, consisting of clouds in the guise of women, daughters of the ether, that is the air (v. 570). They come down to Athens from the Parnes mountain (v. 323). They live near the peaks of snow-covered mountains (v. 269), and they look over the earth just as from the Hephaistion they can look over the surrounding territory, and they praise the temples, cult statues, and festivals of Athens (v. 300 ff.). They pretend that they, not Zeus, bring thunder, lightning, and rain, thus blessings for men and fruit of the field; and therefore the honors given to Zeus ought to come to them (v. 576 ff.). Like Nike they come from Zeus, and therefore fit very well on the roof instead of the usual acroterion. They are called great goddesses and heavenly clouds (v. 316) and they can take all kind of forms (v. 346 ff.). Clouds crowded together can indeed take all kind of forms, also such a one as we have in the Athenian group.

It seems that personified clouds were a popular belief used by Aristophanes and by the master of the Hephaistion acroterion. The water which their rain brings is very necessary not only for the gardens around the Hephaistion, discovered by Dorothy Thompson, but also for the artisans who had their foundries and potteries around this temple of the god and goddess of handicraft. It supplements the fire provided by Hephaistos.

Picard has given to the group a different explanation, as Demeter and Kore.[8] It is not likely that the goddess would be represented on

7. Sauer, B., *Das Theseion*, 233 ff.
8. Picard, *op. cit.*, II, 2, 716 f., Fig. 290.

the roof carrying her daughter back from Hades to Eleusis. One might also think of the individual cloud, Nephele, carrying her daughter Helle in order to save her from the stepmother Ino.[9] Indeed, the only representation of Nephele in art known to me is on a vase signed by Asteas, on which Phrixos and Helle flee over the sea on the ram while their mother Νεφέλη, appears from the hips up out of the clouds as a woman in chiton and a small mantle which she is spreading out with her left hand as if to shield her children.[10] As there is Dionysos on the other side, and sea creatures below in a rather grotesque appearance, this may be a tragicomedy Helle, based on a tragedy with the same name, mentioned by Aristotle, *Poet.* 14 p. 1454 a 8. As, however, both women in the Athenian group are of the same size and apparently of the same age, I do not believe that we have here any mother and daughter, but two equals.

Homer Thompson has convincingly shown that the group of the Hephaistion as well as the many fourth century and Hellenistic marble and terracotta groups with a similar motif cannot represent the game Ephedrismos, the name generally given to them. But there are other similar games, which can explain at least the small groups. Among the different games, where the defeated has to carry the victor, who sat on him as on a horse, ἱππαστὶ καίθζειν,[11] the one best fitted for the groups is "night or day" (νὺξ ἢ ἡμέρα) or ostrakinda.[12] This game is first mentioned in Aristophanes, *Knights* (v. 855), and is described by lexicographers and scholiasts. Two groups of players form in different camps at a line; over this a disk is thrown with one of its sides black and the other white. The party whose color does not show has lost and must flee, the other pursuing it. Whoever is caught becomes a donkey (ὄνος) and has to carry his captor on his back. As the other name "night or day" implies a quick change of fate from dark to light, the group of the Hephaistion may have had a similar idea behind its outer form. Dawn bringing refreshing dew in the morning, Eos and Pandrosos, as on the corselet of the statue of Augustus of Prima Porta, might be a possible interpretation.

Perhaps the scholar, whose seventieth birthday we celebrate, may be able to lighten this rather cloudy explanation with the brilliance of his intellect.

---

9. Friedländer, P., in *RE*, VIII, p. 159-163, s.v. Helle. Göber, W., *ibid.*, XVI, p. 2490, s.v. Nephele.

10. Naples. Mus. No. 3412. Reinach, Salomon, *Répertoire des Vases* I, 498, 2. Patroni, G., "La Ceramica nell'Italia meridionale," *Atti della Accademia di Napoli*, 19 (1897-8) 44, fig. 34. Trendall, A. D., *Paestan Pottery*, 34 f., Pl. VI b.

11. Hug, *RE*, III A, 2 (1929), 1765 ff.

12. Scholia to Plato, *Phaidros* 241 B and *Rep.*, VII, 521 C. Pollux IX, 111 f. Forbes, C. A., in *RE*, XVIII, 2 (1942), p. 1673, s.v. Ostrakinda.

ZU KALAMIS

HERBERT A. CAHN
Basel

Tafeln 42-43

Die oben abgebildete unscheinbare Bleistatuette befindet sich in Basler Privatbesitz und stammt aus dem Pariser Kunsthandel. Das Stück ist 51 mm hoch. Dargestellt ist ein nackter Jüngling, der auf den Schultern einen Widder trägt — der Kopf des Tieres erscheint über der linken Schulter, die linke Hand hält Vorder- und Hinterbeine zusammen. Die Hinterbeine des Widders sind quer über die Brust des Mannes gelegt. Seine Rechte hängt frei herunter, ein Bohrloch darin zeigt an, dass er einen stabähnlichen Gegenstand hielt. Trotz der Kleinheit der Statuette ist die Ponderierung deutlich, besonders in der Rückansicht ist das linke Bein als Standbein, das rechte als Spielbein markiert. Die Füsse fehlen. Eine Bohrung in den Unterschenkeln scheint modern zu sein, die Statuette ist ein Vollguss. Nach dem Guss ist sie nur flüchtig bearbeitet worden. Gesicht und breite Haarkappe sind nicht ziseliert. Die Schädeldecke ist abgeplattet. Kleine antike Einhiebe bemerkt man am Hinterkopf, am rechten Oberarm und an beiden Unterschenkeln; eine moderne Verletzung hat die linke Hand getroffen. Beide Beine sind durch die Einhiebe ein wenig verdreht worden. Eine dicke gelblich-graue Patina bedeckt die Figur, an einigen beriebenen Stellen tritt die ursprüngliche Bleifarbe hervor.

Das Figürchen ist griechische Arbeit; grosszügig, ohne kleinliches Detail, auf die Grundformen konzentriert. Leben durchpulst die Gelenke und Muskeln, es gibt dem kleinfingergrossen Stück eine geradezu monumentale plastische Kraft, wie sie nur griechischer Kleinkunst eigen ist.

Griechische Bleifiguren sind selten. Sehen wir von den archaischen Bleireliefs ab, die in der Peloponnes, namentlich in Sparta in Massenproduktion hergestellt wurden,[1] so hat die Forschung wenig Notiz von Bleifiguren genommen. An rundplastischen Exemplaren aus griechischer Zeit notierte ich nur einen spätarchaischen Silen aus Olympia, einen hochklassischen Hermes aus Marzabotto, sowie eine Reihe von Bleifigürchen, wohl vom 6.-3. Jahrhundert, die aus Klein-

---

[1]. Dawkins, *Artemis Orthia*, passim. Der Vollständigkeit halber seien noch die bleiernen Verwünschungsfigürchen meist italischer Abstammung genannt. Vgl. Nogara, *Ausonia* 4 (1910), 31ff. Dugas *BCH* 39 (1915), 413.

asien stammen und mit der Sammlung Gaudin ins Louvre kamen.[2]
Manche Stücke mögen nicht publiziert sein, weil sie schwer klassier-
bar sind. Unser Widderträger ist nicht die einzige Bleifigur in Basel:
das Historische Museum besitzt eine winzige hochklassische Frauen-
figur,[3] und Frau Prof. Pfuhl-Rhousopoulos ein köstliches Fragment
einer stehenden weiblichen Statue aus dem späten 7. Jahrhundert.
Gewiss is das leicht verderbliche Metall öfter plastisch verwendet
worden als wir wissen, sein tiefer Schmelzpunkt, seine Geschmeidig-
keit, die plastische Dichte und Präzision seiner Oberfläche haben ja
Goldschmiede und Medailleure der italienischen und deutschen Renaissance dazu geführt, sich vorzugsweise des Bleis für Modelle und
unziselierte Güsse zu bedienen. Die Bleioriginale eines Pisanello, eines
Peter Flötner geben die Gussform und damit die künstlerische Intention ihrer Meister am getreusten wieder.

Es bedarf keiner Erklärung, wenn wir unseren kleinen originalen
Widderträger in die Zeit um 470-460 ansetzen. Mit diesem Ansatz ver-
bindet sich sogleich die Frage, ob ein Zusammenhang mit dem Hermes
Kriophoros des Kalamis besteht. Bekanntlich hat Kalamis, mit Myron,
Onatas, Hageladas und Pythagoras in der antiken Literatur als füh-
render Meister der Bildhauergeneration vor Phidias genannt, zwei
Werke für die Stadt Tanagra geschaffen: einen Dionysos und einen
Hermes Kriophoros. Die Tätigkeit eines so grossen Meisters für
eine so kleine böotische Stadt und sein Ammon, den er im Auftrag
Pindars für Theben schuf, haben verschiedene Forscher dazu be-
wogen, in Kalamis einen Böoter zu sehen. Ueberliefert ist über seine
Heimat nichts.[4] Ueber die Aufstellung des Hermes gibt Pausanias
(IX 22, 2) ausführlich Bericht. Die Darstellung des Gottes mit dem
Widder auf den Schultern knüpft an einen alten Lokalmythos an,
nach welchem der widdertragende Hermes, die Mauern der Stadt
umschreitend, Tanagra vor einer Seuche bewahrt haben sollte. Sie
entspricht auch einem kathartischen Ritus: der schönste Jüngling
der Stadt ging als Kriophoros beim Hermesfeste um die Mauern.
Vom Aussehen des Kultbildes geben uns Bronzemünzen der Kaiserzeit eine sehr unvollkommene Vorstellung.[5] Wir können gerade nur

2. Olympia, IV, 69 (T. IX); Hermes Marzabotto: Montelius, *Civilisation primitive* pl. 110, 1; De Ridder, *Bronzes ant. du Louvre* II 195, 3742ff.

3. Inv. 1906/782. J. J. Bernoulli, *Cat. des Antiquariums* (1880) p. 190, 1090.

4. Studniczka, F., *Kalamis* (*Abh.Sächs. Ges.* 25/4), 1907. Furtwängler, *Sitz-
Ber.Bayr. Ak.* 1907, 160. Anti, *Atti Ist.Veneto* 82 (1923), 1105ff. W. Amelung,
JdI 41 (1926), 247. Ch. Picard, *Manuel* II 1, 45. Zum Kriophoros: Svoronos,
Journ.int.num. 16 (1914), 71.

5. Drei verschiedene Stücke — alle Unica — sind bekannt:
a. British Museum, *BMC Central Greece* p. 64, 51, pl. X, 12. Studniczka,
Kalamis, T.6 b 1. Head, *Num.Chron.* 1881, pl. XIII, 14. Imhoof-Blumer and
Gardner, *Numismatic commentary* pl. X, xi (Áv. Pansbüste).

erkennen, dass der Gott unbekleidet und unbärtig war, und dass wie
auf unserer Bleistatuette der Widderkopf auf der linken Körperseite
neben dem Kopf des Gottes hervorlugte. Der Widderträger des Museo
Barracco,[6] einzig erhaltene statuarische Kopie eines frühklassischen
Kriophoros, wurde von Studniczka und nach ihm von Langlotz als
Wiedergabe des Hermes von Tanagra angesehen. Doch schon Helbig
äusserte Bedenken, die von V. H. Poulsen mit guten Gründen bestärkt
wurden: er hält das harte, starre, archaisierende Werk für grossgriechisch. Jedenfalls hat es nichts von der vielgerühmten λεπτότης
und χάρις (Dion. Hal. *de Isocrate* p. 522) des Kalamis und verun-
klärt das nur in Umrissen erkennbare Bild des Meisters völlig. Fällt
also der Kriophoros Barracco ausser Betracht, so müssen wir uns nach
anderen frühklassischen Widderträgern umsehen. Der wichtigste ist
eine wenig beachtete frühklassische Originalbronze der Sammlung
Sabouroff, deren Bedeutung Furtwängler erkannte.[7] Leider ist sie im
Katalog Sabouroff nur mit einer schlechten Zeichnung publiziert.
Diese Bronze stimmt nun in mancher Beziehung mit unserem Bleifigürchen überein: der Gott hat eine gesenkte Rechte, für die Furtwängler ein Kerykeion annahm. Ein Kerykeion in der rechten Hand
der Bleistatuette ist im höchsten Grade wahrscheinlich. Beide Figuren
sind unbärtig, auf beiden liegt ein breiter Haarwulst über der Stirn.
Verschieden ist die Haltung des linken Armes, der bei der Bronze
über der Mitte der Brust des Gottes die Hinterbeine des Widders
hält, während er bei der Bleifigur Vorder- und Hinterbeine des Tieres
ergriffen hat und nach unten abgewinkelt ist. Die Zeichnung erlaubt
leider nicht, das Standmotiv der Bronze Sabouroff zu beurteilen; das
linke Bein war jedenfalls vorgestellt, unklar bleibt, ob eines der Beine
stärker belastet war als das andere.

Es ist hier nicht der Ort, um die ganze sehr vielfältige und nicht
leicht zu deutende Ueberlieferung der griechischen Kriophoroi zu

b. Berlin ex Imhoof-Blumer. Studniczka, *ibid.*, T.6, b2 Imhoof-Blumer, *ibid.*,
pl. X, xii (Av. Büste des Poimandros)

c. Berlin ex Prokesch-Osten. Studniczka, *ibid.*, T.6, b3 (Av. Appollonkopf).

Details sind auf allen drei Stücken kaum zu erkennen. Münzen des Sept.
Severus von Aegina zeigen einen ganz analogen Kriophoros, nur mit dem Widderkopf links (Imhoof-Blumer *ibid.*, pl. L, v). Münzen der Plautilla von Aegina haben
aber einen schreitenden, bärtigen Kriophoros (*ibid.*, pl. L, vi). Dies Beispiel
allein zeigt, mit welcher Vorsicht die kaiserzeitlichen Münzen benutzt werden
sollten.

6. Helbig, *Coll. Barracco* pl. 31, 31a. *Cat.Museo Barracco* 83. Helbig-Amelung
3. Aufl. 1111. Studniczka, *loc. cit.* S.73. Langlotz, *Bildhauerschulen* 50; 174; 181
Anm. 40. W. Amelung, *JdI* 41 (1926), 285. V. H. Poulsen, *Acta Arch.* 8 (1937),
142. Hier anzuschliessen sind etruskische Bronze-Kriophoroi wie *BMC Bronzes*
555 (pl. XIII).

7. Furtwängler, *Slg. Sabouroff* II T.146 (kam nicht in das Berliner Antiquarium).

besprechen. Nur auf einige Typen sei kurz eingegangen.[8] Ein Torso von Korinth und eine Statuette in Wilton House sind Kopien der gleichen Statue: der bärtige Gott steht streng frontal, von seinen Schultern hängt eine Chlamys zu beiden Seiten herunter. Jede Hand hält ein Beinpaar des Widders — nur dessen über der rechten Schulter auftauchender Kopf unterbricht die Symmetrie. Verwandt ist das Relief eines archaistischen Tron-Untersatzes in Athen, auf welchem Hermes in der Linken dazu noch ein Kerykeion hält. Hinter den drei Werken steht vielleicht ein echt archaisches Kultbild.[9] Diese Gruppe steht natürlich in keinem Zusammenhang mit dem Hermes des Kalamis und kann wie der Kriophoros Barracco aus der Diskussion ausscheiden.

Genauer müssen wir uns die Terrakotta-Widderträger ansehen, da sie meist aus Böotien stammen.[10] Von den bei Winter abgebildeten Typen ist keiner früher als das 2. Drittel des 5. Jahrhunderts. Nur der späteste von ihnen, wohl schon aus dem 4. Jahrhundert, zeigt den Gott völlig nackt; die übrigen hier in Betracht kommenden Stücke, davon drei aus Tanagra selbst, haben die gleiche symmetrische Armhaltung wie die Typen Barracco und Korinth-Wilton; diese Kriophoroi sind unbärtig, tragen einen Pileus und eine lange, von den Schultern herabfallende Chlamys; der Widderkopf erscheint bald auf der linken, bald auf der rechten Körperseite. Gerade die böotischen Exemplare sind von sehr einfacher Faktur; Stand- und Spielbein ist bei keinem deutlich. Der Mantel diente dazu, den Rücken mit dem Brennloch ganz flach zu halten, was man oft an böotischen Terrakotten beobachten kann.

Schliesslich sei noch der Torso und Kopf eines hochklassischen Kriophoros, im Liebighaus in Frankfurt, erwähnt, mir nur durch die Umrisszeichnung in Reinach's Répertoire bekannt. Ein kleines Fragment in Korinth mag eine Replik des gleichen Werkes sein, auf das vielleicht die statuarische Fassung des "guten Hirten" zurückzuführen ist.[11]

---

8. Die von Furtwängler sehr abschätzend beurteilte Materialsammlung von Veyries, *Les figures criophores*, war mir leider nicht zugänglich.

9. Korinth: *Corinth* 9 (The Sculptures), p. 28, 21.

Wilton House: Kriophoros aus Slg. Mazarin und Pembroke. Michaelis, *Ancient Marbles* 702, 144. Clarac, IV, pl. 658, 1545 b.

Tron Athen: Svoronos I pl. 23, 54 (p. 97). Hauser, *Neuatt. Reliefs* p. 170. Papaspyridi, *Guide* p. 41.

Eine Münze der Julia Domna von Sikyon, Svoronos, *Journ.int.num.* 16 (1914), 76 gibt ein ähnliches Kultbild wieder, das auf dieser Darstellung zwischen zwei hochklassischen Frauenfiguren erscheint.

10. Winter, *Figürl.Terrakotten* I 180. Robinson, *Olynthus*, IV, 58-59 no. 337; VII, 70 no. 260.

11. Frankfurt: Reinach *Rép.* 4, 97, 4. (Laut brieflicher Mitteilung hält Herr Prof. G. von Kaschnitz - Weinberg die Figur für einen Eberträger.)

Korinth: *Corinth*, 9, p .29, 22.

Ueberblicken wir die hier aufgezählten Widderträger und fragen uns, welche wohl am ehesten ein statuarisches Original der frühen Klassik wiedergeben, so drängt sich sogleich die Bronze Sabouroff und unser Bleifigürchen auf. Gewiss können wir keine der beiden als genaue Abbilder verstehen: es sind zeitgenössische Werke der Kleinkunst, die ein berühmtes Kultbild höchstens widerspiegeln. Was aber eine gleichzeitige Schöpfung der Kleinkunst getreuer verkörpern kann als die trefflichste römische Kopie, ist die plastische Struktur. Und in dieser Beziehung scheint mir die Bleifigur in Proportion und Ponderation mehr von einer Monumentalplastik zu haben als die gleichzeitige Bronze: diese geht wohl vom gleichen Vorbild aus, verarbeitet es jedoch selbständiger, d.h. unabhängiger von der Grossplastik und mehr in der Tradition schreitender Bronzejünglinge. Die Bleistatuette aber spricht eine plastische Sprache von besonderer Eigenart. Die linke Körperseite ist durch das Standbein, durch den Akzent des linken Armes, der die Beine des Tieres zusammenhält, und durch den Widderkopf stark betont, die rechte Seite wird durch Spielbein, gesenkte Rechte und den herabhängenden Schwanz des Widders entlastet. Besonders die Rückansicht drückt diese Gewichtsverteilung deutlich aus, in der Parallelität linker Arm — linker Oberschenkel, rechter Unterarm — rechter Unterschenkel. Denken wir an die symmetrische Gestalt des archaischen Widderträgers, so erfassen wir hier erst recht die durchgreifende Erneuerung, die Originalität des Motivs. Der nackte Götterjüngling, der ein Tier auf den Schultern trägt, war als Thema wie geschaffen, um die neue Auffassung der klassischen Plastik von Belastung und Entlastung, vom organischen Kräftespiel eines ruhigen und doch bewegten Körpers Gestalt werden zu lassen.

So verkörpert unser Hermes eine Entwicklungsstufe zwischen dem Kritiosknaben und dem polykletischen Kanon. Von dieser Bestimmung ausgehend, gewinnt die Vermutung an Wahrscheinlichkeit, dass die Bleifigur unter dem Eindruck des Hermes Kriophoros des Kalamis entstanden sei. Man wird sogleich einwenden, dass weder die Münzen von Tanagra noch die besprochenen böotischen Tonfiguren die Vermutung stützen. Münzen und Terrakotten sind zwar auch unter sich verschieden, denn die Münzen zeigen den Gott völlig nackt und ohne Kopfbedeckung. Doch gemeinsam ist ihnen der symmetrisch-frontale Aufbau, namentlich in Armen und Beinen. Nach meiner Meinung darf aber der Quellenwert der schlecht erhaltenen, vereinfachenden, späten Münzen nicht überschätzt werden. Und die schlichten Tonfiguren sind wie so oft von einem archaischen Schema abhängig, das nur äusserlich erneuert ist.

Gewiss kann unsere Bleifigur nicht als Angelpunkt zum Verständnis von Kalamis bewertet werden, zu dessen Oeuvre bisher eine feste Ausgangsbasis fehlte. Aber gerade weil die Vorstellung von diesem hochberühmten Meister bisher so dunkel war, darf man selbst an einem so unscheinbaren Dokument nicht vorbeigehen.

Zum Schluss sei die Frage zur Diskussion gestellt, wie sich unser Kriophoros zum Omphalos-Apollon verhält. Die Zuschreibung dieses offenbar in der Antike berühmten Werkes ist in letzter Zeit wieder viel erörtert worden. Kaum ein Name der Bildnergeneration vor Phidias fehlt bei diesen Attributionen: Kalamis wird am meisten genannt.[12] Verglichen mit Jünglingsfiguren der Zeit um 460 — etwa den Bronzeknaben von Adernò und Liguriò, dem Diskophoren und dem Adoranten in New York, dem Apollon Béarn,[13] dem Eros Soranzo, dem Kasseler Apollon und dem Omphalos-Apollon, rückt unser Hermes in den Umkreis Athens. Der Omphalos-Apollon hat mit der Bleifigur wesentliche Elemente gemeinsam: die Belastung der einen, die Entlastung der anderen Körperseite sowie die fliessende Schlankheit des Körperbaus. Das erstere Prinzip gilt gewiss auch für den Apollon Béarn, bei welchem wie bei der Bleifigur und wie beim Omphalos-Apollon Arme und Oberschenkel jeder Körperseite parallel gestellt sind. Doch wie anders ist diese peloponnesische Bronze gebaut — straffer, härter, mit mehr Staccato in Umriss und Gelenken. Die Möglichkeit, dass hinter dem Omphalos-Apollon und der Bleifigur des Hermes Kriophoros Originalwerke des gleichen Meisters stehen, bleibt nur eine Vermutung. Die Bleifigur selbst als Reflex des Kriophoros des Kalamis mag als Beitrag zu dem schwer fassbaren Oeuvre des Meisters Geltung behalten.[14]

---

12. Kalamis: Conze, *Beiträge zur Gesch. der griech.Plastik*, 13. Furtwängler *Meisterwerke* 115. Langlotz, *Bildhauerschulen* 174. Amelung, *JdI* 41 (1926) 247. Homann-Wedeking, *RM* 55 (1940), 196. Buschor, *Phidias der Mensch*, 89.
    Onatas: Lippold, *Phil.Woch.* 1930, 139. Pfeiff, *Apollon* 159, Anm. 273.
    Myron: V. H. Poulsen, *Acta Arch.* 11 (1940), 4.
    Kanachos: Beyen-Vollgraff, *Argos et Sicyone* 86ff.
13. Bronze Adernò (Syrakus) Langlotz, *Bildhauerschulen* T.89, 90. Lamb, *Greek and Roman Bronzes* pl. LVI a.
    Bronze Liguriò (Berlin): Langlotz T.27 c. Lamb pl. LII a.
    Diskophor New York: Langlotz T.9, 52. Lamb pl. LII d.
    Adorant New York: Langlotz T.88. Lamb pl. LVI b.
    Apollon Béarn, Paris: Langlotz T.6. Pfeiff, Apollon T.30. Von Lusoi, Arkadien.
14. Für Hinweise und Anregung habe ich Herrn Prof. K. Schefold aufrichtig zu danken.

ATTIC BRONZE MIRRORS

SEMNI PAPASPYRIDI KAROUZOU
National Museum, Athens

Plates 45-53

In the many studies, old and new, that deal with Greek bronze mirrors the student of today will seek in vain for any attempt to isolate examples showing Attic characteristics and to group such examples as the product of an Attic school.[1] This indifference to Attic mirrors may seem an injustice, for many mirrors have with success been attributed to the various Peloponnesian centers of bronze work, and even to those of Southern Italy. When we recall the many representations of women holding mirrors on Attic funerary stelai and on red-figured vases, and also the mirrors which on these monuments are represented suspended on walls, we might feel justified in maintaining that silence on the subject of the bronze originals is inexcusable. In all fairness, however, we should note that this silence is not without a reason. The mirrors seen on Attic monuments belong to the common type of hand mirror with simple decoration, and scholars with reason are interested in the beautiful stand mirrors, whose discs are supported by a female figure. These stand mirrors, however, are in the main the products of the Peloponnesian and especially of the Laconian, Argive, and Corinthian workshops.[2] We may none the less

---

1. General Bibliography:
Mylonas, K., *AZ* 1875, 161 pl. 14; *Ephemeris* 1884, 78 pl. 6, 4-5.
Michon, *Mon. grecs*, 1891-2, 1 ff.
Dumont-Chaplain, *Céramique de la Gr.propre*, 2, 242 ff.
De Ridder, *BCH* 1898, 201-233.
Praschniker, *OJ* 15 (1912) 219 ff.; 18 (1915) 57 ff.
Franck, *AA* 1923-24, 373-5.
Lamb, W., *Greek and Roman Bronzes*, 159 ff.
Langlotz, *Frühgr. Bildhauerschulen.*
Hambidge-Caskey, *The Diagonal* 1 (1920) 55 ff.
Webster, *JHS* 54 (1934) 207-8; *Memoirs of the Manchester Liter. and Philosoph. Society* 80 (1936) 38-40.
Schefold, *Die Antike* 16 (1940) 11 ff.
Konstantinou, *AA* 1938, 543-552.
Poulsen, *Acta Arch.* 8 (1937) "der Strenge Stil."
Beazley, *Proceedings Irish Academy* 45, 5, p. 31 ff. *AA* 1937, 140-143.
Richter, *AJA* 42 (1938) 337; 46 (1942) 319.
Gjödessen, *Acta. Arch.* 15 (1944) 109.
All the photographs of the mirrors in the National Museum were made by G. Tsimas. I am indebted for the translation to Professor George E. Mylonas.

2. I regret that I have to disagree with Miss Richter and Sir John Beazley who, in their recent articles (cf. note 1), question the Lakonian provenience of some of the mirrors which have been attributed to the Lakonian workshop. Langlotz' Lakonian is one of the workshops that will remain firm: cf. also Gjödessen, *op. cit.*, 154.

remedy somewhat the injustice done to Attic works by the present study which will present a number of mirrors which are with great probability Attic.

A simple hand mirror from Athens, now in Munich, has characteristics so clearly Attic that it can without difficulty be attributed to the Attic school.[3] The decoration of the handle is formed by volutes that alternate with anthemia. This decoration, with its sharp contour lines and elegant curves, exhibits Attic strength and grace.

The provenience of mirror No. 16350 in the National Museum at Athens is certain (pl. 45, drawing by Alex. Kontopoulos). It was found some years ago, along with an alabastron in stone, in a grave near the center of modern Athens, not far from Omonoia Square. Alabastra and mirrors are often found in women's graves; this was almost certainly the grave of a woman, and an Athenian woman. We may recall that the well-known bronze stand mirror from Hermione, now in the Louvre, was found attached by a chain to a bronze alabastron.[4]

The disc of our mirror 16350 is broken at the circumference and bears no decoration on its outer surface. The handle ends above in an Ionic capital the volutes of which are rendered plastically and without the help of incision. A single row of leaves is placed between the capital and the peripheral band of the disc. The handle, not preserved in its original length, was without doubt encased in a cover of wood, bone or ivory. The shape of the handle may not have been especially characteristic, but the capital presupposes a column, and handles in the shape of a column are not unknown.[5] With such column-handles in mind we can restore the mirror as illustrated in our figure 1.

When the mirror stood on a table it must have given the impression of a column supporting the disc. Such a base was sometimes enriched by the addition of a female form, as Neugebauer showed in connection with the well-known "Kanephoros" from Paestum, which he argued must have belonged to a mirror support.[6] It is, however, improbable

---

3. Schefold, *op. cit.*, 30 fig. 24.

4. *Mon. grecs*, 1891-92, 19. Lamb, *op. cit.*, pl. LX, c. Poulsen, *op. cit.*, 18, no. 10.

5. Stackelberg, *Gr. Hell.*, pl. 74. Jantzen, *Bronzew.*, pl 29, p. 66, B 3 cf. the mirror from Turowka: Schefold, "Der Skythische Tierstil in Südrussland," *Eurasia septentrionalis Antiqua* 12, 31, fig. 22. The metallic base of these mirrors has been preserved. The disappearance of the base of mirror 16350 is due to the perishable material, bone or ivory, used in its construction. Züchner (*Klappsp.*, 120) on the occasion recalls the inscription of Brauroneia: *(κά)τοπτρον ἐλεφαντίνην λαβὴν ἔχον πρὸς τῷ τοίχῳ. Ἀριστοδαμία ἀνέθηκεν.*

6. Lamb, *op. cit.*, pl. LI, b. Neugebauer, *Berl. Museen*, 51, 1930, 130. *AA* 1930, 519. Langlotz, *op. cit.*, 104, 18. Jantzen, *Bronzewerkst.* 4, no. 27. Langlotz-Schrader, *Akr.* 34, note 27.

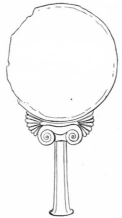

Fig. 1. Mirror No. 16350, restored.

that so over-loaded a support, developed by the Italiote Greeks with their liking for elaboration, would have found favor in Greece proper.

Closely related to our first example, and perhaps the work of the same artist, is a similar mirror in the National Museum at Athens, known from the drawing published years ago by K. Mylonas. His description contained a few sympathetic words: "*Εὐκόλως ἐνορᾷ τις πόσον οἱ Ἕλληνες ἐγνώριζον καὶ εἰς τὰ κατώτερα εἴδη τῆς καλλιτεχνίας, οἷα τὰ κάτοπτρα, νὰ ἐμφυσῶσι ζωὴν οὕτως εἰπεῖν καὶ ἁρμονίαν.*"[7] This mirror was found in Corinth and its provenience induced Payne to incline toward a Corinthian attribution. Not only the spirit of the decoration, however, but also the absence of any relation to other objects of Corinthian workmanship will lead us away from Corinth. We shall discuss later the fifth century type of Corinthian hand mirror that could be considered as parallel to the Attic mirrors illustrated here.

We have no information as to the provenience of our second mirror, illustrated in our plates 46 and 47, b, now in the National Museum at Athens (inventory no. 7683).[8] The main decoration rises above an Ionic capital which finishes the upper part of the handle, a capital so small that it can hardly be distinguished in the photograph. The decoration consists of two large volutes of the "Aeolic" type over which are placed, in a similar manner as in the preceding example, two leaves separated by a triangular space at the centre. These leaves

7. No. 7688. *Ephemeris* 1884, 78, pl. 6, 4. De Ridder, *Br. Soc. Archéol.* 34, no. 135. Payne, *Necrocorinthia*, 247, note 1.

8. *Ephemeris*, 1884, 78, pl. 6, 5. De Ridder, *Br. Soc. Archéol.* 34, no. 135. For the provenience of the type of the handle cf. Andrén, *Opusch. Arch.* 5, 39. Cf. the Acropolis capitals, Raubitschek, *Bull. Inst. Bulg.* 12 (1938) 165 figs. 22-23.

or petals, that suggest palmettes, are not directly attached to the disc, but to a narrow band which is placed between them and the disc. On the back of the mirror, the attachment is effected by means of a triangular leaf prolonged to the disc (pl. 46, after the drawing by Papaeliopoulos). How much more carefully the back is worked is indicated by the concentric circles which decorate the outer face of the disc. On the back, also, close to the top of the disc, faint impressions in the shape of a ring were revealed by the recent cleaning of the mirror. They must be the marks left by the ring by which the mirror could be suspended. The small empty space on the periphery of the mirror (pl. 46) apparently was left for the attachment of this ring.

There are no traces proving the existence of a ring on mirror 16350, and this detail supports the hypothesis that its handle was in the form of a column. On mirror 7683, the capital, reduced to the minimum, has only decorative significance; the ring therefore was indispensable since the disc was not standing on a column, but was to be suspended from the wall. On the other hand, a suspension ring was unnecessary for mirror 16350 where, as we have seen, the craftsman wished to give the impression of a disc supported by a column; that impression would have been destroyed had the disc been provided with a suspension ring.

In spite of the richer appearance of mirror 7683 (pl. 47, b) the work in the volutes and the leaves is less careful. The lines in the interior of the volutes are incised without great care and the broad leaves are separated by grooves drawn in an off-hand manner. The maker of mirror 16350 (pl. 45), from the Athenian grave, took more pains with his work; a feeling of harmony is evident in the softer grooving of the volutes of the capital, which are however, no less fresh and firm because of this. The craftsman did not limit himself to incised lines to indicate the divisions of the leaves but produced these divisions plastically; thus the outer contour line is not sharply abrupt. Were it permissible to employ a classical term for so small a work, we would say, following Riegl's expression, that the decoration of this mirror is "haptisch", in the sense that the full enjoyment of its beauty is impossible without the intervention of touch.

The characteristic Attic use of the capital and the strength and clarity of each line, without any confused softness in the transitions, may help us to collect around this other similar mirrors. Mirror 7683 we would call Attic (pl. 47, b) because of the strength of its decoration. The size of the volutes with their broad empty bands and few revolutions, in general, the simplicity of the volutes and of the sharply opened leaves express a more archaic conception. The melodic contour of the more slender leaves of the first mirror and the more numerous turns of the volutes of the capital, along with the other elements that we have noted already, bring us very near the classical feeling, to the years, let us say, between 450-440 B. C.[9] Mirror 7683, with the "Aeolic" volutes, we may place at the end of the sixth century B. C.

How common this style of mirror was in Attica is indicated by representations on the funerary stelai, and still further by representations on red-figured vases. From among the generally formalized renderings of the vase-painters, the representation on the stamnos by the Eucharides Painter in Copenhagen (pl. 47, a)[10] stands apart. It gives us one of the clearest examples of mirrors we have on vases. The volutes at the upper end of the handle are distinguished clearly, as is also the suspension ring on the upper edge of the periphery of the disc. The type of handle clearly shows that this mirror was not intended to stand; that it was a hand mirror.

The shape of the mirror represented on the stamnos recalls another very similar small example in the Agora Museum. It is made in one piece whereas the mirror on the stamnos is clearly made of two pieces, one for the handle and a second for the disc; here the volutes are turned outwards. It was found, as Miss Virginia Grace kindly informs me, in a grave on Lenormant street in Athens along with black-figured lekythoi by the Haimon Painter, the Emporion Painter and others;[11] it should belong therefore to the years of the battle of Marathon, a time which corresponds well with the date of the stamnos in Copenhagen. We have moreover further confirmation for the prevalence of the shape with the simple volute in late archaic times. The type of mirror illustrated by the Agora specimen is represented with exactitude on two beautiful vases by the Pan Painter (Beazley, *Panmaler*, pl. 15, 2; Feytmans, *Vases Grecs*, pl. XXIII, no. 10).

---

9. The capital of the Italiote mirror with the beautiful, youthful figure represents the immediately preceding phase (*Notizie*, 1913 Supp. 15, figs. 15-16. Buschor, *Olympia*, 39. Jantzen, *op. cit.*, 4, no. 39); the lines connecting the volutes are horizontal and lack the curvatures noticeable on the Athenian mirror. From the figure we can adduce 460 B. C. as the approximate date of the Italiote example. The marble capital of the temple of Athena at Sounium is related to the capital of mirror 16350. (*Ephemeris*, 1917, 184. Weickert, *Archäische Architektur*, 117). Also related to the mirror capital is the one compared by Moebius to the capital from Sounium: *AM* 52 (1927) 170 Beibl. XVIII, 9. Cf. Raubitschek, *Bull. Inst. Bulgare*, 12 (1938) 171 fig. 28-29, and the Ionic capital in Athens, *AM* 55 (1930) 191 ff. (Wrede). On the mirror from Aegina we have a capital of an early Archaic type (*Ephemeris*, 1885, pl. 7. Neugebauer, *Bronzestat.*, fig. 26. Langlotz, *op. cit.*, 99. Schefold, *op. cit.*, 17, figs. 12 and 17).

10. *CV Copenh.* III, Ipl. 134, 1a. Beazley, *ARV* 155, 27. I am indebted to Dr. Niels Breitenstein for the new photograph of the object.

11. For these painters cf. Haspels, *Black-figured Lekythoi*, 130 ff., 165 ff. The attributions of the Agora vases are recorded in the inventories of the Agora Museum.

An amusing example of a similar mirror comes from a Scythian grave (fig. 2).[12] The outward turn of the volutes and the simple shape show so close a relationship to the Attic type that the Athenian origin of this piece is most probable. The local trader corrected the

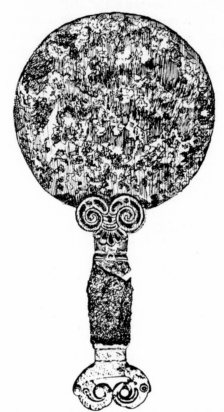

Fig. 2. Mirror from a Scythian grave.

simplicity of the mirror, unbearable to barbaric taste, by adding a golden handle decorated with two animal heads placed antithetically. It is needless to emphasize that the Attic grace, based on the studied proportion between handle, volutes, and disc, was completely ruined. Later on we shall meet with another more complete Scythian metamorphosis of an Attic mirror.

From the examples cited we may conclude that a preference for the Ionic capital to volutes in Attic mirrors begins toward the middle of the fifth century. The type with the Ionic capital, did not, however, enjoy any great popularity either because the capital, presupposing

12. Minns, *Scythians and Greeks*, 191 fig. 83, no. 351 (cf. also pages 65-66).

a column, imposed the form of the stand mirror that was not practical, or because the Ionic capital had become an antiquated form due to its use on monuments of the sixth century. The second half of the fifth century saw, instead, the popularity of the type with the anthemion, a type that we shall now examine.

A mirror handle with engraved ornament, found in the excavations of the "Royal Stables" at Athens, and illustrated in our figure 3, represents an early phase of this type. The volutes have considerable width; the leaves do not as yet show any tendency toward over-refine-

Fig. 3. Fragment of a mirror found in the cemetery of the "Royal Stables," Athens.

ment, nor any outward curve, but preserve the strong $\mathring{\eta}\theta o\varsigma$ characteristic of the anthemia we find on the lekythoi of the Achilles Painter and his contemporaries.[13]

The most important example of the type that is cast in one piece, handle and disc alike, is the heavy, solid mirror 7684 of the National Museum at Athens which, according to the Museum inventory, was found in an Athenian grave (pl. 47, c drawing by Alex. Kontopoulos). On both faces it bears the same decoration: volutes of the "Aeolic" type and between them, at the point where the handle terminates, a lightly engraved anthemion. Beyond the central volutes on either side we find smaller volutes and leaves terminating in an elegant pointed leaf. This decoration is later than the archaic volutes of mirror 7683 (pl. 47, b) and gives the impression that it belongs to the early classical period. To the middle of the fifth century we can likewise assign one of the two mirrors now in foreign collections.[14]

A fourth example we were able to recognize with difficulty below

13. See especially Buschor in *Münchner Jahrb*. 1925, figs. 7, 8, 9, and page 22. Beazley *ARV* 648-9.

14. Orvid Andrén, in *Opusc. Archaeol*. 5, 38, no. 83, pl. XX. The other in Amsterdam: Van Gulick, *Catal. Br. in the Allard Pierson Mus*., pl. 33, no. 148.

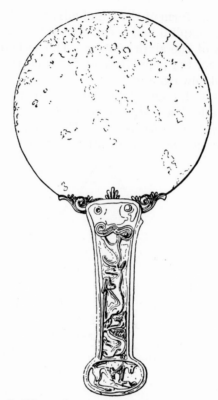

Fig. 4. Mirror from a Scythian grave at Kul Oba.

its heavy Scythian disguise (fig. 4). It was found near a woman's skeleton at Kul Oba.[15] Since the original simple decoration was not considered sufficient to satisfy local taste, the handle of the mirror was embellished with gold leaf crowded with representations. Fortunately this addition did not entirely cover the original decoration; hence the sections of leaves and volutes that can still be seen, like protesting expressive eyes, betray a type of decoration similar to that of the Athenian mirror 7684 (pl. 47, c) It must be recognized that along with the good results of the famous Greek πενία (Herod. VII, 102), it gave birth to forms so difficult to understand outside Greek borders that these forms had to be clothed with golden costumes for the benefit of northern customers. This happened to these Attic mirrors, and in a lesser degree to the red-figured cylix from Klein-Aspergle, in the Stuttgart Museum.[16]

15. *Antiq. Bosp. Cimm.*, 31, 7. Minns, *op. cit.*, 201, fig. 95 (cf. also page 65).
16. Ebert, *Reallexicon für Vorgesch.*, 7, pl. F. Jacobsthal-Langsdorff, *Schnabelk.*, pl. 33. Beazley, *ARV* 551, 18 (the Amymone painter).

The examples enumerated above help to place the Stackelberg mirror, from the Haller Collection, without difficulty among Attic mirrors.[17] This piece brings us to a phase that follows immediately that represented by the handle of figure 3. Another mirror in the National Museum at Athens is only a little later than the Munich mirror, as appears from the anthemion on the handle (pl. 47, d, drawing by Alex. Kontopoulos). The decorative composition instead of being spread lengthwise along the disc, as on the handles of mirrors of an earlier date, has been arranged vertically. The almost vertical volutes, enclosing the anthemion, instead of terminating in leaves that open outwards, acquire extra height by the addition of a second volute. The volutes below the anthemion in mirror 7690 do not protrude as they do in the engraved handle of figure 3 and thus an exceptional elegance is achieved. This characteristic, as well as the narrowness of the volutes, the very slight grooving of the ornament, and the close-set slender leaves of the anthemion bring us to the beginning of the last quarter of the fifth century. We find ourselves near the world of the Eretria Painter where feeling has finally won over ἦθος and over θυμός.[18] The Stackelberg mirror must be placed between the older mirrors and our example 7690; its decoration partakes both of the horizontal and vertical development.

There can be no doubt that the group of these mirrors will become greater since it is only natural that with time many more examples will be recognized as Attic.[19] But it seems rather improbable that Attic hand mirrors enjoyed a significant distribution beyond Attica. The Greek merchants dispatched the two mirrors to the Scythian market rather as companions of Attic vases than because of any special demand, or because of their belief that they would have a magic attraction for the native women. During the entire fifth century the reputation of the Peloponnesian bronze products attracted buyers to that part of the Greek world. It is strange that even in graves in Attica mirrors with decorated handles are not found more often. In the cemetery of the "Royal Stables," near Syntagma Square in Athens, for example, only a few mirrors were found and they were of the

---

17. Cf. *supra*, note 5.

18. Anthemia of the Eretria painter: *JHS*, 1905, pl. VII, 6. Beazley, *ARV* 727, 36, 728, 441. *Mon. Linc.* 24, 883, pl. 5, cf. also the lekythos of the Louvre (Buschor, *Gr. Vasen*, fig. 247. Beazley, *ARV* 832, 8) in *Mon. Grecs*, 1889-90, pl. 9-10. Jacobsthal nevertheless emphasizes the difficulty of a more exact dating of the anthemia on the vase (*Orn.*, 175).

19. Most of the examples cited by Jantzen (*Bronzew.*, 68, nos. 45-53) from workshops of Southern Italy, are distinguished from the "malerisch" conception of the ornament; cf. on the one hand Jacobsthal (pl. 141) (= *Notizie* 1913. Suppl. 31, fig. 35, Lamb, *op. cit.*, 159, fig. 1) and on the other the Attic of our plates. The handles from the Epizephyrian Lokroi that are so near to no. 7690, also exhibit an Italiote feeling. [*AA* 45 (1930) 523, fig. 4 — Neugebauer.]

common type, the disc and the handle cast in one piece and without decoration. This, however, probably indicates a local burial habit, since for the prevalence of mirrors in Athens we have the evidence of fifth century monuments.

Returning to our group of Attic mirrors, we find that we start from our oldest example illustrated in plates 46 and 47, b, proceed to mirrors of the severe style with volutes (the Agora mirror and the vase representations), then to those of the Early Classical period with the Ionic capital (pls. 45 and 47, c) and with the open system of volutes, and conclude with our example of 7690, to be dated about 430 B. C. (pl. 47, d). This last example illustrates a tendency toward reducing the weight of the mirror by shortening the handle and by thinning the disc. The delicate hands of the women of the years of the Peloponnesian war doubtless could not tolerate the older, heavier works of art. These are the years in which the thin Ionic chiton was adopted again because the traditional Doric peplos was found to be too heavy.

The nucleus of the group of Attic mirrors which we have formed can be placed in the following chronological arrangement:

1) Mirror 7683 of the National Museum at Athens. Provenience unknown. *Ephemeris*, 1884, pl. 6, 5. Here, plates 46 and 47, b.

2) The Agora example (Inv. B 475) from Lenormant street. Cast in one piece.

3) Mirror from the Scythian grave. Minns, *Scythians*, 191, fig. 83, 351; cf. pages 65-66. Our figure 2.

4) Mirror 7684 of the National Museum at Athens. From an Athenian grave. Cast in one piece. Our plate 47, c.

5) The example from a Scythian grave at Kul Oba. Minns. *op. cit.*, 202, fig. 95 and p. 65. Probably in one piece. Our figure 4.

6) Mirror in Munich, from Attica, Schefold, *Die Antike*, 16 (1940) 30.

7) Mirror 16350 of the National Museum at Athens. From an Athenian grave. Plate 45.

8) Mirror 7688 of the National Museum at Athens. Similar to No. 7. *Ephemeris*, 1884, pl. 6, 4. De Ridder, *Be. Polyt.*, 34, no. 135. Payne, *Necrocorinthia*, 247, note 1.

9) Handle in the National Museum at Athens. Our figure 3.

10) Mirror in Munich, "aus dem Nachlass der Ex. v. Haller." Stackelberg, *Gr. Hell.* pl. 79. Jantzen, pl. 66, 29; B, 3. Neugebauer, *Berl. Museen* 51 (1930) 136, note 3.

11) Mirror 7690 of the National Museum at Athens. "It was bought from Palaiologos." Our plate 47, d.

Mirror 7706 in the National Museum at Athens (fig. 5) seems to be quite foreign to the Attic tradition. It possesses a flat handle ending below in a rosette, and the transition to the disc is weak, formed by two leaves vaguely traced. A similar mirror now in the National Museum at Athens (No. 15128) was found not far from that Museum along with another, evidently of Attic workmanship, whose handle is in the form of a Siren (National Museum No. 15127. Lamb, *Bronzes*, pl. 60 b). But this circumstance does not force us to believe that mirror 15128 is an Attic work as is the case, most probably, with mirror 15127. On the contrary, the Corinthian provenience of a third mirror

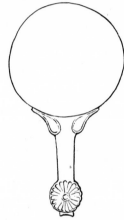

Fig. 5. Mirror 7706 in the National Museum at Athens.

in all respects similar to our examples, with the exception of a hole bored in the centre of the rosette, is not without significance. We meet this type, further, in a simplified form at Perachora (Payne, *Perachora*, pl. 80, 11-14). On the other hand the connection of this group with the archaic mirrors with sculptured handles, collected by Furtwängler and Payne[20] is apparent, as is its connection with the two mirrors from Corinth and Naupactos (*Necrocorinthia* 103 A. B.), dated in the sixth century. But then we have to question whether or not the richly decorated and graceful mirror from Amphanai now in the Volos Museum (*AA* 1932, 158, fig. 28, Jantzen, 67), which is not without relation to mirror 7706, fig. 5, was also made in Corinth. The same could be said for the related but simpler mirror in Munich, with the incised inscription (Jantzen, 67, D 4, pl. 30, 126), and for the fine mirror from Sparta (Lamb, *op. cit.*, 160, fig. 2). The popularity of

20. Furtwängler, *Kleine Schr.* I, 410. Payne, *op. cit.*, 225 ff., figs. 101-102. Cf. Lamb, *op. cit.*, pl. 44 a, c. A very intereseting bond with the last is the undecorated example from Muschowitza Mogila: *JDAI* 45 (1930) 315, figs. 36 and 314, 9.

the type with the rosette among the Peloponnesian workshops is further indicated by similar mirrors from the Argive Heraeum, most probably local imitations of Corinthian works (Waldstein, *Argive Heraeum*, pl. 82, nos. 1560-61 and pls. 93-96).

*   *   *   *   *

Stand mirrors with a female figure instead of a handle, the type developed by Peloponnesian craftsmen, were avoided by the Athenian bronze workers. Because of this it is surprising that a kore belonging to a stand mirror and found on the Acropolis has characteristics so evidently Attic that it was without hesitation attributed to the Attic school (pls. 48 and 50, b).[21] In this figure the left foot is advanced, balancing the right hand, which is extended, holding a flower; in the left hand, which like the right foot is drawn back, the kore holds a pomegranate. The maiden wears a chiton that forms a kolpos, and a light himation falls diagonally across her chest and back. The two ends of the himation, the one in front appearing on the left side and below the slanting line of the cloak and the other behind and over the left shoulder, terminate in beautiful schematized folds (pl. 50, b). On the hem can be seen very refined decorative dots. In the flat parts of the chiton wavy incisions, with a vertical direction, are clearly seen on the chest, the back, and the thighs. At the end of the hair on the shoulders is a row of bead-like curls that strongly differentiates the hair from the shoulders and back over which it falls in tight wavy locks. The ears with the long earrings are not covered by the hair. The craftsman covered the head with a sakkos embroidered with fine linear engraving, to avoid placing the disc of the mirror immediately on top of the head of the maiden.

In spite of the narrowing of the lower part of the body, it is evident that this kore belongs to a later stage than that represented by the archaic korai with legs close together[22] On the other hand it differs so much from the later korai of the Peloponnesian mirrors, that any dependence on them is excluded.[23] And yet the maker of the Athenian kore had in mind a Peloponnesian prototype, and it is worth investigating why he, an Athenian, did not allow himself to copy the prototype without changing it.

---

21. De Ridder, *Br. Acr.*, pl. VII, no. 784. Langlotz-Schrader, *Akrop.*, 80, no. 37. Ashmole, *Greek Sculpture in Sicily and South Italy*, 21, pl. XI, 46. Our photographs were taken after the recent cleaning of the figure.

22. Especially see the Corinthian: Payne, *op. cit.*, 246, 1, 4 and pl. 46 and Schefold, *op. cit.*

23. For the peplophoroi see especially, Langlotz, *op. cit.*, *passim*. Poulsen, *op. cit.*, 16 ff.; cf. Schefold, *op. cit.*, 30 ff.

Beazley has recently published with excellent illustrations the bronze Kore 7464 in the National Museum at Athens (pls. 50, a and 51, a) and has compared her with a similar one, a sister kore, now in Dublin.[24] The stance of this kore, the kind of drapery she is wearing, the projection of the hands, even the vertical folds between the legs, show such close relationships to the same elements in the Athenian Kore 6504 that they warrant the conclusion that the Athenian craftsman tried to imitate Kore 7464, or another similar to her that might have been dedicated as a votive offering. Langlotz, placing Kore 7464 in the Sicyonian School, emphasizes the fact that her long kolpos considerably reduces her height: "Denn das sich bauschende Gewand nimmt der Erscheinung das leicht Aufstrebende und zieht den Körper gleichsam nach unten, worin sich die Vorliebe für gedrungene Formen in den ersten Jahren ausspricht."[25] The Athenian had no liking for this short, square figure. In his desire to represent his maiden as slender and tall, he reduced the length of the kolpos and added the himation with its diagonal arrangement. A simple comparison of the side views of the korai in question (pls. 51, a and 51, b-c) will suffice to prove how far more artistic is the arrangement of the drapery in the Athenian Kore 6504. Two groups of vertical folds, one between the legs and one on the outside, frame the left leg of Kore 6504. The right leg, freed of heavy folds, shows its contour clearly, contrasting with the folds of the kolpos above. The kolpos, however, exhibits no fold whatever in the left side view (pl. 51, c) so that the system of vertical folds carved below it might show to greater advantage. In the Sicyonian example (pls. 50, a and 51, a), the folds, deprived of all plasticity, are only to be found between the legs and the same arrangement is repeated in front and back. The body, although covered with drapery is, with its accentuated lines, what gives this figure its contours, while in the Athenian example we find that in accordance with the point of view sometimes the body, sometimes the drapery, sometimes both help to determine the contour line. And yet it is the drapery that, descending to the base, supports the Sicyonian maiden, while in the Athenian kore it stops at the ankles. This constitutes another element of elegance and grace characteristic of Kore 6504.

The Athenian craftsman chose to make the hands turn inwards, while in the Sicyonian example they are turned out, and this, along with the extended fingers and the bending forward of the body indicate late archaic mannerism. In the Athenian example the pose of the

---

24. *Proceedings of the Irish Academy, l. c.,* 35, pl. X. Langlotz, *op. cit.,* 30, 8. For the related Acropolis kore 683, Langlotz-Schrader, *Akrop.,* pl. 17, cf. Karouzos, Chr., *BSA* 1938-9, 10 ff. and Raubitschek, *BSA,* 1939, 37, fig. 15.

25. *Frühgr. Bildhauerschulen,* 37.

figure is self-contained, the expression of the face is austere, and the chin is emphasized. These characteristics place the kore among the works of the severe style, around 480 B. C. The profile recalls that of the Thracian woman on the white cylix by the Pistoxenos Painter, from the Acropolis, dated about 480.[26] Ashmole compares the kore to the Damareteion coins; Langlotz places her rather early, near the Euthydikos' kore.[27] The elimination of the volutes, that intervene between the head of the figure and the disc of the mirror, appears to be not an archaic feature but rather a conscious simplification. In the Sicyonian example the volutes were necessary to add height and give space to the figure; the Athenian craftsman made his maiden elegant by other plastic means and consequently had no use for the volutes.

One may wonder on what kind of a base the Athenian kore stood. Beazley has suggested that the Sicyonian kore 7464 (plate 50, a) perhaps stood upon a base in the form of an ὀκλαδίας δίφρος, and he further suggested that the small bronze δίφρος found on the Acropolis (De Ridder, Acc. 133, no. 407) served as her base.[28] His suggestion is probably correct in spite of the fact that no traces of feet are distinguishable on the stool, not even after its recent cleaning. Good luck has contributed to the discovery of the base for the Athenian kore, and in this discovery we have an uncommon instance of the verification of an hypothesis by fact.

The small bronze object with the racing colts from the Acropolis (pl. 48, b; De Ridder, op. cit., no. 503, fig. 155) is not, as one could maintain, a throne for a seated figure but rather a base for one who is standing. The two racing colts are connected by a small thin plaque that suggests the carriage of a chariot. The head of one of the colts continues the horizontal line of the body, that of the other, the one that appears in the frontal plane in our illustration (pl. 49), has a sharp outward turn.

De Ridder, in his discussion of this bronze, noted traces of two feet on the plaque: "Le gauche (should read droit) serait en arrière du droit (should read gauche), ce qui confirmerait l'opinion que nous avons faite de la date récente du bronze."[29] These traces, that can be seen more definitely now that the piece has been cleaned, are illustrated in our figure 6. The right foot is close up to the left, which projects a little. This position agrees perfectly with that of the feet of our kore, pl. 48, a. The somewhat greater length of the footprints

26. Diepolder, *Penthesileamaler*, 10, pl. 5. Buschor, *Gr. Vasen*, fig. 196. Graef-Langlotz, pls. 35 and 36. Pfuhl, fig. 416. Beazley, *ARV* 57, 2.

27. *Supra*, note 21.

28. *Proc. Irish Acad., l. c.*, 36.

29. *BCH* 22 (1898) 212.

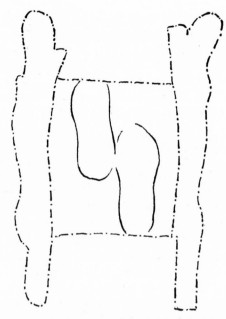

Fig. 6. Traces of feet on the base with colts No. 6549.

is due to the adhesive substance that was used to attach the figure to
its base. It is certain that the figure which stood on the base was
soldered to it, perhaps by means of silver according to the opinion of
the craftsman of the National Museum; no trace of a hole is found on
the base. The later boring of a hole for attachment, a cruder device,
is commonly used today. The examination of the feet of a number of
figures supporting mirrors showed that the method of attaching them
to their bases by some kind of adhesive was rather common; none
shows any signs of a hole for attachment.[30]

When the kore from the Acropolis was placed on the base with the
colts, not only was our hypothesis that they belonged together verified,
but also the maiden gained in impressiveness (pls. 49 and 51, b-c).
Actually the kore, in these illustrations, does not stand on the original
support but on a plaster cast made from it. This was done, first, in
order to avoid the boring of the original bronze, as would have been
essential for the support of the figure since her right foot is missing,
and, second, to make sure that the footprints on the original base
would be available for study at any future time. The footprints on
the base indicate that the maiden stood in such a manner that her

---

30. Among others we may cite figures 6197 in the National Museum (Langlotz,
op. cit., pl. 40.2) and no. 7576 (Langlotz, *op. cit.*, pl. 25, 2 our plate 9).

breast was not parallel to the front horizontal plaque of the chariot, but slightly diagonal to it, with the left shoulder and hand pulled inward and with the head turned slightly to the right. It seems that this placing was intentional. The craftsman apparently wanted to counterbalance the outward movement of one of the colts, and to suggest at the same time, by the two opposite turns, so far as the fixed poses would allow, the movement of the chariot and the undulation of the riding figure.

The period and the style of the colts do not prevent their association with Kore 6504. Their animated expression, τὸ θυμοειδές, places them in the Attic school. The planes of the face, softer than in earlier work, place them in the severe style. Sometime ago De Ridder suggested a date, relative of course, of 500 B. C. for these colts.[31]

The type of support with animals was not invented by Athenian craftsmen. It appears in the stand mirror in the British Museum (pl. 52, a) in which a peplos kore stands on a chariot flanked by two Pegasoi.[32] Although it represents a more advanced type, it is not necessarily much later than our Athenian kore, who still has her knees unbent and who keeps her archaic character. Langlotz has attributed the British Museum mirror to the school of Kleonae. Today Corinth seems to have better claims to this group of mirrors; the Corinthian attribution of the example in the British Museum will explain the choice of Pegasoi as companions to the figure.

The base of another figure in the British Museum, published by De Ridder in the same study, is flanked by two lions; here then the figure is Cybele. De Ridder's hypothesis that the type was created in Ionia is not weakened by the attribution of the work to Italiote schools (Jantzen 67, 8 pl. 20, 11, 8). In the two mirrors of the British Museum, therefore, we have the epiphany of a goddess in a manner similar to that known from examples where another goddess, on a bull, is surrounded by the thiasos of Dionysos.[33]

The Corinthian bronze worker used Pegasoi instead of the Ionic lions to flank his female figure; the Athenian craftsman of the Acropolis kore went still farther. Removing the wings from the Pegasoi, he transformed them into colts and thus transferred them from the realm of myth to that of the life of his city.

---

31. *BCH* 22 (1898) 212. The second support similar to this from the Acropolis is very much oxidized and bears no traces of footprints (De Ridder, no. 503, fig. 154).

32. De Ridder, *BCH* 22 (1898) pl. 1. Walters, *Select Bronzes*, pl. 34. Studniczka, in *Ilberg Jhb.* 1926, 397, pl. 6 c. Langlotz, *op. cit.*, 68, no. 6.

33. Technau *JDAI* 52 (1937) 76 ff. cf. Lehmann-Hartleben, *AJA* 1939, 66 ff. N. Gialouris examines in detail the throne of the Goddess on a chariot in his doctoral dissertation to be published in the *Museum Helveticum*, 1950, under the title *Athena als Herrin der Pferde*.

In the lost bronze maiden from the Troad, which Chapouthier had
the inspiration to restore as a mirror stand, we have another example
parallel to the two just discussed. He based his restoration on the
drawings and descriptions of Choiseul-Gouffier and of Le Chevalier
(fig. 7).[34] We may infer that the lady represented in the example

Fig. 7. The lost mirror from the Troad
as restored by Chapouthier.

34. *BCH* (1929) 42 ff., fig. 5, repeated in *"Les Dioscures aux service, d'une
déesse*, 216, fig. 30.

from the Troad is none other than Helen, since the two riders who accompany her could most probably be considered as the Dioskouroi. Surrounded by wild animals, she is here represented not as a mortal but as a πότνια θεά of nature, a distant descendant of that old and fearful goddess of the Grächwyl hydria, the mistress of all kinds of wild animals.[35]

Chapouthier hesitated between Cybele and Helen as a name for the goddess from the Troad. The probable attribution of the mirror to a Peloponnesian, perhaps the Argive, school seems to favor her identification as Helen. It is a well-established fact that Helen was worshipped as Δενδρῖτις in the Dorian island of Rhodes, and this has justly been taken by scholars to indicate that in the Argolid also her character as a goddess was widely recognized.

The presence of Helen on a mirror could most probably be attributed to another reason, almost magical in significance. The story preserved by Herodotus may perhaps explain the magic effect of Helen's presence. In VI, 61 we read that a nurse would take her charge daily to the sanctuary of Helen and would pray that the goddess take away the child's ugliness. Helen listened to her prayers and with a touch of the hand transformed the child καλλίστην ἐξ αἰσχίστης. As she stood, like an omnipotent goddess, below the disc of the mirror, Helen in a similar way could help the maiden using the mirror to become more beautiful and more desirable. The mirror was placed in the grave to accompany a dead woman in the hope, perhaps, that Helen as an old goddess of vegetation might use her powers to help in some resurrection of the dead.

The probable identification as Helen of the figure from the Troad helps to suggest that perhaps the peplos kore of the very beautiful mirror 7576, found at Corinth and now in the National Museum at Athens, also represented the heroine of the Trojan War (pl. 53).[36] This figure owes its grandeur especially to the epoch which it represents, that is to the Early Classical period. The new ideal is expressed in the easy stance, without the old rigidity of the legs, and the classical spirit is also shown by the elimination of the old formula of the drapery held on one hand. Six, starting from this mirror, long ago pointed out that the placing of the left hand below the ἀπόπτυγμα is found in the Eriphyle of the Nekyia by Polygnotus.

---

35. For the Grächwyl hydria (Lamb, op. cit., pl. XLVIII, b) cf. the illustration and excellent notes of Bloesch, Antike Kunst in der Schweiz, 22 ff. and 148 ff., pl. 3-7. Helen as the Goddess of vegetation: Mannhardt, Wald Feld, Kulte, 22. Kaibel, Hermes 27, 256. Wide, Lakon. Kulte, 343. Nilsson, Gr. Religion, 195, 292, 466, cf. Chapouthier, Dioscures, 143 ff.

36. Dumont-Chaplain, op. cit., 35. Six, AM 19 (1894), 335 ff. Langlotz, op. cit., 20, 55, no. 15, pl. 25b. JDAI 42 (1927) Beibl. 20. Poulsen, op. cit., 24, no. 11.

That Erotes are not only the companions of Aphrodite, but in no less degree of Helen also, is so well known from a great number of works of art that it is unnecessary to give references. The peplos kore 7576 is, as Langlotz recognized, an Argive work and so it leads us, through Rhodes, to the special associations of Helen already noted. We know besides that Helen was worshipped as Kourotrophos at Argos. According to Pausanias (II, 22, 6), it was there that she gave birth to Iphigeneia and built a sanctuary of Eileithyia. A further indication of the relation of mirrors to the story of Helen is shown by her appearance on a great number of Etruscan mirrors where very often we find her represented at her toilet.[37] On the exterior of a red-figured kylix in Berlin she is represented with Eros and a mirror.[38] Again, on the red-figured hydria from Rhodes, now in Berlin, she is represented holding a mirror in a very characteristic manner; so also on an Italiote skyphos in the Museum of Taranto.[39] In front of a seated woman with a mirror painted on a pyxis now in the British Museum we find written the name ʽΕλένη.[40] The peplos kore of a Peloponnesian mirror is surrounded by Erotes, like the one illustrated in our pl. 53, and holds a mirror in her hands in a manner so similar to that of Helen on the Berlin hydria that there can be no great doubt as to her identity.[41] All these indications may perhaps lead us to the conclusion that Herodotus' story of the nurse and the ugly child is not without an aetiological origin. In Sparta especially, but most probably in other places also, the belief was apparently current that besides all the protection that she gave to girls Helen had also the power to transmit to them her beauty. Her special relation to mirrors, as seen on the monuments cited, would further indicate that the mirror was one of the means through which Helen exercised her magic influence, and this would become especially effective if the mirror was supported by Helen herself, sometimes accompanied by Erotes. Perhaps it is not very rash to maintain that Helen was instrumental in bringing about the first association in art of a mirror and a female form. This we shall now try to prove.

The oldest draped figure support of a mirror is to be found in the

---

37. Especially see Gerhard, *Etr. Sp.*, 2, pl. 196-221 5, pl. 79, 83, 107. *Cat. br. Mus.*, no. 626-27. Richter, *Metr. Museum Bronzes*, no. 797. Babelon-Blanchet, nos. 1287, 1292, 1296-9, 1306-1319.

38. *JDAI* 41 (1926) 202; Jacobsthal, *Orn.*, pl. 86c.

39. *Hydria:* Schefold, *UKV* nos. 145, p. 89, fig. 27-28. *KV* 7, pl. 3b. Jacobsthal, *Orn.*, pl. 84b. *Skyphos: CV Taranto* IV, Dr. pl. 32. The presence of Paris on the other side of the vase seems to confirm this identification of Helen.

40. *F. R.*, pl. 57, 1 Beazley, *ARV* 537, 41.

41. Schefold, *op. cit.*, 32 fig. 27. Langlotz, *op. cit.*, pl. 25a ("Argos"). That the ancients connected strongly Helen with mirrors and ornaments is also indicated by verse 1112 of Euripides' *Orestes*.

mirror from Leonidion in Kynouria, attributed to the Laconian school
(pl. 52, b).[42] From the polos which the figure is wearing we can
infer that she is a goddess. Thus the question arises automatically:
although this unsmiling divinity is at a considerable distance from
the beautiful figure illustrated on pl. 53, what other goddess than
Helen of Sparta could in the Archaic period have been used to animate
a Laconian mirror? Stesichoros, in his παλινωδία composed in the
years of the making of the Leonidion mirror, ca. 560-550 B. C., indicates that the people of the Archaic period believed that Helen at times
could be inexorable, and fully expresses the religious conceptions of
the sixth century Spartans in this matter. He was trying, by his poem,
to gain Helen's favor because the goddess had sent word to him from
Leuke, the island in the Black Sea on which she lived with Achilles,
that she and no other deity had blinded him because he had treated
her badly.

Already, therefore, in the Archaic period a myth regarding the
powers of Helen had been transferred to works of art. The beginning
of the myth was the belief in a kind of sympathetic magic, one of the
pre-suppositions of which is that "like produces like."[42a] In our case,
the influence is provoked in a manner usual to magic rites, that is by
means of a figure, the figure of a goddess who could transmit her
legendary beauty, though not without some intermediary. In exer-
cising her influence, she was helped by the object she carried, the
object considered by all peoples as the medium *par excellence* for
magic influence, namely the disc of the mirror. If, then, we finally
agree to see Helen in the figures of the two Peloponnesian mirrors
illustrated above, pls. 52, b and 53, we shall have to decide how
gradually she gave way to Aphrodite, who dominates the wrought
stand mirrors of the fourth century. But even then the suspicion may
linger that perhaps behind the beautiful head which often decorates
fourth century mirrors, and especially Corinthian mirrors (Züchner,
Klappsp., figs. 38, 40-41 and pls. 29-32), is hidden that old goddess of
the Leonidion example, the Laconian Helen.

Let us now return to the Athenian kore from the Acropolis, pls.
48a, 49 and 50b. As far as she is concerned, we have indications that
will enable us to recognize her, too, as a goddess. In the past De
Ridder endeavored (cf. note 32) to interpret the significance of the
support with the two colts. At the same time he was publishing the
British Museum mirror (our pl. 52, a), yet he did not try to find
among the mirror stands from the Acropolis a kore that in a similar

---

42. De Ridder, *Br. Soc. Archéol.*, pl. 1. Langlotz, *op. cit.*, 88, 34. Schefold,
op. cit., 32, fig. 8, 22.
42a. Frazer, *Golden Bough₃*, I, 1, 52 ff.

manner could fit the footprints on the support. Carried along by his survey concerned with religious matters, he ended with the conjecture that perhaps Poseidon Hippios stood on the support. N. Gialouris' suggestion that we may see Athena Hippia in the figure now comes nearer to the truth (cf. note 33).

Is it necessary, however, to equate the kore of the mirror as it has now been restored with a definite goddess? The old theories concerning the korai of the Acropolis have been abandoned and the opinion is prevalent that their beauty and their youth provided the one strong reason why they were pleasing to the goddess to whom they were dedicated.[43]

We shall be closer to this spirit, with respect to the dedications offered on the Acropolis, if we attempt to find a reason for these mirrors in the life of the city itself. Supplementing Miss Sylvia Benton's suggestion that perhaps the colts indicated a victory of the donor in the horse-races, I should incline towards an interpretation that would not be foreign to the psychology of Athenian ladies of the fifth century as we know it from Aristophanes. A mirror of this kind would flatter the vanity of the owner if she belonged to the *genos* of the Knights, and if she did not then it could nurture her dreams that her sons might rise that far.[44] The bronze worker, who had altered the foreign theme of the Pegasoi, kept exactly what was necessary to attract the local market. Yet it is more probable that this mirror never belonged to a mortal woman but was a votive offering, meant as such from the day it was made, to one of the goddesses of the Acropolis. The artist made her, along with the base and the disc, to be an *ἄγαλμα*, an object of admiration and at the same time an ornament.

One wonders whether other Attic korai who support mirrors are hidden under the Argive peplos which their creators borrowed from their prototype and which perhaps makes their recognition difficult. A very beautiful peplophoros, excellently preserved with disc and accessories, was found in the section of Kypsele at Athens; it exhibits, however, characteristics so evidently Argive that it is impossible to assume it to be an Attic copy of an Argive prototype. On the other hand, the importation of mirrors of such quality must have provided strong inducement to the Athenian bronze worker to endeavor to produce similar articles, foreign to the Attic tradition.[45]

---

43. Langlotz-Schrader, *Acrop.* 7 ff.

44. "*Τοῦτον τὸν υἱὸν λαμβάνουσ' ἐκορίζετο:*
   Ὅταν σὺ μέγας ὢν ἅρμ' ἐλαύνῃς πρὸς πόλιν,
   ὥσπερ Μεγακλέης, ξυστίδ ἔχων". (*Νεφέλαι*, 68-70).

45. Mirror from Kypsele: National Museum at Athens no. 7579. Langlotz, *op. cit.*, 80, no. 7. Bieber, Gr. Kleidung, pl. 6, 1. Poulsen, *op. cit.*, 24, 7. *Deltion*, 1933-35, 29 fig. 14. We are inclined to consider the strange bronze kore in Cook's collection

The description of Athenian mirrors does not end at this point. Another type, not the least interesting, remains to be examined, the fifth century mirrors with handles cast in the form of a siren, and Eros or some other winged creature. Among these mirrors a good number can be found that can be attributed to the Attic school because of their provenience and style.[45a] The bronze Attic hydriai with a siren below the main handle, a type related to our mirrors, will help in the examination of the mirrors. The cast handles preceded the wrought handles of the later hydriai and Züchner (*Klappsp.* 192-3) seems to believe that the change to the new technique took place in Athens. If this is true, then the importance of Athenian toreutic art, an art that has been underrated, is considerably increased.[46] Besides the clay copy of the excellent Attic piece at Bonn,[47] we have the silver phiale in New York. Its discovery in an Attic grave and its relation to Attic works of art make probable the conclusion that it was made by an Athenian craftsman toward the end of the fifth century.[48] Besides, we have definite evidence for the activity in Athens of Mys, the collaborator of Parrhasios, and for the contribution of Pheidias to the perfection of toreutic technique.[49]

In spite of this evidence, scholars seem to be held back by some special reluctance from attributing works of this kind to the Attic school. Overlooking the fact that a good many Attic white lekythoi have been found in Eretria, Züchner, influenced by the provenience of the well-known Eretrian bronze hydria (Lamb, *op. cit.*, pl. 71 b), attributes it to his vaguely traced Chalkidic workshop, and this at a time when Chalkis, long the vassal of Athens, must have been stripped

---

at Richmond as the work of an Athenian craftsman (Burlington, *Illustrat. Catal.*, pl. XIV, A 8. *Cook Collect. Catal.* pl. 35. Neugebauer, *Ant. Br.*, fig. 25, Langlotz, *op. cit.*, 30, 5) in spite of her Sikyonian appearance. Her face, strikingly similar to that of the Acropolis kore (see pls. 48, a and 49), indicates that both were made by the same craftsman. The altogether unusual accessories of the disc, Nikai instead of the Erotes of Peloponnesian workshops, indicate an Attic tradition. It seems that in this example too the Athenian bronze worker tried to imitate a Peloponnesian stand mirror.

45a. For instance it is difficult to believe that the mirror of Munich was not made by an Athenian workshop, cf. Buschor, *Musen des Jenseits*, frontispiece (Sieveking, *Antike Metallgeräte*, pl. 21).

46. Züchner, *Klappsp.* 221. But the opposite view is held by Lippold, *RE* s.v. Toreutik, 1762. For the Attic toreutic art see especially D. B. Thompson in *Hesperia* 8 (1939) 283-316.

47. Rodenwaldt, *JDAI* 1926, 191. *Kunst der Antike* 348. Schuchhardt, *Gesch. der Kunst*, 275, pl. 5, fig. 256. Züchner, *op. cit.*, 221, note 5. D. B. Thompson, *loc. cit.*, 309, fig. 17. Langlotz, *Phidiasprobl.*, 85, pl. 30.

48. New York phiale: Richter, G., *AJA* (1941), 363 ff., 375.

49. For Pheidias as a toreutic artist cf. Brunn, *Künstlergesch.₂*, 132; Miss Richter's most interesting article in the *AJA* cited *supra*, p. 337; Langlotz, *Phidiasprobl.*, 87.

of her old traditions and, in the stagnant atmosphere of a dependent state, been completely unprepared for the opening of new artistic paths.[50]

Yet Attic toreutic art, no matter how active it may have been, still is indebted in some degree to those who developed the older tradition, and among others to the lowly craftsmen who made bronze mirrors with decorated handles.

---

50. Züchner, *op. cit.*, 194-95. Recently scholars begin to attribute to the Attic workshop some of the hydrias with wrought handles: Picard, *Mon. Piot* 1940, 90 ff. and Richter, *AJA* 50 (1946) 360 ff. In the near future we hope to present new elements strengthening this opinion. Cf. also Robinson, *AJA* 46 (1942) 172-187.

AN ATTIC GRAVE RELIEF

HAROLD N. FOWLER
Cambridge

Plate 54

It gives me great pleasure to offer a contribution to the volume which commemorates the seventieth birthday of David M. Robinson. Being a little more than two decades his senior, I have watched his career with interest as he grew from a young beginner to his present stature as one of the most distinguished archaeologists in the United States.

The monument which I have the privilege of publishing[1] is a lekythos of Pentelic marble covered with a rather heavy coating of the yellowish-brown patina familiar to all who have seen much weathered marble of this kind. The circular base is of plaster. The height, including the base, is 85 cm., without the base, 73 cm. (pl. 54). The date is approximately 400 B. C., about the same as that of the stele of Hegeso.[2]

Compositions similar to that of the relief here published are not uncommon, though the combination of a seated woman holding a mirror with a standing maid holding a box is unusual, if not actually unique, though both figures occur in other combinations.[3] Here the box held by the maid is larger than that seen on similar reliefs, and probably it is not a jewel-box, but is intended to hold toilet articles. The cover seems too large for the box. The maid is much smaller than her mistress, who would, if standing, overtop her by more than head and shoulders. The lady holds her garment with her right hand in such a way as to expose her right breast. A rather large, flat object which disappears into the background seems to be held (if held at all) in the hollow of the lady's right arm. It may perhaps be a board on which cosmetics were mixed, but that is mere conjecture. The execu-

---

1. I owe this privilege to the kindness of Professor George H. Chase, Acting Director of the Division of Classical Antiquities in the Boston Museum of Fine Arts. I am grateful also to Miss Edith Marshal, Secretary of the Division, for her effective and gladly given assistance.
The lekythos was bought in 1938 of the Brummer Gallery. On account of Mr. Brummer's death, it is at present impossible to obtain any information about its previous history.
2. Conze, *Die Attischen Grabreliefs*, I, pl. XXX. Richter, *The Sculpture and Sculptors of the Greeks*, fig. 429. Fowler, *A History of Sculpture*, fig. 75.
3. Cf. box on the stele of Hegeso, but no mirror, so also Conze, pls. XXXI, XXXII, XXXIII, and XXXIV, lady holding mirror, Conze, pls. XLVIII, LXXVI, and XC.

tion of the relief is excellent, hardly inferior to that of the relief on the stele of Hegeso; but the latter is much larger.

There is apparently no reason to attribute any special significance to the differences between this relief and others similar to it in general composition, but the differences are obvious and worth noting.

The seated lady is not looking into her mirror, nor is she looking at her maid, or indeed at anything. It is tempting to think of her, the deceased, as gazing into eternity, but such a thought is, so far as I know, foreign to the classical Greek mind. She may be simply wondering what ornament or cosmetic to put on next, or the artist may not have wished to indicate any particular thought. At any rate he has produced a charming work of art.

GRAVE RELIEF OF AN ATHENIAN POET

T. B. L. WEBSTER
University College, London

Plate 55

The relief, which is the subject of this article, was found in 1812 in Athens. The discoverer, who brought it back to Lyme Park, Stockport, where it has now become national property administered by the Stockport Corporation, says that it was "in the sepulchres we opened at a short distance from the walls of the city (Athens) on the western side of the road that leads to Thebes."

It has been illustrated several times,[1] but the old photograph from which all the illustrations are taken does not give a true idea of its quality or of the details. Its dimensions are 3 ft. 8½ ins. high and 2 ft. 11 ins. broad (pl. 55). The depth from the surface of the seated figure to the relief ground is about 6½ ins. A diagonal break runs from a point just to the left of the seated figure's head to his knee: the lower half of the mouth and the beard of the frontal mask have been broken off and were perhaps originally an extra piece of marble. The profile mask has lost the bottom right side of mouth and beard and holes in the remaining portion show where it was attached. Except for the foremost drapery of the seated figure the relief is well preserved; the top edge and the right edge seem to be original and a short portion of the left edge at the top. Nothing much therefore is lost at the bottom except the feet, which filled the bottom left corner. I could find no trace of *antae* and am inclined to suppose that the relief had merely a pediment like the gravestone of Dexileos.[2] The following details do not appear at all on the old photograph: the head of the seated man is bearded with the hair of the beard cut quite short and represented by incised lines; there are three short deepish vertical furrows above his nose and two deep cuts on either side of his nose; the corners of his mouth turn down; he held a cylindrical object in his left hand; the diameter is about 1½ inches and it is broken off just where it protrudes from the hand and it is difficult to see what it could have been except a scroll. On the frontal mask the right brow is raised and the left is level; they join in a narrow loop over the forehead; the mouth appears to be absolutely smooth and shows no

1. *JHS* 23 (1903), pl. 13; Robert, *Masken der neueren attischen Komödie*, fig. 127; Winter, *K.i.B.*, 316/3.

2. Athens, *Conze* 1158; Winter, *K.i.B.*, 315/1; Richter, *Sculpture and Sculptors*, fig. 215.

trace of hair. On the profile mask the beard is clearly marked on the
trumpet mouth starting from the outer-sides of the upper lip. The
brows curve evenly on both sides.

As far as I know, the following dates have been suggested. Robert[3]
says Old Comedy; Simon[4] quotes it as an example of the New Comedy;
Luschey[5] dates it to the first half of the fourth century. The last seems
to me to be right, but may be narrowed further. Luschey notes a technical similarity with a relief in Moscow[6] ("in both the Naiskos pediment was worked as a separate piece") and a stylistic resemblance
with a stele from the Peiraeus.[7] Luckily the authorities agree remarkably on the dating of this stele; Diepolder before 377; Curtius about
380 B.C.; Süsserott between 384 and 380; Byvanck before 380 B.C.
If we look at a sequence of three[8] seated figures on grave reliefs,
Theano (dated by Süsserott early in the '90's), the woman on the
Peiraeus stele, and Mnesarete (dated by Süsserott 370/60), our seated
figure is clearly nearest to the Peiraeus stele; compare the treatment
of the drapery over the legs, and particularly the folds in front of the
left hand and on the chair at the bottom behind the back; the body
is swung more into the plane of the relief than on the Peiraeus stele
and only slightly less than Theano's. The eyes are long in proportion
to their height and the lids are evenly stressed and the brows are
sharp; "Praxitelean" eyes and brows are beginning to appear on the
stele of Mnesarete.

We have then a grave relief of an elderly man who died about
380 B.C. According to the original discoverer a red-figured vase was
found in the same spot; this is now in the British Museum; it is a red-
figured pelike by the Villa-Giulia painter (*ARV* 404/43) and must
date from about the middle of the fifth century or soon after; it must
be contemporary with the birth of the dead man but its connection
with his grave may be purely fortuitous. The scroll in the man's hand
proves that he was a poet, and not an actor; this was overlooked in
the original publication and led Robert reluctantly to reject this interpretation, which has been revived by Luschey. The figure therefore
belongs to the series of seated dramatic poets, of which three may be
mentioned. At the beginning of the fourth century the Pronomos
painter (*ARV* 849/1) drew the poet Demetrius seated with a scroll

---

3. *Op. cit.*, 79 n. 2.
4. *Comicae tabellae*, 1938, 77.
5. *Ganymed*, 1949, 74.
6. Diepolder, *Attische Grabreliefs*, pl. 32.
7. Conze no. 69; Diepolder, pl. 26; Curtius, *Antike Kunst*, 2, 351, fig. 520;
Süsserott, *Gr. Pl. des IVten Jhr.*, 110, n. 86; Bijvanck, *BVAB* 19, 20.
8. Theano: Athens, Diepolder, pl. 22; Süsserott, pl. 14/1; Mnesarete: Munich,
Diepolder, pl. 27; Süsserott, pl. 18/1.

in his hand; he needs no mask as identification because his actors
and chorus surround him, holding or wearing their masks. Poulsen[9]
has suggested that the seated Euripides of the Constantinople relief
goes back to a memorial erected in the time of the statesman Ly-
curgus; the likeness of the seated Euripides with a mask in the right
hand and a short scroll in the left hand is obvious. Thirdly on the
Lateran[10] relief Menander sits in the same way with a mask in his
right hand but no scroll.

Sophocles' tomb was decorated with a satyr carrying the mask of
a shorn maiden; the later writer of the epigram (*Anth. Pal.* VII, 37)
did not know whether it was Antigone or Electra. How are we to
interpret our masks? The profile mask is clearly a slave. Without
the painting we cannot tell whether it is the smooth-haired leading
slave or the shaggier wavy-haired leader of Pollux' list; both occur
as early as this on terracottas and vases;[11] the particular stylisation
of the beard and mouth is perhaps seen first on a terracotta herdsman
in Berlin, who wears the bald Maison[12] mask. The frontal mask is
more difficult to interpret as the lower half of the mouth and the
beard are missing. It seems however to be a flat mouth and not a
rounded mouth like the other; there is no trace of hair on the preserved part whereas on the other the beard goes round on to the upper
lip. In the Middle Comedy period the wide mouth is used for free[13]
men as well as slaves, whereas the mouth with the hair marked all
round it seems to be confined to slaves. The sculptor may therefore
have used the difference of beard and mouth to distinguish old man
from slave. Unfortunately the unevenness of the brows (right raised,
left level) does not help us, although Pollux only quotes this feature
for the leading old man and the Lycomedian old man; slave masks
with one raised brow appear in the Old, Middle, and New Comedy[14]
material. The mask has a good head of hair; the only old man in
Pollux' list who can be so described is the Lycomedian (the leading
and wavy-haired old men are excluded because they do not appear

9. *Iconographic Studies* in *From the Collections of the Ny Carlsberg Glyptothek,*
1931, 80, fig. 62; Bieber, *Denkmäler,* no. 29; *History,* fig. 60; Schefold, *Bildnisse,*
162/1.

10. Robert, fig. 96; Bieber, *D.,* no. 129; *HT.,* fig. 223. For further reliefs of
seated poets see Krüger, *AM* 26, 137 f.

11. Examples are given in *Rylands Bulletin,* 32, 130, nos. 22/ii and 27/ii. A
good early example of the first type in Heidelberg is published by Luschey,
Ganymed, 71, fig. 1.

12. Bieber, *D.,* no. 81; *H.T.,* fig. 88.

13. e.g. Bieber, *H.T.,* figs. 89, 90, 95, 111, 113, 125, 133.

14. e.g. Attic r.f. oenochoe, Louvre, L.9; *ARV* 848/22; Pfuhl, fig. 572. Terracottas, Bieber, *H.T.,* figs. 100, 101. Marble mask from Kerameikos, Bieber, *H.T.,*
fig. 266. Cf. also the important discussion of this feature in Rumpf's article on
Parrhasios, *AJA* (forthcoming).

before New Comedy). He may therefore be the Lycomedian and have had painted curly hair.[15] Whether this is right or not, it is certain that the masks differ, and therefore Luschey's ingenious suggestions that we should recognize the poet of a comedy called *Didymoi* or *Homoioi* must be ruled out; in any case we know no play in which twin slaves appeared without twin masters as in the *Amphitruo,* and we know no play with these titles by a poet of the Old Comedy, to which our man by virtue of his age must belong.

The masks of an old man and a slave (with painted inscriptions) could indicate Aristophanes' *Ploutos.* They could however represent mythical characters, since Attic vases show both Zeus and Nike in Comedy with normal comic[16] masks; Daidalos was a character in the *Kokalos* and Daidalos on an Apulian phlyax[17] vase of about 350 B.C. wears a similar slave mask to that held by our poet. We cannot exclude the possibility that this is the funeral monument of Aristophanes. If he wore a large ivy wreath, like the poet on the Pronomos vase, it would cover the "shining forehead." Aristophanes' famous baldness should not be exaggerated; he mentions it himself in the *Knights* (550) and *Peace* (767f.), and Eupolis takes up the jest some five years later (78K); it may merely mean that as a young man he had a high forehead and slightly receding hair. The characteristic features which appear on the various later heads[18] which have been identified as Aristophanes, furrowed, knit brows, deep cuts on either side of the chin, sombre mouth, thin cheeks, short or shortish beard could all have derived from this relief. This cannot be proved; in any case we have a large funeral monument set up in memory of a comic poet who died in Athens, aged 60 years or more, about 380 B.C.[19]

---

15. The terracotta in New York, Bieber, *H.T.,* fig. 133, is also, I think, the Lycomedian.

16. See *Rylands Bulletin,* 32, 126, nos. 2, ii a, and 31, ii, b.

17. B.M., F269; Bieber, *H.T.,* fig. 370. For interpretation see *C.Q.,* 43, 23.

18. The Bonn Herm (Bernoulli, *Gr. Ikonographie,* I, 173; Winter, *K.i.B.,* 320/4; Bieber, *H.T.,* fig. 222; Schefold, *Bildnisse,* 159/4), the Terme Herm (*N.d. Sc.,* 1929, 351 f., pl. XVI/XVII; Poulsen, *op. cit.,* fig. 21), the "pseudo-Seneca" (Naples 5616; Winter, *K.i.B.,* 345/4; Schefold, *Bildnisse,* 134).

19. I should like to acknowledge my gratitude to Mr. B. Ashmole for reading my manuscript and to the Town Clerk of Stockport for procuring me the new photograph.

EIN TOTENMAHLRELIEF AUS SAMOS

OTTO WALTER
Innsbruck

Tafeln 57-58

Das auf Taf. 57a abgebildete Totenmahlrelief habe ich im Jahre 1943 in Athen im Besitz des damaligen deutschen Geschäftsträgers gesehen und bin ihm für die Bewilligung der Veröffentlichung verbunden; inzwischen scheint es verschollen zu sein.

Es stammt, wie einwandfrei feststeht, aus Samos, wurde von dem dortigen deutschen Konsul Herrn Acker vor ca 30 Jahren erworben und soll in der Nähe von Vathy gefunden worden sein. In den Berichten über den Antikenbestand der Insel[1] scheint es nicht auf, doch könnte es mit dem "Totenmahlrelief" identisch sein, das K. Wiegand in seinen Untersuchungen über Thymiaterien, *Bonner Jahrb.* 122 (1913) 70 unter IV 1 erwähnt; es war ihm nur aus einer A. Pfuhl verdankten Photographie bekannt.

Die längliche, genau rechteckige Platte von 0,5075 : 0,2575m ist bis auf die rechte untere Ecke sehr gut erhalten. Das Materiel wird von Fachleuten als pentelischer Marmor erklärt. Die 0,03-0,035m breite Bodenleiste und das obere 0,045m breite Profil — seitliche Einfassungen waren keine vorhanden — ergeben eine ursprüngliche Dicke der Platte von 0,062m, der auch die höchsten Relieferhebungen entsprechen. Die Dicke der stehengebliebenen Grundplatte beträgt jetzt 0,05-0,035m (an der rechten oberen Ecke). Der Reliefgrund liegt ungefähr in einer Ebene, nur unter dem Stuhl der Frau und zwischen ihrem Fuß und dem Tischbein ist weniger tief abgearbeitet. Die Seitenflächen waren fein, die narbige Rückseite grob gepickt. Ueber die Art der Aufstellung läßt sich nichts entnehmen; ein Einlaßzapfen war nie vorhanden.

Mehr als die Hälfte der Platte wird von dem Gelagerten und seiner Genossin eingenommen, die durch die Größe im Verhältnis zu den anbetenden menschlichen Figuren als überirdische Wesen gekennzeichnet sind. Der Kopf der Hauptfigur, des auf der Kline liegenden Mannes, fällt fast genau in die Mittelachse des Reliefs; er hält in der Linken eine napfartige Trinkschale, die er aus dem in der erhobenen Rechten gehaltenen Rhyton gefüllt hat. Vor der Kline steht der dreibeinige Tisch, wie immer mit den paarigen Beinen gegen das Kopf-

---

1. Th. Wiegand, *AM* 25 (1900) 175ff. bes. Nr. 55-87. L. Curtius, *AM* 31 (1906) 151ff. E. Preuner, *AM* 49 (1924) 27ff.

ende der Kline; darauf befinden sich drei große laib- und zwei
pyramiden- oder kegelförmige Kuchen, vier Stück Granatäpfel oder
Feigen, sowie ein Thymiaterion mit dreikantigem Untersatz und
breiter runder Räucherschale. Neben dem unteren Ende der Kline,
also gegenüber der einbeinigen Schmalseite des Tisches, sitzt auf
einem einfachen Hocker, von dem nur ein Fuß zu sehen und der so
wie die Kline mit einem Teppich überdeckt ist, eine Frau in Unter-
gewand und Mantel nach rechts in einer für ein Totenmahlrelief ganz
auffallend bewegten Haltung: der Fuß ihres linken Beines ist auf dem
Boden aufgestellt, über dieses das rechte geschlagen und zwar so hoch,
daß Oberschenkel auf Oberschenkel zu liegen kommt. Der linke Arm
ist quer über den Schoß gelegt, seine Hand hängt über den rechten
Oberschenkel herab; der rechte ist gebeugt vorgehalten, so daß der
Ellbogen in der Nähe des rechten Knies erscheint, aber wohl ohne
darauf gesetzt zu sein. Das starke Vorbeugen des Oberkörpers der
Frau ist offenbar aus dem Bestreben zu erklären, mit der Rechten
möglichst weit nach vorne, d.i. rechts vom Beschauer zu reichen:
tatsächlich hält sie sie genau über das Thymiaterion. Nach der Haltung der Finger — sie sind in den Gelenken so gebogen, daß die
Spitze des Daumens das vorderste Glied des Zeigefingers berührt —
wird man wohl mit Sicherheit annehmen dürfen, daß sie Weihrauchkörner auf das genau unterhalb stehende Thymiaterion streut.[2]

Der aus der Vorderansicht etwas nach rechts gewandte Kopf des
gelagerten Mannes blickt auf die dort herannahenden Adoranten:
einen bärtigen Mann in der üblichen Stellung und Tracht, hinter ihm
eine Frau in auch über das Hinterhaupt gezogenem Mantel; sie erhebt
beide Unterarme mit adorierend gehaltenen Händen. Vor dem
Ehepaar steht unmittelbar am Kopfende der Kline ein kleines Kind,
ganz in den Mantel gehüllt, aus dem auch die Hände nicht heraus-
ragen; der linke Unterarm liegt quer über die Körpermitte, der rechte
abgebogen vor der Brust. Nach der Kopfhaltung blickt der Knabe
schräg nach aufwärts, vielleicht auf die sitzende Frau.

Wenn Totenmahlreliefs, wie Inschriften bezeugen, in späterer Zeit
zweifellos sehr oft auch als Grabdenkmäler verwendet wurden, so sind
in anderen Stücken ebenso sicher Weihgaben zu erkennen.[3] Zu diesen

---

2. Daß die Frau auf Totenmahlreliefs oft in dieser Aktion dargestellt ist, wurde
bereits von P. Wolters, Friedrichs-Wolters, *Gipsabgüsse* 354 zu Nr. 1058 vermutet,
trotzdem aber das in der Linken hochgehaltene Kästchen mit dem Räucherwerk,
das nur in diesem Zusammenhang zu erklären ist, vielfach mißverstanden; richtig
C. Blümel, *Berl. Katalog* III K 98-100. Auch das Mädchen auf der Stele Giustiniani
in Berlin No. 1482, C. Blümel a.a.O. K 19 wird wohl eher Weihrauchkörner aus
einer λιβανωτίς ausstreuen als ein Schmuckstück halten.

3. Die Hypothese von J. N. Svoronos, *Athen. Nationalmuseum* 533ff., daß die
griechischen Totenmahlreliefs auf Asklepios und Hygieia zu beziehen und diese in
dem dargestellten Paar zu erkennen seien, wurde von L. Malten *JDAI* 29 (1917)

gehört auch unser Relief. Aus der Art der Darstellung der sitzenden Frau ist zu erschließen, daß es sich nicht um Gottheiten, sondern um Heroen, also heroisierte Sterbliche handelt. Ihre Benennung ist mangels einer Inschrift unmöglich. Die Anbetung durch ein Ehepaar und der Vortritt des Kindes weisen darauf hin, daß wir in dem Heros den göttlich verehrten Ahnherrn der Familie erkennen dürfen. Er liegt beim Mahle wie seinerzeit bei Lebzeiten und genießt im Jenseits die ihm von seinen Nachkommen bescherten Tafelfreuden. Die Hero-ine — wir wollen annehmen, daß es seine Frau ist, — leistet ihm dabei Gesellschaft. Sie teilt nicht sein Lager, sondern sitzt, wie es einer anständigen Frau ziemt, neben ihm u.zw. nicht wie so oft auf griechischen Totenmahlreliefs auf der Kline selbst, sondern daneben auf einem Stuhl und streut Weihrauchkörner auf das Räuchergefäß. Wenn dieses ebenso wie die anderen auf dem Tisch befindlichen Ge-genstände auch auf ein Opfer an den Heros hinweist, wird man doch nicht unmittelbar an ein Rauchopfer denken dürfen, da die durch ihre Größe als Heroine charakterisierte Frau ein solches doch wohl nicht darbringen kann. Auf griechischen Weihreliefs pflegt alles, was auf das Opfer Bezug hat, Opferknabe, Opfertier, Altar, in seinen Größen-maßen denen der Sterblichen zu entsprechen. So wird man sich wohl besser daran erinnern, daß Räucherungen auch zu profanen Zwecken vorgenommen wurden und bei den Symposien Lebender nicht fehlten; seine Genossin bietet ihm auch im Jenseits diesen Genuß.[4]

Dem göttlich verehrten Ahnherrn führen die Eltern ihr Kind — es ist wohl ein Knabe, also den Stammhalter — vor. Daß derartige Vorstellungen, παραστάσεις, der Kinder vor Gottheiten oder Stam-

---

219 Anm. 1 mit Recht zurückgewiesen. Allerdings läßt sich diese Deutung für einige Stücke gegen P. Wolters Behauptung *Arch. Ztg* 40 (1882) 301 mit Sicherheit beweisen (O. Walter, *Beschreibung* Nr. 312-314 und *JOAI* 26 [1930] 75ff.), zumal wir auch von der στρῶσις τῆς κλίνης und der ἐπικόσμησις τῆς τραπέζης im Athener Asklepiosheiligtum durch dessen Priester wissen. Doch durfte Svoronos daraus keine so weit gehenden Schlüsse ziehen. Schon A. Holländer hatte in seiner 1865 erschienenen Dissertation. De anaglyphis sepulcralibus Graecis quae caenam repraesentare dicuntur 12 richtig erkannt, daß die Stammesheroen in dieser Form verehrt wurden; aber auch dies durfte nicht verallgemeinert werden. Daß diese Annahme in bestimmten Fällen richtig ist, läßt sich an einzelnen Beispielen durch Inschriften beweisen: Berlin, *Beschr. ant. Skulpt.* 819 mit IG II, 3₂ 4686 Ἡγεμὼν ἀρχηγέτης (Svoronos a.a.O. 551 Abb. 254). Triest *JDAI* 29 (1914) 187 Abb. 7 mit Inschrift *IG* II, 3₂ 4645 τῶι Ζευ<ξ>ίππωι καὶ τἓι Βασι<λ>είαι in Verbindung mit meiner Erklärung des Echelos-Reliefs *Ephemeris* 1937, 11. Das tegeatische Re-lief *AM* 39 (1914) 196ff. Taf. XII 2, wenn Rhomaios die Inschrift *IG* V, 2 248 richtig Δερκέτου ἥρωος πατ<ρ>ῴου ergänzt, wozu er *BCH* 4 (1880) 401 aus Halikarnass vergleicht. In anderen Fällen ist der Gelagerte nur als "Heros" bezeichnet.

4. *RE* I A 278. K. Wiegand a.a.O. 69. Thymiaterien auf Symposiondarstel-lungen : H. v. Fritze, *Rauchopfer bei den Griechen* 47f. Vielleicht wurde damit auch der praktische Zweck der Abwehr lästiger Fliegen und Mücken verfolgt, *RE* VI 2746 und XVI 454 mit den dagegen empfohlenen, bezw. angewandten Mitteln.

mesheroen durchaus üblich waren, wissen wir aus literarischer und bildlicher Ueberlieferung.[5] Zur Erinnerung daran und in Verbindung mit der Bitte um weitere Förderung und Schutz ihres Sohnes weihten die Eltern den Stammesheroen den erhaltenen Pinax. Auch viele andere sogenannte Totenmahlreliefs mit ganz ähnlichen Darstellungen, z.B. Berlin K 95 und 97, mögen aus einem derartigen Anlaß geweiht worden sein.

Wenn unser Relief somit auch im Allgemeinen mit anderen ähnlichen Stücken zu einer längst bekannten Gruppe gehört, bietet es doch, wie im Folgenden gezeigt werden soll, in mehrfacher Beziehung Abweichendes und Interessantes, so daß die besondere Veröffentlichung dieser auf ein Familienfest bezüglichen Weihung in der Festgabe für den verehrten Jubilar berechtigt scheint.

Vor allem ist es die Art des Sitzens der Heroine, die auffällt und m.W. bisher auf keinem Totenmahlrelief begegnet. Sie hat das eine Bein über das andere geschlagen, d.h. es sind nicht die Unterschenkel gekreuzt oder der Unterschenkel des eines Beins auf den Oberschenkel des anderen gelegt, sondern Oberschenkel kommt auf Oberschenkel zu liegen. Dieses Motiv der "überschlagenen Beine" ist bereits um die Mitte des 5. Jahrhunderts v.Chr. belegt[6] und besonders im sogenannten Penelopetypus vertreten, der uns auf Stein- und Tonreliefs (den "melischen") sowie auch auf dem bekannten Skyphos von Chiusi mit der Heimkehr des Odysseus überliefert ist.[7] Im späteren 4. Jahrhundert, im 3. und in der Folgezeit wird dieses Motiv häufig benützt und weiter ausgebildet. Es bietet den Künstlern ein willkommenes Mittel, durch die Beinstellung und die dadurch bewirkten Gewandfalten die räumliche Tiefe stärker zum Ausdruck zu bringen. Beispiele dafür finden sich auf den verschiedenen Gebieten der antiken Kunst.[8] In der Großplastik ist das Motiv zuerst in der auf den Lysippschüler Eutychides zurückzuführenden Tyche von Antiocheia fassbar, von der sich zahlreiche Varianten und Weiterführungen auf-

5. O. Walter, *JOAI* 30 (1936) 60 und *Ephemeris* 1937, 103. H. Riemann, *Kerameikos* 2, 140 zu Nr. 209.

6. Auf thessalischen Tetradrachmen um 460 v. Chr. (P. Jacobsthal, *Melische Reliefs* 197 Anm. 2). Bei gelagerten Figuren findet sich dieses Motiv auf Reliefs, z.B. schon bei dem ruhenden Herakles auf der Basis von Lamptrai *AM* 66 (1941) 162f. Taf. 65 und bei der Flötenspielerin der ludovisischen Thronlehne.

7. Steinreliefs: W. Helbig, *Führer* 3. Aufl. I 57ff. Dazu jetzt das nach Persepolis verschleppte Stück *AJA* 54 (1950) 10ff. — Melische Reliefs: P. Jacobsthal *a.a.O.* 192ff. Skyphos: E. Buschor, Furtwängler-Reichhold III 126f. zu Taf. 142.

8. A. Arndt zu Br. Br. 610. G. Lippold *RM* 33 (1918) 72ff. Zu den pompejanischen Gemälden jetzt auch die auf die Erziehung Alexanders des Großen bezüglichen Wandbilder aus dem Haus des Lucretius Carus *RM* 57 (1942) 55ff. mit Abb. 6, 7, 9, 11, 12.

weisen lassen.[9] Einen weiteren wichtigen Anhalt für die Datierung bietet sein häufiges Vorkommen auf den Bildern der Kertscher Vasen.[10]

Die Haltung des Oberkörpers der so sitzenden Gestalten ist verschieden und hängt von dem Ethos der dargestellten Figur ab: nach rückwärts gelehnt, steil aufgerichtet, nach vorne übergebeugt. Dazu kommt manchmal eine seitliche Drehung, wobei dann der mit der Hand auf den Sitz aufgestemmte Arm als Stütze dient. Im Zusammenhang damit steht auch die Kopf- und Armhaltung.

Unter den uns hier interessierenden Figuren mit nach vorne gebeugtem Oberkörper lassen sich im Wesentlichen zwei Gruppen unterscheiden, bei denen dieser entweder schlaff in sich zusammengesunken oder gespannt nach vorne gerichtet ist, je nachdem die Figur ihre Aufmerksamkeit sich selbst oder etwas vor ihr Befindlichem zuwendet, wovon dann auch die Kopfhaltung abhängt. Ersteres geht auf den schon oben besprochenen "Penelopetypus" zurück und findet sich bei Trauernden, Nachsinnenden, Zuhörenden. Oft wird der Ellenbogen des einen Arms auf das übergeschlagene Bein oder den quer über den Schoß oder die Oberschenkel gelegten andern Arm aufgesetzt, der Unterarm zum Gesicht erhoben und Kinn oder Wange in die Hand geschmiegt — also genau die Stellung, wie sie uns der nachsinnende Dichter Walther von der Vogelweide in seinen bekannten Versen schildert.[11] In zweiten Fall kann das Objekt, das die Aufmerksamkeit der sitzenden Figur auf sich zieht, ein Gegenstand, eine Person oder ein Vorgang sein; auf unserem Relief ist es das Thymiaterion, beziehungsweise das Streuen der Weihrauchkörner auf dieses.

Unter den Frauenfiguren, die auf Reliefdarstellungen in dem besprochenen Typus erscheinen,[12] ist das bekannteste Beispiel die so-

---

9. Hedwig Kusel, *Frankfurter Musen*, Diss. Heidelberg 1917, 39 Anm. 15. Besonders sei noch auf die von R. Herbig *JDAI* 59/60 (1944/5) 141ff. nunmehr als Θεὰ Σιβύλλα gedeutete neugefundene Statue im Thermenmuseum hingewiesen. vgl. nunmehr auch B. M. Felletti Maj in *Archeologia Class.* 1 (1949) 46ff.

10. Hedwig Kusel a.a.O. 38 Anm. 11.

11. Walther von der Vogelweide, *Wahlstreit:* Ich saz ûf eine steine — und dahte bein mit beine, — darûf satzt ich den ellenbogen; — ich hete in mîne hant gesmogen — daz kinne und mîn wange. — dô dâhte ich mir vil ange, — wie man zer werlte solte leben. — So sitzt auch der dem Kitharaspiel Apollos lauschende Marsyas auf der Kertscher Pelike Furtwängler-Reichhold 87.

12. G. Lippold a.a.D. 74 Anm. 1. Hieher gehört auch das Bruchstück des schönen attischen Grabreliefs aus der 2. Hälfte des 4. Jahrhunderts in Paris, H. Diepolder, *Att. Grabreliefs* 55 Abb. 12, bei dem zum erstenmal innerhalb der attischen Grabreliefs das Motiv der überschlagenen Beine bei einer sitzenden Frau festzustellen ist — A. Conze hatte das chiaramontische Peneloperelief (*Att. Grabrel.* 471 a Taf. 111 7) nur zweifelnd under die attischen aufgenommen; vgl. dazu jetzt die obige Anm. 7 mit dem neuen Exemplar aus Persepolis. Ferner darf z.B auf das Totenmahlrelief in Konstantinopel G. Mendel, *Cat.* III 1009 aus dem 2. Jahrhundert v.Chr. hingewiesen werden. Auf dem Relief des Lehrers Hieronymos von Rhodos scheint mir die von Br. Sauer Br. Br. 579 gegebene

genannte Diotima auf dem Bronzeblech (Taf. 57, b) einer Truhe aus Pompeji in Neapel, A. Ruesch, *Guida* I₂Nr. 1660,[13] dessen Darstellung auch auf einer Tonsitula in Orvieto, A. Amelung *AJA* 31 (1927) 283, Abb. 2, wiederkehrt. Diesem "Diotimatypus" steht unsere Heroine auch in Körperhaltung und Kleidung sehr nahe, nur in der Armhaltung scheint zunächst ein Unterschied: wohl streckt auch die "Diotima" den rechten Arm, offenbar mit der Kette spielend, nach vorne, der linke ist aber überhaupt nicht sichtbar. Auf unserem Relief erscheint er quer über den Schenkel gelegt, ein Motiv, das einerseits sehr wohl der Natur abgelauscht ist, andererseits aber auch vom Künstler gerade bei derartig sitzenden Figuren gerne benützt wird, da es ihm ein Mittel bietet, den sonst schwer sichtbaren im Reliefgrund befindlichen Arm zu zeigen und, ebenso wie bei den Beinen, eine bessere Tiefenwirkung zu erzielen. Jedenfalls stellt dies aber wegen der erforderten verkürzten Wiedergabe höhere Anforderungen an ihn, denen der Verfertiger des Bronzebleches lieber auswich; er zog es auch vor, den linken Fuß im langen Gewand verschwinden zu lassen.[14] So ist diese scheinbare Abweichung in der Armhaltung wohl nur aus einer Vereinfachung in der Darstellung zu erklären und die Aehnlichkeit beider Figuren ist so groß, daß wir auf ein gemeinsames Vorbild dieses "Diotimatypus" schließen dürfen.

Weiters unterscheidet sich unser Relief von der großen Anzahl der Totenmahlreliefs auch durch die Art der Anbringung der Adoranten. Im Allgemeinen gilt hier folgendes: Der gelagerte Mann stützt sich, so wie es jeder beim Symposion tat, um die Rechte frei beweglich zu haben, auf den linken Arm. Dadurch ist seine Lage auf der linken Seite und weiters mit dem Kopf nach rechts vom Beschauer gegeben

Deutung der rechts von der Nemesis in diesem Motiv sitzenden, "mit ihrem Sitz gleichsam verwachsenen Verhüllten," noch weniger die der "in den Tartaros Versinkenden" daneben als Büßerinnen überzeugend; auch die so breitspurig dasitzende Frau links von der Nemesis kommt mir gar nicht so selig vor!

13. Zuletzt darüber H. Fuhrmann *RM* 55 (1940) 78ff. mit Literatur in Anm. 1. Er lehnt wohl mit Recht die schon oft bezweifelte Deutung der mit Sokrates gepaarten Frau als Diotima ab (Natrop in RE V 1147 erwähnt das Relief nicht) und will in ihr Aspasia erkennen. Ebensowenig wird man in der auf der Schmalseite des Musensarkophags aus Ostia in Louvre Cat. somm. Nr. 475 (*RRR* 3. 196, 2) neben Sokrates stehenden Frau Diotima erkennen dürfen; wahrscheinlich stellt sie wie die auf der anderen Schmalseite eine allegorische Figur dar. Mit viel mehr Recht hat M. Möbius *JDAI* 49 (1943) 45ff. auf dem in Mantinea gefundenen Relief Athen, Nat. Mus. 226, Svoronos Taf. 199, einer Vermutung Fougères folgend, eine Darstellung der heroisierten, durch Platons Symposion berühmt gewordenen mantineischen Priesterin und Seherin erkannt.

14. Eine bezüglich der Armhaltung vollkommenere Parallele bietet der erste Perser links in der mittleren Reihe auf der bekannten Ueservase in Neapel, Furtwängler-Reichhold II 142f. Taf. 88, der in lebhaftem Gespräch mit seinem Nachbarn begriffen ist; die Vase wird von A. Furtwängler a.a.O. in die Zeit Alexanders d. Gr. gesetzt. — Auch der oben Anm. 11 erwähnte Marsyas auf der Kertscher Pelike Furtwängler-Reichhold Taf 87 hält den im Grund befindlichen Arm in derselben Weise.

und damit auch der Platz für die Frau am linken Klinenende; sitzt
sie ausnahmsweise rechts von ihm, z.B. Athen, Nat.Mus. 1515,
Svoronos Taf. 127, dann dreht er sich ihr zu.[15] Da weiters die Adoranten auf den Heros zuschreiten, zu ihm betend, vor sein Antlitz
treten, werden sie weiter links, also hinter der Frau angeordnet, da-
zwichen eventuell Altar und Opferdiener mit Tier.[16] Daß dieses
Heranschreiten der Adoranten von links nicht etwa mit dem Kultge-
brauch oder Aehnlichem zusammenhängt, zeigen etliche Weihreliefs,
wo sie von rechts kommen. Da weiters in den Reliefdarstellungen aus
ästhetischen Gründen das im Grund befindliche Bein vorgesetzt wird,
bietet die Anordnung der Adoranten nach rechts den Vorteil, daß das
linke Bein das vorgesetzte ist, was vermutlich auch althergebrachter
Sitte und dem Ritus entspricht. Abweichend von dieser Regel gehört
nun unser Relief zu den wenigen Ausnahmen unter den Totenmahlreliefs, wo die Adoranten von rechts heranschreiten. Ein weiteres
Beispiel dafür bietet das schöne attische Stück Athen Nat.Mus. 1501,
Svoronos Taf. 83, wo dies aber vielleicht durch den Gegenstand der
Darstellung besonders begründet ist, ferner ein Relief vom Westabhang der Akropolis *AM* 26 (1901) 323 Nr. 2 (Taf. 58, a), auf das wir
gleich zurückkommen werden.

Ferner fällt auf unserem Relief der Adorationsgestus der Frau auf:
sie erhebt beim Beten beide Unterarme. Während wir nach der literarischen Ueberlieferung annehmen müssen, daß man beim Gebet an
die oberen Gottheiten Blick und Hände, die Handflächen nach außen,
zum Himmel erhob,[17] finden wir bei den Darstellungen Betender auf
Weihreliefs fast durchwegs nur e i n e Hand etwa in Gesichtshöhe
erhoben. A. Conze hatte schon im *JdI* 1 (1886) 12 auf diese auffallende
Erscheinung hingewiesen. Daß in den Reliefdarstellungen die Hände
abweichend von dem wirklichen Ritus nicht hoch gegen den Himmel,
sondern nur etwa in Gesichtshöhe erhoben werden, ist voll begründet,
sobald der Gegenstand der Verehrung, d.i. die Gottheit, neben, bezw.
vor den Anbetenden dargestellt erscheint, wie dies ja gewöhnlich der
Fall ist — die Hände werden ihr eben entgegengestreckt. Wenn
weiters statt der beider Hände fast durchwegs nur e i n e erhoben
wird, so ist dies wohl mit C. Sittl, *Gebärden der Griechen und Römer*

---

15. Anders auf dem strengen Relief aus Thasos in Konstantinopel, G. Mendel,
Cat. I 578, wo die Frau auffallend klein gebildet ist.

16. Darum ist wohl auch die Darstellung auf dem Doppelrelief im Akro-
polismagazin, O. Walter, *Beschreibung* Nr. 311 A nicht als Totenmahl zu ergänzen.

17. P. Stengel, *Griech. Kultusaltertümer*[2], 73 mit Anm. 13. So erklärt man
auch die bekannte Jünglingsstatue in Berlin, Mus. Nr. 2 als "betenden Knaben."
—L. Deubner, *JDAI* 58 (1943) 90 Anm. 1, tritt für die Erklärung als ursprünglich
apotropäische Gebärde ein.

291f. auf künstlerische Rücksichten zurückzuführen.[18] Als Ausnahme von dieser bezüglich der griechischen Weihrelief gemachten Feststellung konnte C. Sittl *a.a.O.* 291 Anm. 3 nur das späte Relief aus Philippopel, *Annali* 1861 Taf. S, mit der Weihung an Demeter ὑπὲρ τῆς ὡράσεως anführen, wo die Weihende beide Arme gegen die rechts dargestellte Göttin ausstreckt. In Hinblick auf die Inschrift wurde auch vermutet, daß die Frau dadurch als blind charakterisiert werden soll (*AM* 17, 1892, 235 Anm. 1). Nunmehr kann auch auf ein sicher attisches Beispiel aus dem vierten Jahrhundert v.Chr. hingewiesen werden: das oben bereits erwähnte Totenmahlrelief vom Westabhang der Akropolis *AM* 26, 1901, 323 Nr. 2, das ich hier nach der Photographie des Deutschen Archäologischen Instituts, Athen Varia 184, auf Taf. 3 abbilde (Breite 0,61, Höhe 0,35ᵐ). Auch hier erhebt wieder eine Frau adorierend eide Arme, ohne daß m. W. dies bisher weiters beachtet wurde.

Eine ganz auffallende Erscheinung ist endlich die Art, wie der Tisch auf unserem Relief wiedergegeben ist; es handelt sich um den gewöhnlichen Typus des dreibeinigen rechteckigen Symposiontisches.[19] Während im Allgemeinen die einzelnen Objekte unseres Reliefs, wie dies ja auch sonst in der älteren griechischen Malerei und Reliefplastik üblich ist, in Parallelperspektive dargestellt sind, somit auch die beiden Tischbeine am rechten Tischende in Deckung, ist die linke Schmalseite sowohl an der Tischkante als auch an dem unpaarigen Bein perspektivisch wiedergegeben (Abb. 1). Aehnliches scheint auch an der rechten Klinenecke der Fall zu sein. Wie so oft in der griechischen Reliefplastik hätten wir also auch hier mehrere verschiedene Blickpunkte anzunehmen, u.zw. auch bei einem und demselben Gegenstand, was E. Buschor, Furtwängler-Reichhold III 128 bezüglich der Vasenmalerei für die griechische Raumgestaltung zumindest im 5. Jahrhundert v.Chr. als bezeichnend erklärt. Bedeutend weiter im Versuch der perspektivischen Wiedergabe des Tisches ging der Bildhauer des

---

18. Daß dies fast ausnahmslos der rechte Unterarm ist, u.zw. ohne Rücksicht darauf, ob der Adorant von rechts oder links herankommt — kleine Kinder erheben manchmal ihr linkes Händchen —, kann nur aus kultlichen Gründen erklärt werden; die Linke gilt bei verschiedenen Völkern als unrein. — Es wurde auch versucht, zwischen den Gebärden Betender und Gelobender zu unterscheiden, P. Stengel, a.a.O. 73 Anm. 13 — Auf attischen Grabreliefs römischer Zeit erscheinen wohl beide Unterarme im Gebet erhoben, z.B. A. Conze, *Att. Grabrel.* Nr. 1837. 1939.

19. Daß derartige Tische nur drei Beine hatten, wird wohl aus dem Wunsch nach größerer Standfestigkeit auch auf unebenem Boden zu erklären sein; vielleicht konnten sie auch bei Nichtbenützung bequemer aufeinander gestellt werden. Sehr stabil waren sie jedenfalls nicht, da eine stärkere Belastung an einer Ecke der einbeinigen Schmalseite sie zum Umkippen bringen mußte; trotzdem verwenden sogar Akrobaten solche Tische für ihre Produktionen (*Rev. Arch.* 6, 6, 1935, 23).

Abb. 1. Detail aus dem Totenmahlrelief aus Samos, Taf. 57, a.

Abb. 2. Detail aus einem Totenmahlrelief in Würzburg.

Totenmahlreliefs in Würzburg (K. Sittl, *Würzburger Antiken*, Taf. X; hier Abb. 2), wo die Tischplatte von oben gesehen, das Beinpaar nur in teilweiser Deckung nebeneinander, das unpaarige Bein aber in reiner Seitenansicht dargestellt ist; das Relief dürfte nach sonstigen Anzeichen um die wende des 4. zum 3. Jahrhundert anzusetzen sein.[20]

---

20. Auf dem Heroenmahl der einen Seite des Doppelreliefs Athen. Nat. Mus. 1943, Svoronos Taf. 79, ist der Tisch ähnlich dargestellt; man wäre fast versucht, hier an O. Wulffs "umgekehrte Perspektive" (*Kunstwissenschaftliche Beiträge für A. Schmarsow* 1ff.) zu denken.

Von weiteren Versuchen einer perspektivischen Darstellung auf unserem Relief wurde die verkürzte Wiedergabe des quer über den Schoß gelegten Armes der Heroine schon oben erwähnt. Auch den linken Unterarm des Heros, der mit der Trinkschale nach vorne gehalten gedacht ist, wollte der Bildhauer in perspektivischer Verkürzung wiedergeben. Wenn er auch die gefährliche Stelle mit dem Mantel zu bedecken versuchte, so ist ihm dies doch nicht gelungen: der Unterarm liegt ohne organische Verbindung mit dem Oberarm neben diesem wie eine Prothese und scheint aus dem Kissen herauszukommen.[21] Einen noch kühneren Versuch in dieser Richtung zeigt z.B. das sicher noch ins 4. vorchristliche Jahrhundert gehörende eleusinische Weihrelief des Lysimachides, Athen, Nationalmuseum 1519, Svoronos Taf. 88, wo der liegende *"θεός"* den linken Unterarm, dessen Hand die Schale umfasst, aus der Reliefebene senkrecht herausstreckt.[22]

Im Uebrigen kann hier auf die sehr komplizierte Frage des Eindringens und der Entwicklung der perspektischen Darstellung in der griechischen Reliefplastik nicht näher eingegangen werden. Im allgemeinen ergeben sich ja für den Reliefbildner infolge der Mittelstellung des Reliefs zwischen Rundplastik und Zeichnung bezüglich der Perspektive schwere, vielleicht überhaupt nicht zu lösende Aufgaben: Die Zeichnung gibt vom dreidimensionalen Objekt ein planes, also zweidimensionales Bild, das im Auge des Beschauers wieder als solches erscheint.[23] Bei dem, meist als Giebelschmuck verwendeten, Vollrelief werden die einzelnen Teile wie in der Rundplastik wiedergegeben, also den wirklichen Verhältnissen entsprechend, ohne jede Berücksichtigung der durch die Perspektive bewirkten Veränderungen. Je flacher aber das Relief ist und sich damit der Zeichnung nähert, umso mehr muß der Künstler wie bei letzterer die durch die Perspektive begründeten Veränderungen zur Darstellung bringen. Von diesen Gebilden, die infolge dieser Veränderungen den wirklichen Verhältnissen nicht entsprechen, aber immer noch dreidimensional sind, entsteht nun im Auge des Beschauers ein planes Bild, das natürlich die durch die Perspektive bewirkten Veränderungen zeigt, somit also auch von den bereits im Relief perspektivisch dargestellten

---

21. Ebenso wird die heikle Stelle an der linken Schulter des Kriegers auf der Stele von Pella (Konstantinopel, G. Mendel, *Cat.* I Nr. 39) zu "bemänteln" versucht.

22. Wenn A. Brueckners Annahme (*Friedhof am Eridanos* 84) richtig ist, daß dieser Lysimachides mit dem Inhaber des Grabbezirks IV (mit dem Charonrelief) und dem Stifter des Weihreliefs, Athen, Nat. Mus. 3526, Svoronos Taf. 237, aus dem Athener Amynaion identisch ist, gewinnen wir durch sein Archontat im Jahre 339/8 v.Chr. eine ungefähre Datierung dieser Reliefs.

23. Für die griechische Malerei siehe nunmehr die Freiburger Dissertation von Ludwig Schnitzler, *Ueber Aufkommen und Entwicklung einer perspektivischen Zeichenweise in der griechischen Vasenmalerei*, 1945.

Teilen; bezüglich dieser liegt also gleichsam eine Perspektive zweiten Grades vor.

Es erübrigt noch die Frage nach der Einreihung und Datierung des Reliefs. Obwohl aus Samos stammend, unterscheidet es sich doch wesentlich von den anderen dort gefundenen Totenmahlreliefs (s. o. Anm. 1), die durchwegs zur Gruppe der ostgriechischen Grabreliefs gehören. Schon die äußere Form ist eine andere: es zeigt nicht die naiskosartige Einfassung; auch fehlt das reiche Beiwerk, mit dem auf jenen der Hintergrund ganz oder teilweise gefüllt ist. Andererseits scheinen Thymiaterien, wie wir auf unserem Relief eines unter den Gegenständen auf dem Tisch finden, auf ostgriechischen Grabreliefs nach A. Pfuhl (K. Wiegand a.a.O. 71 Anm. 1) fast ganz zu fehlen. Dafür weist manches nach Attika: vor allem schon das Material, wenn es wirklich pentelischer Marmor ist. Für die äußere Form der länglichen Platte ohne seitliche Einfassung bieten zahlreiche attische Reliefs Parallelen, so gleich das oben S. 600 herangezogene Totenmahlrelief vom Westabhang. Gerade dieses konnte auch als Beispiel für den so auffallenden Gestus der Adoration mit beiden Händen und für das Heranschreiten der Adoranten von der ungewöhnlichen rechten Seite angeführt werden. Desgleichen finden wir die Aktion, in der die Heroine erscheint, das Streuen von Weihrauch auf das Thymiaterion, wie oben ausgeführt, sehr oft auf attischen Totenmahlreliefs dargestellt. Wenn endlich die Heroine auf letzteren in der Regel auch auf der Kline selbst, und nicht wie auf unserem Relief und fast durchwegs auf ostgriechischen auf einem eigenen Stuhl, sitzt, so finden sich doch auch zahlreiche attische Stücke, wo dies der Fall ist; z.B. Athen Nat.Mus. 1505, Svoronos Taf. 85.

Beim Versuch einer Datierung stößt man zunächst auf sich anscheinend widersprechende Merkmale. Die äußere Form der Platte, das flache Relief, die in scharfer Seitenansicht dargestellten Adoranten — zumal die Figur der Frau — und ihre isolierte Anordnung würden eher auf ältere Zeit hinweisen, aber gerade letzteres findet sich ja im Gegensatz zu der gedrängten Darstellung der Reliefs des 4. Jahrhunderts auf jüngeren Stücken wieder (vgl. dazu O. Walter, *Beschreibung* Nr. 46). Als sicherer Ausgangspunkt kann nur der Typus der Heroine dienen, der nach den obigen Ausführungen ins letzte Viertel des 4. Jahrhunderts v.Chr. weist. In dieser Zeit scheint auch der Versuch der perspektivischen Wiedergabe, wie wir ihn an dem Tisch und den verkürzten Gliedmaßen sahen, sehr wohl möglich. Endlich sind für die hier erscheinende Form des Thymiaterion nach K. Wiegand a.a.O. 71 gerade auch für diese Zeit weitere Beispiele nachzuweisen. Es bleibt nur noch der so lebendig wirkende Kopf des Heros.

Daß er als Hauptperson das Gesicht herauswendet, begegnet auf jüngeren attischen Totenmahlreliefs häufig — hier ist seine Dreiviertel-Profilstellung durch die von rechts heranschreitenden Adoranten begründet. Die starke Auflockerung der Haare läßt sich als handwerkliche Weiterführung dessen, was wir auf den großen attischen Grabreliefs der letzten Zeit vor dem Luxusgesetz des Demetrios sehen, wohl verstehen. Da andererseits keinerlei Anzeichen vorliegen, die in hellenistiche Zeit weisen, so bestünde kein Bedenken, das Relief ins ausgehende vierte Jahrhundert zu setzen, wenn nicht ein bisher nicht erwähntes Detail dagegen spräche: Beim Heroenpaar sind die Augensterne durch tiefe Punkte plastisch angegeben. Nach der sorgfältigen Ausführung und der Oxydierung ist kaum anzunehmen, daß es sich um eine moderne Retouche handelt; wohl könnte sie im späteren Altertum anläßlich einer Wiederverwendung des ursprünglichen Weihreliefs als Grabstein erfolgt sein. Andernfalls dürfte man vielleicht an eine Entstehung des Reliefs in hadrianischer Zeit denken. Daß attische Bildhauer die Augensterne bereits vor und um die Mitte des 2. Jahrhunderts n.Chr. auch in der Reliefplastik öfter plastisch angaben, ersehen wir aus einer Anzahl von Grabreliefs,[24] die durch ihre Inschriften in diese Zeit datiert sind. Wie in der damaligen Großplastik und in der Architektur vielfach klassizistisch gearbeitet wurde, kann dies auch in der, wenn auch mehr oder minder kunstgewerblichen, Reliefplastik der Fall gewesen sein und so wären aus dem Eklektizismus jener Zeit vielleicht auch manche uns zunächst altertümlich anmutende Elemente zu erklären.

24. Z. B. A. Conze, *Att. Grabrel.* Nr. 1901. 1902. 2086 mit den Inschriften IG II, 3₂ 9479. 12358. 6299.

EIN TOTENMAHLRELIEF IN PERGAMON

OTFRIED R. DEUBNER
Salem/Baden

Tafel 56

In dem Lokalmuseum von Bergama, das in den Jahren 1932-35 nach den Plänen von Harald Hanson gebaut und seit 1935/36 von mir eingerichtet wurde,[1] befindet sich unter anderen Schätzen ein Relief vom bekannten Typus der Totenmahle (Taf. 56).[2]

Wir blicken gleichsam hinein in die Vorhalle eines Naiskos, in der sich ein festliches Gelage abspielt. Hier lagern zu zweit auf einer Kline hingestreckt zwei fröhliche Festgenossen. Es ist offenbar und trotz der starken Verwitterung auch noch zu sehen, dass es sich um das Fest von wohlhabenden Leuten handeln muss, denn das Bein der Kline, das sichtbar wird, zeigt ebenso wie der Löwenbeindreifuss davor kostbare Schnitz- und Drechselarbeit. Der leere Raum unter der Kline ist mit einem Tuch verhangen, das an der Polsterunterlage unmittelbar neben dem Klinenbein befestigt senkrecht herabfällt.[3]

Die Kline scheint sich ganz in der Ebene des Reliefgrundes vor uns auszubreiten; wo sie nach links hin endet, ist nicht ganz klar; es scheint, als habe der Bildhauer durch die Fortsetzung der Beinlinie des linken Gelagerten hinter dem Rücken der Sitzenden ausdrücken wollen, dass sie über die Bildfäche hinausragt und erst hinter der Säule endigt. Von den beiden Männern, die auf ihr liegen wird der weiter rechts liegende von den Oberschenkeln ab von seinem Genossen überschnitten; diesen verdeckt etwa an derselben Stelle die vor der Kline sitzende Frau.

Der rechte Gelagerte, der nur um den Unterkörper einen Mantel gewickelt hat und im übrigen nackt ist, zeigt sich in einer auffälligen Gebärde. Er hebt nämlich mit erhobener Rechten ein Rhyton genanntes Gefäss[4] hoch, aus dem er Wein in die Schale spritzen lässt, die seine Linke, nach verwandten Denkmälern[5] zu urteilen, gehalten haben

---

1. Ein noch auf Wunsch von Wiegand im Jahre 1936 von mir verfasster Museumskatalog liegt seit 1939 dem türkischen Unterrichtsministerium im Manuskript vor. Unbekannte Gründe haben seine Drucklegung bis heute verhindert.

2. Feinkörniger weisser Marmor; sehr verwitterte Oberfläche. H. = 74 — Br. = 68, 5 — D. = 18, 5 — Relieft. 8 — H. der Säulen 47 cm.

3. Vgl. die Klinen der pergamenischen Reliefkeramik *Alt. v. Perg.* 1, 2 Beibl. 44, 4. — *AA* 1939, 346 Abb. 10.

4. Buschor *MüJb.* 1919, 26ff. — *AA*. 1938, 762 (Luschey).

5. Totenmahlreliefs: Literatur J. Seidl, *Das Totenmahlrelief* Diss. Wien 1943 (mir nicht zugänglich). Sonst Hauptstelle *JdI.* 20, 1905, 47ff. 123ff. (Pfuhl). 50, 1935, 13ff. (Pfuhl). Mendel, *Katalog Konstantinopel* III S.184ff.

muss. Mit dem linken Ellenbogen stützte er sich auf ein Stützkissen. Die Haltung des ebenfalls leider ganz abgesplitterten Gesichts ist auch nur aus analogen Reliefs zu ermitteln: der feiernde Zecher, der den Beschauer grade anzublicken scheint, ist tatsächlich mit grösster Aufmerksamkeit dabei, den Strahl im richtigen Bogen vom Rhyton zur Schale zu leiten. Während aber die meisten vergleichbaren Gelagerten bärtig sind, hatte der unsrige, soweit die Reste ein Urteil zulassen, ein jugendlich bartloses Gesicht.

Versunken in ein anderes Tun, viel weniger einem möglichen Zuschauer zugewandt, ist der zweite Gelagerte, der sich auch äusserlich von seinem Genossen durch die Tracht zu unterscheiden scheint: Man glaubt zu erkennen, dass er einen Chiton anhat (Halsausschnitt, Falten bei der rechten Achsel) ; um seinen Unterkörper ist das Himation gewickelt und offenbar noch über die linke Schulter und den linken Unterarm gezogen. Er streckt seine Rechte nach einem auf dem Tischchen stehenden Gerät aus und scheint es mit den Spitzen seiner Finger zu berühren. Das Gerät ist deutlich erkennbar, ein kleines auf drei Füsschen stehendes Räuchergefäss, dessen zwei Henkel an den Seiten herabfallen: der Genosse bringt ein Räucheropfer dar. Man möchte glauben, dass auch sein leider fortgebrochenes Gesicht ganz diesem Opfer zugewendet war ; seine Linke wird die Büchse mit dem Räucherwerk gehalten haben, die nur noch in Spuren sichtbar ist.

Auf lehnenlosem Stuhl, dessen Beine, trotz der starken Verwitterung, noch eine Drechselarbeit zeigen, die derjenigen des Klinenbeines entspricht, sitzt am Fussende der Kline eine Frau, wie teilnahmlos, die Füsse auf einen Schemel gesetzt, die linke Hand wie sinnend oder trauernd zum Kopfe geführt. Sie trägt einen bis auf die Füsse reichenden Chiton und einen Mantel, der die ganze Gestalt umhüllte und vermutlich auch noch das Haupt verschleierte. Stuhl und Schemel sind wiederum ganz in die Bildfläche gerückt, und auch die Gestalt der Frau selber breitet sich in reinem Profil auf ihr aus. Sie ist erstaunlich klein, wenn man sie mit dem beiden Gelagerten vergleicht, aber darin ist keine Absicht zu erblicken ; sie gehört als nahe Teilnehmerin zu der festlichen Szene, deren Zeugen wir sind, ist nicht etwa durch das Format in eine andere Sphäre gerückt, wie man denken könnte, auch wenn sie weder in Handlung noch in Gebärde mit den Hauptpersonen verbunden zu sein scheint.

Noch muss eine vierte aber wichtige kleine Person unseres Reliefbildes erwähnt werden, die der sinnenden Frau gegenüber, angelehnt an die rechte Naiskossäule, in still abwartender Haltung dasteht, mit übergeschlagenem rechten Bein und vor dem Schoss gekreuzten

Armen, gekleidet in einen bis zu den Knien reichenden Chiton; das vor ihm stehende Gefäss, ein hochfüssiges Mischgefäss, verrät uns, dass wir es mit dem Mundschenken zu tun haben, der auf den Wink seiner Herren wartet, Trinkbecher oder Schalen mit frischem Wein zu füllen. Der Vorderteil seines Kopfes ist ebenso wie es bei den anderen Figuren geschehen ist, offenbar willkürlich abgeschlagen.

Die Betrachtung unseres Banketts wäre unvollständig, wenn wir nicht noch einen Blick auf das Löwenfusstischchen würfen, von dem oben bereits kurz die Rede war; es ist der Speisentisch der Gelagerten; ausser dem Räucherbecken stehen darauf noch einige andere Dinge, die wir bei dem mangelhaften Erhaltungszustand auch nur durch die Hilfe von verwandten Denkmälern wiedererkennen können: deutlich zeichnen sich im Umriss zwei pyramidenförmige Kuchen und neben ihnen, zum Räucherbecken hin, kleinere runde Gegenstände, Eier oder Früchte ab, nach rechts hin dann ein flacher Kuchen und ihm entsprechend links eine Weintraube, die etwas über den Tischrand hängt. Es sind Speisen, die teilweise jedenfalls bei solchen "Totenmahlen" üblich waren.

Das Tischchen selbst ist in konventioneller Weise wiedergegeben mit drei Beinen, aber so, als müsse man sich noch ein viertes vorstellen. Das liegt aber nur an dem Darstellungsschema, die Tischchen dieser Art waren allesamt dreifüssig.[6]

Was wir bisher sahen, steht durchaus in einem festen Sinnzusammenhang, lässt sich als ein zusammengehöriges Ganzes begreifen: Ein festliches Bankett im kleinen Kreise der engsten Familie, das man in einer offenen überdeckten Halle feiert. Nur die Haltung der Frau schien auf den tieferen Sinn dieses Mahles zu deuten; anwesend — nicht anwesend, so schien sie zu veranschaulichen, womit wir es hier zu tun haben, mit einem Denkmal des trauernden Gedenkens an geliebte dahingegangene Menschen.

Gewaltig und schreckenerregend ragt von der anderen Seite, unvermittelt aus dem Innern des Naiskos emporspriessend, ein Baum in diese festliche Szene hinein; knorrig wächst sein Stamm empor und geht in Stumpf und weiter oben in Aeste aus, die dichtes Laubwerk tragen; die Blätter gleichen Platanenblättern. Was den Baum so besonders unheimlich macht, das ist die Schlange, die sich um den Stamm und den Aststumpf des Baumes ringelt und ihren Kopf nach der Schale streckt, die der rhytonhaltende Zecher in seiner Linken hält. Man nimmt aber merkwürdigerweise keine Notiz von ihr, scheint vielmehr mit ihr zu rechnen; sie gehört nämlich zu einer solchen Bankettszene, wie unzählige verwandte Denkmäler zeigen; sie ist das

---

6. Löwenbeine von solchen Tischchen *Alt. v. Perg.* 7, 2 nr. 448f.

dämonische Tier, in dem nach griechischem Glauben die Seele besonderer Toter, der Heroen, weiterlebte, und so empfängt sie bei dieser festlichen Gelegenheit den ihr geschuldeten Tribut.

Wird mit Baumstamm und Schlange der düstere Untergrund unseres Banketts sehr deutlich vor Augen geführt, steht so neben frommem Brauch gleichsam seine dämonische Begründung, so finden wir bei unserem Relief noch ein weiteres Element: das von dem Gebälk herabhängend oder an der Wand befestigt zu denkende Bild des Reiters, der auf seinem Pferde einem Baum entgegenreitet. Dies Bild, kräftig von dem Hintergrund des Naiskos abgesetzt und darüber erhoben, soll ganz offenbar ein Weihepinax sein — gemalt oder in Relief — den einer der Angehörigen zu Ehren eines der Verstorbenen an dieser Stelle angebracht hat. Auch seine Darstellung ist konventionell[7] und von zahlreichen Reliefs bekannt: der Baum deutet dieselbe Sphäre an, die der Baum des grösseren Reliefs kennzeichnet, denn auch um ihn ringelt sich eine Seelenschlange und streckt ihren Kopf dem Reiter entgegen. Es handelt sich auch bei diesem kleinen Pinax um ein Grab- oder besser Totendenkmal besonderer Art: wie die Totenmahle den Toten im Jenseits an den Freuden des Mahles teilnehmend darstellen, so zeigen diese Denkmäler den Toten bei einer anderen Beschäftigung, die dem Edlen gebührte; er reitet im Paradeschritt auf einem wohldressierten Pferd einher und vereinigt sich dabei ganz zwanglos mit seiner Seelenschlange, für deren Ernährung er offenbar Sorge tragen muss.

Die Anbringung der Reiterdarstellung an dieser Stelle ist auffällig; gewöhnlich findet man bei solchen Totenmahlen hier nur einen Pferdekopf, um den ritterlichen Stand des Toten zu kennzeichnen; es sind mir nur zwei weitere Reliefs (davon eines ein Bruchstück) bekannt, wo ebenfalls die Darstellung der ganzen Gestalt des Reiters auf einem Pinax genau an derselben Stelle zu finden ist;[8] und da diese die älteren sind, darf man vermuten, dass der Meister unseres Reliefs sie oder verwandte Stücke als Vorlagen benutzte.

Im Giebelfeld des Naiskos sind zwei Schlangen dargestellt, die sich symmetrisch von beiden Seiten der Mitte zu ringeln, wo eine Schale zu sehen ist — hier helfen wieder Paralleldenkmäler aus[9] — in der Speise für die Seelenschlangen, vermutlich ein Ei, liegt. Dass diese Schale aufrecht auf ihrer Kante im Giebelfeld steht, dass das Ei also aus ihr herausrollen müsste, darf uns nicht stören; das gewiss altüber-

---

7. Grabreliefs aus Pergamon mit dem Typus des Reiters *Alt. v. Perg.* 7, 2 nr. 306ff.

8. Svoronos, *Das Athen.Nat.Mus.* Text 2, 536.

9. *Alt. v. Perg.* 7, 2 nr. 328.

lieferte ornamentale Sinnbild deutet den Inhalt des Reliefs gleichsam in verkürzter Form.

Hat man sich mit der Darstellung und ihrem Sinngehalt beschäftigt, dann verdient auch die rahmende Architektur einen Blick und ein erklärendes Wort. Denn ganz offensichtlich haben wir es hier mit aussergewöhnlichen Formen zu tun, die nicht in die bekannten griechischen Architekturordnungen passen. Die Säulen stehen auf quadratischen Plinthen, wie jonische Säulen, ihre kannelierten Schäfte wachsen aus einfachen Wülsten heraus, die jedoch noch ein verbindendes Glied, einen kleinen Wulst, oder wahrscheinlicher ein glattes Bändchen für den Uebergang in den Schaft tragen, wie es über den Tori attisch-jonischer Basen erscheint. Die Krönung der Säulen bilden nun ungewöhnliche Kapitelle einer Form, die man am ehesten als niedrige Blütenkelche bezeichnen darf. Auf ihnen liegen quadratische Abakusplatten, die aber nicht ungegliedert sind wie die Abaci der dorischen Kapitelle, sondern die ein kleines Bekrönungsprofil tragen. Auf den Säulen liegt ein Zweifaszienarchitrav jonischer Bildung; was darüber folgt, wird man für die Abbreviatur eines Zahnschnittes halten dürfen; ein ebensolcher wird auch in den aufsteigenden Giebelgeisa gemeint sein. Die Akrotere zeigen schematisch derbe Formen. Diese letzten Einzelheiten interessieren aber lange nicht so sehr wie die höchst eigentümliche Säulenform: es wird schwerlich ein Zufall sein, dass in der grossen Architektur Pergamons mehrere Beispiele von ebensolchen Kapitellen zu finden sind,[10] während sie andernorts nur ganz sporadisch auftreten. Bei dem einzigen mit Sicherheit wiederherstellbaren Bau dieser "pergamenischen Ordnung" setzt sich freilich die Architektur über den Kapitellen im Unterschied zu dem, was unser Relief zeigt, in einer Spielart der dorischen Ordnung fort, wodurch jedoch der Zusammenhang nicht weniger deutlich wird.

Die Vorstellung des im Jenseits zechenden Toten war nicht gemeingriechisch, ja vermutlich überhaupt ungriechisch. Das erste Denkmal, das sie vielleicht bezeugt, gehört dem mittleren 5. Jh. an,[11] und die Kammergräber, die mit Klinen ausgestattet sind, wo also der Glaube zugrunde liegt, dass die Toten für ihre Gelage im Jenseits eine solche Ausstattung des Grabes nötig haben, gibt es in Griechenland erst seit dem 4. Jh.

---

10. Z. B. *Dionysostempel am Oberen Markt Alt. v. Perg.* 3, 1 Taf. wiederholt bei Zschietzschmann, *Die hellenist.u.röm. Kunst* 6 Abb. 3. Hallen (?) des hellenistischen Asklepieions O. Deubner, *Das Asklepieion von Pergamon* 40 Abb. 31. *Hallen der Theaterterrasse, Alt. v. Perg.* 4, Taf. 24 Hallen (?) der mittleren Gymnasiumsterrasse *Alt. v. Perg.* 6, Taf. 30.

11. Schede, *Meisterwerke* Taf. 5. Rodenwaldt, *Kunst der Antike*⁴, 284. Ch. Picard, *Manuel* 2. 93, fig. 44 und sonst häufig abgebildet.

Manches spricht dafür, dass die Griechen die Idee des Totenmahles in historischer Zeit von ihren kleinasiatischen Nachbarn[12] übernommen haben. Selten sind solche Uebernahmen jedoch einfach, selten wird das neue Gut vorbehaltlos angenommen; es scheint kaum ein Zufall, dass das thasische Zecherrelief — als Totenmahl — im 5. Jh. völlig alleinsteht.[13] Die Uebernahme des Totenmahles in dieser Form ist zu jenem Zeitpunkt offenbar missglückt, und es mussten 150-200 Jahre vergehen, bis die Griechen den Schritt der Uebernahme aufs neue und diesmal mit bleibendem Erfolg taten.[14]

Dabei kam ihnen zustatten, dass inzwischen, seit dem Ende des 5. Jh., im Bereich der Heroenkulte eine Gattung von Weihreliefs in Schwang gekommen war, die wie ein Präludium des Themas der Totenmahle anmuten.[15] Diese Reliefs atmen die frohe Stimmung, die allen klassischen Weihreliefs eignet, sprechen von schlichter Ergebenheit der Menschen in die göttliche Fügung. Nichts von Trauer um Dahingegangene: es handelt sich um echte Heroen, grosse Männer einer längst verflossenen Zeit, die in diesen Reliefs dargestellt werden, und deren Hilfe man sich mit diesen Gaben einer echten Frömmigkeit versichern wollte. Ihre Namen wechselten mit den Orten.

Der grundlegende Wandel der geistig-religiösen Situation seit dem 4. Jh., der aus unserem Relief spricht, wenn wir es neben die Heroenreliefs und auf der anderen Seite auch neben die attischen Grabreliefs jenes Jahrhunderts stellen, lässt es unmöglich erscheinen, dasselbe unmittelbar an jene Werke, etwa als ein Erzeugnis des frühen 3. Jh., anzuschliessen. Eine beträchtliche Zeitspanne muss verflossen sein, bis aus den ganz schlichten, innigen, garnicht auf einen Beobachter berechneten, im echten Sinne naiven Szenen der Heroenreliefs so raffiniert durchdachte, komplexe, für einen Beschauer berechnete und fast bühnenmässig zurechtgemachte Bilder entstanden sein können, wie unser pergamenisches Totenmahlrelief eines ist. Dabei muss man ihm noch eine gewisse Beschränkung in den Mitteln zugestehen; noch ist hier das Interieurhafte der grossen Masse der hellenistischen Totenmahle nicht überwiegend, es fehlen die vielen,

---

12. S.z.B. E. Akurgal, *Späthethit. Bildkunst* (Ankara 1949) 135.

13. Das Relief im Kerameikos Conze nr. 1173 Taf. 251, auf dem zwei bärtige Männer in Gesellschaft von zwei sitzenden Frauen beim Mahle liegen, während Charon mit seinem Nachen vorgefahren ist, um den Verstorbenen abzuholen, ein Werk der 60er Jahre des 4. Jh. gehört trotz der typologischen Verwandtschaft nicht in den Zusammenhang! Es zeigt eine reine Familienszene, wie die anderen Reliefs und die Lekythen, in die sich die Sphäre des Todes sehr vernehmlich mischt, und hat nichts mit der Heroisierung der Toten und Jenseitsfreuden zu tun.

14. Die früheste Totenmahl-Darstellung des später üblichen Typus scheint auf der marmornen Choenkanne attischen Stils im Louvre aus dem Ende des 4. Jh. v.Ch. vorzukommen. L. Deubner, *Att. Feste* Taf. 15. Photo Giraudon 26304.

15. Zuletzt U. Hausmann, *Kunst und Heiltum* 111ff.

so oft bis zum Ueberdruss vorgetragenen Symbole wie Grabaltar, Grabmal, das Wandbrett mit den Gebrauchsgegenständen, der Geschirrstand mit Trink- und sonstigen Geräten und was sonst üblich ist. Die grosse Masse dieser Totenmahle ist ebenso wie die meisten Grabreliefs des Hellenismus, erst im späteren 2. Jh. und im 1. Jh. v.Chr. entstanden, wie der gleiche Herkunftsort, das gleiche Format und der gleiche Stil genügend beweisen.

Das pergamenische Relief macht aber nicht nur durch die Beschränkung in den Anspielungen auf die Grabesphäre, sondern auch durch die gesamte bildhauerische Arbeit einen günstigen Eindruck unter diesen Werken. Nur selten findet man die Architektur mit solcher Ausführlichkeit vorgeführt, und die Qualität auch in den übrigen Partien bestätigt, dass wir es mit einem besondern schönen Exemplar seiner Gattung zu tun haben. Und dass die Säulenarchitektur mit einem Giebel abschliesst, das gehört zu seinen zweifellos wohl erwogenen Besonderheiten. Der Bildhauer wollte damit wohl sagen, dass die Bankettszene nicht wie sonst meist in der Säulenhalle oder Laube eines Grabbezirks, sondern in der säulengetragenen Vorhalle eines Tempelchens stattfindet, das doch wohl das Heroon, der Grabtempel der in dem Relief geehrten Toten, sein soll.

Diese Deutung führt zusammen mit dem von den Heroenreliefs hergeleiteten Bildtypus, auf die höchst merkwürdige und wohlbekannte Tatsache, dass sich mit dem Fortschreiten des Hellenismus die Vorstellung immer weiter verbreitete, dass alle Toten zu den Heroen versetzt werden; was ehemals Vorrecht von längst verstorbenen Helden und Helfern der Menschheit und allenfalls von einigen wenigen ausgezeichneten Männern war, das beanspruchten im Lauf der Zeit seit dem 3. Jh. v.Chr. immer mehr Menschen für sich: dass sie, als Belohnung für ein tugendhaftes Leben, im Jenseits derselben Freuden teilhaftig würden, die ursprünglich nur den echten Heroen gebührten. Und so errichtete man Grabtempel, die man mit Grabbezirken umgab, nannte diese Tempel ἡρῷα und die Bezirke τεμένη und feierte das Andenken der heroisierten Toten alljährlich mit Gastgelagen innerhalb der Grabbezirke. Man wird mit Hinblick auf das Heroon von Gjölbaschi kaum fehlgehen, wenn man die Ausbreitung dieser Sitte im griechischen Osten — das Mutterland hat sie anscheinend nur in kleinem Umfange mitgemacht — mit starkem kleinasiatischen Einfluss erklärt, der ja auch bereits weiter oben für die Herkunft der sepulkralen Vorstellungen verantwortlich gemacht wurde; das würde gut zusammenpassen.

Wann zum ersten Male Totenmahle sich vom Heroenrelief abgelöst haben und nun als eigene Gattung unter den übrigen Grabreliefs erscheinen, diesen Moment veranschaulichen vielleicht am besten solche Reliefs, wo der Heros nicht mehr in heroischer Nacktheit, sondern in seinem zufälligen bürgerlichen Gewand zu sehen ist;[16] damit soll nicht gesagt sein, dass nicht auch nach dem Zeitpunkt, wo das möglich war, noch nackte Gelagerte vorkommen. Freilich stehen die Datierungen der fraglichen Reliefs noch zu wenig fest als dass man hier eine sichere Grundlage hätte. Kann unser Relief uns zu einem etwas festeren Punkt in der noch sehr losen Gruppierung des Materials verhelfen?

Der architektonisch ausgestaltete Rahmen schliesst sich an die grosse pergamenische Architektur an, wo solche aussergewöhnlichen Formen nicht vor dem 2. Jh. v.Chr. nachzuweisen sind. Die verwandten Grabreliefs mit ausgebildeten Architekturrahmen scheinen allesamt eher dem späten als dem mittleren Hellenismus anzugehören.[17] Die Bekleidung des linken Gelagerten mit dem Chiton deutet auf die fortschreitende Verbürgerlichung der heroischen Sphäre, mit der doch vor dem späteren Hellenismus nicht zu rechnen ist, während der unbekleidete Gelagerte den heroischen Stil wahrt; er mag der gedachte ἥρως κτίστης der Familie sein. Die Vielschichtigkeit des Reliefs, verbunden mit dem Bemühen, die Anstandsregeln in der Reliefbehandlung im Sinne der klassischen Reliefs zu wahren, spricht für beginnenden Klassizismus des 2. Jh. eher als für eine ältere Zeit. Unser Relief wird um die Mitte des 2. Jh. v.Chr. entstanden sein.

Das Denkmal, das uns beschäftigt hat, ist 10 km von Pergamon entfernt an der Strasse nach Dikili gefunden worden.[18] Man wird annehmen dürfen, dass es aus der West-Nekropole von Pergamon stammt. Wie es allerdings in den Grabbezirk eingefügt war, in dem es gewiss keine ganz unbedeutende Rolle spielte, ist noch ungesichert; vermutlich war es, tafelbildartig verwendet, mehr oder weniger zwanglos als Belebung einer glatten Mauerfläche eingefügt, in einem der τεμένη, das einer der wohlhabendsten Familien von Pergamon gehört haben muss; anders ist seine hohe Qualität nicht zu deuten. Dem Vorübergehenden sprach es von Jenseitshoffnungen, deren materialistischer Geist einen echten Griechen fremdartig berührt haben muss, die aber vielleicht nicht unbeteiligt an der Vorstellung von der "Auferstehung des Fleisches" waren; denn hier sah man sie

16. So etwa das Relief *JdI* 50 1935, 40 Abb. 22 unbekannter Herkunft in Istanbul.

17. Z. B. Pfuhl a.a.O. 47ff. Abb. 3, 10 10a, 17, Taf. VI 2. — *Berlin, Beschreibung* nr. 767. — Mendel a.a.O. III 906, 928, 1043, 1021.

18. Nach freundlicher Mitteilung des Direktors der Altertümer in Bergama, Osman Bayatlï.

ja im Jenseits tafeln, voll Blut und Leben, sie, die der Rasen deckte oder die Grabkammer umschloss. Und so wäre denn die geistesge- schichtliche Wirkung, die von diesem Denkmal wie von anderen ähn- lichen ausgegangen sein mag, weiter und tiefer, als ein erster Blick vermuten liess.

ATTIC STELAE

Bas-reliefs of art sublime
From the tombs of olden time,
Spirit of antiquity,
Soul of sorrow that I see
Where the chisel of divine
Inspiration traced the line
On the stone Athena gave
Honoring a hero's grave,

Spirit, grant the power to me
In holy cloak of harmony
Grief eternally to dress
And the tears of her distress
To enclose and sacred hold
In Metre's urn of precious gold.

Kostes Palamas

Translated by
John B. Edwards

LA STELE VATICANA DEL PALESTRITA INTEGRATA

Filippo Magi
Città del Vaticano

Tavole 58-60

Circa mezzo secolo fa, e precisamente nel gennaio del 1902, Orazio Marucchi, mentre era in cerca di antiche iscrizioni, rinveniva in Roma, in un magazzino della chiesetta di San Lorenzo *in foro piscium* presso Piazza San Pietro, una stele funeraria greca del secolo V a.C., che di lì a poco, donata dai Padri Scolopi (allora proprietari della chiesa) al papa Leone XIII in occasione del suo giubileo sacerdotale, diveniva vaticana ed era collocata nel passaggio dalla Galleria delle Statue al Gabinetto delle Maschere, dove tuttora si ammira.[1]

Il monumento fu ritrovato incompleto; mancavano infatti la parte superiore, che poteva essere un coronamento a palmetta soprastante a una cornice di cui resta traccia, la parte inferiore della lastra figurata per circa un terzo, e nella stessa lastra una zona longitudinale a destra, oltre ai due angoli superiori, ma la superficie del rilievo era assai ben conservata, nonostante che il marmo avesse perfino servito, prima d'esser buttato là dove lo rinvenne il Marucchi, a coprire una chiavica.

La scena rappresentata è colta nella palestra: un giovane palestrita (il defunto) e il suo servitorello si guardano, in piedi l'uno di fronte all'altro; il primo, in procinto forse di iniziare il suo esercizio, sembra che stia per afferrare con la destra il vasetto dell'olio che il ragazzo gli avvicina sospeso al suo polso destro (il legaccio era dipinto), accompagnando il gesto con la sinistra alzata, l'altro è ai suoi ordini e nella mano sinistra tiene lo strigile che servirà alla fine dell'esercizio (tav. 59 a, parte superiore).

Fin dalla prima publicazione, per merito dell'Amelung, si riconobbe nel rilievo un pezzo già appartenuto alla ricca collezione d'antichità iniziata dal Cardinale Paolo Emilio Cesi nel 1520 e poi continuata dal fratello Cardinale Federico, e conservata nel possesso che i Cesi ebbero, palazzo e giardino, a sud dell'attuale Piazza San Pietro presso la Porta Cavalleggeri (ove è oggi la curia generalizia degli Agostiniani), in luogo dunque assai vicino alla chiesetta di San Lorenzo. Lo vide in

---

1. *Dissert. Pont. Accad. Romana di Archeologia*, serie II, VIII, 1903, 473 segg. (O. Marucchi, W. Amelung, G. Gherardini); Amelung, W., "Griechische Grabstele," *JDAI*, 18 (1903), 109 seg.; *id., Die Sculpturen des Vatican. Museums*, 2, 1908, n.421. 666 segg.; *id.,* "Zu der Grabstele eines Palaestriten im Vatikanischen Museum," *JDAI* 24 (1909) 191 segg.; Helbig, W., *Fuehrer durch d. Sammlg. klass. Alter. in Rom*, 1912, n.246, 157 seg.; Gerke, F., *Griechische Plastik in arch. u. klass. Zeit*, 1938, n. 142, 239 seg.

quel giardino, infatti, e lo descrisse nelle sue "Statue antiche che in Roma in diversi luoghi e case particolari si veggono" Ulisse Aldrovandi già nel 1556, e Pierre Jacques, uno scultore di Reims, che disegnò antiche sculture in Roma tra il 1572 e il 1577, ce ne lasciò un accurato disegno[2] (fig. 1).

Ma già prima, e cioè nel 1532, la stele era stata riprodotta in quella curiosa ricostruzione di Roma antica che è l' "Antiquae urbis Romae

Fig. 1. Il disegno di P. Jacques.

cum regionibus simulachrum" di M. Fabio Calvo, la cui prima edizione è appunto di quell'anno[3] (fig. 2). Infine, nella prima metà del secolo XVII, troviamo ancora una volta disegnata la stele in un libro di schizzi di proprietà di un certo Dal Pozzo che si conserva a Windsor Castle. Anzi, in quella raccolta c'è anche disegnato a parte il particolare della mano con lo strigile[4] (tav. 59 b).

In tutti e tre questi disegni le due figure ci si mostravano integre, e perciò si ritenne che quanto appariva in più nei disegni rispetto al rilievo non fosse dovuto a fantasia dei disegnatori, ma riproducesse

2. Per la collezione Cesi vedi Huelsen, Chr., "Roemische antike Gaerten d. XVI. Jhrhs.," in *Abhandl. d. Heidelb. Akad. d. Wissensch*, Phil.-hist. Kl. 4. Abhandl. 1917, 1 segg. Ivi pure, a pp. 27 e 39 per le testimonianze di Aldrovandi e Jacques.

3. Cf. *Dissert.*, 478.

4. Cf. Amelung, *JDAI* 24 (1909), 191 segg.

l'originale come era allora conservato, o al più un sapiente restauro, e si preferì giustamente la prima piuttosto che la seconda ipotesi.[5]

Un fortunato rinvenimento, accaduto pochi giorni prima della scorsa Pasqua, ci permette ora di completare questo insigne e avventurato monumento. Infatti, in occasione dei lavori di restauro della predetta chiesa di San Lorenzo, condotti a cura della Santa Sede, si è appunto ritrovata la parte inferiore della stele, divenuta chiusino di sepolcro inserito nel pavimento della seconda cappella di sinistra (tav. 58 b, 59, a parte inferiore). Il frammento,[5a] che conserva le gambe delle

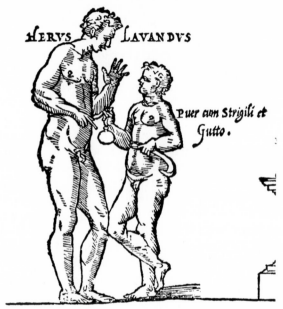

Fig. 2. Il disegno di Fabio Calvo.

due figure coi piedi poggianti su di un largo listello scanalato, combacia perfettamente con il pezzo vaticano dal quale fu segato, ma non giunge a sinistra all'orlo di quello mentre lo sorpassa notevolmente a destra, pur non estendendosi fino all'orlo originario, Vi resta tuttavia, da questa parte, un cospicuo avanzo di quel panno ripiegato e posato su di un pilastro, del quale è pure visibile sul marmo l'orlo anteriore davanti alle gambe del ragazzo, che è riprodotto nel disegno del Jacques (disegno che a fronte del frammento mostra di essere quanto mai esatto); nel disegno di Windsor Castle è riprodotto il solo panno, in

5. Cf. Amelung, *Die Sculpturen*, 667 (non era dello stesso parere in *Dissert.*, 8). In *Berl. Philol. Wochenschr.*, 1902, 787, A. Furtwängler riteneva senz' altro che il pezzo mancante fosse ancora esistente al tempo di P. Jacques.
5a. Alt. 0,665, Largh. 0,705, spess, 0,085-0,09.

quello di Fabio Calvo non c'è né panno né pilastro. Questo panno è evidentemente la veste del palestrita, da lui tolta e deposta su di un pilastrino nella palestra per compiere liberamente il suo esercizio.[6] Nel disegno del Jacques il pilastrino è indicato, a sinistra, con due linee verticali quasi se ne vedesse una faccia in iscorcio; sul marmo non appare che una sola delimitazione dell'oggetto, quella più a destra nel disegno. L'orlo esterno del pilastro non è più visibile sul frammento, essendo stato questo tagliato, forse proprio lungo di esso. Che il ragazzo si appoggiasse col gomito al pilastrino, come pare dalla posizione del braccio sinistro nei disegni e come sembra richiedere il suo insistere quasi soltanto sul piede sinistro, è giusta ipotesi, data anche la torsione del tronco rispetto alle gambe; il nuovo frammento non può dare evidentemente per questo riguardo una conferma diretta, ma bastino a questo proposito i confronti che si possono stabilire.[7] La superficie scolpita del frammento è meno bene conservata che nel pezzo superiore, e ciò si deve probabilmente alle esalazioni della sepoltura su cui fu posto a chiusino, che ne favorirono la corrosione. Tuttavia la scultura può dirsi sufficientemente conservata. Si notino le vene dorsali nei piedi del palestrita, e nel piede destro del ragazzo, oltre l'alluce, il contorno del dito adiacente. Non molto evidente è rimasto il profilo del pilastrino, più netti appaiono nella stoffa, che forma massa compatta, gli orli sovrapposti. I due fori simmetricamente disposti a metà altezza contenevano i bulloni di ferro per manovrare il marmo nella sua funzione di chiusino (uno di essi, al momento della scoperta, era ancora inserito). Le smussature ai lati si debbono anche esse al nuovo ufficio, appunto per meglio abboccare il chiusino alla apertura della sepoltura. Invece ad un tempo anteriore si deve la scanalatura nel listello di base, poiché essa già appare nel disegno di Windsor Castle (in quello del Jacques, per quanto più preciso, il listello è stato omesso perché probabilmente non interessava). È questo un solco insolito, senza una ragione plausibile d'ordine estetico; si dovrebbe pensare soltanto alla scalpellatura di una probabile iscrizione, eseguita con la preoccupazione di sostituirvi quasi una scorniciatura.[8]

Come si è detto, il frammento fu segato dalla stele per farne un chiusino. L' iscrizione che è incisa sul dorso dentro un riquadro (tav.

---

6. Cf. il rilievo attico del IV sec. in H. Th. Bossert e W. Zschietzschmann, *Hellas u. Rom*, 1936, fig. a p. 298 (sopra) (= Conze, A., *Die Attischen Grabreliefs*, 2, p. 223, n. 1046, 2, 2, tav. 203).

7. Mi limito a citare le stele di Orcomeno e Borgia e la cosiddetta Atena Pensierosa (Gerke, *op. cit., figg.* 76, 1 e 2; 146), e la statua di un giovane pugilista da Tralles a Costantinopoli (Bossert e Zschietzschmann, *op. cit.*, fig. a p. 306).

8. Non conosco altro esempio, ma osservo che il listello è di solito più sottile (si veda ad es. Gerke, *op. cit.*, figg. 76, 1 e 2; 79; 80; 81; 144).

60 a) ci dice quando e per conto di chi fu compiuto tanto misfatto. Essa suona: *Pro.devotis/S.Nicolai/Anno.MDCCI/Arbitrio.suo/Religio /Scholar.Piarum.*[9] Evidentemente la stele si era conservata integra fino a quel momento: il taglio lungo il fianco, a scalpello e non a sega, è infatti pensabile solo dopo che la parte inferiore era stata segata dal resto, e fu fatto forse, come quello dell'angolo superiore destro, pure a scalpello, (l'altro angolo è semplicemente rotto) per adattare il pezzo più grande che rimaneva disponibile al poco nobile ufficio di coprire una fogna. Come si sia giunti a un tal disprezzo per questa opera di scultura antica, e proprio nel colto ambiente delle Scuole Pie, non si comprende. Particolare degno di nota sono i buchi nel marmo presso i genitali dell'una e l'altra figura, che ammettono una sola spiegazione plausibile e cioè quella di aver servito a fissare delle foglie di fico metalliche.[9a] Ora, fino al più tardo disegno, noi troviamo le due figure senza foglie, vale a dire fin verso la metà del 1600, quando appunto la collezione Cesi cominciò ad essere dispersa per le mutilazioni che il possesso dei Cesi venne in quell'epoca a subire con la costruzione del colonnato del Bernini. Può darsi che allora insieme ad altre "anticaglie" passasse nella casa degli Scolopi presso la chiesetta di San Lorenzo anche la nostra stele[10] e che allora si provvedesse a renderla più pudica con l'aggiunta delle foglie. Ma si vede che questo non bastò a proteggerla e finì come sappiamo. Qualche anno dopo, invece, nel 1706, i Padri provvedevano ad inviare a Clemente XI in Vaticano per il "Museo Ecclesiastico" un altro pezzo già dei Cesi, l'iscrizione di M. Emilio Barbula (che però poi andò smarrita).[10a] D'altra parte i restauri della chiesetta hanno messo in luce non pochi marmi, anche nello stesso altar maggiore, con iscrizioni che per lo più risultano anch'esse già appartenenti alla collezione Cesi. Il che dimostra che le iscrizioni non ebbero maggior fortuna della scultura, e che si fece tranquillamente scempio di tutti, o quasi, quei marmi che si poterono avere in un modo o nell'altro dalla collezione in rovina. Ed il bello si è che erano proprio stati i Cesi a donare la chiesa agli Scolopi giusto nel 1663, e ad adornarla.[11] D'altra parte siamo proprio in quel tempo nel quale il colonnato di San Pietro, che allora si costruiva, era occasione di rilevanti danni alla raccolta Cesi, come già si è detto; sicché da un lato veniva a cessare la cura per la quale gli antichi marmi erano stati raccolti e conservati, dall'altro, apprento per questo

---

9. Forcella, V., *Iscrizioni delle chiese e di altri edifici di Roma*, 10, 1877, 193, n. 319.

9a. Cf. Amelung, *Die Sculpturen*, 666 e 669.

10. Cf. Huelsen, *op. cit.*, 10 e 27 (n. 98).

10a. Cf. Huelsen, *op. cit.*, 15 (n. 29a).

11. Vedasi l' iscrizione in Forcella, *op. cit.*, 10, 1877, 193, n. 309.

fatto, gente di dubbia cultura e scarso sentire ne profittava per il proprio interesse. Ma i gusti cambiano col mutar dei tempi, e d'altronde sappiamo, per dirla con Orazio,[12] che "quicquid sub terra est, in apricum proferet aetas; defodiet condetque nitentia"; così nella assidua vicenda delle cose, anche la nostra stele, un pezzo dopo l'altro, è riapparsa quasi integra ancora una volta alla luce: buon per essa e per noi che cultura e bellezza siano tornate ad essere parole non vane.

12. *Epist.*, 1, 6, 24.

IN SKIES BLUER THAN VIOLETS

In skies much bluer than violets far
   The traveler clouds trail wisps of rose.
Shy wraiths, fleeting as shadows are,
   The pale mists of the soul disclose.

Like joys that never smile they go,
   Like griefs that know not how to weep;
Nor tears nor laughter can they show,
   But silence deep as death they keep.

They vanish like a shooting star—
   What witch their secret can disclose?
In skies much bluer than violets far
   The traveler clouds trail wisps of rose;

John B. Edwards

Translated by
John Gryparis

LA STÈLE-FRONTON BÉOTIENNE D' ÉRÔTIÔN

R. Demangel

Directeur de l'École française d'Athènes

Planches 60-61

Depuis que M. Ant. D. Kéramopoullos a publié, voici une bonne trentaine d'années, dans ses *Θηβαϊκά*,[1] trois des plus intéressantes stèles-frontons en calcaire jaune du musée de Thèbes, l'attention des archéologues s'est spécialement portée vers l'ornementation végétale stylisée, qui fait le prix de ces documents.[2] Le problème a été largement traité dans le cadre de la décoration des stèles funéraires grecques, en liaison avec celle des grands monuments, et la date, IIIe-IIe siècle av. J.-C., des stèles béotiennes semble avoir été définitivement admise. Je voudrais ajouter ici quelques observations concernant principalement la stèle-fronton d'Érôtiôn (pl. 60 b), en tâchant de compléter les brèves notices qui servent de légendes aux trois figures présentées, sans commentaire ni mesures, par l'heureux fouilleur de la Cadmée.[3]

Les monuments du musée de Thèbes présentés par M. Kéramopoullos appartiennent à une abondante série, en grande partie inédite, de stèles funéraires propres à la Béotie, provenant de Thèbes même et de Tanagra. Essentiellement composées d'un entablement de fantaisie terminé par un fronton décoré, ces stèles ont ceci de particulier qu'elles semblent incomplètes ou mutilées en bas, si on les compare au type normal des stèles à décor architectonique. La cella du naïscos, qui manque en effet, se trouvait pour ainsi dire supplantée par le tertre funéraire surmontant la tombe, dans lequel était fichée une colonnette portant comme une bannière la stèle-fronton elle-même.[4] C'est ce qui apparaît, entre autres,[5] sur le monument d'Érôtiôn, dont le fronton

---

1. *Deltion* 3 (1917) 316 sq., fig. 189-191.

2. Jacobsthal, P., *Χάριτες für Leo*, 451 sq.; Möbius, H., *Die Ornamente der gr. Grabstelen*, 54 sq. et 88 sq.; Karouzos, Chr., *Τὸ Μουσεῖο τῆς Θήβας*, 31 sq., nos. 59-82.

3. Il ne m'a pas été possible, comme j'en avais depuis longtemps l'intention (cf. Demangel, R., *REA* 1940 [*Mélanges Radet*], 102, n. 7; *BCH* 1940-41, 156-7), de mesurer et de photographier sur place les originaux, enterrés hâtivement lors de l'invasion italienne de l'automne 1940 et que la situation politique et la détresse financière de la malheureuse Grèce n'ont pas permis jusqu'à présent d'extraire de leurs abris. On devra donc par nécessité se contenter ici provisoirement de l'illustration déjà connue.

4. Les traces de scellement de la colonnette sont très visibles au centre de la face inférieure des stèles.

5. Cf. aussi le *Guide du musée de Thèbes* de Chr. Karouzos, p. 31 et fig. 28.

est occupé, au centre, par un tumulus en forme d'omphalos,[6] que couronne la stèle-fronton protectrice. De part et d'autre, des démons chthoniens, dont la queue de dragon s'enroule en rinceaux vivants dans les *kerkides,* s'occupent à entourer le *sèma* de bandelettes ou de rameaux. Les mêmes Σπαρτοί ou Tritopatores locaux, dont la légende thébaine intéressait spécialement M. Kéramopoullos pour sa restitution de la topographie cadméenne,[7] se retrouvent ailleurs une main au sol et l'autre sur la stèle ou la statue du mort (pl. 61, a et fig. 1).

Fig. 1. Fragment de la stèle de Philôn.

Le rôle protecteur de ces bisaïeuls chthoniens, au nom significatif, est ainsi bien clairement établi.

Sous ces frontons si parlants, sommés d'acrotères moins lisibles[8] ou d'attiques agréablement décorés de rinceaux, une frise dorique régulièrement ordonnée tient toute la largeur de la stèle. Viennent ensuite, entre deux bandeaux d'épaisseur variable, un long cartouche portant gravé le nom du trépassé,[9] puis, à la zone inférieure, un rinceau

---

6. Les schémas pyramidants, conoïdes ou omphaloïdes constituent les plus naturels des modes d'agencement des masses de terre protégeant une sépulture. On a donc quelque scrupule à parler ici d' "omphalos," malgré l'évidente analogie de forme de ces "tertres" avec le vieil omphalos delphique, dont la mortaise centrale aurait pu, avant la croix dont l'auraient peut-être surmonté les chrétiens, porter ainsi un tout autre emblème. Cf. *BCH* 1940-41, 157, n. 3.

7. *Ibid.,* 315 (le champ où Cadmos "sema" les dents du dragon).

8. Le poros jaunâtre utilisé pour ces stèles, d'un travail aisé mais manquant de finesse, était protégé par une couverte peinte de diverses couleurs, parfois très reconnaissables encore.

9. Ἐρωτίων (et non Ἐρωτίων, Θηβαϊκά, 316), nom spécialement béotien d'homme plutôt que de femme (Ἐρώτιον), peut être un patronymique. Cf. Pape, *s.v.;* Kirchner, *Prosopogr. Att., s.v.;* Bechtel, *Hist. Personennamen des Griechischen,* 167, et *Die att.Frauennamen,* 72. C'était le nom d'un frère de Pindare. Nom de mignard ou de courtisane, il rappellerait la petite esclave morte à l'âge de cinq ans qui inspira les trois exquises épigrammes de Martial V, 34 et 37 et X, 61.

sculpté enserrant des patères ou des rosaces, dont le départ médian
— volutes de part et d'autre d'une palmette — éveille l'idée d'un
chapiteau éolique à larges volutes qui terminerait la colonnette-
support: plantureuse efflorescence végétale du meilleur augure, sans
nul doute, pour le défunt.

L'étage dorique mérite d'attirer particulièrement l'attention. La
frise y est constituée par des triglyphes, parfois privés de *regula*,
qui alternent avec des rosaces, des amphores ou de petites idoles
féminines aux bras levés et à la robe en cloche. Il est évident que ces
divers symboles ne sont pas sans relation avec la destination funéraire
des stèles.

Le rapport des triglyphes avec les puissances souterraines est
attesté ailleurs par les autels à triglyphes bas, par la margelle de la
"fontaine sacrée" de Corinthe, par les socles de sarcophages, etc.[10]
Leur sens funéraire ressort de leur emploi sur des stèles comme celle
de Ziméno, sur la route de Delphes à Livadia,[11] ou sur des vases
destinés à des tombes, comme les cratères peints de Centuripe, où
ils alternent avec des Éros évoquant les noces mystiques avec l'Hadès.[12]
Le sens symbolique connu des vases lustraux, des phiales ou des
rosettes ne requiert non plus aucune explication spéciale. Il n'en est
pas de même des curieuses petites bonnes femmes dans lesquelles le
premier éditeur a cru reconnaître des pleureuses.[13]

Si l'on observe les "pleureuses" typiques des vases géométriques
et archaïques ou celles des tombeaux étrusques, on constate que leurs
bras sont généralement levés au maximum de manière à toucher leur
tête et plus précisément leur chevelure,[14] ou bien que, coudes hauts,
les mains frappent la poitrine ou déchirent les vêtements:[15] dans les
deux cas, les avant-bras se trouvent dans une position se rapprochant
de l'horizontale. Sur la stèle de Thèbes, au contraire, l'attitude est
celle des mains hautes, écartées de la tête, avec les avant-bras verti-
caux. Or, toute une classe de figures féminines, allant de la période
préhellénique à l'époque byzantine, représente en effet une déesse aux
bras levés dans cette position. Le type oriental, qui a connu de nom-

---

10. Cf. notamment Demangel, R., *BCH* 1931, 135, n. 4 et 1937, 429 sq.

11. Contoléon, A. E., *BCH* 1936, 371, fig. 1. Cinq triglyphes peu saillants
apparaissent largement espacés sous un fronton en fort relief, au-dessus du nom
des morts.

12. Libertini, G., *Atti e Mem. della Soc. Magna Grecia*, 1932, 187 et 192, et pl.
II-III. Les triglyphes n'ont pas de *regula;* leur tablette supérieure déborde
notablement de chaque côté.

13. *Deltion*, 3 (1917) 316: γυναῖκας οἱονεὶ δρυπτομένας.

14. Cf. par ex. Buschor, E., *Gr. Vasen*, fig. 12, 15 et 20; *Dict. Ant.*, s.v. *funus*
(nombreuses illustrations).

15. Giglioli, G. Q., *L'Arte etrusca*, pl. 73-74.

breuses variantes,[16] pourrait se matérialiser dans le symbole phénicien de Tanit, très voisin de la représentation béotienne : ⛧

On trouverait surtout dans l'île de Minos une large diffusion de ce genre d'idole, avec sans doute également traduction dans les écritures[17] et transmission aux époques suivantes.[18] On a donné à ces figurines, selon l'aspect essentiel des divers groupes, les noms les plus variés : "casques à cornes" à Cnossos (A. Evans), "robes votives" à Tylissos (J. Hazzidakis), "clochettes" (*bell*, A. Evans) et plus généralement idoles en cloche, auxquelles sont apparentées les idoles en croissant mycéniennes et même certaines figurines archaïques de Sélinonte ou de l'Héraion de Délos.[19] Il y a eu sans doute, pour ce cas comme pour d'autres, une "contamination," une fusion des types, selon laquelle un même objet sacré, à la fois clochette et figurine, est au mieux désigné par le terme d'*idole en cloche*.

En Béotie — et en Attique[20] — les idoles féminines en cloche ont, il est vrai, malgré l'indication habituelle des seins, un aspect qui les rapproche plus de la sonnette que de la figurine aux mains levées. Telles sont celles du Louvre ou du musée de Berlin, publiées autrefois par Maurice Holleaux.[21] Mais M. Kéramopoullos a publié dans ses *Θηβαϊκά*[22] une série de minuscules plaquettes d'argile, couvertes d'un enduit blanc et brûlées, présentant diverses formes : palmettes, rosaces et *petits personnages* (pl. 61, b). Ces *ἀνθρωπάρια*, de 0m.03 à 0m.035 de haut, qui ont l'air de croquignoles ayant reçu un coup de feu, se

---

16. Cf., entre autres, Jean, Ch. F., *Syria* 9 (1928) 292 (inscriptions sinaïtiques, n⁰ 354).

17. Cf. Chapouthier, F., *Mallia*, II, *Écritures minoennes*, 59 sq. (type normal de l'idole pourvue de pieds et type de l'idole sur un trône).

18. Marinatos, Sp., *Αἱ Μινωϊκαὶ θεαὶ τοῦ Γάζι*, *Ephemeris* 1937, 290-291 (idoles de Gazi, "dernière phase de l'époque minoenne", et du Lasithi, sanctuaire de l'époque protogéométrique, Pendlebury, J. (1937). Cf. aussi Kunze, E., *Kret. Bronzereliefs*, pl. 3 et 5 et p. 192 sq. (déesse nue de la fécondité aux bras levés symétriquement, à droite et à gauche de la tête).

19. Cf. Picard, Ch., "Sur un signe d'écriture minoenne: 'casque' (?) ou idole?" *Ephemeris* 1937, 83 sq. On a trouvé aussi une figurine archäique à un bras levé *(bras aileron)* à Kirrha, dans le dépôt d'offrandes.

20. Une nouvelle idole en cloche vient d'être trouvée à Néa Ionia, banlieue d'Athènes, par M. Papadimitriou avec quelques très beaux vases protoattiques. Elle possède ses deux jambes, un trou de suspension dans sa tête d'oiseau, les seins en légère saillie et des amorces de bras (peut-être levés?).

21. Holleaux, M., *Mon.Piot*, I, 21 sq. Les idoles en cloche à pieds mobiles ne pouvaient être posées. Lorsqu'elles n'étaient pas munies de trous de suspension, leurs cous "longs à dessein comme un manche" (Picard, Ch., *op. cit.*, 87) permettaient de les saisir.

22. *Op. cit.*, 228, fig. 164. Les objets ont été trouvés tous ensemble dans la partie occidentale de la tombe, ce qui montre qu'il ne s'agit pas d'ornements du cercueil, mais plutôt de la décoration d'un objet plus petit, coffret ou coussin, déposé à une place déterminée dans la sépulture. Car le grand nombre de débris de charbon répandus dans toute la tombe prouve que l'incinération du mort avait été opérée sur place.

trouvaient au nombre de 42 dans une tombe d'époque assez voisine de celle des stèles-frontons, — non antérieure, en tout cas, d'après les vases recueillis, à la seconde moitié du IVe siècle av. J.-C. Le vêtement ne couvre pas complètement les jambes des petites figures, nettement séparées comme sous la robe des idoles en cloche. Quant à la position des bras levés, moins raides parce que non géométriquement encadrés dans un décor architectonique, elle ne peut pas ne pas rappeler celle des idoles de la stèle d'Érôtiôn. Aussi est-il difficile de ne pas penser qu'il s'agit dans les deux cas de la même déesse, descendante attardée des Terres-Mères primitives de la paysanne Béotie.

L'attitude de l'idole aux mains levées peut s'expliquer comme par un même geste favorable de la divinité féminine essentielle, et M. Sp. Marinatos[23] a sans doute raison de relier à la Grande Mère orante de la Crète minoenne la Bonne Mère chrétienne, la Πλατυτέρα byzantine, priant et bénissant.[24] On y reconnaîtrait peut-être plus précisément une épiphanie divine, apparition ou résurrection, s'il s'agit de tombes, de la grande déesse de la végétation. Toute déesse de la fertilité est naturellement une déesse de la vie et de la mort, si intimement liées, c'est-à-dire qu'elle préside à la transmission de la vie par la mort.[25] Car, comme l'enseigne la science la plus moderne, "si l'une des molécules d'un groupe est perdue, il importe que le groupe la reconstitue. . . . Cette duplication des molécules des chromosomes préfigure la multiplication des cellules elles-mêmes et de tous les êtres vivants."[26]

La déesse de fertilité agraire, dont la représentation sur la stèle-fronton d'Érôtiôn apportait "the hope of participation, for the deceased, in the eternity of life,"[27] pourrait être l'hypostase béotienne de la "déesse aux rinceaux," dont les images répétées se plaisaient à la compagnie des palmettes et des rosettes, et qui se manifestait par l'exubérante profusion des rinceaux recouvrant la plupart des frontons, des attiques et des socles des stèles béotiennes, sur lesquelles j'ai voulu rappeler ici brièvement l'attention des savants.

---

23. *Op. cit.*, 290.

24. Sur ce type de Vierge, Cf. Leclercq, H., *Dict.d'archéol.chrét.*, *s.v. Orante;* Demangel, R., *Le quartier des Manganes*, 155 sq.

25. Jastrow, Elizabeth, "Terracotta Reliefs in American Museums," *AJA* 1946, 67 sq. (petits autels avec tête féminine entourée de rinceaux).

26. Auger, Pierre, "De l'atome à l'homme," *Annales du Centre Universit. méditerr.*, 2 (1947-48) 41.

27. Jastrow, *op. cit.*, 80.

DIE MITTELGRUPPE DES OSTGIEBELS VON OLYMPIA

HANS MÖBIUS
Würzburg

Tafeln 61-62

Der Ostgiebel des Zeus-Tempels von Olympia hat durch zwei Probleme in den letzten Jahrzehnten die Forscher geradezu leidenschaftlich beschäftigt: die Anordnung der Figuren, mit der die inhaltliche Deutung zusammenfällt, und die Frage nach ihrem Meister und der Heimat ihres Stiles. Was die A u f s t e l l u n g betrifft, so waren für den Zeus in der Mitte, für die Gespanne und die Liegenden in den Ecken die Plätze gegeben, aber die anderen Figuren sind in der mannigfachsten Weise herumgeschoben worden. Allmählich zeigte sich, dass teils durch die Fundlage teils durch andere Erwägungen der Platz der sechs Nebenfiguren vor und hinter den Gespannen sich festlegen liess, und nur der Platz der beiden Paare neben dem Zeus blieb zweifelhaft.[1] Abgesehen von den verunglückten Rekonstruktionen Schraders und Weeges,[2] die mit Recht in der späteren Forschung keine Beachtung gefunden haben, sind besonders zwei Vorschläge zu nachhaltiger Wirkung gelangt: Pfuhl[3] stellte Pelops und Hippodameia zur rechten Hand des Zeus auf, Oinomaos und Sterope zu seiner linken, Studniczka[4] ordnete umgekehrt Oinomaos und Sterope rechts, Pelops und Hippodameia links vom Zeus an. (Taf. 62, a.) Die Anordnung Pfuhls, die mit einer geringen Aenderung auf der Kekules beruht, hat sich stärker durchgesetzt, sie ist in die Handbücher und die Real-Encyclopaedie übergegangen, und auch Bulle in seiner besonders ausführlichen Behandlung des Problems[5] bekennt sich als ihr Anhänger. (Taf 62, b.) Dabei ist sie von ihrem Urheber selbst zu gunsten der Studniczkaschen Aufstellung wieder aufgegeben worden.[6] Buschor[7] hat diesen Vorschlag neu begründet und Gisela

---

1. Vgl. die lehrreiche Zusammenstellung bei Becatti, *Il Maestro d'Olimpia* (= *Quaderni per lo studio dell'Archeologia* Nr. 6) 1943.

2. Schrader: *Städel-Jahrbuch* I (1921) 39 und *JOAI* 35 (1943) 65 ff. Weege: bei Dörpfeld, *Alt-Olympia* 2, 456 ff.

3. *JDAI* 21 (1906) 154 Abb. 3.

4. *AZ* 1884, 281 ff. und *Abh.Sächs.Ges.d.Wiss.* 1923 Bd. 37 Nr. 4.

5. *JDAI* 54 (1939) 137 ff.

6. *Phil. Woch.* 1923, 962 ff.

7. Ernst Buschor und Richard Hamann, *Die Skulpturen des Zeustempels zu Olympia*. Marburg 1924. Dazu die Rezension Ferd. Noacks, *Phil. Woch.* 1928, 428 ff.

Richter,[8] Rumpf,[9] Lippold,[10] Schefold,[11] Becatti[12] sind ihm gefolgt. Auch die jetzigen Ausgräber von Olympia, unter ihnen Emil Kunze,[13] sind seine Anhänger. Sie hatten, wie Jantzen berichtet,[13a] vor Abbruch der Arbeiten in Olympia begonnen, die Figuren in dieser Weise neu aufzustellen. Mir scheint ebenfalls die Anordnung Studniczka-Buschors den Vorzug zu verdienen, doch kann die Begründung erst gegeben werden, wenn wir die Beweise, die aus allen Stufen der Methode gewonnen werden, überblicken.

Die beherrschende Mittelfigur des Z e u s hat uns Bulle in der Grossartigkeit ihrer Gesamtkonzeption nahegebracht. Die Einzelbeobachtung hatte schon Treu zur Feststellung von "Pentimenti" geführt, von Aenderungen während der Arbeit: Der Mantel des Gottes ist erst nachträglich bis zu seinen Füssen verlängert worden, um der unteren Hälfte der Gestalt mehr Masse zu verleihen. Der neuerdings gefundene linke Fuss des Zeus, der jetzt mit dem von Treu erkannten rechten vereinigt wurde, hat diese Beobachtung glänzend bestätigt.[14] Die neue Erkenntnis, dass beide Füsse enger zusammenstehen als in den bisherigen Ergänzungen angenommen wurde, ist übrigens von Bedeutung, da die Gestalt aus schmalem Stand noch viel grossartiger aufwächst. Mit der Verlängerung des Mantels hängt eine zweite Aenderung zusammen: die herabhängenden Falten unterhalb der linken Hand des Zeus mussten vermehrt und vergrössert werden, um dieser Seite einen gewichtigeren Abschluss zu geben. Auch hier hat ein neu gefundenes Fragment die von Treu und Bulle gefundene Anordnung der für sich gearbeiteten Mantelfragmente gerechtfertigt.

Schwierig bleibt bei dem Zeus die Deutung seiner Gesten. Bulles eingehende Beschreibung der Durchbohrung der linken Hand gibt keinen schlüssigen Beweis dafür, ob er Blitz oder Szepter in ihr gehalten hat, aber die Wahrscheinlichkeit, dass es der Blitz war. Von der rechten Hand ist sicher, dass sie in die Mantelfalten gegriffen hat, aber wie ist dieser Gestus zu deuten? Bulle sieht in ihm den Ausdruck von "Gelassenheit und Ruhe," aber bei dem schreitenden Dichter in Paris empfindet er ihn—ebenso wie Schefold[15]—als Zeichen der Erregung. Auch Buschor und Kunze[16] deuten das unruhige Greifen in

8. *Sculptures and Sculptors of the Greeks*[1], 94 Abb. 390.
9. *Einl. in die Altertumswiss.*[4], 1931, 30 f.
10. *Phil. Woch.* 1936, 1383 ff.
11. *JDAI* 52 (1937) 68.
12. *Critica d'Arte* 4 (1939) 1 ff., 53 ff. und 6 (1941) 65 ff.
13. *Antike und Abendland* II, 110.
13a. *Ol.Ber.* 4, 1944, 154.
14. Kunze, *Olympia-Bericht* 4, 144 ff. Taf. 55 und 56.
15. *Die Bildnisse der antiken Dichter, Redner und Denker* 66 zu Taf. 67, 1. Anders Deubner, *Marb. WPr.* 1948, 24.
16. Buschor, a.O. 24. Kunze a.O. 110.

den Mantel als Symbol der Ungnade und als Regung verhaltenen Zornes. Auf Vasen und am Parthenonfries[17] kommt die Geste ebenfalls vor, und der Hermes des berühmten Orpheusreliefs hält die Rechte in ähnlicher Weise. Ich glaubte früher, dass hier eine dem 5. Jahrhundert eigene Haltung vorliege, die wir so wenig erklären können wie das Gewandraffen archaischer Koren oder das Halten der Mantelspangen bei Gestalten der Stauferzeit. Aber eine konventionelle Geste würde doch dem Geist der Giebelkunst widersprechen, und ich möchte mich daher der Erklärung von Buschor, Kunze und Schefold anschliessen.

Bei dem O i n o m a o s zeigt sich besonders deutlich, wie stark die Giebelfiguren an Kraft und Ausdruckswert gewinnen, wenn sie genau frontal stehen, besonders wird der sperrige rechte Ellenbogen jetzt nach hinten gedreht. Auch so stösst er in Bulles Aufstellung noch peinlich gegen die linke Seite des Zeus. Stellt man aber den Oinomaos zur Rechten des Zeus auf, so verschwindet jener Ellenbogen hinter dem gehobenen linken Arm der Sterope.[18] Sehr glücklich erscheint die neue Ergänzung des linken Unterarmes—die nicht zugehörige linke Hand ist inzwischen wieder entfernt worden[19]—, der jetzt nicht mehr nach dem Kopf zu abgewinkelt, sondern gerade ausgestreckt die Lanze hält. Dann greift die Hand aber unmittelbar unter den Giebelrahmen hinauf und das Blatt der Lanze wird überhaupt nicht mehr sichtbar. Eine solche Aufstellung, wie sie Bulles erste Abbildung veranschaulicht, kann unmöglich richtig sein. "Eine beabsichtigte Steigerung der Hochwirkung" ist in Wirklichkeit ebenso unwahrscheinlich wie die Annahme, dass Oinomaos und Sterope im ursprünglichen Entwurf zu gross für den Giebelrahmen waren. Stellt man aber den Oinomaos auf die andere Seite, so kann die Lanze in ihrer vollen Länge erscheinen. Freilich meint Bulle, dass ein Stück vom Mantel an der linken Seite des Oinomaos abgeschnitten worden sei, um Platz für den rechten Unterarm der Sterope zu schaffen, aber ebenso gut kann das geschehen sein, um den Mantel nicht zu nahe an den seitlich ausgestreckten rechten Arm des Zeus kommen zu lassen.

Eine starke Veränderung hat durch Bulles Forschungen die Gestalt der S t e r o p e erfahren. Aus der technischen Herrichtung ihres rechten Unterarms, besonders aus der groben Abflachung seiner Innenseite hatte man geschlossen, die Königin habe einen großen Korb oder einen Teller zum Opfern gehalten. Nunmehr ergab eine genaue Beobachtung der Anspannung der Muskeln, dass der Arm nicht waagerecht ausgestreckt, sondern senkrecht erhoben war, er führte

17. Schweitzer, *JDAI* 54 (1939) 20.
18. Vgl. die Oberansichten der Giebelfiguren bei Bulle Abb. 2.
19. Jantzen, *Ol.-Ber.* 4, 155.

also eine ähnliche Bewegung aus wie der linke Arm, dessen Hand den
Kopfschleier fasst. Demnach meint Bulle, die Königin werde in ihrem
Stolz dadurch charakterisiert, dass sie den Schleier fallen lasse. Hier
steht es ähnlich wie bei den antiken Figuren, die mit ihrer Sandale
beschäftigt sind, wobei die Frage lautet: Sandalenbinder oder San-
dalenlöser? Ich glaube, dass Sterope vielmehr im Begriffe steht, den
Schleier über den Kopf zu ziehen, ein viel markanteres Motiv, das
uns doch wieder auf die Deutung der Opfernden zurückführt. Die
rechte Seite der Sterope ist verkürzt und die Partie ihres rechten
Oberarms durch mannigfache Veränderungen verschmälert worden.
Hierin erblickt Bulle den endgültigen Beweis für die Richtigkeit seiner
Aufstellung, da er annimmt, dass Platz für den linken Arm des
Oinomaos geschaffen werden sollte, dessen Mantel aus demselben
Grunde abgeschnitten wurde. Aber wäre es nicht auch möglich, dass
die Schulterpartie der Sterope verändert wurde, damit sie nicht zu
nahe an die Pferde des südlichen Wagens geriet? Becatti empfand
die Geste der Verschleierung als zu momentan und zu bräutlich. Nun
trägt Sterope aber ein "schmales, shawlartiges Gewandstück,"[20] das
kann nur mit beiden Händen aufgehoben oder niedergelegt werden,
die Schale in der Hand der Sterope ist also unmöglich.

Wohl die anmutigste Gestalt des ganzen Giebels ist der vor dem
südlichen Gespann k n i e e n d e K n a b e. Er konnte jetzt von Bulle
und seinen Bildhauern überzeugend ergänzt werden. Man hatte früher
den Knaben als Zügelhalter verstanden, aber mit Recht bestreitet Bulle
die Möglichkeit, dass ein feuriges Gespann gleichzeitig von vorn und
von hinten gezügelt werden könne, vielmehr scheint es sicher, dass
der Knabe in beiden Händen einen Stab trug. Bulle sieht in diesem
Stab das Kentron und im Epheben den Knappen des Pelops, der es
seinem Herrn bereit hält. Nun hält der Knabe den Stab aber ange-
strengt mit beiden Händen; wäre dieser ein leichter Stock, so müssten
wir an Figuren des Barock denken, die mit allen Kräften einen leichten
Gegenstand handhaben. Es muss sich vielmehr um eine eiserne
Stange handeln, die an einem Ende beschwert war, das heisst um einen
Bratspiess, an dem das Opferfleisch steckt, und der Knabe ist ein
zarter Opferdiener, der neben Sterope kauert, während die Königin
sich verschleiert, um das Opfer zu beginnen.[21]

Am P e l o p s ist wenig zu ergänzen, es sei denn, wir müssten uns
den vergoldeten Panzer, mit dem er wohl bekleidet war, in die Phantasie zurückrufen, vielleicht auch das bronzene Schildtuch, das — als
Gegengewicht gegen den von Pfuhl angenommenen Altar — von

---

20. Treu, *Ergebnisse* 3, 51.
21. Dieselben Argumente finde ich nachträglich bei Schrader, *JOAI* 35 (1943)
65.

seinem Rundschild herabhing. Neuerdings ist ihm sein rechter Fuß wiedergegeben worden, und allein dadurch, dass Bulle die Figur in voller Frontalität mit senkrecht aufgestützter Lanze vor uns hinstellt, ist sehr viel gewonnen. Erst jetzt können wir an der Geraden der Lanze die wundervolle Ponderation der Gestalt ablesen. Sein Schild erscheint in starker Verkürzung, vielleicht trug er als Zeichen einen Rennwagen. Freilich muss in Bulles Aufstellung auch Pelops seine Lanze so hoch anfassen, dass er sich an ihrem Eisen schneiden würde, versetzen wir ihn hingegen auf die linke Seite des Zeus, so kann auch diese Lanze in ihrer vollen Länge erscheinen.

Bei der H i p p o d a m e i a ist immer die starke Senkung der linken Schulter aufgefallen. Bulle erklärt sie daraus, dass sie sich unter den rechten Arm des Pelops schmiegen müsse. Aber auch dann bleibt der Bräutigam von der Braut durch die Lanze getrennt und blickt sie nicht an. Vielmehr wird mit Buschor das Tiefstehen der linken Schulter im Vergleich zur rechten aus dem Absteigen des Giebelrahmens zu erklären sein. Unerwähnt bleibt bei Bulle, warum Hippodameia in so auffälliger Weise den linken Fuß vorschiebt.

Die Erklärung gibt wohl die vor dem nördlichen Gespann kauernde k l e i n e D i e n e r i n, wenn sie neben Hippodameia angeordnet wird. Bulle und seine Bildhauer haben sie mit vor dem aufgestellten Knie verschränkten Händen ergänzt, aber dann werden die Arme, besonders der rechte Unterarm, bedenklich lang. Studniczka hatte nach Löwys Vorgang angenommen, dass die Sklavin damit beschäftigt sei, ihrer Herrin die Sandale festzubinden, ein Motiv, das die Braut, die sich zur Wettfahrt rüstet, vortrefflich kennzeichnen würde. Aber dann müssten die Arme der Dienerin noch länger ausgestreckt werden, um den vorgeschobenen Fuß der Herrin zu erreichen. Ich möchte eine Ergänzung vorschlagen, nach der die Dienerin beide Arme mit griffbereiten Händen nach dem Fuß der Hippodameia hin bewegt, ohne ihn zu berühren. Das wäre ein "transitorisches" Motiv ähnlich dem der Sterope, welche mit der linken Hand bereits den Schleier gefasst hält, während sich die Rechte noch nach ihm ausstreckt. Auch Schrader hat richtig beobachtet, dass Bulles Ergänzung der Arme daran scheitert, dass der rechte Oberschenkel vollkommen ausgearbeitet ist und keine Spur von umschlingenden Armen zeigt. Er gibt der Dienerin eine tief gehaltene grosse Schale in die Hände, aber das wirkt geradezu grotesk, denn man denkt an ein Becken für ein Fußbad oder an eine Schüssel mit Hühnerfutter. Es muss also doch bei der Vorbereitung zum Sandalenbinden bleiben, das auch Becatti für das Wahrscheinlichste hält.

Dem W a g e n l e n k e r hinter dem südlichen Gespann hat Bulle einen unbärtigen Jünglingskopf aufsetzen lassen, der ausgezeichnet zu dem erhaltenen Torso passt. Becatti hat mit Recht darauf hingewiesen, dass man den Ostgiebel nicht nur auf Grund von Pindar erklären dürfe, wie das Bulle nach Winters Vorgang tut. Pindar hatte allen Grund in seinem Hymnos auf ein siegreiches Gespann des Hieron die Sage vom ungetreuen Myrtilos zu umgehen. Aber diese Gestalt spielt in Sage, Kult und Dichtung eine so bedeutende Rolle, dass sie unmöglich eine blosse Erfindung des Pherekydes sein kann. Gerade im Zeitalter der Tragödie wird sie in der repräsentativen Darstellung der Sage nicht gefehlt haben. Myrtilos muss also im Giebel vorhanden sein — so auch Rumpf — und kann da nur in dem knieenden Wagenlenker gesehen werden.

Die neue Ergänzung des s ü d l i c h e n S e h e r s gehört zu den bedeutendsten Ergebnissen von Bulles Untersuchung; sie ist auch von den Ausgräbern anerkannt und durch Anfügung der linken Schulter vervollständigt worden.[22]

Der n ö r d l i c h e S e h e r gehört zu den am besten erhaltenen Gestalten des Giebels, zumal nachdem ihm Jantzen den linken Ellenbogen und die dem Oinomaos abgenommene linke Hand wiedergegeben hat.[23] Man hatte ihn als Trauernden verstanden im Gegensatz zum freudig erregten Seher der anderen Giebelseite, solange man jenen noch in stark bewegter Stellung ergänzte. Jetzt zeigte Bulle, dass der Ausdruck trüben Sinnens weniger stark ist als der einer mächtigen geistigen Spannung. Der Ausdruck der Kraft wird gesteigert, wenn der Seher einen senkrecht aufgestützten Stab in die linke Hand erhält wie sein Gegenstück. Freilich wirken jetzt diese zu kurzen Stäbe wie abgeschnitten. Wichtig ist daher Bulles Beobachtung, dass der Seher nach der teilweise schrägen Durchbohrung der Hand vielleicht einen gebogenen Krummstab als Abzeichen seiner Würde trug; ein ähnlicher Stab wäre dann auch dem anderen Seher zu geben.

Gut erhalten ist auch der hinter dem nördlichen Seher k a u e r n d e K n a b e; die Ergänzung seines Kopfes durch Bulle weicht kaum von den bisherigen Vorschlägen ab. Nach ihm hat Rodenwaldt auf Grund neuer Zeichnungen und Photographien die Gestalt nochmals eingehend analysiert und dabei mit Recht auf die Bedeutung der Farbe, gerade bei dieser Figur, hingewiesen.[24] Er wagt keine Deutung, widerlegt aber Bulles Interpretation durch den einfachen Hinweis darauf, dass der Dämon Sosipolis nach der Kultlegende ein kleines Kind war. Es bleibt also dabei, dass wir in dem Knaben den nackten Pais des Pelops

---

22. Jantzen a.O. 155.
23. Jantzen a.O. 158.
24. *JDAI* 57 (1942) 199 ff.

mit dem Mantel seines Herren zu sehen haben, der wartend am Boden sitzt und an seinen Zehen herumspielt.

Noch umstritten sind die b e i d e n   l i e g e n d e n   M ä n n e r   in d e n   E c k e n. Als Pausanias Olympia besuchte, wurde ihm der eine als Alpheios, der andere als Kladeos erklärt, und diese Deutung musste ihm einleuchten, da seiner Zeit gelagerte Flussgötter so geläufig waren wie uns seit der Renaissance. Im 5. Jahrhundert sind sie sonst nirgends mit Bestimmtheit nachgewiesen, auch nicht im Westgiebel des Parthenon, wo wir sie noch am ehesten vermuten könnten. Hingegen wissen wir, dass im strengen Stil der Flussgott mit starken Resten der ehemaligen Stiergestalt, mindestens mit Hörnern, erscheint. Statt dessen sehen wir hier zwei bequem hingestreckte Jünglinge, beide bartlos, denn von dem einen ist der Kopf vollständig erhalten, vom anderen wenigstens das in die linke Hand gestützte Kinn. Bei den neuen Arbeiten in Olympia wurden am "Alpheios" die Fussfragmente mit dem unteren Gewandsaum zusammengesetzt, dem "Kladeos" die zur Faust geschlossene rechte Hand mit Unterarm wiedergegeben, die bisher an der Hirschkuh-Metope angebracht war.[25] Am Gestus ändert sich dadurch nichts, ich möchte für ihn eine neue Deutung vorschlagen: Der Liegende ist im Begriff, mit der Faust den verträumten kauernden Jungen anzustossen, um ihn darauf aufmerksam zu machen, dass sein Herr seiner bedarf. Das wäre ein "transitorisches" Motiv, wie wir es ähnlich für Sterope und die kleine Dienerin erschlossen hatten.

Nachdem Carl Robert die Deutung auf Flussgötter als längst überwundenen Irrtum des Pausanias oder seiner Führer behandeln konnte,[26] sind Bulle und wohl die meisten der heutigen Archäologen noch immer ihre Anhänger, was mir von jeher ganz unbegreiflich gewesen ist.

Den wohlerhaltenen Kopf des "Kladeos" hatte schon Langlotz[27] eingehend beschrieben. Er empfindet im Schnitt des Gesichts, der "Ausdruckskraft des mageren, beinahe geistig zarten Kinnes," der Bildung der übrigen Gesichtsteile eine "Verfeinerung und Sensibilität," die sogar über den Apoll des Westgiebels hinausgehe. Bulle im Banne seiner Deutung auf ein Elementarwesen nennt den Kopf "eine der stärksten seelischen Leistungen im Giebel, der die ewig unruhige, drängende Leidenschaftlichkeit hellenistischer Meerwesenbildungen voraussnimmt." Wenn nun Löwy von demselben Kopf sagt,[28] er sei "von unsagbar gemeinem Typus" und habe "im Gesichtsausdruck

---

25. Jantzen a.O. 158.
26. *Hermeneutik* 58.
27. *JDAI* 49 (1934) 24 ff.
28. *Griech.Plastik²*, 20.

geradezu etwas Blödes," so ist das zweifellos zu hart. Ich glaube, wer
den Kopf unbefangen betrachtet, wird in ihm einen aufgeweckten,
aber recht ungeistigen Burschen erkennen, der sich bemüht, aufmerksam einem bestimmten Geschehen zu folgen. Er gehört zu jenem
"starkknochigen, fast bäuerisch vierschrötigen Geschlecht" von dem
A. v. Salis spricht.[29]

Nun gibt es aber für die beiden Liegenden im Einzelnen wie für
ihre Gruppierung mit einem kauernden Knaben eine schlagend ähnliche Darstellung aus derselben Zeit, auf die auch schon längst hingewiesen worden ist: die Sklaven unter den Zuschauertribünen auf
dem grossen Fresko des Stackelbergschen Grabes von Corneto.[30] Hier
noch mehr als "im olympischen Ostgiebel benimmt sich das Gefolge in
unmittelbarer Nähe seiner fürstlichen Herren im höchsten Grade un-
geniert."[31] Daraus ergibt sich mit voller Sicherheit die Deutung der
Eckfiguren: es sind Stallknechte, der eine in völliger Ruhe, da der
Wagenlenker bereits mit seinem Wagen beschäftigt ist, der andere
voll Aufmerksamkeit der Handlung folgend, da auf seiner Seite das
Gespann ohne Wartung dasteht.

Sind nun diese Diener alle wirklich nur "Füllfiguren," wie L. Curtius
meinte?[32] Gewiss mit Recht nimmt Bulle für den bildnerischen
Schmuck des Zeustempels, also auch für die Giebel, ein genaues
P r o g r a m m an, das von den Priestern ausgearbeitet war. Die
Priester selbst sind vertreten durch die Ahnherren der beiden olym-
pischen Sehergeschlechter, Jamos und Klytios. Das Porträthafte im
Kopf des nördlichen Sehers könnte sich nach einer ansprechenden
Vermutung Bulles daraus erklären, dass "der Jamide und der
Klytiade, die zur Zeit des Tempelbaues amteten, sich auch berechtigt
fühlten, das Bild der Ahnen nach ihrem eigenen gestalten zu lassen."
Seit der Auffindung der Themistokles-Herme von Ostia[33] sehen wir ja
die Möglichkeit des Bildnisses im strengen Stil mit anderen Augen
an als bisher.

Wie die beiden Seher nun Diener des Zeus sind, so können wir die
vier Diener den beiden Paaren neben Zeus zuordnen. Zum König
gehört ein erwachsener Begleiter, also der Wagenlenker, zu Pelops
ein Pais, also der kauernde Knabe. Entsprechend muss die Prinzessin
von einem noch sehr jungen Mädchen bedient werden, also der knieenden Sklavin, während der Königin ein älterer Diener verbleibt,
nämlich der Ephebe mit dem Bratspiess; die Stallknechte stehen

---

29. *Kunst der Griechen*[1], 92.
30. Weege, *JDAI* 31 (1916) 138 ff. Schrader, *Phidias* 180 ff.
31. v. Salis a.O. 92.
32. *Antike Kunst* 2, 217.
33. *A.A.* 1941, 475 ff. Ab. 59-62. L. Curtius *RM* 57 (1942) 78 ff.

natürlich in Beziehung zu ihren Gespannen. Jeder Diener hat seine
ganz bestimmte Funktion zur Verdeutlichung der dargestellten
Sagenszene.

Nach diesem Ueberblick fassen wir die Argumente zusammen,
welche die von uns vorgeschlagene Aufstellung begünstigen:
1.) d i e F u n d u m s t ä n d e . Als methodischen Fehler müssen
wir es betrachten, dass Bulle die Fundumstände der Ostgiebelfiguren
überhaupt nicht erwähnt. Nun sind allerdings einzelne kleine Fragmente wie die beiden Füsse des Zeus an entlegenen und einander ent-
gegengesetzten Punkten der Altis gefunden worden. Die grossen
Torsen aber, zum Beispiel die Gespanne, waren, wie die Fundkarte
im Olympia-Werk ausweist, in Mauern nachantiker Hütten östlich
des Tempels verbaut, teils unmittelbar vor seiner Front, teils nach
Norden oder Süden hin verschleppt.[34] Hierbei zeigt sich nun, dass
alle Bruchstücke der Figuren, die bei Studniczka zur Rechten des
Zeus stehen, vor der Südhälfte der Tempelfront, die anderen vor
seiner Nordhälfte gefunden worden sind. Nur der kniende Opferdiener lag nördlich, aber die Verschleppung dieser besonders leichten
Figur bildet nur eine Ausnahme, welche die Regel bestätigt. Aus
diesem Befund hat schon Konrad Wernicke die richtige Verteilung
der Paare zu Seiten des Zeus erschlossen.[35] Selbst Treu[36] hatte zuge-
geben, dass rein auf Grund der Fundumstände die Aufstellung Stud-
nickas anerkannt werden müsse. 2) d i e B e s c h r e i b u n g d e s
P a u s a n i a s (V 10, 7). Eine diesem Problem eigens gewidmete
Dissertation von Erich Müller[37] ist zu dem Ergebnis gekommen, dass
Oinomaos und Sterope zur Rechten des Zeus gestanden hätten. Dieses
Resultat ist zwar vielfach angezweifelt worden, besonders von
Schweitzer,[38] und auch Bulle schiebt es beiseite. Aber "ἐν δεξιᾷ τοῦ
Διός" heisst nun einmal: "zur Rechten des Zeus"; es folgt "τὰ δὲ
ἐς ἀριστερὰ ἀπὸ τοῦ Διός ἐστι Πέλοψ" also: "was aber nach links
hin vom Zeus kommt, ist Pelops usw." Wie man hieraus schliessen
kann, beide Ausdrücke seien vom Beschauer aus gemeint, ist mir un-
verständlich. Wenn dann der vermeintliche "Alpheios" im Norden,
der "Kladeos" im Süden erscheint, so stimmt das in der Tat nicht zur
Lage der beiden Flüsse in der olympischen Landschaft. Aber eine
solche Uebereinstimmung ist wohl ein moderner Gedanke, abgesehen

---

34. Bei G. Becatti, *Maestro d'Olimpia* ist bei der Beschriftung der Fundskizze
(Abb. 3) ein Irrtum unterlaufen, indem Oinomaos mit Pelops, Sterope mit Hippodameia vertauscht wurden.

35. *JDAI* 12 (1897) 190 ff. mit Beilage zu S. 169.

36. *JDAI* 4 (1889) 269.

37. *Beiträge zu Pausanias* (Erlangen 1921). Auszug daraus: *AA* 1922, 352 ff.

38. *JDAI* 43 (1928) 244 ff.

davon, dass dem Pausanias ganz andere Verwechslungen unterlaufen sind, als wir sie ihm auch hier zutrauen dürfen. 3.) D e u t u n g d e s V o r g a n g s. Zeus wendet sich in unserer Aufstellung dem Oinomaos zu, obwohl er ihn verderben wird. Viele Gelehrte haben das unerträglich gefunden, da sie annehmen, dass durch die Neigung des Gottes der Sieger gekennzeichnet werde. Wir glauben, dass die Wendung des Zeus dem Oinomaos als dem Könige des Ortes gilt. Vor ihn tritt das Königspaar, um sein Opfer darzubringen.

Wenn Winter meint,[39] das von zwei Dienern gehaltene Gespann müsse das des Pelops sein, weil dieser zuerst abfährt, so ist mit Buschor zu entgegnen, dass die Alternative nicht lautet: "Fertiges oder unfertiges Gespann" sondern: "Gespann mit oder ohne Lenker." Oinomaos fährt mit seinem Lenker, Pelops mit seiner Braut, also muss der König auf die Seite gehören, wo der Wagenlenker hinter dem Gespann kniet. Bulle hat zwar die Schwierigkeit gesehen, dass bei seiner Aufstellung der Wagenlenker des Königs fehlt, er sucht aber diese Schwierigkeit durch die Annahme zu umgehen, man habe in Olympia nicht an die Sage vom schändlichen Verrat des Myrtilos erinnern wollen, und den Wagenlenker deshalb einfach fortgelassen, eine wenig überzeugende Auslegung.

Natürlich ziehen nun andererseits der Pais und die kleine Sklavin das jugendliche Paar auf die Linke des Zeus hinüber. Gegen unsere Deutung, dass die Dienerin die Sandale der Hippodameia binde, hat Winter eingewendet, dass dieses "harmlose" Motiv zum feierlichen Ton der Mittelgruppe nicht passe. Aber hier liegt nun eine grundsätzliche Frage vor, über die sich kaum eine Einigung wird erzielen lassen. Mit Recht betont Buschor,[40] dass vor den Werken des Olympiameisters die Frage müssig werde, ob hier der Idealismus grösser sei oder der Realismus. Während A. v. Salis die Olympia-Plastik unter dem Stichwort "Der Wille zur Wahrheit" behandelte, hat Bulle den Giebel mit Oden Pindars verglichen und Schweitzer ihn als eine Stein gewordene Tragödie des Aischylos bezeichnet.[41] In der Tat bestimmt das grosse tragische Ethos den Eindruck, aber zugleich ist jeder Gott, jeder Mensch, jedes Tier scharf in seiner Wesensart erfasst. So vermag ich auch nicht zu sehen, inwiefern das Motiv des Sandalenbindens, das den Aufbruch der Braut so treffend kennzeichnet, dem hohen Ethos der Darstellung Abbruch tun soll.

4.) A e s t h e t i s c h e G e s i c h t s p u n k t e. Ein einziger Grund sollte eigentlich genügen, um Studniczkas Aufstellung als die richtige zu erweisen: nur in ihr haben die Lanzen genügend Platz, um in ihrer

---

39. *AM* 50 (1925) 1 ff.
40. a.O. 13.
41. a.O. 248.

vollen Länge sichtbar zu werden. Zugleich rahmen sie die Gestalt des Zeus und heben sie dadurch mächtig hervor.

An den Figuren des Oinomaos und Pelops, in geringerem Grade auch bei den Frauen, wird sehr deutlich, wie stark sie die tektonische Bindung in sich tragen; diese Feststellung Buschors hätte man nie verleugnen sollen. In Bulles Aufstellung wendet sich Oinomaos betont von Zeus ab, auch Pelops bleibt durch den Schild von ihm getrennt und blickt ihn nicht an. Man muss dann annehmen, dass Zeus als unsichtbar gedacht sei und hat an die Athena in den Aegina-Giebeln und den Apollon des olympischen Westgiebels erinnert. Aber im Kampfgetümmel wirkt der unsichtbare Gott überzeugend, im Ostgiebel erhält man den peinlichen Eindruck, dass Zeus unbeachtet, ja verachtet zwischen den Parteien stehe. Der Ellenbogen des Oinomaos stösst gegen seine linke Seite, während dieser bei der anderen Aufstellung, wie bereits gesagt, hinter dem erhobenen linken Arm der Sterope fast verschwindet.

König und Königin stehen bei Bulle unverbunden nebeneinander und blicken ins Leere, ohne jede Beziehung zu Zeus oder ihrem Gefolge; Sterope erhält so eine übermässige Betonung. Man hat es getadelt, dass Pelops und Hippodameia sich bei unserem Vorschlag voneinander abwenden, und in der Tat schliesst sich die Braut gegen den Bräutigam hin ab. Doch scheint mir das ein besonders feiner Zug des Meisters zu sein; er kennzeichnet das scheue Mädchen, das zugleich die gefahrenvolle Wagenfahrt und das dem Vater drohende Verhängnis bedenkt. Dass bei beiden Paaren die "inneren" Beine die Standbeine sind, schliesst sie ebenso zusammen wie die "inneren" Spielbeine bei Flächenbildern, die Schweitzer zitiert.[42] In all diesen Fragen wird sich freilich eine schlechthin überzeugende Beweisführung nicht ermöglichen lassen, und dem subjektiven Geschmack bleiben die Tore geöffnet. Wie wir uns die Mittelgruppe denken, zeigt Taf. 61, c, deren Vorlage durch Umstellen der beiden Paare aus Bulles Beilage 2 mit Zufügung der Lanzenspitzen hergestellt wurde. Oinomaos kann noch weiter vom Zeus abgerückt werden, wenn man unserer Annahme beipflichtet, dass sein rechter Ellenbogen hinter dem linken Unterarm der Sterope verschwand. Es zeigt sich jedenfalls, dass der verfügbare Platz für diese Umstellung völlig ausreicht, besonders wenn der Opferdiener und die kauernde Sklavin in die Schrägansicht gedreht werden, die für beide wahrscheinlich ist.

Aus der Anordnung ergibt sich nun die G e s a m t d e u t u n g. Sie ist bei Pausanias klar ausgesprochen: Vorbereitung zur Wettfahrt zwischen Oinomaos und Pelops.

---

42. a.O. 237 ff.

Bulle hat im Anschluss an Schweitzer gemeint, der Ostgiebel sei
"der schaubar gestaltete Inbegriff des Zeusglaubens, der die Altis
beherrschte, und die Legende der Wettfahrt nicht viel mehr als ein
loses äusseres Band, das die Gestalten der Mitte zusammenhält." Das
scheint mir zu abstrakt gedacht und zu theologisch formuliert zu sein.
Vielleicht ist das Umgekehrte richtig. Dargestellt ist die Wettfahrt in
allem frischen Realismus des Strengen Stils: Auf der einen Seite der
König, der sich siegesgewiss an Zeus wendet, die Königin, die das
Vorsprungsopfer darbringt, dahinter das Gespann, das aber noch
nicht sogleich abfahren wird, wie der am Wagen beschäftigte Lenker
und der ruhende Stallknecht andeuten. Auf der anderen Seite Pelops,
der sich zum Gehen wendet, Hippodameia, die sich zur Wettfahrt
rüstet, und der Stallknecht, der auf den bevorstehenden Aufbruch
hinweist. Da nun aber diese Sage im Zeitalter des Aischylos und
Pindar dargestellt wird, strahlen die Gestalten zugleich monumentale
Ruhe aus, "ein ernstes, grosses Sein," wie Bulle so schön formuliert.
Sehr wesentlich wird dieser Eindruck bestimmt durch die beiden
Seher, denn inhaltlich verkörpern sie das Walten des Schicksals,
formal bilden sie die Ruhepunkte der Komposition durch ihre breite
Lagerung und ihre Stäbe, welche den Rhythmus der Lanzen zu Seiten
des Zeus wieder aufnehmen.

EIN ARTEMIS-KOPF

ERNST LANGLOTZ
Bonn

Tafeln 63-66

Es gibt für die Festschrift zu Ehren eines Forschers, dem unsere Wissenschaft zu bleibendem grossen Dank verpflichtet ist, kaum ein geeigneteres Thema als die Publikation eines griechischen Meisterwerks. Zwar handelt es sich nicht um ein Ineditum, das hier vorgelegt wird, aber doch um ein Bildwerk, das im wahren Sinne des Wortes erst ins richtige Licht gerückt werden muss.[1]

Der auf Taf. 63 abgebildete Kopf ist in dem Katalog der Ausstellung antiker Kunst in deutschem Privatbesitz im üblichen Seitenlicht aufgenommen, das falsche Licht- und Schattenakzente setzt und dadurch die plastischen Werte verfälschen muss. Der kurze Text der Beschreibung hat wohl auch deshalb wichtige Züge des Werkes verkannt.

Sein Fundort ist unbekannt. Am Ende des vorigen Jahrhunderts hat ihn Max Klinger im Kunsthandel erworben. Der Kopf besteht aus sehr feinkörnigem griechischen Inselmarmor, dessen Herkunft nur petrographisch bestimmbar wäre. Die kristalline Konsistenz des Steines ist nicht sehr fest. Die ganze Haarpartie an der rechten Seite ist deshalb abgesplittert, wie häufig bei pentelischem Marmor. Auch die Epidermis der nackten Teile ist gleichmässig corrodiert. Dass die Wirkung des Kopfes gleichwohl noch grossartig ist, wird seiner starken plastischen Kraft verdankt, selbst in Einzelformen wie der zarten Muschel des Ohres oder den weichen Lippen, die trotz ihrer Corrosion noch lebenerfüllt wirken.

Der Kopf war nicht zum Einsetzen in eine Statue bestimmt, wie behauptet wurde, sondern aus einem Block mit seinem Körper gearbeitet. Der unregelmässig verlaufende Bruch am Hals lässt darüber keinen Zweifel. Eingesetzte Köpfe pflegen den Ansatz der Schultern noch zu zeigen. Auch die Bruchfläche der Unterseite bestätigt dies. Als das Bildwerk zerbrach, hat es beim Sturz den Boden zuerst mit der linken Schläfe berührt. Ein Viertel der linken Gesichtsseite ist dabei abgesplittert.

Mehrfach ist behauptet worden, der Kopf sei Teil eines ruhig stehenden Körpers gewesen. Das ist unmöglich. Denn die Stirn-Nasen-Achse liegt nicht in der des Halses. Der Kopf ist beträchtlich

---

1. Neugebauer, *Ausstellung antiker Kunst in deutschem Privatbesitz* Nr. 5, Taf. 3. Erhaltene Höhe 27 cm. *Berytus* VI S. 9 Anm. 4. *Acta Arch.* 1940, 39. V. H. Poulsen hatte die Güte, mir ein Photo des von ihm als abgeänderte Wiederholung bezeichneten Kopfes zu senden. Ich halte diesen Kopf für jünger.

nach seiner rechten Seite hin geneigt. Es bedarf auch der Erklärung, warum der Umriss der Nackenlinie nicht senkrecht abfällt, sondern leicht konkav nach dem Rückgrat hin ausläuft. Es dürfte daraus vielleicht zu schliessen sein, dass der Kopf nicht steil aufgerichtet war wie bei einer ruhig stehenden Figur, sondern sich etwas nach vorn neigte. Das bestätigt auch das schmale Bruststück oberhalb des rechten Schlüsselbeins. Es steht in einem Winkel von etwa 100° zum Halsumriss. Der Kopf wird also stark zu seiner rechten Seite und etwas nach vorn geneigt auf dem Körper gesessen haben.

Die rechte Wangenseite des Kopfes ist allein leidlich erhalten. Sie wirkt herb durch die wenig bewegte grossflächige Wange, das knochige Kinn und die unwillig "verbissen" vorgeschobenen Lippen, mit den Falten an den Mundwinkeln. Die Arbeit ist hier von grosser Zartheit. Arethusaköpfe syrakusaner Münzen der Frühklassik könnten zum Vergleich herangezogen werden. Jedoch dies herbe Gepräge verliert sich beim Umschreiten des Kopfes. Schon in der Vorderansicht nimmt das Volumen des Gesichtes zu. Der Umriss der im Profil so karg wirkenden Wange scheint aufzublühen und der Mund den schmollenden Zug zu verlieren. Die linke Wange entwickelt sich breiter und voller (Taf. 64, a, b). Der Hals wirkt weicher und runder. In Dreiviertelansicht scheint der Ausdruck des Kopfes noch reifer und weicher, fast üppig und schon an Köpfe der Columna Caelata in Ephesos anzuklingen. Kaum ein Zweifel: der Künstler hat die linke, fast zerstörte Seite des Kopfes als Hauptansicht concipiert. Bemerkenswert ist jedoch, dass der Bildner nicht den im Mutterland üblichen Gesetzen der plastischen Perspektive gefolgt ist.[2] (Unteransicht Taf. 65, a).

Das Haar war über der Stirn gescheitelt und hinten in wenigen breiten Strähnen in einen Krobylos aufgerollt, der wohl mit dem dicken, runden, aus Metall vorzustellenden Bronzereif, der über der Schläfe sichtbar wird, zusammenhing. Die über dem Reif liegende flache Haarmasse ist plastisch nicht gegliedert und war einst bemalt. Sehr flache, mehr fühl- als sichtbare konzentrisch vom Scheitel ausgehende plastische Wellen sind hier noch deutlich zu erkennen, die, seit der archaischen Plastik üblich,[3] allein schon beweisen, dass der Kopf nicht in römischer Kopistenmanier, sondern von einer griechischen Hand des 5. Jh's. gearbeitet ist.

---

2. Meist pflegt die abgewandte Gesichtshälfte schmaler und vorspringender zu sein, als die flachere, dem Blick zugewandte. Es gab in der Antike aber auch eine andere Art, die plastische Perspektive darzustellen (Langlotz, *Phidiasprobleme* 61), die durch die Ansicht von unten veranschaulicht ist (Taf. 65, a). Die Frage bedürfte einer eingehenden Untersuchung.

3. Vgl. Schrader, *Kat. der archaischen Marmorskulpturen im Akropolis-Museum* Taf. 15. 27. 49. 59. 75. 100. 103. Kore aus Garagusa, *NSc.* 1941, 254 Abb. 8.

Auch die Bildung der Lider spricht für die Originalität der Arbeit. Sie überschneiden sich nicht, wie stets seit dem Ende des 5. Jahrhunderts. Die Augäpfel waren wohl aus buntem Glasfluss eingekittet. Ein Bohrloch ist nicht sichtbar. Auch diese Wiedergabe ist seit dem 6. Jahrhundert an griechischen Originalen bekannt[4] und unterscheidet sich von römischer Kopistentechnik, die tiefer höhlt und eingesetzte Augen anstiftet.

Von grosser Schönheit muss das Ohr mit seiner weit gehöhlten Muschel gewesen sein, das auffallend schräg zum Profil gestanden hat. Auch hier dürfte die zarte Form der "Ecke" des Ohres griechischen Ursprung bezeugen.

Die nun nächstliegende Frage nach der Entstehungszeit des Kopfes ist jedoch nicht einfach zu beantworten. Denn der Kopf wirkt in seiner rechten Wangenseite herb und ernst wie ein Werk der Frühklassik, in der vermutlichen Hauptansicht von seiner linken Wange aus aber wesentlich reifer und weicher. Das mag durch die Aufstellung der Statue mitbedingt sein, bei der der rechten Kopfhälfte wohl keine Wichtigkeit zugemessen worden ist. Es gibt manche Köpfe, wie den aus Cumae stammenden im Louvre,[5] die gleichsam zweiansichtig sind, was im griechischen Mutterland nicht zu finden sein dürfte. Die Entstehung des Kopfes wird kaum präziser als zwischen der frühen und reifen Klassik, also zwischen 440-20, zu bestimmen sein.

Noch schwieriger und wohl nur versuchsweise zu beantworten ist die Frage nach der Bedeutung des schönen Kopffragmentes. Dass es zu keinem Standbild einer Sterblichen, also keiner Votivfigur gehört hat, macht die heftige, am Hals noch sichtbare Bewegung des Körpers wahrscheinlich. Auch die hoheitsvollen Züge des Kopfes lassen eher an eine Göttin oder Heroine denken. Sind die Beobachtungen richtig, dass der Kopf in Dreiviertelansicht von seiner linken Seite zu sehen war und dass eine etwas vorgebeugte Haltung des Körpers bei einer leichten Neigung des Kopfes nach rechts hin zu erschliessen ist, so könnte man vielleicht an eine bogenschiessende Gestalt denken, wie sie in dem wunderbaren Torso des Theodoros von Phokaia (Taf. 64c)

---

4. Vgl. Knidierkore *Fouilles de Delphes*, IV Taf. 26. Schrader, *Kat. d. archaischen Marmorskulpturen im Akrop. Mus.* S. 135 Abb. 3 Taf. 50. 53. 105. 120. Kopf Webb im British Museum. *BCH* 1893, 294. Langlotz, *Bildhauerschulen* Taf. 62 b. Kopf aus Girò Ashmole Abb. 60. Der von V. H. Poulsen, *Der strenge Stil*, 141 abgebildete verschollene Kopf ist wohl identisch mit dem von Pacciaudi, *Marmora Peloponnesiaca* XLII abgebildeten. Wo befindet er sich jetzt? Er ist stilistisch verwandt dem Kopf in Cleveland, *Arch.Deltion* 1930/1, 91 Abb. 32 (Karouzos).

5. *MonPiot*, 34, 19 Taf. 2. Wuilleumier 278.

oder in dem Niobidenrelief Albani erhalten ist.[6] Eine bogenschiessende Artemis könnte deshalb nach der Haltung des Kopfes vermutet
werden, zumal das jungfräulich Herbe dieser Göttin den Zügen des
Antlitzes besonders stark aufgeprägt ist. Ja die besondere Wirkung,
die der Bildner dem Blick der einst leuchtenden Augen zugemessen
hat, macht die Deutung auf Artemis nur noch wahrscheinlicher. Bei
dem altertümlicheren Gepräge der linken Gesichtshälfte und der
Beobachtung über den Fall der Figur kann man an eine Gruppe von
mehreren Figuren, vielleicht in einem Giebel denken. Doch darüber
ist vorläufig keine Gewissheit zu gewinnen. Dagegen ist es möglich,
die künstlerische Herkunft des Kopfes zu bestimmen, auch wenn es
nicht mehr gelingen dürfte, die formende Hand an anderen Werken
mit Sicherheit nachzuweisen.

Als stilistisch nahe verwandt wüsste ich freilich nur einen Kopf
in Sammlung Alba zu nennen.[7] Die in diffusem Licht mit zu kleinem
Objektiv aufgenommenen Bilder der Originalaufnahmen fassen nicht
seinen plastischen Gehalt, eher die Heliogravüre im JHSt. 1884 Taf.
45, deren Profilaufnahme aber kaum die Hauptansicht gewesen sein
dürfte (Taf. 65, b). Aehnlich sind die glatte Haarkalotte, die Strähnen
und der allgemeine Charakter der Gesichtszüge, besonders des Mundes.
Jedoch überschneidet das Oberlid das Unterlid, was Korrektur des
Restaurators sein könnte. Die Neigung zur Seite lässt eine gewisse
Bewegung auch des Körpers vermuten. Auch hier fällt die Asymmetrie der Gesichtshälften auf, aus der ich nach den unzulänglichen
Photos allein keine Schlüsse für die Ansicht ziehen möchte.

Die den Ausdruckscharakter beider Köpfe bedingenden plastischen
Züge sind die Einung von Herbheit und weicher Fülle, im Kontrast
der linearen Lider zu dem weichen Mund und den Wangen. Die
formende Hand hat dem Marmor zarte Schönheiten abgewonnen, die
im Gipsabguss verhärtet zur Geltung kommen. Auch jene Besonderheit dürfte griechischen Ursprung der Arbeit wahrscheinlich machen.

Solche Züge begegnen häufig an in Grossgriechenland gefundenen
Bildwerken, dessen Marmorplastik leider noch keine zusammenfassende Bearbeitung gefunden hat. Sie kann hier auch nicht gegeben
werden.

Die 7. und 6. Jahrhunderte scheinen im Westen, wenn die Funde ein
Urteil erlauben, keine grosse Marmorplastik gekannt zu haben. Nur
kleine Tempellampen aus Marmor sind damals importiert worden.[8]

---

6. *Fouilles de Delphes*, IV Taf. 57, 3. Picard, *Manuel*, III 1, 1. 186 Abb. 56.
Abb. 5 nach einer französischen illustrierten Zeitung. Niobidenrelief: *Münchner
Jahrbuch* 1912, 138. *Antike* IV, 31. JdI. 55, 1940, 202 (Schweitzer).
7. *EA* 1784/5. *JHS* 1884 Taf. 45. Friedrichs-Wolters, *Bausteine* Nr. 214.
Berytus VI S. 9. Käufliche Abgüsse im Alten Museum Berlin.

Man hat sich mit dem vorzüglichen Kalkstein benügt. Erst aus dem letzten Jahrzehnt des 6. Jahrhunderts sind Koren, Kuroi und Sphingen erhalten, seit 460 auch Fragmente von Grabstelen.[9]

Die Annahme, diese von Griechen in Südrussland ebenso wie in Aegypten, Sizilien und Gallien aus Gründen des Kultes gebrauchten Skulpturen seien in der Weise entstanden, dass man grosse Marmorblöcke weit übers Meer verschiffte und dann an Ort und Stelle verarbeitete, dürfte dem praktischen und geschäftstüchtigen Sinn der Griechen widersprechen. Da Arbeiten derselben Werkstätten zudem im Osten wie im Westen gefunden worden sind, ist die Annahme, diese Votiv- und Sepulcralskulpturen seien auf den Marmorinseln der Kykladen gearbeitet und dann exportiert worden, wahrscheinlicher sein als die heute übliche Ansicht, nesiotische Bildhauer hätten mit Marmorblöcken ferne Länder bereist, um dort die stereotype Votiv- und Sepulcralplastik anzufertigen. Schon unter dem für Griechen gewiss nicht zu unterschätzenden wirtschaftlichen Gesichtspunkt empfiehlt sich jene Annahme. Der Export grosser Blöcke weit übers Meer für Skulpturen, die man ebenso gut in dem wesentlich geringeren Fertiggewicht exportieren konnte, hätte diese anspruchslosen Votive und Sepulcralwerke zu sehr verteuert. Auch Missbildungen im Stein konnten zu kostspieligen Enttäuschungen führen. Man wird deshalb grosse Figuren in abbozziertem Zustand, wie die Kore in Tarent, exportiert haben. Ein griechischer Bildhauer wird den Transport begleitet und dem Werk die letzte Vollendung vor der Aufstellung gegeben haben. Denn die Arbeit in Marmor erfordert lange Erfahrung und Tradition und eine andere Technik als die in Unteritalien heimische Arbeit in Kalkstein. Die in Unteritalien gefundene Votiv- und Sepulcralplastik in Marmor dürfte deshalb überwiegend von Inselgriechen gearbeitet worden sein, die als Händler diese Serienplastik verkauft haben.

Kuroi: Syrakus 49401. Aus Megara Hyblaea.
  Syrakus. Aus Granmichele. Langlotz, *Bildhauerschulen* Taf. 67.
    Dem Theseus aus Eretria verwandt.
  Syrakus 705. Langlotz Taf. 64 a.

---

8. *JHS* 50, 22 Taf. 5. 6. Gelänge es, die Herkunft des Marmors der Lampen aus Selinunt und Syrakus festzustellen, so hätten wir wichtige Anhaltspunkte für die Kykladenplastik des 7. Jh's. Erinnert der Kopf der Lampe *JHS* 50, 25 Abb. 2. 3 nicht an den Kopf des Sunion Kouros, dessen attischer Ursprung nicht bewiesen und unwahrscheinlich ist? Vielleicht gehört das spätere Köpfchen in Berlin A 3 Taf. 10 in diesen Zusammenhang. — Es ist interessant festzustellen, wie unmodern bisweilen die Exportstücke in den fernen Westen gewesen sind. Der dädalische Kopf in dem 595 gegründeten Agrigent scheint wesentlich älteren Ursprungs zu sein. Marconi, *Agrigento arcaico* Taf. 1, 1.

9. Vgl. *RM* 58, 1943, 208. Langlotz, *Bildhauerschulen* 110. Schrader, *Kat. Akropolis-Skulpturen* S. 37. *Festschrift Salinas* 25. Pace II 68 Abb. 71.

Syrakus 23624. Aus Leontinoi. *EA* 754. Langlotz Taf. 64 c.
Schrader, *Kat. Akropolismus*. S. 37.

Potenza. Aus Metapont. *NSc.* 1941 Vol. II 257 Abb. 15.

Syrakus 8293. Aus Megara Hyblaea. ML I Taf. VI, 7, 8.

Koren: Syrakus 710. Della Seta, *Italia Antica* 148 Abb. 142.
Tarent, nicht vollendet. Wuilleumier, *Tarente* 269.

Berlin 578. Wuilleumier 268 Taf. 4, 4.

Tarent 23. 7. 1900. Statuette. Stehende Göttin, ähnlich Akro 671.

Potenza. Thronende Göttin aus Garagusa. Einen Abguss verdanke
ich der Güte P. C. Sestieris. *NSc.* 1941 Vol. II 254 Abb. 8.

Haag. *Bull. van de Vereeniging* XIV 14 Abb. 1.

Köpfe: Berlin. Köpfchen aus Sizilien. *Festschrift Benndorf* Taf. 6.
Ashmole Abb. 76, 77.

Boston. Kopffragment. Caskey, *Cat.* 6. Ashmole Abb. 17. Wuilleumier 275 Taf. 4. 3.

Rom Forum Museum, unpubliziert. Aus Pozzo A. Vgl. Helbig[3] 1099.

Nike: Syrakus 34136. ML 25, 221. *NSc.* 1915, 180 Abb. 3.

Sphinx: Syrakus 5892, aus Megara Hybläa, parisch. Wie Athen NM.
77.

Lampen: JHS 50, 22 Taf. 5. 6.

Grabreliefs: Syrakus. Misc. Salinas 25. Pace II 68 Abb. 71.

Rom, Conservatorenpalast. Taubenstele. Stuart Jones, *Catalogue* 212
Nr. 5.

Syrakus 35441. 36396. 33271. 237. Pace II 549 Abb. 56.

Boston, Priamosrelief. Wuilleumier Taf. X, 1.

London, Brit. Mus. Totenmahlrelief. Wuilleumier Taf. XI, i.

Anders wird es bei speziellen Aufträgen gewesen sein, wenn die
Priester eines Heiligtums ein grosses Kultbild, Giebelfiguren eines
Tempels oder einen Altarschmuck bestellt haben. Es wird dann mit
dem Import sparsam zugeschnittener Marmorblöcke gerechnet werden
dürfen. Bei der Schwierigkeit der Arbeit in Marmor liegt es weiter
nahe anzunehmen, dass auch die ausführenden Bildhauer Inselgriechen der Kykladen gewesen sind. Bei folgenden Skulpturen wird
mit diesem Arbeitshergang gerechnet werden dürfen.

Berlin. Kultbild thronende Göttin. *AD* III Taf. 37. Ashmole Abb.
19-21. Wuilleumier 269. Blümel, *Kat.* A 17 Taf. 33.

Tarent. Kopf eines Kultbildes. Unpubliziert.

Rom, Thermenmuseum. Ludovisi-Relief. Helbig[3] 1286. *JdI*, 26, 1911,
50.

Tempelplastik:

Syrakus 36218. Laufende weibliche Figur. *NSc.* 12, 1915, 199. Pace
II 44 fig. 43.

Syrakus. Athenakopf. Della Seta, *Italia Antica* 152 Abb. 147. Pace
II 201 Abb. 14. Beides Arbeiten der in Keos (*BCH.* 29, 1905, 344
Abb. 9. 10) arbeitenden Werkstatt.

Palermo. Liegende Frau aus Selinunt. *ML* 32 Taf. 25/6. Ashmole Abb. 80/1.

Palermo. Köpfe der Metopen aus Selinunt von drei Werkstätten gearbeitet, einer älteren, einer jüngeren und einer lokalen. Ashmole Abb. 56. 64. 75.

Rom, Thermenmuseum. Kopenhagen, Ny Carlsberg. Niobidengiebel. Literatur zuletzt *AJA* 43, 1939, 27-47.

Rom, Conservatorenpalast. Nike. Helbig[3] 981. Akroter eines Tempelgiebels? Stuart Jones, *Cat.*, 222 Nr. 16. BrBr. 263.

Kopenhagen. Apollon. Coll. Ny Carlsberg Taf. 33. *JdI* 41, 1926, 146.

Crotone. Giebelfiguren. *NSc.* 8, 1911 Suppl. 101 Abb. 79. 80.

Palermo. Bärtiger Kopf aus Selinunt. Pace II 70 Abb. 72. Verwandt den Köpfen in Halmyros *AM.* 65, 1940 Taf. 63/5, und Cypern, *Guide Cyprus Museum* Taf. 17, 2.

Sonstige Werke:

Catania, Mus. 147. Libertini, Mus. Biscari Taf. 1, 2. Die Formelemente sind die des Theseus in Eretria, aber das sphärische Zusammenwölben der Teile ist dem Künstler nicht geglückt.

Metapont. Schädelkalotte eines mit einer breiten Tänie unwundenen Kopfes. Phot. Deut. Arch. Inst. Rom 77.

Freiburg. Weibliches Köpfchen aus Tarent.

Rom, Villa Borghese. Kopf der dorischen Peplosfigur BrBr. 262. Helbig[3] 1558, dem (echten?) Terrakottakopf *Dragma Nilsson* 5 Abb. 2 ähnlich.

Tarent 3899. Athenakopf, wohl vom Meister der Niobide im Thermenmuseum. Wuilleumier 279 Taf. 4, 1.

Boston. Leda. Caskey, *Cat.* 22. BrBr. 678.

Rom, Mus. Barracco. Athenakopf. Coll. Barracco Taf. 30. V. H. Poulsen, *Der strenge Stil* 106.

Die Verbindung mit den Besitzern der Marmorbrüche musste aufrecht erhalten und gepflegt werden. Vielleicht geschah dies in der Weise, dass ein Teil der Werkgenossen dauernd auf den Kykladen arbeitete, um die Blöcke zuzuschneiden und zu abbozzieren (Löwensimen in Himera und Syrakus). Nur nesiotischer Marmor ist im Westen verwandt worden, da die Brüche bei Taormina noch nicht bekannt waren.[10] Alle diese Bildwerke sind deshalb als nesiotische, vielleicht kykladische Arbeiten anzusehen. Diese Meister dürften reisende Bildhauer gewesen sein, worauf G. M. A. Richter häufig schon hingewiesen hat und wie sie auch das Mittelalter gekannt hat. Ihre Zahl war kaum beträchtlich.

Viele dieser Scapellini werden sich im Laufe der Zeit in Grossgriechenland angesiedelt haben, um die Beziehungen zu ihren Kunden

---

10. Baedeker, *Unteritalien* 1912 S. 389.

in Städten und Heiligtümern aufrecht zu erhalten. Sie werden dadurch unwillkürlich von den gestaltenden Kräften der Westgriechen erfüllt worden sein. Solchen länger im Westen verweilenden kykladischen Bildhauern dürften auch die Marmorteile der Selinunter Heraion-Skulpturen verdankt werden. Die Kalksteinmetopen selbst sind einheimische Arbeiten, an denen die Marmorköpfe in betonter Graecität hervorleuchten. Am Heraion in Selinunt lassen sich vier Gruppen von Marmorbildhauern noch scheiden: Die Köpfe mit noch spätarchaisch anmutenden, aus dicken Lidern vorquellenden Augen (Taf. 65, c). Die knapperen, gleichsam wacheren Gesichter eines bedeutenden nesiotischen Meisters (Taf. 66, a). Eine dritte Hand am Kopf der Artemis, vielleicht identisch mit dem Meister, der das Ludovisi-Relief gearbeitet hat (Taf. 66, b). Und schliesslich einheimische Schüler, die es den Meistern nicht gleich tun.[11]

Vielleicht liessen sich die Oeuvres jener nesiotischen Meister noch zusammenstellen. Es wird unmöglich sein, zu erkennen, wie weit es sich bei den genannten Werken um Importe oder um in Italien ausgeführte Arbeiten handelt. Bei kleinen Arbeiten war es natürlich immer möglich, sie an Ort und Stelle aus einem kleinen Marmorblock zu fertigen.

Als dritte grosse Gruppe von Werken sind die als grossgriechisch im eigentlichen Sinn zu Bezeichnenden zu nennen. Zu ihnen gehört als bedeutendste Leistung der Athenakopf eines Akroliths im Vatikan, der dem Athleten aus Adernò sehr verwandt und deshalb in den Umkreis des Pythagoras gestellt worden ist.[12]

Weniger persönlich muten die Akroterfiguren aus Lokri an. Die Dioskuren gleichen im Bau so sehr lokrischen Jünglingsbronzen, dass hier ein Lokalstil sichtbar zu werden beginnt. Vielleicht fällt von diesen Figuren auch ein erhellendes Licht auf den einstigen Markstein der argivischen Kunst, den Stephanosjüngling.[13] Er ist seit Wald-

11. Benndorf, *Metopen von Selinunt*. Pace II 36. Neue Aufnahmen durch mich machen zu lassen, hatte Frau Bovio Marconi die grosse Güte, für die ihr hier nochmals aufrichtig gedankt sei. *Antike und Abendland* II Abb. 20. 21. BrBr. 292/3.

12. Langlotz, *Bildhauerschulen*, 147 Taf. 89/90. 92. 93c. Pace II 62 Abb. 65. Ashmole Abb. 43. 44. Zu dieser Gruppe von Werken gehört vielleicht das Vorbild der Münze Roscher, *Lex*. I, 2, 2137 und Himera, Ashmole, *Late Arch. Sculpture in Sicily*, Abb. 11. Alda Levi, *Cat. delle terracotte di Napoli* 156 Abb. 121. Die Bronzen 15178 und 15179 im Nat.Mus. Athen. Reinach, *Rép*. II 472. Ist auch der aus Kyrene stammende Kopf BM 1411 hier zu nennen oder gehört er einer archaisierenden Phase der alexandrinischen Kunst an, ähnlich wie die Bronzen Coll. Lambros Dattari 433 und Coll. Khawan Bros. Caire 1924?

13. Helbig[3] 1846. 1909. BrBr. 301. EA 1093. F. Poulsen, *Greek and Roman Portraits in English Country Houses* p. 21 Abb. 24. Berlin Nr. 509. *Kat.d. Skulpturen* IV K 139. *BullComm*. 1901 Taf. 10. Pal. Doria Matz-Duhn Nr. 995. Leningrad, Ermitage Nr. 16. Torlonia Nr. 11. — Zu den Dioskuren aus Lokri, Guida Ruesch 125. Vgl. die Münze von Himera Kat.Hirsch XIII 325. — Ist der Kopf im Lateran *EA* 2127/8 wirklich eine exakte Kopie? V. H. Poulsen, *Der*

steins klärender Beobachtung in Vergessenheit geraten. Da der Lehrer des Stephanos, Pasiteles, aus Unteritalien stammt, könnte vielleicht erwogen werden, ob der Stephanosjüngling nicht ein für den manieristischen Geschmack des 1. Jahrhunderts umgebildetes berühmtes grossgriechisches Werk wiedergibt. Anklänge an grossgriechische Arbeiten zeigen auch manche Marmorkratere und Sphingen als Tischträger, die einer ähnlichen Stilrichtung angehören.[14] Neben jenen persönlich anmutenden Köpfen stehen dann die grossgriechisch provinziellen Werke:

Rom. Thermenmuseum. Helbig[3] 1288. Pace II 47 Abb. Ashmole Abb. 66. 74.

Como, Museum. Kopf. Leicht archaisierend. Kleine Buckellocke. Unterlid überschnitten.

Hannover, Kopf. *JdI.* 35, 1920, 41 Taf. 4. Pace II 63 Abb. 66. Ashmole Abb. 79.

Boston. Relief. *Cat.* Caskey Nr. 17. Ashmole Abb. 29.

Syrakus 16968. Weiblicher Kopf. *Ausonia* 8, 1913, 61 Abb. 8.

Paris, Louvre. Kopf aus Cumae. *MonPiot.* 34, 19 Taf. 2. Wuilleumier 278. Der barberinischen Schutzflehenden verwandt.

Reggio. Nike aus Lokri. Ferri, *Divinità ignote* Taf. 36.

Tarent 3897. Weiblicher Kopf. Alinari 35347/8. Wuilleumier 280 Taf. 5, 1.

Paris, Louvre. Kopf. Archives photographiques 1362. An die Selinunter Köpfe sich anschliessend.

Reggio. Kopf und Füsse eines Kultbildes aus Girò. P. Orsi, *Tempio del' Apolline Alaei* 135 Taf. 16. Ashmole Abb. 60/62. Wuilleumier 277.

Toulouse. Eckvolute, den Selinunter Köpfen verwandt. *Fasti Archaeol.* I 301 Abb. 99.

Maur a.d.Url, Stift Seitenstetten. Relief. *JhO.* XXV Beibl. 62 Abb. 37. Wenn die Abbildung nicht trügt, spätarchaischen Köpfen Süditaliens verwandt.

Madrid. Frau aus Elche. Garcia y Bellido, *La dama de Elche* Taf. 6, vergleichbar der Hera aus Selinunt? Langlotz Abb. 20.

Kansas City. Langlotz 122 Abb. 7. *Pantheon* XII 367. Wuilleumier Taf. 7. 4.

Tarent. Weibliche Köpfe. Wuilleumier Taf. 5.2.

Rom, Thermenmuseum. Relief Reiter, "chalkidisch"? Helbig[3] 1932.

Kopenhagen, Ny Carlsberg 31. Relief *Billedtavler* Taf. 3.

Rom, Thermenmuseum. Relief Tanzende Mänaden.

Rom, Villa Borghese. Kassandrarelief. Wuilleumier Taf. X, 2.

Tarent. Grabrelief. Wuilleumier Taf. XI, 2.

---

strenge Stil S. 126. Vgl. die Bronzen aus Lokri in Reggio 4779. *NSc.* Suppl. 1913, 39 Abb. 49. Jantzen, *Grossgriechische Bronzewerkstätten.* Zu dem herben Stil des 1. Jhs. in Grossgriechenland: Spinazola, *Arte decorativa* Taf. 259.

Ueberblickt man diese wohl für grossgriechische Heiligtümer ge-
arbeiteten Werke — bei manchen, wie den in Rom gefundenen, ist die
Herkunft aus Grossgriechenland nur zu vermuten —, so dürfte der
"Artemiskopf" der zweiten Gruppe von Werken zuzugesellen sein.
Der westliche Zweig der Kykladenkunst gewinnt dadurch einen neuen
Aspekt. Seine Verwandtschaft mit dorischen Schulen wird sichtbar.
Sie zu klären, würde über den Rahmen dieser Publikation hinaus-
führen.

14. *AA* 1928, 203.

ANADYOMENE

In the radiant dawn of a sky a-flush like roses
    With lifting arms up from the waves I rise;
But more than all the sea-depths a deeper repose is
    Calling me up to the blue depths of the skies.

Swift, savage winds against my breasts come dashing
    Out from the shore and trembling is over me;
In the clinging waves, O Zeus, my long hair falling
    Is dragging me down like stones into the sea.

Hasten, ye soft winds, Glauke, Cymothoe also,
    Hasten to hold me up lest I sink below;
How could I dream that ever I should fall so
    Soon into the Sun's embracing arms a-glow!

Angelos Sikelianos

Translated by
John B. Edwards

HEILENDE SCHLANGE

Georg Lippold, Erlangen

Tafel 67

Dem Entdecker Olynths möchte ich als Festgruss ein Denkmal in
Erinnerung rufen, das aus dessen weiterer Umgebung stammt, das
Krankenrelief von der Chalkidike in Kopenhagen[1] (Taf. 67, a) Seit ich
es vor über 30 Jahren veröffentlicht habe, ist es wiederholt der Gegenstand archaeologischer und religionsgeschichtlicher Untersuchung
gewesen, ohne dass ein völlig befriedigendes Resultat erzielt worden
wäre. Da auch die letzte Behandlung ein solches nicht ergeben hat,
lohnt es sich wohl, die Probleme noch einmal darzulegen.

Die Erklärung kann nur von dem Bildwerk selbst ausgehen: keine
Inschrift, keine nähere Angabe über den alten Aufstellungsort kommt
zu Hilfe. Dafür ist die Sprache des Künstlers klar und eindringlich,
er beherrscht die Mittel der Darstellung vollkommen. Wir sehen ungefähr in der Mitte[2] einen Baum — verzweigt, aber blattlos wie auf
älteren griechischen Reliefs üblich. Aus einem Astloch kommt eine
Schlange hervor, die sich um die Aeste schlingt und ihren Kopf (links
von der Astteilung) der Hauptperson im Bild, dem Kranken entge-
genstreckt.

Dieser, ein bärtiger Mann, mit Mantel nur um Unterkörper und
linken Unterarm, erhebt sich mit dem Oberkörper von der Kline, auf
der er liegt, hebt Kopf und rechten Arm der Schlange entgegen, hebt
auch das rechte Bein etwas. Die Kline wird getragen von drei nackten
Jünglingen, einem grösseren am Kopf- und zwei kleineren am Fussende. Beiderseits, von den Tragenden teilweise verdeckt, also in einer
hinteren Raumschicht, der des Baums, dringen zwei Jünglinge vor,
der grössere, mit Mantel um Unterkörper und linker Schulter links,
der kleinere, rechts, mit Chlaina über den Schultern, jeder in der erhobenen Rechten einen Stein, nach der Schlange zielend, auf die auch
die Linke des Jünglings rechts weist. Die Bedeutung des Reliefs im
allgemeinen ist klar. Weihung eines Genesenen, der als Kranker,
Heilung Suchender auf der Kline getragen wird, an die Gottheit, die in
der Schlange sichtbar wird. Zu beachten ist die verschiedene soziale

---

1. Kopenhagen, *Glyptothek Ny Carlsberg* 233 a. Fr. Poulsen, *Katalog* 1940,
S.173 mit Litteratur. Lippold, Brunn-Bruckmann, *Denkmäler* 680 a: *Antike
Skulpturen der Glyptothek Ny Carlsberg* 16, Abb. 14. Eitrem u. Nilsson, *Fra
Ny Carlsberg Glyptoteks Samlinger* II, 77ff. Herzog, *Philologus* Suppl. 22, 3, 79.
Karo, *Weihgeschenke in Epidauros* 3. Hausmann, *Kunst und Heiltum* (1948)
58, Abb. 3.

2. Etwas nach links verschoben, dafür rechts der kräftige Seitenast.

Stellung der Nebenfiguren: die Träger der Kline sind nackt, damit als
dienend, Sklaven gekennzeichnet. Die Steinwerfenden dagegen sind
dem Kranken gleichgestellt, der kleinere als jünger, Ephebe, nur mit
der Chlaina bekleidet, der grössere vollerwachsen in bürgerlicher
Tracht. Nahe liegt, hier die Angehörigen, die Söhne des Kranken zu
erkennen.

Während soweit kaum eine Meinungsverschiedenheit möglich ist,
ergibt schon die Interpretation des rein Tatsächlichen, Sichtbaren
Zweifel. Wird die Kline niedergesetzt oder aufgehoben? Gegen die
erste Deutung hat man eingewendet, die Träger müssten doch auf
dem Weg zum Baum in gleicher Richtung gegangen sein, der am
Kopfende also mit dem Rücken gegen die Kline. Dieser Einwand
setzt voraus, dass der Zug mit dem Kranken "zufällig" an dem Baum
vorbeikommt und beim Erscheinen der Schlange die Kline niedergesetzt wird. Dies die eine Erklärung des Bildes: der Kranke hat
vielleicht vergebens anderswo Heilung gesucht, die Epiphanie der
heilenden Schlange ist ein persönliches einmaliges Erlebnis, der Anlass
zur Stiftung des Kultus. Wenn also die Kline nicht niedergesetzt
wird, muss man annehmen, der Zug habe "zufällig" an dem Baum
gerastet, beim Erscheinen der Schlange habe man entfliehen wollen,
die Kline aufgehoben, der Kranke aber habe den Gott erkannt und
Heilung gefunden.

Anders, wenn der Baum als Sitz der Gottheit schon bekannt war.
Dann konnte nur ein Niedersetzen der Kline gemeint sein. Spricht
dagegen wirklich die Art des Tragens? An sich ist bekanntlich im
ruhenden Kunstwerk eine "bewegte" Haltung doppeldeutig, die Richtung der Bewegung muss der Künstler durch besondere Impulse an-
zeigen, welche die Illusion der Bewegungsrichtung suggerieren. Nun
zielt ja Alles auf die Schlange zu, auch die Träger blicken zu ihr
auf: nichts, was auf eine Gegenbewegung hinweise: da müsste wenigstens einer der Träger einen Schritt vom Mittelpunkt weg machen
oder auf andere Weise irgendwo eine entgegengesetzte Richtung
sichtbar sein. Wie die Kline angefasst wird, wie die Träger mit ge-
beugten Knieen stehen, das deutet auf ein behutsames Niedersetzen,
nicht auf eiliges Aufheben. Natürlich waren die Träger auf dem
Weg in gleicher Richtung gegangen. Am heiligen Ort angekommen,
setzten sie zunächst ab und trugen dann, entgegengesetzt anfassend,
den Kranken genau an die Stelle unter dem Baum, wo die Gottheit
erwartet wird.

Nimmt man also an, dass es sich nicht um ein zufälliges uner-
wartetes Erlebnis handelt, sondern dass der Baum dem Heilsuchenden
als Sitz der heilenden Gottheit bekannt war, die er nur in der Gestalt

der Schlange zu finden erwartete, dann ergibt sich auch die Rolle der Steinwerfenden: nach der einen Erklärung halten sie die Schlange für ein gefährliches Tier, suchen sie zu vertreiben, nach der andern[3] haben sie das Tier durch Steinwürfe auf den Baum herausgelockt — das kann im Bild nur so gezeigt werden, dass sie noch Steine halten. Ich möchte der ersten Deutung nicht mehr wie früher den Vorzug geben. Die Deutbewegung des Jünglings rechts lässt sich doch verstehen als Hinweis: "da ist sie, wir haben sie herausgelockt." Also Parallele zur Geste des Kranken, nicht Gegensatz.

Soviel ergibt das Bild. Können wir mit der Erklärung weiter kommen, die Gottheit benennen, Parallelen aufzeigen? Genau entsprechende Bilder gibt es nicht, auch in den Nachrichten über Heilungen und Heilungswunder findet sich nichts wirklich vergleichbares. Und das ist verständlich. Die bisherigen neueren Interpretationen kranken daran, dass man die Deutung ausschliesslich im griechischen Bereich gesucht, die Schlange als Vertreter des Asklepios oder einer andern griechischen Heilgottheit angeshen hat. Gewiss ist das Relief ein rein griechisches Werk, sind die Dargestellten Griechen oder wenigstens Menschen griechischer Kultur. Aber die Herkunft des Votivs weist über den griechischen Bereich hinaus. In der Chalkidike, wo es nach glaubhafter Angabe gefunden ist, ohne dass natürlich die Händler den genauen Fundort angeben wollten oder konnten, sitzen die Griechen als Kolonisten neben der einheimischen thrakischen Bevölkerung, die natürlich ihre eignen Götter, Daemonen, Vorstellungen ihrer Erscheinungsform und Wirkungskraft hatten. Wir wissen ja, wie stark die griechische Religion von thrakischen und benachbarten religiösen Vorstellungen und Mythen befruchtet worden ist, wie der Grieche überall den fremden Gott anerkennt, wenn er ihn auch mit seinem eigenen gleichsetzt, dem fremden Namen seinen substituiert oder beisetzt. Und gerade Heildaemonen, die geheimnisvoll an einsamem Ort, in der Wildnis hausen und wirken, fremdartig und doch dem Griechischen irgendwie verwandt, mussten Kranke herbeilocken, die bei den eignen Göttern vergebens Heilung erhofft hatten, eine allgemein menschliche und im Grunde immer bis heute wiederkehrende Erscheinung.

Gewiss, die Schlange am Baum kehrt bei Asklepios auch in rein griechischem Bereich wieder: aber da ist sie eben das Tier des Gottes, "herabgesunken" zum Attribut. Bedeutsamer als das attische Relief, das man verglichen hat,[4] ist ein anderes, das man ebenfalls herange-

---

3. Küster, *Die Schlange* (*Religiongesch. Vers.u.Vorarb.* XIII 2) 134 A. 3.
4. Hausmann Anm. 242. Das Relief Athen NatMus. 1335: Rodenwaldt, *Relief* 90.

zogen hat, ohne auf das Wichtigste hinzuweisen: ein Bruchstück, wieder in Kopenhagen (Taf. 67, b),[5] das erst hellenistischer Zeit angehört. Hier ist der Baum mit der Schlange zurückgedrängt, hinter eine Mauer, vor der sich die Darstellung entwickelte. Von dieser ist nur eine Nebenfigur, anscheinend Opferdiener erhalten — neben ihm Spur einer grösseren Gestalt, vielleicht des Weihenden. Die Szene spielt vor dem Temenos, von dem ausser dem Baum wohl noch Weiteres über der Mauer zu sehen war. Echt hellenistische Reliefkomposition. Bedeutsam ist, dass dieses Relief aus Makedonien stammt, also aus dem weiteren Bereich unseres Krankenreliefs.

Nun wissen wir von der besonderen Rolle, die die Schlange in Makedonien spielt. Allgemein bekannt ist die Geschichte von der Erzeugung Alexanders d. Gr., Olympias und die Schlange, die noch auf späten Contorniaten[6] dargestellt ist. Lukian erwähnt sie in der Geschichte des Alexandros von Abonuteichos,[7] als der Prophet durch Makedonien wandert und dort die riesigen Schlangen sieht, die von den Einwohnern gezähmt werden and die mit ihren Kindern zusammen leben. Das ist ein Verhältnis zu dem Tier das über griechische Vorstellungen hinaus geht, wenn sich auch Berührungen finden, die Schlange mit ihrem geheimnisvollen Wesen bei den verschiedensten Völkern eine bedeutende Rolle im Volksglauben spielt, wobei keine ursprünglichen Zusammenhänge angenommen werden müssen.

Ist also die Schlange unseres Reliefs nicht die Erscheinungsform oder das dienende Tier des Asklepios oder eines andern griechischen Heilgottes, sondern hat sie ursprünglich mit griechischer Gottesvorstellung nichts zu tun, so werden wir auch nicht nach einem Namen fragen, ja zweifeln, ob sie einen Individualnamen hatte, nicht nur "die" Schlange war, die eine von den vielen ihrer Gattung, die alle geheimnisvolle Kräfte hatten, die man in hohlen Bäumen hausend wusste und dort zur Heilung aufsuchte.

Dann befremdet auch das Steinwerfen nicht mehr. Ein solches Wesen kann man zur Hilfe zwingen, wie der Gott der Primitiven durch sehr derbe Mittel, durch Schlagen und Peinigen, gezwungen werden kann — Vorstellungen, die ja bis in die Schwänke mit den widerwilligen Heiligen fortwirken. Es geht beides durcheinander: real wirft man das reale Tier mit Steinen und im Ritus wendet man das selbe Mittel gegenüber dem daemonischen Tier an.

---

5. *Glyptothek Ny Carlsberg* 189. *Einzelaufnahmen* 3988.

6. Alföldi, *Die Kontorniaten* 102 (hier auch die Münzen mit der Darstellung erwähnt), Taf. III, 1, 2 usw.

7. Lukian *Alexandros* 7 (215) — Vgl. noch die Schlange in den Bildern des "Thrakischen Reiters": Küster, *Die Schlange* 83; Robinson, *TAPA* 69 (1938), 75-76, Taf. XXIII.

Unser Relief ist nicht das einzige Zeugnis für das Zusammentreffen griechischer und einheimischer Vorstellungen in diesen Gegenden. Ebenfalls von der Chalkidike stammt ein zweites Relief in Kopenhagen, das ich ebenfalls vor Jahren besprochen und gegen Verdächtigung zu verteidigen hatte: das Votiv praxitelischer Zeit mit Staphylos und Athena,[8] dessen nur halb verständliche Inschrift trotz ihrer tadellosen Schriftform auch tüchtige Epigraphiker an Fälschung denken liess. Dass die Verbindung Staphylos-Proxenos durch das Nebeneinander von Proxenos und Botrys in Tegea gestützt wird, konnte ich seitdem nachweisen.[9] Dann kam auch eine Weihung aus Delphi an Proxenos zu Tage, die diesen im Typus des Silens beim Mahl gelagert zeigt.[10] Sie beweist, dass auch Proxenos in den dionysischen Kreis gehört. Der Gott des Reliefs freilich erinnert in Tracht und Typus viel mehr an Asklepios: d.h. der einheimische Gott, dessen Name in dem "barbarischen" Teil der Inschrift stecken muss, wird von den Griechen mit Staphylos und Proxenos, den dionysischen Daemonen, identifiziert, ihr Wesen deckt sich aber nur teilweise, der Einheimische denkt sich den Gott seiner herrlichen Trauben würdiger, er ist ihm wohl auch ein Heilgott gewesen, wie er dem Wein heilende Kraft zugeschrieben haben mag. Ihm steht Athena gegenüber, als Vertreter der Griechen, die seinen Beistand zur Heilung erflehen: daher die für Weihinschriften nicht gebräuchliche Vocativform.

Das Krankenrelief verträgt eine scharfe Interpretation aller Einzelheiten, weil es offenkundig nicht provinziell mit Verwendung entlehnter Typen, sondern wie im Ganzen so im Detail primär gestaltet ist, aus dem Gegenstand, sachlich und formal überlegt und dem Wollen entsprechend gekonnt. Freilich darf man es nicht an attischer Harmonie und Anmut messen, es finden sich störende Härten: mit diesen will der Künstler eben wirken, Ausdruck, Realität geben. "Die Parallele der Tragenden links gibt das gleichmässige Anfassen sehr anschaulich wieder; dafür wirkt es künstlerisch äusserst ungünstig" kann nur vom klassicistischen Standpunkt aus gesagt werden, denn das Anschauliche ist ja eben expressiv "künstlerisch." Dasselbe gilt von der Parallele der drei Beine rechts, dem Zusammendrängen der Köpfe auf den Seiten. Die Komposition ist genau ausgewogen: der Mittelpunkt in dem Dreieck Kopf der Schlange—Hand des Kranken—Knie des kranken Beins — das keineswegs "ungeschickt" wiedergegeben ist — also im Wirkungsraum der Heilung. In dem sehr flachen Relief wird gerade durch die harten Ueber-

---

8. *Glyptothek Ny Carlsberg* 233 b (Fr. Poulsen, *Katalog* 1940, S.175). Brunn-Bruckmann 680 b.

9. *Phil. Woch.*, 1932, 277.

10. *BCH* 60, 359, pl. 44, 1. Picard, *Rev. Arch.* 5, 1935, 262.

schneidungen die Vorstellung der Raumtiefe erweckt. Baum und Steinwerfende sind in der hinteren Schicht, aus der der Kopf in die vordere des Kranken vorkommt der Raum über den Figuren, der im 5. Jahrhundert keineswegs unerhört ist, wirkt für die Komposition nicht leer. In ihn zielen die Bewegungen der erhobenen Arme, durch ihn fliegen die Steine, er gibt zusammen mit dem Baum und der Tiefenstaffelung der Figuren eine Raumillusion, wie sie das griechische Relief schon der klassischen Zeit aus wirklichem Raumgefühl schafft, während der Raum des römischen Reliefs nicht primär erlebt, sondern äusserlich konstruiert ist.

So wenig das Relief als provinzieller Ableger attischer Kunst zu erklären ist, so stark die positiven nichtattischen Elemente sind, so ist es doch nicht ohne den Vorgang der klassischen attischen Kunst denkbar. Mit Recht hat man auf den Parthenonfries u. a. hingewiesen.[11] Am nächsten steht wohl das eigentümliche, allerdings auch nicht typisch attische Jagdrelief von Spata[12]: auch eine Freiraumscene, wenn auch über den Figuren nur knapper, für die Schlagbewegungen allzu knapper Raum ist: die beiden Jäger rechts und links lassen sich gut unsern Steinwerfern vergleichen.

Enger, aber ganz anderer Art ist eine Parallele, auf die ich kürzlich nebenbei hingewiesen[13] habe, der viel besprochene "Laokoon" — Kantharos in London (Taf. 67, c).[14] Hier sehen wir als Gegenbild zur Bestrafung des Ixion eine Darstellung, die sich bis jetzt einer befriedigenden Deutung entzogen hat, obwohl — wie bei unserm Relief — derVorgang sehr klar und eindringlich dargestellt ist: ein bärtiger Mann mit wildem Haar, in Chlamys, ist auf einen Altar geflüchtet. Eine Schlange hat ihn umwunden und beisst ihn in die linke Schulter. Er aber achtet darauf nicht, blickt nach der andern Seite, zückt das Schwert, dessen Scheide die Linke hält, gegen den geflügelten bärtigen Daemon, der einen hinter dem Altar niedergesunkenen toten Jüngling, mit langem Haar, in Chlamys, in der rechten Seite die blutende Todeswunde, mit beiden Händen packt, um ihn wegzuziehen. Rechts vom Altar ein Baum, hinter dem ein königlicher Mann, mit wohl gepflegtem Haar, im Mantel, mit Kranz und Scepter herbeieilt, mit der Rechten einen Stein erhebend.

Die formalen Parallelen zum Kopenhagener Relief sind offenkundig: der Baum, die Schlange, der Steinwerfer rechts, vom Rücken

---

11. Jacobsthal, *Melische Reliefs* 160.

12. Rodenwaldt, *Relief* 71, Abb. 85.

13. *JDAI* 61, 110, Anm. 4. Für das Gegenständliche auch von Poulsen (Anm. 1) verglichen.

14. Br. Mus. E 155. Furtwängler-Reichhold Taf. 163, 2 (Buschor). *CVA.* Gr. Brit., 226, 2 a-b; 228, 2a.

gesehen — selbst der zupackende Flügeldaemon und die Kranken-
träger links. Der Kantharos ist älter als das Relief, das Bild gewiss
nicht Erfindung des Vasenmalers, sondern Nachklang "grosser"
Kunst. Es zeigt sich also, dass der Künstler des Reliefs, so sehr
scheinbar sein Bild primär, ganz aus dem Gegenstand heraus, gestaltet ist, doch ein älteres Kompositionsschema im Sinn hatte.

Oder ist der Zusammenhang nicht nur ein formaler? Wirft er
Licht auf die Deutung des Vasenbildes? Dass die immer wieder vor-
gebrachte Deutung auf Laokoon unmöglich ist, soll hier nicht nochmals ausgeführt werden. Sicher zu benennen ist der Flügeldaemon
mit dem wilden Haar und Bart; das ist Thanatos, genau wie er auf
den attischen Lekythen[15] erscheint. Der Tote, den er packt, ist erwachsen, kaum Sohn, eher jüngerer Bruder oder Genosse des von
der Schlange Umwundenen. Dieser ist ein wilder, ein "böser" Mensch
wie Ixion[16] auf der Gegenseite im Kontrast zu dem König mit dem
Stein. Woher kommt die Wunde des Toten? Ist das der Biss der
Schlange, die zuerst den Jüngling, dann den Bärtigen tötet? Oder,
wie andere Erklärer[17] wollen, rührt sie vom Schwert des Bärtigen
her? Die Sprache der Kunst, der sehr überlegten Kunst dieses Bildes,
erlaubt nur eine Deutung: Wunde und Schwert gehören zusammen.
Der Man hat den Jüngling ermordet, flüchtet auf den Altar, wo die
Schlange, eben die Gottheit des Altars, die Strafe an ihm vollzieht.
Ist also die Schlange ein ähnliches Wesen wie die des Reliefs, dort
freundlich heilend, hier feindlich strafend? Ist die dargestellte Sage
in demselben, nordgriechischen halbbarbarischen Bereich zu suchen?
Gehört das Bild, das der Vasenmaler benutzte und das dem Künstler
des Reliefs vorschwebte, der nordgriechischen thasischen Malerei an,
wie das Relief der Kunst dieses Kreises nicht fern steht?

---

15. Z. B. Pfuhl, *Meisterwerke griech. Zeichn. u. Mal.* Abb. 88.
16. Dass die Aehnlichkeit mit diesem, die übrigens gar nicht so gross ist, nicht
Identität des Dargestellten beweist, betont Buschor mit Recht.
17. Vgl. Waser, *RE.* X, 1378, 42ff.

APOLLON SUR LA MITRA D'AXOS

CHARLES PICARD
Sorbonne, Paris

Planche 69

Depuis que M. Doro Levi a proposé l'interprétation première d'une *mitra* incisée d'Axos, datée de la fin du VIIe s.,[1] et a vu une apparition divine dans la silhouette incomplète représentée là à mi-corps seulement au-dessus de la cuve du trépied,[2] une controverse est née et se prolonge, touchant l'identification de la figure d'épiphanie (fig. 1).

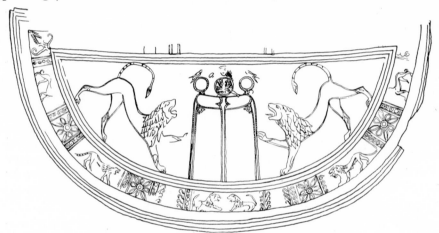

Fig. 1. Mitra d'Axos (Crète).

Au lieu de l'Apollon, $Διὸς προφήτης$, auquel avait pensé d'abord M. Doro Levi, Mlle Marg. Guarducci a cru pouvoir plutôt reconnaître une Athéna.

A son tour, M. Doro Levi est revenu sur la question,[3] et, dans un article de l'*American Journal,* il a défendu son point de vue antérieur. Je n'ai pas la prétention de vouloir intervenir en arbitre dans cette discussion italienne; mais on m'excusera, puisque le débat, né en

---

1. "I bronzi di Axos," *Annuario* 13-14, 61-63, 131-134, pl. 13.
2. Cf. un couvercle de pithos de style géométrique (Cnossos): D. Levi, *Early Hellenic Pottery from Crete*, 29-30, pl. 28, 3; *AJA* 49 (1945) 311-312: Zeus brandissant la foudre s'avance vers un trépied, sur la cuve duquel est posé un oiseau, et entre les montants duquel apparaît à mi-corps une figure humaine.
3. *AJA* 49 (1945) 293-313; *Gleanings from Crete* (cité ci-après: *Gleanings*). Dans son livre récent, *la Crète dédalique*, 1947, M. P. Demargne a bien donné son accord au point de vue présenté par M. Doro Levi (notamment p. 295, n. 6); mais il n'a pas signalé de raisons nouvelles pour résoudre ainsi le problème posé par le décor du document.

Crète, a déjà été transféré en Amérique même, de signaler ici, à l'occasion des *Studies Presented to David Moore Robinson,* quelques observations qui pourraient aider à conclure.

Je dédie bien volontiers ces remarques à notre aimable confrère de l'Université de Mississippi, dont l'activité archéologique brave les fatigues de l'âge, et dont les découvertes en Grèce m'ont si souvent procuré leur précieuse instruction.

La *mitra* de bronze dont l'interprétation est litigieuse a été reproduite en détail, en dernier lieu, en 1945, par l'*American Journal of Archaeology,* dans l'article signalé de M. Doro Levi (fig. 15, à la page 295).[4] On sait que le document provient des ruines du temple d'Aphrodite à Axos, en Crète, et qu'il avait été trouvé par une mission italienne il y a environ une cinquantaine d'années.

Il s'agit de reconnaître et dénommer le petit personnage visible à mi-corps, armé d'un épieu et couvert d'un bouclier dont l'épisème est un poulpe; il jaillit, en quelque sorte, du sommet du trépied central, accosté de deux lions rugissants. La silhouette est équivoque, détériorée, un peu évanide.

C'est, comme je l'ai dit ci-dessus, pour M. Doro Levi, un Apollon; pour Mlle Marg. Guarducci,[5] une Athéna. L'opposition de Mlle Marg. Guarducci aux conclusions du premier exégète a été provoquée par la présence des fauves autour du trépied, et par les armes, inattendues, attribuées ici à la petite figure divine.

S'étonnant devant ces particularités, Mlle Marg. Guarducci a réfléchi qu'on verrait, plus volontiers qu'Apollon, une Athéna, déesse guerrière, armée d'une épée, comme il arrive ici. Déesse importée en Crète par les envahisseurs achéens, Athéna aurait pris, un jour, pour les ajouter à ses pouvoirs, ceux de la πότνια θηρῶν minoenne: on la figurait, au mieux entre des animaux sacrés, fauves et oiseux; or, au-dessus du trépied, deux oiseaux sont perchés encore sur les poignées — anneaux du trépied d'Axos, et ils encadrent hiératiquement la petite apparition d'épiphanie.

Puisque nous avons la preuve d'un culte oraculaire local à Axos, sur le site même où la *mitra* crétoise qui est en cause fut découverte,[6] il paraît à Mlle Guarducci que la figuration discutée pourrait avoir été l'image d'une Athéna, déesse oraculaire à l'occasion, elle aussi; c'est

---

4. La planche donnée dans la *Crète dédalique,* pl. II, en bas, trop petite, trop noire, ne montre pas assez le détail.

5. *Riv. del R. Istituto d'archeologia e storia dell'arte* 6 (1937) 7-12; cf. aussi *Inscriptiones Creticae* II, *Tituli Cretae orientalis,* 1939, 47.

ce que M. Doro Levi a contesté vivement, en 1945, dans l'*American Journal of Archaelogy*.

Le but de cette courte note n'est pas de revenir, dirait-on, vers l'arrière, donc sur l'ensemble des arguments qui ont été présentés de part et d'autre, assez en détail, pour ou contre les deux hypothèses rivales. Ainsi qu'en toute controverse, il a bien pu échoir aux deux savants engagés dans le débat de dépasser, çà et là, la portée limite de certaines des justifications qu'ils découvraient, pour étayer leur point de vue. A ce sujet, par exemple, M. Doro Levi ne m'a pas convaincu lorsqu'il essaye[7] de retirer à l'Athéna de l'Érechtheion, sur l'Acropole d'Athènes, ses pouvoirs prophétiques attestés. Peut-être serais-je porté personnellement à vouloir répondre sur ce point à l'éminent savant italien, car je n'ai pas changé d'avis, depuis qu'en 1930, dans l'article auquel M. Doro Levi a fait allusion,[8] j'essayais d'interpréter le témoignage d'Herodote, V, 72, sur ce qui a bien été, je crois, un essai manqué de consultation oraculaire du roi des Lacédémoniens, Cléoménès, à l'Acropole d'Athènes. L'importance de l'Érechtheion comme *manteion* populaire, attestée historiquement à l'époque des Pisistratides et plus tard, est inscrite sur le terrain même, dans le dispositif du vieux sanctuaire des *martyria*. On s'exposera toujours à l'aventure, en doutant du sens des rites traditionnels qui avaient leur place à l'*adyton*, dans les parages de la "mer d'Erechthée." A travers tout ce qui a été allégué, p. 301 sqq. pour tenter de retirer à Athéna, non seulement à Athènes, mais aussi à Argos, à Delphes, etc., son activité prophétique, il me semble pouvoir dire que M. Doro Levi a voulu, en général trop prouver, ce qui n'es pas le meilleur moyen de convaincre.[9] Il était en droit sans doute, au contraire, de penser que l'association d'Athéna avec le trépied oraculaire n'est guère traditionnelle.

C'est cela qu'il eût été facile d'objecter plutôt à Mlle Marg.

6. Le trépied a figuré sur les monnaies de la ville: *AJA*, 1945, *l. l.*, 300, fig. 19 A-C (d'après J. N. Svoronos, *Numismat. de la Crète ancienne*, pl. II, 30; III, I et III, 10. Le trépied est accompagné là des figures et des emblèmes, tantôt de Zeus, tantôt d'Apollon, comme on verra).

7. *Gleanings*, 302.

8. *REG* 43 (1930) 262-278.

9. Le texte de Zenobius cité par M. Doro Levi (p. 302, n. 155: cf. Παροιμίαι, V, 75 E.) donne à Athéna un rôle qu'il est tout de même difficile de vouloir nier; les études prochaines de M. P. Amandry montreront, à propos de l'oracle delphique, l'importance réelle, à Delphes même, des instruments de la divination, tels que les ψῆφοι. Un témoignage, malheureusement tardif et isolé, prouverait, en ce qui concerne Delphes et plus spécialement le *téménos* réservé à Athéna Προναία (Marmaria) le rôle prophétique de la déesse: cf. Aelius Aristide, *Athena* II, 14 (éd. Dindorf, I, p. 23: ὁ δὲ Ἀπόλλων τῶν αὑτοῦ χρησμῳδίων ταύτην προὐστήσατο καὶ προθύειν ἐπέταξεν). Donc les consultants delphiques s'entendaient signifier par Apollon l'obligation d'une consécration préalable à la déesse.

Guarducci ; et peut-être aussi, eût il fallu observer que, sur la *mitra*
d'Axos, la voltige de la divinité, dans l'épiphanie représentée au-dessus
du trépied oraculaire, dénote une virtuosité de sport qu'on eût plutôt
attendu d'un dieu mâle. Or l'*Hymne à Apollon,* recueilli dans la série
des *hymnes* dits *homériques,* nous donne plusieurs fois les occasions
de voir Apollon se signaler par des épiphanies acrobatiques ou ful-
gurantes, plus ou moins proches de celle que le document crétois nous
invite à imaginer. Soit qu'Apollon *bondisse* en pleine mer sur le pont
du navire marchand venu de Cnossos, avec l'apparence d'un dauphin
énorme qui renverse de tous côtés les marins spectateurs et ébranle
le pont supérieur.[10] Soit qu'à l'arrivée à Cirrha-Crisa, et au sortir
même du navire, le dieu se transforme en astre étincelant, faisant
jaillir de sa personne des feux sans nombre *"pour passer à travers
les trépieds de grand prix"* et entrer dans son *adyton.*[11] Ce passage
en bolide est en rapport assez direct avec l'épiphanie, si mouvementée,
si brusque, de la plaque de bronze à interpréter, et l'on s'étonne un
peu que le rapprochement n'ait pas encore été suggéré jusqu'ici, du
texte littéraire à l'image de la *mitra.*

A Mlle Marg. Guarducci aurait incombé la tâche de bien nous
prouver d'abord, que l'image d'épiphanie de la *mitra* d'Axos est
féminine, et se rapporte bien ainsi à une *déesse.* Je ne crois pas qu'elle
eût pu établir nettement cette démonstration. Si la représentation
donnée dans les *Gleanings,* fig. 15 (p. 295) est fidèle, le personnage
représenté a des cheveux qui foisonnent et retombent en boucles libres ;
ils évoquent plutôt la chevelure calamistrée des *Couroi* archaïques.
Les mèches encadrant la figure sont restées, jusque dans l'art hellénistique, le privilège du jeune dieu du Parnasse, notamment. On ne voit
pas qu'une Athéna, tenant un bouclier (à l'épisème *marin* du poulpe)
et une épée, ait pu manquer d'un casque ; or, il n'en paraît pas sur la
mitra d'Axos. Tout cela eût été propre à faire réfléchir.

Et je voudrais encore signaler que si la *mitra* est bien un couvre-
ventre de guerrier, une plaque protectrice contre les coups qu'on
portait volontiers, dans les batailles, aux parties molles et vulnérables
de l'abdomen, la présence d'un *dieu* protecteur est la plus indiquée.
Qu'Apollon ait paru sur un trépied encadré d'oiseaux — aigles ou
corbeaux, car on ne peut bien décider, d'après le document crétois ici
en cause ! — il n'y a rien là qui surprenne. Les oiseaux antithétiques
autour de l'*omphalos* delphique appartiennent, en tout cas, à une

---

10. *Hymne à Apollon, Suite Pythique,* v. 400 sqq.
11. *Hymne, l. c.,* v. 440 sqq.: J'avais suggéré de reconnaître une "allée de
trépieds" dans les fondations retrouvées d'un monument énigmatique de Cirrha,
au bord de la mer: cf. *RA* 1938, I, 97-99. Si le rapport avec l'épiphanie de l'*Hymne*
n'est pas certain, les allées de trépieds, à Delphes, au Ptoïon, sont, du moins, bien
en rapport avec Apollon.

imagerie ancienne et traditionnelle, et je ne rencontre pas de parallèle qui compte pour l'iconographie d'Athéna.

Peut-être ces quelques remarques critiques, qui se sont efforcées d'être objectives, mettent-elles déjà, du moins, un peu en évidence mon propre point de vue : je penche plutôt en faveur de l'interprétation apollinienne. Mais j'ai dit que je ne tendrais pas surtout à discuter ici les arguments déjà apportés, de part et d'autre, dans la controverse. J'en viens donc à ce qui est mon dessein personnel : ainsi, à l'utilisation d'observations qui n'ont pas encore été mises en cause dans le débat, quoiqu'elles puissent emporter, à mon avis, la conviction et décider de l'interprétation discutée.

Je tire, pour ma part, ces arguments du décor même de la plaque d'Axos, où les *lions,* qu'on aurait grandement tort de considérer comme ornementaux, *prédominent d'une façon fort saisissante :* ce qui, pourtant, ne paraît guère avoir été remarqué par tous ceux qui ont étudié la question jusqu'ici. Il y a d'abord les deux énormes lions, en attaque (de taille surnaturelle, d'après les proportions de la divinité !) qui entourent le trépied symétriquement, hiératiquement. Il eût convenu, à mon sens, de remarquer l'importance donnée à ces présences de fauves, dont la tête est levée, mouvement de soumission plus que de menace, vers le petit dieu jaillissant sur le trépied. On voudra bien prendre garde au fait que les deux grands lions du décor principal, mis à l'honneur, ne sont pas, d'ailleurs, isolés : la petite bande décorative courbe qui cerne en bas la *mitra* fait reparaître six fois encore (Doro Levi, fig. 15) le thème des lions passant ou affrontés — et, par exemple, deux lions sont présentés symétriquement dans l'axe au-dessous du trépied, se faisant face, comme ceux qui encadrent le trépied, au-dessus. — Insistance bien significative !

Ce sont ces remarques qui doivent clore la discussion. Car, autant que je puis savoir, le lion n'est pas un "familier" d'Athéna, et ne l'a guère accompagnée. Au contraire, nous pouvons déduire de bien des monuments, ou documents, qu'Apollon a été, à l'époque archaïque, — en Asie surtout et même en Grèce —, un dompteur de fauves, armé, associé familialement à la πότνια θηρῶν qu'était Artémis ; les lions qu'il maîtrisa formaient son escorte, ou se tenaient près de lui, soumis à sa volonté. Qu'ils aient aussi pu encadrer, à l'occasion, un trépied symbolique et participer à une épiphanie du dieu sous forme humaine, rien qui puisse en tout cela nous surprendre.

Je donnerai, à ce sujet, quelques indications, en commençant par ce que peut nous apprendre la Crète même, d'où vient précisément la *mitra* d'Axos. Imprégnée d'influences orientales à l'époque de l'archaïsme,[12] la Crète a entretenu volontiers les survivances d'un type de dompteur de lions apparu au M.M. I et qui avait été fort répandu dès la fin de l'âge du bronze. Si l'on examine des lamelles de bronze trouvées à Kavousi,[13] à Cnossos,[14] on y remarque des guerriers qui — l'un nu, à Kavousi, et, semble-t-il, sans armes, l'autre, sur la plaque de Cnossos, coiffé d'un casque conique à crinière et armé d'un poignard — tiennent en respect des lions dressés debout; *ceux-ci les encadrent hiératiquement.*[15] Les lions de Kavousi et de Cnossos semblent rugir, comme ceux de la *mitra* d'Axos auxquels ils s'apparentent.[16] Quant au "dompteur," M. P. Demargne a écrit à son sujet: 'Quand il aura abandonné ses lions trop orientaux, ce dompteur . . . ne deviendra-t-il pas le dieu guerrier auquel on dédiait des armes en miniature à Praesos, à Dréros, ailleurs encore?" Et M. P. Demargne pensait précisément, en ce passage, à la *mitra* d'Axos.[17]

Il est possible que le dieu guerrier ait été Arès à Cnossos et à Olonte; mais, à Axos, c'est un Apollon; et sans doute aussi à Dréros, car M. P. Demargne a observé précisément, en accord avec une remarque de M. Sp. Marinatos, que le "Palladion" de Dréros, de la fin du VIIe s., petite image d'une divinité armée découpée dans une feuille de bronze, pourrait bien figurer Apollon, *plutôt qu'une Athéna.*[18] Je le crois volontiers, pour ma part, en raison des analogies, dûment signalées déjà par M. Sp. Marinatos, avec le type de l'Apollon Amyclaeos (Pausanias III, 19); et il pourrait s'agir d'un Apollon *cornu* (protubérance sur le front, en partie brisée!) comme celui qui a été trouvé récemment par la mission anglo-chypriote d'Enkomi-Salamis, à Chypre.[19] Cet Apollon, à dater du XIIe s. peut-être — qu'il soit ou non "Alasiotas," comme on l'a voulu, un peu vite et sans preuves — ressemble en tout cas, de très près, par son costume et sa coiffure conique au guerrier menaçant les lions de la lamelle de Cnossos dont il a été question ci-dessus.[20] Il s'intègre dans une même famille de figurations égéo-crétoises.

---

12. Demargne, P., *La Crète dédalique*, 294 sqq.
13. Demargne, *op. cit.*, 236, fig. 37 (d'une tombe géométrique tardive).
14. *Ibid.*, 237, fig. 38 (en provenance, aussi, d'une tombe: *JHS* 1933, 290-291, fig. 16). M. P. Demargne suppose que l'atelier des decorateurs, pour les lamelles de Kavousi et de Cnossos, se trouvait à Cnossos même (*l. c.*, 236).
15. Pour M. P. Demargne, le guerrier de Cnossos égorge les lions: en tout cas, il les menace.
16. Cf. aussi Kunze, E., *Kretische Bronzereliefs*, fig. 31 et pl. 56 e = *AJA* 1901. 147 sqq., fig. 10-11.
17. Il renvoie précisément à sa pl. XI, 2.
18. Cf. *La Crète dédalique*, 295, n. 6, et Marinatos, Sp., *BCH* 1936, 276-278, pl. 30 (le renvoi à la fig. 41: *Crète dédalique, l. c.*, n. 6, n'est pas nécessaire = objets votifs).
19. *Illustrated London News*, 27 août 1949, 316-317, fig. 4-7.
20. Demargne, *op. cit.*, 237, fig. 38. Remarquer le justaucorps à ceinture des deux personnages.

J'ai rappelé ci-dessus, d'autre part, les rapports possibles avec l'Apollon Amyclaeos, dont l'image doit avoir figuré sur les monnaies de Sparte;[21] mais nous ne manquons pas d'autres rapprochements *àpolliniens* à présenter.

A Delphes même, ce n'est pas au hasard, on l'a dit déjà, que l'épiphanie centrale d'Apollon en char, au fronton Est du temple des Alcméonides, s'accompagne, au VIe s., de *combats d'animaux* symétriques, vers les angles, le *lion* y intervenant deux fois,[22] contre le taureau et le cerf.

De cette grande évocation religieuse, si typique, et qui avait ému l'admiration d'Eschyle,[23] nous avons la chance de pouvoir aujourd'hui rapprocher une image d'Apollon dompteur de lion, qui nous a été rendue en 1939, grâce à la découverte du Trésor de l'Aire sacrée, dans le *Manteion* même d'Apollon (pl. 69, d). C'est le bel ivoire publié en 1944-1945 par M. P. Amandry,[24] qui l'avait trouvé. Tout dans la qualité de ce noble document d'art annonce qu'il magnifie une personnalité supra-humaine: la présentation frontale, qui est celle des statues de culte, l'agencement coquet de la longue chevelure calamistrée, avec les extrémités des boucles conventionnellement arrangées en rosaces: mèches toujours si soignées, à toute époque, autour des visages des Apollons! Etant donné le lieu de la trouvaille, et ce que nous savons maintenant des Apollons archaïques armés, un personnage à la lance, maintenant contre lui un lion mâle devenu son familier (car il a l'air de toucher la hampe de son arme, et de vouloir aussi lui protéger le ventre!) nous porte à penser à une identification qu'il eût été, sans doute, possible de présenter plus fermement.[25] A qui penserait-on avec une meilleure certitude?

En pleine époque classique, le sculpteur Bryaxis, qui avait travaillé au Mausolée et connaissait bien les cultes lyciens et cariens, avait fait, semble-t-il, pour la ville de Patara, en Lycie,[26] un Apollon groupé avec

---

21. Head, V. B., *Hist. num.*, 364, fig. 240.

22. Bibliographie récente dans: Lapalus, E., *Le fronton sculpté en Grèce*, 442-433 et fig. 22; le livre n'ajoute malheureusement rien aux études antérieures.

23. Plassart, A., *Mélanges Radet: REA* 1940, 293 sqq.

24. *Syria* 24 (1944-1945) fasc. 3-4, p. 149-174, et pl. X-XI (haut. actuelle, les jambes étant brisées assez au-dessus des chevilles: 0, 185). M. P. Amandry n'a pas fait état, dans son commentaire, de la *mitra* d'Axos.

25. M. P. Amandry qui a penché pour cette explication, *op. cit.*, 171-172, laisse la question en suspens. Lui-même a eu le mérite de rappeler les monnaies de Tarse (époque impériale), avec un Apollon Lyceios en forme de *xoanon*, contre lequel se dressent deux loups, que le dieu tient par les pattes antérieures: encore un exemple d'Apollon dompteur! Il est parfois environné aussi de taureaux (au pied de la statue): cf. la bibliographie donnée par P. Amandry, *op. cit.*, n. 2 de la p. 172.

26. Clément d'Alexandrie *Protrept.*, 4, 47 (éd. commentée d'A. Plassart et Cl. Mondésert, 1949, p. 107).

Zeus *et environné de lions:* il renouvelait là une tradition archaïque
très répandue, sans doute proprement attestée pour l'Apollon de
Patara, qui avait des affinités avec celui de Claros. Ne quittons pas
l'Anatolie — où sans doute fut créé l'ivoire delphique, dans un atelier,
soit de l'Ionie du Nord, soit de la Lydie[27] — sans avoir rappelé qu'à
Milet, en Carie, le lion était aussi symbole d'Apollon. Des monnaies
autonomes de Milet montrent une figure de style archaïque où l'on a
reconnu l'Apollon de Canachos en archer,[28] avec, sur sa main droite,
un petit cervidé tournant la tête vers son maître. Au revers, il y a un
lion couché. C'est l'occasion de rappeler ici que les lions sculptés ont
été trouvés sur les voies sacrées de sanctuaires apolliniens, tant à
Claros qu'au Didymeion surtout. Et à Délos la voie sacrée primitive
menant vers le Létôon, vers le temple de la mère d'Apollon, s'orne
aussi, de lionnes naxiennes archaïques,[29] les Létoïdes ayant toujours,
à Délos et ailleurs, aimé l'escorte des grands félins.[30]

Enfin, M. Herbert A. Cahn a bien voulu attirer mon attention, en
juillet 1948, sur les monnaies de Cnide, qu'il classe et étudie, et où
la figuration du lion, connue depuis 540, est en rapport avec le culte
d'Apollon du Cap Triopas. Là encore les études de numismatique an-
noncées apporteront bientôt une preuve complémentaire des affinités
d'Apollon, dieu chasseur et dompteur, avec les grands fauves qu'il
passait, en Asie, pour avoir soumis à sa puissance.

Concluons: on ne devrait plus, désormais, discuter sur l'interprétation de la *mitra* d'Axos, pièce d'armement *masculin* qui se rapporte
incontestablement au culte guerrier de l'Apollon crétois.[31] C'est l'argument fourni par la présence *orientalisante* des lions qui tranche le
débat, je voudrais l'avoir montré, de façon décisive.[32] La figuration

---

27. Dès 1922, j'avais signalé la possibilité, en Ionie, d'une identification du
dompteur de fauves avec Apollon: *Ephèse et Claros,* 514.

28. L'Apollon crétois figure en archer sur les monnaies d'Eleutherna,
Rhéthymna, Tylissos, aux V-IV s.; cf. Amandry, P., *op. cit.,* 172, n. 2.

29. Pour les monnaies autonomes de Milet. cf. notamment, Overbeck, J., *Kunst.
Mythol.: Apollo,* 23 (Münztaf.: 22-23); Head, V. B., *BMC, Ionia,* 196, Nos. 134-
141, pl. 22, 9; Babelon, E., *Coll. Waddington,* 1851-1856.

30. L'ex-voto naxien de Nicandra à Délos s'explique si l'on restitue, en laisse,
les lionnes archaïques trouvées en même temps que l'Artémis, ce que j'ai déjà
indiqué depuis longtemps (cf. bibliographie: Plassart, A., *Inscr. Delos, Inscr.
archaïques,* à paraître). Sur les Létoïdes et les lions, Bakalakis, G., *Hellenika
Trapezophora,* 19-20 (pour Artémis).

31. Aly, W., *Der Kretische Apollonkult,* 1908.

32. J'avais seulement annoncé en 1948, dans *Mana, Les religions préhelléniques,*
135-136, mes conclusions (et l'étude ici fournie). *La mitra* d'Axos apparaît un
document important, car elle montre bien le mélange des traditions crétoises (dont
il ne faudrait pas exagérer la prédominance!), avec d'autres plus asiatiques, qu'on
peut qualifier d' *anatoliennes.* Les lions au service d'Apollon correspondent à une
conception *orientale,* fort répandue, comme on peut voir, en Asie-Mineure. Ce

de la *mitra* d'Axos gagne à être regardée dans son ensemble, et c'est aussi le meilleur moyen d'éclairer convenablement ses représentations. Ainsi comprenons-nous un Apollon dompteur de lions qui paraît bondir, tout armé, sur le trépied, instrument de divination et siège sacré, au moyen duquel le dieu migrateur a si souvent voyagé, et auquel on ajoutait parfois aussi les ailes qu'Apollon a portées lui-même, dans l'art archaïque, sur une métope de Sélinonte, ou ailleurs.

Dècembre 1949.

n'est pas, malgré Doro Levi, *Gleanings*, 294, une acquisition à porter au compte de la religion préhellénique.

Pendant la correction des épreuves ont paru plusieurs des ouvrages ci-dessus annoncés; n. 9: Amandry, P., *La mantique apollinienne à Delphes*, 1950, n. 30. Plassart, A., *Inscriptions de Délos*, 1950. A paru aussi la suggestive étude de M. Herbert A. Cahn, "Die Loewen des Apollon," *Museum Helveticum* 7 (1950), 185-199.

L'INVITATION À LA DANSE

W. Deonna
Genève

Planches 68-69

Une toute jeune fille, presque une enfant, est assise sur un rocher; elle est à moitié nue; une draperie ne couvrant que le bas du corps, les jambes en partie seulement, forme d'amples plis qui tombent à terre et dissimulent de côté le support (pl. 68 et 69 a, b). De la main gauche elle s'appuie sur le rocher, et elle croise la jambe gauche sur la droite. Le bras droit, qui manque, était abaissé, pour attacher de la main la sandale du pied gauche. La tête, à la chevelure ondulée et ramenée en arrière, est quelque peu tournée à sa droite, et le visage mutin et rieur semble fixer avec attention quelque objet disparu. Bien que brisée et rajustée au corps, la tête appartient assurément à ce dernier, preuve en soit au revers la chevelure qui se prolonge sur la nuque en un court chignon.[1]

Ce marbre antique appartenait à l'archéologue autrichien bien connu, le Dr. L. Pollak, qui l'avait acheté vers 1909 dans le commerce à Naples[2] et l'avait déposé au Musée de Frankfort.[3] Au début de la guerre, en 1940, son possesseur l'avait remis en dépôt, avec d'autres pièces de sa collection, au Musée d'art et d'histoire de Genève, et celui-ci vient de l'acquérir de ses héritiers. Il est à ma connaissance inédit, et n'a jamais été signalé que par Klein, d'après une photographie que Pollak lui avait communiquée.[4]

Une monnaie de Cyzique, frappée sous Septime Sévère,[5] reproduit un groupe statuaire: un jeune homme nu, le pied droit posé sur un "kroupezion" — petit instrument de musique fait de deux planchettes que réunit une charnière, entre lesquelles des grelots — le haut du corps un peu incliné, le bras droit levé, le gauche abaissé, se tient devant une jeune femme assise sur un rocher, qui le regarde avec attention.

---

1. Manquent: le pied droit, la partie inférieure de la jambe gauche, le bras droit, une partie de la base. La statue était brisée en plusieurs fragments qui ont été recollés. Haut. totale 1.08.

2. Klein, *Zeitschrift für bildende Kunst*, 20 (1909) 104, note 2: "im Neapler Kunsthandel."

3. Klein, *Vom antiken Rokoko*, 179, no. 54 (Klein en possédait une photographie remise par M. Pollak).

4. Klein, *Zeitschrift*, 104, note 2: "Während der Drucklegung erhalte ich von Dr. Ludwig Pollak in Rom die Photographie eines achten im Neapler Kunsthandel aufgetauchten Exemplares unserer Mänade, dessen gebrochener aber zugehöriger Kopf der gleiche ist, wie jener, den wir dem Brüsseler Exemplar hier abgesetzt haben"; *id.*, *Vom antiken Rokoko*, 179, note 54.

Les érudits ont cherché à retrouver les éléments dispersés de ce groupe. Grâce à son attitude et à son attribut, ils ont identifié le personnage masculin,[6] avec un type plastique répété à plusieurs exemplaires, dont le Satyre au kroupezion des Uffizi à Florence est le plus célèbre.[7] Ils ont reconnu la jeune femme, dont l'attitude n'est pas moins caractéristique, dans une série de statues d'une Nymphe,[8] dont certaines avaient été utilisées déjà dans l'antiquité comme motif de fontaine.[9] Mais celles-ci étaient privées de leur tête, où étaient pourvues de tête qui ne leur appartenait pas,[10] et pour identifier la véritable, il fallut de nouvelles recherches;[11] elles furent confirmées par la découverte d'un fragment du Musée du Bardo à Tunis,[12] buste encore muni de sa tête originelle, dont on possède aussi plusieurs répliques.[13]

Ces éléments ayant été successivement repérés, W. Klein a reconstitué en un moulage ce groupe, d'après la monnaie de Cyzique, en éliminant les modifications qu'il avait subies au cours du temps[14] (pl. 69, c). On a libéré les bras du Satyre, supprimant les cymbales; on l'a doté d'une autre tête de jeune Satyre riant, dont l'exemplaire de Venise pourrait répéter celle de l'original.[15] La jeune femme, dont la statue de Bruxelles semble être la meilleure réplique,[16] a reçu la

---

5. Imhoof-Blumer, *JDAI* 3 (1888) 296 sq, pl. 9, no. 29; Klein, *Gesch. d. Griech. Kunst*, III, 235-6; id., *Zeitsch. f. bildende Kunst*, 101, 102, fig. 2.

6. identification déjà faite par Wolters, *JDAI* 8 (1893) 175.

7. Klein, *Zeitschr.*, 101, note 1, liste des répliques, fig. 1 (Florence), fig. 7 (Louvre); Bulle, *Der schöne Mensch im Altertum*, pl. 80 (Florence); Arndt-Amelung, *Photog. Einzelaufnahmen* No. 2641-2, texte (2 ex. Torlonia). Fragment du Céramique, Athènes, *AM* 56 (1931) 87, pl. XXXIX-XL.

8. Klein, *Gesch. d. gr. Kunst* III, 236; id., *Zeitschr.* 101, note 3 (liste de 7 ex.). La statue du Metropolitan Museum, New York, Arndt-Amelung, No. 4717-21, avec tête qui lui appartient, offre des analogies d'attitude, mais est toutefois d'un type différent; on a rapproché à tort sa tête de celle de la Nymphe de notre groupe (Bieber).

9. Klein, *Zeitschr.*, 102; Lippold, *Kopien*, 169; Arndt-Amelung, no. 3878-9 (texte, Bendel).

10. Klein, *Zeitschr.*, 101; id., *Gesch. d. griech. Kunst*, III, 237.

11. Klein, *Zeitschr.* 102; id., *Gesch.*, III, 237.

12. Gauckler, *Musée Aloui*, pl. XII, 16; Reinach, *Répert. de la stat.* III, 119, 6; Klein, *Gesch.*, III, 237, note 2; id., *Zeitschr.* 101, note 3.

13. Klein, *Zeitschr.* 102, note 1 (liste); 103, fig. 5 (Venise); Arndt-Amelung, No. 2641-2 (Venise) et texte; No. 2153 (Rome, Latran). Cività Vecchia, *NScav*, 1933, 398, 409, fig. 6; *AA*, 49 (1934) 432-3; *REG*, 52 (1939), 162—tête de Copenhague, Arndt-Amelung, no. 3878-9.

14. Klein, "Die Aufforderung zum Tanz. Eine wiedergewonnene Gruppe des antiken Rokoko," *Zeitschr.* 1909, 101; reconstitution, 106-7, fig. 9-10, à l'Inst. d'arch. de l'université allemande de Prague; id., *Vom antiken Rokoko*, 1921, 46 sq., fig. 14.—id., *Gesch. d. gr. Kunst*, III, 235 sq.; Bulle, *Der schöne Mensch₂*, 50, fig. 32; Lawrence, *Later Greek Sculpture*, pl. 30 b.; Ducati, *L'arte classica₂* (1927) 537, fig. 668,534; Arndt-Amelung, no. 4717-21 (texte, Bieber, réf.).

15. Klein, *Zeitschr.*, 102-3, fig. 4 (Louvre); fig. 6 (Venise).

16. *ibid.*, 105, note 1, fig. 3, comme l'avait déjà reconnu Furtwaengler.

tête de jeune Ménade riant de Dresde, jadis placée sur une statue de bacchante.[17] Dans le groupe original, les deux statues étaient sans doute placées sur une base commune.[18] Cette reconstitution a été admise par les érudits, et le groupe retrouvé a pris place dans l'histoire de la plastique antique.[19]

La jeune femme — Ménade ou Nymphe —[20] a rencontré le Satyre. Elle vient de s'asseoir sur un rocher, et, dans une position instable, momentanée, elle attache de sa main droite la sandale de son pied gauche, avant d'acquiescer à la demande de son compagnon. Celui-ci, les bras levés, claquant des doigts,[21] pesant de son pied droit sur le kroupezion, tout le corps frémissant et paraissant danser sur place, scande le rythme de la danse à laquelle il invite la jeune femme. Un instant après, elle se lèvera et l'imitera. L' "invitation à la danse," tel est le titre que Klein a donné à cette composition et sous lequel elle est désormais connue.

Le groupe original est une création de l'art hellénistique, du IIe s. av. J.C.[22] On retrouve en lui la préférence de ce temps pour les thèmes dionysiaques des Satyres, des Ménades, des Nymphes, exubérants et rieurs, pour les scènes d'idylles champêtres[23] — on se figure volontiers ce groupe se détachant sur le fond de verdure d'un parc, d'un jardin —, pour les actions momentanées, dont les attitudes laissent présumer celle qui a précédé et celle qui suivra, pour les poses contournées où le corps se tord sur lui-même, comme celui de la jeune femme; on a noté certains traits qui évoquent, avec l'art de Pergame apparenté,[24] la période où le classicisme se transforme en "baroque," en "rococo" hellénistique.[25]

La monnaie de Cyzique, le nombre des répliques, témoignent que ce groupe devait être célèbre. Sans doute se trouvait-il à Cyzique même,[26] et sortait-il d'un atelier de cette cité d'Asie Mineure, dont la

---

17. *ibid.*, 102 et note 1; 105, fig. 8 (Bacchante); Reinach, *Recueïl de têtes idéales ou idéalisées*, 214, pl. 266; Lawrence, *op. cit.*, pl. 31b.

18. Klein, *Vom antiken Rokoko*, 46, fig. 14 (reconstitution sur une même base).

19. voir les réf. précédentes.

20. pour Klein une Ménade; pour d'autres, une Nymphe.

21. Weege, *Der Tanz in der Antike*, 13, place à tort des flûtes dans les mains du Satyre.

22. Klein, *Gesch.*, III, 235, 238 (montre que la date du milieu du IIIe s. est trop haute); 238 (IIe s. et à peine la première moitié de ce siècle); *id.*, *Vom antiken Rokoko*, 47, milieu du IIe s. av. J.C.

23. cf. les exemples donnés par Klein, *Vom antiken Rokoko*.

24. Klein, *Zeitschr.*, 108; *id.*, *Vom antiken Rokoko*, 9 sq.

25. *id.*, *Vom antiken Rokoko*; *id.*, "Studien zum antiken Rokoko," 1921, *JOAI*, 19-20 (1919) 253; sur le rococo et le baroque hellénistique, Deonna, *Du miracle grec au miracle chrétien*, III, 452.

26. Klein, *Zeitschr.*, 108.

production artistique est attestée par de nombreuses oeuvres depuis l'archaisme jusqu'à l'époque d'Hadrien[27] et qui était en relation avec les grands centres créateurs d'alors, entre autres avec celui de Pergame.[28]

La Ménade Pollak s'ajoute à la liste des répliques déjà connues et en est la huitième; elle a le grand intérêt d'être le seul exemplaire à peu près complet, pourvu de sa tête originelle; celui de Tunis, qui a aussi cet avantage, étant réduit au buste.

---

27. sur Cyzique; Hasluck, *Cyzicus;* Lübker, *Reallexikon* s.v. 572, réf.; *RE,* s.v. Kyzikos; Picard, *La sculpture antique,* II, 260, 276.

28. Hasluck, *Cyzicus,* 174; Klein, *Zeitschr.,* 108.—Apollonis, mère d'Eumène et d'Attale II, était originaire de Cyzique.

STATUETTE EINER TAENZERIN

REINHARD LULLIES
München

Tafel 70

Die Terrakottastatuette einer Tänzerin im Mantel, der die folgenden Zeilen gewidmet sind, gelangte mit einer Reihe von anderen
griechischen Terrakotten im Jahre 1907 aus der Sammlung Arndt in
den Besitz des Münchner Museums antiker Kleinkunst (Inv. 6790,
Taf. 70). Schon der erste Eindruck lehrt, dass es sich hier nicht um
eine landläufige Fassung des an sich häufigen Motivs der Manteltänzerin handelt, sondern dass wir es mit einer einmaligen, höchst kunst-
vollen Prägung dieses Vorwurfs zu tun haben. Was an der Statuette
besonders fesselt und zur Bewunderung auffordert, ist die unnach-
ahmliche Art, mit der die Figur im Wechselspiel der Kräfte scheinbar
schwerelos über den Boden dahingleitet und mit der hier der Künstler
im Wirbel der schnell veränderten Bewegungen einem flüchtigen
Augenblick Dauer verliehen hat. Idee und formale Gestaltung haben
sich in dieser kleinen Figur in glücklichster Weise zu gegenseitiger
Steigerung miteinander verbunden. Kein Zweifel, dass nur ein Plastiker von hohem Rang ein solches Werk zu konzipieren, dass nur ein
sehr geschulter Tonbildner es zu formen imstande gewesen ist.

Die Statuette, die Paul Arndt im griechischen Kunsthandel erworben hatte, ist 15 cm hoch und so gut wie unbeschädigt. Der Ton
ist fein geschlämmt, hat eine warme, rötlich braune Färbung, eine
mürbe, verhältnismässig weiche Konsistenz und entspricht seiner
ganzen Art nach so weitgehend demjenigen böotischer Vasen und
Terrakotten, dass die Entstehung der Figur in Böotien als sicher
gelten darf. Wie das in hellenistischer Zeit üblich war, ist die Statuette aus mehreren Negativformen hergestellt. Und zwar werden zwei
Formen für den Unterkörper bis hinauf zum linken Unterarm gedient
haben, zwei für den Oberkörper bis zum Hals einschliesslich der Arme
und zwei weitere für den Kopf. Die einzelnen Teile sind vor dem
Brennen, solange das Material noch bildsam war, aneinandergesetzt,
die Nähte aussen und innen verstrichen. Die Gewandfalten, das Haar
und andere Einzelheiten sind nachgearbeitet. Bemerkenswert ist
noch, dass das wehende Mantelende im Rücken, dessen unterster
Zipfel jetzt fehlt, und der rechte Fuss nicht aus der Form gepresst,
sondern aus freier Hand, nur mit Hilfe des Modelliersteckens, gesondert gearbeitet und dann der soweit fertigen Figur angefügt
worden sind. Von der dunklen, heute schwarzen Bemalung auf

weisser Grundierung sind auf dem Mantel und dem Schuh überall Reste erhalten, jedoch so ungleichmässig, dass es sicht nicht mehr sagen lässt, ob der Mantel ganz oder nur teilweise bemalt war. Nur an einer Stelle, und zwar über dem Fuss, ziehen sich auf dem Mantel abweschselnd schwarze und weisse waagerechte Streifen von fünf bis sieben Millimeter Breite hin. Nur dicht über dem Fuss erscheinen auf dem dunklen Grund ausserdem einige geringe Reste von matter, leuchtend roter Farbe.

Der hohe Reiz der Statuette beruht auf verschiedenen Momenten, die von einer sehr überlegten, wohldurchdachten Kunstprache Zeugnis ablegen. Obgleich der Körper der Tänzerin wie eine Spirale gedreht ist und alle Glieder kontrastreich gegeneinander bewegt sind, wirkt die Figur nicht unruhig oder nervös. Den einzelnen gegensätzlichen Motiven stehen andere gegenüber, die sie in ihrer Wirkung mildern oder auflösen. So antwortet dem nach vorne zu vorgeworfenen rechten Bein mit dem blossen, in der Luft schwebenden Schuh der nach rückwärts gewandte Oberköper mit dem halb verhüllten Kopf und dem über die Schulter zu Boden gerichteten Antlitz. Dabei ist das Gleichgewicht sorgfältig gewahrt. Einzelheiten wie das flatternde Mantelende im Rücken der Tänzerin spielen hierfür eine wichtige Rolle. Dieses Gewandstück hält einerseits dem rechten Bein die Waage und leitet andererseits den mehrfach gebrochenen Strom der Bewegung nach unten zu ab. Kompositionell ist die Figur ganz in sich geschlossen; zugleich ist sie aber auch als eine kleine Welt für sich nach aussen hin von ihrer Umgebung abgegrenzt. Diese beiden einander begegnenden und bedingenden Tendenzen sind durch die Haltung der Arme, die Richtung der Faltenzüge, nicht zuletzt durch den Kranz des Mantelsaums am Boden augenfällig betont. Der plastische Reichtum der Figur ist von einem einzigen Punkt aus nicht voll zu erfassen. Man muss fast im Kreise um die Figur herumgehen, will man die Absichten des Künstlers, will man den ganzen Reiz dieses Kunstwerks in sich aufnehmen. Trotzdem kann man nicht sagen, dass die Statuette mehrere gleichermaßen befriedigende Ansichtsseiten besitzt. Nur von jener Seite her entfaltet sie ihre reichsten Werte, von der aus der grösste Teil des Gesichtes und das Mantelende im Rücken zu sehen sind. Schon eine leichte Verschiebung des Augenpunktes nach der einen oder anderen Seite beeinträchtigt die volle Harmonie des Gleichgewichts, führt zu Unzuträglichkeiten in der ästhetischen Wirkung.

Je ausgeprägter der Charakter eines Kunstwerkes ist, desto eher gibt es sich im allgemeinen als Schöpfung einer bestimmten Zeit zu erkennen, desto eindeutiger lässt sich seine kunstgeschichtliche Stel-

lung bestimmen. Wie sehr auch die Geschichte der hellenistischen
Plastik im einzelnen heute noch umstritten ist, so zeichnen sich doch
gewisse Wesenszüge der Entwicklung dank den Ergebnissen der
neuesten Forschung deutlich ab. Das erste Jahrhundert nach dem
Tode Alexanders des Grossen († 323 v.Chr.) bedeutete für die Plastik
in vieler Hinsicht eine Abkehr von den Tendenzen der klassischen
Zeit, in mancher Hinsicht eine bewusste Reaktion gegen sie. Die fest-
gefügte, in sich geschlossene Vorstellungswelt des älteren Griechentums, in der Staat und Gesellschaft, Gottheit und Mythos unverbrüch-
liche Geltung besassen, hatte sich mit Sokrates und den Sophisten
und in wachsendem Maße seit der Alexanderzeit aufzulösen begonnen.
An die Stelle überpersönlicher Bindungen traten die Bedürfnisse und
Ansprüche des Einzelnen, der sich seiner individuellen Eigenart
zunehmend bewusst wurde. Gleichzeitig mit dieser Entwicklung, die
sich auf alle Zweige des politischen, religiösen, sozialen, künstlerischen
und geistigen Lebens überhaupt erstreckte, veränderten sich Gehalt
und Wesen der plastischen Gestaltung. Der einheitliche Lebensstrom,
der die klassische Figur erfüllt hatte, begann gegen Ende des 4. Jahrhunderts v.Chr. zu versiegen, der grosse Schwung zu erstarren. An
Stelle des klaren Achsengefüges, das den Aufbau der klassischen
Figur bestimmt hatte, kennzeichnen nunmehr Ueberschneidungen
und gegensätzliche Rhythmen den Charakter der plastischen Werke.
Das innere Gefüge der Figuren verfestigt, ja versteift sich und wird
zugleich komplizierter. Ausdruck der Zeit ist nicht mehr eine gross
angelegte und kraftvolle Formengebung. Die Formensprache wird
aufgelöster und kleinteilig. Aeussere und innere Monumentalität
gehören nicht zum Stil der frühhellenistischen Epoche. Auch die
grosse Plastik greift im 3. Jahrhundert gern zum unterlebensgrossen
Format. Hatte die ältere griechische Zeit das Bild des Menschen
immer wieder in seiner allgemein gültigen Erscheinung dargestellt,
so ging der frühe Hellenismus dazu über, das Besondere und Ein-
malige an der menschlichen Gestalt in den Vordergrund zu rücken.
Die verschiedenen Geschlechter, Altersstufen und sozialen Schichten
werden in ihrer Eigenart unterschieden. Entlegene und ausgefallene
Motive, künstliche Haltungen, schwierige Stellungen, geschliffene,
zugespitzte Pointen werden gesucht.

Unter denjenigen Werken, die die allseitig "geschlossene Form" des
3. Jahrhunderts besonders charakteristisch vertreten, sind in erster
Linie Figuren wie das sitzende Mädchen im Konservatorenpalast,[1]

---

1. Orti Lam. 31. Jones, H. Stuart, *The sculptures of the Palazzo dei Conservatori* Taf. 53. — *Arch. Ertesitö* 41, 1927, 6 Abb. 7 — Bulle, H., *Der schöne
Mensch*[2], Taf. 171.

die Budapester Mädchenstatuette,[2] die kauernde Aphrodite des Doidalses[3] und der sein Schwänzchen beschauende Satyr[4] zu nennen, deren kunstgeschichtliche Stellung in den Jahrzehnten um die Mitte des 3. Jahrhunderts vor allem G. Krahmer begründet hat.[5] Unter ihnen wieder ist es der Satyr, der mit der Münchner Manteltänzerin kompositionell weitgehende Beziehungen und Verwandtschaften aufweist. Beide Figuren zeigen die starke Torsion des Körpers, die Ueberschneidung der Glieder, die Konzentrierung um eine Mitte herum, die strenge Isolierung nach aussen hin, die Spannung zwischen Körper und Raum, was darauf hindeutet, dass unsere Tänzerin unter den nämlichen oder doch zum mindesten sehr ähnlichen künstlerischen Bedingungen, dass auch sie um die Mitte des 3. Jahrhunderts entstanden ist.

Ueber die verschiedenen Arten des Tanzes im Altertum sind wir trotz einer umfangreichen antiken Literatur über den Tanz und einer kaum überblickbaren Fülle von Denkmälern im einzelnen nur schlecht unterrichtet.[6] Die grosse Bedeutung, die der Manteltanz in der Antike gehabt haben muss, geht aus den zahlreichen Darstellungen von Manteltänzerinnen in der Terrakottaplastik, auf griechischen Vasen und Reliefs bis in die Kaiserzeit zur Genüge hervor.[7] Wie der griechische Tanz überhaupt im Kult und in religiösen Gebräuchen seine Wurzel hatte, so kann auch die Verhüllung des Körpers im Manteltanz ursprünglich nur kultische Bedeutung gehabt haben. Es sei in diesem Zusammenhang an den Ritus der verhüllten Hände erinnert, dessen Sinn Albrecht Dieterich in einer meisterhaften Untersuchung aufgehellt hat.[8] Dieser Ritus, der aus dem Orient nach dem Abendland eingedrungen und in seiner Wirkung in bestimmten religiösen Zeremonien bis auf den heutigen Tag erhalten geblieben ist, gründet sich auf die Vorstellung, dass man einer geheiligten oder über das gewöhnliche menschliche Maß hinausragenden Person nicht mit den

---

2. *Arch. Ertesitö* a. O. 5 Abb. 1-4. — Hekler, A., *Die Antiken in Budapest* 1 Nr. 76.

3. *Arch. Ertesitö a. O.* 17f. Abb. 10, a-b.

4. *Bollettino d'arte* 14, 1920, 47f. Abb. 8. — *Arch. Ertesitö a. O.* 12 Abb. 9.

5. Vgl. *Röm. Mitteilungen* 38/39, 1923/24, 157f. und *Arch. Ertesitö a. O.* 250ff.

6. Vgl. zusammenfassend Warnecke in Pauly-Wissowa-Kroll, *RE* 2. Reihe, 4. Band, 2233ff. s.v. Tanzkunst. Vgl. auch Séchan, *La Danse Grecque Antique*, 1930; Weege, *Der Tanz in der Antike;* Emmanuel, *Essai sur l'Orchestique Grecque*, 1895 (nicht bedeutend); viele Artikel von Lillian Lawler in amerikanischen Zeitungen über Tänzerinnen. D. M. Robinson hat viele Terrakottastatuetten von Tänzerinnen in Olynth gefunden. Vgl. Robinson, *Olynthus*, IV, 60, 330, 335, 376; VII, 181-189.

7. Vgl. Heydemann, H., *Verhüllte Tänzerin* (4. *Hall. Winckelmannsprogramm* 1879) 5ff. und Weege, F., *op. cit.,* 65 ff. Für den Manteltanz vgl. *AJA* 35, 1931, 374-377; Robinson, *Olynthus*, VII, 52ff.

8. *Kleine Schriften* 440ff.

blossen, unreinen Händen nahen, dass man einen geheiligten Gegenstand nur mit bedeckten Händen berühren darf, um ihn nicht zu entweihen. Frauen, die mit verhüllten Armen und Händen ekstatische Tänze aufführen, erscheinen auf griechischen Vasenbildern durch das ganze 5. Jahrhundert v.Chr. Auf der spät-schwarzfigurigen Lekythos aus Rhodos in Berlin F.2010 tanzen zwei Frauen in leidenschaftlicher Bewegung vor einem Altar einen Festtanz zu den Klängen einer Flötenspielerin. Sie tragen den langen ionischen Chiton und haben die Arme unter weiten Aermeln verborgen. In ähnlicher Bekleidung und Verhüllung umtanzen Frauen auf den Bildern von attisch-schwarzfigurigen und attisch-rotfigurigen Gefässen das Säulenidol des Dionysos,[9] schwärmen Mänaden, oft bekränzt und mit dem Pantherfell über den Schultern, zusammen mit tanzenden und Flöte spielenden Silenen im dionysischen Taumel dahin. Mit dem Kelchkrater des Kleophrades-Malers im Louvre,[10] den Aussenseiten der Münchner[11] und der Pariser Schale des Brygos-Malers,[12] des Briseis-Malers, London E 75,[13] mit dem Kantharos des Amymone-Malers in München[14] und der Berliner Schale des Eretria-Malers[15] sind einige charakteristische Beispiele genannt. Ihre Zahl liesse sich erheblich vermehren.[16] Dass diese Darstellungen tanzender Mänaden Elemente orientalischer Kulttänze enthalten, kann keinem Zweifel unterliegen. Sieht man von den genannten Vasenbildern ab und richtet den Blick auf die Darstellungen des Manteltanzes selbst, so zeigt sich, dass auch dieser immer wieder in Szenen vorkommt, hinter denen der Orient mit seinen orgiastischen Kulten steht. So begegnen Manteltänzerinnen vorzugsweise im dionysischen Kreis, des öfteren auf Vasen in Darstellungen, die von der Bühne beeinflusst sind, zusammen mit tanzenden Komödienfiguren und mit Satyrn und Mänaden, die die Doppelflöte blasen oder in den Händen halten und das Tympanon und

---

9. Zum Beispiel auf einer sf. Schale in Stockholm (*AJb* 49, 1934 1 Abb.) und einem rf. Stamnos des Deepdene-Malers in Goluchow (Frickenhaus, A., *Lenäenvasen*, 72. *Brl. Winckelmannsprogramm* 1912, Taf. 2, 14. — Beazley, *Att. Vasenmaler* 295, 14 = *Attic Red-figure Vase-painters* 327, 15).

10. G. 162. *Corpus Vasorum* Taf. 13, 5 und 8; 16, 3. — Beazley, *AV.* 72, 32 = ARV. 124, 40.

11. 2645 (J. 332). Furtwängler-Reichhold, *Griech. Vasenmalerei* Taf. 49. — Beazley, *AV.* 176, 12 = *ARV.* 247, 15.

12. *Cabinet des Médailles* 576. Hartwig, P., *Griech. Meisterschalen* Taf. 32. — Beazley, *AV.* 177, 13 = *ARV.* 247, 15.

13. Hartwig, *Meisterschalen* Taf. 43. — Beazley, *AV*, 194, 3 = *ARV*, 267, 2.

14. 2560 (J. 240). *Corpus Vasorum München* 2 Taf. 93, 1. — Beazley, *AV.* 319, 6 = *ARV.* 550, 3.

15. F. 2532. Gerhard, E., *Trinkschalen und Gefäße* Taf. 6-7. — Beazley, *AV.* 428, 1 = *ARV.* 727, 39.

16. Vgl. auch. Jahn, O., *Beschreibung der Vasensammlung König Ludwigs*, zu Nr. 240.

Fackeln schwingen.[17] Ein wichtiges Zeugnis für die orientalische
Herkunft und die kultische Bedeutung des Manteltanzes ist weiterhin der Tanz der Frauen beim attischen Adonisfest, das als eine
jährliche Feier der Frauen zu Ehren und zum Gedächtnis für den
toten Adonis begangen wurde.[18] Dass es sich dabei um einen Manteltanz von Frauen zur Doppelflöte handelt, ist durch die Darstellung
auf einer Hydria Kertscher Stils im Britischen Museum E.241[19]
bezeugt. Wichtig sind hier ferner die beiden Manteltänzerinnen, die
auf dem Hauptbild einer apulischen Spitzamphora in Neapel[20]
zwischen Blumenranken das Haupt des Adonis umschwärmen. Das
Flötenspiel und nach ihm der Tanz im Adoniskult hatten, wie Adonis
selbst, den Namen Gingras.[21]

Wahrscheinlich bestand der Manteltanz wie andere antike Tänze
aus festgelegten Tanzschritten. Aus den Darstellungen hat man —
allerdings ziemlich willkürlich — sieben verschiedene Bewegungen
des Manteltanzes erschliessen wollen, vom zierlichen Schreiten bis
zum ekstatischen Wirbel. Getanzt wurde er nur von Frauen, und
zwar sowohl von einzelnen Frauen wie paarweise oder zu dritt oder
auch in grösseren Gruppen. Der Grad der Verhüllung, vor allem des
Gesichtes, schwankt. Die Hände sind fast immer vom Mantel bedeckt.

Die Münchner Manteltänzerin gibt von den religiösen Vorstellungen, aus denen der Manteltanz erwachsen ist, zunächst nur wenig
zu erkennen. Sie mögen auch damals, als die Figur entstand, schon
stark verblasst gewesen sein. Aber man muss sich den Vorstellungs-
bereich vergegenwärtigen, in dem der Manteltanz seine Wurzeln und
seinen Sinn hatte, um eine Figur wie die Münchner Terrakotte in
ihrer vollen Bedeutung verstehen zu können.

---

17. Vgl. Heydemann, *a.O.* 5ff. und Furtwängler-Reichhold, *Griechische Vasenmalerei* Taf. 80.

18. Vgl. Deubner, L., *Attische Feste* 220ff.

19. *Corpus Vasorum* Taf. 96, 4; 97, 4. — Schefold, K., *Untersuchungen zu den
Kertscher Vasen* Taf. 19, 2. — *JOAI* 12 (1909) 96 Abb. 56.

20. Heydemann 3220. — *Annali dell' Istituto* 1843, Taf. O. Q. danach *JOAI*
a.O. 98 Abb. 57.

21. Vgl. *RE* 1. Reihe, 7. Band, 1365 s.v. Gingras.

VORHELLENISTISCHE KOPIEN UND WIEDERHOLUNGEN VON STATUEN

FRANK BROMMER

Marburg

Professor D. M. Robinson, dem diese Zeilen in Verehrung gewidmet sind, hat an dem Beispiel einer attisch-rotfigurigen Vase aus seiner eigenen hervorragenden Sammlung auf einen Fall hingewiesen, in dem klassische Skulpturen von der gleichzeitigen Vasenmalerei wiedergegeben worden sind.[1] Eine Anzahl weiterer solcher Fälle ist unverkennbar, wenn es sich auch selten um ein genaues Kopieren handelt.[2] Diese Tatsache lenkt auf die Frage, ob ein ähnliches Verfahren auch für die grosse Kunst denkbar ist, ob es Kopien, Nachbildungen oder Wiederholungen von Standbildern auch schon in klassischer Zeit, oder vielleicht sogar bereits früher gegeben hat. — Bei einem modernen Kunstwerk aus Bronze ist die Verbreitung in mehreren Exemplaren nichts Ungewöhnliches. Beispielsweise sind Rodins "Bürger von Calais" oder sein "Ehernes Zeitalter" an verschiedenen Plätzen oder in mehreren Sammlungen aufgestellt, ohne dass sich sagen liesse, welches von diesen Exemplaren das "Original" ist. Etwas Derartiges kann für die griechische Klassik nicht vorausgesetzt werden, weil bei dem Wachsausschmelzverfahren die Form verloren ging und also nicht, wie bei den heutigen Gussverfahren mehrere Güsse aus ein und derselben Form gemacht werden konnten. Wegen dieser allgemein bekannten Tatsachen neigt man ungern dazu, Kopien oder Wiederholungen auch für die klassische Zeit anzunehmen. Auch ist über jeden Zweifel erhaben, dass die eigentliche antike Kopistentätigkeit grösseren Ausmasses erst in den beiden nachchristlichen Jahrhunderten herrschte. Es ist aber ebenfalls bekannt, dass schon in hellenistischer Zeit kopiert worden ist. Beispielsweise ist die Athena aus der Bibliothek in Pergamon[3] bekanntlich eine Kopie

---

1. Robinson, *AJA* 38 (1934) 45ff. Taf. 5. — Ders. CVA Robinson Coll. 3 (1938) III I pl.IX. USA 303.

2. Schefold, *JdI* 52 (1937) 30-75. — Langlotz, *Ephemeris* 1937, 606 Anm. 3. — Schweitzer, *JdI* 53 (1938) 85. — Ders., *JdI* 54 (1939) 4. 9 Anm. 5.10 Anm. 1.19 Anm. 2. — Raubitschek, *BSA* 40 (1939/40) 33 zu Wiedergaben der Euenor-Athena auf Vasenbildern, a.O. 34 zum Omphalosapoll. — Bielefeld, *Würzburger Jb* 2, 1947, 172-175. — Langlotz, *Phidiasprobleme* 100 Anm. 3 a. — Zum Miltiades-Teller in Oxford: Schuchhardt in Schrader-Langlotz-Schuchhardt; Raubitschek, *Dedications* 359ff. zu Athena mit Altar, a.O. 497 zur Euenor-Athena, a.O. 513 zur Tyrannenmörder-Gruppe. — Zur Nachbildung der grossen Malerei auf Vasen: Zuletzt E. Bielefeld, *Von griechischer Malerei* 10.

3. *Altert. v. Pergamon* VII 33 Nr. 24 Taf. VIII Beiblatt 2.3.

der phidiasischen Athena Parthenos. Wenn sie uns auch derart vom
Geist ihrer eigenen Zeit getränkt erscheint, dass es schwer zu entscheiden ist, ob sie mehr hellenistische oder klassische Züge aufweist,
so besteht doch kein Zweifel, dass sie ohne das phidiasische Vorbild
undenkbar ist und dass sie dieses wiedergeben will. Die römischen
Kopien sind ebenfalls nicht frei vom Stil ihrer eigenen Zeit. Wenn
auch nicht im Punktierverfahren übertragen, so ist daher die pergamenische Athena doch zweifellos Kopie im weiteren Sinn. Sieht
man von der Kleinkunst ab, so ist sogar für die Frei- und Relief-
skulptur schon des 4. Jh. v. Chr. ein Kopieren in dieser freieren Bedeutung belegt. Die zweite Klassik hat zuweilen gern von der ersten
gezehrt. Polyklets Werke galten insbesondere als kanonisch und
wurden als Vorbilder benützt, bei deren Verwendung aber doch der
eigene Stil zum Durchbruch kam, ähnlich wie später bei der pergamenischen Athena.

Bekannt ist seit langem als mehr oder weniger freie Nachbildung
des Westmacottschen Epheben die Statue aus Eleusis,[4] als Nachbildung des Doryphoros das Relief aus Argos.[5] Ferner wurde ein
richtiges Kopieren für das 4. Jh. verschiedentlich bei den Ersatz-
figuren des Westgiebels von Olympia angenommen.[6] Ein weiteres mit
Sicherheit in das 5. Jh. datiertes Beispiel ist eine Kopie der "Penelope"
aus Persepolis.[7]

Im 4. Jh. und im Hellenismus hatte aber die künstlerische Entwicklung noch Antrieb aus eigener Kraft. Sie setzte sich selbst in solchen
bewussten Rückwendungen durch. Vereinfacht gesagt: Aus diesen
Zeiten könnte man sich die Rückwendungen wegdenken, aus der
römischen Kunst kaum. Insofern unterscheiden sich auch die Kopien
der vorchristlichen Jahrhunderte von denen der nachchristlichen. Die
Frage ist also: gibt es, wieder in einem anderen Sinn, Kopien oder
Wiederholungen schon vor dem 4. Jh.? Die Frage ist bereits gelegentlich bejaht worden,[8] aber die bisher nachgewiesenen frühesten Kopien

---

4. Lippold, *Kopien und Umbild.* 14. — Schuchhardt, *Kunst d. Gr.* Abb. 277. —
Süsserott, *Griech. Plastik 4. Jh.*, 136f. Taf. 29, 2. Für Statuette-Kopien von
Parthenon-Skulpturen vgl. Carpenter, *Hesperia* 1 (1932) 11-16.

5. Athen, Nat.Mus. *AM* 3 (1878) Taf. 13. — Collignon, *Sculpt.* I 491. —
Hauser, *OeJh* 12, 1909, 104 Abb. 60. — Richter, *Sculpture and Sculptors* fig. 649.
— Bianchi-Bandinelli, *Policleto* fig. 31.

6. So vor allem Studniczka, *NJb* 1926, 396. — Rodenwaldt *JdI* 41 (1926) 225.
— Rumpf, *Gnomon* 5 (1929) 16. — Kunze-Weber, *AJA* 52 (1948) 495 Anm. 11,
während andere die Figuren für römische Kopien hielten.

7. Erich F. Schmidt, *The Treasury of Persepolis*, 65f. — Den Hinweis verdanke
ich E. Langlotz einen Auszug des erwähnten Berichtes K. Erdmann. Aber D. M.
Robinson schreibt mir, dass Cleta Olmstead, *AJA* 54 (1950) 10-18, Taf. VIII-XII,
glaubt, dass es zwei Originale gab und dass die drei römischen Kopien von dem
des spät-fünften Jahrhunderts stammen.

8. Furtwängler, *Ueber Statuenkopien im Altertum*, 1896. — Ders., *Griech.
Originalstatuen in Venedig* 1899. — Hauser, *RM* 17, 1902, 254. — Frickenhaus,

oder Wiederholungen stammen erst aus dem 4. Jh. oder aus den letzten Jahrzehnten des 5. Jh.[9] Daher hat die Forschung im allgemeinen diese Frage offen gelassen oder sogar entschieden verneint,[10] weil mit Recht die moderne Art der Wiederholungen als in der Klassik unmöglich erkannt wurde.

Es ist aber doch zu fragen, ob nicht trotzdem Kopien oder Wiederholungen anderer Art schon in klassischer oder früherer Zeit möglich waren. Bei diesen Fragen werden die von Lippold angeführten Werke im Folgenden als bekannt vorausgesetzt und es werden ihnen hier einige neu angereiht, um eine breitere Basis für die Untersuchung zu gewinnen.

Die Statuen des Kleobis und Biton aus Delphi[11] sind einander zwar nicht völlig gleich, aber doch erstaunlich ähnlich. Dies ist hier natürlich mit durch das Thema gegeben, denn beide Dargestellten sind Brüder, auch waren beide Standbilder zusammen, vielleicht auf einer gemeinsamen Basis, aufgestellt. Immerhin zeigen diese Werke, dass sich schon im frühen 6. Jh. Bildhauer nicht scheuten, ein eigenes Werk oder das eines anderen zu wiederholen.[12] Dies wird auch in einer Zeit nicht wundernehmen, die solche Reihungen von gleichen oder ähnlichen Werken vornahm, wie die archaischen Löwen von Delos.[13]

Ebenfalls archaisch — von Schuchhardt um 540 v. Chr. oder wenig

---

JdI 28 (1913) 365f. — Lippold, *Kopien und Umb.* 6. — Langlotz, *Ephemeris* 1937, 607 Anm. 5 mit Beispielen.

9. Es sind dies ausser den in Anm. 4, 5, 7 erwähnten drei Werken vor allem die Standbilder, die von der in Anm. 8 zusammengestellten Literatur behandelt werden. Dazu H. Weber, *Griech. Frauentrachten* 128 und ebenda 135, wo er die Peplosstatue im Piräusmuseum (*RM* 51 (1936) Taf. 18/9) für eine zeitgenössische Kopie des 5. Jh. erklärt. Ferner die Athenabilder, die C. Praschniker, *AB* 1948, 11ff. Nr. 7 behandelt.

10. Lippold, *Kopien und Umb.* 6 meinte: "Nach Analogie anderer Kunstepochen sollte man auch für die griechische Kunst Werkstattwiederholungen voraussetzen, annehmen, dass Werke, die besonderen Beifall fanden, vom Meister selbst oder in seiner Werkstatt in weiteren Exemplaren angefertigt wurden. Beweise, dass dies vorkam, haben wir nicht." Trotz der fehlenden Beweise nahm er (a.O. 9) wenigstens "Schulwiederholungen" an. L. Curtius und G. M. A. Richter nahmen sogar anlässlich der Nike des Paionios scharf dagegen Stellung, dass es in jener Zeit Wiederholungen gegeben habe. S. Anm. 19.

11. de la Coste, *Delphes* fig. 34. — Buschor, *Bildnisstufen* Abb. 98. — Richter, *Kouroi* Nr. 11 Taf. XVIII, XIX, XXIII. Die Zahl der Stirnlocken weicht ebenso wie die der Haarsträhnen auf dem Rücken voneinander ab.

12. G. v. Kaschnitz verdanke ich die mündliche Mitteilung, dass er die beiden Standbilder für von verschiedenen Bildhauern gefertigt hält. Zur Frage der Gegenstücke von verschiedenen Bildhauern in archaischer und klassischer Zeit: Rodenwaldt, *Korkyra* 157 Anm. 1. — Ders., *Olympia*² 46. — Ihm folgt: Akurgal *Griech.Reliefs* 17. Dazu auch Schrader-Langlotz-Schuchhardt, *Arch.Marmorbildw.* zu Nr. 373. — Vgl. auch die Gegenstücke sitzender Frauen aus Prinias (Pernier, *AJA.* 38 (1934) 175) und den beiden Reiter Rampin von der Akropolis, die zu schlecht erhalten sind, um die Frage zu entscheiden, ob es sich um Arbeiten verschiedener Hände bei den Gegenstücken handelte.

13. *Antike* 14 (1938) Taf. 5, 6.

später datiert — sind die Löwen von der Akropolis,[14] zu denen es einen entsprechenden Löwen vom Kerameikos gibt. Schuchhardt schreibt darüber: "In derselben Werkstatt und nach demselben Modell wie die Akropolislöwen ist der Löwe vom Kerameikos gearbeitet (AA.1937, 287 Abb.20). Er stimmt in den Massen, in der Haltung und der Ausführung im Grossen genau mit ihnen überein (vgl. Abb. 310 mit 308 und 309). Nur in Einzelheiten der Anordnung der Zotteln der Ausführung der Augenpartie finden sich Unterschiede, verrät sich eine andere modellierende Hand. Er wiederholt zum dritten Male den nach rechts gerichteten Löwen, gehört also gewiss nicht — etwa als verschleppt — zu den Akropolislöwen. Die Verwendung des gleichen Modells zur gleichen Zeit als Akroter und als Grabmonument ist lehrreich."

Angesichts dieser Beispiele wird man einer weiteren Parallele, die nur durch die antike Literatur bekannt ist, nicht von vornherein misstrauen: Der Bildhauer Kanachos gehört zweifellos auch noch in archaische Zeit. Er hat[15] für Theben einen Apollon Ismenios und für Milet einen Apollon Philesios gemacht. Beide unterschieden sich nicht in Grösse und Aussehen, nur im Material. Der thebanische war aus Zedernholz und der milesische aus Erz. "Wer eins der beiden Werke sah und den Meisternamen erfuhr, der brauchte nicht viel Verstand zu haben, um zu wissen, dass auch das andere von Kanachos sei" sagt Pausanias.

Ebenso sagt der gleiche Schriftsteller zu der Artemis Soteira des Bildhauers Strongylion in Megara, dass sich in Pagai eine ebenfalls eherne Artemis Soteira befunden habe, die ihr an Grösse gleich gewesen sei und sich in der Haltung in keiner Weise von ihr unterschieden habe.[16] Pausanias sagt zwar nicht, dass beide Werke auch vom gleichen Bildhauer gewesen seien, doch ist dies nach dem Beispiel des Kanachos naheliegend. Sind die Werke des Kanachos und Strongylion nicht im Original erhalten, so lassen sich solche "Selbstwiederholungen" im Parthenonfries mehrfach deutlich beobachten[17] Wenn man auch sagen kann, dies sei in künstlerischer Absicht geschehen, und ein zusammenhängender Fries sei etwas anderes als an verschiedenen Orten aufgestellte Freiplastiken, so bleibt dies doch zweifellos ein Fall, wo ein Meister und nicht der schlechteste, sich nicht gescheut hat, seine eigenen Werke zu wiederholen.

---

14. Schrader-Langlotz-Schuchhardt, *Die arch. Marmorbildw.* Nr. 382. 384.

15. Overbeck, *Schriftquellen* Nr. 403 = Paus. IX 10, 2.

16. Overbeck, *Schriftquellen* Nr. 877 = Paus. I 40, 2; I 44, 4. — Dazu Raubitschek, *Dedications*, 524, der eine Kopie durch einen anderen Bildhauer für möglich hält.

17. Schweitzer *JdI* 54 (1939) 24f.

Von hier aus gewinnt auch die Frage der Paionios-Nike neues Licht. Die in Olympia gefundene marmorne Nike gehört zu einem eigenartigen, dreieckigen, hohen und auffallenden Postament. Nach der Inschrift ist dieses Siegesdenkmal von den Messeniern und Naupaktiern errichtet und die Nike von Paionios geschaffen worden. Von dem Kopf der Nike gibt es Kopien.[18]

Angesichts der hohen Aufstellung dieser Nike und angesichts der bekannten Tatsache, dass es von Originalen in Olympia sonst kaum Kopien gibt, nicht einmal vom phidiasischen Zeus, ist es zunächst auffallend, dass vom Kopf der Nike trotzdem Kopien vorhanden sind.

Ein dem olympischen gleichartiges, hohes, dreieckiges, mit Schilden geziertes Monument in Delphi trägt eine Inschrift, aus der hervorgeht, dass es ebenfalls von den Messeniern und Naupaktiern geweiht worden ist. Nichts liegt näher, als anzunehmen, dass das gleiche Postament auch das gleiche Werk, also eine Nike des Paionios, trug. Sie ist nicht erhalten und wird von Pausanias nicht erwähnt. Man hat einleuchtend vermutet, dass sie vor dem Besuch des Pausanias nach Italien verschleppt worden ist und dass dort die Kopien nach ihr angefertigt worden sind.[19]

Angesichts der bisher aufgezählten Fälle wird man die an sich schon durch verschiedene Gründe nahegelegte Möglichkeit, dass in Olympia und in Delphi beidemal eine Nike des Paionios stand, nicht ablehnen können.

Für dieselben Orte ergibt sich noch eine weitere Möglichkeit: die Korkyraier haben nach Delphi und nach Olympia einen ehernen Stier geweiht. Für den delphischen kennen wir den Künstlernamen Theopropos. Der olympische ist wegen eines besonderen Vorfalls, den Pausanias schildert, vor dessen Zeit aus der Altis entfernt worden. Daher kennen wir auch leider den Künstlernamen nicht. Aber die schon von Brunn[20] ausgesprochene Vermutung, dass es sich auch hier

---

18. Beide in Rom. Kopf Hertz und Hermenkopf im Vatikan: Richter, *Sculpture and Sculptors* fig. 639-641. G. Kasdmik-Weinberg, *Sculture del Magazzino del Museo Vat.*, Nr. 47 Taf. 15 und tav. d'aggiunta.

19. Diese Ansicht, dass zwei einander gleiche Werke, beide von Paionios und zwar das in Delphi aus Bronze, das in Olympia aus Marmor, bestanden hätten, wurde vor allem von Pomtow (*JdI* 37 (1922) 60 und ders., *RE.* Suppl. IV 1308ff. Nr. 54) vertreten. Ihm folgten Lippold (*Kopien und Umb.* 69 und ders. vorsichtiger: RE. *s.v.* Paionios) und Wace (*Approach* 33). Bedenken hatte Bieber (in: Thieme-Becker *s.v.* Paionios: "Es ist unwahrscheinlich, dass ein so grosser Künstler wie P. sich selbst so sklavisch wiederholt haben sollte"). Richter und Curtius lehnten die Ansicht energisch ab (Richter, *Sculpture und Sculptors* 243: "not suggested by our present knowledge of Greek sculpture. This applies also to Pomtow's theory that the statue . . . in Delphi was the bronze original from which the Victory in Olympia was copied. The fifth century was an age of original creations, not of replicas." — Curtius, *Gnomon* 1 (1925) 11: ". . . . sei in Delphi die gleiche Nike wie in Olympia aufgestellt gewesen, ein im Griechischen doch ganz unmöglich zu denkendes Verfahren").

20. *Gesch.d.griech.Künstler* I 96.

um ein Werk des Theopropos handelt, liegt immerhin nahe. Dass hier dann wiederum eine Wiederholung vorliegen kann, wird man nur bestreiten wollen, wenn man diese Möglichkeit für die archaische und klassische Zeit überhaupt allgemein leugnet.

Die Möglichkeit, dass wie bei den erwähnten archaischen Löwen, bei Kanachos, Strongylion, Paionios und Theopropos dasselbe Werk des gleichen Künstlers in einer Wiederholung an zwei Orten aufgestellt ist, ist noch ein sechstes Mal gegeben: beim Daochos-Weihgeschenk. Bei diesem mehrfigurigen Weihgeschenk von Marmorstandbildern stellt eins den Agias dar. Wie Preuner entdeckt hat,[21] ist demselben Agias mit einer Inschrift, die der delphischen sehr ähnlich ist, auch in seiner Heimatstadt Pharsalos ein Standbild aufgestellt worden. Das pharsalische trug die Künstlerinschrift des Lysipp, beim delphischen ist keine Künstlersignatur erhalten. Es ist unbekannt, ob in Pharsalos nur Agias allein oder dieselbe Gruppe wie in Delphi aufgestellt war. Mindestens beim Agias entsteht also die Frage, ob beide Statuen vom selben Meister stammten, oder ob die delphische vielleicht eine gleichzeitige Marmorkopie des Originals von Pharsalos war, oder ob trotz der Inschriften beide Werke nichts miteinander zu tun hatten.

Unsere Vorstellung von Lysipp stützt sich fast nur auf die einzige Kopie des Apoxyomenos. Erst in den letzten Jahren haben uns Inschriften gelehrt, die Lebensdauer des Lysipp viel länger anzunehmen, als man bisher glaubte.[22] Man wird daher auch mit einem grösseren Umfang seiner Stilmöglichkeiten rechnen müssen und also bei einem stilistischen Vergleich des Agias mit dem Apoxyomenos nicht von vornherein ausschliessen dürfen, dass Lysipp die Vorbilder dieser beiden Werke gemacht hat. Die Möglichkeit, dass der erhaltene Agias von Delphi lysippisch ist wie der verlorene Agias von Pharsalos, ist also durchaus gegeben. Es liegt allerdings beim delphischen wegen der nicht hervorragenden Qualität näher, eine Werkstattwiederholung anzunehmen, als eine Wiederholung des Meisters selbst.

Auch bei Praxiteles ist die Möglichkeit von Werkstattwiederholungen gegeben. Nach Pausanias I 44.2 und VIII 9.1 hat er sowohl für Megara wie für Mantinea Bilder der Leto mit Artemis und Apollon gemacht. Leider wissen wir über deren Aussehen nichts und können daher keine weiteren Folgerungen ziehen. Dazu kommt schliesslich die Frage des Zusammenhangs zwischen der phidiasischen Aphrodite Urania und der Berliner Frauenstatue auf der Schild-

---

21. Preuner, *Ein delphisches Weihgeschenk* (1900). — Dazu Pomtow, *RE.* Suppl. V *s.v.* Delphoi Nr. 222. — Süsserott, *Griech.Plastik des 4. Jh.*, 167 Taf. 34, 1.

22. Wilhelm, *OeJh* 33, 1941, 44.

kröte. Diese Frage kann auch auf die Annahme von Werkstattwiederholungen im 5. Jh. führen.[23] Die hier erwähnten Werke, ob sie nun
Meister- oder Werkstattwiederholungen sind, entstanden offenbar im
Einverständnis mit dem ursprünglichen Meister. Daneben gibt es andere Fälle, in denen ein überlegenes Werk von geringeren Künstlern
kopiert wurde, ohne dass dieses Einverständnis vorgelegen zu habem
braucht.

Ein solches Verfahren scheint ebenfalls schon in archaischer Zeit
möglich gewesen zu ein. Payne hat auf solche offensichtlichen
Nachahmungen von Statuen oder von Teilen von ihnen hingewiesen,[24]
Lullies hat[25] Beispiele dafür zusammengestellt, wie in der böotischen
Kunst Werke der attischen oder auch solche aus anderen Land-
schaften in archaischer und klassischer Zeit kopiert worden sind. Bei
diesen Werken handelt es sich offenbar um mehr, als um das Aufnehmen der Wirkung, die jedes bedeutendere Werk ausstrahlt, nicht nur
um ein unbewusstes Verarbeiten, sondern um ein bewusstes und
ziemlich genaues Kopieren. Dies ist natürlich am meisten gerade bei
geringeren Werken zu erwarten und ist auch in der Kleinkunst zu
beobachten. Die zahlreichen Fälle, in denen Wiedergaben von Statuen
oder Reliefs auf Vasenbildern und Münzen erscheinen, sollen dabei
noch nicht einmal berücksichtigt werden. Es genügt, sich auf freiplastische Nachbildungen der Kleinkunst zu beschränken.

In einer Kleinbronze in Leningrad ist eine originale Statuette des
5. Jh. erhalten, die eine nicht lange vor ihr entstandene Statue wiedergibt. Die Statue ist verloren, aber es gibt mehrere Kopien des Kopfes,
der in seiner Haltung und Haartracht so auffällig ist, dass kein
Zweifel besteht, dass die Statuette und die Köpfe auf dasselbe Vorbild zurückgehen, das man auf Grund der Statuette geradezu wieder
rekonstruieren kann.[26] In einer Berliner Tonform erkannte Blümel

---

23. Darauf soll an anderer Stelle eingegangen werden. Ferner hat Wace, *An Approach to Greek Sculpture*, 49 für möglich gehalten, dass der Hermes von Olympia eine Werkstattausführung nach einem Modell von Praxiteles ist und dass die knidische Aphrodite des gleichen Meisters ebenfalls in Bronze und Marmor existiert hat. — Die Kopie der Athena Parthenos im Akropolismuseum (Casson II Nr. 1362) wurde von Dinsmoor, *AJA* 38 (1934) 103 noch in das spätere 5. Jh. datiert. Curtius, *Gnomon* 2 (1926) 18 hält sie für eine mässige römische Kopie. Jenkins, *Dedalica* nahm S. 18 Statuenkopien sogar schon im 7. Jh. an, ohne allerdings diese Ansicht zu begründen; a.O. 71 meinte er, dass man auch nach dem 7. Jh. Werke dieser Zeit kopiert habe.

24. *Archaic Marble Sculpture from Acropolis* S.17: the stylization of the dress of the Lyons kore must have been copied from an East Ionic Model. — S. 24 direct inheritance S. 31: Kore 675 is evidently not a work of much originality, perhaps not more than a version of a statue now lost. Ders., *JHS* 54 (1934) 163 Anm. 2. "is probably a Boeotian copy of Corinthian". Siehe auch Raubitschek, *BSA* 40 (1939/40) 22. — Ders., *Dedications*, 481, 483, 513 hält die Tyrannen-mörder von Kritios und Nesiotes nur für eine Kopie nach der Gruppe des Antenor.

25. *JdI* 51, 1936, 148ff. und *Am* 65 (1940) 6 Anm. 2.

26. Zu der Statuette und den römischen Kopien, sowie der Frage ihrer Zurück-

eine Kopie der sitzenden archaischen Göttin des Berliner Museums.[27] Ein weiteres, noch sichereres Beispiel ist der strenge Spiegelträger mit den Schlangen, in dem Jantzen[28] einen zeitlich nahen Nachklang der Schlangensäule aus Delphi erkannt hat.

Langlotz teilt weitgehend die Ansicht, dass schon im 5. Jh. kopiert wurde. Wichtig sind seine Hinweise auf die von ihm vermuteten zeitgenössischen Nachklänge der Athena Promachos und auf das Relief der "Sinnenden Athena" mit seinen Nachklängen.[29] Dass in klassischer, vielleicht sogar schon von archaischer Zeit an Wiederholungen von Standbildern angefertigt wurden, wird auch durch eine andere Ueberlegung nahegelegt: Bei der ausserordentlichen Zufälligkeit in der Erhaltung von Denkmälern ist es sehr unwahrscheinlich, dass wir von demselben Werk sowohl das Original wie auch eine oder mehrere Kopien römischer Zeit besitzen. Und doch scheint es mehrere solcher Fälle zu geben.[30] Nimmt man nun aber an, dass die "Originale" klassischer Zeit manchmal nicht nur in einem einzigen Exemplar bestanden haben, sondern gleichzeitig in Wiederholungen des Meisters oder seiner Schule verbreitet waren, dann wird die Wahrscheinlichkeit, dass sich "Original" und römische Kopie in einigen Fällen zugleich erhalten haben, bedeutend grösser.

Diese Wiederholungen unterscheiden sich von den eingangs erwähnten modernen Fällen grundsätzlich dadurch, dass sie unter einander nie genau gleich sein können, da sie nie aus derselben Form stammen, oft aus einem anderen Material bestehen und offenbar auch nicht immer vom gleichen Meister, sondern zuweilen auch von einem Schüler gefertigt wurden. Diese Wiederholungen gehören oft gerade zu den führenden Meisterwerken, die auch von den Meistern selbst

führung auf den Orpheus des Dionysios: Sieveking, Text BrBr. 698. — Ders., *AA* 1926, 334ff. — Poulsen, *Acta Arch.* 1937, 33,115. — Schuchhardt. *KdGr.* 250. — Langlotz, *JdI* 49 (1934) 43f. — Ders., *Ephem.* 1937, 604ff. — Schefold Text BrBr. 785 S. 24 Anm. 2. — Bielefeld, *Arch.Verm.* 6 Anm. 7 — Bulle, 99. *BWPr.* 16 Anm. 15. — Schweitzer, *Stud.z.Entst.Port.* 54. — Schuchhardt, *GGA* 1934, 313. — Kunze, *Antike u. Abendl.* II 108 Anm. 23a. V. H. Poulsen, *Berytus* 6 (1939-40) 10. Langlotz, *JdI* 61-2 (1946-7) 95-111.

27. AA. 1939, 307 Anm. 1 Tonform aus Tarent: Berlin Inv. 30990. — O. Rubensohn, *AM.* 1 (1948) 21-43 will in einem Tonbruchstück aus Paros eine ungefähr zeitgenössische Kopie der "Nike von Delos" erkennen, die er — allerdings wegen des Knielaufschemas nicht überzeugend — für eine Artemis hält. Buschor, *Altsam. Standbilder*, 48 hält Terrakotten aus Samos (Abb. 178) für Nachbildungen von Marmorwerken. Brooke, bei Casson, *Cat. Acr. Mus.* II, 322, 333 Nr. 1444, 1446 meint dass Terrakotten nach dem "Einführungsgiebel' 'von der Akropolis kopiert seien.

28. *AA* 1937, 336-339.

29. *Phidiasprobleme* 74, ebenda 75 und Nachtrag zu S. 109 Anm. 8.

30. Zuletzt zusammengestellt von H. Götze, *RM* 53 (1938) 225 Anm. 2.; dazu v. Buttlar, *MWPr* 1947, 8. — Die Berliner Statue (Blümel, *Kat.* III K 5) mit der "Melpomene" in Leningrad (Frickenhaus, *JdI* 28 (1913) 365 abb. 8) wäre auch hierin zu rechnen.

signiert oder wenigstens in der späteren Literatur unter ihren Namen gezählt werden konnten.

Neben diesen Wiederholungen gibt es auch Kopien im engeren Sinn. Sie unterscheiden sich von den hellenistischen und späteren dadurch, dass sie innerhalb der gleichen Zeit immer einen Schritt zum Geringeren hin bedeuten: vom führenden Meister zum schlechteren, von der Hauptstadt zur Provinz, von der Statue zur Statuette.

In der Archäologie lässt sich sehr wenig mathematisch beweisen. Daher wird sich auch manches Bedenken gegen das eine oder andere der angeführten Beispiele vorbringen lassen, bei denen die Wahrscheinlichkeit, dass es sich um Wiederholungen handelt, teils gegeben. teils naheliegend, teils nur möglich ist. Andererseits werden sich auch weitere Beispiele finden lassen. Jedoch zwingen vielleicht schon die bisherigen Fälle dazu, die Frage vorurteilsfreier anzusehen und die Möglichkeit, dass es solche Wiederholungen bereits in klassischer, ja schon in archaischer Zeit gab, nicht grundsätzlich abzulehnen. Je mehr solcher Fälle sich finden lassen, desto mehr stützen sie sich gegenseitig in ihrer inneren Wahrscheinlichkeit.

Wenn man also für die Originale der archaischen und klassischen Zeit weder annimmt, dass sie heutigen Wiederholungen entsprechend wie ein Ei dem andern glichen, noch voraussetzt, dass bei der Entstehung von antiken Kunstwerken ein Massstab angelegt wurde, der unsere neuzeitlichen Forderungen, geistiges Eigentum zu wahren, erfüllte, dann wird man wohl dem damaligen Schaffensvorgang am nächsten kommen. Ein griechisches Original war also nicht in allen Fällen ein "Original."

THE THORVALDSEN MUSEUM FRAGMENT NO. 82

GEORGE BAKALAKIS
Anatolia College, Thessaloniki

Plates 72-73

The fragment illustrated on plate 73 has been kept for over a century in the archaeological collection of the Thorvaldsen Museum in Copenhagen.[1] The older scholars generally have classed this relief, along with others not related to it, as "architectural." Arndt more specifically stated that it is a fragment from a marble door.[2] But none of these views can any longer be considered satisfactory. A great number of ancient marble doors chiefly coming from graves are extant. But, they have only one side, that is, the front face decorated. The design is stylized, consisting only of the wooden framework represented in relief with huge nailheads protruding. Thus, they imitate actual wooden doors with their metal sheathing and their ornamental copper nails.[3]

In contrast to these doors, the fragment at Copenhagen is ornamented on both sides. The front face is decorated with a fluted acanthus spiral, vine leaves, and a satyr facing left with his right hand extended. The reverse of the slab has the main fluted trunk of the acanthus spiral and in addition a much more delicate tendril, while in place of the satyr there is a male goat rearing on its hind legs and turning toward the right. How large a part of the original composition is now missing can be deduced from a well-known relief in the Berlin Museum from the Pergamene Asklepieion, although even that relief is not preserved to its original full width. The two fragments have never been considered together, although each is practi-

---

1. The author wishes to express his appreciation to Dr. Constantine G. Yavis, of the St. Louis University, for his translation from the Greek. He is deeply grateful to the director of the Thorvaldsen Museum, Mr. Sigurd Schultz, both for permission to publish the illustrations and for information provided.
   Description: White marble. Original limit not preserved. Extant height 0.25 m., extant width 0.17 m, thickness 0.11 m. Provenience unknown, but probably Italy, since the collection was formed in Rome.

2. Müller, L., *Description des antiquités du Musée-Thorvaldsen*, Sections I and II, No. 82, 141. *EA* 1481 b, (middle fragment) and text by Arndt. Oppermann, Th., *Musée Thorvaldsen, Catalogue illustré*, 71. The other slabs with relief on both sides (index no. 83 and 84; Müller, *ibid.* and Oppermann, *ibid.*) have no connection or relationship to no. 82, being decorative reliefs of Roman date (maskenreliefs).

3. Altmann, W., *Die römischen Grabaltäre der Kaiserzeit*, 14, fig. 8. *JDAI* 26 (1911) 195, figs. 4, 5. Dyggve-Rhomaios, *Das Heroon v. Kalydon*, 338 figs. 43, 44.

cally a replica of the other.[4] Both must have been members of marble
tables.

The front face of the Berlin relief shows acanthus leaves forming
a calyx out of which spring two spirals which undulate upwards and
cross each other so as to form successive connected rings or medallions. Inside the lower ring two seated satyrs gesticulate. The one
to the left is lifting the veil of a maenad who is asleep on the acanthus
calyx and the roots of the spirals. Inside the second ring there are
vine leaves and a bunch of grapes. The entire background of the
relief is decorated by vine leaves, tendrils, and rosettes. But the
lateral continuation of these elements is cut away. The third intersection of the spirals terminates in a palmette with two beautiful
rosettes. On the reverse the same motifs are repeated, but with the
difference that inside the lowest ring two opposed male goats stand
on their hind legs while their fore legs rest on the mouth of a vessel
resembling a kantharos or a krater.[5] In the present case the subject
is, of course, entirely decorative, but its original Dionysiac significance
is clear.

The Copenhagen and Berlin fragments resemble each other very
closely, and show very small differences. In the former relief the
satyr is kneeling, and leans on the fluted acanthus spiral grasping it
in his left hand; in the latter relief he holds a delicate tendril which
starts from acanthus and vine leaves; his arm is further extended,
and his figure is more lively. Further, the hind legs of the goats in
the Copenhagen relief are clearly distinguished, while in the Berlin

---

4. K. Museen Berlin, *Führer durch das Pergamon Museum*, 1904, 41. *Altertüm.
von Perg.*, VII 2(1908) 232, index no. 407, fig. p. 324, suppl. pl. 43. Description:
Marble. Original height 0.71 m. Extant width below 0.34 m., above 0.32 m.
Thickness above 0.11 m., under the frame also 0.11 m.; but in between and above
the frame 0.05 m. Thus the background in the upper part is not at the same
level as below, so that the relief is quite high below and quite low above, changing
gradually. This variation may be due to exigencies of the material, but it suits
well the decorative motif, which requires greater depth and shading below. The
diminution of thickness below did not unduly weaken the slab in its function as
a table support, because in that position it must have had a border extending
right and left. On both sides the original width has been trimmed off, evidently
at a later time. On the analogy of other similar supports, the height of this slab
calls for a width of ± 0.80 m., so that about 0.20-0.23 m. is missing from the sides
of the slab. That the original width was greater than now is confirmed by the
unsmoothed surface of the narrow sides and by the nature of the decorative
motif, which must have been continued laterally on both sides. The upper surface
of the slab is smooth, as is necessary in order for it to receive the covering slab,
which was held in place only with the projections from the now lost sides. Cf.
G. Bakalakis, Ἑλληνικὰ Τραπεζοφόρα, 13, fig. 9 p. 26.

5. On this motif in Hellenistic sculpture see Schwabacher, W., *AJA* 45 (1941)
201ff., notes 54-56. In regard to the origins of the motif I should like to add the
representations inside the medallions of the kylikes of Tleson: Beazley, *JHS* 52
(1932) 176, fig. 10; also the well-known gable relief of the altar-niche of Pan at
Thasos.

relief they are not. Generally, the latter fragment is done in higher relief.

The Berlin slab helps us to understand the function of the Copenhagen slab, since a common interpretation must apply to both fragments. The Copenhagen relief cannot be a door, nor can the Berlin relief with its Dionysiac decoration be a funeral stele.[6] Both slabs must have been supporting members of marble tables of type A.[7] The Dionysiac decoration accords perfectly with such a function.

The original function of these slabs can be further understood from an unpublished fragment of a marble table support from the Athenian Acropolis (plate 72, a).[8] This fragment does not have relief on both faces, and the decorative scheme on its front face is a simplified echo of the luxurious Copenhagen-Berlin relief. In the former the intersecting acanthus spirals do not rise so high; the acanthus on the base consists of deeply furrowed triple leaves, which are less clearly rendered; and the spirals are unfluted. The vessel also rests immediately on the middle leaf of the acanthus, while in the latter relief the spirals and other shoots and a special base intervene. The grapes of the second ring of the Acropolis relief do not have the free feeling of the Berlin relief, but are somewhat compressed. The Athenian fragment has only two tendrils intersecting beneath the upper frame, while in the Berlin relief a very handsome palmette and two rosettes are formed beyond the full ring. In general the Athenian fragment is simplified in design and generally inferior. The Athenian fragment is later, although it is impossible to date it accurately because it is much damaged, especially the ring containing the goats. On stylistic grounds—the four-sided rosette on the left and the vine leaves—which here are our only chronological guide we can assign it to a date as late as that of Augustus. Thus this frag-

---

6. G. Kowalczyk-A. Köster, *Decorative Sculpture*, pls. 59, 60; cf. *AJA* 45 (1941), 201 and note 56. The earlier publication *Altertümer v. Pergamon*, VII 2, 324, explained the slab as part of a parapet between two columns or antae, on the basis of wall pictures.

7. Bakalakis, as cited in note 4.

8. It is still located near the Belvedere, left of the staircase which leads to that point, set up by the north parapet of the Acropolis wall with other ancient fragments. The front face bears decoration somewhat similar to that of the Berlin and Copenhagen slabs, while the reverse face is smooth. The support is of type A, but has borders slanting upwards: Bakalakis, *op. cit.*, 37. I am grateful to my friend Mr. I. Travlos for the photograph of pl. 72, a. Description: Broken into three pieces and joined with clamps; other fragments are indicated by a clamp hole on the left, but I sought them in vain. Original height, extant, 0.775 m.; restored width below 0.66 m. above 0.76 m.; below on the right side are irregular knobs, the remains of broken-off animal claws, which are the usual decoration of table legs; thickness of the slanting frame 0.048 m., thickness at the upper frame 0.15 m. at the background of the relief 0.12 m.

ment is later than the two Hellenistic examples discussed above, but all three must belong to the same class, namely, to table supports of type A.[9]

The dating of the reliefs depends on two criteria: (a) the form of the vine leaves; (b) the carving of the figures, especially of the satyr on the Copenhagen fragment, who is the best preserved. The outline of the Copenhagen vine leaf and especially its clear veins are closely akin to the plane tree leaves of the frieze of Telephos of the altar at Pergamum,[10] which was carved about 180-160 B. C.,[11] although the latter leaves are only engraved. The period immediately after that of the Pergamene frieze suits also the general form of the satyr's body and in particular the head, which recalls the restless and sinewy head of Antiochos III of Syria (221—186 B. C.) in the Louvre.[12] I believe that the Copenhagen and Berlin reliefs date at about the same time.

Another work which dates later than these fragments is the relief from Tralles, now at Istanbul.[13] It has plane tree leaves which are more widely spread; some leaves have single veins rendered by engraving, others have double veins executed in relief; for example, the leaves to the left, two above and two below the branch, but those between these leaves and another leaf to the right have the veins engraved. In the case of the two leaves to the right there is a clear difference, one having the veins engraved and the other having the veins in relief. The Tralles fragment has leaves with double veins, but engraved, instead of in relief. The date of the Tralles relief has been much discussed, and recent opinion favors the first century B. C.[14]

The vine leaves and rosette of the Athenian table support can not date later than Augustus or the Flavians, as can be seen for example by comparing them with the reliefs on the tomb of the Haterii at the Lateran.[15] Actually, the workmanship of the Athenian relief is somewhat earlier than the shaded and fleshy vine leaves of the Augustan Boscoreale silver cup now in the Louvre, and is earlier than the well-known altar in the National Museum at Rome with vine sprays whose

---

9. Bakalakis, *op. cit.*, 36.

10. *Altertümer v. Pergamon*, III, pl. XXXI 4, 5, 6; *JDAI* 15 (1900) 123, figs. 14, 15. Rodenwaldt, *Das Relief bei den Griechen* fig. 116 b, c.

11. The latest bibliography: Dawson C. M. "Romano-Campanian Landscape Painting," *Yale Classical Studies*, IX, 29ff., notes 134ff.

12. Hekler, pl. 123.

13. Dawson, *loc. cit.*, 35 and note 162.

14. *Ibid.*, 36; for a different view, Picard, Ch., *Mélanges Maspero*, II, 1934-37, p. 319; earlier than the frieze of Telephos.

15. Rodenwaldt, *Die Kunst der Antike* (Propylaen Kunstg., III.), pl. 593.

16. *Ibid.*, pl. 572 b; Paribeni, R., *Le Terme di Diocleziano ed il Museo Nazionale Romano*,[2] 830.

leaves have an undulating outline and body. The grave monument of Ti. Claudius Philetus from the time of Nero, now in the Vatican,[17] is a good example of vine leaves whose modelling and general feeling is of the Flavian period.

These considerations indicate that the Copenhagen and Berlin fragments belong to table supports, and are best dated in the middle of the second century B. C. They are beautiful examples of fresh Hellenistic Pergamene art, of the years immediately after the building of the great Pergamene altar. They are replicas of the same prototype which must have been copied many times. The Athenian table support is a somewhat lifeless variation approximately of the time of Augustus.

17. Altmann, *op. cit.*, 268, fig. 203.

EIN SPAETANTIKES KOPFFRAGMENT AUS EPHESOS

GERDA BRUNS
Berlin

Tafeln 71-72

Aus deutschem Privatbesitz erwarben die Berliner Museen 1935 das Fragment eines wenig überlebensgrossen bärtigen Männerkopfes,[1] dessen Herkunftsangabe glaubhaft "die Gegend von Ephesos" lautet (Taf. 71, 72b). In den früheren Veröffentlichungen[2] wurde der Kopf als aus der Zeit des Marc Aurel stammend oder in dieser wurzelnd bezeichnet.

Die bisherigen Bearbeiter haben für die photographische Wiedergabe den Blickpunkt in Höhe des Wangenknochens gewählt. In der Frontalansicht[3] ergibt sich daraus ein sehr unangenehmer Kontur an der erhaltenen linken Kopfseite. Das weitausladende, gelockte Haupthaar fällt steil zur Schläfe ab. Auch die Stirne ist zur Schläfe hin eingezogen, der Wangenknochen darunter lädt stark aus. Der gerade in Höhe des Wangenknochens ansetzende Bart verbreitert das Mittelgesicht noch darüber hinaus, um dann bis zu seinem Ende hin beinahe die Linie eines Spitzbogens zu umreissen. Betrachtet man das Gesicht als solches, so liegt eine trotz der drei Querfurchen leere Stirn über schielenden und dabei etwas stupid blickenden Augen, die Nase ist sehr lang, der dicke Schnurrbart setzt hart und unerfreulich an, die Mundpartie ist flach. Ueber dem Ganzen liegt völlig unorganisch der Haarkranz.

Bei der Profilansicht[4] ist die Verdickung der Wange unerträglich gesteigert, bei der Dreiviertelansicht (Taf. 72, c) ist das Schielen der das Ganze beherrschende Eindruck; das Stück wirkt ausgesprochen unerfreulich.

Das Original aber stellt sich als gute Arbeit der Zeit um 400 n.Chr. dar. Auch bei unseren Aufnahmen (Taf. 71, 72, b) hat das Objektiv noch nicht die nötige Entfernung vom Objekt gehabt,[5] doch ist der Unterschied von den älteren Aufnahmen deutlich, und das Charak-

---

1. Inventar 1863. Höhe 34cm.

2. Heidenreich, *OeJh.* 27 (1932) 43ff. Abb. 66f. Poulsen, Fr., *Syria* 17 (1936) 55ff. Abb. 3f. Neugebauer, *Berichte der Vereinigung der Freunde antiker Kunst* 1936, 22 Abb.

3. *OeJh. a.O.* Abb. 66.

4. *OeJh. a.O.* Abb. 67.

5. Da der jetzige Aufenthaltsort des Kopfes nach dem Abtransport 1946 unbekannt ist, können keine neuen Aufnahmen hergestellt werden.

teristische des Kopfes erscheint so weit, dass seine Einordnung möglich ist.

Ein flaches und zugleich grossflächiges Gesicht ist rings von Haar umrahmt und dem Hinterkopf so vorgelegt, so wenig organisch verbunden, dass der Verlust des Schädels jetzt, bei der Betrachtung von vorn, kaum als wesentlich empfunden wird. Auf dem Kopfe gerade eben angelegt, bildet das Haupthaar über der Stirn einen reifartig aufgelegten Kranz aus unregelmässigen Locken, deren einzelne Strähnen durch Bohrlöcher aufgelockert sind. An der Schläfe setzt unter diesem "Reif" unvermittelt der Bart in ganz kurzen gewellten Strähnen an, sodass mehrere Reihen solcher Locken übereinander liegen. Der Bartansatz ist an der Wange und der bartfreien Unterlippe durch einzelne flüchtige Kerben merkwürdig unorganisch angegeben. Die gleiche Technik ist für die Augenbrauen angewendet. Unter den kurz gespannten Bogen liegen verhältnismässig klein und flach gebettet die Augäpfel, deren Iris und Pupillen wenig nach den inneren Augenwinkeln hin verschoben durch eine dreiviertelelliptische Umrisslinie um eine bohnenförmige Vertiefung gebildet werden. Während das Oberlid sich kräftig über dem Augapfel wölbt, spannt sich das Unterlid nur flach und dünn von Augenwinkel zu Augenwinkel. Das gibt dem Kopf den über den Betrachter hinweg in die Ferne gehenden Blick, der für spätantike Porträts charakteristisch ist. Die in der Wurzel kräftig ansetzende Nase ist schmal und lang, Rücken und Spitze, leider zerstört, dürften nicht allzu klein gewesen sein. Der flache schmallippige Mund ist leicht nach unten gebogen und vom Schnurrbart überschattet. Der Kopf fügt sich gut in das Bild ein, das L'Orange[6] für das theodosianisch-honorianische Porträt entworfen hat.

Die in der antoninischen Zeit ähnlich getragene Frisur[7] wird zum ersten Mal, nun aber voll ausgeprägt, wieder aufgenommen auf den beiden stilistisch späteren Sockelreliefs des Theodosius-Obelisken,[8] doch liegt hier das Haupthaar bedeutend tiefer in der Stirn, etwa so, wie bei dem Arkadius des Berliner Museums.[9] Auch bei den beiden Beamtenporträts aus Aphrodisias[10] umgibt das Haar den Kopf mehr als dass es ihn krönt. Die beste Möglichkeit der Trachtvergleichung bieten die Diptychen. Die flache Haardecke des Probia-

6. L'Orange, H. P., *Studien zur Geschichte des spätantiken Porträts*, 1933, 66ff.

7. Wegner, M., *Die Herrscherbildnisse antoninischer Zeit*, 1939, Taf. 3,9.

8. Bruns, G., *Der Obelisk und seine Basis auf dem Hippodrom zu Konstantinopel*, 1935, Abb. 37ff. 44ff. Kollwitz, J., *Oströmische Plastik der theodosianischen Zeit*, 1941, Taf. 35f. L'Orange a.O. Abb. 174, 176.

9. Blümel, C., *Römische Bildnisse* R. 122 Taf. 79f. L'Orange a.O. Abb. 185f. Delbrück, R., *Spätantike Kaiserporträts*, 1933, Taf. 103f.

10. Kollwitz a.O. Taf. 17f. 38f. L'Orange a.O. Abb. 202f. 205.

nus[11] (um 400) begrenzt die Stirn des Konsuls ebenso hart wie die Lockenfülle unser Porträt. Auch der Schreiber neben Probianus auf der Rückseite des Diptychons trägt die Frisur unseres Kopfes, während bei den Rednern auf den unteren Bildfeldern der Lockenkranz wieder tiefer in der Stirn liegt. Stilicho (um 395)[12] trägt die den Kopf in schönem Bogen umrahmende Frisur wie Arkadius, bei Probus (406)[13] ist das Haar über den äusseren Augenwinkeln in scharfer Ecke nach unten gekämmt. Diese Frisur ist ein Vorläufer derjenigen, die Konstantius III. (um 417)[14] und Felix (um 428)[15] tragen. Trachtmässig steht unser Kopf zwischen diesen beiden Gruppen. Stilistisch ist den kleinen Elfenbeinarbeiten das überlebensgrosse Marmorfragment nicht zu vergleichen.

Noch mühen wir uns um eine feste Datierung der Monumente dieser Zeit und noch ist keine völlige Sicherheit bei der Trennung in östliche oder westliche Reichskunst erreicht. Man hat früher versucht, in heidnische und christliche Werkstätten zu scheiden. Seit geraumer Zeit wissen wir, dass die gleichen Werkstätten für Heiden und Christen gearbeitet haben, von Glauben oder Weltanschauung her also eine Einordnung der Werke nicht durchzuführen ist. Wir sind in der glücklichen Lage, den Fundort des hier besprochenen Kopfes zu kennen; er stammt aus Ephesos, von der kleinasiatischen Küste. Und gerade bei ihm scheint nun deutlich, dass zwischen den Arbeiten aus Ephesos und denen aus dem benachbarten Aphrodisias enge Verwandtschaft aber auch ein gewisser Unterschied besteht, der vielleicht Beachtung verdient.

Grossporig wie bei einer übermässig starken photographischen Vergrösserung erscheint die Haut bei den ephesichen Plastiken. Unser Porträt ist das erste der Reihe, das bekannteste ist der Kopf Wien Inv.Nr. I 880,[16] doch auch Wien Inv.Nr. I 932[17] zeigt deutlich die gleiche Eigenschaft. Dick und ein wenig wollig steht das Haar gegen das Gesicht. Anders die Köpfe von Aphrodisias. Wie bei dem jugendlichen Gesicht Valentinians II.[18] ist auch bei den beiden älteren Männerstatuen, die in das Jahrzehnt vor und nach 400 datiert werden, das Gesicht von einer glattgeschlossenen Haut umspannt; strähnig oder flockig liegt der in Ritztechnik wiedergegebene Bart auf. In

---

11. Delbrück, R., *Die Consulardiptychen*, 1929ff. Taf. 65 (im folgenden *Diptychen* zitiert).
12. *Diptychen* Taf. 63.
13. *Diptychen* Taf. 1.
14. *Diptychen* Taf. 2.
15. *Diptychen* Taf. 3.
16. Kollwitz a.O. Taf. 43. L'Orange a.O. Abb. 216ff.
17. Kollwitz a.O. Taf. 44. L'Orange a.O. Abb. 199f.
18. Kollwitz a.O. Taf. 34. L'Orange a.O. Abb. 181ff.

höchster Vollendung zeigt diese Werkstattmanier der Brüsseler Kopf aus Aphrodosias.[19] Technisch bedingt ist dieser Unterschied darin, dass den ephesischen Köpfen die Politur fehlt; dass diese unterblieben ist, ist nicht Unfertigsein, sondern ein bewusstes Mittel künstlerischen Ausdrucks, das in dieser Werkstatt anscheinend durch ein halbes Jahrhundert gepflegt wird. Wie nahe im übrigen die Werkstattgepflogenheiten der Zeit untereinander stehen, zeigen die kurzen, gebogenen Ritzlinien am Bartansatz des ephesischen Kopfes, die an den Beamtenköpfen von Aphrodisias ihre nächste Parallele finden.[20]

Leider ist die Epidermis des Steines sowohl bei den Reliefs der Obeliskenbasis [21] wie bei den Resten der Theodosiussäule[22] und der Arkadiussäule[23] zu Konstantinopel so zerstört, dass sich für die Behandlung der Haut nichts mehr feststellen liess, als ich aus anderem Anlass die Monumente 1931 daraufhin untersuchte; ein Vergleich mit den gesicherten Werken der Hauptstadt muss also in dieser Richtung unterbleiben.[24]

Man glaubt aber die Frage stellen zu dürfen nach der geistigen Haltung der Porträtierten und nach der Art, wie sich der Künstler seiner Aufgabe gegenüber verhielt.

Es scheinen sich drei Gruppen von einander scheiden zu lassen.

Der Berliner Arkadiuskopf und die Valentiniansstatue, also Kaiserporträts, sind Idealbildnisse, deren Charakter weder mit dem Beiwort klassizistisch, noch mit höfisch ganz erfasst ist. Bereits hier sind die individuellen körperlichen Erscheinungsformen des Fürsten dazu benutzt, die Grundlage für das repräsentative Bildnis des Kaisers abzugeben, nicht um den Menschen zu charakterisieren, der das Amt des Herrschers versieht.[25]

In scharfem Gegensatz dazu stehen die Beamtenstatuen aus Aphrodisias, die ganz bewusst diesseitig (nicht idealisiert) zeitgebunden und zugleich vorwärtsschauend sind.

Man spricht häufig von dem verinnerlichten Blick der spätantiken Köpfe und denkt an die Auswirkung des religiösen Erlebnisses der Spätzeit. Mir scheint, die Nebeneinanderstellung der vier eben er-

---

19. Kollwitz, a.O. Taf. 37. Rodenwaldt, G., *Griechische Porträts aus dem Ausgang der Antike*, 76.BerlWPr. 1919, Abb. 7.

20. Bei dem Kopf Wien Inv.Nr. I 835 (L'Orange a.O. Abb. 219f.) ist die Oberfläche weitgehend korrodiert.

21. s.o. Anm.8 und L'Orange a.O. Abb. 178ff.

22. Kollwitz a.O. Taf. 1f. Schneider, *AA.* 1944/5 Taf. 28,2.3.

23. Kollwitz a.O. Taf. 5ff. L'Orange a.O. Abb. 177.

24. Bei dem qualitativ so ausnahmsweise hochwertigen Arkadiuskopf der Berliner Museen (jetziger Aufenthaltsort unbekannt) ist die Herkunft leider nicht festzustellen.

25. Buschor, E., *Bildnisstufen* 132ff.

wähnten Bildnisse zeigt eindringlich, dass auch hier die Verallgemeinerung eine Gefahr bedeutet.

In dem jüngeren Mann aus Aphrodisias sieht Kollwitz einen Nichtgriechen.[26] Das mag richtig sein, ist aber in unserem Zusammenhang nicht wesentlich, denn das Bildnis des Stilicho auf dem Elfenbeindiptychon[27] zeigt, dass auch ein Barbar durchaus klassizistisch-höfisch als Idealporträt wiedergegeben werden kann. Der "nicht übermässig sympathische" Eindruck beruht vielmehr darauf, dass die Züge einen bedenkenlos zielstrebigen, vielleicht sogar brutalen Charakter verraten. Dem älteren etwas sensibleren Manne dürfte es schwerer geworden sein, sich zu diesem "sacro-egoismo" durchzuringen, doch geht er den einmal beschrittenen Weg mit angemessener Härte. In der Auffassung hier zugehörig aber qualitativ bedeutend höher stehend schliesst sich der Brüsseler Porträtkopf[28] an, der wohl den charakterlich zartesten der drei Männer wiedergibt.

Wiederum eine andere Haltung — die dritte Gruppe — zeigt der ephesische Kopf in Berlin. Auch bei ihm drückt sich ein zielbewusstes klares Wollen, das sich wohl nicht immer nur vornehmer Mittel bedient hat, in den Zügen aus, doch ist das Antlitz bestimmt von dem bewussten Verzicht auf ein zwar nicht zu erreichendes aber dennoch unverrückbar geglaubtes Ideal, das zu jener Zeit stets verbunden scheint mit dem Willen zur Erhaltung der überkommenen Kultur. Es ist in den letzten Jahren des öfteren darauf hingewiesen worden, dass es in der Auswirkung nicht sehr wesentlich war, ob das Ideal als solches das Christentum oder eine der späten Formen antiker Philosophie verbunden mit einem der überlieferten Kulte war.

In Ephesos selbst findet sich in dem Zeitraum von 390 bis 410 nichts unserem Bildnis Vergleichbares, doch tritt die Menge der Beamtenporträts am Sockel des Theodosiusobelisken dafür ein, deren Erhaltungszustand ausreicht, um sagen zu können, dass hier und bei dem ephesischen Kopfe die gleiche Grundhaltung zu verspüren ist. Wir sind damit wieder in der Nähe der höfischen Kunst und erinnern uns des Berliner Arkadiuskopfes, der auf den ersten Blick dem ephesischen Beamtenkopfe so nahe verwandt erscheint. Beide Köpfe gehören zusammen in ihrer klassizistisch-retrospektiven Haltung, doch lebt der Arkadiuskopf, wie auch das Valentiniansporträt in konstantinischer Tradition, deren Form aus einem Wiederaufgreifen julisch-claudischer Stilformen erwachsen war; der Beamtenkopf dagegen lehnt sich an Antoninisches an. Die höfische Kameenkunst des

---

26. Kollwitz a.O. 123.
27. *Diptychen* Taf. 63.
28. Kollwitz a.O. Taf. 37.

4. Jahrhunderts[29] zeigt, dass die Anlehnung an claudische Formen
auf Konstantin I., die an hadrianisch-antoninische auf Julian zurückgeht, die beide politisch-weltanschauliche Absichten damit verbanden.
Von Julian an laufen die beiden klassizistischen Tendenzen neben der
offen "zeitgebundenen" Form her.

Gegen die Mitte des 5. Jahrhunderts scheint in dem Kaiserporträt
in Barletta[30] das zeitgebunden realistische, in dem Wiener Kopf Inv.
Nr. I 880[31] aus Ephesos das idealistisch-klassizistische Porträt —
beide nun in letztmöglicher Ausprägung — noch einmal greifbar.

So steht die offen zeitgebundene Gruppe, deren Hauptvertreter wir
um 400 in Aphrodisias antrafen, einer klassizistisch idealisierenden
Gruppe gegenüber, die in sich zerfällt in Fürstenporträts und solche
von Beamten, die man wohl richtig als offizielle Porträts anspricht.

Solch ein offizielles Porträt eines Mannes, dessen psychische Reife
weit über sein Lebensalter hinauszugehen scheint, das gut erfasst
und sauber ausgeführt ist, mag der hier vorgelegte Kopf sein. Um
400 wird er in der führenden Werkstatt von Ephesos vielleicht vom
Meister selbst hergestellt sein. Ob der dazu gehörige Körper mit der
Toga oder der Chlamys bekleidet war, vermögen wir nicht mehr festzustellen.

Handwerklich und künstlerisch scheinen die Köpfe von Aphrodisias
beziehungsweise Ephesos jeweils zusammen zu gehören. Ob sich
diesen Beobachtungen weitere hinzufügen lassen werden, die erlauben,
daraus Schulunterschiede zu entwickeln, muss spätere erneute Untersuchung der Originale sowie der nicht herangezogenen Stücke, besonders auch der Torsen, zeigen.

---

29. Bruns, G., *Staatskameen des 4. Jahrhunderts n.Chr.*, 104. *Berl.W.Pr.* 1948.
30. Kollwitz a.O. Taf. 42. Delbrück, *Spätantike Kaiserporträts* Taf. 116ff.
31. Kollwitz *a.O.* Taf. 43. L.Orange *a.O.* Abb. 216f.

SUR UN BAS-RELIEF DE CYRÈNE

FRANCOIS CHAMOUX
Paris

Planche 74

En offrant à M. D. M. Robinson ces commentaires sur un bas-relief
découvert à Cyrène, je tiens à rappeler que l'archéologie cyrénéenne
doit au savant jubilaire une contribution d'importance.[1] Puisse-t-il, à
la lecture de cette étude, évoquer le grand ciel et les vastes horizons
du Djebel-Akhdar, les "deux collines jumelles" et les "plaines aux
sombres nuées"![2]

Le document dont il s'agit a déjà été maintes fois publié, décrit et
commenté.[3] Il se présente sous la forme d'une plaque de marbre blanc
à grain fin, longue de 92 cm., haute de 50 cm., 5 épaisse de 19 cm. Elle
est sculptée sur les deux faces. *Face A* (pl. 74, a) : quatre personnages
sont encore visibles, au moins partiellement. A gauche, on a une scène
à deux personnages: un homme glabre, à demi-nu, est assis, face à
gauche, sur un siège du type appelé *klismos*. Il étend les bras en avant
et pose les mains sur l'épaule d'un homme barbu, à demi-nu, qui se
présente presque de face et dont la partie inférieure a disparu. Ce
personnage barbu a l'air d'être assis; de sa main gauche abaissée (qui
a disparu), il tenait peut-être le bord de son siège, tandis que de la
droite il s'appuyait sur un grand bâton noueux tenu verticalement.
Dans la partie droite du relief, il y avait une autre scène à deux personnages: un adolescent nu (dont la tête manque), tourné vers la
droite, présentait sa main droite à un autre homme assis sur un
klismos (le pied antérieur du *klismos* est conservé avec sa courbure
caractéristique). Mais il ne reste de ce dernier personnage que ses
deux jambes enveloppées dans son manteau. En haut et en bas, deux
listels, hauts de 4 cm. environ forment une saillie d'environ 3 cm. Le
listel supérieur a presque entièrement disparu.

Face B (pl. 74, b) : un seul personnage occupe tout le champ. C'est
un homme à demi-nu, étendu la tête vers la droite. Le coude gauche
s'appuie sur des coussins et la main gauche tient une phiale, tandis
que la main droite serre le rebord du lit, qui se confond avec le listel

---

1. *AJA* 17 (1913) 157-200, "Inscriptions From the Cyrenaica"; *A&A* (1915-16)
212-214 (sur l'Aphrodite de Cyrène).

2. Pindare, *Pythiques*, IX, 55 et IV, 52.

3. Oliverio, G., *Documenti antichi dell'Africa italiana*, II, 1, 1933, 100 sq.,
pl. XV; Becatti, G., *Critica d'arte*, V, 49 sq., pl. XVI-XVII; Fuhrmann, H., *J AA*
1941, 706 sq., fig. 160-161; Robert, L., *Hellenica*, II, 142 sq., pl. II.

placé sous le relief. Le visage est tourné vers la droite, mais le corps se présente presque de face. Un large bandeau plat, haut de 13 cm, occupe la partie inférieure de la plaque et porte une inscription dédicatoire. Il n'y avait pas de listel supérieur.

Les parties délicates de la sculpture ont beaucoup souffert. En outre deux angles opposés de la plaque ont disparu avec une partie importante des reliefs. La face B, dont le sujet est simple, n'a pas subi grand dommage, mais la face A, plus complexe, en est devenue plus difficile à interpréter.

L'inscription[4] qui figure sur la face B, après sa première publication par G. Oliverio, a été amendée et commentée par A. Wilhelm et surtout par L. Robert, dont je me borne à résumer brièvement les conclusions. Elle est datée, d'après l'ère d'Actium, en l'an 2 après J. C.; elle se compose d'un texte en prose, suivi d'une épigramme qui reprend en vers le même thème. A l'occasion de la fin heureuse d'une guerre contre les indigènes, le πυλοκλειστής L. Orbius, fonctionnaire subalterne du sanctuaire d'Apollon, a consacré en ex-voto l'image du prêtre éponyme Pausanias, sous le pontificat de qui les dieux avaient accordé la victoire au peuple de Cyrène. Pausanias était représenté en train de présider le banquet solennel qui avait célébré l'événement.

Si ce texte, savamment élucidé par les commentateurs, n'offre plus aujourd'hui de difficulté grave, il n'en est pas de même des deux bas-reliefs, dont la date et le sens ne me paraissent pas avoir été correctement établis jusqu'à présent. Ayant pu les étudier à loisir au cours d'un séjour à Cyrène en 1947, je crois pouvoir en proposer une nouvelle interprétation.

G. Becatti, en publiant le premier les deux côtés du monument, a cru qu'il s'agissait d'un relief à double face, de l'époque du style sévère, sans aucune relation, à l'origine, avec l'inscription: L. Orbius l'aurait simplement usurpé en y faisant graver son épigramme, heureux d'avoir à sa disposition, toute prête, une scène de banquet. H. Fuhrmann a combattu cette opinion. Selon lui, on aurait affaire, des deux côtés, à des pastiches archaïsants d'époque augustéenne, exécutés à la demande de L. Orbius. Cette interprétation n'a pas été contestée depuis lors, à ma connaissance. Elle a même été reçue avec faveur à l'occasion.

Or l'examen du document conduit à rejeter également la thèse de Fuhrmann et celle de Becatti: les deux reliefs ne traitent pas le même sujet et ils ne sont pas contemporains.

Une première remarque s'impose: s'il est certain que, sur la face B,

___

4. Oliverio, G., *loc. cit.;* Wilhelm A., *Wiener Studien*, 56, 71-72; *SEG* IX, 63; Robert, L., *op. cit.*, I, 7-17.

nous avons affaire à une scène de banquet, où a-t-on jamais vu dans les représentations figurées des hommes festoyant assis sur un *klismos?* Dans les pays grecs, ce sont les femmes qui sont assises dans les banquets. Les hommes, eux, sont toujours étendus sur des lits. Donc les scènes représentées sur la face A ne se rapportent pas à un festin. Leur sujet n'a rien de commun avec celui de la face B.

D'autres différences essentielles les séparent. *La mise en page:* sur la face A, deux listels étroits forment cadre en haut et en bas; sur la face B, un seul listel, beaucoup plus large, en bas. *Les dimensions des personnages:* celui de la face B est deux fois plus grand que les autres. *La composition:* sur la face B, un seul personnage occupe tout le champ; la disposition du relief correspond strictement à celle de l'inscription et il semble bien qu'il ne manque rien d'essentiel; sur la face A, au contraire, nous avons deux scènes séparées par une coupure très fortement marquée (les deux personnages centraux qui se tournent le dos); il est probable en outre que la composition primitive s'étendait plus loin vers la gauche, car le coude droit de l'homme barbu n'était sans doute pas directement sur le joint: il apparaît d'ailleurs, quand on examine la tranche, que ce côté a été grossièrement retaillé.

Enfin les deux bas-reliefs diffèrent considérablement par le style. Les analogies superficielles ne doivent pas ici faire illusion. La face A montre, en dépit des mutilations qu'elle a subies, un travail vigoureux, sûr et libre; le relief est franc, bien détaché du fond, qui reste à une profondeur constante; les attitudes sont justes, les gestes souples et naturels; la musculature est bien en place sur des corps bien proportionnés; les plis des vêtements, sobrement indiqués, sont d'un dessin sans aucune mièvrerie. Nous avons là assurément une oeuvre originale de l'époque du style sévère.

Une confirmation précieuse de cette date est fournie par l'étude du *klismos.* Il est en effet d'un type bien caractérisé: des lignes simples, un dossier encore bas, qui prolonge sans interruption la courbe des pieds postérieurs. Un tel siège apparaît précisément sur les représentations à l'époque du style sévère et disparaît bientôt après.[5] Il représente donc un indice chronologique très sûr qui renforce l'impression suggérée par la qualité du travail.

En revanche, sur la face B, quelle mollesse, quelle gaucherie, quelle négligence! Comme l'attitude est sans grâce, les bras courts et patauds, le rendu des muscles sommaire! Quoi de plus raide que ces deux jambes allongées l'une sur l'autre? La technique même de l'exécution est imparfaite: le fond du relief n'est pas régulier; certains

---

5. Richter, G. M., *Ancient Furniture*, 45 sq.

détails, comme les doigts de la main droite, sont plutôt gravés que taillés en relief; quant aux plis de la draperie, ils révèlent une singulière maladresse. L'ouvrage n'est pas de la même veine que celui de l'autre face: au lieu d'une oeuvre originale, nous avons affaire à un pastiche malhabile.

On comprend dès lors ce qui s'est passé. L. Orbius, πυλοκλειστής du sanctuaire, n'était pas, sans doute, un bien grand personnage: il suffit de regarder son inscription médiocrement gravée pour voir qu'il n'avait pas fait appel à un lapicide très qualifié. Comment aurait-il loué les services d'un sculpteur de premier plan? Le praticien auquel il s'est adressé lui a fourni du travail au rabais. Il s'est procuré un vieux relief de marbre mis au rebut et il y a taillé, au revers, l'effigie du prêtre Pausanias, seul sujet qu'on lui demandait de traiter. Il a d'ailleurs soigneusement ménagé la place destinée à l'inscription dédicatoire. Mais, en exécutant son travail, il n'a pas dédaigné de s'inspirer plus ou moins consciemment des restes de sculpture qui figuraient encore sur l'autre face: il a combiné platement la tête de l'homme assis avec le buste du vieillard barbu et il s'est efforcé, sans y parvenir, de reproduire le traitement aisé des draperies que lui fournissait son modèle. Il n'y a rien d'étonnant à cela: à l'époque de L. Orbius, les sculpteurs, depuis un siècle, avaient pris l'habitude d' archaïser pour répondre au goût de la clientèle.[6] Leurs combinaisons éclectiques embarrassent aujourd'hui encore les archéologues. Notre artisan cyrénéen, malgré son inexpérience, n'y a pas trop mal réussi!

Pareils remplois ne sont pas inconnus à Cyrène. S. Ferri a publié[7] une grande statue d'Apollon Pythien qui a été taillée, à l'époque d' Hadrien, sur un Asclépios du IIIème s. avant J. C. Le relief de L. Orbius prendra place désormais à côté de ce document curieux. Bien plus fréquents sont les remplois de bases en marbre, que l'on retournait avant de les utiliser à nouveau: de telles bases se remarquent fréquemment sur le champ de fouilles de Cyrène. Deux longues listes de noms, encore inédites, qui se trouvent dans les magasins du musée, ont été gravées sur la face interne de colonnes sciées en deux. C'est que le marbre était à Cyrène un matériau de luxe, qu'on faisait venir à grands frais de l'étranger. Quand, apporté des Cyclades ou de l'Attique, il avait été débarqué dans le port d'Apollonia, il fallait encore le hisser, au prix de quelles difficultés, jusqu'à la grande cité, à quelque 600 m. d'altitude—autant que Delphes. Or nous savons à Delphes,

---

6. Ces tendances archaïsantes, attribuées d'ordinaire à Pasitélès, Stéphanos et leurs successeurs, sont bien connues. J'ai eu l'occasion d'en traiter à mon tour en étudiant un Dionysos de bronze du Musée du Caire devant le Congrès international de Papyrologie qui s'est tenu à Paris en 1949. Cf. *BCH* 74 (1950) 78 sq.

7. *Africa italiana*, I, 1927, 116 sq.

par les comptes de IVème s., quels prix élevés il fallait payer pour le transport des pierres depuis le bord de la mer. Il n'en était pas autrement à Cyrène: d'où la fréquence des remplois.

*   *   *   *   *   *

Il n'est pas indifférent que nous possédions au dos de l'ex-voto de L. Orbius un bas-relief de style sévère. Il prend place parmi les oeuvres contemporaines d'Arcésilas IV (deuxième quart du V ème s.). La prospérité matérielle était considérable à cette époque dans la métropole libyenne. C'est alors sans doute qu'on achevait, sur la colline orientale, le grand temple de Zeus que G. Pesce a récemment fait connaître[8] et dont les dimensions s'égalent à celles du Parthénon. Plusieurs sculptures, malheureusement à peu près inédites, attestent la présence à Cyrène d'excellents artistes de ce temps: entre autres une admirable tête de déesse au diadème[9] et une belle tête de couros. Notre bas-relief ne leur est guère inférieur en mérite: il a dû être taillé vers les années 475-465.

G. Becatti, dans son étude, a bien marqué les rapprochements avec les sculptures d' Olympie. Toutefois il me semble que cette parenté est plus une parenté typologique qu'une parenté de style. Je crois, pour ma part, que le sculpteur de ce relief regardait surtout vers Athènes: ce ne serait nullement surprenant, car, dans le domaine de la sculpture, la dépendance de Cyrène vis-à-vis de l'art attique est flagrante et continue depuis le milieu du VIème s., comme j'aurai l'occasion de le montrer ailleurs.

Reste à déterminer le sens de la scène représentée, puisque l'exégèse de G. Becatti, qui voulait la rapporter à des Théodaisies, disparaît avec toute allusion à un banquet.

Le personnage principal de notre relief paraît bien avoir été l'homme assis sur un *klismos*, puisqu'il figurait dans chacune des deux scènes que nous pouvons encore y reconnaître. Or le *klismos* est un élément du mobilier quotidien, fréquemment reproduit dans les tableaux de la vie familière. En revanche il apparaît plus rarement dans les représentations divines: les dieux recevaient de préférence pour siège soit le trône, soit le tabouret, jugés sans doute plus dignes de leur condition. Ce n'est pas aujourd'hui seulement que le solennel exclut le confortable!

C'est donc du côté des représentations familières, ou des scènes mythiques qui s'en rapprochent le plus, qu'il faut plutôt chercher. On songera, par exemple, aux leçons de grammaire ou de musique,

---

8. *BCH* 71-72 (1947-48) 307 sq., pl. XLIX-LIX.
9. Cf. *Die Antike,* 19 (1943) 182, fig. 18.

dans lesquelles le maître se distingue souvent par le privilège du *klismos;*[10] ainsi un bas-relief de l'Acropole d'Athènes,[11] lui aussi de style sévère, montre un jeune garçon debout entre deux personnages assis sur des *klismoi.* H. Schrader l'a interprété comme un *agôn* musical, tout en soulignant que l'état de conservation du document ne permettait pas d'arriver à une certitude. Pour le relief de Cyrène, en tout cas, une telle explication est exclue: la scène de gauche ne peut convenir à une leçon et l'homme au *klismos,* étant imberbe, n'est sûrement pas un professeur.

La solution doit être cherchée, plus vraisemblablement, du côté des scènes de médecine.[12] Le *klismos* est fréquemment l'apanage du médecin ou d'Asclépios. Un bas-relief du Musée National d'Athènes[13] montre Asclépios, assis sur un *klismos,* au chevet d'un malade couché. Une base votive dédiée à Delphes par un médecin de Sélinonte[14] le représentait assis sur son siège, tandis que le patient se tenait debout devant lui. Si Asclépios apparaît assis sur un *klismos* sur un relief bien connu d'Epidaure,[15] c'est peut-être parce que, dans la vie courante, ce siège était souvent celui des médecins.

Il faut attribuer une valeur particulière, pour l'intelligence de notre document cyrénéen, à un aryballe attique du Louvre, de style classique, autrefois publié par E. Pottier.[16] On y voit un jeune médecin glabre, à demi-nu, assis sur un *klismos,* en train de soigner le bras d'un malade debout devant lui (pl. 74, c). Nous pouvons restituer sur ce modèle la scène de droite de notre relief: un médecin sur son *klismos* y soignait la main que lui tendait le jeune garçon.

Quant à la scène de gauche, son interprétation a échappé jusqu'à présent aux commentateurs à cause d'une erreur qu'ils commettaient sur le personnage barbu. Ils croyaient y reconnaître un Silène ou un Dionysos, à cause de son masque qui rappelle en effet les figures de ces divinités. Mais le bâton noueux sur lequel il s'appuie n'a rien d'un thyrse et interdit cette exégèse: c'est la canne que portent habituellement les hommes d'âge sur les peintures de vases. Quant à sa barbe

---

10. Cf. par exemple le skyphos Schwerin (Diepolder, *Penthesileamaler,* pl. IV; Buschor, *Griech.Vasen,* fig. 181) ou la coupe de Douris à Berlin (Buschor, *op. cit.,* fig. 178).

11. Musée de l'Acropole, Inv. 3716; Schrader, H., *Marmorbildwerke, Text,* 300, no. 421, fig. 348.

12. La première suggestion dans ce sens m'a été donnée par M.Ch. Picard, que je remercie vivement.

13. *Dict. des Antiquités,* III, 1684, fig. 4882 (*s.v.Medicus*).

14. *Fouilles de Delphes,* III, 1, 330 sq., fig. 48-49.

15. Charbonneaux, J., *La sculpture grecque classique,* II, pl. 66.

16. *Mon.Piot* 13 (1907) pl. XIII-XIV; photo Giraudon 34721 (reproduite ici fig. 3). Je dois la connaissance de ce document à M. P. Devambez, que je remercie vivement.

et à sa chevelure, elles ont l'apparence qu'elles prennent à cette époque chez tous les personnages barbus, et non pas seulement chez les Silènes: que l'on songe aux guerriers d'Egine, ou au Poséïdon de Créüsis,[17] ou encore aux maîtres d'école sur la fameuse coupe de Douris, à Berlin. Nous avons affaire à un bon bourgeois de la ville qui est venu consulter l'homme de l'art pour une luxation de l'épaule ou pour un rhumatisme. Il se laisse aller sur son siège bas, car le patient ne prend pas un siège à dossier, et le médecin, de ses mains expertes, tâte l'épaule malade pour faire un massage ou pour remettre le membre en place. Ce geste si léger et si souple ne peut être destiné, comme on l'a cru, à soutenir un ivrogne qui chancelle: il aurait fallu pour cela montrer les deux bras tendus, et non fléchis. Au reste, le patient barbu, bien appuyé sur son bâton, ne perd pas du tout l'équilibre; il se laisse seulement aller sur son siège et présente l'épaule au médecin.

On pourrait penser aussi à une simple imposition des mains qui aurait une vertu magique. Les exemples ne manqueraient pas.[18] Il faudrait alors considérer le personnage du guérisseur, non comme un médecin ordinaire, mais comme un Asclépios imberbe ou comme un héros. Le type d'Asclépios imberbe n'est pas inconnu: précisément vers l'époque de notre relief, Calamis en avait fait un pour Sicyone.[19] D'autre part on sait qu'à Cyrène le rôle de héros guérisseur fut assumé par Aristée, fils de la nymphe éponyme.[20] Mais son culte n'est attesté sous cette forme qu'à basse époque. La vraie nature de notre personnage, dieu, héros ou mortel, reste donc incertaine.

Rien n'empêche que le bas-relief ait fait partie d'une frise décorant un petit édifice. On imagine bien toute une série de scènes à deux personnages illustrant ainsi l'efficacité d'une divinité secourable. Mais il peut s'agir aussi d'un simple relief votif.

Il est intéressant d'avoir à Cyrène un document attestant dès 470 la prospérité de l'art médical. Nous ne pouvons évidemment savoir où ce relief avait été primitivement consacré: le fait qu'il ait été remployé par un fonctionnaire du sanctuaire d'Apollon est toutefois

---

17. Picard, Ch., *Manuel*, II, 155, fig. 71; Langlotz, *Frühgr.Bildhauersch.*, pl. 22h.

18. Sudhoff, "Handanlegung des Heilgottes auf att. Weihtafeln," *Archiv für Gesch.der Medizin*, 18 (1926) 235 sq.; Herzog, R., *Die Wunderheilungen von Epidauros*, 55; *AM* 35 (1910) 2 sq., pl. I, 2 (relief de Cassel). On trouvera dans Herzog, *op. cit.*, *frontispice*, le relief votif no. 3369 du Musée National d'Athènes (cf. *Ephemeris* 1916, 120), où un malade est soigné pour une plaie à l'épaule.

19. Pausanias II, 10, 3. Autres exemples à Phlionte (II, 13, 5), à Trézène (par Timothéos, II, 32, 4), à Gortys d'Arcadie (par Scopas, VIII, 28, 9). Cf. *RE* II, 1690, *s.v.Asclepios* (Thrämer).

20. *Africa italiana*, II, 17-29 (L. Vitali). Les conclusions de L. Vitali ne me paraissent valables que pour l'époque des Antonins.

une présomption pour qu'il ait appartenu aux offrandes ou à un monument de ce sanctuaire. Pindare, à la même époque, rappelait dans la Vème Pythique le pouvoir guérisseur d'Apollon, le grand dieu archégète de Cyrène.[21] Un passage d'Hérodote (III, 131), qui n'est d'ailleurs peut-être qu'une glose, montre que les médecins de Cyrène jouissaient d'une grande réputation: ils ne le cédaient, nous dit-il, qu'aux seuls médecins de Crotone. A. Balagrai, à quelque 16 km. de Cyrène, il y avait un sanctuaire d'Asclépios, qui existait dés le IVème s.[22] Un compte des démiurges, au IVème s., mentionne au chapitre des dépenses un ἰατρὸς ποθ' ἑσπέραν.[23] J'ai signalé déjà la statue dédiée, au IIIème s., à Asclépios par Thémisôn, fils d'Aristis, statue sur laquelle on retailla plus tard un Apollon Pythien.[24] Enfin l'existence d'un trésor d'Esculape nous est connue au Ier s. de l'empire par un texte de Tacite (*Annales*, XIV, 18).

Le bas-relief réutilisé par L. Orbius vient enrichir ces rares indications sur la médecine à Cyrène. Il nous fait entrevoir combien elle était déjà développée dans cette grande ville africaine, bien des années avant qu'Hippocrate ne lui donnât l'impulsion décisive à travers le monde grec. Lorsque la mission américaine de 1910 tint à s'adjoindre un médecin pour étudier l'état sanitaire des populations libyennes, elle se montrait ainsi fidèle à une très ancienne tradition.

---

21. *Pyth.*, V, v. 63-64.
22. Pausanias II, 26, 9. Sur le sanctuaire de Balagrai, cf. *RE, s.v. Balagrai;* Vitali, L., *Fonti per la storia della religione cirenaica*, 133; Guarducci, M., *Inscr. Creticae*, I, 151; *SEG* IX, 347.
23. *SEG* IX, 13, 17. Autre mention d'un médecin public: *SEG* IX, 1, 43sq.
24. *SEG* IX, 74. Cf. aussi *ibid.*, 75.

A MARBLE HEAD AT UNION COLLEGE[1]

FRANK P. ALBRIGHT
Union College

Plate 81

In 1938 the members of the Psi Upsilon Fraternity of Union College dedicated an ancient marble head of a youth to Walter C. Baker for his benevolent interest in refurbishing the Psi Upsilon house. No information about the head or its provenience is obtainable save what can be gathered from a study of its style and workmanship.

The head (pl. 81) is of a white micaceous marble (probably from the Greek Islands) and shows some cleavage in a plane parallel to the top surface of the nose; a few faults are quite pronounced. The back of the head and a few spots on the face show yellow discoloration from contact with iron oxide. The left side of the face is considerably eroded from behind the ear to the nose and from several inches up in the hair down to the jaw. The neck is broken off immediately under the chin. The nose had been broken off and cemented on with a marble-dust cement. The lips are somewhat chipped, giving the appearance of a harelip, and numerous curls of the hair are broken away.

The heavy head of hair is a mass of curls, wild and high over most of the area but low and flat over the left eye and temple and on the right side of the back (pl. 81), as if the sculptor found his marble too shallow in these places. The curls appear to be piled on rather than to grow naturally out of the scalp. They are cut with a running drill and most of them have deep holes in their centers. The work is very uneven, less extravagant and better executed on the left side than on the right (pl. 81, c, d). The hairline is uneven all around, being lower on the left than on the right. The hair on the front is cut deeper than the forehead. A rectangular hole, measuring about ½ inch by ¾ inch and nearly ½ inch deep, is cut in the hair about three inches above the left ear, with the longer sides aligning downward and just back of the ear. Parallel to it and 2½ inches farther back is a similar cut, though not so readily noticeable. These two cuts are connected by the top ends of a shallow irregular groove in the shape of a Y, the tail of which falls just back of the ear. There are probably similar cuts on the right side of the head although the irregular and broken condition of the hair makes it uncertain. These are the

---

1. Height 24.8 cm (9¾ inches. Width 22.9 cm (9 inches). Depth 20.6 cm (8⅛ inches).

only indications for hair ornaments[2] and they were not planned for when the hair was sculptured. The forehead is very low with an arched hairline and a slight horizontal depression.

The straight nose is rather broad at the bridge and narrow at the tip with small nasal wings (pl. 81, a). It bends slightly to the left. The nostrils are drilled nearly ¼ inch deep at a distance of less than 1/16 inch from the break. The nose is undoubtedly not the original one, though it is of similar stone and has received a heavy percussion on the lower left of the tip. But the original nose could not have differed much from the present one. No eyebrows are indicated other than the rather angular edge of the eye socket. The eyelids are nearly equal in width throughout with sharp edges, deeply undercut at the corners. This deep undercutting, and some recutting on the outside of the lids at the corners, was apparently done after the head had been polished, probably at the time the nose was repaired. The eyeballs are spherical with broken-circle pupils within vague outer circles representing the corneae, almost invisible in the right eye. The tops of the corneae are hidden by the upper lids but the pupils are in full view. The eyes look slightly to the right. The full sensuous lips of the somewhat narrow mouth are slightly parted revealing the upper teeth, which are distinctly marked off. The ears are quite simple, with ample, rounded lobes, and are partly concealed by the hair. This is especially so of the left ear.

The head is evidently a copy or adaptation, from memory, of the "Hermes" of Praxiteles. All the essential features are there as one would take mental note of them: the large proportion of the head taken up by the very curly hair; the low, crescent-shaped forehead with its horizontal depression; the plain and even eyelids; the straight nose with its high and wide bridge and narrow wings; the narrow mouth with full lips; the round-lobed ears. But our head lacks the well modeled facial muscles of the "Hermes"; the jaw is wider and the forehead narrower; edges, such as the eye sockets, nose and the like, are cut more sharply. That flattening of surfaces and sharpening of edges gives the head an archaistic appearance (from the Roman point of time as well as from ours) and is characteristic of idealized statues. The lack of symmetry in the head as a whole and in every feature of it is to be attributed to carelessness and lack of competent ability. The same can be said for the confusion of the hair.

The Union College head was probably made in the time of Marcus Aurelius or slightly later. During the period from Hadrian to Com-

---

2. They could have been metal wings. Cf. the Minturnae Hermes, *AJA* 39 (1935), 448 f., fig. 1 and 2, where the wings are of marble.

modus many Greek statues were copied, usually without the fine
surface modeling, or the feeling of form beneath, of the originals.
The plastic deepening of the pupil of the eye came in under Hadrian,
with the broken-circle pupil in normal use from Marcus Aurelius to
Commodus or Septimius Severus. This type of eye was no new thing
at the time of our head and was used as a matter of course, even
though the original had smooth eyeballs. The bold locks of hair,
effecting a nervous interplay of shadow, and the abundant use of the
drill are also characteristic of the second half of the century, as are
the polished surface (though this is no proof of date *ante quem non*)
and the side-long glance of the eyes. The type is similar to the Diadou-
menos in the Metropolitan Museum[3] in New York with more of a
tendency toward naturalism and less modeling of the facial muscles.
Judging from this quality and from the technique of the hair it is
later in date.

3. *AJA* 39 (1935) 46-52, pls. XII-XV.

A HEROIC STATUE FROM PHILADELPHIA-AMMAN

J. H. ILIFFE
City of Liverpool Public Museums

Plates 75-80

During the early months of 1947 it came to the knowledge of the Department of Antiquities of the Transjordan Government that a find had recently been made in Amman of a full-size ancient marble statue.[1] At first a photograph only of the head was produced, accompanied by some obviously fabricated story of its origin; further enquiries led to the production of piece after piece and eventually revealed the nearly complete statue here published[2] (pl. 75). It appeared that, while clearing a level space for building a house, nearly half way up the S.E. face of the Citadel hill, the owner of the land had come upon fragments of the statue, scattered about along a sort of terrace. A clearance of the immediately adjacent area by Mr. G. W. L. Harding of the Department of Antiquities resulted in the exposure of fragments of masonry, several capitals and other architectural fragments including a Roman Ionic capital with a fillet binding, evidently the remains of an exedra or platform for the group to which our figure belonged.[3] The site occupies a commanding position on the cliff-like S.E. face of the Citadel hill, overlooking the theatre, one of the principal surviving monuments of the Roman City, at a distance of some 300 metres. It would, therefore, have been in full view from the region of the theatre and its approaches. Such a position implies that it was among the chief public monuments of second and third century Philadelphia, "City of the Decapolis". The fragments of the statue were taken to the Palestine Archaeological Museum in Jerusalem, where they were photographed and studied, and a beginning made on the reconstruction of the whole figure, as will be seen from the photographs. Owing, however, to the disturbed state of the country and the cessation of the British Mandate over Palestine, the Transjordan Government requested the return of the statue to Amman, together with all the other Transjordan antiquities hitherto housed in the Museum at Jerusalem. This was done and at

---

1. Cat. No. P.A.M., R. 1381 (Jerusalem), T. J., J. 933 (Amman).

2. Cf. Illustrated London News, 6 Sept. 1947, p. 275.

3. A thorough search along the whole edge of the terrace was precluded by lack of funds. It would have gone beyond the limits of a clearance and developed into a full-scale excavation, very desirable on this Citadel of the former Raboth Ammon and Philadelphia, but which the means available and the circumstances of the time did not permit.

the moment of writing[4] the pieces are still stored in packing-cases in Amman.

The statue is a remarkable and interesting one to have been found in Amman; although a full knowledge of Roman Imperial art in that remote region of Peraea, the Decapolis, would probably remove any grounds for surprise at the existence of such a purely classical work in a Semitic context. The overall height of the figure, excluding any base there may have been, was approximately 1.90 metres; the height of the head 0.27 metres. It was thus rather more than life size. Technically, it is made up of five originally separate pieces, each carved from a separate block, i.e. head and trunk, two arms and two legs, joined together by metal, probably iron, cramps. This practice is common in both Greek and Roman sculpture[5] as a recognized method of economizing marble in figures or groups, especially those involving pronounced movement or separation of the parts; it is however, not so well known as it should be, the handbooks being usually more concerned with style than with technique. Examples are most of the Acropolis Korai, the Demeter from Cnidus, the Farnese Herakles, and the Venus de Milo. It was practiced from archaic Greek down to Imperial Roman times, in the finest marble as well as the coarser limestones and poros; no shame attached to the process. It was a natural treatment for wooden figures, readily put together from separate pieces, while the chryselephantine technique necessarily involved the fitting together of different materials. It is always to be remembered that in classical Greece marble was not the most usual material for statues, bronze being far more common and ivory by no means rare. The head of our statue has at some time been accidentally broken off from the trunk, with which it originally formed one piece. Further than this, however, the right leg, which bore the whole weight of the body, and the left arm, raised aloft and supporting some heavy object,[6] were pierced longitudinally by tubular drill-holes some .05 m. in diameter, into which had apparently been inserted cylindrical metal bars, perhaps encased in or wedged with wood, as supports to strengthen these limbs. (pl. 79a, b, c). This latter is a feature to which so far I have been unable to find a parallel elsewhere, either for the use of such internal supporting bars, or the employment in classical sculpture of a tubular drill and one of such

4. May 1949.

5. Cf. Richter, G. M. A., *The Sculpture and Sculptors of the Greeks*, 111-12; Daremberg et Saglio, *Dict.*, 1143-4.

6. Perhaps the child of which fragments were found with the statue. Cf. below.

considerable size.[7] Casson[8] states that the tubular drill is unknown
in "classical sculpture", after being commonly used in Mycenaean.
Nor is it mentioned in Daremberg and Saglio's article *Sculptura*,
either in reference to Greek or Roman sculpture. May we then conclude that here we have the sole evidence for the practice, and that
in Roman times? If so, we must ask whether this is due to the extreme rarity of the practice or the fact that it has not hitherto been
reported. It would seem improbable that the present statue was an
isolated phenomenon; perhaps, however, the technique may have been
confined to the East. In any event the author of our group must have
been of an experimental turn of mind in regard to the means of supporting statues in different attitudes, since he has also chiselled out
the abdomen of the child to reduce its weight.

Here we have another step, so far unrecorded, in the progress of
Greek Sculpture towards emancipation from the bonds of the first
stiff *kouros* attitude, and a further reason for remarking the originality and versatility of the sculptor of the present work and his school.
Greek we may legitimately describe it, deriving as it patently does
from the Hellenistic background of either Anatolia or Syria. Unfortunately the main portion of both arms is missing, so that one can
only conjecture their exact pose and employment. The cramps connecting the separate pieces of the figure (to judge from the holes for
them) were of square section, which the rods used to strengthen the
two limbs were cylindrical (pl. 79d, e and 80a). At the back of
either shoulder is a rectangular socket or dowel-hole, apparently
for the reception of a metal cramp to secure the figure to the wall
against which it stood (pl. 77). The back would therefore not be
visible, and is accordingly only summarily finished; nor is the crossed
sword-belt on the chest continued right round the back. Of possible
significance in the identification of the statue is the fact that associated more or less closely with the pieces there were found also
several fragments of a youthful, boyish figure, a chubby right arm
from shoulder almost to wrist, with the elbow bent at right angles,
part of a left foot with the toes chipped off, and the left side of a
youthful abdomen, from navel to groin (pl. 80c, d, e). This last, which
was found broken into two pieces, had been hollowed out with a
chisel (pl. 80b), evidently to reduce its weight, indicating that the
youthful figure to which it belonged was either being carried or supported aloft in such a position that weight was a matter of impor-

---

7. See pl. 79, a, b, c, for the tubular drill-holes, espec. pl. 79 a for the tell-tale remains of the broken-off core inside the right thigh. Cf. the traces of a similar drill
on the Lion Gate at Mycenae, Casson, *Technique of Early Greek Sculpture*, 210.

8. *loc. cit.*

tance, another novel detail in the present work. We may add this to the various methods already familiar of lightening or supporting the projecting or insecurely balanced portions of a statue; it would be very appropriate in a marble copy from a bronze original. The upper edge of the abdomen fragment (just visible in pl. 80c) shows a surface finished off flat and square by a saw, suggesting that, like the main figure, this also may have been constructed of several pieces, despite its smaller size.

A single glance at the head and features of this statue enables one to recognize that in it we have a new work of the first importance, an original work of vigorous and arresting style, assignable to the Antonine period or shortly afterwards (pl. 76). The statue represents a man or hero in the prime of life, pressing forward in violent movement, carrying on his upraised left arm someone or something; his agonized gaze is directed upwards and to his left towards some adversary or danger (pl. 78). His whole weight is placed on the right leg, as in running; the left foot does not touch the ground.[9] The right arm is raised to about the horizontal, as if aiming a weapon against an approaching adversary. He leans over to his right to get every ounce of strength behind the blow. He is nude except for a chlamys thrown loosely over his left shoulder, falling transversely in folds across to his right thigh and held by a belt around the waist, and that strange harness of double straps crossing over his chest. The agonized expression on his face is typical of that of the stricken opponents of Zeus or of the other Olympians in various combats of gods and giants;[10] it is the principal element linking our figure in style with the Pergamene sculptors, who notoriously favored subjects in which it might find expression.[11]

The material of which our group was carved is a crystalline, coarse-grained white marble, susceptible of a very high surface polish. In parts it has a greyish-blue tone, e.g. in the trunk; in others, e.g. right leg and arm, there are scattered flecks in the marble. Such marbles with black flecks or veins occur in the N. Syria-Asia Minor region, where these veins are sometimes treated today as an added decorative element.[12] Blue and white marble occur together in quarries close to the ancient Aphrodisias.[13] In the description of one of the statues

9. See pls. 78 and 80 f, showing the sole of the left foot.
10. e.g. Alkyoneus seized by Athena, on a slab of the Great Altar of Pergamon.
11. The resemblance to the "Ludovisi Gaul" in this and other respects is very close. Cf. Beazley and Ashmole, *Greek Sculpture and Painting*, fig. 170; Brunn Bruckmann, *Denkmäler*, 422.
12. I have this on the authority of an Armenian craftsman in Jerusalem formerly resident in the Aintab-Aleppo area.
13. Mendel, *Musées Imperiaux Ottomans, Cat. des sculptures grecques, romaines et byzantines*, II, 179.

from Aphrodisias in the Glyptotek Ny Carlsberg[14] in Copenhagen the marble is described thus: 'le marbe fortement bleuâtre apparenté a celui de Proconnèse qu'on employait à Pergame'. Several of the works of Aphrodisias sculptors[15] in the Glyptotek Ny Carlsberg are carved in Asiatic or other foreign (i.e. non-Italian) marbles. In addition, the well known pair of Centaurs in the Museo Capitolino signed by Aristeas and Papias, sculptors of Aphrodisias, are in black marble, probably to suggest bronze.

The first parallel that leaps to the mind on seeing the statue is the Laocoon. Here is just the same type of subject, the same agony expressed in a very similar pose, the same straining muscles of chest and abdomen, the same emphasis on the contrast between the smooth, highly-polished surface of the face and the wild, snaky locks of hair, a comparable attitude, as far as one may infer from the surviving portions of our figure, and finally, the puzzling fragments of a youth found with it. The sculptor of the Amman group must have had the Laocoon in mind. There are also strong resemblances in pose to the Gauls and Giants of the first dedication of Attalus at Pergamon, and in both style and attitude to figures of Giants on the frieze of the Great Altar. Thus the straining muscles of the trunk may be paralleled in the Gauls of the first dedication,[16] and our figure might almost have stepped out of the mêlée of gods and giants which adorned the "Throne of Satan".[17] It also calls to mind the attitude of the splendid fighting Gaul from Delos in Athens (Beazley and Ashmole, *Greek Sculpture and Painting*, fig. 173). It seems evident that in this direction is the lineage of our statue to be sought. An implication of its being a marble version of a bronze group would be to reinforce the parallel with the surviving figures of the first dedication of Attalus.

A closer examination of the style of the head with its strong contrast between the flesh of the face and the hair suggests an Antonine date: this is borne out by the treatment of the eyes, the pupils of which are indicated by incised circles (pl. 76). The flame-like locks which rise from the forehead and the luxuriant growth of soft down-like curly beard from the smooth cheeks are paralleled in numerous heads of Antonine and early third century date, e.g the so-called

---

14. Arndt, *La Glyptothèque Ny Carlsberg*, 222 ff.

15. On the Aphrodisias School v. Squarciapino, *Afrodisia*; Toynbee, *The Hadrianic School, Appendix* 1, 242ff.; Loewy, *Inschriften Griechischer Bildhauer*, 257ff.

16. Cf. Brunn Bruckmann 80, 421-2, 425, 481-2.

17. Cf. e.g. Rodenwaldt, *Die Kunst der Antike (Hellas und Rom)*, 441ff. (espec. p. 441, head of a giant) in Propyläen-Verlag, Berlin.

"Rhoimetalkes"[18] or the colossal head of Zeus from Aigeira.[19] Despite the loss of chin and with it much of the beard and also the chipping off of part of the moustache, the face has on the whole suffered little damage. It can be seen that the mouth was slightly open in pain, surprise or fear. In particular the surface of the flesh has retained the extremely high degree of polish[20] characteristic of much ancient sculpture after the 5th century B. C., and especially frequent in the early Empire; well-known examples are the Hermes of Olympia and the Aphrodite of Cyrene, but many less known statues show the same treatment, e.g. a fine version of the Cnidian Aphrodite in the possession of the Duke of Bedford.[21] This polish is so high on those parts of the present statue where it has not suffered damage as to give a surface almost like porcelain in its glossy whiteness; a characteristic which also links the main statue with the youthful fragments found with it, among which the bent elbow retains an identical high surface finish. Notable among the tricks of our sculptor are the spiral curls of the beard (pl. 75, 76), and the tiny bridges from lock to lock left by the drill in both hair and beard (pl. 75). This Antonine detail has many parallels, e.g. in heads on the Ludovisi Battle Sarcophagus in the Terme at Rome.[22] On the top of the head at the back the hair has just been roughly blocked out with the chisel.

In pl. 78 the statue is shown as provisonally reconstructed in Jerusalem omitting certain fragments, e.g. of the left arm, which did not connect. These additional fragments are shown in pl. 79, b, c. It is significant that they belonged to the two limbs which were specially reinforced to bear an extra weight. Despite this they broke, justifying the sculptor's fears. The *puntello* on the left thigh (pl. 80, g) indicates a point of support, apparently for some heavy object held on the left arm. Could this be the youthful figure of which fragments were found? If so, what is the subject? Or was it just a shield? The separate portion of the right leg, showing the muscles above the knee strongly flexed, has been restored in approximately its correct position as nearly as calculation permitted. The whole weight of the figure is clearly taken for an instant by this knee, the left leg being directed backwards with the foot quite clear of the ground as in the

---

18. Heller, *Greek and Roman Portraits*, 261: "An unknown barbarian (so-called Christ)": Athens (Nat. Mus.).

19. Walter, *Jahreshefte*, 19-20 (1919) 1ff., *taf.* 1, 2.

20. The γάνωσις ("oiling") mentioned by Plutarch, *cf.* Daremberg et Saglio, *Dict.*, 1147.

21. Included in the Exhibition of Greek Art at the Royal Academy, 1946, *Greek Art: A Commemorative Catalogue etc.* By J. Chittenden and Charles Seltman. No. 152, Pl. 40, 41.

22. Rodenwaldt, *Die Kunst der Antike*, 620, 621.

act of running. This left foot provides an object lesson to the sculptor
in marble or stoneworker, to beware of using iron: the forepart of
the foot had evidently been snapped off anciently and reattached with
a simple iron dowel, which as it expanded with oxidization and rust
had split the forepart of the foot in two again (pl. 80, f): they held
together only by long association. We separated the two parts in
the workshop, removed the iron dowel, and reattached the fragment
to the rest of the foot with cement. From the absence of any iron
oxide or rust marks on the internal surface of the tubular drill holes
except at the ends, and apparently a patch in the centre arm fragment
(pl. 79, b), it would appear that the iron bars may have been cased in
wood, and driven in wedge fashion: there is no trace of e.g. lead.
One of the square iron cramps holding the left arm, however, has left
considerable traces of iron oxidization on the marble of the shoulder,
at the junction.

By whom was our statue made, and where? Whom does it represent? To the first of these questions I would like to suggest that it
is a work of or deriving from the well-known School of Aphrodisias,
which flourished both in Asia Minor and in Italy, from the IInd to
the IVth century A. D. The quality of the work argues it the product
of no minor, local sculptor. The whole breadth of the conception, the
vigorous sweep of its execution and its classic proportions all proclaim it by a master hand. Being made in sections it could easily have
been carved elsewhere, transported to Philadelphia and assembled
there, like several of the sculptures found at Aphrodisias and now in
the Museum at Constantinople. The Aphrodisias sculptors were also
evidently fond of the gigantomachy as a subject and of adding pieces
of a statue separately.[23] It may be a copy of some well-known bronze
figure which has not survived. The subject might well be drawn from
a wall-painting or a vase of the Polygnotan circle. The Pergamene
analogies above noted, the Laocoon, even perhaps something of
Mausolus, would all have been familiar to the sculptors of Aphrodisias.
Such a statue as this would consort well with all we know of their
work.

There should be nothing surprising in the occurrence at this time
of a work of purely Greek inspiration in Raboth Ammon-Philadelphia
of the Decapolis. From neighboring Jerash we have the fine marble
head of a IIIrd century Zeus, possibly re-used in the Christian period
as a representation of Christ,[24] and the hoard from a potter's work-

---

23. Cf. Mendel, *loc. cit.* II, 176ff. (group of sculptures from Aphrodisias).
24. Cf. British Museum Quarterly, 1, 114, pl. LX. *Illustrated London News*
31.7.1926, *pp.* 193*ff.*

shop of IInd century pottery figurines, all in the Classic style of Imperial art, with hardly a suggestion of the Oriental milieu in which they were produced.[25]

No entirely satisfactory identification for the subject of the statue or group has yet occurred to me. An attractive but daring suggestion is Salmoneus,[26] who is represented on the column Krater in the Art Institute at Chicago[27] being struck down by Zeus with his thunderbolts, after he had impiously dared to set himself up in opposition and aspired to hurl the divine thunderbolts himself.[28] But it is a far cry from a 5th century B. C. Athenian vase painting to a 2nd or 3rd century A. D. statue in a remote provincial Syrian town. The chief point of this parallel is that Salmoneus on the vase does wear a similar double harness crossing on his chest, the sole example so far noted. The fate of Salmoneus and his pose on the vase are very similar to those of the giants of the Pergamene sculptors; they might offer an analogy to the attitude of our statue, but neglect entirely the youthful figure which a satisfactory identification must take into account. The series of gods carrying a child, e.g. Hermes or a satyr with the infant Dionysus, must equally be rejected. Here we have no half serious divine escapade: the actors are in deadly earnest. The type of subject which would fit is one from that Pergamene repertory which includes "A Gaul slaying his wife" (Ludovisi Gaul). After some desperate act the man snatches up his infant son and rushes away with him headlong. The Trojan War might perhaps also provide analogous subjects, of the type of Aeneas rescuing his father Anchises. It should be either a heroic episode or a historic one that time has made legendary.

---

25. Quarterly of the Department of Antiquities in Palestine, 2 (1945) 1-26, pls. I-II.

26. A suggestion put forward with reservations by C. T. Seltman, of Queens' College, Cambridge. Mr. Seltman pertinently adds, "But *why* Salmoneus in Amman?!!", and, admitting the improbability reminds me that Salmoneus was father of Tyro (Tyre), not so far away! We are again reduced to the fact that the only analogy is that Salmoneus is the sole heroic (or other) figure we know of wearing those crossing breast straps, not a very secure base for an identification.

27. Cf. *AJA* 1899, pl. 4; Cook, A. B., in *Classical Review*, 17 (1903) 275-6; Roscher, *Lex. s.v.*; Beazley, *Attic Red Figure*, 396, 24.

28. Cf. the story in Virgil, *Aeneid*, 6, 585.

THE PORTRAIT OF PTOLEMY I SOTER[1]

GEORGE H. McFADDEN
University Museum, Philadelphia

Plates 82-85

We are fortunate enough to possess a good number of portraits in stone, marble, and bronze belonging to the early Hellenistic period. Among these, some are contemporaneous Greek originals, whereas others are copies made in Roman imperial times of originals which have been lost. It has always been tempting to see in many of these portraits representations of this or that Hellenistic ruler. It will be the purpose of this paper to survey the evidence on which some of these identifications rest.

It will be remembered how after the death of Alexander in 323 B.C. his generals became independent rulers in those provinces of the Empire where they had established themselves: Ptolemy in Egypt; Seleukos in Babylonia; Antigonos in the greater part of Asia Minor and in northern Syria; and Lysimachos in Thrace. With the death of Antipater, Antigonos was to become the most powerful among the successors. In 306 B.C. his son Demetrios defeated Ptolemy in a great naval engagement off Cyprus, and it was soon after this brilliant and showy victory that he and his father, Antigonos, proclaimed themselves kings. Ptolemy, Seleukos, and Lysimachos followed their example.[2]

It was Ptolemy in Egypt, however, who was the first to strike coins bearing his own portrait, probably not long after he assumed the diadem in 305/4 B.C.[3] He first placed his portrait only on his gold staters (pl. 82, a), but later, after the battle of Ipsus in 301, there appeared a splendid and well executed realistic portrait of him on the obverse of all gold and silver pieces (pl. 82, b).[4] It is a wonderful portrait and one receives the impression that the die cutter faithfully reproduced the outstanding features of this great Macedonian.

---

1. I am greatly indebted to Margarete Bieber for reading the first draft of this paper, for valuable references, and for much helpful criticism. For conclusions drawn, however, I accept sole responsibility.

2. Diodoros, XX, 53, 2-4; 73, 3. Plutarch, *Demetrios*, 17-19. *Mar. Par.*, B, 23. Glotz, *Histoire Générale, Histoire Grecque*, IV, 335-337.

3. Newell, E. T., *Royal Greek Portrait Coins*, 25-28. Milne is of the opinion that Demetrios was the first living man to appear on the coinage of any of the successors. He is referring to the coins struck at Ephesos. See Milne, J. G., *Greek Coinage*, 112. These coins, however, cannot be dated earlier than 301 B.C.

4. Lange, Kurt, *Herrscherköpfe des Altertums*, 1938, Pl. p. 49.

The portrait is, indeed, a fine example of the new realism which is now in vogue, a realism of which perhaps Lysippos was the father. The subject of the portrait is an individual and not an ideal. It presents a likeness but it is the more impressive and memorable features of the man himself that are emphasized. The coin illustrated in pl. 82, b belongs to one of the finest issues ever struck in Ptolemaic Egypt. The hair of Ptolemy's portrait, as we see, is highly stylized. It falls on all sides from the crown of the head in wavy strands. The artist, however, is careful not to conceal what, judging from a comparison with other coin portraits, must have been one of the outstanding features of the king: the baldness over his brow. The front of the diadem rests on the bare forehead with only a few strands of hair slipping up under it. The outline of the brow is composed of two arcs divided by a furrow between them. The short nose is straight down to the tip. The profile then makes a semi-circular turn up toward the nostrils to turn downward again in a larger semi-circular arc to the upper lip. The mouth is slightly open. The lips are full with straight outlines. The chin is firm, strong and round. It projects well in front of the mouth. The eye is wide-open; the pupil fairly protrudes from it giving an effect of keen and intelligent interest. The treatment here is impressionistic. A fold of fat falls across the corner of the eye. A particularly large mass of hair sweeps in a wide arc across the temple to terminate in a counter-swing along the outline of the ear. The style is at once realistic, impressionistic, and highly decorative. There is a strong sense of design throughout. It is a masterful portrait of a man some-what past the prime of life with marked baldness over the brow. The early coin portraits of Ptolemy I vary, but the distinguishing features are realistically emphasized: the baldness; the straight nose; the fold of fat over the eyes; the tuft of hair on the temple; the round, firm protruding chin.[5] It is clear that the die cutter is determined to represent faithfully his outstanding features.

There is in the Pelizaeus Museum at Hildesheim a plaster plaque from Memphis bearing a diademed full face portrait of a king.[6] It is in high relief. The face has few minor blemishes, and there is a rather large air pocket on the tip of the nose; otherwise it is in excellent condition (pl. 82, d). Worthy of particular attention are the following:

---

5. Svoronos, *Τὰ νομίσματα τοῦ κράτους τῶν Πτολεμαίων*, III, 1904, Pls. III-V; VII, VIII.

6. Rubensohn, Otto, *Hellenistisches Silbergerät*, 44, no. 32, Pl. VI. Pelizaeus-Museum inv. no. 1120.

1. The diadem and the way it lies over the incipient baldness of the brow. This can be paralleled only on coins of Ptolemy I Soter.

2. The treatment of the hair like that of the coin portraits.

3. The fold of fat over the corner of the eye also in the characteristic style of the coinage.

As far as one can judge from a full face view, there is nothing in the portrait unlike the impression one receives of Ptolemy I from the coins. It is of him that Rubensohn considers the portrait to be, and there appears to be every reason for accepting his identification.

There is a plaster cast of a silver or bronze medallion belonging to the same collection of finds from Memphis.[7] It carries a portrait also in high relief but in rather poor condition. Here we note again the diadem covering the baldness over the brow and the treatment of the hair. A large tuft of it can be seen on the temple in the style of the coin portrait of Ptolemy I. The fold of fat over the eye is barely apparent, but the eyes slant downward at the corners in a similar way. If seen in profile, they might give much the same impression as the coin portrait. I follow Rubensohn who identified this also as Ptolemy I.

If we take the coin portraits for our profile view, and the plaster plaque, which is in much better condition than the medallion, for our full face view, we should have a sound basis of comparison in the identification of other portraits of the same king.

There is a fine marble head in the Ny Carlsberg Glyptothek at Copenhagen (pl. 82e, f)[8] identified as a portrait of Ptolemy I Soter on the authority of Poulsen,[9] Pfuhl,[10] Rostovtzeff,[11] and more recently of Cahn.[12] The identification, although contested by Dickins[13] in 1914, is generally accepted. The head came from Egypt. It is really

7. *Ibid.*, 24, no. 12, Pl. X, inv. no. 1119. As this paper goes to press I have seen Adriani's publication of a recent acquisition of the Greco-Roman Museum in Alexandria (*Bulletin de la Société Royale d'Archéologie d'Alexandrie*, no. 32, 1938, pp. 77 ff., Pl. VI.). It came from Memphis and belongs to the same group of finds as the plaster plaque and the medallion. It is a relief in a good state of preservation of two jugate heads identified by Adriani as being of Soter and Berenike. The resemblance to the coin portraiture and to the plaque and medallion is so close that I have no doubt but that the identification is correct. See pl. 85 A.

8. Poulsen, F., "Gab es eine Alexandrinische Kunst," *From the Collections of the Ny Carlsberg-Glyptothek*, II (1938), Pls. pp. 12 and 13; *Katalog*, p. 319, no. 455.

9. Idem, "Gab es eine Alexandrinische Kunst," 14 ff.

10. Pfuhl, F., *JDAI* 45 (1930), 6 ff.

11. Rostovtzeff, M., *Social and Economic History of the Hellenistic World*, I, p. 10, Pl. II, no. 2.

12. Cahn, H. A., "Frühhellenistische Münzkunst," *Der Amerbach Bote Almanach*, 1949, 95 f.

13. Dickins, G., *JHS* 34 (1914) 295 f.

little more than a mask. The back was completed in plaster, little of which is extant. This technique is generally considered to be peculiar to Alexandrian sculpture although there is some reason to believe that the process was used elsewhere.[14]

We see that there is no diadem. This, of course, may once have been supplied in plaster; or it may be a representation of Ptolemy before he assumed the diadem. The absence of the diadem does not prove that this portrait is not a royal one but it does greatly widen the field of speculation. Unless, therefore, we see a striking resemblance between this mask and the certified portrait of Ptolemy on the coins, we shall have to discard the identification for lack of confirming evidence. We have, unfortunately, no better basis of comparison.

As the hair and almost all of the brow were supplied in plaster, we cannot compare these with the coinage. The fold of fat over the corner of the eye is absent. The nose, unlike the nose on the coinage, is arched. The tip could hardly be more unlike that of the coins. It falls in a wide arc down to a point below the nostrils, and then without rising the profile falls vertically to the lip. Both noses are comparatively short. They are quite dissimilar in every other respect. The chin, unlike that of the coin portrait, is double and not so round, firm or protruding. It is difficult to compare the mouth of the mask with the coins as we cannot see it in true profile. Poulsen in his discussion of the Copenhagen head finds the likeness between it and the coins not so satisfactory as that between the coins and another head in the Louvre (pl. 83a, b),[15] assigned by him,[16] Wolters,[17] and Wace,[18] with some reservation, also to Ptolemy I. The *taenia* is without the diadem ends. We have, therefore, no proof that it is a royal portrait. The hair has been largely restored; the arrangement is quite unlike that of either the coinage or plaster plaque. The ears, neck and most of the *taenia* have also been restored. The fold of fat over the corner of the eye is lacking; there is not a trace of it even in the profile view. The eyes as seen in full face view do not correspond at all with those of the plaque. The nose is straight, but the tip, almost always the most distinguishing part of the nose, is re-

---

14. Many such heads have been found outside of Egypt, and we cannot assume in all cases that they came from Egypt. The saving in marble where this was not easily available would, of course, have been considerable, and the technique once learnt might well have been used elsewhere.

15. Delbrück, R., *Antike Porträts*, Pl. 23.

16. Poulsen, *op. cit.*, 14.

17. Wolters, *RM* 4 (1889) 33, Pl. III.

18. Wace, *JHS* 25 (1905) 90.

stored. The chin is much like that of the coin portrait. In view of the differences, however, Dickins seems to have been justified in rejecting the identification.[19]

Poulsen in his discussion of the Copenhagen head compares it with a head from Pergamon (pl. 83 c, d).[20] He points out convincingly enough, that Pergamon was a likely place to find a head of Ptolemy in view of the close family ties existing between him and Lysimachos. The head, moreover, is made with the back completed in plaster, a technique characteristic of Alexandrian sculpture. What we have left is also little more than a mask. Some of the hair is extant and this is in plaster. The portrait is that of a young man without a line in his face. The diadem is absent. Of course, if it is a portrait of Ptolemy, as Poulsen believes, it would be one of him before he assumed the diadem in 305/4 when he was over 60 years of age. Again the absence of the diadem does not prove that it is not a portrait of Ptolemy, but it does greatly widen the field of possibility. The nose is unlike that of the coin portrait. The tip, always the most distinguishing part, is not extant. The chin does not protrude beyond the plane of the mouth as it does on the coins, but, on the contrary, recedes slightly from it. It is fleshy, unlike the firm, bony chin of the coins. The fold of flesh over the corner of the eye would be unbecoming to a young man. The head does not resemble the Ptolemy we know as he was in later life. How he appeared in his youth is a matter for speculation.

Poulsen compares the Pergamon head with another head from an art shop in Cairo (pl. 84a, b).[21] There is a striking resemblance between it and the Pergamon head when viewed in profile. The resemblance between the full faces otherwise might not have been noticed. The Cairo head is of a much older man. The chins, however viewed, are quite different. The resemblance between the Cairo head and the Copenhagen head seems closer. Both have the same arched nose and double chin, and the lines on the face are also very similar. What is particularly significant, however, is that they do not share these points of similarity either with the coins or plaster plaque. Not one of these heads identified by Poulsen as Ptolemy Soter, moreover, can be shown to be even a royal portrait.

Pfuhl in his discussion of the Copenhagen head[22] points out that Ptolemy's portrait, even on his own coinage, varies quite consider-

---

19. *JHS* 34 (1914) 295.
20. Poulsen, *op. cit.*, 14 f., figs. 12 and 13.
21. *Ibid.*, 16 f., figs. 14 and 15.
22. Pfuhl, *loc. cit.*, 6 ff.

ably. He illustrates his contention with five coins[23] taken from Svoronos, the British Museum Catalogue, and Imhoof-Blumer.[24] True, they do vary, but the outstanding features of Ptolemy's portrait remain constant throughout: the diadem over the incipient baldness of the brow; the fold of fat over the eye; the profile of the tip of the nose as already described; the protruding chin. The length of the nose varies as Pfuhl says. It is never beaked, although the roundness of the tip occasionally gives this impression as it does in fact in our illustration (pl. 82b). However this may be, the differences between the coin portraits in Pfuhl's illustrations are considerably less than the differences between any one of them on the one hand, and the Copenhagen, Pergamon, and Cairo heads on the other.

Pfuhl, on stylistic grounds, and Poulsen, whom he follows, believe the Copenhagen head to be a posthumous work. Both speak deservedly in high praise of it as a work of art. Poulsen goes so far as to name it among the noblest pieces of portraiture the world has produced. Pfuhl in his study comments that the outstanding features of a man can only provide the raw material for art. True as this may often be, it is not a good apology for an unsatisfactory identification. He believes that the Copenhagen head may have been a copy of the cult statue of Ptolemy I which was set up by Ptolemy II, and that it represented the last stage in the development of Ptolemy Soter's portrait of which the earliest stages, he says, are reflected in the coinage. The cult statue to which he refers is the chryselephantine one mentioned by Theokritos who tells us that Ptolemy II Philadelphos was the first among men to build temples to a mother and father, and that he set up images of them in gold and ivory to be the help of all them that dwell upon the earth.[25]

Ptolemy I died in 283 about the age of 84. If the Copenhagen mask was a posthumous work, how explain so youthful a representation? Poulsen sees in the head a man not more than fifty years of age. He and Pfuhl accordingly, in support of their identification, look upon it as an idealized portrait harking back to the king's comparative youth. The evidence of the coinage does not support this contention. Philadelphos to commemorate the deification of his

---

23. *Ibid.*, Pl. 11, 9-13.

24. Svoronos, *op. cit.*, III, Pls. VII-IX. *Brit. Museum Cat. Ptolemies*, Pl. II f. Imhoof-Blumer, *Porträtköpfe Hellenischer und Hellenisierter Völker*, Pl. I, 2. Pfuhl's no. 9, *loc. cit.*, is much like Imhoof-Blumer's Pl. I, 2. Unfortunately Pfuhl does not give cross references to facilitate the identification of coins in the works cited by him.

25. *Idylls*, XVII, 121-125. See Ditt. *Syll.*³ 309; *Syll.*² 202; *Michel* 373.

parents struck coins (277-270 B.C.)[26] showing on the reverse the
jugate heads of Ptolemy I Soter and Berenike, but Ptolemy's portrait here is that of an old man (pl. 82, c).

There is a head from Thera in Parian marble which Hiller suggested might be Ptolemy I Soter.[27] It is, unfortunately, in very poor
condition (pl. 84c, d). The nose, left side of the chin, and a good portion of the hair are not extant. I note, however, the following similarities between the coin portraiture, the plaster plaque, and this
marble head:

1. The brow divided by a horizontal wrinkle.
2. The comparative baldness of the head over the brow.
3. The fold of fat over the eye.

The ends of the diadem are not mentioned by Hiller in his publication. I assume there is no trace of them. The head, however, belongs probably to the early third century, and Thera is a likely
enough place for a portrait of Ptolemy to have been set up at that
time.[28] The chin is more fleshy than that of the coin portrait. Otherwise the correspondence with the coins is very close wherever the
condition of the head permits comparison. It seems to me that this
piece is the only good candidate that we have in sculpture in the
round for the portrait of Ptolemy I Soter.

---

26. Giesecke, Walther, *Das Ptolemäergeld*, 20, Pl. II, no. 12. Svoronos, *op. cit.*,
11, no. 603; III, Pl. XIV, nos. 15-17. See also Pfuhl, *op. cit.*, Pl. 2, nos. 14-16.

27. Hiller von Gaertringen, *Thera*, I, 245 f., Pl. 21.

28. IG 12, 3, 320, cited by Hiller, *op. cit.*

ASPASIOS I AND II

GISELA M. A. RICHTER
Metropolitan Museum of Art

Plates 85-86

Professor David M. Robinson owns a fine collection of Greek and Roman engraved gems which he has recently described in the Commemorative Studies in honor of Theodore Leslie Shear, *Hesperia*, Supplement VIII. An article on Aspasios may therefore be an appropriate offering for his *Festschrift*.

The signature of Aspasios—in the genitive, *Aspasiou*[1]—appears on a number of engraved gems, ancient and modern. Furtwängler, in one of his articles on "Gemmen mit Künstler inschriften," in the *Jahrbuch des Deutschen Archäologischen Instituts*,[2] and in his *Antike Gemmen*,[3] showed with cogent arguments that three of these stones were undoubtedly ancient, the rest modern imitations. The best known of the genuine ones is the superb red jasper with the head of the Athena Parthenos (pl. 86, d). The other two are also red jaspers. One has a herm of Dionysos and is in the British Museum[4] (pl. 86, e) ; the other is a fragment, with the lower part of a bearded bust, and is in Florence (pl. 86, c).

All three representations are copied from fifth-century sculptures, and in all three the letters of the signatures are identical: the alpha without a horizontal stroke, the sigma lunate, a little ball at the end of each stroke, the whole incised with great nicety. Evidently these three engravings are by the same man. He was probably a contemporary of Dioskourides, who we know worked for Augustus, at a time when copies of Greek sculptural works were particularly popular on sealstones.

An engraved carnelian inscribed *Aspasiou* has recently been given to the Metropolitan Museum by Mr. Rupert L. Joseph (pl. 85, a, b).[5]

---

1. Gem engravers of the Roman period generally sign in the genitive, only occasionally with *epoiei*. On this subject cf. Brunn, *Geschichte der griechischen Künstler*, II, 444 ff.

2. 4 (1889) 46 ff.

3. II, 235 ff.

4. It is not included in H. B. Walters' *Catalogue of the Greek, Etruscan, and Roman Engraved Gems and Cameos*, but is given instead in Dalton's *Catalogue of the Engraved Gems of the Post-Classical Periods*, no. 701. Mr. Ashmole, however, who kindly re-examined the stone for me, reports that in his and Sir John Beazley's opinion it is ancient. Judging from the impression he sent me and the published illustrations, I see nothing to arouse suspicion (see note 9).

5. Acc. no. 50.43; dimensions 1.9 by 1.4 cm.; greatest depth .5 cm. There is some undercutting, as is not infrequently the case in Roman gems.

Nothing is known of its provenance except that the owner acquired it from a dealer in New York. The representation on it is not a copy of a fifth-century work, but a portrait-bust of a middle-aged man, with a mantle on his left shoulder, deeply carved in full front view (the convexity of the stone on both sides made this possible). The style, the beard, the rendering of the locks place the head in the second century A. D. The letters of the inscription are different from those on the other three gems inscribed Aspasiou; the alphas have a horizontal stroke and the sigmas are four-stroked.

The Aspasios who signed this stone must, therefore, have been a different artist from the one who has been known for some time (Aspasios was of course a common name)[6] and he must have lived more than a century later. He too was outstanding, for the portrait is a splendid characterization of a man of perhaps the Antonine age.[7] He bears some likeness to the emperor Hadrian, but the style seems later, and the heavy-lidded eyes and small mouth with their melancholy expression suggest an Easterner.

The historical importance of this newcomer is at once apparent. We have here still another Roman portrait signed by a Greek, and one not of the so-called Graeco-Roman period of the first century B. C. and A. D. but of the second century A. D. Evidently Roman portraits were still being executed by Greeks at that time—on sealstones as in sculpture.

The second engraved gem that I want to discuss in relation to Aspasios is an amethyst ringstone, lent by Rupert L. Joseph to the Metropolitan Museum in 1940 and given by him in 1949.[8] It once formed part of the Wyndham Cook Collection and was exhibited in the Burlington Fine Arts Club in 1904.[9] The engraving represents a

6. Cf. e.g. Pape, *Wörterbuch der griechischen Eigennamen*[3], s.v. Aspasios, and *RE*, II, s.v. Aspasios, cols. 1722 f.

7. The genuineness of the stone is attested by the consistent style, the convincing inscription, and the physical condition. Mr. Meritt wrote me regarding the inscription (in May 1949): "I have very little to say about it. First, there is no reason I can see to believe it is not genuine. Second, the date may well be Antonine, but I don't believe that the letters should be used as a criterion of date." With regard to the physical condition the corrosion around the edge of the face and the little scratches on the surface suggest antiquity. The top of the stone has been broken off, apparently in modern times, to judge by the fresh-looking fracture. The missing portion gives the appearance of a cap or wreath in the impression. At the bottom the stone has been shaved off, evidently to make it fit into a modern ring, and this shaving has removed part of the initial alpha and the bottom of the upsilon.

8. Acc. no. 49.21.1. Convex in front and also at the back, but there with a flattened central area. Dimensions: 2.15 by 1.6 cm.; depth, .8 cm.

9. C. H. Smith and C. A. Hutton, *Catalogue of the Wyndham Cook Collection*, 27, no. 103; Burlington Fine Arts Club, *Catalogue of Ancient Greek Art*, pl. CX, no. M.87.

bearded Dionysos in three-quarter view, with a mantle draped on one side, a single lock on each shoulder, a vine wreath in his hair (pl. 85c, 86a). It is strikingly like the Dionysos by Aspasios I (as we must now call him) except that it is a bust, not a herm, and that there is no broad fillet wound around the head. It also resembles another herm of Dionysos, already connected with Aspasios by Furtwängler,[10] in which, as in ours, much of the hair is visible (pl. 86, b). All three heads are carefully worked by a master of the craft.

The Greek original from which these heads were copied must have been an important sculptural creation, perhaps a bronze statue of the second half of the fifth century. The same composition occurs on a marble disk in the Metropolitan Museum (pl. 86, f)[11] and in two terracotta herms in the British Museum.[12] All evidently reproduce the same Greek original, in a somewhat modified form. Bearded heads of this general type were popular in the fifth century. One thinks, for instance, of Alkamenes' Hermes, of Pheidias' Zeus, of the heads on coins, and of some of the Graeco-Roman gems with profile heads.[13]

That the representations on the three gems were derived from a common source does not necessarily mean that they were executed at the same time, for we know that the same Greek original was copied by sculptors of the Roman period for several centuries. And even if they were contemporary, this would not prove that the two unsigned gems were also engraved by Aspasios. In marble copies, at least, though we know that the same man sometimes reproduced the same Greek statue more than once,[14] we also know that many different sculptors copied the same Greek original. Nevertheless, the fact that in all three stones the head is in the same three-quarter view, presumably copied, as we have said, from a statue in the round, suggests a definite connection between them, especially when we remember that three-quarter views on gems are less common than profile ones. Moreover, though in free copies the criterion of style is difficult to

---

10. *AG*, pl. XLI, 4. The material and the location are not given; so the stone was evidently known to Furtwängler only from an impression.

11. Acc. no. 26.60.27. Diameter 2.1 cm. Not before published. Bought in Paris in 1926.

12. Ellis, *Towneley Gallery*, I, 83; Walters, *Catalogue of Terracottas*, nos. 431, 432. It is the similarity to these herms that cast suspicion on the signed gem in London. But, as Furtwängler pointed out, there is no difficulty in supposing several derivatives from a famous original.

13. Cf. e.g. Walters, *Catalogue of Engraved Gems in the British Museum*, nos. 1553, 1554.

14. Thus Maarkos Kossoutios Kerdon, freedman of Maarkos, signed two practically identical statues of Pan, of fifth-century style, both now in the British Museum (Smith, A. H., *Catalogue of Sculpture*, III, nos. 1066, 1067, pl .VII).

apply, we can at least say that all three gems are carved with the same care and competence.

Who the sculptor was who made the original Greek statue that Aspasios copied we cannot tell. Aspasios is not the only artist of the Roman period who signed his name to a copy of a Greek creation without acknowledging the "source." Plagiarism was not in his time considered a crime. It was the rule rather than the exception, and we of course must be grateful to its widespread practice, since we owe to it much of our knowledge of Greek sculpture.

IONIAN SONG

Though we've broken their statues asunder
   And cast them down from their shrines,
Ionia, thy gods are undying,
   On thee their glory still shines.

They cherish thee still, and their spirits
   Are still ever mindful of thee,
And thine August dawn is a-quiver
   With immortality.

High over thy heaven hovers
   A young god's cloud-poised form;
It passes over thy mountains,
   Wind-winged, a fleeting charm.

Constantine Kavafis

Translated by
John B. Edwards

TWO TERRACOTTA APES

GEORGE H. CHASE
Harvard University and
Boston Museum of Fine Arts

Plate 87

In a volume presented to a scholar and teacher, perhaps only very serious articles should be printed. If the few pages which I have written seem frivolous, I can only offer as an excuse that they were suggested by the work of one of Professor Robinson's pupils,[1] who in the preface to the book, acknowledges his great indebtedness to the master.

Among recent accessions of the Classical Department of the Boston Museum of Fine Arts is an amusing terracotta figure of an ape riding on a donkey (pl. 87, a).[2] Only the left forearm of the ape and the tail of the donkey are missing. The modelling, on the whole, is more careful than is usual in figurines of this sort; especially noticeable is the head of the donkey, with its emphasis on the bony structure, open mouth, wide nostrils, and exaggeratedly long ears, with a forelock between them. The legs, also, are modelled with more attention to anatomical detail than is common in archaic terracottas. But the maker also shows considerable knowledge in the head of the ape, with pointed nose and large ears, though the two holes which must be intended to represent the nostrils seem singularly misplaced.

Although no traces of color are preserved, it may be assumed that the figure originally was covered with the customary white slip, with black (and perhaps red) overcolor for details; surely the eyes, which are hardly modelled at all, must have been brought out by color. The most unusual feature of the group is the right arm raised in a gesture of greeting, which inevitably suggests a Fascist salute.

Although the ape riding an animal is a common archaic type,[3] I have found only one other that exhibits this gesture—the upper part of a terracotta figurine from Perachora.[4] Although Jenkins describes this broken figure as a "standing monkey," surely the curvature of the body is that of a rider. In such mounted types, the rider usually

---

1. Cf. McDermott, William C., *The Ape in Antiquity*, Baltimore, 1938.
2. Acc. No. MFA 49.49. Height, 10.4 cm. From the Carmichael Collection.
3. Cf. McDermott, *op. cit.*, 168-171; Ure, *Aryballoi and Figurines from Rhitsona in Boeotia*, 62, nos. 145.96, 145. 97 (pl. XV), and 96.8; p. 65, no. 112.77 (pl. XVII).
4. Cf. Payne and others, *Perachora*, 229, no. 172, pl. 101.

clasps the neck of his mount,[5] as in another figure in the Boston Museum (pl. 87, b).[6] This has been described as "an ape riding on a dog," and the remarkably pointed face of the rider certainly suggests such an interpretation. But in view of the very crude modelling, I hesitate to include this figure among our apes.

Because of the attention to anatomical detail in the group of the "saluting" ape, I am inclined to date it late in the Archaic period, perhaps not far from 500 B. C. And in view of the popularity of such types at Rhitsona, we may, perhaps, attribute it to a Boeotian maker.

A second "ape" in the Museum collection is of quite a different character (pl. 87, c).[7] Since he is provided with a long tail, he should, perhaps, be called a monkey, but to the archaeologist ape and monkey are interchangeable terms. This ape sits on the ground, holding a two-handled jar between his knees and raising a cake or a fruit to his lips with his right hand. His left hand rests upon a handle of the jar. All details are carefully rendered, with special emphasis on characteristic features—large ears, wide mouth showing the teeth, and well articulated feet. The hairy body is rendered by a series of careful striations and the long tail rests on the ground at the beast's right side. The whole is finished with a thin, hard glaze, light green in color—the usual "faience" technique.

Owing to damage, some details are unclear, but there can be no doubt that this was a vase. The bottom was apparently a separate piece which has broken away; a break at the top of the head makes it uncertain how the mouth of the vase was formed; and something has been lost—cover or ornament—from the top of the jar. What the complete vase was like is suggested by a well-preserved example in the Berlin Antiquarium.[8] In this, the mouth of the vase is modelled in the form of a lotus flower and on the cover of the jar is perched a frog. A fragmentary example, of rather less careful workmanship, was found at Lindos, as well as the head from a similar vase.[9] In discussing these, Blinkenberg lists six other examples, three from Camirus, and one each from Thebes, Carthage, and Caere.

That this type, like the "saluting" ape, is intended as a parody on a similar human type appears clearly from the existence of an even larger number of "faience" vases in which the large jar is held by a

---

5. Cf. the series published by Ure, *op. cit.*, pls. XV and XVI.

6. Acc. No. MFA 90.192. Length, 7.2 cm.; height, 4.4 cm.

7. Acc. No. MFA 01.7918; height, 7.8 cm.; said to be from Cumae.

8. Inv. No. 4877, published by Maximova, *Les vases plastiques dans l'antiquité*, I, 113-115; II, pl. XXXIII, 125.

9. Cf. Blinkenberg, *Lindos, fouilles de l'acropole*, I, col. 363, nos. 1330, 1331, pl. 58.

kneeling woman or rarely by a kneeling man. A well-preserved example from Rhodes in the Louvre is published by Mlle. Maximova,[10] and Blinkenberg[11] lists more than a dozen examples. On these, too, a frog is frequently perched on the cover of the pot.

Of the Egyptian origin of the type there can be no doubt. The squatting servant and the squatting ape holding a kohl pot are found in Egypt both in stone and in faience, and some of these are as early as the New Empire.[12] But the wide distribution of the faience figures makes it probable that they were made by Greek workmen in imitation of Egyptian models. Mlle. Maximova suggests quite plausibly that the motif of the "nibbling" ape is the only contribution of the Greek imitator.[13]

As to the place of manufacture, the two centers which come most readily to mind are Naucratis and Rhodes. Both these cities were actively engaged in the export trade in the sixth century, the period to which our seated ape is surely to be assigned, and the products of both show marked oriental influence. The Egyptian prototype naturally creates a prejudice in favor of Naucratis, but the fact that of the examples of both the human type and the ape type for which the provenience is recorded, more than half have been found in Rhodes[14] favors the theory of Rhodian origin. It cannot be denied, of course, that similar figures may have been made in other places.

---

10. *L.c.*, I, 132; II, pl. XXXIV, 128; cf. Heuzey, *Catalogue des figurines antiques de terre cuite*, 211, 212, nos. 11, 12.

11. *Lindos*, col. 364, no. 1335.

12. Cf. Cairo, *Catalogue générale*: von Bissing, *Steingefässe*, 120, no. 18580, and 121, no. 18582, pl. IX; *Fayencegefässe*, 81 f., nos. 3966, 3968; p. 86, no. 3979; Bénédite, *Objets de toilette*, I, 56, no. 18382, p. 57, no. 18577, and p. 59, no. 3968, pl. XXIV.

13. *Les vases plastiques*, 115.

14. Cf. Blinkenberg, *Lindos*, cols. 363-365.

DEUX STATUETTES DE LA RÉGION DE TYR

R. Mouterde, S.J.
Université St. Joseph, Beyrouth

Planche 90

Une découverte fortuite mit au jour, en 1947, à Khoraïbé, près de Tyr, un lot de figurines en terre cuite. Le Service des antiquités de la République Libanaise entreprit aussitôt des recherches complémentaires, qui dégagèrent toute une officine de coroplaste; le résultat de ces travaux sera analysé dans un prochain tome du *Bulletin du Musée de Beyrouth*. En me procurant ces informations, l'Émir Maurice Chénab, directeur du Service des antiquités, a bien voulu me remettre la photographie reproduite par la pl. 90, B. Il m'aide ainsi à présenter, en hommage à un savant qui a toujours confronté textes et monuments antiques, le bref commentaire de deux statuettes hellénistiques modelées en terre phénicienne.

Quelques pièces de la trouvaille initiale de Khoraïbé ont passé dans le commerce et ne sont point entrées au Musée. Parmi elles j'ai pu photographier la figurine rustique dont ci-joint l'image (pl. 90, A).

Le type est connu. C'est celui du "pédagogue" — d'ordinaire représenté comme il paraissait sur le théâtre grec, sous les traits d'un vieillard décrépit, tenant par la main un enfant. Des figurines modelées ainsi proviennent des tombes de Kertch, comme des ateliers de Myrina et d'Alexandrie.[1] On leur comparera les reliefs des sarcophages d'époque romaine, où le pédagogue est assis près de l'enfant prématurément ravi par la mort.[2] Mais à tous ces modèles la statuette de Khoraïbé s'oppose par un trait essentiel: l'esclave auquel est confié l'enfant n'est plus le vieillard à longue barbe, tout brisé par l'âge — et parfois ivrogne — du répertoire commun; ce n'est pas non plus le philosophe barbu (quoique de rang servile) des sarcophages de Rome et de Beyrouth; c'est un jeune esclave (désigné comme tel par sa demi-nudité) qui porte dans un filet un écritoire et tire par la main son petit maître soigneusement encapuchonné. Un trait de moeurs apparaît ici. Il n'est peut-être pas exclusivement syrien, car une terre cuite du Musée d'Alexandrie représente un esclave imberbe, vêtu d'une simple tunique, qui porte des tablettes et conduit un enfant par

---

1. *Dictionnaire des Antiquités*, s.v. *Paedagogus*, 272-273 (O. Navarre).

2. Cumont, Fr., *Recherches sur le symbolisme funéraire des Romains*, 335 sqq., pl. XXXVII, 1 et 2 (Italie); XXXIX, 1 (Beyrouth).

la main.[3] Pourtant la coutume est bien locale, persistant jusqu'à nos jours au Liban et en Syrie, de donner aux enfants un petit serviteur, plus apte à amuser qu'à conduire et élever. L'usage valait pour les filles comme pour les garçons: une inscription d'Antioche assure que le décès d'une fillette de neuf ans, Nikaia, l'a arrachée "à sa petite gouvernante," ἀρτιφυὴ παιδονόμην.[4] A vrai dire, le gros garçon, à l'air bestial, que le groupe de Tyr présente comme un pédagogue, n'a rien apparemment qui le recommande pour un tel rôle. C'est le lieu de rappeler l'apostrophe de S. Jean Chrysostôme aux gens d'Antioche: "On préfère les animaux aux enfants et l'on prend moins soin d'eux que des ânes et chevaux. Car si quelqu'un possède un mulet, il a grand souci de trouver un muletier excellent, ni malhonnête, ni voleur, ni ivrogne, ni ignorant de son métier; et quand il faut procurer à l'âme de l'enfant un pédagogue, d'emblée et comme par hasard on prend le premier venu."[5]

La seconde statuette (pl. 90, B) est un spécimen unique parmi toutes les figurines que la trouvaille de Khoraïbé a procurées au Musée; un autre spécimen, moins bien conservé, a passé sous mes yeux. C'est une variante du thème de "l'Enfant à l'oie," qui est représenté au Musée par des pièces d'un tout autre type.

L'oeuvre célèbre de Boéthos, dont il existe des répliques au Louvre, à Munich et au Musée du Capitole, est sans doute le prototype de ces figurines; on sait d'ailleurs quelles controverses ont cours au sujet de la date de Boéthos de Chalcédon et de l'attribution éventuelle du morceau à Boéthos de Carthage.[6] Il convient surtout de noter, à propos de la statuette de Tyr, combien l'attitude du bel enfant, debout, vainqueur de l'oie qu'il a domptée, diffère de la véhémence combative du bébé, arcbouté sur ses jambes pour étreindre l'animal, qu'on remarque sur les beaux groupes de marbre cités plus haut. Le modèle qu'ont imité nos coroplastes est autre; alors que nombre des figurines de Khoraïbé relèvent de l'art alexandrin, il pourrait être cherché en Grèce propre et spécifiquement, en Béotie; quelques statues décou-

---

3. A. Adriani, *Annuaire du Musée gréco-romain (1935-1939)*, 1940, 170, Inv. n⁰ 25092, pl. LXXI, 3.

4. *Inscriptions gr. et lat. de la Syrie*, III, 1, 1950, n⁰ 915.

5. *Hom. in Matt.*, LIX, alias LX, ad *finem* = Migne, *P. G.*, t. 57-58, col. 584: Καὶ γὰρ βοσκημάτων οἱ παῖδες ἀτιμότεροι, καὶ ὄνων καὶ ἵππων μᾶλλον ἐπιμελούμεθα ἢ παίδων. Κἂν μὲν ἡμίονόν τις ἔχῃ, πολλὴ ἡ φροντὶς ὥστε ὀνηλάτην εὑρεῖν ἄριστον καὶ μήτε ἀγνώμονα, μὴ κλέπτην, μὴ μέθυσον, μὴ τῆς τέχνης ἄπειρον· ἂν δὲ ψυχῇ παιδὸς ἐπιστῆσαι δέῃ παιδαγωγόν, ἁπλῶς καὶ ὡς ἔτυχε ἐπελθόντα αἱρούμεθα. Dans l'article *Paedagogus* cité plus haut, O. Navarre rappelle les blâmes de Platon, Plutarque, Tacite, à l'égard des parents qui remettent à des maîtres indignes le soin d'élever leurs enfants.

6. Cf. Picard, Ch., *La sculpture antique de Phidias à l'ère byzantine*, 258-259; *RA* 1947, I, 210-219.

vertes à Thespies, qui représentent des enfants debout ou accroupis, parfois jouant avec des oies,[7] donnent à leur héros la même attitude de jeune vainqueur.

L'intérêt de ce rapprochement est que les marbres de Thespies proviennent vraisemblablement, avec une grande statue d'Asklépios, de l'*Asklépiéion* de cette cité. Or il y a cinquante ans que le type de l' "Enfant à l'oie" a été rapproché de la légende d'Asklépios. Le 14 septembre 1900, Salomon Reinach tentait d'établir, devant l'Académie des inscriptions, que l'Enfant à l'oie, tel que le représente le marbre du Louvre, n'est pas un simple sujet de genre; "selon lui, il s'agit d'Esculape enfant, qui, attaqué par une oie sauvage, la réduit à l'obéissance et en fait son animal familier. A l'appui de cette hypothèse, il rappelle qu'il y avait des oies guérisseuses dans les temples d'Esculape, qu'une copie du groupe de Boéthos se voyait dans le temple d'Esculape, dans l'île de Cos, et que Boéthos est précisément cité, dans une inscription grecque, comme l'auteur d'une statue célèbre d'Esculape enfant."[8] En 1907, J. Svonoros proposait de reconnaître, dans l'Enfant à l'oie, l'image de Janiskos, le plus jeune des fils d'Asklépios,[9] et rappelait les nombreux groupes des "enfants d'Asklépios," que l'on connaît à Épidaure et à Agra (sanctuaire d'Ilithyie).[10]

L'hypothèse n'est pas acceptée sans réserves. Les représentations plus graves de Thespies montrent du moins que l'inspiration religieuse, qui fut probablement à l'origine du thème artistique, a pu se maintenir dans les figurines fabriquées à proximité des temples du dieu guérisseur. Or il existait des temples d'Eshmoun-Asklépios en Phénicie — à commencer par le temple de Bostân ech-Cheikh, près Saida.[11] On y venait prier et ces visiteurs comptaient peut-être parmi les clients auxquels les coroplastes de Khoraïbé destinaient leurs produits.

---

7. A. de Ridder, *BCH* 46 (1922) 223-228, fig. 5-6.

8. *Comptes-rendus de l'Acad. des inscr.*, 1900, II, 463. Je n'ai pas retrouvé dans *Cultes, mythes et religions,* ni ailleurs, le texte de cette communication. Le groupe de l'île de Cos est connu par le *Mime IV*, d'Hérondas (vv. 30-31).

9. *Ephemeris* 1908, 133-178 (146-156) ; cf. *BCH* 46 (1922) 224.

10. *Ibid.*, 1917, 78-104, pl. I-II. Cf. Picard, *op. cit.*, 258.

11. Dunand, *Syria* 7 (1926) 3 sq., pl. IV, publie des statues d'enfants (ex-voto) qui y furent trouvées.

ETRUSCA AETERNA

REINHARD HERBIG
Universität Heidelberg

Die auf dem Deckel ihres Sarkophages gelagerte Figur des Verstorbenen ist als künstlerischer Gedanke eine durchaus ungriechische sepulkrale Idee. Sie lässt sich auch in keiner Weise mit den echt anthropoiden Sarkophagen des Orients (Aegypten; Sidon und Karthago: griechisch-phönikische Arbeiten in ägyptischer Manier) zusammenbringen, bei welchen der Leichenbehälter selbst annähernd die Form des menschlichen Körpers annimmt. Die Deckelfigur im etruskischen Sinn erscheint im Altertum vielmehr nur in Etrurien selbst und im Anschluss an diese Gestaltung des Sarges dann wieder in zwei Epochen der kaiserzeitlich-römischen Sarkophagkunst. Die wenigen phönikisch-karthagischen Beispiele der frühhellenistischen Zeit (v. Bissing, *StudEtr.* VII 1933, 83ff.) stehen in keinem Abhängigkeitsverhältnis von der etruskischen Formidee, wie sie auch ihrerseits nicht etwa jene beeinflussen. Die Einzelheiten der formalen Durchbildung sind in beiden Fällen geradezu gegensätzlicher Natur, während die Idee als solche, das Ruhen der Figur des im Sarge Bestatteten auf dessen Deckel, grundsätzlich eine ähnliche ist. Wobei gefragt werden darf, ob dahinter sich ein gemeinsamer Ausgangspunkt verbirgt (Orient), den wir aber in materiellen Hinterlassenschaften nicht zu fassen vermögen. Durch das erste Jahrhundert unserer Zeitrechnung bis in trajanische Zeit hinein finden sich in Rom gelagerte Deckelfiguren auf schlichten Sargkästen, im Anschluss zweifellos an den kurz vor der Zeitwende erst erlöschenden etruskischen Brauch, der sich im etruskischen Gebiet glatt ins römische Bestattungswesen hinübergespielt hatte.[1] Die gleiche Sitte der Anbringung liegender Figuren, nun mit Vorliebe halbaufgerichteter im Gegensatz zum ersten Jahrhundert, wo die Gestalten meist schlafend auf dem Rücken oder auf der Seite lagen, kommt in Rom dann noch einmal seit der Wende vom 2. zum 3. Jahrhundert auf, das letztere ganz erfüllend. Doch stehen in beiden Epochen die zwei Typen durchaus nebeneinander, so dass man in Rom sicher nicht von einer Entwicklung von einem früheren, dem ruhenden, zu einem späteren aufgerichteten Typus sprechen kann. Aber auffällig bleibt unbedingt, in

---

1. Morey, *Sardis* V (1924): *Kleinasiatische Säulensarkophage mit Klinendeckel.* Rodenwaldt, *RM* 58 (1943) 10ff. Derselbe *JDAI* 45 (1930) 138 ff. Collignon, *Stat. fun.* Abb. 225ff. 237ff. Herbig, *AA.* 1934 540ff. Rodenwaldt, *Gnomon* 1 (1925), 125. Weickert, *Gnomon* 3 (1927) 215 (Ferentum). Cumont, *Recherches sur le symbolisme funéraire chez les Romains* (1942) 388ff. liegende, 414ff. aufgerichtete Deckelfiguren.

welch überraschendem Maße die spätrömischen Beispiele bisweilen ihren etruskischen Vorgängern gleichen, so das Paar auf einem Deckel im Louvre[2] in seiner gestaffelten Anordnung und den steil aufgerichteten Oberleibern dem archaischen Prachtbeispiel der Villa Giulia.[3] Das römische Exemplar zeigt freilich organischer empfundene Körperformen, die Gelagerten ruhen mit natürlich angezogenen Beinen, nicht mit so extrem unplastisch empfundenen, wie hingeplätteten Unterkörpern. Erstaunlich ist übrigens auch die Verwandtschaft einer alexandrinischen Deckel-(oder Grab-?) Figur zu den etruskischen Formulierungen der Särge und Urnen,[4] eine Aehnlichkeit, die sich in Haltung, Ausdruck des Gesichtes und Attributen zugleich ausspricht.

Im ganzen kann also kaum bezweifelt werden, dass der jedenfalls für unser Wissen ursprünglich etruskische Gedanke der Anbringung einer gelagerten Bildnisfigur auf den Deckeln der Sarkophage in wiederholt aufgenommenen römischen Bestattungsformen seine nächste Fortsetzung gefunden hat. Mit solchem Neuaufleben hat aber diese ganz zuerst vielleicht wirklich orientalische Idee (die freilich im älteren Orient nie und an keiner Stelle in die gleiche Form geprägt worden ist)[5] in Europa endgültig festen Fuss gefasst und ist im folgenden in der Entwicklung der abendländischen Kunst immer wieder einmal aufgetaucht, nie mehr ganz verschwunden.

Unmittelbare Anknüpfung an etruskische Vorbilder, die an sich gewiss nicht als völlig unmöglich angesehen zu werden braucht, will W e e g e in der Sarkophagkunst des frühen toskanischen Quattrocento erkennen.[6] Die angeführten Formähnlichkeiten sind da sicher nicht gering, wenn W e e g e auch in dem Versuch der Ausdeutung des symbolischen Beiwerks entschieden zu weit geht. Denn die treuen Tiere etwa, welche hier wie überhaupt in der Grabmalkunst des Mittelalters zu Füssen und gelegentlich auch zu Häupten des Toten

---

2. Collignon a.O. Abb. 226.

3. Ebenda Abb. 221.

4. Ebenda Abb. 227. Dazu der trajanische Deckel in Kopenhagen: *From the collections of the Ny Carlsberg Glyptothek,* 3, 1942, 225ff., wo in Abb. 5 der Alexandrinische Deckel besser wiedergegeben ist.

5. Den einzigen Ausnahmefall, einen Klinensarkophag mit gelagerter Deckelfigur im Mausoleum von Belewi bei Ephesos (*JOAI* 29 (1935) Beiblatt Sp. 135ff.) aus dem mittleren 3. Jahrhundert v.Chr. hat Rodenwaldt, etwas kompliziert, aber richtig, erklärt als "seleukidische Zwischenstufe zwischcen den makedonischen Totenbetten und den palmyrenischen Klinen" (*RM* 58 [1943] 12). Die Deckelfigur des Inhabers (Antiochos II. Theos?) sieht in ihrem Lagerungsmotiv ungemein "etruskisch" aus! Zu den Totenbetten in Kammergräbern vgl. Rodenwaldts *RE*-Artikel "Kline." Palmyrenische Klinendarstellungen finden sich neuerdings abgebildet in *Berytos* 2, 1935, Taf. 26ff. (229 n.Chr.) V Taf. 43ff. Ferner u.a. *Syria*, 1936, Taf. 36, 46ff., 1937, Taf. 4.

6. *Etruskische Malerei* 15ff., Abb. 13/14.

seinen Schlummer bewachen, kann man unmöglich mit den Löwen oder Fabeltieren auf den Deckeln der etruskischen Särge in einen Bedeutungsvergleich setzen, denn hier gehören sie nicht zu den Toten im mittelalterlichen Sinnzusammenhang, sondern als Akroterfiguren ausschliesslich zur Architektur der Deckelgiebel. Das Kistenrelief des von W e e g e angeführten und abgebildeten toskanischen Sarkophages, Girlanden schleppende Putten, weist übrigens allein schon eher auf römische Sarkophage mit solcher Verzierung als Vorbild hin[7] als auf etruskische, an denen dieses Ziermotiv gar nicht vorkommt.

Wir können die orientalisch-etruskische Idee des plastischen Totenbildnisses auf dem Deckel des eigenen Sarkophages, hier nicht auf ihrem gesamten Gang durch die Entwicklung der europäischen Kunst verfolgen.[8] So mag nur daran erinnert sein, dass etwa an den gotischen Grabsteinen der Ritter und ihrer Frauen ganz die gleichen formalen Probleme auftauchen wie an den etruskischen Sargdeckeln: der meist ungelöste Widerspruch zwischen den Auffassungen des repräsentativen Stehens und des im sanften Todesschlummer Liegens.

Die Auseinandersetzung zwischen der Auffassung der reliefierten Sarkophagfigur als einer stehenden oder als einer gelagerten hat sich in der Tat das ganze Mittelalter hindurch fortgesetzt,[9] ja bis in die Neuzeit hinein angedauert. Besonders in der Frühzeit des Mittelalters ist sie an fast jedem derartigen Kunstwerk stark spürbar,[10] wenn auch meist dabei die eine oder die andere Interpretation merklich überwiegt. Im 14. Jahrhundert treten die beiden Auffassungen dann stärker auseinander, scheiden sich in ihren beiderseitigen Elementen reinlicher.[11] Aber daneben besteht der alte Konflikt auch seinerseits ruhig weiter fort und spricht sich in einer stattlichen Anzahl von Beispielen deutlich genug aus.[12] Ganz besonders eindrucksvoll in den grossen, mit seitlichen "Sarkophagreliefs" versehenen Tumben in Prag und Querfurt.[13] Die Sarkophagreliefs bestehen in dem einen Fall, am Sarge Ottokars von Böhmen, aus zwei prächtigen Wappen-

---

7. *RM* 1943, 16f., Abb. 7f. *JDAI* 45 (1930), 145 Abb. 22/23.

8. Als lohnende Aufgabe von R o d e n w a l d t bezeichnet *RM* 58 (1943), 25f., der an dieser Stelle andeutungsweise die Verschiedenartigkeit der Tradition aus dem west- und oströmischen Bereich aufzeigt.

9. Panofsky, "Die deutsche Plastik des 11.-13. Jahrh.," *JOAI* 93, 109f. Jantzen, *Deutsche Plastik des 13. Jahrhunderts*, 2. Aufl. 1944, 40ff.

10. Panofsky, a.O., Taf. 13 (1080), 14 (1100), 20 (1130), 23 (1152 und 1200), 46 (1240), 85 (1250), 111 (1270).

11. Pinder, *Die deutsche Plastik des 14. Jahrhunderts*, Taf. 13, eindeutige Darstellung des Todesschlummers, Taf. 47f., ebenso klar dargestellter Stehender.

12. Ebenda Taf. 77/78.

13. Ebenda Taf. 82ff. Ottokar I. um 1377 und Taf. 85ff. Gebhard von Querfurt, um 1383.

bildern, Adler und Löwe im Schild, also heraldisch-symbolischen Motiven, wie sie an etruskischen Särgen grundsätzlich auch vorkommen, in Querfurt dagegen aus Langseitenfriesen je eines Zuges von Trauertänzern, einem inhaltlichen Gegenstück also zu den griechischen Klagefrauen aus Sidon. Von denen ist freilich jede einzelne strenge in ihren architektonischen Rahmen gespannt, während der Zug hier locker und frei nach Art der mittelalterlichen Totentänze durch das Bildfeld marschiert, am Beschauer vorbei. Die äussere Form des Reliefs mit dem ausgesparten Bildfeld, versenkt in den breiten, schmucklosen, balkenähnlichen Rahmen, lässt sich ohne weiteres mit etruskischen Beispielen in formale Parallele setzen. Die "bewusste Derbheit des Rahmenprofils" nennt P i n d e r übrigens "völlig pragerisch."[14]

In die gleiche Zeit und unter dieselbe doppelsinnige Deutung gehören die prachtvollen Grabmäler der burgundischen und französischen Fürsten,[15] wenngleich diese Anlagen als architektonisches Ganzes mehr den Mausoleumsbauten als der Klasse der einfachen Sarkophage zuzuzählen sind. Unter ihnen findet sich eine besonders merkwürdige Lösung, die auch in unserem Zusammenhang der Erwähnung wert sein dürfte. Sie erscheint wie geschaffen, einen grundsätzlichen Unterschied zwischen der antiken und der neuzeitlichen Auffassung der gelagerten Grabfigur zu überbrücken.[16] Die nachantiken Darstellungen geben die liegenden Gestalten stets in der Haltung und Ausstattung parademässig aufgebahrter Leichen (oder Schlummernder, was zum schaustellermäßigen Charakter der Bildwerke schon wieder nicht recht passen will), die Antike dagegen gibt die Sarkophagdeckelfiguren immer, wach oder schlummernd, in der Haltung des Lebens voll natürlicher Bewegung und in bequemer Lage, nicht in einem schaustellungsmäßig künstlich zurechtgemachten Zustand. Das Grabmal in Brou nun hat die beiden Auffassungen vereinigt, in zwei Lösungen an derselben Figur, übereinander angeordnet, ausgesprochen: oben, sozusagen dem Beschauer allein sichtbar vor Augen gerückt, die starre, aufgeputzte paradierende Figur der Verstorbenen, im Tode noch Stand und Würde aufzeigend und wahrend. Unten dann, gleichsam unter der Erde ruhend, das Bild des toten Menschen, der nichts anderes mehr sein will, mit gelöstem Haar dem sanften Schlaf im Leichentuch sich friedlich hingebend. Oben die leere irdische Hülle im Prunk ihres Standes, unten, wie

14. a.O. 65.
15. Philipps des Kühnen von Klaus Sluter. Weese, *Skulptur und Malerei in Frankreich im 15. und 16. Jahrh. (Burgers Handbuch* 20), Abb. 191. Ferner Weese Abb. 192, 195, 201ff.
16. Weese a.O. Abb. 207ff. Grabmal der Margarete von Oesterreich in Brou.

erlöst davon, das rein menschlich rührende Bild der Abgeschiedenen. Im konsequenten Weiterdenken dieses Gedankens, vermischt mit der Vorstellung vom Ablegen aller irdischen Würden im christlichen Sterben, bringt die französische Kunst der zweiten Hälfte des 16. Jahrhunderts dann eine überraschend kühne, fast brutal anmutende Lösung in der Darstellungsreihe der Sargfiguren. Nämlich am Grabmal Heinrichs II. von Frankreich und seiner Gattin, der Katharina Medici.[17] Das hohe Paar ist hier nackt und bloß auf den Sargdeckel gelegt, nur notdürftig mit dem Leichentuch verhüllt und auf Kissen gebettet, aber aller Abzeichen seiner königlichen Würde beraubt und ohne Erinnerung an den Prunk seines irdischen Daseins. Das ist eine konsequent grausame christliche Auffassung, die in der Antike natürlich niemals vertreten worden sein konnte bei der völlig anderen Art der beiderseitigen eschatologischen Anschauungen, auch wenn Heraklit einmal gesagt hat, dass Leichen "wegwerfenswerter seien als Mist."

Im 15. and 16. Jahrhundert spielt dann jener Auffassungskonflikt in der Darstellung der Grabfigur weiter, daneben stehen aber immer wieder Lösungen mit dem Schwergewicht nach der einen oder anderen Seite hin.[18] Seit der Entwicklung der Kunst in den hohen Barock hinein taucht dann im 17. Jahrhundert immer häufiger die antike Formulierung des halbaufgerichteten Liegens auf, als Spätform zu verstehen, genau wie im Altertum auch.[19] Der Typus ist aber in Italien und Frankreich schon in der Hochrenaissance wieder lebendig geworden[20] und hat offenbar von da aus Eingang nach Deutschland gefunden. Der Klassizismus wendet sich unter dem Einfluss der christlich-romantischen Gedankenwelt wieder entschiedener der Vorstellung vom ruhigen ungestörten, an sich sanften Todesschlaf zu[21] und bis auf unsere Tage ist die Wiedergabe dieser Wunsch-

17. 1559 und 1589 gestorben, in der Abteikirche von St. Denis. Weese a.O. Abb. 217/8.

18. Pinder, *Die Deutsche Plastik des 15. Jahrh.*, Taf. 98/99 Konflikt. Taf. 12 stehend, Taf. 47 liegend. Feulner, *Deutsche Plastik des 16. Jahrh.* Taf. 2, 44, 84, 85, 90. Derselbe, *Deutsche Plastik des 17. Jahrh.* Taf. 2.

19. Feulner, *Deutsche Plastik des 17. Jahrh.* Taf. 57.

20. Italien under vielen anderen: Michelangelo, Juliusgrabmal, Figur des Papstes auf dem Sarg, Brinkmann, *Barockskulptur* I 51 Abb. 39; Sansovino, *Grabmal Ascanio Sforza, Rom, Sta. Maria del Popolo;* Schubring, *Propyläen Kunstgeschichte* 9 Taf. 480. Ammanati, *Grabmal del Monte, Rom, S. Pietro in Montorio,* Brinkmann a.O. 107 Abb. 96. Frankreich: Philippe de Chabots Grabmal von Jean Cousin d.Ae., Paris. Weese a.O. 192 Abb. 235.

21. Rauch, *Grabmal der Königin Luise in Charlottenburg;* Pauli, *Propyläen Kunstgeschichte* 14 Taf. 281. Vgl. auch die Skizzen Schadows zu einer ähnlichen Figur (der Gegenstand und die Auffassung waren also vergeschrieben!), ebenda Taf. 227. Ferner Schadows Grabmal des kleinen "Grafen von der Mark" in der Berliner Dorotheenkirche, ebenda Taf. 276.

vorstellung nicht mehr verschwunden. Der im Schmuck seiner Waffen ruhig liegende und von der Mühe des Kampfes ausruhende Kämpfer ist zu einer neuen sympathischen Form des Kriegerdenkmals geworden,[22] die das fatale bürgerliche Pathos der fahnenschwingend Fallenden nach 1870 durch eine menschlich schlichte und ergreifende Form abgelöst hat. Die tiefen und schönen Gedanken solcher Art von Grabmälern hat den Völkern Europas niemand anderes als die immer noch so rätselhafte Nation der Etrusker vorgedacht, vor Augen gestellt und als ein bis heute unzerstörtes Erbe hinterlassen.[23] Vielleicht vermag diese Ueberlegung die Etrusker doch von einem Teil jenes Odiums zu entlasten, welches man immer wieder einmal ungerecht und unter Außerachtlassung wissenschaftlicher Erkenntnisse auf ihr Haupt zu häufen unternahm.

---

22. Ein symbolisches Grab, etwa wie Breekers Mal des Unbekannten Soldaten des Weltkrieges 1914/18 am Münchener Hofgarten: Buschor, *Vom Sinn der griechischen Standbilder* Taf. 46 (Teilansicht). Das Bildwerk, die Figur des Gefallenen, ist längst zu einer wahrhaft mythischen geworden, wie der an ihm geübte "Totenkult" der Bevölkerung beweist.

23. In seiner letzten grossen Arbeit, die zum reifen Vermächtnis eines deutschen Gelehrten geworden i st, der sein Leben an der Ostfront gab, hat Werner Technau (*Die Kunst der Römer*, Berlin 1940, 35) Wesen und geschichtiche Rolle, die hier einmal gespalten nebeneinander hergehen, in knappen Sätzen zutreffend gekennzeichnet: "Hatte das östliche Erbteil der Etrusker das römisch italische Wesen in chthonische Dumpfheit und Magie verstrickt, so hat doch zugleich die künstlerische Abhängigkeit der Etrusker von den Griechen Rom unaufhörlich in mittelbare Beziehung zu Griechenland gebracht. Diese geschichtliche Wirkung darf nicht vergessen werden, wenn man die Ueberfremdung Roms durch die Etrusker als eine Gefährdung und Beeinträchtigung des von nordischen Völkern begründeten Abendlandes erkannt hat."
Darüber hinaus vermochte unser Versuch hier zu zeigen, wie die Etrusker auch einen eigenen fruchtbaren Formgedanken, der ihnen nicht von den Griechen überliefert worden war, zur Weiterentwicklung in der abendländischen Kunst beigesteuert haben.

ETRUSKISCHE BRONZEN IN GRIECHENLAND

EMIL KUNZE
München

Tafeln 88-90

Τίς τῶν λυχνείων ἡ ἐργασία; Τυρρηνική.
Pherekrates bei Athenaios (15, 700c)

Tierbeine oder Tierklauen, die einst als Gerätfüße dienten, haben sich in vielen Heiligtümern Griechenlands gefunden und fehlen auch in keiner größeren Sammlung griechischer Bronzen. Doch schenkt man ihnen im allgemeinen wenig Beachtung. Die Gründe für diese Vernachlässigung liegen auf der Hand. Denn die griechischen Gerätfüße bleiben für uns fast stets Fragment, von dem Ganzen, dem sie zugehörten, läßt sich selten eine präzise Vorstellung gewinnen. Daher kommt man meistens auch über eine recht ungefähre kunstgeschichtliche Bestimmung nicht hinaus. Zumal an einem Ort wie Olympia, wo die Funde besonders reich fließen und die Mannigfaltigkeit der Typen ungewöhnlich groß ist, wird man sich dieser Unsicherheit deutlich bewußt.[1] Um so eher kann es gerechtfertigt scheinen, aus festlichem Anlaß unter den olympischen Gerätfüßen ein Stück herauszugreifen, das mehr auszusagen vermag als seine Gefährten und dem zugleich eine außerordentliche geschichtliche Bedeutung zukommt.

Die schöne Bronze, die wir dem verdienten Ausgräber von Olynth hier vorlegen dürfen (Tafel 88), wurde im Jahre 1939 bei den Tiefgrabungen im Mosaiksaal der neronischen Villa im Südosten der Altis gefunden:[2] eine geflügelte Raubtierklaue, über deren Knie rittlings ein Jüngling sitzt, die Hände in die Hüften gestützt. Der Erhaltungszustand läßt wenig zu wünschen übrig. Gebrochen ist nur der größere Teil des rechten und die äußerste Spitze des linken Flügels, empfindlich beschädigt allein die stark bestoßene Nase des Jünglings. Die von der Zeit kaum angegriffene Oberfläche erlaubt wohl einen Rückschluß auf die Güte der verwendeten Metallegierung. Die hohl gegossene runde Basis, die aus einen Wulst und einer ein-

---

1. Zu den alten Funden (*Olympia*, IV, 126 Nr.811-813 u.137 Nr.855-859 Taf.48 und 51) kommen nicht wenige aus den Jahren 1937-1942, die hoffentlich bald in ihrer Gesamtheit vorgelegt werden können.
2. Grabungsinventar B 1001. Höhe 11 cm. Ueber die Ausgrabungen im 'Mosaiksaal' und seiner Umgebung vgl. *Bericht über die Ausgrabungen in Olympia*, III, 1 und IV, 4. Die Fundstelle unseres Gerätfußes ergibt für seine Datierung nichts weiter, als daß er noch in vorrömischer Zeit unter die Erde geraten sein muß.

springenden niedrigen Deckplatte besteht, gewährt dem Fuß einen
sicheren Stand und legt zugleich dessen Neigungswinkel eindeutig
fest. Er beträgt etwa 60 Grad. Die Klaue ist mit der Basis verlötet,
die Befestigung scheint jedoch noch durch eine Niete verstärkt gewesen zu sein, deren Kopf auf der Unterseite der Platte sichtbar ist.
Das Gerät selbst lag in dem spitzwinkeligen Hohlraum auf, der von
den Flügeln und den beiden breiten Haarbahnen eingefaßt wird, die
von dem nur über dem Scheitel vollrunden Kopf des Jünglings auf
die Flügel herabhängen. Es ergibt sich daraus, daß das Gerät einen
prismatischen, nach oben sich verjüngenden Unterbau hatte. Je zwei
an jedem der Flügel angebrachte Nieten verbanden ihn einst mit
seinen drei Füßen. Der allein erhaltene Fuß muß einmal mit Gewalt
aus seinem Verband losgerissen worden sein, wobei der rechte Flügel
mitsamt den beiden Nägeln abbrach, während vom linken Flügel nur
die Spitze mit dem äußeren Nagel an der Wandung des Gerätes haften
blieb. Am Bruch zeichnet sich hier noch die halbe Rundung des
Nagelloches ab.

Das Löwenbein und die mit ihm verbundene menschliche Gestalt
ist plastisch reich und mit kräftigen Akzenten modelliert. Die Formgebung zeugt von einem reifen Können: man wird dem köstlichen
kleinen Werk das Lob einer vorzüglichen Arbeit nicht versagen. Und
kein Betrachter wird sich dem eigentümlichen Zauber entziehen, der
von der geistreichen, wenn auch seltsam unwirklichen Phantastik der
Konzeption ausgeht. Allein, das an griechischer Form geschulte Auge
wird mit Befremden auch des Mangels an tektonischer Klarheit sowie
der Willkür und inneren Unlogik in der Verschmelzung der Teile
innewerden. So wachsen die Flügel durchaus unorganisch aus dem
Löwenbein heraus, indem ihr Ansatz, die seitliche Beinmuskulatur
verhüllend, bis über die Fessel herabreicht, und erst recht verharrt
der krönende 'Reiter' in unvorstellbarer Schwebe auf seinem Sitz.
Es sieht nicht aus, als könne er sich dort behaupten: von einem
Reiten kann keine Rede sein. Das Verhältnis des Jünglings zu dem
Löwenbein entzieht sich tatsächlich einer Interpretation, wie auch
die enge Verbindung beider Teile auf die natürliche Proportionalität
keine Rücksicht nimmt. Ebensowenig läßt sich das Motiv des Jünglings selbst wirklich erklären. Die in die Hüfte gestemmten Hände
würden zwar zu einer Stützfigur passen.[3] Doch der Jüngling trägt
gar nicht die Last des Gerätes und wäre in seiner prekären Stellung
dazu auch gewiß nicht imstande. Auch die Erinnerung, daß eine

---

3. Vgl. Jantzen *Bronzenwerkstätten in Großgriechenland und Sizilien*, 7f., der
aber nur frühe und in der Haltung der Hände auch abweichende Beispiele für
das Motiv anführt.

ähnliche Armhaltung bei Tänzern begegnet,[4] vermag das Verständnis unserer Figur kaum zu fördern. Man fragt hier nicht ungestraft zu viel: bei dem Versuch, tiefer in Sinn und Struktur des kleinen Gebildes einzudringen, verflüchtigt sich nur seine unmittelbare Wirkung auf die Phantasie, und damit sein ursprünglicher zauberhafter Reiz.

Ein Werk, das sich den Gesetzen tektonischer Logik so wenig fügen will, eine Komposition, deren Sinn sich schlechterdings nicht restlos erklären läßt, kann schwerlich griechisch sein. Und doch steht unsere Bronze auf griechischem Boden nicht allein. Sie hat vielmehr im Heiligtum der Athena von Lindos ein genaues Gegenstück, das leider schlecht erhalten und wohl deshalb bisher nicht bemerkt worden ist. Aber die sonstigen Funde gleichartiger Gerätfüße lassen an deren italischem Ursprung keinen Zweifel. Denn aus Etrurien stammen nicht weniger als drei aus je drei Stücken bestehende vollständige Sätze, für einen vierten ist die gleiche Herkunft mehr als wahrscheinlich. Der Typus unseres Gerätfußes ist also bereits in einer recht stattlichen Zahl von Exemplaren bekannt:[5]

1) Vatikan. Aus Süd- oder Mitteletrurien. *Museo Gregoriano* I Taf.51,3 (A Taf.78,3) ; Helbig, *Führer₃* I Nr.672; Phot.Alinari 35526 links, danach Giglioli, *L'arte Etrusca* Taf.315,4 und *Rendiconti d.Pontif. Accad.Rom.*18,1941/2,252 Abb.16 links; andere Aufnahme Nogara, *Gli Etruschi e la loro civiltà* 107 Abb.57 und Neugebauer, *Bronzegerät d.Altertumes* Taf.12,1. Nach neuer Reinigung und Restaurierung: *Rendiconti a.O.*253 Abb.17 links.

2) Ny Carlsberg Glyptothek H.221. Aus Orvieto. F. Poulsen, *Aus einer alten Etruskerstadt* 37f. Abb. 72-74; *Bildtafeln d. etrusk. Museums d.Ny Carlsb.Glypt.* Taf.95,221.

3) Berlin Fr.697. Aus Vulci. Neugebauer, *Führer* I 103 Taf.30 Mitte; *Röm. Mitt.* 38/9,1923/4,437 Abb.23 Mitte; Giglioli, *L'arte Etrusca* Taf.214,2.

4) New York, Metr.Mus.20.37.1. *Vente Drouot* 11.-13.6.1913 (*Coll. Borelli-Bey*) Nr. 250 Taf.31; G. Richter, *Handbook of the Etruscan Collection* 30 Abb.88. Hier Tafel 89.

---

4. Vgl. Beazley, *Some Attic Vases in the Cyprus Museum*, 41f. Bei unserem Jüngling scheint, wenn die Photographien nicht doch täuschen (ich besitze darüber keine Notizen) der abgespreizte Daumen die Hüfte zu umgreifen: anders z.B. das New Yorker Exemplar, unten S. Nr. 4 Tafel 89. Nach Beazley ist die entsprechende Stellung des Daumens — doch mit lockerer Haltung der Finger — auf den dionysischen Tanz des Satyrspiels beschränkt.

5. Für Aufnahmen des vatikanischen Thymiaterions bin ich F. Magi und H. Speier, für Photos des Berliner Kandelabers C. Blümel verpflichtet, Auskünfte und Photos aus New York, von denen ich hier zwei mit freundlicher Zustimmung der Trustees des Metropolitan Museums abbilde, verdanke ich Miss Richter's nie versagender Güte. Allen diesen Helfern sei nochmals herzlichst gedankt.

5) Olympia. Hier Tafel 88.

6) Konstantinopel. Aus Lindos. Blinkenberg, *Lindos* I 746 Nr. 3217 Taf.151.

Die Füße Vatikan (1) und Kopenhagen (2) gehören zu Thymiaterien, die aus mitgefundenen Resten wiederhergestellt werden konnten. Sie tragen in eben der Weise, die sich aus Form und Befestigungsspuren des olympischen Fußes (5) erschließen ließ, einen prismatischen Untersatz aus Bronzeblech. Bei der New Yorker Serie (4) stimmen die Lage der Nagellöcher und die Zurichtung der Rückseiten genau mit dem Exemplar aus Olympia (5) überein[6]: danach stammt auch sie sicher von einem Thymiaterion. Nur die Berliner Füße (3) stehen in einem anderen Konnex: sie vereinigen sich zu einem Dreibein, von dem der Schaft eines Kandelabers emporsteigt. Nun kann freilich kein Zweifel sein, daß der Typus nicht für diese Verwendung erdacht ist. Lehrt doch schon ein Blick auf die Abbildung des Kandelabers, daß die Flügel dabei ihre konstruktive Funktion verlieren: statt der Befestigung zu dienen, stoßen sie ins Leere. Aber auch der Fuß selbst hat sich gewandelt und seine einheitliche Struktur eingebüßt. Die Klaue endet nämlich, wie die mir vorliegenden Aufnahmen überraschend erkennen lassen, vorne gleich oberhalb des — übrigens auch anders gebildeten — Gelenkes in einer wulstigen Leiste, auf der der Knabe jetzt zu knien scheint. So bleibt der dreieckige Raum zwischen dessen Oberschenkeln leer, während sich die Klaue nach oben nur seitlich in den Flügeln fortsetzt. Den drohenden Zerfall des Gebildes in seine Bestandteile darf man wohl als Zeichen jüngerer Entstehung deuten. Und in der Tat scheint die den Kandelaber krönende feine Gruppe eines Jünglings mit einem Mädchen diesen Eindruck zu bestätigen[7]: ihr Stil ist fraglos jünger als der der Knaben im Vatikan (1), in Kopenhagen (2), Olympia (5) und New York (4), an denen im Gegensatz zu der Berliner Gruppe noch gewisse archaische Züge nicht zu verkennen sind.[8] Das alles führt zu dem Schluß, daß der Typus für das Thymiaterion geschaffen und auf den Kandelaber erst übertragen wurde. Das olympische Weihgeschenk aber muß, wie wir sahen, ein Thymiaterion gewesen sein; für den Fuß aus Lindos (6) dürfte dasselbe gelten,

---

6. Für die beiden antiken Nagellöcher in jedem der Flügel liegt mir eine von Miss Chr. Alexander freundlichst angefertigte Skizze vor; das auf den Photographien allein sichtbare Loch ist danach modern.

7. Giglioli, *L'arte Etrusca*, Taf.215,4; *St. Etr.* 10 (1936) Taf. 7,4.

8. Leider läßt sich der mir zu Verfügung stehenden Aufnahme eines der Füße des Berliner Kandelabers nicht mehr entnehmen, als was oben ausgeführt wurde: sie ermöglicht keinen stilistischen Vergleich des Knaben mit seinen Gegenstücken, weshalb ich auch auf ihre Reproduktion verzichte. Eine Nachprüfung des Originales und die Herstellung einer Neuaufnahme ist zur Zeit nicht möglich.

jedenfalls geht er in seinem einheitlichen Bau mit den älteren Stücken
zusammen, nicht mit den Füßen des Berliner Kandelabers (3).

Die Heimat jener Thymiaterien sucht man jetzt allgemein in
Etrurien, nachdem sich zuletzt auch Neugebauer, der das vatikanische
Stück (1) lange Zeit für unteritalisch-griechisch gehalten hatte,
der herrschenden Meinung zugeneigt hat. Ein Hauptgrund war für
ihn, daß sich Vorstufen für die Form des Weihrauchständers allein
in Etrurien aufzeigen lassen.[9] Doch auch die Füße mit den rittlings
aufsitzenden Knaben, die uns in erster Linie angehen, können ihrem
Stil nach nur etruskisch sein. Zwar bestehen zwischen den einzelnen
Exemplaren unerwartet große Unterschiede nicht nur der Qualität,
sondern auch des Stiles. Gegenüber dem olympischen Stück (5) sind
etwa die Jünglinge der New Yorker Exemplare (4), deren Tierfüße
auch in ihrer Bildung abweichen und eine stärkere Neigung aufweisen, viel gröber in der Ausführung, die Muskeln derber herausge-
arbeitet und starrer gefügt. Die von dem Brustkorbrand giebelig
überdachte Bauchpartie sowie das schmale, hohe Gesicht mit der
maskenhaften Spannung seiner Züge und dem starren Lächeln könnten altertümlicher scheinen, verraten indes in der übertreibenden
Durchführung eher den zurückgebliebenen Werker, der sich von den
selbst in Etrurien bereits überlebten Formeln nicht zu lösen vermochte. Gegen die datierende Kraft solcher 'archaischen' Formen
spricht in diesem Falle ja schon die Haarrolle: eine Haartracht des
strengen Stiles. Die Füße im Vatikan (1) und in Kopenhagen (2)
dagegen kommen stilistisch dem Fuß aus Olympia (5) entschieden
näher. Aber auch dieser, der von allen erhaltenen der qualitätvollste
sein dürfte, verleugnet nicht seinen etruskischen Ursprung, so glücklich auch in Kopf und Körper des Jünglings griechische Formen
nachempfunden sind. Die immer noch etwas schematische Härte der
Bauchzeichnung und der dicke, unartikulierte Hals, den die über der
Brust sich vereinigenden Schlüsselbeinwulste vom Körper förmlich
abriegeln, finden ihre Parallelen unter etruskischen Bronzen[10] und
schließen jedenfalls auch großgriechische Herkunft aus. Der an
griechische Werke frühklassischen Stils gemahnende Anflug von
Strenge und herber Schönheit aber, der Antlitz und Gestalt des
Jünglings adelt, sind vermutlich aus einer Berührung mit der unteritalischen Kunst zu erklären, zu der auch der merkwürdige Haarschmuck eine Brücke schlägt: das mit drei dicken Scheiben besetzte

---

9. *JdI* 58 (1943) 264.
10. Zu den hervorgehobenen Zügen vgl.z.B.Riis,*Tyrrhenika*, Taf.17,3 und 18,2;
JRS 36 (1946) Taf.7. — Zum Stirnhaar vgl.besonders *JdI* 58 (1943) 240 Abb.28.

Band, auf das schon Neugebauer zur Stütze seiner ursprünglichen These hingewiesen hatte.[11]

Unsere Gerätfüße hat kürzlich auch Riis im Anschluß an den Berliner Kandelaber (3) zusammengestellt und sie der Bronze-Industrie von Vulci zugeteilt.[12] Wir halten diese Zuschreibung im Hinblick auf manche Beziehungen, die den Knaben mit etwas älteren Bronzen verbinden, für die Vulcenter Ursprung wahrscheinlich gemacht worden ist,[13] für sehr wohl möglich. Doch herrscht in der Lokalisierung etruskischer Bronzen des mittleren 5. Jahrhunderts, dem der Typus trotz der pseudoarchaischen Formgebung der New Yorker Exemplare (4) angehören muß, noch eine größere Unsicherheit als bei älteren Bronzen, eine Unsicherheit, die zu beheben wir hier nicht versuchen können. Uns mag es daher genügen, auf die alte Archäologenfrage 'Τίς ἡ ἐργασία;' mit dem attischen Komödiendichter summarisch zu antworten: 'Τυρρηνική'.

Der Thymiaterionfuß aus Olympia (5) gesellt sich also mit seinem Gegenstück aus Lindos den wenigen etruskischen Metallwerken zu, die auf griechischem Boden zu Tage gekommen und als etruskisch erkannt worden sind.[14] In erster Linie wären die Reste eines prächtigen Vulcenter Stabdreifußes von der Akropolis zu nennen, der unseren Thymiaterien um mehr als ein Menschenalter, jedenfalls noch vor den Perserkriegen, den Weg nach Osten vorausging.[15] Eher etwas jünger ist eine Eimerattasche aus Dodona mit dem Reliefbild des schlangenbeinigen Typhon, für die Dohrn sicher mit Recht etruskische Herkunft vermutet hat.[16] Und man wird den importierten etruskischen Bronzen jetzt auch getrost die drei Griffe von Siebtrichtern,

---

11. *AA*, 1923/4,326. Ueber diesen Haarschmuck hat Neugebauer, *RM*, 38/9 (1923/4) 423ff. ausführlich gehandelt. Unter seinen Beispielen sind aber nur einige wirklich großgriechisch (für den unteritalischen Ursprung des Schmucks vor allem beweisen die Terrakotten), andere kampanisch (a.O.424 Anm.2, dazu *From the Collections of the Ny Carlsberg Glyptothek* 2,1938,160 Abb. 20 a), wiederum andere etruskisch, wie z.B. der Berliner Kandelaber aus Lokri (Jantzen, *Bronzewerkstätten*, Taf.36,148; Riis, *Tyrrhenika*, 81,Nr.3; dagegen freilich Neugebauer, *JdI*, 58(1943)259) und die Sirenen Riis, *Tyrrhenika*, 90 Anm.2. — Den Jünglingen der Thymiaterionfüße in New York fehlt die mit Scheiben besetzte Binde, sie haben statt dessen aufgerolltes Stirnhaar.

12. Riis, *Tyrrhenika*, 87 mit Anm. 2.

13. Zur Vulcenter Bronze-Industrie *AA*, 1923/4, 302ff. (Neugebauer); *Studi Etruschi*, 10(1936)15ff. (Guarducci); Riis, *Tyrrhenika*, 77ff.; *JdI*, 58(1943)206ff. (Neugebauer).

14. Ueber etruskischen Import in Griechenland zuletzt zusammenfassend Karo, *Ephemeris*, 1937, 316ff.

15. Karo a.O.319; seither sind die Athener Dreifußfragmente mehrfach besprochen worden: Riis, *Acta Archaeol.*10,(1939)22 Nr.2; Riis, *Tyrrhenika*, 78 Taf. 14,1; Neugebauer, *JdI*, 58(1943)231f.Abb.20.

16. Carapanos, *Dodone*, Taf. 13.2; Studniczka, "Zum platäischen Weihgeschenk in Delphi," *Leipziger Winckelmannsblatt* (1928) Abb.5; Dohrn, *Die schwarzfig. etrusk.Vasen*, 103f.; Dunbabin, *The Western Greeks*, 253 Anm.6.

wiederum aus Olympia und Lindos, zurechnen dürfen, für die ich, bedenklich gemacht durch ihre Zahl, seinerzeit die Frage der Herkunft offen ließ.[17] Zeitlich gehört mindestens das Stück aus dem Stadion nach seinen Fundumständen noch vor die Mitte des 6. Jahrhunderts.[18] Es bildet somit das Verbindungsglied zu den älteren etruskischen Denkmälern auf griechischem Boden. Unter diesen aber ragt als Kunstwerk ein reliefgeschmücktes Silberblech aus Olympia hervor.[19] Etwa um die Mitte des 7. Jahrhunderts entstanden, könnte es dem einzigen aus literarischer Ueberlieferung bekannten Anathem eines Etruskers in einem griechischen Heiligtum ungefähr gleichzeitig sein, dem Thron, den der Etruskerkönig Arimnestos in Olympia weihte.[20] Daß jener Thron sehr alt war, oder doch als sehr alt galt, beweist der Zusatz des Pausanias, wonach Arimnestos "als erster Barbar dem olympischen Zeus eine Weihgabe darbrachte." Leider verrät unser Gewährsmann nicht, aus welchem Material der Thron gearbeitet war. Immerhin liegt es angesichts des bekannten Thrones aus dem Barberini-Grab[21] nahe, an Bronze oder ein noch kostbareres Metall zu denken. Träfe das zu, so wäre das Weihgeschenk des Arimnestos technisch den mittelitalischen Bronzeschilden[22] verwandt gewesen, von denen sich gerade in Olympia einige Fragmente erhalten haben. Mit Ausnahme eines orientalisierenden Bruchstücks[23] gehören sie der ältesten, rein 'geometrisch' verzierten Gruppe italischer Schilde an. Zu den zwei schon von Furtwängler in diesen Zusammenhang gestellten Fragmenten[24] kommt jetzt ein drittes aus der neuen Grabung, das wir hier zum erstenmal abbilden (Tafel 90, C).[25] Auf die weitläufige Frage nach dem Ursprung des italischen Metall-

---

17. *Olympia-Bericht*, II,123ff.Abb77/8; *Olympia*, IV, Taf.68,1267; Blinkenberg, *Lindos*, I, Taf.32,798. Zur Gattung zuletzt Magi, *Raccolta Guglielmi*, II, 230f. zu Nr.117 mit einigen Nachträgen zu der Liste von H. Sauer, *AA*, 1937, 285ff.; das New Yorker Exemplar jetzt auch bei G. Richter, *Hb. of the Etruscan Coll.*, 30,Abb.86.

18. *Olympia-Bericht* II, 8ff.

19. *Olympia*, IV, 99 Taf.37,693; Kunze, *Kret.Bronzereliefs*, 166, Anm.67; Karo a.O. 317.

20. Paus.V,12,5; Karo a.O.316.

21. *Memoirs American Academy at Rome*, 5(1925)Taf.32 und 33; Giglioli, *L'arte Etrusca*, Taf.17,1.

22. Zur Gattung zuletzt Akerström, *Der geometr.Stil in Italien*, 102ff., 113f. und 119f.

23. *Olympia*, IV, 163 Taf.62,1007; Lippold, *Münchener Archäol.Studien*, 458, Anm.2 Nr.38.

24. *Olympia*, IV 50 Taf.20,335/6; das erste Fragment auch Akerström a.O.113 Taf.28,5; das zweite ist weniger charakteristisch.

25. *Grabungs-Inventar*, B,1799. Größte Länge 23,6 cm. Rand nach innen eingerollt. Oestlich vom Mosaikraum der neronischen Villa in tiefer Schicht gefunden, dicht bei der hochaltertümlichen Lanzenspitze *Olympische Forschungen* I 150f. Taf.58 d. Gleichzeitigkeit oder gar Zusammengehörigkeit beider Stücke ergibt sich aus diesem Befund natürlich nicht.

rundschildes können wir nicht eingehen. Doch muß wenigsten gesagt werden, daß die Fragmente aus Olympia keinesfalls die mir auch sonst unwahrscheinliche Existenz unmittelbarer griechischer Vorbilder erweisen.[26] Denn sie sind ohne Zweifel aus den gleichen Werkstätten hervorgegangen wie die in Italien selbst gefundenen Exemplare, müssen also wie alle bisher genannten Metallwerke aus dem Westen nach Griechenland gelangt sein. Und sie stehen in ihrer Zeit nicht allein. Reichen doch auch die italischen Fibeln, die in verhältnismäßig großer Zahl in Olympia zu Tage gekommen sind, aber auch in den Heiligtümern der Aphaia von Aegina, der Athena von Lindos und der Hera von Perachora, sowie im argivischen Heraion und in Delphi nicht fehlen,[27] vielfach in das späte 8. oder frühe 7. Jahrhundert hinauf. Als spezifisch etruskisch kann man sie freilich nicht ansprechen, da es sich um Fibeltypen handelt, die meist in ganz Italien und sogar auf Sizilien verbreitet sind.

Die kleine Zahl in Griechenland gefundener etruskischer Metallarbeiten, die wir, ohne irgend auf Vollständigkeit Anspruch zu erheben, doch nicht unbeträchtlich vermehren konnten, führt von dem Jahrhundert, das die Griechen mit den Völkern Italiens zuerst in engere Beziehung brachte, bis an die Schwelle der klassischen Zeit, für die die Kenntnis und Schätzung etruskischen Kunsthandwerks von Seiten der Griechen literarisch bezeugt ist,[28] aus der wir aber noch viel weniger einschlägige Denkmäler besitzen.[29]

Das Bild eines nie ganz abgerissenen 'Imports' etruskischer Erzeugnisse wird indes noch bereichert und ergänzt durch Arbeiten aus anderen Werkstoffen. Zumal an den schlichten und formstrengen

---

26. Für ein Importstück hält auch Akerström a.O.113 das Fragment *Olympia*, IV, Taf.20,335, obwohl er die Theorie verficht, daß sich der geometrische Stil der italischen Schilde aus Griechenland herleitet.

27. Blinkenberg, *Fibules Grecques*, 197ff. Zu einer möglichen Einschränkung des Bereiches italischer Fibeln vgl. Blakeway, *BSA* 33 (1932/3) 191f. Anm.2 und Payne, *Perachora*, I, 170. Ich kann aber die Sanguisuga—, beziehungsweise Kahnfibeln mit ausgeprägtem Kanalfuß nicht für griechisch halten; mir scheinen daher Stücke wie *Perachora* I, Taf.72,10-12 und 73,14-17 italisch zu sein (im Gegensatz etwa zu Taf.73,12), und auch das große Exemplar, Taf.73,1/2, dessen Fuß nicht erhalten ist, dürfte hierher gehören (zum gravierten Schmuck vgl.z.B. Sundwall, *Die älteren ital.Fibeln*, 199,Abb.322). Italische Fibeln mit Kanalfuß sind, wie ich glaube, auch *Fouilles de Delphes*, II,5 (Démangel *Sanctuaire d'Athéna Pronaia, Topographie*) 52f.Abb.60,2 und 61,1.

28. Die Stellen bei Karo a.O.320.

29. Kaum viel jünger als unsere Thymiaterien ein Pfannengriff aus Kertsch, *JHS*, 5(1884)64 Taf.46,9, von Jacobsthal-Langsdorff, *Bronzeschnabelkannen*, 46f.Anm.6 als etruskisch erkannt. Ferner dort genannt ein Helm und eine 'Situla' aus Südrußland: die Abbildung *Eurasia Sepemtrion.Antiqua* I 100 ist mir zur Zeit nicht zugänglich. An der italischen Herkunft des frühen Kammhelmes aus Podolien (*Eurasia*, II,213 Abb.112,5) zweifelt auch v.Merhart, "Zu den ersten Metallhelmen Europas" (30.*Bericht d.Röm.-Germ.Kommission*, 1941) 41, obwohl hier ein Zusammenhang irgendwelcher Art bestehen muß.

Bucchero-Kantharoi scheinen auch die archaischen Griechen Gefallen gefunden zu haben: Ithaka, Korinth, Perachora, Athen, Delos (Rheneia), Naxos, Rhodos und Samos haben solche Gefäße geliefert, ihre Verbreitung hat also einen recht weiten Radius.[30] Bemalte etruskische Vasen fehlen dagegen in Griechenland so gut wie ganz[31]: man begreift, daß ihnen hier keine Liebhaber erwachsen konnten. Seltsam ist nur, daß unter den Funden etruskischer Goldschmuck gar nicht vertreten ist. Sollen die Griechen wirklich die hervorragenden Leistungen der Etrusker auf diesem Gebiet nicht anerkannt haben? Man wird es schwerlich glauben und eher geneigt sein, diese Lücke in unserem Material den dafür besonders ungünstigen Erhaltungsbedingungen zuzuschreiben. Für die verloren gegangenen Kleinodien wäre jedoch ein gewisser Ersatz gewonnen, wenn sich meine Vermutung bestätigen sollte, daß die Reliefplatten eines Elfenbeinkästchens aus der archaischen Nekropole von Ialysos nicht, wie ihr Herausgeber meinte, einheimisch rhodisch, sondern vielmehr etruskisch sind.[32] Jedenfalls wüßte ich ihnen aus dem Bereich ostgriechischer Kunst nichts zur Seite zu stellen, wogegen äußere Form und Stil sie aufs engste mit einer Gattung — freilich meist ein wenig jüngerer — Elfenbeinreliefs verbinden, deren Heimat nur Etrurien sein kann.[33] Zum Schluß sei noch der wenigen auf griechischem Boden aufgetauchten etruskischen Gemmen gedacht: sie gehören meist in spätere Zeit, nur ein archaisches Stück stammt vielleicht aus Korfu.[34]

Es mochte bisher scheinen, als sei in der Frage des etruskischen Imports die literarische Ueberlieferung mit der Aussage der Denk-

---

30. Das Material am vollständigsten bei Jacobsthal und Neuffer, *Gallia Graeca* (Préhistoire 2) 45ff. Zum Kantharos aus Ialysos, *Clara Rhodos*, III,24 Abb. 6, siehe Jacobsthal, *Gött.gel.Anz.* 195,1933,4. Füge hinzu zwei Exemplare aus Korinth, Weinberg, *Corinth*,VII,1, *The Geom. and Oriental.Pottery*, 71, Nr.310/1, Taf.37, und Fragmente aus Ithaka, *BSA* 43 (1948) 103 Taf. 45,601.

31.Italisch-korinthische Scherben werden nur aus Perachora erwähnt: Jacobsthal und Neuffer, *Gallia Graeca*, 45. Bei den in diesem Zusammenhang mehrfach angeführten Tonaltärchen aus Korinth und Perachora (Jacobsthal u.Neuffer a.O. 45; Karo a.O.320) handelt es sich keinesfalls um Import aus Etrurien: vgl. Weinberg, *AJA*, 53(1949)265 und Payne bei Broneer, *Hesperia* 16(1947)221.

32. *Annuario d.R.Scuola Ital.di Atene*, 6/7(1923/4)322f., Abb.216 (Maiuri). Vgl. auch Buschor, *Meermänner* 8. Das Grab durch einen attischen Kothon in das 3. Viertel des 6. Jahrhunderts datiert.

33. *RM*, 21(1906)314ff.Abb.1-6 Taf.15/6 (Pollak); Rumpf, *Katal.d.etrusk. Skulpt.*, 14; Riis, *Tyrrhenika*, 93. Es sei vor allem auf den typischen Rahmen hingewiesen, der sich wie bei den meisten Elfenbeinreliefs aus Etrurien aus Leiste und Kyma zusammensetzt und der ähnlich auch auf etruskischen Aschenkisten wiederkehrt (z.B. Giglioli, *L'arte Etrusca*, Taf.138,2; 139,4/5; 140,1), sowie auf die seltsamen Flossen des Meerwesens, deren willkürlicher Sitz und flügelartige Stilisierung durchaus ungriechisch sind: vgl. *MondI*.VI 46,4 = *RM*21,1906 Taf. 16 oben rechts.

34. Furtwängler, *Ant.Gemmen*, III,193; Jacobsthal-Langsdorff, *Bronzeschnabelkannen*, 46f.Anm.6. Archaisch: Beazley, *Lewes Gems*, 33f.Nr.37 Taf. 3.

mäler schlecht in Einklang zu bringen.[35] Man hat eine Unstimmigkeit vor allem auch darin gesehen, daß die schriftlichen Zeugnisse
die Vertrautheit der Griechen mit etruskischen Erzeugnissen für eine
Zeit beweisen, in der die Funde fast ganz versiegen, während wir
umgekehrt für die archaischen Jahrhunderte wohl Denkmäler, aber
— vom Thron des Arimnestos abgesehen — keinerlei Nachrichten
haben. Tatsächlich besteht jedoch zwischen beiden Zweigen der
Ueberlieferung zeitlich keine Lücke mehr: sie wird jetzt überbrückt
durch die Thymiaterionfüße aus Olympia und Lindos. Denn diese
sind gewiß nicht älter als das älteste Schriftzeugnis, die Stelle in
den 458 aufgeführten Eumeniden, die von der 'tyrrhenischen Trom-
pete' spricht (Aisch.*Eum.* 567f.). Gleichwohl ändert sich nichts
wesentliches daran, daß sich das Schwergewicht der Ueberlieferung
von den Denkmälern für die archaische, auf die literarischen Quellen
für die klassische Zeit verlagert. Es mag nun freilich Zufall sein, daß
in der erhaltenen archaischen Dichtung von etruskischer Kunstfer-
tigkeit niemals die Rede ist. Doch für das Versagen der Funde im
späteren 5. und im 4. Jahrhundert lassen sich immerhin Gründe erkennen. Stammt ja die Mehrzahl der in Griechenland zu Tage ge-
kommenen etruskischen Bronzen und Vasen aus Heiligtümern, als
Grabbeigaben kennen wir sie nur vereinzelt aus Rhodos, Rheneia und
Südrußland. Für Weihgeschenke aber sind die Erhaltungsbedingungen
in nacharchaischer Zeit im allgemeinen unverhältnismäßig viel
ungünstiger.[36] Andererseits sind die mannigfachen Gebrauchsgegen-
stände etruskischer Provenienz, die uns gerühmt werden, die Trom-
peten, Kandelaber, vergoldeten Schalen und $πᾶς \; χαλκὸς \; ὅτις \; κοσμεῖ$
$δόμον \; ἔν \; τινι \; χρείᾳ$, ihren Besitzern gewiß nur selten mit ins Grab
gefolgt. Es ist daher nicht zu verwundern, daß wir für den etruskischen Import in das klassische Griechenland im wesentlichen auf die
Literatur angewiesen bleiben. Beide Quellenkomplexe bilden also,
indem sie sich gegenseitig ergänzen, eine unteilbare und in sich wider-
spruchslose Einheit.

An der Tatsache eines kontinuierlichen Zustroms etruskischer
Erzeugnisse nach Griechenland ist nicht mehr zu zweifeln. Seine
Bedeutung wird man freilich nicht überschätzen. Ganz unvergleich-
lich größer und folgenreicher war die Wanderung griechischer
Künstler und Kunstwerke nach Etrurien. Diese Bewegung, die zur
Hellenisierung Italiens, und damit zur Bildung einer einheitlichen
antiken Kultur einen wesentlichen Beitrag geleistet hat, steht unter
einem weltgeschichtlichen Aspekt. Demgegenüber konnten die Her-

---

35. Jacobsthal und Neuffer, *Gallia Graeca*, 44; Karo a.O.320.
36. Die Ursachen dafür habe ich IV. *Olympia-Bericht* 138 angedeutet.

vorbringungen des etruskischen Handwerks wegen ihrer technischen
Qualität, ihrer ungewohnten Formen oder ihrer reizvollen und
eigenartigen Verzierung unter den Griechen wohl Anklang und
Absatz finden, aber kaum eine tiefere Wirkung ausüben. Von allen
Umwelteinflüssen, denen sich Griechenland öffnete, ist der etruskische ohne Zweifel einer der geringsten gewesen. Und doch ist der
etruskische Import nicht bloß ein Faktum der antiken Handelsge-
schichte. Am Rande interessiert er auch die Kunstgeschichte wenigstens insofern, als er schießlich bewirkt, daß sich für den einen oder
anderen Gebrauchsgegenstand eine bewährte etruskische Form auch
in Griechenland durchsetzt, wie es zum Beispiel für die 'tyrrhenische
Salpinx' oder für eine bestimmte Sandalenart[37] der Ueberlieferung
zu entnehmen ist. Und das mag wohl auch für das Thymiaterion
gelten, dessen stattlicher etruskischer Typus in späteren Zeiten die
schlichteren griechischen Räuchergeräte einigermaßen verdrängt zu
haben scheint.[38] Die hier besprochenen Gerätfüße geben Anlaß,
daran zu erinnern. Bezeugen sie doch, daß solche Thymiaterien schon
einige Jahrzehnte, ehe sie — nach Darstellungen auf griechischen
Vasen zu schließen — auch in Griechenland heimisch werden, aus
Etrurien eingeführt worden sind.

---

37. Karo a.O.320. Pollux, VII,28,86 u.92.

38. Vgl. Wigand, *Bonner Jahrb.*, 122(1912)32ff.u.51ff., im einzelnen freilich
jetzt vielfach zu berichtigen und zu ergänzen.

ON A SMALL BRONZE FROM CERVETERI AND A SERIES OF ETRUSCAN FIGURES

MARCEL RENARD
Universities of Liège and Brussels

Plates 91-92

Among the Etruscan antiquities of the "Musées d'Art et d'Histoire" in Brussels is a small bronze figure from Cerveteri which possesses a certain interest and represents a young man (pl. 91, a). We are happy to present this new document[1] to Professor David Moore Robinson although we are aware how slight our small homage is in comparison to Professor Robinson's contributions to the field of archaeology.

Our statuette belonged to the Ravestein collection[2] and subsequently entered the Museum of Brussels,[3] along with the bulk of the antiquities collected by that lover of art. It is well preserved, despite the traces of damage on the right part of the face and slight grazes on the top of the head. It is cast solid and has a brown patina (here and there green and blackish). The height is 19 cm. Since the bronze is fixed on a modern marble base, it is not possible to see whether it is provided with tenons.

The beardless youth is figured standing in a frontal position. The long and straight hair is carefully indicated by parallel lines. On the forehead it is arranged in a thick round mass and behind this mass of hair a thin and low diadem encloses the whole circumference of the head. In front this ornament presents a series of crankles, each point of which is in the form of a little buckle.[4] At the back the hair goes down to the lower part of the neck. The ears are rather large, a trifle above the correct height. Their relief is much damaged.

The oval face becomes thinner at the chin. The profile is rectilineal in its upper part but recedes in the lower part, where it assumes a triangular aspect. The forehead is not prominent and not very high, the nose is small, the thin lips slightly open, and the chin round.

1. In fact it is unpublished, apart from a poor little drawing three cm. high in Reinach, *Rép.Stat.²*, III, 1920, 176, 2.

2. E. de Meester de Ravestein, *Musée de Ravestein²*, Brussels, 1884, 271, n° 908.

3. Inv. R 908. We are very much indebted to the Direction of the "Musées d'Art et d'Histoire" for permission to publish and for the photograph of the specimen.

4. About this diadem (not visible on the plate) Ravestein, *l.c.*, writes that its "petits boutons (the buckles of the crankles), aux angles alternativement saillants et rentrants, nous démontrent qu'il est en métal et probablement en or." But nothing indicates that the diadem is an inlaid work, unless Ravestein intends to say that the ornament represented on our bronze was actually of metal and often of gold.

The curve of the eyebrows is accentuated. The asymmetric eyes are not on the same level, which produces an unpleasant break in the balance of the face. The right eye is obviously lower than the left. With the injury which it had suffered, the eye resembles a lozenge. But the left eye, better preserved, assumes the same aspect—although less obviously—with its prominent almond-shaped ball between the broken-arched eyelids.

The line of the neck is slender and continues with the descending curve of the round shoulders. The proportions of the body are elongated and its volume is not much accentuated. The outer lines of the nude trunk are curved, especially on the left side, narrowing at the lower part of the chest. The clavicles protrude, and the breast is plainly drawn. The abdominal muscles are excessively delineated. The back has but little relief apart from the spine and buttocks.

The legs are slender and too long for the trunk. The left leg is bent a little at the knee and is placed slightly forward. The nude feet lie flat on the ground with their toes separated.

The two arms, removed from the body, are bent at the elbows. The right fore-arm rises sharply from the trunk to an horizontal position. The hand is half closed and originally held an object now missing; a little round hole is hollowed in the palm near the fingers for the purpose. Moreover the inner part of the hand is rough. The left fore-arm goes back obliquely. The hand is then stretched open, with some exaggeration, the palm being turned back toward the ground. The thumb is removed from the other joined fingers, the details of which appear very clearly on the inside but are very faint on the outside.

A himation covers the lower part of the body in a triangular pattern. The cloth surrounding the waist goes back half-way up the leg while its outer edges rise again obliquely, so that they cover themselves again and wrap around the left fore-arm.

At the waist the edge of the cloth shows three swellings decorated with dots. Two similar lines of dots adorn the other margins of the himation. The reverse side of the cloth hanging from the arm presents a set of folds rendered in lower relief.

The first owner of the statuette regretted that the object held in the right hand was lost because, he said, "il aurait sans doute pu nous aider à donner un nom au personnage représenté par ce bronze."[5]

However, the identification is easy: it is evident that we have to deal with a figure in prayer. In his left hand the youth held an offering —doubtless fruit—as is proved by many examples. His right hand is in a gesture of prayer. To judge by the fact that the palm is turned

---

5. *L.c.*

out towards the ground, it may be conjectured that his prayer is addressed to the chthonic gods.[6]

Among the possible comparisons between our specimen and other evidences of the Etruscan art, a male figure perhaps from Chiusi (Berlin, Antiquarium)[7] may be considered. Of course that bronze figure is entirely nude, is more archaic than ours, and belongs to the VIth century and to the transitional phase from the Orientalizing to the Ionizing period. In spite of these stylistic differences there are strong similarities in the plastic type. Furthermore, the gesture of the two hands is perfectly similar.

The stylistic connexion becomes more evident with another bronze from Palestrina (Rome, Villa Giulia) of the end of the VIth century.[8] Here the treatment of the hair, arranged in three rows of stylized curls, is more affected than in the Brussels figure, and the position of the right hand is not similar. But the chief point is that we already see an important resemblance in the anatomical rendering. We realize that the distance between this statuette and our bronze is not very long.

This distance is traversed in another nude male figure from Monte Falterona (Paris, Louvre; pl. 91, b) of the last years of the VIth or of the first years of the Vth century[9] which may be considered as contemporaneous with our bronze. Not only do the general type and the gesture show a strong resemblance but the hair, the anatomy (note the clavicles, the chest, the abdomen) and the style are similar. The drapery is the only important innovation of the Brussels bronze.

This figure then appears to be a true prototype of the well known bronze from Monte Guragazza in the Apennines (pl. 91, c), now in the Museo Civico in Bologna,[10] belonging to the transition from the late archaic to the early classical period,[11] about 490-480 B. C.

It is true that this bronze which also figures a young devotee is a work in which the anatomy is conspicuous. This attests a more advanced phase of art. However, not only the frontal posture with the left leg forward, but the antithesis between the upper part of the body

---

6. Picard, Ch., "Le geste de la prière funéraire en Grèce et en Etrurie" *RHR* 114 (1936) 137 ff.

7. Mühlestein, H., *Die Kunst der Etrusker. Die Ursprünge*, fig. 189 = Giglioli, G. Q., *L'arte etrusca*, pl. 126, 3.

8. Nogara, B., *Gli Etruschi e la loro civiltà*, p. 124, fig. 69 = Giglioli, pl. 126, 2. The specimen is a little earlier than the beginning of the Vth Century as Giglioli thinks.

9. Giglioli, *op. cit.*, pl. 123, 3.

10. Ducati, P., *Storia dell'arte etrusca*, pll. 102-103, figg. 273 and 275 = Giglioli, pl. 220, 1-2.

11. Riis, P. J., *Tyrrhenika*, 164 and 172.

which is nude and the lower part surrounded with the himation with its edges hanging from the left fore-arm, the intersection of the arm-pit with the lower line of the pectoral, the median fosse of the back, the position of the hands (the right holding an umbilical patera for a ritual libation, the left stretched toward the ground with the palm open), the disposition of the hair, everything attests that this beautiful specimen follows the type offered earlier by the Brussels bronze from Cerveteri.

A figure of Turms, the Etruscan Mercury, found at Uffington (Berkshire, England)[12] and now in the Ashmolean Museum, Oxford, is connected with our series (pl. 92, a). Here again we have the same type, the same build, the same posture, the same style as in the Monte Guragazza devotee. The Turms (about 470 B. C.) and the Bologna bronze had been taken for works "of one master, or at least works of fellow artists."[13]

These three figures and others form a very homogeneous whole in the point of view of type, build, proportions, hair, facial features, and drapery. P. J. Riis thinks that they come from Vulcian workshops.[14] It may be added that the success of this plastic theme is proved by industrial products with no aesthetic value.[15]

Having restored our statuette to its sphere of art, we shall try now to characterize its essential features, its qualities, and its defects.

Our bronze with its frontal posture, its rigid composition, its elongated proportions, its slender hips is still in the archaic tradition. But if we compare it with such "incunabula" of Etruscan art as the stone sculptures of the Pietrera,[16] which go back to the oldest works of the Greek islands, we shall find that there is great progress in the working of our bronze. The arms are no longer hanging down; they no longer adhere to the body as in the Pietrera sculptures. Furthermore we no longer have the primitive technique of the sharply cut lines that we see in the bronze warriors from Brolio.[17]

Of course, our figure is still fashioned to be seen frontally, but the sculptor struggles against the inexorable law of the archaic frontality: not only does the left leg move forward (this is already the case in many archaic kouroi), but chiefly the personage becomes animated by the gesture of the arms which breaks the monotony of the com-

---

12. Riis, P. J., "The Bronze Statuette from Uffington, Berkshire" JRS 36 (1946) 43 ff.

13. Ibid., 44.

14. Tyrrhenika, 90.

15. Cf. Richter, G. M. A., The Metr. Mus. of Art. Greek, Etruscan and Roman Bronzes, 105, n⁰ 185 and 107, n⁰ 190.

16. Ducati, pl. 62, fig 194 = Giglioli, pl. 66, 7, VIIth Century.

17. Ducati, pl. 64, fig. 198 = Giglioli, pl. 84, 3, beginning of the VIth Century.

position. Differences in the masses of light enclosing the figure thus appear in the hollows drawn by the lines of the arms and of the torso. In the Brolio warriors—earlier than our Cerveteri devotee—the movements are more violent (partly on account of the nature of the subject) : the right arm is raised to swing the spear and chiefly the head is vigorously turned toward the left shoulder. But in spite of that, there is in that work a sharpness of movement that has vanished in the Brussels bronze. This latter statuette presents less violent agitation, but on the whole has more life and is not rendered in so primitive a manner.

Finally, on the composition of the whole, we have already observed the intentional opposition between the nude torso and the lower part of the body covered by the himation; this antithesis of the nude and of the drapery enjoyed a great success in Etruscan art.[18]

The details also reveal the developed archaic style. The long hair hanging down in a broad mass upon the neck, as it appears in so many archaic *kouroi*, is found again with the diadem in small Greek bronzes of advanced archaic style, and also in Etruscan statuettes of the same period representing men or women.[19] And the fillet of the forehead in the Monte Guragazza, in the Uffington figures, in the Brussels bronze, and others, shows a marked similarity.

The face of our devotee is somewhat affected, but it is pleasing nevertheless. The prominent and almond-shaped eyeballs recall the bronze from Monte Falterona, cited above, but the line of the eyebrows and of the nose once more recalls the Bologna and Oxford bronzes. The artist has made an effort to release the lips from the archaic smile and to give to the mouth an individual aspect. If he

18. This opposition occurs not only in the male types figured standing but also in the type lying on a *kline* or in the seating type. On a *kline*: Ducati, pl. 91, fig. 250 = Giglioli, pl. 117 (sarcophagus from Cerveteri, about 630 B. C.); Ducati, pl. 76, fig. 225 = Giglioli, pl. 112, 2 (Tomba delle Leonesse, Tarquinia, end of the VIth cent.); Ducati, pl. 88, fig. 242 = Giglioli, pl. 205, 3 (Tomba del Triclinio, Tarquinia, about 475-450 B. C.); Giglioli, pl. 233, 1 (ossuario from Chiusi, Vth cent.); Giglioli, 233. 2 (ossuario from Sarteano, Vth cent.); Ducati, pl. 136, fig. 352 = Giglioli, pl. 234, 3 (sarcophagus from Città della Pieve, Vth-IVth cent.; Ducati, pl. 136, fig. 353 = Giglioli, pl. 235 (sarcophagus from Chianciano, Vth-IVth cent.); Giglioli, pl. 244, 1 (Tomba Golini I, Orvieto, IVth cent.); Ducati, pl. 224, figg. 547 and 548 = Giglioli, pl. 386, 2 and 387 (Tomba degli Scudi, Tarquinia. IIIrd cent.); Ducati, pl. 234, fig. 573 = Giglioli, pl. 346, 2 (sarcophagus from Chiusi, IIIrd cent.); Giglioli, pl. 351 (sarcophagus from Tarquinia, IIIrd cent.); Ducati, pl. 271. fig. 659 = Giglioli, pl. 365 (sarcophagus from Chiusi, IIIrd-IInd cent.), etc. Seating type: Giglioli, pl. 187, 1 (antefix from Cerveteri, Vth cent.); Ducati, pl. 185, fig. 469 = Giglioli, pl. 248, 1 (Tomba dell'Orco, Tarquinia, IVth cent.); Ducati, pl. 212, fig. 521 = Giglioli, pl. 301, 2 (mirror, IVth cent.); Ducati, pl. 212. fig. 522 = Giglioli, pl. 301, 3 (mirror, end of the IVth cent.); Ducati, pl. 260, fig. 635 (terracotta from Luni, IIIrd-IInd cent.). etc.

19. Examples are quoted p. 749 ff. cf. also Richter, G. M. A., *op. cit.*, figg. 76-77 and 71 = *Greek, Etr. and Rom. Br.*, 34, n° 56.

does not succeed, his attempt deserves to be noted. It must also be observed that the jawbones are no longer so accentuated as in the archaic phase. The anatomical modelling reveals that our sculptor still follows analytical conceptions, but that he already tries to restore the details in the whole.

The waist widens under the arm-pits and the hips recede as is the case in many old *kouroi*. But there are interesting attempts to represent the bones and the muscles. The clavicles delineate the base of the neck, the pectoral swells with the vital breath, the vertical line to the navel attempts to mark the divisions of the abdomen, which presents only two horizontal lines, as in the latest *kouroi* of the sixth century.

Of course many details are still wrong. The bony frame-work which supports the flesh is not always very strong. The musculature of the arms is weak. The joining of the torso and the abdomen is faulty. The ribs are not drawn. The relief of the back muscles is deficient. To judge the progress which is still to be achieved, we may compare our bronze with the Monte Guragazza devotee, the Turms figure from Uffington, a warrior of Civita Castellana,[20] a so-called "Apollo" in the Museo Archeologico in Florence,[21] a *criophoros* in the Ny Carlsberg Glyptothek in Copenhagen[22] and the Pourtales vase in the British Museum.[23]

In the rendering of the whole we see more delicacy than strength and vigor. Some sweetness in the modelling, the forms sometimes a little soft in spite of the slender proportions, the wish to avoid the angular schemes, the gesture a little affected, remain echoes of the Ionizing influence which characterizes, for example, the fine devotee from Isola di Fano.[24] On the other hand we see here already a firmness announcing the Attic influence which is soon to prevail.[25]

The drapery of the himation which preludes that of the Bologna and Oxford bronzes is also interesting. The treatment of the cloth is not without defects. It remains ornamental and flat, without flexibility and it adheres to the body, insinuating itself between the legs as if it were moist. The folds of the edge hanging from the fore-arm are drawn in a stepped pattern. However, this drapery is no longer a rigid carapace. There is an attempt to simulate the transparency of the cloth and to indicate its relation to the body.

---

20. Giglioli, pl. 220, 7-8. Beginning of the Vth century.
21. Giglioli, pl. 220, 9. Vth cent.
22. Giglioli, pl. 216, 2. Vth cent.
23. Giglioli, pl. 225, 4. Vth cent.
24. Ducati, pl. 102, fig. 271 = Giglioli, pl. 135, 4. VIth cent.
25. Cf. Riis, *Tyrrhenika*, 172 with respect to the *kore* from Monte Guragazza.

A last word about the himation. Its ornamental borders incised with rows of dots recur frequently in the period of our bronze.[26] Later such ornaments become more complicated.

The plastic type illustrated in our figure continued to enjoy success in the more advanced periods, of course with modifications of style due to the evolution of art. Thus a devotee from Monte Falterona (pl. 92, b) belonging to the end of the IVth century[27] and another bronze of Apollonian type (pl. 92, c) in the Museo Archeologico in Florence[28] are precise continuations of the series of the Brussels, Bologna, and Oxford bronzes which manifest so homogeneous a tradition.

---

26. Cf. Ducati, pl. 81, figg. 231 and 232 = Giglioli, pl. 108, 1, 2 and 3 (painted terracottas from Cerveteri, about 530 B. C.); small bronzes as in Loukomski, *Art étrusque*, pll. 60 and 62, VIth cent.; Ducati, pl. 125, fig. 328 (vase, end of the VIth cent.); Ducati, pl. 86, fig. 240 and pl. 87, fig. 241 = Giglioli pl. 206 (Tomba del Triclinio, Tarquinia, about 475-450 B. C.), etc.

27. Giglioli, pl. 261, 1.

28. Giglioli, pl. 261, 3.

ZUR KAPITOLINISCHEN WOELFIN

FRIEDRICH MATZ
Marburg

Tafeln 93-94

Trotz vieler Erörterungen ist der kunstgeschichtliche Ort der Kapitolinischen Wölfin (Taf. 93a) immer noch nicht genügend geklärt. E. Petersen glaubte ihren griechischen Charakter nachgewiesen zu haben,[1] und Amelung konnte bald darauf feststellen, dass man sich "in archäologischen Kreisen neuerdings fast einstimmig dafür erklärt" habe, in der Wölfin "die Schöpfung eines jener ionischen oder chalkidischen Künstler zu sehen, die in Italien ansässig geworden waren."[2] Wenige Jahre später wurden die berühmt gewordenen grossen Terrakottafiguren in Veii gefunden, die eine neue Vorstellung von der Leistungsfähigkeit der mittelitalischen Kunst im späten 6. und frühen 5. Jahrhundert begründeten. Die Auffassung von der Wölfin schlug in ihr Gegenteil um. Eindruck gemacht hat besonders Giglioli's Hinweis auf Aehnlichkeiten in der Körperbildung zwischen der Hindin der Gruppe aus Veii und der Bronze.[3] Seitdem gilt in der wissenschaftlichen Literatur die Wölfin als italisch.[4] Der energische Einspruch, den L. Curtius dagegen erhoben hat, beleuchtet aber die Situation.[5] Offenbar ist die geltende Meinung doch nicht genügend begründet. Denn allerdings ist der Mangel an geeigneten Vergleichsstücken empfindlich. Daher möchte ich die Aufmerksamkeit auf eine Gruppe von Denkmälern lenken, die in diesem Zusammenhang noch nicht berücksichtigt wurden und denen ich ausschlaggebende Bedeutung dafür beimesse.

Es handelt sich um die kreisförmigen Reliefs aus getriebenem Bronzeblech mit Löwenköpfen, die in Gräbern von Tarquinia gefunden sind. Die ganze Gruppe bedarf noch der Aufarbeitung. Ausser den Löwenköpfen gibt es auch einige Widderköpfe in ihr und namentlich Acheloosmasken.[6] Die älteren Abbildungen sind unzulänglich. Dem

---

1. *Klio* 9 (1909) 30 ff.
2. *Führer durch die öffentlichen Sammlungen klassischer Altertümer in Rom,* 3. Aufl., 1912, 1, 563.
3. *NSc.* 1919, 33 A. 5. *AD.* 3 Text zu Taf. 55 ff. S. 58.
4. Zusammenstellung dieser Literatur bis 1934: Löwy, *St.Etr.* 8, 1934, 77 A. 1. Abgesehen von mehr oder weniger kurzen Erwähnungen sind hinzuzufügen E. Strong, *Scritti in onore di B. Nogara,* 1937, 475 ff.; Technau, *Die Kunst der Römer,* 1940, 8 ff.; P. J. Riis, *Tyrrhenika,* 1941, 30; Jones, *Cat. Pal. Conserv.,* Sala dei *Fasti Cons.* 1; BrBr. 318; Ducati *AE.* p. 261; Giglioli; *AE.* pl. 197.
5. *RM.* 48, 1933, 210 A. 1. 213.
6. Ueber sie zuletzt: M. Pallottino *MA* 36 (1937) 352 A. 5 und Riis,*Tyrrhenika,* 67.

Stilvergleich mit der Wölfin können nur die beiden einzigen bis jetzt zugänglichen fotografischen Wiedergaben zugrunde gelegt werden. Die eine ist nach einem Stück im Museo Gregoriano hergestellt (Taf. 93, b),[7] die andere nach einem der Berliner Museen.[8]

Eine kleine, aber charakteristische Besonderheit verbindet diese Löwenprotomen und die Wölfin: die Bildung des den Kopf umrahmenden Haares.

Hier wie dort setzt es sich als eine Art von Kragen oder Halskrause in betontem Bogen von der Stirn ab. In der Mitte teilt es sich symmetrisch. Die einzelnen Zotteln biegen sich in ihrem unteren, verdickten Teil nach aussen, um sich mit der Spitze in umgekehrter Richtung einzurollen. Die Enden haben bei der Wölfin die Form von Spiralen, bei den Löwenköpfen die von kleinen Buckeln. Dieser Unterschied und das Fehlen der Längsgliederung erklären sich aus der Verschiedenheit der Guss- und Treibarbeit. Jedenfalls sind die kleinen Buckel nur als umgeformte Spiralen verständlich.[9] Einen anderen Unterschied bietet die untere Hälfte dieser Haarkrause. Bei der Wölfin ist sie in derselben Weise gestaltet wie die obere, so dass sie im ganzen das Haupt ringförmig einfasst. Bei den Löwen ist sie als Bart behandelt. Ihre Strähnen verlaufen radial, und nach aussen ist sie durch eine Bogenlinie begrenzt.

Wie ist dieses Verhältnis zu verstehen? Bilden die beobachteten Züge eine etruskische Besonderheit oder finden sie innerhalb der griechischen Ueberlieferung ihren Platz? So gestellt muss die Frage sich beantworten lassen, weil die Löwenköpfe einen Vergleich mit vielen griechischen Werken erlauben.

Ein zusammenfassende Untersuchung über die archaischen griechischen Löwen fehlt noch. So viel scheint aber klar zu sein, dass in der zweiten Hälfte des 6. Jahrhunderts zwei Typen nebeneinander hergehen, ein ostgriechischer und ein helladischer. In welcher Beziehung zu ihnen stehen die Löwenköpfe aus Tarquinia? Zur Beantwortung dieser Frage ist es nötig, die Besonderheiten der beiden Typen und ihre Beziehungen zueinander kennen zu lernen. Ich stelle daher ihre bedeutendsten Vertreter zusammen, soweit sie über die Bildung des Kopfes Auskunft geben.

---

7. Alinari 35541, danach Verf. bei Bossert, *Geschichte des Kunstgewerbes*, 1, 1928, 227. Della Seta, *Italia Antica*, 316, 1. Nogara, *Gli Etruschi*, 1933, 99, 49. Giglioli, *L'Arte Etrusca*, 1935, 97, 2.

8. Mühlestein, *Die Kunst der Etrusker*, 1929, 143.

9. Das Entsprechende beobachtet man an einem der Acheloosköpfe dieser Gruppe: Mühlestein aO. 144. Die Form der Locken zwischen den Hörnern geht auf griechische Vorbilder zurück, wie sie beispielsweise das sog. Waffenläuferrelief und die Aristionstele im Athener Nationalmuseum bieten. Auch in diesem Fall sind durch die etruskischen Bronzearbeiter die Spiralen in Buckel umgesetzt.

A. Oestlicher Typus.

1. Liegend, Marmor, aus Didyma, Istanbul, Mendel Nr. 242. *Br.Br.* Text zu Taf. 641/45 Abb. 13. *RS.* 4, 453, 4.
2. Liegend, Marmor, aus der Nekropole von Milet, Louvre, *BrBr.* aO. Abb. 14. Ed. TEL. 3, 140 A. *RS.* 2, 721, 2. Winter *KGiB.* 201, 7. Foto Marburg 163094.
3. Liegend, Marmor, aus Sardis, Istanbul. Shear, *ArtBull.* 13, 1931, 127 ff. Fig. 1.16.
4. Liegend, Marmor, aus Milet, Berlin. Rodenwaldt, *Antike Kunst* 4. Aufl. 195. Richter, *Animals in Greek Sculpture* Taf. 4, 10.
5. Kopf, Marmor, aus Ephesos, BritMus. 140. *BrBr.* Taf. 642. Winter *KGiB.* 203, 5.
6. Kopf, Wasserspeier, Marmor, aus Ephesos, BritMus. 254, *Cat.* Fig. 163.
7. Liegend, Marmor, Grabrelief, aus Xanthos, BritMus. 286, *Cat.* Taf. 18. Poulsen, *Orient* 152, 180. *RR.* 1, 466, 1.
8. Tierkampf, Andesit, Fries aus Assos, Louvre, Clarke *Assos* 151, 9. 11. 12. *BrBr.* Taf. 412 Ed. TEL. 3,143 F. *RR.* 1, 4. 1-3.
9. Vor dem Wagen der Göttermutter, Marmor, Fries des Siphnierschatzhauses, Delphi. *F. Delphes* 5 Taf. 13 f. Richter aO. Taf. 3, 8.
10. Kopf, Wasserspeier, Marmor, vom Siphnierschatzhaus, Delphi. De la Coste-Messelière, *Delphes* Taf. 92 f. Foto Marburg 135141.
11. Laufend, Bronze, Griffzierat aus Samos, Berlin. Bruns, *Antike Bronzen*, 1947, 33, 21.
12. Caeretaner Hydria, Berlin Inv. 3345. AD. 2, 28. Neugebauer, *Führer* Taf. 18. Rodenwaldt aO. 202.
13. Klazomenische Sarkophage, z. B. Berlin 3352 f. AD. 2, 25 f. Neugebauer, *Führer* Taf. 22 f.
14. Klazomenische Vase, Berlin, *AD.* 2, 55, 3A.
15. Phineusschale, Würzburg, *FR.* 41 (Löwe vor dem Wagen des Dionysos).

B. Helladischer Typus.

1. Liegend, Marmor (Paar), aus Lutraki, Kopenhagen, Glypt. N. Carlsberg. *BrBr.* aO. Abb. 4-11. Payne *NC.* 242 Taf. 50, 3. 4. 8. Richter aO. Taf. 1, 4.
2. Sitzend, Marmor, aus Perachora, Boston. *BrBr.* Taf. 641. Payne aO. Taf. 50, 7. Richter aO. Taf. 1, 3.
3. Liegend, Terrakotta, Korinthisches Salbgefäss, Syrakus, Orsi *NSc.* 1925, 123 Taf. 8.
4. Liegend, Terrakotta, aus Praisos, Herakleion. *BSA.* 8 Taf. 14. Maraghiannis, *AntCrét.* 1 Taf. 45.
5. Liegend, lakonische Löwenfibeln, Bronze. Neugebauer, *Antike Bronzestatuetten* Taf. 20. Blinkenberg, *Fibules Grecques et Orientales* 280.
6. Liegend, Beinrelief, Sparta. Dawkins aO. 216 Taf. 114, 3.

7. Liegend, korinthische Bronzelöwen, zusammengestellt von Payne, *Perachora* 136 f. Taf. 43, 8f. Abb. 19, 1. Dazu die Bronzelöwin aus Korfu im Brit.Museum, Payne *NC.* 252 Taf. 50, 2. 5.

8. Liegend, kretische Bronzelöwen. *RS* 2, 711, 1 f. *MusIt.* 2, 746 unten.

9. Masken, Appliken und vollplastische Figuren an Gefässen und Geräten aus Bronze, deren grösster Teil aus grossgriechischen wahrscheinlich aus tarentinischen Werkstätten stammt, von denen manche aber auch in der Peloponnes entstanden sein werden. Neugebauer, *RM.* 38/39, 1923/24, 341. *AA.* 1925, 177. Politis, *Ephem.* 1936, 147. Jantzen, *Bronzewerkstätten in Grossgriechenland und Sizilien*, 1937, 26 ff. Dazu Filow, *Trebenischte* 1927. Vulic *AA.* 1930, 276. 1933, 459. *OeJh.* 27, 1932, 1. 28, 1933, 164.

10. Sitzend. ausgeschnittene Bronzereliefs in Berlin und New York, das eine aus Makedonien. Neugebauer, *Führer*, 69, 10557 Taf. 6. Payne *NC* 69.

11. Schreitend, liegend und sitzend, Blei, Sparta, Dawkins *AO.* 259 f. Abb. 119-121.

Beschränkt man sich auf die Kopf- und Halsbildung, so sind dieses die Hauptunterschiede:

bei dem östlichen Typus:

1. volle, dichte und buschige Mähne,
2. nach hinten gestrichenes, von der übrigen Mähne nicht abgesetztes Stirnhaar,
3. plastische Bewegung und Auflösung der Mähne,
4. starker Nacken und kurzer Hals;

bei dem helladischen Typus:

1. kurzes Mähnenhaar,
2. nach unten gegen dieses, nach oben gegen die übrige Mähne scharf abgesetzter, den Kopf rahmender Haarkranz,
3. zusammengefasstes Mähnenhaar innerhalb einer gekrümmten Fläche, deren vorderes Ende sich mit dem oberen Rand des Stirnhaares verbindet,
4. enger Hals.

Natürlich gibt es mannigfache Zwischenglieder und Abstufungen. Aber die Zuweisung a parte potiori zu einem der beiden Typen macht keine Schwierigkeit. Den sichersten Massstab für die Scheidung gibt das unter 2) genannte Kriterium. Die drei anderen können verschiedene Verbindungen eingehen. Im allgemeinen sind die östlichen Löwen majestätischer, raubtierhaft- dumpfer und unheimlicher, die helladischen hundeartiger und wacher. Viele von diesen wirken geradezu, wie wenn sie abgerichtet und im Grunde gar nicht so bösartig seien, wie sie sich gebärden.

Der helladische Typus entwickelt sich aus dem von den assyrischen Vorbildern abgeleiteten der frühkorinthischen und frühattischen Vasen[10] durch Straffung und Verdichtung. Dem östlichen Typus geht ein bis gegen die Mitte des 6. Jahrhunderts reichender voran, in dem sich die Einwirkung von Vorbildern der sog. jüngeren hethitischen Kunst fortsetzt.[11] Er gibt sich als dessen Umwandlung unter dem Einfluss des helladischen zu erkennen. In den spätarchaischen korinthischen Bronzelöwen (B 7) macht sich die umgekehrte Beeinflussung bemerkbar. Charakteristisch ist, dass die spätarchaischen attischen Löwen in wesentlichen Zügen dem östlichen Typus folgen.[12] Der in das zweite Jahrhundertviertel zu datierende Poroslöwe aus dem Kerameikos[13] ist dagegen noch ein entschiedener Vertreter des helladischen. Umgekehrt schliessen sich die Tarentiner Bronzewerkstätten (B 9) der mutterländischen Ueberlieferung an. Oestliche Züge machen sich auch hier im späten 6. und frühen 5. Jahrhundert geltend. Namentlich die Auflockerung der Mähne gehört dazu. Auch die kretischen Löwen des 6. Jahrhunderts sind von der helladischen Art (B 4. 8).

Die getriebenen Löwenköpfe der Bronzemedaillons aus Tarquinia gehören nicht zu dem ostgriechischen Typus. Mit dem helladischgrossgriechischen haben sie das gesträubte Stirnhaar gemeinsam. Sie unterscheiden sich von ihm dadurch, dass die eigentliche Mähne dahinter mit ihrer Oberfläche tiefer liegt als der obere Rand dieses Stirnhaars, dass sie also von geringerer Fülle ist und sich enger über den Hals legt. Damit stehen sie abseits von den übrigen etruskischen Löwen des späteren 6. und frühen 5. Jahrhunderts, die dem ostgriechischen Typus folgen.[14] Nur die kleinen Bronzelöwen der Fabrik von

---

10. Payne *NC.*, 67 ff.

11. 1) Liegend, Marmor (?). Smyrna, Aziz, *Guide du Musée de Smyrne*, 1933, 67 f. Nr. 328. FotoDAInst. Athen, Smyrna 20. 2) Sitzend, Marmor, vom Heiligen See auf Delos, Picard, *Manuel* 1, 419 Fig. 117. Leroux, *Rev. de l'art anc. et mod.* 23, 1908, 177 ff. 3) Liegend, Stein, Keos, Savignoni *Ephemeris* 1898, 231 Taf. 14, 1. *RS.* 2, 710, 4) Liegend Kalkstein, früher in Smyrna, Curtius *AM* 31 (1906) 155 Abb. 4. FotoDAInst. Samos 131. Kunze, *AM* 59 (1934) Taf. 6, 1.

12. 1) Delphi, Apollontempel, De la Coste, *Delphes*, Taf. 148. *F. Delphes*, 2 A 1, 104, 82. Foto Marburg 135144. 2) Wasserspeier vom Peisistratischen Athenatempel auf der Akropolis, Schrader 439 Taf. 180 f. 3) Marmorlöwe, Akropolis 382, Schrader Taf. 166. 4) Marmorlöwe, Akropolis 383, Schrader Taf. 167 f. Foto Marburg 124613. 5) Marmorlöwe aus dem Kerameikos *AA* 1933, 287, 20. Foto Marburg 135039. Dazu die rotfigurigen Vasen seit dem Andokidesmaler.

13. Kübler *AA* 1934, 227, 18. Foto Marburg 135038.

14. Nenfrolöwe im Museo Gregoriano, Giglioli aO. Taf. 72, 1. Nenfrolöwe früher im Deutschen Archäologischen Institut, Rom, v. Mercklin, *Scritti in onore di B. Nogara*, 1937, Taf. 31, 7 Bronzelöwe in der Ermitage v. Mercklin aO. Taf. 30. Kleiner Bronzelöwe in München, Mühlestein aO. 171 f. Grabreliefs aus der Nähe

Vulci nehmen eine Stellung ein in der Mitte zwischen beiden Gruppen.[15]

Enge Beziehungen sind dagegen festzustellen zwischen den Löwenköpfen aus Tarquinia und den Wasserspeiern vom Tempel in Himera (Taf 94, a).[16] Gemeinsam ist beiden Gruppen der aus flammenartigen, in der Mitte geteilten Locken bestehende Haarbogen über der Stirn und das im Gegensatz dazu zurückgestrichene Nackenhaar. Die s-förmige ornamentale Gravierung auf der Schnauze verbindet die Bronzen aus Tarquinia mit der älteren Reihe der Wasserspeier von Himera, die an der nördlichen Langseite des Tempels angebracht war. Mit dem radialen Barthaar teilen sie eine Besonderheit der jüngeren Reihe. Diese Aehnlichkeiten sind so gross, dass sie die Annahme eines gemeinsamen Archetypos fordern. Er verband den Haarbogen des helladischen Typus mit der dichten und plastisch aufgelösten Mähnenbildung des östlichen, hat sich also ausserhalb dieser beiden Bereiche gebildet. Bei dieser Lage der Dinge kommt nur Sizilien oder ein Gebiet Grossgriechenlands in Betracht, das abseits von dem tarentinischen Einfluss lag. Die Wasserspeier aus Himera sind in die Jahre bald nach 480 datiert. Wesentlich früher ist also auch die Gruppe der Bronzemedaillons aus Tarquinia nicht.

Eine Abweichung von den Wasserspeiern aus Himera bieten sie in den kleinen Buckeln, in denen die einzelnen Locken des Stirnbogens endigen. Diese stammen überhaupt nicht aus der griechischen Ueberlieferung. In deren Sinn sind sie ein unorganischer Zusatz. Da sie als Ersatz von Spiralen zu gelten haben, fragt es sich, ob dieser Zug auf eine ältere etruskische Quelle zurückgeht und Werke von der Art der Wölfin voraussetzt.

Bei dieser liegt zwar der aus den kleinen Spirallocken gebildete Rahmen, der den Kopf einfasst, dem Halse eng an. Er setzt sich nicht dadurch von der Stirn ab, dass er sich aufrichtet. Als Uebereinstimmung mit dem ionischen Löwentypus lässt sich das aber nicht auffassen, in seiner rahmenden Funktion eher als eine Aehnlichkeit mit dem helladischen. Dessen Vertretern aus der Kleinkunst fehlt es hier meist an einer Gliederung. In einigen Fällen ist sie durch radiale Gravierungen angedeutet. Aber die monumentalen haben auch an

---

von Florenz, Mühlestein aO. 212. Rumpf, *Katalog der etruskischen Skulpturen des Berliner Museums*, E 10. Cippus aus Settimello in Florenz, Mühlestein aO. 238. Bronzereliefs: *RM* 9 (1894) 311, 17. *BrBr*. Text zu Taf. 586 Abb. 14. Taf 588. Giglioli aO. Taf. 91. Grabmalereien: AD. 2, 41. Hilfstafel 41. 42 A. Weege, *Etruskische Malerei*, Taf. 42. 44. 73. 92 Beil. 3. 6. *Pontische Vasen:* Ducati Taf. 2. 11. 12. 17. 23. 25. 27.

15. Neugebauer *JDAI* 58 (1943) 206 ff.

16. Marconi, *Himera*, 1931, 70 ff.

dieser Stelle das Flammenhaar wie ihre östlichen Gegenstücke.[17] Ueberhaupt dürfte es schwer fallen, bei archaischen Tieren aus dem griechischen Bereich ähnliche Spirallocken zu finden, während sie bei der Darstellung von Menschen in der spätarchaischen griechischen Kunst häufig sind. In fast derselben Gestalt wie bei der Wölfin finden sich diese Spirallocken aber bei Gorgoneien tönerner Stirnziegel aus Etrurien, Latium und Campanien, die ihr zeitlich nahestehen.[18] Der verdickte, nicht eingerollte Ansatzteil ist bei ihnen auch der Länge nach gefurcht. Der Unterschied liegt nur darin, dass er gestreckter ist und dass diese Locken sich nicht aufrichten, sondern hängen. Die Löwenprotomen, die Wölfin und die Antefixe erweisen also die Vorliebe der mittelitalischen Kunst für diese Form.

Aber woher stammt sie? Da sie aus dem angegebenen Grund der griechischen Tradition fremd ist, muss sie, in dieser Verwendung jedenfalls, italisch sein. Ein etruskischer Bronzekopf im British Museum, der frühestens in die zweite Hälfte des 5. Jahrhunderts zu datieren ist, beleuchtet diesen Sachverhalt.[19] Er hat noch dieselben Spirallocken. Das ist eine der für die mittelitalische Kunst so charakteristischen Retardationen, gleichzeitig aber auch ein Zeugnis für die Besonderheit des dekorativen Formgefühls dieses Kunstkreises, das für die Annahme einer Entstehung innerhalb dieses Zusammenhangs ins Gewicht fällt.

Die Abhängigkeit der Wölfin von griechischen Löwen ist durch die Gestalt der Hals- und Rückenmähne und durch das Vorhandensein der Halskrause gesichert. Mit Hilfe der Bronzen aus Tarquinia haben sich die griechischen Vorbilder ermitteln lassen. Sie gehören der sizilischen Kunst der Zeit zwischen 480 und 470 an. Die thematisch geforderte Umbildung hat sich, wie namentlich die Spirallocken erkennen lassen, nicht im Sinne der griechischen, sondern im Sinne der mittelitalischen Form vollzogen, geradeso wie bei den bronzenen Löwenköpfen der Medaillons. Den griechischen Löwen ist diese Behandlung der Halskrause fremd. Das erweist die Wölfin als eine italische Schöpfung. Die merkwürdig freie Bildung ihrer Augen, die im Gegensatz steht zur strengen Stilisierung des Mähnenhaars, rät überhaupt zu einem möglichst späten Zeitansatz. Die Wölfin wird ebenso wie die Gruppe der Bronzemedaillons aus Tarquinia eher im zweiten als im ersten Viertel des 5. Jahrhunderts entstanden sein.

---

17. B 1 und 2 und oben Anm. 13.

18. Koch, *Dachterrakotten aus Campanien*, Taf. 5, 5-7. 6, 1. 2. 4. Andrén, *Architectural Terracottas*, 32, Taf. 10, 502 Taf. 144.

19. Riis, *Tyrrhenika*, 89 f. Taf. 17, 2.

MAGNI NOMINIS UMBRAE

FRANK E. BROWN
American Academy in Rome

Plates 95-97

The expediency of Caesar and the policy of Augustus honored both the memory and the effigy of Pompey. In Rome the statues, like the followers, of his great rival were conspicuous objects of Caesar's *clementia*.[1] On his new rostra at the end of the Forum the image of Pompey with that of Sulla regained the place it had held on the old.[2] Pompey's statue in the Curia of his theater was spared to tower over Caesar's corpse.[3] The enrollment of Magnus among Augustus' predecessors in legitimacy may have earned him a place among the worthies of the Forum Augustum.[4] The statue, at any rate, which had witnessed Caesar's death, was not piously walled up in that forbidden place. It was salvaged by Caesar's heir, to be set on a marble arch before the central doorway on the stage of Rome's first and greatest theater.[5]

For this, the most famous of his many portraits, the gift of a grateful city, Pompey must have sat during the years 55-52 B. C., being between 51 and 54 years of age and at the pitch of power and reputation. Whether it was of bronze or of marble, we are not told. About it stood a renowned set of fourteen marble figures, which typified the peoples over whom the great captain had triumphed. Their author bore the homespun Roman name of Coponius.[6]

It is in all likelihood the traits of this portrait, which are preserved by a series of coins and by the remarkable copy in the Ny Carlsberg Glyptotek.[7] The coins were issued in Sicily by Sextus Pompey six to twelve years after his father's death, from 42 to 36 B. C.[8] The various obverse dies consistently render the features of a single notable

1. Suetonius, *Divus Julius*, 75; Plutarch, *Caesar*, 57, 4.

2. Cassius Dio, 43, 49, 1.

3. Plutarch, *Brutus*, 14, 2; *Caesar*, 56, 1.

4. Velleius Paterculus, 2, 29; cf. Syme, R., *The Roman Revolution*, 316f. Further, Suetonius, *Divus Augustus*, 31; Hist. Aug., *Alex. Sev.*, 28, 6.

5. Cassius Dio, 47, 19, 1; Suetonius, *Divus Julius*, 88; *Divus Augustus*, 31.

6. Pliny, *N. H.*, 36, 41; Suetonius, *Nero*, 46: Brunn, H., *Geschichte der Griechischen Kuenstler*₂, I, 420.

7. Schweitzer, B., *Die Bildniskunst der roemischen Republik*, 86.

8. Grueber, H. A., *Coins of the Roman Republic in the British Museum*, II, 560-565; Poulsen, F., *RA*, ser. VI, vii (1936), 17-19; Vessberg, O., *Studien zur Kunstgeschichte der roemischen Republik* (Acta Instituti Romani Regni Sueciae, 8, 1941), 134-136.

original. The same or a closely similar portrait had served two or three years earlier as the model for Sextus' Pompey-Janus asses, struck in Spain in 45-44.[9] Of it the Ny Carlsberg head is a clear but distant echo.[10]

This (plate 95) is the full-blown masterpiece of a great portraitist of the Hadrianic age. Rather than a copy, it is an unequivocal and strongly colored interpretation of the man whose features were recorded in the original. The puffed, complacent face with its pursed, uncertain mouth and small suspicious eyes mocks the carefully wayward tuft of forelocks, which gave Pompey his cherished likeness— more remarked than apparent, as Plutarch observes—to Alexander the Great.[11] The Ny Carlsberg head is an unsparing characterization of the vain and greying dynast, of whom we catch glimpses in the sources.[12]

It is not a portrait to have done honor to Rome's first citizen between his second and third consulships. However merciless the realism of the sculptured faces of those years, they are all possessed of a grave, impenetrable dignity, or, if moved, are moved with the emotions appropriate to *virtus, magnanimitas* and the pursuit of *gloria*. The coin profiles of the same original translate not only the sculptural technique of an earlier day but a vastly different mood of serene and confident power. They have been likened for their ennobled realism to the coins of Ariobarzanes I-III of Cappadocia and Nicomedes II and III of Bithynia.[13]

Of that original itself we may, I believe, form a more adequate impression from the fragment of a portrait of Pompey, recently come to light in Rome and now in my possession (plates 96 and 97). It is the face and frontal portion of the head of a statue somewhat (1 1/5-1 1/6) more than life size. Carved in Parian marble, it measures

---

9. Grueber, *op. cit.*, 2, 371f.

10. Vessberg, *op. cit.*, 136f. It is probable that two other portraits of Pompey are to be recognized as the originals of (a) the portrait on denarii of Cn. Pompey issued in Spain in 46-45 (Grueber, *op. cit.*, 2, 366f. and on a gem, Furtwaengler, A., *Die antiken Gemmen*, 1, taf. L, 43; Poulsen, *op. cit.*, 31, fig. 15; cf. Vessberg, *op. cit.*, 137) and (b) a bust in the Archaeological Museum in Venice, judged by Poulsen to be of Claudian date (Poulsen, *op. cit.*, 22-27; Schweitzer, *op. cit.*, 88f.).

11. Plutarch, *Pompey*, 2, 1-2; Poulsen, *op. cit.*, 35-50; Schweitzer, *op. cit.*, 86-88. V. H. Poulsen, however, in the *Journal of the Walters Art Gallery*, 11 (1948), 10, dates the head, wrongly I feel, to the time of Claudius on the basis of its alleged discovery in the tomb of the Licinii and Calpurnii outside Porta Pia (*RA*, ser. V, 36, 1932, 54-62) and of its possible connection with Cn. Pompeius Magnus, son of Marcus Licinius Crassus Frugi, cos. 27 A. D., d. 47.

12. Cicero, *Ad Atticum* 1, 18; 2, 3, 1; Valerius Maximus, 6, 2, 7; Ammianus Marcellinus, 17, 11, 4.

13. Pfuhl, E., *JDAI* 45 (1930), 14; Vessberg, *op. cit.*, 216f.; cf. L'Orange, H. P., *Apotheosis in Ancient Portraiture*, 52ff.

0.285 m. (11½″) from chin to crown. The masklike fragment was cleanly split away just in front of the right ear and through the left cheek bone. The tips of forelock, nose and chin are chipped away. Broad, shallow chips mar the left side of the hair and the jaw line on either side. The surface, through soil corrosion, has lost its sensitive finished skin, but the underlying quality of the modelling has not been impaired.

The features are those of the coins of Sextus, heavy and ruthless in the flesh, here transfigured. They breathe a calm assuredness, a spirit of majestic and imperturbable benevolence. The eyes are wide and fearless, the mouth decisive and good-humored. The only marks of age and greatness are the thoughtful corrugations of the brow and the firm wrinkles at the corners of the eyes and the edges of the cheeks. The thick cap of hair lies in close, heavy rows of short locks, save for the tidy commotion of the center.

The face is modelled in broad, flat, lightly modulated planes. The clear passages from one to another are slurred and smooth, except as sharply marked by the deep accents of wrinkles. The quality is perhaps best seen about the mouth, where the flesh around the thin, cleanly defined lips is moved by the suggestion of a smile. Here the surfaces are delicately but flatly handled, even to the slight shadow of hair above the lip. The lightly lifted eyebrows are rendered as a high-lit ridge above the deep-cut shadow of the upper lid and the answer-ing wrinkle beneath the lower. About the sharply chiselled edges of the lids the lashes are suggested by a faint incision. The hair is given tightly and flatly as almost uniform, short curving locks, whose sur-faces are broken by parallel, highly regular grooves. All this betrays the hand of a sculptor of the mid first century B. C., a sculptor of the first rank, Greek-trained or well versed in the classicizing hellenism of contemporary eclecticism.

The coins of Sextus Pompey, allowances being made for the simpli-fication and emphasis on salient features inseparable from coin por-traiture and for the hands of various die-cutters, faithfully reproduce not only the traits and the mood of our head, but also in some cases so particular a feature as the rendering of the hair in overlapping rows of short locks.[14] Similarly the Ny Carlsberg copy, abstraction made of the style and interpretative genius of the Hadrianic master, answers to our head detail for detail. It is, in short, either the original itself, from which both the coins and the Ny Carlsberg head were taken, or a contemporary duplicate. Wilhelm Klein a generation ago detected in the Ny Carlsberg head the hand of Pasiteles, and

---

14. For this feature, see Schweitzer, *op. cit.*, 48f.

Schweitzer has tentatively accepted this attribution for its original.[15] The style of our head of Parian marble, differing in so many respects from the emphatic and deeply scored realism of its day, and akin in so many others to the crisp and mannered classicism of the eclectics, aptly confirms the essential rightness of this judgment.

Pasiteles is but a name. Were we to seek another, none would more readily suggest itself than that of the Coponius, who carved the *"quattuordecim nationes quae sunt circa Pompeium."*[16] Roman portraitists are anonymous. Coponius, were he our sculptor, would emerge as a precursor of the great classicizing Augustan masters. If it be overbold, on such slender and circumstantial evidence, to see in ours the very face of the statue, at whose feet Caesar fell, we shall not be far off the mark in forming from it our impression of that vanished masterpiece.

---

15. Klein, W., *Vom antiken Rokoko*, 173f.; cf. C. C. Van Essen, *JRS* 24 (1934) 157; Schweitzer, *op. cit.*, 145.

16. It is perhaps worth considering that the Provinces of the Hadrianeum may have stood in the same relation to the fourteen "Nationes" of Pompey as the Ny Carlsberg copy to its original, a possibility not entertained by J. M. C. Toynbee, *The Hadrianic School.*

FLAVA CERES

Maurizio Borda
Università di Roma

Tavola 98

In un santuario rurale del suburbio di *Aricia,* in un'epoca imprecisabile, molto dopo, certamente, la fondazione della colonia romana ed assai prima che la regione venisse sconvolta dalla guerra civile, un ignoto dedicante offerse, riconoscente della protezione accordata, questo busto fittile all'alma Cerere (tav. 98, a).[1] Donario per forma e dimensioni assai superiore agli altri, più modesti e dozzinali, teste e statuette votive, posti nello stesso santuario.[2]

La figura è ridotta al busto, caratteristica delle figurazioni di carattere votivo di divinità ctonie; espressa con tutti gli attributi matronali e divini di *Demeter-Ceres.* Bene acconciata la capigliatura, con scriminatura sulla fronte che lascia due masse di capelli morbidi e leggeri a cornice del volto, che vanno a raccogliersi in nodo sulla nuca, lasciando sfuggire fluide ciocche sulle spalle e sul petto; capigliatura fermata superiormente da un cercine ad estremità annodate sulla fronte, su cui poggia, come un diadema, la corona di spighe.

Un leggero chitone, ampiamente scollato, abbottonato sulle spalle, ed un mantello più pesante, di cui appare un lembo sull'omero sinistro, costituiscono l'abbigliamento della dea, che essa completa, con gusto un po'provinciale, con fastosi e pesanti gioielli.

Questa figura di Cerere non è un apparizione consueta in un santuario latino, di carattere modesto quale dovette certamente essere questo di Ariccia. Se la confrontiamo con le altre teste e statue fittili verisimilmente raffiguranti la stessa dea, che facevano parte della stessa stipe votiva, la diversità salta subito all'occhio. Si tratta di opere di tecnica quasi sempre scadente, nelle quali appare una sostanziale indisciplinatezza formale, la mancanza di un sicuro e coerente criterio plastico. Sono dei caratteri che riscontriamo in novanta casi su cento nelle manifestazioni della coroplastica etrusco-italica, dove la vacuità formale e la mancanza di organicità strutturale sono in parte surrogate da un vivace naturalismo o da un colorito espressio-

---

1. Notizia di scavo: Paribeni, *NSc,* 16 (1930) 373, Alt. m. O. 73: largh. m. O. 97; privo della punta del naso, di parte della corona e dei capelli nella metà sinistra del capo. Cfr. *AA,* 1931, 551 (Museo Nazionale Romano, Roma. *Antiquarium*).

2. Paribeni, *ibid. passim.*

nismo.[3] Le poche eccezioni che si possono segnalare[4] vanno riferite non già alla modesta produzione anatematica di artigianato, ma alla decorazione templare e sono perciò fuori del campo che a noi interessa.

Al contrario, dunque, di quanto si può notare nella plastica fittile votiva coeva dell'Italia centrale, nel busto di Ariccia le forme non sono soltanto intuite con piena consapevolezza della organicità strutturale, ma rese anche con tecnica affatto diversa. Una lettura accurata del trattamento dei particolari ci avverte subito che ci troviamo di fronte alla traduzione fittile di una scultura bronzea: si notino i solchi aguzzi nella massa della capigliatura, che viene divisa in strie quasi metalliche; il lieve tratteggio delle sopracciglia, i globi oculari sprofondati nelle orbite, gli ampi fori delle cavità nasali, le labbra contornate con una sottile linea incisa; anche gli orecchini e la collana sembrano quasi calcati dall'archetipo bronzeo. E soltanto da questo punto di vista, della derivazione da una statua fusa in bronzo, potremo tentare un'adeguata interpretazione delle forme stilistiche di questa scultura, che nulla ha in comune, per la sua solidità strutturale, per la sua fermezza di piani, per la netta incisività degli elementi fisionomici, con l'immediatezza delle opere coroplastiche, dove sempre si avvertono il pollice e la stecca del modellatore.

Nella forma del busto, in questo singolare elemento tipologico,[5] risiede gran parte del mistero che circonda questa scultura. Elemento indubbiamente italico, poichè completamente ignoto al mondo greco e frequente invece in ambiente siceliota e megaloellenico, riferito normalmente a divinità ctonie, alle quali allude il concetto simbolico della figura emergente dalle latebre del suolo.[6] Proprio in Sicilia, epicentro del culto di Demetra e Persefone, divinità ctonie per eccellenza, si determina una vasta produzione di busti fittili a partire dalla fine del VI secolo a. C. fino all'epoca romana.[6] A questa produzione di carattere votivo corrisponde quella analoga svoltasi nella Magna Grecia,[7] ma più tarda, a quanto sembra, e più limitata. Dalla Sicilia, centro di

---

3. Per la coroplastica etrusco-italica v. Giglioli. *L'Arte Etrusca, passim.* — sui caratteri formali della st. v. V. Kaschnitz-Weinberg, *RM* 41 (1926) 133ff.

4. es. le terrecotte del territorio falisco (Civltà Castellana: Giglioli, *op. cit.*, t. 318-19) e le terrecotte romane di Via S. Gregorio: Stuart-Jones, *The Sculpt. of the Pal. dei Conservatori*, 350.

5. p. il concetto del busto v. Benndorf, *Oest. Jahresh.* 1898, 1ff.; Deonna, *Les statues de terrecuite dans l'antiquité*, 43-47.

6. Pace, *Arte e Civiltà della Sicilia antica*, II, 81; Marconi, *NSc* 1925, 140; *Dedalo*, 10 (1929) 657; Libertini, *Centuripe*, t. 19-21.

7. Busti da Canosa; Levi, Alda, *Le terrecotte del Mus. Naz. di Napoli*, 63, fig. 59; da Pompei: Kekulé, *Die Ant. Terrakotten*, I, 1. XXIX, 3 etc. da Capua prov. busti di defunti: cfr. Schweitzer, *Die Bildnisk. d. röm. Republik*, t. II, fig. 5. Cfr. fig. 8-10.

origine e di diffusione, dobbiamo supporre che il tipo si sia diffuso, attraverso la Magna Grecia, fin nell'Italia Centrale.[8]

Italico è dunque l'elemento del busto e non meno italico è il tipo dei gioielli. Gli orecchini con rosette e pendenti piramidali sono noti specialmente in ambiente tarantino.[9] Anche il monile che la dea reca al collo, sebbene non italico di origine, diviene caratteristico dell'ambiente italico nel periodo a cui il busto va riferito. Si tratta certamente di un *torques*, la collana a verga attortigliata a fune con estremità aperte e avvicinabili grazie all'elasticità del metallo (bronzo, oro o argento): ornamento di carattere barbarico in uso presso le popolazioni scitiche, dalle quali lo adottarono i Greci della Crimea, e quelle celtiche, dalle quali lo adottarono gli Etruschi ed altri popoli italici.[10] Uso non già riservato agli uomini, come ritengono alcuni basandosi su un passo di Isidoro (*Etym.* XIX, 31, II) che va probabilmente riferito solo ai suoi tempi, ma anche esteso alle donne;[11] di che si ha conferma in opere di ambiente etrusco, dalla prima metà del III alla fine del II secolo a.C. La testimonianza più interessante è data da una testa femminile da Volsinii-Orvieto, di trachite,[12] che ornava la facciata di un sepolcro, e che reca, come il busto di Ariccia, la capigliatura allacciata da nastri e pendenti alle orecchie; e da una figura femminile di un cippo della Tomba François, della fine del II secolo.[13] Potrebbe supporsi che in entrambi i casi si tratti di Persefone o di divinità ctonie; ed allora il *torques* potrebbe esere un attributo di queste ultime. Sappiamo però anche dagli scrittori che il *torques* veniva pure offerto, quale consacrazione del bottino di guerra tolto ai Celti vinti, alle divinità, a Giove Capitolino (Liv. 33, 36) o a Marte (Flor. 2, 41).

Uno studio sulla coroplastica italica è ancora da scrivere e certo prima di farlo occorre attendere che venga pubblicato il ricco materiale, ancora per gran parte inedito, della Sicilia e della Magna Grecia. Ma nella copiosità della produzione di queste due regioni è dato fin d'ora ravvisare ben poche manifestazioni che esprimano delle

---

8. cfr. Giglioli, *op. cit. passim.*

9. cfr. una testa femminile (antefissa) da Taranto: Wuilleumier, *Tarente* t. XXXIX, 4; Hadaczek, 27ff.

10. *RE*, XII, s. v.; Daremberg-Saglio, V, 375; Ducati, *Storia dell'Arte Etrusca*, II, 517ff. (non era solo un abbigliamento, ma un insegna).

11. Già in Francia, nell'età del Ferro più recente era recato da donne, come apparve nelle tombe dello Champagne; *RA*, 1886.

12. Museo Barracco, Roma; *Collection Barracco*, t. LXXVII, 53, Giglioli, *op. cit.* t. CCCLXIII (anteriore alla distrusione di Volsinii (265 a. C).

13. Giglioli, *Arte Etrusca*, t. CCCLXIV, cfr. una testa femm. su un vasetto bronzeo configurato da Todi (Museo Gregoriano: ppo. III secolo. Giglioli, *op. cit.* t. CCCX, 2; figura femminile in un fregio fittile da Vetulonia (II metà III secolo): Ducati, *Arte Etrusca*, 479, fig. 557.

possibilità formali che possano essere paragonate con quelle realizzate nel busto di Ariccia. Questo ci induce sempre più a ribadire il nostro punto di vista che si debbano cercare confronti più nel campo della plastica, per così dire, monumentale, di bronzo, che non nell' ambiente coroplastico. Si aggiunga che le sculture fittili di grandi dimensioni sono poco predilette nell'arte della Magna Grecia. I pochi confronti che si possono fare (e si noti che le terrecotte, specie di grande modulo, devono aver avuto, anche nei tempi antichi, un'assai breve durata) si riferiscono ad opere dell'ambiente campano, come le grandi statue di Pompei,[14] ed a quello siceliota (un confronto relativamente puntuale può essere istituito col busto di Aidone del Museo di Siracusa).[15]

Ammesso, dunque, che nel busto di Ariccia si debba vedere la fedele traduzione di un grande bronzo, in quale ambiente stilistico dobbiamo supporre creato quest'ultimo?

Ancora alla Sicilia dobbiamo rivolgerci, per cogliere i più puntuali confronti tipologici e stilistici nei tipi monetali sicelioti e specialmente siracusani. Nella tradizione artistica della bellissima testa di Persefone coronata di spighe, coi capelli annodati sulla nuca e fluttuanti sul collo e pendenti alle orecchie che appare sui tetradrammi coniati nel periodo 310-304 a.C.;[16] tradizione che viene continuata nei tipi monetali di Hicetas (288-79)[17] e di Gerone II (274-216 a.C.)[18] è la testa della giovane dea su un pezzo da 10 litre coniato sotto il governo democratico nel periodo 215-12 a.C.[19] Nel volto pieno, nei grandi occhi, nel naso sensuale, nelle labbra tumide e nel grosso mento, nel collo pieno in cui è segnata la collana di Venere, perfino nella capigliatura con bande laterali rigonfie, riccioletti a virgola sulla fronte e davanti alle orecchie, è una persuasiva puntualità di raffronto fra la testa della Demeter di Ariccia con quella della Persefone siracusana. Il netto, puro ed incisivo profilo della testa fittile (tav. 98b) richiama esso stesso a quello di un conio inciso da un maestro siceliota.

E'un ideale di bellezza femminile del tutto diverso da quello dell'arte classica: pur componendosi le forme del volto in un'espressione di beltà ideale che discende in linea diretta dalla tradizione stilistica del IV secolo, esse appaiono già compenetrate da una nuova concezione

14. Levi, *Le terrecotte*, cit. t. X (Giove), t. XI (Giunone) da archetipi ellenistici. Cfr. a. la bella testa muliebre colossale (Arianna?) a tav IX. (prov. ignota).

15. Libertini, *Centuripe*, 91ff; Pace, *op. cit.*, 110, fig. 103.

16. Hill, *Coins of Anc. Sicily*, t. XI, n. 13-14; *BMC*, 196, n. 381.

17. Babelon, *La Coll. De Luynes*, 1342-43.

18. pezzo da 60 litre: Hill, *op. cit.* t. XIII, 4; *BMC*, 208, n. 514.

19. Head, t. XIII, n. 7; Hill, *op. cit.*, 196; *BMC*, 224, n. 661.

formale. La costruzione sintetica ed unitaria del volto è dominata dalle masse carnose, non nettamente articolate, ma fuse in una morbidae fluida continuità: guance rese a larghi piani nei quali si annullano i particolari, grandi occhi spalancati ed incavati sotto i rigonfi muscoli sopraccigliari; bocca con labbra tumide ed ondulate, mento sporgente ed adiposo, ricca massa della capigliatura.

E'rispecchiata una concezione propria dell'ambiente stilistico dell' alto ellenismo. Gli stessi caratteri appaiono in opere create in ambiente ellenistico asiatico fra la fine del III ed il principio del II secolo a.C. Se osserviamo una testa di Cibele che appare su tetradrammi di tipo alessandrino coniati a Smirne al principio del II secolo,[20] notiamo un analogo linguaggio costruttivo con tendenza alla rotondità ed alla morbidezza, con forme del volto piene ed opulente, dai tratti fortemente segnati. Caratteri che riapaiono in teste femminili da Tralles[21] e da Smirne,[22] e, in parte, anche nella bellissima testa bronzea di Satala (Erzindjan), dello stesso periodo.[23]

Di questo nuovo linguaggio stilistico determinatosi nella *koinè* artistica dell'alto ellenismo, anche l'ambiente occidentale doveva logicamente, pei suoi frequenti contatti con l'oriente ellenistico, partecipare. Ed un riflesso di questa concezione appare infatti nei ritratti della regina Filistide, moglie di Gerone di Siracusa (274-216 a.C),[24] espressione delle possibilità formali degli artisti siracusani ancora in questo periodo.

Tutti gli elementi concorrono dunque a localizzare l'*anáthema* fittile di Ariccia in ambiente siceliota: il tipo del busto,[25] il tipo iconografico, di cui ci sembra di cogliere un riflesso in un'altra manifestazione artistica determinatasi in ambiente laziale, in un rilievo fittile[26] col busto della dea, con analoga acconciatura, recante mazzi di papaveri e spighe: composizione a sua volta derivante dall'ambiente siceliota o megaloellenico. Poi la tecnica, che rivela un coroplasta di esperienza consumatissima ed attivo in un ambiente in cui le forme artistiche erano ancora vive ed operanti; non un modesto artigiano che ricalca pedissequamente una grande opera. Infine l'archetipo bronzeo.

L'esecuzione del busto fittile e la sua dedica nel santuario latino debbono essere cronologicamente compresi fra due avvenimenti che

---

20. *BMC, Ionia*, 237, t. 25, 5ff.; Horn, *RM*, 53 (1939) t. 10, 4-5, 71ff.
21. *RA*, 1904, 349 t. XIII, I (Mus. di Istambul).
22. *AM*, 1912, 307ff. *Abh.* 8 cfr. a. Mendel II, 629, p. 378.
23. *Brit. Mus. Catal.* 266; *Select Bronzes*, XV; Bulle, *D. Schöne Mensch*, t. 266; Lawrence, *Later Greek Sculpture, pass.* (non ant. ppo. II s).
24. Hill, t. XIII, n. 73.
25. cfr. Pace, *op. cit.*, 277.
26. Rohden-Winnefeld, *Arch.Röm.Reliefs d. Kaiserzeit*, Berlino-Stoccarda, 1911, t. XX, I, p. 4, 248ff.; replica scoperta recentem. a Cinecittà: *NSc.* 1943, v. IV, f. I, 28, fig. I.

hanno esercitato certamente un grande influsso sulla vita della regione: la costruzione della Via Appia (312 a.C) che attraversava la zona dei Colli Albani e che, specie dopo l'impianto della prima *mansio* da Roma, determinò uno sviluppo dell'abitato di *Aricia*,[27] e la devastazione della zona intorno a quest'ultima durante le guerre civili, all'inizio del secondo decennio dell'ultimo secolo a.C. L'*acmè* della vita del santuario aricino va dunque riferita al II secolo a.C., il che si accorda pienamente con le conclusioni alle quali siamo giunti dal punto di vista stilistico.

Pur recando in sè dei caratteri non latini, è difficile che il busto sia stato portato di lontano. La produzione fittile votiva deposta nei santuari risulta quasi sempre, da più indizi, fabbricata sul posto. In questo caso non potendosi, per le ragioni già esposte, fare questa ipotesi, dobbiamo ritenere che l'esecuzione sia avvenuta non già in Sicilia, ma tutt'al più in Campania o più facilmente a Roma. La statua bronzea di Cerere che servì da archetipo poteva trovarsi nel suo santuario sull'Aventino, costruito, secondo la tradizione, nel 496 a.C. in occasione dell'introduzione nell'Urbe del culto della dea.[28] Poichè sappiamo che furono chiamati a decorare il tempio due artisti verisimilmente sicelioti, Damófilo e Górgaso, è probabile che anche l'*ágalma* della dea, di bronzo dorato (Liv. 2, 41, 10; Plin. *N. H.* 34, 15) fosse opera di uno scultore siceliota; o addirittura una replica del famoso simulacro bronzeo di Demeter-Cerere che stava nel suo celebre santuario di Enna.[29]

Ma altri simulacri di Cerere dovevano essere in Sicilia, come quel busto radiato che appare in tipi monetali di Leontini,[30] di un periodo tardo, e nella stessa Roma.

Le conclusioni che si possono dunque trarre da un'analisi tipologica e stilistica del busto di Ariccia sono nel senso che esso si debba considerare la replica fittile, ad opera di un coroplasta megaloellenico o siceliota, di un grande bronzo uscito, tra la fine del III e l'inizio del II a.C., dallo studio di uno scultore attivo in un grande centro artistico siciliano, quale può essere stato Siracusa in quel periodo di notevole incremento per le arti figurative rappresentato dal regno di Gerone II. Ci sembra di non essere lontani da quell'ambiente stilistico nel quale si crea quel ritratto della regina Filistide cosi efficacemente caratterizzato nei tipi monetali; periodo in cui la grande tradizione artistica siceliota è ancora in grado di realizzare nuovi valori.

---

27. Sulla topografia di Aricia v. Florescu, in *Eph. Daco-Romana*, 3 (1925) 1ff.
28. Liv. 40, 2, 2; 41, 28, 2; 3, 55, 7. la data tradizionale forse è un po' troppo antica: cfr. Lugli, *Monum. Antichi di Roma e suburbio*, III, 580.
29. Cic. *Verr.* 4, 108; Strab. 6, 272.
30. Hill, *op. cit.* t. XIV-V.

THE COCK AND SCORPION IN THE ORTHONOBAZOS RELIEF AT DURA-EUROPOS

PAUL V. C. BAUR
Yale University

Plate 94

As a tribute to my old friend, Professor David M. Robinson, on his seventieth birthday, I bring this modest little article on the relief of Orthonobazos, the son of Goras. Everybody knows Robinson's excavation of Olynthus and his excellent publication of the material found. I know, as I have followed his other works not only in philology but also in archaeology, how versatile is his talent!

It is my intention to lay special stress on the scorpion and cock, a group in the above-mentioned relief.

Franz Cumont, in his *Fouilles de Dura-Europos*,[1] discusses a series of plaster reliefs found in the temple of Artemis and elsewhere.[2] Since Cumont's book, reliefs stamped from the same mold have been found in private houses, Block D5. Of these, I have six photographs.

As is clear from his pl. LXXXVI = our Fig. 1 (see also our pl. 94, b) the relief consists of two registers, an upper and a lower with a torus between. The height of the upper register is 78mm., of the lower register 25mm., of the torus 18mm. In Greek capital letters there is the following inscription: $M(νησθῇ)$ $'Ορθονόβαζος$ $Γόρου$, which means, "Remembered May Orthonobazos, the Son of Goras, Be". Cumont (p. 227 and especially 405) points out that Orthonobazos and Goras are Persian names.

The date of the Orthonobazos relief is about 200 A. D. The relief was made from many molds, reduced from larger monuments to a size to fit the two registers which were probably painted. Orthonobazos fills the whole background with rosettes of five petals and growing plants, etc. It is highly probable that the Orthonobazos relief was used as a cornice. Some of the isolated scenes are purely decorative.

---

1. Paris, 1926. His excavations cover the year 1922-23. Hereafter I shall refer to this work as "Cumont." To Professor C. Bradford Welles I wish to extend my most sincere thanks for his kindness in sending to me Cumont's *Fouilles* and also the Preliminary Report on the Mithraea at Dura. To Miss Ann Perkins of the Yale Art Gallery I wish to extend my thanks for sending me not only a photograph of Cumont's plate, but also the complete set of photographs for the private houses in Block D 5 at Dura.

2. On Pl. LXXXVI, our fig. 1, Cumont illustrates in outline drawing all the motives known; it is really a reconstruction.

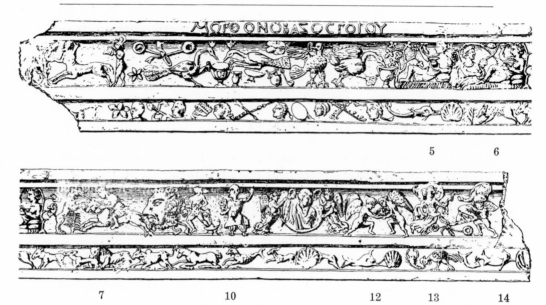

Fig. 1. The Orthonobazos relief (Cumont, *Fouilles de Dura-Europos*, pl. LXXXVI).

In the upper zone, among others we find a young man lying on a couch and resting his left elbow on a cushion (Cumont, No. 5, p. 233; our fig. 1). It is a hot day so he throws off his mantle which he wraps around his legs and reclines under the shade of a highly conventionalized tree. As he is thirsty he pours wine from a rhyton into a cup. According to Cumont, however, he is drinking the beverage of immortality. In Cumont, No. 6, two young women face each other under a grape arbor. The one to the right reclines on a couch; her left elbow resting on two cushions. She is pouring wine from a rhyton into a cup. The other woman, entirely draped, is sitting Turkish fashion and holds a crown. Next, Cumont, No. 7, comes a helmeted warrior carrying a lance and galloping toward a lion. Between the figures is a leaved plant indicating the country. No. 10 is identified by Cumont as a man wearing a tunic with feet ending in claws of a bird as if a siren, but it is without doubt a Parthian wearing a tunic and puttees and standing with heels close together and out-turned toes. In his right hand he holds a large vase, and his left hand is uplifted. Cumont, No. 12, shows two winged Erotes confronted and carrying in both hands a large basket of fruit. This is a motive taken from Greek Art, occurring already in Pompeii (Cumont gives the reference and cites other parallels on p. 236). No. 13, according to Cumont (p. 236), may represent a Maenad holding a piece of cloth, perhaps, but it seems to me, rather, that she holds a snake. Next comes a winged

Eros carrying a draped goddess, probably Aphrodite. I know of no other example of this.

In the lower register are emblems of the Bacchic cult alternating with six masks of the theater: thyrsus, syrinx, crossed flutes, tambourine and again crossed flutes (Cumont, p. 237). Then follows a series of aquatic and terrestrial animals, among whom we find the cock and scorpion (fig. 1, immediately below Cumont's figure 13) which form the subject of our study. That part of the composition of the Orthonobazos relief is also seen on the relief from a house on block D 5 (pl. 94, b, 13).

The cock is looking down at the scorpion. The group is well composed. The cock is very inquisitive, especially when he sees animals too large to eat, as I well know from experience. Here he is looking down much puzzled by the scorpion. The cock originally comes from Persia; and one variety of scorpion is also at home in Persia. That the cock is sacred to Hermes is well known, but that the scorpion is also sacred to Hermes is less well known. I shall come back to this later.

In the Concise Oxford Dictionary of 1944 we find the following description of a scorpion: "The scorpion is an arachnid with lobster-like claws and jointed tail that can be bent over to inflict a poisonous sting on prey held in his claws." The poison is in the last sac-like joint. If the scorpion catches a grasshopper he stings it to death before devouring it. The term "arachnid" is explained in the same dictionary as follows: "The Arachnid refers to a member of the *Arachnidia*, a class comprising spiders, scorpions and mites." Although the scorpion belongs to the same class with spiders, it differs from them in that it does not spin a web. There are many kinds of scorpions in the Near East. Professor Alexander Petrunkevitch informed me recently that in New Mexico and Arizona a very poisonous scorpion occurs whose sting is fatal. All scorpions are more or less poisonous. The sting of those not fatal is not pleasant, but not more unpleasant than the sting of a wasp.

In the same dictionary under the word Scorpio: "The Scorpio is a Zodiacal constellation and also the eighth sign of the Zodiac." In the Dura Mithraea both Middle and Late, occur signs of the Zodiac. The date of the Middle Mithraeum is *c.* 210-240 A. D. and of the Late Mithraeum, *c.* 240-256 A. D.[3]

---

3. *The Excavations at Dura-Europos Conducted by Yale University and the French Academy of Inscriptions and Letters, Preliminary Report of the Seventh and Eighth Seasons of Work*, 1933-34 and 1934-35. For the signs of the Zodiac of the Middle Mithraeum decorations, see p. 103, fig. 36. For the signs of the

In the interpretation of the tauroctone reliefs of the Dura Mithraea, Professor Rostovtzeff (p. 101) writes: "The traits characteristic of and common to Syria and Mesopotamia are the absence of the scorpion . . . ." The scorpion attacking the testicles of the bull occurs in the Mithraea of the West and especially in Germany.

The scorpion in literature and in art is discussed by Steier and Eitrem, to mention only the most important articles.[4]

On a contorniate, illustrated in Dar-Sagl. I, 2 p. 1689, is represented the triumph of Cybele and Attis in a chariot drawn by four lions; in the field above are two signs of the Zodiac, Taurus and Scorpio.

On a gem in Berlin published by Furtwängler, *Ant. Gemmen,* pl. 46, no. 46, is a fly and a scorpion.

On the famous Gemma Augustea of Vienna, illustrated in Furtwängler, *Ant. Gemmen,* pl. 56 and in Reinach, *Rép. de reliefs,* II, 144, a scorpion is a shield device. The shield is hanging on a tree.

On shields of some of the soldiers on the well known floor mosaic of Praeneste are scorpions as shield devices to frighten the enemy. Although the mosaic belongs to the Roman period, the model probably goes back to Hellenistic times.

An allegorical representation of Africa holds a scorpion on his hand or on his head.[5]

Not yet in the general bibliography is a representation of the Evil Eye painted on the outer wall of the Tower of the Archers (illustrated by Cumont, *Fouilles,* p. 138, fig. 31. Cumont gives the bibliography of the Evil Eye). A large eye is pierced by a dagger and a small harpoon. A bird of prey flies toward the eye and on each side, a snake attacks the eye, whereas a third snake, crested and therefore male, rises upward. On this design there is no scorpion, but at Palmyra itself, in a large tomb with paintings, has been discovered a similar figure of the Evil Eye, but much more complicated: a dagger and an arrow pierce the eye. Around it are two birds, two scorpions, a crab, a cock, and a serpent.[6] These are prophylactic images destined

Zodiac of the Late Mithraeum, see p. 110 and Pls. XXIX and XXX. On p. 110, Professor Rostovtzeff writes, "The signs of the Zodiac, symbolizing the celestial sphere, were painted in a counter-clockwise direction around the soffit or reveal."

4. Steier in *RE,* zweite Reihe 6, col. 1807ff., s.v. Spinnentiere, C., "Der Skorpion im Volksglauben und in der Kunst." Eitrem, "Der Skorpion in der Mythologie und Religionsgeschichte," *Symbolae Osloenses,* fasc. 7 (1928), writes that among the animals most common are the scorpion and the cock. Cf. also Tod, M. N., "The Scorpion in Graeco-Roman Egypt," *JEGArch,* 25 (1939) 55-61. In antiquity it was believed that certain silver rings could cure one of a scorpion's bite: Marshall, *JHS,* 24 (1904) 332-335; Mylonas, *AJA,* 49 (1945) 561, note 13.

5. Imhoof-Blumer, *Münzen und Gemmen,* VII, 42-46, Pl. XXIV, 10-16; Imhoof, *Monnaies,* 469; Bernhart, *Antike Münzbilder,* fig. 191. Keller, *Ant. Tierwelt,* 475.

6. Chabot, *Choix d'inscr. de Palmyre,* pl. XVI, 3 and p. 101.

to destroy the Evil Eye. Of great importance to me is the fact that here the scorpion is friendly to man. The date of both the Dura example and the Palmyra one is probably in the first half of the first century A. D.

Now that we have established the fact that the scorpion is the friend of man on certain occasions it is fitting that we discuss Hermes and the scorpion sacred to him.[7] It should be remembered that Hermes is the friend of man.[7a] In the impression of a medallion in Aquincum, Hermes is represented as riding on a ram. In front of the ram is a cock and behind him a scorpion.[8] The date is the middle of the third century A. D.

Much more common, however, is the cock and the tortoise. At Horn, near Roermond, Limburg, is an altar dedicated to *Mercurius Arvernus*, found a little over a century ago. On the main front of this monument, the Arvernian national god is represented as seated with a goat on his knees and a tortoise on which Mercury's feet rest.[9] A cock and a tortoise occur on a mosaic in the church S. Theodore in Aquileia which is, however, later than the destruction of Dura; nevertheless, the cock looking down at the tortoise has exactly the same pose as the cock looking down at the scorpion on the Orthonobazos relief.[10]

The cock and the tortoise group occurs with slight change but with less artistic care, in the Katechumeneum of Aquileia.[11]

On one of the lateral sides of an altar dedicated to *Mercurius, Arvernus,* is the representation of a cock standing on a tortoise.[12] This is sufficient evidence that the cock in connection with the tortoise is sacred to Hermes. Date: third century A. D. On the main front of this altar representing the Arvernian national god, Mercury's feet rest on a tortoise (see above note 9).

The tortoise is usually sacred to Aphrodite, but as we have just seen, the tortoise in its connection with the cock is sacred to Hermes.

---

7. For the scorpion as a device, "Abzeichen," of Hermes see Toutain, *Bull. de la soc. des Antiquaires de France*, 6 (1931), 195; a relief at Tetif in Algeria.

7a. See Brown, N. G., *Hermes the Thief. The Evolution of a Myth*, 1947. Nilsson, M. P., *Geschichte d. gr. Religion*, I, 471-480. These references I owe to the kindness of Professor C. Bradford Welles of Yale University.

8. András Alföldi, *Laureae Aquincenses, Dissertationes Pannonicae*, Ser. II, No. 10 (1939), Pl. LXIII, 1, p. 330.

9. *AJA* 53 (1949) 171.

10. Rudolph Egger, *Römisch-Germanische Kommission*, Leipzig, 1930 *Kultgebäude Konstantinischer Zeit in Aquileia.* Cecchelli, Carlo, *Gli Edifici ed i Mosaici Paleocristiani Nelle Zone Della Basilica di Aquileia*, Bologna, 1933.

11. Egger, *l. c.*, 100, fig. 3, 101, fig. 4.

12. Espérandieu, *Recueil Général*, III, no. 1800, from Fleurieu-sur-Saône.

EL ARA MITHRAICA DE ITALICA

Antonio Garcia y Bellido
Universidad de Madrid

Plate 99

La última guerra de conquista y pacificación que Roma hubo de sostener en España fué la de Cantabria, felizmente terminada por Augustus en el año 19 antes de J. C. La paz que, durante toda la época imperial subsiguiente, reinó en España no hizo necesaria ya la presencia de ejércitos de ocupación ni el movimiento permanente de tropas, que fué una de las características de las zonas de fricción en el Imperio. Para la seguridad de la Península Ibérica fué bastante una sola legión, la Legio VII Gemina Pia Felix, fundada por Galba. Sus cuarteles estuvieron en donde la actual ciudad de León, cuyo nombre deriva, precisamente, del de Legio. Esta única legión fué bastante, durante toda la época imperial, para vigilar de cerca a las tribus galaicas y astures, siempre inquietas, y proteger y custodiar las importantes explotaciones auríferas de la región norte-occidental de Hispania, de la que, según Plinius (NH 33, 78), se venían a sacar unas 20.000 libras de oro al año. Tal "desmilitarización" de Hispania trajo como consecuencia que ciertos credos religiosos exóticos propagados, sobre todo, por medio de los soldados, llegasen a la Península Ibérica no solo con retraso, sino de un modo sumamente atenuado. Tal ocurrió, precisamente, con el mas importante de estos credos orientales propagados durante el Imperio, con el mithraismo. Ya hemos tenido ocasión de tratar de ello mas ampliamente en un articulo no ha mucho publicado[1] en el que recogimos todos los monumentos mithraicos conocidos hasta el presente en España y Portugal. En él pudo comprobarse, una vez más, que, pese a los nuevos monumentos de todo orden surgidos del suelo recientemente (inscripciones de Benifayó y Beja, relieves y esculturas de los mithraea de Mérida y Troia), la Península Ibérica no fué nunca campo fácil para la propagación de las ideas mithraica en la medida que lo fueron las regiones del limes europeo y asiatico.

Con posterioridad a mi trabajo, antes citado, he podido reconocer en el Museo Arqueológico de Sevilla un nuevo monumento de caracter mithraico cuya divulgación creo interesante. A él vamos a dedicar las cortas lineas que siguen.

---

1. García y Bellido, A., "El culto a Mithras en la Península Ibérica," *Boletín de la Real Academia de la Historia*, 122 (1948) 283 sqq.

Trátase del ara reproducida en nuestras figuras adjuntas (pls. 99 a, b, c, d). Es de marmol blanco, grisáceo. Su forma, prismática; de base cuadrangular, y de las siguientes dimensiones: altura 0.23m.; anchura 0.15m.; grosor 0.10m. Procede de Santiponce (asiento de la antigua Italica) en las proximidades de Sevilla. No se conocen las circunstancias en que apareció. Fué entregada al Museo de Sevilla, por la Comisión de Monumentos de la Provincia, en enero de 1926. Inventario General n. 828; Registro de Entradas n. 4326. Hasta ahora inédita, según nuestros informes. Las fotografias fueron tomadas por mi en mayo de 1948.[2]

Su tamaño es, como se habrá deducido de las dimensiones arriba dadas, realmente minúsculo. Carece de inscripción alguna y se halla muy mutilada aunque, afortunadamente, sus deterioros no afectan en nada importante a su decoración relivaria. Esta ocupa los cuatro lados del árula y consta de los siguientes temas o motivos: cara principal, un toro marchando hacia nuestra derecha (pl. 99, a); cara posterior, un árbol que parece ser una higuera (pl. 99, c); cara menor, lateral derecha, un campo de trigo simbolizado en cinco espigas (pl. 99, b); cara menor, lateral izquierda, una vid con sus hojas, pámpanos y tal vez racimos de uvas, aunque estos no se ven por lo deteriorado de este lado (pl. 99, d). Unas molduras sencillas remataban el árula por la parte superior. De la inferior no queda nada. De los dos rollos o volutas (cornua) solo queda uno, el de nuestro lado izquierdo. El arte, en lo que nos es dado ver, parece bueno; la talla es fina, con empleo de trépano, pero muy discreto (cara posterior, con la higuera).

La intencionada asociación en un mismo monumento de caracter religioso, como es un ara, de estas cuatro figuras simbólicas (el toro, la higuera, las cinco espigas de trigo y la vid) es clara alusión a conceptos puramente mithraicos. En la teología de esta religión, el toro es animal que juega un papel primordial, bien perceptible, sobre todo, en los monumentos esculpidos. Se le atribuye, en efecto, una potencia creadora universal. Lleva en si mismo el gérmen de todos los dones primordiales de la tierra nutricia. Cuando el toro muere a manos de Mithras, de su cuerpo y de su sangre se engendra toda la vegetación terrestre. Porphyrios dice que "del mismo modo que lo es Mithras, tambien el toro es el demiourgós y rey de la generación."[3]

En nuestro relieve el lado principal del árula se halla ocupado por

---

2. Damos nuestras gracias al Sr. Lafita y a la Señorita Fernández Chicarro, director y secretaria, respectivamente, del Museo de Sevilla, por las facilidades de todo orden dadas para el estudio y reproducción de esta pieza.

3. ὡς καὶ ὁ ταῦρος δημιουργὸς ὢν [ὁ Μίθρας] καὶ γενέσεως δεσπότης. Porphyr. *De Antro Nympharum* c. 24 p. 73 Nauck; Cumont, *Textes et Monuments figurés relatifs aux Mystères de Mithra*, 2, 41 frag. e 6.

la figura única del toro que, como en los demás monumentos mithraicos, marcha hacia la derecha, según lo preceptúan, tambien, los textos sagrados.[4]

Las cinco espigas que figuran en el lado menor derecho del ara, parecen brotar del suelo. La relación de tales espigas con el toro está atestiguada, no sólo en lo antes dicho, sino tambien en los monumentos esculpidos. En cinco espigas se transforma la cola del toro moribundo en un monumento del Laterano.[5] Aquí, como en el árula de Italica, el número de espigas es cinco. En otros similares, empero, es sola una, o tres, e incluso siete, pero siempre impares, según fórmulas mágicas comunes a casi todas las religiones. Muy significativo es tambien un relieve del British Museum[6] en el que Mithras, al asestarle la mortal cuchillada al toro en el cuello, hace brotar de la herida tres chorros de sangre que salen ya trasformados en espigas de trigo. La relación entre la muerte del toro y el brote de las espigas, es pues, evidentemente, una relación de causa y efecto. Tal interdependencia no es menos patente en un relieve de la Villa Doria Pamphili en el que se representa la consabida escena del Mithras tauroktonos, pero con la particularidad, mucho mas rara, de figurarse a los pies de Cautes un haz de espigas de trigo y a su lado una hoz, símbolos de la cosecha; en el mismo relieve la cola del toro se termina en tres espigas.[7]

En el lado menor de la izquierda del árula figúrase, como hemos dicho, una vid. La vid, según un texto mithraico, nació tambien de la sangre del toro y llegó a sustituir al jugo sagrado llamado haoma, "la principal de todas las bebidas salutíferas," pero que parece se desconoció en el Occidente.[8] En los monumentos mithraicos no es rara la presencia de alusiones y representaciones relacionadas con Bacchos y Liber Pater, y sabemos que Bacchos mismo y el vino, fueron venerados por los sectarios de esta religión mazdea.[9] El reverso del gran bajorelieve de Heddernheim[10] muestra una escena en la que el sol entrega a Mithras un racimo de uvas. En el relieve de Troia, cerca de Setúbal (Portugal),[11] figuran tambien Helios y Mithras en el ágape sagrado teniendo en sus manos sendos rhyta, con el que beben cierta

4. Cumont, *op. cit.*, 1, 187.
5. Benndorf y Schoene, *Das Lateranische Museum*, 5 n. 199; Cumont, *op. cit.*, 2 n. 20.
6. Cumont, *op. cit.*, 2 monum. n. 65.
7. Vide Cumont, *op. cit.*, 2 fig. 48.
8. Cumont, 1, 197.
9. Cumont, 1, 146 s.
10. Cumont, 2, 365 *e*.
11. García y Bellido, *Esculturas Romanas de España y Portugal*, n. 398 lám. 282.

poción que debe ser vino. Asi se ve igualmente en otros monumentos emparentados con el de Troia.[12] A Liber Pater se le cita varias veces en una serie de inscripciones mithraicas recogidas por Cumont.[13] Finalmente, aunque dudoso por su posible restauración, citemos la escultura que estuvo en la Villa Giustiniani; en élla vemos[14] a Mithras surgiendo de la petra genitrix con un racimo de uvas en la diestra alzada, racimo hacia el cual dirige su mirada. La relación de este símbolo con el culto mithraico, y con la presencia del toro y las espigas en el ara de Italica es, pués, evidente, y confirma, por su parte, tambien, el caracter mithraico de nuestro monumento.

La cara posterior del árula, la opuesta a aquella en la que se figura al toro, se llena con la imágen de cierto arbol que parece ser una higuera. La identificación no es muy clara, pués sus frutos, los higos, están imaginados demasiado grandes y las hojas no aparecen del todo evidentes, en parte por la fuerte corrosión con que el tiempo ha dañado a la superficie del relieve. Por otra parte una figuración mas precisa del árbol no es facil encontrarla en todo el arte antiguo, en el que, como es sabido, los árboles suelen aparecer representados con un esquematismo genérico tal, que casi se convierten en meros símbolos, en los que es sumamente dificil, por lo general, poder determinar su especie. Esto ocurre, precisamente, aquí. Por exclusión, empero, y dado que estamos sin duda ante un monumento mithraico, no puede ser sino una higuera, ya que el granado, arbol sagrado tambien en el área del mundo antiguo mediterráneo, con el cual podría identificarse, no es árbol que figure en la religión mithraica. De los demás posibles (peral, manzano, ciruelo, melocotonero, etc. etc.) no es caso por el caracter e historia de ellos en el Mediterráneo. Ha de ser, por tanto, una higuera. Ahora bien la higuera es árbol que parece ser figuró en la teogonia de Mithras. Este hubo de alimentarse, no bien nacido, de los frutos de un árbol que se cree higuera, al tiempo que se cubrió con las hojas del mismo.[15] Desgraciadamente las representaciones mithraicas no son generosas a este respecto, y solo se puede señalar un relieve en el que hallemos algo relacionado con el caso. Es el relieve de Osterburken[16] en el que se ve una escena con la figura de Mithras cortando con un cuchillo una rama de cierto arbol identerminable, que parece sea una

---

12. *Ibid.*, n. 398.
13. *Op. cit.*, 1, 147.
14. Cumont, 1, fig. 62.
15. *Ibid.*, 1, 163 s.; 304.
16. *Ibid.*, 2, 350 f. 20.

higuera. Sería pues Mithras alimentándose y vistiéndo su desnudez con los frutos y hojas de la higuera.

Aras mithraicas de estructura paralela a la nuestra solo conocemos la del templo de Altbachtal, de Tréveris, con cuatro caras esculpidas[17] y en parte la de Wiesbaden.[18]

---

17. Loeschcke, S., *Der Tempelbezirk im Altbachtale zu Trier*, Heft 2 (Berlín 1942) lám. 18, 1*a-d*.

18. Espérandieu, *Bas-reliefs, stat. et. bust. de la Germanie Rom.*, no. 20; Ritterling, E., "Mithras Heiligtum," *Nass. Annalen*, 44 (1916-17) 231 lám. VI.

THEOTOKOS
EINE KOLOSSALPLASTIK AUS DER ZEIT DES
3. EPHESISCHEN KONZILS

WALTER HAHLAND
Linz

Tafel 98

Der bekannten und häufig besprochenen Gruppe spätantiker Frauenköpfe,[1] deren Zahl gegenüber den Männerplastiken der Zeit nach Konstantin d.Gr. auffallend zurücktritt, reiht sich ein Marmorkopf unbekannten Fundorts von etwa dreifacher Lebensgrösse an, den das Museum in Smyrna beherbergt.[2] Er steht im Hof des Museums neben dem Aufgang zum Direktionsgebäude (Taf. 98c). Vor der Katastrophe Smyrnas im Jahre 1922 war er im Konak der Stadt aufgestellt.[3] Mörtelreste im Haar und in den Falten des Kopftuches zeigen an, dass der Kopf in neuerer Zeit in irgendeiner Mauer verbaut gewesen war, und dies lässt wieder vermuten, dass er mit dem einstigen "Wahrzeichen von Smyrna" identisch sei, von dem Stark, *Aus dem Orient* S.189 spricht: "Das Wahrzeichen von Smyrna, der kolossale über dem Westtor eingemauerte weibliche Kopf, ist schon seit Jahren verschwunden und soll in der gewaltigen Kaserne am Südwestende der Stadt irgendwo eingemauert sein."[4]

Der Kopf, aus weissem, grobkristallinischem Marmor, misst 0,68 m vom Bruch unter dem Kinn bis zur Scheitelhöhe. Die Gesichtshöhe vom Kinn bis zum Haaransatz beträgt 0,46 m. Die Grösse des Kopfes

1. In Anbetracht der ausserordentlich beschränkten bibliothekarischen Hilfsmittel, die mir z.Zt. zur Verfügung stehen, bin ich genötigt, für sämtliche im Rahmen dieser Abhandlung gegebene Literaturangaben grösste Nachsicht zu erbitten. Spätantike Frauenköpfe: grundlegend R. Delbrueck, *RM.* 28, 1913, 310ff. Vgl. ferner Arndt-Bruckmann, *Griech.u.Röm.Porträtplastik* zu Taf. 895ff., Oskar Wulff, *Altchristliche und byzantinische Kunst* (Burgers *Handbuch der Kunstwissenschaften*) I, 157f., S. Fuchs, *Die Antike* 19, 1943, 109ff., G. Rodenwaldt, *JdI.* 59/60, 1944/45, 96ff. H. P. L'Orange, *Studien zur Geschichte des spätantiken Porträts*, Oslo 1933, 75 Anm. 5 erwähnt ein noch unveröffentlichtes Frauenporträt theodosianischer Zeit in Saloniki.

2. Inventar-Nr. 173. Foto des Museums 109, 436, 217. Unsere Taf. 98d nach Museumsaufnahmen. Taf. 98c nach eigener Aufnahme. Die Museumsaufnahme des Kopfes in Vorderansicht ist unbrauchbar. — Bei meinen Nachforschungen nach der Herkunft des Kopfes, die leider erfolglos blieben, unterstützte mich in entgegenkommender Weise Aziz Ogan, Generaldirektor der Museen, dem auch an dieser Stelle für seine stets bewährte Hilfsbereitschaft gedankt sei. Der Kopf wird in Aziz, *Guide du Musée de Smyrne*, S.20 erwähnt.

3. Vgl. Arndt-Amelung, *Einzelaufnahmen* Nr. 1345.

4. Vgl. ferner den weiblichen Kopf vom Pagos in Smyrna, Konstantinopel, Mendel *Cat.* Nr. 1133, der ebenfalls mit dem von Stark, a.a.O. 189 genannten gemeint sein könnte.

überragt die nicht geringe Zahl kolossaler Männerplastiken der Spätantike[5] bis auf wenige Ausnahmen, überragt die Kolossalstatuen
Konstantins d.Gr. und des Constantinus Caesar von der Piazza del
Campidoglio in Rom,[6] die Konstantinstatue von der Vorhalle von San
Giovanni in Laterano[7] und reiht sich unter die grössten Plastiken der
Spätantike wie den Bronzekoloss von Barletta,[8] den Konstantinskoloss aus der Basilika des Maxentius[9] und den Bronzekopf im Museo
dei Conservatori in Rom.[10] Ob der Kopf in Smyrna von einer Büste
oder von einer Statue stamme, lässt sich nicht entscheiden. Die Statue
müsste bei aufrechtem Stande, den wir allerdings nicht erwarten
dürfen, über 4½m hoch gewesen sein, ungefähr halb so hoch wie der
Konstantinskoloss. Es handelt sich also um die grösste weibliche
Plastik der Spätantike, deren Grössenverhältnisse sich dem Bronzekoloss von Barletta näherten.[11]

Da die Rückseite des Kopfes stärker, als es sonst bei Freiplastiken
üblich war,[12] vernachlässigt und nur mit groben Hammerschlägen
zurechtgeformt ist, muss die Statue oder Büste ein-ansichtig in einer
Nische oder an einer sonstigen Wand eines grossen Gebäudes aufgestellt gewesen sein. Für die Aufstellung in einem gedeckten Raume
spricht auch die verhältnismässig gut erhaltene Oberfläche des
Kopfes.

Beim Sturz aus dem Standraum wurde der Kopf nicht unerheblich
beschädigt. Die Nase, die Lippen und die vorderen Säume des Kopftuches sind weggebrochen, die Augenlider und Brauenbögen und einzelne Stellen im Haar, vor allem über der Stirn, wurden angeschlagen.
Ein grosser Sprung durchquert in Höhe der Nase fast den ganzen
Kopf, begleitet von einigen kleineren Sprüngen und Rissen.

Der Scheitel ist oben muldenförmig abgeflacht (Taf. 98d), die
Falten des Kopftuches verlaufen bis zum Rande der sehr verwaschenen
Mulde. Es liegt jedoch nicht das geringste Anzeichen dafür vor, dass

---

5. Vgl. H. P. L'Orange, *Studien zur Geschichte des spätantiken Porträts*
sowie J. Kollwitz, *Oströmische Plastik der theodosianischen Zeit* (*Studien zur
spätantiken Kunstgeschichte* Bd. 12), Berlin 1941. Am nächsten kommt dem
Kopf in Smyrna der Kolossalkopf in Wien, L'Orange *Kat.* 105 Abb. 199-200,
Kollwitz Taf. 44: Kopfhöhe 0,59 m, Gesichtshöhe (Kinn-Haaransatz) 0,455 m.
Vgl. ferner L'Orange *Kat.* 11, 27, 38, 41, 46, 55, 58, 71, 73-77, 80-82, 86, 91, 95,
100, 117 and 119.

6. L'Orange *Kat.* 80 Abb. 155,-Kat. 82 Abb. 156.

7. L'Orange *Kat.* 81 Abb. 157, 158.

8. *Antike Denkmäler* III, 20, Arndt-Bruckmann 895ff. Kollwitz 93f. Nr. 21 Taf.
30 und 42. Buschor, *Bildnisshifen*, 146, Abb. 62. Jetzige (ergänzte) Höhe 5,11 m,
Höhe des antiken Torsos 3,55 m.

9. L'Orange *Kat.* 86 Abb. 163.

10. L'Orange *Kat.* 87 Abb. 164.

11. Vgl. oben Anm. 8.

12. Vgl. etwa Kollwitz Taf. 25, 28.

das Scheitelstück gesondert gearbeitet und angestückt gewesen sei, vielmehr dürfte die Blockgrösse für den oberen Teil der Schädel- kalotte nicht ausgereicht haben. Eine Aussparung zur Gewichtser- leichterung wie etwa beim kolossalen Domitianskopf aus Ephesos[13] kann es kaum sein, sie wäre im Verhältnis zum Ganzen auch zu un- bedeutend gewesen. An den Seiten des Kopfes sind etwa in Ohren- höhe drei würfelige Punti stehen geblieben, in den Falten an der linken Seite zwei, rechts einer, die neben ihrem ursprünglichen Zweck möglicherweise auch dazu gedient haben können, beim Versetzen des Kopfes oder beim Einsetzen in den Torso die Seile festzuhalten. Der Kopfwendung entsprechend sind die Falten des Kopftuches an der linken Seite durchmodelliert und bis auf die hinterste geglättet, an der rechten Gesichtsseite dagegen ist das Tuch nur summarisch ange- deutet und die Oberfläche rauher belassen (vgl. Taf. 98, c, d).

Der über das Hinterhaupt gezogene Schleier ist, soweit der kolossale Massstab es ermöglichte, als leichtes Gewebe charakterisiert. Sein vorderer Saum wellte sich, wie an den Bruchrändern noch deutlich erkennbar ist, leicht auf, an der Seite wird das Tuch durch zwei schmale, rundstabartige Falten gegliedert, zwischen denen eine nach oben sich gabelnde Mittelfalte liegt. Es handelt sich um das Schleier- tuch, das von den Marien- und Orantendarstellungen der Katakomben und anderen frühchristlichen Denkmälern her hinreichend bekannt ist, so etwa von den Muttergottesbildern in der Priscilla-[14] und der Domitillakatakombe[15] oder etwa von den Oranten in der 5. Kammer des Coemeterium maius[16] oder der Thrasonkatakombe.[17]

Aus dem Ansatz der Halsmuskel, aus der leichten Asymmetrie der beiden Gesichtshälften, vor allem aber auch aus der verschiedenen Behandlung der Locken auf der rechten, bzw. linken Seite ergibt sich, dass der Kopf etwas zur rechten Schulter gedreht war. Die Augen folgen jedoch der Kopfwendung nicht, sondern sind geradeaus in die Ferne gerichtet. Unter dem Kopftuch tritt ein ungeteilt in die Stirn gekämmter Lockenkranz hervor, der wiederum die durch die Kopf- wendung bedingten Asymmetrien aufweist. Ueber der Stirn und gegen die Schläfen zu schichten sich zwei Lockenreihen über einander,

---

13. Vgl. *OeJH.* 27, 1932 Beiblatt 54ff. Abb. 40 und Taf. 3, *Forschungen und Fortschritte* 7, 1931, 65f. Abb. 1 und 2, A. Aziz, *Guide du Musée de Smyrne* (Istanbul 1933) 39 Taf. 17. Der Kopf befindet sich im Museum in Smyrna, In- ventar-Nr. 670, Foto des Museums 704 (Vorderansicht) 703 (Seitenansicht) 650 (Rückansicht), 711/12 (Arm). Der 1,25 m hohe Kopf ist bis auf eine Wand- stärke von 0,16-0,20 m ausgehöhlt.

14. O. Wulff, a.a.O 72 Abb. 58. S. Bettini, *Frühchristliche Malerei und früh- christlich-römische Tradition bis ins Hochmittelalter*, Wien 1942, Taf. 13.

15. Bettini, a.a.O. Taf. 18.

16. Wulff, a.a.O. 88 Abb. 69, Bettini, a.a.O. Taf. 23.

17. Wulff, a.a.O. 88 Abb. 70 Bettini, a.a.O. Taf. 28 und 29.

zwei mittlere Locken der oberen Reihe rollen sich s-förmig ein. An den Schläfen schliessen sich längere Strähne an, deren Enden sich über dem rechten Auge und über der Schläfe wiederum einringeln, während die Strähne an der linken Seite, die etwas voller durchmodelliert sind, ihre Spitzen gegen die Mitte zu wenden. Von den Schläfen fallen tief gekerbte Ringellocken beide Ohren verdeckend bis in Nackenhöhe. An der rechten Seite werden sie vom Saum des Kopftuchs überdeckt, an der linken Seite tritt eine Strähne frei aus dem Tuch hervor (vgl. Taf. 98d).

Das jugendliche, ovale Gesicht (Taf. 98c) ist maskenhaft-monumental in grossen, gleichmässig gewölbten Flächen angelegt, in die keine einzige Rune individuellen Lebens eingezeichnet wurde, das Kinn kräftig hervorgehoben, der Mund schmal, aber plastisch belebt, wie sich aus den Lippenansätzen im Bruch noch deutlich erkennen lässt. Die Augenbögen verlaufen ohne Braueneinritzung in grossem, scharfkantigem, völlig regelmässigem ornamentalem Schwunge und setzen sich ohne Absatz in den Kanten des Nasenrückens fort. Der Uebergang von der Stirn zur Nase und der erhaltene, obere Teil des Nasenrückens ist völlig flach. Die übergrossen, den Ausdruck des Gesichtes völlig beherrschenden Augen[18] sind von präziser, ornamentaler Härte. Der nach oben gerichtete Blick entspricht der Gebetshaltung wie die alexanderhafte Kopfhebung der Konstantinischen Münzen.[19] Durch die Hebung des Oberlids bildet sich eine tiefgeschnittene Falte, die zwischen Brauenbogen und Lidrand einen dunklen Schattenkontur zieht. Die Unterlidränder werden von einer zarten, flachen Mulde begleitet. Die Innenzeichnung der Augen schwankt zwischen plastischer Wiedergabe und harter Ritzung. Ein hart und kräftig eingeritzter Bogen, der zur Verstärkung der Blickrichtung nach oben vom Unterlid nicht überschnitten wird, umrandet die Iris. Die Pupille ist doppelt umrandet, d.h. sie wird von einer plastischen Sichel gebildet, deren Kern, das Glanzlicht des Auges, vom Oberlid halb verdeckt wird. Auch in den inneren Winkeln sind die Augäpfel noch einmal umritzt. Der Blick ist mit einer Kraft, die sich bei antiken Köpfen selten findet, in die Ferne gerichtet, es ist ein völlig durchgeistigtes Schauen, das an frühgriechische Bilder erinnert, obwohl ihm jene gespannte, naive Bereitschaft zum Staunen mangelt, die der Jugend des Griechentums eigen war. Der entrückte Jenseitsblick dieses jungen Weibes entstammt einer neuen Welt, die mit dem

---

18. Vgl. die Bemerkungen und Belege bei L'Orange, a.a.O. 91 Anm. 1 und Kollwitz, a.a.O. 121 über die Bedeutung der grossen Augen bei spätantiken Porträts und in den biographischen Zeugnissen über das Aussehen spätantiker Männer.

19. Vgl. *Die Antike* 8, 1932, 16 (R. Delbrueck).

blühenden Leib und dem Wunder des Natürlichen nicht mehr einig war und im Prosopon den stärksten, fast ausschliesslichen Schauplatz des Geistigen sah.

Bei dem fast gänzlichen Versiegen der Freiplastik allgemeiner Art seit Konstantin d.Gr. und der vor allem im griechischen Osten immer strenger werdenden Verengung der im Bilde gestaltbaren Welt auf die Repräsentation des kaiserlichen Hofes[20] und des Staates können wir in der Spätantike zunächst nur Bildnisstatuen erwarten. Die Formen des Kopfes, die Gesichtsbildung, die Frisur und das Kopftuch sind aber so allgemein gehalten und entbehren so sehr des individuellen Gepräges, dass es kaum möglich erscheint, den Kopf in Smyrna als ein Porträt anzusprechen. Es soll gewiss nicht vergessen werden, dass der grosse Massstab des Kopfes zu einer erheblichen Vereinfachung der Formen zwang, dennoch aber hätte selbst eine jeder Art von Realistik fern stehende und ausschliesslich von klassizistisch-idealisierenden Tendenzen getragene Kunst die Individualität der dargestellten Person kaum in diesem ungewöhnlichen Ausmasse aufzuheben versucht.

Ueberdies konnte im griechischen Osten eine spätantike Bildnisstatue kolossaler Grösse nur von den höchsten Repräsentanten des Staates in Auftrag gegeben bzw. zu ihrer Ehrung errichtet sein.[21] Aber das von Konstantin d.Gr. eingeführte und sich im Laufe der Zeit noch steigernde hohe Zeremoniell, das jede Erscheinung des Kaisers und seines Hofes vor der Welt regelte und jede Formlosigkeit ausschloss, hätte es niemals zugelassen, dass ein Mitglied des kaiserlichen Hauses in einer repräsentativen Kolossalstatue im schlichten Kopftuch dargestellt worden wäre. Es ist ja hinreichend bekannt und durch Zeugnisse belegt, dass wohl kein anderer Hof mit einer vergleichbaren Bewusstheit und Bestimmtheit der Welt gegenüber getreten ist wie der kaiserliche Hof von Byzanz. Wohl läge es im Bereiche des Möglichen, dass einer dem kaiserlichen Hause nahestehenden und vom Hofe besonders begünstigten Frau, etwa der Gemahlin eines hohen Würdenträgers, eine Ehrenstatue errichtet worden wäre, doch wäre in diesem Falle die ungewöhnliche Grösse des Bildes nicht gerechtfertigt gewesen, dessen Ausmass selbst die meisten Bildnisse der Kaiser überragt, und die entwirklichende Idealisierung des Antlitzes wäre noch weniger am Platze gewesen als beim Bildnis einer Kaiserin. Das zur Verfügung stehende ikonographische Material bietet auch keinerlei Anhaltspunkte, das zur Deutung des Kopfes herangezogen werden könnte.

---

20. Vgl. Kollwitz, a.a.O. 81f.
21. Vgl. Kaschnitz-Weinberg, "Marcus Antonius, Domitian, Christus," *Schriften der Königsberger Gel. Ges.*, Heft 14, S.74.

Da die Deutung als ein repräsentatives Porträt kaum in Frage kommt, ist zu prüfen ob es sich um eine weibliche Idealgestalt allgemeiner, religiöser Bedeutung handle, die — wäre sie als Ausklang der heidnischen, hellenischen Plastik anzusprechen — ausschliesslich in den Jahren 361-363 n.Chr. von Kaiser Julianus hätte geweiht worden sein können.[22] Nach der kurzen Restaurationsbewegung unter Kaiser Julianus konnte ein heidnisches Götterbild nicht mehr aufgestellt werden.

Für die Datierung des Kopfes sind uns einige aufschlussreiche Anhaltspunkte gegeben: seine klassizistische Form, die nur in der Nachfolge der erlesenen Denkmäler theodosianischer Zeit möglich war, — und die besondere Art der Augenbildung, die ihn mit einigen Porträtköpfen der ersten Hälfte des 5. Jahrhunderts n.Chr. verbindet. Der die offiziellen Staatsdenkmäler des ausgehenden 4. Jahrhunderts charakterisierende Klassizismus,[23] der vor allem durch die drei Säulen in Konstantinopel, die des Theodosius,[24] des Arcadius[25] und die Marcianssäule[26] vertreten wird, blieb als die dem oströmischen Hofe gemässe Form bis ins 6. Jahrhundert n.Chr. hinein wirksam. Die privatere Sphäre der Bildniskunst hielt sich von diesen offiziellen Tendenzen jedoch frei.

Von den erhaltenen Porträts ist in erster Linie jene Gruppe zum Vergleich heranzuziehen, die H. P. L'Orange mit der in den Thermen zu Aphrodisias gefundenen Statue Valentinians II[27] zusammen gestellt und trefflich charakterisiert hat.[28] In manchen Einzelheiten verbindet sich der Kopf in Smyrna mit dem gewiss um ein gutes Stück älteren, in seinen Ornamentalisierungstendenzen aber verwandten Kaiserkopf in Berlin,[29] in welchem R. Delbrueck[30] ein Porträt des Arcadius erkannte. Der Berliner Kopf hat dasselbe ausgeglichene ovale Gesicht, jedoch bedeutend flächenhafter gegliedert, eine verwandte Bildung des Mundes, ähnlich ornamental gesetzte Brauenbögen, den gleichen flachen Uebergang von der Stirn zur Nase und die gleiche Abgrenzung der Augäpfel gegen die Tränengruben, die allerdings auch bei zeitlich

---

22. Kaiser Julianus wandte sich besonders dem Kult des Helios, des Apollon und der Göttermutter von Pessinus zu, auch in die eleusinischen Mysterien war er eingeweiht. Belegstellen bei Pauly-Wissowa, *RE* 10, 1, 26ff. (v. Borries).

23. Vgl. L'Orange, a.a.O. 66ff., 72f., Kollwitz, a.a.O. 3ff., 115ff. v. Kaschnitz-Weinberg, a.a.O. 987.

24. Vgl. Kollwitz, a.a.O. 3ff. und die dort zusammengestellte Literatur.

25. Vgl. Kollwitz, a.a.O. 17ff. mit Lit.Verz.

26. Vgl. Kollwitz, a.a.O. 69ff.

27. L'Orange *Kat.* 94, Abb. 181-183, Kollwitz Taf. 16, 34 und Beilage 13.

28. a.a.O. 73ff.

29. L'Orange *Kat.* 96 Abb. 185, 186. Kaschnitz-Weinberg, 102.

30. *Aus den Berliner Museen* 44, 1923, 53f. (um 400 n.Chr.).

weiter abliegenden Köpfen gelegentlich zu finden ist.[31] Die Augenbildung selbst weicht allerdings in entscheidenden Einzelheiten ab.
Die im Berliner Kopf so deutlich zutage tretende Tendenz zur flächenhaften Ornamentalisierung der Formen, die auch in den späteren
Jahrzehnten häufig zu beobachten ist, setzt diesen jedoch in einen
erheblichen inneren wie auch zeitlichen Abstand zum plastisch bedeutend freieren Kopf in Smyrna, bei dem eine gewisse Entwirk-
lichung der Einzelheiten durch die Kolossalität und zugleich, wie es
scheint, auch durch die ideale Sinngebung nahe gelegt wurde. Die
Augenbildung, die Pupillen- und Irisumrandung beim Kopf in Smyrna
ist in ihrer Art vereinzelt. Es handelt sich bei ihr um eine Weiter-
bildung der hufeisenförmigen Pupillenangabe, die bei dem häufig
besprochenen bärtigen Beamten aus Aphrodisias,[32] den Kollwitz[33]
zu Unrecht in die Zeit um 410 n.Chr. datierte, und dem zeitlich nahestehenden, ebenfalls schon dem 5. Jahrhundert angehörigen bärtigen
Kopf in Brüssel[34] zum ersten Male fassbar wird und in einigen Vari-
ationen von recht unterschiedlichem Ausdruckswert (vgl. z.B. den
Porträtkopf aus Ostia, L'Orange *Kat.* 117 Abb. 221, 223 und den
"Eutropius" aus Ephesos in Wien, L'Orange *Kat.* 115 Abb. 216-218,
Kollwitz 128 Taf. 43) bis in die zweite Jahrhunderthälfte in Gebrauch
bleibt.

Eine Besonderheit des Kopfes in Smyrna ist die schmale, seichte
Furche, die die unteren Lidränder begleitet. Sie kehrt in ähnlich
zarter Form nur noch einmal bei dem Kopfe der Theodora in Mailand[35]
wieder, zu dem G. Rodenwaldt kürzlich den ephesischen Männerkopf
in Wien (*JdI* 59/60, 1944/45 Taf. 4) gesellte. Diese Lidrandfurche
bei dem Kopf in Smyrna muss wohl mit den stark vergröberten Falten-
bildungen bei Köpfen der ersten Jahrhunderthälfte verglichen werden
wie etwa dem "Patricius" des Diptychons in Novara,[36] dem schon
genannten bärtigen Beamten aus Aphrodisias[37] und einigen west-
römischen Bildnissen wie dem übertrieben realistischen Porträt aus

---

31. Vgl. z.B. die Porträtbüste des Alexander Severus, L'Orange Abb. 1, Gal-
lienus Abb. 8, Kosmetenherme Abb. 18 u.a.m.

32. L'Orange *Kat.* 107 Abb. 202, 205, Rodenwaldt, 76. *Berliner Winckelmannsprogramm* 15f., Wulff, a.a.O. 153.

33. a.a.O. 96f., 122f. Taf. 17 und 38. Kollwitz übersieht bei seinen Datierungen
den grossen inneren Abstand gegen die Statue Valentinians II oder den Berliner
Arcadiuskopf.

34. Wulff, a.a.O. 157, L'Orange *Kat.* 114, Rodenwaldt, a.a.O. 18 Nr. 11, Kollwitz 121f. Taf. 37. Auch dieser Kopf wird von Kollwitz viel zu nahe an theo-
dosianische Denkmäler angerückt. Gegen die zu hohen Datierungen von Kollwitz
vgl. auch die Bemerkungen G. Rodenwaldts, *JdI* 59/60, 1944/45, 98 Anm. 5.

35. Vgl. Fuchs, a.a.O. 138f. Abb. 23-26.

36. Delbrueck, *Consulardiptychen* Taf. 64, L'Orange Abb. 201, 204.

37. Vgl. oben Anm. 32.

Ostia[38] und den Bildnissen aus Aquileia,[39] die vor der Zerstörung der Stadt durch die Hunnen im Jahre 452 n.Chr. entstanden sein müssen.

Die in der Porträtkunst gerechtfertigten realistischen Tendenzen und das Streben nach psychologischer Durchleuchtung des Antlitzes hatten bei der Formung eines kolossalen Idealbildes zu schweigen. Der grossgliedrige Aufbau des Kopfes in Smyrna, auch die ornamentale Augenbildung, waren durch die Aufgabe gegeben; dennoch ist die ideale Entrücktheit des Kopfes von der plastisch lebendigen Bewegung des Haares umrahmt, die das Göttliche mit der Wärme des Irdischen umspielt.

Fassen wir alle Einzelelemente zusammen und versuchen wir, sie für die Datierung des Kopfes auszuwerten, so ergibt sich als obere Zeitgrenze das zweite Jahrzehnt des 5. Jahrhunderts n.Chr. und als untere etwa die Jahrhundertmitte. Bestimmte historische Erwägungen lassen es wahrscheinlich erscheinen, dass der Kopf kurz nach dem 3. ephesischen Konzil (431 n.Chr.) entstanden sei.

Eine heidnische Deutung des Kopfes scheidet auf Grund der Entstehungszeit im 5. Jahrhundert n.Ch. völlig aus, aber auch die bekannten, aus der heidnischen Welt übernommenen, in der christlichen Aera weiterwirkenden Sinnbilder wie etwa Nike, Eirene oder Personifikationen wie Constantinopolis, Roma usw. kommen nicht in Betracht. Suchen wir nach einer spezifisch christlichen Deutung des Kopfes, so stehen wir vor einem ausserordentlich engen Vorstellungskreis, der in der Kunst Kleinasiens zu jener Zeit gestaltet werden konnte.[40] Der griechische Osten, philosophischer veranlagt und um die Klärung dogmatischer Fragen leidenschaftlicher bemüht als der allzeit realistische Westen, hat sich der Bilderwelt der jüdisch-christlichen Legende gegenüber zunächst zurückhaltender gezeigt als der Westen, der sich der christlichen Legendenstoffe schon in den ersten Jahrhunderten mit naiver Erzählerfreude bemächtigt hatte. Wie weit der Westen dabei von der mit dem Judentum unmittelbar in Berührung stehenden Kunst des syrisch-palästinensischen Raumes beeinflusst war,[41] lässt sich noch nicht voll überschauen. In Kleinasien aber scheinen die spezifisch christlichen Motive erst im 5. Jahrhundert n.Chr. grössere Verbreitung gefunden zu haben, vorausgesetzt, dass die durch den Bildersturm des 8. Jahrhunderts stark beeinträchtigte Denkmälerüberlieferung nicht trügt.[42]

---

38. L'Orange *Kat.* 117 Abb. 221, 223.

39. L'Orange *Kat.* 109, 110 Abb. 206-209.

40. Vgl. Kollwitz, a.a.O. 132ff., 153ff.

41. Wulff, der durchwegs den Einfluss der syrisch-palästinensischen Kunst ausserordentlich hoch einschätzt, wird dem Problem sicher nicht voll gerecht, da er die Kräfte des Westens und ihre Tradition viel zu gering achtet.

42. Vgl. Kollwitz, a.O. 153ff.

Auch von den in Erwägung kommenden christlichen Deutungsmöglichkeiten für den Kopf in Smyrna scheiden die meisten aus, da an die Repräsentation etwa der heiligen Weisheit, der christlichen Hoffnung, der Ekklesia, einer Märtyrerin oder Kirchenstifterin in einer Kolossalplastik kaum gedacht werden darf und eine Darstellung eines Engels in dieser Gestalt nicht in Frage kommt.

Wir haben die Deutung des Kopfes durch die Ueberschrift über diesen Zeilen — Theotokos, Gottesmutter — schon vorausgenommen. Für diese vorgeschlagene Deutung spricht ein geschichtlicher Umstand, dem ganz besonderes Gewicht beizumessen ist.

Ende der Zwanziger und zu Anfang der Dreissiger Jahre des 5. Jahrhunderts war der griechische Osten von Alexandria bis Konstantinopel leidenschaftlich aufgewühlt von dem grossen Dogmenstreit[43] zwischen Nestorius und Cyrillus von Alexandria um das Problem der hypostatischen Union, in den sich auch Kaiser Theodosius II durch einen Vertreter einmischte, und an dem, wie die Berichte über das ephesische Konzil lehren, auch das Volk lebhaften Anteil nahm. Der Streit, der um das Verhältnis zwischen Gott Logos und dem vom Weibe geborenen Menschen Christus ging, endete im Sommer des Jahres 431 n.Chr. zunächst damit, das auf Betreiben Cyrills von Alexandria die nestorianische Lehre, Nestorius selbst und seine Anhänger durch das 3. Allgemeine Konzil zu Ephesos mit dem Anathem belegt wurden. Der kaiserliche Hof, durch das übereilte und schoffe Vorgehen Cyrills verletzt, sorgte dafür, dass bald darauf ein Gegenkonzil einberufen wurde, das nun wiederum Cyrills Lehre verwarf, ihn selbst und seinen Mitstreiter, den Bischof Memnon von Ephesos, absetzte und ihre Anhänger exkommunizierte. Erst im Jahre 433 n.Chr. kam es zu dem vom Papst erstrebten Ausgleich zwischen Cyrillus und seinen Gegnern.

Der Syrer Nestorius, Günstling Theodosius II, seit 428 n.Chr. Patriarch von Konstantinopel, hatte, vom kaiserlichen Hofe zunächst gestützt, gelehrt,[44] dass Jesus, der Sohn Marias, der Person nach ein anderer sei als Gott Logos. Die zwei verschiedenen Naturen, die göttliche und die menschliche, seien aber aufs engste mit einander verbunden, indem Gott Logos im Menschen Jesus wie in einem Tempel einwohne. Jesus könne daher nicht Gott im eigentlichen Sinne, sondern nur θεοφόρος, Gottesträger, sein. Die Verbindung zwischen dem Logos und dem Sohne Marias sei daher keine ἕνωσις φυσική,

---

43. Vgl. A. Ehrhard, *Die griech. und lateinische Kirche im Westen und Osten,* Bonn 1937, II 69ff., J. Hergenröther, *Handbuch der allgemeinen Kirchengeschichte,* 1902, I, 504ff., Pohle, *Handbuch der Dogmatik, neubearbeitet von M. Gierens,* Frankfurt 1932, II 54ff. und die dort angegebenen Belege.

44. Belegstellen bei Pohle-Gierens, a.a.O. II 54ff., 57ff.

sondern eine Verknüpfung (συνάφεια). Bei der Inkarnation handelt es sich demnach nicht um eine Menschwerdung des Logos im eigentlichen Sinne, sondern um eine ἐνοίκησις des Logos im Menschen Jesus.

Die Konsequenz dieser Lehre war, dass die seit den Frühzeiten des Christentums als Gottesmutter verehrte Maria nicht wahre Gottesmutter sein könne. Da sie nur einen Menschen geboren habe, in dem der Logos innewohne, könne sie selbst nicht θεοτόκος, sondern nur ἀνθρωποτόκος, besser χριστοτόκος genannt werden.

Das Konzil zu Ephesos entschied diesen, die Geister des griechischen Ostens tief bewegenden Streit, indem es die nestorianische ἕνωσις προσώπων verwarf, an ihre Stelle die ἕνωσις καθ' ὑπόστασιν Cyrills und seiner Anhänger setzte und die Gottesgebärerin θεοτόκος zur tessera fidei erklärte.

Die Verehrung Marias[45] hatte sich seit Konstantin d.Gr. im Osten wie im Westen, wie es scheint, ziemlich rasch ausgebreitet. Konstantin selbst hatte in Nicäa (328 n.Chr.) und Konstantinopel (330 n.Chr.) dem Andenken Marias geweihte Kirchen errichtet, seine Mutter Helena hatte Marienkirchen in Bethlehem und Nazareth erbauen lassen, nach Mitte des 4. Jahrhunderts entstand in Rom die erste grosse Marienbasilika und auch die Konzilskirche zu Ephesos, in der Maria 431 n.Ch. feierlich als wahre Gottesgebärerin erklärt worden ist, war der Gottesmutter geweiht. Es darf hier daran erinnert werden, dass sich die Legende vom Tode Marias ebenfalls an Ephesos knüpfte.

Mit dem Spruch des ephesischen Konzils und seiner Anerkennung durch Papst Sixtus III gewann die Marienverehrung, die im Westen in den Katakombenbildern ihren ersten volkstümlichen Ausdruck gefunden hatte, ihre feste dogmatische Grundlage und seit jener Zeit fanden die Marienbilder Eingang in die eigentliche, kirchliche Kunst.[46] Für die Marienbilder möchte die Entscheidung zwischen der "Menschengebärerin" und der "Gottesgebärerin" auch insofern von Bedeutung sein, als dem Wunsche des Papstes Sixtus III entsprechend Maria nun im Sinne des ephesischen Konzils dargestellt werden sollte. Im Gegensatz zu den mehr menschlich-natürlichen Marienbildern der Katakomben, etwa der säugenden Maria der Priscillakatakombe,[47] musste nun die unnahbare jungfräuliche Hoheit der Gottesmutter zum Ausdruck gebracht werden, der Proklos, Bischof von Kyzikos,

---

45. Vgl. Pohle-Gierens, a.a.O. II, 313ff., W. Rothes, *Die Madonna in ihrer Verherrlichung durch die bildende Kunst*, 1920, Wulff, a.a.O. passim.

46. Vgl. Wulff, a.a.O. 430ff.

47. Vgl. oben Anm. 14.

seit 434 n.Chr. Patriarch von Konstantinopel, den hohen Titel ἡ ἁγία θεοτόκος παρθένος Μαρία gegeben hat.[48]

Wir glauben nicht fehl zu gehen, wenn wir den Kopf in Smyrna als Marienbild deuten, das durch jene erregenden Ereignisse veranlasst worden ist. Die ἁγία θεοτόκος παρθένος hat der Bildhauer in der Mädschenhaftigkeit des Antlitzes und in der Entrücktheit des grossen Schauens zu fassen gesucht; die monumentale Grösse steigert die Hoheit des Bildes. Noch ist die Gottesmutter mit dem einfachen bräutlichen Schleiertuch dargestellt, wie es in den Katakombenbildern üblich war,[49] noch schmückt sie kein kaiserliches Diadem, das unter dem Einfluss des Hofes bald den Marienbildern verliehen wurde. Der Kopf in Smyrna ist noch frei von der Starrheit byzantinisch-höfischer Würde, mit der das Muttergottesbild vor allem in die Kunst des orthodoxen griechischen Ostens eingegangen und fast unverändert bewahrt worden ist. R. Delbrueck[50] hat auf das allmähliche Uebergreifen des Hofzeremoniells und der Hoftrachten auf die Darstellungen der christlichen Legende hingewiesen und im Hinblick auf die thronende Gottesmutter von Santa Maria antiqua[51] in Rom festgestellt: "Die Mutter Gottes selbst hat das Diadem angenommen und ist sogar einmal in S. Maria antiqua ebenfalls als Gattin eines Kaisers kostümiert, der das Konsulat innehat."

Etwaige Bedenken, in jener Zeit des Theotokosstreites eine Marienplastik anzusetzen, lassen sich mit dem Hinweis auf die weitläufigen und entschiedenen Aeusserungen gerade Cyrills von Alexandria über die Anfertigung von Heiligen- und Christusbildern zerstreuen.[52] Cyrillus rechnete mit zahlreichen Bildern (in erster Linie natürlich mit Gemälden) und hiess sie gut, da sie die Herzen der Gläubigen erregen.

Plastiken werden im Osten wie im Westen freilich immer seltener, doch reichen die Nachrichten über repräsentative Freiplastiken noch bis in die Zeit Justinians.[53] Haben wir auch nur spärliche Zeugnisse, so dürfen wir neben den staatlich-repräsentativen Plastiken doch auch vereinzelte spezifisch christliche Skulpturen[54] annehmen, die allerdings — wie der berühmte Christus von der Chalke in Konstantinopel[55] — dem im Jahre 725 von Kaiser Leo III, dem Isaurier, ausgelösten

---

48. Vgl. F. X. Bauer, *Proklos von Konstantinopel. Ein Beitrag zur Kirchen- und Dogmengeschichte des 5. Jahrhunderts,* München 1919.

49. Vgl. oben Anm. 14-17.

50. *Antike* 8, 1932, 20f., Wulff, a.a.O. 239.

51. Vgl. Delbrueck, a.a.O. Abb. 15.

52. In Psalmos 113, Vers 16, Migne, *P. G.* 69, 1268.

53. Vgl. Kollwitz, a.a.O. 12ff., 113, Wulff, a.a.O. 151f.

54. Nachweise bei Wulff, a.a.O. 150 ff., 180.

55. Wulff, a.a.O. 150, 194f.

Bildersturm zum Opfer fielen.[56] Erhalten blieben lediglich einige
Reste zerschlagener Reliefplatten.[57] Es besteht kein Zweifel, dass
auch der Kopf in Smyrna in jenen Zeiten von seinem Standort entfernt worden und in irgendeiner Baugrube oder sonstigen Versenkung
verschwunden ist. Um darüber Näheres zu ermitteln, wäre die
Kenntnis des Fundorts erforderlich.

Sollte der Kopf in Smyrna von einer Statue stammen, so wäre in
erster Linie an eine thronende Maria zu denken. Dies legen nicht
allein die Katakombenbilder oder etwa das gleichzeitige, vermutlich
ebenfalls aus Kleinasien stammende Relief mit der Magieranbetung
in Karthago,[58] sondern die Mütterdarstellungen aller Zeiten nahe.
Auch Christus erscheint auf den kleinasiatischen Reliefs jener Zeit
meist thronend.[59] Der Typus der stehenden Maria[60] mit dem Kinde
vor der Brust (Hodegetria) entwickelte sich erst im 6. Jahrhundert
und erlangte nie die gleiche Bedeutung wie das Bild der sitzenden
Gottesmutter, das im Osten wie im Westen gleicherweise verbreitet
war. Als Kirchenschmuck war das Bild der thronenden Gottesmutter,
wie es scheint, zum ersten Male, im Apsisbilde des Domes in Capua
vetere,[61] nach Oskar Wulffs Vermutung vielleicht sogar schon vor
dem ephesischen Konzil, als Logotokos war Maria ausserdem in der
Apsis der ersten Basilika S. Maria Maggiore dargestellt.[62] Wie ver-
traut der Osten mit dem Bilde der thronenden Gottesmutter war,
zeigen am deutlichsten die Elfenbeinreliefs des 6. Jahrhunderts wie
die Tafel aus Etschmiadsin in Armenien[63] und die Marientafel in
Berlin,[64] auf denen Maria ebenfalls ohne Diadem, mit dem Tuch über
dem Hinterhaupt, auf dem Throne sitzend und von zwei Engeln
flankiert dargestellt ist. Gerade diese Reliefbilder lassen es als nicht
unwahrscheinlich erscheinen, dass es vereinzelt auch freiplastische
Darstellungen der sitzenden Gottesmutter gegeben habe. Oskar Wulff
vermutete,[65] dass sich der Typus der thronenden Himmelskönigin

---

56. Vgl. Wulff, a.a.O. 362f.

57. Vgl. Kollwitz, a.a.O. Taf. 45-56.

58. Kollwitz Taf. 52/53, Literatur S.178.

59. Vgl. Kollwitz, a.a.O. 153ff. Taf. 51.

60. Vgl. Wulff, a.a.O. 434f.

61. Vgl. Wulff, a.a.O. 432f.

62. Wulff, a.a.O. 432.

63. Strzygowski, *Das Etschmiadsin Evangeliar, Byzantinische Denkmäler* I,
Taf. 1, 2; Wulff, a.a.O. Abb. 185, S.188.

64. Wulff, a.a.O. 196 Abb. 198.

65. a.a.O 430ff. Vgl. ferner die von Kenner, *Jahrb. d. Kunstsammlungen
d. Allerhöchsten Kaiserhauses* IX S.170 Nr. 270 veröffentlichten Goldmedaillons,
welche die thronende Fausta mit dem Kind im Schoße liegend darstellen. Es
scheint, dass die Medaillons das bereits geläufige Motiv der thronenden Gottesmutter übernahmen; Fausta ist jedoch durch Krone und Nimbus als Augusta
charakterisiert (vgl. Kenner, a.a.O., Strzygowski, a.a.O. 39f.).

verhältnismässig früh aus den erzählenden Kompositionen wie etwa der Magieranbetung[66] herauskristallisiert habe. Es wäre durchaus denkbar, dass die Plastik in Smyrna eine bedeutsame Station auf diesem Wege gewesen sei.

Der Kopf in Smyrna kann jedoch ebensowohl von einer Halbfigur stammen, der, um die Theotokos deutlich zu charakterisieren, das Kind beigegeben sein musste.[67] Die Halbfigur könnte im Bogenfeld einer Kirchenfassade oder in einer Nische gestanden haben.[68] Dass plastischer Schmuck der Bogenfelder bei kleinasiatischen Bauten nichts ungewöhnliches war, beweist die Halbfigur Christi im Bogenfeld des Palasttores in Konstantinopel, das auf dem berühmten Elfenbeindiptychon des Domschatzes zu Trier[69] dargestellt ist.

Treffen die oben dargelegten Zusammenhänge zu, so haben wir in dem Kolossalkopf in Smyrna den Ueberrest des ersten und einzigen, grossplastischen Marienbildes wiedergewonnen, das den Bildersturm des 8. Jahrhunderts überdauert hat, ja des ersten und einzigen grossplastischen Marienbildes des griechischen Ostens überhaupt. Es musste in jener von der Plastik abgewandten Zeit durch ein bedeutendes und erregendes Ereignis veranlasst worden sein. Was läge darum näher, als es durch jene feierliche Erklärung der wahren Gottesmutterschaft Marias durch das dritte Konzil zu Ephesos im Sommer des Jahres 431 n.Chr. veranlasst zu denken, die in harten, bis in die höchsten Kreise des Hofes dringenden Auseinandersetzungen erkämpft wurde und den bedeutendsten Anlass geboten haben mag, diese wahre Gottesmutter und Jungfrau auch in einem monumentalen Bilde an geheiligter Stätte darzustellen.

Leider lässt sich die Herkunft des Kopfes nicht mehr ermitteln. Zunächst ist natürlich an Smyrna selbst als Fundort zu denken, doch schliesst ein allgemeiner Ueberblick über die Herkunft der im Museum in Smyrna vereinigten Antiken es keineswegs aus, dass der Kopf etwa aus Ephesos stamme, wo die Marienverehrung ihre kirchlich-dogmatische Rechtfertigung gefunden hat.

---

66. Vgl. Kollwitz, a.a.O. Taf. 53, Wulff, a.a.O. Abb. 171.

67. Vgl. die Halbfigur (Orans mit Kind) aus dem Coemeterium maius in Rom, Bettini, a.a.O. Taf. 23. Ferner wäre auf die in der Spätantike wieder beliebten Büsten von Philosophen und Aposteln hinzuweisen (vgl. Wulff, a.a.O. Abb. 1.— Kollwitz, a.a.O. Taf. 40, 41); auch das Museum in Smyrna besitzt eine noch unveröffentlichte Reliefbüste eines Bärtigen.

68. Vgl. dazu Wulff, a.a.O. 150f., 194f.

69. Delbrueck, *Consulardiptychen* Nr. 67, Wulff, a..aO. 194 Abb. 196.

A IV CENTURY A. D. SILVER STATUETTE

MARVIN CHAUNCEY ROSS
Walters Art Gallery

Plate 100

A silver statuette[1] in the Walters Art Gallery has considerable interest for the study of late antique art. It represents a young man dressed in a short tunic over which he wears a *lacerna*[2] fastened on the right shoulder by a clasp. On his head he has a round cap; he is unshod. In his left arm he carries a cornucopia and in his right hand he holds a patera. The surface shows a certain amount of corrosion due to burial and certain details such as the nose and the fingers of the right hand are somewhat worn; otherwise, the statuette is very well preserved. It is hollow cast with details worked over afterwards. The subject is one of the household gods, whether a Lar or a representation of a Genius (as of Abundance) it is rather difficult to say, for in the late periods there seems oftentimes to have been little distinction, and even contemporary writers appear to have confused them.[3]

The style of the statuette, on the other hand, is so definite that it can be immediately related to a group of well known silver statuettes. These are the Tyches of the four cities, Rome, Constantinople, Antioch, and Alexandria, found in Rome in 1793 on the Esquiline Hill near the Church of Saints Silvester and Martin and known since that time after the name of the findspot.[4] These four statuettes along with most of the rest of the treasure are in the British Museum. Comparison of the Walters' statuette with those found on the Esquiline Hill shows the same modelling of the garments, the same rendering of the hair, but more especially the exact same crude modelling of the hands, and seems to indicate that all five statuettes had issued from the same silversmith's shop.

The Esquiline Treasure contains a marriage casket made for a

---

1. No. 57.1819. H. 3⅞". Acquired at the sale of *Part II of the Notable Art Collection of the late Joseph Brummer*, New York, May 11-14, 1949, lot 157, with previous history.

2. Cf. Wilson, Lillian M., *The Clothing of the Ancient Romans*, 117 ff.

3. Cf. Hild, J. A., "Lares," and "Genius," in Daremberg and Saglio, *Dictionnaire des Antiquités Grecques et Romains*, III, Part II, 937 ff. and vol. II, part II, 1488 ff.; Reinach, S., *Répertoire de la Statuaire Grecque et Romaine*, II, 3rd ed., p. 47 (Genius of Abondance); Rink, Ernst, *Die bildliche Darstellung des Römischen Genius*, Giessen, 1933.

4. Dalton, O. M., *Catalogue of Early Christian Antiquities and Objects from the Christian East in the British Museum*, nos. 332-335.

5. "Spätantike Silberfund von Esquilin," *AM* 45 (1930) 130.

certain Projecta who is thought to have married a member of the
great family of the Asterii who embraced Christianity only late in
the IVth century. Poglayen-Neuwall[5] has shown that Projecta was
married before 380 A. D. The Treasure contains objects which are
decorated with many pagan subjects, the marriage casket having in
addition to its non-Christian design, the monogram of Christ. Thus
the Walters statuette can be dated early in the last quarter of the
IVth century on the basis of comparison with objects in the dated
Esquiline treasure. The subject, a pagan household god,[6] need not
upset such a dating since the contemporary Esquiline treasure made
in the Christian period also contains many objects with pagan subject matter.[7]

A statuette of one of the old Roman household gods which can be
so surely dated in the IVth century has interest for us because a
number of Christian writers spoke of them, stating how even Christians continued to have them around. St. Jerome complained of seeing
them everywhere and a IVth century polemist spoke of them. In 392
Theodosius forbade practices in honor of Lares and Penates, indicating that they were still popular enough to require legislation against
them. Thus the specimen in the Walters Art Gallery is a type of
pagan statuette, made in the first century of the triumph of the
Church, the worship of which continued and disturbed the early
Church fathers.[8]

----

6. For earlier silver statuettes of household gods, see Walters, H. B., *Catalogue
of the Silver Plate (Greek, Etruscan and Roman) in the British Museum*, nos.
6 and 34.

7. For the pagan character of the private houses of the rich in the IV century,
Cf. Kitzinger, E., "A Survey of the Early Christian Town of Stobi," *Dumbarton
Oaks Papers*, no. 3, 127.

8. J. A. Hild in the articles listed under note 3 has gathered the references.
The number might easily be increased but would only give additional proof.

UNA MEDUSA DEL RINASCIMENTO NEL MUSEO CIVICO DI PERUGIA

Bartolomeo Nogara
Direttore Generale dei Musei e Gallerie Pontificie

Tavole 101-102

Tra le terrecotte esposte nel Museo Civico di Perugia ha sempre fermato l'attenzione dei visitatori una formella rettangolare che rappresenta una testa di Medusa.[1] Non vi mancano i consueti particolari dei due serpi attorcigliati che incorniciano il viso, delle lunghe ciocche dei capelli ondulate ai lati, delle alucce sporgenti dalle tempie, degli occhi sbarrati e della bocca spalancata come nelle figurazioni arcaiche; bensì fanno eccezione la faccia non circolare, ma oblunga, le alucce non di uccello, ma di pipistrello, l'occhio particolarmente accigliato, torvo e fisso in avanti, la bocca aperta in atto di urlare, la lingua non sporgente, ma rattrappita, le rughe profonde della fronte e le contrazioni dei muscoli facciali che danno un' impressione mista di dolore e di spavento (tav. 101a). Si è sospettato perciò da qualcuno, che non si tratti di un prodotto genuino dell' antichità classica, in cui, se il brutto e l'orrido hanno pure la loro parte, sono sempre contenuti entro certi limiti di compostezza e di armonia, ma piuttosto dell' opera di un artista del Rinascimento, che, ispirandosi ai modelli antichi della Medusa, ne ha esagerato le forme e in questa esagerazione ha voluto segnare la propria personalità.

Ma, si può sussumere, non è forse uno dei caratteri dell'arte etrusca la riproduzione realistica delle forme in cui si afferma la cosiddetta corporeità e dove hanno risalto maggiore le note che nella natura comune non sono la regola ma l'eccezione? Non si osserva il fenomeno medesimo nella riproduzione delle figure demoniache di Charun e di Tuchulcha? Non si hanno forse nello stesso Museo di Perugia altre teste di Medusa di tipi svariatissimi, tra cui una effigiata sul prospetto di un' urna cineraria lavorata a stecco, in mezzo a due grifonesse scarne e lattanti, modellate a tratti vigorosi, che pare faccia richiamo alla nostra ed è certamente genuina etrusca? (tav. 101b).

Non si sa quando il cimelio sia stato acquistato.[2] Solo dal confronto

---

1. Il prof. G. Bellucci nella sua *Guida alle Collezioni del Museo Etrusco-Romano in Perugia*, 119, dopo averla sommariamente descritta, scrive: "Doveva esser collocata sopra una porta d'Ipogeo, quale mezzo di protezione contro il fascino, fissata mercè de chiodi attraversanti i fori, che si veggono in essa tuttora aperti."

2. Interrogato l'attuale Direttore del Museo Etrusco-Romano, prof. Umberto Calzoni, questi gentilmente mi assicurava che dall' Inventario del Museo non risulta alcuna indicazione circa la provenienza e la data dell'acquisto.

delle Guide a stampa si può dedurre che essa mancava alle collezioni perugine nel 1882,[3] mentre vi figurava già prima del 1900.[4] Tra il 1882 e il 1900 pertanto va cercata la data d'ingresso della Medusa nel Museo. Questo è quanto risultava a me fino all'agosto del 1945, quando, scorrendo per ozio le pagine di un periodico di grande formato "Arte Italiana decorativa e industriale" diretto da Camillo Boito e pubblicato da U. Hoepli nel 1907, m'imbattei in uno studio a firma di Paolo Giordani, dove, fra gli elementi decorativi dell' architettura del Palazzo Apostolico della Cancelleria, sono citate le teste di Medusa scolpite nella fascia trasversale di marmo che maschera le giunture dei due pilastri angolari della loggia del primo piano dal lato di mezzogiorno. Le Meduse della Cancelleria riproducono il tipo comune, calmo, a bocca chiusa, da cui esula il fine profilattico; e che ritorna le mille volte a scopo ornamentale negli scomparti architettonici dal Rinascimento in poi. Ma l'autore dello studio, per dimostrare che il tipo della Gorgone della Cancelleria non era nemmeno per quei tempi un elemento nuovo, riporta un capitello di pilastro e parte della trabeazione della facciata di un palazzetto che si trovava allora in via Arco dei Ginnasi (tav. 102), capitello e trabeazione tutti in cotto, in cui sono riprodotti due tipi di Medusa: l'uno calma nella base del capitello immediatamente sotto l'echino, e l'altro torvo, accigliato, somigliantissimo, anzi identico a quello del Museo di Perugia, nel fregio sovrastante l'architrave, dove le formelle della Medusa si alternano con formelle di foglie d'acanto.

Poichè le Meduse del fregio romano risultano identiche alla formella di Perugia, vien logica la conclusione che questa deriva dal palazzetto di via dell' Arco dei Ginnasi. Nota infattè il Giordani nello studio citato che già ai suoi tempi (a. 1907) le lastre in terracotta erano in parte cadute e tolte e in parte in malo stato conservate. E' facile perciò congetturare che una delle formelle distaccata a bello studio, o caduta, sia stata raccolta dal mercato antiquario dell' Urbe, donde, o per dono o per vendita, passò come cimelio etrusco nel Museo di Perugia.

Dopo Paolo Giordani, vide ed annotò la casa delle terrecotte il prof. Marchetti Longhi nel suo studio sulle "Contrade medioevali della zona del Circo Flaminio" pubblicato nel 1919,[5] dove egli scrive che "a tutti celata, essa è nota a chiunque s'interessi di cose d'arte, per le magnifiche terrecotte cinquecentesche che l'adornano" e delle quali ripro-

3. Vedi Lupatelli, A., *Indicazione degli oggetti più importanti che si trovano nei Musei di Antichità etrusco-romane e medioevali esistenti nell' Università di Perugia.* Perugia, 1882.

4. Margaret Symonds e Lina Duff Gordon, *Perugia la sua storia i suoi monumenti,* 279.

5. *Archivio della R. Società Romana di Storia Patria,* 42, 532 e sgg.

duce un esemplare. E, dopo il Marchetti Longhi, più recentemente ha dato notizia del palazzetto il prof. architetto Giovannoni, il quale lo identifica con la casa dello scultore Guglielmo Della Porta, l'autore del monumento di Paolo III in S. Pietro,[6] basandosi soprattutto sulla pianta del Bufalini dei tempi di Giulio III che porta sulla casa di via Ginnasi, alla piazzetta di S. Lucia, l'indicazione "F. Guglielmus de Plumbo," e sopra una notizia dell' Aldrovandi (*Delle Statue antiche a Venezia*, 1556, p. 115), in cui sono registrate le statue conservate in casa di "fra Guglielmo, a le Botteghe oscure, presso la piazza de' 'Mattei'." Ricorda inoltre il Giovannoni che la casa demolita per l'allargamento di via delle Botteghe Oscure non conteneva più le sculture antiche dell' Aldrovandi, ma "un fregio finissimo in terracotta — cosa assai rara per Roma — che correva intorno al cortile" e che egli teme perduto nelle demolizioni del quartiere e conservato soltanto in una bella fotografia del Moscioni.

Per questo riguardo, sono lieto poter completare la nota del Giovannoni, assicurando che, se il palazzetto fu demolito, sono conservate le terrecotte, che, a cura del Riparto X del Comune di Roma, si possono rivedere nel Museo Comunale a via dei Cerchi, dove, col consenso del prof. A. Colini, potei esaminarle con tutta libertà.

Tanto il Giordani quindi, quanto il Marchetti Longhi e il Giovannoni si accordano nel loro giudizio sulle terrecotte, riconoscendone i singolari pregi artistici ed aggiudicandole al periodo del Rinascimento, ma ignoravano che qualche antiquario, in buona o mala fede, le aveva impreziosite con l'aggettivo "etrusco" e che una di esse, con questa classifica, aveva potuto prender posto in un Museo di molta fama, come quello di Perugia.

Ma qui si affaccia subito un quesito: come spiegare la presenza di queste terrecotte nella zona del Circo Flaminio, e l'oblio in cui sono sempre rimaste, non ostante i loro pregi straordinari come opera d'arte? La riposta non è difficile, quando si pensi alla frequenza dei monumenti civili a religiosi della zona, tra cui, ricorda il Marchetti Longhi, il tempio Rotondo del Largo dell' Argentina, votato ed eretto nel 179 a. C. in onore di Giunone Regina, che era costruito in cotto e dove, tra le antefisse a testa di Giunone, si trovavano altre antefisse a testa di "Gorgone aventi indubbio valore apotropaico"[7] E' ovvio immaginare che qualcuna di queste terrecotte con la testa di Medusa sia venuta tra le mani di qualche artista di vaglia del Rinascimento, che abitava nel quartiere o ne percorreva le strade, il quale ne avrebbe

---

6. *Bollettino del Centro Naz. di Studi di Storia dell' Architettura. Sezione di Roma*, 1945, no. 4, p. 9.

7. Vedi Longhi, G. Marchetti, "Apollinar, Senatus ad Apollinis" ecc., *Rendiconti della Pont. Accademia Rom. di Archeologia*, 30 (3ª serie), p. 477.

ricavato un tipo nuovo, ricalcato sull'antico, ma che ha la freschezza
e la vivacità di un originale. Presentatasi poi l'occasione, il nuovo
tipo sarebbe entrato in composizione con altri elementi architettonici
di sapore classico nella decorazione di una casa prossima all' Argentina: casa di proporzioni modeste e di materiali altrettanto modesti
— il mattone — e che per disgrazia venne a trovarsi in un ambiente
chiuso e quasi soffocato da costruzioni di maggior mole. Si avrebbe
qui il caso non infrequente di un' opera moderna suggerita od ispirata
dall' antico, in cui il modellatore ha trasfuso la sensibilità artistica sua
propria. Basti ricordare la Chimera d'Arezzo che C. Ricci ritrovò in
parecchie figurazioni medioevali[8] e i bronzi a testa di leone e di lupo
delle navi di Nemi, che ricompaiono in affreschi e rilievi del tardo
Rinascimento,[9] segno evidente che bronzi antichi raffiguranti la Chimera circolavano ancora nell' età di mezzo, e che le navi di Nemi, fin
dal Rinascimento furono esplorate e fatte oggetto di studio nei loro
particolari ornamentali.

Esclusa quindi l'ipotesi che le Meduse dell'Arco de' Ginnasi e gli
ornati annessi derivino da un monumento antico, o ne siano la copia
diretta, sorge il quesito dell' autore, della fabbrica e dell' età a
cui appartengono. Per ciò che riguarda la soluzione di siffatti
problemi non ho difficoltà a dichiarare la mia incompetenza e mi
rimetto agli specialisti in materia. Noto soltanto che il tema ha un'
importanza speciale per Roma, dove manufatti artistici in terracotta
si trovano di rado, mentre abbondano in Umbria, Toscana e più
ancora nella città dell' alta Italia. Quanto all'età, l'essersi trovate le
terrecotte nella località medesima, in cui Guglielmo della Porta aveva
casa e bottega, potrebbe sulle prime suggerire l'ipotesi che esse siano
un prodotto dell'arte sua o della scuola. Ma, se pure è dimostrato che
il Della Porta ha lavorato anche in cotto, basta un semplice sguardo
alle sue sculture e ai disegni rimasti di sua mano per accertarci che
non vi è alcuna affinità di stile tra i mascheroni e gli altri ornati usciti
dalla sua bottega, e le terrecotte a cui appartengono le Meduse dell'
Arco dei Ginnasi.[10] Per trovare qualche cosa di analogo all'arte delle
nostre Meduse, dovremmo riportarci indietro due o tre generazioni,
ai tempi del Bregno, quindi alla seconda metà del '400, in quella
fioritura di bassorilievi e di ornati che trovano l'applicazione maggiore
nei monumenti sepolcrali del tempo.

8. *La Chimera* in *Nuova Antologia*, 1⁰ luglio, 1928, 15 e sgg.

9. Ucelli, Guido, *Le navi di Nemi*, 197 e sgg.

10. Vedi Krasceninnicowa, M. Gibellino, *Guglielmo Della Porta, scultore di Papa Paolo III*, per es. Tav. XXII.

Tornando ora al palazzetto di via Arco de' Ginnasi, bisogna riconoscere che l'architetto ideatore e costruttore, nella scelta e nella collocazione delle terrecotte, ha saputo trarre buon partito dagli esemplari dell'arte classica che venivano quasi ogni giorno alla luce. Concludendo: la Medusa di Perugia non è un cimelio isolato, tanto meno l'antefissa di un ipogeo di tarda età romana, bensì un elemento separato della decorazione architettonica appartenente ad un palazzetto del Rinascimento: opera essa pure del Rinascimento, ma che ha probabilmente subito l'influsso dei bronzi e delle terrecotte etrusche.

HELIOS

O Helios, fount inexhaustible
   Of life, more fair than the bright
Immaculate stamp of the beautiful,
   Crown of the infinite night,

Before the legions innumerable
   Of the gods began ever to be,
Thee only the centuries worshipped as
   Their first god, their only god—thee;

And still the god last in eternity,
   Like a funeral torch in flaming white
Of the worship bespoken as ultimate,
   On the cold void shall glitter thy light.

Kostes Palamas

Translated by
John B. Edwards

AUS DEM MUSTERBUCH EINES POMPEJANISCHEN WANDMALERS

W. Kraiker
Kiel

Tafel 103

Für die handwerksmäßige Ausübung der Wandmalerei in Pompeji, Herculaneum und Stabiae hatte Gerhart Rodenwaldt ein Musterbuch angenommen, "das eine Reihe der beliebtesten Kompositionen . . . enthielt und sich in der Hand eines jeden dieser Maler befand, ein richtiges Buch wie Varros imagines, aber hier zum praktischen Gebrauch innerhalb eines beschränkten Kreises." Ferner, "daß dieses Buch nur die Figurenkomposition enthielt, die natürlich einem griechischen Tafelbild entstammte, während die landschaftliche Folie von den Malern hinzugefügt wurde . . . Zunächst kann man annehmen, daß es eine Reihe von einzelnen Figuren enthielt, besonders von Göttern, wie solche sich häufig innerhalb der gemalten Architektur befinden."[1] Er hatte auch einige Wandbilder zusammengestellt, für die er die Benutzung eines solchen Musterbuches wahrscheinlich machen konnte. Die Forschung ist der Frage nach diesem Musterbuch und nach seinem vermutlichen Inhalt jedoch seither nicht weiter nachgegangen. Sie sah sich bemüht, einen anderen Weg einzuschlagen, auf den sie durch eine weitere Feststellung Rodenwaldts gewiesen wurde: "Selbstverständlich benutzten die g u t e n Künstler ein solches Musterbuch nicht, sondern hielten sich bei ihren Vorlagen entweder an die Originale oder an Kopien, die von jenen genommen waren" (S.245). So stand die Wiedergewinnung griechischer "Originalkompositionen" aus den römischen Wandbildern im Vordergrund der Forschung auch da, wo der von Rodenwaldt aufgezeigte andere Weg zu zufriedenstellenderen Ergebnissen geführt und vor manchen Irrtümern bewahrt hätte.

Ein bezeichnendes Beispiel hierfür ist die Beurteilung, die das Wandbild "Pan unter den Nymphen" dritten Stils aus Pompeji erfuhr.[2] Rodenwaldt hatte noch angenommen, daß es als Ganzes nach einem griechischen Tafelbild gemalt wurde, wenn auch die Komposition von dem Wandmaler nicht genau wiedergegeben worden sei (S.73). H. Diepolder hat dagegen später nachgewiesen, daß die Gruppe der beiden Nymphen links im Bilde nicht zu der ursprüng-

---

1. Rodenwaldt, G., *Die Komposition der pompejanischen Wandbilder*, 243.
2. Regio IX Insula 5 Haus 18. Herrmann, P., *Denkm.d.Mal.d.Altert.* Taf. 69. Curtius, L., *Die Wandmalerei Pompejis*, 287 Abb. 169. Rodenwaldt, G., *Die Kunst der Antike*, Farbtafel 37.

lichen Komposition gehörten.[3] Doch bemerkt er: "ausgezeichnet sind die Figuren des Pan und der Lyra spielenden Nymphe. Gerne sind wir geneigt, ein griechisches Vorbild für sie anzunehmen." Wo gäbe es aber ein griechisches Vorbild, in dem eine Nymphe die Lyra spielt? Die Lyraspielerin des Wandbildes muß also wohl eine Muse sein.[4] Damit steht aber die Annahme, der Syrinx spielende Pan und die Leier spielende Muse enstammten demselben griechischen Original, auf unsicherem Boden. Diese "seltsame Begegnung" wäre in einem griechischen Original schwer zu erklären. In der Tat "trennen sich hier zwei Welten."[5] Doch bereitet nicht nur der Inhalt des Wandbildes Schwierigkeiten, sondern auch seine Komposition.

Pan "thront im Heiligtum des Bergwaldes" auf einem Felsensitz. Sein stark bewegter Körper und die ausgreifenden Bewegungen seiner Glieder führen die Dreidimensionalität des freien Raumes in sehr aufdringlicher Weise vor Augen. Die Muse (Taf. 103a) dagegen steht in reiner Profilansicht vor einem "unmotiviert in die Landschaft gesetzten Mauerstück,"[6] sodaß sie "wie auf die Wand aufgemalt erscheint."[7] Dieses Mauerstück ist ebenso wenig oder ebenso gut motiviert wie der rechtkantige Sockel, auf dem die Nymphe links sitzt. Dieser Sockel ist offenbar ein Versatzstück, wie sie die pompejanischen Wandmaler immer zur Hand haben; hier um eine Sitzgelegenheit für die Nymphe zu schaffen, die auf den anderen Wandbilderen auf Felsen sitzt.[8] Gewiß ist bei der Muse dem Maler auch "das Streben nach möglichst unräumlicher Wirkung maßgebend" gewesen, als er ihr diesen Hintergrund gab. Dieses Streben ist an vielen Wandbildern des dritten Stils festzustellen, wie Diepolder nachwies. Inhaltlich könnte man das Mauerstück als Temenosmauer verstehen, und als solche deutet es wohl Herbig, wenn er von einem "Heiligtum des Bergwaldes" spricht.[9] Aber wo gibt es eine Temenosmauer, die oben mit einer

---

3. *RM* 41 (1926) 19ff.

4. Rodenwaldt scheint die Unstimmigkeit empfunden zu haben, denn er spricht von einer leierspielenden "Frau" (Komp. 73). Als Muse jetzt auch von R. Herbig, *Pan*, 26 gedeutet: "Die Musikantin trägt über der Stirne eine aufragende Feder, das Abzeichen der über die musikalische Konkurrenz der Sirenen siegreichen Musen."

5. Herbig a.O.: "Leider verschweigt uns der gemalte Mythos, bei welcher Gelegenheit, aus welchem Anlaß diese seltsame Begegnung der hohen Kunst der Muse mit dem Kreise ländlichen Musizierens stattgefunden hat. Die fast überdeutliche Zäsur zwischen Pan und der Muse beweist aber jedenfalls eindeutig, daß sich hier zwei Welten trennen, daß Pan zwar immer ein ländlicher Musizierer, aber niemals ein musischer Künstler gewesen ist. Der hohe künstlerische Bereich apollinischer Musik ist ihm stes verschlossen geblieben."

6. Diepolder *RM* 41 (1926) 19.

7. Rodenwaldt, *Komp.* 73, der daraus den Schluß zieht, "die Füße müßten weiter vorn aufstehen."

8. Die sogenannten Aktai. Beispiele führt Diepolder a.O. 19ff. an.

9. s. Anm. 4.

profilierten Leiste abgeschlossen ist wie hier?[10] Ueberdies wachsen
Stauden, Gesträuch und ein Baum über ihr auf, als ob sie der Erde
für diese Vegetation als Terrassenmauer diente. Der Maler hat sich
darüber offenbar keine Gedanken gemacht, wie er auch den Zusammenhang zwischen "Heiligtum" und "Bergwald" im Unklaren ließ.
Er hat aber auch ebenso wenig "die Schrägstellung des Hauses (und
was bedeutet dieses Haus?) ausgenutzt, sondern auch hier die Hellig-
keit der Mauermassen nur als Folie für die beiden Nymphen benutzt."[11] Das unmotiviert in die Landschaft gesetzte Mauerstück ist
demnach wohl nicht einmal eine Temenosmauer, sondern ebenfalls
nur eine bloße Folie für die Muse. Die Figur verlangte einen solchen
Hintergrund. Denn betrachtet man sie näher auf ihre Raumhaltig-
keit hin, so fällt es ohne weiteres auf, wie sehr sie als Flächenfigur
gemalt ist. Ganz im Gegensatz zum Pan erscheint sie "wie auf die
Wand aufgemalt." Ihre Körperperspektive ist bei weitem nicht so
entwickelt wie bei diesem. Sie ist überhaupt ganz anders g e s e h e n.
Beide Figuren k ö n n e n daher ursprünglich gar nicht von demselben
Künstler entworfen worden sein. Sie können daher auch nicht auf
ein und dasselbe griechische Vorbild zurückgehen. Der Wandmaler
muß die beiden Gestalten einzeln seinem Musterbuch entnommen
haben, genau so wie die Nymphen links. Erst der pompejanische
Wandmaler also hat alle vier Figuren zu einem Wandbild mit land-
schaftlicher Staffage im zeitgemäßen Stil vereinigt. So lassen sich
auch die Widersprüche in der Räumlichkeit des Wandbildes, die im
dritten Stil nicht ungewöhnlich sind, auf die einleuchtendste Weise
erklären.

Auch ohne diese Beobachtungen wird es heute jedem näher hin-
sehenden Betrachter schwer fallen, Rodenwaldts Folgerung beizu-
stimmen, daß "die stilistische Uebereinstimmung der Figuren empfiehlt, ein gemeinsames Original" auch nur für den Pan und die
Muse vorauszusetzen. Das geht schon darum nicht, weil die Muse
eine ganz andere Atmosphäre um sich hat, die sie seltsam isoliert.
Sie gibt nicht nur "die Stimmung an,"[11] sondern sie ist selbst in
einer ganz besonderen Weise "gestimmt." Diese nur ihr eigene "Gestimmtheit" trennt nicht nur die apollinische Welt, der sie angehört,
von der des Pan, sondern trennt sie von ihm als eine ganz andere
G e s t a l t. Sie hebt sich als eine Gestalt ganz anderer Art von
diesem ab, aber sie hebt sich auch aus a l l e n anderen Gestalten der
römischen Wandbilder heraus. Sie erscheint unter ihnen wie ein

---

10. Eine ähnlich profilierte Mauer auf dem bekannten Europabild Herrmann
Taf. 68 (aus dem gleichen Haus wie das besprochene Pan-Nymphenbild), wo sie
ebenso als Versatzstück, aber nicht als Hintergrundsfläche verwendet ist.

11. Diepolder a.O.

Fremdling aus einer anderen Welt. Wir müssen also nach Ihresgleichen anderswo suchen. Aber wo sonst begegnen wir einer solchen "Gestimmtheit" als in den Gestalten der Parthenonzeit? Man braucht nur die Muse des Achilleusmalers auf seiner weißgrundigen Lekythos in München daneben zu stellen, um die Welt zu erkennen, in der beide Gestalten ihr Leben haben (Taf. 103, b).[12]

Wem dieser allgemeine Hinweis nicht genügt, der vergleiche das Profil der beiden Musen, die allgemeine Anlage des Kopfes und seine Neigung, bei der die lange Nackenlinie so stark mitspricht und so bezeichnend ist, und die Haltung der beiden. Freilich wird sich dabei auch der Einwand erheben, daß an der Muse des Wandbildes alles gelöster und freier ist. Das gleiche gilt von Einzelheiten, etwa der Hand, die in dem Wandbild feiner durchgezeichnet und von größerer Ausdrucksfähigkeit ist, wie überhaupt die ganze Gestalt inniger und stimmungsvoller gegeben ist. Wir müßten schon etwas jüngere Lekythenbilder vergleichen, um einen ähnlich starken Stimmungsgehalt zu finden, etwa die Lekythos mit dem Lyraspieler aus der Gruppe des Schilfmalers in Wien, die mindestens zwei Jahrzehnte jünger ist als die Lekythos des Achilleusmalers.[13] Besser läßt sich vielleicht die Gestalt der Mutter auf einer Lekythos der späteren zwanziger Jahre des 5. Jahrhunderts vergleichen.[14] Sie hat die gleiche Haltung, die gleiche Anlage des Gesichts, die gleiche Neigung des Kopfes und anscheinend auch die gleiche Haartracht (die auf den Meidiasvasen so beliebt ist) mit dem aufgebundenen freistehenden Schopf über dem Wirbel wie die Muse des Wandbildes. Auch die gestreckten Proportionen des Körpers scheinen die gleichen zu sein.[15] Aber für die Musikalität der Falten und ihre malerische Behandlung findet sich in den Lekythenbildern nichts Vergleichbares. Wie ist sie zu erklären?

Die Beobachtungen von A. Rumpf helfen hier zunächst nicht weiter, so groß ihr Verdienst ist, uns eine genauere Vorstellung von der

---

12. Privatbesitz München. Buschor, E., *Grab eines attischen Mädchens*, 39 Abb. 31. *Hellas* (herausgegeben von H. von Schönebeck und W. Kraiker) Taf. 90. Beazley, J. D., *Attic White Lekythoi*, 15f. Taf. 8, 2. Beazley vermutet a.O. in dem Vogel vor der Muse einen wood warbler (= Grasmücke?). Hackenschnabel, lange Schwingen und Krallen kennzeichnen ihn jedoch unverkennbar als Raubvogel. Jedenfalls ist er kein Haustier. Wie mir H. B. Jessen freundlicher Weise mitteilt, möchte er in ihm eine Weihe (oder einen Falken) erkennen, das Tier Apollons (*Od.* XV 526: κίρκος Ἀπόλλωνος ταχὺς ἄγγελος; vgl. *Il.*, XV 237, wo sich Apollon in einen ἴρηξ Falke, Habicht verwandelt).

13. O. Benndorf, *Griech.u.sic.Vasenbilder* Taf. 34. W. Riezler, *Weißgr.att. Lekythen*, 28f. Abb. 17-18. Beazley a.O. 24 mit Anm. 4. Buschor, *Gr. Vas.* 227 Abb. 246. *Hellas* Taf. 91.

14. Früher im Kunsthandel in Athen. Buschor a.O. 218 Abb. 236.

15. Die gestreckte Proportion des Körpers der zwei letzten Jahrzehnte des 5. Jhs. zeigt deutlicher die rechte Frau auf der Lekythos Benndorf Taf. 15. Alle drei Frauen dieser Lekythos tragen den erwähnten Haarschopf.

entscheidendsten Phase in der Entwicklung der griechischen Malerei geschenkt zu haben: dem Aufkommen der Schattenmalerei.[16] Rumpf faßte die Ergebnisse seiner Beobachtungen folgendermaßen zusammen: "Seit dem letzten Jahrzehnt des fünften Jahrhunderts, in das Plinius den Apollodoros, den Skiagraphos setzt, können wir auf einer kleinen Gruppe attischer Lekythen erstmalig reichlichere Schattengebung beobachten. Schattiert werden nicht nur — wie schon früher — leblose Gegenstände und Gewänder, sondern auch die Körper von Männern, hingegen bleibt das weibliche Fleisch schattenlos. Die gleiche Erscheinung kehrt wieder auf allen Originalen, die wir in die erste Hälfte des vierten Jahrhunderts setzen dürfen, auf etruskischen Wandbildern sowohl wie auf polychromen Vasen, ja auf farblosen Spiegelritzungen. . . . Für Polygnot ergibt sich daraus, daß wir bei ihm wohl etwas Schatten an den Gewändern und leblosen Gegenständen annehmen dürfen, nicht aber an Gestalten. Aber auch der Skiagraph Apollodoros war noch weit von der Vollendung entfernt. . . . Er wird auf der Stufe der Berliner Lekythen gestanden haben. Keineswegs kann man ihm zutrauen, daß er einen räumlichen Ausschnitt aus der Natur auf die Fläche gebannt habe. Solche Absichten lagen der klassischen Zeit fern."

Rumpf hat auf "eine an sich billige geistesgeschichtliche Untermalung der beobachteten Erscheinung" verzichtet, und er bemerkt dazu: "die Hauptsache ist, daß wir das Phänomen . . . als gegeben hinnehmen" (S.22). Damit ist zunächst die Tatsache gemeint, daß die griechischen Maler bis zu Nikias die Frauenkörper ohne Schatten wiedergegeben haben. Wichtiger scheint mir aber an seinen Beobachtungen zu sein, daß seit der Zeit des Apollodoros die Schattengebung auch bei dem menschlichen Körper angewendet wird, wenn auch zunächst nur bei dem männlichen Körper. Dies ist zunächst gewiß eine notwendige Folgerung der Maler aus der stärkeren Körperperspektive der Gestalten, die vor allem durch eine neue Konturführung erreicht wird. An den Gestalten des Parrhasios, des älteren Zeitgenossen von Apollodoros, wird gerade der Kontur gelobt mit einer Begründung, die für die neue Körperperspektive der Malerei der hochklassischen Zeit äußerst bezeichnend ist (Plinius, *Nat. Hist.* XXXV, 67-69). Zum Verständnis dieser Konturführung hat R. Bianchi Bandinelli auf den Begriff der *linea funzionale* aufmerksam gemacht, den B. Berenson in die moderne Kunstbetrachtung eingeführt hat, "per definire la linea che, circoscrivendo un corpo . . . crea relazioni di volumi."[17] Zur Veranschaulichung seiner Darlegungen

16. *JDAI* 49 (1934), 6ff. Die oben angeführte Zusammenfassung S. 23.
17. *La Critica d'Arte* 3, 1938, 4ff. besonders 9ff.

wählte Bandinelli ein sehr glückliches Beispiel, die Lekythos aus der
Gruppe des Schilfmalers aus dem letzten Jahrzehnt des 5. Jahrhunderts in Athen.[18] Aber gerade an dieser sind die Farben verloren gegangen und damit auch die farbige Schattengebung. Doch auch auf
den anderen besser erhaltenen Lekythen dieser Zeit scheint die Art,
wie die Gewänder und ihre Schatten wiedergegeben sind, weit entfernt
zu sein von ihrer malerischen Behandlung in dem pompejanischen
Wandbild.[19] Daß die Maltechnik des Apollodoros im großen Ganzen
aber auf der Stufe dieser Lekythen gestanden haben muß, betont
Rumpf wohl mit Recht. Doch ist dabei zu bedenken, daß diese Art
der Farbgebung, die "Schattenmalerei", auf den Tafelbildern des
Apollodoros und seiner Zunftgenossen noch stärker hervorgetreten
sein muß als auf den Lekythenbildern, die notgedrungener Weise auf
die beschränkten Möglichkeiten der keramischen Farben eingeengt
blieben. Wir werden nicht fehlgehen, wenn wir für die Tafelbilder
eine größere und reichere Farbigkeit annehmen, als sie die Lekythenbilder geben können. Das Eine ist jedenfalls sicher, daß diese farbige
Schattengebung darin bestand, die Hell- und Dunkelschattierung in
die Lokalfarbe durch Verdichtung dieser Farbe aufzunehmen. Dadurch mußten die Gestalten einen neuen tonigen Zusammenschluß
bekommen, der ein ganz neues farbiges Element in die Bilder bringt.
Genau so ist aber die Muse auf dem pompejanischen Wandbild gemalt!
Ihr Mantel ist von gleichmäßig blaugrüner Eigenfarbe, mit Ausnahme
eines hellvioletten Saumes unten und im Rücken. In diese blaue Eigen-
farbe sind die Faltenschatten mit der gleichen Farbe in dunklerer
Tönung hineingemalt. Es gibt keine aufgehöhten Töne und keine
Glanzlichter (wie beim Pan!), geschweige denn das Changieren der
Farbe wie in späteren Bildern.[20]

Wollten wir uns allein nach der literarischen Ueberlieferung und
den Lekythenbildern eine möglichst vollständige Vorstellung von der
Farbigkeit und der farbigen Schattengebung der Tafelbilder aus der

---

18. Nat.Mus. Nr. 1817 aus Eretria, a.O. Taf 1. Riezler Taf. 91. Buschor, *Gr.
Vas.* 236 Abb. 256. *Hellas* Taf. 93.

19. Vgl. die von Rumpf *JDAI* 49 (1934) 15 zusammengestellten Beispiele.

20. Wie sie z.B. an dem Gewand der Priesterin des bekannten Stuckgemäldes
aus Herculaneum im Museo Nazionale in Neapel zu beobachten sind: Herrmann
Taf. 3; Curtius, *Wandmalerei Pompejis,* 269 Ab. 160. Wie Curtius anmerkt, geht
das Stuckbild auf ein griechisches Weihebild aus dem 4. Jahrhundert zurück.
Vergleiche mit Gefäßzeichnungen und Grabreliefs datieren das Originalbild in die
Zeit um 340 v.Chr. Die Kopie folgt ihm anscheinend auch in der malerischen
Behandlung genau und stammt offensichtlich von einem jener guten Wandmaler,
"die sich bei ihren Vorlagen entweder an die Originale oder an Kopien hielten,
die von jenen genommen waren." Die Oeffnung des Hintergrundes und der
charakteristische Mittelpfeiler sind offenbar von dem pompejanischen Wandmaler.
So aber auch das Mädchen links, das sich auf die Lehne des Thronstuhles stützt:
sie muß nach einer hellenistischen Vorlage kopiert sein. So erhalten wir für das
Gemälde des 4 Jhs. ein Dreifigurenbild.

Zeit des Apollodoros machen, könnte sie dann anders ausfallen, als sie die Muse auf dem pompejanischen Wandbild zeigt?[21]

Es muß freilich zugegeben werden, daß der pompejanische Wandmaler mit der langen Mantelfalte, die von der Schulter vorn senkrecht herabfällt, ein fremdes Motiv in die Figur gebracht hat, das in der attischen Gefäßmalerei nicht zu belegen und für die Malerei jener Zeit überhaupt unwahrscheinlich ist. Es bringt eine Verhärtung in die Figur, die sich in dem schweren eckigen Faltenwulst auf der Schulter entgegen ihrer ganzen gelösten Haltung störend bemerkbar macht. Hierin ist wohl nichts anderes zu sehen als eine klassizistische Verhärtung, die auch an dem Zickzack-Rand zu beobachten ist, der sich an dem herabhängenden Mantelende im Rücken der Figur viel zu breitflächig entfaltet. Das Motiv an sich ist in der attischen Malerei und Reliefkunst seit der Parthenonzeit sehr beliebt. In beiden Fällen scheint also der Wandmaler Einzelmotive seiner Vorlage vereinfacht und in seinem klassizistischen Streben linear verhärtet zu haben.[22] Man beachte auch, wie hart und schematisch die Falten der sitzenden Nymphe auf seinem Wandbild gemalt sind. Alle anderen vergleichbaren Einzelheiten weisen für das Vorbild der Muse etwa in das vorletzte Jahrzehnt des 5. Jahrhunderts vor Chr. Der Schluß scheint daher gerechtfertigt, daß die Figur der Muse in dem Musterbuch des pompejanischen Wandmalers aus einem geweihten Tafelbild jener Zeit kopiert worden war. Die Vorlage im Musterbuch folgte offenbar der Maltechnik des Tafelbildes so genau, daß sich der Wandmaler — im Gegensatz zu den Vorlagen für den Pan und die Nymphen — auch in der Maltechnik daran hielt. So kann uns die Muse des pompejanischen Wandbildes noch eine gute Anschauung von der Malweise und der Art der Tafelbilder des Apollodoros und seiner Zunftgenossen vermitteln.

21. Für die Schattengebung muß man freilich die Taf. 69 bei Herrmann oder die Aufnahme von Alinari vergleichen, während die farbige Wiedergabe bei Rodenwaldt, *D.K.d.Antike* Taf. 37, hierfür ganz unzureichend ist. Von den Lekythenbildern zeigen ähnliches weniger die von Rumpf zusammengestellten Beispiele (Anm. 19), als etwa die Lekythos in Wien aus den zwanziger Jahren des 5. Jhs., und zwar der untere Teil des Gewandes des Mädchens links: Riezler S.29 Abb. 18. Die Nachzeichnung gerade dieses Gewandteiles bei Benndorf Taf. 34 geht in ihrer modern "malerischen" Interpretation allerdings zu weit.

22. Wir müssen annehmen, daß die Muse unter dem Himation einen ärmellosen Chiton trägt, der den rechten Arm freiläßt, wofür sich Beispiele auf den attischen Lekythen finden: Athen, Nat. Mus. 1937 aus Eretria; Riezler Taf. 73; Buschor, *Münchner Jahrb. d. Bild. Kunst* 1925, 19: "Quadratmeister, gegen 420." Gestalten im Himation und Chiton sind auf den Lekythenbildern selten und daher findet sich dort nichts unmittelbar Vergleichbares. Am ehesten vergleichbar ist die Frau im Mantel mit ähnlichem Rückenmotiv auf der Lekythos Athen, Nat. Mus. 1955 aus Eretria: Riezler Taf. 71; Buschor a.O. 21: "Frauenmeister, nach 425"; Pfuhl, *Mal. u. Zeichng.* III 213 Abb. 550. — Hingewiesen sei noch auf die hohe schmale Form der Lyra, die sich ebenso auf der Lekythos im Louvre Nr. 90 findet: Riezler Taf. 62; Buschor a.O. 21: "Frauenmeister, Frühwerk."

FIGURATA SIMILITUDO

A. Ippel
München

Tafeln 104-106

Pictura fit imago eius quod est seu potest esse — das sind Vitruvs lapidare Worte, mit denen er Aufgabe und Bereich der Malerei umreisst (VII 5), um alsbald die iniquos mores zu verdammen, die sich an Dinge wagen, die nec sunt nec fieri possunt nec fuerunt.

Man lächelt gern über den alten Herrn und schlägt sich gerade mit besonderer Freude auf die Seite der Verdammten, die haec falsa videntes non reprehendunt sed delectantur. Ja, wir fühlen unsere mentes nicht im geringsten iudiciis falsis obscuratas, wenn wir uns an zahllosen jener picturae auf den Wänden Pompejis delektieren, quae non sunt similes veritati.

Aber so ganz unrichtig sind jene ersten Worte Vitruvs gar nicht. Hätte er nur statt des fit ein initio fuit gesagt, so liesse sich schon darüber reden. Und man sollte geradezu vor den pompejanischen Wänden mehr darüber reden und sich neben stilkritischen und ästhetisierenden Erörterungen mehr auch der Frage zuwenden, ob nicht doch hinter vielen picturae, quae falsa videntur, stehe eine imago eius quod erat.

In der Tat bin ich überzeugt, dass sich bei allen, noch so phantastisch anmutenden Architekturen des vierten Stils die ursprünglichen Formen nachweisen lassen, e quibus finitis certisque corporibus figurata similitudine sumpta sunt exempla.

Mit Ueberlegungen dieser Art stand ich auch öfter im Atrium der Casa dell' Ara massima, vor jener Malerei im oberen Teil der Westwand, über dem kleinen Raum mit dem Narcissusbild, die, je länger man sie betrachtet, umso fesselnder und gewichtiger wird. L. Curtius hat das Bild in seiner *Wandmalerei Pompejis* auf S. 45 und 47 abgebildet und zu Anfang des Kapitels über die Stile der dekorativen Architekturmalerei S. 51f. besprochen (Taf. 104).

Auf der als einheitlich nach links und rechts durchgehend angegebenen Wand findet sich in der Mitte ein grosses, von Linien umrahmtes Bild, der Blick in eine Landschaft: ein von rechts her aufgetreppter Fels, auf dem eine nach rechts sich öffnende, schön gerundete, offene, einfache Säulenstellung mit gewaltigem Architrav vor einem heiligen Baume steht, links im Hintergrund ein Heiligtum und darüber ein kegelförmig aufragender Berg. Rechts und links von diesem Bild

wird die Wand von einer Tür durchbrochen. Aus jeder Tür tritt eine
Frau, wohl eine Priesterin, mit heiligen Geräten heraus, mit jener aus
so manchen pompejanischen Bildern bekannten stillen und doch so
erregenden Bewegung, die den Beschauer in geheimisvolle Spannung
versetzt. Die Frauen schicken sich an, die Stufen herabzuschreiten,
die aus der Tür hinabführen. Auf Sockeln neben diesen Stufen erhebt
sich beiderseits eine vor die Hauptwand vortretende Prostas. Ihr
Gebälk und ihre Ueberdeckung ruht hinten auf Säulen, die sich an die
Wand anlehnen, vorn auf zierlichen Stützen über den Köpfen
schlanker Karyatiden, die auf ebenso schlanken hohen, viereckigen
Pfeilern stehen. Aussen neben diesen luftig hohen Vorhallen steht
je eine grosse Götterstatue, links wohl die des Poseidon, recht der
Amphitrite.

Von weitergehender Einzelbeschreibung kann hier abgesehen
werden, da sie nichts für den augenblicklichen Zweck Belangvolles
ergäbe. Wohl aber möchten wir uns der Frage zuwenden, ob auch bei
dieser Malerei vicerit veritatem ratio falsa oder sie nicht auch einen
ganz bestimmten Sinn habe.

Das architektonische Schema, das zugrundeliegt, ist ja im Grunde
ganz einfach: eine Wand trägt in der Mitte ein grosses Bild, rechts
und links von diesem befindet sich eine Tür, vor der je eine Prostas
steht und aus der Stufen herabführen.

Es ist dies keine unbekannte Form. Sie entspricht der Darstellung
auf dem campanischen Krater im Louvre *R V I* 279, 2, die nach Otfried
Müller, *Handbuch*[3] S. 719 Lehmann-Hartleben *JDAI* 42 (1927), 30f.
Abb. 1, 2 als Skenenbau deutete und H. Bulle 94. *B.Wi.Pr.*, 1934,
S. 13ff. weiter behandelt hat (Taf. 105). In der punktierten Linie sieht
Bulle sicherlich richtig die Andeutung eines naturalistisch gestalteten
Bodens zwischen den zwei "Paraskenien," und dieser realistischen
Gestaltung muss auch eine realistische Darstellung des Hintergrundes
in Form einer Hintergrundkulisse entsprochen haben. Als solche wird
man entsprechend die Landschaftsdarstellung in der Mitte des Wandbildes bei Curtius a.O. S.45 (Taf. 104) ansehen dürfen, das damit
wohl die vollkommenste Darstellung dieser Art ist. Tritt ihm doch
erklärend und bestätigend auch das nach einer Würzburger Scherbe
von H. Bulle a.O. auf Tafel II hergestellte Bild zur Seite (Abb. 1).
bei dem die Flügelbauten, zwar einfach, aber im wesentlichen gleich,
in dieser erstaunlichen perspektivischen Ansicht, gegeben sind.

Diese müssen nach den drei sich ergänzenden Darstellungen eine
ganz wesentliche Rolle in den Aufführungen gespielt haben, und es
erscheint notwendig, jenen "Aediculen," die man so häufig auf den
unteritalischen Vasen trifft, etwas nähere Aufmerksamkeit zuzu-

Abb. 1. Bild von einer Würzburger Scherbe.

wenden. Wir meinen, uns hier mit einem Beispiel begnügen zu können,
nämlich einem der Bilder aus der Iphigeniesage, abgebildet bei L.
Séchan, *Études sur la tragédie grecque*, S.385 fig. 113 (Abb. 2). Denn
dass eine solche Aedicula nicht eine belanglose Abbreviatur ist, sondern wirklich einen ganz bestimmten Sinn hat, ergibt sich aus der
Gegenüberstellung mit dem Iphigeniebild aus der Casa di Caecilio
Jucundo, Sogliano 585, abgebildet bei L. Curtius a.O. S.247, nach
Herrmann, *Denkmäler* Tafel 118 (Taf. 106). Der Wandmaler ist doch
nicht so ganz ein Opfer der Unzuverlässigkeit und Taktlosigkeit geworden, die Curtius den Malern des dritten Stils voll Aerger vorwirft,
a.O. S. 234. Wie es mit der Gruppe von Orest und Pylades steht, ist
noch nicht zu entscheiden, Curtius' Urteil a.O. S.249 vermag ich mich
aber nicht anzuschliessen. Auch ob die Begleiterinnen Iphigenies nicht
doch auch schon zu der ursprünglichen Komposition gehörten, ist
nicht mit mehr oder weniger willkürlichen ästhetischen Gründen zu
entscheiden. Aber fraglos ist, dass Vasen- und Wandmaler bei der
Aedicula und der Gestalt der Iphigenie dem gleichen, beiden vorliegenden Original folgten. Die Aedicula darf demnach also nicht
etwa aus dem Wandbild eliminiert werden. Bereits das Vorbild wies
sie auf, ihr kam also nach Meinung des Künstlers innerhalb seines

Abb. 2. Bild aus der Iphigeniesage.

Gemäldes eine wesentliche Bedeutung zu, die auch dem Betrachter des Bildes ohne weiteres verständlich sein musste.

Dies wird es auch uns aus dem Louvrekrater und dem Würzburger Fragment, Bulle a.O. S.15 und Taf. II (Abb. 2 und 3), nämlich als Wiedergabe eines der Flügelbauten; vgl. auch in dem Vasenbild bei Séchan S.384 fig. 112 die halbgeöffneten Türen wie bei Bulle a.O., Taf. II (Abb. 2) — weitere Beispiele liessen sich leicht anführen.

Die Würzburger Vase stellt nicht eigentlich ein Skenengebäude dar, gibt vielmehr das Bild der Aufführung. Die Rekonstruktion des angeblichen Skenengebäudes bei Bulle a.O. S.9 wäre dahin zu ändern, dass lediglich der mit Recht angenommene hintere Längsraum, die eigentliche Skene, mit einem festen Dach zu ergänzen ist, während dies dem ihm vorgelegten Proskenion natürlich fehlen musste.

Die Flügelbauten gehören, was nachzuweisen hier zu weit führte, bereits in sehr frühe Entwicklungsstufen des Theaters. So mag zum Schluss einer Vermutung Raum gegeben werden, die an anderer Stelle ausführlicher begründet werden soll. Es dürfte nämlich durchaus zu erwägen sein, ob nicht bereits auf dem Berliner Amphiaraoskrater die Säulenarchitekturen zu beiden Seiten der Mittelgruppe — auch eine figurata similitudo — als jene Flügelbauten anzusprechen seien und wir das Ganze als Bild einer Aufführung eines Heroenspieles πρὸς τὰ πάθεα τὰ ᾽Αμφιαράου deuten dürfen, so wie sie in Sikyon den Adrast πρὸς τὰ πάθεα αὐτοῦ τραγικοῖσι χόροισι ἐγέραιον (Herod. 1, 23), und Korinths Bedeutung für die Entstehung des Dramas ist ja bekannt. Vgl. E. Bickel, *Die griechische Tragödie*, S.138ff. in "Griechenland," Bonn 1944.

INTORNO ALL'ORIGINE E PER UNA NUOVA DENOMINAZIONE DEI MOSAICI "COSMATESCHI"

GOFFREDO BENDINELLI
Università di Torino

Tavole 107-111

Nella storia dell'arte italiana i mosaici cosiddetti "cosmateschi" sono ornamenti così comuni delle chiese medioevali dell'Italia centrale e meridionale fino in Sicilia, da risultare largamente noti alla generalità degli studiosi non solo nelle loro principali caratteristiche, ma anche nella loro sommaria cronologia. Si considera generalmente che questa cronologia vada dalla metà del secolo XII alla fine del XIII, e comprenda un secolo e mezzo di attività artistica, o più esattamente artigiana. In seguito ad accurati contributi di studiosi romani, tra la fine dell'800 e i primi del secolo presente, è stato pure accertato che quella che prima si riteneva essere una sola famiglia (o come anche si è detto, una "dinastia") di artisti, si scinde praticamente in varie famiglie o "dinastie," di cui le più note e operose, in Roma e nel Lazio in genere, sono appunto quelle dei "Cosmati" e dei "Vassalletti."[1]

Non è dato purtroppo accertare a quale famiglia appartenesse quel *magister Paulus* il quale lavorava a Ferentino ai tempi di papa Pasquale II (1099-1118), col quale nominativo di *Paulus* l'attività dei cosiddetti "Cosmati" può essere riportata sino ai primi del secolo XII. Una cosa certa è però che il mosaicista il quale lavorava a Ferentino, in provincia, a una data intorno al 1100 o 1110, o veniva direttamente da Roma, o (che è lo stesso per la valutazione del fatto artistico) si era venuto educando e formando alla scuola di mosaicisti romani. Per cui non dovrebbe parere illazione arbitraria la tesi che lo stile decorativo musivo denominato cosmatesco, avesse fatto la sua apparizione in Roma già nel corso del secolo XI.

Ora quale fu — ci domandiamo — la genesi, quali furono le circostanze determinanti di uno stile decorativo del tutto nuovo agli occhi nostri, in un periodo storico sostanzialmente così poco favorevole non tanto allo svolgersi, quanto al rinnovarsi di un'arte decorativa purchessia, come dovette essere nell'Italia centrale, e in Roma stessa, il secolo XI? Poichè non si può a meno di ritenere che quello stile decorativo facesse veramente al suo apparire l'effetto di una attraente novità, visto che esso ottenne subito tanto favore e potè diffondersi

---

1. Vedasi in proposito Giovannoni, G., in *Enciclopedia Italiana*, all'art. *"Cosmati"* (vol. VI, 1931, 576 segg.), con la bibliografia precedente.

estesamente nella penisola, e quivi perdurare abbastanza a lungo. Rispondere a una domanda come questa che ci proponiamo, sarebbe stato fino a non molti anni or sono, impossibile. Ma, con la speranza di non ingannarci, si posseggono oggi i documenti utili ad affrontare con qualche probabilità di riuscita una così ardua questione.

Gli scavi genialmente intrapresi e arditamente condotti per un decennio, da D. M. Robinson nel sito dell'antica Olinto, la città radicalmente distrutta nel 348 a. C. da Filippo II di Macedonia, a nord della penisola Calcidica, hanno fruttato alla scienza, colla meravigliosa serie di volumi esaurientemente illustrativi di quegli scavi, risultati cospicui non soltanto dal punto di vista della conoscenza delle antichità classiche, ma qua e là utili anche sotto altri punti di vista. Così una scoperta effettuata nel campo delle antichità medioevali dal Robinson, e da questo pubblicata nel volume XII della serie di "Olinto" (volume dal titolo *Excavations at Olynthus, Domestic and Public Architecture,* 1946), ci induce a riprendere l'interessante questione delle origini del mosaico "cosmatesco," illuminandola col sussidio di materiale del tutto nuovo.

A circa mezzo chilometro da Olinto e dalla zona di scavo sorgeva una moderna e assai modesta chiesetta campestre, dedicata e intitolata a San Nicola: chiesetta che abitanti del luogo asserivano costruita sui ruderi di altra molto più antica. Ottenuta, non senza fatica, l'autorizzazione a procedere alla demolizione della insignificante costruzione moderna, gli scavatori, una volta liberato il terreno da tutte le moderne superfetazioni, riuscivano a riportare alla luce i resti — veramente poco più che la pianta — di una chiesetta medioevale di tipo bizantino, ad abside tricora, interessante sotto varî punti di vista, ma specialmente importante, a nostro giudizio, per l'originale pavimento musivo che occupava e supponiamo occupi tuttora la parte centrale della navata mediana (tav. 107-108).

Il mosaico, di un disegno geometrico abbastanza semplice, risulta di un tondo centrale fiancheggiato da quattro tondi minori e da quattro altri poco più grandi negli intervalli; con altri quattro delle medesime dimensioni posti diagonalmente a contatto dei tondi minori. Tutto quanto il disegno, composto di tredici tondi a cerchi concentrici bianchi e scuri, si iscrive in un quadrato. Più che di un pavimento musivo, si direbbe trattarsi di un emblema musivo di pavimento, poichè questo è fatto per il rimanente di semplici lastre di marmo bianco, salvo avanzi di una fascia scura addetta a incorniciare l'emblema. L'interesse della composizione stellare è dato dal fatto che i tondi sono tenuti insieme da una fascia o nastro, che corre intorno all'uno e all'altro tondo, formando un intreccio. Cosicchè il mosaico presenta tutti i caratteri — come l'egregio autore della scoperta si esprime — proprî di un saggio di stile ornamentale "cosmatesco."[2]

I resti della chiesetta bizantina vengono riferiti dal Robinson al secolo XI (propriamente alla fine del secolo XI). Rifacendoci alle nostre conoscenze, si dovrebbe quindi concludere per l'apparire pressochè simultaneo di forme artistiche di genere "cosmatesco" in regioni assai distanti e del tutto estranee fra loro, come l'Italia (centrale, meridionale e insulare) da una parte, e la Macedonia dall'altra. Conviene tener presente che l'esempio di mosaico pavimentale di Olinto trova dei riscontri assai significativi nella stessa penisola greca, come è il caso del mosaico di San Luca di Stiris nella Focide,[3] giudicato anche questo del secolo XI. Secondo gli storici specialisti di arte bizantina, quei mosaici geometrici rappresentano la diffusione de una moda artistica creatasi e affermatasi in Costantinopoli, e dalla capitale irradiatasi all'intorno nelle provincie. Si spiega in tal modo come la moda di questi mosaici pavimentali siasi estesa ad oriente di Bisanzio almeno fino a Trebisonda.[4] Per località ad occidente della capitale, come appunto Olinto, Iviron sul monte Athos,[5] i paesi della Focide ecc., ancora più di Costantinopoli dovette avere importanza già nel medioevo il centro di Tessalonica (Salonico), fucina artistica di prim'ordine, destinata a servire da mediatrice tra Costantinopoli e i paesi della penisola ellenica. E' noto infatti come Tessalonica fosse nei secoli prima del 1000 (già dal VI secolo) un centro artistico fiorente, con officine specializzate nell'arte del mosaico.[6] I mosaici parietali e absidali delle chiese bizantine di Salonicco godono di una notorietà pari alla loro importanza storica.

Mentre Tessalonica diffondeva i modelli dell'arte bizantina nel territorio più strettamente circostante, e in direzione della penisola greca (il mosaico rinvenuto ad Olinto proviene quasi sicuramente di là), la capitale Bisanzio giovavasi del suo ricco naviglio, delle posizioni militari e della preminenza politica saldamente occupata in Occidente, per diffondere si direbbe specialmente nei centri costieri dell'Adriatico, a partire dall'estuario veneto, quegli stessi modelli.[7] La

---

2. Robinson, *Excavations at Olynthus*, vol. XII, 320 ("opus alexandrinum," "Cosmati work"), tav. 262 segg.

3. Dalton, O. M., *Byzantine Art and Archaeology*, fig. 251 (= *Encicl. Ital.*, vol. XXIV, fig. a p. 85).

4. Dalton, *op. cit.*, 146.

5. *Op. cit.*, 426.

6. Diehl, Ch. et Le Tourneau, M., "Les mosaïques de Sainte Sophie de Salonique," in *Monuments Piot*, 16 (1909) 39 segg.; e degli stessi "Les mosaïques de Saint Demetrius de Salonique," *Mon. Piot*, 17 (1911) 225 segg. Vedasi inoltre Diehl — Le Tourneau — H. Saladin, *Les monuments chrétiens de Salonique*, Parigi, 1918; e Diehl, Ch., *Salonique*, ivi, 1920, *passim*.

7. L'arte bizantina cui qui ci si riferisce, è naturalmente quella del secondo periodo bizantino, cioè dei tempi gloriosi della dinastia "macedonica" (a. 865-1025).

presumibile relativa simultaneità di espressioni artistiche e di documenti artistici in regioni così distanti fra loro, non può forse aspirare a spiegazione più ragionevole e persuasiva di questa.

Ora però, se nel mondo medioevale tardo-bizantino, certe manifestazioni di arte musiva, che tanto per intenderci seguiteremo ancora per poco a chiamare "cosmatesca," assumono l'aspetto di opere ingegnose o addirittura di creazioni originali, considerate invece sullo sfondo e al paragone dei prodotti dell'arte sentuosa e multiforme fiorita e coltivata a Costantinopoli come a Tessalonica, quelle medesime manifestazioni artistiche non possono a meno di apparire e di definirsi come delle povere cose, riflessi modesti, espressioni misere e irrigidite di una civiltà artistica tanto più antica, più smagliante e più ricca.[8]

Ciò che principalmente caratterizza le espressioni di arte decorativa di cui ci stiamo interessando, si è la varia giustapposizione dei tondi, spesso disposti a raggera, riuniti dentro combinazioni variamente complicate, di fasce più o meno policrome, con andamento a treccia. Ma non è questa una novità. Anche restando rigorosamente nel campo del mosaico, il motivo ornamentale della treccia geometrica è così comune e risale a tempi così remoti, che non merita il conto di segnalarne le testimonianze. Forse più degno di studio è il processo per il quale la treccia, allargando circolarmente i suoi anelli, dà luogo all'inserzione di appositi tondi in formelle musive o in semplici dischi di marmi colorati, delle più svariate qualità. Rimane indecisa, e potrà anche sembrare oziosa, la questione se nel campo dell'antica arte decorativa sia stato il motivo della treccia a determinare la creazione del tondo, di carattere altrettanto decorativo, o sia stato il tondo a suggerire l'allacciamento con un altro mediante la treccia. Certo è che la più antica applicazione, finora nota, del motivo ornamentale della treccia e dei tondi, per quanto non ancora perfettamente uniti insieme, si riscontra negli stucchi di vòlte delle Terme Stabiane a Pompei.[9] Segue forse a non grande distanza la decorazione variata

---

8. Il magistero dell'arte musiva di origine bizantina, oltre che nei monumenti di carattere più strettamente locale, si apprezza in documenti artistici cospicui dell'Asia Minore. Così nei mosaici di Damasco: su cui vedasi E. De Lorey e M. Van Berchem, "Les mosaïques de la mosquée des Omayyades à Damas," in *Mon. Piot*, 30 (1929) 111 segg. Come qui si ricorda, i mosaicisti bizantini ai tempi di Cosroe e di Giustiniano, arrivarono sino a Ctesifonte, e fino in Sicilia nel secolo XII, al tempo dei Normanni, dando implicitamente l'impressione di una ininterrotta fioritura del'arte musiva, per tutti questi secoli, sulle rive del Bosforo.

9. Un chiaro saggio dimostrativo di codesti stucchi pompeiani trovasi riprodotto in *Encicl. Ital.*, vol. XXXI, tav. CXXIX. Non mi risulta che gli stucchi delle Terme Stabiane di Pompei, per quanto assai noti (vedasi in proposito anche Bendinelli, G., in *Rivista Architettura e arti decorative*, 1922, 97 segg.), abbiano mai dato luogo, finora, a uno studio e a un'illustrazione accurata e sistematica dell'interessante materia.

dell'ipogeo dei Pancrazi sulla Via Latina;[10] con tondi chiusi entro treccia.

Dallo stucco per decorazione di vòlte il motivo passa, forse direttamente, ai mosaici pavimentali.[11] E per quanto le testimonianze scarseggino, si può dare per certo che già nel I° secolo dell'impero venissero realizzati, in ambienti più o meno di lusso, pavimenti con decorazioni musive del tipo che veniamo studiando. Uno dei più antichi pavimenti musivi di Aquileia, con tondi o dischi intrecciati, non figurati, è giudicato appartenere allo stesso primo secolo.[12] A una fase intermedia tra il primo e il secondo secolo, cioè al periodo di passaggio dal primo al secondo secolo, ci pare possa essere ascritto il frammento di pavimento musivo di Genazzano (Roma), conservato nel Museo Nazionale Romano[13] e qui pubblicato per la prima volta (tav. 109a), risultandoci finora inedito. La decorazione musiva consisteva, qui, di sette medaglioni o clipei circolari, insieme uniti dall'incrociarsi ad andamento sinuoso, di un nastro pieghettato e di un ricco tralcio di foglie d'alloro. A parte la novità degli elementi costitutivi, lo schema geometrico cui la composizione è riducibile, è perfettamente quello in uso e noto nei mosaici "cosmateschi" (fig. 1). Ciò che aumenta il pregio di questo frammento, sono le teste superstiti racchiuse nei clipei: una testa di ridente Satirello ed una di Pan barbato. La decorazione figurata degli altri clipei è andata perduta con tutto il resto: ma non sembra potersi dubitare che nei tondi perduti si trovassero

---

10. Gli stucchi dell'ipogeo dei Pancrazi, oltre che riportati parzialmente qua e là (vedasi ad es. P. Gusman, *L'art décoratif de Rome*, tav. 85., e G. B. art. cit.), trovansi esaurientemente riprodotti in appendice al lavoro di Wadsworth, E. L., "Stucco Reliefs of the I and II Century Still Extant in Rome," *Memoirs of the American Academy*, 4 (1924), 75 segg. e tavv. XXV-XXXV. Importanti per il nostro tema le tav. XXX-XXXII. E' però da avvertire che anche di codesto gruppo di stucchi romani, considerati genericamente e in base a un criterio tradizionale, come "del periodo degli Antonini," manca una analisi stilistica convincente. Le conclusioni cronologiche della Wadsworth risultano poi tutt'altro che sicure, e scientificamente assai poco fondate. Così la celebre decorazione a stucco della Basilica (o piuttosto "mausoleo") di Porta Maggiore, appartenente ad età giulio-claudia (su di che vedasi la mia monografia in *Monumenti Antichi dei Lincei*, 31, 1927), viene datata dalla Wadsworth circa la fine dei I° secolo dell'impero, senza nessuna apparente ragione giustificativa.

11. Già in una mia comunicazione accademica ("Un mosaico dionisiaco africano") pubblicata in *Atti della Accademia delle Scienze di Torino*, 72 (1936-37) 10 segg. dell'Estr. (chiedo venia al lettore, di queste purtroppo inevitabili "autocitazioni"), si rileva come la genesi di svariati mosaici pavimentali classici possa essere rintracciata nella decorazione di vòlte e soffitti di ambienti privati (dipinti o stuccati, oppure dipinti e stuccati, come la vòlta dell'ipogeo dei Pancrazi).

12. *Notizie d. Scavi*, 1927, 275 (fig. 10). La colonia di Aquileia non potendo a meno di essere considerata diretta tributaria, nel campo artistico, della capitale Roma, almeno per la prima età imperiale, anche i suoi pavimenti musivi dovettero essere esemplati su modelli romani.

13. Paribeni, *Le Terme di Diocleziano e il Museo Naz. Romano*, 214 (n. 567). La riproduzione fotografica del mosaico mi è stata molto gentilmente favorita dal Soprintendente prof. S. Aurigemma, che qui desidero ringraziare.

Fig. 1. Ricostruzione schematica del mosaico di Genazzano.

espressi motivi e personaggi affini del repertorio o tiaso dionisiaco, con una testa di Dioniso al centro. La bontà dello stile,[14] cioè la finitezza di esecuzione dei busti superstiti, è la più solida base, se non l'unica, sulla quale possiamo fondarci per assegnare la data approssimativa del mosaico di Genazzano.

Sembra a tutta prima fare il paio con quello di Genazzano il mosaico pure rinvenuto ad Aquileia (nel 1930) e finora pubblicato molto sommariamente,[15] caratterizzato da una doppia treccia svolgentesi circolarmente dentro un apposito tondo (diam. m. 3,26). In codesto mosaico i campi delimitati dagli incroci della doppia treccia, assumono

14. Come appare evidente dalla stessa succinta descrizione redatta da G. Mancini (*Notizie d. Scavi*, 1910, 517).

15. *Notizie d. Scavi*, 1931, 134 segg.

la forma di "triangoli curvilinei di due grandezze."[16] La pura classicità del motivo è qui evidentemente venuta meno, per la ragione che il disegnatore non è più in grado di dare agli intervalli dell'intreccio quell'andamento circolare che è proprio della natura del motivo medesimo. Anzi si manifesta nella stesso disegnatore una certa ottusità di fronte ad elementari esigenze di carattere estetico: al punto che al centro esagonale della composizione trovasi inserito, in maniera del tutto impropria, un emblema quadrato (con una grossolana maschera, a quanto sembra, di Oceano). La data da assegnare all'esecuzione di questo mosaico, non può essere pertanto anteriore all'età severiana.[17]

Di età sicuramente più tarda è un certo riquadro musivo aquileiese, isolato, caratterizzato da un intreccio di elementi curvilinei puramente geometrici, a perfetto riempimento di un clipeo tondo, con quasi assoluto dispregio dei campi intermedi, triangolari, ridotti a ben povera cosa (tav. 110).[18] Ai fini della presente trattazione, i due ultimi saggi di litostrati di Aquileia costituiscono i prototipi di una categoria a parte di mosaici sviluppati nel corso del medioevo avanzato: la categoria dei mosaici a treccia con abolizione dei tondi.[19]

Quella inesauribile miniera di pavimenti musivi romani, che è il suolo di Aquileia, poi, ci ha già restituito, oltre a quelli citati, più d'un mosaico nel quale domina il motivo della treccia, e dove il posto d'onore è occupato da medaglioni con elementi ora figurati ora semplicemente geometrici. Così, materialmente al di sopra del predetto mosaico aquileiese, si rinvenne un altro mosaico, dove il motivo della treccia risulta ancora più largamente sviluppato e applicato.[20] La sostituzione della figura con un ozioso motivo geometrico a mò di riempitivo, induce a stimare come relativamente tarda l'età di quelle composizioni, tra la fine del secondo secolo e il principio del terzo. A questo secolo appunto — forse prima metà — sembra possa essere assegnato un altro mosaico aquileiese, della categoria che c'interessa:[21] dove s'incontrano tondi numerosi con inframmessi taluni emblemi quadrati; questi ultimi occupati da elementi figurativi, i tondi invece occupati da motivi geometrici dentro cerchi concentrici. I medaglioni

---

16. *Ibid.*, 135.
17. La decorazione della ricca fascia di cornice (ib., fig. 7), a grandi volute di tipo classico, parrebbe a tutta prima suggerire una datazione alquanto più antica. Ma (a parte l'incompiutezza dei dati tuttora a disposizione) la composizione del tondo e gli stessi elementi compositivi mal si conciliano con un genuino classicismo.
18. *Ibid.*, 138.
19. Vedasi più oltre, alla tav. 111, il saggio di mosaico di Pomposa.
20. *Notizie d. Scavi*, 1927, 275 seg. e tav. XXII.
21. *Ibid.*, 1922, 188.

tondi non risultano qui uniti da treccia, ma il motivo della treccia è
ben presente alla fantasia dell'artista, che se ne serve per occupare
una parte delle superfici concentriche dei tondi.

Una variante dei disegni musivi a tondi allaccciati da nastri si
osserva in un mosaico dell'Esquilino, conservato nel Museo Nazionale Romano:[22] dove i medaglioni tondi, occupati da rosette, si alternano ad ellissi risultanti dall'intersezione di archi di cerchio. Anche
questo mosaico è stato giudicato — senza che appaiano motivi per una
datazione diversa — come appartenente ai primi del secolo III. Si
appaia a questo, come dello stesso schema compositivo e della medesima età, se non un poco più antico, il mosaico di Ippona (*Hippo
Regius*), oggi Bona in Algeria,[23] con una figura allegorica di giovinetto
nel tondo centrale e otto medaglioni intorno, quattro dei quali tondi,
con maschere sceniche, e quattro ellissoidali, con supposte figure di
Stagioni.[24] Tondi ed ellissi uniti fra loro dall'intrecciarsi di due festoni
di foglie, al posto dei tradizionali due nastri.[25]

Dall'età post-severiana, con circa mezzo secolo d'intervallo, si passa
ai tempi dioclezianei con il pavimento musivo che si conserva a Roma
nel palazzo Almagià al Corso (rinvenuto sul luogo), ritenuto al più
presto, della fine del secolo terzo.[26] Tale mosaico, proveniente, come
pare, dalla locale *Domus Lucinae*, si riduce a una combinazione di elementi geometrici secondari, dove il motivo classico della treccia
appare dominante. Esso occupa infatti, in tutta la sua lunghezza, il
doppio nastro che racchiude i cerchi di varia grandezza formanti
l'ossatura della composizione, e si ripete lungo tutta la cornice
rettilinea, rettangolare o quadrata che fosse, dell'intero disegno.

Il IV secolo ci offre il mausoleo romano detto di Santa Costanza,
celebre non tanto per la sua architettura, quanto per quello che fu già
chiamato "il più bel saggio dè musaici del IV secolo in pubblici
edifici."[27] Tra i varî settori in cui risulta divisa la vòlta anulare del-
l'edificio, ciascun settore distinto da una particolare composizione geometrica, figurata o floreale, due se ne trovano [28] in cui la decorazione è
data da dischi o clipei di due grandezze diverse, alternati e uniti fra

22. *Memoirs of the American Academy in Rome*, 17 (1940) tav. 19, 1.

23. Vedasi *Opere d'arte del R. Istituto di Archeologia e Storia dell'Arte*, fasc.
V (1935), tav. V, 2.

24. Indicate come tali nel testo di A. Levi, *ibid.*, 9. I soggetti figurati del
mosaico trovansi riprodotti in *Mélanges d'Arch. et d'hist.*, 1911, tav. XXIV-
XXV (cfr. Reinach, *RPGR*, 228, 8).

25. Il medesimo intreccio a festoni di foglie, con medaglioni tondi intorno e
uno più grande al centro, caratterizza il mosaico lateranense riprodotto in *RPGR*,
226, 2.

26. *Memoirs* cit., tav. cit., n. 2.

27. Venturi, A., *Storia dell'arte italiana*, 1, 229.

28. *Ibid.*, figg. 99 e 100. Inoltre: *Riv. L'Arte*, 1904, fig. a p. 465.

loro da quel sistema a treccia di cui ci adoperiamo a seguire lo sviluppo storico. I dischi minori hanno un motivo vegetale o floreale a quattro petali, i dischi maggiori presentano figure di genietti maschili o muliebri, variamente concepiti e atteggiati. Gli ottagoni o pseudo-ottagoni (trattandosi di superfici a lati ricurvi) intermedi sono occupati da figure del mondo animale: per lo più uccelli. Il tutto su fondo bianco. Si può pacificamente attribuire il mausoleo di Santa Costanza, con i relativi mosaici, alla metà del IV secolo, rinunziando a proporre una data di poco più antica, come parrebbe suggerito da ragioni storiche, o una data più recente, per altre considerazioni.[29]

Ancora una volta poi — se vogliamo seguire la successione cronologica — dobbiamo rifarci ad Aquileia, dove il grande litostrato di Teodoro, della seconda metà del IV secolo, ci presenta medaglioni o emblemi figurati, alternati a motivi geometrici (riquadri a sezioni di cerchio), evidentemente suggeriti dai noti intrecci di nastri decorativi.[30] All'età immediatamente successiva, cioè al V secolo, si suole datare la vòlta musiva della chiesa di Casaranello, in provincia di Lecce.[31] Anche sulla vòlta di codesta piccola chiesa, di età antichissima, accade di riscontrare una certa varietà di motivi decorativi, eseguiti nella tecnica del mosaico, come si osserva in Santa Costanza. Fra tali motivi si nota quello che possiamo dire classico, dell'intreccio di due nastri — come si esprime lo Haseloff — o meglio forse, quello

---

29. Se infatti la data della costruzione del mausoleo dovesse essere compresa tra gli anni 337 e 351 (v. Toesca, *Storia dell'arte italiana*, 1, nota 57 a p. 143), la decorazione musiva non potrebbe a meno di venire collocata nel tempo alquanto più tardi. Mentre se dovessimo giudicare esclusivamente dallo stile, la stessa decorazione potrebbe essere ascritta alla prima metà del secolo; tanto più che vi è chi, come T. Rivoira (*Architettura romana*, 287), assegna al mausoleo una data anteriore al 350 (anzi circa il 325). Quest'ultima sembra veramente la più verisimile.

30. Prima bibliografia sul grande litostrato di Aquileia, in Toesca, *op. cit.*, v. cit., n. 61 a p. 78. Inoltre v. G. Brusin, *Aquileia* (Guida), Udine, 1929, p. 263 segg. e figg. 201 e 202 (per il motivo della treccia semplice). Nella fig. 201 è facile riconoscere lo schema decorativo, già realizzato negli stucchi delle Terme Stabiane, dei medaglioni non *inseriti*, ma *sovrapposti* all'intreccio dei nastri (ridotti qui a semplici elementi lineari).—Insieme al litostrato di Aquileia sembra opportuno ricordare il mosaico di Grado, edito in *Notizie d. Scavi*, 1920 (p. 11): dove pur senza l'intervento della treccia, si osserva un sistema di tondi (in numero di otto) collocati a raggera intorno a uno più grande, come nel mosaico di Olinto. Con l'avvertenza importante che nessuno dei tondi è monocromo, poiché ciascuno porta inserito o un motivo geometrico (svastica) o un motivo floreale o come nella maggior parte dei casi, una scritta dedicatoria. Il che sarebbe sufficiente ad attestare la maggiore antichità del mosaico di Grado (fine VI secolo) rispetto al mosaico di Olinto. Su Aquileia vedasi inoltre A. Calderini, *Aquileia* (Milano, 1930).

31. Haseloff, A., in *Bollettino d'Arte*, 1907, n. 12, 22 segg. ("Gasaranello .... frazione del paese di Casarano, situata sulle falde delle Murgie Salentine, sulla strada che conduce da Gallipoli al Capo di Leuca".) Ib. (mosaici della vòlta del braccio orientale della chiesa) "Il compartimento mediano è coperto da un ornamento a squame, i due laterali sono decorati da due nastri.... L'andamento dei nastri forma dei cerchi grandi e piccoli, nei quali sono diverse rappresentazioni."

dei clipei o dischi tenuti insieme a mezzo di nastri intrecciati. I dischi sono occupati da motivi figurati animalistici e vegetali ("uccelli acquatici, una lepre, un grappolo d'uva"). Anche la decorazione musiva della piccola, modesta e quasi ignorata chiesa di Casaranello può essere stata ispirata da modelli romani, ed eseguita da artefici venuti da Roma: per quanto la posizione geografica, sulla linea di displuvio tra Ionio e Adriatico, possa indurre l'ipotesi di interventi diretti da parte di artefici bizantini.

Tale ultima ipotesi però non risulta altrettanto giustificabile allorchè dall'estrema punta meridionale della penisola si risalga, coi mosaici del palazzo di Teodorico, fino a Ravenna.[32] E' certo che i pavimenti musivi del palazzo, ritornati alla luce in seguito agli scavi condotti dal 1908 al 1914, non possano a meno di appartenere ai primi lustri del VI secolo (estremo termine *ante quem* il 526, anno della morte di Teodorico). In mezzo al materiale musivo colà rinvenuto, che per quanto cospicuo, non è che una piccola parte di quello originale, si rileva il notevole sviluppo che nella varietà delle composizioni geometriche (non dimenticando la presenza di riquadri musivi figurati) ha qui ricevuto il motivo classico della treccia e dei tondi. Motivo che nello scompartimento centrale del portico *A* risulta riccamente sviluppato, con andamento ingegnoso quanto nuovo per noi, nei due sensi, verticale e orizzontale (o ad angolo retto), con tondi di due diverse grandezze, occupati da rosette, mentre gli intervalli sono occupati da "nodi di Salomone" (tav. 109b). In altra stanza *(Q)* lo stesso motivo ritornava opportunamente variato, dominando tutta la sala. In altri ambienti (esedre contrapposte della sala tricliniare e sala *D*) il motivo della treccia con tondi era utilizzato come bordura od orlatura di altre composizioni geometriche. Tutto considerato, riconoscendo la dovuta importanza anche a spunti decorativi minori, con riferimento alla treccia semplice, si può dire che in tutta la serie dei mosaici del palazzo, la classica treccia, con tondi e senza, costituisca il motivo fondamentale d'ispirazione. Il che è quanto dire che se non una unica mente direttrice, un omogeneo gruppo di mosaicisti presiedette e attese alla realizzazione dei pavimenti d'arte del palazzo imperiale.[33]

---

32. Naturalmente si considera, qui, non il problema storico generale delle origini e vicende dell'arte musiva ravennate, come arte in concorrenza con la pittura, ma soltanto lo sviluppo storico di un motivo decorativo. In quanto a Ravenna, oltre a citare la fondamentale relazione di G. Ghirardini, "Gli scavi del palazzo di Teodorico a Ravenna," in *Monumenti antichi dei Lincei*, 25, fasc. 2º (1918), non mancheremo di ricordare il noto libro di G. Galassi, *Roma o Bisanzio* (Roma, Libreria dello Stato, a. VIII), avvertendo che del materiale musivo tornato alla luce da quegli scavi, è nel volume del Galassi solo un breve accenno a pag. 118 (a commento delle riproduzioni fotografiche ivi riportate alle tavv. CVIII-CX).

33. Gli stessi, identici motivi geometrici si trovano applicati in un pavimento

A parte il problema del centro d'irradiazione — problema per se stesso spinoso — importa rilevare che il motivo geometrico dei clipei uniti da treccia si è venuto, coll'andar del tempo, nobilitando: nel senso che a partire almeno dall'età costantiniana, esso risulta esteso, dalla decorazione di pavimenti, a quella di vòlte, e verisimilmente, in altri casi, anche di pareti.[34] Al punto, però, al quale siamo arrivati, la forza creativa e propulsiva di Roma nel campo dell'arte è venuta scemando, per le mutate condizioni politiche ed economiche del mondo antico. Bisanzio, l'imperiale Bisanzio, ha preso il posto di Roma, e a Bisanzio occorre d'ora innanzi far capo per rintracciare il punto di partenza delle nuove correnti artistiche. E poichè — come pare, nel VII secolo — il motivo ornamentale dei clipei e della treccia lo si vede ricomparire, ad esempio, nella decorazione musiva della chiesa del Calvario a Gerusalemme,[35] appare ormai ovvio che i cartoni preparatorî di quei mosaici dovettero essere confezionati in Oriente, da pittori decoratori bizantini, i quali venivano sviluppando gli insegnamenti di una tradizione artistica che risaliva, in ultima analisi, a maestri romani, cioè a elementi nel campo artistico, più legittimamente rappresentativi del mondo romano.

In confronto della sfarzosa arte bizantina raggiante dalla corte imperiale, e anche della stessa arte ravennate, che seguitava a brillare come di luce riflessa, tra il VII e il X secolo Roma non contava già quasi più che per la suggestione del suo passato. Ma era un passato che affascinava le menti e induceva gerarchie ecclesiastiche e ordini religiosi a incoraggiare un'attività artistica locale; che per quanto in tono minore, non cessava, anche nei secoli più oscuri, di dare luogo a manifestazioni a volte di una certa importanza.[36] Anche

---

musivo rinvenuto presso la chiesa di S. Apollinare in Classe (Toesca, *op. cit.*, v. c., fig. 185; Galassi, *op. cit.*, tav. CVI, e citaz. a pag. 120. Il mosaico non e però da ritenere del secolo V, come ritiene il Galassi, ma almeno di un secolo posteriore.

34. Corrispondono, in fondo, a decorazioni parietali i rivestimenti "cosmateschi" di cattedre vescovili, di pulpiti e simili (vedasi per una rapida e sommaria informazione: U. Oietti e L. Dami, *Atlante per la storia dell'arte italiana*, 93 seg.), nonchè di tombe monumentali (ib., p. 116, tomba del card. Di Braye in S. Domenico di Orvieto), e perfino di facciate di chiese (S. Pietro di Spoleto) sempre per i secoli XII e XIII. A questi saggi di arte decorativa si può associare la composizione geometrica, eseguita in pittura, dal Pinturicchio o da qualche suo aiuto, su una parete di sala dell'Appartamento Borgia in Vaticano (tav. a colori in *Encicl. Ital.*, XXIX, alla p. 764): eloquente dimostrazione della relativa popolarità che quello stile decorativo e quei motivi decorativi godevano ancora in pieno Rinascimento. E ciò senza dimenticare il pavimento cosmatesco, di ottima conservazione, della Cappella Sistina.

35. Come si vede nell'intradosso di un arco della chiesa (v. *Encicl. Ital.*, 25, tav. IX; da Creswell, K. R. C., *Early Muslim Architecture*, Oxford 1932). Vedasi anche il mosaico di Gerusalemme, trasferito al Museo di Costantinopoli, in Reinach, *RPGR*, p. 203, n. 4 e 7.

36. Opere poco note di mosaico e di pittura, di questo periodo, sono ricordate da G. Galassi, in *op. cit.*, pag. 204 segg.

in codeste opere di bassi tempi gli artisti, per quanto di modesta
levatura, non mancarono di ispirarsi a modelli del classico passato,
lasciando qua e là tracce più o meno evidenti delle loro fonti d'ispirazione. Così è delle pitture protoromaniche (del X secolo) conservatesi
sulle pareti del tempio della Fortuna Virile al Foro Boario,[37] cioè
della chiesa medioevale di S. Maria Egiziaca. Su queste pitture (con
i fatti della Vergine e degli Apostoli) i soggetti sono inquadrati
dentro cornici a motivi geometrici i quali rivelano colla massima
evidenza la loro derivazione dall'antico. La cornice superiore e
inferiore dei quadri è data da un tipo di treccia a perline, con delimitazione di cerchi o clipei alternati di due grandezze. I clipei maggiori
contengono rosette o teste umane di fattura squisitamente miniaturi-
stica. Il motivo genuinamente romano classico della treccia, dunque,
seguitava ad imporsi anche in Occidente, sempre però sotto la giusti-
ficazione pratica dell'inquadramento d'immagini (*imagines clipea-
tae*). [37a]

Non si dubita che estendendo e approfondendo le ricerche sarebbe
possibile dare della storia dei mosaici precosmateschi una documenta-
zione più nutrita e meno lacunosa della presente. Ma crediamo pure
che ciò nulla di sostanziale aggiungerebbe all'attuale dimostrazione
e alle prossime logiche conclusioni. Paragonando ora i rivestimenti
musivi precosmateschi di Olinto e di altri paesi del mondo orientale,
con i saggi classici e classicistici passati in rassegna, apparirà evidente la parentela, e con questa appariranno evidenti i rapporti di
derivazione intercedenti tra gli uni e gli altri. Nei mosaici tardo-
medioevali detti "cosmateschi," viene ripreso e applicato largamente
il motivo della treccia,[38] mentre al posto del clipeo variamente figurato
e adorno, a motivi animali, vegetali o anche semplicemente geometrici,
si sostituisce il disco in marmo di colore. L'opera del mosaicista, per
economia di tempo e di lavoro, risulta così sostituita quasi integral-
mente dall'intervento del marmorario; il quale da un semplice frammento o tamburo di colonna è in grado di ricavare, per mezzo della

---

37. Muñoz, A., *I restauri del tempio della Fortuna Virile* (Roma, 1925), e G.
Galassi, *op. cit.*, pag. 234 seg., e figg. 125-127.

37a. E' interessante notare come anche in età di profonda decadenza, quale si
ritiene essere nell'Italia settentrionale il secolo IX, si confezionassero in Venezia
pavimenti musivi con disegni a treccia e con emblemi di fattura che si può dire
senz'altro primitiva (a tessere bianche e nere): come si vede nella citata op. di
G. Galassi, tav. CXXX e seg. Malgrado il carattere imbarbarito di quei disegni
— di derivazione classica — appare tuttavia chiaro come sia estranea alla mente
del mosaicista l'idea di sostituire il classico emblema, ornamentale o figurato, con
una macchia di colore, come si riduce a essere il tondo di marmo, al posto del
l'emblema.

38. Buoni saggi fotografici di mosaici medioevali italiana, in *Encicl. Italiana*,
24, tav. XIII segg. Vedasi inoltre Salmi, M., *La Badia di Pomposa* (Roma, 1936),
tav. X segg.

sega, un certo numero di dischi di dimensioni tutti uguali, da utilizzare per rivestimento di una vasta superficie. Un certo impiego di clipei o dischi marmorei lisci si osserva già nella decorazione parietale di monumenti bizantini del VI secolo, come la chiesa di S. Vitale di Ravenna e la stessa S. Sofia di Costantinopoli. Ma si tratta lì di soli dischi isolati, e non a gruppi.[39] La sostituzione del marmorario al mosaicista, con la conseguente riduzione della treccia classica a rigidi schemi geometrici, deve essere avvenuta a poco a poco, e dovrebbe quindi essersi affermata, insieme con l'aggruppamento a figura stellare di clipei di varia grandezza, sul declinare del millennio, ad opera di artefici di Bisanzio. E' nota infatti la predilezione che costoro — pittori e mosaicisti — dimostrano per il clipeo tondo figurato, tanto da inserirlo in tutte le loro composizioni, mostrando nello stesso tempo di conoscere per tradizione il clipeo marmoreo monocromo, da collocare al posto del clipeo figurato o comunque policromo. Nel X^0 secolo appunto fiorisce in Costantinopoli la gloriosa dinastia macedone, sotto la quale la cultura e l'arte bizantina prendono tanto sviluppo. Una volta realizzato, tale nuovo tipo di decorazione si diffonde sempre più verso occidente (Tessalonica, Macedonia, Grecia, bacino adriatico, Roma), e nello stesso tempo in paesi più orientali (Asia Minore e Siria, fino in Palestina). Quindi avviene di riscontrare il fenomeno di una approssimativa simultaneità di manifestazioni artistiche dello stesso genere o stile, in oriente e in occidente. Il pavimento, o meglio "emblema musivo", della chiesetta di S. Nicola di Olinto, può essere considerato pressochè coevo dei più antichi pavimenti musivi "cosmateschi" di Roma e del Lazio in genere, giunti fino a noi;[40] senza che dagli uni agli altri vi sia luogo di rilevare alcun altro rapporto, se non quello di una semplice affinità formale.[41]

---

39. Dischi di forma rotonda od ottagonale, a colore scuro su fondo chiaro, si trovano già applicati, dipinti, sulle pareti di ambienti pompeiani (*lararia*, banchi di *thermopolia*): probabile sopravvivenza di elementi del primo stile pittorico decorativo, detto "d'incrostazione."

40. Manca un inventario di codesti mosaici medioevali tuttora conservati. Forse i più interessanti mosaici pavimentali, del tipo di cui si tratta, erano però quelli che andarono perduti con la demolizione della più antica Basilica di S. Pietro in Roma.

41. Fuori del Lazio è da ricordare come ai primi decenni del secolo XI (a. 1026) venga attribuita l'esecuzione del litostrato di Pomposa (Galassi, G., *op. cit.*, figg. 156 e 157 a pag. 261, e nota n. 13 a pag. 301; Salmi, M., *op. cit.*, tav. IX segg.) Ricorre qui non soltanto la treccia multipla (come nel caso ora accennato), ma anche la treccia semplice nella composizione stellare più schematica: tondo più grande al centro e quattro tondi minori in corrispondenza degli angoli del quadrato in cui la composizione stellare si iscrive. La decorazione geometrica a bianco e nero, realizzata sia pure a semplici triangoli e rombi, si distende per tutta la superficie dei clipei. Ritenuto che il litostrato di Pomposa si debba a maestranze ravennati sotto l'influenza dell'arte bizantina del secondo periodo ("arte deuterobizantina"), il litostrato medesimo è la prova che lo schema del motivo a mosaico, qui detto "geometrico-bizantino", era stato già introdotto in Italia. Gli artefici ravennati però si astenevano dall'accettarlo di peso, rifiutandosi di sostituire la raffinata

Viene opportuno a questo punto, di richiamare la tradizione vasa-
riana delle origini greche — cioè bizantine — della pittura medioevale
italiana. "I Greci che Vasari poneva alle origini della pittura italiana
del secolo XIII — scrive Charles Diehl — non sono affatto degli
esseri mitici,"[42] ma reali, come se ne hanno le prove. Soltanto è da
aggiungere che la presenza di questi artisti forestieri in Italia risale
un pò più indietro del secolo XIII; e che non si tratta soltanto di
pittori, ma di artisti decoratori in genere. Specialmente poi una
categoria di artisti — quella piuttosto umile dei marmorari — seppe,
malgrado la modesta levatura, compiere opera così efficace di pene-
trazione, da esercitare una profonda influenza sull'arte decorativa
occidentale dei secoli successivi.

Indipendentemente da tutto questo, cioè dallo sviluppo delle vicende
storiche, lo schema geometrico dei clipei uniti insieme da treccia,
sembra essere originario di Roma antica, di Roma imperiale, le sue
prime affermazioni trovandosi sul suolo classico di Roma e del Lazio,
con qualche riferimento alla non meno classica Campania; in modo
che il suo riapparire in Italia, dopo l'oscura parentesi protomedioevale,
si potrebbe considerare un ritorno alle origini. Così come in certo
modo, un ritorno alle origini classiche sono la stessa pittura bizantina
in Italia, e tante altre manifestazioni d'arte, in mancanza delle quali
la civiltà bizantina perderebbe, agli occhi degli occidentali, gran parte
della sua riconosciuta importanza.

Tutto ciò vale dal punto di vista strettamente scientifico. Da un
altro punto di vista, scientifico-pratico, dopo tutto quanto siamo venuti
osservando e riconoscendo, apparirà più che mai evidente il carattere
affatto convenzionale e provvisorio, della denominazione di "cosmatesco" assegnata allo stile di certe composizioni geometriche decorative
tarde, specialmente in territorio orientale. I Cosmati non rappresen-

---

opera del mosaicista col grossolano ripiego dei dischi di marmo pieni, piuttosto
confacente alla tecnica di modesti artefici marmorarî.

Tutto ciò appare confermato da quanto già si conosce in materia. Il citato
mosaico pavimentale di Classe (v. nota 33), attribuibile al VI secolo, presenta,
sia nella treccia della cornice, sia nei riquadri interni, dei motici che per potersi
classificare nel repertorio della produzione artistica "cosmatesca" non avrebbero
bisogno — come a tutta prima parrebbe — che di essere eseguiti un poco più in
grande. In realtà, però, chi ben guardi, il disco o clipeo centrale monocromo, che
è ciò che costituisce il nucleo del motivo di stile cosmatesco, non si trova neanche
lì: poiché o risulta ripartito in settori, o viene poco meno che annullato e, per
così dire, sbriciolato, in un sistema di cerchi concentrici. In entrambi i casi il
mosaicista si guarda, per la dignità della sua arte, dal compiere opera di semplice
marmorario.

42. *Manuel d'art byzantin*, II[2], p. 717 seg. L'affermazione del Diehl non è da
accettare senza limitazioni, come quelle poste da Galassi, il quale (*op. cit.*, pag.
283) accenna ad "importazioni" artistiche, anzi pittoriche, effettuate "alla vigilia
di Giotto." Nè sembra difficile, su questa linea, che possa trovarsi un punto
d'intesa tra "bizantinisti" e "occidentalisti."

tano ormai evidentemente, che la fase di estrema decadenza di un indirizzo artistico, il quale ha alle sue spalle secoli di gloria. Necessita quindi oggi, in sede di terminologia artistica, ricorrere a una diversa denominazione, la quale possa ugualmente essere accettabile per casi affini nella illustrazione di opere musive, in tutti i paesi ad oriente e ad occidente dell'Adriatico e dell'Egeo. Tale denominazione che qui ci permettiamo di proporre, sarebbe quella di "stile geometrico-bizantino"; con la quale denominazione sarebbero indicate chiaramente le caratteristiche formali insieme e quelle geografiche di codesto stile, e si accentuerebbe nello stesso tempo la esatta genesi storica dello stile decorativo diffuso in Italia non soltanto dai Cosmati, ma anche dai Vassalletti, e da chissà quante altre famiglie, più o meno contemporanee, di umili e sconosciuti marmorari.[43]

Non è possibile, allo stato dei fatti, entrare in particolari a proposito delle maestranze che nell'Italia preromanica ebbero il merito di ridestare e di trasmettersi, di generazione in generazione, l'amore dell'arte insieme ai segreti della tecnica musiva. In tanta incertezza di elementi, però, considerando la ricca e continuata produzione di litostrati d'arte nella regione veneto-ravennate specialmente, dai mosaici di Aquileia, Grado e Parenzo, fino a quelli di Ravenna, Venezia e Pomposa, potrebbe farsi strada l'ipotesi che accanto ai mosaicisti venuti da Costantinopoli, riprendessero vigore maestranze occidentali, di origine aquileiese. In ragione del vasto materiale musivo che Aquileia tuttora ci conserva[44] nessun altro ambiente potrebbe essere concepito come più indicato per la formazione sia pure in territorio ravennate, di una "scuola" protomedioevale di arte musiva. Se poniamo a confronto il quadretto aquileiese, di supponibile età severiana tarda, o post-severiana, riprodotto alla tav. 110, con l'altro quadretto musivo del litostrato di Pomposa, riprodotto alla tav. 111, non si potrà a meno di concludere per l'identità, come è già stato rilevato e riconosciuto,[45] del motivo geometrico fondamentale. Motivo sviluppato da una parte, con ricchezza di fantasia e perfetta padronanza di mezzi tecnici; dall'altra semplificato e scarnito, schematizzato ed impoverito al punto da poter essere giudicato lo scheletro di ciò che era prima.

E' questo, in sintesi, il processo che subiscono le forme disegnative in genere, nel loro passaggio dall'età classica all'età medioevale:

43. Lo stesso nome di battesimo "Cosma" è di tipo così spiccatamente bizantino, da offrire buona ansa alla tesi della provenienza dall'oriente — o della prima formazione in oriente — di certe famiglie di artefici marmorarî, divenute così attive e ricercate in territorio italiano.

44. Si vedano le relazioni di G. Brusin sopra cit., e le altre dello stesso, in *Notizie d. Scavi passim*, ai luoghi cit., e 1947, pag. 1 segg.

45. Salmi, M., *op. cit.*, pag. 132 segg.

processo che dà origine appunto allo stile che qui si propone di de-
nominare "geometrico-bizantino." Il che non ci può vietare di riconoscere che mosaicisti di Aquileia si dividerebbero con altri, non meno
anonimi, di Costantinopoli, il vanto di questo primo e prematuro
rinascimento, in Italia, di forme artistiche originarie di Roma imperiale.

MEMBERS OF THE SPONSORING COMMITTEE

John Alexander

James Allen Cabaniss

William B. Dinsmoor

Glanville Downey

A. D. Fraser

George M. A. Hanfmann

Hugh Hencken

Ernest Highbarger

Leicester Holland

Richard H. Howland

Harald Ingholt

L. W. Kosmopoulos

Herbert Lipscomb

Rensselaer W. Lee

Stephen M. Luce

William McDermott

William A. McDonald

Emile Malakis

George E. Mylonas

James W. Poultney

Gisela M. A. Richter

C. A. Robinson, Jr.

Gorham Stevens

Mary H. Swindler

Helen Tanzer

Albert Van Buren

Saul Weinberg

William H. Willis

Constantine G. Yavis

John Young

DONORS

Anonymous
† George H. Allen
Mary E. Armstrong
Walter B. Agard
Anatolia College
W. J. Battle
Paul V. C. Baur
Benjamin A. Beck
Edith A. Beck
Julia Bentley
Harvey C. Bickell
Clarence P. Bill
Edwin M. Blake
Jacob Blaustein
George O. Blome
W. Bourne
Johnston A. Bowman
Mrs. Louise W. Braff
Dericksen M. Brinkerhoff
Mrs. A. E. Brown
Carl D. Buck
William H. Buckler
J. Allen Cabaniss
Joseph Callaway
Lillian C. Canfield
W. Calvin Chesnut
Alex G. Christie
Marcus W. Collins
Elizabeth Conn
John Coolidge
R. F. Cooper
George W. Corner
Cornelia C. Coulter
Molley B. T. Coyle
Irene J. Crabb
Irene M. Cudlipp
Mrs. Don DaCosta
Albert L. Dart
Mrs. Anne M. Davis
Esther De Berg
Alice Diggs
George C. Doub
John B. Edwards
Mrs. Mary Ross Ellingson
Elizabeth Faulkner
Floyd V. Filson
John H. Finley
Benjamin Fitzpatrick

A. D. Fraser
Marvin W. Friedman
Richard E. Fuller
Lady Mabel M. Gabriel
Edward Gans
Leslie N. Gay
Dem. Georgakas
Tom L. Gibson
Mrs. John M. Gilchrist
Miss Hetty Goldman
Mrs. Henrietta S. Gray
Kent Roberts Greenfield
Mrs. Sarah James Gregory
G. H. Grosvenor
Mrs. Elise F. Gumse
Clayton M. Hall
George M. A. Hanfmann
Hazel D. Hansen
Lewis G. Harriman
Raymond D. Havens
Irene R. Hays
Ella S. Hitchcock
Clark Hopkins
Howard University
Archer M. Huntington
Lucy Hutchins
Franklin P. Johnson
William S. Kellner
Roland G. Kent
Mrs. Betty Washburn King
Robert S. Kinsey
W. C. Kirk, Jr.
William C. Korfmacher
Mrs. Alice Walker Kosmopoulos
Franklin B. Krauss
H. C. Lancaster
Mrs. Emma G. Lane
Lillian B. Lawler
Warren H. Lewis
Donald M. Liddell, Jr.
Milton M. Lilien
Thomas O. Mabbott
David I. Macht
Lincoln MacVeagh
Emile Malakis
Gladys Martin
M. Estelle Martin
Johannes Mattern

Florence St. Mayo
Eugene S. McCartney
William C. McDermott
G. H. McFadden
Arthur P. McKinlay
Millard Meiss
Robert G. Merrick
Ulrich Middeldorf
M. V. B. Miller
Mrs. India E. Minshall
C. R. Morey
Francis Murnaghan
George E. Mylonas
Mrs. Edward T. Newell
Eva May Newman
William A. Nitze
Elizabeth C. G. Packard
Charles W. Peppler
James Posey
James W. Poultney
W. Kendrick Pritchett
Mrs. W. Karl Rechfeld
Mary B. Rheude
Richard L. Rianhard
Bessie E. Richardson
Wm. Robbins Ridington
Edward W. Robbins
C. A. Robinson, Jr.
Florence H. Robinson
Helen Sahagian
Katherine Scarborough
Mrs. Isabel W. Schmeisser
Ida Sharogrodsky

L. R. Shero
John R. Sherwood
Emily L. Shields
Elizabeth I. Shoemaker
Joseph T. Singewald, Jr.
Mrs. Gertrude E. Slaughter
Leslie F. Smith
Leslie W. Smith
Mary A. Sollman
Genevieve Souther
Bessie C. Stern
R. S. Stites
Sibyl Stonecipher
Carl B. Swisher
Helen H. Tanzer
Grace H. Turnbull
Eleanor H. Turnbull
Alexander Turyn
A. Morris Tyson
Laura B. Voelkel
Helmut von Erffa
Walters Art Gallery
Evelyn Lee Way
Carl Weeks
Mrs. M. Westington
Mrs. William Wherry
William H. Willis.
J. Scott Willock
Miss Lillian M. Wilson
Emmett R. Wootton
Constantine G. Yavis
C. A. Yeo
Mrs. C. M. Kurrelmeyer Zintl

Special acknowledgment should be made of the generous gift of Anonymous which made possible the publication of many articles in German.

LIST OF SUBSCRIBERS

Walter R. Agard
Alabama, University of
W. F. Albright
Christine Alexander
John A. Alexander
Walter Allen, Jr.
American Academy, Rome
American School of Clasical Studies, Athens
B. Aratowski
Amsterdam University
Axel Boethius
Oscar Broneer
Mrs. A. E. Brown
Brown University
J. Allen Cabaniss
Calvin College
Howard Comfort
Don Da Costa
Lloyd W. Daly
Esther De Berg
William B. Dinsmoor
A. P. Dorjahn
Glanville Downey
Duke University
Ilona Ellinger
Henry Field
Harold N. Fowler
Hetty Goldman
J. Walter Graham
George M. A. Hanfmann
Hazel D. Hansen
Harvard College
R. D. Havens
E. L. Highbarger
Leicester B. Holland
Richard H. Howland
Lucy Hutchins
Harald Ingholt
John H. Kent

R. G. Kent
A. L. W. Kosmopoulos
J. A. O. Larsen
Lillian B. Lawler
Rensselaer W. Lee
D. M. Liddell, Jr.
H. C. Lipscomb
Louis E. Lord
Stephen B. Luce
Lyon University
T. O. Mabbott
Kemp Malone
S. D. Markman
W. B. McDaniel
William C. McDermott
William A. McDonald
George H. McFadden
A. P. McKinlay
Panos P. Morphos
Newberry Library
Mrs. Edward T. Newell
University of New Mexico
Eva M. Newnan
New York Public Library
C. Milton Page
Parker & Son
Pennsylvania, University of
Pittsburgh-Xenia Theological Seminary
Helen Pope
J. W. Poultney
Enoch Pratt Library
Princeton University
A. E. Raubitschek
Doris Raymond
Marcel Renard
Rice Institute
Gisela M. A. Richter
D. S. Robertson
C. A. Robinson, Jr.

Saint Louis University
W. T. Semple
Henri Seyrig
John and Fern R. Shapley
L. R. Shero
Emily L. Shields
E. W. Schweigert
R. S. Stites
E. G. Suhr
Mary H. Swindler
Helen H. Tanzer
Temple University,
    Sullivan Memorial Library
Texas Technological College
A. D. Trendall

Tulane University
B. L. Ullman
Uppsala University
A. W. Van Buren
Virginia, University of
Laura B. Voelkel
Walters Art Gallery
Washington University
West Virginia University
Lois V. Williams
William H. Willis
Harold R. Willoughby
Constantine G. Yavis
John H. Young
H. C. Youtie

INDEX

Doris Raymond
University of Mississippi

PLATE 1

a. Sling bullets from Olynthus.

CENTIMETRES
INCHES

b. Clay sling bullets from Hassuna. "Neolithic phase."

c. Front and side views of Bull's Head "O" as restored.

PLATE 2

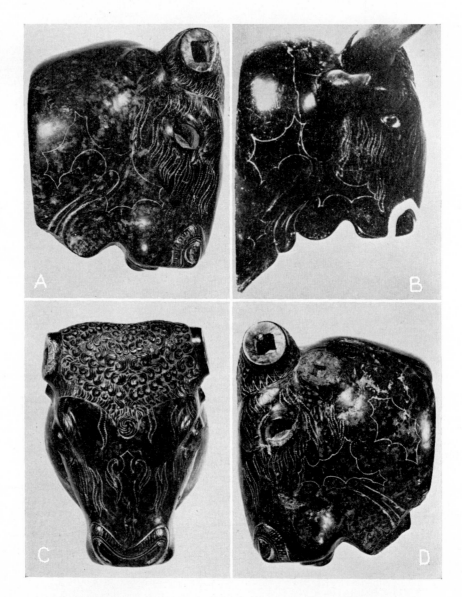

A, C, D. The Olive Bull's head (= O) ; B, the head from Knossos (= K).

PLATE 3

a. Ossuary at Agios Kosmas.

b. Round pit beyond grave 11.

c, d. An early Helladic kitchen utensil.

PLATE 4

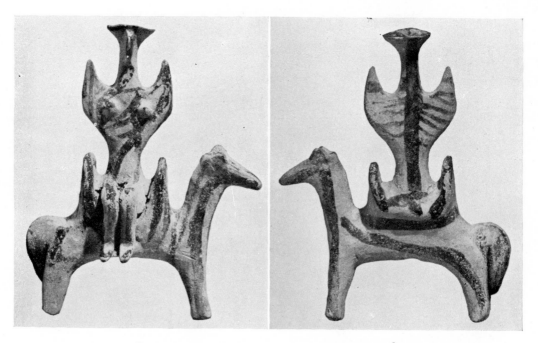

a   b

a, b. Terra cotta figurine of a female figure on horse back.

c. Terra cotta figurine of a rider.

d. Tripod of stone with a bull's head.

c   d

Objects from a grave at Charvati in Attica.
(Collection Mme. Elena A. Stathatos.)

PLATE 5

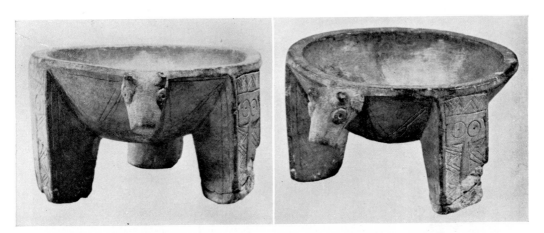

a

Stone tripod from the grave at Charvati in Attica.
(Collection Mme. Elena A. Stathatos.)

1   2   3

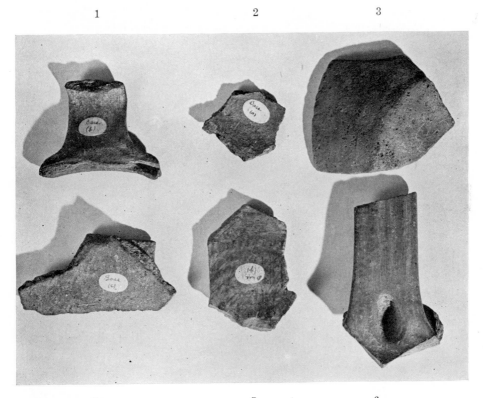

4   5   6

b. Sherds found below the archaic basis of the Temple of Artemis.

PLATE 6

a   b

a. Stone axes from Sardis in the Sturge Collection of the British Museum.

b. Sherds found below the archaic basis of the Temple of Artemis.

c

c. Heads from an Assyrian relief, Paris.

d. Side view of the door-figure from Boghazköy.

d

PLATE 7

a   b
a. Part of the Gudea stele in Berlin.
b. Relief of the Hammurabi stele.

c   d
c. Detail (Head) of the door-figure from Boghazköy.
d. Heads from the relief of the Magi from Ergili (now in Istanbul).

PLATE 8

a

b   c

Egyptian and Cypriot figured-capitals.

PLATE 9

a

b

c

d

e

f

Roman, Egyptian, and Cypriot figured-capitals.

PLATE 10

a

b

c

d

a, b. c. Cypriot and Roman figured-capitals.
d. Double capital in the Egyptian Museum at Florence.

PLATE 11

a b

a. Building model from the Argive Heraeum after Müller.
b. Building model from the Argive Heraeum after Oikonomos.

c d

c. Building model from the Argive Heraeum after Oikonomos.
d. Building model from Perachora after Payne.

PLATE 12

a. Building model from Perachora.

b. Blocks between the pedestal of the Promachos and the North Wall of the Acropolis.

c. Block at the South end of the long flight of steps to the West of the Parthenon.

PLATE 13

a. The Sicyonian Treasury in Olympia.

b. Square altar over round altar at Olympia.

PLATE 14

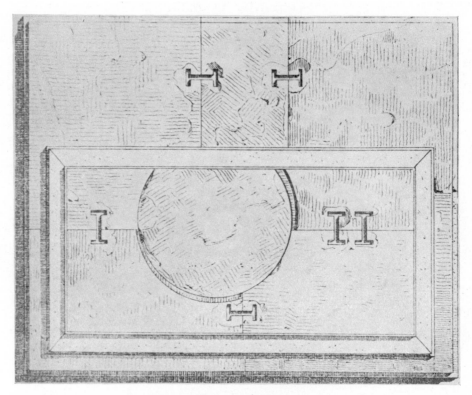

a. Plan of older round altar at Olympia.

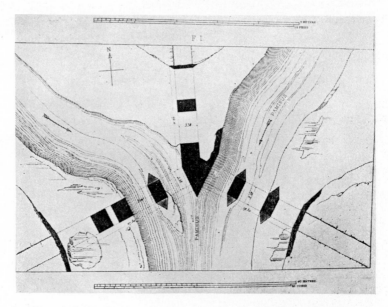

b. Plan of the Bridge over the Mavrozoumenos River. (After Blouet.)

PLATE 15

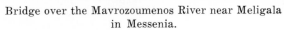

Bridge over the Mavrozoumenos River near Meligala
in Messenia.

A. The southwest and southeast arms from the south.

B. Roadway on the northern arm.

C. Angle of the northern and southwestern arms.

D. The southeastern arm.

E. Greek masonry of the central pier.

F. Side channel in southwestern arm.

G. Vaulting in the southwestern arm.

PLATE 16

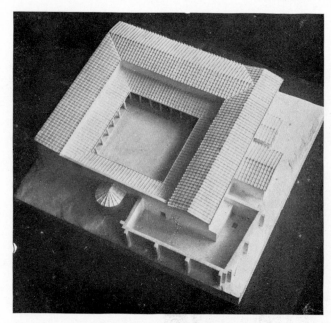

a. The Leonteion at Calydon. Model E. D.

b. The site of Heroon II in the "Kallirrhöe" Valley, as seen
from the terrace of the Temple of Artemis.

PLATE 17

a. Heroon II. Flag-stones above the tomb chamber.

b. Chamber in a tumulus at Mangalia in Dobrudža.
c. The vault in the Mangalia tomb chamber.

PLATE 18

a. A two-storeyed Heroon at Delphi.
(The Museum may be seen in the background.)

b. The vault in the innermost hypogaeum of the
Heroon at the Museum of Delphi.

PLATE 19

a. The site of "Dusae ad Olympum." View from the North.

b. Brickwork with the gate on the South side of the citadel. View from inside.

PLATE 20

c. The Southern wall with adjoining door arch.

d. The door arch on the Southern Wall.

PLATE 21

Λ ΑΟΓ Τ ΛΓΙ
ΓΙΚΥΡΙΛ-ΜΛ ΙΤΟ/
ΚΡΑΤΟΡΙΚΑΙϹΑΡΑ
ΓΟΥΑΛΔΙΟΚΛΗΤΙΑΝΟΥϹΕΒ/

ΚΑΙΜΑΡ ΑΥΡ ΟΥΑΛΕΡΙΟϹ

ΜΑΞΙΜΙΑΝΟϹ

ΛΟΝΙΚΕΩΗΠΟΛΙϹ

ΚΑΙΤΟΙϹΕΠΙΦΑΝΕϹΤΑ
ΤΟΙϹΗΜΩΝΚΑϹΑΡϹΙΝ
ΦΛΑΒΑΙΩΟΥΑΛΕΡΙ
ΩΚΩϹϹΤΑΝΤΙΩ
ΚΓΑΛΕΡΙΩΟΥΑΛΕΡΙΩ
ΜΑΞΙΜΙΑΝΩΟΥΑΛΕΡΙΩ
ϹΕΒΑϹΤΟΙϹΚΑΙΦΛ
ϹΥΜΚϹΕΒΗΡΙΚΑΙΓΑΛ
ΦΛΝΕϹΤΑΞΙΜΙΝΕΠΙ
ϹΑΡϹΙΝΗΘΕϹϹΑΛΟ
ΚΕΙΚΕΩΝΠΟΛΙϹ

Α

0 3 6 9 12 15   27 cm.

The *miliarium* from the Langada Road and its inscription.
(Now in the Museum of Thessalonike.)

PLATE 22

Fig. 13. — Sezione del muro e dell'aggere.

a. Section of the Agger and Grotta Oscura wall in the garden of the Ministero dell'Agricoltura. (*NSc* 1910, p. 511, fig. 13.)

b. Agger and its revetting wall near the railway station. (Parker's photograph No. 151.)

PLATE 23

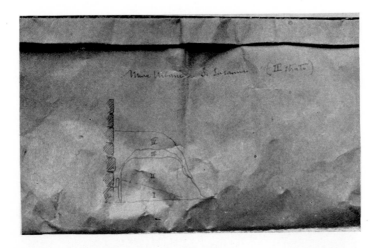

a

b

c

d

e

a. Photo of the envelop containing the finds from Stratum II.
b. Fragment of semi-circular tile.
c. Fragment of flat roof-tile.   d. Red-figured fragment.
e. The Agger seen behind its revetting all near the railway station.
(Parker's photograph No. 793.)

PLATE 24

a. The Agger seen in front of its revetting wall in the
Piazza Fanti. (Parker's photograph No. 3005.)

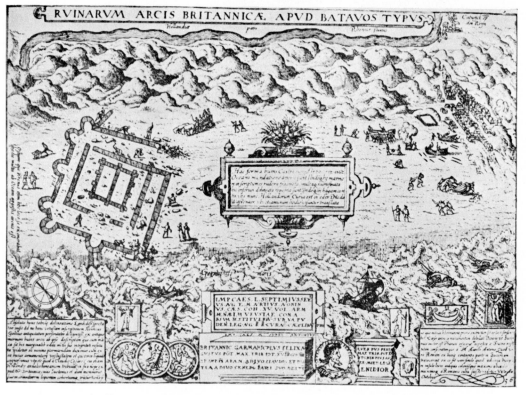

b. Engraving by A. Ortelius of the year 1567. (After Bijvanck.)

PLATE 25

The Atrium and the Tablinum of the Casa dell'Atrio a mosaico. Herculaneum.
(Photograph Filli Alinari No. 43110.)

PLATE 26

Detail of the Tablinum of the Casa dell'Atrio a mosaico. Herculaneum.
(Photograph Filli Alinari No. 43128.)

PLATE 27

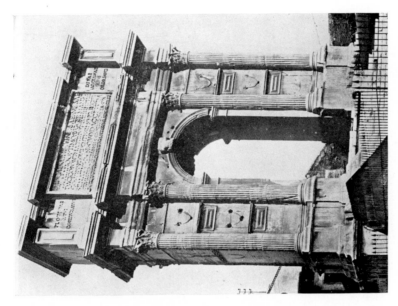

b. Trajan's arch at Ancona.

a. Inscription from Puteoli in Philadelphia.

PLATE 28

The relief from Puteoli in Philadelphia.

PLATE 29

The relief from Puteoli in Berlin.

PLATE 30

Joining reliefs in Philadelphia and Berlin. (Plaster casts—now in Rome.)

PLATE 31

a   b

a. Piazza Giudetta Tarani Arquati (Trastevere).
b. Via Benedetta 19-21 (Trastevere). Two narrow-fronted houses coupled together.

c. Façade of an *insula* in the Aurelian wall between the
Porta Tiburtina and the Porta Maggiore.

PLATE 32

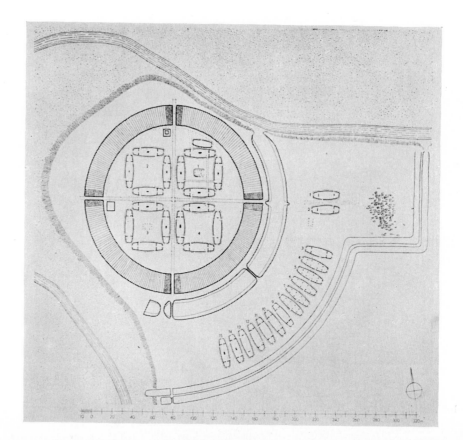

a

b

The Castle of Trelleborg after excavation.
a. Ground plan after P. Nörlund, fig. 11 (Scale c. 1:2500).
b. Aerial photograph after P. Nörlund, fig. 26 a.

PLATE 33

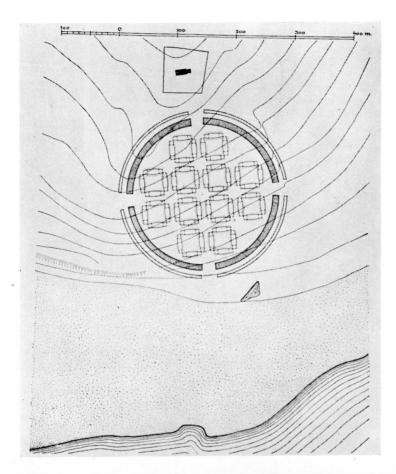

b   c

a. Ground plan of Aggersborg. At the top church and churchyard. At the bottom
   the coast of Limfjord. (After P. Nörlund, fig. 12; Scale c. 1: 5000.)

b. Assyrian fortified camp.   c. A fortified camp. Detail from the
                                          Balawat gate relief.

PLATE 34

a. Aerial photograph of Firūzābād (after R. Ghirshman, pl. VII b).

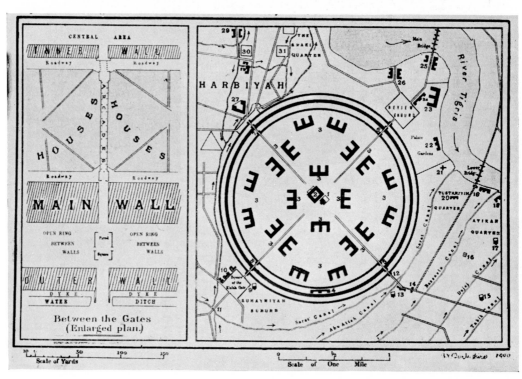

b. Baghdad, the "Round City" in the time of Mansur. (After G. L. Strange.)

PLATE 35

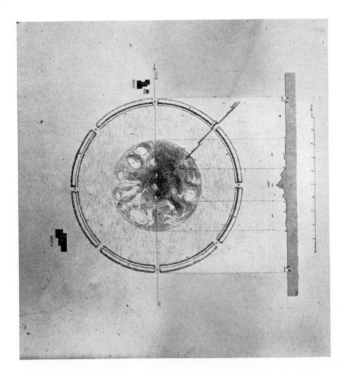

b. Dārābjird.

a. Norwegian design from the 13th century Jerusalem. (After H. Fett, Norges Malerkunsti Middelalderen, fig. p. 218.)

PLATE 36

An archaic marble vase cover with Medusa head.

PLATE 37

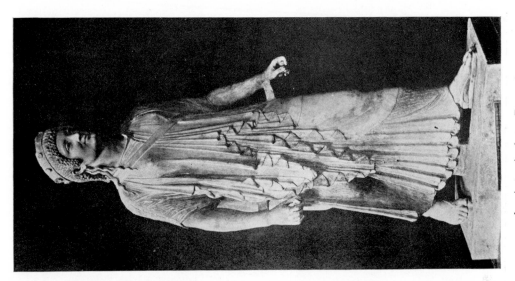

b. *Artemis from Pompeii.*

a. *Archaic Attic Kore.*

a

b

c

d

a. Statuette of a Bodhisattva from Taxila.
b. Book cover in the Bodleian Library.
c, d. Figures on a cross.

PLATE 39

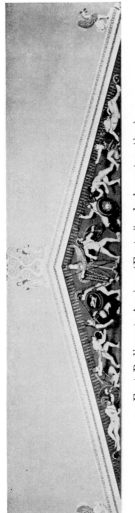

a. East Pediment, Aegina (Furtwängler's restoration).

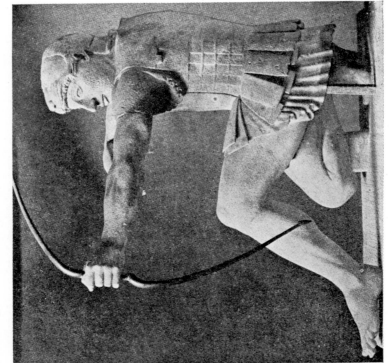

c. Archer from Aegina. (Side view.)

b. Stowitz as archer.

PLATE 40

Archer from Aegina. (Front view.)

PLATE 41

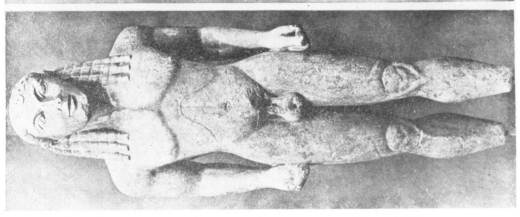

a. The twins of Delphi (De La Coste-Messelière.
    Delphes, pl. 34).

b. Head of a Kouros from Kamiros
    (*Clara Rhodos*, 6-7, fig 51).

b

a

PLATE 42

b. Lead statuette in a private collection
at Basel.

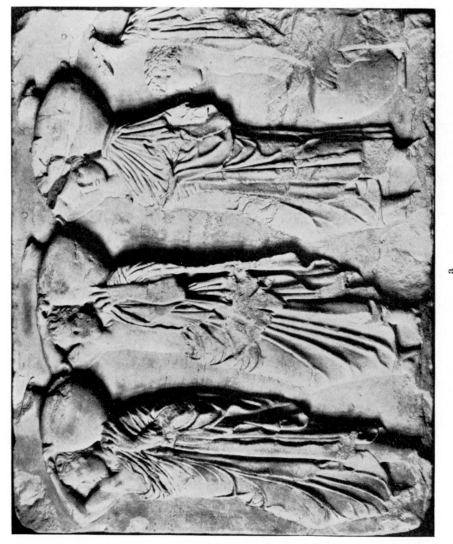

a

a. The three hydrophori from the Parthenon Frieze (Hege-Rodenwaldt,
Die Akropolis von Athen, pl. 47).

PLATE 43

b

b. Rear view of the lead statuette at Basel.

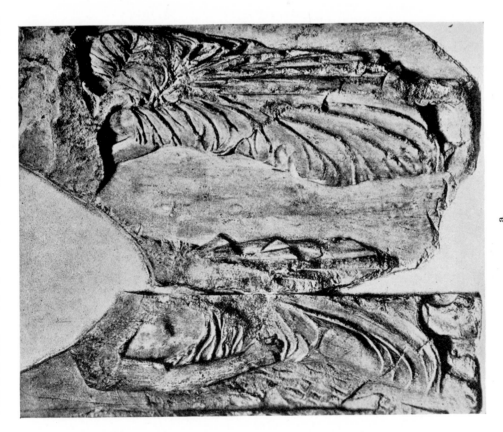

a

a. Figures 12-13 from the North Frieze of the Parthenon.
(Von Lücken, *Parthenonskulpturen*, pl. 19.)

PLATE 44

Group of two women, Athens. (Courtesy of Homer A. Thompson.)

PLATE 45

Bronze mirror No. 16350 of the National Museum at Athens.
(Drawing by Alex. Kontopoulos.)

PLATE 46

Bronze mirror No. 7683 of the National Museum at Athens. Rear view.
(Drawing by Alex. Papaeliopoulos.)

PLATE 47

a. Red-figured stamnos by the Eucharides
painter.

b. Bronze mirror No. 7683 at the
National Museum.

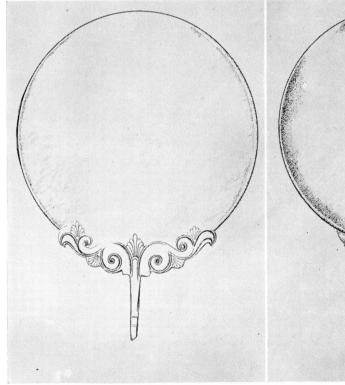

c   d

c. Mirror No. 7684 from an Athenian grave.
d. Mirror No. 7690 at the National Museum, Athens.
(Drawings by Alex. Kontopoulos.)

PLATE 48

a. Bronze maiden from the Acropolis No. 6504.

b. Bronze base from the Acropolis Museum No. 6549.

PLATE 49

Mirror stand from the Acropolis.

PLATE 50

a

a. Bronze mirror in the National Museum No. 7464.

b. Rear view of the Bronze mirror from the Acropolis.
(Illustrated on plate 48, a.)

PLATE 51

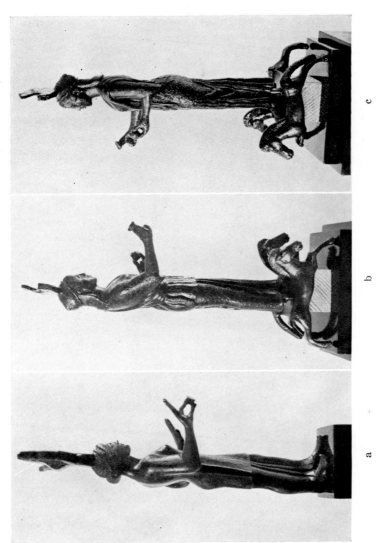

a
b
c

a. Side view of Maiden No. 7464.

b. and c. Side views of the support of the Acropolis mirror (Kore No. 6504).

PLATE 52

a

b

a. Bronze Mirror in the British Museum.

b. Bronze Mirror from Leonidion now in the National Museum at Athens.

PLATE 53

Bronze Mirror from Corinth in the
National Museum, No. 7576.

PLATE 54

Marble lekythos in the Boston Museum of Fine Arts.

PLATE 55

Grave relief of an Athenian poet at Lyme Park, Stockport.

PLATE 56

A marble relief in Pergamon.

PLATE 57

a. Marble relief from Samos

b. Bronze relief from Pompeii. *RM* 55 (1940) 79, fig. 1.

PLATE 58

a. Relief from west slope of the Acropolis.

b. The discovered fragment of the Stele of Palestrita.

PLATE 59

b

a

a. The Stele of Palestrita as completed.

b. The drawing of Windsor Castle.

PLATE 60

a. Inscription on the back of the fragment of the Stele of Palestrita.

b. Funerary stele of Erotion (*Deltion* 1917, fig. 189).

PLATE 61

a. Fragment of a funerary stele (*Deltion* 1917, fig. 190).
b. Small clay ornaments from a cremation burial at Thebes (*Deltion* 1917, fig. 164).

c. East Pediment of the Temple of Zeus at Olympia (Figures after Bulle,
arrangement after Studniczka).

PLATE 62

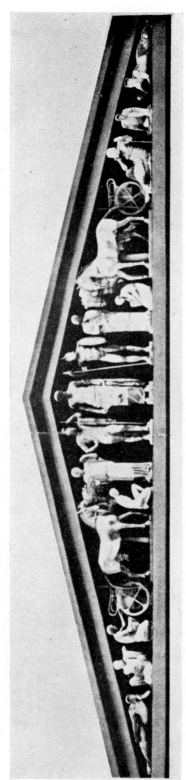

a. East Pediment of the Temple of Zeus at Olympia (Studniczka).

b. East Pediment of the Temple of Zeus at Olympia (Bulle).

PLATE 63

Marble head of Artemis in a private collection.

PLATE 64

c. Torso of Theodoros in Delphi.

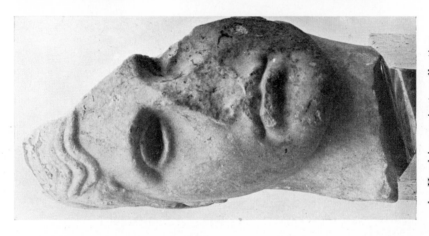

b. Head in a private collection.

a. Head in a private collection.

PLATE 65

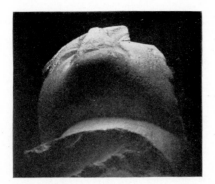

a. Detail from below the chin.

b. Head in the Alba collection in Madrid.

c. Head from Selinus.

PLATE 66

b. Artemis head from Selinus.

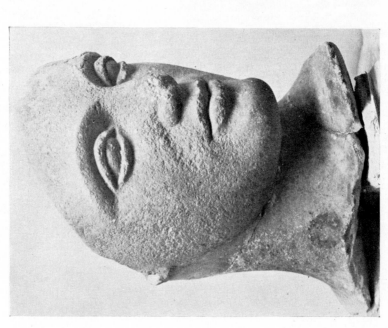

a. Head from Selinus.

PLATE 67

a. The Relief in Copenhagen.

c. The "Laokoon" kantharos in London.

b. Fragment in Copenhagen.

PLATE 68

Youthful dancer in the Geneva Museum of Art and History.

PLATE 69

a

b

c

d

a-b. Details of figure Plate 68.
c. Restoration of the group of dancers by W. Klein.
d. Ivory statuette of Apollo with lion.

PLATE 70

A terra cotta statuette of a dancer in the Munich Museum.

PLATE 71

A fragment of a head from Ephesos.

PLATE 72

a. Table support from the Athenian Acropolis.
b-c. Marble head from Ephesos.

PLATE 73

The Thorvaldsen Museum fragment No. 82

a. Face B. b. Face A.

a

b

PLATE 74

a. Low relief from Cyrene. Face A.

b. Low relief from Cyrene. Face B.

c. Attic aryballos in the Louvre: medical consultation.

PLATE 75

Heroic statue from Philadelphia—Amman. (Front view.)

PLATE 76

Statue from Philadelphia—Amman. Head: detail.

PLATE 77

Head and torso; rear view.

PLATE 78

Provisional reconstruction of the statue.

PLATE 79

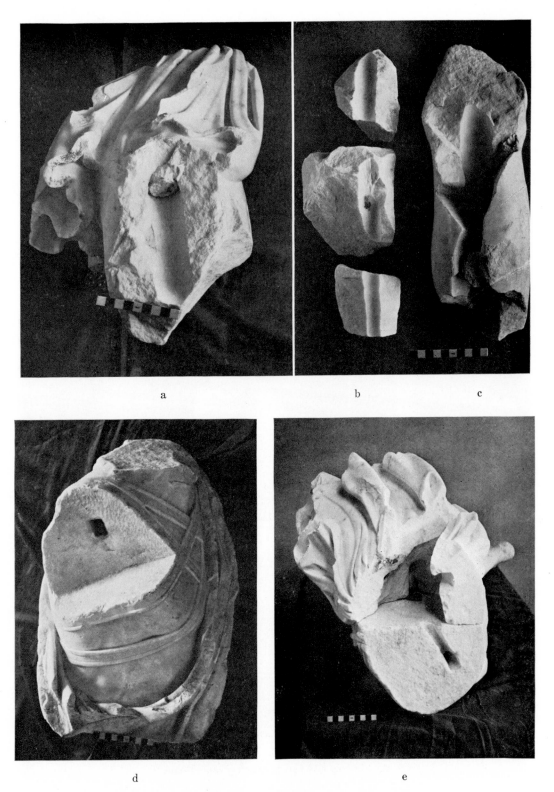

a. Upper right thigh, showing tubular drill-hole and remains of core.
b. Fragments of left arm. c. Fragment of right leg.
d. Junction of right shoulder showing cramp-hole. e. Section through waist showing
junction of both legs and cramp-holes. From above.

PLATE 80

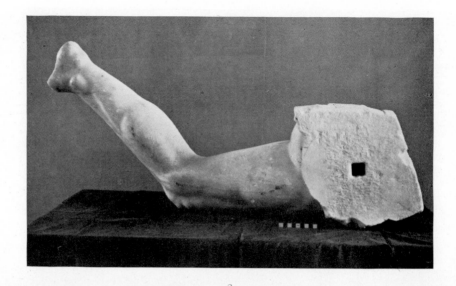

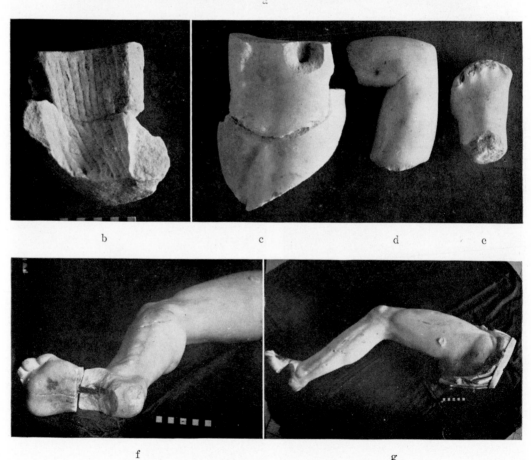

a. Left leg and thigh, showing cramp-hole.
b. Interior of abdomen fragment shown in c.
c, d, e. Fragments of a youthful figure; c. abodmen, d. arm, e. foot.
f. left foot, showing repair. g. Left leg and thigh, showing puntello.

PLATE 81

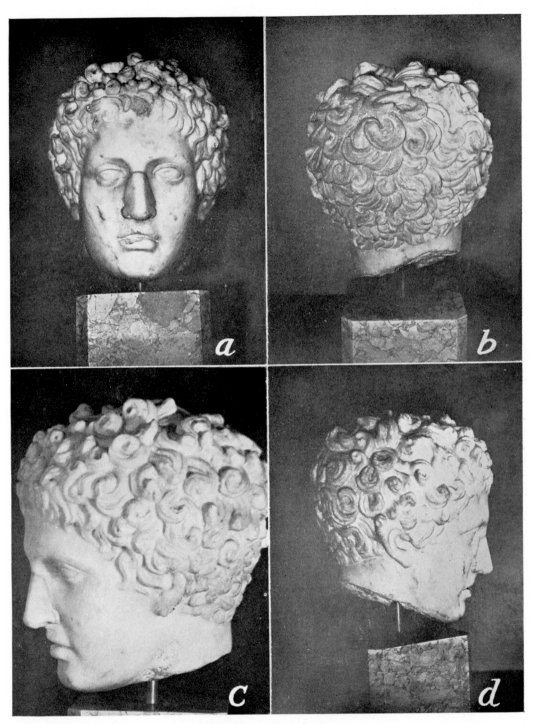

Marble head at Union College.

PLATE 82

a. Gold stater, Ptolemy I Soter (Courtesy, American Numismatic Society).
b. Silver tetradachm, Ptolemy I Soter (Courtesy, British Museum).
c. Gold stater bearing jugate heads of Ptolemy I and Berenike.
d. Plaster plaque from Memphis at Hildesheim.
e, f. Marble head from Egypt at Copenhagen.

PLATE 83

a

b

c   d

a, b. Marble head from Greece in the Louvre (Courtesy of the Museum of the Louvre).
c, d. Marble head in the Pergamon Museum at Berlin.

PLATE 84

a

b

c

d

a, b. Head from Cairo.
c, d. Head from Thera.

PLATE 85

A. Jugate Heads of Ptolemy I Soter and Berenike in Alexandria
(Courtesy, Royal Society of Archaeology, Alexandria).

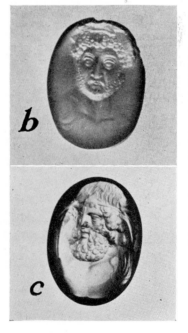

a, b. Engraved carnelian in the Metropolitan Museum inscribed *Aspasiou*.
c. Amethyst ring stone in the Metropolitan Museum.

PLATE 86

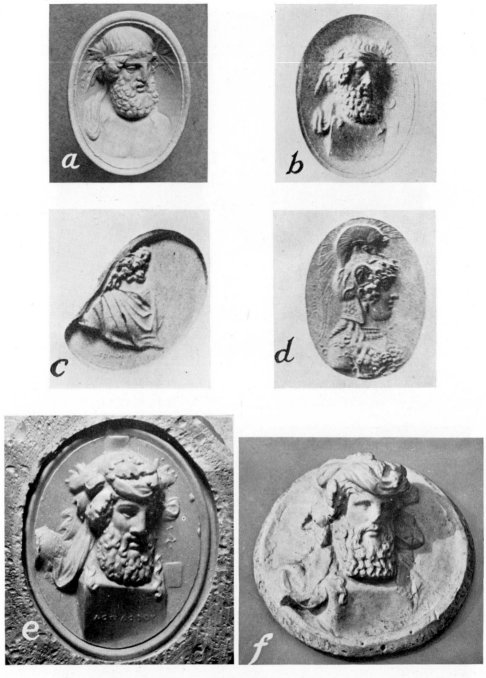

a. Amethyst ringstone in the Metropolitan Museum (cf. pl. 85, c).
b. Gem with herm of Dionysos. c. Fragment of a gem by Aspasios in Florence.
d. Red jasper with the head of Athena Parthenos by Aspasios.
(Formerly in Vienna, now in Rome.)
e. Red jasper with herm of Dionysos in the British Museum.
f. Marble disk in the Metropolitan Museum.

PLATE 87

a

b

c

a. Ape riding on a donkey.
b. Ape (or man) riding on a donkey.
c. Seated ape holding a large pot.

PLATE 88

Foot of a Thymiaterion from Olympia. (Inv. B 1001.) Front and side views.

PLATE 89

Foot of a Thymiaterion in the Metropolitan Museum. Front and side views.

PLATE 90

A-B. Terracotta figurines from the Tyre region.

C. Shield fragment from Olympia. (Inv. B. 1799.)

PLATE 91

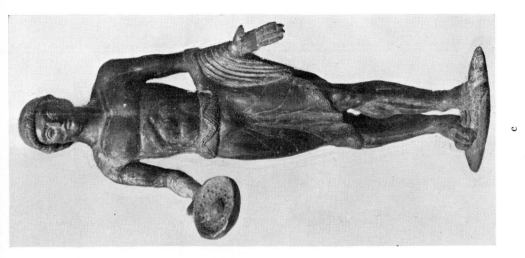

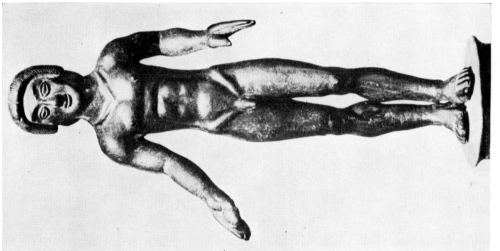

a. Bronze statuette in Brussels.
b. Bronze statuette from Monte Falterona in the Louvre.
c. Bronze statuette from Monte Guragazza in Bologna.

a

b

c

PLATE 92

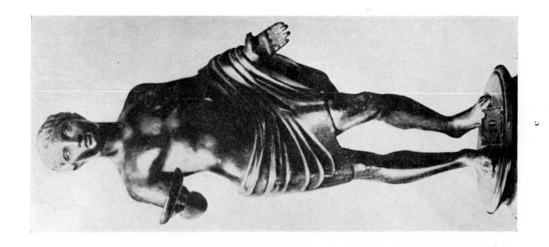

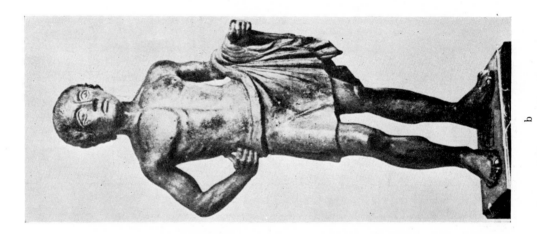

a. Bronze figure of Turms in the Ashmolean Museum.
b. Bronze statuette from Monte Falterona in Florence.
c. Bronze statuette in Florence.

c

b

a

PLATE 93

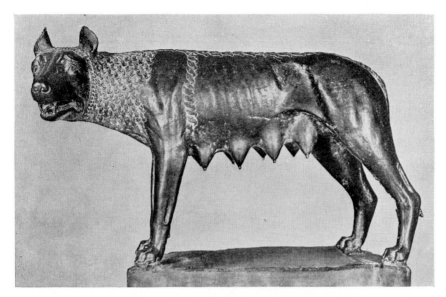

a. The Capitoline wolf.

b. Bronze lion medaillon from Tarquinia.

PLATE 94

a. Lion water spout from Himera.

b. Relief from a house on block D5 at Dura-Europos.

PLATE 95

Portrait head of Pompey in the Ny Carlsberg Glyptotek.

PLATE 96

Portrait head of Pompey in the collection of Frank E. Brown.

PLATE 97

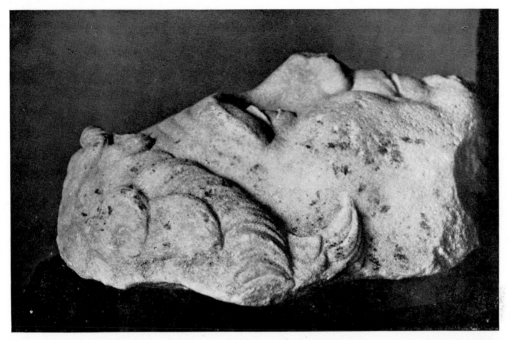

Portrait head of Pompey in the collection of Frank E. Brown.

PLATE 98

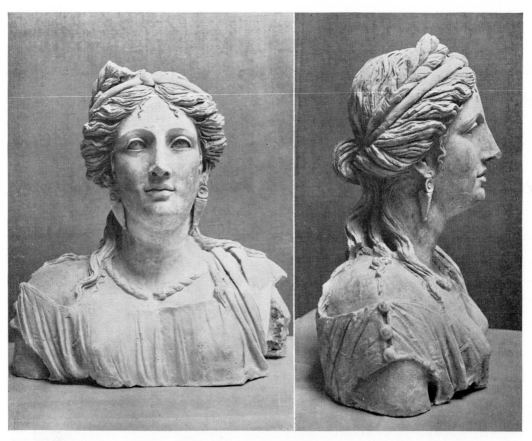

a-b. Terracotta bust of Demeter in the Museo Nazionale Romano.

c-d. Theotokos, a colossal head in Smyrna.

PLATE 99

Mithraic altar of Italica.

PLATE 100

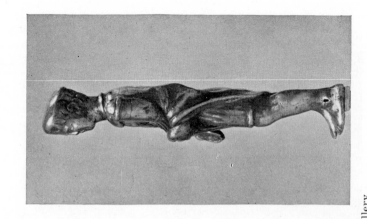

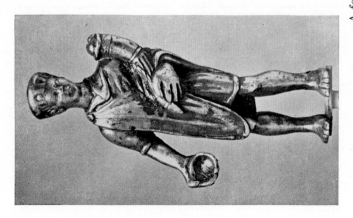

A fourth century A. D. silver statuette in the Walters Art Gallery

PLATE 101

a. Head of Medusa in the Museo Civico of Perugia.

b. Terracotta cinerary urn in the Museo civico of Perugia.

PLATE 102

Terracotta decoration from a Renaissance house in Rome.

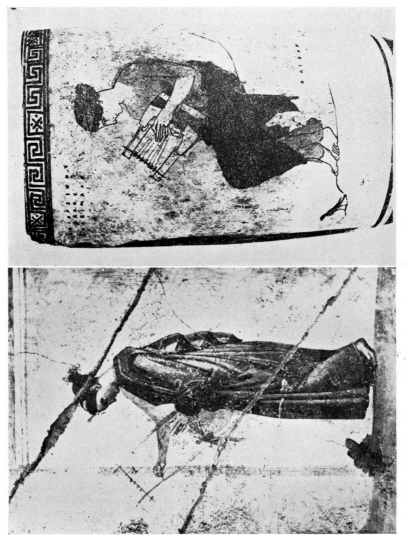

PLATE 103

a. The Lyreplayer from a Pompeian wall painting.
b. The Lyreplayer on a lekythos in Munich.

PLATE 104

Painting of Narcissus in the atrium of the Casa dell'Ora massima.

PLATE 105

Painting on a Campanian Crater in the Louvre.

PLATE 106

Iphigeneia and her attendants in the Casa di Caecilio Jucundo.

PLATE 107

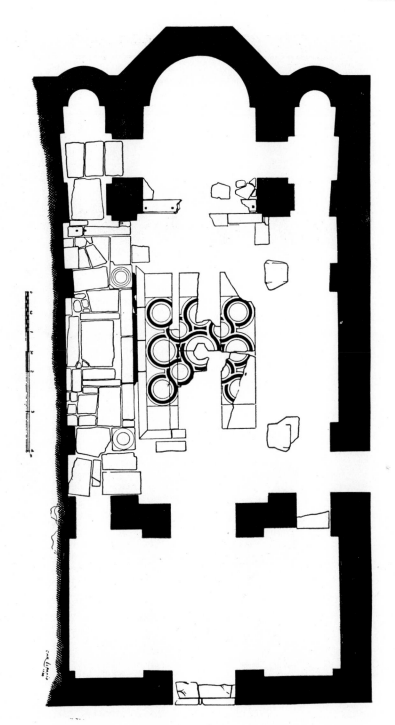

Plan of the Byzantine Church of St. Nicholas. (*Olynthus*, XII, pl. 262.)

PLATE 108

The Byzantine Church of Olynthus from the West. (*Olynthus*, XII, pl. 263.)

PLATE 109

a. Mosaic of Genazzano in the Museo Nazionale Romano.

b. Mosaic pavement from Ravenna.

PLATE 110

Mosaic pavement of Aquileia.

PLATE 111

Pavement of Pomposa.